W9-CTW-424

Contemporary
Literary Criticism

Guide to Gale Literary Criticism Series

For criticism on	Consult these Gale series
Authors now living or who died after December 31, 1959	*CONTEMPORARY LITERARY CRITICISM (CLC)*
Authors who died between 1900 and 1959	*TWENTIETH-CENTURY LITERARY CRITICISM (TCLC)*
Authors who died between 1800 and 1899	*NINETEENTH-CENTURY LITERATURE CRITICISM (NCLC)*
Authors who died between 1400 and 1799	*LITERATURE CRITICISM FROM 1400 TO 1800 (LC)* *SHAKESPEAREAN CRITICISM (SC)*
Authors who died before 1400	*CLASSICAL AND MEDIEVAL LITERATURE CRITICISM (CMLC)*
Black writers of the past two hundred years	*BLACK LITERATURE CRITICISM (BLC)*
Authors of books for children and young adults	*CHILDREN'S LITERATURE REVIEW (CLR)*
Dramatists	*DRAMA CRITICISM (DC)*
Hispanic writers of the late nineteenth and twentieth centuries	*HISPANIC LITERATURE CRITICISM (HLC)*
Native North American writers and orators of the eighteenth, nineteenth, and twentieth centuries	*NATIVE NORTH AMERICAN LITERATURE (NNAL)*
Poets	*POETRY CRITICISM (PC)*
Short story writers	*SHORT STORY CRITICISM (SSC)*
Major authors from the Renaissance to the present	*WORLD LITERATURE CRITICISM, 1500 TO THE PRESENT (WLC)*
Major authors and works from the Bible to the present	*WORLD LITERATURE CRITICISM SUPPLEMENT (WLCS)*

ISSN 0091-3421

Volume 103

Contemporary Literary Criticism

Excerpts from Criticism of the Works
of Today's Novelists, Poets, Playwrights,
Short Story Writers, Scriptwriters, and
Other Creative Writers

Deborah A. Schmitt
EDITOR

Jeffrey W. Hunter
COORDINATOR

Tim Akers
Pamela S. Dear
Daniel Jones
John D. Jorgenson
Jerry Moore
Polly Vedder
Timothy White
Thomas Wiloch
Kathleen Wilson
ASSOCIATE EDITORS

GALE

DETROIT · NEW YORK · TORONTO · LONDON

Library of Congress Catalog Card Number 76-46132
ISBN 0-7876-1193-X
ISSN 0091-3421

Printed in the United States of America
10 9 8 7 6 5 4 3 2 1

Contents

Preface vii

Acknowledgments xi

Preface

A Comprehensive Information Source
on Contemporary Literature

Named "one of the twenty-five most distinguished reference titles published during the past twenty-five years" by *Reference Quarterly,* the *Contemporary Literary Criticism (CLC)* series provides readers with critical commentary and general information on more than 2,000 authors now living or who died after December 31, 1959. Previous to the publication of the first volume of *CLC* in 1973, there was no ongoing digest monitoring scholarly and popular sources of critical opinion and explication of modern literature. *CLC,* therefore, has fulfilled an essential need, particularly since the complexity and variety of contemporary literature makes the function of criticism especially important to today's reader.

Scope of the Series

CLC presents significant passages from published criticism of works by creative writers. Since many of the authors covered by *CLC* inspire continual critical commentary, writers are often represented in more than one volume. There is, of course, no duplication of reprinted criticism.

Authors are selected for inclusion for a variety of reasons, among them the publication or dramatic production of a critically acclaimed new work, the reception of a major literary award, revival of interest in past writings, or the adaptation of a literary work to film or television.

Attention is also given to several other groups of writers-authors of considerable public interest—about whose work criticism is often difficult to locate. These include mystery and science fiction writers, literary and social critics, foreign writers, and authors who represent particular ethnic groups within the United States.

Format of the Book

Each *CLC* volume contains about 500 individual excerpts taken from hundreds of book review periodicals, general magazines, scholarly journals, monographs, and books. Entries include critical evaluations spanning from the beginning of an author's career to the most current commentary. Interviews, feature articles, and other published writings that offer insight into the author's works are also presented. Students, teachers, librarians, and researchers will find that the generous excerpts and supplementary material in *CLC* provide them with vital information required to write a term paper, analyze a poem, or lead a book discussion group. In addition, complete bibliographical citations note the original source and all of the information necessary for a term paper footnote or bibliography.

Features

A *CLC* author entry consists of the following elements:

- The **Author Heading** cites the author's name in the form under which the author has most commonly published, followed by birth date, and death date when applicable. Uncertainty as to a birth or death date is indicated by a question mark.

- A **Portrait** of the author is included when available.

- A brief **Biographical and Critical Introduction** to the author and his or her work precedes the excerpted criticism. The first line of the introduction provides the author's full name, pseudonyms (if applicable), nationality, and a listing of genres in which the author has written. To provide users with easier access to information, the biographical and critical essay included in each author entry is divided into four categories: "Introduction," "Biographical Information," "Major Works," and "Critical Reception." The introductions to single-work entries—entries that focus on well known and frequently studied books, short stories, and poems—are similarly organized to quickly provide readers with information on the plot and major characters of the work being discussed, its major themes, and its critical reception. Previous volumes of *CLC* in which the author has been featured are also listed in the introduction.

- A list of **Principal Works** notes the most important writings by the author. When foreign-language works have been translated into English, the English-language version of the title follows in brackets.

- The **Excerpted Criticism** represents various kinds of critical writing, ranging in form from the brief review to the scholarly exegesis. Essays are selected by the editors to reflect the spectrum of opinion about a specific work or about an author's literary career in general. The excerpts are presented chronologically, adding a useful perspective to the entry. All titles by the author featured in the entry are printed in boldface type, which enables the reader to easily identify the works being discussed. Publication information (such as publisher names and book prices) and parenthetical numerical references (such as footnotes or page and line references to specific editions of a work) have been deleted at the editor's discretion to provide smoother reading of the text.

- Critical essays are prefaced by **Explanatory Notes** as an additional aid to readers. These notes may provide several types of valuable information, including: the reputation of the critic, the importance of the work of criticism, the commentator's approach to the author's work, the purpose of the criticism, and changes in critical trends regarding the author.

- A complete **Bibliographical Citation** designed to help the user find the original essay or book precedes each excerpt.

- Whenever possible, a recent, previously unpublished **Author Interview** accompanies each entry.

- A concise **Further Reading** section appears at the end of entries on authors for whom a significant amount of criticism exists in addition to the pieces reprinted in *CLC*. Each citation in this section is accompanied by a descriptive annotation describing the content of that article. Materials included in this section are grouped under various headings (e.g., Biography, Bibliography, Criticism, and Interviews) to aid users in their search for additional information. Cross-references to other useful sources published by Gale Research in which the author has appeared are also included: *Authors in the News, Black Writers, Children's Literature Review, Contemporary Authors, Dictionary of Literary Biography, DISCovering Authors, Drama Criticism, Hispanic Literature Criticism, Hispanic Writers, Native North American Literature, Poetry Criticism, Something about the Author, Short Story Criticism, Contemporary Authors Autobiography Series,* and *Something about the Author Autobiography Series.*

Other Features

CLC also includes the following features:

- An **Acknowledgments** section lists the copyright holders who have granted permission to reprint material in this volume of *CLC*. It does not, however, list every book or periodical reprinted or consulted during the preparation of the volume.

- Each new volume of *CLC* includes a **Cumulative Topic Index,** which lists all literary topics treated in *CLC, NCLC, TCLC,* and *LC 1400-1800.*

- A **Cumulative Author Index** lists all the authors who have appeared in the various literary criticism series published by Gale Research, with cross-references to Gale's biographical and autobiographical series. A full listing of the series referenced there appears on the first page of the indexes of this volume. Readers will welcome this cumulated author index as a useful tool for locating an author within the various series. The index, which lists birth and death dates when available, will be particularly valuable for those authors who are identified with a certain period but whose death dates cause them to be placed in another, or for those authors whose careers span two periods. For example, Ernest Hemingway is found in *CLC,* yet F. Scott Fitzgerald, a writer often associated with him, is found in *Twentieth-Century Literary Criticism.*

- A **Cumulative Nationality Index** alphabetically lists all authors featured in *CLC* by nationality, followed by numbers corresponding to the volumes in which the authors appear.

- An alphabetical **Title Index** accompanies each volume of *CLC*. Listings are followed by the author's name and the corresponding page numbers where the titles are discussed. English translations of foreign titles and variations of titles are cross-referenced to the title under which a work was originally published. Titles of novels, novellas, dramas, films, record albums, and poetry, short story, and essay collections are printed in italics, while all individual poems, short stories, essays, and songs are printed in roman type within quotation marks; when published separately (e.g., T. S. Eliot's poem *The Waste Land),* the titles of long poems are printed in italics.

- In response to numerous suggestions from librarians, Gale has also produced a **Special Paperbound Edition** of the *CLC* title index. This annual cumulation, which alphabetically lists all titles reviewed in the series, is available to all customers and is typically published with every fifth volume of *CLC*. Additional copies of the index are available upon request. Librarians and patrons will welcome this separate index: it saves shelf space, is easy to use, and is recyclable upon receipt of the next edition.

Citing *Contemporary Literary Criticism*

When writing papers, students who quote directly from any volume in the Literary Criticism Series may use the following general forms to footnote reprinted criticism. The first example pertains to material drawn from periodicals, the second to material reprinted in books:

[1]Alfred Cismaru, "Making the Best of It," *The New Republic,* 207, No. 24, (December 7, 1992), 30, 32; excerpted and reprinted in *Contemporary Literary Criticism,* Vol. 85, ed. Christopher Giroux (Detroit: Gale Research, 1995), pp. 73-4.

[2]Yvor Winters, *The Post-Symbolist Methods* (Allen Swallow, 1967); excerpted and reprinted in *Contemporary Literary Criticism,* Vol. 85, ed. Christopher Giroux (Detroit: Gale Research, 1995), pp. 223-26.

Suggestions Are Welcome

The editors hope that readers will find *CLC* a useful reference tool and welcome comments about the work. Send comments and suggestions to: Editors, *Contemporary Literary Criticism,* Gale Research, Penobscot Building, Detroit, MI 48226-4094.

Acknowledgments

The editors wish to thank the copyright holders of the excerpted criticism included in this volume and the permissions managers of many book and magazine publishing companies for assisting us in securing reproduction rights. We are also grateful to the staffs of the Detroit Public Library, the Library of Congress, the University of Detroit Mercy Library, Wayne State University Purdy/Kresge Library Complex, and the University of Michigan Libraries for making their resources available to us. Following is a list of the copyright holders who have granted us permission to reproduce material in this volume of *CLC*. Every effort has been made to trace copyright, but if omissions have been made, please let us know.

COPYRIGHTED EXCERPTS IN *CLC*, VOLUME 103, WERE REPRODUCED FROM THE FOLLOWING PERIODICALS:

African American Review, v. 27, Summer, 1993 for "Alice Walker's Vision of the South in 'The Third Life of Grange Copeland' by Robert James Butler. Copyright © 1986 Indiana State University. Reproduced by permission of the publisher and the author.—*American Indian Culture and Research Journal,* v. 18, 1994; v. 19, 1995. Copyright © 1994, 1995 The Regents of the University of California. Both reproduced by permission.—*American Indian Quarterly,* v. IX, Winter, 1985. Copyright © Society for American Indian Studies & Research 1985. Reproduced by permission of the publisher.—*American Literature,* v. 66, December, 1994. Copyright © 1994 Duke University Press, Durham, NC. Reproduced with permission.—*The Antigonish Review,* Autumn 1984 for "Craig Raine & Co.: Martians and Story-Tellers" by Michael Hulse. Copyright © 1984 by the author. Reproduced by permission of the publisher and the author.—*Black American Literature Forum,* v. 20, Winter, 1986 for "In Search of Our Fathers' Arms: Alice Walker's Persona of the Alienated Darling" by Philip M. Royster. Copyright © 1986 by the author. Reproduced by permission of the publisher and the author.— *The Black Scholar,* v. 12, March/April, 1981. Copyright 1981 by *The Black Scholar.* Reprinted by permission of the publisher.—*Book World—The Washington Post,* February 19, 1978; January 16, 1994; January 2, 1996. Copyright © 1978, 1994, 1996, Washington Post Book World Service/Washington Post Writers Group. All reproduced with permission.—*boundary 2,* v. V, Spring, 1977. Copyright © boundary 2, 1977. Reproduced by permission.—*British Book News,* January 1985. Copyright © The British Council 1985. Reproduced by permission.—*Camera Obscura,* n. 11-15, Fall 1986 for "Metropolis: Mother-City—'Mittler'—Hitler" by Roger Dadoun. Reproduced by permission of the author.—*Centrum,* v. 6, Spring, 1978. © Minnesota Center for Advanced Studies in Language, Style, and Literary Theory 1979. Reproduced by permission.—*Chicago Review,* v. 39, 1992. Copyright © 1992 by *Chicago Review.* Reproduced by permission.—*Chicago Tribune,* April 30, 1995 for "The Woman Who Went Away in Anne Tyler's 13th Novel, An Unhappy Wife Seeks A New Life" by Roberta Rubenstein. © copyrighted 1995, Chicago Tribune Company. All rights reserved. Reproduced by permission of the author.—*Chicago Tribune—Books,* October 16, 1994 for "Into Troubled Waters: Novelist Tim O'Brien Probes Our Lurking Taste for Violence" by William O'Rourke. © copyrighted 1994, Chicago Tribune Company. All rights reserved. Reproduced by permission of the author.—*Contemporary Literature,* v. 32, Spring, 1991. © 1991 by the Regents of the University of Wisconsin. Reproduced by permission of The University of Wisconsin Press.—*Critique,* v. XXXV, Fall, 1993; v. XXXVI, Fall, 1994. Copyright © 1993, 1994 Helen Dwight Reid Educational Foundation. Both reproduced with permission of the Helen Dwight Reid Educational Foundation, published by Heldref Publications, 1319 18th Street, NW, Washington, DC 20036-1802.—*Dutch Quarterly Review,* v. 15, 1985. Reproduced by permission of the publisher.—*Essays in Literature,* v. XVIII, Fall, 1991. Copyright 1991 by Western Illinois University. Reproduced by permission.—*Film Quarterly,* v. XXVII, Summer 1974 for "Structures of Narrativity in Fritz Lang's 'Metropolis'" by Alan Williams; v. 43, Spring 1990 for "Fritz Land and Goebbels: Myth and Facts" by Gosta Werner. Copyright © 1974, 1990 by The Regents of the University of California. Both reproduced by permission of The Regents and the respective authors.— *The Hudson Review,* v. XLVIII, Summer, 1995. Copyright © 1995 by The Hudson Review, Inc. Reproduced by permission.—*Journal of Aesthetics and Art Criticism,* v. XLI, Fall, 1982. Copyright © 1982 by The American Society for Aesthetics. Reproduced by permission.—*Journal of American Culture,* v. 18, Summer, 1995. Reproduced by permission.— *The Kenyon Review,* v. VI, Summer, 1984 for "Bloom, Freud, and 'America'" by David Wyatt. Copyright 1984 by Kenyon College. All rights reserved. Reproduced by permission of the author.—*Kirkus Reviews,*

Harold Bloom
1930-

American critic, editor, and novelist.

The following entry presents criticism of Bloom's work through 1995. For further information on his life and career, see *CLC,* Volume 24.

INTRODUCTION

As important to literary criticism as he is controversial, Harold Bloom has been a major contributor to academic scholarship for over thirty-five years. His work has been influenced by a wide variety of sources, ranging from Freud and Nietzsche to Gnosticism and Judaism. Most of Bloom's books are concerned with the development of his theory of poetics, which centers on the notion that poets engage in a constant struggle with their literary forebears. This "anxiety of influence," as Bloom has termed it, has been alternately referred to as "genius" and "idiosyncratic" by his scholarly peers. Denis Donoghue, who holds the Henry James Chair of English and American Letters at New York University, frequently reviews Bloom's books and has ambivalent feelings regarding his work, saying in one review that he finds Bloom "quite wondrous, even when I don't believe him."

Biographical Information

Harold Bloom was born in New York City in 1930 to William and Paula Lev Bloom. Even at an early age, Bloom was a voracious reader; it has been said that he read English before he spoke it. He lived in New York City until he entered Cornell University, where he earned his B.A. in 1951. In 1955, he earned his Ph.D. from Yale University and has been a member of the faculty since that time. In 1958, Bloom married Jeanne Gould, with whom he has two sons, Daniel and David. His first book, *Shelley's Mythmaking* (1959), began as his Ph.D. dissertation and was awarded Yale's John Addison Porter Prize in 1956, the first of many awards. Bloom has been awarded a Guggenheim Fellowship (1962-1963), a Morton Dauwen Zabel Award from the National Institute and American Academy of Arts and Letters (1981), and the 1985 MacArthur Foundation Award. While Bloom has written on a variety of literary topics, it was with the publication of *The Anxiety of Influence: A Theory of Poetry* (1973) that he first brought widespread attention to his work. Bloom was a distinguished literary critic before the publication of this book, but as Helen Requeiro Elam wrote in *Dictionary of Literary Biography,* "it has been impossible to discuss theories of in-

fluence without reference to Bloom" since its appearance on the critical scene. Most of Bloom's writings following *The Anxiety of Influence* have either extended or revised his ideas. His most recent work, *The Western Canon* (1994), is a departure from his theory of poetics, but has produced just as much critical debate as any of his prior writings. Bloom is currently the Sterling Professor of the Humanities at Yale University.

Major Works

At the center of Bloom's "anxiety of influence," the focus of his theory of poetics, is the notion that modern writers (poets, in particular) wrestle with the writers of the past in an effort to create something new and original. Since the Enlightenment, Bloom contends, writers have suffered from a feeling of "belatedness." As Denis Donoghue writes: "Born too late, they find everything already said and done; they cannot be first, priority has by definition, and the indifference of fate, escaped them." The weak writer fails to find his own voice while the strong writer challenges his precursor, willfully "misreading" him so as to clear a space for himself. In books such as *A Map of Misreading* (1975), *Kabbalah and Criticism* (1975), *Poetry and Repression: Revisionism from Blake to Stevens* (1976), and *Agon: Towards a Theory of Revisionism* (1982), Bloom further refines his theoretical approach, utilizing psychoanalysis (Freud), philosophy (Nietzsche and Vico), and Jewish theology (Gnosis and Kabbalah) to create an intricate theory of poetics that continues to spur critical debate.

Critical Reception

Not unlike Jacques Derrida and Michel Foucault, Harold Bloom is a literary critic who, as a writer, has received a great deal of critical attention of his own. His work is reviewed widely, attacked critically, and often praised. Many critics have lauded his daring, "antithetical" approach, while others have called him "willfully offensive to the profession." Bloom's reply to these praises and criticisms is, as Alvin Rosenfeld states, "perhaps the most outrageous thing of all: *he writes another book.*" Rosenfeld goes on to refer to Bloom's work as a "theory in progress," noting that as new volumes appear, new influences are brought to bear on his ideas, such as with *A Map of Misreading,* in which Bloom turns to Lurianic Kabbalism (a form of Jewish mysticism) as "the ultimate model for Western revisionism from the Renaissance to the present." In addition to the books devoted to his theoretical model, Bloom has written on a variety of other topics, including works devoted to Wallace Stevens and William Butler Yeats.

PRINCIPAL WORKS

Shelley's Mythmaking (criticism) 1959

The Visionary Company: A Reading of English Romantic Poetry (criticism) 1961

Yeats (criticism) 1970

The Anxiety of Influence: A Theory of Poetry (criticism) 1973

A Map of Misreading (criticism) 1975

Kabbalah and Criticism (criticism) 1975

Poetry and Repression: Revisionism from Blake to Stevens (criticism) 1976

Wallace Stevens: The Poems of Our Climate (criticism) 1976

The Flight to Lucifer: A Gnostic Fantasy (novel) 1979

Agon: Towards a Theory of Revisionism (criticism) 1982

Ruin the Sacred Truths: Poetry and Belief from the Bible to the Present (criticism) 1989

The Western Canon: The Books and School of the Ages (criticism) 1994

CRITICISM

Howard Eiland (essay date Spring 1977)

SOURCE: "Harold Bloom and High Modernism," in *Boundary 2,* Vol. V, No. 3, Spring, 1977, pp. 935-42.

[*In the following essay, Eiland discusses Bloom's theory of repression and revisionism as creative forces for poets.*]

In *The Anxiety of Influence* Harold Bloom claims for his theory a "deliberate literalism", yet in that book and its successors his interpretations of poems have been hardly "literal." In *Poetry and Repression,* in fact, the motivating critical question is: "What is being repressed here?"—and it stimulates a search for meanings that are *latent,* more or less concealed from the poet himself. "Literal" or manifest meaning is usually a self-deception, a defense against an anterior poetic stance or "fathering force." Poets don't necessarily "mean" what they think they do or what they overtly say; their writing deviously "voices" a dark psychic drama emanating from an ambiguous preconscious realm of contending forces, voices a text of images that resemble those of Freud's psychology, and that, like all archetypal tropes, keep merging into one another without ceasing, however, to embody distinct general principles of opposition or exchange. This submerged but indeterminately graspable drama is thus essentially dualistic or dialectical (the distinction is never completely clear in Bloom), expressing an eternal and eternally multiform "agon" between the body in nature and abstract consciousness. It is doubtful that psyches are texts, Bloom observes in swerving from Jacques Lacan, but texts are surely stratified psyches, are "psychic battlefields."

To any fairly faithful reader of Bloom's recent criticism, this encapsulated argument should sound familiar. He has often been accused of repetitiousness, but one could as well point out in the succession of his books a steady, increasingly bold and technical elaboration and differentiation of certain basic theoretical tenets which I shall try to identify before I conclude. Like other powerful theoretical minds, he seeks to assimilate various disciplines—perhaps most saliently psychology (*Anxiety of Influence*), rhetoric (*Map of Misreading*), and theosophy (*Kabbalah and Criticism*)—into his own systematic. *Poetry and Repression* obviously presupposes these three earlier works in its subtle, difficult associations of tropes, defenses, and divinations. To trope is to turn away from, to fend off, it is a sublimely or grotesquely hyperbolized divergence from "proper meaning," and as a psychic defense mechanism it is a repression or "forgetting" of the idea that one must die: it is thus a supremely fictive prophecy of one's own immortality. Figuration is divination against death, and "proper meaning" for Bloom is death; the imagination, as Vico said, is a faculty for self-preservation. "Meaning in poems," Bloom says, "is always a matter of survival." As the title suggests, *Poetry and Repression* elaborates the key idea of repression. Using Freud's notion that what is repressed is an *image* of a drive, Bloom suggests that the anxious poetic ego of the ephebe or latecomer "absorbs" the too well-loved precursor poem into the ephebe's id, from which the internalized precursor later rises, phantom-like, as a menacing primal image or impulse. The ego is thus trapped in a "strange area of identity and opposition," burdened by what seem to be its own images, and consequently provoked to escape this burden by "misreading" the image of the precursor poem and thereby defining itself:

> For the post Enlightenment poet, identity and opposition are the poles set up by the ephebe's self-defining act in which he creates the hypostasis of the precursor as an Imaginary Other.

In a kind of conflation of this Lacanian terminology with that of Jacques Derrida Bloom goes on to view repression as "a difference in contending forces," and to this he adds Paul Ricoeur's summary of primal repression as meaning "that we are always in the mediate, in the already expressed, the already said." The principle of reciprocity or mediation or difference between conscious and preconscious forces, "fire" and "flood," is thus central to the concept of repression. The alert reader in this context will doubtless recall the extended dialectic of "limitations" and "representations" in Bloom's mapping of the process of poetic "creation-by-catastrophe":

> Limitations turn away from a lost or mourned object towards either the substitute or the mourning subject, while representations turn back towards restoring the powers that desired and possessed the object. Representation points to a lack, just as limitation does, but in a way that re-finds what could fill the lack.

Limitations (which are really concentrations into the self) and re-presentations are connected by processes of substitution, or "crossing," to use Bloom's term from his recent striking essay "Poetic Crossing: Rhetoric and Psychology," *Georgia Review* (Fall 1976). Identity with and opposition to the image of the precursor, as we have just seen, are similarly dialectical functions; repression is a kind of substitution or crossing. And so finally is criticism itself.

> The function of criticism at the present time, as I conceive it, is to find a middle way between the paths of demystification of meaning, and of recollection or restoration of meaning, or between limitation and representation.

Opposed equally to the reductiveness of synchronic structur-

alism (that is, of Paul de Man and J. Hillis Miller) and the mystical autotelism of New Criticism (not autonomous texts but *relations* between texts is Bloom's subject), this criticism will "re-center" our notions of poetic meaning.

Lest this all sound too melioristic, Bloom is also concerned, as in the past, to defend a principle of "revisionism" or "antithesis," directed primarily against the more benign, pseudo-objectivist, high-church view of canon-formation propounded by T.S. Eliot and Northrop Frye. He claims to de-idealize relations between tradition and the individual talent, and at the least, we might say, his is the more dramatic and compelling vision. But I would add that in the context of his basic Romantic premises, we must look askance at this claim to de idealize. For despite the biological vocabulary of strength, survival, and territorial imperative, the general tenor of this critical system is clearly toward *transcendence* of the biological and temporal: toward, as we have seen, "the only victory worth winning, the divinating triumph over oblivion." From *Ringers in the Tower* on to *Poetry and Repression*, Bloom has been relatively frank in his rejection of Freudian "wisdom," or the "reality principle," and one wishes only that he would call his actual pervasive (one hesitates to say banal) idealism by its right name. His wavering between biological and transcendental ("supermimetic") frames of reference furthermore seems tied to a number of other inconsistencies in his system. He has grudgingly admitted the point of John Freccero and others that Petrarch and Virgil, along with other *pre*-Enlightenment poets, are legitimate instances of the anxiety of influence, that the fundamental nature and concerns of human discourse don't seem to change so much after all (see *Map of Misreading*, p. 77); and yet he continues to conceive post-Enlightenment poetry as distinctively anxious and radical, continues to imply an entropic theory of literary history, continues to emphasize the idea of *discontinuity* as integral to his concepts of troping and originality, and as antithetical to the idea of *continuity,* which leads back to the bitter eternal return of cyclic nature. He argues, as we know, a criterion of strength and a method of "creative misprision," and yet he implicitly asks—and actively works—to be understood *fairly,* even as he asserts that his "misreadings" are "more adequate to the text" than the weak misreadings now available, and that there are in any poem "definite patterns" of tropes or images. "Misreading" comes more and more to sound like "reading," and "strength" like "accuracy," and it is as if a critic can afford to be "creative" only after he has attained to something like Bloom's great scholarly learning.

These apparent inconsistencies boil down, it seems to me, to a basic hedging between dualistic and pluralistic modes of thought. He is attracted, on the one hand, to the pluralistic relativism of a Derrida, who following Nietzsche substitutes the concept of "freeplay" for that of "center," and who orphically suggests in his essay "White Mythology: Metaphor in the Text of Philosophy," *New Literary History* (Autumn 1974), that all thought/language is metaphoric or figurative. "There is only interpretation," Bloom declares in *Poetry and Repression,* echoing not only Derrida but his own earlier virtual identification of "poetry" with thought. But if all is interpretation or poetry, it is difficult to know how "figurative" is supposed to differ from "proper" or "literal" (in his recent *Georgia Review* article, p. 513, he finally denies this distinction), or "imagination" from "nature." If all is poetry, then all potentially sublime, unless "sublime" comes to mean only negation, as it does in some "advanced" forms of French Symbolism. It would seem that Bloom cannot logically maintain his pluralistic conception of reality (with its suppressed democratic implications, such as the idea of play) alongside his privileged and tragic conception of imagination. Terms like "universe of death" or "barrenness of experience" can have only a "figurative"—a nominal or formal—sense, expressing not contentual or descriptive "truth" but rather the polemical will and temperament of the critic of which Nietzsche was so complexly suspicious. "Strong" means "it pleases me," or "it impresses me, bends my ear." In other words, Bloom is not writing a Logic but a Rhetoric, and it perversely follows that he should exalt the oxymoron, the necessary circle ("Criticism is the discourse of the deep tautology," *Anxiety*), the "saving lie." He is more than half-conscious of his own ambivalence toward origins, centers, mothers, oceans, bodies, and he knows that "originality" (like "life" as Freud defines it in *Civilization and Its Discontents*) means fighting against conditions even while questing for them. All this makes one feel that Bloom's real, profoundest subject is *evasion*—the necessary complement of "influence"—a subject that could conceivably take him to the study of novels, except that he appears bored by human relations in anything but the abstract.

Such ambivalence or evasion, at any rate, is the focus of his interpretation of individual poems. As almost always, these interpretations are richly suggestive, and it should be clear by now that Bloom stands in a long line of Yale critics who excel at the close reading of poetry. The essays in *Poetry and Repression* are largely concerned with applying or testing the terms and schemes of his theoretical map, while those collected in *Figures of Capable Imagination* (written during the period 1970-74) are more conventional and perhaps, like the essays in *Ringers in the Tower,* more conventionally satisfying. My personal favorites are the brilliantly etymological analysis of Blake's "London" in *Poetry and Repression* and the fascinating, affectionate, wry consideration of Coleridge—that "high-jumper of the Sublime"—in *Figures*. In *Poetry and Repression,* as I indicated earlier, Bloom uses his quasi-Freudian method to suggest how a poet's manifest intentions tend to be undermined by repressive processes. Thus, he argues interestingly, the deep subject of "Tintern Abbey" is memory—"the one great myth of [Wordsworth's] antimythological poetry"—memory as a defensive "lie"

against time, which is to say against the looming figure of Milton. He observes in the poem a struggle, similar to one in Blake's "London," between "prophetic voice" and "demonic writing," between hearing and seeing, a struggle "in which visible traces usurp the hopeful murmur of prophetic voice"—"murmur" here subtly alluding to the voice of waters, which, as Bloom has shown in earlier essays, one keeps hearing as "the oceanic sense" throughout Wordsworth's belated—that is, "inland"—poetry. Again Bloom argues for an essentially solipsistic, or "apotropaic," Wordsworth: "the love of that answering subject, nature, is a love that distances and estranges nature." His essay on Tennyson is one the whole more honorific than the earlier essay in *Ringers in the Tower,* though I believe he still slights—not unexpectedly—*Idylls of the King*. His earlier point about Mariana's suffering as "the disease of Romantic self-consciousness" he now elaborates: her sexual anguish is only secondary, a mask for—what else?—influence anguish. No bridegroom, real or imagined, could ever assuage this malaise, and the inevitable antithetical conclusion is that Mariana the poetess represses an actual controlling desire to remain solitary and narcissistic. His essay on Browning attempts rather briefly to explain his own preoccupation with "Childe Roland" as a fascination for that poem's representation of power, but in my opinion, neither here nor in *Map of Misreading* does he substantially add anything to his dazzling interpretation of Roland's "Gnostic" quest in the well-known essay in *Ringers*. There is a discussion of "Song of Myself" in his essay on Emerson and Whitman, where once again he tries to show the latter battling against the specter of the former. Whitman's swerve takes the form of denying Emerson's distinction between Soul and Nature, leading him to "overproclaim" the body:

> The "real me" or "me myself" in Whitman could not
> bear to be touched, ever, except by the maternal trin-
> ity of night, death, and the sea, while Walt Whitman,
> one of the roughs, learned from Emerson to cry:
> "Contact!"

Blooms adds, extraordinarily: "Emerson had no sexual problems," while "Whitman, gloriously and plangently, always had much too much to say about sex and death." One cannot help wondering if the easy confidence of these assertions—"much too much"—conceals some deep uneasiness with "sex and death" in the critic himself.

What is one to make of interpretations that a priori refuse to take a writer "at his word?" Surely it is possible to object that Wordsworth and Whitman, to mention the most obvious examples, are being distorted here. Although in *Figures* Bloom refers in passing to "the primordial, Tolstoyan power" in Wordsworth, as manifest in poems like "Michael" and "The Old Cumberland Beggar," he prefers, as I have indicated, to portray the poet as an alienated visionary and a solipsist, dismissing as mere rhetoric, so to speak, the passage in "Tintern

Abbey" about half-creating and perceiving, and never dealing with a strong anti-solipsistic poem like "Peele Castle." By the same token, could not one accurately as well as persuasively read in the tropes of "Song of Myself" an underlying rhetoric or "drift," such that "pointing" becomes a kind of "infolding" and "embracing" a kind of "launching," such that "singing" becomes a "gathering" and "listening" and "mimicking"? Doesn't it seem more interesting to talk about this poem as an *invocation* (with all the far-reaching implications of this term that Heidegger discusses in *What is Called Thinking*?), a musical meditation on the very idea and bodily process of voice, voicing, giving voice to? There may well be a visionary Whitman in later poems like "Passage to India," but certainly "Song of Myself" is still "in nature."

Bloom's interpretations suggest how we keep having recourse to *masks* in our relations with others, including the Others that people our imagination.
—*Howard Eiland*

At the very least, Bloom's interpretations suggest how we keep having recourse to *masks* in our relations with others, including the Others that people our imagination. It is striking, in fact, how so many of his interpretations come to sound like *exempla* for the Nietzsche who writes, in his most movingly deconstructive work, *Beyond Good and Evil,* of "an irresistible distrust against the very possibility of self-recognition"—the Nietzsche who was an "aesthetic man" despite himself; striking, moreover, how so many of Bloom's texts come to echo, not only one another, but Nietzsche's stoical masked inquiries into himself:

> Wanderer, who are you? I see you going your way, without scorn, without love, with unfathomable eyes, damp and sad like a plummet which has returned to the light from every depth without finding satisfaction. What was it seeking down below? I see your breast which does not heave, your lips that hide their nausea, your hands which are slow to touch anything—who are you? What were you doing? . . . What will serve to refresh you? Just name it . . . . What? What? Tell me! "Another mask! A second mask!"

If we look closely, we can see a general pattern running through most of Bloom's interpretations: initial anxiety and debilitating self-consciousness, after reaching an abysmal nadir, gradually give way to an upward surge of creative power, by which a new mask, a more confident self, is constituted in the very act of articulating this sense of power. No doubt I simplify—or misread—grossly. My purpose nevertheless is to indicate how closely Bloom's portrayal of poetic creation resembles Nietzsche's conception of self-overcoming, and how intimately both of these theories turn about the familiar dichotomy of self-consciousness and belief. Nietzsche's philosophy can be seen very broadly as an analysis of the nihilistic and entropic consequences of Western individualism, what Nietzsche calls "the Alexandrian spirit": the detachment of the individual from the organic or mythic or universal by means of an increasingly scientific and historical self-consciousness. As a solution to the impasse brought about by "the *principium individuationis,*" which is precisely the impasse of "belatedness," Nietzsche paradoxically proposes, as we know, an even more radical individualism, a deeper questing into the abyss of self for the sources of all man's heretofore falsely conceived "objective" values. The quester "misreads" God as subjectivity; he "introjects" the idea and image of divinity. Self overcoming means "self-begetting." The superman is a "saving lie."

With its roots specifically in Schopenhauer's paradoxical notion of the Will's deliverance from itself into Knowledge, and in Kleist's equally paradoxical notion (in his essay on the Puppet Theatre) of a "later reason" both self-conscious and spontaneous, Nietzsche's conception of self-overcoming is, after all, only a climatic instance of a perennial "modern" preoccupation with descent and regeneration, inevitably combining a "nostalgia for origins" with a skepticism toward the possibility of ever transcending time or language. All such preoccupations revolve around the myth of a fall from original integrity of Being; they all simultaneously celebrate and lament what Erich Heller—another brilliant, aphoristic, perhaps more classically lucid, Nietzschean critic—has called "the tragedy of knowledge." Bloom is quite explicit in his use of the myths of fall and regeneration, and, like Heller before him (compare *The Ironic German: A Study of Thomas Mann*), he argues for a continuity between "Romantic" and "Modern" as both essentially *Gnostic*. What we have here, I believe, is nothing other than the controlling myth of "High Modernism," a grand composite trope (indeed, by now a cliché) extending from the Gnostic Faust of the Renaissance to the failed Faust, Stephen Dedalus, with his phobic dreams of flight and his looming phantoms and his embarrassed theories of self-begetting, on to the Nietzschean Faustus of Thomas Mann's late novel, which, as Bloom has noted in ***Anxiety of Influence,*** has as its conscious, all-too-conscious subject the spiralling difficulty of belatedness, and the hoped for "breakthrough." That this mythic complex of ideas is not really or exclusively *modern* but rather is rooted in the dualistic strains of earlier systems of thought, is made clear by the researches of Bloom and others into Kabbalah, Gnosticism, Manicheanism, Neoplatonism, Orphism, Shamanism, and so on back into the obscurities of the past. These philosophically poetic systems can all be viewed as figural anticipations of Romanticism/Modernism, or rather as the moving image of itself which Romanticism eternally casts. They bespeak a permanently recurring "antithetical" strain in human thought, antithetical in the sense of being "eternally hungry," not at home in the body or nature, temperamentally bent on transcendence (whether religious or aesthetic—and the distinction ultimately is unreal), incurably—though uneasily—condescending to the *Leopold* Blooms of the world. (Which is perhaps to say that in truly representative literature this higher strain usually co-exists with a less apocalyptic one.) Writers such as Heller and Bloom, both of whom tend to interpret particular texts as revealing "moments" in a more general psychic drama—a journey into the interior, a narrowing struggle for priority—such writers may be seen as literary critical embodiments of this High Modern mythic tradition. And in the case of Bloom, one must ask whether the anxiety he describes so compulsively is not finally the "Alexandrian" anxiety of the ambitious *critic* who is not a poet.

Alvin Rosenfeld (essay date Summer 1977)

SOURCE: "'Armed for War': Notes on The Antithetical Criticism of Harold Bloom," in *The Southern Review,* Vol. 13, No. 3, Summer, 1977, pp. 554-66.

[*In the following essay, Rosenfeld explores the various influences involved in the development of Bloom's antithetical criticism of poetry.*]

> A good critic . . . is armed for war. And criticism is
> a war, against a work of art—either the critic defeats the work or the work defeats the critic.
> —Jacob Glatstein

It is a duty of critics, as Harold Bloom has recently defined it, to make a good poet's work harder for him to perform, for it is only in the overcoming of genuine difficulties that strong poetry emerges. A corollary of this view—never stated as such but clearly implicit in Bloom's writings—is that a critic should do his work in such a way as to make a *reader's* work also more difficult for him to perform, and for much the same reasons, namely, to achieve interpretations strenuous enough to be adequate to the age. "Strength" is a central term in Bloom's critical vocabulary, just as it is the goal of all of his intellectual labors. The designation "reader" must, in this case, apply to the professional reader—fellow critics, among whom Bloom values, and increasingly seems to write almost exclusively for—those relatively few "deep readers" of poetry who, in various independent ways, are attempting to formulate a theory of literature that might serve as the basis for a new practical criticism. Certainly that is Harold Bloom's aim, yet those who have been encountering him in his latest and most difficult phase, more often than not, have been finding him perplexing and extravagant in his views, with the result that Bloom has emerged as not only the most powerful but also

the most provocative and controversial critic of the day. More and more, in fact, the argument over his theories is set forth in personal terms: is Harold Bloom truly "brilliant" or just "mad"; "outrageous" by temperament or willfully "offensive" to the rest of the profession; "serious" or merely "putting us all on"?

Bloom's reply to such questions—and they are increasingly *ad hominem* in nature, increasingly polemical—is perhaps the most outrageous thing of all: *he writes another book. The Anxiety of Influence* (1973), the small volume that first presented the author's formulations of an antithetical criticism, was followed two years later by the companion volume. *A Map of Misreading* (1975), an effort at developing a new practical criticism based on a revisionist theory of poetic creation. If the first volume provoked a good deal of dismay in academic circles and generated a controversy in criticism rather rare in recent times, the second one heightened perplexity and exacerbated the dispute. For in *A Map of Misreading* Bloom not only extended his earlier view that "the meaning of a poem can only be another poem" but pronounced against the very existence of the poem itself: "there are *no* texts, but only relationships *between* texts." In an attempt to discover and clarify the intricate nature of these relationships, Bloom developed, in *The Anxiety of Influence*, a set of six "revisionary ratios" that might aid the critic in traversing "the hidden roads that go from poem to poem." In the companion volume, these ratios were not only tested in a series of close readings of individual poets but drawn together into a "map of misprision," where they combined with coordinating sets of psychic defenses, poetic images, and rhetorical tropes to form the most elaborate apparatus for literary interpretation given us since the early work of Northrop Frye. Bloom's affinities with Frye have often been noted, but inasmuch as his evolving subject is now clearly in the realm of psychopoetics, or the philosophy of composition, he seems closer at this point to Kenneth Burke, our most gifted and perhaps most advanced rhetorician to date. Finally, though, Bloom seems destined to find a direction for his work independent of both Frye and Burke, a direction quite possibly that will move him to approximate or even partake of the most formidable system of textual commentary yet devised—Bible commentary, or, as Bloom would understand it, interpretation as a struggle for priority with Text Itself. This prospect was hinted at in *A Map of Misreading* when the author turned to Lurianic Kabbalism as "the ultimate model for Western revisionism from the Renaissance to the present" and stated his intentions for further study along just these lines. With *Kabbalah and Criticism* (1975) and *Poetry and Repression* (1976) he has sought to make good on these promises.

Bloom has set himself a three-fold task in *Kabbalah and Criticism:* one, to offer an exposition of the rich but complex system of Kabbalistic thinking; two, to relate this thinking, and especially that branch of it formulated by Isaac Luria, to a theory of reading poetry; and three, to explain and defend the adoption of a Kabbalistic model for literary interpretation and to show its value for the practice of an antithetical criticism.

Antithetical criticism is a means of understanding poetry from within the long tradition of poetic history, which is to say, it is a non-reductionist attempt at appreciating poetic lineage. Poems, as Harold Bloom would have us see them, descend from and are "about" other poems before they arise from and are about the poet's reactions to life; as such they share a "family relationship" not unlike human relationships. To grasp the essential character of poems, therefore, it becomes necessary to perceive a poetic text in terms of its formative precursors—those antecedent and influential texts that help to shape and misshape the literature that follows them. Creation is always a function of influence, and the "anxiety of influence" suffered by later poets in relationship to their forebears is the hidden but motive force behind all poetry. Bloom sees this anxiety of influence as especially acute in the Post-Enlightenment period, where to write poetry at all means to wrestle for living space with the mightiest of the dead—principally Milton and Wordsworth in the British line, Emerson and Whitman in the American line—who among them not only defined but largely occupied the central ground of poetic tradition. Those who come after suffer the limitations of an inevitable belatedness, which they try to throw off in complex but identifiable ways. It becomes the goal of criticism to perceive and explain these moves to resist or offset a crippling influence, to expound poetry's life struggle with its own grand but limiting past. Antithetical criticism, dedicated to observing and clarifying the procedures of influence as it forms and malforms poets, is Harold Bloom's important theoretical contribution to such a practical criticism.

Bloom, an uncommonly learned and prolific scholar, has worked ambitiously in these four books to formulate and refine his ideas, yet it must be stressed that his theory is still very much a theory-in-progress, one beset by its own searchings and anxieties. The thinkers who have contributed most to it are Vico, Nietzsche, and Freud. But while these continue to exert their influence, it is apparent that Bloom has been attempting of late to assimilate a more ancient system of thought, namely Gnosticism—more specifically, Jewish Kabbalism. Why align criticism with the Kabbalah? Because, in Bloom's view, Kabbalah, while generally valued as a form of mysticism, is most interesting as the embodiment of "a theory of writing" and, as such, "offers both a model for the processes of poetic influence, and maps for the problematic ways of interpretation." Accordingly, the author sets out in *Kabbalah and Criticism* to investigate the Kabbalistic system in terms of its rhetoric, to see it even as a *theory* of rhetoric, a mode of speculation whose ultimate importance lies less in the doctrines it announces than in the stance it takes against "not only a closed Book but a vast

system of closed commentary." More than anything else, it was the ability of the Kabbalists to accept such a formidable system of canonical texts and, at the same time, to find the means for an independent spiritual assertion that moves Bloom to admiration in this book.

> **In Bloom's view, Kabbalah, while generally valued as a form of mysticism, is most interesting as the embodiment of "a theory of writing."**
> —*Alvin Rosenfeld*

Basing himself on the life work of Gershom Scholem, as any student of this subject must, Bloom offers brief but reliable and wholly readable accounts of the evolution of Kabbalah from the *Sefer Yezirah* ("Book of Creation") and the *Sefer ha-Bahir* ("Book of Brightness") to the masterpiece of Jewish esoteric thinking, the *Sefer ha-Zohar* ("Book of Splendor"). Along the way he registers lucid and personally-felt appreciations of Moses Cordovero (1522-1570)—"the best example of a systematic thinker ever to appear among the Kabbalists"—and his pupil, Isaac Luria (1534-1572)—"the archetype of all Revisionists." The burden of exposition in this part of the book is carried with remarkable ease, and the resulting essay will stand for many as a most convenient and clarifying brief introduction to Kabbalah. Bloom works his way knowingly through powerful but recondite texts to offer an explanation of the ten *Sefirot,* the mystical names or emanations of God, in terms of poetic images and rhetorical tropes. To Bloom, the *Sefirot* are, in fact, very much like poems, and since to him poems are essentially commentaries on or readings of earlier poems, he advocates an appreciation of Kabbalism as among "the first Modernisms." The characteristic impulse in Modernism, as Bloom understands it, is revisionism, in this case "a reaction to the double priority and authority of both text and interpretation, Bible and the normative Judaism of rabbinic tradition." The importance of Kabbalah and its interest for literary interpretation, therefore, are to be found in the answers it managed to give to an abiding question, one that all new creativity of whatever kind must struggle with:

> The Kabbalists of medieval Spain, and their Palestinian successors after the expulsion from Spain, confronted a peculiar psychological problem, one that demanded a revisionist solution. How does one accommodate a fresh and vital new religious impulse, in a precarious and even catastrophic time of troubles, when one inherits a religious tradition already so rich and coherent that it allows very little room for fresh revelations or even speculations?

Accepting the challenge of this dilemma—and in terms of

poetic tradition every new poet must face something similar to it—the Kabbalists "developed implicitly a *psychology of belatedness,* and with it an explicit, rhetorical series of techniques for opening Scripture and even received commentary to their historical sufferings, and to their own, new theosophical insights." The genius of this development, and consequently the hero of *Kabbalah and Criticism,* is Isaac Luria, whose revisionary theory of creation as a *regressive* process is adopted by Bloom as "the classic paradigm upon which Western revisionism in all areas was to model itself ever since."

Just what was the system that Luria worked out? In brief, it stated that the world came into being as the result of a divine contraction—in Hebrew, *zimzum,* or God's withdrawing into Himself. What fell off or remained after this event was world—in Kabbalistic terms, an unredeemed fragment or vessel of divinity. Luria and his followers thereafter introduced an involved ethical system to coordinate with this startling version of genesis-as-catastrophe, but since Bloom's subject is origins and not ethics, he chooses to concentrate attention solely on the processes of creation. Nevertheless, he does adapt the ethical language of Lurianic Kabbalah to his concerns with writing and the problems of original genius and introduces two more basic terms to the discussion— *shevirat ha-kelim* and *tikkun,* the breaking apart and mending, or restitution, of the vessels. Taken together with *zimzum,* these comprise, in Bloom's summation and translation of Luria, a triple rhythm of "limitation, substitution, and representation," the model of Bloom's own dialectic of revisionism and, as he sees it, "the governing dialectic of Post-Enlightenment poetry."

The claim will startle, both for its boldness of assertion and its extravagant esotericism. Most poets and readers of poetry, after all, will never have heard of Isaac Luria; how then can Harold Bloom possibly expect them to give assent to Luria's sudden centrality? Bloom is willing to answer that question, but only in terms of his own working formulations of poetic influence. Digesting these from several separate passages this is what results:

> The center of my theory is that there are crucial patterns of interplay between literal and figurative meanings in post-Miltonic poems, and these patterns, though very varied, are to a surprising degree quite definite and even over-determined. What determines them is the anxiety of influence . . . . I do not say that these patterns produce meaning, because I do not believe that meaning is produced *in* and *by* poems, but only *between* poems . . . . A modern poem begins with a *clinamen* that depends upon the renunciation of an earlier poem . . . . The creation through contraction of an internalized precursor text, which is the Kabbalistic mode, is precisely the dia-

lectical mode of belated or Post-Enlightenment poetry . . . . The hidden roads that go from poem to poem are: limitation, substitution, representation; or the dialectic of revisionism.

To chart these hidden roads as they move through English poetry—from the great Romantics; through the major Victorians; to the American giants Emerson and Whitman; and finally to their modernist inheritors, Yeats and Stevens— Bloom has given us *Poetry and Repression,* a mapmaker's guide to poetic revisionism. The subject of this book is once more the psychopoetics of literary origins, although this time Bloom depends somewhat less on the Kabbalistic model of creation than he does on some of the theories of Nietzsche and Freud. His method is that of antithetical criticism, although by now this has become far more than a procedural means of literary investigation and amounts to a hermeneutical passion; indeed, Bloom has moved from an initial position that asserted the usefulness of an antithetical *approach* to the study of poetry to a point where he now views poetry in the Post-Enlightenment period as possessing an essentially antithetical *character.* One major consequence of this shift is that, more and more, the distinctions between poet and reader have begun to dissolve. As he stated it in *Kabbalah and Criticism,* the "ephebe's [or later poet's] misreading of the precursor is the paradigm for your misreading of the ephebe," a formula that renders all poetry a kind of errant criticism and all criticism, errant poetry. In his own words, which upon reflection are not in fact as mystifying as they may first appear, "reading is mis-writing and writing is mis-reading." The most notable element in *Poetry and Repression,* however, and the one that is certain to trouble most readers of the book, is its strongly deterministic stance, as illustrated in such assertions as these:

> In studying poetry . . . we are studying a kind of labor that has its own latent principles, principles that can be uncovered and then taught systematically . . . . [The patterns of any poem] are as definite as those of any dance, and as varied as there are various dances. But poets do not invent the dances they dance, and we *can tell* the dancer from the dance . . . . I am afraid that there does tend to be one fairly definite dance pattern in Post-Enlightenment poetry, which can be altered by strong substitution, but still it does remain the same dance.

Attendant upon this view, Bloom sets out, in a series of intricate readings, "to uncover the pattern of revisionism" in key poems by ten different authors. His aim in each case is to "trace the network of ratios, tropes, defenses, and images" in the poems and, in such a manner, to answer the question that he finds at the center of all new poetic creativity: "*What is being freshly repressed*? What has been forgotten, on purpose, in the depths, so as to make possible this sudden elevation to the heights?" Such questions arise inevitably because "a poem's true subject is its repression of the precursor poem." What necessitates this repression? The fact that "poetry lives always under the shadow of poetry," so that in order to come into being at all, a new poem must find the means to translate its own belatedness into an earliness, must necessarily contend with and attempt to neutralize or escape the overriding power of priority. The history of poetry, in this view of it, is "an endless, defensive civil war," in which new poets engage the strongest of their precursors in a contest for and against canonization, "the final or transumptive form of literary revisionism."

Since Bloom understands poems themselves as "acts of reading"—instances not so much of fresh writing but of *re*writing—he turns his major attention to what he perceives to be the essential intertextual relationships that comprise poetry. Thus, in interpreting the well-known lyric "London," Bloom focuses on Blake and Ezekiel, the biblical text identified as the crucial antecedent for Blake's revisionary or antithetical poem. In the cases of Wordsworth, Shelley, and Keats, the dialectical pairings are with Milton; in the case of Tennyson, with Keats; of Browning, with Shelley; of Yeats, with Browning, Blake, and Pater, etc. Bloom's emphases throughout are on the way poems originate and behave, or rather misbehave, for he has posited misprision as a basic principle of poetic existence and likes to concentrate particularly on the necessarily *wayward* behavior patterns of poems vis-a-vis their precursors. The results of his interpretive mappings are time and again startling, especially as he contends with works so central to the tradition that not only they but by now some of their readings have become "received" as basic. It is certain that there will be arguments with Bloom's analyses of such poems as "London" and "Tintern Abbey," "Prometheus Unbound" and "Song of Myself," for following his persistently revisionist impulse, Bloom has pitted himself, strength for strength, against all previous commentators on these works— including the earlier Bloom! The largest point of issue will come, however, not so much over particular differences in opinion between Bloom and other critics but over the method chosen to study poems in *Poetry and Repression*.

For it is clear that Bloom has turned away from the admirable insistence to avoid all reductionism in criticism, first voiced in *The Anxiety of Influence*, to a critical practice that now demands reduction—in this case to his network of "ratios, tropes, defenses, and images," as well as to certain fixed areas in which he finds poetic language invariably centering itself: "presence and absence, partness and wholeness, fullness and emptiness, height and depth, insidedness and outsidedness, earliness and lateness." These, he concludes, "are the inevitable categories of our makings and becomings," and although individual poets can give them a various emphasis, none can escape them. The dance pattern may alter, but it does remain the same dance.

The new gains for Bloom's practice as a critic must be carefully weighed against the losses, for while his critical cartography does unquestionably allow him some exceptionally challenging insights, it also tends to break down into the formulaic repetitions of a new jargon and, hence, to become monotonous; worse yet, it threatens to make the poetry itself appear severely limited and monotonous. Bloom would contend, of course, that it is not his interpretive method that restricts poetry but the consequences of poetry's own belatedness. This assertion will not easily be accepted by most readers, who will rightly resist the tendency to flatten poems into predetermined schemes, however ingeniously conceived. More than anything else, it is this reductionist, or algebraic, character of Bloom's critical method that must be questioned.

What accounts for it? Is reductionism an unavoidable consequence of Bloom's critical revisionism? At the time of *The Anxiety of Influence*, it seemed not to be, but, with the publication of *Poetry and Repression*, a book that completes a tetralogy of the author's studies in antithetical criticism, we are confronted by such an unexpected and sorrowful acknowledgement as this: "All reading is translation, and all attempts to communicate a reading seem to court reduction, perhaps inevitably." If that is so, then why reduce to the Kabbalistic paradigm and not some other?

Bloom reached this dilemma, it seems, when he turned to a hermeneutical principle that projects the reader as a commanding, even controlling, figure in the life of poetry—the critic suddenly elevated to a level that acknowledges him as equal in importance to and virtually one with the creator. That is a Gnostic turn—Gnosticism being in this case a defense against the blinding force of textual antecedence and a challenge to its authority. In the history of literature, there is only one Text with that kind of overpowering force, just as there is only a single Creator grand enough in conception to be responsible for it. Gnosticism, whose *stance* Bloom values as the central model for literary interpretation, was a thrust against this primacy, an exercise of the will-to-power over the Prime Precursor Himself. In its Jewish expression, the Kabbalah, this strain of revisionary defiance was greatly feared by the rabbis, who correctly understood its antinomian impulses. For to the Gnostic, knowledge is always knowledge of origins, ultimately *a rival claim* upon origins, which in human terms inevitably means an attempt to transform man into God. The means to this magical and forbidden end? A radical or revisionary hermeneutics, interpretation conceived as an effort to reach some equivalence with Original Text through substitution or displacement.

Now what, it can legitimately be asked, does all of this Jewish esotericism have to do with English and American poetry? In Bloom's case, just about everything. What, after all, is the ambition of "strength" in his work if not to reach an equality of power and place with textual priority? In his own words, "according to the strong reading, it and the text are *one*." A Talmudist could never say that, but a Kabbalist (at least in Bloom's conception of him) could and does say *only* that. The issue, once more, is one of stance—the Talmudist arguing for the maintenance of a proper piety, the preservation of some human distance from not only a canonized Text but a canonized Commentary; while the Kabbalist must argue—in revisionary, antithetical, and finally anti-textual terms—that the Text is no more than the mirror of his own making, his own *mis*-making, as Bloom likes to call it, his Necessary Error. Reduced to the secular plane, here is how Jacob Glatstein, the modernist Yiddish poet, formulated one side of this ongoing contest between reader and text: "The poet writes not only his poem, but in fact also his own criticism. The critic only transcribes the poet's criticism of himself, rewrites it and expands it. The poet puts the words in the critic's mouth, and tells him: 'This is what you will say.'" One can hardly imagine a situation more intolerable than this for a critic of Harold Bloom's disposition and drive. To accept the attitude of *secondariness* implicit in these words is tantamount to accepting servility, which may be all right for the pious but clearly is all wrong to one who maintains, with Bloom, that "a theory *of* poetry must belong *to* poetry, must *be* poetry, before it can be of any use in interpreting poems."

Now Bloom knows that criticism, however imaginative or "inspired," is *not* poetry, and that if it aspires to the condition of poetry, it is bound to find itself locked in a futile and unequal conflict which *it* can never win. If poets are not as self-begotten as they would have us and themselves believe—and no one has argued more forcefully and persuasively against the idealization of poetic origins than Harold Bloom—critics are even less independent and self-originating. It is in the nature of things that the critic depends upon and follows a primary text—for most critics, a normal enough state of affairs and the cause for no special anxiety. Yet just as there resides a *critic* within the soul of every powerful *poet*—a proleptic or forward-vaulting spirit that wants to dictate to others the interpretations of its own makings—so there resides a *poet* within the soul of certain powerful *critics*—a restless, contentious sprite that looks to traduce poetry and make of it a mere illustrative metaphor for theory or interpretation. Bloom is such a critic, one who comes to his work armed for war, for he understands that reading is "always a defensive process," even a form of "defensive warfare," a counter-thrust against an antecedent hegemony of mind that condemns the reader to the melancholy position of one-who-comes-after. In visionary or intellectual terms, that is tantamount to being expelled from paradise. No wonder, then, that Bloom has aligned himself with the Kabbalah, a paramount part of the elaborate Jewish defense system against expulsion and exile.

In adopting Kabbalah as a metaphor for the act of reading—reading here understood as an attempt to reclaim centrality

by *undoing* the priority, autonomy, and singularity of text—however, Bloom has courted not only hyperbole but reduction. While he has revealed much of the heretofore unknown dynamics of the intertextual, he has overleapt the bounds of the critically plausible by denying the legitimacy or even the existence of individual texts. On the strictly literal, even grammatical, level, he would surely acknowledge that there are both poems *and* relationships between poems. On this same level, he would have to grant as well the obvious and more sober distinctions between poetry and criticism, an acknowledgement that must see reading for what it is—an act that necessarily, even if reluctantly, follows upon the act of writing. Bloom has convincingly argued that the writer is a kind of reader, that there is no creative work that is not also interpretive, but that is not the same as proving that a critical reading of a poem, however "strong," and the text are *one*. To argue that point is to make a claim for solipsism—a claim not only for survival but for the solitary and exclusive right to survive. Poets, as Bloom has by now amply demonstrated, *may* be solipsists of this order, at least at their most "anxious," but there is no reason why critics *must* be, unless, of course, the poets within them become anxious for a fuller and freer release than they normally enjoy.

In adopting Kabbalah as a metaphor for the act of reading, . . . Bloom has courted not only hyperbole but reduction.
—Alvin Rosenfeld

Actually, if Bloom is able to adjust his new hermeneutics a bit—modify his sense of the reader's ability to affect or determine meaning in poetry—he can retain the major emphases of antithetical criticism and perhaps escape the cul-de-sac of reductionism into which he has recently been led. Moreover, he can continue to do this form within the sphere of Jewish thinking—and from his earliest adaptations of Buber to his more recent expropriations of Luria and Freud his work is recognizably Jewish in its origins—a thinking which, in the Post-Biblical period, he correctly recognizes to be predominantly interpretive and commentative.

Biblical hermeneutics, in its most normative Jewish expression, maintains a continual dependency of text upon commentary, commentary upon text. To be sure, the world and all that flows from it rests upon the centrality of Torah, but far from being a closed text, the Torah remains open to study and commentary, without which it simply cannot exist intelligibly or be transmitted through the generations. "No interpretation of the Bible of the various traditional kinds," as Simon Rawidowicz has written, "means no expansion, no continuation of the *people* of the Bible." Consequently, "*interpretatio* is Israel's *creatio continua* . . . . *Interpret or perish* is the voice Israel hears incessantly since Sinai." According to at least one line of rabbinic thought, God Himself, the eternal Creator, is also an "eternal learner," whose passion it is to study the teachings of His interpreters. In a fine revision of Leviticus 19:2 that must delight any critical heart, Rawidowicz offers us this imperative: "Ye shall be *interpretatores* for I am an *interpretator*." Interpretation in this view of it is clearly more than an adjunct to text but provides the necessary language for its setting and transmission, its ongoing life.

Nevertheless, while interpretation is invested with an immense authority—to the point where it at times even takes for itself some of the power of the primary source that is its occasion—it can never fully wrest priority of place from the text but must coexist with it in a mutually reinforcing continuum:

> What did God give to Moses and Moses bring to Israel? A "text" for *interpretatio;* not a finished, independent, self-sufficient text, but one which is open and has to remain open to *interpretatio;* more than that, one which demands *interpretatio,* obliges Israel to go on interpreting, thus discovering in the process of learning the Torah the duty of *interpretatio;* also of *interpretatio* as a secret of the account Israel was able to give of itself in history.

Rawidowicz, himself a considerable master of interpretation, even if a generally unknown one, has described the dynamics of this interdependency in a way that both illuminates and confirms much of the thrust of Harold Bloom's theory of antithetical criticism while at the same time providing a necessary balance or corrective to it:

> *Interpretatio* lives by crisis in various degrees . . . . [It] can be characterized by a particular attitude of the *interpretator* who struggles between preserving and rejecting some forms or content of the world at his interpretive "mercy," by a tension between continuation and rebellion, tradition and innovation. It derives its strength both from a deep attachment to the "text" and from an "alienation" from it, a certain distance, a gap which has to be bridged. *Interpretatio* is the "way out" when man is compelled to "take it" or "break it."

Within the Post-Enlightenment period, Harold Bloom would say, this "crisis" has heightened to the point where "breaking it" has become the familiar first option to succession, the "way out" of the tradition being a radical one for most aspiring poets. There is much in the four books considered here to bear him out. These writings also contain evidence of a hermeneutical crisis, however, the critic himself subjecting the canonized works of poetic tradition to a radical "breaking." There is a certain amount of good in that, for a closed thing is a dead thing, but the heavy critical determinism that

marks the readings in *Poetry and Repression* seems calculated not so much to revive or "open" poetry as to reduce it, and hence to deprive it of much of its natural primacy. When that happens, when the interpretive stance takes precedence over the text at its mercy, the loss is near total for both.

What is needed now is some greater distance between poem and reader. That need not diminish the authority invested in criticism, which will remain considerable, but it may help to bring back into equilibrium the vitalizing tension that must exist for reading itself to exist—the tension between continuation and rebellion, tradition and innovation, preservation and loss. Bloom has shown us the awesome power of *shevirat ha-kelim*—"the breaking of the vessels." If he can now adjust his critical stance in a way that will allow for restitution, a new power may be his. The most humanizing move at this point would have to be *tikkun*—in critical terms, the restoration of those conditions of possibility that permit the poem to be in the difficulty of what it is to be: a poem among poems, even a poem among commentaries, but also "a thing final in itself and, therefore, good."

Denis Donoghue (review date 15 September 1977)

SOURCE: "Stevens at the Crossing," in *The New York Times Book Review,* September 15, 1977, pp. 39-42.

[*In the following review of* Wallace Stevens: The Poems of Our Climate, *Donoghue provides a brief synopsis of Bloom's theory of poetry and how it applies to Wallace Stevens's poetry.*]

Harold Bloom's new book is not only an interpretation of Wallace Stevens's major poems but a sustained application of the theory of literary history which he first outlined in *The Anxiety of Influence* (1973). It may be useful to recite the theory before considering its bearing upon Stevens.

Bloom's first books were powerful but relatively straightforward interpretations of the major Romantic poets. *Shelley's Mythmaking* (1959), *The Visionary Company* (1961), and *Blake's Apocalypse* (1963) were written on the understanding that the central act of Romanticism is the transformation of natural life into human life. The necessary mode of this transformation is "myth-making, the confrontation of life by life, a meeting between subjects, not subjects and objects." The last phrases indicate that Martin Buber's vocabulary of I-Thou and I-It relations helped Bloom to describe the mythopoeic mode not only in Shelley but in the Romantic poets generally.

I am not sure that he continues to find Buber's terms inspiring. In the preface to the 1969 edition of *Shelley's*

Mythmaking he described his theme as "Shelley's internalized quest to reach the limits of desire." I take this gloss as a revisionist gesture on Bloom's part, pushing the book away from Buber toward an idiom of desire and will. Bloom's *Yeats* (1970) now seems a transitional book, mainly because its chapters on Gnosticism have more to do with Bloom than with Yeats. Gnosticism is marginal to Yeats, but central to Bloom in the development of a theory of literary history which owes more to certain Gnostic texts and the Kabbalah than to its official sources in Vico, Nietzsche, Emerson, and Freud. The gist of the theory is given in Bloom's tetralogy: *The Anxiety of Influence* (1973), *A Map of Misreading* (1975), *Kabbalah and Criticism* (1975), and *Poetry and Repression* (1976).

Since the Enlightenment, according to Bloom, writers have suffered in one degree or another from a feeling of belatedness: born too late, they find everything already said and done.
—Denis Donoghue

Since the Enlightenment, according to Bloom, writers have suffered in one degree or another from a feeling of belatedness: born too late, they find everything already said and done; they cannot be first, priority has by definition, and the indifference of fate, escaped from them. Before the Enlightenment, there was no such anxiety; to Ben Jonson, art was merely hard work, a craft without shadow. Bloom concedes that there are some post-Enlightenment writers whose genius is compatible with nonchalance. Goethe, like Milton, "absorbed precursors with a gusto evidently precluding anxiety." Nietzsche shows no sign of the *Angst* of influence in his relation to Goethe and Schopenhauer. But the shadow is nearly universal. Poets under that shadow are either strong or weak; weak if they merely idealize, strong if they wrestle with their precursor angels and define their genius by that struggle. Strong poets, challenging their precursors, misread them willfully so as to clear a space for themselves. Blake wrestles with Milton, Mailer with Hemingway.

The rules of wrestling are called tropes, they are the official gestures, turnings, strategies, defense mechanisms. Bloom calls them revisionary ratios and describes six of them under the names clinamen, tessera, kenosis, daemonization, askesis, and apophrades. Presumably there are far more than six; the available turns and swerves are as numerous, I suppose, as the tropes of Elizabethan rhetoric. But Bloom's six make a working typology of evasions, a set of exercises by which the new poet, the "ephebe," enters into a tense relation, at once cooperative and aggressive, with his precursor or precursors. Clinamen is the poet's swerve away from his precursor, a corrective gesture to make change possible and desire

continuous; without clinamen, the new poet is doomed to imitation and weakness.

Tessera names the gesture by which the new poet, retaining his precursor's terms, uses them in an independent or heretical sense and thinks of himself as completing the work his precursor left unfinished. Kenosis is a break away from the precursor in a spirit of self-abasement, an emptying of the poetic self. In daemonization the new poet finds something in the precursor's poem which he thinks the precursor did not know. Askesis is self-purgation performed in a special mood; the new poet separates himself from others, including his precursor, and thus attains to solitude. In apophrades the poet holds his poem open at last to his precursor, and we are compelled to feel that he has written the precursor's poem, we find it suffused with his spirit. In *Kabbalah and Criticism* Bloom attempts to relate these revisionary mechanisms to the six active phases or *behinot* of the Kabbalah's *Sefirot*.

It follows that the exemplary poem in post-Enlightenment literature is "the Wordsworthian crisis-poem," which is obsessively turned upon the fear that the poet has lost his imaginative power. In recent books culminating in *Wallace Stevens: The Poems of Our Climate* Bloom has been charting the scenes of crisis in particular poems, marking certain "Crossings" or representative crisis-moments, crucial places where the poet's language leaps the gap "between one kind of figurative thinking and another." He has distinguished three major Crossings—the Crossing of Election, which faces the death of the creative gift; the Crossing of Solipsism, which struggles with the death of love; and the Crossing of Identification, which faces death itself, total death. These crossings are sought in particular poems because Bloom's theory requires them to be there. A major crisis is bound to be mediated through local crises, turns of fear.

The first Crossing is situated between irony and synecdoche, "or psychologically between reaction formation, where one defends against one's own instincts by manifesting the opposite of what one both wants and fears, and turning against the self, which is usually an exercise in sado-masochism." The second Crossing is between metonymy and hyperbole, "or defensively between regressive and isolating movements of one's own psyche, and the massive repression of instinct that sublimely augments one's unconscious or inwardness at the expense of all the gregarious affects." And the third Crossing takes place between metaphor and metalepsis, or "psychoanalytically between sublimation and introjection, that is between substituting some labor for one's own prohibited instincts and the psychic act of so identifying oneself with something or someone outside the self that time seems to stand still or to roll back or forward."

Bloom finds these Crossings most clearly but not solely in Stevens's long poems, especially *The Auroras of Autumn* and

An Ordinary Evening in New Haven; and also in the poet's career as a whole. He points to the Crossing of Election in the Stevens of 1915, "when his first strong poems were written." The Crossing of Solipsism "lasted a long time in Stevens, but its crux was in 1921-22, and it was not resolved until 1934-36." The Crossing of Identification "took place in 1942, and gave him *Notes Toward a Supreme Fiction.*" The later poems, especially *The Auroras of Autumn* in 1947 and *The Rock* in 1950, were resolved on the basis of formulations already reached in *Notes.* Sometimes, as in "Domination of Black," the three Crossings occur in one poem: but not always. Two poems may place themselves at different points or stages along the path of crisis, with correspondingly different recourse to tropes and figures. If the chosen stage is late, presumably the earlier phases are taken for granted: the exact "moment" of the poem depends upon the conjunction of the poet's will and the factors which have provoked it on this occasion. Generally, the Crossings seem to occur in the order in which I have given them.

I have referred to Bloom's sources, but it is more accurate to speak of his models. In **Poetry and Repression** he asserts that "negative theology," even where it verges upon theosophy, provides the likeliest discipline for revisionist or antithetical critics:

> But so extreme is the situation of strong poetry in the post-Enlightenment, so nearly identical is it with the anxiety of influence, that it requires as interpretative model the most dialectical and negative of theologies that can be found.

Kabbalah, especially as mediated through the doctrines of Isaac Luria, provides "not only a dialectic of creation astonishingly close to revisionist poetics, but also a conceptual rhetoric ingeniously oriented toward defense." And in **Kabbalah and Criticism** Bloom refers to "the Gnostic formulation that all reading, and all writing, constitute a kind of defensive warfare, that reading is mis-writing and writing is mis-reading." Of course there are helpful texts nearer home. In several books Bloom quotes the passage in the *Letter about Mallarmé* in which Valéry, writing of influence, says that what a man does either repeats or refutes what someone else has done, "repeats it in other tones, refines or amplifies or simplifies it, loads or overloads it with meaning; or else rebuts, overturns, destroys and denies it, but thereby assumes it and has invisibly used it." As for Vico, Nietzsche, Emerson, Pater, and Freud: Bloom's recourse to these masters is frequent but opportunistic. My own guess is that his true precursor is Blake, and I find the first trace of Bloom's revisionary ratios in his account of Blake's distinction between States and the Individuals in those states. The chapter on Blake's *Milton* in **Blake's Apocalypse** could easily be translated into the idiom of **The Anxiety of Influence.**

Bloom's aim is "not another new poetics, but a wholly different practical criticism." He urges us to learn to read any poem, or at least any strong poem, "as its poet's deliberate misrepresentation, *as a poet,* of a precursor poem or of poetry in general." Criticism is either primary or antithetical. Primary criticism vacillates "between tautology—in which the poem is and means itself—and reduction—in which the poem means something that is not itself a poem." Antithetical criticism denies both tautology and reduction, "a denial best delivered by the assertion that the meaning of a poem can only be a poem, but *another poem—a poem not itself.*" The precursor, according to antithetical criticism, admonishes his ephebe: "Be me but not me." Bloom speaks of "my own addiction to a Romantic and prophetic humanism," but generally he allows his commitments to issue between his lines.

I hope this synopsis of Bloom's theory of poetry will be regarded as fair and decently accurate. Now I want to indicate some of the reservations I would find myself urging in a discussion with Bloom: some of these are so obvious that I would express them only if our discussion neglected to take them for granted.

One: Bloom presents literary history since the Enlightenment as one story and one story only, a struggle of gods and demiurges; the character of the struggle issues from obsession, trespass, defense, and revenge. The only narrative is a "family romance." The story has nothing to say of time, history, the world, society, manners, morals, chance.

Two: Bloom's interest in the poem expires with the disclosure of its plot; it concentrates upon certain disjunctive moments in the poem and insists upon finding there the local phases of anxiety and crisis. His practical criticism is not much concerned with the structure of an individual poem except as an embodiment of crisis; it has little to say of diction, the metres, rhythm, syntax, or tone, it is mainly concerned to isolate the defensive gesture which it anticipates. Like Desdemona, Bloom understands a fury in the words, but not the words; a fury of revisions and evasions directed against the precursor poem.

Three: much of this concentration arises from Bloom's insistence that modern poets are either "strong" or "weak." I cannot see much point in saying that the strong poets are Hardy and Stevens if this means, as it does, that Eliot and, say, Frost are weak. Eliot is weak, presumably, because his relation to Dante was not a Freudian struggle of son against father; it was rather a sustaining relation, based upon Eliot's feeling that "there is no competition":

> There is only the fight to recover
>   what has been lost
> And found and lost again and
>   again: and now, under conditions

That seem unpropitious. But
  perhaps neither gain nor loss.
  For us, there is only the trying. The
  rest is not our business.

For Eliot, "trying to learn to use words" means wrestling with words, with the whole body of the language, rather than with Laforgue, Donne, Milton, Shakespeare, or Dante. Frost is weak, presumably, because his relation to Emerson and William James was not a family romance, a war between rival states of feeling. In *A Map of Misreading* Bloom seems to accept Emerson's principle that literary energy, as Bloom phrases it, "is drawn from language and not from nature, and the influence-relationship takes place between words *and* words, and not between subjects," but in practice by "language" he means not the whole body of speech, the thew and sinew of the language (to use Hopkins's terms), but a precursor's language; he ignores the pressure of the language which did not embody itself in the precursor's poem. The relation between Blake and Milton is clearly remarkable, but it does not account for everything in Blake's language, even in his *Milton*. Bloom's theory is of far more limited application than he claims.

To Bloom, poetry is not a form of knowledge but of action.
—*Denis Donoghue*

Four: to Bloom, poetry is not a form of knowledge but of action. I do not object to this view, but I think Bloom does not take its consequences seriously enough. The explanation is that he refuses to distinguish between will and imagination: will subsumes imagination in every case. Bloom wants to find in the poem an *agon* rather than a structure, so he forces the poem away from knowledge toward action, gesture, and desire. Imposing orders not as he thinks of them but as he has already thought of them, he prescribes one official plot, a crisis to be evaded, resolved, or transcended. The motto is given in the new book on Stevens: "where the will predominates, even in its own despite, how much is there left to know?" But knowing is not the point, despite Stevens's desire "to make a new intelligence prevail." Imagination, Bloom asserts, "as Vico understood and Freud did not, is the faculty of self-preservation." But so is the will; there is no difference. Yeats, who insisted upon the difference, reflected sharply upon situations in which the will tries to usurp the work of imagination.

What is the difficulty with Bloom's procedure? Simply this: if you allow the imagination to be subsumed in will, you set aside or relegate to some Limbo the association of imagination with creativity, the making of poetic objects, signs distinguishable from the poet's self. The basic point here is that

Bloom is not interested in the supposed autonomy of signs or structures. His theory of poetry requires the subordination of imagination to will because it reads the poem only as the figurative manifestation of self. The center of his interest is the self, the poet, the psychic drama disclosed in the poem. He is a psycho-biographical critic, it appears, after all, interested in the poem not as artifact but as evidence. In his aesthetic there is no need to invoke the poetic imagination, since the will is always enough: nothing more than will is required for self-preservation.

Wallace Stevens can be the poet Bloom wants him to be only in the conditions Bloom ascribes to Schopenhauer's account of the Sublime: that is, "when the objects of contemplation have a hostile relation to the will, when the power of objects menaces the will." A strong poem begins when the poet's will feels itself provoked or threatened by an object of attention, a situation in the world at large, a world not ourselves ("Today the leaves cry . . ."), a reified circumstance, the "stale intelligence" of others, an alien landscape, a "litter of truths," but most of all by a precursor poem which tells the poet that he is too late. The will is the self in its resistance. Poetic history is reduced to the story of that resistance: the events in the story are tropes.

Five, and last of these reservations: to Bloom, the entire lexicon of tropes is nothing more than a set of defense mechanisms, and criticism is nothing more than a rhetoric of will. Tropes "are primarily figures of willed falsification rather than figures of unwilled knowledge: there is willed knowing, but that process does not produce poems." In *Wallace Stevens: The Poems of Our Climate* Bloom says that "there are only two fundamental tropes, tropes, of action and tropes of desire." A trope is therefore the will, so far as it translates itself into a verbal act or figure of *ethos;* if the will fails to translate itself, it abides as a verbal desire or figure of *pathos*. The tropical life cannot take any other form.

Bloom's new book is an elaborate exposition of his theory: the gist of his interpretation of Stevens is already available in *A Map of Misreading, Poetry and Repression,* and *Figures of Capable Imagination,* where Stevens is presented as "the authentic twentieth-century poet of the Sublime, surpassing even Rilke in that highest of modes." The main object of the new book is to devise a critical procedure, based upon Stevens's major poetry written between 1942 and his death in 1955, for describing "disjunctions or crossings in the rhetoric of poetry, because Stevens is the most advanced rhetorician in modern poetry and in his major phase the most disjunctive." The richest evidence is in the long poems, especially *Notes Toward a Supreme Fiction, The Auroras of Autumn,* and *An Ordinary Evening in New Haven.* In these poems the Supreme Fiction turns out to be not poetry, as Stevens said, but the poet, "a fiction of the self, or the poetic self as a transumption, an audacious trope undoing all previous tropes." Stevens's chief precursor is Whitman, but he also wrestles with Emerson, and exercises himself upon Schopenhauer, Valéry, William James, Santayana, and others.

His *agon* is the one story of crisis, but it may be regarded as a drama in three acts. In the first act, lest he be charmed or deceived by illusions, the poet reduces the object of attention to what he calls the First Idea, the condition in which the object is merely what it is in its essential poverty. The idea is such because without the poet a sense of the poverty of the object would be impossible; the willed reduction makes the object an idea. This marks the first act of will, and it is deemed to be candid and ascetic. The second act is the discovery that the First Idea is intolerable, the poet cannot live with it, its poverty is monstrous: it is not even the ground of our beseeching, it is not the Truth because if it were we would be content to live with it as animals live with nature. So in the third act the poet reimagines the First Idea, resorts to it again in his full plural humanity; transforms it by a flick of feeling, turns it into an acceptable fiction; acceptable now because he has made it, knowingly and willfully.

What intervenes between the first alien object of attention and the ultimate fiction is the poet's feeling, desire, defense, transgression, will; to the post-Nietzschean Bloom, these are the essential qualities of human life under the shadow of belatedness. Tropes are old strategies, turns which have proved themselves useful: the new poet uses them again, like a dancer going through the official steps but giving them the nuance of his will and grace. Bloom's version of this drama in three acts recites Emerson's terms to say that "Fate in Stevens is the First Idea, Freedom is the realization that the First Idea cannot suffice, and Power or Will is a finding of what may suffice, a revision of the First Idea." The entire book gathers evidence for this reading.

Does this involve distortion of Stevens to make the story come out right? Even if it does, Bloom has already taken out insurance by asserting that misreading and misprision are essential to the strong reader wrestling with his strong poet. But if you decline to be charmed by this assertion, you are likely to report that the book is best, soundest, wisest when it glosses those poems in which the power of objects menaces Stevens's will: "Esthétique du Mal," "The Man on the Dump"; or poems like "Domination of Black" in which Bloom's rhetoric of will and crisis shows that urbanity on the surface is consistent with turbulence beneath. The book is sullen when it has to admit that there are poems in which Stevens's will is gratified rather than threatened by the power of objects: "Evening without Angels," "Nomad Exquisite." In such poems the mind lays by its trouble and relents. Bloom seems bored or embarrassed by the peaceful poems, mostly in *Harmonium,* and in a hurry to see the war taken up again. But it is remarkably invigorating to see Bloom's terms deployed upon a poet like

Stevens who often seems offensively bland. This is Bloom's major skill, or the most formidable consequence of his theory, that the reader of Stevens is forced to register turbulence in poems which seemed to have no other design upon him than to caress him out of thought.

The same reader, however, if he finds himself swerving or clinamening away from Bloom's interpretation, is likely to recall other things that have been said of Stevens and insist upon reciting them. Let me quote three. Blooms' criticism, I have remarked, is not much interested in Stevens's words except as stage directions for an internal drama, but another reader has argued that "if any poems have been simply confected from words, words shaggy, smooth, humdrum, exotic, words stroked and smoothed and jostled, words set grimacing, they would seem to be Stevens's poems." Fine: and here is another sentence: "you will search Stevens's canon in vain for human actions with agents good and bad." And a third extends the second: "In Stevens's world there are no actions and no speeches, merely ways of looking at things."

Now I am not asserting that these three sentences speak the deepest truth about Stevens, but I think it a limitation in Bloom's criticism that it would not allow itself to say, or even to think, any of them. He would veto the first because it would testify to an interest in Stevens's diction and syntax, in the principles by which he chose words and put them together, an interest likely to divert the reader from the *agon* in progress. Bloom would find the second sentence beside the point and its Aristotelianism irrelevant because, according to his interpretation of Stevens, there is only one human action, one agent, the poet himself in the throes of belatedness. The third sentence, "merely ways of looking at things," would be alien to Bloom because it imprisons Stevens in problems of epistemology, a Vaihinger in verse. I have quoted the three sentences, from Hugh Kenner's *A Homemade World,* partly to resist Bloom's rhetoric, an urgent motive because readers of Bloom find it hard to assure themselves that they have minds of their own; and partly to bring forward again some themes which Bloom's antithetical criticism would suppress.

There are wonderful perceptions in Bloom's new book: that goes nearly without saying. I do not know any other critic of Stevens who would say of the comic heroine of the poem "Mrs. Alfred Uruguay" that "she represents what Stevens now knows to be the most dangerous element in his own poetic mind, the Snow Man tendency that says no to everything in order to get at itself." I assume that a lively reader would ask Bloom to describe the danger and to explain why it does not constitute yet another revisionary ratio. Bloom's arguments must be met with the vigor they deserve. One hint to end with: the word "evade" is crucial to his rhetoric, and indeed to his entire theory of modern poetry. Where Hugh Kenner and many other readers are bored with Stevens's long poems and cry out, "Ideas, ideas!" Bloom answers: "No, Stevens never stays philosophic for very long; he is himself only when he is most evasive." And watch out for the same verb two hundred pages later, when Bloom says that "Stevens was a man 'to whom things spoke,' as they spoke to Wordsworth and to Ruskin, but he emulated Ruskin more than Wordsworth in seeking to evade this speaking." Evasion plays no part in knowledge, and is a scandal to epistemologists, but it is crucial if you want to escape or refute your fate. This is Bloom's theme.

Jonathan Arac (essay date Spring 1978)

SOURCE: "The Criticism of Harold Bloom: Judgement and History," in *Centrum*, Vol. 6, No. 1, Spring, 1978, pp. 32-42

[*In the following essay, Arac examines Bloom's earlier works and traces the development of his theoretical stance in order to locate Bloom's "concerns and gestures in the continuing contests of literary criticism."*]

I

Of our critics who have defined their identities in the post-war years, Harold Bloom is one of the most useful. I have learned much from Bloom about reading the poems of the last two hundred years, but such individual readings only extend New Criticism, which Bloom has helped in other ways to bring us beyond. Northrop Frye's archetypal criticism made the totality of literature, rather than the individual poem, the unit of effective wholeness, but Bloom challenges both Frye and New Criticism in opening for exploration a middle range, a human scale: individual poets rather than single poems or all poetry. For understanding the dynamics of literary careers, his work and Edward Said's have been the most useful to me, and for thinking about literary history as made by writers' responses to earlier writers, Bloom and Reuben Brower have offered me the most concrete instances. Bloom's work, however, still lacks any single achievement comparable to *The Mirror and the Lamp, Anatomy of Criticism, John Keats* by W.J. Bate, and *Wordsworth's Poetry* by Geoffrey Hartman. Bloom's work is hard to grasp because it is not systematized. After discovering through Blake how to read all literature, Northrop Frye produced a series of exploratory essays, publishing *Anatomy of Criticism* ten years after *Fearful Symmetry*. Bloom similarly found through Yeats his fundamental insight into the revisionary process, but the result has been a flurry of books, each both amplifying and revising what came before.

I hope to locate Bloom's concerns and gestures in the continuing contests of literary criticism, extending from the current scene and the recent past a long way back. By looking at Bloom's early work for his starting-points and by relating these points to the larger history of criticism, I hope to show of Bloom what he has shown of Shelley: the irrelevance of the esoteric. Like Blake, like Frye, Bloom scorns mystery. To place him in his own tradition, as he did Yeats and Frye did Blake, will help us both to use and to judge Bloom. I therefore avoid the intricate schemes and terms of the recent work, and I rejoice to note that the six revisionary ratios, after being Kabbalistically elaborated, appear in *Wallace Stevens* as transformations of the classical rhetorical "places." The way now lies open for Bloom to prove his "mappings" no more outlandish than the Renaissance studies of Rosemund Tuve or Louis Martz.

To point to a possible absurdity, or self-contradiction, and walk away smiling and wiping one's hands, is the privilege of the press consultant. Once works have appeared and had an impact, it seems necessary to suggest their appeal, their use, and their growing points. The typical attraction of Bloom's writing is assertiveness, the powerful phrase that makes him so fine a writer of introductions as well as of polemics. Let me offer not a slogan but the summary interpretation of Blake's *London* as "a Jonah's desperation at knowing he is not an Ezekiel." Following analysis of the poem's figures and movement in relation to a passage from Ezekiel, this phrase moves out from the poem to a sense of a man and of a history, the history not only of prophetic poetry but also of the English 1790s, when the French Revolution awakened both apocalyptic hopes and the repression that made it worth a person's life to voice those hopes. Blake abandoned voice for the silence and cunning of his art, but at a cost that he felt and that long kept his work from any place in the public life of English poetry. Here I run ahead both of Bloom and my exposition, because Bloom does make you run ahead. I will return to these issues at the end in looking towards a possible future course for Bloom.

Bloom is a fine reader of poems, but does not grind them into bits; rather he finds just the right passage to persuade you of the excellence of a writer or work. Bloom's power of quotation suggests that he is haunted by phrases from his reading and keeps trying to make a context that will give them the full weight he feels they contain. Thus in *Fearful Symmetry*, Frye mentions Lucretian *clinamen* to characterize the fall of Los, which swerves into creation. Years later this term appears as the cornerstone of revisionism. Sometimes, however, the assimilation is less complete and yields dismal pastiche: a full paragraph about Bloom's changed views on Keats wears the language of Wordsworth's *Elegiac Stanzas*. It's like *Play it Again, Sam:* the greatest success is suddenly to be in the position to repeat words you have long hallowed. For a critic, such abdication is costly, but I suspect that thinking about his own need to do this aided Bloom's perceptions about influence.

Such compositional problems, like the boulders from Freud

or Nietzsche that often necessitate detours, all suggest a great virtue: Bloom's "brooding." He is a rethinker. He will not rest with achieved positions, but is always ready to return upon himself. I find admirable energy in Bloom's reformulations in response to others. He shows no sign of closing off before intelligent criticism.

One fascinating movement in Bloom is the drama of reduction, as a Shelleyan skepticism drives him to question, and abandon, his cherished earlier positions. How much can you give up and still have something? Bloom has given up the imagination; from the apocalyptic autonomy of Blake, it becomes an effect of repression or an illusion, Hobbesian "decaying sense." So Blake, prophet of the future, yields as the father of modern poetry to Wordsworth, with his Freudian sense of the past. Bloom once found in Keats and Stevens a naturalistic acceptance of death, but now has lost this consolation. Death is all we have, immortality all we want, and this split is our life. Finally Bloom has also given up the idea that a poem can fulfill an earlier poem or tradition; it can only revise it. Therefore, poetry always declines. Only this cost could buy assurance of poetry's continuation. Culminations exhaust poetic lines, but while falling, one can keep swerving.

What does Bloom keep? In exchange for his losses, Bloom grasps the self. Revisionism has brought "the man who suffers" back into relation with the poem, from which Eliot and Frye alike barred him. Despite many qualifications ("to be a poet is to be an inter-poet"), this notion remains fundamental. The self, the natural embodied person, once Blake's Spectre of Urthona, is now our only defense against two sets of enemies: spiritualists, whose totalized view of tradition would murder all desire by showing a culture complete without us into which we nonetheless mysteriously fit; mechanists, who would disintegrate us into shards of language. Bloom's second possession, held even longer, is Abrams's "heterocosm," the assurance that literature enjoys autonomy as a world elsewhere. These two premises keep Bloom in touch with humanistic traditions and account for much of his appeal. I wonder whether he can maintain them against the Nietzschean and Freudian challenges to the self and against the growing necessity to link literature to history.

II

From this overview, I turn to the historical situation. Bloom enjoys a privileged place in the major critical event of the postwar period: the revival of Romanticism and displacement of New Criticism, a process encapsulated in the books I've cited by Frye, Abrams, Bate, and Hartman. Bloom studied with Abrams at Cornell; has worked with Hartman at Yale; was among the first reviewers of Frye's *Anatomy;* and has carried on in print a continuing dialogue with Bate. Bloom had also to reach terms with New Haven formalism, most

formidably embodied in W.K. Wimsatt, and this necessity may account for Bloom's attention to individual poems in his first three books. The effectiveness of these books as teacherly commentary established the goodwill and authority that made Bloom's voice heard when he launched the revisionary series.

Bloom enjoys a privileged place in the major critical event of the postwar period: the revival of Romanticism and displacement of New Criticism.
—Jonathan Arac

How did Bloom see the critical situation when he began? It was an "odd and unnatural . . . time": "A formidable array of minor poets-turned-critics convinced the academies that twentieth-century verse had somehow repudiated its immediate heritage, and mysteriously found its true parentage in the seventeenth century." Only Yvor Winter had the "descriptive accuracy" to recognize that "almost all poetry written in English since the age of sensibility . . . was inescapably Romantic," but Winters saw only to condemn.

Bloom's earliest significant collected essay engages at once with this condition. In "Lawrence, Eliot, Blackmur, and the Tortoise" (1958), Bloom sets Frye against the principles and judgments of New Criticism. Through the *Anatomy*'s critique of literary evaluation, Bloom exposes the "social . . . dialectic" informing Blackmur's dismissal of Lawrence. That dialectic systematically excludes the "Protestant, romantic, radical" (Frye's inversion of Eliot). Frye offered a new tradition to oppose that established by the New Critics: prophecy and romance against wit. Bloom could thereby rescue Yeats and Stevens from New Critical standards and join them to the Romantic tradition.

Three further issues of continuing importance emerge, the first of which is evaluation. From Frye's position, Bloom could scorn Blackmur as "a judicial critic" who "approximates the Arnold of our day" and "ranks poets" into a "new scriptural canon." The need for a canon, for rank and exclusion, motivates Bloom's later break with Frye, after which Bloom calls Frye "the Arnold of our day." Our second issue, then, is "Why Arnold?" which also means "What about the touchstones?" The third issue comes in a question, asked rhetorically, which still awaits Bloom's real answer: "Why should the order of institutions be more valid for poetry than the order of a gifted individual?" At the time of asking, the answer was, it should not be and is not. By now for Bloom the "gifted individual" is involved with other individuals, but the question remains how institutions operate in the canon-formation at which his theory increasingly aims.

I begin, however, with Arnold. To define his significance as a bogey will clarify some of Bloom's premises about literary history. Arnold, I suspect, clearly manifests for Bloom a process that began with Coleridge and runs through Eliot and Blackmur: defeated poets propounding a view of literature that stifles the radical extremities of Romanticism, the individuality of Protestantism. Arnold's career moves in three phases that mark a retreat first from Romantic poetry, then from any poetry. His 1853 "Preface" tries to correct the *practice* of poetry. A poet speaking to poets and reviewers polemically sacrifices his major work and calls upon his fellows to join him in preferring their art to themselves. Such sacrifice brings only further retrenchment in "The Function of Criticism at the Present Time" (1864). Arnold speaks as a critic who by sacrificing the practice of poetry altogether, hopes to establish the preconditions for a future poetry written not out of romantic, individual ignorance but from common knowledge. In "The Study of Poetry" (1880) the writing of poetry disappears. The "future" of poetry is immense, but only as read. The notorious touchstones will free the reader from personal or historical bias by showing the perfect adequacy of Shakespeare and Milton. Arnold shows that to give up Romanticism is to give up the self is to give up any future writing of poetry.

Arnold repeats Coleridge's idolatry of the great dead and his turn to public cultivation. The great lost word for Bloom is Shelley's; his *Defence* is "the most profound discourse on poetry in the language." Strikingly, Bloom's scattered references to the *Defence* bear on time, the future, the process of history, not "platonic" immutability. Shelley offers, indeed, a basis for the "catastrophe theory of creativity" that Bloom now seeks. Poetry in Shelley entails recreative discontinuity: we build our "paradise . . . out of the wrecks of Eden." There is no creation, only transformative reperception. The poet always comes *after*; we compose only when the breeze has already departed, the coal is fading. If Dante forms a "bridge" between ancient and modern poetry, the crossing is strangely discontinuous, for he is also a "Lucifer" whose every "burning atom" bears an even more disruptive "lightning." Shelley hopes for a progressive poetic history, in which all poets contribute to one "great poem," but he fears that the first poem already contains all that poetry offers. Only the endless unveilings of interpretation will make it differ from itself over time. From this aspect of Shelley's theory, which follows from the impossibility of creation, Earl Wasserman concluded, as has Bloom, that poetry is only possible if every poem is a criticism of a previous poem.

In contrast to Shelley, Frye lacks *bite*. There is no negative moment in his understanding of literature. Poetry, like dreams, works through the dialectic of desire and repugnance, but the repugnance is inessential. It only produces the displacements which criticism must undo to reveal the total form of literature as fulfilling desire. Frye is like the early Freud who found

no "no" in the unconscious, only an erotic will to union. But Freud's later instinctual dualism makes aggression as fundamental as eros and thus explains competition and exclusion, the world of Bloom's later work.

Now why do touchstones continue to worry Bloom so? In one of the latest essays in his first collection he cites several passages beside some lines from Ammons but warns that this is "not to play at touchstones, in the manner of Arnold or of Blackmur." Finally, however, Bloom has self-consciously given in. To illustrate Stevens's greatness as a poet of sublimity, he offers some "Arnoldian or Blackmurian touchstones." Why the fuss? This issue marks Bloom's break with Frye and Frye's optimistic view of human nature. Arnold took his touchstones from the *paragoni* of Italian Renaissance criticism, set pieces of comparison that readily became rivaly (*paragone*, from Gr. *parakone*, touchstone, confused with *agon*, struggle, competition). Touchstones set poetry against poetry rather than like Frye integrating poetry with poetry. Furthermore, citation of short passages out of context fragments the unity of a work, violating principles on which Wimsatt and Frye could both agree with Aristotle.

The locus classicus of literature as fragmentary and competitive is Longinus's *On the Sublime*. Longinus helped extricate the Romantics from the dilemmas of eighteenth-century poetry and is crucial to Bloom's new Romantic criticism. Longinus is extravagant and difficult, and since Bloom rarely cites him, many readers do not appreciate his place in Bloom's work. The sublime is disjunctive, a power that "scatters everything before it like a thunderbolt," in a moment. This power derives from the grandeur of the human mind, "the echo of a great soul," and is freed from any natural mimesis. It offers a theory of inspiration that goes back to no divinity. Men become gods to one another, as the "effluences" of past greatness fill the young writer. To achieve full power, however, one must leave such passivity and emulatively combat one's predecessor, as Plato did Homer, "entering the lists like a young champion matched against the man whom all admire." Thus Bloom's agonistic metaphors join a tradition of discourse. Likewise another of Bloom's important, apparently idiosyncratic, notions: the Scene of Instruction. To achieve the sublime, one may conjure up the great past writers as judges and exemplars; the "ordeal" of this ghostly "tribunal" will yield us the power to immortalize ourselves, or will quell us if our spirits are inadequate.

For Longinus the eternity of literature is not dead monuments, empty pyramids that testify to the vain hunger of the imagination; it is human encounter, both pedagogic and competitive, that mysteriously bridges time. Bloom finds the sublime an archaic mode that is nonetheless "always available to us again, provided a survivor of the old line comes to us." Thus the sublime is associated not only with demonization, repression, and hyperbole, but also with the final position in Bloom's map: return of the dead and transumption. This context defines one of Bloom's most provocative undertakings. His analysis of "transumptive allusion" attempts a precise rhetorical explanation of the eternity effect of great literature, since classical times a puzzle more invoked than explored. The Romantic theory of the symbol, and its New Critical inheritors, could only explain this effect metaphysically, through the participation of a temporal part in an eternal whole. Transumption, however, "murders time" only "figuratively." It is only "troping on a trope" and enforces a "state of rhetoricity" at the expense of the "presentness of the present," in contrast to the presence necessary to the symbol. The rhetoric of sublimity allows Bloom to evade the critical line from Coleridge to Blackmur, from which his thought takes its oppositional beginning.

III

From this large view, I turn to Bloom's own career. Read now, *Shelley's Mythmaking* proves astonishingly at one with revisionism in its concerns, though not in its positions. The basis from which Bloom defines and analyzes Shelley's myths, the Buberian personalism of "I-Thou" confrontation, continues to inform the dialectical, "subject-centered . . . person to person" relations of influence, defending against both linguistic reduction (it-it) and the oppressions of tradition (I-it). The work already emphasizes the "corrective competition" between Shelley and Milton, and Bloom hears the uncanny echoing between *The Witch of Atlas* and Yeats's "Byzantium" years before the ratio of *apophrades* could account for it.

Even problems of method in reading emerge reflectively. Yeats's observations on Demogorgon suggest that the "misunderstandings of one great poet by another" are valuable; Wilson Knight exemplifies the danger that criticism may become "independent vision," an "individual and inferior poetry." The term "misreading" occurs often in *Shelley's Mythmaking*, always negatively. *The Visionary Company*, however, begins Bloom's self-revision toward "the necessity of misreading." Robert Graves is "the most persuasive of modern misreaders," "more imaginative" than other critics on Keats's "La Belle Dame." Bloom's first three books maintain his initial loyalty to Frye, but his break begins late in *Blake's Apocalypse*: "I don't believe that Blake's reading of the Bible was as imaginatively liberated as Frye takes it to have been." Since Frye had begun our whole current attention to "reading" by defining the key to Blake as his reading of the Bible, this disagreement is fundamental. Bloom cannot accept Blake's Christian understanding of the New Testament as purifying and completing the Old Testament. From this will follow the general impossibility of "fulfillment" in literary tradition, the recognition that fulfillment involves invidious judgments, that Frye's criticism depends upon decisively evaluating the relation of the two testaments. Thus Frye is a canonizer, another Matthew Arnold.

Yeats, which occupied Bloom for most of the sixties, marks his crisis. He had to recognize his own activity in making the canons of literature. He too was ranking, making judgments, invoking a tradition in order to diminish Yeats by it. His earlier work could be seen as wholly positive (though it has its polemic), offering only descriptive appreciation of misunderstood works. But now like any Leavis—or Arnold—he was engaged in "scrutinoid" revaluation, performing acts not only of love but of aggression toward poetry, undoing much of Yeats in order to clear our view of the Romantics. Revisionism is the means to comprehend and justify the double process by which Bloom discovered what Yeats has done to Blake and Shelley and what he himself was doing to Yeats. Reflection upon this experience would suggest literary history as an activity simultaneously individual and exclusive, competitive and delusive. Elaborating these qualities would produce the apparatus of precursor and canon, Freudian psychology and Nietzschean rhetoric.

Leaving Coleridgean formalism and the archetypes of Frye, Bloom turned source-study "inside out," humanizing it as Frye's Blake had nature. The "organic analogue" yields to the "human analogue": "To say that a poem is about itself is killing, but to say it is about another poem is to go out into the world where we live." My last pages pursue this "world" and question its relation to history, exclusion, power.

No sooner does Bloom offer engagement with the world than he retracts it: "Mature creation, for a poet, rises directly from an error about poetry rather than . . . about life." Some **indirect** process might be crucial and interesting, but not to Bloom. So far is poetry from the world that it "transcend[s] mimesis." Poets confront "not the universe, but the precursors." I await Bloom's promised "literary history as canon-formation," but his positions erode this goal: "There is no literary history . . . only biography," individual "defensive misreadings." No dialectic of "art and society" but only of "art and art" fuels the process of poetry.

Such unwillingness to come to disciplined terms with the world produces the extreme variation of Bloom's claims for the applicability of his theory. At first it was scrupulously limited to post-Enlightenment poetry. So Shakespeare was exempt by living in "the giant age before the flood." But such dualism is obviously mythical, not historical. Discovering the dialectics of influence in earlier contexts forces the alternative, equally unhistorical, assertion of universality. Only precise attention to the place of poetry in society—the opportunities offered for voice, script, and instruction, by whom, to whom and for what purposes—will allow the nuance, detail, and differentiation that make a history, and set proper limits to a theory.

Bloom, however, denies himself the means needed for his end. He has abandoned many idealizations but still maintains that "canon-formation is not an arbitrary process" and therefore "not, for more than a generation or two, socially or politically determined." This is still faith in the mystic agency of Shelley's "redeemer and mediator, Time." To assert that "poets survive because of inherent strength" is to neglect the subordination of the Old Testament to the New, the centuries long suppression of the Gnostics and Kabbalists, Blake's lament, "I am hid." Against such political, social, ideological repression, Bloom insists upon the psychological: "A strong reading is the only poetic fact, the only revenge against time that endures." But what of the material basis of such facts? How do I **enforce** my reading? Such questions fall outside Bloom's thought: "The idea of a 'finished' poem . . . depends upon the absurd, hidden notion that reifies poems from relationships into entities." But what if we replace "finished" with "published"? Isn't such reification exactly what publication performs and what we value it for? Replace "finished" with "censored"; the purity of relationship is compromised by the material vulnerability of the poem's existence. Replace "finished" with "vanished." If its reified traces disappear, we have no relationship at all, except in a Blakean imagination that lets no act of humanity perish.

Bloom knows the kind of thing I'm talking about, and in *A Map of Misreading* his remarks on the current role of American teachers began to work with them, but to no consequence as yet. Bloom's position lacks any imaginative form for organizing what he knows about poetry in the world. For psychology he has Freud as precursor, Lacan as transatlantic contemporary, and Geoffrey Hartman as colleague; for rhetoric, Nietzsche as precursor, Derrida as transatlantic contemporary, and Paul de Man as colleague; for history, Marx and Foucault would make a start. To take on one more reduction, to give up at last the heterocosmic autonomy of literature, will enrich and complicate the story Bloom has to tell and join it fully to the world where we live.

Robert Alter (review date 31 January 1982)

SOURCE: "More Wrestling With Forebears," in *The New York Times Book Review,* January 31, 1982, pp. 8, 14.

[*In the following review, Alter discusses* Agon, *"the latest installment in Harold Bloom's elaborate theory of poetic creation."*]

"As soon as a man begins to see everything," G.C. Lichtenberg observed in an aphorism Harold Bloom sets at the head of an essay on Emerson, "he generally expresses himself obscurely—begins to speak with the tongues of angels." The statement surely applies as aptly to Mr. Bloom as to Emerson, and, indeed, Mr. Bloom is so shrewdly self-conscious a writer

that it seems altogether likely he intended to hint at the personal application.

Agon is the latest installment in Harold Bloom's elaborate theory of poetic creation as a desperate wrestling with forebears, inaugurated in 1973 by *The Anxiety of Influence.* The new volume, it would seem, is a collection of literary and cultural essays written for different occasions, but just as the half-dozen books Mr. Bloom has published over the past nine years are really chapters in one long book (the end of which is not yet in sight), these sundry pieces make one tightly clenched argument, for the author is committed to pursuing the manifestations of a single master idea in whatever he touches. *Agon,* as far as I can determine, does not depart significantly from the doctrine of the earlier books, but in several respects it makes clearer the character and purpose of Bloom's project and in particular what it might mean for him to be a man who "begins to see everything."

To begin with, it is apparent in the new book that Mr. Bloom, despite his notion that both poetry and interpretation emerge from the willful misprision of earlier texts, is not a Deconstructionist. He and his colleagues at Yale, it must be said, have a certain complicity in the general confusion about this, having published together—the other contributors were Geoffrey Hartman, Paul de Man, J. Hillis Miller and Jacques Derrida—a volume called *Deconstruction and Criticism* that hovers ambiguously between being an expression of divergent opinions and, despite a disclaimer, a manifesto of the so-called "Yale School." Mr. Bloom is not a Deconstructionist, because in his vision of literature the personality of the author is primary, the text secondary; writing is always ancillary to voice, and consequently, poetic texts are not merely an endless dance of linguistic signifiers but have a referential aspect, rooted in the experience of the poet and reaching toward the experience of the reader. Language for him is a means of expression, not the basis of an ontology, and in the lead essay of the new volume he speaks with appropriate disdain of "a currently fashionable shibboleth, Franco-Heideggerian and monolithic, that is another usurpation, language-as-Demiurge replacing the self-as-Abyss or even the self-as-Jehovah."

> **Bloom is not a Deconstructionist, because in his vision of literature the personality of the author is primary, the text secondary.**
> **—Robert Alter**

It would seem a peculiarly American literary fate to seesaw between a sense of the self-as-Abyss and of the self-as-Jehovah, with the preponderant weight usually on the Jehovah side, and another aspect of his own enterprise that Mr. Bloom clarifies here is its profoundly American character. "The language of American criticism," he observes, "ought to be pragmatic and outrageous," two qualities his own writing seeks strenuously to achieve. By "pragmatic," I take it that he means opposed to metaphysical theorizing of the Franco-Heideggerian sort and, in particular, something that might be of urgent practical use to the struggling self of the critic and his readers. The outrageousness in Mr. Bloom's stance, perhaps his most winning quality, needs no comment, but I cannot resist offering two brief illustrations:

> "Most of my own readers will have confronted revisionism primarily in their erotic lives, which are quite simply now our spiritual lives."

> "I have come to the conviction that the love of poetry is another variant of the love of power."

The first statement looks like a provocative throwaway; the second is central to Mr. Bloom's whole doctrine, and I should like to reflect on it presently.

The essays of *Agon* shuttle among the major figures of what is obviously conceived of as an American canon. It begins with Emerson, runs through Whitman to Hart Crane and Wallace Stevens, and, latterly, to John Ashbery. If Mr. Bloom were also inclined to grapple with the novel, he would undoubtedly have included Melville and probably Hawthorne, perhaps Faulkner as well, but would have had trouble with Mark Twain and Henry James, just as he has no real place for poets like T.S. Eliot, Ezra Pound, and William Carlos Williams, who do not aspire to what he calls the American Sublime. He makes the refreshing suggestion that his exemplary American texts will prove resistant to deconstruction, an analytic-associative technique honed on the glinting self-referentiality of the poetry of Mallarmé, because both criticism and poetry "in the American grain" affirm "the self over language."

Mr. Bloom's idea of revisionism is, as he is well aware, a radically idiosyncratic theory or, rather, a theory of radical idiosyncrasy as the key to identity and creativity, and this he presents here as an essentially American theme. For the American writer isolation and freedom are absolutely connected, and Mr. Bloom sees in America "the literary culture of the isolate individual, the solitary construer, a Dickinson or Thoreau or Whitman." America becomes the supreme instance of what Bloom calls belatedness. Coming after nearly three millennia of European literary tradition, Americans seek to evade the crushing burden of the past by repeatedly conjuring with the fiction of an absolute beginning, an American genesis, the American self-as-Jehovah, and Emerson is the first revealer of this New World truth. "Emerson's American Gnosis denies our belatedness by urging us not to listen to tradition . . .; he is the authentic prophet-god of discontinu-

ity, of the breaking of tradition, and of reinscribing tradition as a perpetual breaking, mending, and then breaking again."

A good deal of space is devoted to an exposition of Gnosticism, an esoteric doctrine that flourished in the early Christian centuries in certain elite Christian circles and apparently among Jews as well; the most powerful Jewish version of Gnostism, however, surfaced only with the Kabbalistic thinkers of the late Middle Ages and the early modern period. The chief emphasis of Gnosticism was on the mystic knowledge of a paradoxically unknowable God, Who was conceived to be removed from the world we inhabit; the world itself was not His creation but that of an ambiguous or rebellious Demiurge. For Mr. Bloom, the principal appeal of the sundry Gnostic systems is their daring "revisionism"—that is, their assertion of intellectual freedom through a radical reversal of the basic terms of authoritative religious or philosophic tradition, whether embodied in the cosmogony of the Book of Genesis or in Plato's ontology. Mr. Bloom sees Gnosticism as a paradigm of the process of breaking tradition, and has two bold disquisitions on Freud as an inadvertent Gnostic.

It is particularly in these disquisitions on Gnosis that Mr. Bloom speaks in the tongues of angels, in antithetical response to the received body of Revelation which, according to the rabbinic dictum, "spoke in the language of men." What is evident in the new volume is that these theological matters have become increasingly substantive rather than metaphorical for Mr. Bloom. He now speaks of himself as someone "working at the outer limits of literary criticism," and says even more explicitly, "I write this book as a Jewish Gnostic, trying to explore and develop a personal Gnosis and a possible Gnosticism, perhaps even one available to others." Mr. Bloom, trained as a literary scholar and passionately engaged in a certain line of post-Enlightenment literary texts, is less and less a critic or even a literary theorist, more and more a kind of aspiring heresiarch. (He is, however, less grim than this makes him sound; despite his sense of spiritual crisis, he has a good deal of wry self-irony.) As a man who has begun to see "everything"—self and cosmos and will and death in an eternal drama of origins in catastrophe and an effort to overpower one's antecedents—he can discover in any given literary work mainly an illustration of that compelling everything. Denis Donoghue has argued this last point acutely in his recent book, *Ferocious Alphabets:* "Bloom's practical criticism is indifferent to the structure, internal relations, of the poem, or to its diction, syntax, meters, rhythm, or tone: it is chiefly concerned to isolate the primal gesture which the critical paradigm has predicted."

Agon offers occasional exceptions to this stricture, the most extended being the fine essay on John Hollander's "Spectral Emanations," which, despite some rhetorical gestures toward revisionist theory, is precisely devoted to structure, internal relations, diction and so forth. But for the most part, Mr. Bloom, a first-rate critic, knowingly chooses not to practice criticism, and so the moments of real critical illumination are largely accidental, occurring when the submerged structure of the poem happens to correspond perfectly to the Gnostic paradigm, as in some passages from Hart Crane discussed here. Elsewhere, the Bloomian tongues of angels tend to overwhelm the poet's still small voice, which is, of course, what he says criticism should do. When, for example, I read Mr. Bloom on John Ashbery, I find a confirmation of the theory of revisionism that has little to do with my own experience of the poems—in contrast, say, to reading Helen Vendler on Ashbery, where I find my own perceptions given better focus, my imperceptions persuasively called to my attention.

The ultimate issue for me is that the kind of critical exposition I like to read and would like to practice presupposes the existence of a community of shared literary experience, which is to say, literary tradition, while for Mr. Bloom tradition is "the trope of usurpation and imposition," a course of internecine warfare carried out under a facade of continuity. Mr. Bloom's single truth about conflict has considerable explanatory power in regard to certain writers, and it surely has instructed us all that neither literary creation nor interpretation is so innocent as we once thought. But I wonder whether it is really true that all reading and all writing, as he so vehemently argues, are undertaken out of the individual's claustrophobic need to usurp the text and make a place for himself in its stead. Agreeing with Mr. Bloom that most criticism has an aspect of hidden autobiography, I will say that his description does not accord much with my own experience of reading, or with my perception of many eminent interpreters, from Abraham Ibn Ezra on the Hebrew Bible to A.C. Bradley on Shakespeare and Cleanth Brooks on Donne, in all of whom I think I can detect rather a reverence before the astonishing fullness of the text, a patient loving desire to unpack its riches.

As for the possibility of a literary tradition that might be a genuine passing on (Latin *traditio,* Hebrew *masoret*), no one has argued the case more persuasively than Mr. Bloom's friend John Hollander in his 1975 study, "Vision and Resonance." I refer in particular to Mr. Hollander's splendid essay on Ben Jonson, which shows through analysis how Jonson "believed in a vital tradition embracing the poetry of the ancient and the modern worlds" and, shaping a supple poetic corpus through that belief, sought to "create discourse in an ideal community, within which the literary dialect would be as speech." Mr. Hollander's modern instance of this conception of poetry as civilized continuity rather than permanent revolution is Auden, another uncanonical poet for Mr. Bloom. Since Blake and Coleridge, we have often been encouraged to think of the making of poems as the making of new worlds, and it is on this Romantic bias that Mr. Bloom builds his new theosophy. But poetry has not entirely lost hold of an older sense that to make a poem is to fashion something cunningly in words, according to established procedures, that may reflect and heighten nonverbal experience. At the end of his essay on Jonson, John Hollander nicely catches this sense, reminding us that Gnosticism is not the inevitable paradigm for literary creation, in the most un-Romantic reversal of a Yeatsian motto. Speaking of Auden, he writes: "In craft began, for him as well as for his predecessor Jonson, responsibilities."

Dan O'Hara (review date Fall 1982)

SOURCE: A review of *The Breaking of the Vessels,* in *Journal of Aesthetics and Art Criticism,* Vol. XLI, No. 1, Fall, 1982, pp. 99-101.

[*In the following review, O'Hara contends that* The Breaking of the Vessels *is "both more extreme" and "more predictable" than Bloom's other works, and that the author seems to have moved from "precocious and prolific youth to decadent and despairing ancientness without ever having attained critical maturity."*]

Harold Bloom has been a controversial figure in American literary criticism for some time. His first book, *Shelley's Mythmaking* (1959), set itself squarely against the ruling critical orthodoxy of the time which denigrated the great Romantic poet as (in Arnold's notorious phrase) "an ineffectual angel" beating his golden wings vainly in a void of idealistic abstraction. Bloom argued instead that Shelley was much more of a self-conscious visionary craftsman in the style of Northrop Frye's Blake than he was ever given credit for by Arnold's New Critical heirs and fellow-travelers. Ever since, no matter what the dominant opinion in critical circles has been, Bloom has repeatedly adopted an antithetical stance. Consider the first and still most original of his theoretical utterances, *The Anxiety of Influence* (1973). Just when such colleagues of his at Yale as Paul de Man, Geoffrey Hartman, and J. Hillis Miller were adapting Derridean deconstruction and Lacanian psychoanalysis to the interpretation of literary texts within an American context; and such former mentors of Bloom's as M.H. Abrams and Walter Jackson Bate were either defending the conventional methods of doing literary history against the neophyte deconstructors or refining their own well-established views of the Romantic tradition and its Christian and humanistic origins: Bloom returned to Nietzsche, Freud, and occult forms of speculation (Kabbalah and Gnosticism) to propound a radically subversive position on why and how poetry gets written and literary traditions, especially the Romantic tradition, impose themselves so effectively on our minds. In essence, then, Bloom in *The Anxiety of Influence* attempted to trump the hands of all the leading figures, old and new, in the critical profession by redefining the context of the various debates in his own eccentric fashion.

The poet, for Bloom, must wrestle with all the specters of his elected and partially repressed precursors, in order to win the right to his own distinctive imaginative identity. Consequently, every poem is another strategic move in the great match with the mighty dead, an achieved anxiety concerning the difference in priority and spiritual authority between the belated poet and his precursor, a defensive invention of the former's necessary stance in relation to the latter's sublimity. That is, Bloom's theory is a kind of literary judo intended to turn the formidable strength of one giant of the imagination after another to one's own advantage. Since the discordant notes of *The Anxiety of Influence* Bloom has added to, revised, refined, elaborated, and relentlessly applied his theory in a series of volumes that have made him the first literary critic in the American tradition to rival the greatest of the nineteenth-century masters of English prose, such as Carlyle, Ruskin, Emerson, Arnold, and Pater—truly cultural presences. The irony of Bloom's achievement, for all its curiously representative status, is, however, that given our highly compartmentalized disciplines, Bloom can never exercise the kind of influence in our time that these earlier figures once could and did. But, as we shall see, this irony is, perhaps, really a fortunate one after all.

The poet, for Bloom, must wrestle with all the specters of his elected and partially repressed precursors, in order to win the right to his own distinctive imaginative identity.

—Dan O'Hara

For Harold Bloom's latest volume, *The Breaking of the Vessels,* represents as *Agon* does (his other production for this year) his drive for originality in its decline. The book strikes a series of antithetical poses both more extreme than struck in the past and more predictable given the general outlines of his theoretical project as found in *The Anxiety of Influence* and the speculative books that followed it in the mid-seventies. It is as if the perennial "bad boy" of American literary criticism has suddenly become old overnight, moving from precocious and prolific youth to decadent and despairing ancientness without ever attaining critical maturity along the way. Bloom's concern in *Vessels* is, as usual, "neither self nor language but the utterance, within a tradition of uttering, of the image or lie of voice, where 'voice' is neither self nor language, but rather spark or pneuma, as opposed to self." Consequently, for this self-confessed Jewish Gnostic, a poem can only be "spark and act" and criticism must ape its subject or "else we need not read it at all." Bloom's concern, that is, is all for *image:* "How can one measure the disruptions of a tradition as they occur within an individual poem? . . . What was the poet attempting to do for himself by writing this particular poem?" One can measure those disruptions with

Bloom's six-fold revisionary ratios (*clinamen, tessera, kenosis, daemonization, askesis, apophrades*), his strange amalgam of traditional rhetorical figures of speech and Freudian mechanisms of defense, which *A Map of Misreading* most successfully articulates. And one can discover what the poet was trying to do for himself if one remembers that "the figure that a poet makes, not so much in or by his poem but as his poem relates to other poems," is the figure one must seek "to isolate define, and describe by adequate gradations." This spectral figure, part poet's phantasmagoria, part reader's projected phantasm, haunts those interstices in a text, those spots of rhetorical disjunction and semantic indeterminacy, which have always been and always will be Bloom's critical focal point, since his exclusive wish is to learn how to become *exnihilo* an influence himself, and so achieve the status of symbolic immortality as a cultural monument. Thus Bloom would become, if only he could through his theoretical exertions, one of those spectral figures he conjures up in his antithetical readings of canonical texts.

If this makes Bloom sound like the critical descendant of Yeats with all his occult aesthetic speculations, this is as it should be. Bloom openly confesses that his critical project is "an aestheticism," one that endorses "the language of Gnosis" and private visions over the language of reason and social effectiveness. But it is a curious aestheticism to which he confesses, because unlike Yeats and the other aesthetes such as Oscar Wilde and Lionel Johnson Bloom does not care overly much about the basic principles of poetic form. For example, Bloom quotes Emerson from "The Oversoul" with obvious enthusiasm: "The soul is superior to its knowledge, wiser than any of its works. The great poet makes us feel our own wealth, and then we think less of his compositions." In other words, Bloom's critical vision must be considered a belated form of Romantic irony, that self-conscious post-enlightenment form of the sublime, in which the literary work exists almost solely for the opportunity it gives its author to imagine himself superior to the various conflicts he has dramatized, parodied, and so apparently overcome in his text. The most famous modern instance of such a vision of Romantic irony is, ironically enough, put in the mouth of a failed poet. In Chapter Five of *A Portrait of the Artist As a Young Man,* Stephen Dedalus waxes visionary and compares the artist to "the god of creation" indifferently paring his fingernails, a vision of the Demiurge enshrined by the very New Critics who hated Shelley for being pinnacled in the intense inane and with whom Bloom still continues to war even as he also continues to echo them, when he argues repeatedly in *Vessels* and in *Agon* that the strong poet necessarily becomes the latest version of the Demiurge who first produced the creation-fall in the Gnostic cosmology.

The most significant new wrinkle that *The Breaking of the Vessels* puts into Bloom's theory emerges from his discussion of the three paradigms of poetic invention that he proposes the critic should use to measure the effectiveness of the poem he is reading. These paradigms are 1) a catastrophe theory of imaginative creation drawn from Gnostic speculation concerning the origins of the cosmos; 2) Freud's understanding of the workings of what he termed "the family romance"; and 3) Bloom's own rhetorical transcription of Freud's notion of the transference. In brief, Bloom believes that each strong or truly successful poem must be seen on the model of the original creation-fall proposed by the Gnostics; sparks of the unknown Alien God fell and were ensnared in the forms of this world when the anxiety-ridden and envious Demiurge made the cosmos to contain his fear of the primal abyss. Similarly, each strong poem, Bloom contends, must be seen as another re-invention of the literary father the poet would like to revise and appear imaginatively greater than, as if the later poet were, somehow, the earlier poet's spiritual progenitor. Finally, Bloom also argues that each strong poem enacts a transference of power from earlier to later poet, primarily by means of a "transumptive" interplay of images of earliness and belatedness, in which the later poet introjects the former quality and projects the latter fate back on his poetic father: "When a strong poet revises a precursor, he re-enacts a scene that is at once a catastrophe, a romance, and a transference . . . . The catastrophe is also a creation: the romance is incestuous; the transference violates taboo and it ambivalences."

In this fashion, Bloom revises himself and his own earlier understanding of the dialectic of revisionary interpretation found in *A Map of Misreading* and *Poetry and Repression*. For Bloom then the belated poet ironically limits himself, in order to substitute his own image of the precursor for the established one, an act of interpretive sleight-of-hand which actually results in the precursor's imaginative diminishment even as it beefs up the later poet's own self-representation. This revisionary dialectic of limitation, substitution, and representation has become in *Vessels* the three full-scale paradigms of poetic originality—catastrophe creation, family romance, and transference—previously discussed. The consequence of such self-revision is that Bloom's dialectic of revisionism appears now to be less indebted to contemporary continental versions of the Hegelian dialectic. In fact, as conceived here, Bloom's dialectic is less of a reductive system of interpretation and more of an imaginative revisionary paradox. One surmises that all this coincides with Bloom's intentions in *The Breaking of the Vessels,* a volume ultimately about the cost of such self-criticism.

This last notion—the cost of self-criticism—really stands at the heart of any evaluation of Bloom's work. For the cost seems to involve the necessity of ruthless self-parody, a baleful prospect that Bloom repeatedly invokes in *Vessels*. The reason that Bloom's kind of criticism must end in a demonic celebration of self-parody, of radical and interminable self-revision, lies in his operating assumption that poetry speaks

the language of the will, with the will being an apocalyptic antithetical force at odds with all that is not itself, even with its own earlier representations, since this antithetical will desires the impossible: above all else to be itself alone, the great original to top all great originals, like that Alien God the Gnostics relentlessly attempted to envision. "By uttering truths of desire within traditions of uttering, the poetic will also gives itself a series of overdetermined names." Such a vision of the motive for metaphor overlooks entirely the interpersonal and social functions of poetry, pinnacling the would-be visionary critic not so much in the intense inane as on the barren heights of his own guilty solitude, a self-tormenting creature who is unable to tell his desire from his despair:

> Any mode of criticism, be it domestic or imported, that would defraud us of this true context of [suffering] must at last be dismissed with a kind of genial contempt. Perhaps there are texts without authors, articulated by blanks upon blanks, but [the strong poet] has the radical originality that restores our perspective to the agonistic image of the human which suffers, the human which thinks, the human which writes, the human which means, albeit all too humanly, in that agon the strong poet must wage, against otherness, against the self, against the presentness of the present, against anteriority, in some sense against the future.

The human-all-too human who would be a god—can we really afford this silly vision of literary creation any longer?

Ulrich Horstmann (essay date March 1983)

SOURCE: "The Over-Reader: Harold Bloom's Neo-Darwinian Revisionism," in *Poetics,* Vol. 12, No. 2/3, March, 1983.

[*In the following essay, Horstmann takes issue with various elements of Bloom's work.*]

Harold Bloom embarked on his scholarly career in 1959 when he published his dissertation on *Shelley's Mythmaking* and reached notoriety fourteen years later with *The Anxiety of Influence: A Theory of Poetry*. This book formulated the Magna Charta of Bloom's poststructuralist doctrine of 'antithetical revisionism', and its author has since expounded and consolidated his highly controversial poetics with unremitting zeal and missionary ardour in such studies as: *A Map of Misreading* (1975), *Kabbalah and Criticism* (1975), *Poetry and Repression: Revisionism from Blake to Stevens* (1976), *Figures of Capable Imagination* (1976), *Wallace Stevens, The Poems of Our Climate* (1977), *Agon: Towards a Theory of Revisionism* (1982).

Bloom's more recent work does not only propagate the heuristic principle of antithesis; more importantly it embodies and exemplifies it by reacting antithetically to the norms and expectations of the academic community it addresses. In vain do we look for annotations, index, or bibliography in his books, as Bloom defiantly parades his disregard for the ideals of philological accuracy and verifiability by constantly referring to exotic and unorthodox systems of thought such as Kabbalah and Gnosis and by revelling in linguistic idiosyncrasies that substantiate McGann's criticism:

> The book [*Anxiety of Influence*] has become notorious for its obscurity, yet I do not think that the ideas of the book are obscure but that it has been written in a private language. Its rhetorical conventions seem the common property of a small literary club whose only permanent and full-fledged member is Bloom himself. To read Bloom, we have to learn *his* language.

To these animadversions Bloom turns a deaf ear in his contribution to *Deconstruction and Criticism,* where he waves good-bye to the regulative idea of intersubjectivity:

> I don't believe that I ever could be clear enough for others, since for them "clarity" is mainly a trope for philosophical reductiveness, or for a dreary literal-mindedness that belies any deep concern for poetry or criticism.

And in his latest publication *Agon* he takes up the issue again, this time to declare:

> In expounding my own critical theory and practice, I neither want nor urge any "method" of criticism. It is no concern of mine whether anybody else ever comes to share, or doesn't, my own vocabularies of revisionary ratios, of crossings, of whatever. What Richard Rorty cheerfully dismisses as "the comfort of consensus" I too am very glad to live without, because I don't wish to privilege any vocabularies, my own included.

The two quotations in defence of an "aggressive personalism" seem to document a strategic shift from an early ex-cathedra stand to a more modest and 'withdrawn' position which even smacks of a rearguard action. But Bloom's invocation of an unlimited methodological pluralism and relativism must not be taken at face value. In spite of his rhetoric of mutual toleration Bloom has never been a pluralist, because this attitude would have prevented him from ever assuming his role as prophet of the interpreter's unscrupulous 'will-to-power' over literary texts. Bloom's revisionism is as monistic as is possible, and like all heresies it derives its intellectual momentum, penetrative power, and feeling of superiority

from an unshaken belief in the truth of its own privileged insights.

Thus Bloom's initiation into the 'true nature' of poetry begins with an anti-pluralistic revolt against the father-figures of his academic noviciate: Abrams, Wimsatt, and Frye. In order to "know" he must first escape from "the impasse of Formalist criticism" as well as from "the barren moralizing that Archetypal criticism has come to be." Eliot and Frye have mythologized tradition into an all-inclusive simultaneity, into a pantheon freely accessible to practically every 'newcomer poet', whose freedom consists in the freedom of being integrated into a pre-existent tradition:

> Freedom, for Frye as for Eliot, is the change, however slight, that any genuine single consciousness brings about in the order of literature simply by joining the simultaneity of such order. I confess that I no longer understand this simultaneity.

This lack of understanding is based on a total reversal of Bloom's view of history, which not only plays off the violence of diachronic processes against an idealized synchronism, but which also substitutes a *competitive* for a *cooperative* matrix and consequently looks upon literary history as a Darwinian cultural medium in which only the fittest have a chance to survive.

Bloom's revisionism aims at dispelling 'illusions': "One aim of this theory is corrective: to de-idealize our accepted accounts of how one poet helps to form another" and the most pernicious illusion of all is that of a continuous and harmonious tradition which enables every poet to contribute to what Shelley once called "the great poem of mankind." According to Bloom there is no "great poem" and no harmony, no joint enterprise of common heritage either; as the fog of wishful thinking clears, all that remains is a battlefield covered with the dead and the dying. That "the history of poetry [is] . . . an endless, defensive civil war" is the message of *Kabbalah and Criticism,* and in his introduction to *Figures of Capable Imagination* Bloom declares:

> The dialectics of influence, if examined without over-idealizing, reveal that literature itself is founded upon rivalry, misinterpretation, repression, and even plain theft and savage misprision. [. . .] To see literature for what it is, the dark mirror of our egoism and our fallen condition, is to see ourselves again as perhaps eternity sees us, more like one another than we can bear to believe.

What a critic needs under these circumstances is a kind of ideological survival kit and a "War Game Manual," both of which Bloom is willing to provide. The very first thing such a manual has to do is to give reasons for the unappeasable bellicosity of the literary combatants.

Bloom obliges with a double answer. Poets enter the arena of literary history because of the tempting prize at stake: "the greatest of all human illusions, the vision of immortality." And they fight to the finish, because their fear of defeat and cultural oblivion forces them either to overcome their opponents or to die in the last ditch.

For Bloom their literary 'fear of death' is equivalent to their apprehension of not being able to escape from the shadow of a classic precursor and thus of succumbing to the immense and absorbing pressures of the cultural stock, to a stifling over-abundance which seems to leave no breathing space whatsoever to the 'latecomer poet' and which threatens to make every poet's nightmare—"that no proper work remains for him to perform"—come true.

This so-called "anxiety of influence"—a concept which Bloom took over from W. Jackson Bate, who had outlined the modern cultural experience of the paralysing presence of the past as early as 1970 in his book *The Burden of the Past and the English Poet*—is a necessary concomitant of a highly developed historical consciousness that no longer harbours any doubt about its own posteriority and tries in vain to acquiesce in the fatal consequences resulting from this awareness:

> The poet of any guilt culture whatsoever cannot initiate himself into a fresh chaos, he is compelled to accept a lack of priority in creation, which means he must accept also a failure in divination, as the first of many little deaths that prophesy a final and total extinction. His word is not his own word only, and his Muse has whored with many before him. He has come late in the story, but she has always been central in it, and he rightly fears that his impending catastrophe is only another in her litany of sorrows.

In the given cultural situation the 'latecomer poet' or 'ephebe' has no choice but to rise against the predominance of his precursor, and this is why, for instance, Wordsworth's harmonizing view of poetry has to be discarded: "A poet . . . is not so much a man speaking to men as a man rebelling against being spoken to by a dead man (the precursor) outrageously more alive than himself." What the above quotation labels as rebellion may be circumscribed on a psychological plane as a kind of mental processing following the lines of Freudian repression and aiming at the deconstruction of the latecomer's literary-historical super-ego represented by the precursor. This deconstructive activity which will ultimately result in the latecomer's usurpation of his precursor's cultural aura unfolds within the medium of the ephebe's literary work and manifests itself in a series of highly complex tropological

transformations that Bloom analyses and charts in *The Anxiety of Influence* and *A Map of Misreading*.

These operations are essential for the young poet's survival because on the one hand the existence of an idealized precursor is the prerequisite of poetic initiation whereas on the other only a gradual diminution of the precursor's role will enable the ephebe to develop his own talents. Bloom compresses the dialectics of emancipation into a single statement, "if we have been ravished by a poem, it will cost us our own poem," and thus makes it clear that only an antithetical and revisionist attitude towards preexisting paradigms and models, only the 'will-to-power' over the precursor's work, and the demolition of its uniqueness and aesthetic transcendence, will guarantee the latecomer's survival.

As poems are acts of self-defence, they cannot possibly be isolated from their origins. The New Critics are oblivious of this fact and consequently their techniques of decontextualisation have always been doomed to failure. Bloom draws the conclusion: "Let us give up the failed enterprise of seeking to 'understand' any single poem as an entity in itself" and propounds a dynamic and 'open' counter-notion of what we mean when we talk of 'texts':

> A poetic "text", as I interpret it, is not a gathering of signs on a page, but is a psychic battlefield upon which authentic forces struggle for the only victory worth winning, the divinating triumph over oblivion.

Thus every poem is necessarily an "inter-poem" coming to life within an intratextual and intertextual field of conflict and is characterized not by "benighted meanderings after truth," but by its author's 'survival instincts' and violent revisionism:

> Poetic influence—when it involves two strong, authentic poets—always proceeds by a misreading of the prior poet, an act of creative correction that is actually and necessarily a misinterpretation. The history of fruitful poetic influence . . . is a history of anxiety and self-saving caricature, of distortion, of perverse, wilful revisionism without which modern poetry as such could not exist.

'Tradition' and 'literary history' are merely euphemisms which gloss over a remorseless struggle for existence that smothers and buries the weak "as the hungry generations go on treading one another down." There is only one kind of person that can exist in a pandemonium like this without coming to grief: the 'strong poet', a poetic duplicate of Nietzsche's Over-man, who will stand the test of "wrestling with the greatest of the dead" and thus make the dream of the modern man of letters come true and realize his deep-felt desire "to beget one's own self, to become one's own Great Original."

Bloom distinguishes six phases of the poetic psychomachia: Clinamen, Tessera, Kenosis, Daemonization, Askesis, and Apophrades, and draws elaborate parallels between these 'revisionary ratios' on the one hand and psychic defence mechanisms, rhetorical tropes, and the images in the poem on the other. As we cannot here discuss his esoteric categorical apparatus in detail, suffice it to say that in spite of the schematic shape that may at first dazzle the reader, there is a syncretic haphazardness below the polished surface that rapidly undermines our confidence in the heuristic potential of the more intricate constructions of Bloomian "psycho-aesthetics." In addition, wherever Bloom applies his categories directly to poetic texts, as in the second part of the *Map of Misreading*, the irritating sterility of his model interpretations will de-idealize his own poetics rather than an orthodox view of poetry.

Bloom certainly is more a theoretician than a critic.
—Ulrich Horstmann

Bloom certainly is more a theoretician than a critic, and in contrast to 'strong poetry', 'strong interpretation' is not his forte. Therefore let us return to his broader notion of the literary over-man who is practicing a constant poetic revisionism that prevents him from further developing a precursor text and who does violence to it instead. For Bloom a poem is a pragmatic rather than an ephistemological event, a product of semantic activities that make no claims to truth whatsoever. All the strong poet strives after is an *innovation* which implies his triumph over his precursor's literary prototypes, the demolition of the integrity of his texts, and the annihilation of their literal presence:

> If death ultimately presents the earlier state of things, then it also represents the earlier state of meaning, or pure anteriority; that is to say, repetition of the literal, or literal meaning. Death is therefore a kind of literal meaning, or from the standpoint of poetry, *literal meaning is a kind of death. Defenses can be said to trope against death, rather in the same sense that tropes can be said to defend against literal meaning,* which is the antithetical formula for which we have been questing.

Thus Bloom's critical 'survival kit' mainly contains a number of tropological devices that act as semantic defenses against literal meaning, thus allowing the poet to transform and dissolve a classic text into a work of art all his own. Writing poetry is described by Bloom as responsive and reactive behaviour, as "a relational event, and not a substance to be analyzed." Consequently, a poetic text 'has' no meaning that a good interpretation will distill from it, but 'is' its

relation to another text: "The meaning of a poem [can] only be another poem. Not, I point out, the *meaning* of another poem, but the other poem itself, indeed the *otherness* of the other poem." Poetry represents a continual process of antithetical rewriting, of the fearful transmutations of an oppressive tradition that only he can get rid of who is strong enough to pervert it:

> Every poem is a misinterpretation of a parent poem. [. . .] Poetry is anxiety of influence, is misprision, is a disciplined perverseness. Poetry is misunderstanding, misinterpretation, misalliance.

And it is the same strategy of tropological annexation that for Bloom becomes the guiding principle of criticism and scholarly exegesis, too. As Bloom has abandoned the concept of meaning, the critic's traditional task of translating a literary 'message' into discursive prose turns into an absurdity, and the only option left to him is to adopt the interactional patterns which characterize his former object of investigation (poetry). With this 'poetization' of criticism the time-honoured barriers between primary and secondary literature collapse along with their hierarchical superstructure. According to Bloom there is no fundamental difference between the act of writing poetry and that of writing about poetry; the two activities are but the two sides of the same coin, two modes of reading so much akin that the same prestige value should be allotted to either of them: "A poet attempting to make his language new necessarily begins by an *arbitrary act of reading* that does not differ in kind from the act that *his* reader subsequently must perform upon him." 'Strong critics' or 'over-readers' read as antithetically, arbitrarily, and distortingly as 'strong poets', and they do it for the same reason, that is to avoid tautological repetition and to explode the petrifications of literary history:

> The influence-relation governs reading as it governs writing, and reading is therefore a miswriting just as writing is a misreading. As literary history lengthens, all poetry necessarily becomes verse-criticism, just as all criticism becomes prose-poetry.

This convergence of poetry and criticism is based on the hypothesis that all comprehension is, at bottom, nothing but "creative misunderstanding," a concept which points back to Giambattista Vico's philosophy of language, which has become quite influential in recent American thought. In accordance with the Vichian definition of language as an endless process of tropological transformation and substitution Bloom finally arrives at the conclusion: "Tropism of meaning compels tropes themselves *to be meaning.*" This statement, from *Kabbalah and Criticism*, denies that there can be any ontological 'feed-back' between language and reality as such, for 'reality' is merely a configuration of sedimentary tropes that seem to be meaningful not because 'meaning' presupposes an *adaequatio intellectus ad rem,* but because it is itself a tropological operation, the result of an interplay of certain rhetorical patterns, some of which have been grouped together under the heading of 'logic' and constitute our so-called 'scientific rationality'.

The critic who has traded in the search for truth for "salutary acts of textual violence," who holds that "common rules for interpreting words will never exist," and who reduces primary to secondary literature, because in both cases texts generate new and antithetical texts can hardly claim truth and validity for his own theory of poetry, one which is little more than a meta-interpretation and is therefore, in its turn, obliged to comply with the methodology it propounds.

Bloom is well aware of the anti-scientific and self-subverting tendency of his theorizing and consequently characterizes his poetics in *The Anxiety of Influence* as "a severe poem, reliant upon aphorism, apothegm, and a quite personal . . . mythic pattern." In his contribution to *Deconstruction and Criticism* he calls his work "an allegory of reading" and translates his approach in *Kabbalah and Criticism* into a methodological directive:

> I knowingly urge critical theory to stop treating itself as a branch of philosophical discourse . . . A theory *of* poetry must belong *to* poetry, must *be* poetry, before it can be of any use in interpreting poems.

Of course, the clear-cut parameters of exactness, inter-subjectivity, and logical consistency have lost their validity under these circumstances and are replaced by their exact opposites. Bloom's project can do without the "careless habits of accuracy"; it appeals not to objective criteria of truth, but to "the preferences of an individual reader" instead, and establishes the aporia as the vanishing point of all knowledge:

> The proposal then is to enrich criticism by finding a comprehensive and suggestive trope for the act of interpretation, a trope antithetical not only to all other tropes but to itself in particular.

This new para-science of criticism, which presupposes its own permanent self-erosion and self-deconstruction, can absorb more traditional and constructive systems of meaning only after they have been metamorphosed into argumentative 'playgrounds' first. Bloom's authorities Nietzsche and Freud are thus turned into "two of the strongest poets in the European Romantic tradition" and their work is deliberately 'misread', that is exploited for fitting fragments and concepts with a casual justification: "Freud's life-work is a severe poem, and its own latent principles are more useful to us, as critics, than its manifest principles." From this perspective

anything read into a text (as its 'latent principle') is more relevant and interesting than what the text actually says, and those texts which show the least resistance to arbitrary semantic projections are the most fascinating. This is why Bloom looks back to the gnostic and kabbalistic traditions with unparalleled enthusiasm and regards them as forerunners of his own wilful revisionism: "Kabbalah offers both a model for the process of poetic influence, and maps for the problematic pathways of interpretation."

Just like Bloom Kabbalists fight the anteriority of a tradition based on the truth of the letter:

> The Talmud warns against reading scripture by so inclined a light that the text reveals chiefly the shape of your own countenance. Kabbalah . . . reads scripture only in so inclined or figurative a defensive mode.

And in accordance with his revisionist poetics they are engaged in the production and dissemination of meaning and not in its reduction to a hard core of eternal truths.

For Bloom both his own revisionism and kabbalistic speculation are "machine(s) for criticism," systems of semantic transformation which promise not only liberation from the monolithic past but also an endless freeplay of meaning.

As this freeplay is instantaneously blocked by any truth principle, its dynamic center is dominated by the counter-principle of inescapable error which in its turn has become the 'ultimate truth'. Thus 'misinterpretations' provoke opposition, that is further 'misinterpretations', and the highest error even comprises this antithesis in itself and derives its immense productivity from the tensions inherent in self-contradiction. This is the reason why Bloom foregrounds not only the inconsistencies of the texts he interprets but also those of his own interpretations, thus fomenting polemical disagreement and controversy:

> A critical theory and *praxis* that teaches the defensive necessity of "misprision" or strong "misreading" cheerfully accepts even the weakest misreadings of its doctrines and techniques. If they persist in their folly, all these outraged reviewers will become wise.

There is an air of methodological exhibitionism and a parading of "splits of gaps in my [Bloom's] own theorizing" in several of his books, as error, self-contradiction, and misinterpretation indicate an unbroken interpretive vitality rather than philological failure, they constitute liberating acts, are manifestations of an indomitable "will-to-power over a text" beyond good and evil, and mark yet another defeat of a paralyzed and paralyzing truth.

Although the official purpose of Bloom's theory of revision is the defossilization of criticism and the dissemination of meaning, its second and equally important function consists in immunizing Bloom's poetics against any attempt at falsification. Bloom's strategy in this respect deserves to be called ingenious because it erodes the epistemological basis of refutation itself by turning every well-grounded opposition to his theory into a welcome 'misreading' and thus automatically into a demonstration of its validity. But all his ingenuity does not save Bloom from paying a price for this impregnability of his doctrine, which consists in its cognitive sterility. As there is no longer any possibility to refute the theorems of antithetical criticism, there is no longer any possibility to learn—learning being a process of falsification and the spotting of errors—and the theorist will forever discover what he has always known:

> Bloom's absorption in his imaginative critiques tends to leave him without the ability to be critical of *his own* judgments, which he is not disinclined to pronounce. The object, as a result, tends to disappear into the construction that is put upon it.

Thus the tautological character which is so conspicuous in Bloom's interpretations of 'strong' poetry reemerges on the methodological level and manifests itself in the contention of irrefutability. In spite of all the lip-service he pays to flexibility and perpetual revision, Bloom is a dogmatist at heart and is determined to uphold his axiom of the anxiety of influence in the teeth of highly compromising evidence:

> The theory, deliberately an attempt at de-idealizing, has encountered considerable resistance during my presentation of it in a number of lectures at various universities ... I take the resistance shown to the theory by many poets, in particular, to be likely evidence for its validity, for poets rightly idealize their activity; and all poets, weak and strong, agree in denying any share in the anxiety of influence.

Whatever the practitioners of poetry may say, Bloom knows better—and he knows more, for the critic and not the poet is in command of the machinery of revisionism. The concept of the precursor's influence on the latecomer poet provides a striking example for this imbalance.

According to Bloom 'influence' does not designate a process of the superficial adoption of the precursor's peculiarities of style or structure. On the contrary, such similarities indicate a weak and epigonous response:

> The greatest apparent puzzle in poetic influence [. . .] is that the deepest or most vital instances are almost never phenomena of the poetic surface. Only weak poems, or the weaker elements in strong poems,

immediately echo precursor poems, or directly allude to them. The fundamental phenomena of poetic influence have little to do with the borrowings of images or ideas, with sound-patterns or with other verbal reminders of one poem by another.

Poets do not have to look like their fathers either, as "the anxiety of influence more frequently than not is quite distinct from the anxiety of style." But how, then, do the kinship and poetic dependance make themselves known? Bloom's answer is that they do not manifest openly, but in a common "fundamental stance," a "spiritual form" or—even more cryptically—in a delicate latency:

> A poem is a deep misprision of a previous poem when we recognize the later poem as being absent rather than present on the surface of the earlier poem, and yet still being *in* the earlier poem, implicit or hidden *in* it, not yet manifest, and yet *there*.

To put it bluntly: Bloom's ultimate proof of the precursor's presence in a strong poem is his demonstrable absence from it. The logical absurdity of this argument is quite clear, because lack of evidence is regarded as the *conditio sine qua non* for its validity. But Bloom, whose antithetical revisionism has transformed poetic into theoretical licence, does not stop there: not only does he make the precursor vanish from the poem his influence has called into being, but he also eliminates the very text the ephebe is said to have reacted to from the latecomer poet's memory:

> Antithetical criticism must begin . . . [with] *another* poem [. . .] And not a poem chosen with total arbitrariness, but any central poem by an indubitable precursor, even if the ephebe *never read* that poem.

Thus the ephebe misreads a poem he has never known. This is the final paradox of Bloomian aesthetics and its saga about the initiation, struggle, triumph, and transfiguration of strong poets, a saga expanding the "magical theory of language" Bloom propounds in his paper "The Breaking of Form" into a magical theory of poetry. This theory may well result in what Frank Lentricchia once called "a 1001 nights of literary analysis," but it is a far cry from the historical reality literary scholarship still has to reconstruct, not deconstruct.

David Wyatt (essay date Summer 1984)

SOURCE: "Bloom, Freud, and 'America'," in *The Kenyon Review*, Vol. VI, No. 3, Summer, 1984.

[*In the following essay, Wyatt uses Bloom's own theoretical approach to examine the significance of Freud and American literature in Bloom's work.*]

Harold Bloom's theory of poetic influence is the most controversial and influential of our time. It is an overtly psychological theory: in *Agon,* published in 1982, Bloom asserts that we live in the Age of Freud. Bloom argues that the relations between poets are the true subject of literary history, and that these relations are characterized by all the envy, guilt, ambivalence and love that create the Oedipal family. Strong poets suffer in particular an acute anxiety of belatedness. Their writing consists of a series of defenses against the sense that they have been born too late to do any truly original work. In twelve books published over nearly three decades, Bloom has almost single-handedly transposed Freud's theories of intrapsychic and generational conflict into the realm of poetic careers. By doing so he has also assured that any critic of poetry in English lives now in the Age of Bloom.

Harold Bloom's theory of poetic influence is the most controversial and influential of our time.

—David Wyatt

Bloom is a student of rhetorical figures—or tropes—and of the way that poets organize their poems and careers around them. To "trope" means to turn, as Bloom often reminds us, and when he does so he means to suggest that a poet takes up a trope as a defense, as a way of lessening or transforming some psychic burden. I would like to train Bloom's method on Bloom himself in order to examine the central turn in his career. It is my thesis that the key turn in his work is away from England and toward America, from his adopted and imaginative fatherland and back to his natural and mother country. The reason he needs to make this turn, I will argue, is to protect a crucial notion in his theory of influence: the notion of the *self.* For Bloom literature is not organic or semiotic or decentered but agonistic. It is a struggle for priority among egos joined in a great game. The literature that reduces most purely to such a struggle is American literature. Finally—and this is the third phase of my argument—in this turn from England to America Bloom must adopt in his exposition of the self one indispensable ally: Sigmund Freud.

Bloom's first four books were on Shelley, the English Romantics as a group, Blake, and Yeats. Each of these but the last argues for the unity of the human imagination and the continuity between English and American Romanticism. The tradition has one term which stands for a god—the Imagination. Here is a typical quote from *The Visionary Company,* published in 1961: "The inner problem of *The Prelude* is that of the autonomy of the poet's creative imagination . . . it is the single most crucial problem of all that is most vital in

English Romantic poetry." This is the credo of what Jerome McGann has recently called *The Romantic Ideology,* which advocates an escape from the limits and history of the social world "through imagination and poetry." Bloom has certainly been the most successful critic at promulgating this ideology; it is fair to say, I would venture, that Bloom has succeeded in passing off this version of Romanticism as the truth in most quarters. It is an ideology which makes no distinction between national origins. Bloom's early project was to show, against Eliot and the New Critics, that modernism is a Romanticism, and that a line extends through Milton, Blake, Wordsworth, Yeats, and Stevens in which the recurring subject of the poem is the poet's own relation to his poetic vision.

The appeal of such an ideology may be obvious: for all those dispossessed of authoritative social communities, it makes of literature a secular church at which we can worship, a place where imagination becomes the supreme transgressor of boundaries in a kind of United Nations of the mind. Unfortunately for all unified field theories of the imagination, this was an imaginary organization from which America, in Bloom's mind at least, was destined to withdraw.

Bloom was required to turn toward the American Imagination because of the swerve which the British tradition took away from him. Bloom sees twentieth-century British literature as a "modernism" devoted to a cult of the "Impersonal" best articulated by Eliot, the renegade American:

> the more perfect the artist, the more completely separate in him will be the man who suffers and the mind which creates . . . . The poet's mind is in fact a receptacle for seizing and storing up numberless feelings, phrases, images, which remain there until all the particles which can unite to form a new compound are present together . . . . the poet has, not a 'personality' to express, but a particular medium, which is only a medium and not a personality, in which impressions and experiences combine in peculiar and unexpected ways . . . . Poetry is not a turning loose of emotion, but an escape from emotion; it is not the expression of personality, but an escape from personality.

If modernism in Britain is represented by Joyce, Woolf, Pound, Lewis and Eliot, then it adds at least three crucial strategies and attitudes to the suppression of personality: discontinuity in syntax and narrative; the fiction of all times being simultaneous (the mythic method); a fascination with words rather than story. The literature which results affirms that language is a system inclusive of the producers of it. For a modern, the author is the scribe who is inscribed, an amanuensis dictated to by the conventions and permutations of the text-producing game that language always already is. The basic premise in all these assumptions is that writing is not an expression of a self.

Bloom has been noticeably uninterested in American writers who are radically modern. He has never produced a major essay on Williams or Pound, and his work is particularly dismissive of Eliot. Eliot not only forsook his native land (no matter that he would later tell Donald Hall, "I'd say that my poetry has obviously more in common with my distinguished contemporaries in America than with anything written in my generation in England"), but deliberately obscured his literary debts. In the notes to *The Waste Land* you will find mention of Nerval and the Upanishads, but none of Tennyson, from whom Eliot borrowed the grail quest and the desert imagery, of Browning, who taught him all about speaking, like Prufrock and Gerontion, in dramatic monologues. Eliot attempts to escape the pressure of what Northrop Frye calls "the English Romantic tradition" and persists instead in a kind of Tory resistance. Frye is eloquent on this point:

> I have not thought of trying to prefer one kind of English culture to another, and I regard all value-judgments that inhibit one's sympathies with anything outside a given tradition as dismally uncritical. I say only that this combination of Protestant, radical, and Romantic qualities is frequent enough in English culture to account for the popularity, in every sense, of the products of it described above. There has been no lack of Catholic, Tory, and Classical elements too, but the tradition dealt with here has been popular enough to give these latter elements something of the quality of a consciously intellectual reaction. During the twenties of the present century, after the shock of the First World War, this intellectual reaction gathered strength. Its most articulate supporters were cultural evangelists who came from places like Missouri and Idaho, and who had a clear sense of the shape of the English tradition, from its beginnings in Provence and medieval Italy to its later developments in France.

Eliot and Pound are, in the words of Milton's God, "ingrates." "Ingrate, he had of mee / All he could have." If God is a disappointed parent, so is the Romantic tradition when defended by Frye or Bloom.

Eliot's behavior as a literary historian proves in fact a kind of perverse exaggeration of all that Bloom sees as true about how poets face the past. Eliot's career is a massive reaction-formation against his anxiety of influence. Instead of robustly confronting this anxiety, Eliot converts it into a fantasy of receptivity and potential "conformity":

> No poet, no artist of any art, has his complete meaning alone. His significance, his appreciation, is the appreciation of his relation to the dead poets and artists. You cannot value him alone; you must set him, for contrast and comparison, among the dead. I mean this as a principle of aesthetic, not merely historical, criticism. The necessity that he shall conform, that he shall cohere, is not onesided; what happens when a new work of art is created is something that happens simultaneously to all the works of art which preceded it. The existing monuments form an ideal order among themselves, which is modified by the introduction of the new (the really new) work of art among them. The existing order is complete before the new work arrives; for order to persist after the supervention of novelty, the *whole* existing order must be, if ever so slightly, altered; and so the relations, proportions, values of each work toward the whole are readjusted; and this is conformity between the old and the new.

This was written in 1919, and much of Bloom is latent here: the confidence that a tradition can be articulated; the belief that poems have their meaning as found among other poems; the sense that talent exists in tension with tradition, even if tradition is finally the inclusive term. What Bloom cannot abide—and this marks an important debt to Freud—is the idealizing passivity of the poet's stance. It is an active and aggressive struggle with the past that Bloom sees as the mark of any strong poet. Since all relations are Oedipal, we cripple ourselves to pretend otherwise, and weakness is the only crime. Bloom faults Eliot for inventing a bogus legacy and for refusing to wrestle openly with his true fathers. Through his continual allusion to and pillage of the past, Eliot actually promotes the central illusion of modernism: that it is possible to be new, in the "modo," *now.* Thus the poet who starts as the most acute clinician of the anxiety of influence proves its most self-deceived victim, and thereby becomes the key figure in Bloom's understanding of modernism in literary history.

In the year in which America decided to commit ground troops in Vietnam, Bloom divined but did not deduce the concept of a national imagination. This was the year he published his first major essay on Emerson: "The Central Man: Emerson, Whitman, and Wallace Stevens." In this essay he writes about "the starting-point of Romantic poetry in America." In this quote and throughout the essay, the word "Romantic" is capitalized and retains a priority over and a power to encompass any transatlantic deviations. The American imagination is characterized as "extreme and ironic," but the extremity and irony are seen as differences in degree rather than kind. Important here, rather, is the surfacing of Emerson in Bloom's thought. In his most recent book, ***The Breaking of the Vessels*** (1982), Bloom has written that it was "Emerson . . . who changed my mind about nearly everything when I was in the middle of my journey, back around 1965 . . . . " By the early

70s Emerson would come to rival Milton as the origin of an imaginative tradition.

Milton had been a convenient *point d'appui* for the Romantic tradition because of his passionate conviction that living and reading involve a continuous testing of the free self. His is a poetry of choice which shapes the reader into a figure of the educated will. In *Paradise Lost* we are free to choose our place of rest, but we are also aware that every such act, from the moment that pilot anchors his "night-founder'd Skiff" to Leviathan, is part of a process of soul-making with mortal consequences. Any poet in the tradition of Milton stands on a definite line which it is easy to swerve away from. Emerson, on the other hand, deploys a rhetoric of surprise which continually undercuts its previously held positions. The "noble doubt" which suggests itself in *Nature* is only the most famous instance of this. It is, however, the separateness of his sentences rather than the unpredictability of his argument which most effectively releases us from the authority of time. To read Emerson is to experience what he called a "plenteous stopping at little stations" in which rhythm and style argue for each moment as a new departure. The stance enjoyed is readiness, not righteousness, an elasticity rather than an integrity of soul. Any poet in the tradition of Emerson occupies a sphere from which it is impossible to wander. What Bloom couldn't have known in the middle 60s was that in turning toward Emerson he had struck a blow not only against Milton but also at the tar baby—in his blithe willingness to occupy contradictory imaginative stances. Emerson has grasped Bloom as the ubiquitous precursor who refuses to let go.

While I want to argue that the theoretical rationale for Bloom's turn toward America has to do with his interest in the concept of the self, it was probably dictated as well by the shape of recent literary history. To embrace Emerson is to embrace the inescapable fact that the best poetry written in English in this century has been written by Americans. The critic of influence, carried inevitably backward from present incarnations to past origins, is compelled to invent a precursor who can account for this belated renaissance. After all, Bloom has said that if he were allowed two books to take to a desert island, they would be the poems of Stevens and Frost. While Bloom has ignored the latter, he has championed Stevens as the poet of the century. He even had to write an ill-tempered book about Yeats in order to clear the ground of Stevens's most significant competitor. Bloom discovered Stevens in an Ithaca bookstore in 1947, at the age of seventeen. "I think that I am not unrepresentative of a generation of critics," he writes, "that learned to read and reread all other poetry by learning the various ways of reading Wallace Stevens." The oft-leveled charge that he reads all of American literature through Stevens is not only one to which Bloom admits here, but also one which he has codified as the sixth revisionary ratio by means of which later poets struggle against earlier

ones. Bloom hears Stevens everywhere in the American strain, and in doing so he converts Stevens's work into a vast metalepsis in which the later poet is felt to have actually preceded all earlier poets and to have written their characteristic work.

While this argument supplies Bloom with a strategic motive for embracing Emerson, the discovery of Emerson also allows Bloom to defend an essential theoretical position. It is one that required Bloom to become a central apologist, during the 70s and early 80s, of a canon of values that lies hidden within the term "American." For it fell to Bloom to discover the uniqueness of American literature at the very time that the concept of the author, national identity, and even determinate meaning were under attack from the newest new critics—the deconstructionists. While Derrida and the continent of the Old World argued for the indeterminacy of the text and the self as a mobile desiring fantasy, Bloom argued that the literature of the New World calls us into a "recentering," a repeated affirmation of Emerson's eternal "ME." Emerson's marvelous and ungainly eyeball—"I am nothing; I see all"—becomes Stevens's self-assertion: "I have not but I am and as I am, I am." The later poet's affirmation may be minimal, but the repetition of the personal pronoun has become even more insistent. It is this stubborn and lonely insistence upon the uniqueness of the self—this "anxiety of originality"—that finally sets American poetry apart from a European tradition. In his best essay on Emerson (from *A Map of Misreading*), Bloom tries eloquently to distinguish Emerson's project from all Europeanisms:

> Nietzsche ... delighted in Emerson, and seems to have understood Emerson very well. And I think Nietzsche particularly understood that Emerson had come to prophesy not a de-centering, as Nietzsche had, and Derrida and de Man are brilliantly accomplishing, but a peculiarly American *recentering,* and with it an American mode of interpretation.

What is continually recentered in America—and this is what Bloom celebrates—is the agonized, desiring, named, Freudian self.

Why does Bloom need to believe in the self? Why do any of us? It is a construct whose time seems to have passed, and yet one to which many of us stubbornly cling, as if believing would make it so. Bloom certainly needs the concept to preserve his system, since only a poet with a fairly continuous and coherent identity could continue to wage with such pride the struggle against other poets which some have labelled Bloom's War in Heaven. Whatever his reasons, Bloom cleaves to a belief in "the agonistic image of the human which suffers, the human which thinks, the human which writes, the human which means" as the author and origin of the poem. The author is not, as Foucault says, "the principle of thrift in the proliferation of meaning"; the author is a more primary and assumed element of Bloom's system than the poem.

Bloom's invention of America is also a story about Family Romance. A critic who feels born into one tradition (albeit not a native one) invents for himself a more spacious tradition and discovers that he is its native after all. Bloom's invention of America is certainly subject to a Freudian interpretation, the possible lines of which I have tried to lay down. But I now want to turn to his overt use of Freud as the major theoretical support for his system. Bloom reads Freud as the last great exponent of the fiction of the self, and it is fair to say that in his recent work, his theory of America and his theory of Freud have become fused in his mind.

If Emerson supplies the content of Bloom's vision (there is a self and only a self), Freud supplies the form. He is the scientist of tropes who codifies the ways in which the self defends against the priority of other selves. It did not take Lacan to tell us that the Unconscious is structured as a language: we could have found the point most readily made in *The Ego and the Mechanisms of Defense*. It is no small irony that Bloom owes the symmetry of his system less to a book by the father than to one by the pious daughter. For when Bloom comes to enumerate his revisionary ratios—the stances through which a later poet joins the contest against an earlier one—he does so by lining up his terms against Anna Freud's. In *The Anxiety of Influence* and more systematically in *A Map of Misreading*, Bloom argues that poets confront other poets through six basic stances. Each stance corresponds to one of the six major mechanisms of defense: reaction-formation, reversal, isolation/undoing, repression, sublimation, introjection/projection. These defenses correspond to six major tropes of rhetoric: irony, synecdoche, metonymy, hyperbole, metaphor, and metalepsis. A poet's characteristic choice of defense/trope/revisionary ratio determines the kind of poet he will be. No wonder that Bloom has recently questioned whether defense may not be the most fundamental concept of psychoanalysis.

A curious aspect of this map—and Bloom calls it a "map"—is how unoriginal it is. The idea for lining up psychic defenses beside rhetorical tropes is one Bloom borrowed from another interpreter of Freud, Lionel Trilling. In a sentence of remarkably compressed lucidity, Trilling anticipates much of Bloom's project. The quotation is from *Freud and Literature,* published in 1940:

> It was left to Freud to discover how, in a scientific age, we still feel and think in figurative formations, and to create, what psychoanalysis is, a science of tropes, of metaphor and its variants, synecdoche and metonymy.

So Trilling saw what Bloom was to capitalize on: that Freud

was a student of the psyche's twistings, of the isomorphism between turns of mind and turns of phrase. That Freud saw the mind as troping against its inadmissible drives is a fact that cannot be stressed often enough, since it is a view that defends the mind's active power against all behaviorist reductions.

> **Where Bloom revises Freud is in the content rather than the form of his vision.**
> —*David Wyatt*

Where Bloom revises Freud is in the content rather than the form of his vision. For Freud the great secret is sex; for Bloom, it is time. Freud saw our task as one of attachment to objects, even if they prove only substitutes for earlier objects. It is a task that admits of no literal but considerable figurative satisfaction. Bloom sees our task as the transumption of earlier achievement. It is a task that admits of no literal and small figurative satisfaction. Our lives are spent not trying to refind the mother but to precede the father. The problem is not desire but belatedness. I quote here from *Agon,* Bloom's most succinct attempt to shift the human project away from Freud's ground and onto his own. He has been talking about his obsessive subject, "the poetic will to an immortality." It is that will, he suggests, "that may seem some day the truest definition of the Freudian Eros: the will's revenge against time's 'it was' is to be carried out by the mind's drive to surpass all earlier achievements." In one fell swoop Bloom here redefines human love as the anxiety of influence. By so defining our project Bloom renders it entirely agonistic, since it is a game, unlike Freud's, which we cannot win.

What survives in Bloom's account of Freud is, of course, the hegemony of the self. Whether the self is engaged in the pursuit of happiness or the revenge against time, it is still a psyche-centered world that Bloom and Freud share. Bloom has on occasion gone so far as to imply that even this essential construct may be only a trope: "the *psyche,* the image or trope of the self, has an inevitable priority, for Freud, over reality or the object-world." This way of talking about the psyche as a trope strikes me as a ploy, Bloom's way of letting continental skeptics know that he, too, is playful enough to admit that everything is rhetoric. The fact is that Freud and Bloom are linked in their belief that the psyche is not a trope, that it is the organizing reality of our lives which it is possible to experience and gather evidence about. For Freud, defenses are the man, and the idiosyncrasy and complexity of our defenses provide the best evidence that there exists behind them a shaping self. For Bloom, *stance* is the key word. By focusing upon a poet's stance as his peculiarly distinguishing characteristic, Bloom lays emphasis upon an elective act performed by a human form. In reading Bloom, we are continually asked to picture poets as bodies assuming fundamental positions. The imagination and its stances compose the self, and the self is prior to whatever discourse it takes up. Rhetoric is a means of self-expression which we possess, not an independent system of discourse which we are possessed by. We live in a world constituted of will rather than language.

Bloom would argue that Freud, gazing upon the current critical scene, would complain that it divides the objects of its attention into units of significance which it is impossible to care about. How does one summon concern about the path between a stimulus and a response, or the relation between a signified and a signifier, or the mounting series of aporia that, for some readers, constitute a poem? The essential measure must be poetic, Bloom asserts, and by this he means one scaled to the dramatic encounters between and within people in everyday life. Poetry renders us understandable through concepts like fate, choice, character, epiphany, and plot; it gives us a world in which man is the *modus,* the measure of things. It was because Freud approached his data through the inherited stories of the race that he has become not the greatest scientist but, in Bloom's words, "*the* greatest mythologist of our age." His tropes have replaced all other tropes because he knew the tropes, and he so sublimated this learning that it emerged as a system which many of us are tempted to take as the truth. Bloom can pay no greater tribute to Freud than to nominate him as the Great Replacer, and it is with the quote in which he does so that I would like to end:

> Freud has usurped the role of the mind in our age, so that more than forty years after his death we have no common vocabulary for discussing the works of the spirit except what he gave us.

Charles Molesworth (essay date 1984)

SOURCE: "Promethean Narcissism," in *Partisan Review,* Vol. LI, No. 1, 1984, pp. 155-58.

[*In the following essay, Molesworth discusses the roles of Freudianism and theology in Bloom's criticism.*]

Bloom now offers criticism based on his own religious experience, defining this experience in terms of gnosticism.
— *Charles Molesworth*

In the last three decades, literary critics have struggled to retain their field as the center of cultural understanding. Criticism has been a hybrid, unstable amalgam since the rise of a mass readership. Not surprisingly, the recent struggle has seen criticism try to strengthen and clarify itself by mergers with other disciplines and subjects. From popular culture to structural linguistics, the nets of literary analysis have been flung far and variously. What has increased the extraordinary complexity of this phenomenon is that everywhere literary criticism searched, it found another discipline equally mired in self-doubt and in the "problematic of language." All the disciplines—philosophy, psychoanalysis, Marxism, social science—felt the crisis of interpretive confidence caused by several factors, chiefly the question of how to ground authority in interpreting texts. In this context, Harold Bloom's work takes on a poignant typicality. Two main but contradictory thrusts unite the books he has published in the last decade: first, he centers literary analysis on the literary canon, rejecting humanistic disciplines such as history as little more than the work of knaves and fools. Second, he borrows much of his authority from Freud, but a literary Freud, a writer and interpreter of texts, not a practitioner of healing. Bloom also has revivified a method (almost an anti-methodology) of analysis long discredited, namely, expressionistic criticism, the spectacle of the critic recording the struggle of a lonely soul among masterpieces. Bloom's polemics obscure his strategy, which borrows interpretive authority from Freudianism while making Freud into a sublime poet in the Romantic tradition. Thus Bloom ends with a self-enclosing sense of literature paradoxically close to the formalism he so actively despises.

In two new books this strategy is extended from psychology to religion. Bloom now offers criticism based on his own religious experience, defining this experience in terms of gnosticism (more of which in a moment). The paradox persists, however, since his central insight—that all poems exist in and cry against their own temporality—actually equates belatedness with fallenness. If the first prophets of the diaspora were belated, looking back to previous authority to define themselves, then there is really no "firstness," no ancient truth on which to ground authority. Everything rests on personal will and persuasiveness, and so Bloom is condemned to contentious struggle with enemies and supporters, despite his hunger to be unique. Bloom contradictorily celebrates his religious vision at the same time that he insists no social arena is necessary or sufficient. The critic *agonistes,* he looks in remote, unimpeachable places for the very authority he claims can come only from the genius of the self.

In *Agon* Bloom employs gnosticism as his framework, and admits gnosis is hard to define and radically unhistorical. Borrowing from Hans Jonas's *The Gnostic Religion,* Bloom wields gnosis as a master term that includes, but is not restricted to, poetic knowledge, Romantic imagination, mystical utterances, and early and late versions of the sublime. With a term so many-sided, one makes many claims. (Note that Bloom redefines gnosis as a form of *literary* experience.) But Bloom's obscurity comes not from ambiguity, since he seldom hesitates or qualifies. First he introduces gnosticism as a historical phenomenon, before he dehistoricizes it and finds a gnosis in Whitman, Stevens, and Ashbery. This gnosticism has a familiar core: "The primary teaching of any gnosis is to deny that human existence is a historical existence." If so, how do gnostics avoid the atemporality that leads to formalism? By struggling against predecessors, thus containing and eradicating them. History is no more than a search for self-knowledge. Bloom mediates between the hollow pieties of enervated liberalism (all poetry is not sweetness and light, but struggle and darkness), and the social values that are entangled in the struggles of history. As he says, somewhat smugly, he delights in deconstructionists calling him a sentimental humanist while academicians call him a deconstructionist. But both groups are partly correct. If the self envelopes all conflict and knowledge, then the critic who interprets the self must be all-knowing. But more important, he must not be bound by any historical or social framework or value, using such values only to dramatize and justify the long, all-encompassing agony of self-definition.

Insisting his view of poetry is pragmatic, Bloom says poetry is useful "for whatever poetic and critical use you can usurp" it to. Bloom's use is not any use whatever, but the bringing into action (though largely affective, never social action) of "concepts of being." Bloom here seems to tolerate pluralism, but not really. His concepts are limited and are all versions of belatedness. Whether poetry is a "catastrophe creation, agonistic strife, [or] transference of ambivalence," it always protests against the universal truth of temporality, time's insistence that "it *was*." What poems do in resisting and revising the "it *was*" resembles Eros and Thanatos, but is finally a distinct and equal drive. Bloom claims Freud's two drives are defense reactions and are "indistinguishable from the resistances they supposedly invoke." Poetic will, unlike Freud's negation, negates a negation, and insists on the godliness of the self. (What else would we expect from a being who has no history?) This will is also Emerson's gnosis, the cornerstone of the American religion. Bloom thus mediates between American pragmatism and American idealism.

All of this is the doctrine, or the enabling process, that all strong poems embody. Strong poems appear autochthonous and yet are misread by later poets needing proof of self-generation. (Everything strong is both temporally at strife and self-generated.) Critics know this more clearly than poets, since critics discover the paradox in their textual will-to-power: poetry was there before criticism. And before the poem was, there were prior poems, themselves acts of criticism. Bloom claims great power for critics, a power virtually greater than that of poets. "I mean that I can observe . . . *patterns of forgetting* in a poem." Bloom sees past the poet's influences (his allusions) to his real (real because hidden) struggle. As critic he rewrites the poem as every poet rewrites his precursor poet. Again, in circular logic, though Bloom ostensibly writes prose criticism and not verse poetry, since poetry is criticism and vice versa, Bloom emerges as that which not even he is bold enough to claim directly: our most sublime poet.

What if we take him as we take poets at their highest, as guides to spiritual truth? Bloom writes out of religious experience, though he says explicitly he is content not to convert anyone. Religious in an American way, he is a sect of one. Bloom writes in part about poetry as rhetoric, but his chief paradox is that for all his obsession with the persuasiveness of rhetoric (for where else does power come from?), he claims not to need to persuade others. This inverts the American sublime: I alone escaped to tell you, though I know you won't believe me. (Gnosticism is an inverted religion, an antithetical theodicy.) Bloom boasts, "If you don't believe in your reading then don't bother anyone else with it, but if you do, then don't care also whether anyone else agrees . . . or not." Bloom is a Nietzschean *übermensch,* a polemical, imperious reader, and comico-pathetic solipsist. The implicit call, as in Emerson's "Self-Reliance," is that we all become like this, a mass of imperial selves denying other selves: "When you have life in you . . . you shall not see the face of man."

Bloom bases his will-to-power on ever larger proofs until finally he invokes a theology. Yet, an American, he eschews all authority except the self. What follows is a theologizing of the self. This leads to several things, for example, the canonization of Freud, and the claim that Freudianism is now the language in which we conduct our spiritual lives. It also produces ridiculous claims, such as that Milton's *Paradise Lost* "is the most Freudian text ever written." Poetry is not meant to liberate, "but to define, limit, and so defend the self against everything that might destroy it." Poetry's action is greater than poetry's being; the poem is a process, not an object, just as a self is. (Again, gnosticism is a religion of process, not of being.) Bloom's radical Freudianism says the self is a process that constantly wards off its own redefinition, though it is without definite identity. Society and history never enter. Self, poet, and critic: all are self-generated and self-regarding.

With Promethean narcissism, Bloom's project answers the social moment in America. All is struggle and self-searching, denial of authority and an obsession with it, longing for fulfillment and dread of communal responsibility. How this criticism is valued in the largest terms should be clear; you must take Bloom as you find him, he will be no other. As for how effective he is as a critic, my verdict is mixed. His reading of *Miss Lonelyhearts* is an (unwitting) self-parody, moldy fig academicism, and sterile methodology. The paragraph on page forty-six of **The Breaking of the Vessels** is as badly written as any major critic has published in some time. On Freud and Emerson, Bloom is good indeed: fresh, cogent, even persuasive. On the cultural prospects for Jews in

America, Bloom writes intelligently about social issues (though with a tendency to genuine despair). As a practical critic he descends the admirable heights of *The Visionary Company* to the erratic brilliance of *Yeats,* to the murkiness of his book on Wallace Stevens. One last paradox: Bloom insists on the socially transcendent role of literature and criticism, but his own work is less and less about literature, and more and more a reflection of, and a failed corrective to, our social and cultural malaise.

Denis Donoghue (review date 2 May 1989)

SOURCE: "The Sad Captain of Criticism," in *New York Review of Books,* Vol. XXXVI, No. 3, March 2, 1989, pp. 22-4.

[*In the following review of* Ruin the Sacred Truths: Poetry and Belief from the Bible to the Present, *Donoghue explores Bloom's discussion of the influence of religious forms in Romantic literature.*]

One of the many histrionic vivacities in Harold Bloom's book is its title. Ruin the sacred truths: apparently an admonition, the verb an imperative. But why would Harold Bloom, hitherto not known as a vandal, urge his readers to do such a dreadful thing? The point of the title, but not the justification of the ruin it proposes, emerges on page 125, where Bloom alludes to Andrew Marvell's poem on *Paradise Lost,* in which Marvell, referring to Milton, feared

> *That he would ruin (for I saw him strong)*

> *The sacred Truths to Fable and Old Song.*

I assume, then, that *Ruin the Sacred Truths,* the text of Bloom's Charles Eliot Norton Lectures at Harvard for 1987-1988, is his riposte to T.S. Eliot's *The Use of Poetry and the Use of Criticism,* the Norton Lectures for 1932-1933, in which Eliot, in turn, proposed to discredit an account of poetry and belief which he found in Matthew Arnold and I.A. Richards.

Bloom's project is, in fact, the same as Arnold's, though I would be afraid to mention the latter's name in the former's presence. "For Arnold," as Eliot said, "the best poetry supersedes both religion and philosophy." So also for Bloom, the gist of whose lectures is to say: reduce the once sacred truths to mere fables and old songs, and then let us, like Wallace Stevens, construct in poetry our own romantic tenements. If Arnold's criticism had succeeded in its object, it would be unnecessary for Bloom to trouble himself further. But here he is, trying yet again to show not only that great literature is independent of belief but that it is supremely great when it

has triumphed over belief. In that sense, his new book is a reply not only to Eliot but to M.H. Abrams's *Natural Supernaturalism* (1971), which undertakes to show the continuing power of religious and especially of Christian forms of experience in Romantic literature.

If Bloom is the saddest captain of criticism, the reason may be that, thinking he had disposed of Arnold, he now finds himself belatedly practicing much the same subversion as Arnold's, and with instruments not significantly different. These lectures on the Hebrew Bible, the *Iliad,* Dante, Shakespeare, Milton, Wordsworth, Freud, Kafka, and Beckett have the same moral as Arnold's meditations on translating Homer; that in the absence of religious belief, poetry can save us. Not that Bloom is without beliefs. I might say of him, as Eliot said of Bertrand Russell, that he believes more than Augustine did. Bloom believes in American individualism, in Emerson as founder of the American religion called self-reliance, in Freud as strong theorist of the psyche, and in virtually every further consequence of these beliefs. The essential loneliness of one's being in the world is the culmination of these assumptions. But Bloom's beliefs are not, as I recognize them, religious: their emotions do not include awe. For that reason I cannot say, if poems are to save me, what form of salvation Bloom has in mind for me to hope for.

Bloom is a man of many attributes: he is by birth and I presume on principle an American, by heritage a Jew, by more deliberate affiliation a Gnostic, and in his critical procedures a Pragmatist. On his being an American, he has little to say, apart from his celebration of the Emerson of "Self-Reliance" and the "Divinity School Address," and his repudiation of the smiling Ronald Reagan as false domestication of that Emerson. Bloom's Judaism, I gather, is not normative; he reads the Law but does not otherwise observe it; the Torah is literature to him, but a powerful provocation even in that diminished or absented state. All strong writing is sacred, according to Bloom; an assertion I find shocking since it makes Milton's Satan the paradigm of sacredness, whereas I regard him as a spoiled brat. The significance of the Bible, to Bloom, is that it "invented our literary sense of human personality" and thus prefigured Shakespeare and Freud. Perhaps I do Bloom an injustice; there may be more to his Judaism than I can see. Whatever I know of Gnosticism—to me, a strikingly alien heresy, as deplorable in its repudiation of nature and history as the Manichaeism which it anticipated—I have learned from Hans Jonas's *The Gnostic Religion* and Plotinus's *Against the Gnostics, or against those who say that the Creator of the World is evil and that the World is bad.* According to Bloom, Milton's Satan is a Gnostic because he sees God and Christ as mere versions of the Demiurge, ruler of the cosmological emptiness in which we live:

> In Gnosticism, there is an alien, wholly transcen-

dent God, and the adept, after considerable difficulties, can find the way back to presence and fullness. Gnosticism therefore is a religion of salvation, though the most negative of all such saving visions.

As for Pragmatism: since Bloom values words as deeds and for that reason alone, and since the Pragmatist lodges the process of knowing within the process of conduct, Bloom resorts to Pragmatism to get things done, not to pose ultimate questions. In a sentence that Bloom loves to quote, William James says that "theories thus become instruments, not answers to enigmas, in which we can rest."

Reading Bloom's books as they appeared, I interpreted them as mainly engaged in the recovery of the poetry of Romanticism, against the opposition then represented by Eliot and his pupils, the English and American New Critics. The recovery of Romanticism emerged as a major project in Northrop Frye's study of Blake, *Fearful Symmetry* (1947), M.H. Abrams's *The Mirror and the Lamp* (1953), Geoffrey Hartman's *The Unmediated Vision* (1954), Georges Poulet's *The Metamorphoses of the Circle* (1961), Bloom's ***The Visionary Company*** (1961), and Abrams's *Natural Supernaturalism*. More recent work by Paul de Man and several other critics has made Eliot's dismissal of Romantic poetry—as distinct from his specific recognition of certain poets, notably Poe, Whitman, Tennyson, and Swinburne—seem opportunistic.

Bloom's influence in the restoration of Romantic poetry to an unashamed readership has been, and continues to be, immense.
—Denis Donoghue

Bloom's influence in the restoration of Romantic poetry to an unashamed readership has been, and continues to be, immense. But I have only recently come to understand the scope of the claim he is making for Romanticism: not merely that it is one creative procedure among many or that it marks the site of some great poems, but that the particular kind of poetry it has produced is poetry-as-such, the sole type and model of true poetry. In the vertigo of his most exalted paragraphs, we are to find ourselves persuaded that every poem, however decisive in its apparent character, from the Bible and Homer to Dante, Shakespeare, and Milton has been a precursor of the definitive type or mode of poetry as we find it in Wordsworth's "Immortality" Ode and the two-part *Prelude* of 1799.

The model for this mode of reading is Borges's "Kafka and His Precursors," according to which your reading of Kafka makes you feel that certain earlier works—Borges mentions Han Yu, Kierkegaard, and Browning—are best understood as prefigurings of Kafka. It is no wonder that Bloom reads the early masterpieces much as the Romantic poets read them, and later works chiefly in their diverse relations to Romanticism. No wonder, too, that in Bloom's hands all great poems tend to become one and the same, the exemplary act of Narcissus: only minor poems keep their differences. Stevens's *Notes Towards a Supreme Fiction* comes out sounding like Wordsworth's "Tintern Abbey": both are alike and equally Emersonian acts of power, the proclamation of divinity within oneself; to me an empty or Pyrrhic victory.

Bloom's central concern, from his earliest writings, has been with "the poetical character," otherwise known as poetic genius. To retain the mystery but not the mystification of that power, he resorts to an Emersonian distinction between psyche, the subjectively perceived mind, and pneuma—the divine spirit or spark that transforms the mind. Prematurely, as it seems to me, Bloom is prepared to take Freud's word for our psychic lives. "Our father Freud," as he charmingly calls him, stands unquestioned in his prescription of ego, id, and superego. In *Agon* (1982) Bloom refers to "the strong self, by which Emerson means the Gnostic *pneuma* or spark and not the mere psyche." The pneuma is "spark-of-the-primal-Abyss," the true soul in its fullness of presence.

In ***The Breaking of the Vessels*** (1982) Bloom speaks of "the Orphic or Gnostic or Kabbalistic spark, the pneuma of the poet and of the knowing reader." In ***Ruin the Sacred Truths*** he says that Kafka refused "the Gnostic-quest for the alien God, for one's own spark or *pneuma* rejoining the original abyss somewhere out of this world." If the pneuma, spark, or "inmost self" is, as Bloom insists in *Agon*, "absolutely alien to the cosmos, to everything natural," it follows that it must seek salvation, whatever that entails, within itself. Poetry becomes—in Arnold's phrase—"the dialogue of the mind with itself." Or rather, the dialogue of the pneuma with itself. It follows, too, that when a poet deals with anything "natural"—a landscape, for instance, which the poet cannot claim to have made—he must deal with it as if it were himself or at last became himself.

I recall Bloom, a few years ago, making a comparison between Elizabeth Bishop's "The End of March" and Robert Lowell's "Skunk Hour." The comparison was much in Bishop's favor because her poem offered "the overwhelming self-revelation of a profoundly subjective consciousness," while Lowell's poem remained "an opacity," presumably because the "natural" in it remains grimly resistant. I recall, too, his positing that John 1:14 says (or should say): "And the Word became Pneuma [spirit] and dwelt among us"; rather than "became Flesh"; a conceit entirely consistent with Bloom's reluctance to see the Old Testament book yielding in the New Testament to an incarnate person, Jesus Christ.

Bloom concedes that poetry cannot continuously be the dialogue of the pneuma with itself. There are obstacles: contingency, the given, necessity (Ananke). But he insists on gathering every obstacle together and giving the sum of them a personal form, the form of a contest with the past. A great poet meets his necessities in the form of his forerunners, and especially of one of them, his fated and chosen precursor, who must be taken on, removed, completed, evaded, or otherwise transcended. The predicament is like the one described in Walter Jackson Bate's *The Burden of the Past and the English Poet* (1970), but I take Nietzsche to be Bloom's immediate source.

In *Zarathustra* and more fragmentary writings Nietzsche recurs to the agon between a writer and his precursor. In "Homer's Contest" Nietzsche speaks—the passage is quoted in *Ruin the Sacred Truths*—of the relationship of Xenophanes of Colophon to Homer, and of the "overwhelming craving to assume the place of the overthrown poet and to inherit his fame." Even a dead man, Nietzsche says, can "still spur a live one to consuming jealousy." In Bloom's terms, the anxiety caused in the strong poet by the overbearing force of his precursor is the epitome of the poetic character. If he is strong enough, the later poet will triumph: he will master anteriority by remembering rather than by repeating the past, and he will make the past seem the creation and consequence of his will. I would add that the strong poet also protects his consciousness against the ennui of having nothing to encounter but its own devices. Narcissus can imagine that his predicament and Satan's agon are one and the same.

Is this agon characteristic of great artists by virtue of their daimon? Or is it a relatively recent, perhaps post-Renaissance symptom of certain historical conditions? Bloom has not been consistent on this question. Dante and Shakespeare seem to embarrass any theory of anxiety, since they show no sign of having felt anxious about authority or about recapitulating the work of the artists of genius who came before them— what Bloom calls their own "belatedness." In *Ruin the Sacred Truths* Bloom refers to the agon between Aeschylus and Euripides, and claims that Euripides is "a severe case of the anxiety of influence." Virgil apparently suffered the double anxiety of having Lucretius as his precursor and Homer as his "daunting father." Dante is "Virgil's daemonic son"; though the assimilation of Dante to Bloom's theory of influence still seems to me implausible because there is simply no evidence of it. He also refers, more convincingly, to Milton's "loving but fierce competition with the Bible and Homer, Virgil and Dante, Spenser and Shakespeare." So I suppose he has come to the conclusion that the agon is categorical to strong writers: weak writers evince their weakness by not recognizing their situation as agonistic.

The aim of *Ruin the Sacred Truths* is to disengage the poet from any belief that would create an obstacle to his poetry.

Bloom does this by assigning such beliefs to the mere psyche, where presumably they work mischief or good. Belief to Milton, for instance, meant "the liberty exercised by his own pure and upright heart," so it didn't get in the way. If a belief threatens to get in the poet's way, it can be nullified by showing that while the poet-as-psyche may have held the belief, the poet-as-pneuma entertained it only nominally or speciously. Milton's pneuma therefore merely entertained the God of *Paradise Lost,* his true self being of Satan's party throughout. In any case a belief can't intimidate the pneuma. If belief continues to assert itself, it can be disabled by calling it "a weak misreading of literature." Ambition for immortality, a clear sign of the pneuma, "takes priority over belief of any kind."

A genius, according to Harold Bloom, lives and works to overcome his precursor; to transform every obstacle into himself, his own inwardness. The supreme emotion of this transformation is "the sublime," irrefutable mark of victory. In a strong poet, every merely contingent, historical, political, or economic condition, including one's religious belief, is consumed and nothing much is left of it.

The origin of *Ruin the Sacred Truths* is clearly the distinction, proposed in various forms by Hazlitt, Coleridge, and Keats, between two types of imagination. One type, found in Shakespeare, sequesters itself in favor of its creations. Hazlitt said of Shakespeare:

> He was just like any other man, but that he was like all other men. He was the least of an egotist that it was possible to be. He was nothing in himself; but he was all that others were, or that they could become.

The other type was ascribed now to Milton, now to Wordsworth; as in Keats's famous account, in a letter of October 27, 1818, to Richard Woodhouse, of the impartiality of the poetical character, as distinct "from the wordsworthian or egotistical sublime." Under the sway of this Wordsworthian type of imagination, nothing perceived by the poet's mind is allowed to retain its apparent independence, it must yield itself to the subjective power of the poet which in the end overwhelms it.

To clear a vast space for the egotistical sublime, Bloom not only dumps every apparent nuisance on the poor psyche, but follows Hazlitt in establishing Milton's Satan as the archetype of "heroic vitalism." Those passages in which Satan appears to some readers a mere casuist, Bloom interprets as expressions of nothing less than the majesty of self-assertion. In *Paradise Lost* (Book V, lines 856-864) Satan, who has evidently been reading Wallace Stevens, rounds upon Abdiel, who has been insisting that Christ was God's agent in the Creation:

Who saw
When this creation was? rememberest
thou
Thy making, while the Maker gave
thee being?
We know no time when we were not
as now,
Know none before us, self-begot,
self-raised
By our own quickening power when
fatal course
Had circled his full orb, the birth
mature
Of this our native Heaven, Ethereal
Sons.
Our puissance is our own ....

This passage sends Bloom into an *altitudo* of eloquence, on the assumption that here Satan is the poet Milton, magnificently claiming to be, as pneuma, self-begotten. But the gorgeousness of the lines in a Stevensian way can't conceal the fact that Satan's argument is nonsense. Adam meets it when he says (Book VIII, lines 250-251):

For Man to tell how human life
began
Is hard: for who himself beginning
knew?

In the end, *Paradise Lost* isn't about the poet Milton and his pneuma, though in responding to Bloom's satanic eloquence I find myself wishing for a while that it were. Bloom rarely convinces me of anything, except that in a differently constituted world the beauty of his sentences or of the lives he quotes would make them true.

I have the same feeling again, reading Bloom's account of *Paradiso,* Canto XV, where Cacciaguida addresses Dante. Bloom says that Dante, through Cacciaguida, "salutes himself as that unique one, all but messianic, who beheld the truth in his own image before ever he began to think." Cacciaguida, according to Bloom, "gives Dante the principle of the poet's prophetic vocation, which establishes the authority of the *Comedy:* 'You behold the truth, for the small and great of this life gaze into that mirror, in which, before you think, you behold your thought.'" In fact, this is the opposite of what Cacciaguida says. It is not for Dante a matter of beholding the truth in his own image, but of believing the truth that comes from God: it is "Tu credi" in line 61, repeating the "Tu credi" of line 55. What Cacciaguida says to Dante is:

You believe that your thought flows to me from Him
who is First .... [*Tu credi che a me tuo pensier*
mei/da quel ch'é primo ....] *You believe the truth,*

because the lesser and the great of this life gaze into that mirror in which, before you think, you display your thought .... [*Tu credi 'l vero; ché i minori e' grandi/di questa vita miran ne lo speglio/in che, prima che pensi, il pensier pandi. . .*]

Cacciaguida's address to Dante supports a theory of poetic inspiration, and therefore of prophecy, but not one of prophetic self-begetting. Bloom is so entranced by the figure of a self-begotten pneuma that he sees what is not in the poem, and refuses to see what is. He reads *Paradiso* Canto XXXI as if it ended with Beatrice, not Mary; and as if Beatrice, when Dante looks up to see her, is found to have "made for herself a crown, reflecting from her the eternal beams." Not so: Beatrice reflected the eternal rays as they came to her from God.

A motto for **Ruin the Sacred Truths** might well be Stevens's: "God and the imagination are one." They are one in a sense which Stevens often but not always settled for, the egotistical sublime which converts every ostensible object into subjectivity. Bloom is devoted not to Pure Poetry but to the poem as Pure Act and its ideal model, the act of self-begetting. Freud seems to be Bloom's authority for this notion. In Bloom's **Yeats** (1970) we read:

Freud thought all men unconsciously wished to beget themselves, to be their own fathers in place of their phallic fathers, and so "rescue" their mothers from erotic degradation. It may not be true of all men, but it seems to be definitive of poets *as poets.* The poet, if he could, would be his own precursor, and so rescue the Muse from her degradation.

Wordsworth, surprisingly, becomes the truest poet, a conclusion Bloom has reached by ignoring Blake's complaint against him, that his commitment to memory held him back from true vision. Bloom's Wordsworth is Keats's and Hazlitt's, not Blake's. "Wordsworth celebrates his own godhood," Bloom says, reading him as if he were reading Milton's Satan and ignoring, too, the fact that in the sublime passage from the two-part *Prelude* that he quotes as evidence, Wordsworth says that the power he felt within was

for the most
Subservient strictly to the external
things
With which it communed.

Subservient? That doesn't sound like Bloom's Wordsworth.

How then does Bloom deal with Shakespeare? Surely Shakespeare, of all writers, can't be appropriated to a theory of the egotistical sublime? No, but he allows his greatest characters to change by becoming egotistical sublimists. The hint for this notion comes from Hegel's remark, in *The Philosophy of Fine Art,* that Shakespeare confers intelligence and imagination on his choice characters and, "by means of the image in which they, by virtue of that intelligence, contemplate themselves objectively as a work of art, he makes them free artists of themselves." Bloom argues that Shakespeare, acting upon the example of Chaucer in developing the Pardoner and the Wife of Bath, set his characters to contemplate themselves and by doing so to change and to manifest the process of change. Hamlet, Edmund, Iago, Falstaff: these are Bloom's examples, and he writes of them with exhilarating zest, especially of Falstaff. It is old-fashioned criticism, indeed, somewhat Wagnerian, contiguous with A.C. Bradley's *Shakespearean Tragedy* and other works similarly unabashed about subjectivity. Indeed, only a critic with Bloom's authority and verve could use without fuss or apology or definition the words he uses: mimesis, will, ego, being, voice, author, self, personality. Faced with "current flight from individuality in literary critical circles"—in which authors and selves supposedly have no place—he is *content to see these* neo-Gallic tourists buy a one-way ticket to Paris. How can I fail to enjoy the spectacle of Bloom sending these youngsters on their bon voyage? He is the Satan of criticism, in the sense that he is heroic even in those passages in which we are permitted to suspect that he may be a charlatan. He is not a charlatan, and in that—in my view—he differs notably from Satan.

But there is a cost to every merit. I have implied that Bloom is impassioned in his sense of words, but only because he thinks of words as deeds and wishes to see them fulfill their destiny as deeds without equivocation. "The Yahweh-Word is an inward fire, however raging," he says, "as are the Yahweh-Act and the Yahweh-Thing, since word, act, and thing are blent in the Hebrew for 'word.'" They are blended, too, in every word of Bloom's criticism. As a result, he has little to say about words in any of their other capacities: perhaps he denies that they have any. My own prejudice is that in poetry, words are so chosen and ordered as to delay their resolution as deeds, and to prolong the contemplation of them in every other respect. But I suspect that Bloom, in a hurry to see the poets triumphant in the sublimity of their self-assertions, would regard my prejudice as pusillanimous, a mere urbanity. He speaks, in a tone I associate with the great actor-managers, of "the best of all critics, Dr. Johnson." I am more regularly persuaded by Johnson than by Bloom, but I think a comparison between the two not at all absurd. Bloom's puissance is not entirely his own; for some of it, he is indebted to Nietzsche, Freud, Schopenhauer, Gershom Scholem, and other masters. But enough of it is his own to constitute a distinctive form of splendor.

Nannette Altevers (essay date Spring 1992)

SOURCE: "The Revisionary Company: Harold Bloom's 'Last Romanticism'," in *New Literary History,* Vol. 23, No. 2, Spring, 1992, pp. 361-824.

[*In the following essay, Altevers argues that Bloom's "psychopoetic model" does not constitute "a fundamentally historical mode of interpretation."*]

My sense of Harold Bloom's critical importance would not alone seem enough to justify this essay since others have explicated the essentials of his revisionary poetics at substantial length—Frank Lentricchia's *After the New Criticism* (1980), Elizabeth Bruss's *Beautiful Theories* (1982), and Jean-Pierre Mileur's *Literary Revisionism and the Burden of Modernity* (1985) are three examples that come immediately to mind. Despite their strength in other ways, however, these efforts seem to me finally to lack any real understanding of Bloom's project, any sense of its underlying significance. The same, I believe, can be said of certain influential forms of feminist criticism (most famously that of Sandra Gilbert and Susan Gubar) which would posit against Bloom's so-called gender-restrictive Oedipal theory of literary relations a counter-patriarchal, noncombative, matriarchal tradition of women writers precursors. Focusing on the female literary tradition of the nineteenth century in their monumental *The Mad Woman in the Attic* (1979), Gilbert and Gubar aim to articulate a historical feminist poetics modeled on Bloom's patriarchal poetics of the male tradition. Instead of an "anxiety of influence," female writers experience an "anxiety of authorship"—an anxiety and rage resulting from the confining backdrop of male literary authority which keep them from attaining literary autonomy. But as I shall argue in the following pages, Bloom's psychopoetic model is *not* an Oedipal model. Nor does it constitute, as the critical consensus would have it, a fundamentally historical mode of interpretation.

In a recent interview Frank Lentricchia reasserts his (influential) claim in *After the New Criticism* that in his revisionary tetralogy Bloom "has put forth bold and important ideas which threaten to make the moribund subject of influence the pivot of the most satisfying historicism to appear in modern criticism." Citing the "historical, self-conscious sophistication" of Bloom's theory, Lentricchia again maintains that it "is the historicist character of his project" that makes Bloom's an "'exemplary career.'" And it is this view of Bloom, I believe, that has kept alive an interest in his project. No reasonably attentive reader of the major journals in literary criticism and theory, after all, will be unaware of the new enthusiasm for a rhetoric of referentiality, of the current fascination with something called "history," whether under the specific rubric of a "new historicism" or as part of a commitment to the development of polemical and political applications, in the present, of scholarly research done about the past. Books and articles that have "politics" or "history" in their titles are in fact proliferating. So much so that one is perhaps tempted to sympathize with Lentricchia's exasperation: "Bandwagons. Christ! . . . everyone wants to be political; every other word is 'politics this' and 'politics that,' 'history this' and 'history that.' It makes me want to say I'm not interested in that any more . . . . It's a fashion." Bloom's case, however, is somewhat different. Although he *appears* in his texts on revisionism to revitalize and historicize his view of the romantic tradition—romanticism begins to split into a new temporal polarity as Bloom "historicizes" the imagination into a tension between its early, original manifestations and its later derivative ones—his new historicism turns out, as I shall argue, to be barely skin deep and amounts finally to a distrust of the historical more thoroughgoing than any he had evidenced before. Though most of his critics have recognized (Lentricchia among them) that Bloom's is "romantic" criticism, none has recognized the extent to which this is so. Bloom's theory of influence ultimately rests on the hope (and the possibility) of a self that can rise above its historical situation to a state where the false imperatives of merely institutional forms will be exchanged for the true imperatives that can now be spied by a newly cleaned vision— that is, by a newly free self. In other words, his revisionary poetics is of a piece with his earliest theoretical pronouncements.

In fact, the first of Bloom's revisionary texts implicitly announces his own belated membership in the "visionary company" itself. *The Anxiety of Influence* "offers a theory of poetry that presents itself as a severe poem, reliant upon aphorism, apothegm, and a quite personal (though thoroughly traditional) mythic pattern." The "pattern" on which Bloom's "severe poem" is "reliant" is not, however, that of the Freudian family romance. In *The Ringers in the Tower,* a book published one year earlier but in which the phrase "anxiety of influence" already appears tangentially throughout, Bloom had respectfully dismissed Freud as the prisoner of a reality principle the romantics had left behind. And although in *The Anxiety of Influence* his reading of Freud has gained in complexity, he is still discarded as "not severe enough," his wisdom outranked by "the wisdom" of "the strong poets": "If *Wordsworth's Ode: Intimations of Immortality from Recollections of Earliest Childhood* possessed only the wisdom found also in Freud, then we could cease calling it 'the Great Ode.'" Freud's "poem, in the view of this book is not severe enough, unlike the severe poems written by the creative lives of the strong poets."

Again, in *A Map of Misreading*—Bloom's theory of influence is of course an evolving process, with each text repeating and amplifying the scheme of its predecessor—Bloom associates, though even more explicitly, his own "severe poem" (or theory of revisionism) with those written by the visionary company (and particularly by Wordsworth, whom Bloom refers to as "the exemplary Modern Poet, the Poet

proper"): "I will follow the order of my own revisionary ratios from *The Anxiety of Influence* because their movement is founded both on the Lurianic model of the myth of creation (though I did not know this consciously when they came to me) and also on the model of the Wordsworthian crisis-poem." Of course the "Wordsworthian crisis-poem" which, according to *Kabbalah and Criticism,* set "a pattern" that all "subsequent strong poems [including Bloom's we can assume] seem doomed to repeat" is but another name for the poetic genre M.H. Abrams long ago christened "The Greater Romantic Lyric." Moreover, the structure of such lyrics as the "Intimations Ode" and "Tintern Abbey" is but an abbreviated version of the romantic "Circuitous journey" documented by Abrams in his now-classic *Natural Supernaturalism:* "Wordsworth's *Prelude* [which for Abrams is paradigmatic of the journey] can be viewed as an epic expansion of the mode of 'Tintern Abbey,' both in overall design and local tactics." I thus propose that the "thoroughly traditional mythic pattern" upon which Bloom's "poem" is "reliant" is in fact that of the romantic circuitous journey. Though there are of course many versions of the journey, the most useful paradigm for Bloom's own "personal" version is, as I seek to demonstrate, Wordsworth's incredibly involuted masterpiece. Thus, although I maintain that Bloom's theory of revisionism is *not* a theory of literary history in the sense that critics continue to view it, it does in fact constitute a history of sorts. Like Wordsworth's *Prelude,* Bloom's "severe poem" is a psychological autobiography which narrates the history or growth of the poet's own mind.

> **The structure of Bloom's journey, like Wordsworth's, is circular and radically achronological.**
> **—Nannette Altevers**

The structure of Bloom's journey, like Wordsworth's, is circular and radically achronological; it starts not at the beginning but at the end, and it reaches at its end the very stage in time at which it in fact begins. In the Introduction to *The Prelude,* as in that to *The Anxiety of Influence,* the narrator is confirmed in his vocation as poet. Wordsworth then narrates his life, not as a simple narrative in past time but as the present remembrance of things past, in an effort to determine what forces molded him to poetic utterance. The title of Bloom's Prologue to his "severe poem"—"It was a Great Marvel That They Were in The Father Without Knowing Him"—metaphorically hints at the poet's unusual birth: he "begets" himself. The "Father" or precursor, I suggest (though admittedly such a suggestion appears rather fanciful at this point), is the practical critic of *The Visionary Company* who gives birth to a son, the poet/theorist of the "revisionary company," who, if Bloom's poetic is to be believed, will be forced to revise or "misread" his strong precursor. The poet then begins, like Wordsworth, to recollect his earlier years and the process of his development as a poet:

> After he knew that he had fallen, outwards and
> downwards,
> away from the
> Fullness, he
> tried to remember what the Fullness had been.
> He did remember

I. The Visionary Company: "Paradise"

Dedicated to M.H. Abrams, *The Visionary Company* (1961) is informed throughout by Abrams's "romantic approach" to the subject of romanticism and its works. According to Bloom, the romantic poets are aggressive humanists who "have the same enemy . . . the universal and enduring vulgarization of the myth of the Fall." And like Abrams, he assumes that the high claims made for the romantic imagination as the guarantor of man's innocence over his corruption constitute what is truly revolutionary in the romantic movement. Although Bloom's visionary company inhabits a universe already recognized as discontinuous rather than organic (they are not "naive" but "sentimental" poets, to borrow Schiller's terms), they refuse to embrace the nihilistic implications of the "unromantic" doctrine of the Fall. Bloom claims in essence that the romantics repress a "causality" explanation of the universe by substituting a teleological explanation—the myth of the creative imagination. Based on the Kantian assumption that the mind in perception is always creative or constitutive, this myth undermines the prevailing Lockean epistemology, allowing man to become his own original as he breaks the chain of causality. Thus the romantic poet "escapes" from the fallen world into the myth-making world of his own imagination which *wills* the universe to be a good and happy place, a "postlapsarian" paradise of enthusiasm and organic creative process.

So the romantic imagination puts mind and world, subject and object, back together again—at least in mind. Which brings up the age-old question of aesthetic representation. If the poet's symbolic vision expresses itself in sublunary language, it becomes secondary, trapped in a prior network or medium, rather than a true moment of origin. Hence the romantics' inevitable deference to the phenomenology of consciousness over the status of discourse, which results, as Thomas McFarland points out in a recent book, in their curious tendency to distinguish between the terms "poetry" and "poem." Because the word "poetry" suggests, like consciousness, "something unbounded, a current only adventitiously caught in words," while "poem" suggests "something closed and delimited, a verbal artifact," in romantic "formulations the conception of 'poem' is devalued." The visionary critic's own commitment to the prelinguistic theme or "argument" of a poem (the "poetry") leads likewise to a profound disdain

for the poem's figurative language. Towards the end of *The Visionary Company,* for example, Bloom explicitly states his purpose in writing the book: "I am studying Romantic argument in these pages, and the argument of *To Autumn* is largely implicit, that is, 'obscured' by its own verbal imagery."

Because the poet's idea is "obscured" by its "imagery," Bloom opts for a transparent language that will reflect clearly the poet's consciousness which, by definition for a phenomenologist, is visionary and not linguistic: "Wordsworth and Wallace Stevens," for instance, "are at one in forsaking the image when they wish to tell their truths, and it is precisely then that they write some of their highest poetry." Similarly, after citing a passage from the Prospectus to *The Recluse,* Bloom assures us that "Image and metaphor are not wanted here; this kind of poetry has a palpable design upon us, and does not disguise it." Interestingly, Bloom here anticipates, albeit inversely, the "anti-deviationist" claims for poetic language expounded by Derrida and the deconstructionists. Bloom implicitly blurs the distinction between philosophy and the "highest poetry" because the latter is also logocentric, a conveyer of "truths" written (so Bloom believes) in a perfectly clear or literal language bereft of metaphor, while Derrida blurs the distinction between literary and philosophical discourse precisely in the opposed direction by pointing out the original "metaphoricity" of *all* discourse. Although this is perhaps to get ahead of myself, the so-called deconstructive strategy underlying Bloom's texts on revisionism—he admits no distinction between philosophical and literary discourse ("all criticism is prose poetry" [*AI* 95])—is, as I shall later argue, of a piece with his strategy here and thus remains diametrically opposed to Derrida's notion of "écriture." However, *The Visionary Company* anticipates "the revisionary company" in a more fundamental and crucially important way. Bloom's visionary company is, in fact, *already* a revisionary company.

Though one could cull from Bloom's text numerous examples of one poet's "revision" of his precursor, I cite merely a representative few: "Byron claimed to have little use for Wordsworth's poetry, though he did not escape its influence. Shelley and Keats acknowledged Wordsworth's poetic ancestry, but both repudiated the later poetry of their great original"; "The key to *The Prelude* as an internalized epic written in *creative competition* [emphasis added] to Milton is to be found in those lines (754-860) of the *Recluse* fragment that Wordsworth prefaced to *The Excursion* (1814)"; "Behind Coleridge's" *Kubla Khan* is "Collins' masterpiece of a poet's incarnation, the *Ode on the Poetical Character*." We find in *The Visionary Company,* moreover, an ominous foreshadowing of Bloom's willful "misreading" of poets in the texts on revisionism. Aside from his "debts" to Coleridge, Bloom focuses on Keats's unpalatable notion of "disinterestedness," which is of course the reverse of his own extremely "interested" poetics. Citing a passage from *Sleep and Poetry,* he notes that Keats protests "Promethean expressionism . . . . The nature of poetry is to be disinterested . . . . A poem is neither thought nor personality; it does not affirm anything, not even the poet himself." Bloom promptly adds, however, that "Keats is more himself when, in the remainder of his poem, he considers his own destiny as poet." But if Bloom's commitment to the psychology of the poet's imagination or "self" (and concomitant valorizations of the phenomenology of consciousness over the status of discourse) is explicit throughout *The Visionary Company*, it becomes surprisingly even more pronounced, despite the emergence (close to home) of radically new and influential critical movements, with the passing years.

In 1970 J. Hillis Miller published "Geneva or Paris," an article perhaps indebted to one published the previous year by Paul de Man—"The Literary Self as Origin: The Work of Georges Poulet"—that sounded the death knell for phenomenological criticism. In any event both critics, now followers of Derrida, systematically "deconstruct" Poulet (whose work of course greatly influenced Bloom's at this time). What most troubles Miller is that Poulet takes "language for granted" as a "perfectly transparent medium . . . . All the apparent assumptions of Poulet's criticism are interrogated by Derrida and found wanting." As it turns out, however, Poulet is only "apparently" wanting; Miller tells us that "Poulet's exploration of the 'cogito' of each of his writers leads to the recognition that the 'cogito' is the experience of a lack of a beginning, of an irremediable instability of the mind." It is clear, ultimately, that Poulet is not "really" a privileger of the silent origin (as phenomenological voice which is identical with itself) but is rather a connoisseur of "écriture" and the absence of presence. This accords nicely with de Man's earlier discovery, through a "certain amount of interpretative labor," that Poulet's "criticism is actually a criticism of language rather than a criticism of the self." Astonished but undaunted by such critical feats, Bloom published one year later (in 1971) his "revision" of *The Visionary Company* which, it turns out, is actually not a revision at all.

Though Bloom claims in his Preface that "Where I am persuaded I was mistaken, I have made revisions, and I have tried to eliminate redundancies," the contents of the text proper remain virtually unchanged. The only revisions consist in the addition of a one-page preface, an introductory essay, and an epilogue—all of which, though they reveal an emergent "anxiety" resulting from Bloom's "demystified" awareness of his own previously "mystified" state, reveal simultaneously and paradoxically a deepening commitment to subjectivity. In his Epilogue ("The Persistence of Romanticism"), for example, Bloom claims that "Wordsworth was the inventor of modern poetry, and he found no subject but himself . . . . Our disease is not so much alienation as it is solipsism, and the subject of modern poetry is endlessly solipsism." Clearly repulsed by the structuralists reduction of

the author to a mere function of language, Bloom maintains in the epilogue, moreover, that "Romantic poetry has survived several varieties of reduction, and so will survive the structuralists, against whom it offers a fierce countercritique. In the structuralist view, myths have no authors and come into existence only when incarnated in a tradition, but the myths of Romanticism have authors, and then are embodied by tradition." Claude Lévi-Strauss is "Our contemporary Peacock . . . whose respect for mythical thought extends to music, but not to poetry: 'Music and myth are languages which, each in its own way, transcend the level of articulate speech.' Poetry, he tells us, is a descent from words to phonemes, a fall into language, a failure to transcend daily limitation. The meaning of a myth, he finds is only to be conveyed by another myth, as the meaning of music is in other music, but Lévi-Strauss does not want to know what all the Romantics knew, that the meaning of any poem can only be another poem." Though Bloom's notion that the meaning of a poem is a relational event ("the meaning of any poem can only be another poem") appears to derive from the structuralists' concern with the interdependence of all structures, the relations among things rather than things in themselves (a concern rooted ultimately in Saussure's linguistic principle of the differential character of signs, in his theory that meaning is differentially or diacritically produced), his implication that, like myth and music, poetry too transcends, "in its own way," "the level of articulate speech" clearly suggests that he is interested in the relations among structures of consciousness rather than the relations among structures of discourse, in intersubjectivity rather than intertextuality.

In the final section of the epilogue Bloom claims that "From our current perspective" we cannot read "Romantic poetry" as that poetry "was meant to be read" because "a freedom to know appears to have been lost." "Wordsworth meant to renovate his readers," but "Our readings are swervings or falls into language, and not the completions these poets rightfully expected." Of course the phrase "rightfully expected" carries with it an implicit *ought* about the kind of reader required by Bloom (and Wordsworth before him), thus short-circuiting his grant to us, in the texts on revisionism, of subjective freedom. Clearly, what the "visionary company" (and its new member) "rightfully" expect is that their poetry be read by other visionaries (whose "readings" are *not* "swervings or falls into language"). Indeed, Bloom himself had claimed in his Introduction—ominously entitled "Prometheus Rising," thus reminding us of his advocacy in the original *Visionary Company* of "Promethean expressionism" while simultaneously alluding to the imminent birth of the "severe" poet ("The Promethean Quester every ephebe is about to become")—that, because of Milton's conservatism (he ultimately rejected "a Satanic idolatry of self"), the romantics were forced to misread their great predecessor: "one of the great characteristics of the Romantic period" was "that each major poet in turn sought to rival and surpass Milton" which "could only mean to correct his vision by humanizing it."

Thus, although we learned in the original version that the visionary company was *already* a revisionary company, we now learn that they are "re-visionaries" as well as revisionaries. What the romantics "correct" or "revise" is not Milton's poem but his "vision," which they must "re-see." Similarly, though the "aim" of Bloom's forthcoming "severe poem" is "to try to provide a poetics that will foster a more adequate practical criticism", it is the poet's consciousness that Bloom's "practical criticism" aims to help us read; his concern is with "*the poet in a poet,* or the aboriginal poetic self" rather than with the poet *as* poet, as maker-in-language. Bloom is concerned with how the reader can recuperate his [Bloom's] "vision": "This book's main purpose is necessarily to present one reader's critical vision in the context both of the criticism and poetry of his own generation, where their current crises most touch him, and in the context of his own anxieties of influence." Bloom's desire "to renovate his readers" thus parallels Wordsworth's and is just about as "practical." Moreover, the second stage of Bloom's "Prelude" parallels Wordsworth's: the paradise of Wordsworth's childhood is lost in his wrong turn to the persuasive lures of the French Revolution, while Bloom's is lost in his turn to those of the French "theoretical revolution."

II. The Revisionary Company: "Paradise Lost"

We thus circle back from the past to the "point de départ" of Bloom's dialectical journey—his birth, in *The Anxiety of Influence,* as poet/theorist. We remember, however, that, according to the romantic version of the journey, one's birth is also a fall. As Abrams notes, the romantic circuitous journey "has a clearly defined plot: the painful education through ever expanding knowledge of the conscious subject as it strives—without distinctly knowing what it wants until it achieves it—to win its way back to a higher mode of the original unity with itself from which, by its primal act of consciousness, it has inescapably divided itself off." Bloom's "birth" is a "fall" from the mystified phenomenologist's unified consciousness into the demystified poet/theorist's divided self-consciousness, a fall into an intensified awareness of the world of temporal process and hence of the diachronic nature of language. He has fallen away from the "Fullness" ("he knew that he had fallen outwards and downwards, away from the Fullness") of the womb and of "the Word." This decentering of the poet's consciousness apparently causes him such anxiety that he becomes schizophrenic. The discourse throughout the revisionary tetralogy (the four intertextual volumes that record the second stage of Bloom's journey) is dialogical, narrating the "agon" between his two antithetical "consciousnesses"—the mystified phenomenologist's and the demystified poststructuralist's. Of course Bloom, like the other members of the visionary company, knows that there is progression

only through contraries; hence his claim that this type of anxiety is, in poets at least, actually a sign of health: "Schizophrenia is disaster in life, and success in poetry."

Though Bloom is seemingly preoccupied now with poststructuralist theory—his new code word in *A Map of Misreading* is "text"—it is hardly surprising that his use of the word "text" is in fact antithetical to the poststructuralists. While the opening sentence of *A Map of Misreading* informs us that "This book offers instruction in the practical criticism of poetry, in how to read a poem, on the basis of the theory of poetry set forth in my earlier book, *The Anxiety of Influence*", the epigraph provides a metaphorical description of what Bloom means by "reading": "As wine in a jar, if it is to keep, so is the Torah, contained within the outer garment. Such a garment is constituted of many stories; but we, we are required to pierce the garment." The "real" text ("the Torah") is transcendent; the Word is contained in the words of the apparent text ("the garment") which constitute not a medium but a transparency that we can "pierce" in order to see the truth. And while Bloom also claims on the opening page that the "strong reader" is "placed in the dilemmas of the revisionist, who wishes to find his own original relation to truth, whether in texts or in reality (which he reads as texts anyway)," his "strong reader" is not to be mistaken for the poststructuralist who is confronted with a world of wall-to-wall discourse (who "reads" reality "as texts"); he is the phenomenologist whose vision "pierces" the language of texts or of reality in order to see "truth." Still, it is not that difficult to understand how a typical example of Bloom's deceptive rhetoric—"If not to have conceived oneself is a burden, so for the strong poet there is also the more hidden burden: not to have brought oneself forth, not to be a god breaking one's own vessels, but to be awash in the Word not quite one's own"—might result in the claim that, "Despite" his "ostensible disagreement with Derrida," Bloom "clearly recognizes" the "fundamental intertextuality of writing." Of course, as the capitalization of "Word" suggests, the "strong poet" is *not* "awash" in écriture.

Indeed, despite the "ventriloquist's" unrestrained tendency to decenter his own argument, to undermine the notion of "logos" through his "dummy's" deconstructive jargon, the wary reader ultimately discovers that even Bloom's most obviously poststructuralist formulations actually underline the fact that his "disagreement with Derrida" is fundamental rather than "ostensible." He informs us, for example, that "A single text has only part of a meaning; it is itself a synecdoche for a larger whole including other texts. A text is a relational event and not a substance to be analyzed"; or again, "Influence, as I conceive it, means that there are *no* texts, but only relationships *between* texts." He does not mean, however, that a text is not a discrete verbal entity because every text is itself already an intertextual event, a part of the vast sea of écriture. For Bloom a text is "not a substance to be analyzed" because it is a prelinguistic rather than a verbal entity: "a poet's consciousness of a competing poet is itself a text." He is no advocate of the "intertextuality of writing" because the "texts" between which meaning wanders are *not* written: "A poetic 'text,' as I interpret it, is not a gathering of signs on a page, but is a psychic battlefield" on which the belated poet/critic/reader struggles with his precursor. The "meaning" of these prelinguistic texts wanders between subjects on a "psychic battlefield." And make no mistake; there is nothing in Bloom to suggest that he shares Lacan's notion that the psyche is *itself* a signifying machine.

Bloom does not believe that language determines consciousness but explicitly the reverse.
—*Nannette Altevers*

Bloom does not believe that language determines consciousness but explicitly the reverse: what Emerson knows "is that his language, language itself, always fails his soul, or rather the Oversoul, which indeed transcends the dance or interplay of tropes." What Emerson "knows then is something about adequacy or inadequacy, something about agon, about the struggle between adverting subject or subjectivity and the mediation that consciousness hopelessly wills language to constitute." For Bloom, "influence remains *subject-centered, a person-to-person relationship, not to be reduced to the problematic of language . . . poetry, despite all its protests, continues to be a discursive mode, whose structures evade the language that would confine them*" (emphasis added). He clearly insists on a preverbal "psychic" warfare, which argues for a deep-structure beyond the manifest contents of text/writing/language: the "fundamental phenomena of poetic influence have little to do with the borrowings of images or ideas, with sound patterns, or with other verbal reminders of one poem by another"; the "most vital instances of influence are almost never phenomena of the poetic surface." Thus for Bloom, as for Poulet (whose influence clearly extends to Bloom's latest work), "A text is a relational event" between two consciousnesses. His so-called "intertextuality" is in fact the intersubjective dynamic hermeneutics of the belated and besieged phenomenologist, his "psychopoetics" but another version of the expressivism which informed *The Visionary Company*. But even a phenomenologist who offers a specific methodology, a "map" by which to read poems, must eventually confront actual poems ("a gathering of signs on a page"), and here is where Bloom's real problems begin.

Though he claims that his "theory of influence" has nothing to do with theories of influence "Old Style," that "poetic influence cannot be reduced to source study . . . to the patterning of images" or to verbal echoes, Bloom ends up relying precisely on source study and on the descriptive, mimetic

criticism that characterizes his "readings" of poems (dismissing "irrelevant analytical techniques" [*VC* 153], he summarizes selected passages) in *The Visionary Company*. Thus when we examine his "practical analyses," we can extract no principles that do not inevitably contradict his theoretical claims. Blake's "London," for instance, is fathered by the book of Ezekiel. We recognize this because the "central image" is the same in both, even the key rhyme of "'cry'" and "'sigh'." Indeed, though one could cull from Bloom numerous examples that attest to the accuracy of de Man's claim that "For the most part," Bloom's "examples" are "*a priori* assertions of influence based on verbal and thematic echoes and stated as if they spoke for themselves," insufficient space here requires that I cite but a representative few. Bloom chooses Stevens's "The Snow Man" as a poem which, though "central and quite thoroughly original . . . reveals itself as another version of the apotropaic litany that poetry has become." In fact, "this apparently least restitutive of poems moves . . . to the hyperbole of pathos in the misery of the Shelleyan wind, on to the introjective metalepsis of the final 'beholds,' where the 'nothing' that is there and the 'nothing himself' of the beholder both are effectively equated with the greatest of American epiphanies: 'I am nothing; I see all'." Despite the clogged syntax and Bloomian jargon, the point is simple enough. Two of the obvious precursors whom Stevens echoes are Shelley and Emerson. Often finding the Shelley in Whitman, Bloom compares Whitman's "As I Ebb'd" to Shelley's "Ode to the West Wind": "For Shelley's leaves Whitman substitutes 'those slender windrows, chaff, straw, splinters of wood, weeds' and the rest of his remarkable metonymic catalog. For Shelley's 'trumpet of a prophecy,' Whitman gives us 'that blare of the cloudtrumpets'." And so it goes.

Behind the arbitrariness of the psychological plot, the wary reader ultimately senses that Bloom's texts on revisionism actually deal with something else, that he has some other not so hidden agenda. In fact, one becomes increasingly suspicious about the usefulness of his "methodology" as, with each successive text, he increases the intricacy of his "map," while simultaneously decreasing his actual usage of it. And despite the fact that the eighteen categories of the map which have accumulated by the publication of *Poetry and Repression* actually reduce to the original six "revisionary ratios" set forth in *The Anxiety of Influence*, we are ultimately confronted with statements such as the following: "This is the Lurianic pattern of *Zimzum Shevirath ha-kelim Tikkun,* and is enacted again (in a finer tone) in the next dialectical pair of ratios, *kenosis* (or undoing as discontinuity) and *daemonization* (the breakthrough to a personalized Counter-Sublime)." Yet while the unwary asks himself what such private language (Bloom has clearly said good-bye to most of the conventions of modern critical discourse) might possibly mean, the astute reader knows the answer: This is nonsense; it doesn't mean anything. Nor, for that matter, does Bloom's "map."

Though de Man rightly claimed in his review that *The Anxiety of Influence* "is by no means what it pretends to be," that "the main interest" of the book "is not the literal theory of influence it contains," he is quite wrong in claiming that its main interest is rather "the structural interplay between the six types of misreading, the six 'intricate evasions' that govern the relationships between texts." It is, of course, hardly surprising that he should focus, as does Hayden White, who claims in a recent article that "Tropology" is for "Harold Bloom" a "primary problem of discourse analysis," on what appears to be the historical and linguistic side of Bloom. But although the substantial emphasis in Bloom's description of the six ratios falls on temporal priority—a polarity of strength and weakness (Bloom consistently speaks of "strong" and "weak" poets) is correlated with a temporal polarity that pits early against late—the sixth ratio curiously undermines not only any notion of temporality but, in fact, Bloom's whole methodology. "Apophrades" (also referred to as "metalepsis" and "transumption"), which Bloom informs us is "the revisionist trope proper", is, ultimately, the *only* revisionist trope. It rightly figures in the climactic last place as the sixth ratio, because it destroys the principle on which the system is patterned: it substitutes early for late in a metaleptic reversal. That Bloom's "rhetoric of temporality" is empty, his "map of misreading" a throwaway, is in fact attested to in the chapter of *A Map of Misreading* entitled "Testing the Map: Browning's *Childe Roland*," where Bloom offers "a reductive and therefore simplified total interpretation of the poem, firmly based on the model of misprision I have been tracing." We have, of course, come to expect such reductiveness from a theorist who claims that "poets do not invent the dances they dance, and we *can tell* the dancer from the dance. The stronger poet not only performs the dance more skillfully than the weaker poet, but he modifies it as well, and yet it does remain the same dance. I am afraid that there does tend to be one fairly definite dance pattern in post-Enlightenment poetry, which can be altered by strong substitution, but still it does remain the same dance." Clearly, this one "dance pattern" is that of the "Wordsworthian crisis-poem": "Hegel says that History ended in October, 1806, with Napoleon's victory at the Battle of Jena. Let us say that Poetry ended just about then also, with the Wordsworthian crisis-poem setting a pattern that subsequent strong poems [including Bloom's own, we can assume] seem doomed to repeat, whatever the variations of rhetorical substitution." Like the "Wordsworthian crisis-poem." Browning's *Childe Roland* provides an example of the "Romantic quest or internalized romance" which takes the form of a dialectical or circuitous journey in "three parts."

The first stage of Roland's journey ("Stanzas I-VIII") constitutes "the induction, during which an initial contraction or withdrawal of meaning is gradually redressed by a substitution or representation of the quest." The poem's "second movement (IX-XXIX)," its "long middle," enacts Roland's fall into nature (his "ordeal-by-landscape") and temporality. In this crisis-stage Roland inhabits "a landscape of repetition, but in the deadliest sense, one in which all questions of genesis have yielded to mere process, to one-thing-after-another." Though he "describes his landscape like Zola describing an urban scene, yet Roland's world is wholly visionary, its 'realism' a pure self-imposition." Roland's "misprision or mistaking of his inherited quest-pattern culminates in stanza XXIX, which ends the second movement of the poem . . . . In the nick or crucial moment of giving up, which would be the prolongation of a wholly negative repetition, Roland is suddenly startled into a climactic recognition, which is that he is trapped, yet paradoxically this entrapment alone makes possible a fulfillment of his quest." According to Bloom, the poem's final three stanzas (XXII-IV) enact a metaleptic reversal, "a transumptive scheme or figure of a figure, *which undoes the figurative assertions of Roland throughout the entire poem before them*" (emphasis added). In the previous chapter Bloom had explained that metalepsis, which "overcomes temporality by a substitution of earliness for lateness", is a "trope-reversing trope" to which Quintilian applied "the Latin name transumption." In the poem's "final stanza" Roland "negates the larger part of his poem." Thus the temporal, fallen stage of Roland's journey—the landscape of "mere process" and "continuous metonymy"—is transcended; indeed, Bloom now informs us that "Roland's time-sense in the long middle part of the poem is a delusion." Roland "ends in strength": "What remains is vision proper, as the once ruined quester is transformed into a seer." Though Bloom assures us that "we have read *Childe Roland* as a revisionary text, on the model of our map of misprision", it is clear that we have left behind neither *The Visionary Company* nor its visionary critic.

Towards the end of his reading of *Childe Roland* Bloom asks, "If Roland is alone at the end, as he is throughout the poem, then who is the antagonist? Certainly not 'The Band' of brothers and precursors, for they stand ranged in vision, at the close." His answer is that the agon of the poem's "long middle" takes place in *intra*subjective rather than in *inter*subjective terms (between Roland and "'The Band' of brothers and precursors"): "There is only Roland himself to serve both as hero and as villain . . . . Roland sees himself at last as what he is," the "dangerously internalized" solipsist, "the solitary poet-quester, the penseroso." Bloom reminds us a few chapters later that "Internalization of the precursor is the ratio I have called *apophrades* [transumption/metalepsis]," and "Romantic internalization, as I have shown in another study, 'The Internalization of Quest Romance,' takes place primarily in intra-subjective terms, the conflict being between opposing principles *within the ego*." He explains, moreover, that "Roland is giving us a parable of his relation to his brother-knights, which becomes a parable of Browning's relation to the poets who quested for the Dark Tower before him." And thus, by implication, a parable of

Bloom's relation to *his* precursors. Indeed, Bloom's allusion to his earlier essay reminds us that the precursor who most concerns him is not Frye, Bate, or Abrams, or contemporary rivals ("'The Band' of brothers and precursors"), but Bloom himself (he had in fact suggested a few pages earlier that a writer's work exists in anxious relation to 'the youth he was', in other words to *his own* prior works); it reminds us that the subject of his revisionary tetralogy (his own "severe poem") is not the history of literary influence, but the history of his own mind.

Moreover, Bloom's claim in "The Internalization of Quest Romance" (the opening essay in *Romanticism and Consciousness* [1970], a now-classic encomium to phenomenological criticism) that "what Blake and Wordsworth do for their readers, or can do . . . is to provide both a map of the mind and a profound faith that the map can be put to a saving use" obliquely foreshadows his forthcoming "practical" map of misreading. Indeed, such a Blakean/Wordsworthian "map of the mind" was mentioned by Bloom as early as 1961, in the original version of *The Visionary Company*. We can read "*The Four Zoas* as a Freudian allegory" in which "Urizen was a kind of superego, Thormas an id, with Luvah-Orc rising from him as libido; but Los, the fourth Zoa, is hardly a representation of the Freudian ego . . . . Los has no part in this scene, which is deterministic and clearly indisputable as an act of psychic cartography." This "act of psychic cartography" is described as "the intense warfare of consciousness against itself within a psyche." Of course Bloom describes metalepsis, the "revisionist trope proper" which "overcomes temporality by a substitution of earliness for lateness" and thus destroys the principle on which his "map" is patterned, in precisely the same way: metalepsis "takes place primarily in intrasubjective terms, the conflict being between opposing principles within the ego." I thus suggest that Bloom's "map of misreading" is itself "a map of the mind"—a psychic map of the agon (between the mystified phenomenologist and the demystified poststructuralist) within Bloom's ego as he revises his own mind. Furthermore, Bloom's own "severe poem," like Browning's and like all "Wordsworthian crisis-poems," is destined to end metaleptically ("from the Renaissance through Romanticism to the present day metalepsis has become the major mode of poetic allusion, and the figure without which poems would not know how to end"), with "a substitution of earliness for lateness." The final lines of his poem must enact a metaleptic reversal, "a transumptive scheme or figure of a figure" which "negates the larger part of his poem."

For all Bloom's talk throughout the revisionary texts about "wandering signification," this final stage of his dialectical journey was anticipated in one of them:

> Though I am myself an uneasy quester after lost meanings I still conclude that I favor a kind of inter-

pretation that seeks to restore and redress meaning, rather than primarily to deconstruct meaning. To de-idealize our vision of texts is a good, but a limited good, and I follow Emerson, as against Nietzsche, in declining to make of de-mystification the principle end of dialectical thought in criticism . . . . And I think Nietzsche particularly understood that Emerson had come to prophesy not a de-centering, as Nietzsche had, and as Derrida and de Man are brilliantly accomplishing, but a peculiarly American *re-centering* . . . that remains stubbornly logocentric.

The epigraphs to *Poetry and Repression,* the final volume of the revisionary tetralogy, foreshadow the "American *re-centering*" of "wandering signification" by depicting metaphorically Bloom's move from "The Revisionary Company" ("Paradise Lost") to *Agon* ("Paradise Regained"):

> O earth, how like to heaven, if not preferred
> More justly, seat worthier of gods, as built
> With second thoughts, reforming what was old!
> For what god after better worse would build?
> *Paradise Lost*

> The past and present wilt—I have fill'd them, emptied them,
> And proceed to fill my next fold of the future.
> *Song of Myself*

III. Agon: "Paradise Regained"

The first two lines of *Agon*'s Preface attest to Bloom's now recentered consciousness: "A book might seem an anomaly that offers itself as a unity in design and theme, but includes chapters on the ancient religion of Gnosticism, on Freud, on Emerson and Whitman and Hart Crane, on American Jewish cultural prospects, and on the author's own theories of fantasy, of the Sublime and of poetry and its interpretation. What, beyond the aggressive personalism of the author, can hold together so eclectic a range?" Surely nothing but Whitman's intentionality ("I am large, I contain multitudes"). More importantly, Bloom claims in his first chapter that "When Whitman revised the first line" of *Song of Myself* "he made explicit his antithetical relationship to epic tradition. *But his more vital revision was of himself, since he had come to understand that his truest contest was with his own earlier text*" (emphasis added). And despite his claim on the opening page of his Preface that "these chapters direct themselves towards the theory of revisionism its author hopes to live to write," *Agon* is, in fact, the final revision of Bloom's earlier texts on revisionism. This claim is but a variation on the romantic poet's traditional largeness of ambition and self-imposed inclusiveness of scope, his striving after the infinite ("something evermore about to be"). "Revisionism," Bloom tells us, "is this book's subject," and "Revisionism pragmatically has become only a trope for Romanticism." Revisionism is a form of "agon," and while the "first theologians of agon were the Gnostics of Alexandria," the "final pragmatists of agon have been and will be the Americans of Emerson's tradition . . . . that is the center [the end as new beginning] of this book."

Agon, Bloom tells us, "searches for the revisionary gift that Emerson called 'self-reliance' and made into the American religion, a purified Gnosis. Against its only apparent eclecticism, this book proclaims a religious intention"; it constitutes "a personal blend of my individual religious experience with my own literary theory and criticism." Thus we return to the impassioned defenses of the visionary, religious values of poetry that characterize Bloom's earliest work. In the original version of *The Visionary Company* Bloom had claimed that "What Wordsworth is giving us" in the final book of *The Prelude* "is his vision of God . . . . Here, as he gathers *The Prelude*'s many currents together, he shows a confidence both in his art and in his personal myth of natural salvation. In this confidence he has created a major poem." This of course parallels exactly Bloom's description of *Agon,* the final book of his own "Prelude." And although the book's Introduction is entitled a "Prelude to Gnosis," it is no more a "Prelude to Gnosis" than Wordsworth's *Prelude* is a "prelude" to *The Recluse.* In *Kabbalah and Criticism* he had already urged "a Kabbalistic model, which means ultimately a Gnostic model" for the interpretation of poetry. Bloom explained that he turned back to the Kabbalah, seeking an interpretive "paradigm for reasons akin to those that led Emerson back to Orphism and Neoplatonism. Emerson accepted the necessity of misreading, or the active figuration of the strong reader, and he accepted it with joy and confidence, as befitted the prophet of Self-Reliance. He read for the 'lustres,' he insisted, and he saw those lustres as emanating from His own Reason . . . . The Kabbalists read and interpreted with excessive audacity and extravagance; they knew that the true poem is the critic's mind, or as Emerson says, the true ship is the shipbuilder." Clearly, "misreading" is but a variation on the phenomenology of reading as described by Poulet in his essay of that title. It is, of course, not Poulet but Emerson (Bloom's new visionary hero and the president of the visionary company's American subsidiary) on whom Bloom focuses in *Agon.*

Indeed, the nascent Emersonianism of Bloom's early work becomes strident in this text where he insists that the "strongest of all texts urging strong misreading is Emerson's *Self-Reliance,*" which "I have evaded until now": "'Man is timid and apologetic . . . he dares not say "I think," "I am," but quotes some saint or sage. He is ashamed before the blade of grass or the blowing rose. These roses under my window make no reference to former roses or to better ones . . . . There is no time to them'." To this Bloom responds: "I call this theo-

retical literary criticism, or the theory of strong misreading." And to this we respond: So much for Bloom's rhetoric of referentiality, his theory of literary "history." Similarly, after comparing a couple of passages from Carlyle's two essays on history with one from Emerson's, of which I quote only the concluding line—"'The student is to read history actively and not passively; to esteem his own life the text and books the commentary'"—Bloom responds: "So much then for Carlyle on history; so much indeed for history. The text is not interpretable? But there is *no text*! There is only your own life, and the Wordsworthian light of all our day turns out to be: self-reliance" (emphasis added). That Bloom was never interested in literary history or influence is in fact suggested again, in a more indirect, though perhaps even more telling manner, earlier in *Agon.*

Emersonian transumption (misreading/revisionism/gnosis) is more whimsical than Nietzschean transumption because "Nietzsche remains a rhetorician . . . and has more in common with Carlyle, whom he loathed, than with Emerson, whom he adored." Nietzsche, like Carlyle, "cannot do without the old descriptions of the world" (that is, of history and of language). Both Nietzsche and Carlyle "remain Protestants, however displaced, but Emerson has entered upon the American religion, Orphic and Gnostic, rather than Protestant." Emersonian transumption, moreover, derives from Milton. "Like Milton, Emerson establishes as the basis of his figuration three temporal Zones [which parallel the three stages of the romantic circuitous journey]: the true origins, everything false ever since, and the truth of the eternal now." Bloom explains that "The Miltonic or American text is true [here read *Agon*]; what happened at the start is true [here read *The Visionary Company*]; all of literature and history and religion, all text in between is false [here read the tetralogy on literary influence]." Clearly, Emerson's version of "Gnosis" or "strong misreading," with which Bloom has already identified his own, could just as easily serve as Bloom's:

> Emerson's Gnosis rejects all history, including literary history, and dismisses all historians, including literary historians . . . A discourse upon Emerson's Gnosis, to be Emersonian rather than literary historical, itself must be Gnosis . . . . it will not speak of epistemology, not even deconstructively of the epistemology of tropes, because it will read Emerson's tropes as figures of will, and not figures of knowledge, as image of voice and not images of writing . . . . I am suggesting that what a Gnosis of rhetoric, like Emerson's, prophetically wars against is every philosophy of rhetoric, and so now against the irony of irony and the randomness of all textuality. The Emersonian Self, "that which relies because it works and is," is voice and not text, which is why it must splinter and destroy its own texts.

Thus Bloom implicitly encourages his reader not to deconstruct the words on the page but to destruct them, to invent his own text.

Bloom implicitly encourages his reader not to deconstruct the words on the page but to destruct them, to invent his own text.
                                        —*Nannette Altevers*

After Emerson "the literary, indeed the religious mind of America has had no choice, as he cannot be rejected or even deconstructed . . . . Since he will not conclude haunting us, I evade concluding here, except for a single hint. He was an interior orator, and not an instructor, a vitalizer and not an historian". The same could of course be said of Bloom, according to whom, "Criticism is the discourse of the deep tautology—of the solipsist who knows that what he means is right, and yet that what he says is wrong." The solipsist is a "voice," but not the words he speaks; his are the unspoken words *behind* the spoken words. There *is* origin, identity, truth, but it remains locked in the subjectivity of the "interior orator" (in "the orator's word, the transparency as proclaimed by Emerson" [*A* 272]). I thus "evade concluding" my citation of Bloom's Prologue to *The Anxiety of Influence*. Bloom's poetic birth was a tragedy: when the poet emerged

> from the Fullness, he tried to remember
> what the Fullness had been.
> He did remember, but found he was silent, and
> could not tell the others.
>
> . . . .
>
> Sometimes he thought he was about to speak, but
> the silence continued.

There is, finally, no "severe poem" because there is "no text." Bloom's "theory" calls for the growing solipsism of the poet, and so, in the final analysis, for the "death" of his own poem in the "birth" of "poetic" criticism ("The poem we write as our reading" [*AI* 96]).

It should by now be obvious that Lentricchia is mistaken not only about Bloom's offering "the most satisfying historicism to appear in modern criticism," but also about his managing, "once having brought the issue of the active reader forward, to avoid the extremes represented by Fish and Gadamer." The idea of meaning being somehow immanent in the text's language, awaiting its release by the reader's interpretation, is, for both Fish and Bloom, an objectivist illusion. Bloom, like Fish, simply carries the implications of phenomenology to their logical extreme, relocating meaning in the "intending subject." But Bloom is, in fact, *more* extreme than Fish. Fish's key concept of "interpretive communities" guards against the hermeneutical anarchy to which his theory appears to lead.

Not any old reading response will do: the reader in question is an "informed" reader bred by the academic institutions, whose responses are thus unlikely to prove too wildly divergent from each other to forestall all reasoned debate. Bloom is, like Emerson, much more "democratic"; his theory allows no criterion by which to distinguish the validity of a reading: all readings are, apparently, equally valid. In light of the foregoing argument the title of Lentricchia's chapter on Bloom— "Harold Bloom: The Spirit of Revenge"—takes on a new meaning. Though Murray Krieger's *Theory of Criticism* may be *his* "Last Romanticism," surely Bloom's is *the* "Last Romanticism."

Denis Donoghue (review date 6 January 1995)

SOURCE: "The Book of Genius," in *Times Literary Supplement,* No. 4788, January 6, 1995, pp. 3-4.

[*In the following review, Donoghue questions Bloom's choices and methods in the formation of a literary "canon".*]

In 1970, W. Jackson Bate published *The Burden of the Past and the English Poet,* in which he argued that the crucial predicament of English poets since the eighteenth century has been their conviction of belatedness: they feel that they have come into poetry too late and are forced to look with envy and dismay upon, "the Giant Race, before the Flood". Keats told his friend Richard Woodhouse that "there as nothing original to be written in poetry; that its riches were already exhausted—and all its beauties forestalled". Not that every poet was daunted by giants. Blake, in a more spirited mood than Keats, wrote: "Drive your cart and your plow over the bones of the dead." But the dead masters persisted, darkening the living.

In *The Anxiety of Influence* (1973), Harold Bloom took up Bate's theme and turned it into a general theory of poetic influence. The sense of belatedness, he maintained, disables the weak poet but provokes the strong poet to challenge his precursors, thereby increasing his strength. Anxiety, he argued, is not to be avoided; the canon is its fulfilment:

> A canon, despite its idealizers from Ezra the Scribe through the late Northrop Frye, does not exist in order to free its readers from anxiety. Indeed, a canon is an *achieved anxiety,* just as any strong literary work is its author's achieved anxiety. The literary cannon does not baptize us into culture; it does not make us free of cultural anxiety. Rather, it confirms our cultural anxieties, yet helps to give them form and coherence.

In some of his books Bloom has followed Bate in thinking

the anxiety of being influenced a modern phenomenon, but in other books, and now in *The Western Canon*, he writes of it as if it were perennial, the one story and one story only of great literature. Blake challenges Milton, Milton confronts Shakespeare, Shakespeare overcomes Chaucer and Marlowe, Chaucer engages with Reccacio, and so on till we find Pindar in primal conflict with Homer.

Bloom's extension of the theory of anxiety to cover all strong writers completes the logic of his theory of poetry: it is a theory of genius, and genius scorns every condition except that of the belatedness on which, we see, it thrives. Bloom's books since *The Anxiety of Influence* have been elaborations of this theory. No circumstance or force at large, religious, political, social, or economic, is allowed to circumscribe genius. If you think that Wordsworth respects the energy of the natural world and is often enthralled by its manifestations, you err: he is most powerfully Wordsworth when he enforces his imagination against "the strong enchantments of nature". If you agree with Coleridge that we receive but what we give, you are still in error. Nature, culture, history, society, the pleasure of being in the world: none of these matters to genius, of which therefore we can say nothing. In the presence of genius and its works, we can express only wonder, awe, admiration, Bacon's "broken knowledge". The spark of *pneuma* which a strong reader recognizes as genius is unconditioned except for one consideration, the fact that it has to sustain the burden of being late. Genius knows how to deal with that.

Genius is Bloom's choice word, but he surrounds it with a few more accessible ones. Personality, will, self, subjectivity, introspection: these are his main terms of reference and admiration:

> Shakespeare invented the perpetually changing, endlessly growing inner self, the deepest self, all-devouring, the self first perfected in Hamlet and still ravening on in Satan.

The true use of Shakespeare "or of Cervantes, of Homer or of Dante, of Chaucer or of Rabelais", according to Bloom, "is to augment one's own growing inner self". Elsewhere he writes:

> When I read, say, "The Poems of Our Climate", by Stevens, or "The End of March", by Bishop, I encounter eventually the overwhelming self-revelation of a profoundly subjective consciousness. When I read, say, "Skunk Hour", by Lowell, or one of Berryman's sonnets, I confront finally an opacity, for that is all the confessional mode can yield.

It never occurs to Bloom—or rather, he never lets it stay in his mind for long—that a poet's scruple might consist pre-cisely in letting a grain of sand remain opaque, irreducible. Bloom insists that every constituent of reality be dissolved by one's subjective consciousness: he is evidently a convinced philosophic idealist. In "Notes towards a Supreme Fiction", Stevens writes:

> From this the poem springs that we live in a place
> That is not our own and, much more, not ourselves
> And hard it is in spite of blazoned days.

No doubt. But while Stevens is writing superb poems that brood upon this quandary, Bloom is feeling exasperated. His mind resents meeting anything in the world of a different order from itself, and he requires poets to appear to remove the opaque phenomenon for his satisfaction. He admits that Kafka accepted "the primacy of fact", but apparently that is no reason why Bloom should. He is appeased only by flares of "the egotistical sublime", to which he thinks himself, it would seem, the last elegiac witness:

> All that the Western Canon can bring one is the proper use of one's own solitude, that solitude whose final form is one's confrontation with one's own mortality.

In other words: good readers are returned to "the autonomy of imaginative literature and the sovereignty of the solitary soul, the reader not as a person in society but as the deep self, our ultimate inwardness".

It follows that genius expresses itself in two forms. One of these is self-creation, uttering itself as prophecy, whether in Milton's Satan or in Blake. Bloom writes of "the aesthetic anguish at not being self-begotten", and he quotes with exhilaration one of the passages of *Paradise Lost* in which Satan seems to me most absurd:

> We know no time when we were not as now;
> Know none before us, self-begot, self-raised
> By our quickening power . . . .

The other form of genius expresses itself in the creation of characters. A motto for this might be taken from Hamm in Beckett's *Endgame:* "Then babble, babble, words, like the solitary child who turns himself into children, two, three, so as to be together, and whisper together, in the dark". This should make a difficulty for Bloom, to begin with, because the creation of characters is not inherent in a subjective consciousness. Keats and Hazlitt clearly understood this in relation to Shakespeare and Wordsworth. Bloom is not deterred. Contradicting himself freely because he contains multitudes, he says that "literary character is an imitation of human character", and that "the meaning and value of every character in a successful work of literary representation depend upon our ideas of persons in the factual reality of our lives". But he reduces the difference between the two modes of genius by saying that Shakespeare, following Chaucer's Pardoner, makes Lear, Macbeth, Hamlet and Othello change, modify themselves "not only by their actions, but by their utterances, and most of all through overhearing themselves, whether they speak to themselves or to others". Bloom writes of Shakespeare's plays and of other works of literature as if they contained nothing but their characters; and of these as if their supreme form of communication were the soliloquy. His theory, in its bearing on Shakespeare, amounts to this: by acts of the objective or histrionic imagination, presumably, Shakespeare invented Hamlet; but then he endowed him with a great subjective imagination, making him, more than anyone else in the plays, "the free artist of himself". Bloom quotes that phrase from Hegel's *The Philosophy of Fine Art,* and it gives the gist of his own chapter on Shakespeare.

Bloom describes himself as a literary critic, but in *The Western Canon* he has chosen not to be one. What he practices is the psychology of authorship, ego psychology for which literature supplies the occasions. No wonder Shakespeare is "the major psychologist in the world's history". As for aesthetic considerations: the aesthetic and the agonistic are one, Bloom asserts. But the agonistic is a psychological premiss, not a literary one. I don't understand why Bloom continues to call himself an aesthetic critic; he shows no interest in literary form, structure, questions of narrative, style, or tone, the fellowship of word and word, syllable and syllable. He doesn't seem perturbed by having to quote Dante in English prose, or by the multiplicity of misquotations that disfigure *The Western Canon.* If one is a literary psychologist, the verbal detail doesn't matter much; one quickly translates the words on a page into an approximate gesture of the self, and discusses that instead of the words.

I am not the first to remark that the substance of Bloom's work is psychology. Reviewing *The Anxiety of Influence,* Paul de Man noted that the book marked a relapse on Bloom's part "into a psychological naturalism". From a relationship between words and things, or words and words, as de Man said, "we return to a relationship between subjects". De Man tried to save Bloom from himself, drawing him back from the "agonistic language of anxiety, power, rivalry, and bad faith", but the effort has failed. In *The Western Canon,* Bloom is more a psychologist than ever. So the contradictions in his books hardly count. Reading great literature will do you neither harm nor good, he says at one point, but it may teach you how to overhear yourself when you talk. On the other hand, in his introduction to *Odysseus/Ulysses* (1991), he refers to "the healing work of a literary culture, which implicitly seeks to cure violence through a normative mimesis of ego, as if it were stable, whether in actuality it is or is not". I don't understand how a society which apparently can't be redeemed by "religion, science, philosophy, politics, social movements"

can be brought to peace by ego psychology, in my view a justly discredited myth.

Bloom's version of the Western canon is meant to sustain this myth. He ascribes canonicity to authors rather than to works, and to authors in only one disposition:

> Most simply, the Canon is Plato and Shakespeare; it is the image of the individual thinking, whether it be Socrates thinking through his own dying, or Hamlet contemplating that undiscovered country.

Later it turns out that "the Western Canon is Shakespeare and Dante". Separate chapters are given to Dante, Chaucer, Cervantes, Montaigne, Shakespeare, Molière, Milton, Johnson, Goethe, Wordsworth, Jane Austen, Whitman, Emily Dickinson, Dickens, George Eliot, Tolstoy, Freud, Proust, Joyce, Kafka, Woolf, Neruda, Beckett, Borges and Pessoa. After Wordsworth, the names become somewhat arbitrary. We have Jane Austen and George Eliot but not Balzac, Henry James, Flaubert or Conrad. We have Virginia Woolf, represented by *Orlando,* a novel not at all canonical, rather than a greater writer, D.H. Lawrence. We have Joyce but not Yeats or T.S. Eliot. How the chosen writers rather than some mute inglorious Miltons succeeded in entering the canon Bloom doesn't say. "The authentically daemonic or uncanny always achieves canonical status", he insists, but he has nothing to say about the process which leads to that result. Or about the readers who have joined to make the writers canonical. "L'oeuvre propose, l'homme dispose", according to Roland Barthes, but Bloom has no time for such a notion. Indeed, on the large question of canonicity, he has little to contribute. I am surprised that he has not intervened in this debate, in which many wise things have been said during the past two centuries. My favourite writers on this theme are David Hume in "Of the Standard of Taste" and Frank Kermode in *The Classic, Forms of Attention* and *History and Value.* Hume's values may be hard to recover, but Kermode's argument that certain works of art become canonical by being "patient of interpretation" has the great merit of acknowledging the work of readers as well as of writers. Bloom is content to say that certain writers are canonical because of their originality and strangeness, a variant of Pater's "strangeness and beauty"; but that is all he says.

When the flurry of assertions has passed, we return to the particular chapters of *The Western Canon,* some of which are wonderfully perceptive while others are disappointing. The chapter on Shakespeare has a certain grandeur of eloquence, especially on *Hamlet* and *King Lear,* which we have not heard since A.C. Bradley's *Shakespearean Tragedy.* But I wish Bloom would condescend to do some close work. He asks us to contrast a passage in *Othello* (III, iii) with a passage from *Paradise Lost,* but he doesn't lead the way. "You can hear John Keats and Walter Pater in Iago's crooning", Bloom says, quoting:

> Not poppy, nor mandragora
> Nor all the drowsy syrups of the world
> Shall ever medicine thee to that sweet sleep
> Which thou ow'dst yesterday.

Iago is not crooning. What we really hear in those lines, for the one and only time in the play, is Iago speaking in the voice of "the Othello music". Why Shakespeare gave Iago a few moments of that music is a question Bloom hasn't asked.

The chapter on Emily Dickinson is one of the best, an entirely fresh reading which draws attention to three or four poems normally ignored. The claim Bloom makes for Dickinson—"the best mind to appear among Western poets in nearly four centuries"—is difficult either to establish or to refute. Unfortunately, he misquotes poems 419 and 761 from Thomas H. Johnson's edition of Dickinson, and acts interpretatively on the misquotations. Of the modern chapters, the best is on Beckett. Bloom ignores Beckett's later fiction, but his commentary on *Waiting for Godot, Endgame* and *Krapp's Last Tape* is superb.

The most disappointing chapters are on Whitman and on Joyce. That Whitman's imagination was autoerotic and onanistic is a standard view and mildly interesting, I suppose. There are poems, notably "Spontaneous Me" and the twenty-eighth section of "Song of Myself", which are regularly quoted to make the case. But the matter is far more complex than Bloom allows. A full commentary would require a close reading of "Song of Myself" and would take into account many difficult passages, such as Whitman's reference to "the sick-gray faces of onanists" in the first version of "The Sleepers", and the line in "I Sing the Body Electric" that reads: "Have you seen the fool that corrupted his own live body? or the fool that corrupted her own live body?" Meanwhile Bloom says, not surprisingly, that "Whitman's ultimate romance is with Whitman".

The problem with the chapter on Joyce, "Joyce's Agon with Shakespeare", is that Joyce did not conduct an agon with Shakespeare. Bloom's sole evidence is the National Library chapter of *Ulysses,* in which Stephen Dedalus elucidates his theory of Shakespeare as father and son. Bloom takes this theory with amazing gravity, but in fact it is high comedy, a lark shared between Stephen, Lyster, Russell, Eglinton, Best, and Mulligan. The proper response to the theory is Mulligan's shout, "Eureka!" Bloom's commentary on this chapter of *Ulysses* is not helped by further misquotations. Twice on the same page he botches one of Joyce's most ravishing sentences: "We walk through ourselves, meeting robbers, ghosts, giants, old men, young men, wives, widows, brothers-in-love, but always meeting ourselves." In Bloom's transcription, "meet-ing" becomes "meet" and "brothers-in-love" becomes "brothers-in-law".

I was surprised to find Bloom regarding *Finnegans Wake* as "Joyce's greatest achievement". H.C. Earwicker, Anna Livia, Shem and Shaun are hardly characters, at least in the sense in which Falstaff, Hamlet, Rosalind, Iago, Macbeth and Lear—Bloom's paradigms—are characters. Nor are they Satanic self-begetters. Bloom spends only a few pages on the *Wake* and in the end merely says that it is "the most successful metamorphosis of Shakespeare in literary history". He seems uneasy with the book, as well he might be, and he returns to Leopold Bloom with relief and pleasure. Of Leopold as a character—whom he calls Poldy, as Molly Bloom does—he says:

> Poldy has a Shakespearean inwardness, far more profoundly manifested than the interior life is in Stephen, or Molly, or anyone else in the novel. The heroines of Jane Austen, George Eliot, and Henry James are more refined social sensibilities than Poldy, but even they cannot compete with his inward turn. Nothing is lost upon him, even though his reactions to what he perceives can be humdrum. Joyce favors him as he favors no one else in his work.

This is fair, though "profoundly" prejudges the question: there is no way of knowing what, if anything, is lost on Leopold, since we can read only what he found or fancied.

The Western Canon should have ended on page 514, with Beckett's Krapp saying:

> Perhaps my best years are gone. When there was a chance of happiness. But I wouldn't want them back. Not with the fire in me now. No, I wouldn't want them back.

But Bloom wouldn't leave well alone, he had to accost his opponents—"all six branches of the School of Resentment"—and put them to shame: Feminists, Marxists, Lacanians, New Historicists, Deconstructionists, Semioticians, "the rabblement of lemmings". I am sorry that he confronts these people with mere oppugnancy. He doesn't name any of them or report their arguments. I am impelled to wonder how assiduously he has read their work. He dismisses Edward Said's *Culture and Imperialism* without naming its author. Looking on the dark side of our profession because it is less trying on the eyes, Bloom keeps alluding to "our current squalors". He sucks melancholy out of any song, and writes as if he were all alone unhappy. "The shadows lengthen in our evening land", he intones, "and we approach the second millennium expecting further shadowing." It is all very odd.

Bloom adds to the canon three American writers, John

Ashbery, James Merrill and Thomas Pynchon. There must be something good and right in a cultural situation that has brought to prominence three such splendid but difficult writers. There must also be something to be said for the cultural forces that have published *The Western Canon* and gained for it a vast readership, far larger than any exemplar of the School of Resentment has ever enjoyed. I assume that darker forces have compelled Bloom to add to *The Western Canon* an appendix setting out a list of writers canonical and not yet canonical. He has divided the list chronologically into the Theocratic Age, the Aristocratic Age, the Democratic Age and the Chaotic Age. I want to believe that Bloom himself did not compile the list, a gathering so eccentric that it includes Gloria Naylor but not Cavalcanti. This part of the book belongs to the history of marketing.

It is unlikely that I will read *The Western Canon* again for its official programme, the assertion that there is indeed a canon and that the substance of it will prevail against much folly. The book is too personal to be read in that way. But I will read it again to hear Bloom's voice. The book is best read, I think, as his autobiography. Setting aside its mere argument, we can warm to its eloquence, even to its grandiloquence. Bloom loves literature. Furthermore, he prefers great literature to merely good literature, and good literature to bad literature. He is also right to say that "expanding the Canon tends to drive out the better writers, sometimes even the best, because pragmatically none of us (whoever we are) ever had time to read absolutely everything, no matter how great our lust for reading". Strange, then, that he names for the Chaotic Age many books that are most unlikely ever to become canonical. But enough: let us think of Bloom not as a legislator or a polemicist but as a writer. At his frequent best he is a lord of language, and while I grow tired of his neo-Nietzschean clatter and the accelerated grimaces by which he associates himself with Zero Mostel, I keep relishing his art of surfeit. I find him quite wondrous, even when I don't believe him. The tragic style suits him, he has grown into it, with Johnson as his chosen master. But I smile when I hear Bloom, two years younger than me, saying that "in early old age, I find myself agreeing with Nietzsche, who tended to equate the memorable with the painful". That has not—not entirely—been my experience.

David Dooley (essay date Summer 1995)

SOURCE: "Bloom and The Canon," in *The Hudson Review,* Vol. XLVIII, No. 2, Summer, 1995, pp. 333-38.

[*In the following review, Dooley notes that* The Western Canon *marks a "significant change of direction" for Bloom.*]

Consider the two following kinds of critical writing:

1) I must admit that each time I reread [*Bleak House*], I tend to cry whenever Esther Summerson cries . . . .
2) [T]here are *no* texts, but only relationships *between* texts.

The first quotation may seem naive or at least old-fashioned, not only pre-Derrida but pre-New Criticism. The second kind of writing is immediately recognizable as a specimen of academic deconstruction or literary "theory"; the source is the first page of Harold Bloom's *A Map of Misreading* (1975). Surprisingly, the first quotation is later, not earlier, than the second; it comes from Harold Bloom's new book, *The Western Canon*. Part of the interest of *The Western Canon* lies in measuring the distance Bloom has traveled from books like *A Map of Misreading* and *The Anxiety of Influence* (1973).

One cannot understand Bloom's criticism, especially *The Anxiety of Influence,* without imagining the situation of a very bright, very well-read young graduate student and teacher at Yale in the 1950s. No other university was then so closely identified with the New Criticism, which had by then securely established close reading of the self-contained art object as method and the Modernist and Metaphysical canons as preferred subject. Most of the prominent New Critics were at least sympathetic to high church Christianity. Bloom was Jewish, and he mentions in the new book, the son of a garment worker. Eliot and Pound, gods for most of the New Critics, had on occasion written anti-Semitic poems. Is it any wonder that Bloom sought to overturn most of the pieties of his elders, or that a key concept in his work has always been "belatedness"?

Yet another well-known critic must be mentioned in any discussion of Bloom's work: F.R. Leavis, perhaps the most prominent English-language critic during the fifties and sixties. Although Leavis was no Tory in either politics or religion, like the American New Critics he advocated the Metaphysical poets at the expense of Milton and the Modernists at the expense of the Romantics. Part of Bloom's career seems to have been devoted to changing Leavis' pluses to minuses and minuses to pluses. Leavis attempted to lower the reputations of Milton and Shelley; Bloom worked equally hard to raise them again. Leavis placed Hopkins far above Browning and Tennyson; Bloom just the reverse. Leavis praised Blake's *Songs of Experience;* Bloom preferred the prophetic books. If for Leavis, Yeats became a great poet by outgrowing his Romantic origins, for Bloom, Yeats ended as a stronger Romantic poet than he began. However well or ill Bloom's theory in *The Anxiety of Influence* applies to any pair of poets, it definitely sheds light on the sense of oppression Bloom felt because of Leavis and because of his New Critical elders at Yale.

If poetic originality is difficult, and it is, how much more difficult is critical originality. Even his chosen subject of poetic influence was not new; W. Jackson Bate's *The Burden* of the Past and the English Poet (1970), though it primarily deals with eighteenth-century writers, offers a more comprehensive and less reductionist guide to the subject than Bloom has yet given us. What enabled Bloom to lessen his burden of belatedness, both in *The Anxiety of Influence* and in subsequent books, was the creation of a vocabulary and frame of reference unavailable to, and no doubt unwelcome to, his predecessors: Gnosticism, Orphism, misprision, the Covering Cherub, revisionary ratios, Lurianic Kabbalah, all creating a Bloomspeak before which any reader must feel "belated."

The Western Canon marks three significant changes of direction for Bloom: he has changed his mind about the significance of Freud for literary criticism; he has reoriented his stance toward the common reader; and, whereas his work from *The Anxiety of Influence* at least through *Agon* (1982) was perceived to be generally friendly to deconstructionism, he has now joined battle with the deconstructionists and their allies.

Bloom writes in *The Western Canon* that "The anxiety of influence is not an anxiety about the father, real or literary." Twenty years ago he wrote that "the anxiety of influence, from which we all suffer, whether we are poets or not, has to be located first in its origins, in the fateful morasses of what Freud, with grandly desperate wit, called 'the family romance.'" Bloom's "revisionary ratios" of influence were not only "tropes" but "psychic defenses," though he granted that his "transfers from Freudian theory to poetry" might seem "curiously literal." Bloom now speaks of "Freud's curious overvaluation of what he called the Oedipus complex." Freudian literary criticism, like the old joke about the Holy Roman Empire, is "not Freudian, not literary, not criticism." A Shakespearean reading of Freud illuminates and overwhelms Freud; a Freudian reading of Shakespeare reduces Shakespeare. Whereas Bloom previously invoked the authority of Freud (in part, perhaps, to be able to accuse his critical opponents of being in denial), his chapter on Freud in the new book emphasizes Freud's borrowings from and blunders about Shakespeare—for example, Freud's belief that the Earl of Oxford wrote Shakespeare's plays.

Equally as remarkable as Bloom's change of mind about Freud is his new opening to the common reader. Most of Bloom's earlier books were seemingly written to impress other academicians, with many sentences like "*Daemonization,* as a revisionary ratio, is a self-crippling act, intended to purchase knowledge by a playing at the loss of power, but more frequently resulting in a true loss of the powers of making." The chapter on *kenosis* in *The Anxiety of Influence* and the fifth chapter of *A Map of Misreading* could almost have been written by Nabokov's Professor Kinbote in *Pale Fire.* Despite Bloom's Kinbote-like ability to find Gnosticism in most of his favorite authors, he states quite accurately that his new

book "is not directed to academics, because only a small remnant of them still read for the love of reading." Such an "old-fashioned sense of reading," in which one identifies with characters like Esther Summerson in *Bleak House,* now seems to Bloom "the only sense that matters."

Keeping the common reader in mind has significantly improved Bloom's prose. Many readers will enjoy the wit of "[Whitman's] poems of heterosexual passion have convinced no one, including Whitman himself" and the deeper wit of "Ibsen had the mysterious endowment of the true dramatist, which is to be able to lavish more life on a character than one possesses oneself." Bloom shows a welcome insight into human behavior in suggesting that "a secure faith in theater may have given [Molière] a certain detachment or serenity."

The Western Canon defends the validity of the traditional literary canon and celebrates some of its most prominent authors. Bloom does not define the canon theoretically, but offers numerous descriptive metaphors. The canon is "the relation of an individual reader and writer to what has been preserved out of what has been written." The pragmatic function of the canon is "the remembering and ordering of a lifetime's reading:" The canon is "a standard of measurement that is anything but political or moral." It is "a gauge of vitality." Writers elect themselves to the canon by wagering on their writing. Bloom suggests that "The strength of the canonical is manifested in the quiet persistence of the strongest writers." Ultimately, "the Western Canon is Shakespeare and Dante," a judgment with which Pound and Eliot would have agreed. One test for the canonical is that "unless it demands rereading, the work does not qualify." Bloom places particular emphasis on the original strangeness of the canonical work: "works are appropriated by [the canon] for their singularity, not because they fit smoothly into an existing order."

Bloom ably upholds the canon against attacks by the six divisions of what he calls "the School of Resentment: Feminists, Marxists, Lacanians, New Historicists, Deconstructionists, Semioticians," whom he excoriates as "amateur political scientists, uninformed sociologists, incompetent anthropologists, mediocre philosophers, and overdetermined cultural historians." He observes that "left-wing critics cannot do the working class's reading for it." Indeed, if someone believes that aesthetic value "is only a mystification in the service of the ruling class, then why should you read at all rather than go forth to serve the desperate needs of the exploited classes?" We all know the answer to that one: a purported concern for the exploited classes is a status symbol for a subclass of bourgeois intellectuals, not intended as a principle for actually altering one's own life.

Bloom further argues—rightly, I think—that "primarily each ambitious writer is out for himself alone and will frequently betray or neglect his class in order to advance his own interests." Great writers, he suggests, "are influenced by one another without much regard for political resemblances and differences." The devotion numerous left-wing American poets have felt for Ezra Pound offers a striking confirmation of Bloom's thesis. Bloom demonstrates that although Samuel Johnson and William Hazlitt were diametrically opposed politically, they praised Milton in similar terms. He points out that those who contend that the canon is arbitrary must be able to show why the "dominant social class" selected Shakespeare rather than Ben Johnson to center the canon. I would add that they must also show why *As You Like It* was assigned a higher role in the canon than *The Two Gentlemen of Verona* and why no English-language play between Farquhar and Shaw has been admitted to the canon. They must also show why popular authors like Judith Krantz—and there have been scores of such authors since the eighteenth century—who do represent the world-view of the dominant social classes have not been admitted to the canon.

Some of Bloom's most eloquent words concern the decline of his profession due to the School of Resentment. He writes that

> many of the best students will abandon us for other disciplines and professions, an abandonment already well under way. They are justified in doing so, because we could not protect them against our own profession's loss of intellectual and aesthetic standards of accomplishment and value.

He suggests that literature and teaching depend on "people who were fanatical readers when they were still small children," and fears there may be "no more generations of common readers, free of ideological cant." Departments of English and American literature, as opposed to "cultural studies," may become as small and beleaguered as classics departments are now. Obviously *The Western Canon* is written in the hope that this will not be the case.

As strong as the polemical sections are, most of *The Western Canon* is devoted to celebrating canonical authors from Dante to the present (oddly, Bloom includes no essays on Greek or Roman authors). Bloom offers many interesting and provocative ideas: that Shakespeare's characters develop by overhearing themselves talk; that most critics underestimate the intellectual complexity of Emily Dickinson's poems; that the autoerotic is an important component of Whitman's work; that Hedda Gabler is a troll-like character no societal possibilities could satisfy; that an asexual aestheticism pervades even Virginia Woolf's seemingly political writings. The sections on *Persuasion*, *Bleak House*, and Tolstoy's *Hadji Murad* catch the tone of each novel especially well. Noting that Chaucer rarely writes an unironic passage, Bloom suggests that Chaucer's irony is his principal instrument for discovery, by compelling readers to determine for themselves precisely what he has invented. Curiously, given his interest in writerly anxiety, Bloom mentions in passing but does not discuss the theory that the relationship of Clov and Hamm in *Endgame* reflects the real-life situation of Beckett and Joyce. The Shakespearean references Bloom finds in *Endgame* seem extremely far-fetched by comparison. Like many critics, Bloom finds more merit than I do in the work of Borges, who seems to me the most overrated fiction writer of the twentieth century. Borges' reputation may result less from his charming if slight fictions than from his implicit reassurance to professors that literature is, after all, only an intellectual game.

Perhaps the most controversial part of *The Western Canon* is the list of canonical authors and works at the end of the book. In general, Bloom's lists through the nineteenth century should cause relatively little disagreement, although the medieval section omits the splendid Anglo-Saxon poems *The Wanderer*, *The Seafarer*, and *The Battle of Maldon*, along with *Sir Gawain and the Green Knight*, *The Pearl*, and *Piers Plowman*. The twentieth-century selections will occasion the most debate. The list, though absurdly long, still leaves out notable works. According to Bloom, the Western Canon includes *Myra Breckinridge* but not *Lord of the Flies*, *Brideshead Revisited*, *Steppenwolf*, *Siddhartha*, *Zorba the Greek*, *Franny and Zooey*, or *Lord of the Rings*. Bloom omits the short stories of Doris Lessing and William Trevor (which demand comparison with the short fiction of James, Lawrence, and Hemingway), as well as the remarkable nonfiction of Robert M. Pirsig, Annie Dillard, and Peter Matthiessen. Matthiessen's Conrad-like novel *At Play in the Fields of the Lord* is also left out.

The most egregious omission is probably Edward Albee. As often happens with canonical works, the weaknesses of *Who's Afraid of Virginia Woolf?* were apparent from the beginning but have proven to be much less important than the energy and vitality of the whole. Albee's Martha is one of the four classic stage roles for American actresses, along with Amanda in *The Glass Menagerie*, Blanche Dubois in *A Streetcar Named Desire*, and Mary Tyrone in *Long Day's Journey into Night*. Albee is not the only important dramatist omitted. While one can imagine arguments against including Noel Coward, John Osborne, Caryl Churchill, William Inge, Lanford Wilson, Peter Shaffer, Christopher Hampton, or Brian Friel, to ignore all of them while choosing David Rabe, David Mamet, and especially Edward Bond seems peculiar, to say the least.

An inevitable difficulty of attempting to define a canon is deciding when to honor one's own critical judgment and when to defer to received opinion. Some works *are* in the canon; some works *should be* in the canon. The categories overlap considerably but are not identical. I dislike John Marston's *The Malcontent*, but it is part of the canon of Elizabethan drama. I think Thackeray's novel *The Luck of Barry Lyndon* is a brilliant tour de force, every bit the equal of *Vanity Fair,* but *Vanity Fair* is canonical, and thus far *The Luck of Barry Lyndon* is not. Bloom notes that he is including the poetry of Robert Lowell and Philip Larkin against his own taste. In other instances he might also have deferred to critical consensus. He may wish that Irving Feldman, Alvin Feinman, and Allen Grossman (all of whom he includes) were canonic and that Allen Ginsberg (whom he does not) were consigned to oblivion, but such is not the case.

Bloom describes some of the writers included in Samuel Johnson's *Lives of the Poets* as "fit precursors for many of our prematurely canonized poetasters and inchoate rhapsodists." This quotation came to mind often when I read Bloom's long list of twentieth-century American poets. Does Bloom seriously believe that Kenneth Koch, Jean Garrigue, and J.D. McClatchy—to choose only three examples—are canonic authors? Such better-known poets as Hayden Carruth, Sylvia Plath, Adrienne Rich, Kenneth Rexroth, and Anne Sexton are all missing from Bloom's list, as is Jack Gilbert, the contemporary poet not in the canon who most surely belongs there. To Bloom's choices from the admittedly weak interregnum generation (b. 1934-1943), which include Charles Wright, Mark Strand, Charles Simic, and Alfred Corn, I have no hesitation in preferring Robert Hass or the Louise Glück of *The Wild Iris.* I was amused to discover in Bloom's canon two books published in 1994 that I greeted less than rapturously in the Winter 1995 *Hudson Review.* To Bloom's credit, he includes some worthy writers I would not have expected him to like: Weldon Kees, Edwin Muir, and Donald Hall, for example.

At the very least, Bloom's list of canonical authors and works provides a useful starting point for discussion. *The Western Canon* is an intelligent, stimulating, and, wonder of wonders, readable account of both the crisis facing English departments and the literary inheritance which proponents of the School of Resentment are eager to discard. Just as some people believe that only Nixon could have changed American policy toward China, perhaps Bloom is now exactly the right person to make the case for literature, aesthetic value, and the Western Canon.

FURTHER READING

Criticism

Alter, Robert. "Beauty and the Best." *The New Republic* 211, No. 15 (10 October 1994): 36-42.
    Review discusses Bloom's criteria for choosing authors for the literary canon.

Berman, Jaye. "Harold Bloom and Judaism." *Midstream: A Monthly Jewish Review* XXXIII, No. 8 (October 1987): 42-44.
    Examines Bloom's use of Judaism in his theoretical structure.

Brown, Erella. "The Ozick-Bloom Controversy: Anxiety of Influence, Usurpation as Idolatry, and the Identity of Jewish American Literature." *Studies in American Jewish Literature* 11, No. 1 (Spring 1992): 62-82.
    Discusses the differing theoretical views of Cynthia Ozick and Harold Bloom regarding Jewish-American literature.

Caruth, Cathy. "Speculative Returns: Bloom's Recent Work." *MLN* 98, No. 5 (December 1983): 1286-96.
    Essay discusses *Agon* and *The Breaking of the Vessels* and their contribution toward the development of Bloom's theories.

Donoghue, Denis. "Creation from Catastrophe." *Times Literary Supplement,* No. 4139 (30 July 1982): 811-12.
    Review provides a brief summary of Bloom's theory and its development over the course of his publications.

Edmundson, Mark. "Bloom's Giant Forms." *London Review of Books* 11, No. 11 (1 June 1989): 13-14.
    Review of *Ruin the Sacred Truths* in which Bloom is discussed in terms of the Romantics.

Godzich, Wlad. "Harold Bloom as Rhetorician." *Centrum* 6, No. 1 (Spring 1978): 43-9.
    Essay explores reasons why Bloom is sometimes disregarded by his peers.

Hollander, John. "The Anxiety of Influence." *New York Times Book Review* (4 March 1973): 27-8.
    Review of *The Anxiety of Influence* in which Bloom is credited with enriching the study of Romantic poetry.

Norris, Christopher. "Harold Bloom: A Poetics of Reconstruction." *British Journal of Aesthetics* 20, No. 1 (Winter 1980): 67-76.
    Essay discusses the challenge presented to the traditional school of "New Criticism" at Yale by Bloom's theory of poetics.

Robinson, Douglas. "Dear Harold." *New Literary History* 20, No. 1 (Autumn 1988): 239-52.
    Essay takes the form of a letter to Harold Bloom explaining Bloom's influence on the author and his theoretical approach.

Silver, Daniel J. "The Battle of the Books." *Commentary* 98, No. 6 (December 1994): 60, 62-3.
    Review of *The Western Canon* that questions Bloom's methods in making canonical selections.

Additional coverage of Bloom's life and career is contained in the following sources published by Gale: *Contemporary Authors,* Vols. 13-16R; *Contemporary Authors New Revision Series,* Vol. 39; and *Dictionary of Literary Biography,* Vol. 67.

Susan Daitch
1954-

American novelist and short story writer.

The following entry presents an overview of Daitch's career through 1996.

INTRODUCTION

Until the late 1970s, Susan Daitch worked as a painter producing what she calls "narrative drawings." Her artistic background has come into play in her writing by providing her with a visual basis for her work. The translation from a visual to written format has intrigued Daitch and led her to inspect how meaning changes with translation—a recurring theme in her writing.

Biographical Information

Born in New Haven, Connecticut, Daitch graduated from Barnard College in 1977. She then attended, and later worked for, the Whitney Museum of Modern Art's Independent Study Program. The late '70s marked a turning point in her career as she moved away from art and towards fiction. Her background in art, her work at the Whitney, and her husband's experiences in the Berkeley riots all contributed to her first book, *L.C.* (1987).

Major Works

Daitch uses history as a springboard for her work because, according to her, it is a "kind of ready-made that can be reinterpreted or misinterpreted, and translated." Her first novel, *L.C.,* is an example of Daitch's re-invention of history: the novel centers on a diary, written by the title character in 1848 France, which is subsequently found, translated and retranslated by two other authors. Dr. Willa Rehnfield first finds and translates the novel in 1968. Rehnfield's translation is affected by her own life and the riots at Berkeley. Likewise, Rehnfield's assistant retranslates the last section of L.C.'s diary to correct Rehnfield's "mistakes," only to add her own biases. Just as *L.C.* has a book as its central narrative frame, so too does Daitch's second work, *The Colorist* (1990). *The Colorist* centers around a comic book entitled *Electra*. After the comic book folds, Julie, the colorist, and the book's inker, Laura, take it over. Julie's and Electra's lives begin to parallel each other and lead the reader down a path of complex storylines. Kate Lynch calls *The Colorist* a "literary shell game" with "drop-dead writing." Most recently Daitch has published a collection of short stories entitled *Storytown* (1996).

Critical Reception

Daitch's works have been variously received as either brilliant or trite. Most critics agree that Daitch has unique descriptive talents and have praised her storytelling abilities; *L.C.* was recognized as a promising first book from a new postmodern writer. Leslie Rabine calls it "an important first novel . . . well worth reading for its ingenious interweaving of narrative threads"—a sentiment expressed in the bulk of critical reaction to Daitch's first work. *L.C.* has, however, been criticized for historical inaccuracies and narrative imbalance. *The Colorist*'s reception has followed much the same path. Elizabeth Judd calls it a "breath-taking second novel" and asserts that Daitch has again succeeded in producing a well-told, complex storyline. However, the story's complexity and Daitch's technique of situation-driven writing have resulted in what some critics see as weak characters, though Richard Katrovas says that the narrative imparts "the powerful sense of a woman gazing into the heart of things."

PRINCIPAL WORKS

L.C. (novel) 1987
The Colorist (novel) 1990
Storytown (short stories) 1996

CRITICISM

Laura Marcus (review date 20 June 1986)

SOURCE: "Herself as Others," in *Times Literary Supplement,* June 20, 1986, p. 682.

[*In the following review, Marcus contends that Daitch's first novel,* L.C., *is a "promising" book with writing that is understated and intelligent.*]

It is an unusual pleasure to be able to say of a first novel not just that it is promising but that it delivers the goods. Susan Daitch's *L.C.* is an important book, in part because it works with materials that are proliferating in feminist publishing—diaries, memoirs, historical reconstructions—and, through complex novelistic strategies and acute historical imaginings, produces a form which encourages us to rethink both fiction and history.

The major part of the novel is taken up with the diary of Lucienne Crozier, a young woman living in Paris immediately before and during the 1848 revolution. The diary, whose entries vary from the elliptical to the highly detailed, records the merging of a private with a public life. Her arranged marriage does not so much disintegrate as slide from view when her husband leaves on a business trip. She begins a series of affairs, the first with the painter [Eugène] Delacroix, the last with the revolutionary Jean de la Tour. Her story is not important merely because she is the mistress of famous men, however, nor is hers a sentimental education. Through Delacroix, she comes to understand and question the romantic and aesthetic idealism which motivated the revolutionary fervour of the previous generation, now transmuted into Delacroix's opaque allegorical representations, With de la Tour she meets [Pierre-Joseph] Proudhon, becomes involved with the revolutionary 14 Juilletists and watches Paris burn. The first part of the novel ends as she prepares for exile in Algiers.

Surrounding this narrative is a double layer of contemporary historical reconstruction. Dr. Willa Rehnfield, an archivist and biographer, finds and translates the diary in 1968. On her death, her assistant Jane Amme discovers it and re-translates the final section, in which Lucienne is in Algiers. "Translation is a filter, there is always some refraction", Jane writes. In Willa Rehnfield's version, Lucienne ends the diary because she is dying; in Jane's translation Lucienne is silenced by impending arrest for her continued political activities. One hundred and twenty years of history are elided as Jane records her own story; campus revolution in Berkeley in 1968, involvement in the killing of a man who exploits countries in the name of American imperialism and rapes women for thrills, and her subsequent fugitive existence. The history of revolutions has certain constants, she asserts, not least of which is the way in which women are both implicated and marginalized, their labours employed but their own political interests dismissed as at best secondary to the larger class struggle. She translates Lucienne's story because it is her own.

Daitch succeeds both in producing a series of compelling narratives, and in raising central questions about the contemporary endeavour to speak for hitherto silent women. The novel's labyrinthine structure works against any simple notion of the "discovery" of a buried past; the found manuscript, that staple ingredient of archival history and of Gothic novels, cannot simply speak its own truth. The translation that takes place in *L.C.* is more than a matter of conversion from one language, or one era, to another. History is violent, and women have been involved in that violence; a women's history cannot occupy a benign space outside wars and revolutions. 1968 is crucial to the novel because subsequent views

have tried to reduce it to an outbreak of youthful frenzy: Daitch, through Jane's narrative, superimposes it on the past to show how much was at stake.

The writing is for the most part understated, but what shines through the novel is intelligence. There have been many worthy practitioners of historical fiction, and a depressing number for whom it is a romp in fancy dress. When, as in Georgette Heyer's costumed fantasies, historical authenticity is aimed for with the entrance of Beau Brummell, usually around page 100, the reader knows the game is up. Daitch is rather more subtle. Her Delacroix does not stalk through the diary entries being bohemian, lecherous or famous. Instead, through his shadowy outline and his art, Daitch interrogates the representations which are our only access to the past:

> Drawings as recordings, documents of human and animal motion, a way of producing and fixing graphic memory. The pencil as a precursor of [Louis] Daguerre's invention. Odalisques stretched out on divans: these are Eugène's mental daguerreotypes. Erotica, chapters of. He confessed the existence of a private notebook filled with such drawings as would help him pass the hours of loneliness.

Daitch's sure tone moves effortlessly from the language of the past to that of the present, transforming romantic historical fiction and the romance of women's history in the process. Hers is a highly original first novel which could mark a new development in women's writing. *L.C.* is not concerned with that female self which, in too much recent feminist fiction, has endlessly rehearsed its traumas, twitches and comings into its own. Such sanctioned egotism is rejected in this novel, in which politics is about commitment, history is elusive but essential, and writing means learning about all that is not yourself.

Leslie W. Rabine (review date 13 December 1987)

SOURCE: "Feminism in 1848 and 1968," in *Los Angeles Times Book Review,* December 13, 1987, p. 10.

[*Rabine, in the following review, finds Daitch's novel* L.C. *worth reading for its interwoven plot, despite its occasional historical inaccuracies.*]

Few people have even heard of the feminists active in France in the 1830s and '40s. But contemporary feminists who do know them, like historian Claire Moses (*French Feminism in the 19th Century,* SUNY Press, 1984) or biographer Dominique Desanti (*Flora Tristan: A Woman in Revolt,* Crown, 1976) experience an uncanny spark of recognition and identification.

Now novelist Susan Daitch has built upon that elusive sense of identification a fictional relation between Lucienne Crozier, a young woman who records in her diary her participation in the Revolution of 1848; Willa Rehnfield, a scholar who finds and translates the diary in the 1960s, and Jane Amme, a Berkeley radical of 1968. After Willa's death, Jane solves the mystery of Lucienne's missing diary, and in saving Lucienne's story from oblivion, feels compelled to record her own parallel journey from middle-class *Angst* to extralegal action: "My epilogue is a Book II, a running commentary in the margins of the diary."

Lucienne, married off to industrialist Charles Crozier in order to pay the bills of her impoverished aristocratic family, grows increasingly appalled at the wretched fate of workers exploited by men like her husband. But in 1848, her attempts to change the lives of workers and women force her to flee with her lover to Algeria. Jane, a participant in Berkeley's Vietnam-era antiwar movement, is raped by a wealthy weapons manufacturer and then abused by disbelieving police. Compelled to take justice into her own hands, she too must become a fugitive. Daitch leaves it up to the readers to draw their own conclusions about the complex patterns of similarity and difference, historical change and continuity that she has woven between her two characters.

Both Lucienne and Jane trace the conflicts of women engaged in radical struggle, who resist both being in complicity with an all-pervasive social injustice they find intolerable and being used by Socialist men who lead that struggle. Doubt suspends them between an all-too-sure knowledge of what they are fighting against and an ironic mistrust of any attempt to define what they are fighting for. Both have been stranded beyond the place where they could have been "duped ... into believing sides were simple: X against Y; clean, neat, unambiguous."

The novel, ingeniously constructed, raises questions about truth and deception in Lucienne's representation of herself, in Rehnfield's translation of Lucienne's writing, and in the reconstitution of history. But these questions also reflect upon Daitch's writing.

As a reconstitution of 1848, *L.C.* does not ring true. The names of streets and cafes of 19th-Century Paris are there, but the ambiance and mores are out of kilter. Lucienne's daily actions lack historic accuracy. Upper-class women, even if they were eccentric rebels, did not, as Lucienne so casually does, go to cafes with each other, or go to parties at restaurants with men.

Anachronism also infuses the writing itself. The style, the tone, the psychology, the terminology do not fit those of an 1840s French rebel woman. Women writers of the period, like George Sand, Marie d'Agoult [who, under the name of

Daniel Stern, wrote the first authoritative history of the Revolution of 1848], Flora Tristan, Pauline Roland [who was also exiled to Algeria], Claire Demar, and Suzanne Voilquin all write with a certain similarity. Their accounts of their sexual and political involvements ring with a romantic intensity and passion that Daitch does not catch in the voice of her cool, ironic heroine.

Lucienne's narrative voice is almost indistinguishable from Jane Amme's, but the lack of effect that makes Lucienne a somewhat vague figure succeeds compellingly for Jane. Jane's point of view is retrospective, looking back from the other side of the loss of idealism. Steeled by living underground, she has kept her memories crystal clear, frozen in a fine-edged, delicate, icy anger, expressed with concise elegance: "The Governor [Reagan] continued to call in the National Guard, saying, 'If it takes a blood bath to end the violence, let's get it over with.' The words seemed like a toxic spot in my notebook, but I wanted to keep a record of them. Stuck in the world of fried eggs, side orders of fries and men who treated waitresses badly, blatant brutality fascinated me." But Lucienne, who is supposed to be recording events as they happen, from the time she marries Charles Crozier as an innocent young girl, seems inexplicably always/already disillusioned and jaded.

Despite this imbalance between the two narratives, *L.C.* is an important first novel by a promising young novelist, well worth reading for its ingenious interweaving of narrative threads, for its uncompromising treatment of sex and politics, and for the questions it raises about truth and deception in representing self and history. But even more does it lay claim to praise for its courageous excavation of the issues raised in Berkeley, 1968, in an age when many would rather smother them under nostalgia.

Julie Wheelwright (review date March 1988)

SOURCE: Review of *L.C.* in *The Women's Review of Books*, Vol. V, No. 6, March 1988, p. 16.

[*In the following, Wheelwright discusses the parallels that Daitch has created in her first novel,* L.C.]

Popular representations of women's role in both world wars often indulge in romantic images. Khaki greens, tartan kilts, greatcoats, braided suits, ribbons and medals are the most current manifestation of this nostalgia. The height of this winter's European fashions reflect a renewed fascination for things military. "As the world contemplates laying down its arms," as the Irish women's magazine *It* cheerfully claims, "the fashion world seems to celebrate this notion with a whole battalion of military inspired clothes." As the war years recede into the mists of time they become safe, a fantasy landscape to be raided for its exotic value.

New novels and films—among them John Boorman's film *Hope and Glory* and Marge Piercy's novel *Gone to Soldiers*—also reflect a recurring interest in the subject. Piercy supplies a vast, panoramic feminist reading of World War II, Boorman a nostalgic vision of his childhood surrounded by female family in London. Both are attempts to make better sense of an era that profoundly affected their lives. These highly personalized readings offer an intriguing insight and a discovery of lost voices.

Valerie Miner's most recent novel, *All Good Women*, is part of this trend. It aims to shed light on the experiences of American women on the home front in the 1930s and 1940s. Susan Daitch's first novel tackles difficult questions about women's role during periods of war, linking the revolutions of Paris in 1848 with the student demonstrations of Berkeley, California in 1968. Both novelists examine what happens to women pulled into the maelstrom of male-created events whose lives are profoundly altered by forces over which they had no control. They grapple with the profound contradiction that in the horror of war some women find a transitory but exhilarating liberty and become aware of their female oppression. It is this irony that Daitch confronts in an invigorating and highly readable manner without succumbing to nostalgia for either period.

Daitch's debut novel, *L.C.* is a bold and refreshing treatment of some extremely perplexing questions about women's experiences with both warfare and violence. Through an inventive structure Daitch weaves three spellbinding stories of women separated by time and space, caught up in and definitively changed by the storm of revolution. A fictional American historian, Willa Rehnfield, writing in 1968, opens the novel with an introduction to her translation of a woman's diary kept during the 1848 French revolution. The diary tells the story of Lucienne Crozier—the L.C. of the title—and her transformation from a restless bourgeois wife to a hunted revolutionary.

> **Daitch's debut novel, *L.C.* is a bold and refreshing treatment of some extremely perplexing questions about women's experiences with both warfare and violence.**
> **—*Julie Wheelwright***

Daitch drops tantalizing hints about the rewriting of L.C.'s diary through Rehnfield's occasional footnotes and jarring anachronisms of language (according to Lucienne, "it's a puke world"). The third strand of the novel is the story of Jane

Amme, who comes across the diary while working for Rehnfield. Jane is on the run from Berkeley because of her part in the political assassination of an arms dealer-cum-rapist and arrives in New York under an assumed name. It is she who brings the story full circle. Rehnfield merely acts as "the connective tissue" between Lucienne and Jane, drawing the two narratives together.

Daitch compares their interlocking relationship to women watching each other across the air-shaft of a tenement building—"abstractly, like the lines of women's vision at their windows, zig-zagging from one to the next, the first knows of the invisible third through the second." This is a rarity—a historical novel that deals with the fiction of history and the struggle to remain true to the spirit of a subject. History, Daitch recognizes, is not a given set of facts but a subjective process of selection and interpretation.

As Jane Amme, the radical, the revolutionary and exile completes Lucienne's story, it becomes her own. Opening the diary, Jane explains:

> This space, these margins Dr. Rehnfield would probably claim were hers by virtue of the acts of translating and introducing, but I think she's wrong because Lucienne's story and mine run in tandem, then mine keeps going where hers leaves off.

Both Jane's and Lucienne's lives are shaped by political commitment and born of a belief that consciousness demands action. Willa Rehnfield's resistance to political commitment or awareness, says Jane, is the resistance of a passionate voyeur, and Rehnfield's translation of L.C.'s notebook—manufacturing Lucienne's death from consumption—a deliberate falsification of history.

Daitch explores a central contradiction of warfare. Both Jane and Lucienne are propelled into the male-controlled actions, and it is through the tumult of political events that they become aware of their oppression as women. Their part in revolution destroys their bourgeois identity, only to force them into exile and further onto society's margins. As Lucienne writes of her inevitable transformation from observer to participant, she speaks for Jane as well: "our fate grabbed us by the collar, shook us by the lapels and bounced us down the stairs into the street . . ." But it is in the street, in the heat of confrontation, that the myth of political neutrality evaporates and the women's strengths are revealed.

This is a beautifully crafted novel which demands attention and offers the rewards of an intelligent and thought-provoking read. The revolutions of 1848 and 1968 are not reduced to romantic backdrops but pose the contradictions that Daitch tackles in a highly stimulating manner. She recognizes that political commitment, exile and love-affairs are the stuff of passion as well as bone-numbing boredom and alienation. Her characters are not good women, but humanly flawed; they refuse to simplify the agonizing realities of revolution and the female condition. This is an exceptional first novel.

Steven Moore (review date Fall 1988)

SOURCE: Review of *L.C.,* in *Review of Contemporary Fiction,* Vol. 8, No. 3, Fall 1988, p. 166-67.

[*In the following, Moore looks at the manipulation of text and claims that Daitch "brilliantly" connects the women of 1848 and 1968 in her novel* L.C.]

This intriguing and very accomplished first novel [*L.C.*] is concerned with the efforts of three women to redress personal and political inequality through the manipulation of texts. The novel begins with an editor's introduction to her own translation of a journal kept by one Lucienne Crozier, a proto-feminist witness to the February 1848 Revolution in Paris. All seems well at first, but irregularities begin appearing: the language is not that of a twenty-four-year-old Frenchwoman of the last century but of an older one of this century; the editor's signature to the annotations shrinks from Willa Rehnfield to W.R., then expands back to the full name, then is joined by annotations by a Jane Amme (a nom de guerre), writing fourteen years after Rehnfield's 1968 translation. When Lucienne's diary comes to an end halfway through the novel, Amme steps in and explains Rehnfield's reasons for doctoring her translation. The fact that Rehnfield wrote in 1968, a year of revolutionary activity as futile as that in France 120 years earlier, points to the identification the reclusive Rehnfield feels for Lucienne. Amme, on the other hand, was a participant in the Berkeley riots of 1968 and consequently has her own reasons for identifying with L.C. She offers her own translation of the last section of L.C.'s diary—radically different from the Rehnfield version—and as text competes with text, questions arise concerning the recording of history, the nature of translation, and the ultimate subjectivity of all texts.

Dozens of cross-references link L.C. with her twentieth-century annotators, and Daitch brilliantly underscores the similarities between the socio-political injustices that led to the revolts of 1848 and 1968. She's clearly done her homework in both eras (she was only fourteen in 1968 herself) and demonstrates a vivid historical imagination. The role of woman vis-a-vis history—from spectator and victim to participant—runs through this tale of two cities, a stunning debut by a young writer clearly worth watching.

Michiko Kakutani (review date 16 February 1990)

SOURCE: "The Lives of New Yorkers, Uptown and Down," in *The New York Times,* February 16, 1990, p. C33.

[*In the following review of* The Colorist *and a work by another author, Kakutani provides a synopsis of Daitch's* The Colorist *stating that the "narrative tends to be . . . unstructured" but praises Daitch's ability to capture the flavor of Manhattan.*]

The New Yorkers in these two new novels are young, hip, disoriented and self-involved. The ones in *The Colorist,* live on the Lower East Side in grungy studios and lofts, wear colored streaks in their hair and wonder how they'll pay the rent. The ones in *Leap Year* live in appliance-laden apartments in SoHo and on the Upper West Side, shop at Barneys for their clothes and spend a lot of time talking about happiness and self-fulfillment. Though the characters in both novels are pretty casual about sex—a woman in *The Colorist* takes up prostitution as a way of earning pocket money: a man in *Leap Year* shuttles back and forth between the beds of his ex-wife and his male lover—no one seems to worry about AIDS.

Julie, the narrator of *The Colorist,* Susan Daitch's second novel, works at a comic book company, coloring in the panels of a strip called "Electra"—a space-age fantasy about a warrior girl, who's constantly getting into trouble. "Two fates, happy marriage and death, could be approached but must never actually be met," writes Ms. Daitch. "For anyone or anything in space to fall, even superficially, in love with Electra was useless. Love for Electra was doomed, and death a subject of close brushes, but never the big end."

When the strip is discontinued, Julie loses her job and she begins making up her own version of "Electra" at home, a version in which Electra falls to earth, becomes a homeless person and feels lost and confused—a state of mind that mirrors Julie's own.

In fact Julie's entire existence seems aimless and random. After a frightening encounter with a would-be mugger, she moves in with a man she barely knows—a photographer named Eamonn, whose work oddly complements her own cartoons. Eamonn disappears for long periods of time—he seems to be on some sort of secret mission in Ireland—and Julie passes some of that time dating Martin, a former office colleague, who may or may not have a mysterious half-brother. She desultorily looks for a new job, postpones a date with the unemployment office and ends up helping a friend who has borrowed a call girl's little black book.

Although Ms. Daitch's narrative tends to be as unstructured and improvisatory as Julie's messy life—the novel suffers from an all-inclusiveness that causes the reader's attention to wander—she demonstrates an observant eye and a gift for capturing the hectic rhythms of the trendy downtown Manhattan of Susan Seidelman's movie *Desperately Seeking Susan.* Her vision of New York is one of a cartoon city, where anything is possible, where real-life adventures resemble the antic happenings of a comic strip, where nothing is permanent and nothing is too far-fetched.

Elizabeth Judd (review date April 1990)

SOURCE: Review of *The Colorist,* in *Village Voice Literary Supplement*, No. 84, April, 1990, pp. 9-10.

[*The following is a positive review of Susan Daitch's* The Colorist.]

The Colorist, Susan Daitch's breathtaking second novel, is more than just another postmodern story about a wannabe artist zigzagging through downtown New York (although at one point the narrator does wangle her way onto her lover's lease). Reading it is like unwrapping a stack of presents from someone witty and wise who knew just what you wanted.

The setting and tone of *The Colorist* distinguish it from Daitch's first book, *L.C.,* the diary account of a Frenchwoman who has an affair with Eugène Delacroix and is swept up into radical politics as the 1848 revolution approaches. Lucienne's diary inspires two 20th century women, one a scholar and the other fleeing the Berkeley riots of the late '60s, to annotate her political and personal observations with their own. What follows is a historical tale refracted through various times and temperaments, a novel demonstrating that politics is perspective. *L.C.* also probes one of *The Colorist*'s major themes—the symbiotic relationship between artist and art—through Lucienne and Delacroix's sketching one another as a form of courtship. But although well written, *L.C.* doesn't make good on its ambitious promises because the characters are colorless and indistinct.

Daitch is still short on characterization in *The Colorist,* but she turns this weakness to her advantage by making the question of character a cornerstone of the story. In the first paragraph the narrator, Julie Greene, declares herself invisible, and the process of acquiring and losing traits is traced throughout the book. Julie earns her living coloring in the frames of a serial comic about a superheroine with the supercharged name of Electra. In Julie, Daitch has created a character as mild-mannered as Batgirl in her librarian guise or Clark Kent outside the phone booth; she's the perfect alter ego for a superheroine. But Julie is not the only staffer who feels possessive about Electra. The scripter, aptly named Loonan, regards her as his "test-tube child" (and Julie as Clytemnestra). When the comic is canceled, Julie and her friend Laurel, the inker, appropriate Electra, starring her in their own more feminist fantasies of a superheroine in Manhattan.

Susan Daitch writes gorgeously, winking at the reader as she pulls the rug out from under one idea after the next. At first the episodes Julie concocts weave and dart around her own experiences; she invents an exploitative photographer who turns Electra into a pornographic image, only to have Laurel object that she has written her own lover, photographer Eamonn, into the story. At other times Electra's situation foreshadows that of Julie and Laurel; imitating Electra's degradation, Laurel tries her hand as a prostitute, with Julie hidden in the closet as guardian voyeur.

> **Susan Daitch writes gorgeously, winking at the reader as she pulls the rug out from under one idea after the next.**
> —*Elizabeth Judd*

Daitch plays with layers of language as she does with layers of plot, elegantly turning linguistic questions into mild farce. "One person doesn't control definitions," Julie points out, an idea that sends her dashing to the dictionary every time someone's words don't match her expectations. When Eamonn tells her that he missed her inordinately, Webster's brings her no relief: "If he thought inordinately meant something else, what word could he have meant? I missed you occasionally? I thought about you at night? I missed you like a hole in the head?"

Daitch's sentences are punchy, packing a thwack and kaboom on the grand scale of a Lichtenstein canvas. But for all its Pop Art playfulness, *The Colorist* is about the straight-faced issues of mothering, memory, and domination. Just as Electra is determined by scripters and colorists, Julie is increasingly dominated by chance actions and memories.

Despite the intimacy of her observations, Julie views her own life at a safe distance—preferably through someone else's eyes. As she tells of being attacked in her East Village apartment, she muses about [Alfred] Hitchcock's *Frenzy* and the camera angles that would best capture the scene, before cutting back to her own plight: "Here it is the twentieth century, and cities, for a moment, appear just as self-contained [as in medieval times], especially in a long shot during a movie. I was a woman on a roof looking at the pointed end of a screwdriver." Daitch has come a long way since *L.C.* Unlike Lucienne, who perceives herself without irony, Julie is able to observe herself on several levels.

Born of the brightly lit big city familiar to readers of current fiction, *The Colorist* is quirkier than its peers and travels well beyond New York City limits, ranging from ancient Egypt to outer space with no sign of strain. The novel also distinguishes itself by Daitch's erudition; she mixes anecdotes from art history and philosophy with the objects of daily life. What *The*

Colorist demands from its readers is epitomized by Julie's comment about Eamonn's photographs: "No crystal-clear scandal, no shock, no gun to the head. You had to come to these pictures with some information first. You might have to know geography and a little history."

Not only do the loops and paradoxes that entangle Electra illuminate the ambiguity of emotions, but they shed light on how Julie sees her creation and, in turn, on the relationship between artist and art. While Eamonn is shadowboxing, a photographer on a political mission he can only guess at, Julie is attempting to understand a disordered universe through Electra. At one point, Julie speculates about how Orion, Electra's obsessed admirer, must feel when he realizes that she has landed on Earth, where he can no longer pursue her. "The disappearance of the object of his desire turned the universe into a dull, barren place inhabited only by early life forms, evolving slowly." That Julie can so perfectly imagine the empty feel of a galaxy without Electra reveals the intimate bonds of creator and creation.

Kate Lynch (review date 13 May 1990)

SOURCE: A review of *The Colorist,* in *New York Times Book Review,* May 13, 1990, p. 24.

[*In the following review, Lynch commends Daitch on her storytelling and the complex story lines of* The Colorist.]

The timing of Susan Daitch's second novel couldn't be better. Now that we're in the midst of a renaissance of interest in cartoons and comics, here's a story set in the comic book industry, complete with workaday details. But *The Colorist* has little in common with the breathless cliffhangers that mention of the genre may conjure; there is some borrowing from the "graphic novel" and a lot of reflection of fantasy literature, but Ms. Daitch aims more to confound comic clichés than to copy them. The novel is a complex of refracted story lines that rewrite and revive the tales of a few "discontinued" characters: the superheroine Electra, whose series of comic books is written off; Julie, the artist who fills in the colors of the panels, and her pal the inker, who are then laid off; and Julie's photographer roommate, an Irishman who slowly fades off into the mists of I.R.A. intrigue. Although it ranges geographically from deep space to Belfast, the story is centered squarely in Manhattan's East Village, which helps account for its downtown literary sensibility. The book contains references to "an object called a cinema hat," a boxy headpiece with an interior that looks like a theater and an opening where the movie screen would be. "Your life as it happens, that's the film," explains Julie. "You are the leading actor and the audience at the same time." This is one of Ms. Daitch's less inspired metaphors, but it pretty well sums up

the insularity that characterizes her storytelling. *The Colorist* is not to be read for its two-dimensional plot or characters, but for Ms. Daitch's drop-dead writing style and the pleasure of joining her literary shell game. While looking for a story, readers will discover instead a not-so-brave new world of permanently reduced expectations and psychic desolation.

Leslie Camhi (essay date Summer 1993)

SOURCE: "Uncertain Physiognomies: Susan Daitch's *L.C.,*" in *Review of Contemporary Fiction,* Vol. XIII, No. 2, Summer 1993, pp. 97-100.

[*In the following essay, Camhi examines the questions that arise when a text is translated and re-translated in Susan Daitch's* L.C.]

Political progress for women is frequently tied to the disintegration of an existing social order. The chance to grab at a bouquet half-tossed and half-forced from the hands of power is a dubious opportunity at best; but in the realm of hope, the dispossessed will often take what they can get. Political revolutions rarely strike at the heart of tyrannies of gender, and their momentary disordering of property relations may be expiated by a more rigid reinforcement of bodily regimes. Susan Daitch's novel *L.C.* interweaves portraits of three women and two historical moments in which gender was a fellow traveler in social revolutions whose promise for women remains largely unfulfilled.

In 1968, a scholar named Willa Rehnfield translates and edits the diary of Lucienne Crozier, an unknown bourgeois woman who witnessed, survived, or participated in the February Days of the 1848 revolution in Paris. The questions surrounding the nature of Lucienne's political involvement are central to both the document and to its scholarly transmission. In translating and annotating a text, do we witness, survive, or participate in the making of a historical record? These questions become acute midway through the diary, when a second editorial voice, in a distinctly post-'68 idiom, suddenly intervenes. The scholar's assistant, Jane Amme (a pseudonym), is a fugitive from the Berkeley student riots who has gone underground in New York. After Willa's death, Jane "completes" the manuscript, offering her own annotations and retranslating its final pages.

In writing about 1848, [Karl] Marx (citing [Wilhelm Friedrich] Hegel) notes that history repeats itself twice: the first time as tragedy, the second time as farce. *L.C.* is structured around such repetitions, though the novel declines to distinguish between tragedy and farce. Jane Amme and Lucienne Crozier are both disaffected daughters of single-mother homes, in search of identities that are only oppositionally defined. In 1968, as in 1848, women revolutionaries tend to follow men's lead.

If Jane and Lucienne are related by temperament and inclination, Lucienne's diary is a material link in a chain of circumstances unknowingly binding Willa to her assistant. Jane Amme and her Berkeley friends, in their final incendiary act, bombed the house of a California industrialist. Luc Ferrier was at once the perfect date and the perfect target, a dealer in art and arms, a suspected Berkeley rapist, and man-about-town in New York and Paris. The same man was also Willa Rehnfield's source for the original *L.C.* manuscript.

The scholar dutifully translates a text lent to her by an old acquaintance, a man of dubious culture and character, whose intentions, however, she barely questions. Her notes to [Honoré de] Balzac and Montmartre contain the manuscript in historical terms. After the scholar's death, her assistant (having already blown up the tainted means of cultural transmission) retranslates the end of the diary with a distinctly defiant twist. At stake are the politics of translation and the means of transmission of a culture produced by women as it is filtered through institutions, networks, and economies defined primarily by men.

Jane's footnotes reclaim Lucienne as historical precursor. In the tradition of Walter Benjamin's historical materialism, Jane brings the revolution up to date. "The true picture of the past flits by. The past can be seized only as an image which flashes up at the instant when it can be recognized and is never seen again. . . . For every image of the past that is not recognized by the present as one of its own concerns threatens to disappear irretrievably." Yet Lucienne is an uncomfortable figure upon which to stake revolutionary claims. She marries for money, according to the wishes of her fallen bourgeois family, a speculator on the Bourse. She begins to write, with characteristic passivity, because her best friend gives her a diary. At the outset of the novel, she is a likely candidate for *Bovarisme*, that popular nineteenth-century diagnosis (named for [Gustave] Flaubert's heroine) for the disaffection and depression which frequently affected recently married middle-class women. Instead, her husband leaves Paris for business reasons during the mounting social unrest which culminates in the February revolution. In the margins of this larger history, Lucienne recounts a series of *petits histoires* with men, from the aging and illustrious Delacroix, to a minor revolutionary, Jean de la Tour. Each affair is a step in the process of her political formation, a gradual turning toward radical socialism, on the one hand, and a vague feminism informed by the publication of first feminist daily, Eugènie Niboyet's *La Voix des Femmes*, and various radical women's organizations.

Yet for Lucienne, the roles of bourgeois wife, artist's lover, and revolutionary companion are a series of mistaken identities. Each is essayed, and proves only slightly less ill-fitting than the others. If "Jane Amme" is a nom de guerre, "Lucienne Crozier" is similarly pseudonymous, the married name of a woman who lived only momentarily with an indifferent husband. Lucienne refers to "the Croziers" as if the name did not include her. The initials on the cover of her diary ("L.C.") express only the necessary alienation of women under patriarchy, the guise of an identity whose "truth" is still to come.

For Marx, the 1848 revolution in France displayed with particular clarity the difficulty of defining a revolutionary identity in opposition to the past.

> The tradition of all the dead generations weighs like a nightmare on the brain of the living. And just when they seem engaged in revolutionizing themselves and things, in creating something that has never yet existed, precisely in such periods of revolutionary crisis they anxiously conjure up the spirits of the past to their service and borrow from them names, battle crises and costumes in order to present the new scene of world history in this time-honored disguise and this borrowed language.

Eighteen forty-eight was a revolution of citation; borrowing words and gestures, rhetoric and public figures, from 1789 and its revolutionary traditions. The ghosts of received ideas and established forms were summoned to calm the anxiety accompanying a radical break with the past. The revolution promised an unmediated relation to presence, a change not only in the names of months in the calendar, but in the relation of people to time. Yet this promise of presence was constructed from layers of history, riddled with ghosts from the past.

Lucienne, we learn in the first pages of the novel, is a woman who "mourns for the present," for whom each gesture in 1848, whether revolutionary or otherwise, is tinged with its own transience. She is a woman of her time only to the extent that she is acutely aware of its passing. In Marx's terms, she mourns for a present tense which is evacuated between the conjured ghost of the past and an uncertain future.

[Alexis de] Tocqueville, in writing his *Souvenirs* of the 1848 revolution, describes his project as seeking "to catch and engrave on my memory those confused features that make up the uncertain physiognomy of my time." Both Tocqueville and Lucienne seek in the "uncertain physiognomy" of revolution a reflection of themselves. For each, the problem is to distinguish their own identity, as landed aristocrat, or gendered subject, from the complexion of their time. Identities are at issue in revolutionary moments, when all the old markers of social definition suddenly become radically unstable. Women, as members of a perennially disaffected social class, may find in such moments a reflection of their perpetual estrangement from established codes.

Alienation has a specific economic meaning, as a transfer of property. When the Crozier home is sacked during the general looting in February, Lucienne accepts the loss of property with almost total equanimity. By then impoverished and in hiding with Jean because of their affiliation with a banned political organization, she regrets only that she hadn't sold more of the Crozier property previously, to support their coming exile. As an afterthought, she searches the house for a sketch she made of Delacroix one day while he was drawing her, a mirror reflection of the artist as seen through the eyes of his object. But this reverse image, all that (with the diary) had properly belonged to her, had disappeared.

My sense is that for Susan Daitch, writing is a kind of exile, a literary space of cross-gendered exchanges, and the end of *L.C.* questions the relation of that space to political action and social change.
—*Leslie Camhi*

Where is Lucienne in these events? She notices that in spite of the revolution, business as usual continues on a street of prostitution.

> Girls who do it part time are seamstresses, laundresses and domestic servants, usually those who don't live in. Revolution or not, business on the Rue de Langlade will continue as before.... Women's work: sewing, scrubbing, peeling potatoes, legitimate work sanctioned by religion, pays just enough to starve slowly and gives you enough time to think about how unfair life is while you're in the process of attenuated dying.

What is the relation of these daily forms of oppression to a history of events, and to a revolutionary promise of radical change? Aligned neither with property, nor strictly with the people (revolted by Proudhon's misogyny), Lucienne's place is with the improper: the margin of her gender, which is variously elided from both sides of the struggle; and with space of writing, which offers her a minimum critical distance from both her own position and events.

My sense is that for Susan Daitch, writing is a kind of exile, a literary space of cross-gendered exchanges, and the end of *L.C.* questions the relation of that space to political action and social change. Lucienne's diary accompanies her into exile in Algeria, where her challenge to property has led her to a radically sex-segregated society. According to Rehnfield's translation, she dies of tuberculosis, abandoned by her lover in an Algerian brothel. In this version, questioning the established order leaves Lucienne hopelessly dependent on the failed revolutionaries who are her companions.

According to Jane Amme's revision, she circulates in Arab men's clothing in Algerian society and, fearing arrest, disappears defiantly, sending her diary back to France to avoid incriminating her friends. "In my translation I've tried to be true to the original," Jane contends. Yet how true was this "original" to herself, and how true were 1848 or 1968, in Paris or Berkeley, to the promises of change? These are questions that remain open when the covers of *L.C.* are closed.

Richard Katrovas (essay date Summer 1993)

SOURCE: "Into the Heart of Things: Passion and Perception in Susan Daitch's *The Colorist*," in *Review of Contemporary Fiction*, Vol. 13, No. 2, Summer 1993, pp. 121-26.

[*The following essay examines how the female narrator of Daitch's* The Colorist *functions in a male-centered world.*]

With *L.C.*, Susan Daitch established herself among the more gifted novelists of her generation, and in *The Colorist*—actually an elaboration of a novella that preceded *L.C.*—she again marshaled impressive erudition to the service of a considerable writerly talent. The speaker of this clipped, hip, urban narrative ruminates at the nexus of passion and perception, and maintains that ground by addressing the former wholly in terms of the latter. I shall say a few words about the effect of this orientation, how it is achieved, and the feminist worldview it illustrates and reinforces.

Alienation defines the tone of many "serious" first-person narratives in modern literature, just as piety had defined the tone of so many premodern first-person narratives. Modernist first-person fictions and confessions have been notes from underground, and indeed there have been few such works deemed serious that have not expressed an orthodox, if you will, alienation. What is "serious" then in modernist terms equates with what in a previous era's paradigm had been appropriately serious, that is, pious. Perhaps in this regard an important, indeed defining ideological feature of modernity is that alienation, especially in first-person discourses—the most fundamental rhetorical condition of prayer—became the new piety.

That this modernist piety, this alienation, has been a male province is true to the extent that the resulting status of the anti-hero may only be understood in the context of a male tradition that is powerfully anti-female. Aeschylus's problematic sounds through the ages: Clytemnestra and her Furies are emblems of female power and who must in their turn be murdered and domesticated. Butch Athena as judicator participates in the suppression of matriarchal authority. The problematic, of course, is that females may only act in their own interests in a "masculine" sense; yet when they do, unless they have burst from the brow of God Himself, they are destroyed or, like the Furies, stuck in the ground and demoted to wimpy goddesses of the hearth.

The Colorist, in the modernist tradition of *Nightwood* and *Mrs. Dalloway*, explores female interiority in a predominantly male fictive context, that is, relative to humanist assumptions of a heroic ideal defining the rhetorical parameters of subjectivity. In addition, though, Daitch hits all the right keys in the postmodernist scale, and tips her (cinema!) hat often to such heavyweights of postmodern theory as [Michel] Foucault and [Louis] Althusser; yet it is the extent to which her second novel seems an old-fashioned modernist allegory of alienation that I find most interesting, especially as it touches on the Aeschylean problematic of female power necessarily working Athena-like against its own gender interests. Whereas, say, the Joycean or even Dostoyevskian anti-hero's is (in [W. H.] Auden's phrase) a "self-observed, observing mind," and this self-reflexivity colors perception with a libidinal passion turned grotesquely upon itself, in Daitch's fiction, as in that of her modernist female precursors Woolf and Barnes, libidinal passion seems channeled into the act of perception, and the orthodoxy of self-reflexive alienation/piety is thereby reconfigured within the larger male/heroic tradition. In *The Colorist* to a greater extent than in the works of [Virginia] Woolf and Barnes there is an allegorical dimension reinforcing what is otherwise a function of dramatic situation and voice.

Julie, Daitch's narrator, "had a job coloring empty frames for a serial comic called *Electra*", which might have been a source of wry humor regarding the absurdities of specialization in the mass-market workplace if playing it straight, so to speak, over the course of the fiction did not produce such an attractively odd tonal effect. The colorist does not lack self-irony, and certainly does not glorify the importance of her role in a production mode the end result of which is a relatively unpopular popular-art commodity. Indeed, like a typical wage-earner, she contrives reasons to avoid her tedious tasks, sometimes going on "color searches" that are "often a ruse . . . for leaving work". Yet throughout she otherwise exhibits a professionalism suggested by attention to detail, sensitivity to nuance, and general appreciation of colleageal interaction on particular projects that determine her social identity. Julie is a colorist, and this gets highlighted when she is let go from her job because of *Electra's* diminished popularity, and for a good deal of the story is no less an unemployed colorist than the victims of Detroit plant closings bear long after their job terminations the identities of unemployed auto-workers.

The colorist's exploration of identity is set primarily against that of her beleaguered comic-book heroine whom she reappropriates to eventual sad effect, and that of her conspicuously passionless primary love interest, a peripatetic photographer originally from Ireland who is "no longer an immigrant but not yet a citizen," a man who "sometimes made a profession out of the role of displaced person". There is much conceptual play throughout regarding aesthetic, philosophical, and ideological distinctions between modes of imaging to artistic ends; and indeed questions centered on artistic modes of production are explored with tantalizing suggestiveness and a light touch. But it is the power relation of the male seeker/adventurer to the female narrator's own fixed circumstances that resonates most memorably, and it is this aspect of the dramatic situation that supplies impetus for an allegorical reading of the fiction and that reinforces the Aeschylean problematic played out by the comic-book character Electra (temperamentally similar to Aeschylus's own mournful and conflicted character of the same name), and by the colorist herself in the activity of covertly reauthoring Electra's "adventures."

The colorist's alienation is implicit in the circumstances of her life as detailed in the narrative, not in a pervasive tone; indeed, her tone throughout is colorless. Her agony within the Aeschylean problematic seems at first flush a paradoxically dispassionate one, yet this small trick of tone speaks proverbial volumes—volumes of male-produced first-person narratives expressing a hysterical nostalgia for access to discourses of heroism and to the pious tones in which they were always couched. "Heroism" is of course the paradigm of the Western subject, a phenomenon that, as Althusser among others posits, exists only in ideologies as sources of initiative tethered to imaginary identities. The colorist's own identity gets configured relative to two males, her aforementioned occasional housemate Eamonn, who "had been in countries where he risked his life just getting off the plane carrying a camera", and Martin, a dreamy co-worker with whom she has a brief flirtation, a comic-book letterer and aspiring screenwriter who "made up foreign-sounding scenarios while foreignness lay outside his window". Both the man of action who captures images of experience the other is compelled to imagine imperfectly, and the teller of tales who poorly imagines life *in extremis* rather than acknowledging its imminence and close proximity are in fact agents of the same ideological apparatuses, the same institutional apotheosis of phallocentric authority, the same heroic ideal.

Julie's friend and colleague Laurel is even more dour than the colorist and considerably more assertive, more the woman of action. Early on Laurel participates in the reappropriation of Electra, an activity both women engage in at first with humor and irony, but with increasing desperation, especially as the colorist continues the project more or less alone. Because they must proceed from where Electra was terminated, much of their project entails wrenching the character's voluptuous-outer-space-vixen identity from the male imaginations that had spawned it (the *Electra* text had been written by a pathetic little man) and then consumed it (adolescent males were the target audience). If Eamonn "lent himself well to comics" it was because "he knew how to act heroically," and Laurel, actually more heroic by nature than Electra, matches Eamonn's willfulness. Electra, by contrast, seems always the victim of circumstances, forced into a heroic role to which she is not temperamentally suited. Of course, being male-imagined for the imaginations of young males, she must hold out the possibility of relenting to a male will, of giving in, finally, to her male nemesis in space, or any pimple-faced kid on Earth, or even to a man like Martin who, if "incorporated into the strip . . . might be that wrong man, the one met accidentally, the disaster who leaves Electra obsessed with the most trivial memories. Or he might be the one who straightens her out, marries her, teaches her the meaning of money, instructs her in the idiomatic twists and turns of the English language, and this would turn into another kind of domination".

> The colorist's phenomenology of passion should be understood in the context of a feminist allegory of empowerment, of a woman refusing to play either Isis-in-search or Electra-in-mourning, or any "heroic" role necessarily in male drag.
> —*Richard Katrovas*

It is a commonplace that the chief project of the postmoderns is the dismantling and irretrievable scattering of the humanist (heroic) subject. It is hardly surprising, then, that *The Colorist*'s allegorical drift has Laurel securing a position with Jack Ladder, "a man who made reproductions for the Metropolitan Museum," and eventually arranging a position for the narrator due to the "great demand for Egyptian hieroglyphics". This seems appropriate because the popular subject from the Pyramid Texts on which they work at home, copying onto fake papyrus, is "Osiris, god of the underworld," who "was often placed standing between his wife, Isis (who was also his sister), and her sister, Nephthys," both of whom "were in love with him". The narrator notes that the three deities were often portrayed together: "each woman had one wing, and Osiris stood between them, as if they were some kind of moth". This god of the underworld thus becomes by ancient reckoning a figure suggestive of the post-modern subject, the latter so semiotically problematized as to seem more shattered than scattered over creation. But it is not Isis's search for the pieces, particularly the phallus, of the subterranean god that transfixes Julie's imagination. It is rather the fixed image of the three figures that troubles her, the heroic god flanked by single-winged female deities:

> In every picture we copied, they appeared, the three of them, bound together with no hint of tension. They were symbolic, all tied together, but of what I didn't know. The picture hadn't arrived yet which showed

Isis beaning Osiris with a frying pan or a brick. If I were Isis, I'd find it difficult not ever being able to get away from the other two. There was a preponderance of serenity in the pictures. I was instructed to take a heavy hand with the green oxide and Nile blue. Remember, it's the underworld, Laurel said. The greens and blues you think symbolized serenity might have actually implied passivity, boredom, or sleep. No one is supposed to have a good time, and the three of them are stuck with each other. Blues and greens can be deceiving.

Emblems of feeling determine the aesthetic nature of any mimetic system, whether primitive or sophisticated. Even the most abstract, non-representational system is negatively defined by traditional assumptions of mimetic efficacy. That these systems are *not* unitary and archetypal, but highly relative, even unto themselves unstable, is the bane of a humanism that in its aesthetic dimension must suffer to conceal the enormous contradiction that the feeling subject, self-consciousness aspiring to heroism, acts upon but more importantly *feels* within an overdetermined system that, once scrutinized, admits neither feeling nor action. The transcendent passion implicit in heroic willfulness is itself an aesthetic construct, whether regarded in terms of action or expression. Blues and greens can indeed be deceiving, and Julie's lack of passion is an absence signifying (as Eamonn's merciless black-and-white photos signify by their lack of color) a surfeit of those passions ("blues and greens") associated with color—not a repression, but a compulsion, indeed a passion for noting the nuances of perception.

> Delacroix had a passion for two colors which are the most condemned, lemon yellow and Prussian blue. . . . I bought colors to lay out side by side, looking for clues to a passion or an obsession generated by this impossible combination. I anticipated a hostile reaction between the two which would have been spontaneous, like the splitting of an atom. Perhaps he hadn't meant they were condemned in whatever separate state they might be found. I rarely did see them together. Like paint itself, color experiments seem to lose their stability over time.

The colorist's phenomenology of passion should be understood in the context of a feminist allegory of empowerment, of a woman refusing to play either Isis-in-search or Electra-in-mourning, or any "heroic" role necessarily in male drag. Heroic piety (ranging from the self-aggrandizement of the man of action to the condescending humility of the supplicant) and anti-heroic alienation (ranging from the unrelenting self-examination of the self-loathing ironist to the dyspeptic musings of the sexually repressed misanthrope), two sides of the same humanist coin of subjectivity, get revealed as such and dismissed as options for the narrator's own passage. She wears, metaphorically, a "cinema hat," that is, a "box-shaped object" the inside of which "looks like a small movie theater. . . . Your life as it happens, that's the film. You are the leading actor and the audience at the same time", but one is also outside a "fixed story" and outside the strictures of mimesis, the codes within which and by which images and their values get reproduced. If we cannot feel ourselves to be anything other than overdetermined "subjects," we may at least peer into the mechanisms by which feeling gets constituted. The result is a kind of fresh perspective on the self-as-construct, but not in the psychoanalytical sense of self-revelation. Psychoanalysis is the final blossoming of the heroic tradition, and as such largely defines anti-heroic self-absorption. The colorist does not seek a cure but a perspective:

> As I walked to his studio, I was stopped by a man with a walkie-talkie. He was part of a film crew, and from the east side of the avenue I watched a movie being shot. I had no idea what the story was about. Production assistants would tell you where to stand but would say nothing about the script. You could spot the actors from a mile away almost. As I walked back and forth during the course of the day, buying paint, picking up more fake papyrus from Jack Ladder, I walked in and out of what the movie version of my life might look like. . . . The movie was full of clean strangers wearing the wrong clothes and too much orange make-up. Extras playing homeless men and women were covered in paint that was supposed to look like dirt. . . . I stepped in and out of the movie. . . . I prefer the cinema hat.

The colorist's own passions, her sense of loss and betrayal, her sexual fantasies, her desire and terror as such are not expressed, though the narrative remains entirely within her point of view. This first-person narrative does not impart a revelation of feeling but a feeling of revelation, the powerful sense of a woman gazing into the heart of things.

Larry McCaffery (interview date Summer 1993)

SOURCE: "An Interview with Susan Daitch," in *Review of Contemporary Fiction,* Vol. XIII, No. 2, Summer 1993, pp. 62-82.

[*In the following interview, Daitch discusses the structure and creation of her novels. She discusses her interest in meaning as dependent on context and her interest in "thought language" versus "spoken language."*]

[*Larry McCaffery:*] *What sort of writing have you been do-*

ing recently? In an interview a while back you mentioned you were working on a series of interrelated novellas . . .

[Susan Daitch:] I've put those aside and have been working on a novel about Georges Méliès, the early filmmaker, and the [Alfred] Dreyfus trial. Dreyfus isn't a character in the book, but there were elements surrounding his trial, questions of representation and reproduction, that I'd explored in *The Colorist* and other pieces. The camera had already been invented at the time of the trial, but photography as a means of documenting evidence was used only in a fairly rudimentary way, almost as an afterthought. An enormous number of forgeries were produced and copies of copies. I was interested in some of the characters who had been only tangentially connected to the affair. Around 1899 Méliès made a film about the Dreyfus trial which was an early version of a docudrama. He hired an ironmonger to play Dreyfus, and he himself performed two roles—a lawyer who is assassinated in one scene, and in a later part of the film, as a journalist. He dramatized the trial as opposed to Lumière's straight-man realism.

Sounds like we are already in the realm of Baudrillard's "simulacra"—the "stand-in" for reality.

Méliès called these films "reconstructed actualities." He divided his work into two categories: actualities and preconstructions. The preconstructions are more well known and involve fantastic metamorphoses, puns, transformations, dismembered body parts with lives of their own and what André Maugé called "salvoes of comic go-getting." He didn't make many of these reconstructed actualities, but the ones he did—the film about Dreyfus, about the American invasion of Cuba and the Philippines, and the wreck of the *Marne*—were very different from the preconstructions. They tended to comment on what he saw as the political aggression; they were very convincing, if not incendiary, when they were shot. The film about Dreyfus caused riots when it was shown and was banned in France until 1973. Documentaries about the affair were banned until 1951.

Other than Méliès, who were these tangential characters in the Dreyfus affair? And what got you interested in them in particular—their roles in the ways the trial got represented?

I was intrigued by a character who was called the "Ordinary Track," a woman who emptied the wastebaskets from the German embassy. She worked for what was called the Section of Statistics (which was like the French CIA or FBI). After surreptitiously collecting the scraps of paper, torn-up letters, apple cores, and so on, she would bring the embassy trash (called "cones") to a church in the sixth arrondissement for someone from the Section of Statistics to pick up. It was usually Colonel Henry, one of the forgers. The garbage did contain what has been described as "lewd and erotic fantasies" attributed to the German and Italian attachés, and from these bits of garbage, some of the evidence used against Dreyfus was constructed.

They were fabricating this scenario against Dreyfus even though they must have already known who the real spy was? This almost sounds like Coover's take on the Rosenberg case in The Public Burning*: history as paranoid political fantasy.*

Yes. I was interested in the role the Ordinary Track played in the trial because she was illiterate. The Section of Statistics was putting together its forgeries from bits of rubbish they found in her "cones," yet she couldn't read any of them. I've been interested in how people learn language or, in her case, how they survive without the written signs of language. The Section of Statistics was all about language and the more I read about it, the more inevitably [Franz] Kafka-esque it appeared. Whole freight cars full of files were constructed in order to present a picture of false guilt. It is the architecture of all these fictions that my book focuses on, not Dreyfus himself. He doesn't appear at all except though his traces, a series of very tangential and indirect fictionalized versions and references. There's been very little fiction written on the Dreyfus affair, apart from *Remembrance of Things Past* and a satire by Anatole France, *Penguin Island*, which refers to "The Affair of 80,000 Bales of Hay." Susan Rubin Suleiman has written that "the novelistic quality of the real story may account for its relative lack of fictional representation, since the facts themselves are so gripping what need is there to fictionalize them?" I think she's right. My book is really Dreyfus without Dreyfus. As I've said, he's not in it, some of the tangential characters are.

Several different threads of connection unified the concerns you developed in your first two novels L.C. *and* The Colorist—*for instance, your interest in the idea of representation, storytelling, the ways that reality gets "translated" into words, images, stories, and the ways people use this process for their own subjective needs or ends. Based on what you're saying, it sounds as if these concerns are central in your new book as well. What kinds of factors have contributed to your interest in these general areas?*

I started out as a painter, sort of. Actually, what I was doing were more like narrative drawings than paintings, so when I began writing fiction it seemed very natural to be thinking of texts in visual terms. This was especially true in *L.C.,* which is about how something (a text or a story) changes hands, and how it graphically or visually changes when that happens. When the provenance changes, the meaning changes as well. That led me to start thinking about the next step— how translation changes a passage, or a series of narratives.

At what point did Delacroix enter the "picture"?

I was interested in Delacroix because he was so much a man *not* of his political moment in 1848. I'd been reading his notebooks, and the idea of using a notebook as the core of another story seemed worth trying. The notebook or diary is such a subjective form, to use it pulls all the obvious questions about point of view out of the hat. Who's telling the story? What kind of ax do they have to grind? How do they know what they know? Are they reliable? Probably not. Reading Delacroix's notebooks suggested the idea of a traffic in documents: notebooks or letters, going through different translations within a fictional frame. What happens to texts, for both readers and translators, when the original goes through this transformation into another language? That was an important part of what I wanted to do in the book almost from the beginning. The journal is invented but would only be represented to readers through other versions, translations, never directly.

What you were saying just a moment ago about exploring the way the "meanings" attached to an object change depending upon the context (who owns it, what the subject biases and reading practices are over different periods, and so on) sounds almost like a gloss on some of the main deconstructionist ideas. Were you in fact reading theory during this period?

I was reading a lot of Henry James, as well, and so many of his books involve stories within stories, or you have a situation in which someone is telling a story which was repeated to him or to her by someone else who heard it from someone else before that. When I was writing *L.C.* I was working for the Whitney Museum Independent Study Program which I had also participated in as a student. The program was very involved in Marxist theory, psychoanalytic theory, feminism, and deconstruction. All these ways of thinking about narrative and taking narrative apart have seemed important to address in one way or another. Many feel the case for theory and fiction is a case that rests on a bucket of eels. It puts you outside the mainstream certainly.

How do you mean that—simply that the sort of built-in self-consciousness about narrative that theory generates goes against the grain of most fiction?

There is a desire to sink into a book and pretend that the experience is coming to you directly, to take the devices, plot, character, form, certain kinds of content for granted. The world of narrative or mainstream writing or whatever you want to call it has a lot of trouble with that idea of advancing the form but that seemed important to me. Harry Mathews wrote that "the experience is the experience of a book and not looking through a window at life. . . . Books which complete themselves more or give more apparent satisfaction to the reader by bringing things to a conclusion are much easier to put aside. The guy will go down to the ground floor and retrieve the book because he's interested in the *process* and not the conclusion." Which I agree with although if you're a woman, rather than a generic guy, and you live in an apartment you can't go downstairs anyway. You have a different set of problems.

You once told me that Hans Haacke's text-and-visuals pieces had a big impact on you in a certain way that might have affected your thinking about writing. Why was that?

There was a kind of turning point for me in the late seventies when I stopped making art altogether, and there were many nails hammered into that particular coffin, most of which aren't worth going into. I remember seeing Haacke's work, especially one piece in which he had lined a gallery with reproductions of [Édouard] Manet's *Bunch of Asparagus* and underneath each painting was the date of purchase and a paragraph about the owner. When you looked at the first reproduction, you'd read that the first owner was a friend of Manet's who paid him 1000 francs for the painting, 200 francs over the agreed price. In gratitude Manet sent him another painting with a note that read, "There is still one missing from your bunch." The painting changed hands over the years increasing in value. One owner committed suicide, others fled from the Nazis. By the last frame the painting is in a museum in Cologne that, in 1968, paid $260,000 for it. Haacke documented the lives of several other paintings as well and so by tracing their provenance, a narrative is unraveled. World wars, the Rockefellers, Interpol, and so on come and go. The viewer/reader rides along the paintings' coattails—these sorts of "tags" of history and politics that fall behind as the story is told. The diary in *L.C.* traces a similar sort of trajectory: the February revolution, the Berkeley riots, the Vietnam War. At the Whitney Biennial in 1977 I saw Juan Downey's video Trans Americas installation which also made a big impression on me. The installation was set up so that video monitors were arranged on a north/south/east/west axis. One was a taped performance by a Chilean group of actors who called themselves The Aleph. I think it was in part a sort of comic performance, but at the end of the tape you were told that the actors had all been disappeared. The tape had the quality of being made five minutes ago, and then the words rolling across the screen inform you that all the performers have been murdered. On another monitor was a video based on the Velasquez's *Las Meninas*. Actors played the parts of King Philip and Queen Mariana, Velasquez himself, the Infanta Margarita, court dwarfs, maids, and so on. The voice over narration quoted Foucault, Kubler, described Downey's trips to the Prado to see *Las Meninas* when he lived in Madrid, and explained what was going on in Spain in 1656, placing the painting in a historical context (the revolution of Portugal and Catalonia, the loss of the Spanish Netherlands—issues of colonization). It seemed to me that this was what I wanted my work to do: address historical and political meanings, and if possible, garner "salvoes of comic go-getting."

When Lucienne writes in her diary early in the novel, "How is a book like a life?" she seems to present a justification for **L.C.***'s elaborate, ambiguous structure of meaning/translation/false translation, and so on (a "straightforward" narrative simply wouldn't portray the complexities of this book-life relationship). Was that in fact one of the reasons you didn't consider developing a more straightforward narrative?*

That would be like writing a linguistic white elephant. I'm not interested in writing a straightforward fictional narrative about historical and political events because it creates a false conversion. To simply recreate history you court the world of historical fiction, tipping the scale toward the romance even. Foucault writes about using history paradigmatically to understand the present in *Discipline and Punish: The Birth of Prisons*.

> **I'm not interested in writing a straightforward fictional narrative about historical and political events because it creates a false conversion.**
> **—*Susan Daitch***

What kinds of parallels did you begin to uncover between the 1848 and 1968 periods? You must have been too young to have had firsthand access to what was taking place in Berkeley.

I was, yes. My husband and many of his friends went to school there and were teargassed, arrested, and went to jail. He deserves a lot of credit for providing me with details about what had happened. His stories were terrific, and listening to them was one way the parallels started to become clear to me.

L.C. *very much has to do with class and power, the ways that ferment gets started—and the relationship of the artist to all of this. Lucienne presents Delacroix and some of the other people she meets—artists and observers of what is taking place—as having a theoretical interest in what's going on, but as finally being only observers and artists. They seem a bit like certain "tenured radicals" or theoretical Marxists at universities today whose commitment is limited to lecturing and explaining but who never get directly involved in anything or have any deeper connections to these things. I'm reminded of the scene where Lucienne is describing the political debates she hears at cafés and dinners by saying, "For many of the guests, political debate is heavily laced with gossip, transformed to reactionary opinion and 'Did you hear this?' It is, for them, like discussing a play. They're removed from the action." This sense of distance is lessened in the later scenes with Jane in Berkeley but it seemed to come up again in* **The Colorist***, with Julie and her photog-*

*rapher boyfriend's different relationships to political con-
flict (and to the art that represents this conflict).*

In both books I was trying to question how one writes or
produces art in situations of conflict. With Lucienne in **L.C.**
I had an interest in observing the observer, while Jane is the
one who actually gets involved 120 years later. Eamonn in
The Colorist is also an observer and while remembering how
he had photographed the troubles in Northern Ireland, he realizes he no longer knows who he's working for, and goes
through a period of paralysis that's a kind of crisis of representation.

*Is the "flattening" effect of television one of the main things
producing this crisis for artists wishing to represent contemporary conflicts? A tank battle in Iraq, or a bomb set off in a
Belfast restaurant, or a television movie with Arnold, or a
local newscast about a kitten being rescued—all these things
are presented so they somehow effect viewers equally. We're
encouraged to invest the same emotions on all them because
they're all part of this society of the spectacle.*

I wasn't really thinking specifically about television and the
society of the spectacle, but it's difficult to talk about film
and photography without these issues rearing their heads. My
own position, writing these things, is by definition voyeuristic,
but so much American fiction is about sentimental realism,
very personal and domestic in a claustrophobic way, and that,
for me, has been something to avoid.

*I don't think it's any accident that so many writers of your
generation are very self-conscious about this issue of how to
find an honest perspective once you're no longer trying to
create the illusions of realism. And this is a key area of concern specifically for you, Bill Vollmann, and David Foster
Wallace, both in content (the constant focus on image-making and the ways language constructs "reality," the presentation of the self or identity as a linguistic concept, etc.) and
in the refracted formal structures and metafictional features
of your work. Wallace, of course, has been very vocal about
the limits of metafiction, but my own view is that writing about
writing is often more than a rarefied activity divorced from
the world within the word. There's very real political and
practical implications to attempts by writers who want to
engage the world but to do so in a way that's not, as you say,
just sentimental realism. You could even say that this current
crisis of representation is basically what "postmodernism"
is all about. Certainly this sense of the variety of representations we encounter (and the confusion this brings, for both
artists and ordinary citizens) is part of the whole texture of
The Colorist—it even seems to inform the way its plot unfolds, the elaborate "layering" structure we were talking
about earlier.*

I think of **The Colorist** as being like an accordion falling off

a chair. One of the reasons it's a plotless book is that it's
about thinking different kinds of representation through,
whether comics or photography or Egyptian hieroglyphics.
Everything that happens in the book goes through different
filters or frames, so "plot" in the usual sense has taken a walk.
Conditions of moral ambiguity, for example, might be conveyed in four different scenarios: movie, photograph, comic,
museum reproduction. A resolution of that ambiguity might
not be possible, but the condition itself is presented through
different frames.

*What's been your response to frustrations some reviewers
seemed to feel about your refusal to fulfill readerly demands
for plot and character development and so forth? One of
them quoted the character of Loonan (the scripter of
Fantomes Comics), then criticized his notions about an audience being "extraneous." The* New York Times *took exception to the fact that your narrative in* **The Colorist** *"tends
to be as unstructured and improvisatory as Julie's messy life."
What's your sense of obligation to your readers in terms
of providing them with a reading experience that is structured, plotted, and so on? (Clearly this has to do with the
issue of what literary "realism" means—maybe* **The
Colorist***'s refusal to provide these things is what makes it
"realistic.")*

Was her life messy? I thought Julie was living the life of Reilly.
I think I've explained that the structure wasn't improvised at
all. Accusing critics of coming to your work with the wrong
set of expectations, for criticizing your books for reasons that
have nothing to do with your intentions may be a cry against
misjudgment, but also has the ring of hard cheese. The only
disturbing criticism of **The Colorist** occurred in the *New York
Times*, a paper which has been criticized by ACT-UP and
Queer Nation for its coverage of the AIDS crisis as being too
little and too late. The reviewer charged that the book contained a lot of sleeping around in "the age of AIDS." There
was virtually no sex in the book, and this was deliberate. I
never write about sex. It's embarrassing. I don't know how
others do it. Absence of characterization can be infuriating
but what is it we talk about when we talk about characterization? Characters who "come alive on the page"? What emotions are being produced? Is the reader being manipulated?
Toward what end? Part of the pleasure of reading comes from
these paper tigers capable of engendering strong emotion,
but "character" is a concept often batted around, taken for
granted, rarely explained.

In response to your question about audience, I have little idea
of who my audience is or what they want, so obligations to it
are up for grabs. Henry Green compared his books to newborn babies whose necks he'd like to wring. I feel a certain
amount of embarrassment, lack of preciousness about my
work, and would rewrite all of them given half a chance, or
wring their necks. Once the books are in print I have to turn

the spines against the wall. I can't look at them without seeing a million things wrong.

You've mentioned the influence that visual artists had on your literary sensibility when you were starting out. Were there any writers other than James and Green who had a significant impact on your work?

They're different with each book. It would be an eclectic and disconnected list. Peter Handke and Heinrich Böll, Nathalie Sarraute on language and characterization. Carlo Ginzburg and Robert Darton on which histories are recorded and why, Italo Svevo for pulling the rug out from under. Walter Benjamin, too, although I've been told I should probably get off that Benjamin dime already.

You said you had the conception of the successive transformations of Lucienne's diary more or less in mind early on. Was the idea of a three-part structure also part of your original conception?

The three sections, the triptych structure of **L.C.** was also soon fixed, whereas **The Colorist** began differently. After having written a book that required research at every turn, I wanted to write something which was more immediate. One of my sisters, who is an animator, gave me drawings from the end of *Spiderwoman*. I think she knew the inker. The serial was being discontinued, Spiderwoman terminated in the last frame, and that, with all its implications, seemed interesting in terms of a narrative situation. I spoke with Françoise Mouly at Raw Comics and visited Marvel as well. **The Colorist** was sort of like a *photo-roman* whose sections might be: episodes that have been elided from comics, the daily life of the man who makes reproductions for the Metropolitan Museum, and different uses of photography. **The Colorist** was also a record of my neighborhood, which was changing, rapidly becoming a locus for the GAP and crack.

Did you feel more comfortable with one method rather than the other—or which has seemed to work best for you with your recent writing?

I've sort of gone both ways with the things I've worked on since. With the Dreyfus-without-Dreyfus novel, I began with five characters who had or who have varying degrees of connection to the affair. They are: Méliès's assistant, who builds the sets for the Dreyfus film and becomes caught in the riots that follow its screening; a con artist blackmailed by the Section of Statistics into creating a false correspondence for Dreyfus while he is imprisoned on Devil's Island; a character based on two of Esterhazy's mistresses whose chapter takes place in 1934 when the Maginot Line was being established. The fourth section is devoted to the Ordinary Track many years after the trial when she is living on the street. The fifth chapter set in contemporary Los Angeles focuses on the re-

storer of Méliès's Dreyfus film and a character named Jack Kews. The sections aren't as separate as they sound. There are connections between chapters and the characters.

How would you describe the initial impulse that tends to get you started with a particular work—is it a character or narrative concept, or something more abstract like a formal structure or a metaphor?

A situation or narrative concept. It seems like many writers tend to choose character when they're asked this question, but I remember Henry Green and [Jean-Paul] Sartre both saying in their *Paris Review* interviews they start with a situation every time.

When you say "situation," do you mean in a very large sense—something like an historical or political context with certain types of people in it? Or something more particularized?

I think about who sweeps [Joseph] Stalin's tomb.

The women in your first two novels defy the usual stereotype of women being trained (or brainwashed, or coerced) to fit in to society—the whole business about women's identities being created in response to men, the role of "the male gaze" in constructing sexual identity or image, and so on. In fact, your heroines are revolutionaries; rather than trying to accommodate society-as-is (i.e., patriarchal society), they're trying to change things. But they are never able to escape from imbalances of power that govern their culture's attitudes. If anything, once they have "escaped" and wind up in Algiers, they're exposed to even greater extremes of patriarchal control.

In Algiers their mobility was even more limited. There was truly no Spiderwoman escaping through air ducts in 1848. Given the restrictions in Algeria, most action had to be thought action—if you believe Willa Rehnfield's translation.

When you're in the process of writing, do you find that "themes" or "content" seem to arise "naturally" out of the narrative structure you're working out? Or are you more consciously pursuing thematic possibilities that you anticipated beforehand?

I guess the answer is that I'm consciously developing thematic material. The more you write the more you begin to find things about your own work that repeat. In everything I've written I found myself repeating certain things—ideas about translation and representation and how language is acquired, stories within stories.

Are there other aspects of your writing that you've been consciously pursuing or avoiding?

I've avoided writing about family relationships. My characters are usually people without family ties.

In everything I've written I found myself repeating certain things—ideas about translation and representation and how language is acquired, stories within stories.
—*Susan Daitch*

Is the source of this reluctance primarily autobiographical (some dark family secrets upstairs in the locked bedroom) or aesthetic? For instance, having a character with strong family ties would usually drastically limit your options from a plot standpoint.

We lived in a ranch house. There was no upstairs. It's an aesthetic decision, based partly on the influence of [Samuel] Beckett as well as the writers I've mentioned earlier. The situations I map out and put characters into aren't usually ones that emerge of family engagements, so they don't merit dragging in aunts, uncles, and bath mats (though there are a few exceptions within what I've set out).

Right—family relationships seem to figure fairly prominently in **The Colorist.** *I'm thinking of things ranging from Electra's relationship with Orion right on down to the relationships many of the contemporary characters have; and the problems various characters seem to have that are specifically associated with their mothers. It seems to me that in* **The Colorist** *you were providing a kind of psychological background for some of your characters; but rather than providing this by the usual novelist means, you gave us this through the framing devices. So we understand what's going on inside Julie better by reading about her presentations of Electra—who's almost her alter ego—in the comic book. And so on.*

Bits and pieces of this creep in. I'm still struggling with the problem of how to construct something out of language once you've decided not to be involved with issues generated by developed characters or whatever it is we think about when we think about characterization. Characters might be vehicles for getting the job done, telling the story, but at the same time, I have doubts about them as main architects.

Certainly the old-fashioned, linear means of character presentation seem simply naive to us today. Writers have always enjoyed creating that illusion of being able to understand the character—and it's what readers have come to expect in a novel. But it was always an illusion.

There are also practical considerations (including financial pressures) that make it difficult to choose not to provide char-

acters. Sometimes it's as if I have two homunculi on either side of the screen. One is always saying, "Three-dimensional characters, please!" while the other says, "No way, forget it!" I'm still not sure which one has the right answer. I appreciate how seductive it is to get wrapped up in certain kinds of characters.

Again, I felt that you created a "real" sense of character for the main characters in both **L.C.** *and* **The Colorist,** *even though you were introducing your psychological "portraits" so readers could recognize the ironies and ambiguities involved in your presentation. It's the kind of thing that James, and maybe especially [Vladimir] Nabokov, do so well. I'm wondering, though, if you don't feel that the whole issue of "character" has basically changed for today's authors simply because the concept of "identity" has been so radically undermined and mediated by the media-blitz that inundates everyone today?*

Yes. The camera never lies, right? I don't write very much dialogue. I don't think there's any dialogue in **L.C.** and very little in **The Colorist.** Dialogue, a feature of a certain kind of characterization, often seems to produce something that sounds like an echo of a film script. The columns of type, spoken language, seem much less engaging to me than thought language. There are a lot of "ready-mades" out there, signifiers found in the world of images: film, television, and advertising. These create a lot of instant identification, and I've tried to avoid some of that.

Dialogue, a feature of a certain kind of characterization, often seems to produce something that sounds like an echo of a film script. The columns of type, spoken language, seem much less engaging to me than thought language.
—*Susan Daitch*

You frequently present your characters' thoughts through visual imagery—and in the case of **The Colorist,** *visual imagery drawn from the media (comic books, movies, television, and so on). That seems to be an appropriate way of rendering how completely the media interpenetrates the thoughts of people living in our world.*

I was trying to set up a kind of intertextuality, a dialectic between the identity of the character and everything going on around him or her.

This seems to be literalized in **The Colorist** *by the "cinema hat" that you describe—the one you can wear around, with the cutouts, so that everything you see is part of your own* *private movie. Your acknowledgment at the beginning implies that this isn't just a metaphor.*

The cinema hat was actually constructed by a friend of mine. It was a box you could put on your head. The structure was built to resemble the interior of a miniature theater. If you wore this box as you walked around, it would look like your life was the movie. He told me it's since been lost or fallen apart.

It had the little curtains that lifted up so that everything was framed?

No curtains.

Of course people literally see the world this way—as a movie. This general area is something I feel separates your generation from the sixties postmodernists ([Robert] Coover, [John] Barth, [Thomas] Pynchon, and so on). You're more aware of the ways these media-generated "ready-mades" have been integrated into the world, and are effecting people's sense of their own personal (if it is that) identity. It's significant to me that, say, both you and Vollmann are so meticulous about presenting your fictions within a context of verifiable references to historical and geographical details (in your case, say, the details surrounding the Dreyfus case, or the situation in Paris in 1848, and so on). And of course some of the familiar references—to Pocahontas or Leif Ericson (for Vollmann) or (in your case) to Dreyfus or the French Commune have reverberations that your readers are going to bring to this new textual situation—it's almost a shorthand that saves you from having to present this through another form of exposition.

It also can allow history to finish the story. In Richard Powers's *Three Farmers on Their Way to a Dance* and [Aharon] Appelfeld's *Badenheim 1939*, for example, the title almost tells you the whole story.

At the opening of **L.C.** *there's an anecdote about the three shepherdesses who are said to be "in perpetual mourning. One longed for the past, one for the future, and a third for the present." Like so many other things in* **L.C.** *this seems to be a reflection or refraction of something else—the narrative process involved in your writing the book, for instance, specific hints about the relationship your three narrators are going to have to time. Was this anecdote something that you went back and reinserted after you'd finished the rest of the book?*

I don't remember where that story came from or what part of France it's from. I worked on each part of *L.C.* somewhat concurrently rather than sequentially, but that story wasn't tacked on as a sort of afterthought. The three sections of the book (introduction, notebook, epilogue) can be read in any order.

Did you also write the different sections of **The Colorist** *in this concurrent (nonlinear) way?*

There's always a lot of going backward and forward, partly because I'm a chronic rewriter at every stage, so it's difficult to say what came first and what was written later on. A friend once suggested my grave should read, "Don't bother me— I'm rewriting!"

You mentioned earlier that the kinds of art you were doing were mostly drawings, but not really paintings.

They were sort of narrative drawings, episodic, with drawn sequential frames, all kinds of things glued on to the surface of the paper: unfolding Xeroxes of car parts, plastic body parts, calendars. Some were based on books I'd read. Some were made to fall apart over time. Most were accidentally thrown out the last time we moved. I drew a cartoon strip when I was in high school.

Did that background doing comic strips make you aware of the very interesting (and sometimes genuinely sophisticated) kinds of things being done recently in graphic novels and related materials (I'm thinking of everything from Shade the Changing Man *to the works of Lynda Barry and Art Spiegelman)?*

I'd read Spiegelman and Barry, went to Marvel Comics and spoke to people who had been colorists. Even though Electra is clearly an invention and has a life no comic superhero could ever have, I looked at comparable comics. *Somerset Holmes, Ms. Tree, Laser Eraser*, and others to determine what kinds of situations Julie would have been coloring at Fantomas Comics while she still had her job. The name Fantomas came from Fantomas, the fictional criminal popular in France in 1911. Julie is a kind of Inspector Juve, the only character capable of unmasking Fantomas.

There seems to be a definite sense of patterns repeating themselves in different forms in **The Colorist,** *whereas in the original* Top Stories *version you had introduced the main elements but not developed these "variations on a theme." Was that pretty much the nature of what you wound up doing in your revisions?*

Yes. Top Stories is a small press in New York whose books rarely exceed about fifty pages, I think, except when they do collections. When I first wrote *The Colorist* it was as a Top Story, but also, as I said, emerging from years spent in Paris 1848 and Berkeley 1968. I wanted to write something that was more an immediate reflection of what was around me.

With the Top Stories version, the main elements were established: art in the age of mechanical reproduction.

Was it your interest in the narrative situation you found there transferred somehow into your novel?

I knew there would be several stories within the story and there would be a serial comic character who would be terminated and revived. The comic book, like the notebook in *L.C.,* was a formal means of establishing this structure.

Were you aware that Daredevil had an Elektra character (she was a martial arts heroine trained in mysticism or something like that) in one of its series for awhile?

When the book was in galleys one of my students showed me the other Elektra. (The name is spelled differently.) I did read some comics to determine what kind of stories would be produced at Fantomas Comics, but not that one as far as influences on Electra might have been concerned. Most of her appearances in the book are in the stories Julie invents for herself, which are a departure from the standard superheroine situations. Electra, as she appears in Julie's rewritten versions, is more like one of Peter Handke's anomies. The figure of Wonder Woman on the cover was unfortunate and misleading since she in no way figures in *The Colorist,* nor does Electra have anything to do with her.

When you introduce a character named "Electra" into a novel, obviously at least some of your readers are going to immediately bring to that character certain sets of associations drawn from high culture, while others are going to be bringing in very different sorts of pop cultural resonances— one of those potentially rich circumstances that postmodern artists seem increasingly willing to take advantage of.

One of the frustrating things in writing *L.C.* and a few other pieces about history was that it was difficult for me to point to the tension between popular and high cultures. These were periods when, perhaps because of the infancy of print media and photography, popular culture seems less accessible.

Most of your works could be described as being "historical novels" in the sense of being set within a specific historical period that forms a significant backdrop to your own story (I [am] thinking of the Dreyfus period, the Paris and North African scenes of the late 1840s, their parallel in 1968 Berkeley, and the seventeenth-century period of war between the Austrians and Turks). Is there any commonality among these historical periods that drew you to them?

It was different in each case. My impulse to use history has something to do with storytelling itself, the need to create comparisons. History as a kind of ready-made that can be reinterpreted or misinterpreted, and translated.

So your interest has less to do writing "historical fiction" so much as using the original "ready-mades" as a springboard to your own re-interpretations.

Yes. In each I tried to somehow set up a relationship between the historical sections and the parts in the present, and to chart the process of how meanings become attached to historical objects, people, events, as well as how these meanings change.

How does this work in terms of the sequence of novellas you were working on there for a while?

One of these was based on an event that occurred during one of the last battles between the Austrians and the Turks in the late seventeenth century. The Turkish sultan was so confident he was going to win that he brought his entire harem (about four hundred women) to the battlefield. When he lost, all the women—who had lived in purdah all, if not most, their lives—were taken by the Duke of Savoy to Vienna and "freed." "Harem" seems like an inaccurate word because of its implications in English, so I never used it. It means hidden, which exactly expresses the conditions of the women who lived in it, but I'm afraid many people see the word and think *I Dream of Jeannie.* All the women lived in the inner palace whether they were cooks or the sultan's wives, and they were all taken to this particular battle which took place in Slovenia. The story contains many echoes of what is presently going on in the Balkans. These women would have come from every part of the Ottoman empire, from Ethiopia to Iran. I wasn't particularly interested in this period historically, but I wanted to write about how people would recreate a language and culture starting from zero, an abstract situation. I never found out what happened to them. There were many sources on Vienna and Istanbul, but when the doors opened and the characters found themselves in Vienna, the road ended, so I had to make the rest up.

Your finding the popular cultures of that period so inaccessible to research seems very significant. The tendency of artists and historians from earlier periods to draw references almost exclusively from "high culture" turns out to be a major aesthetic and cultural limitation in certain ways. If those women had wound up in Hollywood or Bombay today, you can be sure there would be a trail of tabloid articles, interviews, docudramas, and B-movies left behind. Score one for postmodern culture. Without access to these sorts of popular forms, you aren't able to access the particular kind of milieu that these women would find themselves in.

Actually, I'm not sure that's true. These people have found themselves shipwrecked in Europe today, and they're greeted by neo-Nazis, not B-movies, so the situation is much the same as it was three hundred years ago. I was able to do some research in the library of the British Museum. I don't read

German or medieval Arabic, but I could read a few French accounts. There were great lists of things taken from the battlefield: camels, cannon, ostriches, and eighty women from the inner palace who'd never stepped outside of it except in shuttered carriages. I was interested how they would read baroque culture, manners, how language might be reconstructed. It's as if they'd been taken off an island and then plunked down on an entirely different one.

Your decision to use "Electra" as your comic book heroine in **The Colorist,** *along with the many other references to mythical figures and events (the references later on to Egypt, for example, with that whole sequence of things having to do with Osiris and so forth) brings to your presentation a lot of the kinds of associations and resonances we were discussing earlier. Why not invent a completely new character—or one whose mythic "baggage" would be drawn purely from the realm of pop culture? In other words, is it important to you in developing intertextualities to combine elements from both high and low culture?*

The mythic baggage wasn't a problem and making up a character, since many comic characters have obvious ties to mythology, seemed contrived. When Jack Ladder appears, the man who makes museum reproductions, the connections are self-evident. He represents other terms of the marketplace and concerns with profit margins. Without these connections, he would appear to come out of the blue, just a man hacking ears off fake Egyptian artifacts.

Your background as an artist has affected your work in terms of its "content" in certain obvious ways—i.e., your two novels, as well as the book you're working on right now, all have visual art and artists as central figures, and all three seem to be exploring issues of sight, perception, and meaning. Do you see any analogous sort of influence that painting or the visual arts might have had on your notions of form in any way?

I spend a lot of time at the movies, and parts of the books are cinematic as if I was looking at the characters through a camera. The Electra sections were written almost as if they were storyboards, and I found it useful to read what Hitchcock wrote (or said during his interviews with [François] Truffaut) about suspense, how it's constructed through a certain sequence of events.

Back in the seventies, when you were starting out as a writer, were you reading the innovative works being written by the first wave of postmodernists—Coover, Barthelme, Gass, Morrison, Pynchon?

No.

Do you feel any sense of being "plugged in" to a literary scene here in New York City—the kind of thing Robert Siegel was pointing to in Suburban Ambush, *his book about Manhattan authors? Or do you feel as if you're working more in a vacuum?*

When I hear the word *scene* I imagine people in black, smoking Chesterfields, and talking about the *Evergreen Review.* There are so many people desperately clamoring for every scrap of attention they can possibly get, as if the whole purpose of writing, or of doing anything, is to ensure the spotlight is fixed in their direction. I admire writers like Pynchon and [J. D.] Salinger who won't grant interviews and shun publicity. I've turned down some, wouldn't do television (although they're not exactly banging on my door), avoid radio, don't like to do readings or interviews. (This may be the last one). No, I don't feel I'm working in a vacuum at all, or maybe it is a vacuum and that's the only way to get anything done.

Kirkus Reviews (review date 15 February 1996)

SOURCE: A review of *Storytown,* in *Kirkus Reviews,* Vol. 64, February 15, 1996, pp. 242-43.

[*The following review calls Daitch's first collection of short stories,* Storytown, *"fundamentally lifeless" with two notable exceptions.*]

[*Storytown,* a] first collection, from the author of *L.C.* (1987) and *The Colorist* (1989), brings together 15 fictions, some of which have appeared in the edgier small-press mags, which is not surprising given the postmodern play of ideas that defines most of Daitch's work.

Many of the meta-level narratives here, full of references to pop culture and cinema, are fundamentally lifeless, more concerned with notions of art and interpretation than with telling stories. Two exceptions stand out from a relatively dire bunch. In the long story **"Doubling,"** a courtroom artist is visited by her cousin from Italy, who slowly takes over her apartment and sets up shop as an art forger. The two become partners, eventually inventing a lost artist whose work they churn out for European art markets. Equally intriguing is the title piece, set in a Lake George theme park, where young people act out roles from children's books. While both stories play with the relation between art and reality, they also rely on character and texture, which can't be said for many of Daitch's deliberately more abstract pieces, including a series of very short takes on print culture in France, a dialogue between Walter Benjamin and Bertolt Brecht, and a triptych including descriptions of a mutilated painting by Correggio, massacred bodies in El Salvador, and the Soviet exhibit at the 1939 World's Fair. Many of Daitch's self-reflexive narratives concern the fringes—and substrata—of the art world. A number of them take off from real and imaginary historical episodes: Eleanor Marx's trip to the States; Oscar Wilde in Coney Island; spies and conmen in Barcelona during the Spanish Civil War. At her worst, the author plays with some Burroughs-like techniques, randomly quoting from newspapers or simply itemizing surreal images.

Daitch explores the nature of art and the meaning of defacement, destruction, and duplication in fictions that invite their own deconstruction.

Rosellen Brown (essay date July 1996)

SOURCE: "Bleak Encounters," in *The Women's Review of Books,* Vol. XIII, Nos. 10-11, July 1996, pp. 32-33.

[*In the following review of* Storytown, *Brown finds the collection stimulating and describes Daitch's stories as "effectively unnerving."*]

It's no news that many moods and mysterious landscapes are hard to evoke through the rational progression of foursquare realistic narrative. Susan Daitch, author of the novels *The Colorist* and *L.C.,* presents an unsettling view of the world by less orderly means in her first collection of short pieces. *Storytown* contains a script for a video and a text for the catalogue of an art show as well as stories that, like a shaken kaleidoscope, tirelessly reconstitute random events in weirdly isolated lives.

Like the elements of composition in an abstract canvas, bled of connection, casually violent, brittle with the anomie of city life, the particulars that overtake Daitch's characters are less central than the color, the texture, of the encounters that compose them. This bleak world is shot through with collages of unreadable signs and provocations, false signals, random juxtapositions; it teems with unpredictable energies and lifelike gestures. Hunks of essay fragments and historical fact float through the stories like icebergs and vanish into cartoon business; a photo from the video shows a hand, spread in what looks like desperation, and a shadowy ghost of a figure, faceless.

Though she doesn't need to be so explicit, Daitch spells out in **"Incunabula #3"** the way "ordinary" stories look to her. "People used to read everything as if it were a story. Readers looked for moral tales ... It was a way of imposing logic on mishaps ... to avoid appearing like a city of helpless victims hit by random catastrophe ... People wanted to recognize the end of a story in its beginning." In contrast, her scenarios are impossible to summarize because most are a succession of accidentally-linked events; event related to character and motive seems their least significant aspect. They

feel like an intellectually tantalizing collaboration between Jim Jarmusch and Krzysztof Kieslowski, random and menacing, amusing and, here and there, like a lot of "downtown" art, chilly and occasionally pretentious.

Daitch's characters, mostly young women, work at an ingeniously chosen set of professions devoted to counterfeit or forged, doubled or mirrored—copied—objects. There are art restorers, one of whom works in a studio in a sub-basement, "a thick walled cell immune from vandals and most catastrophes ... a hospital, a cultural auto body shop." Others translate film subtitles, sketch courtroom scenes, examine pornography for the censor. There are counterfeiters and forgers; there is a transsexual who will "never get it right." And finally, in the eponymous **"Storytown,"** a whole cast of teenagers, the most socially connected of Daitch's isolates, impersonate Alice and Dorothy, Robin Hood and Captain Hook and a host of other storybook personalities at an amusement park.

Everyone is involved in a kind of fraud, though not necessarily with criminal intent, bent on some aestheticized form of re-creation in another mode—which only serves to remind us how unreliably our senses can be trusted to guarantee (or value) "reality." "Why," asks a counterfeiter, "should there be a hierarchical relationship, between the genuine currency and copies? Why is one more valuable than the other?" Isn't he asking the same question of a customer about to fork over millions for an allegedly genuine Van Gogh at Sotheby's?

As if their peculiarly destabilizing work and their general isolation were not sufficiently disorienting to these characters and to the reader, a vague air of threat hangs over almost every scene in *Storytown.* "A group of men standing in front of a laundromat didn't seem aware that she existed.... A few of them laughed, but she couldn't tell if they were laughing at her. She couldn't tell which one, if any, had threatened." Subjective or objective? It's hard to know what to call the tension that constantly ripples beneath the surface of these encounters.

Daitch's carefully maintained manipulation of her semi-abstract surfaces makes her stories effectively unnerving. Caring about these fates (these fakes) would be naively over-earnest. Only in the title story do we actually meet up with characters who seem nearly "real"—which is paradoxical, since the point of view is that of Alice in Wonderland crossed with Dorothy of Kansas, one of the teenagers who play fictional characters until a friend is killed under suspicious circumstances. Funny, sinister, edgily political, **"Storytown"** mocks a setting that is like the other side of the looking-glass, by seeing through the sleazy adult characters who use these disguises cynically. Daitch's writing has comic possibilities she hasn't begun to mine yet.

Like a good bit of post-modern art, I found this a stimulating book to visit, though I doubt I'd like to live in its highly intellectualized environment for long. But readers who also reject what Daitch dismisses as "hierarchies of meaning" will love traveling miles from conventional fiction with Eleanor Marx and Oscar Wilde, Brecht and Walter Benjamin, and a character perfectly named for these elegant tales of disconnection and pseudo-representation: Desiderio Mendacio.

FURTHER READING

Criticism

Allen, Esther. "Sentimental Educations." *The Review of Contemporary Fiction* XIII, No. 2 (Summer 1993): 117-20.
>   Examines the many layers of translation in Daitch's *L.C.*

Nericcio, William Anthony. "Rend[er]ing *L.C.:* Susan Daitch Meets Borges & Borges, Delacroix, Marx, Derrida, Daumier, and Other Textualized Bodies." *The Review of Contemporary Fiction* XIII, No. 2 (Summer 1993): 101-16.
>   Studies the textualization of Daitch's novel *L.C.* and how it relates to itself and other meta-textual novels.

Fritz Lang
1890-1976

Austrian-born director, screenwriter, producer, and actor.

The following entry presents criticism of Lang's work through 1994. For further information on his life and career, see *CLC*, Volume 20.

INTRODUCTION

Lang is considered by many critics to be one of the cinema's finest directors. From his technical accomplishments in the films from his German period to his experimentation with genre in Hollywood, Lang has influenced many directors. He is best known for the suspense, conflict, and violence inherent in his work.

Biographical Information

Lang was born in Vienna on December 5, 1890. His father was an architect and wanted Lang to pursue the same career. Lang studied engineering at the College of Technical Science in Vienna from 1908 to 1911 and then studied architecture at the Academy of Graphic Arts in Munich. However, his interest was in other artistic pursuits. Lang spent some time in Paris working as a cartoonist, fashion designer, and painter. At the outbreak of World War I Lang was forced to flee France, which was then at war with Austria. He returned to Vienna and served in the army from 1914-16. After his discharge from the army, he worked as a scriptwriter and an actor, and then moved to Berlin where he worked for Decla as a reader and story editor. Lang wrote and directed his first film, *Halbblut* (*Half Caste,* 1919), in 1919. In 1920, he married Thea von Harbou, a writer and former actress who collaborated with him on the films of his German period. One of these films was *Metropolis* (1927), which brought Lang to the attention of Adolf Hitler. After the Nazis took power in Germany, Joseph Goebbels offered Lang the position of supervisor of German film production; both Goebbels and Hitler admired his work and were willing to overlook the fact that Lang's mother was Jewish. Lang fled Germany in 1933 soon after the offer was made. When he left Germany, von Harbou remained and made movies for the Nazis. Lang spent a short time in Paris and London, then relocated to Hollywood. He became a U.S. citizen in 1939. In 1945 he became the co-founder and president of Diana Productions, which subsequently folded. He finally left Hollywood in 1956, citing continuing disputes with producers. He made several more films in Germany and then retired in California. Lang died in Beverly Hills on August 2, 1976.

Major Works

The silent films of Lang's German period are monuments of narrative technique. Lang's main theme is the link between the decline in morality to the technological advances of capitalism. *Dr. Mabuse, der Spieler* (*Dr. Mabuse, the Gambler,* 1921) follows the activity of a master criminal, but also shows the depravity of the society around him. In the film Lang criticized post-war Germany, which he depicted as plagued by economic chaos, political extremism, and a loss of values. Next, Lang made *Die Nibelungen,* Part I: *Siegfrieds Tod* and Part II: *Kriemhilds Rache* (*Death of Siegfried* and *Kriemhild's Revenge,* 1924) which focused on the heroic past of German mythology. The film relates the exploits of German mythological figures such as Siegfried, Brunhild, and Kriemhild. Lang went from contemporary Germany to Germany's mythic past, then to the future in *Metropolis. Metropolis* is a science fiction vision of a future in which technology is used to oppress, instead of liberate, the masses. In Lang's version of the future, men have built a glittering city, but it is built upon a subterranean factory and city of workers. The workers become part of the dehumanized technology of the factory and are not allowed to enter the city. The film showed Lang's continued interest in architecture, even though he had not pursued it as a profession. The studio spent $2 million on the film and the architectural design and scope of the picture was unprecedented. *Die Frau im Mond* (*The Girl in the Moon*, 1929) was the culmination of Lang's German work. It combined elements of mysticism, architectural motifs, and melodrama in a story about a flight to the moon to search for gold on the moon's crust. *M, Morder unter Uns* (*M*, 1931) was the first film Lang made with sound, enabling him to turn his attention to more psychological themes. The film is the study of a child killer and uses a changing point of view, with the killer at different times portrayed as horrifying or pitiful. Lang's last German film, *Das Testament des Dr. Mabuse* (*The Testament of Dr. Mabuse*, 1933) was banned in Germany because of its anti-Nazi overtones. Lang experimented with different genres while in Hollywood, including a few successful westerns and war movies, but most of his work from this time consisted of crime thrillers. His first American film was *Fury* (1936), an anti-lynching drama. His *You Only Live Once* (1937) is a drama about the consequences of wrongful conviction. In the 1940s he directed several pictures in the film noir style. These films dealt with such themes as guilt and innocence, and the role of the femme fatale. One of Lang's common concerns in both his German and American work was the impact of the decline in patriarchal authority on both the individual and society. In Lang's films the lack of a strong male figure creates feminized men, such as the killer in *M* and the characters of Manners and Walter Kyne in *While the City Sleeps* (1956). In *Scarlet Street* (1945) Lang also shows how the family and the corporation depend on a certain form of masculinity, and the disaster that follows from its absence.

Critical Reception

Critics praise the silent films of Lang's German era for breaking new ground and setting new standards for the industry. Lang was on the edge of technological accomplishment, using the most skilled artists in the German film industry. The films from his Hollywood period are generally less well-regarded because they are more conventional, typical of films made in the Hollywood studio system. However, some reviewers find the Hollywood films more important because of their emphasis on plot and psychological drama. Another important difference noted by critics is that in his German silent films, Lang wrote, or cowrote with von Harbou, his own scripts. Therefore the films were singular in vision from the start. In Hollywood Lang directed the scripts of studio writers. Even with this difference, however, some critics see a consistent vision in all of his work. Reviewers comment that Lang is concerned with character and how it affects human fate, and that he is preoccupied with the dark side of human nature.

PRINCIPAL WORKS

Halbblut [*Half Caste*] (film) 1919
Die Spinnen [*The Spiders*] (film) 1920
Der mude Tod: Ein Deutsches Volkslied in Sechs Versen [*Between Two Worlds*] (film) 1921
Dr. Mabuse, der Spieler [*Dr. Mabuse, the Gambler*] (film) 1921
Die Nibelungen: Part I, *Siegfrieds Tod* [*Death of Siegfried*]; Part II, *Kriemhilds Rache* [*Kriemhild's Revenge*] (film) 1924
Metropolis (film) 1927
Spione [*Spies*] (film) 1928
Die Frau im Mond [*The Girl in the Moon*] (film) 1929
M, Morder unter Uns [*M*] (film) 1931
Das Testament des Dr. Mabuse [*The Testament of Dr. Mabuse*] (film) 1933
Liliom (film) 1934
Fury (film) 1936
You Only Live Once (film) 1937
You and Me (film) 1938
The Return of Frank James (film) 1940
Western Union (film) 1941
Man Hunt (film) 1941
Confirm or Deny (film) 1941
Moontide (film) 1942
Hangmen Also Die! (film) 1943
Ministry of Fear (film) 1944
The Woman in the Window (film) 1944
Scarlet Street (film) 1945
Cloak and Dagger (film) 1946
Secret beyond the Door (film) 1948
House by the River (film) 1950
An American Guerrilla in the Philippines (film) 1950
Rancho Notorious (film) 1952
Clash by Night (film) 1952
The Blue Gardenia (film) 1953
The Big Heat (film) 1953
Human Desire (film) 1954
Moonfleet (film) 1955
While the City Sleeps (film) 1956
Beyond a Reasonable Doubt (film) 1956
Der Tiger von Eschnapur [*The Tiger of Bengal*] (film) 1959
Das Indische Grabmal [*The Hindu Tomb*] (film) 1959
Die Tausend Augen des Dr. Mabuse [*The Thousand Eyes of Dr. Mabuse*] (film) 1960

CRITICISM

Alan Williams (essay date Summer 1974)

SOURCE: "Structures of Narrativity in Fritz Lang's *Metropolis*," in *Film Quarterly,* Vol. XXVII, No. 4, Summer, 1974, pp. 17-24.

[*In the following essay, Williams discusses the narrative structure of Lang's* Metropolis *using A.G. Greimas's system of analysis.*]

This study will attempt a narrative analysis of Fritz Lang's **Metropolis** using concepts developed by A.-G. Greimas, particularly those of his "Eléments d'une grammaire narrative." Greimas's system analysis posits three fundamentally distinct levels in any text: a "deep" structure of meaning (similar to Levi-Strauss's notion in myth analysis but based on a dynamic model of generation rather than a static set of paradigms), an anthropomorphic level (shifts generated by the model become "actions" performed by "characters"), and finally the level of inscription in which the narrative is presented in whatever matter of expression chosen (in this case the filmic text as "read"). Rather than explain in detail Greimas's theory and then proceed to Lang, we will begin the analysis of **Metropolis,** introducing theoretical points as they become relevant. To this end—we will begin with a preliminary "reading" of the film in Greimasian terms (primarily at the "anthropomorphic" level), then proceed to an attempt at formalization of the narrative structure (the "deep" level), and finally place the text in other systems of discourse, the "texts" of culture and ideology (using mainly the level of the inscription).

Metropolis begins with a segment (a self-contained bit of expression read as a separate unit) which appears totally expository—having, however, a definite function in the narrative. Greimas points out, after Propp, that all narratives must begin with a *manque,* a lack of some sort. In many of Perrault's fairy tales this is a lack of food; in the Russian folk-tales analyzed by Propp it is the kidnapping of the king's daughter. Lang's film begins with a depiction of the totally alienated condition of the workers, their lack of control or even contact with their own conditions of existence. This lack marks the workers as the film's first "subject" or hero (as a collective unit), although their function as actant, as performer of a set of operations, changes in the course of the film, as we will see. (The lack posited by Greimas is, of course, similar to the "problem" considered as the root of narrative in texts on the short story or on scriptwriting. Greimas's notion has the advantage, however, of being more concrete from the point of view of analysis and comparison, if not of storywriting. It is easier to compare the lack of two specific objects than to compare two problems defined in different terms, giving a greater power of critical generalization.)

One of the other major devices of all narrative is also introduced in this first segment, but in a non-operative manner: the film is divided into various "spaces," making possible various transfers or disjunctions. The workers are seen descending from the machine rooms to their homes, using the giant elevators which form part of one of the film's ruling oppositions, movement by machine/self-movement, one aspect of the central opposition Machine/Human in the film's structure of meaning.

This notion of space is central to the most daring aspect of Greimas's theories of narrative, his definition of all narrative events as some sort of real or attempted *transfer* of an *object,* accompanied by or implying a spatial discontinuity. By this criterion the first narrative function in **Metropolis** occurs in the film's second autonomous segment. Maria, as "subject," takes the group of children (the object of value) from the worker city to the "pleasure garden" on the upper level. She is forced to leave, and the unit of narrative (and the segment) is ended by the failure of this attempted transfer. This narrative unit, isolated though it seems, does not remain unconnected with the narrative as a whole, by its creation of another hero, Freder, and its anticipation of the penultimate transfer of an object in the film, which is the return of the children to the upper level (again to the "pleasure garden") by Maria, assisted by Freder and Joseph.

This second segment of the film also introduces a second lack, this time individual rather than collective. This *manque* produces Freder as a "hero" of the narrative, for he discovers his lack of *knowledge* of the workers, which institutes the next portion of the narrative in which he descends to the machine rooms to observe the workers and witnesses the accident at the central power room. This constitutes, however, only the first stage of his acquisition of the knowledge which will enable him to act as a hero or subject in the film. The end of this portion of the narrative (and the third autonomous segment of the film) is indicated by his leaving the space of conflict, the machine rooms, to return to the upper levels with his (still incomplete) knowledge.

When Freder returns to the upper city, the residence of the ruling class, he attempts to give his father, John Frederson, his understanding of the workers' condition. Frederson at this point is simultaneously the intended destination of the object of value, knowledge, and anti-subject (traitor) who prevents its transmission. With the introduction of Frederson at this point the narrative must be interpreted simultaneously on two levels, for as an actant Frederson is the "subject" of another "story," in which the object of desire is the control (later the elimination) of the workers. For the discovery of the maps in the dead workers' clothing reveals another lack, similar to Freder's: the ruler of Metropolis lacks knowledge of the meaning of the maps, of the workers' intentions. From this point until the segment of the film in the catacombs the objects of desire sought by both father and son will be types of knowledge, which will enable them to function as hero and traitor in the decisive later stages of the narrative. In each case the knowledge will be acquired in stages. Thus, following the interview in Frederson's office, Freder redescends to the machines and Frederson goes to the inventor Rotwang's house, each in search of more adequate knowledge. At the level of expression the film emphasizes this similarity by the use of parallel editing.

Their acquisition of knowledge, this stage of which is delineated by the spaces in which both hero and traitors remain, brings them both closer to the full knowledge necessary to the power to act. Freder discovers the grueling effects of time and repeated effort by taking charge of a machine deserted by a failing worker. Frederson is shown the Robot by Rotwang, who also partially deciphers the mystery of the maps, which are revealed to be guides to the catacombs below the worker city. Again parallels are established expressively between these acquisitions of knowledge by intercutting.

In the first segment in the catacombs (which we would number as seventh segment of the film) the acquisition of knowledge for both sides is completed. Freder, his father, and Rotwang observe Maria speaking to the workers. The initial lacks of knowledge are eliminated, but reveal in each case another lack: Frederson discovers that he lacks control over the workers and Freder discovers his responsibility as "mediator." The new object of desire for both Freder and his father (through Rotwang) will be Maria, although she is desired by both as a means of obtaining another object, the workers, for their elimination (father) or liberation (son). Although Maria is still a subject or hero in the film, at this point she also becomes an object of desire.

The next narrative function in the film is the abduction of Maria by Rotwang from the catacombs to his house—a typical narrative transfer complete with spatial discontinuity. In the implied confrontation in the inventor's house between Freder and Rotwang (in the segment which follows) the latter triumphs by using machinery, which serves as helping agent to the traitors throughout the film. Freder is thus denied access to Maria whose features are transferred, quite literally, to the Robot. This is done in order to deceive Freder and the workers, that is, to transmit to them a *false knowledge.* The deception of Freder, in his father's office, removes his power to act. The function of the acquisition of knowledge in narrative is the creation of an ability to act, a *power.* Transmission of false knowledge is the classic means of neutralizing this power.

The individual deception of Freder is followed by the collective deception of the workers in the catacombs; this deception does not merely neutralize their power but converts them temporarily into traitors, allies of Frederson and Rotwang. The Robot, contrary to the real Maria, convinces the workers to act by violence for themselves, not peacefully through oth-

ers, a frequent distinction made in Western narratives between traitor and hero. The children left behind in the lower city will assume the workers' actantial function as hero, as metonymic representatives of the proletariat. In these deceptions, the Robot, though a machine, is an actant and fills the role of anti-subject or traitor.

The deception of the workers, however, is followed by the restoration of Freder's power to act, by his acquisition of the knowledge that the Robot is not Maria. The workers, as traitor, subdue him. Their object, the destruction of the machines, entails the destruction of their own children, who are the final object of value in the narration. The restoration of power to the heroes continues as Maria achieves her release from Rotwang's house and prevents the destruction of the children by moving them to the upper city with the help of Freder and Joseph. The restoration of power to Freder and Maria is followed by the undeceiving of the workers and their return to the status of hero. The knowledge given them by the foreman of the powerhouse frees them from the traitors' domination. With this new status they seize and destroy the Robot, who becomes simultaneously anti-subject and object, as Maria was previously subject and object.

The second abduction of Maria by Rotwang creates one final lack to be dealt with by the hero Freder who by killing Rotwang eliminates the last of the traitors—John Frederson being transformed from traitor to hero by his son's actions. It is Freder's having saved the children which saves his father from being killed by the workers. At the end of the film, therefore, the lacks (of the subjects, not the anti-subjects) are removed, the traitors destroyed, and the imbalance which set the narrative in motion eliminated.

We should add parenthetically that some of the problems raised by the narrative structure of *Metropolis* stem from the fact that much of the original version of the film is missing from the copies currently available. Nonetheless the film as it exists has coherence and has been "read" easily enough by its audiences; thus our analysis has taken as its point of departure the text as we have it and not as it "should have been." In any case there is ample evidence that the original version has most of the inconsistencies which trouble the film in its current state. For a summary of these problems see Jensen, *The Cinema of Fritz Lang.*

Despite the apparent complexity of our preliminary reading, *Metropolis* does not have an inordinately complicated narrative design. The major difficulties of analysis come from the division of the functions of hero and traitor among six principal actants, with two of these switching function in the course of the film. The heroes appear in what we have considered the film's first two autonomous segments: the workers, Freder, and Maria. The traitors appear in segments five and six (in the office and Rotwang's house): John Frederson,

Rotwang, and the Robot. The distribution of actants and also their order of first appearance in the text is thus symmetrical—Frederson and the workers will at times be both subject (anti-subject) and object, and Freder and Rotwang will function unambiguously as hero and traitor. This tripling of hero and traitor is maintained through a tripartite division of objects of value: the knowledge wholly human. The robot is, obviously, a machine, but Rotwang is also in part, having lost his right hand and replaced it with a mechanical one during the robot's construction. Thus the inventor is an embodiment of this central tension: he is half human and half machine, on the metonymic level of the hands. It is, significantly, his right, mechanical hand which Frederson shakes after first seeing the robot in action. Shortly afterward, Frederson also shakes the robot's hand: his transformation to hero will be signalled at the end of the film by his shaking for the first time a fully human hand, that of the foreman.

This master opposition is also present in a less consistent manner in methods of transportation depicted in the film. When the workers, oppressed by the ruling class, go to and from work they use the elevators, helping agents for the traitors, whereas when they descend to the catacombs to hear Maria they do so on foot. When the workers go as traitor to destroy the machines, their position as actant is underlined by their use of the elevators—the very sort of machinery which they wish to eliminate. Freder, Maria, and Joseph take the children to the upper levels by purely "human" effort. These oppositions inscribe themselves in an almost Marxist discourse; they therefore contribute to the paradoxical nature of the film. The deep narrative structure, which we can justly characterize as reactionary, belies the contexts into which the production of this meaning is inserted.

A second sort of discourse alluded to in *Metropolis* is of a religious dimension. This is most evident in the names of the protagonists, Joh Frederson ("John" in the English titles does not suggest "Jehova" as well as the German), Maria, Joseph, and Freder, who is most often referred to simply as "the son" or "Joh Frederson's son." (Joseph, we might add, has a less important role than Maria, the Father, and the Son, as befits the Western religious tradition.)

But there is a consistent opposition present between the vague Christianity present in so much of the film and another tradition, mystical and alchemical, most evident in the connotations produced by the presentation of Rotwang. He is portrayed as a sort of medieval sorcerer (and his robot will be burned like a witch); compared to the archtypically Aryan appearances of Freder and Maria the inventor looks distinctly Semitic. On his door and above the robot in his laboratory is a five-pointed star. He lives alone in a curiously distorted, old-fashioned house, set apart from the rest of society. His "science" is occult and solitary.

The opposing, Christian tradition is most apparent in Maria and Freder. The latter, working at the curious circular machine during his second visit to the machine rooms, is quite clearly crucified on the hands of the clock face which appears behind the controls. Maria is clearly and uncomplicatedly associated with Christian teachings. In the catacombs, when she relates the tale of the Tower of Babel there emerges a curious juxtaposition of the Christian and mystic elements opposed in the text. Maria stands in front of numerous crucifixes, viewed reverently from below by the workers. As the shots appear which illustrate her story (differentiated from surrounding shots by a circular masking) it is apparent that the builders of the tower are visually and verbally equated with the tradition represented by Rotwang, that of the arrogant and occult "scholar." Even the clothing worn by the planners of the tower is similar to that of the inventor.

There is also a third manner in which the text, though less directly this time, may be viewed as inserting itself into larger contexts, into an "intertextual space." This aspect of *Metropolis* is composed of structures analyzable in psychoanalytic terms. We will mention here only Oedipal aspects of the film and the presence of elements suggesting a sort of "death wish." Through the cultural and political grids we have referred to above a three-membered "family" is created. Frederson, as leader of society and as a "Jehova" figure, becomes the Father. Freder, as the ruler's son, as representative of the workers, and as Christ, is the Son. Finally Maria, in her religious context and as spiritual creator of Freder and the workers—for it is she who reveals to them their respective *manques*, creating them as individual consciousness—is the Mother. Freder, to negate and assume the power of the Father, must have access to the Mother—which is precisely what is prevented by the abduction of Maria. He will see the robot in Maria's image in the hands of his father, which of course produces his lack of power (castration). Thus the film portrays an individual and collective, Oedipal and primal revolt against the Father, for Maria is also Mother to the masses. The father is retained at the end of the film only in a partially castrated form (he *kneels* on the ground while his son fights Rotwang). That Frederson is not killed outright, but merely stripped of some of his power which is transmitted only to the Son and not to the workers indicates the repressed, compromised nature of the Oedipal conflict in *Metropolis.*

But the film, and indeed most of Lang's work, lends itself also to an analysis in terms of life and death instincts. The preservation of culture itself is at stake in the prevention of Frederson's projected destruction of the workers. There is a persistent identification in the film of the machines and hence the traitors with death, both of the individual and of the structure of society. This is further identified with the pagan/mystic tradition, as when Freder sees the accident in the central power room as a sacrifice to the god Moloch. In a curious way this death tendency is portrayed as belonging to nature as opposed to culture (this of course is perfectly consistent with Freud's thought). Thus when the central powerhouse is destroyed, it is the released *water* which threatens to kill the children. Culture is always dangerously near a breakdown under the forces of nature. The maintenance of culture is the responsibility of the heroes. In most of Lang's work, particularly in his German silent period, there exist powerful forces for the end of culture, individuals whose goal is total destruction: Mabuse in *Dr. Mabuse the Gambler* or Haghi in *Spione* are perhaps the clearest examples.

In most of Lang's work, particularly in his German silent period, there exist powerful forces for the end of culture, individuals whose goal is total destruction: Mabuse in *Dr. Mabuse the Gambler* or Haghi in *Spione* are perhaps the clearest examples.
—*Alan Williams*

Whether one wishes to consider these cultural and psycho-analytic contexts of the inscription of narrativity in *Metropolis* as primary or secondary as compared to "deeper" structures of the text depends purely on the perspective chosen for the analysis. In this study we have attempted to give more or less equal weight to the various levels of elaboration posited by Greimas. At the "deepest" level are the elementary structures of meaning which, anthropomorphized, produce the notions of "actions" and "characters" which with insertion into larger contexts are elaborated into the immediately accessible narration. In this analysis we have stopped short of considering the nature of the inscription of the film itself, how the text produces meaning from moment to moment: codes of lighting or representation of actions, the function of titles, methods of editing and composition, etc. This would be another aspect of the study of the text and an extremely interesting one. Hopefully, however, through this limited work on the profoundly resonant text of *Metropolis* we have suggested some of the levels of structuration involved in the analysis of the production of meaning through narration.

Raymond Bellour (essay date 1974)

SOURCE: "On Fritz Lang," in *Substance,* No. 9, 1974, pp. 25-34.

[*In the following essay, Bellour provides an analysis of Lang's common cinematic techniques used throughout his career.*]

An amazing fate, Fritz Lang's, and fraught with paradox.

Like Stroheim, he was one of the foremost directors, yet not an actor embellished by the surprising prestige accorded every wretched performance; he was like Sternberg, yet without a woman like Marlene at his side; like Murnau, dying (forty years ago) a death wrapped in mystery; in a sense, Fritz Lang was the first in his day, solely for his work as a filmmaker, to have become cinematic legend. There is Welles, of course, again an actor, whose reputation (being at least mythic) rests upon having provoked America. And there is Hitchcock. But the myth here is concealed beneath a sociological facility, an imagery which hides the essential man. In a sense Lang alone incarnates, decisively yet abstractly, the concept of direction or *mise-en-scène.* Nor is his life foreign to this idea: his opposition to Goebbels, his flight from Germany and his disillusioned return after twenty years of exile in America; the way he visibly poses, from the filming of *Siegfried,* as scenarist of destiny—all this gives Lang a quality of violent compaction. This is the horizon which protects the pure and rigorous image of cinema *par excellence.*

From *Les trois Lumières* in 1922, each of Lang's films confirms his status as a great artist—the greatest, with Murnau, of the German filmmakers. Twelve years later he is in Hollywood enmeshed in the gears of the American machine, he produces twenty-three films: a little more than one per year. Even though he often turns down one project and chooses another, he films every possible Hollywood subject: psychological and social drama, detective and adventure stories, war films, Westerns; he does everything but American or musical comedy, and he touches on that in *You and Me.* Lang becomes a Hollywood director; the independent author of *Métropolis* reluctantly shoots a remake of *La Bêté humaine.* He is a great director, praised for his exceptional rigor and keenness. Nothing more. The grandeur of Hollywood amply rewards the absence of critical distance.

But when Lang leaves America in 1958, his reputation has already been forming in France. For Astruc, Rivette, Rohmer or Douchet, Lang is no longer just like other filmmakers. Not that he is the greatest; it's quite another matter: Lang embodies, in a sense, the very possibility of cinema—what is ambiguously called direction or *mise-en-scène.* In the double set of his American and German works, he shows a particular faithfulness, rather explicit, and more and more strict. The paradox of Lang's American films, set back to back as they are to their German counterparts, rests in this: they properly show how a vision of things takes form; what one might call ultimately, if vaguely, a vision of the world which Lang showed unequivocally in his earliest films. Thus Lang acknowledges, through his own singular method of comparison, a primacy of vision; it is not by chance from *Fury* on, both in the script and the picture, Lang implicitly stages the vision itself, using every possible technique, especially the presence of the inquisitor, the reporter, and the photographer—the man who sees the image and retains its appearance in the narrow rectangle of his movie camera. Every film-maker, in a sense, defines the essence of his art; but is there a single one of them for whom, as for Lang, the film is the ultimate metaphor, stark and beyond all circuity? When a Sternberg film opens the possibility of vision, we are sent back, as soon as we look for a reference point, to Woman, the visible subject and object; with Hitchcock, we are sent beyond a moral system bound to appearances to a dizzying duplication of a symbolically doubled subject; in Eisenstein's work, to a theatrical and visual potential of the historical dialectic. But what can be said precisely for Lang: vision of vision? This has none of the ineffective redoubling which would deplete Lang's art, ensnaring it in its own myth; on the contrary, the horizon is enlarged at every point, corroborating Lang's reply to the question: "What is the most indispensable quality for a filmmaker?" "He must know life." By this we must understand: life as a place where vision is experienced. It remains to discover what lies beneath this word, "vision," how exactly Lang endows it with force; and, finally, in what form it shows or shows through.

> The paradox of Lang's American films, set back to back as they are to their German counterparts, rests in this: they properly show how a vision of things takes form; what one might call ultimately, if vaguely, a vision of the world which Lang showed unequivocally in his earliest films.
> —*Raymond Bellour*

This is what explains the passion, which some find peculiar, of certain of Lang's admirers for his last three films. Made in Germany by a man whom the American experience made master of all the artifices of fiction (with one theme and subjects from his first period), *Die tausend Augen des Dr. Mabuse, Der Tiger von Eschnapur,* and *Das indische Grabmal* offer this paradox: they are at once surprisingly disguised and misleadingly frank. Naive and almost puerile on the surface, they are not unlike the Hindu doublet; for beneath the conventionality and gratuitousness of the serial, the last *Mabuse* reveals a particularly urgent gravity of theme. These extremely theoretical films reject the reassuring alibi of Lang's American work while transposing its basic facticity into a Germany where nothing has survived; they disavow the certainty of the myths which subtend the German period and thus bring them to the level of a double adventure, individual and collective, of film and historical conscience. Lang's destructive-reflective irony belies utmost integrity: he makes a game of the hackneyed subjects he is offered, as if through a derisory faithfulness to himself, but in his third *Mabuse* he foils the ultimate games of vision and life, precipitating the myth into a reflection which guides it towards its ultimate reality: the cinema as possible. The metaphor for this is evi-

dent not only in the symbolic title *Die tausend Augen* ("The Thousand Eyes"), but in the dazzling visual multiplication of television screens which Louxor Mabuse, reincarnated in his son, places in the hotel lounge—as if to imply (it has often been noted)—the director himself. As for the two Indian films: they are precarious, penetrated by blinding moments; they speak only of a beautiful and just stubbornness where despair blossoms; where the *mise-en-scène* and even its idea (as Blanchot said of writing) seems, in the silence which encloses it, a dissociation of its components, an inability to lie which reaches the tragic.

It is therefore not surprising that these films—the last of perhaps the only *oeuvre* which covers nearly fifty years of filmmaking—constitute the vital matter by comparison with the myth. For in France today, where Fritz Lang is becoming legend (far from America which was not able to recognize him, and his native Germany which didn't know how to rediscover him), those who flock to the *Cinémathèque* come more or less consciously to admire the man who in his work saw film as the ultimate metaphor, and whom Godard, by a happy decision, has precipitated in the double game of *Le Mépris.* Lang's only trump cards are the statues colored violently with Greek legend, just as in *Le Tombeau hindou* his trumps are the gardens, the palaces, and the actors placed there like huge marionettes around whom beauty has been suddenly born. Despised by the producer who pays him, despising everything which is not life or the power to tell the life which vision masks, Lang—alone, disillusioned, but always anxious to retain truth within and around himself—does not finish shooting *The Odyssey,* does not finish relating the life which is already woven into the threads of his own fiction.

Lang plays, then, a refined and skillful game with his stories and with each element of his material: varied, assertive, and more or less disguised, a game which it would be fitting to formulate visibly through his forty films. He himself, as one might expect, offers little help. In the handsome documentary book put together by Alfred Eibel, Lang contradicts himself, jokes, limits his discussion to questions of ideas and story, to thematic, political and social aspects of each of his films, or confines himself, with seeming irony, to remarks about technique. But the testimony of his many collaborators invites us to ask, if indirectly, the question of form about which Lang always claims ignorance. For all of them—actors, scriptwriters, cameramen, set designers—describe an extraordinarily attentive man, concerned with the smallest gesture, demanding from each frame of film a rigorous life which quite often defies the illusory banality of his tale. From his book (sparsely written in impassioned episodes which trace Lang's steps—illuminating him and making him more accessible), the certainty is born that the more Lang insists on the apparent meaning of his films, the more the enigma of that meaning must be determined through a systematic exploration of the form through which multiple correspondences are presented and which alone illuminates the irreducible feeling of totality.

It is surprising, then, that no text has yet thrown full light on an author so intimately bound to the essence of his art—as Claude Ollier has done, for example, in his very beautiful study (if only on a single film) of Josef von Sternberg; and, considering the infinite diversity and rigor of Lang's films, that no one has sought to define the paradoxes and the strange, broken unity which show through both the entire documentary book devoted to him and his recent confession which he entitles **"La nuit viennoise"** in memory of his birthplace; a statement so admirable in tone, in details, ambiguities and challenge.

I intend here only to bring together haphazardly some of the very numerous elements which, when described, analyzed in detail, and arranged according to the series of connections which they demarcate, would be the basis for a systematic approach to the Langian universe. Notes, of a sort, for a "cinemanalaysis."

1. The position of an author is defined by the relationship which he maintains with his characters. In the film, one form of this relationship rests on the systems of vision which the pictures reveal: how the author fragmentarily indicates and encloses the viewpoint of his characters within the continuity of his own viewpoint constitutes the viewpoint of the film. Minnelli, for example, generally remains external to what he shows; Hitchcock, inversely, makes the clearly defined vision of his characters a part of the system of his own vision. In this regard Lang himself shows a weighty and decisive ambiguity.

There is one strictly univocal manner of framing a character's vision: to enclose the shot of the seen object between two identical shots of the seeing subject. Lang seldom does more than indicate the possibility of such certitude, and then only to challenge it immediately and to plunge it into an equivocality. This occurs with the three looks of the assassin in *While the City Sleeps.*

—At the time of the first murder, he is framed from the waist up, in front of the door: one feels that the assassin is watching something in particular, but cannot say what; a very brief close-up of the door latch follows, but the shot which comes next is itself divergent in terms of the assassin's gaze.

—The assassin enters the studio of Dorothée Kyne: he sees her in a mirror smoothing her stocking with a long and very gentle movement; the close-up which follows, showing the assassin in the middle of the room, says nothing about his supposed point of view.

—Later he leaves the house and moves towards a low win-dow which looks into the bar; he bends down, one sees a long shot of the barroom; we are assured the camera is outside the room by the deformation of the glass; everything clearly indicates that the shot reflects the assassin's exact view, but nothing proves it; for instead of reframing the assassin, Lang passes to something else.

In a different manner (using three methods of non-disclosure) Lang allows ambiguity to hover over the relationship which unites character and director in the vision. An attitude which one finds again and again in almost all his films, and which is completely manifest, for example, in the twice-repeated leper sequence of *Le Tigre du Bengale* and *Le Tombeau hindou.* And which Lang deliberately plays upon in *The Blue Gardenia,* where Norah's waking gives way to deformations in the substance of the frame, again leaving us faced with two possibilities: either Lang is showing that only an artifice can precisely situate a viewpoint—that vision of the real alone cannot; or he is deliberately moving to a symbolic level, making an assertion of this trick shot which, far from identifying the author with the characters even for a moment, distances him from them even more.

2. The author defines himself by his point of view towards the objects he unveils. This point of view is manifest in the first place by the distance at which the camera is held. The distance of the camera from its objects varies; this variation constitutes a first level of cinematographic reality (or unreality) and of all analysis. With Lang it seems to be either vivid or disguised in manner, keeping constant (by his multiple detours) the fascination and the difficulty one experiences in watching his films.

From a thousand possible examples, here is an almost theoretical one from *The Blue Gardenia:* Lang devotes three shots to evoke his three heroines in bed in their shared apartment:

—The camera frames a comic-book in close-up, then draws back, revealing Rose sprawled on her bed, seen in the light from the night lamp which she has not put out.

—With a wide still-shot, the camera frames Crystal who is murmuring her lover's name in her sleep.

—The camera frames in long-shot the corner of the room where Norah's bed is placed, and advances with a travelling-shot until she is isolated; thus only Norah is shown closely (for she is the main character); she is listening to the radio beneath her sheets.

The distance, the impression of distance, also depends essentially upon the interplay of forms within the picture. Hence, (a constant with Lang), the deepening of the vision through an unforeseen opening. In Mrs. Robby's office in the shadowy house of *Le Secret derrière la Porte,* an engraving with sharply defined and fleeting lines catches one's eyes, as if multiplying the view. Similarly, in *Le Testament du docteur Mabuse,* when Kent and his friend Lilli sit down in a café to confide their confusion to each other, the camera frames in the upper part of the shot a window which looks out on a long, white, almost unreal avenue whose dizzying depths are made more vividly manifest when a passer-by (only his head is visible) appears and crosses the frame. I shall note another such shot in *La Mort de Siegfried,* drowned almost totally in white; young newlyweds are conversing charmingly near a bench which is placed against a background of foliage; but above the trees, five wide arches caught in shadow appear to tear the frame; this contrast leaves a feeling of distance which unbalances the vision and secretly announces the fatal outcome of the plot.

Let us also note the interplay of distance which hinges not on the distribution of fixed masses but on movements within the frame. Thus, almost thematized—so often do they lend support to the story—are the opening and closing doors. They constantly vary spatial relationships as they reveal more or less hidden depths—according to the light and the terrain. Such are the doors which one encounters in each of Lang's films, most particularly in the Chinese quarter in *Les Araignées,* the cemetery in *Les Trois Lumières,* in *Le Tigre du Bengale* and *Le Tombeau hindou*—everywhere, with a violence that multiplies when Henri Mercier, going down the corridors as the doors are closing ends up in the tigers' pit.

Similarly, the queen's cloaks in *La Vengeance de Krimhilde* (cloaks with wide skirts) billow and fall endlessly, sometimes radically modifying the distribution of forms in the shot: Krimhilde (addressing the horde of Huns from the top of a staircase) with her cloak—black and dull on the inside, brilliant and adorned on the other—subjects the frame to a strange play of shadows and surfaces as she raises or lowers her arms against her body. A configuration which Lang will remember, and which will occur again (though less theatrically and more closely bound to the narrative adventure of the picture) in *Die Spione,* where the beautiful Sojia unfurls her immense black and silver lamé cape around Haighi in the same game of oppositions.

3. There are innumerable formal and thematic references, configurations which come into play from film to film and organize the enigmatic web of Langian knotwork. Hence the sign, the token, around which the narration is organized, the significant object Lang always indicates with a close-up which is the first easily located link between the chain of shots and the thematic chain. From the seal affixed to the fateful act in *Les Trois Lumières* to the grease pencil mark on Mercier's shirt in *Le Tombeau hindou,* there is a lengthy inventory of maps, plans, letters, photographs—multiple references which stake out Lang's forty films. These establish a definable series throughout the script; what might be called a series of

events of the script which are manifested in one or several formal series in the picture: the close-up is followed almost invariably in this situation (for example, in the talking films and especially the American ones) by a movement of back-travelling starting with the brusquely introduced object. This short, precise movement, which reveals the object in its surroundings, breaks and demarcates the sudden fascination of the close-up.

I shall cite only three examples of this, all taken from the same film, *Scarlet Street.* The sequence begins with a close-up of a flower; the movement reveals Christopher lovingly painting the flower offered by Kitty. Later, a letter rests on a table among other objects: the movement which reveals Kitty's studio for the first time accurately defines the relationship between the young woman and Christopher—one immediately understands it is a letter from him. The travelling shot which brings to light Johnny's hat, hidden in Kitty's new apartment, states with ironic insistence and without the aid of a single word, the respective situations of the three characters in this harsh and cruel remake of Jean Renoir's *La Chienne.*

4. The generally intensified partialization of space which disrupts the viewpoint in order to lead it to its more rightful place which carries to an extreme, in cinematographic space, a dialectic of subject and object finding its origin in the German cultural tradition and its achievement in the fundamental materialism of industrial civilization. If the object possesses a particular importance in the unfolding of the action, it seems to recapture in the intensity of the film something of the symbolic life of the bewitched objects of Hoffmann or Arnim. The subject is often a vagrant body, only one object among other objects. One finds a particularly striking inversion of this order in the flight sequence of *La Femme sur la Lune,* between the rocket (which seems to be the only actor) and its interpreters (its accessories) and, in *Human Desire* between Jeff Warren and the locomotive, when he drives it down the track into the depot.

This subject-object game, when divided, provokes the eye, making an incredible fissure in Fritz Lang's films which is balanced with a type of shot that is particularly frequent and meaningful, multiplying the dialectic of continuity/discontinuity proper to the system of the Langian vision: the fragmented body of the subject and object, united as two mechanisms in a single frame, offers a perfect example of partialization of space. Thus, in *Man Hunt,* the hero's hand which hesitates again and again on the trigger of the rifle, is shot in extreme close-up. And in *Les Espions* are shown two forearms and the heavy, round handle of a chest which the hands want to turn; the muted light of the black leather raincoat answers the clearer steel one, and both of these reply to the whiteness of the hands: from the beginning of this film (this is the first shot) Lang places it beneath the sign of the enigmatic division of space.

5. Lang, like every filmmaker (but more precisely and more insidiously than others) bases the possibility of his narrative on the richness and the perversity of oppositions in the series of identical configurations.

From film to film one can follow the marks of a perpetual game of similar questions and different replies; one can evoke their rigorous nature extracting the types of opposition which are simultaneously arranged in the picture, the sound, the interpretation and the narrative, sufficient material for an unprecedented inventory whose very limits and meaning are difficult to define. But this game is the logical outcome of the writing and the vision. Here are two examples briefly summarized from a single story, *While the City Sleeps.*

—Walter Kyne, Jr., and Edward Mobley are conversing in the manager's office. In a fixed long shot, appearing from left to right, are: Kyne, Jr., standing, dressed in black; higher, against the wall, the portrait of his father, Walter Kyne, also dressed in black; then, through the window, the city, with its sharp and regular gray masses; finally, Mobley, seated, dressed in gray. Each of the four principal elements of the shot is placed at a different distance from the camera; the colors are distributed two by two. Some moments later, after brief detail shots of the various protagonists, Lang returns to the same long shot, from a slightly different angle. But the elements have changed. From left to right: Kyne, Jr., Mobley, the portrait, the city. The distances have changed. Mobley gets up; the camera follows his movement. A triple opposition is at work in two shots which are formally identical: an opposition between the distribution of the actors, between tonality and distance (each element sustains the two others) setting up the third opposition (immobility/movement), effecting the forward movement of the narrative.

—The bar where the New York Sentinel journalists gather. Again, a fixed long shot. We see Mobley sitting at the counter and the bartender standing; in the back of the room is a barely perceptible staircase, going up to the left. We wait; Lang prolongs the silent irritation of the shot, until Mildred appears on the staircase, with the intention of making advances to Mobley. Why does he hold such a simple shot for so long? Because Lang, some sequences earlier, had already filmed exactly the same space, in the same manner; because he had already lingered there in an almost casual way, and because no one had then appeared at the bottom of the stairs.

6. Lang thus keeps the point of view in perpetual hesitation; for the event, whether it is foreshadowed or has already occurred, always seems linked to something else whose force is arresting even though one does not know how to delimit it but which could not be sustained alone. The film plays sub-

tly on an incessant disequilibrium by means of this dyssymetrical expectancy. This flagrant and deliberately abstract waiting in a shot (a visual and narrative sign) marks all of Lang's work. Its principle is simple. It is a matter of a fixed long shot with three terms: two actions which separate a dead time. A character goes out of the shooting angle; the camera remains facing the set; a second character enters the shooting angle by another entrance (this could be—though it rarely is—the same character who returns, and by the same entrance). The set, at this moment, is always particularly beautiful and heavy with meaning and possibilities: the commissary office in the first *Mabuse,* the corridor outside the doctor's office in the second, the staircase landing leading to the apartments of the two young women in *While the City Sleeps,* caverns beneath the castle in *Le Tigre du Bengale* and *Le Tombeau hindou.* The characters are bound by the imminent event: this shot almost always intervenes in the moments of greatest dramatic intensity. Thus in his own way Lang breaks the ideal hurried flow of the action, wounding his story and distorting time apparently for the benefit of a visual purity; thereby imparting a strangeness to the action (as if spreading it out) and likewise to the vision which becomes suddenly too heavy and insistent. Then he recaptures or almost recaptures what he is doing for a single vision, in a much briefer and tighter shot, when he assembles the elements in such a way that the viewpoint always seems badly placed—either too close or too far away. Thus in *La Mort de Siegfried:* three warriors occupy the near totality of the screen's surface; they are so close that one cannot see them in their entirety; between them are some blank spaces and a bare wall in the background. The frame is perfectly flat; one would believe the soldiers cut out of cardboard. When Krimhilde passes behind them, followed by her women, the perspective is brutally reborn—so vividly that one feels it too deeply, and it seems to be another illusion.

7. For Lang plays the most perverse of games. It is by means of the fissures—by means of the gaps which he sets up—that he can be understood. That is what must be deciphered, and at each of its levels. Thus Lang, more than anyone else, works with counter-shots. Here begins the quest which reveals that at the other extremity of his films, Lang also manifests this "counter" game—this time of the counter-script. As he strains the shot and unbalances it, he loses sight of his narrative, obscuring his characters. And thus he works (as Luc Moullet has clearly seen) in counter-genre; even in America, he simultaneously espouses and insidiously transgresses the laws of the most traditional art. He incorporates the principle and destroys it. Indeed, what are *Frau im Mond, Rancho Notorious, Moonfleet, Beyond a Reasonable Doubt, Der Tiger von Eschnapur* and *Das indische Grabmal* to the science-fiction film, the Western, the adventure film, the police story and the exotic film, if not enterprises of violent perversion?

It remains for us to understand why Lang persists in this disjunction. Persists in often leaving in his films the mark of a subtle defeat which is revealed by the impossibility of a closed system, actually closed upon itself. Lang's films are so dense that they seem to have cracked, as if the author always wanted to leave a tenuous reality visible and evident, and to show the illusory nature of the idea of a harmony through an entire autonomy of representation. From shot to shot, from one end of the film to the other, a writing unfolds that is strictly defined, divided, always anxious to maintain, in each constituent operation, the effort which constitutes that operation; to mark the permanent turning of creation upon itself with the density of its material; and to do this with all the more rigor, as cinema conquers, with its technical mastery, new possibilities of expression. The camera possesses that magical ability which makes it so difficult for us to follow it: to be "an actor full of importance, mobile, alive," on the surface of life to which it always weds itself in order to capture life. Thus, with Lang, in a sense, the film always seems to be in the process of creating itself. One feels effort, the temptation of the possible, the distance between desire and its object, something like the typical experience of a book assured of its strength, but always a little defeated and wearied as well. Hence the fascination and the impression of distancing which his films—so beautiful—always leave. And the feeling that, for Lang, the *mise-en-scène* alone, attains the mythic.

Joseph S. M. J. Chang (essay date 1979)

SOURCE: "*M:* A Reconsideration," in *Literature/Film Quarterly,* No. 4, 1979, pp. 300-08.

[*In the following essay, Chang discusses the role that Schranker plays in the narrative of Lang's* M, *and questions the character's purpose in the film.*]

In the almost fifty years since its release, Fritz Lang's *M* has attained deserved status as a classic, and on a number of points a consensus of critical opinion has emerged. Observers have commented on the similarities which exist between society, as exemplified by Inspector Lohmann and the forces he marshalls and directs, and the underworld, no less efficient under Schranker. At a more general level, the film's moral dualism, which almost approaches Manichean proportions, has been noted. The connection between the two sets of characters, the police and the criminals, and the thematic dualism has not received adequate comment, however. Unresolved is the question of whether the police and the underworld represent contrary forces contesting for the right to exercise their respective wills on the murderer, or whether they are variant forms of the same force against which the murderer must contend. What are the elements of the dualism, and how are they related to the three corners of the plot: the murderer, the police, and the criminals? There is additionally the curious

rupture of tone in the film. On the face of it, the film's many comic elements are incompatible with the seriousness of the concluding scene of the murderer's trial, conducted by Schranker.

The critical problem may be stated in formal terms, though the solution will necessarily transcend formulas. Lang has combined two conventional narrative forms, the story of a psychotic killer and the story of a master criminal. In the first, rationality confronts irrationality; in the second, convention has it that superior resources and deductive powers triumph over an adversary who uses similar modes of operation. Schranker, after all, is himself a murderer who has eluded capture on two continents for six years.

Within the conventions of the standard story of the psychotic killer, the audience is permitted to alienate itself from aberrations which make him what he is. As is revealed in the coda to *Psycho,* he is a creature formed by extraordinary circumstances. However it may have been horrified by Norman Bates's atrocities, because of the clinical analysis of his schizophrenia, the audience is permitted to view the killer with some detachment. The containment of the killer thus goes beyond the simple fact of his apprehension and detention. Not only is the audience (and the characters with whom the audience shares identification) secure from his assaults, it is further detached from the energies which propel him. As normal and integrated people, spectators are inoculated from the killer.

In the conventional detective story, the audience is easily distanced from the crime because that fact is the *donne* from which the narrative evolves. Interest lies in the method of detection. Details which escape observation by others are culled from irrelevancies. Technology, whether in the methodical inquiry of the investigator or in the laboratories at his disposal, defines the significance of the clues gathered. The tale progresses from a chaos which offends the intelligence; the moral indignation aroused by moral disorder may color the narration, but it does not form the center, for one does not expect the investigator to explain why evil exists in the world.

The two species of crime fiction sketched do not of course describe all which fall within the genus, but they help to define a critical problem with respect to *M.* If the film's concern is with the killer's apprehension, then the incorporation of Schranker's role is superfluous. The resources Schranker brings to the search are essentially of the same kind available to the police. The motivation is the same; the murders have had a disruptive influence on society and must be brought to a halt. In the trial scene, the arguments for Beckert's death are those which any prosecutor would have urged. The underworld carries the burden of society's legitimate instruments, the only difference being in its status as a society of outlaws, and to that extent, their unwillingness to accept the possibilities of paragraph 51.

As in the conventional detective story, the dominant question is established early in the film with the poster which asks, "Wer ist der Morder?" As Elsie's ball bounces against the poster, M's shadow slides across the text, effectively restating the question, "What malignancy gives substance to this darkness?"

In the process of identifying the murderer by name, Hans Beckert, the film presents a series of possibilities for defining what the murderer is. The prevailing assumption is that the murderer, as evident in his crimes, is unlike the people who fear him. An alien creature, he nevertheless can move among men unnoticed. The early emphasis on the killer is that he is in disguise, that he may be one's neighbor or any person on the street. The hysteria depicted in the cafe and street scenes wherein innocents are abused because they are mistakenly identified as the killer indicates that the accusers are unprepared to deal with the assailant as one of themselves. The unstated assumption is that which is later, in the trial scene, explicit. The defendant's appointed counselor appeals on behalf of "this man," and his plea is discounted by a penetrating voice: "He isn't one." The premise from which the film moves forward is that the unknown force does not share in common humanity.

The point is repeated with vigor by the underworld. Although both Beckert and Schranker are sought by the law, the master criminal denies anything in common exists between the two. The murderer is not a member of the association; he is not on the same level as the criminals; an abyss separates the two; there is simply no comparison. The judgement is that "We are doing our job because we have a living to make. But this monster has no right to live. He must disappear. He must be exterminated, without pity, without scruples."

The argument has become sophisticated. Beyond the fact of the murders which attest to the perpetrator's monstrosity, there is the point of motivation. What distinguishes the two criminals is that one operates within a rationale: crime is a way of life. The necessity to live dictates and sanctions deviations from law. The child-murderer presumably can offer no such defense.

If Schranker dissociates his organization from the murderer, Lang strengthens the underworld's alliance with the police. Quite apart from the fact that both groups work toward the same end in scenes which are presented in parallel cutting, there is the obvious rapport which exists between them even when they are at cross purposes. The raid on the Crocodile is disruptive, but with the appearance of Lohmann the congregation of thieves and whores is set at ease. It is as though they understand that with Lohmann, they will come to no

serious consequences, and he in turn is solicitous, addressing them as his children. It may only be a symbiotic relationship, but it is a relationship. As Lohmann interviews each person caught in the dragnet, all participate in a game. That identity cards are always forged is mutually understood. The only thing that matters is how well the forgery is made.

The relation between the police and society at large—a city of 4,000,000—is more problematical. When suggestions are made that the police elicit the cooperation of the general public, Lohmann contemptuously reminds his colleague that the public has provided no clues and a mountain of baseless accusations. While it may be that the police are society's instrument against lawlessness, the people themselves are in an anarchic state, quite incapable of coping with the murders in a systematic fashion. The sequence which shows the people first accusing a harmless old man and then reversing their flow to heap abuse on a thief under police arrest not only presents the ambiguity of M's identity either as a normal citizen or as a criminal, it shows the population as motivated by fear and anger, eager to vent their outrage on any plausible target. In doing so, they adumbrate the pressures which Schranker seeks to exploit in the trial scene.

As the film proceeds, Lang enlarges the opportunities to discover who the murderer is. While it is true that Beckert's capture by the beggars and thieves is independent of any efforts by Lohmann, it is nevertheless significant that identification of the suspect is possible only after a colleague suggests that except for the moments when driven by his fits of madness, the killer is "a man who looks like a peaceful little family man, who wouldn't harm a fly." Probably insane, he is capable of functioning in society. For the landlady from whom Beckert rents a room, the man is unextraordinary. His single eccentricity is that he never buys his own newspaper. For the second child he befriends in the film, the prospective ninth victim, he is a man who can inspire innocent trust. She can twice address him as "Uncle."

The most important identification which Lang establishes for Beckert is with the film's spectators. At first, Beckert is only a cipher, the object of a game, a man to be captured. While it is a commonplace of film criticism that Lang's restraint in the murder of Elsie Beckmann heightens the audience's sense of horror by freeing its imagination to conjure the worst possible atrocity, and Lang himself has taken this position, the effect is otherwise. To be sure, the audience understands that something terrible has happened, but it is not enslaved to that fact. The murder is purely conceptual: that a child should be destroyed is vile. The audience is, however, spared the spectacle of the child's growing perception of its peril, its feeble efforts to escape, the savagery of the attack. For this reason, the audience is not energized by the blood lust of the citizens and their criminal counterparts.

Lang's decision not to depict the crime itself modifies the context for the audience's understanding in another way. The audience is not even permitted a glimpse at the murderer until after Elsie is killed. For this reason, it cannot begin to understand his motivations, his satisfaction or his compulsion. For apart from the horror of the act, the killing of a child, the depicted scene would necessarily reveal something about the murderer—an expression on his face, the movement of his body. Does he strangle his victims? Is he swift, or does he let the child hover near death? The audience, and perhaps the screen characters who as well search for the murderer, must not only learn his nominal identity but must discover the totality of his being. Actually, the killer and his deeds at the film's beginning exist at the same barely denoted level of the labels, "murderer" and "murders." At the outset, we can be satisfied with these terms because the film appears to demand nothing more. In a sense, the audience is like Henry, content to follow the branded creature, believing that in the simple "M" all that needs to be known is revealed—the murderer is exposed. However, as the film progresses, we move from such labels to more profound levels of being. The shadow is supplanted by the silent figure held by the lantern's accusing glare, who in turn emits the anguished confession of his tortured soul.

In the film's second phase, the attempt on the next child and the chase which leads to Beckert's being trapped in the office building, the audience begins to learn more about the killer than do the searchers. Very simply, we see him on the street; we can watch his face as he notes details in the world about him. We sense the struggle within him as he catches sight of the child. Much of this is still superficial and stylized, of course, and the limitations of the audience's perceptions are suggested by the vine-covered trellis which obscures the killer from peering eyes as he drinks his brandy. Little as we see, we still can see more than the blind beggar who identifies the murderer by his tune, and from this point forward, a gap separates the audience from the screen characters. In answering the question, "Wer is der Morder?" the advantage lies with the audience.

Coincident with the audience's growing understanding of who the murderer is is the reversal of his role from agent to victim. Lorre's handling of the role is extraordinary, for until the bravura performance of his defense, Lang's economy allows the actor the sparest opportunities in the film's second section. The shock on M's face as he discovers the chalked "M" on his coat—one might even speak of the horror which strikes him—marks the turning point: the stalker is now the quarry. What Lorre brings to this remarkable reversal is the experience of compounding fear as Beckert turns to catch sight of Henry, appraise his situation and flee in terror, only to discover that all avenues of escape are closed. Equally effective is the camerawork, particularly in the high angle shot of the street, composed in the frame as a diagonal, with Beckert

darting up the street, pausing as if to turn into an alley, then wheeling back to stop in the center of the street. All paths are closed.

As the net inexorably tightens in the film's third section, which takes place in the office building, M's fear grows more specific. He is given less room in which to move; his resources diminish steadily. He is not yet a round character, in that the unrevealed aspects which give a character unexpected dimensions remain hidden. We still know nothing more of Beckert than say Lohmann does as he awaits the report of his arrest. However, we have an opportunity to observe and perhaps participate in Beckert's increasing desperation. His helplessness is documented in the snapping of his knife as he attempts to open the lock, and in the use of his knife as a hammer to forge a key. In short, Lorre manages to suggest that there is indeed a character buried under the soft flesh and overly large eyes. The film, then, moves in two directions. The criminals and Schranker remain consistent with their initial portrayals. The murderer promises emotional depths.

From the outset, the injection of comic incident serves to alienate, in the Brechtian sense, the audience. The confrontation between the small, timid, elderly man and the burly citizen; the dispute over the murdered child's hat as either red or green; the slanderous accusation in the cafe and the ensuing hubbub; the pickpocket's pulling out of three watches to fix the time; the "blind" beggar's peering over his dark glasses; the petty criminal, his forged papers exposed by Lohmann, throwing them down in disgust—such elements fictionalize the work and suggest to the audience that the film is no more realistic than any other of the genre, the detective story. And for the pursuers, official and criminal alike, Lang maintains this tone right up to the final scene in the warehouse. Discounting the shots involving Beckert's frantic efforts to escape, the search of the office building maintains the tone by such elements as the carrying of the second (or third) guard across the background, the long run down the stairwell to Schranker to inform him of M's discovered location, and the vanity of the fellow who made the discovery. There is to be sure, a sense of urgency, but it is different from Beckert's. In the same comic vein are the capture of the safecracker, calling for his ladder, his interrogation by Lohmann, and Lohmann's double take when he learns the object of the break-in, all capped by the rinsing of his hair.

This is the stuff of *The Lavender Hill Mob,* of the Rat-pack caper films, the demi-monde of Damon Runyon's imagination. It has less and less to do with Beckert as his role enlarges and is modified to the point of its final development, wherein he would seem to fit better in such worlds as Dostoievsky created. In the second section, cutting between the meeting of the officials and that of the criminals provides a truly parallel movement. In the third section, cutting from the criminals to Beckert results in a divergence of tone. Because the texture of the final phase in the warehouse is established by Beckert's agonized self-revelation, Lang necessarily abandons the use of comic elements. There the divergence created in the second and third sections will be repaired when Beckert's captors will be forced to deal with him in the same manner that the audience has begun to. There the audience will find better validity for its instinctive sympathy for the victimized killer, and for a split second so, too, will his accusers.

The function of the ambivalence established by the comic elements must be fully appreciated before extensive consideration of the final section is possible. The distancing of the audience encouraged by the comic intrusions in a work of uniform tone and texture defines the point of view to be taken: this film is a divertisement, amusing in its own right, but not to be regarded seriously. However, the attention paid to Beckert's situation violates the comic tone and draws the audience into involvement. Even before the audience can know why Beckert deserves some sympathy, it senses his desperation and fear. His helplessness is concrete whereas Elsie's was only to be inferred. Instead of alienating the audience from the film as a whole, the comic elements cause the audience to dissociate itself from the two sets of pursuers. Where at the outset we are willing to assume that M is a monster and we gladly accept the pursuers' goal as our own, if only for the sake of the genre's dialectic, by the time Lohmann thrusts his head under the faucet, we understand the superficiality of our original interest in the apprehension of the killer. The level of response to the cornering of the murderer demonstrated by Lohmann's gesture is at odds with that already experienced by the audience, a sympathy to be amplified in the fourth section, the trial.

The comic quality of the cafe and street scenes only mildly violates the tone of the film as established by the plaintive calling out of Elsie's name by Mrs. Beckmann. In the second and third sections, the continued development of the story in two veins is almost inexplicable, and the closing scenes with Lohmann and the safecracker are astonishingly out of keeping with the image of the terrified murderer. The significance of the contrapuntal movement becomes clear in the final section. For there, the audience appreciates the fact that its sympathies lie with Beckert, not as M, the faceless childkiller, but as the troubled man not much more threatening than was the old man on the street who had been thought the villain. Lang first allows his audience to adopt the point of view sanctioned by detective stories, that the killer should be apprehended. But he uses slapstick to arouse an uneasiness about what is going on. The vague sense of impropriety anticipates the ultimate realization that the murderer is indeed a person worthy of some compassion. Furthermore, the uneasiness inspired by the comic elements prepares the way for the ultimate perception that Schranker's trial does not meet the requirements of the situation. Thus, the comic elements which

violate tone signal the reversal of the audience's sympathies when Beckert's full story is laid bare. They prepare for the audience's rupture from the will and desire of the murderer's pursuers. The severing of the alliance is completed in the fourth section's violent tone, which, in turn, exceeds the audience's own level of response.

In the warehouse the full force of Beckert's agony is released. The developing sense of his victimization is completed with the revelation of his own horror borne of self-knowledge. The man is a victim of his crimes to the extent that he is as repulsed by his deeds as any of his accusers are. His pain may be more acute, because as perpetrator of those atrocities, he must be more offended than they can be, and to the extent that he is powerless over his compulsion, he is a victim. One does not need to explore the legal ramifications which Schranker introduces—paragraph 51—to understand that Beckert, as realized by Lorre, is helpless. All that we need to acknowledge is the fact that the man is incapable of self-control in certain situations; there is no inference that this fact provides valid grounds for permitting him to go free. Besides, the dilemma of society's response to his crimes is dependent on the film's persuasive presentation of the man as psychotic. Before his captors worry themselves about a legal defense of insanity, that aberration must be convincingly demonstrated.

The presentation of Beckert as victim is effected in two ways. The temper of the scene is violent. The brutality of those pulling him from the door, the shrieks of those demanding his death, and the terror manifest in his face and gestures make clear that the assembly thirsts for vengeance and blood. For the first time in the film, the will to violence which makes murder possible is evoked. It is palpable. For the third time in the film, the threat of death is brought to the screen, but this time, the motivations and passions of the killer—here, a crowd—are made specific.

The threatening atmosphere forces Beckert to make his appeal, which is his confession of guilt. His defense is undeniably inadequate in the simple light of fact; he is demonstrably dangerous and cannot be permitted to go free. But as he pleads for his life, his struggle is revealed to be as much against himself as it is against his captors. The pressure created by the assembly is supplanted by the intense monstrosity he constantly struggles against.

For the barest moment his accusers understand, and in that moment, they see the same man we in the audience see, that is, Beckert as he sees himself. He is able to sound responsive chords as he describes the darkness haunting his soul. Where the initial premise that the murderer could not be one of them was reinforced by Beckert's indictment of their crimes as fully willful and unlike his, his plea wakens memories of their share of his anguish. Distinctions between murderer and victim have become blurred: the murderer is victim, and those who have pursued him have been stirred by violent instincts.

The intensity of their rage has been foreshadowed in Schranker's characterization as cold, utterly self-willed. The shot of his face as he demands the gate be opened and the brief spasm of violence when the guard is tortured hint at the energies set free in the warehouse. The criminals are restrained only by their confidence in Schranker's ultimate purpose. Actually, it may be more precise to say that they extend into fact the metaphor of his gloved hand overwhelming the city map. They are his power; he is their embodiment.

The structure of the film employed two modes, the movement from simple identification of the murderer to the revelation of the unseen life within, parallel to the progress from the expanse of the city to the confines of the locker and the subsequent descent down the stairs to the astonishingly cavernous warehouse. Similarly, by the film's end, the question, "Wer is der Morder?" must be enlarged to the more significant one, "What is a murderer?" The models are there before us: Schranker, who operates, if he is to be believed, within a code understood by his adversaries. In a showdown, either he or the arresting officer may have to yield his life. There is reason here, there is choice, and the risks are accepted. In Beckert, there is only chaos. His disordered soul struggles with itself, and only chance dictates his crimes. Thus, the ambiguity of the film's close. As the hand grasps Beckert, in the name of the law, there is, simultaneously, arrest and redemption. He is freed from terror, and Schranker's arms are raised.

What then are we to say about the relationship between the criminals and the police? To all that has been said, that Lohmann is not permitted to make the arrest is worth adding. It is to the law that all parties must submit, and perhaps that ought to include the police as well. What law itself is may be difficult to define, but it can be inferred from the film. The initial premise of the child-murderer as alien is destroyed. Dangerous as he is, he is not radically unlike all others. Prostitutes can share the concerns of motherhood; a child-killer's fascination with those innocents he destroys may spring from confused feelings of warmth and hatred. The appeals for Beckert's death are, Schranker aside, those of society at large. In an actual court of law, that is, law as it is practiced by mortals, the same bases would be urged against the accused.

With the erasing of differences between the murderer, criminals and legitimate society, the film's thematic center emerges. It is not about the capture of a killer, nor is it about the legal problem presented by the criminally insane. It is about the currents of violence which run unseen in society, chaotic and irrational forces which coexist and sometimes merge with order and reason. The dualism of Lang's vision, in *M,* is not that of discrete and contrary realities; it is in the paradox of mutually exclusive instincts and values within the same entity. There is perhaps a richness of suggestion we have failed to note in Lang's bromide that mothers must protect their children from these jackals.

> **The dualism of Lang's vision, in *M*, is not that of discrete and contrary realities; it is in the paradox of mutually exclusive instincts and values within the same entity.**
> **—*Joseph S. M. J. Chang***

Schranker believed that he was entitled to act in the name of the law, and the appointed defense reminded him of his own crimes. The dilemma of the film is that when the reality behind the murderer is revealed, we find more than can be subsumed under so fixed a label. And the same is true of the law. Lang did not seem to find it possible to pursue the full symmetry of his theme by the more direct means of penetrating the superficial lawfulness of the police. His solution was to render the embodiment of the law as a stereotype and to develop Schranker as the implicit counterpart. Just as was asked of the unknown killer, "Is he one of us or an alien?" Schranker in disguise as a policeman poses the similar question, "Are officers of the law a breed apart?" The distinction between "murder" and "law" is absolute and irreconcilable. The differences between Beckert and Schranker exist, but they do not sort out very neatly.

Ann Kaplan (essay date 1980)

SOURCE: "Patterns of Violence Toward Women in Fritz Lang's *While the City Sleeps,*" in *Wide Angle,* Vol. 3, No. 4, 1980, pp. 55-9.

[*In the following essay, Kaplan asserts that while Lang correctly assessed the decline in male authority in the public and private spheres, he puts forth only one solution: a return to the old-style patriarchal authority, instead of a move toward something new and positive.*]

Several feminist theorists have recently argued that, viewed historically, violence against women changes according to transformations in the traditional bourgeois family. Oppressive as it was, the cult of womanhood, entailing the protection of bourgeois women by their husbands, circumscribed violence against this female group. Poor, lower-class women and children have always been subject to violence (viz Jack the Ripper) and abuse by all kinds of masters, but in the modern period (particularly after the two World Wars) more classes of women became vulnerable as they adopted independent lives and began to exist without the protection of men.

The extension of violence toward women upward through the classes is reflected in representations of women in film. As early as 1919, Griffith dealt with child abuse in his startling *Broken Blossoms,* but significantly his little girls are always poor, orphaned and outcast. In the post World War II era, men's fear of women, and the violent impulses toward them that result from this fear, is expressed in the sinister film noir heroines who, frigid and castrating, obstruct the male hero on his quest until exposed and violently murdered.

In the Fifties, representations of violence become more complicated because of a shift in the image of men. In noir films, the investigator was still tough, virile and traditionally masculine, but increasingly in the Fifties images of weak, feminized men appear. The representations no longer carry the attributes that signify masculinity, but instead the gestures, stance, voice and values of male characters carry significations usually assigned to women. Film narratives often expose the consequences of feminized men in the domestic sphere, relying on Oedipal formulations (e.g. *Rebel Without A Cause*), but attention is rarely paid to the effect of declining male authority on public institutions.

Fritz Lang is particularly interesting because of his concern with the problem of male authority in both the public and private spheres. As early as the Mabuse films, and then more clearly in *M,* Lang had shown the increase of violence toward women and children as patriarchal structures weakened and as male authority in the public realm waned. Inherently conservative as is Lang's vision from a feminist point of view, his work is nevertheless fascinating in its presentation of an imaginative realm where women's worst fears are enacted. Always sensing intuitively subtle changes in the tenor of his times and tuned in to future developments, Lang's representations tap aspects of human behavior centered around violence because of its personal interest for him. In the films made between 1922 and 1932, Lang's main theme is the link between the decline in morality and the technological advances in capitalism. His Mabuse films show the corruption and decadence that emerge inevitably from advanced capitalism; *Metropolis,* a negative vision of the future, shows technology used to oppress, not liberate, the masses, while in *Frau Im Mond* we see disinterested scientific advances co-opted and ruined by greedy capitalists.

But *M,* which looks directly toward *While the City Sleeps* in its concerns, exposes the psychosis that modern civilization has spawned and which has become an increasingly frightening aspect of our lives today. The world of this film, as we've seen already, suggests a link between the breakdown of the family and violence. Beckert, the sick hero of the film, lonely and alienated, clearly represents the "feminized" male in his stance and appearance, although there is no explicit analysis of this in *M.* He has a soft, round face, large sensitive eyes and a high whining voice. His tentative, halting manner betrays his lostness, and we later realize that he is trapped by impulses, buried deep in his unconscious, that he cannot control. The violence against the little girls who are Beckert's powerless victims is peripherally linked to the absence of men in that Frau Beckmann's husband is dead and she lives alone with Elsie, bowed down by hard work. But in this film Lang is more concerned with showing that male authority has degenerated to the point that society is no longer efficiently run. Only in the underground can one find the old style patriarch, Schränker, who can control his men and establish an effective, if undesirable, organization.

Lang shows the inadequacy of modern society to deal with a certain kind of psychosis—there are no legal structures capable of containing Beckert's violence and no moral frameworks within which it can be explained. Lang shows the complex situation of his psychotic "feminized" hero, driven to assert his masculinity through raping and killing young girls, paralyzing his community through his attacks, but as much a victim as victimizer. Lang offers no insight into his condition—the level of the unconscious is repressed in the film in order to allow the social issues, which concerned Lang more at the time, to surface fully.

The result of this is an unnatural split in the film: on the one hand there are the extraordinarily powerful, often haunting, scenes with the murderer which draw our sympathies to him (a sympathy, of course, increased through Lorre's sensitive performance) and on the other, the scenes of rather easy social satire that the critique of authority assumes. Lang establishes no link between these two levels of the film other than that authority is too inept to track down and capture Beckert without the help of criminals. There is no larger analysis that accounts for Beckert's behavior as part of the breakdown of social institutions and traditional codes. Alternately appalled by and attracted to Beckert, we are given no insight into what underlies his violent impulses against girls.

Although *While the City Sleeps* lacks, as a work of art, the haunting power of *M* (this for reasons too complex to go into here but having at least in part to do with Hollywood as an institution), Lang does return at the end of his American career to the themes of *M,* made twenty-six years earlier. Significantly, Lang now links the theme of the decline in male authority to that of violence against women in a chilling representation of the results of transformations in the nuclear family in advanced capitalism. But this liberal-humanist position is undercut by Lang's own participation in the violence against women in the way he uses his camera in the film and in his reliance on the film noir conventions that present women as faithless, manipulating and corrupt. There is no female discourse undercutting or exposing the dominant male one as there was, for instance, in *The Blue Gardenia.* This is a role that Nancy Leggett, Mobley's girlfriend, could conceivably have played, representing, as she does, the only innocence (good) in the film; but Lang is evidently too embittered at this point to give credence to her alternate discourse and present it as a value against the clearly bankrupt male one. The "revolutionary" aspects of the film, then, lie in the exposure of the bankruptcy of established male values in capitalism; but while he exposes abuse of women once they are no longer protected by the bourgeois family, Lang does not allow women to speak for themselves or to assert a discourse in the face of the repressive and corrupt male one; nor does he seek viable alternatives to the decline of the family, suggesting rather that modern society's ills stem from the decline of patriarchal authority.

Let me deal first with Lang's demonstration in *While the City Sleeps* that violence against women is integrally linked to the decline in patriarchal authority. This theme emerges clearly first in the figure of the young murderer, Manners, played by John Barrymore, Jr. The film opens with Manners' brutal and unmotivated murder of a young career woman living alone in an apartment house. The words "Ask Mother" scrawled in blood on the mirror take on meaning, after Manners has murdered a second young professional woman, when we learn that Manners is the adopted son of an over-protective mother who had wanted a female child and had often treated Manners like a girl. The father is weak and absent in this family, leaving Manners in the hands of his mother. At one point in the film, Mobley actually presents this psychological profile of the boy on his television show, suggesting that Manners, a "mommy's boy," came to displace his hatred of his mother onto all women and is driven to murder them. Like Beckert, Manners' behavior and the words he leaves suggest that he is asking for help but is powerless to prevent the acting out of his strong inner compulsions. In this case, however, Lang gives a psychoanalytic interpretation of Manners' impulses in revealing the boy's over-identification with his mother and his lack of the solid, masculine identity that, Lang suggests, can only come from a strong father.

A similar psychological profile is presented for Walter Kyne who, while not himself a murderer, is linked to Manners by analogy. Here again the son has turned out weak and effeminate, this time because of an indulgent father. But now Lang deals with this as it effects leadership in the public world. While Manners reflects the violence toward women that emerges from a weak, absent father, Walter Kyne shows the projection of this violence on to the people he has to deal with in the Kyne firm, once he becomes the new leader.

Walter's father, Amos, represented the old-style patriarch who built a flourishing newspaper business from scratch, who had strong moral and liberal sentiments and who was passionate, energetic and socially involved. His death at the start of the film symbolizes the end of an era, since we soon learn that none of the younger men shares Amos Kyne's commitment and integrity. The old-style authoritarian leader, who had a humane side, is replaced by young men who are cynical, disillusioned and out only for themselves. No longer believing in social responsibility, they seek only to outwit others on the way to success.

Walter typifies the new kind of leader. Not having built the business himself, he is uninterested in maintaining what it stands for. He is mainly concerned with obtaining revenge for his father's refusal to bring him into the business earlier, and he particularly dislikes Mobley, senior journalist, since Amos had favored him.

Immature, childish and vain ("feminine" significations), Walter is further "feminized" by his high, whining voice and his loose, drooping stance. He plays a stereotypically female game with his staff, gaining control by making them compete for a newly established post of executive director, suggesting that the one who gets the first story about the murder will have the job.

The weak father is thus seen by Lang to produce disastrous results in both the private and public worlds. But the "fall" of men is equally clear in the depiction of Ed Mobley, the investigator figure who in traditional noir films is the one we identify with as capable of unravelling the mystery and restoring order. Usually tough, virile and relentless in his pursuit of the criminal, the investigator manages to turn aside the women who seek to obstruct his quest, triumphing over them in the end. Mobley is far from this ambitious, aggressive heroic figure. He rather recalls both Eddie from *You Only Live Once* and Svoboda from *Hangmen Also Die* in his moral ambiguity. On the surface he seems the most trustworthy figure in the newspaper office, particularly since we learn at the start that he had won Amos Kyne's respect. His link with Nancy also makes us think well of him, as does his refusal to become involved in the scramble for the executive position.

Yet we soon learn that Ed is by no means the hero he appears to be. To begin with, Mobley's refusal to take on the responsibility for the firm makes us wonder about him: why would he not want to head the business? Is he lazy? Does he shun responsibility? Secondly there is something distasteful in his drunken attempts to force himself on Nancy at the start of the film and in his trick of fixing the door so that he can return to surprise her. He here links himself to Manners, whom we have just seen murder a woman, using the same trick with the door. If Kyne and Manners are linked by analogy, Ed and Manners come closer to the romantic Doppelgänger. While pretending disinterest in the murder, Ed in fact becomes very interested in it and apparently not out of ambition for the post or out of a moral responsibility like Amos Kyne. He rather seems to have a unique understanding of the murderer—an understanding that can only come from his sensing a similarity to himself. While most people, including the police, try to pin the murder on the janitor, Ed learns, with the help of his police friend, that there is little evidence on which to convict him; his friend talks about the effect of the mass media—television and comic books—on young impressionable minds, and Ed concludes that the murder must have been done by a psychopath calling for help, asking to be caught.

But the most dubious light is cast on Ed by his method of trapping the murderer which involves risking the life of his girlfriend, Nancy, whom he has just deeply offended by allowing himself to be seduced by Mildred. So not only is Ed unfaithful, but he is also willing to put his lover's life in jeopardy. His willingness to risk so much suggests that he needs to capture Manners because Manners represents a part of himself that he fears.

The link between Ed and Manners is suggested through the filming of the scene in which Ed appeals to the killer on his television show. The camera begins focusing on Ed within the television screen, although we do not know this yet, then pulls back gradually as Ed talks, analyzing Manners' psychology—his being a "mommy's boy" who hates his mother and her entire sex. Finally, the same shot brings us outside the screen and into a bedroom where we find Manners watching the program. Ed ends his show with the bait that is to catch Manners: he announces his engagement to Nancy, knowing that, angered by Ed's analysis of him, Manners will be seeking revenge and will most likely try to kill Nancy.

Manners does indeed fall for Ed's manipulation and begins to go after Nancy. Ed has given Nancy a bodyguard, but nevertheless Nancy would have been killed had she not been so mad at Ed that she refused to open the door to Manners when he feigned Ed's voice. Finally guessing that Manners is so desperate that he may try to kill Nancy even when she's protected, Ed rushes to Nancy's apartment, sees Manners running away and chases him. Manners goes down a subway and Ed follows in hot pursuit; the scene parallels that in *Manhunt* when Thorndike is chased by his double on the dark subway tracks. Ed forces Manners to leave by an exit and he falls into the hands of the police.

Ed only just manages to succeed in his quest as investigator, his moral ambiguity reflecting Lang's departure from the traditional noir hero. Lang is unable to believe anymore in the tough, virile, ambitious male representation. The conservative nostalgic longing for the patriarchal male figure is evident here as it is in his disillusionment in relation to women. This latter conservatism is clear in the treatment of the three main women in *While the City Sleeps*—Dorothy Kyne, Mildred and Nancy Leggett. Dorothy and Mildred are variations of the noir femme fatale, but even Nancy, the one supposedly "good" presence in the film, is viewed negatively. It is true that the depiction of Dorothy and Mildred is part of the larger cynical vision of the film, reflecting yet one more example of betrayal and the impossibility of trust between people, but these representations weaken Lang's other theme about women's sexual vulnerability. Lang links the moral degeneration of women to the decline in male authority as he had previously linked the decline in leadership to the "feminized" male.

In the case of Walter and Dorothy Kyne, Lang suggests that if men are no longer real men, taking charge of their wives sexually and demanding obedience, then women will no longer respect their husbands and will cheat on them. Walter, weak and effeminate, seems uninterested in his wife physically, although a dedicated husband on the surface. He is too preoccupied with his petty revenge to relate to Dorothy in any other than the most superficial way, so she is able to carry on an affair with one of Kyne's employees, Harry Kritzer, right under his nose.

Lang's representation of Dorothy renders her a disturbing, unpleasant presence in the film; seductive, often lustful, she flaunts her sexuality in her husband's and lover's faces. Conventionally attractive in the terms of the period (Dorothy has blonde curls, pert nose, full mouth and shapely figure), she is seen constantly making up her face, peering at her image in the mirror, cool and confident of her effect on men. She is particularly unpleasant in three scenes: that where her lover, Kritzer, comes to dinner at the Kyne house—she and Harry, hungry for each other, can hardly wait for Walter to leave the room to embrace; that where she and Walter are exercising in their home and Kritzer calls—here we see Dorothy coolly act as though she is talking to a girlfriend and then lie to Walter about going shopping when in fact she goes to meet Kritzer; and finally that where Dorothy and Harry are seen love-making and then bickering in Harry's apartment. Lang's sympathies are clearly with the men, and this undercuts the effectiveness of our horror at Manners' near assault on Dorothy.

Mildred is an example of the scheming, seductive, single woman. Brilliantly played by Ida Lupino, this representation suggests that a career woman, if not monogamously attached to a man, becomes promiscuous, manipulative and scheming. Not actually working in the office when the film opens, Mildred flounces in to meet Mark Loving, whom she is helping win the post of executive director. She stops by Ed Mobley's desk to flirt with him, while Mobley's "steady" girlfriend, Nancy, looks on disapprovingly from the glass-walled office where she is taking dictation. The tension between the women surfaces later when Mildred meets Ed and Nancy in the local bar; the sniping shows their dislike of one another—a dislike occasioned at least in part by jealousy for what the other has chosen. Underlying Mildred's scorn of the "straight," girl-like Nancy, is her envy of Nancy's apparently solid relationship with Mobley; while Nancy is clearly threatened by Mildred's overt sexuality.

Mildred's lover, Mark, is as cynical and manipulating as she is, and he ultimately sends the willing Mildred off to seduce Ed in the hopes of winning Ed's support for Mark as executive director. Mildred finds Ed forlorn in the pub because Nancy is, significantly, at a Red Cross meeting, being a "good" girl. Mildred likes being "bad" and seizes the opportunity to get Ed drunk and in bed with her. Mildred's general deception and manipulation is nicely highlighted when she teases Ed with a slide viewer, pretending to be looking at nude women when in fact the pictures are only of babies.

By the end of the film, Mildred has managed to reinstate herself on the newspaper staff, seen to it that Kritzer was fired (she happened to find Kritzer and Dorothy Kyne together one night) and that Mobley has been promoted. Although married, presumably Ed will still be fair game.

If Dorothy and Mildred are variations on the noir femme fatale, Nancy is presented far more negatively than the "good" girls usually are in the genre. We expect the sexual women to have a compelling presence; the good girl is usually warm, soft and humorous. But everything about Nancy is hard, tight, clipped, prissy. She has cropped hair, wears tight dresses up to her neck and walks with short, jerky steps. She is clearly no match for the sexual women, and seems rather ridiculous when one night she refuses to sleep with Ed on their return to her apartment. Her hurt reaction to Ed's flirtation with Mildred also seems misplaced in the world she moves in, a pathetic stance against moral corruption.

Lang's treatment of both Nancy and Ed reflects his concern about social changes in both the private and public spheres. The traditionally positive characters—the male investigator and the "good" woman who usually helps him—are now seen ambiguously because of the more general disturbance which is the decline in male authority. The dual movement—the possibility of a woman living independently and of the new "feminized" male—has shaken the balance that preserved a certain order. While apparently in favor of women's participation in the social sphere (as we can see from his attitude to Manners in the film), Lang is aware of its consequences in the potential unleashing of hitherto restrained violence toward women.

But Lang's representations do not imply any simplistic, psychoanalytic correlation between the decline in male authority and women leaving the home. While he presents certain male fears about and hatred of women, he also gives us images showing changes in the public realm resulting from the decline of the dynastic family. The success of family businesses was premised on fathers molding sons in their patriar-

chal image, but as this no longer happens the businesses falter. A larger structural change is of course behind all this, and it is felt if not explored in the film—namely, that of the new corporate society with its needs for a different male type: the manager as opposed to the patriarchal owner and president.

Lang's representations have some validity, given changes occurring in the nuclear family and business institutions; he correctly represents the decline in male authority and its dangerous results (a decline that had, of course, been going on ever since the two World Wars). What he does not do is expose the undesirable aspects of what had been destroyed or consider viable alternatives. While women may be more vulnerable without the protection of men and the cult of womanhood, this does not necessitate a return to dependency on men and to the old-style patriarchal authority. How do we know that the "feminization" of men may not be healthy and have entirely different, possibly beneficial results in non-capitalist social structures? This is a question that Lang never asks. But his films are useful in helping us see the complexity of the problems and the transitions taking place, even when all that Lang offers is a return to a past we have long abandoned.

E. Ann Kaplan (essay date 1980)

SOURCE: "The Place of Women in Fritz Lang's *The Blue Gardenia*," in *Women in Film Noir,* BFI Publishing, 1980, pp. 83-90.

[*In the following essay, Kaplan presents three ways in which the male discourse in Lang's* The Blue Gardenia *is undercut by Norah, the female protagonist, even though Lang restores the order of the film noir at the end of the film.*]

In the typical film noir, the world is presented from the point of view of the male investigator, who often recounts something that happened in the past. The investigator, functioning in a nightmare world where all the clues to meaning are deliberately hidden, seeks to unravel a mystery with which he has been presented. He is in general a reassuring presence in the noir world: we identify with him and rely on him to use reason and cunning, if not to outwit the criminals then at least to solve the enigma.

By contrast, the female characters in film noir stand outside the male order and represent a challenge to it. They symbolise all that is evil and mysterious. Sexuality being the only weapon women have in relation to men, they use it to entrap the investigator and prevent him from accomplishing his task. Dangerous because their sexuality is so openly displayed and so irresistible, women become the element that the male investigator must guard against if he is to succeed in his quest.

The Blue Gardenia is a challenge to critics, because in it Lang does not simply follow noir conventions in the manner that he does in two other films (*The Big Heat* and *Human Desire*) made about the same time. Lang rather turns noir conventions upside down in *The Blue Gardenia* by presenting two separate discourses—that is, two modes of articulating a vision of reality. There is the usual male discourse familiar from noir films and represented here by Casey Mayo, journalist playing investigator, and the police; but alongside this, Lang has inserted the discourse of Norah, a young telephone operator—a discourse that presents the confusion and alienation of women in a male world. As I'll show, Lang's treatment of Norah exposes male assumptions about women in noir films; by juxtaposing the male discourse, with its noir conventions, to Norah's point of view, Lang reveals elements of that discourse that generally go unquestioned.

The film opens in an apparently traditional manner, with Mayo driving up to the West Coast Telephone Company and leaving his sleepy photographer in the car. Inside, we find Prebble flirting with Crystal, a friend who lives with Norah and who is also a telephone operator. Prebble, called to the phone, is irritated with demands being made by an hysterical woman. Visually, the men dominate the frames in the expected manner. Prebble is shot lounging beside Crystal, sitting above her and facing the camera. Mayo dominates by standing up and both men act seductively to the women, Mayo in a less sinister and offensive way than Prebble.

The second scene, set in the apartment that Crystal, Norah and Sally share, is in striking contrast to the first. The female discourse is now evident, although the women are still placed symbolically in a subordinate way to men. The cosy relationships among the working women and the sense of a female world recall Arzner's films and other so-called 'women's films,' like LaCava's *Stagedoor* and Bacon's *Marked Woman*. Visually, the women occupy the centre of the frames and face the camera. Within the privacy of their home, they have more confident gestures and body postures, and freely extend themselves in the space they are in as was not possible when men were *physically* present. There is friendly repartee between the women and obvious support and caring for each other.

But, as in the 'women's films' mentioned, the symbolic importance of men assures their domination even when absent. Men provide the main topic of interest and although presented from the women's point of view, their centrality to the women's lives is clear. Each woman has made her own accommodation to the need to have a man: Sally finds real men boring, and lives a vicarious but passionate love life through pulp fiction; Crystal is dating her ex-husband, Homer, having discovered that she gets much more out of the relation-

ship this way; Norah at the beginning of the scene is in love with her soldier in Korea, and lives for his return.

Norah's sudden discovery of her soldier's infidelity sets the narrative in motion and conditions her behaviour on the fatal night of Prebble's murder. Earlier on in the evening, her friends had ridiculed Norah for preferring a lonely birthday supper with her fiance's photograph to a night out. Anticipating that the letter she has saved for this moment will be full of his love for her, Norah is cruelly disappointed by an abrupt announcement of the soldier's imminent wedding to a nurse. At this point, Prebble telephones for a date with Crystal, whose number he had finally obtained earlier in the day. Pretending to be Crystal, Norah accepts the date herself, out of a desperate need to drown her hurt.

Taken aback at first to see Norah instead of Crystal, Prebble quickly adjusts to the situation, the implication being that the particular girl does not matter that much to him. He sees that Norah gets thoroughly drunk at the Blue Gardenia club, where Cole Porter sings the Gardenia song and a blind woman sells gardenia flowers. He then takes Norah back to his apartment where he begins to make love to her. Norah goes drunkenly along at first, pretending her lover is her fiance, but on realising her mistake, she wants to leave. Prebble insists, and in defence against being raped, Norah grabs a poker and strikes out at him, fainting before she can see what she has done. Waking up some time later, she rushes out of the house without her shoes, and goes home.

When Norah gets up the next morning, she has no memory of the events that took place in Prebble's apartment. While on the level of the surface narrative, this is a clumsy device for providing the enigma that has to be solved, it has symbolic importance in relation to the placing of women. Norah's inability to 'remember' or to say what actually happened represents the common experience of women in patriarchy—that of feeling unable to reason well because the terms in which the culture thinks are male and alien. Women in patriarchy do not function competently at the level of external, public articulation, and thus may appear 'stupid' and 'uncertain.' Norah's 'forgetting' dramatically symbolises her lostness in the male noir world of the film; she experiences a nightmare-like feeling of not knowing whether she is innocent or guilty, and of being therefore vulnerable to male manipulation.

The *mise en scène* of the opening sequences underscores Norah's vulnerability; the male world is presented visually as a labyrinth through which she cannot find her way and which is fraught with danger for her. There is a dramatic contrast between the *mise en scène* in scenes representing the women's worlds (the telephone company, the women's apartment), and that in the male worlds (The Blue Gardenia Club, Prebble's apartment, and, later on, Mayo's office). While the scenes in the telephone company and the apartment are brightly lit, the atmosphere cheerful and bustling, those in the male locations are shot in noir style, with looming shadows, unusual camera angles, objects awkwardly placed in the frame, etc., to create a sinister, claustrophobic atmosphere. The first scene in the women's apartment demonstrates the threatening aspect of the male world for Norah in the dramatic change that takes place once the other women have left, and Norah discovers her soldier's betrayal.

Even before we know this, however, Lang has prepared us for something unpleasant. Norah is dressed in a black taffeta dress, and has darkened the room, supposedly to create a romantic candle-lit, atmosphere, but as she sits down the shadows loom ominously. She sits opposite her fiance's picture almost as if before an icon, the candle-light adding to the sense of something unnatural going on. Lang seems to be deliberately exposing the excessive nature of Norah's devotion here, as if to increase the shock of the soldier's infidelity. Once his voice is heard, Norah translating the letter to her lover's spoken speech, the scene becomes even more sinister and ominous, the shadows darkening to the point of seeming almost to invade the light. When the phone rings, and Norah crosses the room to answer it, the music becomes sinister and the screen is almost black.

The women's apartment, thus, is seen to change dramatically, to become sinister and threatening, once men symbolically invade it. The Blue Gardenia Club next presents the male world as manipulative, seeking to trap unaware women. We first see Prebble at the Club setting up his seduction and making jokes about women with Mayo, who is at the bar on the pick-up. As Norah enters, she is seen in long shot, a tiny figure lost in the maze of the elaborate Hawaiian decor of the Club. Guided to Prebble's secluded table, she is seated in a wicker chair with an enormous back that seems to swallow her up. Things become more sinister again as the couple drive home in the pouring rain and thunderstorm. The shots of the car hood closing over the couple suggest that Norah is being trapped, as does the corresponding shot of the skylight window in Prebble's apartment with the rain beating down on it from the outside. Once the couple move into the living room, the *mise en scène* becomes even more sinister; there is a large mirror on the wall, surrounded by plants that cast eerie shadows over the room. It is as if Norah is lost in a jungle, the decor symbolising male traps and wiles.

It is important to note that it is only at this point that Prebble begins to appear in a sinister light. The section of the film up to this point has merely presented the alternating discourses of the men, on the one hand, and Norah (and to a degree the other women) on the other, both being shown as equally 'valid'. As the film goes on, however, and as we come to identify increasingly with Norah rather than the men, so the male discourse begins to be undercut by that of Norah. Reversing the situation in most noir films, where women are seen only within the male discourse, here that discourse is demystified through the fact that Norah is allowed to present herself directly to us. There are three main ways in which the male discourse is challenged.

The first way in which the male discourse is undercut is through Norah's knowing more than the male investigators about what went on the night of the murder. As already noted, in most noir films we identify with the male investigator and rely on him to bring at least some coherence in an essentially chaotic world. Here, however, we identify with Norah and have been present, as Mayo and the police have not, in Prebble's apartment the night of the murder. Although neither we nor Norah know all the facts, we at least know that she was the girl in Prebble's room who left her shoes and handkerchief there, and who was wearing a taffeta dress. On the evidence we have, it seems likely that Norah did kill Prebble in self-defence, but we are sympathetic to her hesitation in giving herself up to the police. Because we are seeing from Norah's point of view, we identify with her, not the investigators, whom we perceive from the outside trying to piece together parts of a puzzle that already fit for us.

A second way in which the male discourse is undercut is through the perspective we acquire, by being placed in Norah's consciousness, on the hypotheses that Mayo and the police develop about the woman who was with Prebble on the night of the murder. They automatically assume that she was no good (most likely a prostitute, since what decent woman would go out with Prebble), and that she deserves all she will get for murdering Prebble. (There is, however, no condemnation of Prebble's seductions, no suggestion that he may have exploited women for his own ends, or taken advantage of women's loneliness.) The disjunction between Norah, whom we experience as a gentle, warm and honest person, and the 'fictional' woman the men and society in general conjure up, highlights the harsh stereotype that women must deal with and the sexual double standard.

Particularly painful for Norah is the way even her close friends assume that the woman with Prebble was no good, and is to be despised and punished. Through the device of Norah's increasing identification with the heroines of Sally's pulp fiction, Lang notes Norah's growing self-hatred as she hears the comments about the 'Prebble woman'. Earlier on, Sally discussed with zest her latest book about a 'red debutante [who] is hit on the head, stabbed in the back, and shot in the stomach'. Norah's increasing identification with these pulp fiction women is made clear after an upsetting conversation with Sally and Crystal about the murderess. When the two friends leave Norah in the kitchen, she picks up a knife and holds it suggestively toward her stomach. We cut to a cover of one of Sally's books, showing a woman brandishing a knife with a terrible grimace on her face; the image echoes Norah's growing frustration as she feels condemned, trapped and helpless.

Norah's increasing sense of being trapped comes from her inability to withstand a definition of herself imposed by an alien and indecipherable male discourse. She does not trust her own sense of what she is, or is not, capable of, uncertain as to where male definitions end and her own begin. As the events of her night with Prebble are reconstructed for her by the police, Norah suffers a terrifying dislocation from reality. Not having evidence to the contrary, she comes to accept their definition of her as a murderess, despite an underlying sense that something is amiss. She is reduced to a state of hysteria, acting like a criminal, jumping when she sees the police, burning evidence like the taffeta dress, listening secretly to the radio in the dead of night. Her personality changes, and she becomes irritable with her friends. She thus folds up under the weight of the male structuring of things, succumbs to their view of her, and takes the guilt upon herself.

The third way in which the male discourse is undercut is through the perspective we develop on Casey Mayo. Identified as we are with Norah, the alternation between the discourses 'places' what Mayo is doing and allows us to see it for what it is. In the ordinary noir film, the investigator's trapping of the murderess would be a demonstration of his triumph over sexuality and evil. Here, Mayo is seen to engineer a despicable betrayal of the murderess whose dilemma he exploits for a publicity stunt. He pretends to be the killer's friend, seductively offering help and secrecy but all along intending to give the girl up to the police once she has revealed herself to him. Norah resists Mayo's appeals for a long time (while, by the way, the audience is 'entertained' by a series of false responses by desperate women, who are made ridiculous), but her isolation finally wears her down. She is unable to confide in her women friends (although we sense that at least Crystal would be sympathetic), partly because they have spoken so badly of the Prebble 'women', but also because Norah presumably does not see them as being able to help. She assumes that only men, those in the place of power, can get her out of her fix. She thus turns to Casey Mayo, who has been presenting himself over the radio as someone able to make reason out of chaos.

Because of the total trust with which Norah turns to Mayo, his treatment of her is shocking. When she comes to him posing as the murderess' friend, Mayo responds warmly to her, partly because he is attracted to her but also because he is anxious to be the first to discover the murderess. When Norah finally reveals that she is herself the supposed murderess, Mayo's response is terrifying: she is now repulsive to him, someone to be shunned, cast off. He does not quite decide to turn her in himself as originally planned—because of his attraction—but is glad to be sent off on another job.

Lang's visual treatment of the meeting between Mayo and Norah underscores her vulnerability, and Mayo's manipula-

tion. He asks Norah to meet him late at night in his office. Norah's arrival is shot from Mayo's point of view: when he hears the elevator coming, he shuts off the lights, presumably so that he will be able to size her up before she has a chance to see him. Also, perhaps, to frighten her. We see Norah emerge from the lit elevator in the back of the frame; she is a tiny figure in black, in the lit corridor, with the threatening blackness of Mayo's office looming in front of her. Mayo watches silently as she slowly makes her way up the dark room, lit only from outside. The visual presentation of the scene expresses Mayo's power over Norah, her dependence on him and his unworthiness to be trusted, since he thinks only in terms of power and not of human vulnerability. Mayo is exposed as incapable of pity or empathy, and as bound by stereotypes of women as either 'good' or 'bad' girls.

The progressive elements of *The Blue Gardenia* that I've been discussing are, as so often, undercut by the way the film ends. Mayo has to be 'redeemed' by being the one who finally *does* solve the mystery of who murdered Prebble. By noticing a discrepancy between the record Norah said was on the phonograph at the time of the murder and that found by the police on the turntable when they arrived, Mayo tracks the murderess down; she turns out to be the hysterical woman Prebble had rejected at the start of the film. Mayo's reward for liberating Norah is of course to win her for himself; he now has the 'good' woman and can throw over his black book to his delighted photographer.

> In turning noir conventions upside down, *The Blue Gardenia* has revealed the place that women usually occupy in these films. We see that the view men have of women is false in that the set of implications about Norah generated from the male world turn out to be invalid.
> —*E. Ann Kaplan*

Although by the end of the film all the structures defining men and women are safely back in place, Lang's achievement remains. In turning noir conventions upside down, *The Blue Gardenia* has revealed the place that women usually occupy in these films. We see that the view men have of women is false in that the set of implications about Norah generated from the male world turn out to be invalid. While the male discourse tried to define Norah as a *femme fatale,* we see rather that she is a victim of male strategies to ensnare her for something she did not do. Norah's submissive placing of herself in relation to the male world is also exposed. She accepts the male view of her and then experiences the world as a riddle that she cannot solve. In this way, *The Blue Gardenia* exposes the essential contradiction between the dominant male discourse and the subordinate (repressed) discourse of women in patriarchy.

E. Ann Kaplan (essay date 1983)

SOURCE: "Ideology and Cinematic Practice in Lang's *Scarlet Street* and Renoir's *La Chienne*," in *Wide Angle,* Vol. 5, No. 3, 1983, pp. 32-43.

[*In the following essay, Kaplan compares how different cultural contexts affect Lang's* Scarlet Street *and Renoir's* La Chienne, *two films made from the same literary original.*]

A comparison of *La Chienne* and *Scarlet Street*—two films made from the same literary original but in different nations, periods and institutional settings—allows us more easily than usual to isolate the effects of political, historical and economic context as these can be read off from each work. The cinematic devices in each film express the ideology of its cultural context—Popular Front France on the one hand, post-World War-II America on the other—and it is thus not surprising to find more elements subversive of dominant bourgeois ideology in Renoir's film than in Lang's. But, given a spectator not committed to bourgeois values, *Scarlet Street* may be read in a progressive manner, while *La Chienne,* for all its criticism of certain aspects of bourgeois society, assumes the dominance of patriarchy and represses the female discourse.

The discussion of each film is organized around three main concepts: first, the idea of the family (domestic space) in contrast to the work world (public space), particularly as this relates to the notion of the individual versus the community; second, the construction of sexual difference as it functions to drive the narrative forward; finally, the idea of class in each film.

The cinematic form of *Scarlet Street* is for the most part that of dominant (classical Hollywood) cinema. The potentially subversive elements that are evident (particularly in the final section of the film) are a result of its falling, roughly, into film noir. For most of the film, Lang follows the rules of classic cutting: he fragments filmic space through montage as the organizing principle of shot change, but preserves the illusion of narrative continuity by disguising the fragmentation. The transition between shots through dissolve helps further to disguise the division between private and public space that is largely responsible for Chris' misery. This division, of course, is routinely structured into classic narratives, and has an ideological base in that the separation of domestic and work worlds has (at least to date) served the interests of capitalism. The polarity reinforces the concept of individualism on which bourgeois culture is founded, and represses the notion of community that could work to undermine capitalist structures. The myth that the home is the haven to which the weary (male) worker returns for spiritual and personal sustenance enables the public world to be defined, without prejudice, as non-supportive and non-nurturing. Hollywood narratives reflect, without question, this division between private and public spaces, and use montage to make it seem "natural," the way things are supposed to be.

The supposedly "natural" separation between home and work worlds is particularly interesting in *Scarlet Street* since the hero, Chris Cross, gets into trouble precisely because his home is not the haven it is ideologically supposed to be. The narrative is structured in typical fashion around a series of juxtaposed sequences that set up polarities, contrasts and oppositions. In the opening section of the film, Chris is seen in a series of separate spaces, none of which connect with each other, but whose disconnection is masked, made to "seem natural." The opening use of montage establishes an apparent contrast between the lonely, noir world of the street and a superficially "warm" business dinner commemorating Chris Cross' twenty-five years with his firm. The street scene is so darkly lit that one barely sees the passers-by, the beggar with the barrel organ, or the sleek shiny car that pulls up outside of the Club, lit with a neon sign, where the dinner is being held. The organ grinder plays "Santa Lucia," a romantic love song that prepares for the shot of the glamorous woman in the car, her white furs and jewelry briefly breaking the blackness. We cut to the scene inside as the chauffeur comes to fetch J.J., Chris' boss, who represents the patriarchal order and is obviously much admired by Chris. Chris is significantly introduced by a shot of the back of his head, as the camera focuses along the table to J.J. making a speech and presenting Chris with the commemorative watch. When we finally cut to Chris' face, we see his boyish joy at being made the center of attention, clearly an unusual circumstance.

J.J.'s manhood is established by his having the glamorous girl waiting for him in the car. The diners leave the table to crowd around the window and gaze down at her, while Chris and his friend take the opportunity to creep out, obviously not at home with this group despite the surface togetherness. Once out on the dark street, now deserted and rainswept, Chris confides his loneliness to his friend and wonders bemusedly what it would be like to be loved by a young girl. He admits that no woman has ever looked at him as that girl looked at J.J.

Paradoxically, the lonely street shortly thereafter offers Chris the "gift" of Kitty, but it is in effect a gift as false as the watch in terms of what it really signifies; the watch, simply a routine recognition of service, did not signify the love Chris needs, and Kitty also offers "false" love.

We cut to a bar where Chris begins to fall in love with Kitty, enchanted by her youth, beauty and her apparent interest in him. Ashamed to say he is indeed the cashier Kitty nearly "mistook" him for, he allows her to believe he makes his living by painting, while in reality he merely paints as a hobby, a way to relieve his empty, painful existence.

The noir street thus mirrors Chris' "true" existence, while the two "warm" spaces are illusions. We cut from the scene with Kitty to a closeup of the flower Kitty gave Chris in the bar and which he is now painting in his kitchen, trying to stay out of the way of his hostile wife. Chris' home is, as already noted, far from the haven it is ideologically meant to be; on the contrary, it is a place where Chris is made to feel unworthy, unloved and inadequate.

The next series of scenes continues this juxtaposition of disconnected spaces that Chris inhabits. The "romantic" scene between Chris and Kitty in an outside cafe (it is the one and only time in the film that nature is shown—there are trees, birds, sunshine) is placed next to a dark shot of Chris in his workplace, tempted to steal the money Kitty has begged for. Chris is alone in his box-like cashier's office, the lighting is shadowy and the camera so close in as to produce a claustrophobic sensation. Chris is then seen arriving home to shrill abuses from Adèle about not buying her a house or even a radio, and for not being a "proper man" like Homer, her former husband, whose portrait dominates all the domestic shots. When Adèle goes to listen to a soap opera at a friend's place, Chris takes his revenge by stealing some of the insurance bonds she obtained through Homer's supposed death. When Adèle returns, Chris goes in his usual beaten fashion to wash the dishes.

In this opening series of sequences, then, the use of montage has shown Chris in a series of disconnected worlds, two of which clearly give him little satisfaction. His alienation in the work world, however, is not seen as being a problem (it is how things are meant, to be), while his miserable home life with his bitchy wife is a sign of unhappiness, of things *not* being as they are meant to be. The spectator is made to identify with Chris and to hate Adèle as much as he does. Since his home is not the haven it is ideologically supposed to be, Chris experiences a lack, a void that has to be filled, and thus arises his first need for Kitty. But secondly, his need for her emerges from his "feminization," exacerbated by Adèle's shrewishness: he must "prove" that he is a man by taking a young mistress. Finally, in the hierarchically structured work world in which Chris is relegated to a low slot, Chris again finds his manhood on the line. He talks of himself as a failure later on in the film, and in terms of the competitive, achievement-oriented society he lives in, he can be described in this way. (Ideologically, we are made to assent to this view of himself.) Falling in love with Kitty seems to place Chris on the same footing as his boss, J.J., and thus fills yet one more need in relation to manliness.

After this introduction establishing Chris' vulnerability to Kitty's manipulations, the narrative focuses on the relationship between Kitty and Johnny, and on their plan to exploit Chris' supposed fame as a painter. Johnny, and to a lesser degree, Kitty, has been briefly established as up to no good in a short scene in Kitty's apartment near the start of the film. The full depth of his evil emerges as the film progresses, but is of course (in accordance with the rules of classical narrative) never ideologically accounted for in any terms other than implicit Christian ones. Cross' name suggests that he is some kind of Christ figure, prey to the "devil" that Johnny personifies. That Lang means Johnny, not Kitty, to be the "serpent" in the Garden of Eden (despite the sex-role reversal involved), is clear from the superimposition of Johnny's face and a snake in one of Chris' paintings at a later point in the film. Johnny, like many characters in more typical noir films, is a "fallen" creature in a world view that sees evil as a matter of individual distance from God rather than as something socially conditioned.

The traumatic discovery of his betrayal by Kitty (through Johnny's urgings) leads Chris to murder his beloved in a fit of jealous passion. From that point on, his tenuous place in normal bourgeois society ("tenuous" because of his low work status and unhappy marriage), is fatally ruptured. Because of the divisions between private and public space, and his enmeshment in worlds that refuse community or proper friendship, Chris, even before he commits murder, has nowhere to turn for help with his miserable marriage, with his newfound love, or with his need for money. Once he has done the deed he is completely, irrevocably isolated. Cross' alienation (masked by the montage in most of the film through cutting from Adèle's rejections to joyful meetings with Kitty) is fully revealed in the final sequence of the film. Film space is now fragmented in an expressionist manner (there are jarring cuts from witness to witness, oblique angles, figures silhouetted against white, empty spaces, distorted sound as in a dream). For a moment, there is a break in the smoothly contained, bourgeois ideology. When Chris is allowed to go free, it seems that public morality briefly follows private morality; for although Johnny is technically innocent, he is morally guilty, and society is shown to honor that guilt in its false reliance on circumstantial evidence.

However, bourgeois morality is hastily recuperated in that Cross, while allowed to go free physically, is not left spiritually free. As the newspaper reporter ominously warned in the train on the way to Johnny's execution, the guilty man never goes free, no matter what faults there are in the judicial system. Chris falls lower than ever after having committed murder; haunted by the persistent voices of Kitty and Johnny, mocking him and declaring their undying love for one another, Chris begins to go mad. In a scene that brilliantly reproduces through lighting, sound and editing, his inner experience of unbearable guilt and frustration, Chris finally tries to hang himself. Although he is saved just in time, he is forever morally and psychologically destroyed. Lost in his pain, Cross is stunned to see his painting of Kitty being moved into a van as he passes the art gallery. After staring at it uncomprehendingly, Cross continues on his way, haunted as ever by the jeering, seductive voices of Johnny and Kitty. He must suffer inner torment forever for having committed a murder—no matter how justified in personal terms—and in this way Lang brings Chris back safely within the bourgeois world, ultimately viewed as a trap from which there is no escape. Within the limits of Hollywood narrative conventions, breaking the rules is no solution.

We see thus how in Lang's film the division between public and private space is built into the structure of the cinematic world as a given, as completely "natural." The cause of Cross' tragedy is not the division itself (i.e., of the way social institutions are constructed), as it might be viewed in a "progressive" reading, but rather it is seen as first, the result of Adèle's not performing her wifely role in the manner prescribed (i.e., as nurturing, supportive, loving toward her husband); second, the result of Cross' lacking the kind of manliness patriarchal capitalism demands and expects of its men. Cross' tragedy is thus viewed as an individual tragedy rather than as a result of social organization or cultural demands.

Renoir's use of cinematic space reflects a very different ideology than does the bifurcation through montage found in Lang's film. This is not to argue, as have critics since Bazin, that Renoir brings us closer to "reality" through his on-location shooting, his devices of loose framing, panning camera, long takes and eye-level, medium-long shots, or through his use of deep focus. But rather it is to say that Renoir constructs an image of "reality" strikingly other than that constructed in classical Hollywood narratives. He presents a new way of seeing bourgeois "reality" a way that is not more or less "real" but simply *different* from that which we are used to in traditional narratives. To the average spectator, indeed, Renoir's use of cinematic space seems less, not more, "realistic" because it is so unfamiliar and not in accord with the constructions Americans have in their heads as "the way things naturally are."

To begin again with the treatment of private/public space: we find here a striking difference from *Scarlet Street,* since instead of setting up the two spaces as disconnected, separate, polarized, Renoir rather shows the connections between the spaces. It is not so much that Renoir links the work space and the domestic space specifically (Legrand is perhaps even more alienated at work, although for significantly different reasons than Cross), but that instead of showing his hero as isolated in an isolated domestic unit, Renoir places both Legrand and his domestic space in a community context. This is done through the techniques of deep focus, long takes, and a panning camera as against the placing of characters in a

shallow field, the use of relatively short takes, and montage instead of camera movement, that we find in Lang.

Thus the community is present and dwelt upon in all the key scenes, as for instance when Legrand steals Adèle's bonds, when Alexis comes to the house, when Legrand murders Lulu, and finally when Dédé is convicted of the murder he didn't commit. And the connections are made not through intercutting (a separating device) but through use of deep focus, with the action being developed within one shot. The effect of the community presence is different in each case, but the technique suggests a view of reality where actions of moment are seen not as happening to isolated individuals but to people in a very specific cultural, social and institutional context. The individual is presented as a *social* being, as necessarily a part of a structure beyond himself.

In general, Renoir's editing establishes a method of sequencing unlike that in Lang's film and in Hollywood films in general. In *Scarlet Street,* we saw that the editing was used to mask disconnections, or to present disconnections as quite "natural." The sequences are set up as separate, complete and rather long units, and the spaces are constructed in accordance with our cultural expectations. Where Lang constructs the film with sequences acting like building blocks, Renoir moves from one short interaction to another in a quite jarring fashion. That is, we experience disconnection, fragmentation, and even have some difficulty in following the narrative at times. Thus we have the paradox that Lang actually presents a disconnected, fragmented world but smooths it over and masks the disconnections through continuity editing; while Renoir presents a more unified, connected set of spaces and a view of people as linked to their surroundings and their community, but does not disguise fragmentation between sequences.

The different constructions of public versus private space in the Lang and Renoir films leads in turn to contrasting constructions of sexual difference. In *Scarlet Street,* the ideology underlying the private space/public space dichotomy implies a specific construction of gender roles. J.J. in the public space, and Homer in the domestic space, signify the ideal of manliness that capitalist structures demand: J.J. bears the voice of authority as patriarchal leader in his firm, and his phallic power is demonstrated by his possession of the glamorous young girl; in Chris' domestic space, Homer stands as the voice of authority and possessor of the phallus (at one point Adèle notes proudly how Homer used to be attractive to other women since *he* was a real *man*). Cross' tragedy arises on one level from his lack of the manliness required in his culture; this lack disturbs the sex gender organization and creates disease. Adèle is dissatisfied and disappointed in Chris as a husband (she complains overtly about his failure to provide adequately for her financially, and from Chris' hint that he has never seen a woman naked, we can assume that he does not perform adequately in the bed either). As a result, she sees Cross as lacking the phallus, as symbolically "female," and therefore relegates him to tasks traditionally carried out by the wife.

Adèle in turn takes on the dominating role usually occupied by the husband, but we assume (from her comments about Homer) that she would have been willing to occupy her gender role had Cross been suitably "manly."

While Adèle pits Cross against Homer and finds him lacking, so Kitty pits him against Johnny and also finds him inadequate. Johnny's masculinity is of a construction the opposite of the benign patriarch J.J., and closer to that found in noir figures. He is the tough-talking, greedy, criminal type who manipulates his woman and is not beyond beating her up occasionally so as to keep her in line. This manly assertiveness, in addition to his implied sexual prowess (e.g., Kitty: "I don't know why I stay around a guy like you." Johnny: "You *know* why you do"; or the scene, that within the rules of the code is meant to indicate sexual passion, where we find Johnny sprawled out on the bed and Kitty's belongings all strewn around the floor), is what attracts Kitty to him. She is thus constructed as masochistically preferring the man who brutalizes her to the man who genuinely dotes on her and who is gentle to her. This is clearly revealed in the murder scene where Kitty finally allows her repressed scorn for the "feminized" Cross to emerge; "*You* kill Johnny?" she yells; "Why he'd break every bone in your body; he's a *man*." And "Me marry you? Why, you're old and ugly!" Cross, unable to endure the double pain of his shattered romantic illusions about Kitty and the attack on his masculinity, is driven to assert his maleness by killing what he had loved.

The two couples, Kitty/Johnny and Adèle/Chris, then, are juxtaposed so as to expose the "correct" and "incorrect" construction of sexual difference (although part of Millie's function as Kitty's friend is to show us that Johnny has overstepped his masculine role and will deserve punishment for this); Kitty can be properly "female" (seductive, worshiping her man, willing to sacrifice anything for him) because Johnny is properly "male" (dominating, assertive, sexual). The "trouble" in the narrative that drives the plot forward emerges from Chris' lack of sufficient masculinity. This failure causes domestic unhappiness, causes Cross to feel inadequate both at work and at home, and leads him to fall in love with Kitty and become vulnerable to her and Johnny's exploitation. His weak sense of himself as a man makes him unable to endure her brutal betrayal and leads to the murder, which in turn destroys his inner peace.

The problem of sexual difference takes on another cast in *La Chienne* because of the different conceptions of the hero's "problem," which is here related to the notion of the individual versus his community. Much more ambivalence surrounds the construction of all the characters, except Adèle, in their relation to moral absolutes of good and evil. While Cross' vulnerability to the absolute evil of Johnny and Kitty is linked to his lack of sufficient masculinity, the same is not true for Legrand.

Legrand's main problem is not seen as being one of inadequate maleness; rather, he is set up as a condescending man who considers himself above his peers. He is cultured and well read, while they are philistines; he is the artist with refinement and sensibility, while they lack culture and a taste for the finer things of life. Legrand thus separates himself from the others, and to this degree, since Renoir values community, is criticized by Renoir for arrogance. Legrand is not posed in the opening scene as in awe of a more "manly" boss, but is instead presented as a man who likes to keep himself to himself, and who refuses to go along with the silly exploits that his colleagues indulge in.

Although there is reference to Legrand's not daring to visit a whorehouse because of his wife, Legrand in fact seems self-possessed and used to being the butt of jokes. If he has a sin, it is one of pride (analogous to that of Professor Rath in *The Blue Angel*) as opposed to one of sexual inadequacy. Legrand's behavior results from a kind of snobbish bourgeois lifestyle which leads him to set himself up above others and to separate himself from the community. In a very painful way, Legrand has to learn humility; he has to be brought down to the level of the common man he so scorns, a "lowering" that Renoir views as a liberation from a stuffy, artificial way of being. His obsession with Lulu is thus caused by the bourgeois structures Legrand is locked into; once released from those oppressive structures, he is released from his passion and free to simply "be"—a state far different from the doomed, continual haunting by the past that Chris endures in *Scarlet Street*. Where Cross seems tentative about Kitty's love for him and keeps questioning her, Legrand assumes that because he loves Lulu, she must love him. Much more than Cross, he identifies himself as an artist, a special being set apart, as is revealed in his conception of himself in his paintings as a Christ figure, bearing the "Cross" of having to endure Philistines. Cross' paintings, on the other hand, deal with his sense of a world beset with dangers, a world where evil lurks in common places, like the Village streets (namely the snake around the El supports in one painting), where the human figure (as in the portrait of Kitty) assumes alarmingly vacant, distanced, threatening features.

Renoir's refusal to separate private and public space enables him to critique the separation that Legrand makes deliberately. As we have seen, in Lang's film the separation is an essential part of the film's structure and is never questioned. By contrast, the unquestioned assumption in Renoir's film is a patriarchal view of sex relations. While a feminist reading of *La Chienne* would expose the pitiful exploitation of Lulu by all the men in the film, there is nothing in the way the film is constructed to suggest that Renoir deplores the exploitation.

It is interesting to see that Lulu has been given many more traditionally feminine traits than Kitty in Lang's film; she is small, blonde and round—a figure and presence that cries out to be cuddled. She wears flowing shiny clothes with soft, feathery collars and cuffs that frame her little face, and which she pulls around her in a coy, retiring manner. This is very different from the brash, confident gestures of the dark-haired Kitty, who, sure of herself and her beauty, deploys her body in deliberately seductive ways. While Kitty is knowing, worldly-wise, and (except for her fatal blind spot regarding Johnny) has her head screwed on the right way, Lulu is more traditionally "innocent," despite her supposed role as prostitute. She behaves as if she hardly knows that is what she is doing, and her whole being exists to please Dédé. She is thus much more the traditional woman-as-victim (and accepted as such) than is Kitty.

Lulu receives far greater abuse than does Kitty; she is constructed as masochistically involved in a relationship that offers little more than beatings. For instance, immediately after being beaten up by Dédé, she is worrying about him. While Dédé is in some ways (particularly morally) a less obnoxious character than Johnny, he is much more brutal to Lulu.

While Kitty is equally involved with Johnny in the exploitation of Chris, Lulu stands outside of it all, hardly aware of what is going on. At least Kitty gets some acclaim as the supposed great artist, while in *La Chienne* Lulu ends up being a sexual object to physically distasteful art dealers. Her function as object of exchange between Dédé, her lover, the men selling her work, and the buyers is presented graphically in the scene where Lulu goes to a party arranged by her agents and is literally passed from one man to another, prodded by Dédé, who, thinking only about the money, is anxious for her to please all the other men. Lulu reluctantly complies, and the scene ends with a cut to Lulu signing over her hard-won earnings to Dédé.

Lulu's discourse is completely suppressed in her life with Dédé, and she functions as a mere economic signifier, reduced to the level of a piece of paper. Her function is hardly better in relation to Legrand, for whom she is the receptacle of fantasies and wish fulfillments, there to provide for his pleasure—very much on the level of the pets and flowers with which Renoir's imagery frequently associates her.

The varying construction of sexual difference in the two films creates quite different resonances in the murder scene. Legrand destroys what he loves not so much out of jealousy as out of disappointment that the woman he thought perfect could stoop so low as to love an unrefined man like Dédé. The techniques used to film the murder underscore this interpretation. First, there is the intercutting between the room where the murder is happening and the community outside where people have gathered to listen to a violinist playing a haunting old melody. The people Legrand so scorns are presented as capable of appreciating good music, while he, ironically, stoops to the level of murder. Their presence suggests a deliberate link between Legrand and those he has tried to rise above.

Second, Renoir's method of filming the action from outside the window establishes a necessary distance between the spectator and the action; we are deliberately placed as voyeurs, and are forced to think and judge, rather than simply participate in the horror. The flowerpots and the frilly curtains, along with the soft lighting suggest the tragic loss of Lulu, an innocent victim of men's desires. Legrand looks foolish for killing impulsively and needlessly.

The murder is represented in quite another mode in *Scarlet Street.* To begin with, the phallic imagery suggests that Cross' sexuality is involved in a way that Legrand's is not. The murder scene is linked to an earlier scene that foreshadowed it, both in its phallic imagery and in the rage toward women that Chris experiences because of his submission to them. This earlier scene takes place in Chris' kitchen, where he is seen, complete with apron, cutting up some meat with a huge knife. Adèle walks in scornful because, having seen Cross' paintings with Kitty's name on them, she assumes that he has simply copied the paintings. Cross at first thinks Adèle has discovered his affair, and holds the knife up ominously in center frame as she talks. When he realizes something else is going on, he lets the knife drop, and we get a closeup of it significantly right between Cross' feet.

In the murder scene, the ice pick is similarly focused on. Cross knocks it out of the ice barrel by mistake when talking to Kitty, and absent-mindedly picks it up. He holds it in his hand as he listens to Kitty and then plunges the knife in several times when he realizes that she is laughing at him—deriding his manhood and comparing him negatively to Johnny. In both scenes, the knife stands for the phallus Chris lacks—a lack that he tries to compensate by using the knife murderously.

There is no such emphasis in *La Chienne.* The paper knife that we assume is the murder weapon is only briefly seen, and then Renoir's camera cuts significantly down to the community below, listening to the violinist. The camera then pans slowly up the wall of the house outside to the window of Lulu's room, where it pans right, keeping us outside; from our position, we see Legrand apparently caressing Lulu's body, in great distress about the loss he has brought upon himself.

We are, again significantly, placed very much as voyeurs at this moment in *La Chienne*. We want to see what is going on inside the room, and Renoir's refusal incites our curiosity; one finds oneself peering into the screen, hoping each time to see a little more into the room. Paradoxically, Renoir's hero, while not motivated to murder through sexual inadequacy, nevertheless has a sexual reaction to his self-imposed loss. Chris, motivated through the desire to assert the phallus, is destroyed by his assertion, experiencing no tragic sense of loss and no relief. Legrand, motivated rather through social/class reasons, experiences loss, followed by the final renewal.

We can now see how the construction of sexuality and of public/private space is governed by the construction of class in the two films; and further how the construction of class is related to the political, historical and intellectual milieu in which Renoir and Lang were working. Issues of class were being foregrounded in Popular Front France, while in postwar America they were mystified. While this is partly always the case in America and in Hollywood films, it was particularly true following a successful war in which, ideologically, class interests had been subordinated to patriotism. For the moment, laborers and bosses were working toward the same end, united in their wish to win the war.

That this ideology continued in postwar America may be seen in the mystification of class in *Scarlet Street.* Everyone is leveled to a comfortable middle-class mean, and the narrative avoids inserting class as a cause for anything that happens. While at the start Kitty and Johnny are clearly living a rather sordid existence (although they are always dressed in a thoroughly middle-class style), this is seen as caused by individual laziness and greed rather than by economic or class systems. The conversation between Millie and Kitty early on establishes the fact that Kitty could earn a good living by modeling if she wanted to; a later conversation with Millie and Johnny establishes Johnny in turn as an indulgent dreamer who wants to get rich quick (note his fantasy of overnight success in Hollywood) without doing any work.

Very quickly, through exploiting Chris, Kitty and Johnny are set up in a fancy apartment. Their use of language alone betrays their class origins, and this is neatly masked by Kitty's legitimate adoption of a "refined" accent to seduce both Chris and the art dealers. Her kind of beauty and her poise, sophistication and elegance establish her iconographically as middle class. Johnny is for his part defined not in terms of class so much as of morality (i.e., he is evil incarnate). Finally, although Chris' work world is in fact hierarchical, this is again masked by J.J.'s stance as "one of the boys." Genial and jolly, he is sympathetic rather than aloof when Chris gets into trouble.

But underneath the surface of postwar America sex and gender issues were causing dis-ease. Again, one can look back at the history of literature in America and discover from early on a difficulty (on the part of the almost exclusively male authors who made up the dominant literary tradition) in relation to sex and women. But as the veterans returned and found that their places had been filled competently by women, ongoing problems of male sexual identity were exacerbated. It is for this reason that sexual difference is foregrounded in *Scarlet Street,* and takes precedence over class. Cross' family situation, indeed, reflects one that must have faced many a veteran: the "other man" in the background; the demand that he be a full-fledged provider; the assertive, confident woman, able to take care of herself, yet feeling that she has earned the right to be taken care of. Cross himself is in a sort of shell-shocked state, and, unable to deal with the demands, suffers a crisis in his masculine identity.

The context of Popular Front France resulted in a very different emphasis on the same original in *La Chienne*. Renoir's anti-bourgeois bias dominates his construction of the narrative and is the reason behind his drawing attention to the process of illusion through the device of the puppets, and the constant framing of the action through windows, doors, etc., that replace the proscenium arch. Renoir wants to avoid our identification with Legrand so that we can think about who he is and what he is doing, and also so that we can have some sympathy for Dédé. The distance enables Renoir to set up Legrand as a petit-bourgeois man who, because of his superior culture (he is a painter who understands great art) sees himself as above everyone else in his community, both at home and at work. Dédé, meanwhile, is thoroughly working class in his clothes, hair style, stance, gestures, speech, and is filmed in locations (the bars, the clubs) that reflect his class origins. Although we only glimpse him briefly, Legrand's boss is much more the aristocrat than is J.J. in *Scarlet Street*; he separates himself from his workers, thus completing the sense of a strong class hierarchy, rigidly adhered to.

Significantly, Lulu is the character least tied to class because of what Renoir intends her to represent in the film—namely, the eternal feminine. (In feminist terms, as we've seen, she is a mere projection of male fantasies with no voice of her own.) Adèle, on the other hand, is a comic stereotype as old as comedy—the working-class, shrewish wife, emotional, violent, abusive.

Renoir's narrative is thus driven forward by issues having to do with class. Legrand's misery is presented as due to oppressive, bourgeois structures; forced out of them by his murder of Lulu, he achieves a kind of existential anarchic freedom, living happily on the street, released from the cares and desires that bourgeois society entails. Dédé, meanwhile, is seen as the pitiful victim of his class status. Despite his brutality to Lulu, he retains our sympathy as a man who knows no better; lacking the education needed to think more deeply about things, he pushes on in the only way he knows how, not deliberately intending to hurt people, but acting out of a sad ignorance of human possibilities.

This analysis of cinematic practice and ideology in *Scarlet Street* and *La Chienne,* films made from the same original but in different nations and political periods, has allowed us to see how cultures speak through texts, shaping the means of expression, conditioning what can be said, and affecting the focus given the narrative. The bifurcation of cinematic space in Lang's text, smoothed over by continuity editing, reflects an accepted division between public and private worlds, and a view of the individual as alienated without, however, his being aware of this as something abnormal. The narrative focuses on the problem of sexual difference, reflecting a deep-rooted concern in American culture generally, but one that is of special significance in the post-World War II era. Cross' lack of sufficient masculinity causes the "trouble" in the narrative, and brings about his destruction. The film suggests that capitalist structures like the family and the corporation depend on a certain form of masculinity, and that disaster follows from its lack. Women cannot be properly feminine if their men are not sufficiently masculine, and a man leaves himself open to exploitation if not aggressively male. The film, that is, offers a series of warnings around sexuality in a period when sex roles were in a confused state as a result of the upheavals the war entailed.

Renoir's film, by contrast, structures cinematic space quite differently, relying on long takes, deep focus and a panning camera that probes space. Renoir shoots on location, and his gray, grainy image lacks precise definitions; it stands in sharp contrast to the deliberately stark black/white polarity of Lang's images where mise-en-scène is all important, and definition clear-cut. Renoir's camera seeks to explore spaces beyond its purview, drawing attention deliberately to its own inherent voyeuristic properties; these are properties that Renoir exploits by using windows, doors, buildings and the dumbwaiter as framing devices that enhance our position as spectators.

The spectator in Renoir's film is thus addressed in such a way that he/she must stand at a distance from what is occurring on the screen; fragmentation is not masked by continuity editing, so that we have a sense of Legrand as alienated. But the refusal to separate private and public space makes us see that Legrand's alienation is of his own making rather than being inherent in the state of things. The way space is structured endows value on the community that Legrand himself scorns, and ensures that Legrand's bourgeois values are critiqued.

Since class was foregrounded in Popular Front France, it is this concern that drives the narrative forward, rather than problems having to do with sexual difference. In Legrand's

world, Lulu is inserted as a fantasy, representing all his dissatisfactions, his yearning for more than his narrow bourgeois life can offer. In her own world, on the other hand, Lulu functions as the scapegoat for Dédé's frustrations, the means for his release of tension, and is exploited for her market value. She has no status, no voice of her own, and in placing her thus Renoir implicitly accepts patriarchal culture. The upshot of the film is a devastating critique of the ways *men* are bounded by, trapped in, bourgeois culture, but it leaves women out of the critique. If the ending is politically unsatisfying in being anarchic rather than revolutionary, that is Renoir's choice.

What my analysis has revealed is that while, paradoxically, the overall ideology in Lang's film is more conservative (it does not question accepted bourgeois structures), his film, in foregrounding sex roles, exposes (this is not to say that it critiques) the assumptions about sexuality that underlie bourgeois capitalism.

Roger Dadoun (essay date Fall 1986)

SOURCE: "*Metropolis* Mother-City—'Mittler'—Hitler," in *Camera Obscura,* Nos. 11-15, Fall, 1986, pp. 137-63.

[*In the following essay, Dadoun discusses Lang's* Metropolis *in terms of its moral ideology and presents possible reasons why Hitler admired the film.*]

Metropolis is a German film made by Fritz Lang in 1926. It is commonly held to be a "classic" of cinema; some even call it a "masterpiece." Apart from the stylistic qualities that make it, for many viewers, one of the masterworks of expressionism, it is chiefly the film's moral, or ideology, that has been singled out for praise. The final sequence, a model of the "happy ending," depicts the emotional reconciliation of the employer with his workers, brought about by the employer's son, who, with the blessing of Maria, the pure young woman who is soon to become his wife, assumes the role of Mediator (*Mittler* in German). The film drew harsh words from some critics. H.G. Wells pronounced it "an amalgam of all the nonsense and platitudes we have ever heard, upon which is ladled a sentimental sauce like no other." More significantly, some critics have seen parallels with, not to say instances of, Nazi ideas, values, and fantasies. For Francis Courtade, "*Metropolis* is a fascist, pre-Nazi work." Siegfried Kracauer's analyses in *From Caligari to Hitler* provide valuable evidence in support of this judgment, in particular Lang's own statements to an American newspaper. When the Nazis came to power, Lang was summoned by propaganda chief Goebbels, who told him that he and Hitler had seen the film together some years earlier in a small provincial town. ". . . Hitler said [to Goebbels] at that time," Lang recounted, "that he wanted me to make the Nazis' pictures." The theme of destiny being a recurrent favorite of Lang's, it is curious to note here the Nazi historical "destiny" of *Metropolis.* Before elaborating further on this point, I will briefly review the film's scenario. My main point, however, will be to demonstrate the need for, and pertinence of, psychoanalytic concepts in investigating the specifically filmic content of the work.

Abbreviated to the bare minimum, the film's credits are as follows.

> Producer: UFA, 1926. Director: Fritz Lang. Cameramen: Karl Freund, Günther Rittau. Special effects: Eugen Schüfftan. Set design: Otto Hunte, Erich Kettelhut, Karl Volbrecht. Music: Gottfried Huppertz. Cast: Brigitte Helm (Maria), Gustav Fröhlich (Freder), Alfred Abel (Joh Fredersen), Heinrich George (foreman), Rudolf Klein-Rogge (Rotwang the inventor), Theodor Loos (Joseph, Fredersen's secretary), Fritz Rasp (an employee of Fredersen), Erwin Binswanger, Heinrich Gotho, Margarete Lanner, Georg John, Walter Kuhle, Erwin Vater, Grete Berger, Olly Böheim, Helene Weigel, and Anny Hintze.

Briefly summarized, the story goes like this:

> Metropolis is a gigantic city of the future, filled with enormous skyscrapers. Workers are housed below ground, along with factories and machinery. There they live a hellish existence as slaves subservient to the needs of mechanized production. Above ground, in the Upper City, are the vast offices of industrialist Joh Fredersen, master of Metropolis, who dictates his orders to squads of secretaries; complementing the office building is an Edenic Garden, where the master's sons frolic.

> Into this garden, which is protected by an imposing gateway, wanders Maria, the daughter of a worker, surrounded by a group of wretched children. She stares long and hard at Freder Fredersen, the employer's son, who stands transfixed, as though hypnotized. "These are your brothers," she says, pointing to the children. She is then driven out of the garden, but her visit has revealed to the son the horrible conditions in which workers live. As though walking in his sleep, Freder descends into the machine room. We see a tableau of workers on the job. An explosion takes place, killing some and injuring others. Freder then goes to see his father, who curtly informs him that class division is inevitable and that the worker must toil for his daily bread. The worker's place is "down below." A secretary, Joseph, is fired for not keeping an adequate guard. He contemplates

suicide, but Freder prevents him from going through with it and they become friends.

Freder returns to the machine room and assumes the place of a worker. For ten long hours he submits to the torture of labor. Along with other worn-out laborers he then descends into the catacombs, where he finds Maria, immaculately white and gleaming, preaching patience and prophesying the coming of a "mediator." Meanwhile, the father, to whom a foreman has handed over plans found on the bodies of dead workers, turns for advice to the inventor Rotwang, who describes his masterpiece: a robot that never tires and never makes an error, designed to replace the human worker. The two go down into the catacombs and observe Maria's preaching from a hiding place. The father asks Rotwang to make the robot look like Maria. Thus disguised, the robot could be used to incite the workers to rebellion.

Rotwang, alone, continues to watch Maria. She approaches the kneeling Freder and kisses him. When Freder leaves, Rotwang pursues Maria and after a fierce struggle seizes her and carries her off. He ties her down and forces her to undergo a transformation. The mechanism of the robot is concealed beneath an outer shell that exactly resembles Maria. Thus the robot becomes her double. (I shall refer to the robot thus disguised as the False Maria, to distinguish it from the Real Maria.) Freder sets out in search of Maria but is caught and imprisoned in Rotwang's house, where he hears the girl's cries.

The False Maria is shown to the father. Fascinated by the resemblance, he takes her by the shoulders. The son arrives, witnesses the scene, and falls ill. The False Maria is presented to an audience of employers dressed in tuxedos and performs an extraordinary, erotic dance. She then returns underground and incites the workers to rebellion. A frenzied mob invades the machine room and wreaks havoc. There is fire and flooding. The Real Maria manages to escape and heads for the workers' city to save the children. Freder joins her in this task. The workers, suddenly aware of the situation, lay hold of the False Maria, tie her to a stake, and set her afire. The flames destroy her human covering but leave the inner mechanism intact. "Witch!" cries the mob. Rotwang pursues the Real Maria to the top of the cathedral, himself pursued by Freder. The two men fight and Rotwang falls. The father, on his knees, says, "Praise God!" On the porch of the cathedral the father advances, flanked by his son and Maria. Ahead of them a disciplined troop of workers in triangular formation also advances. The foreman steps out ahead and walks toward the boss. The son takes his father's hand and joins it to the foreman's. Thus the "heart" completes its mission of "mediating" between "hand and brain."

This summary, which may seem rather drawn out, is necessary for my purposes. Readers who have not seen the film need to know the main points of the plot. Those who have seen the film generally recall only brief snatches. Even the few who have seen *Metropolis* numerous times fail to recall all its details. Film criticism operates under an essential handicap: the raw material is evanescent. Fleeting images are lost forever (occasioning what has been called *le deuil cinématique*, or mourning of the lost image). When the substance of a film is rendered in words (as it must be in criticism), images are systematically eliminated. Hence the narration of a film plot always sounds like a rather tedious anecdote. The analogy with the psychoanalytic patient's account of a dream is obvious.

No film is unaffected by the material and ideological conditions under which it is produced. This is especially true of *Metropolis,* a film that played an important part in the ambitious plans of UFA (Universum Film Aktiengesellschaft), "one of the most powerful political filmmaking trusts that Europe has ever known." The corporation was set up with government capital made available by Ludendorff, a proponent of pan-Germanist policies for whom the war had amply demonstrated "the power of images and film as a means of educating and influencing the masses," and with private capital provided by a number of well-known trusts: Krupp Steel, I.G. Farben (chemicals), A.E.G. (electrical equipment), and Deutsche Bank, to name a few. The firm's mission was to produce films that would distract attention from reality ("escapist pictures," or *Traumfilms*) and in various ways cast doubt on the prospects for revolution. Later, under the Nazis, the film industry carried this policy even further, producing a mix of love comedies, elaborate production numbers, and Viennese operettas, apparently with great success: the *Encyclopédie du cinéma* reports that "in 1942 more than a billion movie tickets were sold in Hitler's Greater Reich." At the time *Metropolis* was made, the president of UFA was a publishing magnate by the name of Alfred Hugenberg, who was also the leader of the extreme right-wing "Steel Helmets" group and a financial contributor to Hitler's Nazi Party. Lang's wife, Thea von Harbou, approved of the Nazis's ideas; after Lang's departure in 1933, she remained active, making films for the Nazis.

UFA wanted *Metropolis* to be "the greatest film of all time." Advertising for the picture (which should be taken with a grain of salt) underscored the colossal character of the project: 310 days and 60 nights of shooting, from 22 March 1925 to 30 October 1926; 6 million marks; 750 actors; 26,000 male extras, 11,000 female extras, and 750 children; 1,300,000 meters of positive film and 620,000 meters of negative film; as well as 2,000 pairs of shoes, 75 wigs, 50 automobiles, and so on. The film followed the *Nibelungen,* an ambitious vehicle for traditional mythological themes, written and directed by Lang and Thea von Harbou in 1923-1924. The gargantuan size of the *Metropolis* project, in keeping with its overall ideological aims, could hardly fail to elicit a certain "gigantism" not only in the treatment of scenery and architecture and the use of extras but even more in the nature of the filmic discourse that was developed—a discourse of the paranoid type. To put the point in somewhat different terms, there is a certain accord or unity or interaction between the historical, political, financial, and existential or personal circumstances in which a film is made and the fantasy materials that shape or enter into the composition of the filmic text. In other words, the various elements that make up the film (characters, situations, forms, technical procedures, and so on), though in a sense circumscribed by history and politics, cannot be adequately articulated and organized except in terms of the unconscious processes and fantasy structures discovered by psychoanalysis. This, at any rate, is what I shall attempt to show in the remainder of this essay.

Etymologically *Metropolis* means "mother-city" (from the Greek *meter, mother + polis,* city). This historical residue of meaning is structurally embodied in the title, with all its cultural overtones; these overtones are marshalled into waves of meaning that animate the film as a whole (making it literally a "moving picture").

Metropolis is, superlatively, the City. The ranks of massive skyscrapers in the opening frames make this quite clear (these images were supposedly suggested to Lang by his first sight of New York City). Yet the masses of stone punctuated by square black openings in cold, geometric patterns do not stand erect like the Empire State Building in *King Kong,* for example, where the image of phallic erection is driven home by the lengthy scene in which the ape laboriously climbs the tower. In *Metropolis,* by contrast, oblique spotlights play over the buildings' naked facades and seem to lift or remove their skin; the moving spotlights weave the fabric of the city and, from the film's opening moments, suggest a stripping, skinning, or peeling away.

The city is sealed, closed in on itself, like a womb. The only movement we see (apart from the symmetrical, sublimating ascent in the cathedral) proceeds along tortuous, bowel-like passageways into the lower depths, the catacombs, to the central, altar-like structure where the two Marias stand and preach. Nature is almost totally absent; it is alluded to twice, once in the story of Babel, which is retold in the film (through a gray and barren landscape endless columns of slaves haul huge building stones—nature is thus petrified in myth and in stone), and again in two brief sequences. One of these depicts the Edenic garden, which is treated in painterly fashion with a pool, fountains, vegetation, and great white birds. But this garden stands behind an imposing gateway; it is a hot-house, an *objet d'art,* an artificial production. The second sequence reinforces this interpretation of nature: the sumptuous room occupied by the son, Freder, has walls covered with stylized plant motifs. Nature is reduced to a decorative sign, crushed and flattened against the surface of stone. These motifs (in all senses of the word) of petrifaction establish a complex of fantasies that plays an important part in the film's libidinal economy.

The film's opening frames consist of long, static shots of building models. These are immediately followed by more dynamic, animated shots, with impressive close-ups of machines, or, more precisely, of parts and pieces of machines, partial objects, cogs and complex mechanisms that throb, churn, reciprocate, or rotate. Looking at the image from close up, one might say: it is moving, it is turning within. One point should be made at once, before these images are subsumed in subsequent social and technological totalities: within this city of surfaces, this tissue of stone, there is something—the id (*ça*)—moving, working mechanically, like a machine. And since there is nothing in these frames but pieces of machines working without either raw materials or finished products, we can say: it (*ça*) is working on itself. Now, the usefulness of theory is that it enables us to transform this last statement as follows: the id (*le Ça*), the unconscious, asserts itself as a productive drive or mechanism; it is formed by or takes the form of machinery, a complex, repetitive, articulated interaction of various operations and processes. These quick opening images make it perfectly clear what the film's ideological and cultural position concerning mass production, exploitation, and alienation will be. More than that, they give the key to the production and development of images and signifiers; we might even say that they reveal the film's id: together, the work of the id and the work of the film are intertwined, as cinematographic technique and unconscious processes cooperate in the animation, development, deployment, and organization of figures and forms.

The first and perhaps the primordial operation is the division of the city into two radically different parts, which are kept separate by edict of the father/owners. This hierarchical division is strongly influenced by mythological and religious tradition (God began the creation of the world by separating the "upper" from the "lower" waters). The Upper City is that of the masters and owners, the superior place of supreme and total authority. Here, thought is magisterial. (Fredersen's huge office reflects the enormous size of his brain, which is indicated in the film by pointing: in one frame he is shown lying on his back, and before continuing with his speech he moves two fingers close to his head.) Here pleasure is as readily available as it was in the Garden of Eden (not unlike the garden in which the sons of the owners cavort). This is the "good" city. "Good" means that it is the owners who establish the

law and name all things; we are reminded, too, of the Kleinian notion of the "good" mother.

The Lower City, where the workers work and reside, lies in the "lower depths." It is composed of three rather different layers, one lying more or less above the next: the machine room, the vast territory of labor, suffering, and death (which appears as Moloch in a hallucination experienced by Freder, the son); the workers' dwellings, which are seen, briefly, only from the outside, densely packed around an empty central square; and finally the catacombs, decorated with skeletons and bones. This is clearly the "bad" part of the city.

The spatial division of the city is mirrored in various ways, including the striking, indeed frightening and spectacular division of the Maria character into two quite distinct, indeed antagonistic, parts (the same actress, Brigitte Helm, plays both). Maria is clearly a maternal figure in two senses: the Real Maria is the "good" mother, and the False Maria is the "bad" mother.

In her first appearance, when she enters the garden of the sons after hurdling, as if by miracle, all the obstacles, Maria—the Real Maria, the Good Maria—is surrounded by a host of small children over whom she extends her arms, creating a sheltered zone outlined by the placenta-like veil that hangs from her shoulders. When she points to the children and says to Freder, "They are your brothers," he is so thunderstruck that he stops his lovemaking and places his hand on his heart, a gesture that will be repeated throughout the film; Maria thus turns him into a "child," an "infant." He becomes, in a sense, one of "her" children. Maria's maternal protective function is clearly in evidence in the catastrophe near the end of the film. She saves the children from the flood, rescues them from the water. A deliberately theatrical image, elaborate and decorative, shows her standing on a sort of pedestal in the small square at the center of the workers' city, surrounded by clusters of children who clutch her body. The central object, the gong that she sounds to give the alarm, is circular in shape with a protrusion at the center, exactly like a breast. What is more, Maria occupies, or is identified with, yet another central space that obviously resembles a uterus: the cave at the bottom of the catacombs, reached at the end of a laborious and somber "descent into the underworld." There stands a sort of altar, bristling with tall crosses and candles, a typical place of meditation. Maria's name here takes on its full religious significance. Like Mary she is an immaculate virgin all dressed in white, a virgin mother with arms extended in a cross as she raises her veil, and her evangelical speech soothes the pain of the workers and announces the coming of a messiah, the Mediator (*Mittler*). In this closed, mystical space, Maria's speech evokes and opens up, through a fantastic process of infinite regression, another, still deeper region, a more primordial mythical space, built around the story of the Tower of Babel. This provides Fritz Lang with the opportunity to indulge in (or reveal himself in) various fantastic, large-scale directorial effects: huge, crushing blocks of stone, endless staircases rising toward infinity, gray, antlike slaves emerging in interminable columns from the gray earth, great circles of light that swallow up the sky. In this hallucination, however, the Tower of Babel itself is nothing but a scale model, a paltry thing, a humble erection around which the masters gather to meditate. To all this colossal imagery Lang attaches, in grandiose letters as on an advertising billboard, the principle of a spectacularly inflated religious humanism: "Great is the Creator and Great is Man!"

A clearly more complex, extraordinary, and disturbing figure than the Real Maria, the False Maria (the robot disguised beneath Maria's skin and sharing her appearance) stands out immediately as an image of the "bad" mother, flaunting herself as a de-naturation of the "good" Maria with her lascivious winks and smiles, her stiff arm, and so forth. Significantly, it is the False Maria, far more than the would-be terrifying gestures of Rotwang, who frightens children aged five or six who see *Metropolis.* The False Maria systematically repeats in the "wicked" mode all that the Real Maria does in the "good" mode. She occupies the same key points in space and enters into relations with the same objects (Rotwang, Freder, the mob, etc.), each time inverting or subverting the system of values, that is, turning them upside down so as to reveal an archaic and repressed layer. We, too, must subvert this figure, turn it over, in order to discover its primordial meaning. The appearance will turn out to be the deeper meaning: the human skin that covers the metallic robot is precisely what the robot is trying to hide. The progress of the narrative itself suggests another reversal of this figure: born a mechanical contrivance wreathed in the prestige of science, a science fiction robot, the False Maria ends up a witch, burned at the stake.

The distressing and horrifying primitive maternal dimension of the False Maria is established chiefly in the various primal scenes that occur at intervals throughout the film. Before examining them, let me point out the notable absence of any individualized, homogeneous, and named maternal figure. Freder, the hero of the film, has no mother that we know of. When he falls ill, it is always his father that we see at his side. The fact that the institution of motherhood is so thoroughly expunged from the film makes it clear that the whole burden of maternity is carried by the two Marias, and that the maternal dimension underlies (*fonde*) and merges into (*se fond dans*) the totality of Metropolis, the mother-city.

Fusion, diffusion, and scrambling of figures, forms, and values beneath apparently solid, one-dimensional entities: therein lies part of the wealth and originality of *Metropolis.* So complex are the displacements and overdeterminations that there is scarcely an image in the film that cannot occupy the most surprising positions at any of the forty-nine levels of Talmudic interpretation. Yet the unusual abundance of signifiers is powerfully polarized by an organizing structure: the primal scene, which through a series of frequent reiterations occupies nearly the entire film. The most typical sequence occurs near the middle, as if in the center or "heart" of the film, and it brings into play a cinematographic rhetoric of rare virtuosity. Rotwang, the scientist, has made a robot that looks like Maria and sends it off to be examined by Fredersen. The latter is struck, moved, and seduced by the resemblance. He stares hard at the young woman, moves closer to her, places his hands on her shoulders. The woman plays the seductress with eyes, smile, and body. At that moment the son, looking for Maria, bursts into his father's office. He sees his father and Maria locked in a quasi-embrace. Dumbfounded, he feels the ground fall away; he staggers, and to his eyes, deluded by madness, the couple seems to draw together and begins to whirl about. The two figures—two parents now—are linked together in a rotation, caught up in a blur in which dark and light lines seem to merge. This geometry, these crossed and rotating figures create—do they not?—a swastika: two entwined bodies with four arms. Transfixed as by the sight of Medusa, the son sees an immense, expanding black hole dotted with glowing spots of light (phantasms in the strict sense) and experiences a sense of falling into a void, a loss of consciousness or, better, of a loss of the unconscious, as horror takes refuge in illness: Freder falls ill. After the spectacular image of the fall, we return to Freder lying in bed, racked by fever and hallucinations.

Furthermore, these hallucinations, indicated by Freder's haggard look of fright and horror, establish a link to another version of the primal scene, which is characterized not by traumatic effects but by an extreme, frantic voyeurism, lavishly filmed. The father leaves the room of his sick son to attend the dinner given by Rotwang. We see a crowd of employers, masters, all wearing tuxedos. All are men, who can be considered doubles of the son, because a very effective parallel montage alternates between, and hence identifies, the son and the guests, portraying their common vision of the scene. The purpose of the dinner is to introduce the False Maria, to present her to the public. In a very precise sense, therefore, she is re-presented. A large, glowing object, a sort of basin or cup, slowly rises. An enormous cover is raised, and the False Maria, splendidly dressed, slowly emerges. She spreads her veils, exhibits her almost naked body, and begins to dance. Her whole body revolves at a dizzying rate, turning faster and faster until all that can be seen is a moving, sinuous, serpentine line. Intensely, totally absorbed in voyeurism, the audience is all eyes, all stares—quite literally (or, since it is an image that is involved, iconically): a repeated frame shows a series of huge eyes, a mosaic of fascinated stares, of eyes popping out of heads. Plucked from their sockets, these eyes leave the spectator's tense bodies and voluptuously attach themselves to the spectacle. This is a hallucinatory voyeurism in two senses: it is a hallucination created by the technical means of the cinema, with the shot of a mosaic of eyes, and it is a psychological hallucination of the son, who, lying unconscious in his bed, follows the action. What this complex scene of the dancer watched by voyeurs reveals is that the False Maria is more than just a simple figuration of the "bad" mother. The choreographic rotation, which confuses the feminine shapes of the body and links belly, breasts, thighs, shoulder, and head in a brilliant serpent-like coil, together with the sumptuous display of the hot and smoking cup or basin, suggests that the False Maria should be seen as a condensed, pantomime representation of the primal scene. Recall that the False Maria is in fact composed of two radically different parts, joined together and perfectly fused (and the crucial importance of the process of fusion in the primal scene can hardly be overstated): a rigid metallic form, the robot, and a soft, feminine envelope of lovely flesh, extorted by Rotwang from Maria's body. In other words—to reduce it to the simplest possible conceptual terms—the robot is part phallus, indeed a sort of phallic principle. I say phallic principle because it cannot be clearly defined as either father or son: after the coupling with the father, he and the robot separate, and the robot goes off to serve as provocateur, sowing discord. At one point, when the mob believes that it has won a victory, the robot is even brandished like a trophy, a totem erected on the shoulders of all the sons, workers and bourgeois alike, joined together in communion. The robot is also the object in which the socio-political paternity of Fredersen couples and combines with the technological-scientific paternity of Rotwang. Thus the robot assumes the paternal functions of tyranny, repression, and punishment. But it also assumes the filial functions of criticism, accusation, resistance, and rebellion. (Here the robot is like the severed phallus of Rotwang, who has been symbolically castrated, his hand cut off, for having dared to lay hands on Mother Nature, for having "had" her, to use a slang term [French: entuber] that suggests the tubular machinery that fills his laboratory. The Promethean nature of Rotwang's enterprise is underscored by the shot that shows him, in the presence of the frightened Fredersen, claiming victory by raising his stump covered with a glove whose black color links it to the black shell of the Robot that stands motionless behind him. Like the liver of Prometheus eternally regenerating itself, the black form of the robot, which the hysterical crowd has accused of witchcraft, survives the flames at the stake, cackling with the witch's blasphemous phallic laughter. The son's phallus is structurally heretical; no hell can annihilate it, and no mutilation, castration, or Inquisition can do away with it. (Neither the robot nor Rotwang really dies in the film, as we shall see.) Thus the robot is in part the phallus, a mobile, inner core. But it is also—the second aspect of the construct known as the False Maria—the primordial maternal skin, the placenta, the hot, protective envelope, swollen by the heat, engorged as Hermann would say, and detached from Maria's body: pure intumescence, then, which returns to the bonfire in the ritual consummation of the burning forest (to borrow again from Hermann). This montage of mother-upon-phallus is a traditional but always impressive and fecund condensation, source of monsters from the Sphinx to the Gorgon: the False Maria is a monster of this type, a splendid mythological creation of cinema, baby sister of the formidable King Kong and a woman who no doubt seduced and aroused her own creator, Lang himself, who was able to find the precise shot to express his fascination: a montage of dazzled eyes exploring as a louse might the voluptuous woman's skin (voluptuous and—if the reader will permit—voluptueuse, or curvaceous, flesh; the latter word, through its Latin roots volvere, volutum, suggests vulva or volva, vulva or womb). The primal dance, which the son hallucinates in his neonatal bed while his doubles, the men at the dinner, look on as voyeurs, is wonderfully amplified by the scenery. The vast smoking tub—pelvis of what phylogenetic mother?—from which the False Maria emerges (inwardly armed, one might say) is one of many circular shapes, along with its cover and the circle that surrounds Maria's head, and the curves of the veils and the hairdo and the woman's body. The tub itself is decorated with a motif of hydra-headed serpents upon which the dancer rests her body. The polymorphic sensuality of the dance and the use of redundant signifiers produce a powerful image of the primal scene. (It is not without interest to note that the spectator can easily miss various shots in the sequence just described, particularly the guard of hydra-headed serpents that surrounds the False Maria. In analyzing a film, what was not seen is just as important as what was.)

For the unconscious, of course, no amount of repetition is enough, nor can the variety of repetition be exhausted. In the major scenes analyzed above, sight and its hallucinatory representation of reality are the key elements. This is perfectly consistent with the rest of the film, in which eyes and gazes are powerfully omnipresent. In yet a third version of the primal scene, we are given highly dramatic "shots" of auditory perceptions. (I do not think that it is a misnomer to speak of "shots" of sound in this silent film, because the pantomime and gesticulations are so eloquent, not to say piercing.) These shots accompany, or more precisely herald, a sumptuous technological and "scientific" treatment of the fantasy. As further evidence of the film's innovative style and depth of comprehension of fantasy, primitive memories of the primal scene are given material embodiment in a very theatrical way: an unusual architectural form, a sort of curved or swollen triangle, like a grubby wart grown up, oddly (and insolently) enough, in the vicinity of the great cube-like workers' dwellings and the cathedral. The text says: "In the midst of the city stood an old house." Meaningful paradox: this old building houses the futuristic laboratory of Rotwang, "the genius inventor." Redundancy always multiplies the meanings of an image. Here, the notions Old, Ancient, Primal are emblematically inscribed in what we see as the label or trademark of occultism and the esoteric tradition, the five-pointed star or pentacle, which appears on the entrance to the house, on various inner doors, and, in a more monumental way, on the wall against which the robot's seat is placed; the head of the robot seems to fit inside the star's lower triangular cavity.

Freder hears Maria's cries as Rotwang drags her through the dark corridors of his house, which, given his predatory behavior and the nature of his victim, might also be called his den or lair. The son enters the house in a strange way. Rage and magic mingle and alternate as all doors resist Freder's blows only to open and close suddenly of their own accord—an imperious determinism that suggests both the omnipotent magic of infantile thought and the perfectly ordered structure of fantasy, which here requires a son caught in a trance and trapped in an enclosed room entombed in stone, petrified, while all around the alchemist continues with his work.

In a technological forest bristling with tubes swollen with black sap, with throbbing balloons, quivering levers, thermometers, measuring devices, and rotating coils (*serpentins*), Rotwang bustles about, rapidly moving his hands—the black and the white—over all his "gadgets." This energetic overexcitation centers on and culminates in a sort of glowing white sphere, a sun-like globe mounted high up in the room, which its radiant energy makes "fertile." Maria lies in a glass coffin, her body girded or encircled by black metal rings which create around it something like a space of pregnancy. Waves or rays or filaments of nervous electricity traverse this region and penetrate the body of the passive victim. The other Maria, the robot, mirrors this composition exactly. Motionless in a seated position, the robot is connected to the Real Maria by numerous filaments that slither across the floor like serpents. Large, glowing, white rings circle the robot's body and rotate around it, rising and falling as they turn in an accelerated masturbatory motion. Merely by changing the sign, we can view the black robot as engaged in frenzied copulation, moving rapidly in and out of its hot white sheath. Excitation reaches its peak in the orgiastic atmosphere of the laboratory. Rotwang, after his period of intense activity, is nothing but a gaze contemplating the miraculous impregnation. The robot acquires vessels, nerves, and organs and begins to move; a human skin now covers its structure. Maria, drained, lets her head fall to one side, in a primal gesture suggesting both orgasm and death. The creative act is done. A door opens, freeing the son and allowing the story to proceed.

This is a scene of remarkable density, and it is instructive to compare it with a similar sequence, also depicting the creation of a woman, in *The Bride of Frankenstein,* where the same battery of signifiers is used: electrical charges and discharges, light waves, ringlike forms, mechanical motions of the robot gradually changing to more supple human movements, and so on. In ***Metropolis*** a subtle movement and interplay of forms makes the scene unusually arresting. Inventor, creator, and impregnator, Rotwang is single, double, and multiple all at once: he is the paternal and divine One, symbolized by the solar globe from which all energy emanates (a globe heated until it glows red, suggesting the inventor's very name—Rot-wang, or red cheek; *Wange* also designates clay and hands). He is sovereign over the empirical realm as well as the realm of reproduction. Yet he is a man who not only desires, conceives, orders, and carries out the experiment but also contemplates it: after conceiving it and then carrying it out, he follows its progress with his eyes, in a state of anxious fascination. Thus he assumes the role of the voyeuristic son, the passive witness of the scene. He is the double (in both senses of the word) of the excluded and banished son. Prostrate, the son is castrated; his entire body fails to achieve erection. Rotwang takes on this aspect of castration. His severed hand is punishment for his filial curiosity and establishes a female component of his personality, clearly indicated by his black gown. Finally, Rotwang is multiple in that he disintegrates into the innumerable objects that he manipulates and operates; he is one with his devices (for it is these that we contemplate in his laboratory-lair). The mother herself is double, Maria and the robot. This split is pregnant with sexual dualities, moreover: both figures exhibit a phallic rigidity (Maria in her catatonic state and the robot with its stiff black metal structure, which also allows the phallic axis to be inscribed on the anal register) while the rings and circles suggest feminine and maternal curves. Add to this the plethora (of energy as well as forms) evident in the wires and filaments that fill the zone of copulation with waves and rings, which one cannot fail to recognize as the nerve rays imagined by Judge Schreber in his paranoid fantasy of sexual action at a distance.

Rotwang's dual function—as paranoid father and creator and as rebellious rival son—is also apparent in two more or less symmetrical sequences, one of which ends in triumph, the other in failure. The first precedes and lays the groundwork for the great technological primal scene analyzed above: Maria, having finished her sermon and bestowed her kiss upon Freder, is left alone when Freder departs. Nearby, Rotwang, having concluded his alliance with Fredersen, is left alone when Fredersen departs. In the dark, primitive depths of a cavern, he follows Maria by focusing the beam of his lamp on her. Lang's stylistic virtuosity is given free rein to indulge the expressionist taste for effects of light and shadow, for contrasts of black and white that set off, engulf, or heighten actual forms. In her flight Maria runs into jagged walls, gazes in horror upon skulls and skeletons, and finally succumbs to Rotwang's attack. Duration is here an important part of the meaning: the scene clearly lasts longer than is required by the narrative or the representation of a fantasy. The insistence on these effusions of the imagination is more than just aesthetic license. A principle is laid down, made explicit by images of pursuit, confinement, and death: psychic mechanisms are inflexible, overwhelming, and inexorable. Indeed, I would call the whole sequence principled. It establishes, first, the principle that fantasies are causal, which governs the progress of the entire film. Second, it lays down a general principle of fate (pursuit, confinement, death), which is so important an element in all of Lang's work and which is masterfully expressed in the psychopath's confession scene in *M.* Maria stands with her back to a wall as Rotwang slowly and almost sensually raises the beam of his lamp over her body. In a close-up her face appears to be divided in two: the dark upper portion endures the hypnotic power of Rotwang's sparkling eyes, while the lower portion gleams white in the light cast by Rotwang's lamp, held at mouth level. Maria is thus the object of a hypnotic stare and the focus of a rigid beam of light. Both touch her and hold her still, cover or penetrate her. Sexual action at a distance takes place thanks to an upward displacement of the phallic power. Rotwang's barred phallus (*phallus barré*) moves off (slang: *se barre*) in two directions at once, establishing Rotwang's extreme ambivalence. Intellectual sublimation invests the eyes with a power of penetration-fascination of a hypnotic type, which literally holds the object at a distance: this is the scientist's expert gaze. On the other hand, a process of regression tends to polarize and structure various libidinal investments around the mouth, producing a sexual syncretism (mouth as anus, urethra, phallus, etc.) characteristic of Hitler's libidinal structure (as we shall see in a moment). The sadistic element implicit in this displacement (piercing eyes, mouth spewing forth its luminous jet) is underscored by several shots of skeletons and finally triumphs in the aggressive posture of Rotwang, who dominates Maria and brutally holds her against and beneath him in an embrace-rape that is almost a preliminary take of the great scene of impregnation that follows.

In the final part of the film, Rotwang revives his aggression against Maria, but now every effort ends in failure. The triumphal birth of the False Maria is offset by the robot's immolation at the stake. The depths of the cave in which Maria was caught are countered by the heights of the cathedral to which she escapes. The alliance with Fredersen that was sealed in the cave is broken off. Above all, the lonely, diabolical work of the scientist now gives way to public confrontation with the hero Freder. For this battle a mythological atmosphere is created by a striking low-angle shot. This, together with gargoyles and a Manichaean handling of shapes, confirms Maria's maternal function by distinguishing, in that complex of forms named Rotwang, the grimacing figure of a "wicked," incestuous son, diabolical brother of the "good," angelic Freder, who is set up as the protector of the "good" mother. Rotwang, the "bad" son, symbolizes the "bad" mother with his black gown and black robot. The whirl of images is dizzying: the "bad" son engenders the "bad" mother as much as she engenders him. The themes are Hitlerian: "bad" sons— intellectuals, homosexuals, rebels, Semites, and so forth— have created a bad Germany. Purification will come through extermination and fire.

The "good" son triumphs as Rotwang plunges into the abyss. The father, on his knees, says "Praise God!" This suggests that Rotwang's fall is to be interpreted as the fall of Lucifer. Indeed, in the glowing globe and the beams and coils of light we have seen Rotwang as *luci-fer,* bearer of light; hence he is cast out of Heaven, where God reigns. But the images tell the story: the "wicked one" is not destroyed. The flames may destroy the False Maria's outer covering of flesh, but they leave the robot's inner structure intact. Rotwang falls, but we know not where. The "black nakedness of wickedness" (Michaux) regains the shadows, where it may carry on with its evil work. To track him down the "good" sons dress in black and, as they set out to eradicate evil amid the sound of bonfires and marching boots, tirelessly repeat that the battle is never-ending, that the extermination of the wicked knows no respite or remission or end. If "wickedness" can assume the guise of the "good" mother herself, it can hide anywhere. But here I am extrapolating in terms of known history the unconscious tendencies that Lang's film obscures, precisely with regard to Rotwang's fall. The slate must be wiped clean before the supreme displacement can occur: once the figures of fantasy are gone, the subjects of ideology can make their entrance—theater of representation, elevation of the Representatives.

The final sequence is shot in a theatrical way. We first see a deserted, empty space in front of the cathedral, a stage waiting for the play to begin. Then an audience arrives: the army of workers, in close triangular formation, moving forward in disciplined ranks (or rows), rises from the bottom of the screen. The cathedral serves as backdrop, frame, and enclosure of the final scene. Fredersen, Freder, and Maria pass through a narrow door and are somewhat surprised to find themselves at the dawn of a new day, so to speak, beneath the maternal arch of the porch. The foreman steps out ahead of the group of workers, brawny and awkward in his respect for authority. A pantomime (with movements of the arms, looks, hesitations, and signs of awkwardness and embarrassment) makes it clear that something seeks to be represented, and that the characters do not yet perfectly embody their roles. Perhaps this scene should be called a "super-representation": before us we see not mere circumstantial characters playing to a passive audience, but well-defined socio-economic and ideological entities identified by name. The foreman represents labor (the hand); Fredersen represents capital (the brain). Freder, along with his double, the white shadow of Maria, represents mediation (the heart). Thus the heart, composed, as in sentimental postcards, of two curves, links capital to labor. Hands that had groped tentatively toward one another join in a handshake, and linked arms stretch horizontally across the frame in a composition now in a sense egalitarian, all angles, volumes, and vertical differentiations having been eliminated in the general leveling. Such is the ideological platitude of this happy ending in the form of a handshake; the vast, heterogeneous, contradictory spaces explored by the film are relegated to a place somewhere behind the screen. But they can be brought back in full delirium, by a mere squeeze of the hand: Hitler's manacles, brutally applied, will give the madness a new lease on life.

The triangular structure of the final scene repeats the triangles and diagonals that delimit figures and movements throughout the film. (To meet Maria in the triangular hollow of the catacombs, for example, the workers descend along a left-to-right diagonal, while Rotwang and Fredersen follow a right-to-left diagonal.) Particularly spectacular is the black triangle formed by the army of workers as it moves into center screen; heads lowered, the workers move in lock-step, a black sea of slaves. The robot, seated on its chair with wires coming down diagonally on both sides, also formed a black triangle, repeated once more in the pyramid of the bonfire and in certain of Rotwang's attitudes. Rotwang, the robot, and the workers are thus parts of the same triangle, which rises from below (energy rises into the robot's body, just as the flames of the bonfire mount the stake and the workers' formation moves up toward the cathedral). This lower triangle is the "bad" triangle, as is indicated by stiffness and blackness—in a sense phallic, as we have seen. And just as the robot's head penetrated the lower triangular cavity of the pentacle, so, too, do the square workers' platoons penetrate Moloch's wide-open mouth, and Rotwang the inventor raises his black hand to begin the impregnation of the robot. But this interpretation conflicts with too much of the evidence: the femininity of Rotwang, the castrated male dressed in a black gown; the fact that the robot's head does not so much penetrate the cavity of the star as reinforce it; the robot's female flesh, destroyed by the flames; and so on. Accordingly, the phallic interpretation of this hardware seems rather misleading to me, valid and pertinent though it may be in some respects. It is a smokescreen, an overestimation, intended to conceal a more fundamental truth, something especially frightening, indeed truly horrifying, which can now be revealed simply by inverting the form or relation: turned upside down, belly up, the black triangle turns out to be the V shape of the female genitals. Recall that the False Maria consists of two parts, internal and external. A feminine skin, a swollen womb, materially covers the robot's phallic metal structure. But we can now say, at an even deeper level, in fantasy, that it is the phallic robot that hides and covers the female sex organ in the very act of exhibiting it. Rotwang's complex figure also requires reinterpretation: his spectacular powers as impregnator and father, his aggressive virility, are mere pretenses designed to distract our attention from such less visible or striking signs as his black gown and missing hand-phallus. These signs point to a rich vein of hidden femininity in this highly ambivalent figure. Hence it follows that the black triangle stands primarily for the female genitals, and that the determination to deny, denigrate, camouflage, repress, and destroy it (by crushing the workers, crushing Rotwang, burning the robot, and so on) indicates horror of the female or-

gan, and, since the female organ stands for sex in general, horror of sexuality. This is perhaps both a primal level of the film and an important piece of information for understanding the Nazi imagination.

Apart from the oppressive, destructive context of the primal scene, sexuality is depicted in the film several times as amusement or recreation. In the masters' lovely garden, Freder laughingly skips around a gay fountain in pursuit of a cavorting damsel decked out with jewels, flowers, and feathers. In general, however, the black sexual triangle is crushed: it is always pushed into the depths, the abyss of Moloch, the void, or the flames by a symmetric and antagonistic triangle—white, placed higher up, and opening upwards. This is evident in the final scene: while the black triangle of workers penetrates from below, from the bottom of the screen, the upper portion of the screen is occupied by the cathedral porch, on which two symmetrical rows of saints' statues converge toward a vanishing point, or vertex, where the Fredersen trio makes its appearance, as though it were a holy family sent from on high. The sublime, transcendental, angelic nature of this holy triangle is evident (from the cathedral, whiteness, goodness, and so forth); it reminds us of the spectacularly white and glowing triangle formed in the black depths of the catacombs by Maria's angelic figure, flanked by a fan-shaped array of candles and crosses. The purpose and composition of the structure are further highlighted by Maria's gesture as she raises her arm and spreads her veil—her wings. The kiss that she then bestows on Freder's face can only be an extension of this sexual "whiteness," this chastity; later, Maria herself falls victim to Rotwang's black aggression.

The first thing that makes Freder stand out is his white clothing, and Lang exploits this in a systematic and even brutal way by contrasting the son's glaring white garb with the black suit worn by Joseph the secretary, the gray fumes and huge black bulks in the machine room, the black uniforms worn by the workers, and so on. When Freder rejoins his "brother" workers, he trades his white clothing for a black uniform, since whiteness is now superlatively embodied in Maria (who appears to be radiantly white). In a third stage, we see Freder recovering from his illness (the whiteness of the bed and the sickroom represent the digestive process, the catabolism of the blackness and evil that accompany disease) and again putting on his white clothes, which will henceforth survive every adversity. This three-part chromatic composition (white-black-white) is by itself sufficiently strict and homogeneous to distinguish the three major segments of the film. If the primal scene is the fundamental and motivating structure of the film, then the son's role as mediator can be seen as the primary axis of the narrative and the key to the elaboration of an ideology.

Freder becomes aware of his vocation as mediator in a revelation of messianic type: Maria assumes the role of inspired

Annunciatrix. Obviously this has Christ-like overtones, not only in the quasi-osmotic relationship between Freder and the Virgin-Maria (light is transferred osmotically through the gaze, among other things) but also in an image that occurs at a particularly dramatic moment in the film: when Freder is crucified on the needles of an electrical gauge of some sort (like the hands of a clock) and, in the midst of his torture, invokes the name of the Father. But beneath the reference to Christ lies a rich lode of mythological material. The biblical Babel in the background points to still deeper images (from the architecture of the tower to the huge gray furrows of human beings excreted by the earth). The narrative structure is based on traditional mythological models, in which certain sequences occur in a fairly constant order: annunciation of the mission, vocation, trial, failure, symbolic death and rebirth, confrontation with the monster, triumph and resurrection. In terms of manifest content, composed primarily of elements of narrative and ideological messages, the film essentially follows the actions of the mediator. Indeed, Freder is the only character who appears in all the spaces represented in the film (the Edenic garden, the father's office, the machine room, the catacombs, Rotwang's house, workers' city, cathedral, and so on). He is also the only character who touches (to the point of grabbing or embracing) all the major characters (Fredersen, Maria, Rotwang, Joseph, and so on). Freder's trajectory is one of circular or cyclic totalization rather than a dialectical one of mediation or mediatization. Adversity is seen not as a historical or present contradiction but as an accursed survival of archaic material (the pentacle, the witch) or a sudden unleashing of natural forces (the flood). When Freder encounters Rotwang's opposition, he is immediately forced to take evasive action or to rely on magic to refuse and flee the challenge. Recall, in particular, the spectacular sequences in which Rotwang orchestrates first the technological primal scene and then the choreographic one, thereby in a sense causing Freder to fail to perform. We see him first lying prostrate in a dark room in Rotwang's house and then lying on his bed hallucinating in his sickroom. The contradiction is neither analyzed nor pondered, and no response is made that would exploit its dynamic; it is simply abandoned, hidden, and if possible crushed in a burst of feverish activity that might be classed as activism.

The mediator's mission is accomplished when he reunites Capital and Labor, Brain and Hand, in holy wedlock in the holy church (and recall that re-uniting, re-tying, comes form *religare,* the probable root of the word religion). He brings the opposing parties together and unites what has been separate, fragmented, and antagonistic by placing himself in the middle, in between, that is, by acting as intermediary: in German, the word is *Mittler,* which means "mediator" but is also the comparative of *Mittel,* meaning middle, central, intermediate. (*Mittel* is also the word for "means," in the sense of "means and ends," which suggests a cultural and economic instrumentalism characteristic of Nazism.) Freder's position

is crucial in the strict sense of the word: he is at the center, the crossroads, the crossing, the crux. He encounters (*croise*) everyone in the film; in his hallucination he believes that he has witnessed the copulation (*croisement*) of his parents; he is crucified on the cross formed by the hands of the factory's time clock; he is the crusader (*croisé*) who confronts the heretic Rotwang; and finally he is the one who effects salvation by joining (in a *croisement,* a crossing of hands) capital and labor in the final reconciliation-resurrection. Freder is also the one who believes [in French: *celui qui croit—croit,* the third person singular of *croire,* to believe, being a homonym of *croix,* cross—Trans.]. Freder believes in his father, in the "good" Maria, and in his revealed mission. And I would add, freely associating in a manner inspired by the frenetic history of the times, that after 1926 he also became the person who would grow (*croître:* with the Nazi victory in the 1933 elections) as well as crow (*croasser*), as Hitler crowed in his speeches.

> **Hitler may have been especially likely to see himself or read himself into the *Mittler* of *Metropolis* because his own name was (according to Langer) a subject of uncertainty, frustration, and confusion.**
> **—Roger Dadoun**

At this point it should be noted that Hitler was enthusiastic about **Metropolis** and a great admirer of Fritz Lang. Superficially, the reason for his interest is easy to see: the film's ideology coincides with the Nazi vision (set forth by Hitler in *Mein Kampf,* the book he finished in the same year, 1926, in which the film was made) of a national and cultural harmony transcending class divisions. This explanation is no doubt correct as far as it goes. To see the film as an apology for class harmony, a constant of conservative and reactionary thought, can no doubt account for some of Hitler's pleasure, but it is not really likely to elicit the deep and passionate commitment we know he felt (a commitment so passionate that he was prepared, we are told, to overlook Lang's Jewish background and put him to work making Nazi films). But the essence of the film's power lies not in its rather tiresome didactic themes (apparently a specialty of Thea von Harbou, Lang's wife and collaborator) but in the images that Lang created and constructed, produced and directed (to use film jargon that is perfectly appropriate here)—images rich in libidinal investment and fantasy and capable of seducing or horrifying the viewer. Ideological allusions and references cannot by themselves win a film a special and highly significant place in history and politics. For these references must themselves be carried, traversed, weighted down, interpenetrated by work that informs and figures—that is, gives form and figure to—the unconscious. And that is what Lang achieved. Perhaps this work of informing form is the much-sought place where history and fantasy meet.

To explore this meeting place would, I suspect, require considerable multidisciplinary and interdisciplinary effort aimed at drawing together analyses of style, rhetoric, historical pressures, social and economic data, politics, psychoanalysis, and so on—nothing less than a program for a new anthropology, one possible model of which has been outlined in the journal *Psychoanalysis and the Social Sciences,* founded by Geza Roheim in New York. My purpose here is much more modest: by bringing together the figures of Hitler and *Metropolis,* I want to draw out some parallels, which prove nothing but suggest areas for further research; in this I am indebted to Walter C. Langer, whose book *The Mind of Adolf Hitler* collects many useful documents. One is immediately struck by the similarity between the name *Hitler* and the title *Mittler,* which is attached to the hero of the film. Although the process by which identification through names, or even through the letters of names, takes place remains rather obscure, it has been shown to occur in too many, often quite spectacular cases to be ignored as a major factor in the shaping of the imagination. Hitler may have been especially likely to see himself or read himself into the *Mittler* of *Metropolis* because his own name was (according to Langer) a subject of uncertainty, frustration, and confusion. Early party documents were signed *Hittler*; Adolph's father, Alois Hitler, was an illegitimate child who until age forty, when he was recognized by his father Johann Georg *Hiedler,* used the name of his mother, Maria Anna Schicklgruber. Yet owing to a common ancestor, Hitler's maternal grandmother was also named *Hitler.* The nominal foundations are even more severely shaken (just as Freder feels the ground give way under him as he sees the figures of his parents whirl about) by the suggestion that Alois was actually the son of a Rothschild. (Maria Anna Schicklgruber became pregnant while working in Vienna in the home of the Austrian branch of the Rothschilds.) Whatever the basis for this theory (which seems rather far-fetched), the important fact is that Hitler was aware of it, and that it may have stamped his paternal line with a sign of infamy extending far back into the past (just as the diabolical image of Rotwang is marked as ancient by the sign of the pentacle). Hitler's feeling that his ownership of his last name was fragile was compounded by the fact that his father's various marriages were to women of widely varying ages. Alois's first wife was thirteen years his elder; she died in 1883 without having given birth. His second wife, Franziska, died in 1884, leaving two children: Alois, born in 1882, and Angela, born in 1883. His third wife was his own cousin, Klara Poetzl, who had earlier been adopted by the couple and was twenty-three years younger than Alois. Of six children born to her, four died in early childhood. The only survivors were Adolph Hitler and a sister named Paula, who was apparently slightly retarded. What is more, Adolph's half-sister Angela, the manager of a Jewish student restaurant in Vienna, married a man named Raubal and had a daughter, Geli, with whom Adolph had a long and tortured affair that ended when Geli died in 1930, killed by a bullet fired from her uncle's pistol. This confused family history, frequently punctuated by death, may have heightened Hitler's sensitivity to the primal scenes in *Metropolis,* in which confusion of the figures plays such an important role. Death appears in Freder's hallucination (the same one in which the choreographic primal scene occurs) as a statue moving against a background of the seven deadly sins; to Hitler, death must have been a familiar figure, and he was to ensure that it would enjoy a triumphal future.

There are rather remarkable similarities in the early experiences of Lang and Hitler. Both were born in Austria, Lang in Vienna in 1890, Hitler in Braunau in 1889. Both later moved to Germany, indeed to Munich. Both aspired to become architects; Lang actually studied architecture, but Hitler, who lacked a diploma, could not. Subsequently, both became painters in a minor way, selling postcards and watercolors in order to live, Lang in Brussels in 1910 and Hitler in Vienna from 1908 to 1913. When war was declared in 1914, both felt a surge of patriotism. Both were passionate about the movies, cinephiles in the full sense of the word, and both were attracted to women who worked in theater or film: Thea von Harbou and Eva Braun were former actresses. For our present purposes, the most important similarity is the almost obsessive interest in architecture: in terms both of concrete accomplishments, political in the one case and aesthetic in the other, and of the formation of the imagination, the aptitude for projection, for turning fantasies into spatial constructions and architectonic volumes, is manifest in the two men. As many people have pointed out, *Metropolis* is an architect's film; I earlier alluded to the etymological sense of the word, mother-city. Hitler, Langer writes, "believes himself to be the greatest of all German architects and spends a great deal of his time in sketching new buildings and planning the remodeling of entire cities." Thus the "modeling" of the maternal figure as the mother-city in *Metropolis* corresponds to Hitler's desire to "remodel" his mother, to remake or repair (*Mittler* also means "one who repairs") her damaged body, dismantled by a violent and brutal father (just as the "good" Maria is dismantled, taken apart, by Rotwang). In *Metropolis* the "bad" part of the father is almost entirely invested in the figure of Rotwang. The real, social father, Fredersen, while always good to his son, remains an ambivalent figure (he plots with Rotwang, lays hands on the False Maria, and plays with fire by toying with the destructive rage of the workers) until the son's heroism and Rotwang's fall enlighten and purify him, liberating his essential "goodness" and thereby safeguarding the paternalist social model, the basis of order and discipline. The conclusion of the film, in a milky discharge of "goodness" by father, mother, and son on the cathedral porch, seems to correspond to (and therefore to satisfy) a syncretic vision of Hitler's in which he attempted to combine the maternal figure with a dominant father imposed by German tradition (as well as by western paternalism in general). In this connection, Langer notes that "although Germans, as a whole, invariably refer to Germany as the "Fatherland," Hitler almost always refers to it as the "Motherland.""

Freder rescues Maria from Rotwang's clutches. He saves the children from the catastrophic flood. All in all, then, he saves the entire city, the mother-city, as the final, summary image of universal marriage suggests. The story of the film is obviously one of salvation, and no word better describes Hitler's political and historical vocation. Thus communication and correspondences between the film's images and various aspects of Nazi ambition are permanent. The sequence that shows the rescue of the children from the flooded workers' city readily lends itself to "Hitlerian" political interpretation. In the small square at the center or heart of the city the waters rise (mounting perils menace the victim Germany); Maria sounds the alarm and calls for help (Hitler, we know, felt that he had a calling, that he was merely responding to the appeal, the voice, of the mother country—his vocation); the children, abandoned by their unworthy parents (compare Hitler's attraction to children; his anti-familial feelings; his ability to address the childlike populace and shape their behavior; etc.), unite (as the populace united around Hitler, ending "partisan" divisions) around Maria, toward whom they extend their arms in a gesture of supplication (did not Hitler see the innumerable outstretched arms, the Heil Hitlers, as a gesture of supplication addressed to him, expressing a desire to be saved?); at the height of danger, Freder arrives in the role of savior; he clasps Maria to his bosom (Hitler declared that he was "wedded" to Germany) and leads Maria and the children (Germany and her people) out of danger; he is their guide, their *Führer*.

Those responsible for the disaster have already been identified: Rotwang, the "ingenious inventor," whom Hitler must have numbered among those whom he denounced as "overeducated, stuffed with knowledge and intelligence yet devoid of all healthy instincts," representing "the intellect [which] has swollen to the point of becoming autocratic" (the troubling autonomy of Rotwang's house) and which "now resembles a disease" (the morbid hypertrophy of Rotwang's intellect, indicated by his huge forehead and vast library); to some extent Fredersen himself, the father and industrialist who pays too little heed to his son's voice and who (at Rotwang's gala party) is associated with a decadent, soft, and effeminate bourgeoisie symbolized by the revelers in tuxedos and evening gowns who, while dancing, allow themselves to be led into the abyss by the False Maria; the working class, too, is guilty of impatience, of having heeded agitators (the False Maria) who incited rebellion—the mob is impulsive, irresponsible, "feminine" in a word ("the mob is a woman," Hitler said, and "the vast majority of people are so feminine"). Like Maria, Hitler comes to "possess" the mob through oratory and leads it back to the straight and narrow: rectitude is

nothing less than an obsession in *Metropolis.* Behind all these figures of guilt and sin (the statues of the seven deadly sins) looms the False Maria. It is in fact quite correct to say that she looms, and looms constantly: over the shoulders of Rotwang as he shows her to Fredersen; above the luminous cup from which she emerges; above the crowd of workers and bourgeois who carry her in triumphal processions; and even above the flames of the bonfire that consumes her. If, as I have suggested, she is, above and beyond her various avatars, sexuality itself, seen or treated as a profound, ultimate power, as danger, anguish, and horror; then omnipresent and ubiquitously reborn she becomes something that cannot be tolerated, that must be tracked down, eradicated, annihilated, and burned—the interminable Nazi extermination.

Many other traits typical of Hitler find counterparts in *Metropolis,* "I move forward with the infallible accuracy of the sleepwalker," Hitler wrote; in the film we see Freder receiving Maria's revelation and then proceeding toward his destiny with both arms outstretched in the manner of a sleepwalker. The Christ-like aspect of *Metropolis* has its parallel in the history of Hitler and the Nazi movement, which for a time had a quasi-religious dimension; according to Langer, Hitler cited the Bible and drew "comparisons between Christ and himself." The obsession with architecture that we find in *Metropolis* has its counterpart in Hitler's construction of the "eagle's nest" at Berchtesgaden, reached through "a long underground passage . . . enclosed by a heavy double door of bronze. At the end of the underground passage a wide lift, panelled with sheets of copper, awaits the visitor. Through a vertical shaft of 330 feet cut right through the rock, it rises up to the level of the Chancellor's dwelling place. . . . The visitor finds himself in a strong and massive building containing a gallery with Roman pillars, an immense circular hall with windows all around. . . . It gives the impression of being suspended in space, an almost overhanging wall of bare rock rises up abruptly." The first part of this description accords remarkably well with some of the images of the underground city in *Metropolis,* while the latter part describes the precipice from which the paranoid King Kong surveys his empire. In citing these lines by [then ambassador] François-Poncet, Langer notes that "Hitler often retires to this strange place to await instructions concerning the course he is to pursue." The images of petrifaction that we noted in *Metropolis* (the Tower of Babel, the enormous blocks of stone dragged by the slaves, Freder immured in stone during the impregnation scene), along with the constant presence of eyes and intense stares (Freder staring at his father embracing Maria, Freder hallucinating the erotic dance of the False Maria), were associated with the figure of the "bad" mother and its primal sexual dimension, both represented by the head of Medusa, I therefore find the following note by Robert Waite (from the epilogue to Langer's book) particularly striking: "He was infatuated with the head of the Medusa, once remarking that in von Stuck's painting the flashing eyes that turned men to stone and impotency reminded him of the eyes of his mother." As Hitler watched *Metropolis,* how could he not have been fascinated and hypnotized by the repeated hypnotic stares (of Fredersen and Rotwang and Maria and Freder), so like his own gaze, filled with the magical and paranoiac omnipotence of the stare that petrifies, engulfs, and penetrates, the gaze that wishes it were a disembodied orgasm, which in a frightening reversal injects its venom and like a vampire sucks the blood of its victim in an ersatz of displaced and disfigured sexuality. Langer speaks accurately of the "diffuse sexual function" of Hitler's eyes and notes: "When he meets persons for the first time he fixates his eyes on them as though to *bore through* them. There is a peculiar *glint* in them on these occasions that many have interpreted as an *hypnotic* quality" (my italics).

The Führer's speeches shaped the Nazi imagination, which ultimately produced the crematoriums of Auschwitz: from Hitler's mouth to the "world's anus." Hitler's mouth, all observers agree, was capable of casting a spell over multitudes, producing what Langer, citing Axel Heyst, calls a "veritable orgasm": "In his speeches we hear the suppressed voice of passion and wooing which is taken from the language of love; he utters a cry of hate and voluptuousness, a spasm of violence and cruelty." Auschwitz, anus of the world, enjoys the dubious honor of symbolizing the extremity of horror. In *Metropolis* these images are fused in a layer of destructive and sadistic anality, concretely and compactly expressed in Freder's hallucination of Moloch. As human operators fail to watch over their machines, a series of explosions takes place in the machine room. Liquids and gases are set free, bursting forth with destructive energies. Injured workers roll about on the ground or plunge into the void, so much dark debris. On a buckled, melted screen Freder's hallucination of Moloch's head takes shape. He sees an enormous, fiery mouth framed by huge teeth, into which diabolic creatures toss human beings with their pitchforks. But this fiery fantasy of consumption—the "bad" mother with her tongue of flame swallowing her young, the head of Medusa (flames as serpents) leaving Freder petrified—is further complicated, indeed contorted, into an anal scene of sadistic domination: if we reverse the motion, the unbending black columns of workers who climb toward the mouth-hole become streams of fecal matter expelled or excreted from the anal orifice. A hallucinatory fusion of organs and functions gives rise to a monstrous chiasm, which the Nazis put into practice: the mouth excretes ("filth" flowed from Hitler's mouth) and the anus devours (Auschwitz).

The head of Moloch can serve as emblem for a reinterpretation of the signifiers in *Metropolis* in anal terms: the corridors and labyrinths are like viscera; the blacks and whites are expressive (expressionist) of filth (the material of the walls, partitions, ground, and clothing); the glossy blackness and mechanical rigidity (relative sublimation) of the robot

and of Rotwang's prosthetic hand; the character structure of Fredersen; the explosions and destructions by gas, smoke, liquids, and so on. The phallic organization of *Metropolis,* which serves to cover the primal scenes and, in my view, to mask the horror of sexuality, incorporates this strong anality and thereby reinforces itself (as one says of concrete, but also of billy clubs) with fecal power in order to enclose the libidinal economy (the walls of the mother city are more visceral than uterine) within a rigid structure and orient it toward destruction.

P.S. If we view *Metropolis* as primarily a "spatialization," a shaping and figuration of fantasy, then we may speak of a Langian traversal or exploration of the unconscious, whose existence is recognized in aesthetic terms through an intuitive elaboration and construction of concrete forms, yielding a specific type of ecstasy (*jouissance*) in which knowledge of the unconscious remains trapped. The author plays on (*joue*), and takes pleasure from (*jouit de*), a magical commutability of differences (the two Marias). The Hitlerian exploration is quite different: the existence of the unconscious is recognized, but it is constantly displaced and exploited through active, activist miscognition (*méconnaissance*) of structures, of the intrinsic productivity and lawfulness of the unconscious, all mixed in with the ideological pap (along with a parallel political-economic fusion of social differences—bourgeois, petit bourgeois, workers, peasants— through an outpouring of nationalism and racism). Instead of knowledge we have "acting out," on a historical scale. The imaginary architecture of *Metropolis* becomes Berchtesgaden, Nuremberg, Berlin, Auschwitz. The nation wants all differences to be effaced. Radically different is the Freudian exploration: here the existence of the unconscious is recognized for the first time as a field open to the understanding, to the elaboration of theories and concepts; Freud envisioned a science, a critical rationality, and attempted to establish a praxis for liberating otherness. Here differences are spelled out and called forth (childhood, neurosis, arts, etc.) in order to be articulated.

It may be of some interest to point out that all three explorations, divergent as they are in many respects, start, along with innumerable other explorations of other realms, from the same place: another rich but identical mother-city, Vienna.

Gosta Werner (essay date Spring 1990)

SOURCE: "Fritz Lang and Goebbels," in *Film Quarterly,* Vol. 43, No. 3, Spring, 1990, pp. 24-7.

[*In the following essay, Werner traces the facts surrounding Lang's departure from Germany and the banning of his* The Testament of Dr. Mabuse.]

Myths are born and grow and flourish. Those who unthinkingly pass them on end up believing that they are facts. Repetition creates a cloak of seeming veracity which confuses gullible minds so that they cannot detect the truth underneath.

Thus every knowledgeable member of the film trade believes in the story of film director Fritz Lang's precipitate flight from Germany following on the banning of his film *The Testament of Dr. Mabuse.* The story goes that Dr. Goebbels, who was responsible for the banning, offered Lang the post of managing director of the entire German film industry. He stuck to his offer, maintains Lang himself, even after being told by Lang that he was a Jew—in actual fact Lang was half Jewish, his mother being Jewish. The story then goes on to say that Lang was given 24 hours to reconsider Goebbels's generous offer. Before nightfall Lang fled Berlin for Paris. He did this so precipitously that he did not even have time to draw money from the bank—banks closed in those days in Germany at half-past two.

But is this the true story? Thanks to material recently made available by the *Deutsche-Kinemathek* in Berlin—which placed it at the disposal of the German Film Museum (*Deutsches Filmmuseum*) in Frankfurt and its young and very able program director Ronny Loewe—we are now able to discover the facts. These are as follows.

The Nazi seizure of power occurred on 30 January 1933. For some time traditional German censorship continued without a break as if nothing had happened. It was not until six weeks later, on 14 March, that the *Ministerium für Volkserklärung und Propaganda* was set up, with Dr. Joseph Goebbels as its head. At that time the *Testament des Dr. Mabuse* was not quite completed, so the film had not been submitted to the censors.

No one expected the film to be banned, however, and on 21 March the official film journal *Der Kinematograph* was able to report that the première was to be on Friday 24 March at the large picture palace called *Ufa-Palast am Zoo.* Two days later, i.e., 23 March, *Der Kinematograph* informed its readers that the première had had to be put off as the film only that same day would reach the censors. The day after, 24 March, the same journal wrote that the postponement of the première had been due to "technical reasons."

Nothing further was revealed about the film until not quite one week later. On 30 March *Der Kinematograph* announced that the German Board of Film Censors had banned the film on the preceding day. The decision had been reached at a meeting of the Board, "under the chairmanship of Counsellor Zimmerman." The reason given was that it constituted a threat to law and order and public safety—in accordance with a regulation to be found in the Law of Censorship.

The film was passed, however, for distribution abroad—there was both a German and a French version. The German version was first shown in Vienna on 12 May 1933, but the French version had had its première a month earlier in Paris. The cutter of the film, Lothar Wolff, had even earlier taken the French-speaking material to Paris during the final stages of the making of the film and had completed the editing of the French version there. This gives the lie to the story that appears from time to time about the negative of the film having been smuggled to France in suitcases filled with dirty linen.

The film had also been sold to a number of European countries (besides Austria and France). Among them was Sweden, where, however, on 26 April 1933, the German version of the film was banned by the Swedish Board of Film Censors in accordance with paragraph six of the Royal Ordinance for Cinema Productions, the paragraph against the depicting of violence on the screen.

In Germany the last week of March 1933 turned out to be an eventful and momentous one for the German film industry. Goebbels had lost no time in preparing a large-scale drive to "renew" German film production as a whole. On March 28th, the day before the banning of the *Testament des Dr. Mabuse,* Goebbels had invited in the entire top personnel of the German film industry to a *Bierabend* in the Hotel Kaiserhof. Among those present were producers, directors, and technical staff. Certain reports have it that Fritz Lang was among those present.

It was in the course of this private party that Goebbels expressed his admiration for four films: he said they had made an indelible impression on him. The four were Eisenstein's *The Battleship Potemkin,* the American *Anna Karenina* (with Greta Garbo in the lead), Fritz Lang's *Die Nibelungen,* and Luis Trenker's *Der Rebell.* The last-mentioned film, whose motif is the struggle for freedom of the Tyrolese, had been released in Berlin two months earlier and was still being shown. Goebbels professed his admiration for Eisenstein's film for the power with which a political idea permeated the film. This, he thought, should set an example for the new, ideologically conscious and politically engaged film that he expected from all German producers, directors and manuscript writers—though of course the political overtones would have to be different!

It is very likely that Lang was present at this party. He was known to be a fierce nationalist and had at this time no intention of leaving Germany. The day before, 27 March, he had taken part in the founding of the "direction group" of the NSBO (= *Die Nationalsozialistische Betriebsorganisation*). Three other major film figures were also involved: Carl Boese, an experienced and highly successful director of comedies; Viktor Jansen, a young director of comedies for whom Billy Wilder had written a number of scripts; and Trenker, an actor and director reknowned for his dramatic "mountain pictures" with strongly nationalistic undertones.

Thus Lang can hardly have been surprised when, one day in April, shortly after the Kaiserhof party, he was summoned by Goebbels and offered the leadership of the entire German film production—instead of being only one of the four placed at the helm of the NSBO. It was not just a highly attractive offer. It was a logical [one] as well.

It was at this point, according to the story, that Fritz Lang, penniless and with Goebbels's offer ringing in his ears, fled headlong to Paris, only to return to Berlin and the Fatherland after the end of World War II.

Which parts of this story are facts and which are the "story"?

(A) The contact between Goebbels and Fritz Lang: Even though it is highly probable that Goebbels *did* offer Lang the post as head of the entire German film production, there is not a word about it in Goebbels's usually meticulous diary for the year 1933. Lang is not mentioned there at all.

(B) Lang's headlong flight to Paris:
The answer is to be found in Lang's passport. The passport, numbered 66 11 53.31, was issued in Berlin on 11 September 1931, and valid until 11 September 1936. It contains a large number of stamps and Fritz Lang's name is to be found alongside nearly every one of them. There are no visas or exit stamps for the months of February, March, and the beginning of April 1933. There is only one exit visa for Fritz Lang. It is made out by *Der Polizeipräsident in Berlin* and dated 23 June 1933. It is valid for exits for a period of six months. Up to that date Lang had therefore never left Germany.

The passport also contains several visas for entry into Belgium, every one issued in Berlin and at the end of June and July 1933. Further, during the same period Lang purchased foreign currency repeatedly at the *Weltreisebureau Union* in Unter den Linden in Berlin, totalling 1,366 *Reichsmark*. All these transactions are duly registered in the passport in dated stamps: 26 June, 27 June, 20 July. These days Lang must have been in Berlin.

According to the testimony of entry and exit stamps, in June and in July 1933 Lang visited England and Belgium, inter alia by air. He had a two-year visa for repeated entries into France. It was issued in London 20 June 1932 and was valid until 20 June 1934. The entry stamps for 1933 are all from June and July 1933, the first being dated 28 June, the last 31 July.

The foreign currency stamps from Berlin testify, as do the various entry and exit stamps, that between the journeys abroad in the summer of 1933 Lang returned to Berlin, which city he left finally only on 31 July 1933—four months after his legendary meeting with Goebbels and supposed dramatic escape.

Dr. Goebbels did not forget Lang and his films. When in October 1933 he celebrated his thirty-sixth birthday in his new and elegant official residence in Berlin he entertained himself and his guests in the evening by showing them the banned *Testament des Dr. Mabuse.* Lang, meanwhile, was in France, where he was shortly to begin filming *Liliom.*

Dietrich Neumann (essay date 1994)

SOURCE: "The Urbanistic Vision in Fritz Lang's *Metropolis*," in *Dancing in the Volcano: Essays on the Culture of the Weimar Republic,* Camden House, 1994, pp. 143-54.

[*In the following essay, Neumann discusses the urban architecture of Lang's* Metropolis *in light of contemporary thought about monumentalism, technological progress, and skyscrapers.*]

Fritz Lang's *Metropolis* is widely considered one of the great classics of the cinema, celebrated and described in every anthology on the history of the motion picture. It was the first feature length science fiction film ever and had an enormous influence on later productions. It has rightly been regarded as a paradigmatic product of Weimar culture, reflecting the rich variety of its contemporary discourse.

When the film was finally released in January 1927 after two years of a well orchestrated advertising campaign, it was considered a major cultural event all over Europe and in the United States. In New York thousands lined up on Broadway in April 1927 to see it, and the *New York Times* alone printed seven different reviews of it. The reasons for its fame, however, are curiously difficult to determine. The majority of contemporary reviews were in fact critical, and the public success was not sufficient to compensate for the losses that Europe's most expensive film production to that date had caused.

Metropolis is set in a city of the future, ruled by the almighty John Frederson from his office at the top of a gigantic central tower, called the "New Tower of Babel." The buzzing skyscraper city with its many layers of traffic is kept alive by the machinery underground, which is operated under dangerous conditions by an army of slaves living in monotonous buildings situated even deeper underground. Fatal accidents seem to be frequent, and in one dramatic sequence the central machine turns into a hungry, man-eating monster. The son of the city's emperor, Freder, spends his time leisurely at sporting events and in a harem-like pleasure garden with his friends. One day, however, he meets Mary, a woman from the underground, who acts as the quasi-Christian priestess of some primitive cult, preaching peaceful change to the workers in ancient catacombs deep beneath the city. Freder falls madly in love and suddenly becomes aware of the injustice around him. His father, concerned about the awakened conscience of his son, secretly plots, with the help of a mad scientist, to keep control of his son's emotions through a robot look-alike of Mary; Mary is kidnapped, and her features are duplicated onto the metallic machine. This robot soon gets out of control and preaches violent revolution to the workers. The ensuing uproar leads to the destruction of the machines and the flooding of the underground housing quarters. In the meantime the evil robot with Mary's features has made its way to a party in the city above, where it engages in an elaborate dance performance promising sexual pleasures to upper class businessmen. Finally the masses discover that they have been misled and burn the robot Mary at the stake in a fire fueled by technological debris. Only at the last minute can the real Mary escape from the scientist's laboratory and, reunited with Freder, save the children from drowning in the flooded subterranean houses, survive a dramatic fight with the mad scientist on the roof of the cathedral, convert Freder's father into a conscientious and humane ruler and appease the revolutionary masses with the slogan: "The heart has to be the mediator between the hand and the mind."

It comes as no surprise that many contemporary critics pointed sarcastically to the weaknesses of this plot. Some of them were especially disappointed by the unconvincing reconciliation at the end; others claimed that the love story should have received more attention. Critics in the immediate postwar period, such as Lotte Eisner in *The Haunted Screen* and Siegfried Kracauer in *From Caligari to Hitler* emphasized protofascistic elements in the people's quiet submission under a dictator and the treatment of the masses in a purely ornamental fashion. In recent years *Metropolis* has frequently been examined for its Freudian connotations and its rather obvious sexual metaphors. Anton Kaes has discussed the film's fascination with the vices and virtues of technology and compared it to other contemporary voices, such as the expressionist theater of Georg Kaiser, Ernst Toller, or Karel Capek, and the writings of Ernst Jünger and H.G. Wells. I would like to add to this the possible connection to the almost entirely forgotten film *Algol,* which was released in Germany in 1920, telling the story of a miner, who accepts a miraculous perpetual-motion machine from a stranger. This devilish contraption enables him to build a world-embracing empire based on unlimited industrial power. Robert Herne, the miner who makes the Faustian bargain, gains fame and wealth but loses his love and his happiness and finally destroys the machines in order to keep them away from his evil and decadent son. *Algol* not only shows striking similarities to *Metropolis* in its set design, but also seems to anticipate elements of *Metropolis'* story line.

The long-lasting interest in the film *Metropolis* and the diversity of interpretations show that the movie is by no means easy to categorize or analyze. It has many layers of meaning, speaks different languages, and in no way offers a coherent picture. Its interpretation can never be complete. One of the reasons for this is the simple fact that it is the product of a collaboration, of many compromises and coincidences. Apart from Fritz Lang, the director, there was his wife, Thea von Harbou, who wrote the novel and the film script; the imaginative cameraman Karl Freund also contributed to the film along with several set designers under the leadership of Erich Kettelhut. When the film was finished it was three hours long and had to be edited heavily for a general audience with a limited attention span. These cuts were apparently not carried out under Lang's supervision. Fritz Lang later explained away the incoherence of the film's plot by attributing the much-criticized ending of the film to his wife Thea von Harbou. In a famous interview with Peter Bogdanovich he declared: "I was then not as politically conscious as I am today. You cannot make a socially responsible film by saying 'the heart has to be the mediator between the hand and the mind.' I mean that is silly, really. But I was interested in machines." Lang used to illustrate his matured political consciousness by telling the famous anecdote of how in 1933 Joseph Goebbels, Hitler's Propaganda Minister, told him that Hitler had been very impressed by the *Nibelungen* and *Metropolis,* and that he wanted Lang to become the official film director for the future propaganda movies of the Third Reich. Fritz Lang told Goebbels he would think about it, but instead he packed his bags and left Germany on the evening of the same day. Lang's former wife Thea von Harbou, however, remained in Germany and joined the National Socialist Party.

> **The long-lasting interest in the film *Metropolis* and the diversity of interpretations show that the movie is by no means easy to categorize or analyze. It has many layers of meaning, speaks different languages, and in no way offers a coherent picture. Its interpretation can never be complete.**
> **—*Dietrich Neumann***

From the beginning the film's critics have almost unanimously expressed great admiration for *Metropolis'* impressive set design. The young Spanish film critic Louis Buñuel, soon to become a famous director himself, wrote in 1927:

Metropolis surpasses all expectations and enchants

us as the most beautiful picture album imaginable. Hunte overwhelms us with his grandiose vision of the city of the year 2000. . . . Now and forever the architect is going to replace the set designer. The movie is going to be the faithful translator of the architect's boldest dreams.

Astonishingly, the film's architecture is one of the few features that has not been analyzed in any detail up to now; and yet the urbanistic vision of Metropolis offers a glimpse of the intense discussion of Americanism and issues of monumentality in contemporary German architecture.

The film set was designed in 1925 and 1926 by the architects Erich Kettelhut and Otto Hunte in close cooperation with Fritz Lang himself, who had originally planned to become an architect and was an excellent draughtsman. More than once he overruled Kettelhut's decisions. The architecture of the film set was apparently among those parts of the film that suffered only slightly from the heavy cuts made after the first screening. Research in this area is also made easier by the fact that Kettelhut's personal recollections have survived and many of his sketches are preserved in archives in Berlin, Frankfurt, Paris, and London.

What do we know about this city of the future? There are several spatial layers underground: the ancient catacombs, where Mary reigns; gigantic caves with housing quarters for the workmen and their families; and the halls with the mighty machines. Above ground there are the towering buildings and many layers of traffic, overshadowed by the sublime "New Tower of Babel" in the center. Somewhere in this city are a gothic cathedral, a sports stadium, a nightclub, and the pleasure gardens of the "jeunesse doré." The haunted house of Rotwang the inventor has survived between skyscrapers and highway overpasses. It is, as the novel tells us, "older than the city," older than its cathedral, dark, threatening, and forbidding.

Fritz Lang asserted that the original idea for the movie *Metropolis* was conceived on a trip to the United States which he undertook with his producer Erich Pommer in 1924 in order to study American film production and to promote his most recent film, the great medieval epic *Nibelungen.* Lang stayed in New York and Los Angeles and met Ernst Lubitsch, Charlie Chaplin, and Mary Pickford. But in the end it was not U.S. film production that impressed Lang most, but the American landscape and the sight of New York city by night.

After Lang's return in November 1924 he shared his ideas and impressions with the leading German film journal:

> Where is the American film of the "Grand Canyon," the film of the "Yellowstone Park," or the film about one of those Babels of stone which are the Ameri-

can Cities? The view of New York by night is a beacon of beauty strong enough to be the centerpiece of a film. . . . There are flashes of red and blue and gleaming white, screaming green . . . streets full of moving, turning, spiraling lights, and high above the cars and elevated trains skyscrapers appear in blue and gold, white, and purple and still higher above there are advertisements surpassing the stars with their light.

What Lang had witnessed here was not only the progress that had been made in advertising technology, but also the newly emerging fashion of an "architecture of the night," colored floodlight illumination of the tops of skyscrapers, often carefully planned and orchestrated by lighting engineers and artists. Fritz Lang's enthusiastic descriptions of this phenomenon are still palpable in Thea von Harbou's account of Metropolis as a city "bathed in an ecstasy of brightness, built from squares of light." Fritz Lang tried to capture the overwhelming impression of the multitude of lights on Broadway with his camera by exposing the film twice.

The general interest in science fiction and in views of the future had been greatly enhanced by the success of H.G. Wells's novels, such as *The Time Machine* and *War of the Worlds,* which had sold millions of copies since the turn of the century and were already considered classics by 1924, when Lang started thinking about his new film. It is not surprising that H.G. Wells was asked for his opinion of this new German science fiction movie by the *New York Times,* for which he commented regularly on current events. Wells published a long essay about *Metropolis* in the *Times Sunday Magazine* on 17 April 1927. That essay has remained the only analysis that dealt with *Metropolis'* urbanistic vision in any detail.

H.G. Wells was clearly not amused. He thought *Metropolis* was by far the "silliest film he had ever seen." He was annoyed because he recognized in *Metropolis* "decaying fragments" of his own juvenile work *The Sleeper Awakes* (1897), where he had described the London of the future as a monstrous skyscraper fortress in the middle of a destroyed landscape which contained on varying levels dark factories, living quarters for the workers, and in the higher, lighter regions the apartments of the privileged. H.G. Wells was convinced that such a vision was by now outdated. He argued that the real estate market would lead to the location of industry and housing for the poor in suburbs instead of underneath the city. He wrote, "This vertical social stratification is stale old stuff. So far from being a hundred years hence, *Metropolis* in its forms and shapes is already as a possibility a third of a century out of date." Wells argued that if Lang had talked to some contemporary architects his vision would have been more accurate.

Such accusations are not entirely fair. Of course Lang had *not* intended to produce a realistic projection of urban development or even an ideal city, because such a utopia would have provided an unlikely background for a dramatic battle between good and evil. And given Lang's interest in the architectural profession, we can assume that he was familiar with the visions of contemporary architects, such as Antonio Sant' Elia's Città Futurista of 1914, Auguste Perret's skyscrapers of 1921, Corbusier's Plan Voisin of 1922, and Hugh Ferriss' visions of a future New York, which he developed from 1922 onwards. All of these images had recently been published in Germany and might have informed the design of the film set in 1925 and 1926. Lang's city, however, was planned not on a grid like that of Manhattan or Corbusier's vision, but grouped around one dominating central tower.

This central building is worth closer inspection: it not only houses the headquarters of the almighty ruler, but also functions as central intersection for all traffic in the city. As we know from the film script, all the different means of transport were to flow together in the building's lower stories, and batteries of elevators, partly visible on the outside, would also connect it to the central airport on the top and to the halls for machinery underground. Among the abundant allusions to Christianity and the Old Testament in the film, the most obvious is to the Tower of Babel. The biblical story of this building's erection and destruction is told by Mary in a visionary sequence. *Metropolis'* central tower reveals knowledge of the numerous illustrations of this biblical motif throughout the history of art, such as Peter Bruegel's painting of 1563. Central towers had also been an occasional feature in utopian renaissance cities by Perret, Filarete, and others.

But there are also contemporary German sources. In the years immediately following the Great War, a group of young architects, such as Bruno Taut, Hans Scharoun, and Walter Gropius had published sketches showing a glowing central religious building hovering high above the roofs of a city. Bruno Taut had coined the term *Stadtkrone* (citycrown) for these designs, and in 1919 Walter Gropius had written in the first Bauhaus Manifesto:

> Together let us desire, conceive, and create the new structure of the future, which will embrace architecture and sculpture and painting in one unity and which will one day rise toward heaven from the hands of a million workers like the crystal symbol of a new faith.

All these designs were clearly meant as religious buildings and cannot be directly compared to the central office tower of *Metropolis,* although there are some obvious formal similarities. The missing link here is to be found by examining a chapter in German architectural history that has so far been widely overlooked: between 1920 and 1925 German architects, politicians, and citizens were gripped by what contemporaries called a skyscraper mania. In a wave of enthusiasm unparalleled by anything else at that time and by far surpassing the attention given to the Bauhaus and the Modern Movement, conservative architects in Germany designed thousands of skyscrapers for all major and minor cities. Such designs were entirely unrealistic given the economic constraints of the time, and none of them was built. Office space was not nearly as badly needed as housing, but one frequently repeated argument in favor of skyscrapers claimed that huge office towers could help to relieve the enormous housing shortage by opening up apartments in the center city that had been used as offices. Surprisingly, this skyscraper craze was far removed from Weimar Americanism and infatuation with U. S. mass culture. Quite the contrary, it served as a platform for the anti-Americanism of conservative architects, citizens, and journalists. Innumerable statements had accused American skyscrapers of depriving their neighbors of light and air and of being the most vulgar symbols of rampant capitalism. Even Siegfried Kracauer, in 1921, called them "towering monsters, owing their existence to the unlimited greed of beastly capitalism, assembled in the most chaotic and senseless fashion, clad in a luxurious fake architecture, which is far from appropriate for its profane purpose. . . ." Kracauer and many others, however, seemed determined that Germany should build skyscrapers anyway, as long as they were different from the American examples. Several architects went as far as to announce a "Germanization of the skyscraper" and claimed that the Germans were destined to create, on a higher cultural level, a valid alternative to this American invention, revealing for the first time "the true inner meaning of the skyscraper." The German high-rise building, such critics claimed, would be less historicist than the American skyscraper, and, as a result of highly restricted and socially responsible city planning, there would be just one huge building in the center of each city, a modern version of the medieval cathedral. "By celebrating the idea of labor, the skyscraper aspires to continue the role of the cathedral, which dominated the cityscape and was a symbol for the metaphysical longings and the spiritual tenure of the Middle Ages," wrote a critic in 1923. Some architects took this reference to the cathedral literally; they employed a gothicizing verticality in the facades and demanded, that their design should be executed in a common effort by the whole populace, in a fashion similar to the building of a gothic cathedral, and should be conceived and executed through the collaboration of different masters.

Many of the architects' statements show that these skyscraper projects owed their attraction to a large degree to their apparent symbolic and political potential. Many conservatives believed that the erection of skyscrapers could "prove visibly that the Germans are not a dying populace, but able to work and able to build new paths to a new ascent." The lost war and the enormous reparation payments of the Versailles treaty led to a desperate nationalism and to the idea that a monumental symbolic gesture could demonstrate the undestroyed German will to reemerge after the war and offer a reconciliation with the lost spirituality of the Middle Ages. In the disguise of a twentieth century building type, these designs continued a tradition of gigantic national monuments that had culminated for the first time in Karl Friedrich Schinkel's 1814 plan for a cathedral to celebrate the victory over Napoleon. This event had caused a wave of nationalist sentiment and the first prospect of German unification, pursued by many with an almost religious fervor. Karl Friedrich Schinkel wanted his monumental cathedral for this new religion to be placed in the center of Berlin, at the Leipziger Platz. It would have had a cruciform plan and a central neo-Gothic spire at an unprecedented height of 1000 feet. Gothic was then considered the most original German style, evoking reminiscences of allegedly happier medieval times. Nothing came of Schinkel's project, but the idea remained strong and eventually led not only to the completion of Cologne Cathedral but also to the subject of a commemorative monument in Leipzig, where the famous Battle of Nations against Napoleon had taken place. Finally, in 1897, a competition was held for the so called *Völkerschlachtdenkmal* (Monument to the Battle of Nations) in Leipzig, and this contest was won by Bruno Schmitz, an architect who already had a solid reputation as a designer of monuments. The competition had asked for a monumental building in a new German style which was not historicist but powerful, simple, and heroic. Between 1897 and 1913 Bruno Schmitz erected an artificial mound and on top of it a looming, towering structure 91 meters high out of bare concrete and rock-faced German granite. With its dimly lit chambers inside, its artificial lake, and a seemingly endless approach on the outside, the monument became a temple of fame and a symbol of national power and self-confidence.

At the same time that Bruno Schmitz was supervising the final work on the *Völkerschlachtdenkmal,* in the year 1910, he designed a building for Berlin that became known as the first German skyscraper design. As a monumental round tower it not only drew heavily on the forms developed for the *Völkerschlachtdenkmal*, but was also designed for precisely the same spot where Schinkel, a century earlier, had suggested his cathedral. Schmitz's compact tower design provided a second important prototype for the formal solution of the skyscraper craze in the early Twenties. It clearly influenced designs such as Leipzig's highly popular 1920 'Messeturm' (Trade Fair Tower). The heavy forms of the Leipzig Monument also provided a formal model for the final version of Lang's and Kettelhut's design for their New Tower of Babel.

Left wing avant-garde architects in Germany, such as Walter Gropius, the director of the Bauhaus, Mies van der Rohe, and Hans Scharoun did not share the enthusiasm for skyscrapers. They felt that these structures represented the forces of the past. After a short infatuation with crystal cathedrals directly after the war, most of them were interested in social housing, prefabrication, and the truthful display of structural elements. The famous critic Adolf Behne articulated their opinion: "Most of the suddenly appearing Ideal-Skyscraper-Designs are reminders of the epoch of the Bismarck memorial towers and the Leipzig Battle of Nations Monument: monumental arts and crafts kitsch." And he continued: "There is no reason to turn the skyscraper into a symbol with much rigor, seriousness, and dignity. It is merely a building for offices and stores, no reason for any pathos whatsoever." The few skyscraper projects that the avant-garde architects provided were clearly antihistoricist and as unmonumental as a skyscraper could be. Walter Gropius, for instance, in his design for the Chicago Tribune in 1922 gave up the idea of a unified and coherent geometric form in favor of an asymmetrical stack of building blocks and a facade that only displayed the structure of its steel frame. Mies van der Rohe was even more radical, designing a curvilinear skyscraper in 1922 without any reference to traditional architecture. The building had a reflective glass surface and was to be transparent, which meant a complete negation of the building as such—probably the most powerful possible rejection of the monumental dreams of the time. The avant-garde clearly rejected the centralized approach to city planning and favored instead an arrangement of endlessly repeatable housing blocks that would be carefully distanced from each other to ensure the same amount of sunlight for everyone.

The extent to which set designer Erich Kettelhut was aware of the ongoing discussion about high-rise buildings and town planning both in the U. S. and in Europe becomes apparent from his numerous preliminary sketches for *Metropolis,* which have been preserved in the archives of the *Cinematheque Française* and the *Deutsche Kinemathek* in Berlin. A wealth of imaginary sketches flash up for only seconds in the film, showing fantastic versions of visionary setback skyscrapers or rigid structural steel skeletons with enormously protruding floors. Kettelhut worked in different media, providing simple ink line drawings as well as lavish watercolors and skillfully shaded pastels.

In his first version for the central area of *Metropolis* in 1925, Kettelhut showed a skillfully designed central urban intersection with several layers of traffic for pedestrians, cars, and railroads. The pedestrians stroll leisurely, there seems to be ample parking space, and bright sunlight hits the southern side of the street. An old Gothic cathedral serves as the centerpiece in the distance, surrounded by a densely grouped range of medieval buildings.

As if to support the conservative architects' contention that the skyscraper should take over the role of the cathedral as a new temple of labor, Lang or Kettelhut crossed out the cathedral in the original drawing with the note: "To be replaced by the Tower of Babel."

In a second version, the cathedral is gone, replaced by a functional skyscraper with a gigantic landing platform on its top, a common motif in science fiction since the turn of the century. This tower seems to have almost 50 stories, thus easily surpassing the buildings around it. The adjacent buildings in this version clearly display Kettelhut's knowledge of current architectural discussions. The skyscrapers are set back, nonmonumental, and unadorned, and they display their structural frame of steel or reinforced concrete. Some even seem to recall Mies van der Rohe's curvilinear skyscraper, or the structural rationalism of Walter Gropius' highrise design. The somewhat pleasant view of a future city displayed in both of Kettelhut's preliminary drawings is far from the apocalyptic vision that Thea von Harbou had described so vividly in her novel. One can only speculate that after the second version was designed there must have been an encounter between Lang and Kettelhut, in which Lang made it clear that such a pleasant vision was not what he had in mind: The city should be dark, threatening, overwhelming, nightmarish. At any rate, Kettelhut's final version provided what Lang wanted.

In that final version, the buildings had developed considerably. The street had become the dark and narrow abyss that the critics of the skyscraper had always prophesied. And the standpoint of the viewer had been lifted into the air, far away from any visual contact with the people who crowded the streets below.

The most important metamorphosis was that of the central tower, which had grown from about fifty stories to almost 200. Instead of the slender forms of a conical support for the elegant landing platform, we now have a looming, heavy mass, whose landing platforms have shrunk to nonfunctional wings. The similarity of this tower to the *Völkerschlachtdenkmal* is striking.

For anyone familiar with architectural debates in the Weimar Republic Kettelhut's final version not only stood for the most conservative approach to skyscraper design and city planning, but also clearly harked back to the German empire with its connotations of nationalism, imperialism, and a centralized system. Such a dark vision had been adopted by Lang and Kettelhut to represent the regime of the merciless John Frederson.

Conservative critics obviously did not notice the irony in Kettelhut's choice. They drew enthusiastic parallels between the film and the symbolic content of the *Völkerschlacht-denkmal*. After the first screening on 11 January 1927, one critic wrote: "This film is German in its metaphysical and technical boundlessness, in the immoderateness of its will and the chaotic stream of its ideas. This is monumental, out-

ward-pressing expressionist film of the most fantastic technique. It is a tower of Babel to the world." And another critic declared: "The film *Metropolis* is a matter of the material, it is the *Völkerschlachtdenkmal* of the movies."

By taking this part as a symbol for the whole, the critics overlooked the fact that the film *Metropolis,* especially in its architecture, was by no means a simple celebration of conservative hopes and values. On the contrary, the set contains many clues that its designers sympathized with the opposite side of the political spectrum. The most striking antithesis to the looming tower with its reference to the *Völkerschlachtdenkmal* is to be found in the workers' living quarters underground. In the central square is a monument with a huge gong which calls workers to work, a symbol of repression. Significantly, the base for this gong is appropriately modeled on Walter Gropius' dynamic monument for striking miners who had been shot dead in Weimar during riots in the year 1921. Right-wing politicians had heavily criticized Walter Gropius for this monument. Thus in both levels of the city, one finds references to current debates on monumental architecture and the architecture of monuments.

> ***Metropolis* had an almost immediate impact on urbanistic visions in other films and in popular culture, where the discussion on monumentality and the role of the skyscraper continued.**
> **—*Dietrich Neumann***

The only references to contemporary expressionist architecture in Germany are to be found in the places of vice, such as the "Yoshiwara Nightclub" and the pleasure gardens of the elite's sons, thereby successfully labeling expressionistic architecture as decadent. It is no coincidence that "Yoshiwara," the name of Tokyo's red-light district, was chosen for this temple of vice; Thea von Harbou's novel contains numerous openly racist allusions to Asians being connected to gambling, crime, and prostitution. In contrast, the old Gothic Cathedral, where the final reconciliation takes place, clearly identifies the city as German, or at least northern European. (The scenes in the medieval cathedral also reflect the impression that the recent American production of *The Hunchback of Notre Dame,* after Victor Hugo's novel, had made on its German audience in 1924.)

Metropolis had an almost immediate impact on urbanistic visions in other films and in popular culture, where the discussion on monumentality and the role of the skyscraper continued. The first such response was the American science fiction comedy *Just Imagine* of 1930 by Stephen Goosson. This film's gigantic set of a future city reflected Hugh Ferriss's recently published drawings for a "Metropolis of Tomorrow" featuring high-rise buildings spaciously located on a grid which extended endlessly.

In 1936 H.G. Wells became involved in creating a science fiction movie according to his own ideas, which turned out to be a somewhat belated comment on Fritz Lang's *Metropolis.* H.G. Wells wrote the screenplay and called it *Things to Come.* The film traces the story of "Everytown" from 1936 through the following 100 years, when after a devastating war (Wells clearly anticipated the Second World War) and long decades of suffering under diseases and despotic rulers, technology and reason finally lead to the erection of a new "Everytown" in 2036, where a new dispute over the vice and virtue of progress and technology is fueled over the launching of a rocket to explore the moon.

Although Alexander Corda was the producer and William Cameron Menzies the director, H.G. Wells seems to have been a constant presence at the production. He circulated a memorandum to the members of the film crew in which he wrote: "As a general rule you may take it that whatever Lang did in *Metropolis* is the exact contrary of what we want done here."

Wells hired former Bauhaus-member Lászlò Moholy-Nagy as set designer. Moholy-Nagy responded to Wells's challenge by designing a city of the future consisting of transparent cones and glass-clad skeletal towers. The towers are clearly reminiscent of Mies van der Rohe's curvilinear glass skyscraper of 1922, thereby adopting Mies's consciously antimonumental response to the heavy towers of his conservative colleagues. As Lászlò Moholy-Nagy's wife Sybil later remembered, he wanted to "eliminate solid form. Houses were no longer obstacles to, but receptacles of man's natural life force, light. There were no walls, but skeletons of steel, screened with glass and plastic sheets."

H.G. Wells decided in the end, however, that this design was still not radical enough as an antithesis to the skyscrapers in *Metropolis.* He asked another designer, Vincent Korda, the producer's brother, to create a city of the future which was even more literally the opposite of Lang's skyscrapers. Instead of pursuing the discussion of monumental and nonmonumental skyscrapers, Wells and Korda returned to the fundamental dichotomy between the gendered spaces of a skyscraper city and their counterpart in the subterranean caves, which Fritz Lang had already explored. In the final section of *Things to Come,* the old city of "Everytown" has completely vanished, the surface of the earth has been returned to nature, and instead Everytown of the year 2036 is entirely dug into the ground in a gigantic womb-like cavern. The skyscrapers of New York, which had been the departure point for Fritz Lang, shine up as a faded memory in *Things to Come,* only to be seen on films for educational purposes.

"What a funny place New York was," says one little girl, "all sticking up and full of windows."

Metropolis' central looming tower with an airport on top enjoyed a lasting popularity on the covers of science fiction magazines. More recently the film has found an echo in the sets of such contemporary movies as *Bladerunner* and *Batman.*

The urban architecture of *Metropolis* seems both to embrace and undermine the current notions of monumentalism, technological progress, and Americanism. The film will continue to elicit new readings and serve as a tool to unfold the rich texture of contemporary discourse in Weimar Germany. Its complexity and contradictions will continue to serve as a powerful example against the vision of a coherent, unifying notion of modernity.

FURTHER READING

Biography

Bernstein, Matthew. "Fritz Lang, Incorporated." *Velvet Light Trap,* No. 22 (1986): 33-52.
> Provides an overview of the development and downfall of Lang's independent production company Diana Productions, Inc.

Rolfe, Hilda. "The Perfectionist." *Film Comment* 28, No. 6 (November-December 1992): 2-4.
> Provides a personal view of Lang as the perfectionist behind the camera.

Criticism

Anstey, Edgar. A review of *Scarlet Street. The Spectator* 176, No. 6140 (1 March 1946): 219.
> Complains that *Scarlet Street* does not live up to its imaginative opening.

Burch, Noel. "Fritz Lang: The German Period." In *Cinema: A Critical Dictionary: The Major Film-makers,* edited by Richard Roud, pp. 583-99. New York: The Viking Press, 1980.
> Outlines the different stages and achievements of Lang's German period.

Conley, Tom. "Writing *Scarlet Street*." *Comparative Literature* 98, No. 5 (December 1983): 1085-1109.
> Discusses the use of letters and words in Lang's *Scarlet Street.*

Cooper, Stephen. "Sex/Knowledge/Power in the Detective Genre." *Film Quarterly* XLII, No. 3 (Spring 1988): 23-30.

Discusses Lang's *The Big Heat,* John Huston's *The Maltese Falcon,* Roman Polanski's *Chinatown,* and Alan Parker's *Angel Heart* in terms of their place in the detective genre.

Green, Graham. A review *The Fury. The Spectator* 158, No. 5636 (3 July 1936): 15.
    Praises the extraordinary achievement of Lang's *The Fury.*

Huyssen, Andreas. "The Vamp and the Machine: Technology and Sexuality in Fritz Lang's *Metropolis.*" *New German Critique,* No. 24-25 (Fall/Winter 1981/2): 221-37.
    Discusses how Lang fuses the expressionist fear of technology to man's fear of a threatening female sexuality in *Metropolis.*

Insdorf, Annette. "A Silent Classic Gets Some 80's Music." *The New York Times* CXXXIII, No. 46,127 (5 August 1984): 15, 20.
    Asserts that purists might be upset at the disco rhythms added to Lang's *Metropolis,* but that others may enjoy the new life that the music adds to the director's film.

Johnston, Sheila. "Video/Dr. Mabuse the Gambler." *Film and Filming,* No. 334 (July 1982): 32-3.
    Calls Lang's *Dr. Mabuse* "extremely accessible to anyone prepared to accept the different conventions and slow pacing of the German silent period purely and simply as a finely crafted and enthralling piece of cinema."

Jubak, James. "Lang and Parole: Character and Narrative in 'Doctor Mabuse, der Spieler.'" *Film Criticism* IV, No. 1 (Fall 1979): 25-34.
    Asserts that Lang's *Doctor Mabuse, der Spieler* "questions the dominant ideology of character in the classical film. It suggests a view of character as unstable, inconsistent, and only fitfully in control of its own destiny."

Kaplan, E. Ann. "Fritz Lang and German Expressionism: A Reading of *Dr. Mabuse, der Speiler.*" In *Passion and Rebellion: The Expressionist Heritage,* edited by Stephen Eric Bronner and Douglas Kellner, pp. 398-408. New York: Universe Books, 1983.
    Analyzes Lang's *Dr. Mabuse, der Spieler* in terms of German expressionism and looks at the film as art, beyond the political implications of the time.

Kuntzel, Thierry. "The Film-Work." *Enclitic* 2, No. 1 (Spring 1978): 39-62.
    Presents different methods of reading Lang's *M.*

Mellenkamp, Patricia. "Oedipus and the Robot in *Metropolis.*" *Enclitic* 5, No. 1 (1991): 20-42.
    Discusses Lang's *Metropolis* and how it fits into German Expressionism.

Prawer, S.S. "The Cost-Effective Visionary." *TLS,* No. 3906 (21 January 1977): 61-2.
    Discusses the control that Lang exerts over his films, and how that control makes each of his films his own, focusing specifically on *Lotte Eisner.*

Stiles, Victoria M. "Fritz Lang's Definitive Siegfried and Its Versions." *Literature Film Quarterly* 13, No. 4 (1985): 258-74.
    Outlines and compares the different versions of Lang's *Siegfried* that have been released by distributors.

———. "The Siegfried Legend and the Silent Screen . . . . Fritz Lang's Interpretation of a Hero Saga." *Literature Film Quarterly* 8, No. 4 (1980): 232-36.
    Analyzes the literary aspects of Lang's *Die Nibelungen,* "specifically on the function of symbolic imagery."

Thomson, David. "Lang's Ministry." *Sight and Sound* 46, No. 2 (Spring 1977): 114-18.
    Praises Lang for "compress[ing] so much into 85 minutes and mak[ing] a work more lucid than the novel" in *The Ministry of Fear.*

Wood, Robin. "Fritz Lang: 1936-60." In *Cinema: A Critical Dictionary: The Major Film-makers,* edited by Richard Roud, pp. 599-609. New York: Viking Press, 1980.
    Provides an overview of Lang's films and career.

Additional coverage of Lang's life and career is contained in the following sources published by Gale: *Contemporary Authors,* Vols. 77-80; *Contemporary Authors New Revision Series,* Vol. 30.

Tim O'Brien
1946-

(Full name William Timothy O'Brien) American novelist, short story writer, and journalist.

The following entry presents criticism of O'Brien's work through 1995. For further information on his life and career, see *CLC*, Volumes 7, 19, and 40.

INTRODUCTION

A veteran of the Vietnam War, O'Brien is best known for his fiction about the wartime experiences of American soldiers in Vietnam, often combining the realism of war zone journalism with the surrealism of a soldier's daydreams. The novel *Going after Cacciato* (1978), which won the 1978 National Book Award, and the short story collection *The Things They Carried* (1990), which was nominated for a Pulitzer Prize and a National Book Critics Circle Award in 1991, are valued by many as definitive fictional works about the war. Most of O'Brien's writings deal with the Vietnam War and his stories commonly blend memories of his own experiences with fictional treatments of such themes as courage, heroism, brutal violence, and emotional upheaval in the face of death and destruction by impersonal, global forces. O'Brien's interweaving of fact and fiction has generated much commentary, particularly about the ambiguous nature of his narratives and the metafictional quality of his storytelling techniques. Pico Iyer remarked that "O'Brien's clean, incantatory prose always hovers on the edge of dream, and his specialty is that twilight zone of chimeras and fears and fantasies where nobody knows what's true and what is not."

Biographical Information

Born in 1946 in Austin, Minnesota to William T. O'Brien, an insurance salesman, and Ava Schulz O'Brien, a teacher, O'Brien moved with his family to Worthington, Minnesota, when he was ten years old. As a youth, he studied the techniques of magic and then practiced the art, fascinated by the mystery of illusion. In 1968 O'Brien graduated summa cum laude from Macalester College in St. Paul, Minnesota, with a bachelor's degree in political science. Soon after he was drafted into the U.S. Army. He completed basic and advanced-infantry training at Fort Lewis, Washington, and arrived in Vietnam in 1969. He served with the 198th Infantry (Alpha Company) in the Quang Ngai region, near the South China Sea, where he earned a Purple Heart for wounds suffered at My Lai a year after the infamous massacre. During this time, O'Brien began writing vignettes about his army experience. Following an honorable discharge as an infantry sergeant in

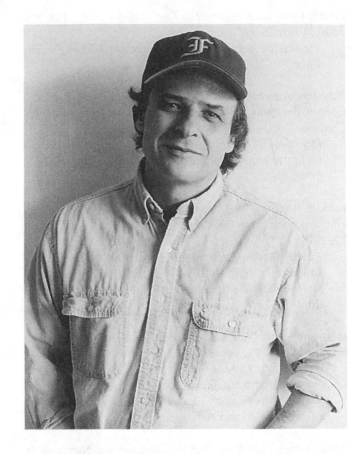

1970, O'Brien accepted a scholarship to attend Harvard University as a graduate student in government studies. In 1971 he received an internship at the *Washington Post* and continued to work there as a national-affairs reporter until 1974. Meanwhile, O'Brien continued to write stories, publishing some of them in national periodicals. These he collected into his first book, *If I Die in a Combat Zone, Box Me Up and Ship Me Home* (1973); two years later he published his first novel, *Northern Lights* (1975). After leaving Harvard in 1976 without a degree, O'Brien devoted himself to writing fiction full-time, regularly contributing to numerous magazines and often submitting selected stories to anthologies. The publication of *Going after Cacciato* in 1978 established O'Brien as a major voice of war literature, although his next novel, *The Nuclear Age* (1985), was generally not well received. The critically acclaimed *The Things They Carried* earned the 1990 *Chicago Tribune* Heartland Award and a listing in the *New York Times Book Review* as one of the six best works of fiction published in 1990. Since then, O'Brien has published the novel *In the Lake of the Woods* (1994).

Major Works

Classified as both a novel and a memoir, *If I Die* concerns the initiation of an inexperienced and bemused young man into the harsh realities of war. The newspaper and magazine vignettes collected here relate incidents that occurred before and during the war, including an account of the social pressures and traditions that led the youth to fight in Vietnam despite his personal objections. *Northern Lights* centers on the conflicts between two brothers—one a wounded but still physically powerful war hero, the other intellectually and spiritually motivated—who bond while they attempt to survive natural threats during an outing in the wilderness. *Going after Cacciato* reflects the surrealistic atmosphere of war as narrated and dreamed by Paul Berlin, a young soldier on guard duty in Vietnam. Blurring the present tedium and horrors of war with memories of a past pursuit of an AWOL soldier, Berlin imagines his patrol team chasing the soldier on foot from Vietnam to Paris, where peace talks are being held. The blend of realism and fantasy leaves the reader to ponder which events actually occurred. *The Nuclear Age* relates the anguish of a man acutely sensitive to the threat of nuclear annihilation as the narrative shifts from his childhood during the 1950s to a future set in 1995. *The Things They Carried,* a collection of linked stories about a platoon of soldiers who lack any understanding of the reasons for their involvement in the Vietnam War, features a character named Tim O'Brien who comments on the process of writing the stories—twenty years later. The interplay between memory and imagination, again, makes it difficult for the reader to distinguish the truthful elements of the story. *In the Lake of the Woods* tells of the mysterious disappearance of the wife of a politician after the two retreat to a remote lakeside cabin in the Minnesota woods.

Critical Reception

The enormity of critical acclaim bestowed upon *Going after Cacciato* and *The Things They Carried*—Robert R. Harris, for instance, has recommended the inclusion of the latter on "the short list of essential fiction about Vietnam"—has extended subsequent commentary beyond pure literary concerns and into the realm of morality and philosophy, especially where O'Brien explores the nature of courage and the writer's interest in transcending reality to represent the truths of experience. Much discussion of O'Brien's body of fiction examines such topics as the relationship between reality and dream in O'Brien's works; whether a connection between the "magic realism" of Borges and Marquez exists in O'Brien's style of writing; structural analyses of O'Brien's fiction to illuminate the ramifications of war and its effects on the individual; and the significance of O'Brien's overriding concern in his writings with the relationship between fiction and experience. Some scholars have addressed the problems associated with the generic classification of individual works in O'Brien's multi-faceted canon, while others have attempted to determine which elements constitute a "true war story";

still others have challenged O'Brien's belief that "stories can save lives." Suggesting the reason for O'Brien's allure, Iyer remarked: "No one writes better about the fear and homesickness of a boy adrift amid what he cannot understand, be it combat or love."

PRINCIPAL WORKS

If I Die in a Combat Zone, Box Me Up and Ship Me Home (memoirs) 1973
Northern Lights (novel) 1975
Going after Cacciato (novel) 1978
The Nuclear Age (novel) 1985
The Things They Carried (short stories) 1990
In the Lake of the Woods (novel) 1994

CRITICISM

Robert Wilson (review date 19 February 1978)

SOURCE: "Dreaming of War and Peace," in *The Washington Post Book World*, February 19, 1978, p. E4.

[*In the following review, Wilson favorably comments on O'Brien's realistic descriptions of war from a footsoldier's perspective in* Going after Cacciato.]

Fantasies must have fed the spirit of the American infantryman in Vietnam just as the canned peaches he carried in his knapsack nurtured his body. Hell means no escape; but in dreams the soldier can escape his fear and dread, and war can become, merely, a ghastly purgatory.

That is why Paul Berlin, an intelligent, sensitive foot soldier in Tim O'Brien's novel about Vietnam [*Going after Cacciato*], spends so much time fantasizing. On patrol, his eyes may be focused on the ground in front of him, as he looks for the enemy mine which could blow off his legs, but his thoughts are somewhere else: home, or places he might visit after the war. And on a particular night, as he keeps watch in an observation tower near the South China Sea, he conjures up a fantasy of escape to a place as distant geographically and in every other way from wartime Vietnam as it is possible to be: Paris.

The dream journey begins in reality, as a mission to find an AWOL soldier named Cacciato (in Italian, "the pursued"), a member of Paul Berlin's platoon whose own fantasy has been to walk away from the war, westward, until he reaches Paris. The search party sets off in that direction, picks up Cacciato's trail, and traps him on a small hill near the Laotian border.

Paul Berlin remembers this much, a month later in the observation tower, and then his imagination takes over: What if Cacciato had slipped away, he asks himself, and we had followed him to Paris?

Well, for one thing, Paul Berlin might get a chance to meet a woman. (A soldier's fantasies are not exclusively of escape, after all.) And improbably, as suits a dream, the search team does overtake a beautiful young Vietnamese woman, a refugee, who is going their way through Laos. It's his dream, so Paul Berlin claims her. Dream journeys tend to the picaresque, and Paul Berlin imagines several episodes in this mode. Having reached Iran, the soldiers are (accurately) accused of being deserters themselves, and barely escape execution by firing squad. They hitchhike through Eastern Europe, where they are picked up by an American flower child. She offers them her mindless sympathy (not to mention her body), and they take her van instead, leaving her behind.

It's a long way to Paris, but Paul Berlin has a long watch to pass that night. And we pass it with him as he weaves the boredom of the watch and the horrible memories the war has produced with the potential pleasures and dangers of dreams.

Tim O'Brien was an infantryman in Vietnam, and his first book, *If I Die in a Combat Zone,* a nonfiction account of his year there, shows how closely Paul Berlin is patterned after himself. In the earlier book, O'Brien writes, "Do dreams offer lessons: Do nightmares have themes, do we awaken and analyze them and live our lives as a result? Can the foot soldier teach anything important about war, merely for having been there? I think not. He can tell war stories." War is one of fiction's great subjects, but the soldier who can tell war stories is a rarity. Merely for having been there, the soldier, like the journalist, can describe war. But the storyteller aims at something more, a knowledge so perfect that the reader can be there, too. Anyone who has read Tolstoy's account of the battle of Borodino knows that this is not too grand a claim for what fiction can do.

Cacciato approaches these heights at times, when O'Brien describes a helicopter assault or a soldier who dies of fright after being wounded by a mine or any of the deaths that Paul Berlin remembers witnessing. For example after the partly headless body of one soldier they called Buff was carried away by helicopter, there was this to witness:

> Very carefully, keeping it steady and close to his stomach, Cacciato picked up the helmet and carried it down the ditch to a patch of high grass.

> Life after death, Paul Berlin thought. It was a stupid thought. How could it be? Eyes and nose, an expression of dumb surprise—how could this promise anything? He tried not to look. He wanted to feel

grief, or at least pity, but all he could feel was curiosity. So he looked.

> He watched as Cacciato stepped over a log, stopped, and then, like a woman emptying her wash basin, heaved Buff's face into the tall, crisp grass.

This is the reality out of which a soldier's dreams of escape arise. (Several of these extraordinary realistic chapters have appeared in publications as different as *Redbook* and *Shenandoah,* the literary magazine; one was an O. Henry award winner.) But it is Berlin's dream—with its fantasy elements—which often seems out of place, hard to reconcile with the evocative realism of the rest of the narrative. Of course, a realistic account of war need not ignore the dreams any more than it can ignore the horrors. Nonetheless, the reader and writer of fiction must strike a bargain in order for the reader to be transported to Borodino, say, or Vietnam. If the writer earns his trust, the reader suspends his disbelief, as Coleridge put it. He doesn't say to himself, "This is only a story." Unfortunately, when the fantasy intrudes, that is just what the reader says. The bargain has been broken.

However, that failure is a minor one; and at its best, *Going After Cacciato* is a telling depiction of the footsoldier's war. Most of what we know about Vietnam we've learned from journalists, and some of the best books to come out of Vietnam are essentially about the journalist's experience there. But it is the experience of the soldier that is important. Tim O'Brien knows the soldier as well as anybody, and is able to make us know him in the unique way that the best fiction can.

Grace Paley (review date 17 November 1985)

SOURCE: "Digging a Shelter and a Grave," in *The New York Times Book Review,* November 17, 1985, p. 7.

[*Below, Paley offers a mixed review of* The Nuclear Age, *faulting O'Brien's characterizations but praising his choice of "disparate and essential themes."*]

What subjects! The probable end of the world, survival, madness. Whose madness? One-person madness or world-madness. Fear. When Tim O'Brien's new novel, *The Nuclear Age,* begins, the year is 1995 and a man is digging a deep hole in his backyard. Why? Because the world hasn't changed too much and neither has he. The world is still accumulating its thousands of nuclear death heads. And he, although he now owns the blonde wife and clever child any American male assumes is his due, is still the boy we meet in flashbacks. About 40 years earlier, William Cowling was a child suffering such extreme clear-sightedness that he was unable to put on the soft cloth of faith threaded with reason and common sense with which most children begin to dress their terror as soon as they hear the bad news we grownups have to tell them.

In books, in real life, we say to them, "Well it's true what you learned in the street the other day, there are these thousands of bombs. There is the possibility that people could get awfully angry and push some button somewhere. Yes, it has happened before, but no one's that crazy and anyway (we may add if we happened to have signed a couple of antinuke petitions) *we* won't let it happen." Since children have to thicken their little bones, get meatier and absorb tremendous amounts of difficult knowledge, they're happy to think, of course no one is *that* crazy and besides my body doesn't have time for so much fear.

Still, the information is there and for this child, William, the pinkest, fattest cloud of parental love can't obscure the fact that it did happen once, no twice, and he can see clearly how, out of the middle of Kansas a missile is rising, rising. No one is paying attention.

His knowledge is so sure that he begins to build a bomb shelter under the Ping-Pong table in the basement. He hears about the usefulness to this enterprise of lead and buys lots of pencils. His father has to say sadly when he sees the dozens of lead pencils covering the table, "I hate to break the news, kiddo, but pencils don't contain real lead."

In the sections dealing with William's childhood there's kind of gentle but rugged play with the American family—with the *idea* of the American family. Because Mr. O'Brien is truthful, not mean or vengeful, he is able to be pretty tough though kind.

Time passes. William acquires a strategy of silence, a natural arrogance. There is no one worth speaking to. He's the only one who knows or cares. He lives through the famous 60's which burn into the 70's the way they really did, with the American bombing of Cambodia, the fall of Saigon. In the course of these years he becomes a member of a group of antiwar campus radicals who with their mixed agendas, guns, armor dreams, disturb the purity of his vision but not the clarity. They all eventually descend into a military underground in Florida and Cuba. When the Vietnam War ends they rise as he does into big money, real estate, uranium.

Suddenly I'm angry with Tim O'Brien. What's wrong here? Is it my sense of the history of that period, my own experience of the deep-in and far-out women and men I knew and still know? It seems as though Mr. O'Brien has become afraid of the political meaning of William's sensible madness. Where William is consistently clear-sighted (which means he is more and more not out of his mind but out of the world's mind), Mr. O'Brien becomes devious and settles for mockery which

usually means easy narrow characterization. In the case of the women this was particularly painful to me. William's love of Bobbi, the blonde poetry-writing stewardess, and his long pursuit of her seem fictionally just right. But the other women, his political comrades, are overly unattractive or extraordinarily beautiful. They seem to be the interfering author's clichéd decision. This is a tack a writer would take who is not particularly interested in the life and art of the nuclear age—or in any age for that matter. I believe that Mr. O'Brien is profoundly interested and probably dark with grief because of it, so I'm sorry to see these easy flaws.

What to do? What to do? William older, richer, madder, trying to be as American as possible owns a shovel and a stewardess wife. The hole he is digging in his backyard has become deeper. He has barricaded his wife and little girl in the upstairs bedroom. He is now using dynamite to deepen the hole when necessary. We begin to wonder whether he's digging for protection or burial.

I wish the novel could have been either more surreal or less. It falls into an untranscending middle which muffles the important cry of "Doom, doom." I do wonder with William why we are not all out on the street corners and village greens crying "Stop!" I wish either William or Mr. O'Brien had been more thoughtful about the powerful places from which the real madness radiates; I know it's not from my worried next-door neighbor. Is this because of the general discomfort American writers have confronting political complexity, or the way we are all stuck (even against our will) in a trough of private, individualistic complaint? Still, I thank Tim O'Brien (who wrote that wonderful, inventive novel, *Going After Cacciato*) for pouring these important concerns into fiction, which is not fed often enough with such disparate and essential themes.

Tim O'Brien with Martin Naparsteck (interview date 20 April 1989)

SOURCE: An interview in *Contemporary Literature,* Vol. 32, No. 1, Spring, 1991, pp. 1-11.

[*In the following interview, originally conducted on April 20, 1989, O'Brien talks about his literary influences, characters and thematic concerns, and the relationships between memory, imagination, and literature.*]

Tim O'Brien is widely considered the best of a talented group of Vietnam veterans who have devoted much of their writing to their war experiences. Sections of his most recent book, *The Things They Carried,* have won a National Magazine Award and an O. Henry Prize and have been included in *Best American Short Stories.* It follows by twelve years his National Book Award-winning *Going After Cacciato,* which until recently was often called the best work of fiction to come out of the war; the critical reaction to *The Things They Carried,* however, now makes it a prime candidate for that accolade. The latest book resists easy categorization: it is part novel, part collection of stories, part essays, part journalism; it is, more significantly, all at the same time. As O'Brien indicates below, he may have created a new literary form. His other books are *If I Die in a Combat Zone,* a memoir of his year in Vietnam; *Northern Lights,* an out-of-print novel about two brothers who become lost on a cross-country skiing trip in Minnesota; and *The Nuclear Age,* about a man who, while building a bomb shelter in 1995, recalls his life as a radical.

This interview took place at O'Brien's home in Boxford, Massachusetts, about twenty-five miles north of Boston, on April 20, 1989. O'Brien had completed writing *The Things They Carried* and was working on some final revisions.

[Naparsteck:] *You have two Pauls in your fiction, Paul Perry in* Northern Lights *and Paul Berlin in* Going After Cacciato. *Is that just a coincidence?*

[O'Brien:] I doubt it's a coincidence, though I can't explain it. The first Paul, the *Northern Lights* Paul—that's a terrible book. I'm embarrassed by it; it's hard to talk about it. It's the first novel I ever tried to write, and unfortunately it was published. It was done logically. Paul was chosen for Paul on the road to Damascus, the Damascus Lutheran Church [which appears in the novel], all the imagery of light throughout the book. The same thing with his middle name, Milton—you know, blindness. Whereas Paul Berlin: just sound. No reason for it.

Why do you say that you're embarrassed by Northern Lights? *It seems to me to have a lot of things that an early book has, a lot of easy Hemingway references, for example.*

That's part of it. I was under two influences: one was Hemingway, one was Faulkner. They both penetrate that book every which way, but beyond that there are a lot of other flaws with it. Overwriting is probably the chief flaw of the book. It's maybe a hundred pages too long. Too much gratuitous repetition. I continue to use repetition in my work to this day, but not so that it's done just for its own sake. I think that if at some point I were to run out of ideas for a new work I might go back to *Northern Lights* and rewrite it. I've done that with *Cacciato* over the last year and a half or so; I've rewritten substantial portions that are appearing in the latest edition. *Northern Lights* would require at least two years of work. The story is O.K., the essential story, that wilderness stuff. The rest of it needs a lot of work, and someday I think I may do it.

The ski trip is what you see as the heart of the book, then?

Yeah, the essential story. I like some of the other stuff, but the other stuff is out of proportion to the narrative heart of the book, I think. I know.

The opening strikes me as in many ways very appealing, with Harvey coming back from Vietnam. I think a lot of stories about returning veterans oversentimentalize the return, which Northern Lights *doesn't do; it's one of the very few stories about a veteran coming home that seems to get things right.*

Yeah, I think those parts I do like. The story about two brothers and the father is solid, and Harvey's not sentimentalized. He's a good, hard character; I like his character. Still, it's a question of language. Language equals content. Unfortunately, there are so many echoes that are Hemingwayesque—language coming out of Harvey's mouth and descriptions and things that get in the way.

Were you conscious of writing with these Hemingwayesque influences?

I was trying to parody Hemingway. I wrote the book not knowing it was going to be published. I was just a beginner, and I was sort of having fun with it, so I tried to spoof *The Sun Also Rises, A Farewell to Arms,* and I thought I did a pretty neat job of doing the spoofs, but unfortunately good literature should be more than just gamesmanship, and I think there is too much gamesmanship in that book.

Let's move to a book you like better. Is Cacciato's decision to leave the war related to his refusal to touch the grenade? You never specifically say that.

It's never said directly, because Cacciato is never there to say it, but, yes, I think it's related pretty directly. The chronology of the book—of which I am fond—is all scrambled throughout the narrative. You can actually map that this event happened first, second, third, and his departure follows pretty quickly after. Refusing to touch the grenade is the first war event prior to his departure. I don't think it's necessarily the only reason for his running, but in a way it's got to be so. I try to keep him off in the horizon and try to keep his motives as removed as he is physically from the rest of the men; they can never figure out precisely what his motives were.

There's something else that's never said directly: is that the grenade that kills the lieutenant?

Again, definitely the lieutenant's off-stage; there's no scene where they kill him. No, maybe it's a different grenade; the grenade is symbolic. I've always pictured it as being the same grenade, but it doesn't necessarily have to be.

And it would be the black guy, Oscar, who throws the grenade?

I think that once they've all touched it, it doesn't much matter. It's like naming the executioner of Ted Bundy; who killed Bundy? It was the state, the whole judicial system. I don't know who threw the grenade; I don't think it very much matters.

Except that a guy like Berlin might be able to touch the grenade, but I have a hard time seeing him being able to throw it.

I have a hard time seeing him do it, too, but I don't have a hard time, for example, seeing Stink do it. He's the sort of guy you'd expect to throw it. Oscar certainly would be a main candidate. But, as I say, I don't think it really matters. If I had to take a guess, it would probably be Oscar who's done it.

Not answering questions like that in the book, is that deliberate?

Yes. It's a question of what matters, I guess, both to the writer and the reader. It doesn't matter to me who did it. It's like if you were doing a scene of the execution of Bundy and you suddenly were to concentrate on the executioner, who's really a stand-in character. The key thing is that touching.

Do you ever feel that you've written so much about Vietnam that you've been typecast, like the town drunk?

Yeah, I do. I can't deny it's part of my material, my life, things I care about. Even if I don't write often, specifically, about Vietnam, a lot of the stuff, for example in *The Nuclear Age* and in *Northern Lights*—courage and obligation and so on— flows from that experience. Beyond that, I think all writers get typecast. I think Melville is typecast as a sea writer. And Conrad certainly is. Updike is a suburban-hyphen-domestic affairs writer. Shakespeare is a king writer. That has to happen, because an author like any other human being naturally gravitates toward a center of concerns that are particularly his or hers. Being typecast still irritates me at times, but not enough to make me say I'm not going to write about Vietnam, because I am, and I'm sure I will in the future.

Your characters spend a great deal of time thinking about courage, which is a fairly common subject for Vietnam stories, but you handle it differently. One symbol that comes up a lot in other writers is John Wayne; Ron Kovic, for example, implicitly rejects that symbolism. You never mention John Wayne, and you do not write of courage as something that drew you to Vietnam. You handle courage in a more realistic way.

It's such a complicated subject, it's hard to know what to say. It's easy to break down courage into categories. There's moral courage versus physical courage and so on. Even that seems oversimplifying it. To break it down into categories of John

Wayne and Socrates, for instance, seems to me to be really artificial. Like everything else, courage interpenetrates the whole fabric of a life. To take a strand out and say this is courage and this is something else violates a central humanness. In my own particular case, I hated the war in Vietnam and didn't want to go. I had no desire to test my capacity to charge a bunker; I had no desire to do that. Some guys did. And I never really understood it, from the moment of basic training. Why would guys want to die? Take the chance of dying? I just didn't get it. So I think my perspective on the issue probably varies a lot from that of a guy like Kovic who wanted to test himself. My concerns aren't those of other people, and the writing probably echoes that.

It seems that your characters are very much concerned about courage, but they typically don't reach conclusions about it. You're not really making a statement about one type of courage being better than another.

The best literature is always explorative. It's searching for answers and never finding them. It's almost like Platonic dialogue. If you knew what courage is, if you had a really wonderful, philosophical explication of courage, you would do it as philosophy, as explication; you wouldn't write fiction. Fiction is a way of testing possibilities and testing hypotheses, and not defining, and so I think that more than anything the work is a way of me saying, yes, courage is clearly important in this character's life; he thinks about its importance in circumstances; the work is a way of searching for courage, finding out what it is. That's especially true in *Cacciato,* I think, where it's both a search for courage for him to walk away from that war and also a kind of search for what courage is, what the courageous thing to do is.

> **The best literature is always explorative.**
> **It's searching for answers and never**
> **finding them.**
> **—Tim O'Brien**

Your first three books differ from the fourth in the treatment of courage. Courage doesn't seem to be a major theme in **Nuclear Age,** *which is more about figuring out what sanity is and is not. Do you think it was inevitable that in moving away from Vietnam you would move away from courage as a dominating topic?*

It's the same issue. It's like the other side of the coin in that this guy in *The Nuclear Age* had the courage to do what I didn't and a lot of other people didn't, which is to risk embarrassment and censure and endure humiliation about walking away from the war. If there's a courageous character in that book, it's that William character, who despite his service in a kind of Waspism and his wimpy attitude toward the war manages to do for the most part what he thinks is right. So I think it's not a departure from the earlier work but a looking at it from another angle. To me, he's the only hero I've written.

It seems to me that in your first three books you were dealing with philosophical issues, such as courage, while **The Nuclear Age** *is more political. Do you feel that way?*

Not really. I see all four books as political in that they all deal with the impact of global forces on individual lives. In my own life and in *If I Die,* this huge thing—global politics—pushed me into the war, and similarly in *The Nuclear Age,* William Cowling is pushed into hiding and pushed away from his own life by global politics. I think anything I've ever written has that as its center theme, even more than issues of courage—how individual human lives are influenced by global forces beyond the horizon.

I sensed in reading **The Nuclear Age** *that you were coming close to making a statement there, saying we should do something about this nuclear madness.*

I don't think I was making a statement; I certainly wasn't trying to. I was trying to write a comedy, basically, and a book that was funny, and I think the real difference between *The Nuclear Age* and the earlier works is tone. It had a more comedic tone to it. I'm not sure people cared for that. But my intent was to be different—like Shakespeare saying, "My subject may be life and death, but I want to have a comedic perspective on it."

The reviewers were not always kind to **The Nuclear Age.** *Do you think a lot of them missed the comedic intent?*

That's probably it. I was trying to write a funny book. I think it is funny. But it's up to the ages. *Cacciato* may, a hundred years from now, not be read at all, while *The Nuclear Age* could be. The best road for most writers is to turn them out at the time. *Moby Dick*, for example, was trashed, worse than *Nuclear Age.* It was "the most hideous piece of garbage ever written," and what happens is that over time, I think, these things straighten themselves out. You can't as a writer defend your work or knock it. You have to say, "Let time take care of it." So I don't get too excited about bad reviews or good ones. I feel happy if they're good, feel sad if they're bad, but the feelings disappear pretty quickly, because ultimately I'm not writing for my contemporaries but for the ages, like every good writer should be. You're writing for history, in the hope that your book—out of the thousands that are published each year—might be the last to be read a hundred years from now and enjoyed.

Was the story **"Speaking of Courage"** *originally intended to be part of* **Cacciato***?*

Yes. It was a piece I took out. It's kind of an orphan. I've since rewritten it for *The Things They Carried*—pretty substantially rewritten it, in fact, changing everything except the lake, driving around the lake, but all the war stuff has been completely changed, and now I'm really fond of the story. I didn't care for it at all when it was originally written.

Is that why it was left out of **Cacciato***?*

Partly that and partly because it just didn't fit. It's a postwar story; *Cacciato* was a war story, and it just didn't have a proper home in that book.

In rewriting it, you changed the character from Paul Berlin to Tim O'Brien.

The character becomes Tim, even though the Tim character is made up entirely, and then the Tim is transformed again into another guy, another character in *The Things They Carried* named Norman Bowker.

Is the Tim character Tim O'Brien? In **"The Lives of the Dead"** *there's a Timmy O'Brien.*

Yeah, it is, in part. It's made up, but I use my own name. *The Things They Carried* is sort of half novel, half group of stories. It's part nonfiction, too: some of the stuff is commentary on the stories, talking about where a particular one came from. **"Speaking of Courage,"** for example, came from a letter I received from a guy named Norman Bowker, a real guy, who committed suicide after I received his letter. He was talking to me in his letter about how he just couldn't adjust to coming home. It wasn't bad memories; it was that he couldn't talk to anybody about it. He didn't know what to say; he felt inarticulate. All he could do was drive around and around in his hometown in Iowa, around this lake. In the letter he asked me to write a story about it, and I did. This was after I published *If I Die.*

Was this somebody you knew?

Yeah, in Vietnam. I sent him the story after it was published, and he said he liked it. Then I didn't hear from him for a long time. His mother finally wrote me. I wrote her and she wrote back saying he committed suicide by hanging himself in the locker room of a YMCA. So that's the terrible-happening anecdote that I include after the story in *The Things They Carried.* The commentary is partly about writing sources and partly about the writing itself.

The Things They Carried is my best book. There's no doubt in my mind about it. When I was writing *Cacciato* I had that feeling; I have that feeling now. I can tell by the strangeness of it. It's a new form, I think. I blended my own personality with the stories, and I'm writing about the stories, and yet everything is made up, including the commentary. The story about Norman Bowker is made up. There was no Norman Bowker. The point being, among others, that in fiction we not only transform reality, we sort of invent our own lives, invent our histories, our autobiographies. When Melville wrote *Moby Dick*, he was inventing himself, for posterity.

Have you ever been approached about doing movies?

Cacciato and *The Nuclear Age* have both been taken by the movies. I've seen a few scripts. I've seen three on *Cacciato,* none of which are any good. There are some good parts in them, but by and large they tend to take all the dreamlike, fantastic, surrealistic elements of the book out and tell a pretty straightforward, realistic story, which to me violates the whole aboutness of the book. The book is about the interweaving of memory on the one hand and the imagination, how one frees the other and back again, and that's gone. To me you don't have *Cacciato* anymore; you've got some new thing. I was asked to write a screenplay of the book, and I said "No," because you end up having to do what they did. You have to, the way movies are made. You have to screw up your own work, and if it's going to be screwed up, I would prefer that somebody else do it, not me.

I've seen the term "magical realism" used in connection with your writing. Do you think Cacciato *fits into that grouping?*

I don't know. I think the term is a shorthand way of saying something that's much more complicated than that. No writer wants to be grouped in any category. Writing is being an individual; it's a creative enterprise, and a writer wants to make an individual, creative statement that's unrelated to anything that's been said before or afterward yet is simultaneously totally related not just to one thing but to everything. "Magical realism" is shorthand for imagination and memory and how they interlock, for what realism is, for what's real and not real.

"How to Tell a True War Story" in **The Things They Carried** *seems to me to be very directly about the interlocking of memory and what actually happened. It also strikes me that this story is as much an essay as it is a story. Did you have that sense in writing it?*

It's a mixture, yes. It's like the rest of the book, in that it's part story, just raw story—six guys go up to the listening post in the mountains—and also a discussion about the making of the story, not a discussion by me as much as by the guys themselves. In a way it's part essay and part fiction, but in a way it's neither. I think that when you're reading the thing you have a total effect. To me, it has a singleness or unity to it. Rather than being part this and part that, it's all those things together. That story is the genesis for the idea for the whole book. When I'm talking about a happening, it seems essayish,

but that stuff is invented and imagined; it isn't true in a literal sense. I don't, for example, believe that war is beautiful in any aesthetic way whatsoever. Even though the character sounds like me and says pretty pointblankly that war is beautiful, the harmonies and shapes and proportions, it's not me saying that. The guy who's narrating this story has my name and a lot of my characteristics, but it isn't really me, I never felt or thought that war's pretty, even though I can see how people such as Bill Broyles have said that. My personal feeling is that it's pretty ugly. I was in danger, and my perception never let me see any beauty. All I felt was fear. What I'm saying is that even with that nonfiction-sounding element in the story, everything in the story is fiction, beginning to end. To try to classify different elements of the story as fact or fiction seems to me artificial. Literature should be looked at not for its literal truths but for its emotional qualities. What matters in literature, I think, are pretty simple things—whether it moves me or not, whether it feels true. The actual literal truth should be superfluous. For example, here's a story: four guys go on a trail, a grenade sails out, one guy jumps on it, takes the blast, and saves his buddies. Is it true? Well, yeah, it may have happened, but it doesn't feel true, because it feels stereotypical, hackneyed; it feels like Hollywood. But here's another story: four guys go on a trail, a grenade sails out, one guy jumps on it, takes the blast, and dies; before he dies, though, one of the guys says, "What the fuck you do that for?" and the dead guy says, "The story of my life, man," and starts to smile. He's dead. That didn't happen. Clearly, ever, and yet there's something about the absurdity of it and the horror of it—"What the fuck you do that for?"—which seems truer to me than something which might literally have happened. A story's truth shouldn't be measured by happening but by an entirely different standard, a standard of emotion, feeling—"Does it ring true?" as opposed to "Is it true?"

The narrator of "How to Tell a True War Story" comes to a different understanding of what happens at the end of the story than he had at the beginning. At the end he climbs into the tree to pick out parts of his friend, who's died in an explosion, giving the impression that he didn't quite understand the truth at the beginning, maybe because it was too difficult to remember, too hard on him. It's the exercising of his imagination that gets him at the truth.

Yes, I think it is. I think exercising the imagination is the main way of finding truth, that if you take almost any experience of your own life that means something to you, that really hits you, let's say the death of your mother, over the course of time your imagination is going to do things with that experience to render it into something that you can deal with and that has meaning to it. You're going to select some details and forget others: she's lying in bed dying for five weeks; you're not going to remember every detail of that; you're going to pick out of your memory, pluck out, certain conspicuous elements, and then you're going to reorder them.

The experience that you remember is going to have a power to it that the total experience didn't have. You went to fix breakfast while she was dying, the phone rang, you had to deal with it—all that random stuff that you've forgotten will be rearranged by your imagination into a new kind of experience. I think in war we tend to block out the long, hard moments of boredom, standing around, sitting around, waiting, which is a lot of what war is. It's ninety-nine percent monotony, and what the imagination does is to push that away and take what's left and reorder it into patterns that give meaning to it.

In **Cacciato** *you have the observation post scenes, which seem to be almost directly essays, and in one of them you talk about how to use imagination. There are a lot of dream sequences in literature, but Berlin is not really dreaming; he's wide awake, and he's controlling what he's thinking about, and what he thinks about makes up half the novel.*

Dreams are dangerous. I don't think I've ever used a real dream. Berlin is awake the same way you and I are now, only alone, and he's staring at the beach and thinking; he's imagining in a way we all do at times. It's a kind of daydream, but it's not an *Alice in Wonderland* or Hobbity sort of thing where events happen at random that come only from the subconscious. It's a mixture of the subconscious and the directed, the same way stories are written. What Berlin is doing is what I do with a typewriter: I'm half living in a rational world and half living in a kind of trance, imagining. Berlin's process in the observation post was meant, at least in part, to echo my own process of imagining that book—not dreaming it and not just controlling it, but a trancelike, half-awake, half-alert imagining.

A lot of guys from Vietnam go to the Breadloaf writers conference in Vermont because they know you teach there every summer.

There are always some, which is good.

They usually try to select you as their teacher.

They try to. They don't always get me. I think of myself not as a soldier anymore. That's all over. I think of myself as someone who now and then writes about the war, but my daily concerns are just the same as yours. When you're writing a book about Vietnam you don't think of yourself as a soldier; you think of yourself as a writer. The subject matter is war, and you're trying to make a sentence that's graceful, you're trying to make a character come alive, you're trying to make a scene shake with meaning and also with a dramatic feel; your attention is on writing that matters. I feel bad when I meet a vet who thinks that because we both shared this soldiering thing we can also share the other thing, writing, without work, and to me writing is really hard work. Anybody

who's done it knows that just making a simple sentence is work. My chief asset as a human being, as a writer, is that I'm tenacious; I work just constantly, stubbornly, and like it. I mean I really like it—I get angry, I feel rotten, if somebody calls me in the middle of work and says, "Let's go play golf," because I like writing that much. If you want to be a writer, you've got to learn to be an eagle soaring up above and a mule who keeps climbing and climbing and climbing.

Robert R. Harris (review date 11 March 1990)

SOURCE: "Too Embarrassed Not to Kill," in *The New York Times Book Review,* March 11, 1990, p. 8.

[*In the following positive review, Harris commends the war stories in* The Things They Carried, *suggesting that the work merits inclusion on "the short list of essential fiction about Vietnam."*]

Only a handful of novels and short stories have managed to clarify, in any lasting way, the meaning of the war in Vietnam for America and for the soldiers who served there. With *The Things They Carried,* Tim O'Brien adds his second title to the short list of essential fiction about Vietnam. As he did in his novel *Going After Cacciato* (1978), which won a National Book Award, he captures the war's pulsating rhythms and nerve-racking dangers. But he goes much further. By moving beyond the horror of the fighting to examine with sensitivity and insight the nature of courage and fear, by questioning the role that imagination plays in helping to form our memories and our own versions of truth, he places *The Things They Carried* high up on the list of best fiction about any war.

The Things They Carried is a collection of interrelated stories. A few are unremittingly brutal; a couple are flawed two-page sketches. The publisher calls the book "a work of fiction," but in no real sense can it be considered a novel. No matter. The stories cohere. All deal with a single platoon, one of whose members is a character named Tim O'Brien. Some stories are about the wartime experiences of this small group of grunts. Others are about a 43-year-old writer—again, the fictional character Tim O'Brien—remembering his platoon's experiences and writing war stories (and remembering writing stories) about them. This is the kind of writing about writing that makes Tom Wolfe grumble. It should not stop you from savoring a stunning performance. The overall effect of these original tales is devastating.

As might be expected, there is a lot of gore in *The Things They Carried*—like the account of the soldier who ties a friend's puppy to a Claymore antipersonnel mine and squeezes the firing device. And much of the powerful language cannot be quoted in a family newspaper. But let Mr. O'Brien explain why he could not spare squeamish sensibilities: "If you don't care for obscenity, you don't care for the truth; if you don't care for the truth, watch how you vote. Send guys to war, they come home talking dirty."

In the title story, Mr. O'Brien juxtaposes the mundane and the deadly items that soldiers carry into battle. Can openers, pocketknives, wristwatches, mosquito repellent, chewing gum, candy, cigarettes, salt tablets, packets of Kool-Aid, matches, sewing kits, C rations are "humped" by the G.I.'s along with M-16 assault rifles, M-60 machine guns, M-79 grenade launchers. But the story is really about the other things the soldiers "carry": "grief, terror, love, longing . . . shameful memories" and, what unifies all the stories, "the common secret of cowardice." These young men, Mr. O'Brien tells us, "carried the soldier's greatest fear, which was the fear of blushing. Men killed, and died, because they were embarrassed not to."

Embarrassment, the author reveals in **"On the Rainy River,"** is why he, or rather the fictional version of himself, went to Vietnam. He almost went to Canada instead. What stopped him, ironically, was fear. "All those eyes on me," he writes, "and I couldn't risk the embarrassment. . . . I couldn't endure the mockery, or the disgrace, or the patriotic ridicule. . . . I was a coward. I went to the war."

So just what is courage? What is cowardice? Mr. O'Brien spends much of the book carefully dissecting every nuance of the two qualities. In several stories, he writes movingly of the death of Kiowa, the best-loved member of the platoon. In **"Speaking of Courage,"** Mr. O'Brien tells us about Norman Bowker, the platoon member who blames his own failure of nerve for Kiowa's death. Bowker "had been braver than he ever thought possible, but . . . he had not been so brave as he wanted to be." In the following story, **"Notes"** (literally notes on the writing of **"Speaking of Courage"**), Mr. O'Brien's fictional alter ego informs the reader that Bowker committed suicide after coming home from the war. This author also admits that he made up the part about the failure of nerve that haunted Bowker. But it's all made up, of course. And in **"The Man I Killed,"** Mr. O'Brien imagines the life of an enemy soldier at whom the character Tim O'Brien tossed a grenade, only to confess later that it wasn't "Tim O'Brien" who killed the Vietnamese.

Are these simply tricks in the service of making good stories? Hardly.

Mr. O'Brien strives to get beyond literal descriptions of what these men went through and what they felt. He makes sense of the unreality of the war—makes sense of why he has distorted that unreality even further in his fiction—by turning back to explore the workings of the imagination, by probing his memory of the terror and fearlessly confronting the way he has dealt with it as both soldier and fiction writer. In doing all this, he not only crystallizes the Vietnam experience for us, he exposes the nature of all war stories.

The character Tim O'Brien's daughter asks him why he continues to be obsessed by the Vietnam War and with writing about it. "By telling stories," he says, "you objectify your own experience. You separate it from yourself. You pin down certain truths." In **"Good Form,"** he writes: "I can look at things I never looked at. I can attach faces to grief and love and pity and God. I can be brave. I can make myself feel again." You come away from this book understanding why there have been so many novels about the Vietnam War, why so many of Mr. O'Brien's fellow soldiers have turned to narrative—real and imagined—to purge their memories, to appease the ghosts.

Is it fair to readers for Mr. O'Brien to have blurred his own identity as storyteller-soldier in these stories? "A true war story is never moral," he writes in **"How to Tell a True War Story."** "It does not instruct, nor encourage virtue, nor suggest models of proper human behavior, nor restrain men from doing the things men have always done. If a story seems moral, do not believe it. If at the end of a war story you feel uplifted, or if you feel that some small bit of rectitude has been salvaged from the larger waste, then you have been made the victim of a very old and terrible lie. There is no rectitude whatsoever. There is no virtue. As a first rule of thumb, therefore, you can tell a true war story by its absolute and uncompromising allegiance to obscenity and evil." Mr. O'Brien cuts to the heart of writing about war. And by subjecting his memory and imagination to such harsh scrutiny, he seems to have reached a reconciliation, to have made his peace—or to have made up his peace.

Richard Eder (review date 1 April 1990)

SOURCE: "Has He Forgotten Anything?" in *Los Angeles Times Book Review,* April 1, 1990, pp. 3, 11.

[*In the favorable review below, Eder relates O'Brien's memories of war to the actual writing of* The Things They Carried.]

Why is he still writing about the Vietnam War, Tim O'Brien's 10-year-old daughter asks him. Why not write about a little girl who finds a million dollars and spends it on a Shetland pony?

The reader may ask the same question, though probably not about the pony. Writing that commands the graceful and unsparing strength that O'Brien used in *Going After Cacciato* a dozen years ago is rare. How we need writers to give us an equivalent strength and discrimination for the more inchoate puzzlement of our own days!

O'Brien, whose reflections and comments run through this new chain of Vietnam stories [in *The Things They Carried*], faces the question. He takes it up, puts it down, takes it up again. He tells us that you get your material where you find it. That's off-hand, even crude. Then, later:

> I'm 43 years old and I'm still writing war stories. . . . The remembering makes it now. And sometimes remembering will lead to a story which makes it forever. That's what stories are for. Stories are for joining the past and the present.

If you are in prison, you write to get out; O'Brien's memories still encircle him. But the fuller justification for *The Things They Carried* is the writing itself. Some of it does seem like the most acute of second thoughts. Some of the less interesting pieces do seem like a harking-back in order to re-live the extra aliveness that came with the horrors.

But the best of these stories—and none is written with less than the sharp edge of a honed vision—are memory as prophecy. They tell us not where we were but where we are; and perhaps where we will be.

O'Brien draws upon his own experience in Vietnam, of course, but the characters and incidents are fictional, he writes. He casts himself, though, both as a fictional member of the platoon where the stories are set and as the narrator meditating upon them years later.

His voice advances, halts, doubles back. An incident will be told in two or three different ways; it will be interrupted, it will peter out, and resume. Sometimes it will deny some of what it has told us, or tell us that it happened differently.

"How to Tell a Story in Wartime" is the title of one set of story fragments, reflections and comments. A story cannot be told straight, it informs us. What is to be told is so hideous, unpredictable and absurd that the narrator has to manipulate it, duck away and invent. In war, you tell a story to escape or change the thing you have to tell.

These 19- and 20-year-olds, plucked from their ordinary lives and hijacked into a nightmare, have to invent themselves as well as their stories. Jensen and Strunk get into a fight over a jackknife; Jensen smashes Strunk's nose so badly he needs to be hospitalized. When Strunk returns a few days later, Jensen begins to worry that he may use one of innumerable opportunities to kill him. He breaks his own nose with his pistol butt; now they're even.

Not only are they even, but they are buddies. They sign a contract that if either is so badly wounded as to become a wheelchair case, the other will kill him. Strunk's leg is blown off; Jensen comes over to comfort him. "Don't kill me," Strunk begs. "Swear you won't kill me." Jensen swears. All this is told, in fact, in two successive stories, the first called **"Enemies,"** the second **"Friends."** The two, in this unhinging light, are synonymous.

A patrol goes up to a highland to stay a week and listen for enemy activity. It is foggy up there; listen is all they can do. And they begin to hear music: string quartets, choirs, the tinkling glasses and chatter of a cocktail party. One of the patrol describes it to the narrator:

> The rock—it's talking. And the fog too, and the grass and the goddamn mongooses. Everything talks. The trees talk politics, the monkeys talk religion. The whole country. Vietnam. The place talks. It talks. Understand? Nam—it truly talks.

They radio for air strikes; all night long, the empty hill is hit with napalm, incendiaries, fragmentation bombs. It is irrational and utterly rational at the same time. To these farm and city boys, all explanations of why they are there are no less imaginary than the hills talking.

There is beastliness, and there are odd, invented moralities. The platoon goes through a village where an air strike has silenced everything. Only a 14-year-old girl is left, dancing crazily outside the house where her dead parents lie. That night, one of the soldiers does an obscene burlesque of her movements. "Dance right," another screams at him.

The most extraordinary piece in the collection is the first, which bears its title. **"What They Carried"** begins as nothing but a list, it seems. It is a list of everything that the members of a platoon carry, and the weight of each item.

Knives, heat tabs, wristwatches, dog tags, mosquito repellent, chewing gum, candy, salt tablets, packets of Koolade, C-rations, water and so on—15 to 20 pounds. Helmets—5 pounds. Boots—2.1 pounds. Rifle—8.2 pounds, loaded. Extra ammunition, 14 pounds. Grenade launcher, 5.9 pounds. Twenty-five grenades—16 pounds. A machine gun—23 pounds. A medic's kit—20 pounds. And then a host of individual choices: foot powder, canned peaches, comic books, condoms, dope, a Bible, a slingshot, brass knuckles. And much more.

O'Brien goes on and on, gradually extending the verb "to carry."

The soldiers carry love letters, photos, fungus, lice and each other when wounded. They carry lucky charms and the thoughts they cling to. They carry grief, terror, confusion. And gradually, a haunting picture is assembled.

They are as heavily equipped as Tweedledum and Tweedledee. Each item has its purpose: for killing, protecting, preserving. Yet all the purposes add up to a grotesque purposelessness. These soldiers are not so much warriors as carriers of war, pack mules on which firepower is placed and among which a terrible mortality is inflicted. This absurd cargo of purposes they carry through a land and a war from which they are utterly divorced, and through which they move in a state between dream and nightmare.

It is an ultimate, indelible image of war in our time, and in time to come.

D. J. R. Bruckner (review date 3 April 1990)

SOURCE: "Storyteller for a War that Won't End," in *The New York Times,* April 3, 1990, pp. C15, C17.

[*Below, Bruckner assesses O'Brien's storytelling abilities in* The Things They Carried, *especially the way he interweaves fact and fiction.*]

For the first time since his Army tour of duty in Vietnam ended 20 years ago, Tim O'Brien will be going back in June. The official reason for the trip is a conference of American and Vietnamese writers in Hanoi. A more personal one for Mr. O'Brien is to return to the area around the village of My Lai.

"When the unit I went in with got there in February of 1969," he said the other day, "we all wondered why the place was so hostile. We did not know there had been a massacre there a year earlier. The news about that only came out later, while we were there, and then we knew. There is a monument in My Lai now and I want to see it."

Vietnam has never left Mr. O'Brien. The country, the war and the men who fought it have filled most of his published fiction, and his latest volume, *The Things They Carried,* is a series of interconnected stories about the war and its victims—and about the whole business of concocting stories.

There will probably be more war stories. In a telephone interview from Minneapolis, where he was promoting *The Things They Carried,* Mr. O'Brien said: "After each of my books about the war has appeared, I thought it might be the last, but I've stopped saying that to myself. There are just too many stories left to tell—in fact, more all the time. I suppose that for the sake of my career, I ought to turn in another direction. And the novel I am working on now is about life in

the north country of Minnesota. But I know more war stories will come out. They have to."

For Mr. O'Brien the stories are larger than the war, and considerably more important. Those in *The Things They Carried* are at least as much about storytelling as about men at war. Some retell in a different way stories already told. Narrators dispute the accuracy of what they themselves are saying. Occasionally a narrator will come to the end of a harrowing tale and then insist that the protagonist did not do the terrible or heroic things he has just recited, but that he himself did them.

Characters snatch stories from one another's mouths and tell them in a different way, with different incidents. A character may take part of a story away from a narrator and refashion it. A first-person commentator who intervenes to critique or correct a story just told, and who can easily be mistaken for Mr. O'Brien, may turn out to be a character in a later story. The stories themselves eventually seem to be engaged in a dialogue about invention. "As you play with stories you find that whatever is said is not sufficient to the task," Mr. O'Brien said.

In 1978, when Mr. O'Brien's third novel, *Going After Cacciato,* appeared, some critics said his tale of an American soldier who simply walked away from the Vietnam War had strong elements of the Latin American school of fiction called magic realism. In his new work the magic is in the storyteller's prestidigitation as the stories pass from character to character and voice to voice, and the realism seems Homeric. Mr. O'Brien seems a little startled when he is asked about that, but he admits that the Trojan War epics of the ancient Greek poet keep drawing him back. There is not a line in *The Things They Carried* that imitates Homer, but at times he is such a presence that he might be included as an unnamed character—in the underlying assumptions about fate, in the enmity of the earth itself toward men in battle, in the sheer glory of fighting, in the boasting of young men.

Storytelling preceded war for Mr. O'Brien, or at least some kind of writing did. He grew up in the southern Minnesota town of Worthington—"the Turkey Capital of the World"—and was there, a month out of Macalaster College in St. Paul, when his draft notice arrived. He had always liked fiction, and books, but he had majored in political science and certainly had no intention to be a writer.

His reaction to the draft notice still surprises him. "I went to my room in the basement and started pounding the typewriter," he recalled. "I did it all summer. It was the most terrible summer of my life, worse than being in the war. My conscience kept telling me not to go, but my whole upbringing told me I had to. That horrible summer made me a writer. I don't know what I wrote. I've still got it, reams of it, but I'm not willing to look at it. It was just stuff—bitter, bitter stuff, and it's probably full of self-pity. But that was the beginning."

He tried to abort the impulse. After he returned from Vietnam in 1970 he went back to political science, doing graduate work in government at Harvard University—"I think I thought I might become the next Henry Kissinger," he said—before a brief stint as a reporter for *The Washington Post.*

But the stories would not be stopped. So far they have filled five books; his impression is that they are multiplying all the time in his head. He talks about them like an evangelist or a prophet. "My life is storytelling," he said. "I believe in stories, in their incredible power to keep people alive, to keep the living alive, and the dead. And if I have started now to play with the stories, inside the stories themselves, well, that's what people do all the time.

"Storytelling is the essential human activity. The harder the situation, the more essential it is. In Vietnam men were constantly telling one another stories about the war. Our unit lost a lot of guys around My Lai, but the stories they told stay around after them. I would be mad not to tell the stories I know."

The stories, then, live on their own, and their relationship to reality is not direct. Mr. O'Brien uses his infectious laugh to punctuate his confession that the insistent reality of characters he has been imagining for 20 years often makes him impatient with people he has not imagined: "I live in my head all day long and the world is a little dreamy."

The intense reality of his characters explains a puzzle in *The Things They Carried.* The book begins with a disclaimer: except for a few details all the characters and incidents are imaginary. But then there is a dedication to a company of soldiers, especially to six who are named. Then these six turn up in the stories. "Well, yes, I dedicated the book to my characters," Mr. O'Brien said. "After all, I lived with them for five years while I was writing. In Vietnam people were being rotated constantly, so men you served with you would know six or eight months. These characters are the people I know best."

Where do they come from? Invariably they begin with "a scrap of dialogue, a way of saying something, in one form or another always with language. There's a whisper inside the ear that begins each of them." They spring from spoken words, even those who are quite inarticulate. In *The Things They Carried,* the central character of one story, **"The Man I Killed,"** is, as Mr. O'Brien puts it, "offstage," and writing a story about a character who is not there was "a wonderful technical challenge."

But the character's voice, the "way of saying something" that

inspired his creation, is not silenced. He turns up elsewhere as a narrator. His name is Tim; other people call him O'Brien. And therein lies another tale. A reader is well advised to heed the book's opening caution that "this is a work of fiction" in which all the characters are made up, as are all the disputes the narrators have about the truth of the stories. This Tim, like Mr. O'Brien, comes originally from Minnesota and is 43 years old. Everything else, even most of the convincing personal details about his life and family, is made up.

It is disappointing to find that Tim's 9-year-old daughter is an invention, not just because she is appealing but because her father's feelings about her role as an interrogator of his conscience are so powerful. She was the most difficult of all the characters to create, Mr. O'Brien said: "I had to keep going back and cutting a lot for the verisimilitude. But, you see, in a way she is real, the child I do not have. Storytelling can even do that for you."

But stories are not all he dreams about. Several years ago he told a reporter he wanted to have a best seller, "not just read in English classes." Now, he said: "I want both. After all, I don't write just for myself. It's really annoying to be on a plane coming out here and see the guy in the next seat reading someone else. So, sure, best seller. I'd love to knock Stephen King off the top of the list. I know I won't but, after all, I spend my life inventing a different reality."

Julian Loose (review date 29 June-5 July 1990)

SOURCE: "The Story that Never Ends," in *Times Literary Supplement,* No. 4552, June 29-July 5, 1990, p. 705.

[*In the following review of* The Things They Carried, *Loose examines some elements of what constitutes a "true war story" in O'Brien's fiction.*]

For nearly two decades Tim O'Brien has written about the impossibility of telling stories true to the American experience of Vietnam, and he is getting better all the time. In his latest sequence, *The Things They Carried,* the narratives O'Brien brought back from the war are enlivened by an increasingly sophisticated sense of genre. A "true war story", O'Brien argues, has no moral; it exhibits an absolute and uncompromising allegiance to obscenity and evil; it is never really about war, it is about love and memory and sorrow. Above all, a true war story may never have happened:

> Four guys go down a trail. A grenade sails out. One guy jumps on it and takes the blast, but it's a killer grenade and everybody dies anyway. Before they die, though, one of the dead guys says, "The fuck you do

that for?" and the jumper says, "Story of my life, man," and the other guy starts to smile but he's dead.

O'Brien convinces us that such incredible stories are faithful to the reality of Vietnam. Courage, always an unpredictable and unreliable response to the moment, often seems absurd in a war so grotesquely misconceived—O'Brien actually charges himself with cowardice for not having evaded the draft. The foot soldiers staved off fear, and the greater fear of seeming afraid, by turning the conflict into a tragicomedy, with themselves as the actors. The terrible softness of human flesh was disguised by a language "both hard and wistful", which turned the Vietnamese into "dinks" and "slopes", transformed lethal mines into "Toe Poppers" and "Bouncing Betties", reduced a Vietcong nurse and a dead baby, fried by napalm, to a "crispy critter" and a "roasted peanut", and left a fellow soldier (or "grunt") not dead but "greased", "offed", "lit up" or "zapped".

In his first two books, the memoir *If I Die In A Combat Zone* and the novel *Northern Lights,* O'Brien was indebted to Hemingway's depictions of war and its lingering aftermath. He then adopted a manner later ascribed to one of his characters who, when he told a story, "wanted to heat up the truth, to make it burn so hot you would feel exactly what he felt". *Going After Cacciato* employed the framing fantasy of a soldier who goes seriously AWOL and walks overland from Vietnam to Paris: *The Nuclear Age* was the fable of a pacifist who dodges the draft, joins a gang of terrorists and makes his fortune selling uranium. *The Things They Carried* includes a few tales similarly "heated up", such as that of the man who brings his girlfriend from hometown America to a quiet outpost in Vietnam, only for her to slip off into the jungle with a sinister group of Green Berets: she discovers that proximity to death brings a new proximity to life, and is last seen wearing a necklace of human tongues.

Fantasy, however, is only one element of the present collection, and many stories impress by their bleak immediacy: a member of Alpha Company steps on a booby-trapped 105 round while playing catch, another drowns in a field of human excrement during a mortar bombardment, a third breaks down and shoots himself in the foot. O'Brien fully exploits the freedoms offered by the sequence, a form which encourages variety and experimentation. A number of the twenty-two "stories" are not conventional narratives at all—**"The Things They Carried"**, for example, vividly evokes the war through a simple naming of parts: the soldiers carry steel helmets, flak jackets and bandages; they hump assault rifles, fragmentation grenades and anti-personnel mines; for good luck they may take letters, a girlfriend's pantyhose or the thumb from a VC corpse: invariably they bring with them infections and the powdery orange-red dust of Vietnam; but they also carry unweighed fear, shameful memories, all the emotional baggage of men who might die.

Long passages of commentary and reflection, which had seemed to interrupt the action of the author's earlier books, are crucial to the success of the new sequence. **"The Man I Killed"** combines a stunned description of a Vietnamese torn apart by O'Brien's grenade with a detailed, imaginary biography of the dead man. **"Ambush"**, which follows, fills in the circumstances of the killing and gives voice to the author's retrospective guilt ("There was no real peril. Almost certainly the young man would have passed by.") In **"Good Form"**, some pages later, O'Brien reveals this all to be a fiction, stating that he only witnessed the man's death, although "presence was guilt enough". Yet then comes a further, irresolvable twist: "But listen. Even *that* story was made up." A confession develops into an exploration of authorial responsibility ("Almost everything in this book is invented. It's not a game. It's a form"), but the sustained urgency of tone marks O'Brien's distance from a merely fashionable reflexivity. By creating a work which so adroitly resists finality, O'Brien has been faithful both to Vietnam and to the stories told about it—for, as he says, "you can tell a true war story by the way it never seems to end".

Catherine Calloway (essay date 1990)

SOURCE: "Pluralities of Vision: *Going After Cacciato* and Tim O'Brien's Short Fiction," in *America Rediscovered: Critical Essays on Literature and Film of the Vietnam War,* edited by Owen W. Gilman, Jr., and Lorrie Smith, Garland Publishing, Inc., 1990, pp. 213-24.

[*In the following essay, Calloway contrasts different versions of the same events and characters represented in O'Brien's fiction in terms of the author's concern with the "problematic nature of reality."*]

Tim O'Brien's second novel, the critically acclaimed *Going After Cacciato,* has long been considered one of the best works to have emerged from the canon of Vietnam War literature, due in part to its emphasis on the subjective nature of perception. Like other postmodernist writers, O'Brien questions the problematic nature of reality itself, a process that engages both the protagonist and the reader. Can there be any definite objective reality in the war? Does absolute truth really exist? Like the elusive Cacciato, the soldier on whom the imaginary journey from Vietnam to Paris is centered, *Going After Cacciato* taunts us with many faces and angles of vision. The protagonist Paul Berlin cannot distinguish between what is real and what is imagined in the war just as the reader cannot differentiate between what is real and what is imagined in the novel. As O'Brien writes, "It was a matter of hard observation. Separating illusion from reality. What happened, and what might have happened." Paul Berlin is forced, as is the reader, into an attempt to distinguish between illusion and reality and in doing so creates a continuous critical dialogue between himself and the world around him.

The impossibility of simplistic judgments—of knowing the reality of the war in absolute terms—is further illustrated in a number of short stories that O'Brien published shortly before *Going After Cacciato.* These stories contain many of the same events and characters as the novel, but differ somewhat from the novelistic versions. While some stories reveal only minor stylistic changes, others contain major differences that serve to provide another perceptual dimension to *Going After Cacciato,* another window on the ever-elusive reality of war or war of reality.

That reality is an on-going process is first illustrated by seemingly minor details that O'Brien changes between the publication of the short fiction and the novel. For example, in the short story entitled **"Going After Cacciato,"** the mileage from Vietnam to Paris is noted as being exactly 6,800 miles, but in the novel by the same name the distance is precisely 8,600 miles. O'Brien further mocks the reader with mathematical discrepancies in the story **"Where Have You Gone, Charming Billy?"** There only 26 soldiers go on a night march, while 32 go in the novel, and Paul Berlin counts to 3,485 to keep his mind off of the war, not to 8,060 as in the later version. Similarly, in **"The Way It Mostly Was,"** the soldiers number 58, in the novel only 38. Such shifts in detail include characters as well as figures. Whereas in the novel *Going After Cacciato* only Lieutenant Sidney Martin is mentioned as having died in a tunnel, in the short story **"Going After Cacciato,"** a Lieutenant Walter Gleason dies as well. Also, when Paul Berlin thinks of the death of Billy Boy of a heart attack on the battlefield, he is comforted in the story **"Where Have You Gone, Charming Billy?"** by a character named Buff. However, in the novel, Buff is mentioned as having died face-down while in a praying position in a ditch, and it is Cacciato, not Buff, who comforts Paul Berlin while on the night march the evening after Billy Boy's death. O'Brien even adds details to Billy Boy's accident. **"Where Have You Gone, Charming Billy?"** reveals not only that Billy Boy dies of a heart attack when his foot is blown off by a mine, but also that his body suffers further abuse when it falls out of a helicopter removing it from the combat zone:

> the helicopter pulled up and Billy Boy came tumbling out, falling slowly and then faster, and the paddy water sprayed up as if Billy Boy had just executed a long and dangerous dive, as if trying to escape Graves Registration, where he would be tagged and sent home under a flag, dead of a heart attack ... Later they waded in after him, probing for Billy Boy with their rifle butts, elegantly and delicately probing for Billy Boy in the stinking paddy, singing—some of them—*Where have you gone, Billy*

> *Boy, Billy Boy, Oh, where have you gone, charming Billy?* Then they found him. Green and covered with algae, his eyes still wide-open and scared stiff, dead of a heart attack ...

Such differences in versions draw the reader into the text, leading him to question the ambiguous nature of reality. What really is the exact distance between Vietnam and Paris? How many soldiers actually go on the march? Who was Lieutenant Gleason, and what was his story? Which soldier comforts Paul Berlin when he thinks of the dead Billy, and did Billy's body really fall out of the helicopter? The questions posed are, of course, far more important than any definite answers or resolutions.

Even more significantly, O'Brien's denial of a fixed, objective reality in *Going After Cacciato* and the short fiction is revealed through inconsistencies in characterization. Many of O'Brien's characters are ambiguous, and he heightens this ambiguity by changing details about the characters from the short fiction to the novel. A good illustration is Lieutenant Sidney Martin whose view of soldiering differs considerably from that of Paul Berlin. Through Sidney Martin's observation of Paul Berlin, O'Brien makes the point that no two people may know what goes on in the mind of the other, especially in warfare. In *Going After Cacciato,* Lieutenant Martin is a professional soldier who believes in mission and in war. War, he feels, was invented "so that through repetition men might try to do better, so that lessons might be savored and applied the next time, so that men might not be robbed of their own deaths." Lieutenant Martin watches Paul Berlin march on the way to battle, seeing Paul Berlin "as a soldier. Maybe not yet a good soldier, but still a soldier." From his perspective, Sidney Martin admires Paul Berlin with pride, thinking that the youth is steady and persistent:

> Lieutenant Sidney Martin watched him come. He admired the oxen persistence with which the last soldier in the column of thirty-nine marched, thinking that the boy represented so much good-fortitude, discipline, loyalty, self-control, courage, toughness. The greatest gift of God, thought the lieutenant in admiration of Private First Class Paul Berlin's climb, is freedom of will. Sidney Martin, not a man of emotion, felt pride. He raised a hand to hail the boy.

However, O'Brien points out that Paul Berlin does "not have the lieutenant's advantage of perspective and overview and height." Paul Berlin is not thinking of mission or of winning battles; instead, "He knew he would not fight well. He had no love of mission, no love strong enough to make himself fight well." It is ironic that Paul Berlin lacks the very qualities that Lieutenant Sidney Martin thinks he possesses: "He marched up the road with no exercise of will, no desire and no determination, no pride ... moving, climbing, but without thought and without will and without the force of purpose." What O'Brien states in this passage is that the reality in a person's mind, his own subjectivity, may have no connection with what is happening in the external world. People project their own personal misunderstandings onto the world at large, just as the pragmatic Lieutenant Sidney Martin projects his heroic attitudes about war onto the unsuspecting Paul Berlin, who really has no will, no heroic goals. In fact, long before this passage, the reader is told that Paul Berlin's "only goal was to live long enough to establish goals worth living for still longer." He is more interested in survival than in a military victory.

This concern with the problematic nature of reality is revealed even further in O'Brien's short story version of the same march. **"The Way It Mostly Was"** contains the same ironic contrast between Sidney Martin and Paul Berlin as *Going After Cacciato,* but adds details that make Sidney Martin a more ambiguous figure. In the novel, Sidney Martin is portrayed as being so unprofessional that he lacks a human element. He makes his men undertake dangerous tasks such as searching Vietnamese tunnels, and he marches his men "fast and hard." According to a paragraph included in the novel but omitted in the short story, Sidney Martin advises his men prior to the march that "if a man fell out he would be left where he fell." **"The Way It Mostly Was"** also reveals that the men must suffer hardships; for instance, they must carry "forty-pound rucksacks" and march until "Their legs and feet were heavy with blood." Sidney Martin, though, is never directly blamed for placing the men under these adverse conditions, and they demonstrate no hostility toward him. The beginning of "The Way It Mostly Was" chapter in the novel indicates that the soldiers are not happy with their lieutenant. There, one character comments that Lieutenant Martin "always looks for more trouble. He want it? Is that the story—do the man *want* trouble?" Sidney Martin also hopes that someday his men will understand why he believes "in mission first . . . that in war it is necessary to make hard sacrifices." In contrast to the novel's soldiers, the short story's characters seem more understanding of Sidney Martin's view about mission and do not complain about their leader or hint of threatening him.

Thus, in spite of his strict view of soldiering, Captain Sidney Martin of **"The Way It Mostly Was"** is presented as being somewhat more humanistic than the Lieutenant Sidney Martin of *Going After Cacciato.* Certain passages in the story add a new dimension to the character and challenge the reader to try to determine which version, if either, is accurate. We are told in O'Brien's novel that Sidney Martin is "*not* [emphasis added] a man of emotion," yet in the story we are told just the opposite—that the captain is "a man of emotion." He is so emotional, in fact, that watching Paul Berlin march makes him want "to cry." There is no mention of the extremely dangerous tunnel searches. This Captain Sidney Martin believes,

"in human beings deeply" and feels "sad and defeated when one of the human beings in his company of soldiers died or got maimed."

Another character whose nature O'Brien leads us to question is Jim Pederson, a Texan who appears in two short stories as well as in *Going After Cacciato.* Paradoxically, Pederson is described as both a good missionary and a "fine" soldier, and he seems to inspire both good works and evil deeds in his fellow soldiers. In *Going After Cacciato* and the short story **"Landing Zone Bravo,"** Pederson is perhaps best remembered as the soldier who is shot and killed by American helicopter gunners who fire into the same rice paddy where they have dropped the soldiers. The gunners become annoyed when Pederson, who has a real fear of helicopters, is too frightened to exit the aircraft. After throwing Pederson out and then shooting him in the legs, the gunners do not stop but continue to fire methodically until Pederson collapses. Pederson's reaction to being gunned down by his own countrymen is to take careful aim and return fire at the gunship in an effort to make it crash and kill the pilots on board.

This incident demonstrates well the moral ambiguity that confronts Pederson and his fellow squad members in the war. O'Brien uses the characters' recognition of the problematic nature of evil to exemplify problems in the nature of reality itself. Eleven chapters after Pederson's death, the novel presents an image of him that totally denies an inherently violent nature. In Chapter Twenty-two, Pederson is portrayed as a peaceful figure, one whom the other soldiers see as having a "Moral Stance." Pederson "gave first aid to a dying VC woman" and wrote a letter of condolence to the parents of a dead soldier. He also treated the Vietnamese villagers kindly. Yet Pederson's death at the hands of his fellow American soldiers serves only to incite Paul Berlin's squad to violence. After Pederson's body is removed, the soldiers reduce a Vietnamese village to rubble. Ironically, while Pederson had previously prevented the squad from burning a village, they now channel their frustrations over his death into emotionlessly doing just that. They are, in fact, not content with just burning it, but must savagely fire into it as well:

> They lined up and fired into the burning village.
> Harold Murphy used the machine gun. The tracers
> could be seen through the smoke, bright red streamers, and the Willie Peter and HE kept falling, and
> the men fired until they were exhausted. The village
> was a hole.

The duality of Pederson's own nature is demonstrated further in a short story **"Keeping Watch by Night"** that develops Pederson's character much more fully than does the novel. O'Brien tells us that "Jim Pederson had been a missionary in Kenya before he was drafted, and was fond of witnessing to the powers of Christ as Healer." Pederson ironically narrates a story about his involvement in religious faith and healing to Doc Peret and Paul Berlin as he plants Claymore mines on a road and sets up an ambush against the Viet Cong. Therefore, as he is telling the story of the saving of the life of an Indandis woman, he is constructing an L-shaped ambush, "a reliable killing zone" designed to take a number of lives. Pederson is also portrayed as being trustworthy, yet possibly untruthful. The story reveals that Pederson has been selected to prepare such a difficult ambush because he is particularly trustworthy, and the comment that "no one had better eyesight in the dark" than Pederson implies that he can see both physically and spiritually better than the other soldiers. However, the soldiers to whom Pederson tells his supposedly true story of faith healing, his miracle of vision, question its validity: "there were too many uncertainties, too many spots for misinterpretation. . . ."

Perhaps the most significant textual changes deal with the characters of Cacciato and Paul Berlin. In *Going After Cacciato,* O'Brien offers only a segmented portrait of Cacciato, the character in the imaginary journey who is described frequently, yet who is not really described fully. Cacciato is as elusive in description as he is in action. O'Brien deliberately omits any fine detail about Cacciato in order to keep him from being too familiar. We know only that he is "A smudged, lonely-looking figure" with a "broad back" and "a shiny pink spot at the crown of the skull." He has "big and even and white" teeth, "short, fat little fingers with chewed-down nails", and a "pulpy" face "like wax, or like wet paper. Parts of the face, it seemed, could be scraped off and pressed to other parts." Cacciato is "curiously unfinished," lacking "fine detail," and the images surrounding him are always fuzzy. Most frequently, Cacciato is described in negative terms. As "Dumb as a month-old oyster fart," he "missed Mongolian idiocy by the breadth of a genetic hair." Furthermore, he is a "dumb slob," as "Dumb as milk," "a dumb kid," a "sleazy little creep," and a "gremlin." "But who was he?" asks Paul Berlin.

The short story entitled **"Going After Cacciato"** continues the same segmented portrait as the novel. Cacciato is a "rockhead" and a "blockhead" who is "tolerated" by the other soldiers "The way men will sometimes tolerate a pesky dog." He is not only going bald, but is as "Bald as an eagle's ass" and as "Bald as Friar Tuck." Whereas we learn little, if anything, about how the novelistic Cacciato feels about himself, in the short story version we learn of another side to this problematical character, one that is somewhat sensitive to his own ugliness. O'Brien tells us that "Cacciato always took great care to cover the pink bald spot at the crown of his skull."

Ambiguous images of Cacciato permeate O'Brien's fiction. For example, in Chapter One of *Going After Cacciato* when the squad begin their pursuit of the real Cacciato, he waves

to them from the summit of a mountain, flapping his arms with "wide spanning winging motions." Cacciato's flying motions have been interpreted as Christ-like, although Cacciato also exhibits the traits of an anti-Christ. His actions can be compared to those of Satan, the great tempter, who must beat his wings in Canto 34 of Dante's *Inferno* while crunching traitors in his mouth. And, in a sense, Cacciato is a Satanic figure. While he guides the squad and rescues them from perils on their imaginary journey, he also serves as the temptation which leads them further into their possible desertion of the war, an act that would condemn them as traitors to their country. Consequently, Cacciato can be viewed as both a symbol of good and evil. How does one distinguish between the two polarities? Such ambiguities draw the reader into the search for Cacciato along with the characters. As Cacciato's face appears, only to metamorphosize into the moon or a Halloween jack-o-lantern, the reader creates his own version of the mythical soldier, the same process of constituting reality that is undertaken by the individual members of Paul Berlin's squad.

Cacciato's ambivalence is complicated even further by the appearance of different details in the short story. Whereas in the novel Cacciato's palms are down when he flaps his arms to signal the squad, in the short story his palms are up, another reinforcement of a Christ-like image. Yet the reader of both the novel and the short stories learns that Cacciato is both compassionate *and* unfeeling. On one hand, he is kind to Paul Berlin in the novel, offering him gum and talking to him after Billy Boy's death. He is also the one soldier in the squad in both the novel and the short story **"The Fisherman"** who does not want to see Lieutenant Sidney Martin die, stating that Martin is "not all that bad." However, O'Brien makes Cacciato even more problematical by showing us a horrific side of him that coexists along with the compassionate part. While Cacciato does not want to participate in the fragging of Lieutenant Sidney Martin, evidence indicates that he is certainly not adverse to atrocity. His perverse nature is revealed in the photograph of "Cacciato squatting beside the corpse of a shot-dead VC in green pajamas, Cacciato holding up the dead boy's head by a shock of brilliant black hair, Cacciato smiling."

Paul Berlin's attitude toward Cacciato also varies somewhat between the novel and the short story. In the novel we are told that Paul Berlin has "nothing" against Cacciato, but in the short story we are told that he has "nothing *special* [emphasis added] against him," implying that he does indeed have something against Cacciato. Some readers of the novel have concluded that Paul Berlin would like to harm Cacciato. Peter Roundy, for instance, suggests that Paul Berlin wishes to kill Cacciato, his double, in "an act of symbolic suicide," because he feels guilty that he himself has not left the war, a war in which he has never believed. Katherine Kearns advocates that the novel implies that Paul Berlin really kills

Cacciato. Certainly the novel contains statements that could be interpreted that way. In Chapter One, Paul Berlin experiences "a vision of murder. Butchery, no less: Cacciato's right temple caving inward, silence, then an enormous explosion of outward-going brains." Then in Chapter Two, an observation post chapter, Paul Berlin thinks of the possibilities, the many ways in which the pursuit of Cacciato could have ended. At one point, he questions, "Had it ever ended in tragedy?" Yet, at the same time, he posits, "Had it ever ended?"

The ambiguity is heightened even further in the short story when Paul Berlin elaborates on his "vision of murder." "It was no metaphor; he didn't think in metaphors," he states, indicating that the murder is real and not imagined. However, he also adds, "it was a simple scary vision . . . Nothing to justify such a bloody image, no origins. . . . Where, he thought, was all this taking him, and where would it end?" He further thinks that Cacciato does deserve to die:

> Murder was the logical circuit-stopper, of course; it was Cacciato's rightful, maybe inevitable due. Nobody can get away with stupidity forever, and in war the final price for it is always paid in purely biological currency, hunks of toe or pieces of femur or bits of exploded brain. And it *was* still a war, wasn't it?

Is Paul Berlin suggesting that he wishes to kill Cacciato or merely that Cacciato may take so many risks that he will be killed in the war? This ambiguity is important because such a technique potentially involves the reader in the process of creation. The "deep, jagged, complex country" in which the squad travels as Paul Berlin has these thoughts perhaps suggests that Vietnam contains no simple answers or resolutions.

The fate of Paul Berlin is left as uncertain as that of Cacciato. At the end of the novel, Paul Berlin is still in Vietnam, and we never learn whether or not he survives his tour of duty, just as we never learn whether or not certain events in the novel actually take place. O'Brien, however, has written a story, **"Speaking of Courage,"** which focuses on Paul Berlin after his return home from the war. While the story is not included in *Going After Cacciato,* it plays off of Chapter Fourteen, "Upon Almost Winning the Silver Star," where Lieutenant Sidney Martin orders someone to search a Vietnamese tunnel. None of the men, including Paul Berlin, will volunteer for the dangerous task, so Lieutenant Martin forces Frenchie Tucker to search the tunnel by threatening him with court martial. Frenchie Tucker enters the tunnel only to die of a gunshot wound. In **"Speaking of Courage,"** Paul Berlin is thinking about how he might have won the Silver Star for bravery in Vietnam had he managed to rescue Frenchie Tucker himself.

Although the story begins by stating that the war is over, we have no way of knowing whether Paul Berlin's return to the

United States really takes place or whether it is conceived in the mind of Paul Berlin as he "pretends." In fact, Paul Berlin makes it clear that he is "pretending" in certain parts of the story. He imagines a conversation with his father:

> "How many medals did you win?" his father might have asked.
>
> "Seven," he would have said, "though none of them were for valor."
>
> "That's all right," his father would have answered, knowing full well that many brave men did not win medals for their bravery, and that others won medals for doing nothing. "What are the medals you won?"
>
> And he would have listed them, as a kind of starting place for talking about the war . . .

The use of indefinite verb forms such as "might" and "would" in specific passages provides a clue that Paul Berlin is more than likely fantasizing once more, even though the story itself is told as if Paul is really at home and only thinking about the war in his past. Again, though, we are left with no definite answers or resolutions. While **"Speaking of Courage,"** supposedly takes place after Vietnam, it by no means answers the question of whether or not Paul Berlin survived the war.

It is O'Brien's refusal to allow us final knowledge, the suspension of final judgment through all of his works, that contributes to his fiction's distinction. Both *Going After Cacciato* and the short fiction are arguments against viewing reality in terms of fixed perceptions. How in life and in literature can one distinguish between what is real and what is not? By raising issues and by still not resolving them, O'Brien continues to resist simplistic answers while portraying the complex tangles and nuances of actual experience. Even more importantly, he demonstrates the need of American culture to reject any oversimplifications of the Vietnam War's inconsistencies and discrepancies and shows us the dangers of imposing final definitions on this elusive and on-going chapter of our American history. *Going After Cacciato* and the short fiction are significant in that they are postmodernist works that carry their readers far beyond a one-dimensional view of reality or the war. Not only do they project the war's pluralities of vision, its moral complexities, and its unsolvable oppositions, but they also prove that there is no one definite way in which to tell a war story. In both theme and technique, Tim O'Brien allows for what he terms "a million possibilities."

Albert E. Wilhelm (essay date Spring 1991)

SOURCE: "Ballad Allusions in Tim O'Brien's 'Where Have You Gone, Charming Billy?'," in *Studies in Short Fiction*, Vol. 28, No. 2, Spring, 1991, pp. 218-22.

[*In the essay below, Wilhelm observes a difference in use of allusions to the ballads "Billy Boy" and "Lord Randal" in O'Brien's short story and the version that appeared in* Going after Cacciato *as "Night Watch."*]

Before being joined and published as a novel, several chapters of Tim O'Brien's *Going After Cacciato* appeared as individual short stories. Frequently these stories were much shorter than the corresponding chapters in O'Brien's novel, and they usually bore different titles. For example, in the October 1977 issue of *Esquire*, O'Brien published a story entitled **"Fisherman."** Subsequently he expanded this piece to form two separate chapters in *Going After Cacciato,* and he renamed these chapters "Lake Country" and "World's Greatest Lake Country."

Critical commentary on *Going After Cacciato* is, of course, both extensive and illuminating, but O'Brien's early short stories have been largely ignored. Even though many of these stories were absorbed into a longer work, the individual stories are significantly different both in text and in context from corresponding chapters of the completed novel. Indeed, several of the stories won prizes as pieces of short fiction and thus deserve attention as examples of that genre. In order to illustrate the distinctive features of O'Brien's short stories, this note will focus on a story entitled **"Where Have You Gone, Charming Billy?,"** which was first published in the May 1975 issue of *Redbook*. After much revision it reappeared with the title "Night March" as Chapter 31 of *Going After Cacciato.* In its original version, O'Brien's story contains persistent allusions to folk ballads, and these allusions provide significant clues for interpretation.

With his change of title to "Night March," O'Brien shifts his focus from the plight of an individual to the joint activities of a military unit. In its original form, however, the piece is a very moving initiation story, and its allusive title works nicely to reinforce important themes. This title refers, of course, to the old folk song "Billie Boy," and lines from the song appear at several points in the account of Paul Berlin's "first day at the war." Even though O'Brien's title alludes to the second line of the folk song, his phrasing is distinctive. Bertrand Bronson has identified twenty-nine variants of "Billie Boy," but none of them exactly matches the wording of O'Brien's question. Numerous versions of the song ask, "Where have you been, Billie Boy," and five versions ask, "Where are you going?" O'Brien's use of the verb go with a shift in tense may appear insignificant, but it establishes an elegiac tone not present in the lighthearted song. On his first day in battle, Paul has witnessed the bizarre death of Billy Boy Watkins. As he reflects on the death of his fellow soldier, he also mourns the loss of his own innocence—especially that sense of himself "when he was a boy . . . camping with his father in the midnight summer along the Des Moines River." In O'Brien's story, then, the question from a comic folk song becomes a plaintive reiteration of the *ubi sunt* motif.

The text of the *Redbook* story (but not that of the novel) quotes part of the folk song's description of Billie Boy's girl. Each stanza of the song typically ends with a line affirming that she is "a young thing and cannot leave her mother." This "young" girl's actual age remains indefinite, but in various versions of the song she is said to be "twice forty-five eleven" and "a hundred like and nine." Even though these ages may be difficult to calculate precisely, it seems clear that the girl is far from young. Indeed, the folk song's outrageous math may imply a triple-digit age. If, at this stage, she is still too young to leave her mother, what can be said of the confused adolescents who populate O'Brien's story? The reader is invited to transfer the song's comic assertion about a young girl and see its more painful relevance in describing the dead Billy Boy, Paul Berlin, and all the youthful soldiers who are suffering the shock of separation from mothers and motherland.

O'Brien's *Redbook* story depicts Paul's painful initiation, but it also shows his attempt to deal with that pain by means of an imaginative transformation. During the march Paul "pretended he was not a soldier" and "that Billy Boy Watkins had not died of a heart attack that afternoon." By the end of the march he has transformed tragedy into comedy by creating a parody of a death notification:

> He imagined Billy's father opening the telegram: SORRY TO INFORM YOU THAT YOUR SON BILLY BOY WAS YESTERDAY SCARED TO DEATH IN ACTION IN THE REPUBLIC OF VIETNAM, VALIANTLY SUCCUMBING TO A HEART ATTACK SUFFERED WHILE UNDER ENORMOUS STRESS, AND IT IS WITH GREATEST SYMPATHY THAT . . . He giggled again. He rolled onto his belly and pressed his face into his arms. His body was shaking with giggles.

In the last paragraph of the story, Paul copes with his immediate pain by projecting into the future. The horror of Billy's death is reduced to "a funny war story that he would tell to his father." The bizarre episode will become the basis for "a good joke."

If allusions to the song "Billie Boy" are useful in emphasizing the theme of initiation, they are equally apt in reinforcing this idea of imaginative transformation. According to Bronson, "Billie Boy" is a "spirited parody" of the tragic ballad "Lord Randal." Just as Paul Berlin takes the horrors of war and recreates them in a ludicrous and hence more tolerable form, this song takes a tragic episode of courtship and transforms it into a comic series of questions and answers.

To understand how "Billie Boy" functions as a parody, one must examine the grim materials on which it is apparently based. Like O'Brien's story and the song "Billie Boy," the ballad "Lord Randal" begins with a question addressed to a young man: "O where have you been, Lord Randal, my son?" Later stanzas of the song focus on the source of the poison Lord Randal has consumed and the various legacies he will leave his survivors. These narrative elements, although they have been radically altered in "Billie Boy," provide an additional subtext for O'Brien's story about the war in Vietnam. "Lord Randal" emphasizes betrayal by one who should be worthy of trust, and O'Brien's soldiers in Vietnam feel equally betrayed and abandoned. The murderer of Lord Randal is identified differently in various versions of the ballad. Typically the villain is Randal's sweetheart, but some of the 103 variants collected by Bronson place the blame on his wife, sister, grandmother, and even his father. In all cases, however, the betrayal is even more devastating because it is executed by one who is presumably so close and loving. Still another detail that suggests misplaced confidence is the specific source of the poison consumed by Lord Randal. Here again the many versions of the ballad differ greatly. Most of the variants printed by Bronson identify the poison source as eels or fishes, but some versions specify "dill and dill broth," "sweet milk and parsnips," "eggs fried in butter," and bread with mutton. The common element in all these cases is a deceptive wholesomeness. What appears healthful and nutritious is in fact deadly. Such are the lessons that Paul must rapidly learn in **"Where Have You Gone, Charming Billy?"** A path that looks safe may be planted with "land mines and booby traps." His fellow soldier Watkins may seem "tough as nails," but he suffers a fatal attack of fear. The mission in Vietnam may at first appear grand and glorious, but soon Paul will see only hollowness and horror.

Among the legacies that Lord Randal will leave his survivors, the most notable are those intended for the one who betrayed him. In various versions of the ballad, these bequests include "the rope and the gallows," the "keys of hell's gates," "hell fire and brimstone," and a "barrel of powder, to blow her up high." If the prevailing tone of "Lord Randal" is bitter and vengeful, that of "Billie Boy" is outrageously comic. Instead of brutal legacies left to a false lover, we find in the later song a list of singular achievements attributed to one who will apparently remain endlessly faithful. For example, in the version of the song that Bronson identifies as number 26, Billie's sweetheart "can bake a cherry pie / As quick as a cat can wink her eye." She can "sweep up a house / As quick as a cat can catch a mouse" and even "make up a bed / Seven feet above her head." In "Billie Boy" then, hyperbolic comedy displaces the cynicism and bitterness of "Lord Randal."

In a similar fashion Paul Berlin's comic telegram uses hyperbole to keep the horrors of war at bay.

Other differences between **"Where Have You Gone, Charming Billy?"** and "Night March" could be noted, but this difference in use of ballad allusions is central. While some ballad allusions are retained in the novel, such references are more persistent and more significant in the *Redbook* story. Throughout O'Brien's story the ballad subtexts provide ironic resonance. With its references to cherry pies and protective mothers, the song "Billie Boy" conjures up an image of home and family that contrasts sharply with the dangerous world into which Paul is initiated. Descriptions of Billie Boy's sweetheart and her remarkable domestic skills suggest fidelity and invincibility—qualities prominent in the rhetoric but seldom in the reality of Vietnam. The ballad "Lord Randal" offers a subtext that is more deeply submerged but equally important in O'Brien's story. Most versions of the song focus on the last words of a young man who courted unwisely and suffered death at the hands of his treacherous lover. Such materials echo the American dilemma in Southeast Asia where idealistic commitments turned bad and left behind a bitter legacy.

James Griffith (essay date Spring 1991)

SOURCE: "A Walk through History: Tim O'Brien's *Going after Cacciato*," in *War, Literature, and the Arts*, Vol. 3, No. 1, Spring, 1991, pp. 1-34.

[*In the essay below, Griffith explicates the meanings of both the characters' actions and the narrative's events in* Going after Cacciato *by situating them in their historical context.*]

Going After Cacciato, Paul Berlin's surname would (or used to) suggest that he is a soldier divided against himself. His immediate circumstance finds him on watch duty atop an observation post at Quang Ngai, Vietnam, from midnight to six a.m. in late November 1968. It is "a bad time," for several of his comrades have been lost. Unmentioned is the frightful history of the year: the Tet offensive and siege at Khe Sanh, the massacre at My Lai, the assassinations of Martin Luther King, Jr. and Robert Kennedy, the riots in Chicago during the Democratic convention, and, finally, the prospect of peace talks in Paris—with the shape of the table first on the agenda. Bad time, indeed. Nevertheless, these particular facts of history do not explicitly occupy Paul's mind.

In *If I Die in a Combat Zone,* a memoir of his participation in the history of that time, O'Brien writes that he was persuaded that "the war was wrong." Even so, when he was drafted in the summer of 1968, doubts about his ability to understand the issues, and feelings of duty to family and country, prevented him from going to Sweden by way of Canada: "I simply couldn't bring myself to flee. Family, the hometown, friends, history, tradition, fear, confusion, exile: I could not run." Although O'Brien served his tour of duty in 1969, he places Paul in Vietnam a year earlier—a time of several important tides' turnings, whether Paul thinks about them or not. The personal issue of moral courage remains, though, and the novel thereby becomes what O'Brien has called a fictional "flip side" of the memoir in which he can imagine the consequences of running. The novel, however, does more than revise personal history: it confronts and struggles with history, personal and national.

As Dennis Vannatta has correctly observed, the novel has three kinds of chapters. First are those chapters marking Paul's hours on the observation post where he tries to think through his fears and doubts and recollect the order of terrible experiences since arriving in Vietnam. Second, in no particular order, are his flashbacks, some of home and youth, but mostly of terrible experiences of fear and death in six months of combat, including the deliberately indirect memory of his complicity in the platoon's fragging of Lt. Martin because of Martin's insistence upon searching tunnels. Last are the fantastic chapters in which Paul imagines a mission to pursue and capture Cacciato, the rather simple-minded soldier who, profoundly disillusioned by Martin's murder, has left the war to walk to Paris. (Even in this fictional world, then, Paul contemplates running only as a fanciful possibility; moreover, feeling the same doubts O'Brien mentions in his *If I Die in a Combat Zone,* Paul cannot even imagine desertion without the excuse of pursuing a real deserter, Cacciato.) This fantastic journey raises the questions I wish to address: Why Paris? For such a desperate plan, would not Hong Kong or even Rome be closer? What purpose do the several characters met along the way serve? And why does Paul encounter certain kinds of events?

In broad terms, Eric James Schroeder has described the journey as more than an escape: when Paul plays solitaire and pretends he is winning in Las Vegas, "This type of 'pretending' is simply escapism. . ."; but when he imagines the journey, his "'working out of the possibilities' represents a mode of not only coping with the war's reality (paradoxically, through the illusion of escaping it) but also of coming to terms with his identity as a soldier." Thomas Myers notes that, even if Paul did wish for escape in the imaginative journey, the "pursuit of Cacciato is filled with the same hazards, personal fears, and moral quandaries offered by the reality experienced in unfiltered Vietnam daylight." Instead of a replay of actual conflict, Edward Palm finds a contemporary morality play in the journey: Cacciato's "nondescript quality" represents the idea that

> the idealistic concepts of honor, courage, and patriotism we traditionally pursue in time of war are

vague and without substance. Seen in this light, the pursuit of Cacciato becomes an ironic allegory for the Vietnam War itself with yet another character, a young Vietnamese girl named Sarkin Aung Wan, serving as foil to Cacciato and representing the tempting expedient of simply abandoning a futile and pointless quest.

Each of these views suggests points worth pursuing, but none specifically addresses the questions raised above about the particular characters and events. The answers lie in seeing that, as Schroeder writes, the journey turns into more than a wishful escape: to be precise, Paul tries to imagine a walk to Paris, but the implied author directs his route through history, a six-hour fantasy that blends six months of Paul's history with the country's; if not the literal allegory that Palm claims, the fantasy certainly places mimetic details of Paul's life in a much larger context of political issues. That is, the itinerary and events force Paul to relive some of his recent, chaotic past—as Myers suggests—and, unconsciously, to retrace some of the war's history. Along the way, Paul confronts the difficulty of making sense of his role in the war's moral and political confusion, for he has no settled ideas about the conflict. An implied author, on the other hand, "will never be neutral toward all values. Our reactions to his various commitments, secret or overt, will help to determine our response to the work." In this instance, the implied author, quite aware of the contesting parties' histories and the war's outcome, hopes to show how this war cruelly forced soldiers personally to face terrible issues—with sometimes heroic and sometimes ignoble results—for politically vain reasons.

The sense of history holds much importance in the novel. Along the road to Paris, Paul's squad spends a night in Ovissil, Afghanistan. The town's mayor, their host, is a "history-teller" (whose stance resembles the implied author's over Paul's story): "Fortune telling is for lunatics and old women. History is the stronger science, for it has the virtue of certainty without the vice of blasphemy." He then tells Lt. Corson's history but refuses to tell Paul's: "You are young. . . . I cannot tell unmade histories." Paul feels slighted, insisting he has a history, and the ensuing chapter recounts—in fewer than two pages—his life up to the age of twenty when he was drafted.

Although Paul does not realize it, his first two decades were the easy part. His last six months present the difficulties and hardly reflect any "virtue of certainty": "Keeping track wasn't easy. The order of things—chronologies—that was the hard part." This confusion will never disappear for Paul or for the reader. Careful attention allows us to put many events in order, but we cannot resolve the contradictory facts that Pederson is present when Bernie Lynn dies in Chapter 14 and that Bernie Lynn is present when Pederson dies in Chapter 20. (In addition to questions brought on by Paul's confused memory, we might also ask how his imagination, in November 1968, could accurately predict that Dwight Eisenhower would die about the time the squad arrives in Paris on April Fools' Day 1969.) Nevertheless, the imaginary trek gives Paul the opportunity to review and, at least, attempt to comprehend his recent past.

Fear dominates that recent past, and Paul feels ashamed of his lack of courage. In fact, he knows he could have killed a comrade in panic, actually firing the rounds himself—quite a different matter from his passive complicity with the squad's murder of Lt. Martin. The mission to capture Cacciato ends on a hill where the squad thinks they have Cacciato surrounded. As they charge, Paul begins firing uncontrollably, even setting the grass on fire. Fortunately, Cacciato has decamped, for otherwise he would certainly have been caught in the fusillade of Paul's automatic weapon. Soon thereafter, in Paul's imagined continuation of the mission, Stink's capture of some refugees imaginatively revises the act. Stink shoots suddenly, without warning, "without aiming," on automatic fire—"It was Quick Kill. Point blank, rifle jerking"—and slaughters two water buffalo while miraculously missing the three women on the cart. Stink boasts of his quick reactions, but the others call him stupid, much as they were disgusted with Paul on the hill. At the end of the imaginary mission, however, Paul cannot displace the responsibility onto Stink, nor displace his panic with something like Stink's bravado: when the squad bursts into Cacciato's Paris apartment, Paul shoots up the room uncontrollably. Paul realizes that the room, like the hill, "was empty," but he knows that he could not have stopped his panicky firing in any case. Paul calls the charge up the hill the "last known fact," but in his imagination, the fear that ensues is the first and lasting fact—a fear that can cause one to turn on innocents and comrades.

Of course the war has much that anyone would reasonably fear. For instance, the elaborate system of tunnels led soldiers to believe that the enemy could pop up and just as suddenly disappear anywhere. Also, for a platoon under the command of a Lt. Martin, finding a tunnel entrance requires, according to Standard Operating Procedure, dispatching one man into the tight, dark hole to search it. On the fantastic journey, when "a hole in the road to Paris" spills the squad into an international network of tunnels, the lone Vietcong, Li Van Hgoc (a Southeast Asian "Leewen' oek?"), pushes Paul to look through a periscope, forcing him to examine that particular fear out of the recent past. Through the mouth of a tunnel, Paul watches a replay of two comrades' deaths, those of Frenchie and Bernie Lynn: having been threatened with court martial, Frenchie has crawled into the tunnel and been shot; when no one volunteers to go in after him (although Cacciato is willing), Bernie Lynn swears, drops his gear, and goes in where "his feet were still showing when he was shot." Paul also sees himself standing aside, "careful not to look at anyone" when Lt. Martin is asking for volunteers. As Li Van

Hgoc tells him, "From down below, or from inside out, you often discover entirely new understandings."

By force of imagination, Paul manages to escape this tunnel with his remaining comrades, but reminders of fear and death persist along the road to Paris. In Tehran, they witness the beheading of an Iranian soldier who had gone AWOL. Besides reminding Paul that running is a crime, the execution also recalls a kind of shame and futility surrounding death in combat. Buff, another comrade killed in action, is found dead in the "unpretty" position of kneeling face-down: ". . . all hunched up on his knees, ass stickin' up in the air. . . . like the way Arabs pray. . . ." After a helicopter removes Buff's body, the rest of the platoon notices his face has been left in the helmet. Doc says it is "not decent. . . . not respectable" to leave Buff's face that way, and Cacciato casually disposes of it in some tall grass, "like a woman emptying her wash basin—." The Iranian soldier, kneeling face-down before the chopping block, as Paul observes, shows no emotion until a fly settles on his face: "It was not fear. It was shame. . . . The boy's tongue was still groping toward his nose when the axe fell." The fear of death grips deeply enough, but the cruel feelings of ridiculous futility, embarrassment—the literal loss of face—linger for those whom death spares.

The squad's escape from Tehran—they have been arrested for desertion—recalls another fearful sensation Paul would have felt in combat: the feeling of chaos. Cacciato springs them from *Savak's* jail and sends them off in a Chevy Impala, but they soon find themselves surrounded in a traffic circle:

> The sounds of the rifle fire were lost in the deeper sounds of artillery, but the soldiers were firing, and red tracers made pretty darts in the wind. The car bucked. There was the sudden smell of burning metal, then tearing sounds. The red darts made holes in the door. A window crashed open and the wind sucked in.
>
> . . . Stink's door had come open. He was weeping, hanging on to the elbow rest, but spinning forces kept the door open, dragging Stink out. He screamed and clawed at the door. . . . Paul Berlin tried to get his eyes to close.

Details of this chaotic ambush—the sounds of gunfire and the wind, the holes shot through metal, the burning smell, the inability of one soldier to maintain his balance, and the inability of another to watch—come directly from memory of the hot landing where Pederson was eventually cut down by the indiscriminate "friendly fire" of the helicopter's door gunners:

> Then there were new sounds. Like dog whistles, high pitched and sharp. . . . Holes opened in the hull, then

more holes, and the wind sucked through the holes, and Vaught was shouting. A long tear opened in the floor, then a corresponding tear in the ceiling above, and the wind howled in all around.

. . . There was a burning smell—metal and hot machinery and the gunners' guns. Harold Murphy was still on the floor, smiling and shaking his head and trying to get up, but he couldn't do it. He'd get to his knees and press, and almost make it, but not quite, and he'd fall and shake his head and smile and try again. Pederson's eyes were closed. He held his stomach and sat still. He was the only one still sitting.

This bedlam in combat brings about the death of Pederson. In the imaginary replay of the scene as they escape from Tehran, no casualties from "friendly fire" occur, but Paul's mind quickly turns to another self-inflicted defeat, the fragging of Lt. Martin: "The way events led to events, and the way they got out of human control." Paul does not want to fight in Vietnam, and Cacciato does not want to kill Lt. Martin, but both are "pressed" into service: the draft brings Paul to Vietnam, and, as one event uncontrollably leads to another, he presses Cacciato's hand onto the grenade that the squad has touched to signify their votes for Lt. Martin's murder.

Paul thinks now that "Cacciato was dumb, but he was right." Thus, even if Paul cannot simply walk away from the war, he cannot completely dismiss this response in anyone else. In Paris, the men never actually lay hands on Cacciato, and even before their final attempt to capture him, Lt. Corson and Sarkin, the refugee whom Paul loves, disappear as well: "Heading east. A long walk but we'll make it." Out of Paul's recent, chaotic history, then, the imaginary trek leads to difficult resolutions: the first and last fact is fear, and the first and last escape is walking away—unless he can face that dominating fear.

These imagined events sort out and rehearse Paul's recent past the way dreams may refashion events and feelings from waking life: some leave tremendously awful impressions—such as the hot landing that ends with Pederson's death—or strangely minor ones—such as Cacciato's getting "bites" while fishing in rain-filled craters, a detail that transforms into Stink's getting bitten by Cacciato on the road to Paris (that is, a bite from something that is not there). Thus, to the extent so far discussed, the daydream's fearsome events, as those in a nightmare, have no more motivation than the emotion of fear and the reaction of flight. On another level, however, above the concerns of the character, the implied author uses Paul's imaginative escape to dramatize some of the larger historical issues about which Paul is ignorant. Paul seems, as mentioned earlier, unaware of the extraordinary turmoil that marked 1968. With no knowledge of current events, he certainly will have little understanding of their historical context, a circumstance that, Myers states, raises the difficult question of "how to act properly within a configuration that affords the entrapped soldier little historical understanding or moral justification as he experiences the most jarring imagery of waste and death." James C. Wilson emphasizes that *Going After Cacciato* succeeds because, like so few other novels set in Vietnam, it perceptively "explores the problem that arises from the absence of historical perspective." The chapter "The Things They Didn't Know" neatly summarizes this ignorance:

Not knowing the language, they did not know the people. They did not know what the people loved or respected or feared or hated.

. . . [Paul] didn't know who was right, or what was right; he didn't know if it was a war of self-determination or self-destruction, outright aggression or national liberation; he didn't know which speeches to believe, which books, which politicians; he didn't know if nations would topple like dominoes or stand separate like trees; he didn't know who really started the war, or why, or when, or with what motives; he didn't know if it mattered; he saw sense in both sides of the debate, but he didn't know where truth lay; he didn't know if Communist tyranny would prove worse in the long run than the tyrannies of Ky or Thieu or Khanh—he simply didn't know.

. . . They did not know even the simple things: a sense of victory, or satisfaction, or necessary sacrifice. They did not know the feeling of taking a place and keeping it, securing a village and then raising the flag and calling it a victory. . . . They did not know how to feel when they saw villages burning. Revenge? Loss? Peace of mind or anguish? . . . They did not know good from evil.

The imaginary walk to Paris does not resolve such doubts for Paul, but in the arrangement of incidents that refer to larger historical issues, we can perceive the shape of O'Brien's belief.

The simple act of crossing the border out of Vietnam should recall the expansion of the war into Laos and Cambodia—incursions that were more common than the public realized until Nixon made the operations public in 1970. The squad's mission is to pursue Cacciato who is seeking respite from the war by fleeing Vietnam; the American military's tactics were to pursue Vietcong who sought sanctuary in neighboring countries. If the objects of pursuit differ, the national strategy and the squad's mission yield similar results. The squad's mission is doubly fruitless: Cacciato always eludes them, and inasmuch as Paul wishes to escape the war, his imaginative journey keeps returning him to the war, its sensations and its issues. Crossing borders solves no problems; in fact, it leads to confronting them instead, for Paul, unlike Cacciato, cannot simply walk away from the war.

For the US, the incursions into Laos and Cambodia were fruitless and even destructive. In Laos, proxy bombing raids in the early 1960s and then actual US bombing, in a decade's time, forced over 140,000 people off the Plain of Jars and onto the road as refugees. Another proxy incursion by Army of the Republic of Vietnam (ARVN) troops to cut the Ho Chi Minh trail within Laos resulted in disaster when the troops were drawn in, surrounded, and then cut up despite heavy American air support; the ARVN suffered a 50% casualty rate, and supply traffic along the trail returned, not only to normal, but reached even higher than previous volumes within three months. All along, the diplomatic struggles of Souvanna Phouma, favoring the North Vietnamese and later turning a deaf ear to the bombing of their supply routes in his country, came to naught when, upon the US's general withdrawal from southeast Asia, Phouma had to negotiate for a coalition government that the Pathet Lao quickly abandoned and overran.

Similarly, the more infamous invasion of Cambodia yielded no real benefits. US troops destroyed plenty of materiel but inflicted relatively few casualties, thereby delaying the "North Vietnamese offensive by no more than a year." Prince Norodom Sihanouk, like Souvanna Phouma, allowed the bombing of enemy supply lines without complaint, and his political life fared as well as his neighbor's in Laos. Faced with contending ideas on how to handle the challenge of the indigenous Khmer Rouge, Sihanouk's government was overthrown by Lon Nol; Lon Nol first adamantly condemned all foreign intervention in Cambodia but soon asked for help—which came in the form of the US incursion that the Nixon administration had planned already. Of course, when the secrecy of Nixon's Cambodian moves was revealed, the backlash at home was politically costly and even incendiary at Kent State where four students died during protests on campus. As for Cambodia, in the intervening years 1970 to 1975, Lon Nol's government relied on the support of the US, and the American withdrawal from Southeast Asia left Cambodia powerless to repulse Pol Pot's Khmer Rouge and the coming of what we know as the "killing fields." For Paul Berlin's squad's military mission and America's military policy, then, crossing borders solves nothing and even creates additional problems; what begins as pursuit of Cacciato becomes a running from the original conflict. The fictional squad's motives may be understandable, but the larger US policy shows blundering and shame.

Once into Laos, Berlin's squad encounters the refugee problem, personified in Sarkin Aung Wan. Paul has always considered the native population with sadness and regret: "He wanted to be liked. He wanted them to understand, all of them, that he felt no hate. It was all a sad accident, he would

have told them—chance, high-level politics, confusion." He cannot explain himself because he cannot speak their language. With Sarkin, though, Paul can talk and even fall in love. Their different problems keep them separate, however. Sarkin needs to find peace by any means to survive; Paul needs to find peace in the means by which he survives. As he would confess to the people, he is "guilty perhaps of hanging on, of letting myself be dragged along; of falling victim to gravity and obligation and events, but not—not!—guilty of wrong intentions." In the end, Paul has almost nothing to offer Sarkin that can help. Long before Paul arrived in Vietnam, the policy of the Diem government was to move the villagers out of hamlets and into refugee camps, and American strategy "completed the process the Diem regime had begun." Michael Huynh, of the Southeast Asia Resettlement Program, underscores the final impact of uprooting so many:

> . . . more than a million people were forced out of Vietnam at the end of the war. . . . Even during the famine of 1945, when more than two million people died from lack of food, we did not leave our country. The results of this war displaced a whole population.

Paul loves Sarkin and wants to save her, but the common soldier's lot is to be frustrated in such humane desires. Not surprisingly, therefore, out of their "peace talks" in Paris, "there is no true negotiation."

Of course, even if Paul could speak to the people, many may not care to listen, for the issues escape him as surely as Cacciato does. Paul knows how he feels but cannot understand how the Vietnamese feel: how and why they suffer. Paul assumes that only the war's killing and destruction oppress the people. This assumption proves to be naive once Paul spots Cacciato among a crowd of monks in Mandalay. Paul wades into the crowd, apparently believing that an American soldier can count on the passivity of monks everywhere. But these monks administer quite a thrashing to Paul, for as Sarkin explains, he is "disturbing Cao Dai. Disrupting evening prayers. Touching the untouchables." Paul's blunder ought to remind the reader of American ignorance concerning the religious issues in Vietnam: early on, the US was supporting Diem, a Catholic who was suppressing Buddhism. Frances Fitzgerald points out that reporters who discussed protests in terms of religious versus political motivations "were so entrenched in their Western notion of the division of church and state that they could not imagine the Vietnamese might not make the distinction." In addition, the Vietnamese monks hardly behaved with total passivity: during protests, they carried signs in English, which they did not speak or understand, and they quickly "came to know which TV crews to phone when a self-immolation was scheduled, and how much time to give them to get to the appointed place and set up their cameras." These visual records of monks burning themselves in protest against Diem dealt American viewers a severe shock, and the naivete of the reporting only added to the bewilderment.

These political martyrs were Buddhist whereas Paul confronts Cao Dai monks. Aside from general religious issues, this reference to a specific sect carries other implications. The Cao Dai show western influence insofar as their worship is eclectic: they reverse Jesus and Buddha, but also "saints" such as Joan of Arc, Victor Hugo, and Sun Yat-sen. Their political loyalties would have baffled Paul all the more had he known the Cao Dai's history. In the late fifties, the US ambassador forestalled a possible overthrow of Diem by bribing, along with other leaders, influential members of the Cao Dai; Diem survived, but thousands of the Cao Dai soon joined the opposition that would become the Vietcong. Of further interest, in terms of problems O'Brien considers, the Cao Dai, in the early fifties, attracted many youths who joined in order to avoid a military draft. Paul Berlin cannot realize that he takes a beating from people who might share his feelings of resistance—without the confusion—regarding the war.

Paul, like most Americans, knows little about such historic forces in Vietnam and, further, knows just as little about the historic force he represents himself. Whatever the morality of American policy, the presence of such a large military commitment meant dislocation for the Vietnamese culture anyway. The causing of destruction and the meddling in foreign affairs aside, America's presence in Vietnam precipitated changes that appear less obvious. In the novel, Paul Berlin confronts these changes in the person of Hamijolli Chand (whose name means "jolly moon," which recalls the characterization of the happy, moon-faced Cacciato). In Delhi, she houses the squad in her hotel and clearly enjoys their company. Jolly Chand, as the Americans call her, tells of how she once lived in America and fell in love with its shopping malls, televisions, and other temptations: "'Corrupted,' she said brightly. 'That's what my husband contends—corrupted by hamburgers and french fries and Winston One Hundreds.'" As if the materialistic desires were not condemning enough, Jolly has a taste for beef and, soon, a taste for Lt. Corson—appetites in a country that reveres sacred cows and supports the tradition of purdah, the practice of keeping women secluded from men not their husbands.

Just so, entering Vietnam involved more than a military presence; the American presence represented a cultural invasion whose soldiers brought their language, their music, their food, and much other "artillery" in the war to make a home away from home. The US, however, was not alone in initiating such corrupting influence. Archimedes L. A. Patti quotes a French report criticizing the High Commissioner for turning Saigon into a place "where gambling, depravity, love of money and of power finish by corrupting the morale and destroying willpower. . . ." Frances Fitzgerald states, however, that the

French occupation and war at least left the family intact, but with the American war came a complete cultural death: "'That is, above all, what the Vietnamese blame the Americans for,' said one Vietnamese scholar. 'Willfully or not, they have tended to destroy what is most precious to us: family, friendship, our manner of expressing ourselves'"; in addition, those peasants who moved into the cities and became "used to the luxuries of the West and the freedoms" were all the more destitute when the Americans left. Don Luce describes the cultural collision bluntly, noting that South Vietnam suffered more than the North, for it was "faced not only with the physical problems of rebuilding but also with the problems of readjustment for most of its citizens." On the one hand, "'Country Fairs' brought rock-and-roll music, hot dogs, and Kool-Aid to remote villages. . . ." On the other hand, those Vietnamese who fled to the cities, farm boys turned to crime for survival, "became addicted to the drugs they were pushing" and forgot all about the necessary occupation of farming; and the young women also fell out of the true work force, for after "working in the bars and brothels. . . . two-thirds of these women had venereal disease, and many were addicted to hard drugs." Jolly Chand claims to be happy with her western outlook, but such an outlook puts her at odds with life in Asia. The confrontation must be harsher for the actual populace of Southeast Asia for whom the cultural clash was unwelcomed and unexpected.

These matters of religion and culture have to do only with the "friendly" population. Meeting the enemy raises an even more immediate issue: the strategy and tactics of the war. The interlude with Li Van Hgoc forces Paul Berlin to relive the incident when two comrades die in the tunnels, but that fanciful meeting also exhibits the fundamental level of battle. When the squad asks Li for directions out of the tunnel, he is almost embarrassed to inform them, ". . . according to the rules, I fear you gentlemen are now my prisoners." Li's arresting statement points out how all soldiers, captured or not, suffer as prisoners in this kind of seemingly fruitless war. The squad has no time for this philosophizing, though, and is in fact incredulous:

> "Outmanned, outgunned, and outtechnologized." Lieutenant Corson tapped his finger against the weapon's plastic stock.

> "Well spoken," the enemy said. "A neat summary of the issues. Very well spoken."

In response, the Americans point their guns at the unarmed Li, tie him up, and set out to find their own escape from the tunnels—to find the proverbial light at the end of the tunnel, and to accept a simple "exit" sign as light enough. Now, Li is incredulous: "Violence will not—. . . . Please! The puzzle, it cannot be solved this way." The Americans get away, but Li has a point.

Earlier, Li told the squad that they are fighting the land: the traps, the tunnels, and the paddies all present danger because the land is fighting back. He describes the force as Xa, meaning "that a man's spirit is in the land, where his ancestors rest and where the rice grows." According to Fitzgerald, the term also conveys the sense that a Vietnamese is connected to the land in such a way that it embodies one's "face" or personality. Hence, the ease with which the Vietnamese could blend into the landscape. On the surface, American soldiers saw primitive villages, but beneath them were networks of tunnels holding not-so-primitive supplies. The enemy's retreats were thereby "doubly invisible: invisible within the ground and then again invisible within their own perspective as Americans." North Vietnam's General Giap promulgated this guideline of evasion: "Concerning tactics, practice guerrilla methods: secrecy, speed, initiative (today in the East, tomorrow in the West); appear and disappear by surprise, without leaving a trace. . . ." Analysts on both sides retrospectively agreed that American firepower and manpower reflected strategy appropriate to some earlier combat: the Americans were big, burdened by equipment, and therefore clumsy and slow to adapt. Ho Chi Minh described his revolution, before the Americans arrived, as "grasshoppers that dare stand up to the elephants." He showed some prescience about American involvement when he added, "Tomorrow, it's the elephant that leaves its skin behind." Paul Berlin's squad, too, fails to understand from Li's pleading that having more troops, more guns, and more technology will not avail in Vietnam; anyone who comes into the country thinking otherwise condemns himself to being a prisoner of that war and that strategy.

Such war by attrition displays an ignorance of the enemy and the issues—the kind of ignorance that leads the promotion board to push Paul into answering that the reason for fighting the war is only "To win it" and that the death of Ho Chi Minh will affect the North Vietnamese population only to the extent that it will "Reduce it by one, sir." The enemy does not foist this problem on Paul Berlin's squad, nor does the problem come from the location or circumstances of the war. The problem comes from within, and within himself is where Paul has his toughest confrontations.

Paul plays out his confusion about the tactics and the overall mission of the war in the dialogue between Doc and Fahyi Rhallon, the obsequiously polite security officer the Americans meet in Tehran. Over drinks, Doc states that the war is like any other war:

> "Politics be damned. Sociology be damned. It pisses me off to hear everybody say how special Nam is. . . . I'm saying that the *feel* of war is the same in Nam or Okinawa—the emotions are the same, the same fundamental stuff is seen and remembered."

In terms of horror and fear, Paul's experience would tend to fit Doc's analysis; however, in terms of purpose and motivation, Rhallon's position speaks for Paul as well:

> " . . . but I understand that one difficulty for you has been a lack of purpose. . . . An absence of aim and purpose, so that the foot soldier is left without the moral imperatives to fight hard and well and winningly."

Like the meeting in Paris between Sarkin and Paul, this exchange produces statements of position without any true negotiation. When the conversation turns to desertion—a sensitive subject for Paul and the others—Rhallon repeats that purpose keeps men from running: "Without purpose men will run. They will act their dreams, and they will run and run, like animals in stampede." Doc replies, "Maybe purpose is part of it. But a bigger part is self-respect. And fear." This "debate" exposes Paul's inner divisions, reflecting his imagined actions so far and anticipating his imagined resolution to come. As always, the issue boils down to fear: fear of facing death or fear of facing a cowardly self.

In pursuit of Cacciato, Paul imagines that others would question the squad's motives. Paul subconsciously enacts these questions by having the squad, before they can vindicate their actions by capturing the deserter, run into other deserters. Li Van Hgoc resisted the war and deserted, for which he is sentenced to the tunnels; in Tehran, just before meeting Rhallon, the squad sees a young man beheaded for, they later learn, being AWOL—"For true deserters the punishment is not so kind." Paul wrestles with this question in his mind, but he is hardly alone in actuality. Until 1968, military absenteeism remained below rates for World War II and Korea. Then, in the next three years, the rate doubled twice:

> These desertions were both in Vietnam and at US bases world-wide indicating the wider military demoralization. . . . The combined desertion and AWOL numbers meant that about one in four of the US forces had mutinied or were defying military orders. . . .

One British draft counselor claims that in one of the war's peak years, "seventy-three thousand soldiers deserted—the equivalent of three full combat divisions with supply units." These deserters certainly had numerous motivations, but in many cases, the war's lack of clear or moral purpose may have given running from it an apparent sense of purpose. Michael Novak, with a group that interviewed several dozen deserters in Paris and Stockholm, reports that, like Paul, these former soldiers arrived at such a sense only after being in the war:

> Although in the small towns from which most of them come they had no tradition for examining and

questioning American political life, and particularly American foreign policy, they were acute enough to see through the Army and its propaganda. . . . Their resistance to the war grew out of their own guts, in confrontation with the army. . . . To accept induction was the easy, natural path of the conformity and docility it is the business of American grammar schools and high schools to teach them: not critical, not questioning. Almost all of those who spoke to me were not pacifists; they were not absolutely against war, or the army; except for the peculiar nature of the Vietnamese war, a war on the poor, on civilians, in support of a vastly unpopular Saigon government, they would still be in the army, getting their term of duty over with.

In short, the announced purpose of the war could not bear scrutiny, especially under fire, and another purpose—survival, obviously, or honor—filled the void.

Cacciato, for one, has more than survival as a reason for running. Pressed into cooperating with Lt. Martin's assassination, he must feel the war has no identifiably moral goal anymore. Cacciato displays great sensitivity, but again, the history of the war shows he was not alone in encountering the issue:

> The term fragging derived from the use of a fragmentation weapon, usually a hand-grenade, as the surest way of dispatching an unpopular officer. . . . Prior to 1969 "fragging" was apparently so rare that official statistics do not record any incidents. Between 1969 and 1971 assaults on officers in Vietnam averaged 240 a year, eleven percent fatal.

In other words, doubts about the war effort spread through much of the military, even if soldiers such as Paul agonized over them seemingly alone. In the novel, Paul's squad encounters the revolutionary woman from California outside Zagreb. Wearing her politics like a latest fashion, she presumes that the American squad's courage resides in the ability to witness "evil firsthand" and walk away in guilt. But her views show no more sophistication than those of Paul's promotion board. At the time of the novel's events, antiwar sentiments held sway because the media's coverage of the Tet offensive showed what many Americans viewed as enemy resilience:

> The pictures of corpses in the garden of the American embassy cut through the haze of argument and counterargument, giving flat contradiction to the official optimism about the slow but steady progress of the war. Those who had long held doubts and reservations now felt their doubts confirmed.

In any case, the revolutionary woman from California still represents division, and division represents most of the doubts examined in the novel. Paul Berlin is a soldier divided against himself, fighting in a force divided against itself, on behalf of a country divided against itself, over another country divided against itself.

The revolutionary from California can argue these issues in a flip manner, but for Berlin's squad, the issues involve life or death—which to Paul's frightened mind means death. Paul imaginatively mulls over this feared inevitability in the scene wherein he witnesses the beheading in Tehran. Myers calls the incident "a grisly symbol of the true inertia on the road to Paris," but the symbolism should bring more specific ideas to mind. The execution, for being AWOL, includes a ceremony that recalls the beginning rather than the end of military involvement. The platform has patriotic decorations, martial music plays over loudspeakers, and several officers attend in full dress uniforms; before the ax falls, the young man's neck is shaved, his cheeks are kissed by the officers, and speeches are made. In sum, the whole spectacle parodies a ceremony to send new draftees to the front: first comes a haircut, then comes the final cut.

The history of the home front, of course, included plenty of anti-draft agitation. For the protest movement, tactics to avoid the draft included deferments, exile, conscientious objection, and sometimes jail. Until 1969, when deferments were abolished, the result, according to Arthur Schlesinger, Jr., was that "the war in Vietnam was being fought in the main by the sons of poor whites and blacks whose parents did not have much influence in the community." For Paul, the choice is academic and, to his way of thinking, cruelly rigged against him: running may be a capital offense in the military, but simply being drafted is tantamount to kneeling before the chopping block anyway.

Accordingly, Paul runs, but only in his imagination, and his hoped-for destination is clarity of mind. The trek leads to Paris because Cacciato said he was going there, but the city suggests a historical destination also. As Sarkin says in leading the squad out of Li's tunnels, "The way in is the way out." Paul knows almost nothing about Vietnam, so he does not know that the way into the modern history of the war in Vietnam leads through Paris. As early as 1856, Napoleon III proceeded with plans to take Vietnamese territory as retribution for Vietnamese abuse of French missionaries; in 1887, despite violent resistance, the fall of Napoleon III, and internal debate, France consolidated all of present-day Vietnam and Cambodia into the Indochinese Union, a "pacified" colony. The area remained in French hands, with a brief Japanese interruption during World War II, until the siege at Dien Bien Phu in 1954 when the French command "woefully miscalculated [Vietnamese General] Giap's intentions and capabilities even before the shooting started," largely because they "had wrongly disregarded intelligence that did not fit their prejudices, and instead 'substituted their preconceived idea of the Vietminh for the facts.'" If Paul remains ignorant of this preview of American involvement in Vietnam, he must know of the contemporary role Paris was playing in the war as the site for the peace talks. Those talks, which began just one month before Paul came to Vietnam, took "seven months just to resolve the seating arrangements (so that the Saigon and N[ational] L[iberation] F[ront] delegations could avoid face-to-face recognition and discussion)"; in fact, according to Michael Novak, the NLF even suspected their North Vietnamese allies would sell them out and negotiate in ways that "would benefit the North at the expense of the South." In any event, the United States certainly did not prevail at the table, despite the table's shape or its seating arrangements. The 1973 treaty the U. S. signed allowed 150,000 North Vietnamese troops to remain in the South while US troops withdrew. One of our negotiators, John Negroponte, stated,

> We got our prisoners back; we were able to end our direct military involvement. But there were no ostensible benefits for Saigon to justify all of the enormous effort and bloodshed of the previous years.

Thus, even some of America's political leadership finally saw the futility of the war, and they had adopted Sarkin's other maxim of escape: "We have fallen into a hole. Now we must fall out." Similarly, Paul's imaginary negotiation with Sarkin offers neither of them any benefits from the effort to walk all the way to Paris, but Paul's adherence to duty, whether out of honor or fear, is more genuinely face-saving than the historical treaty.

So how much has been accomplished in Paul's six hours of dreaming on the observation post? James C. Wilson offers a negative view of Paul's resolution, seeing it as a failed effort: "Even in his imagination, Berlin retreats into official slogans and platitudes, unable to either imaginatively or intellectually transcend the propaganda of his own government." Schroeder responds that "personal politics blinkers critical assessment" in the view that the "peace conference" fails. "Rather," Schroeder continues,

> resolution is realized morally and aesthetically both within the text and without it. . . . The question which Paul Berlin asks (and answers) at the peace table is the one which O'Brien leaves unresolved in *If I Die*: "If inner peace is the true objective, would I win it in exile?"

Myers agrees that Paul's outcome bodes well for Paul's mental and spiritual stability:

> The willed ingenuity in the observation post produces finally a classical boon—self-knowledge

within travail, the partial ordering of chaos that even a statement of positions can provide, the move toward, if not the attainment of, a proper peace.

Dale W. Jones adds that Paul has learned more about the true nature of fortitude:

> . . . courage is not genuine when it is divorced from either wisdom or fear. . . . If he has not actually become a hero after his nightlong vigil, he has at least come a step closer in attaining courage, wisdom and self-knowledge. By the end of the novel, Paul Berlin has integrated the disconnected fragments of his experience and transcended the chaos in his own mind.

The chaos may not be completely overcome, for some memories still overlap while others remain unexamined. As for courage, though, Paul at least imagines a heroic journey, and in order to complete it, he performs a slight, but real-world, act of bravery: remaining on duty atop the observation post, even through the "dangerous time" of the "darkest hours" when attack is most likely.

Occupying a middle ground, Vannatta thinks that O'Brien's novel ends in "indefiniteness": Paul may have asserted "an existential commitment to one's own choices," but

> . . . there is no reason to believe that flight will not once again become an attractive alternative to Paul. For that matter, even the seemingly vanquished goal of heroism, of fighting for God, country, and family, has an obstinate resiliency.

The novel's motifs of irresolvable conflict and Paul's divided mind would support such ambiguity. In the encounter with Li Van Hgoc, both sides are right: Li correctly calls Paul's squad prisoners, and the squad correctly shows its intent and ability to escape. In the debate between Doc and Fahyi Rhallon, Doc may be more cynical, but both positions could find vindication in Paul's experience. And in the final negotiation between Sarkin and Paul, both statements of commitment show nobility, but Paul speaks for himself and thereby takes a stand on one side of the division. No sense of irony accompanies this scene, for although the implied author knows more than Paul knows, Paul's actions are not treated in a condescending or disdainful manner; Paul Berlin's stand then does not, as Wilson would suggest, rest on something so flimsy as mere "slogans and platitudes." Nonetheless, the victory of the one side, like most victories in Vietnam, could yet prove temporary; taking a stand and holding to it could be no more attainable for Paul than "taking a place and keeping it, securing a village and then raising the flag and calling it a victory." In any case, the important point remains that, for the solitary soldier such as Paul, this kind of moral, if temporary, victory can sustain him rather than wear him out.

Paul's qualified triumph must stand in contrast to the verdict of history as represented by the implied author. Vannatta sees ambiguity on this level as well: "O'Brien exposes the horror and suffering of war, but he stops short of saying that war is ultimately without meaning or justification—even the Vietnam war." The narrative will not, I think, support the phrase after the dash. On the way to Paris, the lessons are several. For instance, superior firepower cannot prevail over committed manpower. And: when the land itself becomes the enemy, deadly conflict follows wherever troops go, virtually imprisoning them before putting them to ignominious flight. And: if an enemy cannot be defeated, then war serves only to destroy the people and culture allegedly being defended. Such conclusions carry no endorsement of the North Vietnamese goals, only the point that, if noble goals of freedom and prosperity merely decorate a policy supporting a government that offers little hope of freedom and prosperity, then war waged is simply for winning and no higher purpose. Furthermore, simply winning in Vietnam, prevailing by attrition, O'Brien's novel instructs clearly, is impossible. Sending soldiers into such combat may prompt speeches of the proper sentiments but will result in the practical execution of troops: the Vietnam War had been fought and lost before by the French; the US brought only new faces to its involvement in Vietnam, not new policies.

Paul encounters such lessons in the persons of Sarkin, Li Van Hgoc, the Cao Dai, Hamijolli Chand, Fahyi Rhallon, and others, but he needs only to face himself, not answer for his country's policy. If Paul Berlin knew the political history of the war beforehand, perhaps he would have avoided the draft; if he absorbed accurate political history while in the country, perhaps he would have deserted with Cacciato. Either way, Paul would still need to confront himself and need to justify himself in his own mind. Knowledge may alter choices, but it does not necessarily secure confidence in those choices. Vietnam made choices on all sides insecure. In other wars, the American soldier could sometimes know that, whatever his own involvement, the war's goal was correct and honorable. Not so in Vietnam. The implied author's introduction of several fantastic teachers of history suggests that, regardless of the enemy policy, the allied policy offered no hope of an honorable outcome. Cacciato, in despair, walks away from the war to Paris, prefiguring the American decision to walk away in Paris also. Paul feels fear more than despair, and under the circumstances, his resolution—finding a modicum of personal honor in a terrible enterprise—exhibits an imaginatively humane response to an absurdly vain combat.

Steven Kaplan (essay date Fall 1993)

SOURCE: "The Undying Uncertainty of the Narrator in Tim O'Brien's *The Things They Carried*," in *Critique,* Vol. XXXV, No. 1, Fall, 1993, pp. 43-52.

[*Below, Kaplan examines the emphasis on ambiguity behind O'Brien's narrative technique in* The Things They Carried, *noting the relation between "real truth" and uncertainty.*]

Before the United States became militarily involved in defending the sovereignty of South Vietnam, it had to, as one historian recently put it, "invent" the country and the political issues at stake there. The Vietnam War was in many ways a wild and terrible work of fiction written by some dangerous and frightening story tellers. First the United States decided what constituted good and evil, right and wrong, civilized and uncivilized, freedom and oppression for Vietnam, according to American standards; then it traveled the long physical distance to Vietnam and attempted to make its own notions about these things clear to the Vietnamese people—ultimately by brute, technological force. For the U.S. military and government, the Vietnam that they had in effect invented became fact. For the soldiers that the government then sent there, however, the facts that their government had created about who was the enemy, what were the issues, and how the war was to be won were quickly overshadowed by a world of uncertainty. Ultimately, trying to stay alive long enough to return home in one piece was the only thing that made any sense to them. As David Halberstam puts it in his novel, *One Very Hot Day*, the only fact of which an American soldier in Vietnam could be certain was that "yes was no longer yes, no was no longer no, maybe was more certainly maybe." Almost all of the literature on the war, both fictional and nonfictional, makes clear that the only certain thing during the Vietnam War was that nothing was certain. Philip Beidler has pointed out in an impressive study of the literature of that war that "most of the time in Vietnam, there were some things that seemed just too terrible and strange to be true and others that were just too terrible and true to be strange."

The main question that Beidler's study raises is how, in light of the overwhelming ambiguity that characterized the Vietnam experience, could any sense or meaning be derived from what happened and, above all, how could this meaning, if it were found, be conveyed to those who had not experienced the war? The answer Beidler's book offers, as Beidler himself recently said at a conference on writing about the war, is that "words are all we have. In the hands of true artists . . . they may yet preserve us against the darkness." Similarly, for the novelist Tim O'Brien, the language of fiction is the most accurate means for conveying, as Beidler so incisively puts it, "what happened (in Vietnam) . . . what might have happened, what could have happened, what should have happened, and maybe also what can be kept from happening or what can be made to happen." If the experience of Vietnam and its accompanying sense of chaos and confusion can be shown at all, then for Tim O'Brien it will not be in the fictions created by politicians but in the stories told by writers of fiction.

One of Tim O'Brien's most important statements about the inherent problems of understanding and writing about the Vietnam experience appears in a chapter of his novel ***Going After Cacciato*** appropriately titled "The Things They Didn't Know." The novel's protagonist, Paul Berlin, briefly interrupts his fantasy about chasing the deserter Cacciato, who is en route from Vietnam to Paris, to come to terms with the fact that although he is physically in Vietnam and fighting a war, his understanding of where he is and what he is doing there is light-years away. At the center of the chapter is a long catalogue of the things that Berlin and his comrades did not know about Vietnam, and the chapter closes with the statement that what "they" *knew* above all else were the "uncertainties never articulated in war stories." In that chapter Tim O'Brien shows that recognizing and exploring the uncertainties about the war is perhaps the closest one can come to finding anything certain at all. Paul Berlin, in his fantasy about escaping the war and chasing Cacciato to Paris, is in fact attempting to confront and, as far as possible, understand the uncertainties of the Vietnam War through the prism of his imagination. Once inside his make-believe world, Berlin has the opportunity to explore all of the things that he did not know about the war: The elusive enemy suddenly becomes his partner in a long debate about the meaning of the war; he explores the mysterious tunnels of the Vietcong; one of the victims of the war becomes Berlin's tour guide as he and his fellow soldiers go after Cacciato; and, most important of all, Berlin is given a chance to test and ultimately reject his own thoughts of desertion by imagining how he would react to the desertion of another soldier.

In his most recent work of fiction, ***The Things They Carried,*** Tim O'Brien takes the act of trying to reveal and understand the uncertainties about the war one step further, by looking at it through the imagination. He completely destroys the fine line dividing fact from fiction and tries to show, even more so than in ***Cacciato,*** that fiction (or the imagined world) can often be truer, especially in the case of Vietnam, than fact. In the first chapter, an almost documentary account of the items referred to in the book's title, O'Brien introduces the reader to some of the things, both imaginary and concrete, emotional and physical, that the average foot soldier had to carry through the jungles of Vietnam. All of the "things" are depicted in a style that is almost scientific in its precision. We are told how much each subject weighs, either psychologically or physically, and, in the case of artillery, we are even told how many ounces each round weighed:

> As PFCs or Spec 4s, most of them were common grunts and carried the standard M-16 gas operated

assault rifle. The weapon weighed 7.5 pounds, 8.2 pounds with its full 20-round magazine. Depending on numerous factors, such as topography and psychology, the rifleman carried anywhere from 12 to 20 magazines, usually in cloth bandoliers, adding on another 8.4 pounds at minimum, 14 pounds at maximum.

Even the most insignificant details seem worth mentioning. One main character is not just from Oklahoma City but from "Oklahoma City, Oklahoma," as if mentioning the state somehow makes the location more factual, more certain. More striking than this obsession with even the minutest detail, however, is the academic tone that at times makes the narrative sound like a government report. We find such transitional phrases as "for instance" and "in addition," and whole paragraphs are dominated by sentences that begin with "because." These strengthen our impression that the narrator is striving, above all else, to convince us of the reality, of the concrete certainty, of the things they carried.

In the midst of this factuality and certainty, however, are signals that all the information in this opening chapter will not amount to much: that the certainties are merely there to conceal uncertainties and that the words following the frequent "becauses" do not provide an explanation of anything. We are told in the opening page that the most important thing that First Lieutenant Jimmy Cross carried were some letters from a girl he loved. The narrator, one of Cross's friends in the war and now a forty-three-year-old writer named Tim O'Brien, tells us that the girl did not love Cross, but that he constantly indulged in "hoping" and "pretending" in an effort to turn her love into fact. We are also told "she was a virgin," but this is immediately qualified by the statement that "he was almost sure" of this. On the next page, Cross becomes increasingly uncertain as he sits at "night and wonder(s) if Martha was a virgin." Shortly after this, Cross wonders who had taken the pictures he now holds in his hands "because he knew she had boyfriends," but we are never told how he "knew" this. At the end of the chapter, after one of Cross's men has died because Cross was too busy thinking of Martha, Cross sits at the bottom of his foxhole crying, not so much for the member of his platoon who has been killed "but mostly it was for Martha, and for himself, because she belonged to another world, and because she was . . . a poet and a virgin and uninvolved."

This pattern of stating facts and then quickly calling them into question that is typical of Jimmy Cross's thoughts in these opening pages characterizes how the narrator portrays events throughout this book: the facts about an event are given; they then are quickly qualified or called into question; from this uncertainty emerges a new set of facts about the same subject that are again called into question—on and on, without end. O'Brien catalogues the weapons that the soldiers carried, down to their weight, thus making them seem important and their protective power real. However, several of these passages are introduced by the statement that some of these same weapons were also carried by the character Ted Lavendar; each of the four sections of the first chapter that tells us what he carried is introduced by a qualifying phrase that reveals something about which Lavendar himself was not at all certain when he was carrying his weapons: "Until he was shot. . . ."

Conveying the average soldier's sense of uncertainty about what actually happened in Vietnam by presenting the what-ifs and maybes as if they were facts, and then calling these facts back into question again, can be seen as a variation of the haunting phrase used so often by American soldiers to convey their own uncertainty about what happened in Vietnam: "there it is." They used it to make the unspeakable and indescribable and the uncertain real and present for a fleeting moment. Similarly, O'Brien presents facts and stories that are only temporarily certain and real; the strange "balance" in Vietnam between "crazy and almost crazy" always creeps back in and forces the mind that is remembering and retelling a story to remember and retell it one more time in a different form, adding different nuances, and then to tell it again one more time.

Storytelling in this book is something in which "the whole world is rearranged" in an effort to get at the "full truth" about events that themselves deny the possibility of arriving at something called the "full," meaning certain and fixed, "truth." By giving the reader facts and then calling those facts into question, by telling stories and then saying that those stories happened, and then that they did not happen, and then that they might have happened, O'Brien puts more emphasis in *The Things They Carried* on the question that he first posed in *Going After Cacciato*: how can a work of fiction become paradoxically more real than the events upon which it is based, and how can the confusing experiences of the average soldier in Vietnam be conveyed in such a way that they will acquire at least a momentary sense of certainty. In *The Things They Carried,* this question is raised even before the novel begins. The book opens with a reminder: "This is a work of fiction. Except for a few details regarding the author's own life, all the incidents, names, and characters are imaginary." Two pages later we are told that "this book is lovingly dedicated to the men of Alpha Company, and in particular to Jimmy Cross, Norman Bowker, Rat Kiley, Mitchell Sanders, Henry Dobbins, and Kiowa." We discover only a few pages after this dedication that those six men are the novel's main characters.

These prefatory comments force us simultaneously to consider the unreal (the fictions that follow) as real because the book is dedicated to the characters who appear in it, and the "incidents, names, and characters" are unreal or "imaginary."

O'Brien informs us at one point that in telling these war stories he intends to get at the "full truth" about them; yet from the outset he has shown us that the full truth as he sees it is in itself something ambiguous. Are these stories and the characters in them real or imaginary, or does the "truth" hover somewhere between the two? A closer look at the book's narrative structure reveals that O'Brien is incapable of answering the questions that he initially raises, because the very act of writing fiction about the war, of telling war stories, as he practices it in *The Things They Carried,* is determined by the nature of the Vietnam War and ultimately by life in general where "the only certainty is overwhelming ambiguity."

The emphasis on ambiguity behind O'Brien's narrative technique in *The Things They Carried* is thus similar to the pattern used by Joseph Conrad's narrator, Marlow, in *Heart of Darkness,* so incisively characterized by J. Hillis Miller as a lifting of veils to reveal a truth that is quickly obscured again by the dropping of a new veil. Over and over again, O'Brien tells us that we are reading "the full and exact truth," and yet, as we make our way through this book and gradually find the same stories being retold with new facts and from a new perspective, we come to realize that there is no such thing as the full and exact truth. Instead, the only thing that can be determined at the end of the story is its own indeterminacy.

O'Brien calls telling stories in this manner "Good Form" in the title of one of the chapters of *The Things They Carried*: This is good form because "telling stories" like this "can make things present." The stories in this book are not truer than the actual things that happened in Vietnam because they contain some higher, metaphysical truth: "True war stories do not generalize. They do not indulge in abstractions or analysis." Rather, these stories are true because the characters and events within them are being given a new life each time they are told and retold. This approach to storytelling echoes Wolfgang Iser's theory of representation in his essay "Representation: A Performative Act":

> Whatever shape or form these various (philosophical or fictional) conceptualizations (of life) may have, their common denominator is the attempt to explain origins. In this respect they close off those very potentialities that literature holds open. Of course literature also springs from the same anthropological need, since it stages what is inaccessible, thus compensating for the impossibility of knowing what it is to be. But literature is not an explanation of origins; it is a staging of the constant deferment of explanation, which makes the origin explode into its multifariousness.

> It is at this point that aesthetic semblance makes its full impact. Representation arises out of and thus entails the removal of difference, whose irremov-

ability transforms representation into a performative act of staging something. This staging is almost infinitely variable, for in contrast to explanations, no single staging could ever remove difference and so explain origin. On the contrary, its very multiplicity facilitates an unending mirroring of what man is, because no mirrored manifestation can ever coincide with our actual being.

When we conceptualize life, we attempt to step outside ourselves and look at who we are. We constantly make new attempts to conceptualize our lives and uncover our true identities because looking at who we might be is as close as we can come to discovering who we actually are. Similarly, representing events in fiction is an attempt to understand them by detaching them from the "real world" and placing them in a world that is being staged. In *The Things They Carried,* Tim O'Brien desperately struggles to make his readers believe that what they are reading is true because he wants them to step outside their everyday reality and participate in the events that he is portraying: he wants us to believe in his stories to the point where we are virtually in the stories so that we might gain a more thorough understanding of, or feeling for, what is being portrayed in them. Representation as O'Brien practices it in this book is not a mimetic act but a "game," as Iser also calls it in a more recent essay, "The Play of the Text," a process of acting things out:

> Now since the latter (the text) is fictional, it automatically invokes a convention-governed contract between author and reader indicating that the textual world is to be viewed not as reality but as if it *were* reality. And so whatever is repeated in the text is not meant to denote the world, but merely a world enacted. This may well repeat an identifiable reality, but it contains one all-important difference: what happens within it is relieved of the consequences inherent in the real world referred to. Hence in disclosing itself, fictionality signalizes that everything is only to be taken *as if* it were what it seems to be, to be taken—in other words—as play.

In *The Things They Carried,* representation includes staging what might have happened in Vietnam while simultaneously questioning the accuracy and credibility of the narrative act itself. The reader is thus made fully aware of being made a participant in a game, in a "performative act," and thereby also is asked to become immediately involved in the incredibly frustrating act of trying to make sense of events that resist understanding. The reader is permitted to experience at first hand the uncertainty that characterized being in Vietnam. We are being forced to "believe" that the only "certainty" was the "overwhelming ambiguity."

This process is nowhere clearer than in a chapter appropri-

ately called **"How to Tell A True War Story."** O'Brien opens this chapter by telling us "THIS IS TRUE". Then he takes us through a series of variations of the story about how Kurt Lemon stepped on a mine and was blown up into a tree. The only thing true or certain about the story, however, is that it is being constructed and then deconstructed and then reconstructed right in front of us. The reader is given six different versions of the death of Kurt Lemon, and each version is so discomforting that it is difficult to come up with a more accurate statement to describe his senseless death than "there it is." Or as O'Brien puts it—"in the end, really there's nothing much to say about a true war story, except maybe 'Oh.'"

Before we learn in this chapter how Kurt Lemon was killed, we are told the "true" story that Rat Kiley apparently told to the character-narrator O'Brien about how Kiley wrote to Lemon's sister and "says he loved the guy. He says the guy was his best friend in the world." Two months after writing the letter, Kiley has not heard from Lemon's sister, and so he writes her off as a "dumb cooze." This is what happened according to Kiley, and O'Brien assures us that the story is "incredibly sad and true." However, when Rat Kiley tells a story in another chapter we are warned that he

> swore up and down to its truth, although in the end, I'll admit, that doesn't amount to much of a warranty. Among the men in Alpha Company, Rat had a reputation for exaggeration and overstatement, a compulsion to rev up the facts, and for most of us it was normal procedure to discount sixty or seventy percent of anything he had to say.

Rat Kiley is an unreliable narrator, and his facts are always distorted, but this does not affect storytelling truth as far as O'Brien is concerned. The passage above on Rat Kiley's credibility as a storyteller concludes: "It wasn't a question of deceit. Just the opposite: he wanted to heat up the truth, to make it burn so hot that you would feel exactly what he felt." This summarizes O'Brien's often confusing narrative strategy in *The Things They Carried*: the facts about what actually happened, or whether anything happened at all, are not important. They cannot be important because they themselves are too uncertain, too lost in a world in which certainly had vanished somewhere between the "crazy and almost crazy." The important thing is that any story about the war, any "true war story," must "burn so hot" when it is told that it becomes alive for the listener-reader in the act of its telling.

In Rat Kiley's story about how he wrote to Kurt Lemon's sister, the details we are initially given are exaggerated to the point where, in keeping with O'Brien's fire metaphor, they begin to heat up. Kurt Lemon, we are told, "would always volunteer for stuff nobody else would volunteer for in a million years." And once Lemon went fishing with a crate of hand grenades, "the funniest thing in world history . . . about twenty zillion dead gook fish." But the story does not get so hot that it burns, it does not become so "incredibly sad and true," as O'Brien puts it, until we find out at the story's close that, in Rat's own words, "I write this beautiful fuckin' letter, I slave over it, and what happens? The dumb cooze never writes back." It is these words and not the facts that come before them that make the story true for O'Brien.

At the beginning of this chapter, O'Brien asks us several times to "Listen to Rat," to listen how he says things more than to what he says. And of all of the words that stand out in his story, it is the word "cooze," (which is repeated four times in two pages), that makes his story come alive for O'Brien. "You can tell a true war story by its absolute and uncompromising allegiance to obscenity and evil." This is just one way that O'Brien gives for determining what constitutes a true war story. The unending list of possibilities includes reacting to a story with the ambiguous words "Oh" and "There it is." Rat Kiley's use of "cooze" is another in the sequence of attempts to utter some truth about the Vietnam experience and, by extension, about war in general. There is no moral to be derived from this word such as war is obscene or corrupt: "A true war story is never moral. It does not instruct." There is simply the real and true fact that the closest thing to certainty and truth in a war story is a vague utterance, a punch at the darkness, an attempt to rip momentarily through the veil that repeatedly re-covers the reality and truth of what actually happened.

It is thus probably no coincidence that in the middle of this chapter on writing a true war story, O'Brien tells us that "Even now, at this instant," Mitchell Sanders's "yo-yo" is the main thing he can remember from the short time encompassing Lemon's death. This object, associated with games and play, becomes a metaphor for the playful act of narration that O'Brien practices in this book, a game that he plays by necessity. The only way to tell a true war story, according to O'Brien, is to keep telling it "one more time, patiently, adding and subtracting, making up a few things to get at the real truth," which ultimately is impossible because the real truth, the full truth, as the events themselves, are lost forever in "a great ghostly fog, thick and permanent." You only "tell a true war story" "if you just keep on telling it" because "absolute occurrence is irrelevant." The truth, then, is clearly not something that can be distinguished or separated from the story itself, and the reality or non-reality of the story's events is not something that can be determined from a perspective outside of the story. As the critic Geoffrey Hartman says about poetry: "To keep a poem in mind is to keep it there, not to resolve it into available meanings." Similarly, for O'Brien it is not the fact that a story happened that makes it true and worth remembering, anymore than the story itself can be said to contain a final truth. The important thing is that a story becomes so much a part of the present that "there is nothing to remember (while we are reading it) except the story." This

is why O'Brien's narrator is condemned, perhaps in a positive sense, to telling and then retelling numerous variations of the same story over and over and over again. This is also why he introduces each new version of a story with such comments as: "This one does it for me. I have told it before many times, many versions—but here is what actually happened." What actually happened, the story's truth, can only become apparent for the fleeting moment in which it is being told; that truth will vanish back into the fog just as quickly as the events that occurred in Vietnam were sucked into a realm of uncertainty the moment they occurred.

> **What actually happened, the story's truth, can only become apparent for the fleeting moment in which it is being told; that truth will vanish back into the fog just as quickly as the events that occurred in Vietnam were sucked into a realm of uncertainty the moment they occurred.**
> —*Steven Kaplan*

O'Brien demonstrates nothing new about trying to tell war stories—that the "truths" they contain "are contradictory," elusive, and thus indeterminate. Two hundred years ago, Goethe, as he tried to depict the senseless bloodshed during the allied invasion of revolutionary France, also reflected in his autobiographical essay *Campaign in France* on the same inevitable contradictions that arise when one speaks of what happened or might have happened in battle. Homer's *Iliad* is, of course, the ultimate statement on the contradictions inherent in war. However, what is new in O'Brien's approach in *The Things They Carried* is that he makes the axiom that in war "almost everything is true. Almost nothing is true" the basis for the act of telling a war story.

The narrative strategy that O'Brien uses in this book to portray the uncertainty of what happened in Vietnam is not restricted to depicting war, and O'Brien does not limit it to the war alone. He concludes his book with a chapter titled **"The Lives of the Dead"** in which he moves from his experiences in Vietnam back to when he was nine years old. On the surface, the book's last chapter is about O'Brien's first date, his first love, a girl named Linda who died of a brain tumor a few months after he had taken her to see the movie, *The Man Who Never Was*. What this chapter is really about, however, as its title suggests, is how the dead (which also include people who may never have actually existed) can be given life in a work of fiction. In a story, O'Brien tells us, "memory and imagination and language combine to make spirits in the head. There is the illusion of aliveness." Like the man who never was in the film of that title, the people that never were except in memories and the imagination can become real or alive, if only for a moment, through the act of storytelling.

According to O'Brien, when you tell a story, really tell it, "you objectify your own experience. You separate it from yourself." By doing this you are able to externalize "a swirl of memories that might otherwise have ended in paralysis or worse." However, the storyteller does not just escape from the events and people in a story by placing them on paper; as we have seen, the act of telling a given story is an on-going and never-ending process. By constantly involving and then re-involving the reader in the task of determining what "actually" happened in a given situation, in a story, and by forcing the reader to experience the impossibility of ever knowing with any certainty what actually happened, O'Brien liberates himself from the lonesome responsibility of remembering and trying to understand events. He also creates a community of individuals immersed in the act of experiencing the uncertainty or indeterminacy of all events, regardless of whether they occurred in Vietnam, in a small town in Minnesota, or somewhere in the reader's own life.

O'Brien thus saves himself, as he puts it in the last sentence of his book, from the fate of his character Norman Bowker who, in a chapter called **"Speaking of Courage,"** kills himself because he cannot find some lasting meaning in the horrible things he experienced in Vietnam. O'Brien saves himself by demonstrating in this book that the most important thing is to be able to recognize and accept that events have no fixed or final meaning and that the only meaning that events can have is one that emerges momentarily and then shifts and changes each time that the events come alive as they are remembered or portrayed.

The character Norman Bowker hangs himself in the locker room of the local YMCA after playing basketball with some friends, partially because he has a story locked up inside of himself that he feels he cannot tell because no one would want to hear it. It is the story of how he failed to save his friend, Kiowa, from drowning in a field of human excrement: "A good war story, he thought, but it was not a war for war stories, not for talk of valor, and nobody in town wanted to know about the stink. They wanted good intentions and good deeds." Bowker's dilemma is remarkably similar to that of Krebs in Hemingway's story "Soldier's Home": "At first Krebs . . . did not want to talk about the war at all. Later he felt the need to talk but no one wanted to hear about it. His town had heard too many atrocity stories to be thrilled by actualities."

O'Brien, after his war, took on the task "of grabbing people by the shirt and explaining exactly what had happened to me." He explains in *The Things They Carried* that it is impossible to know "exactly what had happened." He wants us to know all of the things he/they/we did not know about Vietnam and will probably never know. He wants us to feel the sense of uncertainty that his character/narrator Tim O'Brien experiences twenty years after the war when he returns to the place where his friend Kiowa sank into a "field of shit" and tries to find "something meaningful and right" to say but ultimately can only say, "well . . . there it is." Each time we, the readers of *The Things They Carried,* return to Vietnam through O'Brien's labyrinth of stories, we become more and more aware that this statement is the closest we probably ever will come to knowing the "real truth," the undying uncertainty of the Vietnam War.

Richard Eder (review date 2 October 1994)

SOURCE: "Vanishing Act," in *Los Angeles Times Book Review,* October 2, 1994, p. 3.

[*In the following review, Eder calls* In the Lake of the Woods *"an artistic botch."*]

The German writer Theodore Adorno questioned whether art could survive the Holocaust. The new novel by Tim O'Brien, author of *Going After Cacciato* and *The Things They Carried,* raises a similar question. It carries the suggestion that no human project can survive the contamination of exposure to the Vietnam War: not the political ambitions and private sanity of the veteran who is the novel's protagonist, and perhaps not even the possibility that O'Brien, who wrote so brilliantly about the war, will be able to write his way out of it.

In the Lake of the Woods tries to tell the story of John Wade, a young Minnesota politician whose promising race for the Senate is stopped dead by the revelation that he covered up his membership in the Army company that butchered the inhabitants of My Lai. As a child, Wade was a dedicated practitioner of magic and disappearing tricks. His candidacy, in what it concealed, was another disappearing trick. And when he and his wife, Kathy, retreat to a lakeside cabin in the north woods to recover, Kathy disappears.

When I say O'Brien "tries" to tell the story, I do not mean that he has necessarily failed in his intention. In a sense, he may have intended to fail. He sets up two related stories: that of a political chameleon who does not so much violate the truth as make it vanish, even for himself; and a darkly gruesome mystery about what happened to Kathy. But the two stories are hostages of the bloody presence of Vietnam, waiting in a back room.

They speak under constraint. The story of Wade's childhood, marriage and career is formulaic and desultory; whereas the mystery of the disappearance, written more powerfully, blurs in the nightmarish mutter from behind the door. It is as if O'Brien were telling us that even fictionally, there is no possibility of connecting Vietnam with anything that follows; as if it were a kind of antimatter that annihilates any story that tries to build from it.

O'Brien's back room is a group of chapters that alternate with the story of Wade and Kathy. They consist of pages of quotes. Some are from fictional witnesses to the fictional story. Others consist of press reports and trial testimony about the My Lai affair, and of passages from books about the stress of combat and from memoirs of atrocities committed in other American wars.

Underneath these, as footnotes, comes O'Brien's own passionate voice; not as narrator but as a man who was there. He comments on his story, at least on that part of the story in which the fictional Wade takes part in the historical massacre. And the book's key passage occurs not in the fiction, but in the footnote. Here it is, in part:

> I know how it happened. I know why. It was the sunlight. It was the wickedness that soaks into your blood and slowly heats up and begins to boil. Frustration, partly. Rage, partly. The enemy was invisible. They were ghosts. . . . But, it went beyond that. Something more mysterious. The smell of incense, maybe. The unknown, the unknowable. The blank faces. The overwhelming otherness. This is not to justify what occurred on March 16, 1968, for in my view, such justifications are both futile and outrageous. Rather, it's to bear witness to the mystery of evil. Twenty-five years ago, as a terrified young PFC, I too could taste the sunlight. I could smell the sin. I could feel the butchery sizzling like grease just under my eyeballs.

Such a voice drastically overshadows the fiction designed to embody its message. Except in his nightmares, Wade is an uninteresting, sketchy cliché; and Kathy exists thinly as someone who sees through him but loves him anyway. He is not, in fact, one of the real villains of My Lai. He shoots one civilian, but it was because he mistook a hoe for a gun. The other man he kills is one of the bloodiest of his fellow soldiers, who approaches him after he collapses into a ditch, sickened by what he has seen.

If Wade is loathsome, in fact, it is insofar as he is designed to represent the slickness and superficiality of a national public morality. Wade as the soldier who re-enlists after the massacre, gets a spot as battalion clerk and expunges his own company records, as a politician who conceals his past: all these are part of the universal spin that depends on obliterating history in order to be able, comfortably, to repeat it.

Wade pays for his cover-up by being found out and losing shamefully his race for the Senate. But the real price is internal. He no longer is capable of remembering, of distinguishing what he has done from what he wants to appear to have done. His punishment comes when Kathy disappears. As the sheriff cautiously and fruitlessly investigates, O'Brien dramatizes a series of hypotheses. They range from the routine—she has simply decided to leave him, taking their boat—to the bloodier—she has struck a shoal and drowned—to the monstrous—in a Vietnam-vintage nightmare, Wade has killed her in a manner too horrible to describe here—to the possibility, after Wade himself vanishes, that they have staged a two-part flight.

To disappear and to make truth disappear is to enter a wasteland of moral anarchy in which even the most hellish actions are conceivable. O'Brien narrates each version of what Wade has done in equally firm detail. Thematically, this is appropriate, but it makes for an artistic botch. Suspense, like suspension bridges, needs pillars to rest on. With his memory x'd out—and with O'Brien, in order to emphasize his character's spiritual anomie, refusing to supply a memory for him—what Wade has or has not done is of relatively little interest. This is particularly so, since the author has taken so few pains to make him, before and after the killing field, in any way distinctive.

Verlyn Klinkenborg (review date 9 October 1994)

SOURCE: "A Self-Made Man," in *The New York Times Book Review,* October 9, 1994, pp. 1, 33.

[In the favorable review below, Klinkenborg praises O'Brien's ambitious efforts in In the Lake of the Woods, *especially his characterization of John Wade.]*

"What stories can do, I guess, is make things present." That's how Tim O'Brien put it in *The Things They Carried,* which was published in 1990 and which is one of the finest books, fact or fiction, written about the Vietnam War. I don't remember ever hearing a novelist make a more modest claim for the power of stories, at least not a novelist of Mr. O'Brien's stature. The statement itself—stories make things present—is unassuming and it is offered to the reader diffidently, as if the writer were about to deny the possibility of saying anything useful at all about stories. Perhaps it suggests the discomfort of a storyteller who has, for the moment, slipped outside his story, except that outside his story is where Tim O'Brien has nearly always been, taking refuge—as he says in his striking new novel, *In the Lake of the Woods*—"in the fine line between biology and spirit," between some literal, if unknowable, truth and the truth whose only evidence is the story that contains it.

These are important matters in Mr. O'Brien's previous works. In the 1978 novel *Going After Cacciato,* the reader comes to worry about the difference between a story that is merely impossible—a platoon of soldiers following a man on foot from Vietnam to Paris—and a story that is unbelievable precisely because it is true, a story of the Vietnam War itself, a war that seemed to contain every likelihood of improbability. In ***The Things They Carried,*** the storyteller's indeterminacy has grown. The narrator of those stories distinguishes between "story-truth" and "happening-truth," and he plays one against the other. For Mr. O'Brien, as for many other Vietnam veterans, the "happening-truth" is a terrible thing: it is too powerful to look at, though you are forced to witness it. And yet, in Mr. O'Brien's case, it has dwindled over time into what he calls "faceless responsibility and faceless grief," which story-truth has the power to help him accept and alleviate.

In his new novel, he turns these matters of truth, time and responsibility inward, letting them weigh on an individual character in a manner he has never done before. This is a story about a man named John Wade and his wife, Kathleen, who disappears one day from the cottage they are renting at the Lake of the Woods in northern Minnesota, an enormous reach of water and wilderness that divides the United States and Canada. Wade is a Minnesota politician, and he has just lost a primary election for his party's nomination to the United States Senate. He lost big because his opponent uncovered the fact that Wade was present at a massacre in the Vietnamese village of Thuan Yen, which is the local name for a place better known to history as My Lai, where on March 16, 1968, between 200 and 500 civilians were butchered by a company of American soldiers commanded by Lieut. William Calley. Wade's presence there was a secret Wade had kept from his wife, from his campaign manager and, in a sense, from himself.

At Thuan Yen, Wade had been responsible for the deaths of one old man and an American soldier. But in this novel, it is never clear whether culpability can be parceled out like that, whether it belongs to the deed or the doer or merely to what the narrator calls the poisonous sunlight of Vietnam. In the end, Wade also disappears on that northern lake, gone in search of his wife, leaving behind only a sympathetic narrator, an author who tries to reconstruct the tale after it has already come to its mysterious close.

There are three kinds of story in ***In the Lake of the Woods.*** The first is a conventional, remote third-person account of plain facts, the events that can be reconstructed without conjecture, more or less. The second kind of story appears in several chapters called "Evidence": collections of quotations, excerpts from interviews and readings that bear on the Wade case. The third kind of story appears in chapters called "Hypothesis"; it tries to suggest what might have happened to Kathleen Wade in the days after she disappeared. But with these stories, Mr. O'Brien is also building a character, John

Wade, whose inner architecture is more emblematic than personal. Wade is the son of an alcoholic father who hanged himself in the family garage. As a child, Wade consoled himself—isolated himself—with magic. In Vietnam he came to be called "Sorcerer," and one of his last acts before returning stateside was to make himself vanish from the company rolls. To become a politician was an act of atonement for him, but it was also the practice of magic by other means. Mr. O'Brien quotes Dostoyevsky: "Man is bound to lie about himself." The lie John Wade constructed, as man and boy, was intended to avert the loss of love.

At the center of Wade's character is a problem of vision. When he was young, he practiced magic tricks in front of a mirror perfecting illusions. When his father died, Wade discovered that he could escape from his rage by slipping behind a mirror in his head, making himself invisible. And that was precisely what he did on that climactic day in Vietnam, when he found himself lying in a muddy trench while all around him, in some too-explicable exorcism of small-arms fire, an entire village was put to death. Mr. O'Brien has always insisted on the special quality of the things that happened in Vietnam, not to deny their reality, but to suggest that seeing was never adequate proof. You could look and look and look, staring down a trail where a platoon member had just that moment been killed by a mine, and yet seeing would register no reality, at least none that could be accounted for emotionally in that instant.

Incapacity to register reality has become a principle of character in ***In the Lake of the Woods.*** "We are fascinated, all of us, by the implacable otherness of others," says the narrator, who appears from time to time in footnotes. "And we wish to penetrate by hypothesis, by daydream, by scientific investigation those leaden walls that encase the human spirit, that define it and guard it and hold it forever inaccessible."

I have been trying to decide where the ambition lies in this grim, telling novel. It does not lie in reconstructing the events at My Lai, although it is deeply unsettling for the reader to find them reconstructed from within; nor does it lie in a particularly vivid grasp of the political impulse Mr. O'Brien has allowed himself only to suggest the magnitude of the story here, the nature of its psychological and historical depths. The quotations that appear in the chapters called "Evidence"—quotations from the court-martial of William Calley, from biographies of politicians, from magicians' handbooks, from the other characters in the novel—are like tentacles reaching into the unknown, adumbrations of a fuller narrative.

But it may be that ***In the Lake of the Woods*** is the kind of novel whose ambitions are less important than its concessions. Joan Didion has said that narrative is sentimental, and in his own way Mr. O'Brien concurs. One of the most powerful chapters in *The Things They Carried* is the one called "**How to Tell a True War Story,**" which is, in effect, an essay, with examples, on the limits of narrative. The one question that chapter doesn't ask is: Once you've learned to tell a true war story, how do you tell any other kind? *In the Lake of the Woods* asks that question in a different way. It is a novel about the moral effects of suppressing a true war story, of not even trying to make things present, a novel about the unforgivable uses of history, about what happens when you try to pretend that history no longer exists.

Jon Elsen (review date 9 October 1994)

SOURCE: "Doing the Popular Thing," in *The New York Times Book Review,* October 9, 1994, p. 33.

[*Below, Elsen relates O'Brien's personal reasons for writing fiction about the Vietnam War, specifically* In the Lake of the Woods.]

Like the protagonist of his new novel, *In the Lake of the Woods,* Tim O'Brien has been driven to do what be considers terrible things because of his need for love.

For Mr. O'Brien, the commission of sin began in earnest in 1969, when he decided to go to Vietnam instead of to Canada after he was drafted into the Army, he said in a recent telephone interview from his home in Cambridge, Mass. He believed the war was wrong—he had even protested it—but he served anyway. "I went to the war purely to be loved, not to be rejected by my hometown and family and friends, not to be thought of as a coward and a sissy," he explained.

Once in Vietnam, he committed what he considers to be sins to gain the love and respect of his comrades. "If friends are burning houches, you don't want to be thought of as a bad person, so you burn along," he said. "You'll do bad things to be loved by your friends, realizing later you've made a horrible mistake."

A year after the My Lai massacre, which he recounts in *In the Lake of the Woods,* Mr. O'Brien was stationed in the village. He understands the fury felt by the soldiers who did the killing, though he says their actions can never be justified. "There's a fine line between rage and homicide that we didn't cross in our unit, thank God," he said. "But there's a line in the book about the boil in your blood that precedes butchery, and I know that feeling."

When he returned home, he said, he compounded his sins by keeping them secret, fearing that otherwise he would lose people he loved. "The deceits I write about in the book are magnified versions of the secrecy and deceit I practice in my own life, and we all do .We're all embarrassed and ashamed of our evil deeds and try to keep them inside, and when they come out, the consequences are devastating." He added that he wanted to "write a book where craving for love can make us do really horrid things that require lifelong acts of atonement. That's why I write about Vietnam. It was given to me, and I'm giving it back."

Now he plans to make some changes. Writing *In the Lake of the Woods,* which took him six years, was a start. He said he decided to put a mystery at the heart of the story and to break away from a straight narrative (though he feared that critics would object) because that is how the novel worked naturally. "This book is a way of helping myself to start to say, 'No, I'm not going to do things I think are wrong and stupid so people will like me.'"

He also plans to stop writing fiction for the foreseeable future. "The object of writing is to make a good piece of art," he said. "As you're making that art, you're tussling with the wicked self inside. That can get depressing, when you tussle with it for six years."

For now, he aims to stick with writing essays, working out, quitting smoking and improving his golf game. "I feel like I've gone to the bottom of a well with this book," he said.

William O'Rourke (review date 16 October 1994)

SOURCE: "Into Troubled Waters," in *Chicago Tribune Books,* October 16, 1994, Section 14, pp. 1, 8.

[*In the review below, O'Rourke concludes that* In the Lake of the Woods *is "a risky, ambitious, perceptive, engaging and troubling novel, full of unresolved and unresolvable energies and powerful prose."*]

Tim O'Brien is one of his generation's most deservedly acclaimed authors. O'Brien's writing career has recorded both hits (*Going After Cacciato, The Things They Carried*) and peculiar misses (*Northern Lights, The Nuclear Age*)—his novels set in America having alternated with, and fared less well than, books that use Vietnam as their subject.

The challenging and provocative *In the Lake of the Woods* follows that pattern in part. Coming after the widely praised, Vietnam-based *The Things They Carried,* the new novel is set in the States, but it combines both worlds—doing so with mixed but ultimately satisfying results.

The protagonist of *In the Lake of the Woods,* John Wade, is a middle-aged politician who had been a member of Charlie Company when it ran over the number of small Vietnamese villages now collectively known as My Lai, killing most every man, woman, child and animal they found there—though it was mainly, in descending numerical order, women, children and old men. *In the Lake of the Woods* is Wade's biography; but the problematic premise of the novel is that it is written by a fellow veteran who has set out to discover the mystery of Wade's life: "Biographer, historian, storyteller, medium—call me what you want—but even after four years of hard labor I'm left with little more than supposition and possibility. John Wade was a magician; he didn't give his tricks away."

These interpolations, which come at chapters' end, are done by means of footnotes (other secondary source materials are also footnoted with standard bibliographic references). But O'Brien is giving away some fictional tricks with this choice, and it is hard not to question his methods.

The story, without footnotes, is in another tradition of American fiction, bringing to mind Dreiser's *An American Tragedy,* which also makes potent, criminal use of an isolated body of water. Lakes have played a metaphoric role in our literature that is both benign and malevolent, a medium always mysterious and unknowable. And O'Brien fills the novel with that quality:

> It is by the nature of the angle, sun to earth, that the seasons are made, and that the waters of the lake change color by the season, blue going to gray and then to white and then back again to blue. The water receives color; the water returns it. The angle shapes reality. Winter ice becomes the steam of summer as flesh becomes spirit. Partly window, partly mirror, the angle is where memory dissolves.

After losing a primary election for U.S. senator, Wade and his wife, Kathy, rent a cabin in the Minnesota wilderness: "They needed the solitude. They needed the repetition, the dense hypnotic drone of woods and water, but above all they needed to be together." Wade had become lieutenant governor of the state at 30. He seemed to be a shoo-in for senator until his presence at My Lai was uncovered during the campaign. (It was a fact he had hidden from everyone since he had left military service.)

Wade's life unravels still more: His wife "disappears" near the end of their vacation, lost in the Great North. Or was she murdered by Wade? The unnamed biographer can't decide.

O'Brien has set two contradictory narratives forward: one a compelling mystery, the other a investigation into the nature of mystery, of knowing itself. They do conflict. Readers hooked on one are likely to be irritated by the other.

Wade is a compelling character; his wife, Kathy, is much less

so. As Wade's life history is revealed, O'Brien recounts step by step the killings at My Lai. These pages are shocking after 25 years, even if one knows the facts. (O'Brien makes liberal use of a 1992 nonfiction book, *Four Hours in My Lai,* which is equally unsettling to read).

I suspect O'Brien's novel will be the first account of My Lai many younger readers will encounter. O'Brien, it appears, wants to place his fact-based fiction in the service of history (rather than the more usual history in the service of fiction), and he is for the most part successful. Even mainstream Hollywood, not especially reticent these days, has shied away from depicting My Lai.

After the carnage is revisited, O'Brien invents a most cruel and grotesque death for Kathy—he does seem compelled to top the violence already described. "Finally it's a matter of taste, or aesthetics," the "biographer" informs us. In chapters labeled "Hypothesis" we get different versions of what may have occurred. It is clear that O'Brien wants to understand violence, not exploit it.

As hideous as the possibilities are, history provides Wade (and O'Brien and the reader) with contemporary counterparts. The convicted Green Beret slayer of his wife and two children, Jeffrey MacDonald, floats unnamed (along with others) in the ether of Wade's darkest impulses.

Yet, O'Brien, in the eleventh hour, seems to have pulled back from the logic of his character's character. Reviewers were supplied with a rewritten ending for the book long after the bound galleys were distributed, a rare occurrence. The difference was small, a matter of a few lines, but the lines lead the reader to favor a verdict of not guilty for John Wade.

O'Brien himself might still be unsettled about the matter. What is clear, however, is that he has written a risky, ambitious, perceptive, engaging and troubling novel, full of unresolved and unresolvable energies and powerful prose, a major attempt to come to grips with the causes and consequences of the late 20th Century's unquenchable appetite for violence, both domestic and foreign.

Pico Iyer (review date 24 October 1994)

SOURCE: "Missing in Contemplation," in *Time,* October 24, 1994, p. 74.

[*In the following positive review of* In the Lake of the Woods, *Iyer comments on "the time-released traumas of Vietnam," which the critic marks as "the elemental theme" of O'Brien's fiction.*]

Some writers are born with a theme, some acquire a theme, and some have a theme thrust upon them. But however writers come by it, their great subject provides a surge of intensity to their work that no other material can. The novels of Mona Simpson, for example, go electric as soon as she touches on the figure of a mother; Amy Tan's fiction reaches its heights the minute she turns to China. For Tim O'Brien, who deferred his admission as a graduate student at Harvard in order to serve in Vietnam, the elemental theme is his experience there as a shy and questioning infantryman. O'Brien's *Going After Cacciato* (winner of the National Book Award in 1979) is perhaps the finest imaginative reconstruction of that war; and his story **"Speaking of Courage"** (from *The Things They Carried,* 1990), the most poignant evocation of a Vietnam veteran's displacement upon returning home. In his latest novel, *In the Lake of the Woods,* O'Brien turns once again to the time-released traumas of Vietnam, writing about them bravely and often brilliantly.

Lake is mostly the story of John Wade, a boyish, idealistic politician who retreats to a cottage in the Minnesota woods to recover after a humiliating election defeat. There, with Kathy, his longtime wife and college sweetheart, he looks into the mist over the lake and plays hide-and-seek with his unwanted memories. For Wade is not only an earnest man of principles, he is also a spooked vet who wakes up yelling in his sleep recalling the horrors he was part of—and party to—in Vietnam. Kathy is guilty of her own betrayals, and the wary husband and wife tiptoe around each other until eventually Wade is left by himself to dwell on her secrets and his own. Both of them slip through the trapdoors of their minds, down into the subterranean passageways where we all escape when we're missing not in action but in contemplation.

O'Brien's clean, incantatory prose always hovers on the edge of dream, and his specialty is that twilight zone of chimeras and fears and fantasies where nobody knows what's true and what is not. In Vietnam, of course, he locates the ultimate "spirit world," an eerie land of shadows where kids shot at phantoms, unable to tell friend from enemy, uncertain what they were fighting for. "The jungles stood dark and unyielding. The corpses gaped. The war itself was a mystery. Nobody knew what it was about, or why they were there, or who started it, or who was winning, or how it might end." Wade is an amateur magician nicknamed "Sorcerer" by his unit, and Vietnam becomes a place where he tries to make reality go away; it is a perfect training ground for the subterfuge and surveillance tricks people also use in love.

Expertly crosscut with Wade's life is a series of chapters called "Evidence" into which O'Brien throws psychological theories, passages of presidential biography, even accounts of battlefront atrocities in 1776. Here are quotations from Dostoyevsky and George Sand; selections from *The Magician's Handbook* and the Nuremberg Principles; an item

about the 30,000 people who go missing every year. Thus, for example, as we travel deeper into Wade's battlefront memories, we are also given hard-and-fast, nonfiction testimony from the men who perpetrated the My Lai massacre. The "Evidence" chapters broaden the book's focus and prevent us from dismissing the horrors described in the novel as pure make-believe or peculiar only to the war in Vietnam.

With *Lake,* O'Brien manages what he does best, which is to find the boy scout in the foot soldier, and the foot soldier in every reader. No one writes better about the fear and homesickness of a boy adrift amid what he cannot understand, be it combat or love. O'Brien shows us Wade as a lonely, pudgy 10-year-old, practicing magic tricks before the mirror, hoping to conjure a callous father's love out of thin air. "The mirror made his father smile all the time. The mirror made the vodka bottles vanish from their hiding place in the garage, and it helped with the hard, angry silence at the dinner table." At his father's funeral the 14-year-old boy "wanted to kill everybody who was crying and everybody who wasn't."

O'Brien's suggestion that people enter politics in search of the love they've never had seems reductive. And he remains much better at exploring mystery than at explaining it ("There is no end, happy or otherwise; nothing is fixed, nothing is solved"). Yet if he is no psychologist, he is a masterly evoker of shadowy psychological states. And what remains in the mind from this book is an unsparing depiction of the moral and emotional nightmares of Vietnam, made more unsparing by O'Brien's rigorous refusal to write them off as the craziness of the moment. "This was not madness, Sorcerer understood. This was sin." *Lake* looks head-on at those unfashionable old friends, morality and evil.

Maria S. Bonn (essay date Fall 1994)

SOURCE: "Can Stories Save Us? Tim O'Brien and the Efficacy of the Text," in *Critique,* Vol. XXXVI, No. 1, Fall, 1994, pp. 2-15.

[*In the essay below, Bonn discusses the significance of O'Brien's persistent concerns about the relationship between fiction and experience throughout his writing career, highlighting "the effective potential of the stories" related in* If I Die, Going after Cacciato, *and* The Things They Carried.]

Tim O'Brien tells us at the beginning of the final story in *The Things They Carried,* an installment of his literary exploration of the terrain of the Vietnam War, "But this too is true: Stories can save us." But the Vietnam veteran and prize-winning author has spent two decades in skirmishes with the question of just what kind of stories might be able to effect this rescue. O'Brien's Vietnam War works persistently examine the function of stories. Throughout a memoir and two novels he has investigated the polarity of fact and fiction, lived experience and texts, documentation and art, memory and imagination. In the creative space between these poles he locates "story" and "truth" as agents of reconciliation and education.

At times, O'Brien has expressed concern that the literature of the Vietnam War, a literature dominated by author-veterans, might be "held prisoner by the fact of [the authors' own] Vietnam experiences. The result is a closure of the imagination, predictability and melodrama, a narrowness of theme and an unwillingness to stretch the fictive possibilities." He argues that writers must be less concerned with the facts than with the truth and that "lying is a way one can get to a kind of truth . . . [not] a definitive truth, but at a kind of circling . . . hoping that a kind of clarity emerges, not a truth . . . issues can be clarified sometimes by telling lies." In his pursuit of artistic lying to clarify the truth O'Brien has written the two Vietnam War novels *Going After Cacciato* and *The Things They Carried. Going After Cacciato* with its careful blend of picaresque fantasy, magic realism, and combat realism and *The Things They Carried,* a mix of war parables and highly self-conscious metafiction, are novels that could never be accused of failing to explore fictive possibilities.

But O'Brien's espoused belief that fiction has greater potential for conveying essential truth than does nonfiction is one he has arrived at by working through his own personal experience. His first book was the autobiographical narrative *If I Die in a Combat Zone . . . Box Me up and Send Me Home,* in which he questions the efficacy of literature and the relationship between experience and understanding in a different light than he will later in open discussion and in his novels.

O'Brien is self-effacing and ambivalent about setting forth his project in *If I Die.* Early in the book he tells us:

> I would wish this book could take the form of plea for everlasting peace, a plea from one who knows, from one who's been there and come back, an old soldier looking back at a dying war.

> That would be good. It would be fine to integrate it all to persuade my younger brother and perhaps some others to say no to wrong wars.

> Or it would be fine to confirm the old beliefs about war: it is horrible, but it's a crucible of men and events and, in the end, it makes more of a man out of you.

> But, still, none of that seems right. . . .

> Do dreams offer lessons? Do nightmares have

themes, do we awaken, and analyze them and live out our lives and advise others as a result? Can the foot soldier teach anything important about war, merely from having been there? I think not. He can tell war stories.

O'Brien is very conscious of his position as an intermediary between those with personal knowledge of the war and those without. He is the one who has been there and back; he has lived to tell the tale. Yet at the end of this statement he denies the educational potential of such a position. He cannot advise or teach. All he can do is tell his war stories.

But he is not always reductive about war stories. In an Asia Society forum on the literature of the Vietnam War, he asserts "I'm a believer in the power of stories, whether they're true, or embellished, and exaggerated, or utterly made up. A good story has a power . . . that transcends the question of factuality or actuality." It is not clear whether O'Brien has changed his mind about the power of war stories or whether this apparent contradiction is a rhetorical stance, but the disparity between these two statements reflects a divided attitude about the adequacy of art for revealing and teaching.

This division is suggested throughout the pages of *If I Die* and becomes one of its driving tensions. Throughout the memoir O'Brien repeatedly privileges the written text and the story; but throughout the memoir O'Brien also undermines that privilege, until it is ultimately unclear whether he embraces or rejects the power of the story and the storyteller.

If I Die is an educated and literate man's response to war. As O'Brien attempts to make sense of his circumstances, he is continually interpreting them through a structure of texts ranging from Plato to *A Farewell to Arms.* His attitude toward the written text initially seems uncomplicated. The good guys read books and the bad guys don't. We see this at work early in *If I Die* as O'Brien forms his first real friendship in the army—with another recruit, Erik Hansen (to whom he will later dedicate *Going After Cacciato*). Their bonding begins when O'Brien sees Erik reading; the book is T. E. Lawrence's *The Mint,* which Erik is reading because "'He [Lawrence] went through crap like this. Basic training. It's a sort of how-to-do-it book.'" Erik shares the book with O'Brien and, with Lawrence as their guide, the two recruits struggle to maintain their humanity in the face of basic training. We see another attitude altogether toward books when O'Brien discusses his serious reservations about going into combat with the battalion chaplain. The chaplain, incensed at what he sees as O'Brien's lack of courage and patriotism, blames O'Brien's hesitations on reading: "'I think you're very disturbed, very disturbed. Not mental you understand—I don't mean that. See . . . you've read too many books, the wrong ones, I think there's no doubt, the wrong ones. But goddamn it—pardon me—but goddamn it, you're a soldier now, and you'll sure as hell act like one!'" The battalion commander, whom O'Brien goes to see next, similarly blames O'Brien's difficulties with the military system on an over-reliance on books. He complains: "'But you're hearing this from an old soldier . . . I suppose that you've got to *read* it to believe it, that's the new way.'" Our protagonists know how to make use of literature as interpretive schema; their enemies deny the ability of literature to cast any relevant light on real experience.

If I Die is an educated and literate man's response to war. As O'Brien attempts to make sense of his circumstances, he is continually interpreting them through a structure of texts ranging from Plato to *A Farewell to Arms*.
—Maria S. Bonn

There are numerous examples in *If I Die* of O'Brien's reliance upon literary and philosophical texts to provide a structure for his time in Vietnam. He describes his platoon leader, Mad Mark, as working by an Aristotelian ethic; his company commander, Captain Johansen, becomes his hero, a hero he examines in the light of Plato, Hemingway, and Melville (as well as Alan Ladd as Shane and Humphrey Bogart in *Casablanca*); a night ambush reminds him of *The Legend of Sleepy Hollow*, "of imminent violence and guileless, gentle Ichabod Crane." While O'Brien is in the field, Erik writes him a letter that quotes *The Wasteland*: "'April is the cruelest month, breeding / Lilacs out of the dead land, mixing / Memory and desire, stirring / Dull roots with spring rain'" and asserts explicitly that there is a practical lesson to be learned from the poetry: "'Take care. For it is not a fantasy.'"

Even as he contemplates escaping the army, O'Brien relies upon the written text. To make a decision about deserting he goes to the library and researches the question. When he eventually commits himself to going AWOL, he also commits all his plans to paper—so he can check and recheck his vision of escape against the documented plan he carries with him. When at the last moment he backs out of desertion, his first act is to burn the plans—as if destroying the text will destroy the idea.

The central question that O'Brien explores through texts, especially through Plato and Hemingway, is about the nature of courage. *If I Die* revolves around this question and its relationship to O'Brien's decision not to desert the military. Throughout the memoir—and indeed throughout his novels that will follow it—O'Brien relentlessly works over the problem of which choice represents true courage: to desert to keep faith with his moral and political principles or to fight out of obligation to his duties as a citizen and a son of an American family. This choice is embodied in the actions of O'Brien's

greatest heroes—Socrates and Hemingway's Frederic Henry.

Very early in *If I Die* O'Brien considers his position in terms of his reading of Plato: "I remembered Plato's Crito, when Socrates, facing certain death—execution, not war—had the chance to escape. But he reminded himself that he had seventy years in which he could have left the country, if he were not satisfied or felt the agreements he made were unfair. He had not chosen Sparta or Crete. And, I reminded myself, I hadn't thought much about Canada until that summer." Much later in the book he lists his heroes, "especially Frederic Henry. Henry was able to leave war being good and brave enough at it, for real love, and although he missed the men of war, he did not miss the fear and killing." O'Brien tries to reconcile these two mentors by positing that "courage, according to Plato, is [only] one of the four parts of virtue," and that "Henry, like all my heroes, was not obsessed with courage; he knew it was only one part of virtue, that love and justice were other parts," but the fundamental choice between departing and enduring remains unresolved.

Because O'Brien elected to remain with the army, we assume that, at least in part, he chose to follow the model of Socrates rather than Frederic Henry, and thus opted for a Platonic ethic. This ethic appears to be affirmed late in the book, when O'Brien returns to the question of courage, in the chapter entitled "Courage Is a Certain Kind of Preserving." The chapter opens with a long quotation from *The Republic* (Book IV):

> "So a city is also courageous by a part of itself, thanks to that part's having in it a power that through everything will preserve the opinion about which things are terrible—that they are the same ones and of that same sort as those the lawgiver transmitted in the education. Or don't you call that courage?"
>
> "I didn't quite understand what you said," he said. "Say it again."
>
> "I mean," I said, "that courage is a certain kind of preserving."
>
> "Just what sort of preserving?"
>
> "The preserving of the opinion produced by the law through education about what—and what sort of thing—is terrible. . . ."

If O'Brien embraces these reflections on the nature of courage, then his purpose in telling his war stories is simultaneously affirmed and complicated. If we are to come to understand courage through education, then it is essential that we have educational texts. This is how O'Brien arrives at his definition of courage—through his reading. Thus his book, rather than merely telling war stories, can begin to serve some of the moral function that he earlier abnegated.

But the Platonic model also has adverse ramifications for O'Brien as a writer, because there is no place for O'Brien as a writer in the Platonic state. At the end of Book II and the beginning of Book III of *The Republic* Plato makes it clear that the place of the poet and the teller of tales should be a very limited and controlled one. Poets should be subject to censorship and not be permitted the egregious fault of telling lies; they must only represent truth—truth that is advantageous to the state. A little later on in Book III we read "if any one at all is to have the privilege of lying, the rulers of the State should be the persons; and they, in their dealings either with their enemies or with their own citizens, may be allowed to lie for the public good." As a writer, particularly as a writer of Vietnam War literature, a literature that has been so concerned with creating fictions that counter all the officially sanctioned public lies of that war, O'Brien *must* have difficulty with Plato's sentiments here. O'Brien believes in lying as a way to get to a kind of truth. And true courage may not come through education.

In his first book O'Brien was writing literature that would be acceptable in the Platonic model, by creating a straight historical text rather that a fictional one. In an interview with Eric James Schroeder O'Brien says of *If I Die,* "'it's just there as a document. It's not art.'" Yet, as Schroeder points out in a later article, in that same interview he tells about how he had written many of the episodes in *If I Die* when he was in Vietnam, and that upon returning to the United States he "'stitched it together into a book and sent it off.'" O'Brien also admits to fictionalizing dialogue: "'Often I couldn't remember the exact words that people said, and yet to give it a dramatic intensity and immediacy I'd make up dialogue that seemed true to the spirit of what was said.'" In addition to creating dialogue O'Brien tampered with chronology. "'I didn't follow the chronology of events; I switched events around for the purposes of drama.'" This "stitching" combined with the fictive dialogue and rearranged time scheme, as well as a formal structure that begins the story *in medias res* and then moves back to O'Brien's childhood, education, and basic training, suggest considerably more artistry than O'Brien is perhaps willing to admit.

The contradictions between O'Brien's creation of a text fitting for education in the Platonic model and his ideas about the role of fiction suggest a contradiction that is pointed to throughout the memoir. For most of the book, reading is portrayed as a worthwhile activity; books are friends and guides. But there is a thread throughout *If I Die* that contravenes this theme. After O'Brien has quoted the letter from his friend Erik that contains excerpts from *The Wasteland* and stresses that it "is not a fantasy," O'Brien immediately follows the

letter by reporting "April went on without lilacs. Without rain" suggesting that perhaps the poem is not so pertinent after all. In describing guard duty at night, O'Brien once more uses texts to structure his present experience: "Then the guard started, the ritual come alive from our pagan past—Thucydides and Polybius and Julius Caesar, tales of encampment, tales of night terror." But the paragraph ends: "all the rules passed down from ancient warfare, the lessons of dead men." If the rules did not succeed in keeping their creators alive, perhaps they are not useful for the Vietnam soldier either. Similarly, O'Brien dismisses the relevance of "Horace's old do-or-die aphorism—'Dulce et decorum est pro patria mori'" as "just an epitaph for the insane."

The suggestion that texts may complicate as much as they clarify is present as early as the basic training section of the book. At the exact same time as he is gaining understanding from T. E. Lawrence, other texts are perpetuating a lack of understanding between O'Brien and his absent girlfriend. His thoughts dwell on his girlfriend as a way of escaping basic training, and he tells us:

> I memorized a poem she sent me. It was a poem by Auden, and marching for shots, and haircuts, and clothing issues, I recited the poem, forging Auden's words with thoughts I pretended to be hers. I lied about her, pretending that she wrote the poem herself, for me. I compared her to characters out of books by Hemingway and Maugham. In her letters she claimed I created her out of the mind. The mind, she said, can make wonderful changes in the real stuff.

Here the texts obfuscate instead of enlightening. Literature may give O'Brien a clearer understanding of the experience of boot camp, but it is also becoming a replacement for the real experience of another human being.

O'Brien also begins to doubt the applicability of works written about other wars to his positions in Vietnam. He wonders "how writers such as Hemingway and Pyle could write so accurately and movingly about war without also writing about the rightness of their wars." To O'Brien it seems that soldiers in war stories are all convinced of the rightness of their causes, or, at the least, "resigned to bullets and brawn." But for O'Brien, who likens his own position as similar to that of a "conscripted Nazi," the stance taken by legendary warriors may be impossible for him to assume.

O'Brien finds his reliance upon texts inadequate to create an ethical system suitable for Vietnam. His old, fictionally inspired notions about courage and battlefield behavior simply do not withstand the experiential assault of the war. He reports "it is . . . difficult, however, to think of yourself in those ways. As the eternal Hector, dying gallantly. It is impossible. That's the problem. Knowing yourself, you can't make it real for yourself. It's sad when you learn you're not much of a hero." As he arrives at this knowledge, O'Brien also begins to dismiss the fictions that he has used to direct his life:

> Grace under pressure, Hemingway would say. That is how you recognize the brave man. But somehow grace under pressure is insufficient. It's too easy to affect grace, and it's too hard to see through it. . . . Or the other cliché: a coward dies a thousand deaths, but a brave man only one. That seems wrong too. Is a man once and for always a coward? Is a man once and for always a hero?

As he rejects these too-easy ways of understanding courage, O'Brien replaces these written texts with a text of physical, lived experience. For him this new definition of courage comes when "you look at the other men, reading your own caved-in belly deep in their eyes. The fright dies in the same way the novocain wears off in the dentist's chair. You promise, almost moving your lips, to do better next time; that by itself is a kind of courage."

By opting for the text of a fellow-soldier's eyes over a Hemingway novel, for the flesh rather than for the word, O'Brien appears to have arrived at the point from which he begins the book. War stories are only stories; they do not have any practical ramifications. But we know that the issue cannot be allowed to rest there. O'Brien does write the book, a book that is an actively created and ordered thing, a book presumably written to comprehend his own experience. He returns to the written text for structure. The question that *If I Die* poses it leaves largely unanswered.

Going After Cacciato is a return to those questions and a re-opening of the issues. Schroeder posits that the book is a long answer to the question O'Brien posed for himself in *If I Die*: "Do dreams offer lessons?" Certainly *Cacciato* returns to the question of courage. But even more than that it is a return to a consideration of war stories. O'Brien again takes up the question of the relationship between fiction and experience, this time in a more explicit and self-conscious manner; and he attempts to discover the kind of stories that we must tell for them to have a real efficacy in our lives.

The structure of *Cacciato* emphasizes the disparities between experiential realism and fantastic imagination as a way of understanding lived experience. *Cacciato* is written using a tripartite structure. The narrative present is contained in a series of chapters entitled "The Observation Post," where the novel's protagonist, Paul Berlin, spends a quiet night of guard duty remembering and imagining—a remembering and imagining that are the substance of the rest of the novel. A series of flashback chapters detail many of the events that he remembers from the first part of his tour in Vietnam—a tour that is now about halfway over. Finally, "The Road to Paris"

chapters make up Paul Berlin's elaborate imaginative voyage overland from Vietnam to Paris. The scheme of the novel is such that not until about a third of the way through the book is the reader able to sort out this structure and be certain about what is present, past, and dreamed, what is the book's fiction, and what is its reality.

The "Road to Paris" is Paul Berlin's fiction, a fiction that he creates as an alternative to the untenable life of war that is recorded in several flashback sections. These flashbacks are Paul Berlin's war stories. But for this young soldier these stories do not offer adequate lessons. Memory alone proves inadequate for Paul Berlin. As he concludes the flashback sections near the end of the book he muses:

> Out of all that time, time aching itself away, his memory sputtered around those scant hours of horror. . . . Odd, because what he remembered was so trivial, so obvious and corny, that to speak of it was embarrassing. War stories. That was what remained: a few stupid war stories, hackneyed and unprofound. Even the lessons were commonplace. It hurts to be shot. Dead men are heavy. Don't seek trouble, it'll find you soon enough.

In language almost identical to that which he uses in *If I Die* O'Brien once again denies war stories any heuristic function. But Paul Berlin pursues another alternative. Instead of relying upon memory alone to arrive at truth, he transforms memory through his imagination. He alchemizes his experience in Vietnam into a picaresque voyage in search of Cacciato, Paris, and understanding.

If the narrative past in *Cacciato* is the realm of "fact" and reality, and the trip to Paris is the territory of fiction and imagination, then "The Observation Post" chapters are best described as metafiction. In these chapters Paul Berlin deliberates both on the nature of his memories and on the course that his fiction is taking, and the complex interplay between the two. It is through these chapters that we come to understand Paul Berlin's purpose in creating his elaborate journey and that although the imaginative escape to Paris is a way of mentally escaping the facts of war that he cannot confront, the journey is also a way of arriving back at the war, but this time with a greater degree of moral comprehension and a clear definition of courage.

For Paul Berlin, Vietnam is an unreadable and unknowable text. He arrives in Vietnam without the historical or political sense that would enable him to understand the United States position in Vietnam and his part in that position. O'Brien explicates Paul Berlin's sense of lostness upon the protagonist's arrival in country: "He was lost. He had never heard of I Corps, or the Americal, or Chu Lai. He did not know what a Combat Center was." To try to rectify his ignorance, Paul Berlin writes home to ask his father to look up Chu Lai in the world atlas, confessing "'Right now . . . I'm a little lost.'"

This geographic dislocation is symptomatic of the American soldiers' lack of any sort of historical or moral bearing while fighting the Vietnam War, a moral dislocation that is elaborated upon in the chapter "The Things They Did Not Know." Here O'Brien enumerates the many kinds of ignorance that compound the predicament of Paul Berlin and his fellows. They do not know the language, and therefore they cannot know the people of Vietnam. They do not know the political circumstances that have brought them to Vietnam. They do not know "even the simple things: a sense of victory, or satisfaction, or necessary sacrifice." Perhaps most significant "they did not know what stories to believe. Magic, mystery, ghosts and incense, whispers in the dark, strange tongues and strange smells, uncertainties never articulated in war stories, emotions squandered in ignorance. They did not know good from evil." O'Brien's soldiers are mired in their lack of knowledge; they have no geographical context within which to locate themselves and no textual guides to lead them to greater moral understanding.

What knowledge Paul Berlin does have is only superficial because he is unable to relate it to the reality of Vietnam. His expectations that have been formed by the texts that he has read before coming to Vietnam obscure any ability to theorize about his experience of the war. O'Brien tells us:

> He had seen it in movies. He had read about poverty in magazines and newspapers, seen pictures of it on television. So when he saw the villages of Quang Ngai, he had seen it all before. He had seen before seeing, hideous skin diseases, hunger, rotting animals, huts without furniture or plumbing or light. He had seen the shit-fields where villagers squatted. He had seen chickens roosting on babies. Misery and want, bloated bellies, scabs and pus-wounds, even death. All of it he'd seen before. So when he *saw* it—when he first entered a village south of Chu Lai— he felt a kind of mild surprise, a fleeting compassion, but not amazement. He knew what he would see and he saw it. He was not stricken by it; he was not outraged or made to grieve. He felt no great horror. He felt some guilt, but that passed quickly because he had seen it all before seeing it.

Paul Berlin's reliance upon texts to confront the violence he is complicit in here takes him into some dangerous moral waters. He replaces the experience he is undergoing with the vicarious experience of books and magazines, a substitution that inures him to the very real and painful suffering of Vietnam and its people. The violence is familiar, even though now it is unmediated. At the same time Paul Berlin is unable

to see past the suffering and poverty that he expected to any other aspect of Vietnamese life. He can only make his experience conform to categories that he had established well before arriving in Vietnam. Because he is over-reliant upon textual surrogates, he is unable to alter his epistemology in response to new experience.

Paul Berlin does not resolve his relationship to texts nor the uneasiness about his courage that prompts his imaginative odyssey until the climactic section on "The End of the Road to Paris" wherein Paul Berlin and Sarkin Aung Wang, the Vietnamese refugee he has fallen in love with, debate the location of Paul Berlin's deepest commitment. This scene consolidates the issues of courage and fiction that have driven O'Brien through both *If I Die* and *Cacciato.* Sarkin Aung Wang demands that Paul Berlin step out of his imagination and make his fiction real. For Paul Berlin this is tantamount to desertion, and thus he must resolve the question that O'Brien has been pondering since his own incomplete desertion: might desertion be the real act of courage? For Sarkin Aung Wang it is clearly embracing peace. She urges: "Having dreamed a marvelous dream, I urge you to step boldly into it, to join your own dream and live it. Do not be deceived by false obligation." For Paul Berlin it is not so simple, and he must ultimately reject Sarkin Aung Wang's offer. He declares "by my prior acts—acts of consent—I have bound myself to performing subsequent acts. . . . These were explicit consents. But beyond them were many tacit promises: to my family, my friends, my town, my country, my fellow soldiers."

Paul Berlin's resolution is also the resolution of his fiction, and of the moral questions that perpetrated that fiction. Some readers argue that Paul Berlin's inability to embrace his dream is the true failure of the imagination in the novel. A failure of the imagination has been presaged earlier in the fiction when the reality of the war threatened to bleed through into the trip to Paris: the disappearance of Harold Murphy and Stink Harris along the road to Paris, and the squad's near execution in Tehran are more a part of the wartime world than Paul Berlin's fantastic journey. But Paul Berlin's decision does not really seem like *failure* of the imagination—the fiction brings him to the point where he wished to arrive. He has discovered the values he wishes to live for. If the resolution he finds in Paris is not a triumph of the imagination either, this may well be a commentary on the American failure to imagine a happy ending out of Vietnam.

Paul Berlin's dream has finally offered him a lesson; but it may not be the lesson that we, as readers, want him to learn. O'Brien in part affirms a sensibility that he said in *If I Die* did not seem right. War "is horrible, but it is a crucible of men and events, and in the end it makes more of a man out of you." By refusing to step into his dream, Paul Berlin acquiesces to his position in Vietnam. He rejects the fiction that he has created and embraces the reality of his tour of duty—but this time it is a reality informed by fiction. Memory informed by imagination.

If Paul Berlin ultimately refuses to let the fiction be reality, is this the resolution of O'Brien's uneasy relationship to texts that we have seen at play throughout *If I Die* and *Cacciato*? If so, how do we balance that against the indications earlier in *Cacciato* that war stories are simply not adequate to teach us what we need to know about war? On which does O'Brien finally place a higher premium, experience or fiction, memory or imagination? On the one hand Paul Berlin's resolution and Tim O'Brien's own writing come out of autobiographical experience. But on the other it is clear that one cannot learn from experience unless one sets imagination to work upon it. Although the ending of *Going After Cacciato* is more conclusive than that of *If I Die*—through Paul Berlin O'Brien seems to affirm his own decision not to desert—the novel still leaves many open questions. If we cannot learn about courage from Hemingway or Captain Vere, if we cannot learn about Vietnam from television and magazines, if Paul Berlin cannot create an acceptable alternative to his reality, then why write at all? Despite this pending question, Paul Berlin does seem to have achieved moral understanding from fiction. And O'Brien seems to have made a truce—albeit an uneasy one—between memory and imagination.

It is the terms of this truce that he re-examines twelve years later in *The Things They Carried*. O'Brien returns to the material of his experience as a foot soldier in Vietnam. In this novel, the relationship between truth and fiction and the consideration of the effective potential of stories has moved to center stage. In person and in interviews O'Brien presents himself as a bluff ordinary guy, who claims his literary influences are "'the books I read as a kid. *The Hardy Boys* and Larry of the Little League'" and who has little interest in aesthetic theory. But his work belies this stance. When asked if *The Things They Carried* is nonfiction O'Brien appears startled by the question and says off-handedly that every bit of it is fiction. Yet the narrator of *The Things They Carried* is a forty-three-year-old Vietnam veteran named Tim O'Brien who has previously written a memoir called *If I Die in a Combat Zone* and the novel entitled *Going After Cacciato*.

An examination of even the prefatory material to *The Things They Carried* reveals that O'Brien is far more of a literary trickster than he acknowledges. The title page asserts the novel is "a work of fiction by Tim O'Brien." It is followed by a disclaimer that "this is a work of fiction. Except for a few details regarding the author's own life, all the incidents, names, and characters are imaginary." So far this is clear enough. But by the dedication page O'Brien is already beginning to muddy the textual waters. The book is dedicated to "the men of Alpha Company"; the dedication goes on to list their names. They are the names of the characters of *The Things They Carried.*

In and of itself this dedication to fictional characters might be passed over as whimsy on O'Brien's part, but it is soon revealed as part of the novel's elaborate interlocking pattern of truth and fiction. For example, in **"Notes"** O'Brien tells us that the story **"Speaking of Courage"** was written at the suggestion of Norman Bowker, one of those fictional men of Alpha Company, who wrote to O'Brien after reading *If I Die in a Combat Zone.* **"The Sweetheart of the Song Tra Bong,"** one of the most apparently fictive of the twenty-one pieces that make up *The Things They Carried,* is based, according to O'Brien, on a story told to him by a battle-field medic in Vietnam, who was "'desperate to make me believe him.'" The instructive piece **"How to Tell a True War Story"**—which begins by helpfully reporting "this is true"—explicates: "a true war story cannot be believed. If you believe it, be skeptical." Clearly O'Brien is nudging his readers to question some of their assumptions about fiction and truth.

The three consecutive pieces **"Speaking of Courage,"** **"Notes,"** and **"In the Field,"** exemplify O'Brien's relentless investigation of how to tell a true war story. The first story relates how the character Norman Bowker is unable to save Kiowa, a comrade who suffocates in the muck of excrement when Alpha Company is pinned down in a field full of night soil. In **"Notes"** the author-character Tim O'Brien tells us that the story was originally written at the suggestion of Norman Bowker who was dissatisfied with *If I Die In a Combat Zone.* As originally published the story featured Paul Berlin of *Going After Cacciato* and was only about the after-effects of the night in the night-soil field and did not discuss the incident itself. The intertextuality thickens. The fictional Norman Bowker expresses further dissatisfaction; he later kills himself. Prompted by the suicide, the author-character O'Brien rewrites the story for inclusion in *The Things They Carried.* The record is set straight—until the conclusion of **"Notes"** where O'Brien reports: "in the interests of truth, however, I want to make it clear that Norman Bowker was in no way responsible for what happened to Kiowa . . . that part of the story is my own." **"In the Field"** then is the final elucidation, the story in which O'Brien explains that he, not Norman Bowker, was the friend unable to save Kiowa that night.

Lest his readers should be tempted to believe that with **"In the Field"** they have at last been granted a definitive or foundational story, O'Brien follows that story with **"Good Form,"** another authorial commentary by the character Tim O'Brien. It opens with the statement "it's time to be blunt"—surely an alarming declaration to readers that have been struggling through the book's labyrinth of truth. He then goes on:

I'm forty-three years old, true, and I'm a writer now,

and a long time ago I walked through the Quang Ngai Province as a foot soldier.

Almost everything else is invented.

But it's not a game. It's a form. Right here, right now, as I invent myself, I'm thinking of all I want to tell you about why this book is written as it is. For instance, I want to tell you this: twenty years ago I watched a man die on a trail near the village of My Khe. I did not kill him. But I was present you see, and my presence was guilt enough. . . . I blamed myself. And rightly so, because I was present.

But listen. Even *that* story is made up.

So much for being blunt. But the dizzying interplay of truth and fiction in this novel is not solely aesthetic postmodern gamesmanship but a form that is a thematic continuation of the author's concern throughout his career with the power and capability of story.

The Things They Carried is more polished and manipulative even than the sophisticated triple play of *Going After Cacciato.* But for all its interrogation of the liminal space between lived experience and imagination and for all its insistence on abjuring any notion of static truth it is still finally more definitive about the potential of the story than either of O'Brien's earlier Vietnam War works. At the end of *Going After Cacciato* Paul Berlin has found a way of making use of war stories to define his moral position, but *The Things They Carried* makes a renewed attack on war stories: "A true war story is never moral. It does not instruct, nor encourage virtue, nor suggest models of proper behavior . . . as a first rule of thumb, therefore, you can tell a true war story by its absolute and uncompromising allegiance to obscenity and evil."

Yet at the same time that O'Brien strongly rejects any didactic moral function for war stories he clarifies his position on just what stories *can* do. Early on he declares that "sometimes remembering will lead to a story, which makes it forever. That's what stories are for. Stories are for joining the past to the future," and he later muses "what stories can do, I guess, is make things present." Story's ability to "make things present" is O'Brien's apparent resolution of the ambivalence toward fiction that has driven him through his Vietnam War books. He has been troubled by the question of whether dreams offer lessons. In *The Things They Carried* he sees his dreams and stories not as lessons but as elegies; they do not teach, but they do preserve.

In Vietnam, O'Brien tells us, "we kept the dead alive with stories." **"The Lives of the Dead,"** the novel's final story, contains O'Brien's most definitive articulation of the relationship between memory and story. O'Brien recalls the death of his childhood sweetheart and how night after night he would invent dreams to bring her back. He recalls a conversation in one such dream:

> "Right now," she said, "I'm *not* dead. But when I am, it's like . . . I don't know, I guess it's like being inside a book that nobody's reading."
>
> "A book?" I said.
>
> "An old one. It's up on the library shelf, so you're safe and everything, but the book hasn't been checked out for a long, long time. All you can do is wait. Just hope somebody'll pick it up and start reading."

So stories can save us, but through preservation rather than through salvation. In *If I Die in a Combat Zone* O'Brien rejected "the lessons of dead men," and in *The Things They Carried* reading becomes a way of dreaming those dead men back to life. The flesh is made back into word.

O'Brien's Vietnam War works persistently deconstruct the distinctions between memory and imagination, lessons and dreams, truth and fiction, and reality and the text. But the final movement in *The Things They Carried* is toward reconstruction—not of distinctions but rather of a creative connection that draws together experience and art. For O'Brien, stories are that privileged connection that can lift us out of the quagmire of a dualized reality and fantasy and place us on the solid ground of truth. But even this apparent resolution is finally suspended. Because the novel offers us a double lesson: Stories can save us. But if O'Brien's readers have truly accepted his wiley postmodern perceptions of the reader's relationship to the text then they know that they must reject any lessons. O'Brien warns "if at the end of a war story you feel uplifted, or if you feel that some small bit of rectitude has been salvaged from the larger waste, then you have been the victim of a very old and terrible lie." So any sense of conclusion or epiphany must be its own undoing. And as O'Brien might say, "this is true."

Michael Kerrigan (review date 21 April 1995)

SOURCE: "Memories of War," in *Times Literary Supplement*, No. 4803, April 21, 1995, p. 20.

[*In the following review, Kerrigan suggests that* In the Lake of the Woods *reveals "a people at ease but never at peace," referring to the impact of Vietnam on the American psyche.*]

For Wilfred Owen, apparently, the poetry was in the pity; for America's Vietnam literature it is in the irony. The tone of swaggering cynicism we recognize from so many novels and films is that of men who feel utterly confused as to where—and ultimately who—they are. "What's the name of this goddamn place?" asks one man in O'Brien's memoir *If I Die in a Combat Zone* (1973). "I don't know. I never thought of that", replies his comrade: "Nobody thinks of the names for these places." The military institution, non-combatant readers know from *Catch-22*, is absurd enough without having to function in the context of a war whose fundamental "mistakenness" has now, thanks to Robert McNamara, been given all but official confirmation. If the grand geopolitical point of the war was obscure, the "search and destroy" tactics appointed for US troops on the ground amounted to a sort of systematic purposelessness. As the narrator of *Going After Cacciato,* O'Brien's novel of 1978, remarks:

> They did not know even the simple things: a sense of victory, or satisfaction, or necessary sacrifice. They did not know the feeling of taking a place and keeping it, securing a village and then raising the flag and calling it a victory. No sense of order or momentum. No front, no rear, no trenches laid out in neat parallels. No Patton rushing for the Rhine, no beachheads to storm and win and hold for the duration.

Nor was there an identifiable enemy: indistinguishable from the general populace, the Vietcong seemed at once pervasive and maddeningly elusive.

And maddened, notoriously, they were—though as John Wade, the protagonist of *In the Lake of the Woods,* realizes as he watches, appalled but uncondemning, the massacre at My Lai, "this was not madness. . . . This was sin." The main action of O'Brien's new novel opens many years after these events and unfolds in backwoods Minnesota, yet it is all the more a Vietnam novel for that. Time has only made John Wade more completely a creature of his combat experience, though it has been internalized, suppressed until now through a successful political career and an outwardly successful marriage. War was a nightmare—horrific but unreal. Only when the veteran is back in "the world", does Vietnam begin to assume its grim if unacknowledged reality. As the novel begins, Wade is with his wife Kathy in a woodland retreat, trying a pick up the pieces after a crushing defeat in the polls. It is clear that Kathy is about to leave her husband: what we don't know is exactly how or given that she has stayed with him through what is gradually revealed as having been a purgatorial couple of decades, why. Though "Hypothesis" chapters flash forward to explore the possibility that Kathy may indeed be leaving her husband, and back to consider some of her possible motives for doing so, there remains the inescapable suspicion that something more sinister may have befallen her. Will Kathy be alive at all? The soldier kills innocent civilians: why should he not have killed his wife? The at-

tempt to piece together the answers to this question involves the quasi-legalistic assembly, in "Evidence" interchapters, of snatches of testimony, not only from Wade's friends and relations but from non-fictional sources including the transcripts of the Calley trial and the veteran's self-help literature. But it is an attempt to piece something together. Some novels may revel in postmodern fragmentation and centrifugality: *In the Lake of the Woods* would dearly love to recover its lost centre. "For me, after a quarter of a century, nothing much remains of that ugly war", O'Brien reports in an authorial footnote towards the end of the novel. "My own war does not belong to me." Vietnam remains in the memory incoherent but ineradicable, a set of "splotchy images" which must be brought into focus if the experience is to be apprehended. Aesthetics here are no more than a means to an ending. Combat offers multiple encounters with death but leaves the surviving soldier with a need for closure life cannot meet. So it is that the world becomes Vietnam, and the beautiful woods and lakes of Minnesota come to stand in for the jungles and paddies of South-east Asia.

Yet perhaps the North American wilderness has always contained its Vietnam, at least for as long as the United States has existed. "It had been Indian land", recalls O'Brien of his Minnesotan birthplace in *If I Die in a Combat Zone.* "Ninety miles from Sioux City, sixty miles from Sioux Falls, eighty miles from Cherokee, forty miles from Spirit Lake and the site of a celebrated massacre. . . . The settlers must have seen endless plains and eased their bones and said, 'here as well as anywhere, it's all the same.'" Vietnam. O'Brien implies, is just one more stop along the trail for a nation which has indeed "celebrated" massacre in its western tradition but has never come to know the soil it has so ruthlessly conquered. It is significant that O'Brien includes the testimony of a Native American witness at My Lai, a witness who looks on with something like resignation but nothing like involvement. It is significant too that Wade's problems pre-date Vietnam. The humiliated son of an alcoholic and thus largely absent father, he had a boyhood passion for conjuring tricks, and while the tips from conjuring manuals offered in evidence here may suggest the manufacture of consent for an indefensible war by government and media, they provide more immediate insight into the mind of an individual with a mania for control: a boy who will grow up incapable of trust in himself or others and who will find no adequate confessor for the sins of adulthood. Themselves the products of war, born into the baby boom that followed victory in 1945, the Vietnam generation is in some sense sterile: in some sense arrested in childhood. More disturbing than John and Kathy Wade's marital difficulties is the barren infantilism of their marital happiness; more alarming than their conscious decision to abort their baby to further John's political career is the clear subconscious motive that they themselves should remain the children. Foreigners tend to be impatient of the notion that Vietnam was "an American tragedy", pointing out that the war was a sight more tragic for the Vietnamese. Yet it remains interesting that in this, for all its haunting beauty perhaps O'Brien's bleakest novel yet, the most chilling passages are not those which deal with guns and gore in Vietnam but those set in Minnesota many years later, revealing a people at ease but never at peace. Just what is it that American fathers do to their sons that gives them this need to kill and conquer in nameless places abroad? Whatever it is, it robs them of any sense of belonging at home and makes of America itself an indeterminate, disorientating wilderness.

FURTHER READING

Criticism

Johnson, George. Review of *The Things They Carried,* by Tim O'Brien. *The New York Times Book Review* (14 April 1991): 32.

> Places O'Brien's *The Things They Carried* "high up on the list of best fiction about any war."

Ridenhour, Ron. "Riding the Night Winds." *London Review of Books* 17, No. 2 (22 June 1995): 12-14.

Reviews *In the Lake of the Woods,* asserting that O'Brien produced "a mystery so clever and so mysterious that few reviewers appear to have understood it."

Schweninger, Lee. "Ecofeminism, Nuclearism and O'Brien's *The Nuclear Age.*" In *The Nightmare Considered: Critical Essays on Nuclear War Literature,* edited by Nancy Anisfield, pp. 177-85. Bowling Green, OH: Bowling Green State University Popular Press, 1991.

> Proposes "to define a ecofeminist ethics as it relates to nuclearism in general and literature about nuclearism in particular," illustrating "a practical application of these speculations by applying this heuristics to O'Brien's novel."

Smith, Lorrie N. "The Things Men Do: The Gendered Subtext in Tim O'Brien's *Esquire* Stories." *Critique* XXXVI, No. 1 (Fall 1994): 16-40.

> Argues that five stories, which first appeared during the 1980s in *Esquire* and later formed the core of *The Things They Carried,* offer "no challenge to a discourse of war in which apparently innocent American men are tragically wounded and women are objectified, excluded, and silenced." Smith uses this subtext "to position *The Things They Carried* within a larger cultural project to rewrite the Vietnam War from a masculinist and strictly American perspective."

Additional coverage of O'Brien's life and career is contained in the following sources published by Gale: *Authors and Artists for Young Adults,* Vol. 16; *Contemporary Authors,* Vols. 85-88; *Contemporary Authors New Revision Series,* Vol. 40; *Dictionary of Literary Biography,* Vol. 152; *Dictionary of Literary Biography Documentary Series,* Vol. 9; *Dictionary of Literary Biography Yearbook,* 1980; and *DISCovering Authors Modules: Popular Fiction and Genre Authors.*

Craig Raine
1944-

English poet, critic, and editor.

The following entry presents criticism of Raine's work through 1995. For further information on his life and career, see *CLC*, Volume 32.

INTRODUCTION

Widely regarded as among the foremost of England's contemporary poets, Raine writes allusive, erudite poetry stylistically characterized by dazzling wordplay, startling imagery, and strange metaphors. Many critics believe that he has revitalized modern British verse by leading the so-called "Martian" school of poets, a loose literary movement which takes its name from the title of Raine's book of poetry, *A Martian Sends a Postcard Home* (1979). Martian poetry, like Raine's early verse, features unexpected imagery, unique and metaphoric language, and an emphasis on an alien point of view that makes the familiar, everyday world seem fresh, newly discovered, and sometimes humorous. Thomas Lux has declared Raine "a poet of rare wit, originality, and humanity."

Biographical Information

Raine was born December 3, 1944, in Shildon, County Durham, to working-class parents. He attended Exeter College at Oxford University, where he earned an honors degree in English language and literature in 1965 and a bachelor's degree in nineteenth- and twentieth-century studies in 1968. Raine attempted to write a doctoral dissertation about English poet Samuel Taylor Coleridge's poetic philosophy, but abandoned the project in 1971 when he received a one-year appointment as lecturer at Exeter. After his 1972 marriage to Ann Pasternak Slater, the grand-niece of Russian author Boris Pasternak, Raine continued to lecture at various colleges at Oxford until 1979. During the late 1970s, poems that Raine submitted to English periodicals began attracting attention: he twice took the Cheltenham Poetry Prize and received second prize in the 1978 National Poetry Competition. The publication of his first poetry collection, *The Onion, Memory* (1978), generated such controversy in the English poetry establishment that Raine promptly published *A Martian Sends a Postcard Home,* which includes the award-winning title poem. From 1981 to 1991, Raine served as poetry editor at Faber & Faber publishers, which made him the first poetry editor for that firm since T. S. Eliot to publish his own works, including the poetry collection *Rich* (1984), the never-performed libretto *The Electrification of the Soviet Union* (1986), and a collection of astute critical essays, *Haydn and the Valve*

Trumpet (1990). Since 1991, Raine has taught as a fellow at New College, Oxford, and has completed the epic poem *History: The Home Movie* (1994).

Major Works

Possessing deep affinities with early twentieth-century modernist and imagist poetics, Raine's poetry represents a continuous but often witty questioning about "whether seeing *is* believing," according to Michael Hulse, but his later verse expands to include personal, autobiographical observations about the human condition. The poems—some have called them conceits—in *The Onion, Memory* feature the poet's intensely metaphoric descriptions of daily, ordinary objects and phenomena: animals, insects, gardens, vegetation, butchers, barbers, grocers. Similarly, *A Martian Sends a Postcard Home* contains the eyewitness accounts of an imagined visitor from Mars who describes various things used every day on Earth and amusingly reveals his incomprehension of their purpose. *Rich* marks Raine's movement toward a more narrative style in his poetry and furthers his experimentation with wordplay. Divided into three sections—the second consisting of a prose memoir of his father and his family background through age sixteen—the poems in *Rich* depict episodes in the lives of his parents, himself, and his young daughter. This volume also displays Raine's personal, autobiographical impulses and presents several poems about love and sex. *History,* identified by the publishers as "a novel in verse," chronicles the history of most of the twentieth century in Europe through events selected from the family histories of the Raines and the Pasternaks. Comprising dozens of individual parts written in three-line stanzas, the poem makes use of riddling metaphors, graphic sexual language, and violence.

Critical Reception

Reactions to Raine's first two poetry collections initially polarized the English critical community, represented equally well by the extremes of infatuated enthusiasm and near-hysterical dismissal. Most critics have marveled at "Raine's odd rightness of perception," as Lux put it, but others have claimed that his poetry is "superficial and escapist ... [seeming] slickly clever rather than artistically accomplished," according to Martin Booth. John Bayley has observed that Raine's poems "frequently pull off the really difficult feat of not sounding like 'poetry' at all, but just seeming a very clever way of saying something arresting." Although most critics immediately recognized Raine's enlivening and significant impact on English poetry, some have faulted his earlier work for not addressing human emotions or concerns. Since *Rich,* however, commentators have detected a humane, more personal approach in Raine's writings, and they have continued to comment on his linguistic and metaphoric pyrotechnics, often mentioning the influence of Pound, Lowell, or Stevens along the way. Once relatively unknown in the United States, Raine has gained a growing audience since the publication of *History.* Hulse has suggested that "Raine's future development must be of great interest to anyone seriously concerned with the future development of the poetic imagination."

PRINCIPAL WORKS

The Onion, Memory (poetry) 1978
A Martian Sends a Postcard Home (poetry) 1979
A Journey to Greece (poetry) 1979
*A Free Translation (poetry) 1981
Rich (poetry and prose) 1984
**The Electrification of the Soviet Union (libretto) 1986
Haydn and the Valve Trumpet (essays) 1990
1953: A Version of Racine's 'Andromaque' (verse drama) 1990
History: The Home Movie (poetry) 1994

*This work was published as a pamphlet containing six poems, which were later included in *Rich.*

**This work is based on Boris Pasternak's novella *The Last Summer.*

CRITICISM

Gavin Ewart (review date 30 June 1978)

SOURCE: "References Back," in *Times Literary Supplement,* June 30, 1978, p. 728.

[*In the following review, Ewart finds* The Onion, Memory *"intellectually so satisfying that some triviality of theme can be overlooked."*]

[*The Onion, Memory*] is Craig Raine's first book. At the age of thirty-four he is no infant prodigy and it is clear at once that there are qualities of thought and control here which a younger writer might not have been able to command. It is also clear, from the very first poem, that metaphor and simile rule OK. A butcher "duels with himself" and offers "heart lamé-ed from the fridge, a leg of pork / like a nasty bouquet". The new customer in a barber's shop is "another piece / of sheeted furniture to sit there and be dusted". There is also some verbal trickery—"the slap and trickle of blood", "tired as a teapot" (alliteration, in my view, is a technique by no means yet exhausted; the more nonsensical the better, in a certain kind of poem). Perhaps **"The Ice Cream Man"** is a little too contrived; the connection between the Darwin quote and the kids watching an ice cream man is a bit tenuous. **"The Tattooed Man"** (not bad) is a Hugo Williams poem from start to finish. All these are in the first section, **"Yellow Pages"**, and they establish a pedigree, Hamiltonian minimalist, with a really remarkable sensitiveness to hidden parallels (usually visual). The kennings are everywhere.

To appreciate this cleverness, very enjoyable and original, you need an education. You have to know about *esse* and *percipi* and Berkeley, and what misericords are or might be and who Casaubon is or might be (a famous Late Renaissance Classical scholar or a character in *Middlemarch*). Sometimes, as in **"An Enquiry into Two Inches of Ivory"** (otherwise very pleasing), where chess pieces are watching a man in the kitchen, the method over-reaches itself. "The giant puts a kettle on the octopus." The eight flames of a gas ring? Or its eight metal bars? If you have to puzzle too long, some of the surprise is lost.

"Houses in North Oxford" adds human emotional involvement to the ingenuity (the houses are compared, in complicated detail, to soldiers on parade or standing by their beds): "Who would guess from this the timid heart— / the wounded professor, nuns on their knees, / the dear old thing afraid of a khaki envelope?" This makes better use of the cumulative cleverness than just leaving it there to be wondered at, but these final lines also sound like a small piece of early Auden, tacked on. And in **"Bed & Breakfast"** the line "Tea and toast with cunty fingers" is direct (and he knows it) from Henry Green (an amorous butler's idea of perfect happiness). Also: "five pink farrow suckle at each foot". When the Meta-physicals went too far, weren't they a bit like this?

"The Book Of The Market" is sheer description, though very good description ("The raspberries are nursing nipples", carrots "each bunch an old Elizabethan gauntlet, / the tapered fingers creased with wear . . ."), and our final comment might still be: so what?

There is aural as well as visual felicity: "customers break / the rifles in two, nuzzle the stocks / like hungry cats and fire (miaow!)", "A helicopter comes and canes the sky". Sometimes the visual images are very beautiful—"a river is the grey silk dress, / because a mallard pulls a puckering strand". Most of these poems are unrhymed. Often the rhyme doesn't add much—"without palaver", to chime with "cadaver", cheapens the poem.

The later poems are more dramatic. **"Reading Her Old Letter About A Wedding"**, a piece extremely exactly observed, creates a situation. So does **"Invalid Convalescing"**, but less well. **"Gethsemane"** is a good idea mishandled; "and night flings back / its doors of black" isn't very helpful. **"On the Perpetuum Mobile"**, though, where the rhymes work well, as in a [T. S.] Eliot "Prelude", is one of the best poems in the book, seeming more relaxed and human.

The rhymes in the "Rhyming Cufflinks" section are often unobtrusive. In **"The Behaviour of Dogs"** (a charming poem) it hardly exists at all. **"Defective Story"** and **"Beware . . . The Vibes of Marx"**, reminding me formally of Eliot's early rhyming quatrains, are great fun; but the really large-scale metaphor of **"Two Circuses Equal One Cricket Match"** is not so successful.

The final sequence, **"Anno Domini"**, is ambitious but fails, I think, because it is too disjointed; and sometimes the brilliance of language and image is a distraction, suiting some subjects and not others. From this stricture **"The Corporation Gardener's Prologue"**, the first poem, must be strongly exempted:

> Is moder add im layde in live—
> a nonely child an cymbal—

Translated, "His mother had him late in life—an only child and simple". The whole of this poem is in the Lewis Carroll class.

The best work here makes it obvious that Raine is a poet of more than promise; intellectually so satisfying that some triviality of theme can be overlooked. When he can twist more of his iron pokers into true love knots (something that comes with time and not with trying) he will be good indeed.

John Bayley (review date 4 January 1980)

SOURCE: "Making It Strange," in *Times Literary Supplement,* January 4, 1980.

[*In the following review of* A Martian Sends a Postcard Home, *Bayley detects similarities between Raine's poetic technique and that of the Russian formalists.*]

Who but Donne would have thought a good man like a telescope? asked Dr. Johnson, and who but Craig Raine would want to wipe away the sorrows of a new laid egg?—and in so doing sympathize even with the bowl into which it has been shoved.

> To want to wipe away
>
> From this one smudged face
> the mucus and the excrement,
>
> so many final straws
> and the dirt of all dried tears?
>
> Cold beyond comfort, it rocks
> in a kitchen bowl.
>
> And what about the kitchen bowl?
> Poor dogsbody,
>
> its hard enamel
> is chipped like a dalmation. . .

As the last word of the poem shows, spelling is not important in the world of conceits—Donne and his friends would not have been particular about that, however exquisite their sense of connection. In fact both Donne and Raine produce in their different ways popular and highly individualized versions of poetry's most ancient device for turning the unforgiving facts of existence to favour and to prettiness—the riddle.

Such poetry can always and effortlessly go back to childhood, making us purr or cringe with forgotten animisms (Donne on the way to an amorous appointment disciplines his whispering clothes—best silk suit no doubt—like children, and imagines his shoes as dumb even under the torture of being walked on). But in such ploys begin responsibilities. Donne's conceits are cerebral—good men do not actually remind us of telescopes—yet out of the boxes of such ingenuity a world of absolute resemblance and meaning is crouching to jump, for the language of poetry does not distinguish between the physical and the metaphysical, good conceits leaping like electricity across what F. W. Bateson called the "semantic gap" between the one and the other. Raine's stunned trout executed on their mechanized farm, become "rigidly ridiculous" "shocked as a Bateman cartoon / when some bounder mentions death".

If ingenuity comes off in such poetry it is automatically a part of the moral world in which all good art has its natural being. Shakespeare's Isabella imagines "the poor beetle that we tread upon" finding "a pang as great as when a giant dies", and the predicament of Raine's insect equally forces us to identify.

> a glinting beetle on its back
> struggled like an orchestra
> with Beethoven.

The real world is always saving Raine's talent from the concentration of comparison, rather as it appears over the shoulder of a child whose tongue protrudes as he draws it. His is the funniest version of what might be called the New Animism in English poetry. **"The New Hospital"** is a space ship "invented for nothing / but the longest journey / to a different world", but it is also alive in the ancient terms of legend and bodily function, which intermingle without hygienic pieties in the acceptance of terminal meaninglessness.

> Even the lavatories
> create a myth of peace—
> porcelain pelicans
> repeat to infinity,
>
> glittering mermaids sit
> side-saddle on basins
> and each urinal calmly
> sucks its peppermint

(An odd thought that the full beauty of that comparison can only be appreciated by one half of the poetry reading public.)

"Flying to Belfast 1977", the best poem in *A Martian Sends a Postcard Home,* creates a whole climate of feeling out of the simplest possible repetitions and connections. The sea is dark linen, the ships faults in it; the town, looked at from above, a transistor with its back taken off; the plane's windows like drops of solder and everything "wired up". A faceless, imagined bride at the end is laughing

> at the sense of event, only
> half afraid of an empty house

with its curtains boiling
from the bedroom window.

Haiku-like, the verb recalls mutely its equally unexpected fellow in the first stanza, where jet engines "whistled to the boil".

Raine has far too tight a grip of things to need to display feeling: it would be the most unfortunate thing if he felt he had to go on to do so, in the same way that every novelist today is required to be "compassionate" as well as clever. Some of the poems which do not come off, for example one about an ex-guard from a concentration camp, show that he may have qualms about this. One can only hope that he suppresses them firmly. The blurb observes with careful piety that "guileless comic vision" is "finally displaced by a sombre view of commonplace human tragedy", which in the context of the actual poems means absolutely nothing whatever. But readers appear to find it irresistible that the poet should deepen and develop a heart. Most poetic talent has an obstacle race before it, not a Pilgrim's progress, and this seems specially true of Raine.

Manipulation of comparisons and verbal echoes is of course a stock-in-trade, especially of poetic coteries, as much today as in Donne's and Shirley's time. But there is an exoticism in the way Craig Raine does it that is decidedly intriguing. His poems don't sound like those of any contemporary, even those who use the same tricks, and they frequently pull off the really difficult feat of not sounding like "poetry" at all, but just seeming a very clear way of saying something arresting.

> **[Raine's] poems don't sound like those of any contemporary, even those who use the same tricks, and they frequently pull off the really difficult feat of not sounding like "poetry" at all, but just seeming a very clear way of saying something arresting.**
> **—*John Bayley***

The absence of the poetic goes with the absence of sentiment, and both with the odd fact that English does not seem the wholly necessary language for these poems: they could be literal translations from some other tongue, possibly the Martian in which the hero of the title poem sends his postcard home. "Mist is when the sky is tired of flight / and rests its soft machine on ground" or "the lighthouse stands / like a salt cellar by Magritte" could go equally strikingly into another language. But which? The clue is in the particular way these theses "make things strange", the recipe of the Russian formalists, and the closest parallel to Raine's kind of inspiration seems to me the youthful [Boris] Pasternak, who in *My Sister, Life* and other early collections verbalized perception with the same style of lens and focus. It depends on an individual domestication of "strangeness" rather than on any specific linguistic idiom, and poems of Raine's like **"The Meterological Lighthouse at O"** and **"Mother Dressmaking"** could go into another language without losing so very much of their special dimension of seeing and meaning. Pasternak's very early poems made it strange in a manner equally accessible internationally.

It is an interesting singularity that while it is virtually impossible to borrow or to imitate inside one's own tradition of poetry, and still appear original, it can be done by learning from a foreigner. The French poets—incredibly—learnt from Poe, Housman from Heine, Pound and Empson from translations of Chinese and Japanese, Charles Johnston, the admirable translator of *Eugene Onegin,* has also in his own poetry been a judicious student of Russian models. Raine's poems are very much his own, but part of the electricity of connection is this affinity, whether conscious or not with that related brand of acuteness and innocence of which the first couplet of **"Karma"** is a good example.

> Rubbish smokes at the end of the garden
> cracking its knuckles to pass the time.

All ingenuity in poetry is a hit-or-miss affair. When Raine's works, it puts us in new touch with life as unexpectedly and joyfully as the early Pasternak did, or the young Betjeman, but when it does not quite come off it seems like a closed circuit on a cassette, fixed up for the private pleasure of cronies. The Metaphysicals are just the same. Conceits can be worth the carriage, as Johnson observed, but only if they fetch us far enough into a new dimension of awareness. Raine's aperçus are frequently too pleased with themselves, as in **"Facts of Life"**.

> Wasps with Donald McGill bathing suits
> were learning to swim in my cider glass . . .
> yards away, on the cellar steps,
> a thrush jiggled a snail in its pram

But at their best they draw attention not to themselves but to an unfamiliar pleasure of familiar consciousness.

Michael Hulse (essay date Autumn 1984)

SOURCE: "Craig Raine & Co.: Martians and Story-Tellers," in *The Antigonish Review,* Vol. 59, Autumn, 1984, pp. 21-30.

[*In the following essay, Hulse provides an overview of the so-called "Martian" poets, discussing the different emphases on imagery and narrative technique of individual members.*]

John Fuller, to whom I devoted the first article in this series, has a good title to be considered the father of that movement in poetry which has dominated the British scene since the end of the 70s: the Martian school. In *The Mountain in the Sea* (1975), Fuller's parlour-game approach to verse at times produced witty results that anticipate the riddle-making fecundity of the Martians, as in these lines from 'Thing from Inner Space':

> Lumbering, dreamy, pig-headed: like a smooth
> Cauliflower or ribbed egg it would offend
> If not armoured and decently hidden.

After a moment's pause we think: of course, the brain! The aha!-effect is typical of the reading experience we have come to associate with Craig Raine and Christopher Reid's work, as is also Fuller's reference in the same poem to "the daily theatre of objects": Raine's poem **'An Enquiry into Two Inches of Ivory'** programmatically posits "Daily things. Objects / in the museum of ordinary art" as his subject matter, at the same time ostentatiously appropriating to himself something of Jane Austen's modesty (her letter of 16th December, 1816, is alluded to in Raine's title—Austen suspects she "produces little effect after much labour").

Daily things, but daily things seen anew, from a new and unexpected angle, fitted into new patterns, yoked into new relationships: this is the core of the Martian method. The inventiveness of Craig Raine's imagination is more than equal to Fuller's when he writes that the barber's "scissors scandal-monger round the ears," that fields are "ploughed neatly as a fingerprint," that foliage in autumn is "full of broken windows," that the snakes at the zoo "endlessly finish spaghetti," or that dogs "pee like hurdlers, / shit like weightlifters, and relax / by giving each other piggy-backs . . ." These playful images, by the zestful emphasis they place on the values of poetry as sheer fun, might alone identify Raine as an Oxford poet of the Fuller class, and indeed Raine taught there at various colleges after completing his first degree (a doctoral dissertation on Coleridge was abandoned) and in his poetry at times betrays a lightly-worn donnishness, as well as a love of Oxford localities.

Craig Raine was born in Co. Durham in 1944, but it was not until the second half of the 70s, after Fuller's *The Mountain in the Sea,* that his poetry began attracting attention. He twice took the Cheltenham Poetry Prize and his work was promoted by Martin Amis, then literary editor of the *New Statesman,* and in 1978 a first volume appeared, ***The Onion, Memory.*** Reactions to this collection—from which all my Raine quotations have come so far—polarized the poetry established in Britain, with the extremes of infatuated enthusiasm and near-hysterical dismissal equally well represented. Swift to capitalize on the sales value of controversy, Raine brought out a second book in 1979, and it is from this collection—

something of a best-seller, as far as poetry is capable of such a thing—that the school takes its name: *A Martian Sends a Postcard Home.*

The title poem—to which Walker Percy's Martian in *The Message in the Bottle* may well have stood godfather, rather than any science fiction reminiscence—exemplifies both Raine's imaginative vigour and the flashiness to which he is often prone. His Martian has difficulty interpreting the signs on our planet:

> Model T is a room with the lock inside—
> a key is turned to free the world
>
> for movement, so quick there is a film
> to watch for anything missed.
>
> But time is tied to the wrist
> or kept in a box, ticking with impatience.
>
> In homes, a haunted apparatus sleeps,
> that snores when you pick it up.
>
> If the ghost cries, they carry it
> to their lips and soothe it to sleep
>
> with sounds. And yet, they wake it up
> deliberately, by tickling with a finger.

The car with its ignition and rear-view mirror, the wrist-watch, the telephone: here again a riddle-maker's fancy is being brought to bear upon the everyday, and throughout his second volume Raine again exhibits an unsurpassed fertility in simile and metaphor. Thus "a glinting beetle on its back / struggled like an orchestra / with Beethoven." "Dolphins darn the sea." "Mosquitoes drift with paraplegic legs." In Athens he views "weatherworn / lions vague as Thurber dogs." And in a public toilet "each urinal calmly / sucks its peppermint"— an image the full rightness of which, as has been pointed out, can only be appreciated by half the population . . .

A similar imaginative drive can be seen in the poetry of Christopher Reid (born 1949) and of a third member of the school, David Sweetman (born 1943). Reid's *Arcadia* was published in 1979—the year can be seen as the Martians' *annus mirabilis*—and is as abundantly sprinkled with simile and metaphor as Raine's work. His "smutty pigeon on a parapet / pecks for crumbs like a sewing-machine." His weightlifter "carries his pregnant belly / in the hammock of his leotard / like a melon wedged in a shopping-bag." "Your hair is Japanese / with heated rollers." Ginger-root is "arthritic" and chilies are "red leather winklepickers." So too with David Sweetman, who in 'Coasting' writes: "A lazy length of hawser can't spell / even one of the names of Allah correctly."

Elsewhere he observes "the thatched huts lying as still as shells / clustered in an abandoned rockpool."

Clearly, then, these three poets share their most distinctive characteristic of image-making vitality, and it is this which has won them the widest readership enjoyed by any poets in Britain since the much-derided Liverpool poets pushed their pop products—this, and the fact that they (and Raine in particular) have been courted by the media. Ample newspaper features and a half-hour film on television's arts programme *The South Bank Show* have probably done more to make Craig Raine's name nationally familiar than his inclusion in John Haffenden's *Viewpoints,* a collection of ten interviews with established poets, or in *The Penguin Book of Contemporary Verse* (1982). Reid and Sweetman were also included in the Penguin anthology, edited by Blake Morrison and Andrew Motion; the Penguin, indeed, was conceived largely in the belief that—primarily through the Martians—"a new confidence in the poetic imagination" had come into being, that "a body of work has been created which demands, for its appreciation, a reformation of poetic taste." I shall have more to say about the Penguin anthology presently.

But Craig Raine, Christopher Reid, and David Sweetman, though closely linked both by qualities of imagination and by the love the media bear them, prove on closer inspection to be writers with distinct tones of their own. David Sweetman's only collection to date, *Looking into the Deep End* (1981), reveals a more sombre, morally intense cast of mind than Raine's or Reid's. Historical and political factors determine Sweetman's conceptual range, whether he is looking back to Nazi Germany ('The Unhappy Inventor') or the Hiroshima bomb ('The Art of Pottery, 1945'), or writing of more contemporary evils, whether the suffering in South East Asia ('Love in Asia') or our fears of a nuclear holocaust ('0900hrs 23/10/4004 BC'). The economy, the anger, and the compassion of 'Stories to frighten children with,' which I quote in full, are all equally beyond the scope of Raine and Reid:

> Remember the Spartan boy, a snapping fox in his lap
> curled as if his own guts had spilled out, grown hairy?
> Today it shines in metal coils, sprouts wires, is hugged
>
> by a lad in black nourishing a foetal terror silently.
> But others speak, myths are made—in an Asian city,
> tarts wound themselves with lipstick, impatient
>
> for the crew shooting a recent war. Away on location,
> a make-up girl squints at a photograph

before painting the acne of napalm on a child's face.

David Sweetman is uneven, but in such work he achieves poetry of a high order.

Christopher Reid too is uneven, and his writing is as complete a contrast to Sweetman's as we could wish. In his first book, *Arcadia,* the prevalent note was that inventive playfulness which—as in Fuller and Raine—is his most evidently Oxonian characteristic, as in 'Strange Vibes':

> That seven-octave smile, those ten
> chomping cigars, one with a golden band;
>
> nicotined eyes, and someone's squiggly hookah,
> fendered in levers, wheezing the blues;
>
> those three hypodermics pumping in a row;
> men groaning and swooning: well, it all went to show
>
> we'd stumbled by chance on an opium-den.
> Only the front man kept his cool,
>
> stiff as a waiter and stooping to lay
> such infinite knives and forks on a dazzling table.

No need to mention that a big band is being described: the reader's enjoyment of the riddle-making would be impaired by anything so specific. But Reid's poems, perhaps more than Raine's, have seemed open to the charge that merely to concentrate on attractive imagery is somehow to sell poetry short and trivialize it, and it was with relief that one found *Arcadia* also contained a poem like 'The Life of the Mind', a mock-metaphysical account of the passage of a thought or idea through the mind:

> Samuel heard the voice of God at night,
> but I used to see an Edwardian bicyclist,
> a roly-poly man with a walrus moustache.
>
> Since it was always summer, he wore
> a blazer with Neapolitan ice-cream stripes,
> a yellow boater, made of the crispiest wafer,
> and plimsolls, marshmallow-white.
>
> The rules of the game were easy:
> to set the man on his bicycle-seat,
> and let him balance there, without moving
> forward.
>
> He never remained for long, and every time
> his fall was as terrible as the fall of Eli.

This seemed to promise development along Empson/Wilbur lines, with a dab of Marvell, so Reid's second collection, *Pea Soup* (1982), came as a disappointment. Rather too happy to remain in a world of brand-new discoveries, in which daily things were insistently seen afresh, Reid continued to exclaim that "everything was bogus" or "the galaxy reads like a rebus," or that he found himself in a "playground of impromptu metaphors."

Craig Raine has been less prone to the potential pitfalls of self-parody. The manifesto-like statement in **'Shallots'** in the second volume—"images provide / a kind of sustenance, / alms for every beggared sense"—has a wholer, more human tenor than Reid's pedantic maxim, in 'The Ambassador' (*Pea Soup*), that "through a studious / reading of chaos we may / arrive at a grammar of civilization." Raine's poetry has wrongly been accused of lacking either human warmth or a moral centre, but in fact it demonstrably has both: in Raine more than in Reid or Sweetman, the image is the instance of human experience, as in these lines from **'Flying to Belfast, 1977'**:

> I thought of wedding presents,
> white tea things
>
> grouped on a dresser,
> as we entered the cloud
>
> and were nowhere—
> a bride in a veil, laughing
>
> at the sense of event, only
> half afraid of an empty house
>
> with its curtains boiling
> from the bedroom window.

'In the Dark,' one of Raine's finest poems to date, is a narrative of a girl and her unwanted child: his images succinctly present the familial and religious pressures which are brought to bear on the girl and ultimately lead to tragedy:

> God danced on his cross
> at the foot of her bed
>
> like Nijinsky having a heart attack . . .

A pamphlet of six poems, *A Free Translation* (1981), showed Raine writing powerfully, with no slackening of his image-making fecundity but with a notable advance in his readiness to confront the recurring facts of human existence, particularly in **'A Walk in the Country,'** from which these lines come:

> They are burning

the stubble
in the fields ahead,

which is why
the graveyard seems
ringed with fire

and somehow forbidden.
Is it fear
halting my child

so that her thumb,
withdrawn for a second,
smokes in the air?

Of the three writers of the Martian group, Craig Raine has the most substance. I have shown elsewhere (*Critical Quarterly,* vol. 23, no. 4) that his method has affinities both to that of the Imagists and of the Rilke of the *Neue Gedichte.* Beyond both there is in Raine an affection for the French symbolists, as also for Joyce. His writing is intelligent, witty and rewarding, and his forthcoming collection (**Rich,** due at the end of 1984) will be essential reading for anyone concerned with current British poetry.

Raine's **'In the Dark'** tells a story: the girl, after two suicide attempts, kills her child, and is found by the police with a shoe-box under her arm. John Fuller published *The Illusionists,* a long verse tale, in 1980, and a first novel, *Flying to Nowhere,* in 1983. James Fenton and David Sweetman often have a strongly implied narrative background in their work, and the Northern Irish poet Paul Muldoon, whose strongest work of the 70s was in shorter vignettes of Irish life, included a long Chandleresque narrative poem, 'Immram,' in his 1980 collection *Why Brownlee Left.* D. M. Thomas, who first made his name as a poet, is now better known for fiction. Geoffrey Hill turned to narrative in his recent long poem 'The Mystery of the Charity of Charles Péguy.' Among less established but clearly important writers, Jeffrey Wainwright, Andrew Motion and Michael Hofmann all have a strong narrative content in their poetry. The trend to story-telling in British poetry has in fact been visible for some years now and across a wide spectrum of talent, so that Blake Morrison and Andrew Motion, in their introduction to *The Penguin Book of Contemporary Verse,* were able plausibly to identify narrative as an important component in what they termed the extension of the imaginative franchise.

Anthology introductions, by virtue of their need to sell the new, are often one-sidedly propagandist, and Morrison/Motion's Penguin introduction is no exception: both their choice of poems and poets and their view of developments in poetry have very properly been found deficient by critics of the anthology. However, it is interesting to consider their argument for seeing the narrative trend as more than a brief

fashion. "Where other poets make the familiar strange again through linguistic and metaphoric play," they write, alluding to the Martians, "the young narrative poets perform a similar function by drawing attention to the problem of perception." They claim that the "fact of fictionalizing," and the "artifice and autonomy" of the text, are central to the strategies of the new narrative poetry, which they say exhibits "something of the spirit of post-modernism." And so on.

Though there is some truth to this, I can't help feeling we'd be disappointed indeed if it were the whole truth, since it would mean no more than that a worn-out perception of self-reflexive prose fiction had been imported into poetry. But I don't think this is the case. Rather, the new narrative can most persuasively be seen as sharing more with modernist (or even *pre*-modernist) than post-modernist practice, and as being more endearingly tainted with trust and confidence than anything we have seen since Eliot. Andrew Motion's own poetry, which has been widely praised, demonstrates this point. Motion (born 1952) published his first book, *The Pleasure Steamers,* in 1978, and took the Arvon/*Observer* poetry prize in 1981, but it was only with *Independence* (1981) and *Secret Narratives* (1983) that his work achieved a larger maturity of narrative power. The title of his most recent collection, like John Fuller's *Lies and Secrets* or John Hartley Williams' *Hidden Identities,* seems rather self-consciously intent on mystery, but in fact there is nothing secret about Motion's narratives at all, and their modernity is that of the first quarter of our century, as in these lines from 'One Life':

> Up country, her husband is working late
> on a high cool veranda. His radio plays
> World Service News, but he does not listen,
> and does not notice how moonlight fills
> the plain below, with its ridge of trees
> and shallow river twisting to Lagos
> a whole night's journey south. What holds
> him instead are these prizes that patience
> and stealthy love have caught: *papilio
> dardanus*—each with the blacks and whites
> of simple absolutes he cannot match.

It is their openness rather than any mystery that makes such lines so attractive; reading them is like being returned to an Edwardian world of confident sequence and understood tempo. The best poems in *Secret Narratives*—'Anne Frank Huis,' 'West 23rd,' 'On Dry Land'—could be read with scarcely any loss by the naivest of readers.

The world of Motion's narratives is a product of that nostalgia which has given the British *The French Lieutenant's Woman* and *The Siege of Krishnapur* and *The Raj Quartet,* or—in poetry—Thwaite's *Victorian Voices,* Raine's **'In the Kalahari Desert,'** or Hill's 'The Mystery of the Charity of Charles Péguy.' It is an ironized, fictionalized world which paradoxically reinforces its own safe knowledge of itself through the very reflex of doubt. The irony is a gesture the sophisticated writer makes to legitimize his own newfound trust in the Real World beyond himself; what results is often attractive, intelligent and even charming in ways that no longer depend on irony. Implicitly, the writing of narrative poets like Andrew Motion, as also the writing of Craig Raine or John Fuller, panders to that right-wing, nostalgia-oriented readership which in Margaret Thatcher's Britain is if anything still growing, and it panders to this readership even at moments of the greatest irony. This is perhaps the greatest shortcoming of what has been the most zestfully imaginative twin movement British poetry has seen in many years; but there are signs, in the work of John Ash, Michael Hofmann and other new writers, that this amiable if complacent guard is about to be changed.

POSTSCRIPT

Since this article was written, Craig Raine's *Rich* has been published, and indeed fulfills the promise of Raine's earlier work. *Rich* is divided into three sections: 'Rich', 'A Silver Plate', and 'Poor'. The middle of these is a twenty-page prose memoir mainly concerned with the poet's father, an ex-boxer turned faith healer and a colourful character who had had brain surgery, could peel an apple with the skin in one piece, and had other qualifications for winning a son's hero-worship. Raine senior appears in two of the poems here, in the third part: **'Plain Song'** and **'A Hungry Fighter'**. Critics who have accused Raine of writing with too impersonal a remove from human reality might do well to attend to the noticeable autobiographical content not only in this new book: earlier poems such as **'Listen with Mother'** or **'Mother Dressmaking'** drew upon the poet's family life and childhood too, with fondness and a nice judgement in recreating mood.

'Poor', that third section of the new book, looks back to Raine's earlier life and to fictionalized lives of others (in poems such as **'The Season in Scarborough 1923'** or **'The Man Who Invented Pain'**), but 'Rich' focusses more directly upon his present life, as city editor, married man and father. Raine recreates perspectives of the very young child in **'Inca'** or **'In Modern Dress'**, or writes persuasive love poems (**'Rich'**, **'A Free Translation'**, **'Words on the Page'**); at the same time he permits himself Joycean word games in **'Gauguin'**, or adapts Rimbaud in the once controversial poem **'Arsehole'** (see *The Observer* of 10th and 17th April, 1983). Raine has extended his range and his ability to unite a poem around one complex of related imagery; the earlier ingenuity which won him his wide readership is undiminished, as he writes of "the bidet / and its replica, / the avocado" or "eggshells / cracked on the kitchen table / like an umpire's snail / of cricketers' caps".

David Bromwich (review date 19 October 1984)

SOURCE: "Tricks and Treats," in *Times Literary Supplement,* No. 4255, October 19, 1984, p. 1193.

[*In the following review of* Rich, *Bromwich considers the autobiographical aspects of the poetry reminiscent of the confessional poets' technique, but reserves his highest praise for the prose section.*]

Craig Raine's early poems belonged to a subgenre that the Germans call "thing-poems". They dealt with such things as **"Misericords"**, **"Houses in North Oxford"** and, making allowances for compound entities, **"The Fair in St. Giles"** and **"Demolition with Tobacco Speck"**. Other poems, close to these in simplicity, made up a sequence on tradesmen, including **"The Butcher"**, **"The Barber"** and **"The Ice Cream Man"**. A second sequence took as its subjects Pre-Raphaelite paintings with self-explanatory titles: **"The Horse"**, **"Sports Day in the Park"**, **"The Home for the Elderly"** and so forth. The mode that Raine adopted for these flat-sounding topics was not quite naturalistic. And yet, one never came to know the poet himself through the traits or associations of the things he described. The preferred tone was abstract, with an occasional reassuring touch of intimacy; and when a poem reached a climax of some sort, it gave notice with a mildly out-of-place simile: the barber who "massages the scalp like a concert pianist"; the grocer who "smiles like a modest quattrocento Christ". Elsewhere the same effect was produced with a more self-conscious air: "the cobs of corn / are similes for nooses neatly tied"—which is very like saying, "Look, this is how poetry gets written".

From other poems in his first book, *The Onion, Memory,* it appeared that Raine was also a confessional poet. But, though in certain respects his work was modelled on Lowell's and Plath's—in diction, cadence and the routine use of hyperbolic figures—it adapted their procedure to essentially different ends. Plath aimed to be a repulsive writer: "I am a lantern— / My head a moon / Of Japanese paper". Whatever one made of the style, it had a motive. The "I" claimed attention as a special case. Yet here is Raine, in what seems to be a similar key: "Bread develops slowly under the grill, / a Polaroid picture of desert: / above it, the air is almost in tears". He has taken over the sensitive-heartless style, but without the motive: for him it is a way of being clever about a piece of toast. Indeed, Raine's poetry from the start affected to be affectless. But the title poem of his second book, *A Martian Sends a Postcard Home,* offered a new set of credentials for his usual practices, by presenting a fair specimen of the author's own voice as an interplanetary monologue. In this way the slightly strange borrowed the gravity of the estranged. The "Postcard", however, was only the earlier **"Enquiry into Two Inches of Ivory"**, under a gimmicky wrapping. Thus between his first two books, Raine's chief advance was a deepening facility. In both "I" was mostly absent. When he did appear—"It is the onion, memory / that makes me cry"—he was apt to sink into bathos.

In avoiding, as far as possible, the risks of confessional poetry, Raine up to now has avoided most of its vices and virtues. One is therefore surprised to find that the longest single item in **Rich** is a prose memoir of his childhood and family. The pattern for this, in a fairly obvious but unimportant way, is Lowell's memoir in *Life Studies*. Yet here the differences all work in Raine's favour. He writes from a steadier attachment than Lowell, and his prose is much less mannered. He is able to treat his parents, not as queer obstacles to his development, who must accordingly somehow be talked about, but rather as persons altogether discrete from himself, whose uniqueness he comes to feel the more strongly as he writes. His father was a boxer when young, and then a bomb armourer for the RAF, before being invalided out with epilepsy ("the result, we think, of an explosion in a munitions factory"). The description of a fit is vivid, without either callousness or sentimentality:

> I was never aware of being frightened as a child because I saw his fits many times. My mother would take the three heavy cushions from the hide sofa and lay them on the floor. Then, her arms under his and locked on his chest, she'd drag my father's dead weight from wherever he'd fallen over to the cushions. She'd take off his shoes and his tie, open his shirt and loosen his waistband. Then we'd wait. For ten to twenty minutes he would lie there without moving, except for one eyebrow which jigged up and down while his mouth twitched sideways. Suddenly he'd arch his back like a twig in a furnace, scraping his stockinged feet for purchase, then take his head in both hands and try to smash it on the floor, only prevented by the cushions. And he would scream. The screams were the worst part. A priest who happened to be visiting my mother volunteered to stay on one of these occasions, but the screams drove him out.

> When he subsided after five minutes, he'd lie with his eyes wide open but unfocused, weeping. My mother would hitch up her skirt and straddle his chest. With her face close to his, she's say, "Knobser, Knobser, Knobser, Knobser," in a gentle voice until his eyes focused and he came back to her with a groan of recognition. "Knobser" was my father's fighting name. "Young 'un", he'd say, and she'd go off to make him a cup of tea.

The writing is sustained like this, calm, disciplined and free of cliché, for twenty-two pages.

> **The prose that takes up Part II of *Rich* is a success in a venture that simply defeats many writers, and it contains the best work of any kind that Raine has done.**
> **—David Bromwich**

The memoir comes to a stop arbitrarily, in the middle of Raine's school days, but it ends with a recognition. His father had protected him throughout childhood from every outside assault, with the result that he felt answerable only to his family, and looked on his father as a hero. But among other tricks, "my father had taught me to do a proper somersault", and, away in boarding school, he broke the frame of a bed. The bursar told him that he must be careful thereafter: he was different from the other boys, for his parents could not afford to pay for a new bed. He then took to replying to questions about his father by calling him a football manager, or a brain surgeon: "I was at school for seven years. It wasn't until my second year that I told anything like the truth about my father." In its less abrupt fashion, the memoir itself is a delayed effort to come to grips with the truth. It has perhaps two false touches: an allusion to the town Raine grew up in as "a typical, ugly small town in the north of England" (a judgment more stereotyped than even the town can have been); and an assertion that his father's good stories were "useless as raw material" for poetry (a rather stiff answer to a question nobody asked). Still, the prose that takes up Part II of **Rich** is a success in a venture that simply defeats many writers, and it contains the best work of any kind that Raine has done.

By contrast, Parts I ("Rich") and III ("Poor") for the most part confirm the methods of his earlier poetry. The exceptions are autobiographical pieces, some covering, at a lower intensity, the incidents sketched in the memoir, and some extending the narrative to include Raine's own activities as a father:

> Washing hair, I kneel
> to supervise a second rinse
> and act the courtier:
>
> tiny seed pearls,
> tingling into sight,
> confer a kind of majesty.
>
> And I am author
> of this toga'd tribune
> on my aproned lap.

It is a pleasing picture. But "confer a kind of majesty" is at once vague and a little hackneyed; and in this instance, the corresponding passage in Lowell does qualify one's esteem for the later poem: "After thirteen weeks / my child still dabs her cheeks / to start me shaving. . . . Dearest, I cannot loiter here." At any rate, the more personal poems stay clear of the carefully extravagant phrases that have been planted at regular intervals elsewhere. These need as a rule to be decoded rather than imagined: a "trout / tortured with asthma", for example, is nothing more than a trout gasping out of the water. Once we have seen that, its interest is exhausted.

There is other evidence here that Raine still associates seriousness with the on-purpose effects of difficulty. His preface sounds a note of high candour about this, copied from the preface to Lowell's *Imitations:* "As most readers will realize, I have freely adapted to my own purpose work by Dante, Marina Tsvetayeva, Rimbaud, the anonymous Anglo-Saxon poet of 'Wulf and Eadwacer' and Ford Madox Ford. My debt to these authors is very general: they were inspirations, not detailed models." That "work by Dante" is good (as "mobled queen" was good). In fact, the allusions are scarcely audible, and certainly less imposing than this makes them sound. At times, Raine seems to believe that a poem is a moderately fanciful, moderately stimulating, procession of words knocked half a notch out of their prose order. This accounts for the satisfying monotony of his verse—almost all of it free verse of five-to-ten syllables per line. It also helps to explain the nicely calculated quality of the few interruptions that his policy allows: words like "frenum" and "plosive", or "obliterate" and "ejaculate" used as particles; and occasionally, the metaphor that inverts itself by overemphasis—"She felt excitement / like a dying salmon in his lap." Since Raine alludes respectfully to Salvador Dali, it may be added that he shares with Dali a thoughtless fondness for the well-contrived shock.

Apart from the poems about family and memory, *Rich* contains several oblique meditations on history and some expert pornography, both oblique and explicit. **"An Attempt at Jealousy"** is among the best of this group; it begins in resentment and ends in self-pity; but in the meanwhile the deserted lover wonders why he should be jealous of the man who replaced him:

> Tell me, is he bright enough to find
> that memo-pad you call a mind?
> Or has he contrived to bring you out—
> given you an in-tray and an out?
>
> How did I ever fall for a paper-clip?
> How could I ever listen to office gossip
> even in bed and find it so intelligent?
> Was it straight biological bent?

And so it goes on, amiably, for nine more stanzas. The poem on the next page is **"Gauguin"**, a Tahitian child's monologue about the things that men and women do with each other in secret, which ends: "*Handmake Kodak man, come back, / my secrets are sorry with oil.*" It is all managed in this sort of pidgin English; but these last lines are poetry all the same. The style and incidental details of **"An Attempt at Jealousy"** and **"Gauguin"** are arrived at naturally, and together they show Raine's versatility with a single theme. In certain other poems, he sounds like a man trying hard to be drawn to what is repellent, and in his preface he mentions an expression he has tried to admire: "'to wipe someone's face', meaning to kill someone—a deceptive euphemism that deserves wider currency". The expression has not caught on because the idea is not tolerable; and who would want to belong to a life that gave it much currency? Raine's worst moments come from deceptive euphemisms of just this kind. But the prose of *Rich* seems to point in an opposite direction, and it is the direction that he ought to pursue.

Paul Muldoon (review date 1-14 November 1984)

SOURCE: "Sweaney Peregraine," in *London Review of Books,* Vol. 6, No. 20, November 1-14, 1984, pp. 19-21.

[In the excerpt below, Muldoon concludes that Rich *is a "substantial collection, [Raine's] best so far."]*

Raine's third collection follows the procedures of *The Onion, Memory* (1978) and *A Martian Sends a Postcard Home* (1979): his poetic strategy is to present a series of striking similes or metaphors with the hope of forcing his reader to admire the justice of those similes and metaphors. Christopher Ricks need look no further (certainly not across the Irish Sea) for textual substantiation of his theory of the self-reflexive image.

Here, as before, the best of Raine's poems present something more than a concatenation of metaphors; effective though these may be. They are most effective when drawn from one area of experience, grouped around a single event or figure, or unified by a strong narrative. The tradesmen from the '**Yellow Pages**' of *The Onion, Memory*, '**In the Kalahari Desert**' (for me, his most successful single poem), '**Memories of the Linen Room**' and the title-poem from *A Martian Sends a Postcard Home*: in all these cases, Raine has learned an important lesson from the 17th-century concettists: that the *sustained* metaphor in the service of an argument is the most satisfying, if the most difficult, *modus operandi,* that a conceit bears the same relationship to a string of metaphors as the Bayeux tapestry to a line of washing. A successful conceit, that's to say. In '**A Free Translation**', for example, Raine sees lots of Eastern promise in a domestic setting, and the details amass gently and persuasively:

> we have squeezed

a fluent ideogram
of cleansing cream
across the baby's bottom.

The ending of the poem (endings always pose a problem to
the necklace-maker, even if the beads are all of the same size,
shape and colour) is less than original, however:

time to watch
your eyes become
Chinese with laughter
when I say that
orientals eat with stilts

My favourites from *Rich* are **'The Season in
Scarborough 1923'**, **'The Gift'**, the marvellous
'The Man who Invented Pain'—

the kind of day
a man might read

the Sunday paper
by his pigeon cree,
or nervously

walk out to bat
and notice the green
on a fielder's knee—

the excellent versions of Rimbaud and Tsvetayeva, and the
quite brilliant **'Inca'**:

Now, there is only this:
the long, unwritten poem

which almost celebrates
a daughter's parsnip heels
and her pale, perfect nipples
like scars left by leaves.
Inca. How her nightdress rides up.

How she comes, a serious face,
from every corner of the garden,
cupping a secret
she wants me to see,
as if she had somehow

invented the wheel. O Inca.

In a review of ***The Onion, Memory,*** I accused Craig Raine
of a certain lack of feeling, a surface dandyism. I suspect I
was wrong even then. **'Inca'** alone would now prove me
wrong. Note, though, the qualities which are not always so
evident in Raine's work but which contribute to the success
of **'Inca'**: the irony implicit in the words 'unwritten' and 'al-

most', a line-length corresponding to a perceptible rhythm
rather than the short Lego sections he more commonly builds
from, and, Heavens above, an almost total absence of other
than appropriate and discreet simile and metaphor. The least
said the better, by the way, about that Sunday reviewer's wet-
dream—The Martian School, The Metaphor Men. Who are
they? Christopher Reid, perhaps? David Sweetman? Norman
MacCaig? Philip Larkin? Seamus Heaney, perhaps? Doesn't
Heaney's description of a lobster—

articulated twigs, a rainy stone
the colour of sunk munitions—

vie with Raine's

scraping its claws
like someone crouched
to keep wicket at Lord's.

Like [Heaney's] *Station Island,* though for less obvious reasons, *Rich* is divided into three parts. Parts One and Three
are subtitled 'Rich' and 'Poor', while Part Two consists of a
prose meditation on Raine's childhood in the North of England, as if **'91, Revere Street'** formed a junction with **'Terry
Street'**: **'A Silver Plate'** is, to say the least, helpful to a reading of poems in *Rich* (**'The Season in Scarborough 1923'**,
'A Hungry Fighter') and to autobiographical poems in the
earlier books—**'Mother Dressmaking'**, **'Listen with
Mother'** and, above all, **'Anno Domini'**. **'Anno Domini'**
was called 'the fragmented biography of a faith-healer, whose
greatest miracles are imaginative'. We now discover that the
faith-healer is Raine's own father, who, after an accident in a
munitions factory, underwent brain surgery: 'My father remembers the whirr and bite of the saw that took off the top of
his skull. They removed part of his brain and inserted a silver
plate.' And that's not all: 'He was and is a brilliant raconteur,
with a large repertoire of brutal boxing stories, in which he is
always the hero. He turned professional when he was sixteen
and fought for the featherweight title of Great Britain, a bout
he lost to Micky McGuire.' Raine writes fluently, always
entertainingly, sometimes movingly, about his childhood: 'A
Silver Plate' fills out an already substantial collection, his
best so far.

John Lucas (review date 7 December 1984)

SOURCE: "Prodigal Son," in *New Statesman,* Vol. 108, No.
2803, December 7, 1984, pp. 32, 34.

[*In the following excerpt, Lucas senses Wallace Stevens' influence in* Rich, *but criticizes the rhythmic structure and
sometimes the language used by Raine.*]

Rich comes in three sections. The first contains poems about Craig Raine's immediate family and is called 'Rich'. Then there is a prose section, 'The Silver Plate', in which he writes about his boyhood and especially his extra-ordinary father, an unemployed and unemployable epileptic with a gift of tongues and overwhelming personality, someone who seems to be all appetite. The third section, 'Poor', contains poems which sometimes draw on the same material as the second section and which are about suffering of various kinds. What links the three sections is best expressed in Wallace Stevens's dictum that the greatest poverty is not to live in a physical world. Raine does not quote this, although he quotes from a great many other writers, but you feel that Stevens hovers over many of the pages of *Rich.*

I do not mean this to be a criticism. After all, Stevens's appetite for reality always had something slightly theoretical to it which is hardly the case with Raine. In fact, probably enough has already been said about the veracity and voraciousness of his visual appetency and it is certainly true that he is more willing than Stevens ever was to see the world again with an ignorant eye.

This kind of intensity of vision becomes its own morality, especially in the opening section and above all in **'Pornography'** and the already-famous **'Arsehole'**. Raine's taking and giving of the world—to borrow from a more recent poem—is the spendthrift prodigality of careless riches which at times degenerates into Mammon-like catalogues. More interesting, I think, are the poems which celebrate the catching of tigers in red weather, and which vindicate Raine's use of his father as a hero of the imagination. There is for example a poem called **'Again'**, in which Raine remarkably attempts to capture or suggest how a brain-damaged boy constructs a life out of the ways he hears and sees: 'If he utters the sound for pain, / the one with cardboard clothes // will punish his pillows / and let him listen to the heart // she wears outside on a safety pin, / the better to show her love // when she holds his hand.'

There is nothing soft or sentimental about this poem. Instead, it has about it the imaginative gaiety which is also there in **'The Season at Scarborough 1923'**, a poem which invents his mother's perception of her work as a hotel chamber-maid, and that also shows in **'The Man who Invented Pain'**, although this poem about a wartime soldier who loosens pigeons and who is sentenced to be shot, can hardly get beyond its opening. For this is the absolute poem, the purely gratuitous act of celebrating a releasing imagination as the pigeons 'poured / past his hands, // a ravel of light / like oxygen / escaping underwater'. Where can you go from there?

The direction is by way of fables about the imagination, with which the book closes. Of these the finest seems to me to be **'The Grey Boy'** which, because it can't fully be understood

by an effort of intellect, haunts me as few recent poems have. A group of children are camping beside the river . . . But to try to say what the poem is about is absurd. Yes, it's about different urgencies of the imagination and without the example of Stevens I do not think it could have been written. But it is also an entire and seamless creation.

Yet to say this brings me to the two criticisms I have of *Rich.* The first is that Raine's ear isn't always adequate to his imaginative energies. The short, three-line stanza form he has developed often moves with the kind of spasmodic jerkiness that comes near to spoiling such otherwise excellent poems as **'A Walk in the Country'** and **'Widower'**. And on other occasions poems seem to me to break up into detachable bits or simply not to have the accomplishment of rhythmic control they cry out for. This is especially true of the misbegotten **'An Attempt at Jealousy'**.

Secondly, and less emphatically, while I can see the force of Raine's wanting to find fresh ways of speaking the dialect of the tribe, I am not sure that the programme will lead anywhere but to the kind of sport poem exemplified by **'The Sylko Bandit'**, in which he stakes his claim for a poetry of new, extravagant mintings: 'he is the unexpected thyng, / who values not those laws / long passed enforcing playnesse . . . Sick affrayd of sumptuary police, / we do fear his flambouyance . . .' But language is surely as much a matter of rhythm, of stress and inflection, as it is of vocabulary?

Martin Booth (review date January 1985)

SOURCE: A review of *Rich,* in *British Book News,* January, 1985, p. 53.

[*In the review below, Booth blasts Raine for the "basically vacuous" poetry in* Rich, *although he concedes that the prose section contains "genuine attempts at true artistic achievement."*]

The latest collection from Craig Raine, his first verse book for five years, is entitled *Rich*; sadly it is a weak addition to this famous poetry list. Previously, Raine's work has appeared from Oxford University Press (*The Onion, Memory,* 1978, and *A Martian Sends a Postcard Home,* 1979) but his appointment as poetry editor at Faber has him bringing out his own work, making him the first poetry editor for that firm since T. S. Eliot to publish himself.

One of the leaders of the 'Martian' school, the loose movement in modern British verse which has its nickname from the title of his second book, Craig Raine writes poetry characterized by its wordplay and density of image and idea, much of which is so compounded by intellectual arabesques as to make it nebulous. He is not so much a poet as a wordsmith who is captivated by the relationships of word to word rather than word to reality, understanding or readership. The result is a poetry that is superficial and escapist in that it seeks not to enter the intrinsic experience of poetry, but to bounce off it, absorbing little of its life but much of its veneer. His poetry seems therefore slickly clever rather than artistically accomplished:

> Something apt to garden,
> he does plant those naked boys,
> the finest in Holland,
> along the length of windowe box.
>
> Were it not for the Buddha,
> the which he hath acquired
> from out of Angkor Wat,
> stone melted lobes intact
>
> he does much resemble a poet,
> one that ekes out guilders
> in payment for his rented room,
> hard by the station.

Some of Raine's poetry is frankly lacklustre and not all of it is original: his poem '**Arsehole**', for example, is a poor rendering of a sonnet by Rimbaud and Verlaine creating together, unacknowledged when Raine first published it and only vaguely acknowledged now. When the writing does strive for higher levels, it is lost in arty verbosity:

> The captain takes a swig
> at scratched binoculars,
> while we light the fires
> with Act One of Lear.

Only in a lengthy, yet still very self-indulgent, autobiographical prose section, somewhat out of context in the volume, is this inelegant and contrived 'literary' diction permitted to lapse, allowing genuine attempts at true artistic achievement to glimmer through the murk.

One of the leaders of the 'Martian' school, the loose movement in modern British verse which has its nickname from the title of his second book, Craig Raine writes poetry characterized by its wordplay and density of image and idea, much of which is so compounded by intellectual arabesques as to make it nebulous.
—*Martin Booth*

Throughout the book, one is confronted by a deliberate ig-noring of the central tenets of poetry. Raine seems to delight in being obscure and denies his verse lyricality, beauty and simplicity of purpose for an attempted scintillating eccentricity that is basically vacuous and survives in print only because of his reputation.

Charles Forceville (essay date 1985)

SOURCE: "Craig Raine's Poetry of Perception: Imagery in *A Martian Sends a Postcard Home*," in *Dutch Quarterly Review,* Vol. 15, No. 2, 1985, pp. 102-15.

[*In the following essay, Forceville discusses the imagery of selected poems from* A Martian Sends a Postcard Home, *focusing particularly on the implications of Raine's metaphors and similes.*]

Craig Raine is one of those contemporary British poets whose achievements have attracted considerable attention. Several of the poems in his second collection *A Martian Sends a Postcard Home* are first-rate, and the title poem supplied the name for what has come to be known as the "Martian" school in contemporary British poetry, of which Raine may be considered the initiator. The most striking feature of this kind of poetry is no doubt its imagery, to which the epithet "Martian" refers. In what follows I propose to discuss a few representative poems from the collection, focusing on this Martian element in the imagery and its effect on the poems as a whole.

It is no coincidence that the poem **"A Martian Sends a Postcard Home"** has both given its name to the whole collection and is the first one printed in it. In many respects it constitutes the key to how to read the other poems, and can be said to exemplify its author's poetic conviction that

> images provide
> a kind of sustenance,
> alms for every beggared sense.
> [**"Shallots,"** ll.16-18]

It seems to be a reasonable procedure, therefore, to scrutinize this poem first and subsequently examine other poems in the light of what has been discovered.

Once the reader has understood the implications of the poem's title and has overcome his initial puzzlement, he perceives that he is confronted with what in fact is a series of riddles. The Martian reports via interplanetary mail a number of earthly phenomena which to us, humans, are perfectly familiar, but which he, failing to understand their meaning, describes in a highly original, "poetic" way. It is our task as readers to "reconstruct" the phenomena the Martian describes by fusing *our* knowledge of the world with *his* perception of it. Or, to put it differently, Raine wants us to look at our already too familiar world with the unprejudiced eyes of a Martian in order to perceive it afresh. This, he implies, is exactly what a poet ought to do and, by extension, his readers. This notion of the poet's function to make his readers aware of the world is, of course, by no means new. In fact, Coleridge draws attention to a very similar idea when he explains Wordsworth's contributions to the *Lyrical Ballads:*

> Mr. Wordsworth . . . was to propose to himself as his object, to give the charm of novelty to things of every day, and to excite a feeling analogous to the supernatural [Coleridge's realm], by awakening the mind's attention from the lethargy of custom, and directing it to the loveliness and the wonders of the world before us; an inexhaustible treasure, but for which, in consequence of the film of familiarity and selfish solicitude we have eyes, yet see not, ears that hear not, and hearts that neither feel nor understand. (*Biographia Literaria,* Ch. 14)

Or, to quote [Victor] Shklovsky, a critic with a very different background, whose ideas are even more closely akin to Raine's:

> The purpose of art is to impart the sensation of things as they are perceived and not as they are known. The technique of art is to make objects "unfamiliar", to make forms difficult, to increase the difficulty and length of perception because the process is an aesthetic end in itself and must be prolonged.

Being a Martian, then, is like drawing away the "film of familiarity" clouding objects, making them "unfamiliar", so that our sense of perception is fully restored.

In **"A Martian"** Shklovsky's "defamiliarization process" is exemplified in its purest form. Some ten earthly concepts are defamiliarized by being concealed in an alien's perception of them and the reader has to make a conscious mental effort to retrieve the Martian's innocent and flawed view of these concepts. There can be no doubt that Raine succeeds brilliantly in finding striking descriptions for these objects, but his predominant concern with creating surprising images has resulted in a poem which in other respects suffers from certain weaknesses. In the first place the reader needs to surrender to a considerable suspension of disbelief—to invoke another Coleridgean coinage. In order to be capable of making his observations at all, the Martian must have at his disposal a number of sublunary concepts. Consider, for instance, the poem's opening lines:

> Caxtons are mechanical birds with many wings
> and some are treasured for their markings—

> they cause the eyes to melt
> or the body to shriek without pain.

> I have never seen one fly, but
> sometimes they perch on the hand. (ll. 1-6)

Obviously the Martian must be familiar with, among other things, the notions of "mechanicalness", "quantity", "flying animal", "weeping", and of course be able to frame correct English sentences. Inevitably a degree of arbitrariness is involved on the poet's part in selecting the phenomena with which the Martian is acquainted, and those with which he is not. As this arbitrariness is inherent in the whole idea underlying the poem, however, the poet must be granted this freedom. Therefore, no sympathetic reader is likely to complain that the Martian uses words like "mechanical" (l.1), "machine" ("Mist is when the sky is tired of flight / and rests its soft machine on ground"—ll.7-8), "apparatus" ("In homes a haunted apparatus sleeps, / that snores when you pick it up."—ll.19-20), and even "television" ("Rain is when the earth is television"—l.11), but is, as ll.19-24 show, apparently unaware of the use of a telephone. Neither will anyone be seriously bothered to learn that the visitor from outer space marvels at "Model T", which is a "room with the lock inside" (l.13), while disregarding this oddity in the

> punishment room
> with water but nothing to eat.
> They lock the door and suffer the noises
> alone. (ll.26-29)

After all, the "punishment room" is also a "room with the lock inside".

It is a more serious matter, however, when this kind of irregularity takes a form which justifies the qualification "inconsistency". Thus, whereas the Martian needs six lines to explain his "caxtons" (l.1), he describes the world as "dim and *bookish*" (my italics) in l.9, and, moreover, in the final lines shows that he is familiar with the concept of reading:

> At night, when all the colours die,
> they hide in pairs

> and read about themselves—
> in colour, with their eyelids shut. (ll.31-34)

Similarly, while our Martian uses the circumlocution "when all the colours die" to indicate that it gets dark, he employs the verbal phrase "to make darker" in l.12. Finally, it is at least highly unlikely that the Martian would be mystified by the fact that at night humans "hide in pairs" (l.32), when he effortlessly uses concepts like "being tired" (l.7), "sleep" (ll.19 and 22) and "to wake up" (l.23). These inconsistencies suggest a lack of internal coherence in the poem; the poet has not consistently shown the world from the Martian's point of view. As the poet of all the other poems in the collection he could have used "when all the colours die" as another way of saying "when it gets dark"—and we would have admired the poeticality of the expression. But in this poem the narrator is not the poet—the "implied poet" if you wish—but a Martian, whose descriptions, by sheer coincidence, happen to be highly poetical.

The lack of internal coherence can be founded on yet another aspect of the poem: both its length and the order in which the "riddles" are presented, are completely arbitrary. Arguably, the last four lines, with their description of sleeping and dreaming, suggest a faint air of finality (the end of the day), but that would be as far as we can go. The other riddles (Clusters of ll.1-6; 7-10; 11-12; 13-16; 17-18; 19-24 and 25-30) could be read in any order. Furthermore, the poem could theoretically have been indefinitely extended, or alternatively shortened by one or two riddles without its "structure" suffering any serious damage.

It might sound a bit like splitting hairs to dwell so long on the poem's flaws. After all, the poem functions as a kind of prologue to all the poems that follow, which necessitates a clear, unmodified exemplification of the poet's artistic creed. Indeed, one could even consider the poem as a kind of manifesto—and that it has been taken as such is proved by the now widely used adjective "Martian". And as in a manifesto nobody expects carefully balanced stances, we can, as long as we consider the poem in isolation, wink at what, after all, are minor faults and let ourselves be carried away by its extraordinary imagery. A purely imagistic poem like this—titled in such a way as to collect all the images under one heading and bring the message home—should be taken in the same spirit as Pound's "In a Station of the Metro": "The apparition of these faces in the crowd; / Petals on a wet, black bough".

The main reason, then, why I have nonetheless chosen to go into such detail examining the implications of the imagery in this poem is that it provides us with some important touchstones for the analysis of the imagery in other poems in the collection and enables us to judge their relative merit.

There are several more poems which are very similar in pattern to **"A Martian"** in that they are predominantly strings of images with little connection between them, which gives them a very static character. All of these poems share the feature, though not all in the same degree, that they not only lack a neatly elaborated internal development, but also internal coherence. The first characteristic in itself, of course, can hardly count as an objection. As Morrison and Motion point out in the introduction to their anthology [*Contemporary British Poetry* (1982)]: "The new poetry is often open-ended, reluctant to point the moral of, or conclude too neatly, what it chooses to transcribe". But the second feature, the impaired

internal coherence, is, as noted before, of a more dubious nature. Turning to **"The Meteorological Lighthouse at O—"** as a representative of the poems which are flawed in this respect, we are presented with a—presumably short—trip by speedboat to a lighthouse;

> The speedboat ducks and drakes
> through quiet seas to where
>
> the lighthouse stands
> like a salt cellar by Magritte,
>
> dwarfing the keeper
> who figure-eights our rope
>
> around the bleak iron bollards. (ll.1-7)

We might assume from l.17, "the whole place is homesick", and from the fact that the trip is made by boat, that the lighthouse is situated on an island. There the narrator is shown around by the keeper.

Arguably, the poem can be divided into several parts, very much like **"A Martian"**. It is possible to distinguish five clusters—ll.1-12; 13-22; 23-27; 28-34 and 35-38—with, however, only the weakest possible links between them. The second part is connected to the first only by the repetition of the word "keeper" and by a certain basic logico-temporal sequencing (one first sets off to an island and then arrives there, rather than vice versa). That Raine himself is aware of the weakness of the transition from the first to the second part is suggested by the dots in l.12 ("like an opened envelope . . ."), a device which he frequently employs and which, though occasionally it has a clear-cut function (e.g. "passage of time" and "tension" both in **"In the Dark"**), often seems merely to be used to mask an uneasy, insufficiently motivated, transition. Part three (ll.23-27) is joined to the preceding passage by the notion of "sleeping". Raine's use of the contrastive "but" in l.23, however, seems to be not quite justified, for with it he equates the content of the vehicle of a simile ("as if he'd fallen asleep / outdoors and only just woken"), that is, an element from the imagination of the narrator, with a direct quotation of the keeper ("But the lighthouse is insomniac / *he says*", ll.23-24—my italics). In other words, the keeper could never have used the word "but", because he cannot have been aware of a contrast in the first place. Despite the fact that the break between parts three and four occurs within one couplet, there is again no clear connection between them, except that the computer is one more phenomenon the keeper can show to his guest. The last lines, too, are open to the objection that they are not really worked into the texture of the whole poem:

> He shows me a garden
> through his telescope—

> wearing its greenhouse
> like an engagement ring (ll.35-38)

—although one could see in the mentioning of the garden (if it is on the mainland) a reinforcement of the idea of homesickness worked out in ll.17-22.

But still, a unifying imagery could have saved the poem. As in **"A Martian"**, the poem abounds in original and striking images. However, instead of welding the poem into a whole, the images attract so much attention to themselves that they, on the contrary, emphasize its very fragmentariness. The images have been selected from completely different registers—games, surrealist painting, sleep, knitting, etc. Each image has been chosen because it vividly and originally evokes a certain situation, whereas no attempt has been made to have the images reinforce each other—as in for instance the poem **"Floods"**, where the key theme "argument" knits the images together. Even in cases where a phenomenon arouses strong expectations as to its further development we are disappointed. Consider the following lines:

> One side of the keeper's face
> is so badly disfigured
>
> he looks at my feet
> when he talks about the lighthouse.
>
> The whole place is homesick—
> even his scalded cheek,
>
> with its pallid impression
> of ferns and grass
>
> as if he'd fallen asleep
> outdoors and only just woken.

Whereas at first we trust to be told more about the keeper's badly disfigured face, we find we are given no further information, and it is difficult to escape the feeling that this feature was mainly introduced to prepare for the comparison with the "pallid impression / of ferns and grass" as of one who has "fallen asleep / outdoors and only just woken". Admittedly there is some justification for this simile; after all the narrator sees even in the scalded cheek a sign of homesickness, suggesting that the "ferns and grass" are a token of home—but surely this link is too tenuous to warrant the use of such a heavily loaded feature as a badly disfigured face.

It seems imperative at this stage in the argument to investigate more closely the nature of Raine's imagery, in order to avoid the trap of criticizing the poet for what he did not try to achieve in the first place. Following [Geoffrey N.] Leech's terminology and definitions, we can conclude that Raine employs metaphor slightly more often than simile, the use of formal indicators ("like", "as if") between tenor and vehicle distinguishing the latter from the former. Although he concludes that each metaphor can be turned into a simile, Leech warns the reader to remain aware of their important differences. He emphasizes that a simile is generally more explicit than a metaphor and that, unlike metaphor, it can specify both the ground and the manner of comparison. It is the greater implicitness which accounts for

> the tendency of metaphor to explain the more undifferentiated areas of human experience in terms of the more immediate. We make abstractions tangible by perceiving them in terms of the concrete, physical world; we grasp the nature of inanimate things more vividly by breathing life into them; the world of nature becomes more real to us when we project into it the qualities we recognize in ourselves.

It is illuminating to consider Raine's imagery in the light of the preceding remarks. If we return to the "manifesto" Martian poem we discover that its images exemplify neither metaphor, nor simile proper. On the one hand formal connectors are entirely absent—which points to metaphor—on the other hand we are in all cases supplied with manner and ground of comparison—characteristic of simile—and, in the last resort, none of the implicitness of metaphor survives. This oddity finds its origin in a very simple fact: in all cases tenor and vehicle are completely co-referential, identical. Thus, once the riddles have been solved, we are left with an entirely unambiguous rendering of tenor (= vehicle) and the ground of comparison. The fact that the "tenor" is initially unknown explains why (as in simile) the ground of comparison is always included—it is indispensable for construing the tenor. And due to the identity of tenor and vehicle the images lose every hint of the suggestiveness characteristic of metaphor. The result is a poem which through its very transparency precludes any further interest once it has been "reconstructed".

Raine's imagery, then, because of the identity of tenor and vehicle, has an even greater explicitness than that usually associated with simile. While this is particularly true of **"A Martian"**, the same feature can be witnessed in **"The Meteorological Lighthouse at O—"**, though admittedly to a less marked extent. The main difference is that in this last poem we are faced with real similes. However, the potential tension between tenor and vehicle hardly materializes because of two things. In the first place Raine mostly compares concrete, material things in terms of other concrete, material things. Secondly, in most cases the ground of comparison is restricted to only one element: the visual similarity. The speedboat ducking and draking; the taut ropes, "leaving the sea / like an opened envelope"; the computer output; they all evoke a vivid picture—nothing less, but certainly nothing more, either. It is this tenuousness of the link between tenor and vehicle, together with the already mentioned lack of coherence between parts within the poems under discussion which account for their rather static and shallow character.

The question we will have to face now is to what extent we may hold all this against Raine. After all, Raine, in most of the more "orthodox" Martian poems, has no intentions whatsoever of explaining "the more undifferentiated areas of human experience in terms of the more immediate". On the contrary, he wants to draw attention, as we have noted before, to the process of perception itself. Perceiving the familiar in terms of the unfamiliar is a joy in itself and need not lead to a greater (metaphysical) understanding of the world.

This, of course, is a legitimate view. Unfortunately, however, Raine's ideas about the importance of perception clash in a number of his poems with an essential poetic principle. As I have tried to demonstrate, the poet has only been able to indulge freely in imagery by sacrificing internal coherence and consistency. Both by the standards of a "traditionalist" critic like [Graham] Hough, who stresses the necessity of a work of art's "integrity—the almost universal requirement that the work shall be a whole, not a slice, a chunk, a collection or a heap", and by those of a well-known structuralist critic [Jonathan Culler]—"[a] fundamental convention of the lyric is what we might call the expectation of totality or coherence"—we therefore cannot but conclude that a number of the poems in the Martian collection are seriously flawed.

However, Raine has written some outstandingly good poems as well and I would like to end this exposé with a discussion of a poem in which the poet has successfully integrated his perceptive flair in an overall structure. **"Laying a Lawn"** is as full of imagery as any of the poems dealt with before, but in this case a unity has been achieved which makes it one of the best of the collection. Concentrating on the imagery as before, we notice how the grass chunks—books simile with which the poem opens, informs it throughout. We will therefore take it as the starting point for our analysis, then consider other elements, and come full circle again. Let us first take a closer look at these opening lines:

> I carry these crumbling tomes
> two at a time from the stack
>
> and lay them open on the ground.
> Bound with earth to last,
>
> they're like the wordless books
> my daughter lugs about unread
>
> or tramples underfoot. I stamp
> the simple text of grass
>
> with woodwormed brogues (ll.1-9)

Unlike many similes in other poems by Raine, this simile does not hinge on a single point of resemblance, but is a very rich one indeed. In the first place there is the physical similarity between the (probably rectangular) chunks of grass and the poet's daughter's books. Both are "laid open" on the ground; the grass chunks—carried two at a time, thus resembling a jacket and six "pages"—to form the lawn; the books (children's books, so probably with few pages, too) scattered around with a child's carelessness. The little girl's books are presumably of a firm quality as they are meant for children who are still to young to read ("*wordless* books", l.5—my italics). Similarly the grass "tomes"—a very felicitous choice of word—are heavy and meant to be relatively enduring; both books and grass chunks should be able to bear being trampled upon.

In the second place there are less tangible resemblances, where it should be noticed that meaning elements of tenor and vehicle magnificently interpenetrate on different levels. Whereas the books are "wordless", the chunks are "a simple text of grass" (l.8), but neither can be "read" in the literal sense of the word. Furthermore the two meanings of "brogue" (1. strong outdoor shoe; 2. dialectal accent) hint at significant interrelationships. The second meaning in the phrase "woodwormed brogues", when applied to "text", suggests the imperfectness of the earthly tomes, as does "crumbling" (l.1), a feature to which we will come back presently.

The blending of the connotations of the grass tomes and those of the books assume an added significance when juxtaposed to the father-daughter relationship. While the father is busily working with the grass chunks (which, as has been argued, are invested with the "book" connotations), the little girl is passively looking on. She is still innocent, not yet really involved with worldly things; she cannot yet be expected to help her father, just as she cannot yet be expected to be able to read books. Neither is she consciously aware of the fact that her doll is maimed, something which does not escape her father's notice. The idea of her innocence is further emphasized by her primeval nakedness. The father sees

> only the hair on her body
> like tiny scratches in gold,
>
> her little cunt's neat button-hole,
> and the navel's wrinkled pip . . . (ll.21-24)

The child's innocence, concentrated in her body's intactness, is linked to the grass chunks theme by the hint of decay which inheres in both: the grass tomes are crumbling and contain woodwormed brogues, while the girl will change teeth (l.15) and go through the full circle of life. But there is a more profound connection: the girl's decay will ultimately end in her death and she will be buried under the very "tomes" she is now playing on—she will become part of the earth again.

"All go unto one place; all are of the dust, and all turn to dust again" (Eccl.3.20). But for the moment the father refuses to think of all this. He is glad he "needn't see / the thin charcoal crucifix / her legs and buttocks make", ll.18-20. He suppresses thoughts of his daughter's future suffering—the black crucifix is a symbol that leaves no doubt as to its interpretation— and focuses on her innocence instead, marvelling at the perfection of her young body. The poem superbly culminates in its final lines:

> For the moment, our bodies
> are immortal in their ignorance—
>
> neither of us can read
> this Domesday Book. (ll.25-28)

If we read these lines in the light of what has become clear so far, it does not seem to be too fanciful to establish one other connection between the books and the earth, one which fuses the poem into a brilliant whole. For there is more to "reading the Domesday Book" than a witty joke. Not only does the Domesday Book refer back to the detailed survey King William I had drawn up, for tax purposes, of the precise state of England's lands and cattle; an Old English poem of that title, "Doomsday", has invariably been equated with the Day of Judgment, too. Once we have assessed these connotations, I think we are fully justified to be reminded of the medieval notion of the two books God bestowed on man: the Holy Book and the Book of Nature. The already mentioned themes of innocence versus experience, the transience and decay of human life, visions of suffering and the implications of the complex grass tomes simile resolve themselves in this aspect of medieval epistemology. Thus, whereas the father can "read" in the literal sense, which reflects his experience of life and suffering and his knowledge of the inevitability of decay and death, his daughter, who cannot read, is still blissfully unaware of all this—which constitutes her innocence. But neither the father nor his daughter can read "the Book of Nature" and in this respect the father is innocent, too. Focusing on this part of the innocence which he shares with his daughter, the father "for the moment" stops Time's wingèd chariot with its decay and death and completely identifies with her, feeling "immortal in [his] ignorance".

I hope the above analysis has convincingly shown that, unlike in the other poems discussed, the imagery in **"Laying a Lawn"** is not the result of a loose jumble of brilliant but unconnected perceptions, but the red thread welding the poem into a harmonious whole. The central simile is an incredibly rich one: instead of a single point of visual resemblance between tenor and vehicle, areas of comparison abound and trigger off an ever-extending degree of interpenetration of meaning-elements between them. The result is the ideal combination of maximum tension balancing maximum similarity characteristic of the best imagery. The images which are not

directly dependent upon the earth-books simile—for example "the caterpillar, rucked like a curtain" and the "little cunt's neat button-hole"—are not overly conspicuous and are consistent with the dominant themes in the poem.

We already noted that the categories of figurative language do not always hold very precisely in Raine's poetry, so we are hardly surprised to find that the richness of the central simile gives it a very metaphorlike quality. Although many similarities between tenor and vehicle can be made explicit, the horizon keeps receding and new vistas come into view. Notwithstanding the fact that here, as in other poems, Raine compares two concrete things, each has such a vast range of connotations that none of the shallowness, characteristic of his weaker similes, results. Moreover, it is worth noticing that in none of the other poems does Raine so closely approach symbolism. In view of these observations, then, I would like to venture the idea that it is perhaps not entirely coincidental that the imagery in this splendid poem is not so much a celebration of sheer perception, as indeed an exploration into "the more undifferentiated areas of human experience in terms of the more concrete world".

Blake Morrison (review date 20 November 1986)

SOURCE: "Tales of Hofmann," in *London Review of Books*, Vol. 8, No. 20, November 20, 1986, p. 11.

[*In the excerpt below, Morrison reviews* The Electrification of the Soviet Union, *noting that it is "well worth reading."*]

Craig Raine's libretto *The Electrification of the Soviet Union* might be seen as a further strand in his continuing argument with Tom Paulin over *The Faber Book of Political Verse*. On the one hand, Raine here shows himself to be a writer who can step out of the domestic tunnel into the stadium of politics and history: He takes [Boris] Pasternak's novella *The Last Summer,* set in 1916 with flashbacks to 1914, and lets the shadow of the Russian Revolution fall across it, adding an epilogue set in 1920 or 1921. It becomes a far more overtly political work in his hands than in Pasternak's (or in the translation of the novella by George Reavey), with Pasternak himself putting in an appearance to comment on the sacrifice of lives to political causes. On the other hand, all the imaginative sympathies here are with those who stand for the preservation of family life. The central character is Serezha, a poet, too naive to be either Pasternak or Raine, but sensitive and gifted and more to be admired than his hard-headed sister, whose song in praise of the New Man, 1917 model, is undermined by the facility of its rhyming:

> He's broken away from the past.
> The old world has spoken its last,

the fleshpots,
the despots,
the old world is broken at last.

The repressed Nordic Mrs. Arild, who refuses Serezha's love and ends up—gun in holster and jargon on her lips—in the uniform of a Party official, is also unsympathetic, though her behaviour is 'explained' by her moving widow's lament 'I died the day my husband died.' Considerably more warmth goes into Raine's portrayal of Sashka, a prostitute, the third woman in Serezha's life, who is seen peeing on a chamberpot and who talks of clients who 'come all over my face'. One of Raine's most attractive qualities is his readiness to give offence, especially where the sensibilities to be offended concern reticence about bodily functions. Sashka is otherwise characterised with impeccable conventionality (she has drifted into prostitution after being seduced) and the scenes in which she appears, and which include her drunk, Edmund Heep-ish husband, are those which carry most voltage. The Epilogue, about the Revolution's aftermath, seems crude in comparison, as do most of the politics, the current scarcely switched on at all. Nonetheless, it's fascinating to observe what Raine drops or develops from Pasternak, and if the theatrical power of the piece must remain in doubt until next summer (by which time the composer Nigel Osborne should have got his act together), three or four of the lyrics make the libretto well worth reading.

Craig Raine with Mary Karr (interview date 1987)

SOURCE: An interview in *Ploughshares*, Vol. 13, No. 4, 1987, pp. 139-48.

[*In the following interview, Raine discusses Martianism, the evolution of his poetry, his audience, poetic technique, and literary influences.*]

Craig Raine's new kind of poetry has yet to reach a substantial audience in the United States. But, if the reviews can be believed, Raine's reputation in Britain exceeds that of any contemporary poet on this side of the Atlantic. Raine's four books—***The Onion, Memory, A Martian Sends a Post Card Home, Rich,*** and his recent opera libretto, ***The Electrification of the Soviet Union***—have prompted an upheaval in British poetic tastes and tempers, but not a single thoughtful article in the American literary press.

Raine's poetry still bears the label—Martianism—pinned to it by British critics several years ago. In Martian poetry, one encounters the world afresh, as an alien might, through unexpected images: "And then Belfast below, a radio / with its back ripped off"; "the lawn sprinkler's dervish"; "a fluent ideogram / of cleansing cream / across the baby's bottom."

Like cold water on a hot day, such lines startle at first, then resonate through the senses: one must swim in them for a while before actually feeling wet. Raine described the process in an article called **"Babylonish Dialects"**:

> The initial obscurity, the moment of non-sense, puts us in touch with our non-verbal thoughts, or their simulacrum. And even after the necessary translation is effected, the strangeness lingers.

Raine's work recalls the early gems of two master experimenters, Pound and Williams. And just as Pound bridled against the confines of the Imagism box, so Raine resists the Martian pigeonhole today. Such restlessness befits a true inventor, and in an age when American critics trumpet something oxymoronically called "the new formalism," Raine's inventions deserve celebration.

[*Karr:*] *For American readers who haven't yet read* **A Martian Sends a Postcard Home,** *can you describe the Martianism that caused such a hubbub in the British press?*

[Raine:] "Ignorance, Madam, pure ignorance." Dr. Johnson's famous reply to a woman who asked him why he had defined *pastern* as the *knee* of a horse, contains an additional, inadvertent definition—of Martianism.

Ignorance, the mere absence of knowledge, need not detain us. But *pure ignorance* is the condition to which Descartes aspires in the *Meditations*. It doesn't just happen. You have to work at it until it is second nature, until you habitually question what Arnold called "the old straw of habits, especially our intellectual habits."

Our first nature is tidy. The mind is a know-all. It classifies. It is experienced. It is well-supplied with labels. It finishes our sentences for us. It lays down the law.

But Martianism is intellectually delinquent. Try telling it something indisputable, like a rose is a rose is a rose—and it will tell you that rosebuds are "tight pink cupolas" or "careful turbans." Caught pink-handed, it always pleads innocence and asks for the bouquet to be used as evidence. It has been led astray by French Symbolist poetry, by Mallarmé's injunction to Cazalis: "Peindre non la chose mais l'effet qu'elle produit" [Don't paint the thing but the effect that it produces]. In Rimbaud's diagnosis ("Il s'agit d'arriver á l'inconnu par le dérèglement de *tous les senses*" [It's a question of arriving at the unknown through the disordering of all one's senses]) it divines something more than an invitation to drugs and general excess—namely, the austere condition of pure ignorance, a refusal to know what everyone knows. The tidy given world is leading a double life where things are less tame, even a bit deranged. Seeing is believing. But you have to look twice. The first time you see the cooked. The second time you see the raw. Both are "true" but the latter is always fresh and the former is sometimes overdone.

Call Henri Matisse to the stand: "To see is itself a creative operation, requiring an effort. Everything that we see in our daily life is more or less distorted by acquired habits, and this is perhaps more evident in an age like ours when cinema posters and magazines present us every day with a flood of ready-made images which are to the eye what prejudices are to the mind. The effort needed to see things without distortion takes something very like courage; and this courage is essential to the artist, who has to look at everything as though he saw it for the first time: he has to look at life as he did when he was a child and if he loses that faculty, he cannot express himself in an original, that is, personal way." Thank you, M. Matisse; no further questions.

How is the lingering strangeness of your poems like the Symbolist obsession with mystery?

Valéry has an essay called "L'Existence du Symbolisme" in which he maintains that the *only* unifying factor from Baudelaire to Verhaeren is the desire to tease the bourgeois reader with difficulty. I think, however, that the point of this poetry is not only that it is difficult, but that understanding should come, as Mallarmé said, "par une série de déchiffrements" [by a series of decodings]. Reading is like undressing someone you love—very slowly: "Two hundred to adore each breast: / But thirty thousand to the rest." The reader has to participate. It isn't television.

I draw the line between the seemingly non-personal narratives of **A Martian Sends a Postcard Home** *and* **Rich,** *in which the poems and the prose piece seem overtly autobiographical. Where do you stand now in terms of writing personal poetry?*

It is impossible to keep your personality out of what you write. Even writers who copy other writers display their own personalities—weak, colorless, touching, eager, anonymous.

But I know what you mean and I can explain—up to a point. It was really an accident, like so much to do with writing. Aged 16, I gave two poems to my very charismatic English master. We pretended they had been written by a friend. He said they were like pimply Dylan Thomas—a kind judgment, I now realize. And he gave me some advice which I followed faithfully. First, learn about meter and rhyme. Never trust your ear; train it; and keep it in training. Second, avoid the first-person pronoun. The result is that I don't feature in my first two books, directing, interjecting, intervening, in the way most young poets do. And I still find it difficult to use "I" with freedom—which is why my first answer has so much citation. If I were to speak for myself, I would be less coherent because I really don't know how my mind works. I agree

with Gilbert Ryle that honest introspection doesn't produce what Descartes called clear and distinct perceptions. When I look at my thought processes, they are in complete darkness. On the other hand, I do have clear and distinct perceptions: "I noticed how each rose / grew on a shark-infested stem." How this happens, I don't know. It doesn't feel like thought. It's more like discovering a new erogenous zone. Pure pleasure from my point of view. So I always found it difficult to understand what Eliot meant by the dissociation of sensibility. Surely a thought is an experience for everyone—not just Donne.

Where do I stand now in terms of writing personal poetry? Right now I'm engaged in writing an epic. Whenever anyone in the poem behaves badly, selfishly, unfeelingly, insensitively, I know who to study for details. The danger in writing directly about yourself is that you tend to present the best profile. But I'm interested in the complete works.

It's a shame that your publisher has not released **Rich** *or your new libretto in the U.S. In writing your poems, do you ever think of the American reader?*

Don't blame my publisher. It's me who's been playing hard to get.

I can't honestly say I take the U.S. reader into account. I once changed a reference to Durex, at the suggestion of an American editor, to Trojan. But that's as far as it goes. Inescapably, my frame of reference is bound to be English—cricket rather than baseball. But I'm not sure this is a great handicap. In Ireland, people read me without expecting references to hurley rather than hockey.

Generally, it's impossible to think about the audience when you're actually writing. Afterwards, you might make some adjustments—clarify an allusion, say—but the process itself requires total concentration. It's too erotic to tolerate much in the way of distraction.

You've said that there's no such thing as translation, that "translation is impossible because you change the words." If so, how do you read foreign poetry? Can you address the translation problem between British and American readers?

Frost said that poetry is what is lost in translation. Sometimes, though, poetry is what survives the process of translation. Clearly, some translations work: Keeley and Sherrard's Cavafy, Theiner's Holub. Cook an egg and you change its molecular structure, but it's still an egg. The best translation can only hope for that—poached Dante, scrambled Rimbaud, fried Baudelaire, hard-boiled Hofmannsthal. Whenever possible it is better to work from the original, using a prose crib and a dictionary. I have three recordings of Mussorgsky's *Pictures at an Exhibition*—the original piano score, Ravel's orchestration, and Yamashita's arrangement for guitar. The original and two translations, in other words. Without being completely different, they *are* completely different—distant cousins at the most.

American and English are not the same language. A *trucker* isn't a *lorry-driver*. The connotations are different. Even place-names reverberate differently. The old Gene Pitney song "24 Hours from Tulsa" was written for truckers. In England, there is no equivalent. "24 Hours from Peebles" is a joke and no one ever left his heart in Bognor Regis. But what do Americans make of Eliot's reference to the Edgware Road in "The Dry Salvages"? Probably about as much as we make of the Dry Salvages.

Poetry teaches the language to sing. It uses language consciously and carefully. In this sense, it is the very opposite of everyday unreflexive speech. As Eliot/Mallarmé said, the aim is "to purify the dialect of the tribe." But poetry must also and always grow out of the language of ordinary living men and never settle into poetic diction. Poetry, then, is Peter Quince at the conservatoire. Now, let me hazard a generalization: faced with these two apparently opposed imperatives, American poetry prefers to hang out with Peter Quince, whereas English poetry is endlessly practicing scales. In fact, the two imperatives aren't logically opposed at all.

You've been compared to Pasternak. Is that an apt comparison?

My wife is Pasternak's niece so it will seem disingenuous when I say that I do not know Pasternak's work. I speak a little house-Russian which I have picked up. I know the Russian word for *snot*. I can tell a child to wipe its bottom. But I don't know the Cyrillic alphabet and I could not even begin to read Russian. Obviously, given my family milieu, I have picked up ideas about Pasternak's poetry—that it is metaphorical, that its sound patterns are lush and intricate and assonantal, so rich, in fact, that these effects are more or less impossible to translate.

I also wonder if one of Pasternak's influences—the Russian Formalist Victor Shklovsky—influenced you. Shklovsky's dicta seem tailored to your work: "Art exists that one may recover the sensation of life. . . . It exists to make the stone stony. . . . It removes objects from the automatism of perception." Marjorie Perloff elaborates this quote for an American audience, "[Art] defamiliarizes objects by presenting them as if seen for the first time, or by distorting their form . . . so as to make the act of perception more difficult, and to prolong its duration."

I have not heard of Shklovsky, but I agree totally with the quotation that poetry "exists to make the stone stony." In England now (and perhaps in the States) vivid imagery is

perceived not as an illumination of the object but as an obstacle placed in front of it. In this argument, I side with Dickens: "I sometimes ask myself whether there may be occasionally a difference of this kind between some writers and some readers; whether it is *always* the writer who colors highly, or whether it is now and then the reader whose eye for color is a little dull?"

*You've proven yourself a poetic experimenter, yet you obviously borrow from the English tradition, often irreverently twisting it. (I'm thinking of the sonnet "**Arsehole.**") In contrast to your iconoclastic streak, you received an Oxford education and hold a respectable post as poetry editor of Faber. Can you discuss both the traditional and iconoclastic sides of your work?*

In art, the only interesting thing to do is to discover the rules—and then break them. Attack the orthodoxy. All successful revolutions are founded on the understanding of tradition, its strengths and its weaknesses. But erudition isn't enough. There has to be time to do nothing but *think*. Look at *Troilus and Cressida:* Shakespeare may have had small Latin and less Greek, but he knew a bogus heroic tradition when he saw it. Challenge the influential master, said Cézanne.

*In terms of line, how did you settle on the couplet for **A Martian Sends a Postcard Home** and the octosyllabic line for **The Electrification of the Soviet Union**?*

Broadly, I agree with Saul Bellow: "A writer should be able to express himself easily, naturally, copiously in a form which frees his mind, his energies. Why should he hobble himself with formalities?" And I once wrote, in a similar spirit: "Many critics are impressed by technical virtuosity—by which they mean the dead perfection of the sestina and other futile fifteen-finger exercises. The couplet I use is essentially a flexible instrument capable of accommodating a huge variety of subject matter. The sestina strikes me as the poetic equivalent of an instrument for removing Beluga caviar from horse's hooves—bizarrely impressive, but finally useless. The unrhymed couplet, on the other hand, is more like a tin-opener—so useful that one is inclined to overlook its cleverness."

Meter is capable of extremely subtle effects when it is violated. Take Donne's *Elegy on His Picture*—to be left with his mistress until he returns from an expedition, perhaps terribly changed:

> My body'a sack of bones, broken within,
> And powders blew staines scatter'd on my skinne;
> If rivall fooles taxe thee to 'have lov'd a man,
> So foule, and course, as, Oh, I may seeme than,
> This shall say what I was: and thou shalt say . . .

I love the crammed mimetic elision of "body'a sack" and the

inverted foot of "broken" which breaks the meter within the line. I love the forceful equality of stress on "blew staines scatt . . ." before the meter itself suddenly and appositely fades. Donne has one bravura touch after another.

Both free verse and meter have their strengths. They also have their attendant dangers. Meter can quickly become automatic, a kind of poetic Morse code. Free verse can degenerate into a rhythmic desert where the poet's unrestrained voice turns like tumbleweed.

Free verse, if it is any good, is never without rhythm. But its patterns are strange, less predictable, and listening for them is as absorbing as waiting to hear the tap of someone buried alive. Or the tap of some thing buried alive.

In addition to mentioning Hopkins and Ted Hughes as influences, you've also mentioned Lowell. Which Lowell poems most affected you? Have any contemporary American poets impressed you?

•*Life Studies* is a great book. Exact, humorous, vivid, honest, unconcerned about its dignity. Lowell had his eye on the object, rather than on the idea of what a great poem might be. If we're not careful poetry comes to resemble some exclusive club full of stuffed shirts. Ideas and objects aren't admitted unless they're wearing evening dress. So all the really interesting things wind up in the novel and poetry makes polite conversation about the weather or landscape. The artistic ideal for me is the opening of *The Marriage of Figaro:* "*cinque . . . dieci . . . venti . . .*" Numbers. Measurements. Mozart gets them in. Lowell also gets things in and, by implication, attacks the idea that some objects are more suitable for poetry than others. Personally, I don't see why literary criticism shouldn't be a subject for poetry.

I can answer the second part of your question about contemporary American poetry by referring to Lowell again. I once heard him read at the Oxford Union. He was asked which British poets he liked. "Well," he began, "I like Ted Hughes, Philip Larkin, Seamus Heaney, Alan Brownjohn, Geoffrey Hill . . ." Five minutes later, he closed the list with the mischievous observation, "I hope I didn't leave anyone out."

Thomas Lux (essay date 1987)

SOURCE: "On Craig Raine," in *Ploughshares,* Vol. 13, No. 4, 1987, pp. 149-53.

[*In the essay below, Lux gives a close reading of "In the Mortuary" and "The Trout Farm," marveling at Raine's poetic skill.*]

I discovered Craig Raine's work (first his remarkable second book *A Martian Sends a Postcard Home* and then his first book *The Onion, Memory*) about eight years ago. I was immediately struck by its eloquence, which is never stuffy or merely decorative, by the sharpness of its tone, and by the odd rightness of its metaphors/figurative language. The poems are intensely written, never wasting a syllable and using all of the tools available to a poet. They are serious, yet there is a vein of humor that runs through both books. There's a fierce poignancy, a fresh and lucid compassion in a poem such as **"In the Mortuary"**:

> Like soft cheeses they bulge
> sideways on the marble slabs,
>
> helpless, waiting to be washed.
> Cotton wool clings in wisps
>
> to the orderly's tongs,
> its creaking purpose done . . .
>
> He calls the woman 'Missus,'
> an abacus of perspiration
>
> on his brow despite the cold.
> And she is the usual woman—
>
> two terra cotta nipples
> like patches from a cycle kit,
>
> puzzled knees, finely
> crumpled skin around the eyes,
>
> and her stomach like a watermark
> held up to the light.
>
> Distinguishing marks: none.
> Colour of eyes: closed.
>
> Somewhere, inside an envelope
> inside a drawer, her spectacles . . .
>
> Somewhere else, not here, someone
> knows her hair is parted wrongly
>
> and cares about the cobwebs
> in the corners of her body.

The opening of this poem, in its absurdity as well as its tactile exactness, sets the tone and announces the elements of technique for the whole: the softness of the cheese vs. the hardness/coldness of the marble, a sensory immersion into the scene, simple and specific, that carries an emotional reverberation. The *b* and *l* sounds of "bulge" and "marble" and "slab" are a kind of sonic, onomatopoeic equivalent to the imagery. The second couplet changes the effects to the softer *w* and *s* sounds which are more appropriate to the powerlessness of the corpse. This kind of subtle rhyming—assonance, consonance, and other music-making—goes on through all of Raine's poems, internally as well as at the end of lines. He has an excellent ear, a dying or often ignored poetic gift. In the third stanza he uses more aural imagery: the cotton "creaking." That's a sound that is also felt. "Tongs" and "done" off-rhyme and eye-rhyme. Needless to say, all this action—of sound, of imagery, of implicit emotion—in just three relatively short-lined couplets, is not accidental. The reader is now sensorially and humanly involved in this poem and with its (thus far) two characters—the dead woman (it switches to the feminine and the singular in the next line) and the orderly. The next particular detail is a good example of Raine's metaphorical intelligence: "an abacus of perspiration." It works not only literally, visually (beads of an abacus, beads of perspiration) but it also suggests her lack of humanity (she is just a number) plus it suggests the hard manual labor and perhaps even the nerves of an orderly: he sweats despite the cold, which is more sensory information, which places the reader further inside the world of the poem. The next several lines comment on simple, obvious body parts, all external, yet each one is presented in such a way as to make her, in her death, come alive: the particular color suggested by "terra cotta" and again the tactile and visual synesthesia of the tire patches, the "puzzled knees" suggesting a face, the "crumpled skin around the eyes" suggesting age and expression, and the odd transparency of the watermark suggesting lines, scars, stretchmarks, the things which individuate our bodies. This description, very fresh, very lucid, adds up to a depiction of the human (in both the individual and the larger sense of that word) that rings beautifully here. These seven lines, all one sentence, so lyrical, rhythmic, are followed by two short, terse sentences clearly meant to snap us back to the reality of the death, the ultimate coldness of the scene. This kind of syntactical variation is smart and perfectly timed. The first one about the distinguishing marks contradicts, deliberately, what has just been said. The second is serio-comic, bitter. The poem now, in its final three couplets, takes an abrupt turn and risks a great deal—sentimentality, primarily—but I feel it is a risk taken and won. I am moved by the ending because it is both a surprise and, somehow, inevitable, and because he dared to make this corpse even more human, in that she was loved.

Another poem in this collection (*A Martian Sends a Postcard Home*) that I like very much, also in tightly-written couplets (most of the poems in this book are in unrhymed or off-rhymed couplets) is **"The Trout Farm"**:

> The trout are silent choristers,
> singing for our supper
>
> a cold-blooded requiem mass,
> though every one's throat is cut.

> Death is a young Elizabethan lad
> who shambles across the yard,
>
> his waders shrunk to buckets
> round each ankle. For him,
>
> the trout are stacked in rows
> like a crate of open-mouthed empties,
>
> waiting to be carted away.
> He doesn't see their soft Vandykes
>
> or the beautifully tarnished mail
> as glorious as a silver spoon
>
> that changes to sombre indigo
> at the touch of an ordinary egg . . .
>
> He kills them scientifically.
> At the touch of a switch,
>
> they become rigidly ridiculous,
> aristocrats with monocles,
>
> shocked as Bateman cartoons
> when some bounder mentions death.
>
> The boy turns to offer me
> a miniature organ of cigarettes . . .

The trout in their artificial pools sing not for their supper but for ours because they will *be* our supper. The puns in the first two couplets might not be as strong as some of his metaphors but still are very fresh. It would be very dangerous to be too serious here—after all, we raise, kill, and eat animals all the time. He wants us to see the scene not as bloody, chaotic, or noisy, say, as a slaughterhouse but somehow stranger: the fish passive, almost spiritual, and the executioner a "lad" who "shambles" in floppy, water-filled rubber boots. The lad in this poem is somewhat like the orderly in the previous poem— doltish rather than cruel, ordinary rather than a monster, i.e., more real. The next simile, comparing the fish to crates of empty bottles, is particularly apt and again displays Raine's odd rightness of perception. The trout are just another commodity and not a very valuable one at that. The next five lines combine visual and tactile imagery plus a few carefully chosen abstractions: "glorious" and "sombre" and even an oxymoron, "beautifully tarnished." As is the case in so many of these poems, there is a lot going on, a rich verbal and sensory texture, in relatively few lines. The fish are killed, apparently, by electric shock (which makes sense: no damaged flesh) and "they become rigidly ridiculous / aristocrats with monocles" (which strikes me as a wonderfully accurate as well as comic depiction of a dead fish's eye) and shocked like a character in a Bateman cartoon. The Bateman reference I don't get exactly—I assume he's a well-known English cartoonist—but Raine's basic point is clear. He's being careful to avoid the sentimental here, but he is not afraid to risk, again, sentiment with the final couplet, the last line of which is an example of his metaphorical brilliance. We've all seen cigarettes offered that way but have we made the connection ourselves to the church organ? The organ, of course, brings the poem back to its beginning, the silent choristers singing, and there is also the suggestion of death in that offering.

These are only two short poems from one of Craig Raine's books. To me they make it clear he is a poet of rare wit, originality, and humanity. May his poems continue to arrive on our shores.

Sean French (review date 8 June 1990)

SOURCE: "Getting Dirty," in *New Statesman & Society,* Vol. 3, No. 104, June 8, 1990, p. 38.

[*In the review below, French cautiously admires Raine's critical abilities in* Haydn and the Valve Trumpet.]

In my local bookshop I recently saw Clive James's collection of literary essays, *Snake Charmers in Texas,* among the travel books. Craig Raine's eccentric title for his own essays [*Haydn and the Valve Trumpet*] will almost certainly guarantee them a place in the musicology section of most bookshops.

The title derives from an essay exploring Haydn's use of the valve trumpet, which was published in the *Listener* in 1972. The following week a letter was published pointing out that the valve trumpet had been invented nine years after Haydn's death.

Raine himself is at his most carnivorously enjoyable when catching other critics in the act. In response to the critic A. Alvarez's accusation that John Betjeman indulges in "the nostalgia of public schools", Raine points out that "there are 130 poems in *Collected Poems* (1958) and of them only one refers to school—a day-school, as it happens. What bone-idle, irresponsible mendacity."

For Raine, a poem or a novel is like a machine. The job of the critic is to get dirty peering among the pistons and cogs establishing how everything fits together. If they fail to do this, it is because they are lazy, or incompetent, or corrupt.

Trusted artists can fail as well. One of Raine's best qualities as a critic is the freshness of his response. Even a favourite writer won't just receive automatic praise. Looking under the

bonnet of Saul Bellow's latest novel, *More Die of Heartbreak,* Raine discovers that many of the components have been hastily lifted from its predecessors and they barely fit together. In a detailed analysis that seems to be based on a complete re-reading of the Bellow *oeuvre,* Raine demonstrates with daunting authority "how inattentive and incompetent Bellow has become in this novel"—and this is Raine speaking of his favourite modern novelist.

> **For Raine, a poem or a novel is like a machine. The job of the critic is to get dirty peering among the pistons and cogs establishing how everything fits together. If they fail to do this, it is because they are lazy, or incompetent, or corrupt.**
> **—Sean French**

At some point in analyses of difficult poets like T. S. Eliot and Wallace Stevens most people lapse into generalisation and obfuscation where, if they were really honest, they would simply admit that they weren't sure what the poetry means. (Christopher Ricks's confession that a William Empson poem left him "unhelpfully perplexed" is all too rare.) Raine is good at pointing out when other critics are bluffing and brave himself about always attempting to say what a work is really about.

This means that Raine leaves himself more exposed than most critics and sometimes he can seem very wrong indeed. His insistence on common-sense readings of oblique poetry can lead him to interpretations that are both perverse and reductive, as in his account of Eliot's "Mr. Apollinax". For him the lines, "I heard the beat of centaur's hoofs over the hard turf / As his dry and passionate talk devoured the afternoon" means that "as far as his American-audience is concerned, Mr. Apollinax is *flogging a dead horse.* Hence the 'centaur': what horse could be more definitively dead . . .?" If you believe that, you'll believe anything.

His suspicion of the vagueness and evasiveness of so much literary appreciation can lead him to over-statement. We will all agree that there are difficulties in making literary evaluations of works in languages we don't understand but does he have to take it as far as this: "Let us have no more non-Russian-speaking experts *and enthusiasts*"? (My italics.)

Ought we not to read *Anna Karenina* any more? And must we do without the marvellously suggestive criticism that Seamus Heaney has produced in recent years about eastern European poetry?

Raine can be infuriating in his rudenesses and his summary dismissals, but he always has the engagement of the practitioner, of the man for whom poetry is an activity and a craft as well as an elevated art form. This is a book that will encourage readers to get their hands dirty.

Peter Kemp (review date 6 July 1990)

SOURCE: "Matters of Decorum," in *The Times Educational Supplement,* No. 3862, July 6, 1990, p. 26.

[*In the excerpt below, Kemp praises Raine's "exhilarating and engrossing" criticism in* Haydn and the Valve Trumpet, *concluding that "it is almost always stirringly alive to the procedures and possibilities of creativity."*]

[Anthony] Powell's Pall Mall prose, meticulous concurrence with the conservative, and pained recoil from the irreverent lower-class energies of Wells, Twain and their like [in his *Miscellaneous Verdicts: Writings on Writers, 1946-1989*] put him at the opposite extreme as a critic to Craig Raine. Where Powell exudes commendation for the genteel, Raine cordially abominates it. One of his most elegantly edged pieces in *Haydn and the Valve Trumpet* slices into the petrified propriety and frigid diction of Augustan poetry to expose stultified responses.

The imitative and remote from life regularly incur cutting comment. An elevated 18th-century poem about a washerwoman's day—"At length bright Sol illuminates the skies, / And summons drowsy mortals to arise"—is brought crashing down to earth with the remark "Perhaps she 'did' for Mr. Pope". Grandiose abstractions, generalities and standardized utterance—from neoclassical periphrases to the jargon of contemporary literary theory—are seen as the enemies of art and the imagination.

What characterize the authors Raine writes most admiringly and admirably about—Dickens, Joyce, Bellow, Larkin—are a converse fascination with concrete, indeed earthy, detail, and a tellingly individual voice. Idiosyncrasy enthralls him. "All great poetry", he contends, "is written in dialect": by which he means it has a distinctively personal timbre and idiom.

Poets who parrot others' effects are deftly winged with high-calibre bursts of critical marksmanship. At the other extreme, Raine has an especial flair for illuminating the techniques by which gifted writers revitalize cliché. Behind a scene in which a shamed V. S. Naipaul character looks into a mirror and sees nothing there, lies the phrase "to lose face", he shrewdly points out. The gaps between the ill-fitting clothes Dickens's Miss Tox wears manifest her inability "to make ends meet".

Such insights into the way a lurking lively image can be conjured out from a seemingly inert phrase vivify Raine's pages.

Alert to the inventive, he is also keenly attentive, sensitive even to how an over-dramatic exclamation mark "quivers like a javelin on the page". In particular, he is acutely attuned to give-away tremors of affectation: Geoffrey Hill's use of "the Yeatsian 'but' for 'only' . . . like the sob in a pub tenor's top note", arty syntax that leaves him feeling "Inversion on the scale of these poems the reader admires not".

Bogus afflatus is pin-pointed and punctured. Pomposity and stiltedness are nimbly mocked. Raine's distaste for the decorous frequently expresses itself in cheeky, clever puns: noting how books about Johnson re-cycle the same stories, he quips that there's "a limit to how often it is possible to turn Johnson's choler". Homely images sometimes supply satiric sparkle; a horse in one of Henri Rousseau's less successful paintings bares teeth "fresh from a tumbler of Steradent". Among the authors under review, there's even room for Barbara Cartland who makes a memorable appearance "in the pink, nay, the cerise of health".

Given Raine's antipathy to the orotund, it's surprising to find him as appreciative as he is of Arnold and Eliot (quotations from whom almost oversaturate some essays). Even more curious is his dislike of Wilfred Owen who, he claims, "associates poetry with the merely poetic" and is "insensitive to the possibilities of understatement". Taking "Dulce Et Decorum Est" as an example of this, Raine writes off its lines "bitter as the cud / Of vile, incurable sores on innocent tongues" as "the rhetoric of Speakers' Corner". In fact, they contain instances of the quiet effects he thinks absent from the poem. Subliminally pervading Owen's lines is the folk-tale motif of liars being punished by sores on their tongues. In the horribly inverted world of war, his poem intimates, the opposite occurs: it's not the liars—pro-war propagandists—who now get sores on their tongues; it's the young men who, heeding them, end up on the Western Front in a gas attack whose noxious fumes hideously blister their "innocent" tongues.

Raine's inadvertence to Owen's subtle puns, muted word-play and use of deliberate dissonance to echo the discords of war is highly uncharacteristic, though. What makes his criticism both exhilarating and engrossing is that it is almost always stirringly alive to the procedures and possibilities of creativity.

Barbara Everett (review date 12 July 1990)

SOURCE: "Being All Right, and Being Wrong," in *London Review of Books,* Vol. 12, No. 13, July 12, 1990, pp. 11-12.

[*In the following excerpt, Everett identifies the "journalistic" quality of Raine's criticism in* Haydn and the Valve Trumpet, *concluding, however, that his essays are "genuinely literary."*]

Men of different generations and presumably social worlds, Anthony Powell and Craig Raine aren't much alike as writers. But the novelist's *Miscellaneous Verdicts* and the poet's **Haydn and the Valve Trumpet** are both very good, solid selections of occasional writing. The five hundred pages to which they both run are mainly literary journalism, with some illuminating essays on the social-historical from Powell, and vivid side-glances at painters and painting from Raine. With all their differences, the two writers have one thing in common. Both dislike most kinds of academic literary criticism. And this antipathy can't be disentangled from the effective virtues of their work.

It seems safe to assume that academics have as much right to discourse on books as have poets and novelists to write them. Nor do minds as able as Powell's and Raine's need telling that in modern society the arts depend on a current of ideas which it is the universities' task—at least in theory—to provide and protect. The trouble comes with the theory.

Nobody could pretend that universities are at present, or were ever, especially alive with applied intelligence. In addition, we are in a difficult phase of academic literary criticism, which has the air of getting cleverer and cleverer while simultaneously moving close to *pointlessness*. The new quasi-theoretical modes as often as not find a use for Shakespeare or Jane Austen or T. S. Eliot by exposing them, morally or politically or otherwise, as no good. This is annoying for writers and farcical for readers.

Though sometimes plainly motivated, this effect is basically incidental. Academic life is now governed by the thesis; and a thesis is required to show an authoritative mastery of its literary subject easily converting to a stance of superiority on the part of the researcher. Moreover, such research techniques have managed almost universally to demand of all literary criticism that it have what is referred to as 'system'. This seems reasonable. Unfortunately, what passes for system academically is often no more than mechanism, producing results painfully shallow in comparison with the real systems of high-powered human intelligence.

Defending literature now can place the liberal academic in positions which it's not altogether ludicrous to relate to that of the trapped liberal of the Thirties, confronted by competing totalitarianisms. And those positions are inherited by university-trained writers like Powell and Raine. Both enunciate principles as congenial as they now sound dated: Powell's civilised 'plea for mutual tolerance among authors writing on the same subject', Raine's brave 'nothing is more difficult than being open-minded.' Any liberal reader reads and admires and sympathises with their impassioned defence

of the writer as against the academic. And of course poems and novels are better and more vital than critical essays. But at the moments when both try to find a way of saying why this is so, they get curiously trapped between the philistine and the Romantic-aesthetic. Thinking about the arts is at once more important than they sometimes make it sound, and harder. . . .

Powell and Raine come together in a peculiar and very interesting Britishness, their sense of art an English one. This is what makes both, for all their late-Romantic aestheticism, simultaneously risk the philistine in leaning backwards towards an Augustan lack of cant. (Johnson's often misunderstood attack on the corruptive power of arrogant pretension, 'No man but a blockhead ever wrote but for money,' is the great text for journalism. And both Powell and Raine can take on a special sharp-edged no-nonsense realism which shows them as Sons of Sam.) . . .

Miscellaneous Verdicts is itself 'all right' in any number of different ways: its greatest distinction may be the dance which Powell made his reviewing perform for years around the idea and the fact of a writer's rectitude. Craig Raine's **Haydn and the Valve Trumpet** is as gifted and richly entertaining as Powell's volume. But it offers one contrast in style so marked as to be almost ideal. Raine isn't, in a sense, concerned with being 'right'. In fact, he reveals that if a critic is good enough, he can afford to be wrong.

Being wrong is his general theme. A fine brisk essay on Joyce (**'New Secondhand Clothes'**) surveys an earlier stage of the current battle over Joyce texts by stating the principle that misprints occur and don't matter. This is true up to the point that meaning is more important than text. But Raine gives his theory more space in his opening essay. He mentions a critic who recently made the mistake of arguing that Haydn was influenced by a form of the trumpet which proved not to have been invented until after the composer's death. Raine's point is that, in this case as everywhere else, it's the music that counts, not the nonsense we talk about it. Hence Raine's choice of a title for his book which works by a kind of triumphant wonkiness. Interestingly different from the amused offhand anonymity of *Miscellaneous Verdicts,* the attractively nubbly **Haydn and the Valve Trumpet** is a short Raine poem in itself.

Raine's tough commonsensicality, his respect for real life and for the serious 'game' which he takes poetry to be, and most of all the intelligence of his good-natured gusto and rage, all work-together to give integrity to his arguments. Yet in the simplest possible way he can get things wrong in a manner that may dent his case just a little. The dust-jacket of Raine's book sets his title in a box against a fine etching by Rembrandt one perhaps even too fine to have been used to sell a book ('there are perhaps worse places to read about Melancholy than a publisher's office'). The inside of the jacket identifies this beautiful image as *The Young Christ Disputing with the Doctors.* This is a naming which Raine defends in one of his later essays, **'At a Slight Angle to the Universe'**, which rebuts sentimental linking of the artist with the child. The artist may be childlike, he suggests, only in his or her capacity to correct stale and sedate quasi-philosophies, like the young Christ in his dispute with the Doctors of the Temple; and Raine turns to the etching by Rembrandt usually known as *Joseph Telling his Dreams,* claiming that its true subject is that of Christ with the Doctors. If Raine had been right, there might have been even less to be said for using it as a dust-jacket: identifying critics with Jesus just must be a mistake. But luckily Raine is wrong. The subject is what it has always been taken to be, 'Joseph Telling his Dreams'.

Rembrandt left behind at least two real treatments of the topos of Jesus with the Doctors, in each case leaving the subject iconographically unmistakable: brief but definite indications of monumental masonry show that the location is the Temple. The print on Raine's cover is no vast stone edifice filled with Scribes and Pharisees: it is an intimate domestic interior. The old lady behind the boy is in a bed, perhaps a day-bed—you can see bed-curtains, not to mention a night-cap; she is conceivably Joseph's mother, Rachel, who bore him very late in life (though she was actually dead by this stage of Joseph's existence). The figure surely can't be the young Mary, mother of Jesus, and she wouldn't lie around in a Jewish temple anyway. The loving old man on the left isn't a Pharisee but Joseph's adoring elderly father, Jacob; the sullen averted faces to the right aren't intellectuals but his embittered older brothers, soon to attempt his murder in jealous rage. And the wonderfully intent boy at the centre has the face of a poet, not of God; he is dressed not in sanctity but in the very best and most expensive possible 17th-century boy's topcoat—the many-coloured dreamcoat, in short.

The mixture of great virtues and great mistakes is an essential part of what Raine is doing and saying. At one point, he lays down the sturdy affirmation, 'Eliot is a poet by whom critics are judged'—and this is certainly true. But Eliot was a critic himself, as many poets are. He goes on to argue that the general theme of Eliot's verse 'from first to last' is 'Live all you can. It's a mistake not to.' Even Henry James, whose novel *The Ambassadors* is the source of this phrase, wouldn't have said it in propria persona: it's odder still from Eliot.

Raine is a splendid critic of the textures of language, the 'pidgin' or 'Babylonish dialect' that each artist makes his own. On Dickens, on Joyce, on Elizabeth Bishop and John Betjeman—perhaps the best essays—he has things to say both brilliant and new. But he wouldn't have said them, paradoxically, had he not been a critic capable of mistakes. In all his essays he brings virtues easy to class as 'journalistic' up to the level of the genuinely literary. He does so from a strong

refusal to cut the arts out of life. 'Poets hate the sanitised, sentimental, overly spiritual version of what they do. They always want the unpoetical.' And: 'If there isn't the sustained effort to accommodate the unpoetical, poetry is likely to revert to the poetical.' This is a poet speaking, a voice too individual to be mistakable for Jesus. But Joseph is quite good enough.

Carol Rumens (review date 9 September 1994)

SOURCE: "Local Heroes," in *New Statesman & Society,* Vol. 7, September 9, 1994, p. 37.

[*Below, Rumens disputes the publishers' claim that* History: The Home Movie *is a verse-novel.*]

In "Epic", Patrick Kavanagh is consoled by Homer's ghost. So what if the Monaghan poet spent the "year of the Munich bother" arguing about "who owned / That half a rood of rock?" The *Iliad* itself was made from "such / A local row". *History: the Home Movie* doesn't seek the epic in the ordinary quite in this way. The technique is to show us both History *and* the Home Movie, the "Munich bother" as it infiltrates the "local row", the local-row element in the Munich bother.

These poems document the entwined history of two families during the current century, the English Raines and the Russian Pasternaks. There are 87 poems, compactly built in the slightly noun-bound, three-line, two-or-three-beat-a-line stanza form that is one of Raine's old favourites.

His hand-held camera is an enabling device, like his earlier "Martian" persona. It permits revelation through apparent incompetence. It is drawn to the erotic and the bizarre. It catches the players off-guard, peers from an odd angle, unembarrassably stares. When Oswald Mosley lectures at Olympia, Jimmie Raine observes more of the side-show than the main event: a woman in the audience having an epileptic fit, a heckler whistling the Internationale in the roof. Applause "swells and subsides" as does the erection produced by the sight of a suspender-nub; the seats, in long shot, are "a home perm".

The fictional convention, whereby a character shows qualities of perceptiveness that belong, strictly speaking, to his creator functions smoothly enough, given that the other psychological details are right. As they usually are: Raine was never merely the virtuoso of imagism, and these poems reveal his ability to observe a mind's interiors as well as a body's surfaces. His writing-up of that well-known scene in which Stalin phones Pasternak and demands to know Mandelstam's poetic credentials is a good example of his imaginative strategy. Pasternak, taking the call in the hall of a communal block of flats, finds himself staring through a pinhole onto the wet breasts of a bathing neighbour ("Each tit / tipped like a billiard cue / with pink Morocco plush").

Asked if Mandelstam is a genius, he feels *profoundly* that there must be some mistake. "What about me?" he wonders. It is a new angle on the old moral conundrum, an exposure of poetic insecurity, warts and all. Poets always think "What about me?" It takes one to know one.

Clearly, *History: the Home Movie,* is not fiction. Its real impulse is not narrative. For all its imaginative liberties, it deals with actual historical figures and facts. Norman, the poet's father, and other English "players" will be familiar to readers who enjoyed the autobiographical essay, "A Silver Plate", in Raine's last collection of poems, *Rich.*

This is a sequence of poems—at its best when it proceeds by epiphany and pauses for some playful linguistic dabbling, puns and so forth, and at its weakest when it feels obliged to inform. Having got a Booker-ish gleam in their eyes, the publishers may call it a verse-novel, but let's give credit to the right muse here. Poetry is not just shy confessional muttering. It can give you the local row *and* the *Iliad,* and put real toads in imaginary gardens, and vice versa. The publishers may claim fictitiousness as a legal protection, but to suggest the work is thereby fiction is a breathtaking act of philistinism.

Adam Thorpe (review date 11 September 1994)

SOURCE: "Adding Assonance to the Ancestors," in *The Observer Review,* September 11, 1994, p. 20.

[*In the following review, Thorpe admires* History: The Home Movie, *focusing on the "glittering little links" of the poem sequence.*]

Billed as a fiction/poetry hybrid, Craig Raine's *History: The Home Movie* wilfully dispenses with the Pushkinian elements of strong narrative, deeply drawn characters, and a bustling, involved narrator—and there is no complex verse form, either. Home movie, yes: or perhaps an evening at the music hall.

The first 'chapter' arranges the Pasternaks—Russian, renowned—in a filmic family group at a Black Sea dacha in 1905. The second shows Queenie Raine's peeing-toff act flopping at the Victoria Palace in front of King Edward. The ensuing reels, or numbers, or 'chapters', show us the Pasternaks and the Raines shunted and buffeted by the century across various geographical and mental spaces and getting maimed in the process. Secondary characters include Lenin, Churchill and Haile Selassie in pleasantly incongruous situations, as

well as a philandering Russian turned Oxford rapist with a vitriol-damaged, quarter-masked face. He seems a totemic, phantasmal presence in this epic sweep, both ruined and ruining.

Images and incidents flicker charmingly if bewilderingly across the screen, but a narrative presence is felt mostly in the lavish use of vivid and incredible comparison. This is a Raine trademark which once went by the name of Martianism but owes a lot to Donne. In the context of this 300-plus-page poem, when great forces are surging through small lives, this obsession with the exactness of things is curiously effective.

> **Images and incidents flicker charmingly if bewilderingly across the screen, but a narrative presence is felt mostly in the lavish use of vivid and incredible comparison. This is a Raine trademark which once went by the name of Martianism but owes a lot to Donne.**
> —*Adam Thorpe*

For Raine, the past is a rummage of discarded objects; to experience it as anything other than a costume drama is to double-take on things once general, but now invested with the burnished particularity of the antique, the oddity of junk. The process kicks off with the print on the page: a pince-nez is 'like the letter g'; in 1921, a telephone is 'an earwig of brass and bakelite'; a rough midwife's rubber gloves 'cackle . . . like hot fat' in 1929; in 1937, SS officers salute on a train with 'a croquet click of heels'. Raine is equally good on bodies. The Lucian Freud of poetry, Raine particularises his characters by their fleshly parts, eternally pillaged by time and history and other people. Medical appliances abound alarmingly. Sex is generally self-abuse.

In the grander schema of the poem, it's the families that are likened and linked, resembling the two sides of 'the symbol for infinity', with the spying poet at the junction. Craig Raine is married to Boris Pasternak's grand-niece, and in the printed (part-fictional) family tree she becomes his first cousin by Eliot Raine, a second-rate doctor who spends the Thirties as a genetic researcher in Hitler's Germany. The Raines are depicted as a somewhat fickle, muddled lot with a streak of madness—the signwriter Jimmy ends up 'nuts', Norman's hands turn from a boxer's fists to a faith-healer's palms after a terrible war wound, Eliot hides his spanking magazines in a deed box.

The Pasternaks' higher culture and lightly bohemian contentment is swiftly shattered; the ominous opening image of Leonid the painter-father's discarded newspaper stirring and blooming 'as if the letters lived' prepares us for the fraught set-pieces of private and public dispersion across Europe. Here, nuttiness is politically imposed. Boris Pasternak himself, much troubled by his teeth and his women, never really grows beyond biopic grittiness. There are, however, some secretive references to his poetry; in 1950 his exiled sister Zhonya (like Craig Raine)

> . . . pays attention to particulars.
> The line of drips left on the cup
> sometimes makes a book of matches.
> Her lipstick sometimes leaves
> a segment of blood orange
> on her glass of orange juice.
> She cares about coincidence,
> things coming together.

Pasternak's own marvellous poem 'From Superstition' opens with an image of his room as 'a matchbox with an orange'. It closes with the idea of himself as a book taken down from the shelf by a lover, the dust blown from his name. In 1919, Queenie Raine, mourning for her dead daughter Alice, does just the same with *Alice's Adventures in Wonderland.*

History: The Home Movie is a vast and at times immensely enjoyable poem sequence stuffed with glittering little links like these, within and without itself. The broad buckling bands of the novel are exactly what it lacks.

Frank Kermode (review date 22 September 1994)

SOURCE: "Yoked Together," in *London Review of Books,* Vol. 16, No. 18, September 22, 1994, p. 3.

[*In the review below, Kermode traces the narrative movement in* History: The Home Movie, *observing the poem's literary precedents.*]

'There is hardly a stanza in the long poem which is not vivid, hardly one which is not more or less odd, and the reader feels as if he had been riding on the rims over an endless timber bridge.' As I read Craig Raine's new poem [*History: The Home Movie*] (a novel, an epic, a film, says the ebullient blurb) something stirred in the depths of memory, and I found myself thinking of *Theophila,* a very long poem published by Edward Benlowes in 1652. *Theophila* is written in three-line stanzas, a pentameter, a tetrameter and an alexandrine, all on a single rhyme. The judgment on *Theophila* quoted above comes from *The Oxford History of English Literature,* which rightly regards Benlowes as representing the giddy limit in 17th-century attempts to write 'heroic' poetry in the high metaphysical manner. And this must surely seem an unpromising way to tackle extended argument or narrative. Benlowes was a devotee of the far-fetched conceit, in the by now de-

generate tradition of Donne, perhaps with some input from the smoother baroque *concettismo* of Marino and his followers. (On the evidence of some of his delightful earlier poems I had privately awarded Craig Raine an honorary position in the company of the *marinisti.*) Marino produced narrative in this style, but in more fluent stanzas, and without proceeding to the metaphorical extremes of the English. Though often eloquent, Benlowes is neither fluent nor moderate, and clearly it formed no part of his plan to make it easy for his readers to know exactly what he was on about.

Later poets with stories to tell normally preferred to use pentameter couplets or blank verse, which allowed the narrative or the argument to be followed with less effort, and did not encourage wild flights of baroque wit. Milton, a contemporary of Benlowes and an admirer of Spenser, not only freed his narrative of 'the modern bondage of rhyming', but after a youthful fling more or less gave up conceited poetry. It would not do for real epic.

However, if you hold that lucidity and what the philosopher W. B. Gallie called 'follow-ability' aren't everything, that they may be sacrificed in a good cause, then admirable precedents are not wanting. Conceits can be combined with stories at acceptable cost to the stories. A narrative line can be more or less sustained through complex verse-forms and under repeated pressure from centrifugal interests. Think of *The Faerie Queene,* with its awkward nine-line stanza and its heavy concluding alexandrine: in this unlikely form Spenser undertook a huge narrative poem combining a great many stories, only more or less germane to one another and required to bear a considerable weight of philosophical and historical allegory. How well he succeeded is a point that has always been disputed. 'Every stanza,' wrote Spenser's 18th-century editor John Hughes, 'made as it were a distinct paragraph, grows tiresome by continual repetition and frequently breaks the sense, when it ought to be carried on without interruption.' Others contrast Spenser's heavy pace and patches of opacity with the more athletic movement of Ariosto. C. S. Lewis, on the other hand, thought the whole poem moved along pretty briskly. Other critics, without necessarily denying either view, waste their lives, though they may also secure tenure, in trying to explain just what is really going on in Spenser's poem.

These historical reminders are meant to contribute to an understanding of what Craig Raine is attempting in his new long poem [*History: The Home Movie*]; it seemed important to do that instead of saying 'Post-Modernism' and putting that familiar stop to all sensible discussion. He has presented an episodic history (one reason for his subtitle: you don't expect narrative continuity in home movies) and he has done so without serious modification of his normal conceited manner. The history is primarily that of two related families, Raines and Pasternaks (a second reason for calling the book a home movie). I first read the work in a proof copy which lacked the dual family tree now found in the opening pages, so that it was not easy for me to tell with any precision how apparently disparate episodes were related. Readers of finished copies will fare better, though there remain many passages that are not obviously or not closely related to the families or explained by the family tree, and others that may be so related but are still rather obscurely elliptical. Since Raine's three-lined stanzas (much simpler than Benlowes's) must serve as vehicles not only for the discontinuous narrative but for a great payload of Martian similes, in their nature at least as centrifugal as those baroque conceits, the poem is far from instantly intelligible, and is not meant to be.

But it's no use getting into an argument as to whether this is the best way to tell a tale, even if the tale makes some sort of claim to be some sort of history of Europe from about 1905 to 1984. As we have seen, there are precedents of some grandeur for a certain darkness and obliquity of treatment; there are also more modern exemplars, not only in poetry but in fiction and cinema. If you feel a need to hold the entire thing in a single thought, you have to satisfy that need yourself. Or, the sequence of historical occurrences, real and fictional, doesn't make sense in the old way, and it is a disabling mistake to suppose it should.

Interviews and press leaks of various kinds have offered hints on how to read the poem, but it may be best to ignore them and stick to the text. The narrator is a fly on the wall, a secret policeman, a pencil on a desk. He begins with a scene in a Black Sea dacha, date 1905, where the Pasternaks, children of the painter Leonid and his Jewish wife Rosa, are at play. Boris makes his first appearance. The 1905 Revolution is in progress offstage. The painter's palette is compared to a latrine,

> turds of fresh pigment
> fresh from their bolsters,

and the painter himself wipes his hands on a newspaper, thus carelessly disposing of the history it doubtless records. In the next episode, **'1906'**, a male impersonator, whose act includes pretending to have a pee, disgraces herself before Edward VII, incognito at the Victoria Palace. Now skip to 1915, when Henry Raine, the grandfather of Craig Raine (family tree), is writing from the trenches. His letter contains an inadequate attempt to console his wife on the death of their eight-year-old daughter Alice from 'diptheoria'. He then masturbates, a favourite occupation of the characters in this book. Indeed the narrator is extraordinarily interested in their sexual behaviour generally; this private eye stares hardest at everybody's genitals. Meanwhile, all around are corpses wearing gas-masks:

> fixed, like horse-flies

> feeding on filth
> with a black proboscis'
> and bulging perspex eyes.

Raine is very good at noticing that things are unexpectedly like other things, a power certified by Aristotle as an indication of high intelligence: 'a good metaphor implies an intuitive perception of the similarity in dissimilars'; he adds that the gift is innate and cannot be acquired. It was valued just as highly by the 17th-century *concettisti,* some of whom thought they were demonstrating what the world was like, a vast network of resemblances waiting for poets and other persons of genius to discover them. The Rainean conceit depends on the perception of similarity in dissimilars, which in turn calls for a gift of careful and curious observation. This Raine certainly possesses. Henry in his trench is set amid much expertly-noted military detail, each item wherever possible resembling something else.

Next we are moved to Moscow in 1917 for a domestic view of the October Revolution—here begins a long process of persecution and exile—and to Oxford in the same year, where Henry's wife Queenie is assaulted by a pervert. He wields a razor, and 'A nervous moth of light / Flits over the ceiling.' The war ends, Henry returns home, Lenin orates, but Stalin is thinking of sex and does not listen. A wheelchair and the hammer and sickle both resemble an ampersand (which, being an instrument for yoking things together, also resembles Raine's poems). What is memorable here is not the story, though it continues, but the notation of resemblances you would never have dreamed of: a glass of beer is 'a bulging leather gleam / like a farmer's legging'. The same eye can observe the resemblance between a certain kind of sofa and a boxing glove, which in turn resembles a toffee apple. It perceives a light bulb dangling from its flex as being 'like a suicide', or a dangling telephone brushing the carpet as 'like the arm of an ape'. Can you imagine teeth aching 'like testicles / after hours of foreplay'?

Some of the characters emerge recognisably, if dimly, from the plot: Henry is a boxer, also, apparently, an Oxford scout; his son Eliot, not, it seems, a competent doctor, becomes a psychiatrist (probably the most fully presented character, he is not very likeable). The Pasternaks get exit visas, marry and fornicate. Meanwhile History, more largely considered, continues, punctuated by lower-case, domestic history: the Germans experience hyperinflation, the young Raines masturbate, Mosley rants, the Nazis enact their eugenic laws, Pasternaks in England dig air raid trenches, Henry Raine fights, the death camps begin, some Jews escape. Norman Raine, father of Craig, gets a bad prognosis after an RAF accident. And so on till, in 1984, we reach the final ampersand and encounter Craig, grandson of Henry, son of Norman, and Craig's wife, Lisa, great-niece of Boris Pasternak, great-granddaughter of Leonid. They are momentarily amused by two Chinese, speaking comical English, and then visit the art gallery at Dahlem, where the more memorable pictures seem to share the anal interests of the author; even the word *Drücken* on a door reminds the latter of the trials of constipation. But there they are, ampersanded amid all this variety of scene and language, and accompanied by a photograph of Eliot Raine, the pornography-loving doctor who, according to the family tree, married Lydia Pasternak and begot Lisa. The photograph was 'taken on his deathbed' and he seems to be 'Straining to relieve himself'. So it goes; everything sort of comes together in the end.

A considerable number of famous people float anecdotally through the poem, Lord Northcliffe crazy, Lenin in the process of being mummified, Lady Conan Doyle getting in touch with her dead husband, Haile Selassie in exile, his gas bill unpaid. Stalin quizzes Pasternak on the telephone about Mandelstam, Pasternak refuses to sign the letter commiserating with Stalin on his wife's suicide, Churchill jeers at Chamberlain in the Commons. Edward, Prince of Wales, is cosy with his lady, Mussolini has a play on in the West End, Eisenhower is challenged by Jimmy Raine on sentry-go, Yeats lectures tediously at Oxford and has his Steinach operation. The Mandelstams, Akhmatova and Tsvetaeva make appearances. Rilke drops in, mocked by Karl Kraus. Dante and Wallace Stevens are silently cited. Obviously there is never a dull moment, though the sum total of those moments seems duller than they are.

There is an old argument about texture and structure in poetry, and John Crowe Ransom thought that although you had to have the second the first, however irrelevant to the structure, was more important because, for one thing, it is what makes poetry different from prose. Of course there can be recurrent elements in the texture which help to constitute structure; but these, and possibly other structural agents the poet prefers to keep quiet about, can be in some degree occult. Craig Raine has demonstrated elsewhere, when writing for the opera, that he has architectonic ambitions, and they exist here, though in large measure occulted. His short lines and often truncated syntax are capable of narrative load-bearing, and are often tersely effective, even when straitened, as they sometimes are, to aposiopesis (to use one of his own many learned words); but their main business is with texture, in its nature irrelevant to structure.

So we return to the questions posed at the beginning of this notice. Poets care most about texture but understand that poems, and especially the more ambitious kinds, need structure. It has always been a problem, and modern solutions have been authoritatively offered, notably by Eliot and Pound. For Post-Modernists, structure, in the old-fashioned sense, is an outworn myth, one of those *grands récits* that have to go and the sooner the better. But so is the very idea of history as consecutive narrative, an idea to which this poem, in however qualified a way, subscribes. Perhaps that final episode in the art gallery suggests, in addition to what it says more obviously, that the real structure of the poem is occult, accessible only through the details of texture. In Rembrandt's *John the Baptist Preaching* it is not the saint who attracts attention but

> a woman in the foreground dusk . . .
> holding her little girl trussed
> so she can shit in the river.

Of the gallery itself what is remembered is the door marked *Drücken,* which Craig mistakenly pulls, perhaps to avoid the memory that this was the word used to exhort children in the throes of constipation. Admittedly that condition is almost antithetical to the style of this poem, with its splendidly lavish textural scatterings. These are what one remembers: 'a squirrel shudders up a pine. / Tines of sunlight through the trees'; or, in a gale, 'Yachts like Hassids in the harbour'. What they are doing in a novel is a different question from whether they are worth having. They can cleanse one's way of seeing things; why should they also have to tell us what to think?

Mick Imlah (review date 7 October 1994)

SOURCE: "History by Hindsight," in *Times Literary Supplement,* No. 4775, October 7, 1994, p. 31.

[*Below, Imlah assesses the poetic and narrative strengths of* History: The Home Movie, *emphasizing Raine's anal and genital preoccupations.*]

Auden observed of the Old Masters (he had Bruegel principally in mind) that they understood how ordinary life carries on in the corners, regardless of the momentous event that is the painting's subject; how, for instance, in one (unidentified or imagined) picture, "the torturer's horse / Scratches its innocent behind on a tree". Since his sonnet **"Arsehole"** of 1983 ("I fed that famished mouth my ambergris")—which made A. N. Wilson feel "sorry for *Mrs.* Raine"—Craig Raine has committed his poetry and criticism to the promotion of that unheroic "behind" and its kin.

In the final section of his long-awaited *magnum opus,* Raine depicts himself visiting the Gemäldegalerie in Berlin, where he focuses on a similar tiny detail in each of two pictures. In Rembrandt's *St. John the Baptist Preaching,* what he notices is "a woman in the foreground dusk // . . . holding her little girl trussed / so she can shit in the river"; in Bruegel's *Netherlandish Proverbs,* he picks from dozens of competing details the one "where two pair buttocks / loom from a lean-to loo". Raine rightly prides himself on looking where other writers have blinked ("Cancer. Black blood in her cunt", etc.);

though he may seem at moments like this always to be looking for the same sort of thing. If you were to turn for relief from the groaning store of genital and anal groceries on show in *History: The Home Movie*—from the "foreskin crinkled / like the unforced crown of rhubarb shoots" and the "inner labia // like chicken livers, / the segmented anus inside / out, a blood orange"—to the current issue of the *Spectator,* you would find a review by Raine of a volume of Dr. Johnson's letters, which begins with a quotation: "The testicle continues well. . . ." It is Raine's instinct to put the genitals into, and take the Great Man out of, Johnson, just as it is to elide St. John from the Rembrandt. It would be going too far to present *History* as a debagging job on the whole twentieth century; but part of its design is plainly to evict the heroes and torturers from the centre of "historical" narrative in favour of the shitters on the margin.

It opens with a poem set in a *dacha* by the Black Sea in 1905. Across the water, the Kronstadt mutiny is brewing, the subject of Eisenstein's *Battleship Potemkin* (1925) and of Boris Pasternak's cinematic verse "chronicle" *Nineteen Five* (written in the months after he'd seen the film). Here, though, the big-screen drama is kept, like Bruegel's fallen Icarus, "far out to sea"; and Raine's hidden camera plays instead on a family scene: a little boy (Pasternak's brother, as it happens) tucking his "cock and balls" back between his legs. (When we do see a battleship—and it's not until nearly half-way through the book—it's immediately disarmed and domesticated by having its rivets likened to "mangetout".)

The "movie" gathers unauthorized footage from the lives of two families, whose stories—if such calculatedly miscellaneous fragments can be called that—are intercut: the "Pasternaks", bourgeois Russian Jews who migrate to Germany and then to England, though leaving their famous brother at home; and the "Raines", a lower-middle-class family from Oxford. The resolution of this scheme would seem to be the union of Craig and his wife, the woman we know as the scholar Ann Pasternak Slater; but the book also marries fact and fiction in pursuit of clearer symmetries and richer stories. The identities of the three Raine brothers of the middle generation will suggest the blend. "Craig"'s father "Norman" is broadly compatible with the (only mildly incredible) boxer and brain-wounded faith-healer of the prose memoir, **"A Silver Plate"** (*Rich,* 1984); but "Jimmy", a sign painter and masturbator, has a fantastical knack of brushing with the Great (Churchill, Mosley, Haile Selassie, Eisenhower); while "Eliot Raine" is a highly unflattering appropriation into his own bloodline of the poet's father-in-law, the psychologist Eliot Slater.

But a little invention doesn't make this formally unique book a novel, as the blurb corruptly claims it to be (while no less "an epic history of Europe", "the best film you'll ever read", etc.). There is more point in considering how Raine—whose

achievements in verse until now have all been in the miniature mode—has adapted his technique to the requirements of the very long poem.

In a note for a Soviet journal, Pasternak wrote that "in the book *Nineteen Five* I move across from lyrical thinking to epic, though this is very difficult". To Pasternak, lyric utterance had grown inadequate to the times ("this sort of writing no longer has a place in present-day aesthetics"); for Raine, making a similar transition in terms of scale, it is epic that has had its day. Hence the difficulty of *History* is rather the reader's, who has to make more general sense of the whole than Raine's piecemeal and cryptic procedure immediately allows. It consists of eighty-seven poems, between twelve and 135 lines in length, each labelled with a year and a title. The medium throughout is an irregular, unrhymed unit of three short lines, whose avoidance of fixed metres and larger rhythms embodies Raine's purge of "stale cadences" and his abrasive contention elsewhere that "all good poetry is anti-poetry". All is *seen,* in the present tense, with something less than the minimum of explication; so that on one level *History* resembles a huge collection of the sort of poem that Craig Raine has always written.

And it is a snag that, for all their various strengths, what the poems are mostly made of is a superabundance of Raine's old stock-in-trade, the kind of simile or metaphor that wants to startle and can sometimes be caught admiring itself rather than working for the good of the poem. It must be said that in *History* much of the metaphor is perfectly adapted to the narrative context, as in the emblem of a shy man struggling to talk to his wife about their son in pain upstairs;

> There is an obstacle:
> love he feels as furniture,
> as a three-seater sofa
>
> stuck in the stairwell,
> its hessian underside on show,
> its castors comically prim . . .

But a good many of the similes can still seem stubbornly parenthetical, local satisfactions of an excess of what a pupil of Joyce's called his master's "descriptive lust". It is beside any worthwhile larger point, for example, to turn the head of a minor character into fruit, like something out of Arcimboldo-"one eye like a Victoria plum. / Unshaven weak brown bristles / like a kiwi fruit". And while Raine would scorn any notion of *good taste,* surely a full moon hanging up "her radical mastectomy" fails on another count or two.

But read between them, and the similes are not all that *History* has to offer. The reconstruction of so many different Russian and European rooms (the laboratory where Lenin, and Lenin's genitals, are embalmed, for one) is done with thorough mastery of their worlds of strange detail; but Raine is understandably more at home in the Raine household, even if it is invented. The best of the English pieces are tightly paced, sharply realized narrative poems of a sort he has not often attempted before; and if it has required the whole project to get these written, then they justify the whole. The storytelling thrives when the action is most violent—in fight sequences, asylum visits, rape scenes; but there are more delicate successes too, like the beautifully particular **"1919: Back from the Front"**, where Henry Raine spends an evocative evening "opening cupboards and drawers" before confronting the sexual tensions of his homecoming. Some of the poems involving Norman are very funny. And there is any amount of specifically narrative wit at work throughout: to select arbitrarily, in the way a nonsense name is made part of the postponement of the cheerless acceptance of a marriage proposal (though I suppose this depends on a simile):

> Like the frozen hunting horn
> of Baron Karl Friedrich
> Hieronymous von Munchausen
>
> thawing out beside the fire
> after an epic silence
> she speaks: "So I'd better say yes"—

—or in the way the episode of Pasternak and Tsvetaeva having their fling is done as a series of index entries, to convey its perfunctory, instantly "historical" status.

And yet, if it asks to be considered as one thing, *History* is structurally inefficient. Chronology aside, there is no gain to be had from reading its sections consecutively, and therefore no compulsion to read them all. Certainly one catches echoes and recurring motifs—flies, spiders, acronyms, arseholes, quarter-faces, club feet, and a dozen other systematic implants; but these rhymes, the marks of history repeating itself, can as easily be registered backwards as forwards; and if there is a key to their deployment, it's not one that yields itself up to an averagely attentive third reading. Strangest of all, whatever the poem's private business, it seems to have exhausted itself by the end of the Second World War. While the forty-four years from 1905 to 1949 generate 300 pages, the forty-four from 1950 to the present day get only thirty. In the absence of a historical explanation, it feels, and fair enough, as though the poet is simply knackered.

Still, we were never to expect a choral climax. The book's last words—". . .an ampersand. / An ampersand. An ampersand"—do refer to the yoking of Craig and his wife; but they also reprise a lonely, spiritless rhythm that beats through several earlier episodes. It is heard in the noise of trains on the tracks, of needles stuck in the groove, in the ubiquitous "click click" of male masturbation; and in mixtures of these, such as old Leonid Pasternak "doing" a train:

> . . . Merde. De. Te. Merde. De-te.
> Merde-de-te. Merde-de-te-merde-de-te.
>
> He might be masturbating.
> He shakes on the sofa, rigid,
> gripped, unable to stop.

"Merde-de-te", dum-di-ti. It would be something if *History* is showing us, in the face of the modernist ambition it otherwise fulfils, that all we share with former generations is the pulse of this runaway dactyl; that what will survive of us is self-abuse and *metre*.

Richard Tillinghast (review date 11 December 1994)

SOURCE: "Poets Are Born, Then Made," in *The New York Times Book Review,* Vol. 99, December 11, 1994, pp. 25-6.

[*In the following excerpt, Tillinghast reviews* History: The Home Movie, *summarizing the salient points of Raine's poetic technique.*]

Craig Raine has been known in Britain as the chief exemplar of a late-1970's movement in poetry known as "the Martians," in whose work quotidian elements of life were seen as if through the eyes of a visitor from another planet. In *A Martian Sends a Postcard Home,* for example, "Rain is when the earth is television / It has the property of making colors darker." Now he has written a bold; ambitious chronicle of life in Europe, chiefly in England and Russia, from 1905 to 1984. His method in *History: The Home Movie* is to chronicle events—some evidently fictional—from the history of his family, the Raines, and his wife's family, the Pasternaks. The publisher calls it "a novel in verse." Though the two world wars, Stalin, Lenin, various English monarchs, Halle Selassie and literary figures like Yeats appear in passing, what we have is not "official" textbook history, but rather a demotic, home-movie take on this period.

The home-movie analogy is apt. We get flickering glimpses of family dramas; and, as with someone else's home movies, the viewer's attention is not always riveted to the screen. The English characters are fairly well defined, but for the Russians I found myself flipping back to the family trees provided in the front of the book as I tried—often unsuccessfully—to distinguish Zhonya and Fedya and Zhenya (not to mention Zhenya's child, also called Zhenya).

It is as if Mr. Raine were making the point that some of life's commonest activities are those that hardly ever get written about. What we see of life in the trenches in World War I, in a section called **"1915: The Queen's Own Oxfordshire Hussars,"** is grandfather Henry Raine writing a letter to his wife and then masturbating. It is evidently a family tradition, because about 60 pages on we encounter Mr. Raine's Uncle Jimmy, who has a go "while he reads *Film Fun,* / his mind on Harold Lloyd, / Mack Swain and Fatty Arbuckle."

Mr. Raine has other obsessions: the deflation of bourgeois values, sexual transgression and violence, excretion. His anal preoccupations alone might be reason enough to call this book *History: The A Posteriori View.* If his poetry were architecture its style would be Brutalist. His fierce determination to demythologize history is typified in **"1924: Lenin Takes a Long Bath,"** where we are treated to a discussion of the embalming of the Soviet leader: "He'll soon be permanent. / Old ways work best. Evisceration / Those pharaohs knew about meat."

There are one or two tender moments in the book—when Henry Raine returns from the war, for example

> He spends the evening
> opening cupboards and drawers,
> finding the wary napkin rings,
>
> A set of six, like smokers' teeth.

Our response to Henry's safe return is compromised by our awareness that his wife, Queenie, has been violated six pages earlier by a pervert calling himself Mablethorpe: "She does it like domestic chores / making them both a cup of tea / before the shaving and the sodomy."

To be fair to Mr. Raine, however, he is a poet with at least one spectacular gift: the metaphoric or transforming faculty. The book is worth reading if only for the originality, and sometimes the brilliance, of its comparisons. In a catalogue he calls "a cubist quarry," cigarettes and hollow licorice sticks become "Wild Woodbines in packets of ten, / or loose in fives, sherbet fountains / fused like sticks of dynamite." The sound of water flows through a gravel pit "like a little girl / wearing her mother's shoes." Elsewhere "The boy lounges / between his mother's legs / like a cello."

Tom Clark (review date 12 March 1995)

SOURCE: "The Private Life of Our Century," in *Los Angeles Times Book Review,* March 12, 1995, p. 11.

[*In the following review, Clark emphasizes the narrative aspect of* History: The Home Movie, *while praising Raine's choice of verse as appropriate for "an age trained to think in images."*]

This challenging, innovative, unsettling novel in verse [*His-*

tory: The Home Movie] relates the history of 20th-Century Europe through the interlocking private lives of two families—the author's own English family of Raines, and the Russian family of Pasternaks, to which the Raines are linked by accident of intermarriage. Poet Craig Raine here brilliantly melds the tonal authenticity of autobiographical memoir with novelistic modes of structuring, historical scoping and character-building, fleshing out fact with imaginative speculation of a most vivid, graphically immediate and intense kind.

No less distinctly contemporary in method than in subject matter, *History: The Home Movie* revives and updates the lost art of verse narrative to fit an age trained to think in images.

History is not just a serial poem (those are common enough these days), but a serious, full-scale philosophical novel, "modern" in the post-Joycean sense. Raine's montage technique reveals a spectacle of history as largely pointless suffering. Viewing through the peephole of private experience the true facts of a century of war, totalitarian terror and death camps, Craig Raine takes the only course open to a conscientious modern novelist, sacrificing the false "public" order of events (history as "progress") for the uncomfortable, disturbing chaos of what is.

His narrative proceeds via a chain of sharply focused movie-like vignettes. Each stanzaic "chapter" recaptures some telling lost moment from the life of a family member; each of those moments is fraught with both obscure personal significance and oblique, surprising "public"—historical points of contact.

The three generations of English Raines chronicled here descend from Henry Raine, a sergeant of the Oxfordshire Hussars whom we encounter in a regimental tackroom amid shellshocked trenches of the Western Front, and his wife Queenie, a music hall artiste, raffishly performing at Victoria Palace before the king in an early chapter.

The Russian line is introduced with the painter Leonid Pasternak and his wife the pianist Rosa née Kaufman, members of the Moscow middle-class Jewish intelligentsia under the czarist regime of the turn of the century; the Pasternaks first appear here at their *dacha* by the Black Sea in 1905, their tranquillity overshadowed, when their older son, Boris, spots the red flag of a naval squadron far out to sea, by ominous premonitions of upheavals and trials to come.

In keeping with *History's* highlighting of the role of accidents of desire in the course of human events, the poet Boris Pasternak's sexual dalliances and curiosity receive as much attention here as his better-known literary achievements and frustrations. An "excitement almost sexual," provoked by the sudden proximity of power, overcomes him when he's phoned by Stalin from the Kremlin to be interrogated about his fel-low poet, Osip Mandelstam. Distracted by a peephole vision through the collective apartment wall of a young neighbor girl bathing, Boris stumbles into the well-meant but insuffi-ciently cautious comments that inadvertently seal Mandel-stam's awful fate of exile.

In the confusing, entropic unfolding of Raine's *History,* tragic destinies are more often than not enacted by the common-place, and large-scale consequences repeatedly spring from little embarrassments, apparently inconsequential failures to communicate and all-too-human personal misunderstandings. The ancient burden to which the flesh is heir, Raine seems to be saying, fosters far more of history than we might at first glance care to acknowledge.

The novel's corollary figure to Boris on the English side is the author's uncle Eliot Raine. Eliot, with his inquiring, ar-tistic temperament, his bizarrely diversified sexual pursuits, and the checkered medical career that brings him to Germany and marriage with Boris's exiled sister Lydia Pasternak, is perhaps the most complicated and compelling character in *History.* (One suspects that Eliot's private journals provided this project an invaluable research source.)

Less developed dramatically, Eliot's brother Jimmy, an ami-able, rather simple-minded itinerant sign painter, serves as a useful onlooker, providing fleeting glimpses of several of the large-scale political figures who pass like flickering news-reel images through the novel's chapters on the '30s and '40s.

It's through Jimmy's eyes that poet-novelist Raine often ma-nipulates his zoom-lens-like ironic technique of exploding scale. Bringing us up close to discern the large through the small, Jimmy's mute, unwitting witnessing produces some of *History*'s cleverest comic touches.

On a chilly January morning in 1931, the legend on one of Jimmy's billboard paintings for a fairground sideshow ("The Boneless Wonder") draws the eyes of a strolling Winston Churchill ("Burly, bowler-hatted, / breathing brandy hard"), who opportunistically incorporates that phrase later that day in a House speech attacking the prime minister. And in 1942, re-posted with his Black Watch battalion to Gibraltar after a disgraceful failure of nerve at Dunkirk, Jimmy is out on sen-try duty when the magic hand of chance (and/or the poet's fictive art) confronts him with a suspicious night prowler, "some jerk in a jerkin and chinos" who turns out to be the Allied supreme commander, Gen. Dwight Eisenhower, out for an after-hours tour of the Rock. (Ike surrenders to Jimmy with white hankie waving nervously aloft.)

Graphic scenes of physical violence—attempted ax-murder, electrocution, garroting, shooting, flesh-scarifying beatings, etc.—litter these pages. But Raine's images of violence serve a serious thematic purpose. A dark, shadowy stain pervasively emerging like a faint negative watermark on every page, the pain inflicted by modern people upon each other and upon themselves is soaked through this poetic history of the pri-vate life of our century.

In *History: The Home Movie,* the matter-of-fact, tight-focus dwelling on intimate, sometimes repulsive physical detail is not mere shock tactic. Raine's hard-edged images particular-ize objects and situations that surround, and, by their con-tiguous reflections, define the human. A teasingly discontinuous narrative, refusing not only obvious sentiment but explanatory statement, thrusts those images into the fore-ground with unexpected immediacy, at times leaving the reader gasping for breath in the heady spaces between them.

Craig Raine's *History* admirably reclaims poetry's narrative function, its capacity to fictionally propose a world as com-plex and mysterious as reality itself. Its techniques demand extra work of the reader. In the end, though, Raine's choice of verse proves a fitting expressive vehicle for the history of this bewildering century—in which public truth gives way to private impulse, and human beings torn from one another and from themselves must look to poetic fiction to decipher the enigma of a chaotic and unintelligible life.

Additional coverage of Raine's life and career is contained in the following sources published by Gale: *Contemporary Authors,* **Vol. 108;** *Contemporary Authors New Re-vision Series,* **Vols. 29 and 51; and** *Dictionary of Literary Biography,* **Vol. 40.**

Anne Tyler
1941-

American novelist, short story writer, critic, nonfiction writer, and editor.

The following entry presents criticism of Tyler's work through 1995. For further information on her life and career, see *CLC,* Volumes 7, 11, 18, 28, 44, and 59.

INTRODUCTION

Tyler is best known as the award-winning author of the novels *The Accidental Tourist* (1985) and *Breathing Lessons* (1988). She writes fiction depicting tense family situations that result in lonely, confused members who long for connection and meaning in their lives, focusing on everyday occurrences instead of more dramatic events. While family history has a strong influence on her characters, she rarely puts them in a historical or social context. Known as a representative of a new generation of Southern writers, Tyler is often compared to Eudora Welty, William Faulkner, and Flannery O'Connor.

Biographical Information

Tyler was born in Minneapolis, Minnesota, on October 25, 1941, to an industrial-chemist father and a social-worker mother. Her parents were members of the Society of Friends and long-time activists in liberal causes. Tyler lived her childhood years in various communes in the Midwest and the South with her parents and three younger brothers. She received her early education at the communes, but at the age of eleven she began attending public school. The alienation she felt at this time became a consistent theme in her work. Tyler attended Duke University on scholarship, graduating Phi Beta Kappa at the age of nineteen with a degree in Russian. While she was at Duke she twice received the Anne Flexner Award for creative writing, and she began publishing her short stories in magazines. She then studied Russian at Columbia University for a year. In 1962 she worked as the Russian bibliographer in the Duke University Library. She married Taghi Modaressi, a psychiatrist, in 1963, and the couple moved to Montreal so he could continue his medical studies. While looking for a job in Montreal, Tyler wrote her first novel, *If Morning Ever Comes* (1964). This was followed a year later by *The Tin Can Tree* (1965), but her writing slowed while she raised her two daughters. Tyler and Modaressi moved to Baltimore in 1965. With her daughters in school, Tyler began to focus on her writing full time. Starting with *The Clock Winder* (1972), Baltimore became the setting for her fiction.

Major Works

Tyler writes narratives that deal with the internal strife and relationships of families. Family communication, or lack of it, is an essential element in her fiction. While generational influence is important to Tyler, she excludes social or historical context as an influence on her down-to-earth characters: there are no fancy surroundings or sophisticated speech, and generally the people who inhabit her novels are not concerned with material wealth. One continuing message in Tyler's fiction is that clutter in one's life is inescapable. Characters such as Morgan in *Morgan's Passing* (1980) and Delia in *Ladder of Years* (1995) try to escape from life's baggage only to find themselves in the same life all over again. This pull between returning home and running away occurs often in Tyler's work. Tyler also asserts the importance of differences in life and she frequently brings opposites together, a circumstance she considers nourishing and integral to the ongoing health of the family. In *Dinner at the Homesick Restaurant* (1982), for instance, Pearl Tull holds herself and her children together through valuable relationships with outsiders when her husband abandons them. *The Accidental Tour-*

ist, which earned her the National Book Critics' Circle Award, brings together many of Tyler's themes. The main character, Macon Leary, must choose between the security of loneliness and the uncertain comforts of human love. Tyler again takes up the theme of difference in the Pulitzer Prize-winning *Breathing Lessons.* The novel traces a day in the married life of Ira, a realist, and Maggie, a dreamer, with flashbacks showing the importance of their shared past. Tyler shows the compromises, disappointments, and love found in a marriage, and once again shows how differences can be nourishing in a relationship.

Critical Reception

Tyler's earlier novels were not given much critical attention, being most often noted as indicators of the author's potential. It was not until novelist Gail Godwin reviewed *Celestial Navigation* (1974) and John Updike called readers' attention to *Searching for Caleb* (1976) that Tyler gained widespread acclaim. Critics praise Tyler for her wit and her ability to render detail. While some reviewers complain that her characters are implausible, even bizarre, others assert that she presents them with such compassion that their oddities become simply human. Many reviewers point out the connection between tragedy and comedy in Tyler's fiction, and praise her talent at dealing with both. However, some critics complain of the lack of a moral dimension in Tyler's novels: characters are not good or evil; they are just mistaken or confused. There is much debate over Tyler's relationship to the Southern literary tradition, but there are obvious influences in Tyler's fiction from Faulkner, O'Connor, and Welty. Reviewers point out that Tyler, like Faulkner and O'Connor, emphasizes the importance of personal history. Critics often compare Tyler to Welty in the way she writes about everyday people and their lives, instead of just chronicling major events. However, Tyler's novels do not contain the Gothic overtones typical of her Southern predecessors.

PRINCIPAL WORKS

If Morning Ever Comes (novel) 1964
The Tin Can Tree (novel) 1965
A Slipping-Down Life (novel) 1970
The Clock Winder (novel) 1972
Celestial Navigation (novel) 1974
Searching for Caleb (novel) 1976
Earthly Possessions (novel) 1977
Morgan's Passing (novel) 1980
Dinner at the Homesick Restaurant (novel) 1982
The Accidental Tourist (novel) 1985
Breathing Lessons (novel) 1988
Saint Maybe (novel) 1991
Ladder of Years (novel) 1995

CRITICISM

Mary F. Robertson (essay date 1985)

SOURCE: "Medusa Points and Contact Points," in *Contemporary American Women Writers: Narrative Strategies,* The University Press of Kentucky, 1985, pp. 119-42.

[*In the following essay, Robertson analyzes how Tyler changes traditional ideas about family and its interaction with outsiders in her novels.*]

John Updike, a fan of Anne Tyler's work, remarked in a review that "Tyler, whose humane and populous novels have attracted (if my antennae are tuned right) less approval in the literary ether than the sparer offerings of Ann Beattie and Joan Didion, is sometimes charged with the basic literary sin of implausibility." Indeed, Tyler's novels do not seem a promising hunting ground for critics, who seek advances in the experimental surface of fiction. Her most palpable narrative virtues are by and large traditional ones: memorable characters, seductive plots, imaginative and hawk-eyed descriptions. Tyler is adept with the simile, acute as a psychologist, and quite good at the meditative pause in dramatization, although the reflections usually come as ruminations of a character rather than as autonomous philosophical sorties like George Eliot's.

On first opening Tyler's novels—and perhaps until having read several—a reader is apprehensive that he or she has only encountered still more domestic dramas, seemingly oblivious of the public dimension of the life of men and women in society. A social critic might feel that Tyler's very limitation of subject matter confirms an ideology of the private family to the detriment of political awareness, and a feminist reader might think that only female actions having more public importance than Tyler's seem to have can help the cause of women. In this essay, however, I shall argue that Tyler's unusual use of narrative patterns accomplishes much that should interest the feminist and the social critic alike. To see how, perhaps Updike's word *implausibility* should be examined. This trait in Tyler's work might be a sticking point for some serious readers because of prejudices about what is realistic in the plots of novels about families. Words such as *zany* and *magical* that appear regularly on her book jackets amount to labels that are likely to encourage such prejudices, to invite readers to resist the uncomfortable psychological and political seriousness of Tyler's vision, and to settle for a "good read" instead. Such prejudices, however, are ultimately thwarted by Tyler's fiction; in fact, thwarted prejudices are exactly the point. Tyler's implausible narrative form is a door through which the reader passes to a deeper sense of realism.

Families are, of course, a traditional subject of fiction. Novels about families can be divided into two groups: those that explore the interior psychology of a family—*Mansfield Park, Sons and Lovers,* and *To the Lighthouse* are diverse examples—and those that use family sagas to represent larger historical changes—works ranging from *Absalom, Absalom* to *Giant* and *The Thorn Birds.* In either case, the genre depends traditionally on features that produce certain narrative expectations in the reader. Foremost, perhaps, is a clear conception of the boundary between the insiders of a family and its outsiders. The typical family novel reserves its emotional center for the insiders. No matter how many forays or entanglements the members of the family have with outsiders, such a novel gains its power from a clear definition of the traits of both the individual members and the family as a whole. One narrative consequence of this conventional boundary that a reader, accustomed to it, might not notice is that dialogues or interchanges among members of a family are usually more portentous for the themes and outcomes of the book than those between members of the family and outsiders. Even if family problems are not solved thematically in such moments, these moments are the points in the narrative at which the significance of the story accrues. There is a centripetal impetus in such interchanges in the traditional family novel that the narrative design does nothing to question.

This conventional attachment of weight to family interchanges produces a preference for formal purity in the narrative shape of the novel as a whole. The strategy of maintaining the boundary between insiders and outsiders is reflected in the reader's awareness of what is plot—action concerning the family history—and what is subplot—contingent action concerning outsiders who function thematically and narratively to push a character to some momentous choice as he or she develops the family's destiny but who then either recede or are absorbed into the family, for example, through marriage. Such peripheral matters as affairs or business dealings function, if anything, to make clear by contrast the central skein of reciprocal effects of members of the family on one another. Often, too, the chapters of such novels are organized according to the points of view of insiders to reflect the central significance of the family.

Independent of the particular thematic content of individual family novels, such generically conventional narrative patterns constitute a second-order system of signs. They imply a certain ideological relationship among family, identity, and history. The family is shown or implied to be the principal determinant of adult identity and the primary social unit. In conventional family novels a kind of binary thinking rules the narrative. The characters can either submit to or reject the family's ways and values; the family as a whole can either triumph or be destroyed. In either instance the concept of the private, inward-turning family remains coherent and ideologically definitive. Something about families, happy or not, makes them one of the very names of narrative order. If they "break down" in divorce, miscommunication, betrayal, or catastrophe, the reader is as uneasy as if people spoke to him or her in disrupted, nonsensical syntax. If families survive in even some good measure, the reader feels that something has been set right with the universe. In addition, even when the family is historically representative of general cultural movements, such an emphasis on the power of the family projects a certain idea of history. History is implicitly reduced to a narrative about families of unquestioned centrality. Families are perhaps the human race's oldest mode of plotting history, and long after more primitive family chronicles have been outgrown as the dominant mode of recording history, the family survives metaphorically in political histories of monarchies and nation-states.

Anne Tyler's narrative strategies disrupt the conventional expectations of the family novels, and thus the disruptions themselves also constitute a second-order system of signs that helps to dislodge the ideology of the enclosed family and the notion that the family is the main forum for making history. These disruptions are undoubtedly responsible for the feeling of implausibility in Tyler's fiction; Tyler does not respect the usual patterns of the genre. The first "itch" caused by her narratives comes at what I shall call Medusa points. These are points at which a certain pattern obtains in the dialogues and interchanges among members of the family. The second itch arises from Tyler's unwillingness to manage the narrative so as to form a clear line of demarcation between insiders and outsiders. The outsiders assume roles that are more than contingent yet not quite surrogates for family roles. The points at which this ambiguity occurs I shall call contact points. The third itch, the result of the first two, is that the pure narrative shape of the family novel is upset. Because the boundary between insiders and outsiders is continually transgressed, the progress of Tyler's novels is felt more as an expansion of narrative disorder than as a movement toward resolution and clarification. This larger narrative movement of disorder usually includes both negative and positive moments. A member of the family typically both sheds—somehow becomes unencumbered from his other family relations—and incorporates—forms significant new relationships with outsiders. If the reader is alert to the meaning of the disruptions of usual expectations of the genre, it becomes clear that Tyler's most pervasive structural preoccupation is with the family as a sign of order or disorder in personality and society.

This structural obsession with the family as a contender for the signs of identity manifests itself especially in Tyler's three most recent novels. In *Earthly Possessions* a middle-aged housewife named Charlotte, who has been thinking of leaving her preacher-husband, Saul, and her two children, goes to the bank to withdraw money for that purpose and is taken hostage by a bank robber, Jake Simms. Until the end of the book she is held captive in this stranger's peripatetic stolen car, which he has chained shut on the passenger's side, and is allowed out only under close surveillance. This sudden traumatic intimacy, symbolized by the closed space of the car, is a parody of the very familial claustrophobia Charlotte had planned to throw off. Yet it proves to be an important opportunity for revelations about otherness and helps her to arrive at some mature distinctions she had not been in the habit of making. Since Tyler interweaves flashbacks to Charlotte's childhood and married life throughout the book, the implications of her eventual choice to risk at gunpoint leaving the robber and returning to her family can be appreciated fully.

In *Morgan's Passing* the overall tone is more lighthearted, but the structural pattern is similar. The two chief characters are Gower Morgan, an eccentric—who cannot resist impersonating others—with seven children and an unflappable wife, and Emily Meredith, a young married woman. The story opens with Morgan's delivering Leon and Emily Meredith's baby in a car after telling them untruthfully that he is a doctor. At first Morgan haunts the Merediths in a creepy way by trailing them; finally he is let into their lives as a valued friend. After a few years he reciprocates by allowing them into the life of his family. Later yet, he and Emily fall in love, have an affair, leave their marriages for each other, and produce a new child. This account does not begin to do justice to the disorder to be found in either of Morgan's households, nor to the ambiguous way his presence confounds the distinction between insider and outsider, no matter where he resides; but for the moment it is enough to show that, once again, a stranger disrupts a family's ordered life and alters its self-definition irrevocably.

In *Dinner at the Homesick Restaurant* the action takes us from the time when Pearl Tull, the self-sufficient mother, is dying, back through the history of her marriage and her children's adulthood, full circle to her funeral, when her long-lost husband, Beck, shows up for the day. This book might be read only as a dramatization of what one therapist calls the family crucible; Tyler is very good at showing how neurotic traits ricochet off one another in a family and are passed on to the next generation. If that were all, however, the novel would be nothing special. Its particular virtue lies in the way it places the family's children, Jenny, Ezra, and Cody, in various exogenous relationships that prove as formative and valuable to them as do their family ties.

On numerous occasions in these novels there is a pattern of misconnection—what I call a Medusa point in the narrative—such as this one between Ezra Tull and his mother:

> "I'm worried if I come too close, they'll say I'm overstepping. They'll say I'm pushy, or . . . emotional, you know. But if I back off, they might think I don't care. I really, honestly believe I missed some

rule that everyone else takes for granted; I must have been absent from school that day. There's this narrow little dividing line I somehow never located." "Nonsense: I don't know what you're talking about," said his mother, and then she held up an egg. "Will you look at this? Out of one dozen eggs, four are cracked."

Here is a similar interaction between Morgan and his wife, Bonny, who tries to assume the role of bride's mother for her engaged daughter:

> "Morgan, in this day and age, do you believe the bride's mother would still give the bride a little talk?" "Hmm?" "What I want to know is, am I expected to give Amy a talk about sex or am I not?" "Bonny, do you have to call it sex?" "What else would I call it?" "Well . . ." "I mean, sex is what it is, isn't it?" "Yes, but, I don't know . . ." "I mean, what would *you* say? Is it sex, or isn't it?" "Bonny, will you just stop *hammering* at me?"

In *Earthly Possessions* the pattern is not dramatized but revealed through Charlotte's memories. A stubborn separateness at the center of the relationship of Charlotte with each member of her family—mother, father, husband—is emphasized. Though Charlotte's father adores her in one way, he makes her feel she can never please him. She cares all her life for her grotesquely obese mother, but never breaks through to her candidly about her fears and feelings. She is separated most from her husband, whom she plans to leave almost from the beginning and did not even really make an active decision to marry. Here is the way they become engaged:

> In May he bought me an engagement ring. He took it out of his pocket one night when the three of us were eating supper—a little diamond. I hadn't known anything about it. I just stared at him when he slipped it on my finger. "I thought it was time," he told me. "I'm sorry, Mrs. Ames," he said. "I can't wait any longer, I want to marry her." Mama said, "But I—" "It won't be right away," he said. "I'm not taking her off tomorrow. I don't even know what my work will be yet. We'll stay here as long as you need us, believe me. I promise you." "But—" Mama said. That was all, though. I should have refused. I wasn't helpless, after all. I should have said, "I'm sorry, I can't fit you in . . . But I didn't."

None of these characters tries maliciously to damage his or her family interlocutors; in general, they try to help each other in the mundane ways of life. But in their minds and hearts they feel cut off, paradoxically because each feels suffocated by the other. After exposure to several Tyler novels a reader learns to bypass themes of the individual novels and understands that such nonsequiturs as occur in the conversation between Morgan and Bonny and such failures of communication as Charlotte's are best not read as individuals' character problems but as a narrative pattern drawn by Tyler to make a point about family relations in general. These points in the narrative assume a significance that stands apart from their particular content. Through them Tyler shows that situations calling for responses considered proper in certain spousal and filial roles petrify people in both senses of the word: the constant intimate gaze threatens to turn people to stone and also scares them into stratagems to evade the threat, just as Perseus could not look at the Medusa directly but mediated the slaying with the mirror. Thus the phrase "Medusa points" seems useful for such moments in Tyler's narratives when a character refuses or is unable to respond to a family member in the way that member desperately needs or desires. These Medusa points are registered, if not in the reader's petrification, at least in exasperation, because what is "supposed to happen" in a family novel—that is, connection between intimates or at least a definitive antagonism—does not happen. Thus the narrative pattern is mirrored in the reading process as resistance.

The Perseus-Medusa image is appropriate for *Dinner at the Homesick Restaurant* in an even more special way. Tyler seems deliberately to invoke Eudora Welty's *The Golden Apples,* in which this myth is quite important. The connection becomes explicit when Beck Tull, who leaves his wife and children early in the book, just as King McLain does in *The Golden Apples,* returns to Pearl's funeral—King returns to Katie Rainey's funeral; Tyler writes: "King-like, he sat alone." *The Golden Apples* is itself a mysterious and complex book, far more dreamlike and mythical than *Homesick,* but the two books dwell on the same two problems: people's existence in time and the profound ambivalence of human beings about identification with others. People suffer from their separateness and are especially drawn to merging with strangers who are exotic to them; yet, no sooner have they done so than they feel the petrification begin to set in and they fantasize evasion, abandonment, wandering. At the end of *The Golden Apples,* Virgie Rainey remembers the picture that hung on her piano teacher's wall of Perseus holding the Medusa's head. She thinks:

> Cutting off the Medusa's head was the heroic act, perhaps that made visible a horror in life, that was at once the horror in love—the separateness. . . . Virgie saw things in their time, like hearing them—and perhaps because she must believe in the Medusa equally with Perseus—she saw the stroke of the sword in three moments, not one. In the three was the damnation . . . beyond the beauty and the sword's stroke and the terror lay their existence in time—far out and endless, a constellation which the heart could

> read over many a night. . . . In Virgie's reach of memory a melody softly lifted, lifted of itself. Every time Perseus struck off the Medusa's head there was the beat of time, and the melody. Endless the Medusa, and Perseus endless.

Tyler shares with Welty the modified view of the heroic Perseus and Medusa reflected in this passage. The principal difference from the classical view lies in Virgie's recognition that the struggle is never finished. Likewise the Medusa is never really killed in Tyler's novels. Indeed, in Tyler's fiction the Medusa points signify primarily by their irony because they are the points in the narrative at which the occurrence of climactic movements, connections, and definitive severances is expected but never witnessed. Thus in and of themselves these Medusa points signify Tyler's refusal to regard the family as the most significant agent of character development and social representation. A crucial stylistic difference between Tyler and Welty aids this narrative message. Welty's poeticizing style, uplifted and abstract, creates a transcendent aura somewhat at odds with the content of Virgie's insight about time. The style itself has a way of lifting and resolving what is unresolved in the subject. In contrast, Tyler's more ordinary prose stylistically places the Medusa syndrome in real historical time. Her prose enacts stylistically the full force of the "fall into time" of those potential Perseuses—characters or readers—who would finish off forever the Medusa of a too complete family communication or would be totally vanquished by it.

In each of the Tyler novels mentioned certain characters are identified most strongly with the Medusa influence. In *Homesick,* Pearl Tull, after being left with three young children and forced to become the breadwinner, defensively develops a rigid, claustrophobic family style. She has no friends, does not visit with the customers at the store where she works, does not encourage her children to bring friends home. For years, in her stubborn pride, she refuses to admit to her children that their father has left them—the abandonment was simply never mentioned as such during all the time they were growing up. Besides this steely silence, Pearl encourages an unhealthy self-sufficiency and iron discipline. When the young Ezra, who is the most sensitive of the three children and the one who takes on the role of family nurturer, asks Pearl whether she would let him stay home from school one day if on that day alone money grew on trees, she answers with a severe "No," and in response to further pleading erupts, "Ezra, will you let it be? Must you keep at me this way? Why are you so obstinate?" A thousand such exchanges in the life of the family produce personalities inclined to give up on real candor and expression of feelings in the family arena. We see this when Cody, the oldest son, is about to leave for college. Pearl has finally brought herself to mention the most pervasive fact in each of their lives—their father's absence:

"Children, there's something I want to discuss with you." Cody was talking about a job. He had to find one in order to help with the tuition fees. "I could work in the cafeteria," he was saying, "or maybe off-campus. I don't know which." Then he heard his mother and looked over at her. "It's about your father," Pearl said. Jenny said, "I'd choose the cafeteria." "You know, my darlings," Pearl told them, "how I always say your father's away on business." "But off-campus they might pay more," said Cody, "and every penny counts." "At the cafeteria you'd be with your classmates, though," Ezra said. "Yes, I thought of that." "All those coeds," Jenny said. "Cheerleaders. Girls in their little white bobby sox." "Sweater girls," Cody said. "There's something I want to explain about your father," Pearl told them. "Choose the cafeteria," Ezra said. "Children?" "The cafeteria," they said. And all three gazed at her coolly, out of gray, unblinking, level eyes exactly like her own.

In time Tyler's reader learns that the trick at such moments in the narrative is not to read them conventionally as the portrayal of psychological cripples and tragic family failures. The Medusa points are semantically complex because, while they depict the characters as stony to others in the family, they show at the same time (in the children's oblique comments just quoted, for example) the healthy partial escape from total petrification. Such points show characters who have learned to turn their eyes away from the monster of family self-absorption and to seek their maturity and identity by means of other resources.

The second generic disruption in narrative form that develops an independent significance in Tyler's novels is the altered treatment of outsiders. Pushed, like the characters, to swerve from the inconclusiveness of the Medusa moments and denied the satisfaction of the partial closures usually provided in the family interchanges, the reader must look closer at the supposedly marginal characters of the novel to find a new pattern of significance. The reader then realizes that Tyler shapes an unusual nexus of characters that forces him or her to take seriously Morgan's remark that "our lives depend on total strangers. So much lacks logic, or a proper sequence." If said in a certain tone, of course, this statement *could* suggest an alienation like that of Joan Didion's characters and might reflect anomic acceptance of provisional but meaningless encounters with strangers—even intimates who feel like strangers. But alienation is not the contract offered by Tyler through such a thought. The concept of alienation depends on a firm conceptual boundary between the strange and the familiar, inside and outside; Tyler's narrative disposition of characters transgresses this boundary without eradicating it. The outsiders take over some of the usual functions of family, but their ultimate difference from family is their most significant trait. Such characters are signs of permanent hu-

man strangeness, but Tyler's work presents this strangeness as the very resource by which to prevent alienation.

Throughout her life an alienated woman, Pearl Tull, on her deathbed, reflects on the foolishness of holding herself inviolate from disruption: "It was such a relief to drift, finally. Why had she spent so long learning how? . . . She kept mislaying her place in time, but it made no difference." This drift is not a feckless passivity such as that which leads Jenny, Emily, and Charlotte into their first marriages, but an ability to open oneself to the disorder and uncertainty that strangers bring into one's life; it is the ability to be enriched by these strangers, even to be derailed by them, without trying to erase their radical difference from oneself. Narratively, this theme of disorder is registered in a tension produced by Tyler's blurring of the boundary between insiders and outsiders. In their surface organization, whether linear or flashback in manner, her novels give the impression that she is interested in tracing chronological developments of certain families; but the real movements—spiritual, emotional, even material—occur in the marginal relations of members of the family with outsiders. Eventually, the image of the family in each novel becomes an empty presence. The reader feels like a person in a canoe who, while being carried forward by the straight-running current, is also swept sideways by a strong crosswind. In the phenomenological movement of reading, the reader, like the characters, is forced to drift into supposedly contingent, incomplete relations that nevertheless prove to be the most important sources of meaning—the "real story," as a Sherwood Anderson character would say. The reader must be willing to "mislay his or her place" in the ostensible generic order of the novel. The family shape remains in some form to the end of each of these three Tyler novels, but the significant spiritual, emotional, and material movements are produced by the crosswinds of strangeness.

Thus Tyler differs from many radical contemporary writers who give us fragmentary texts in order to challenge us to find the unity beneath them. Hers is an opposite vector. She gives us the semblance of order in the overall family design of the novels, but hollows out such order from within by means of the relations of the family with strangers, thereby suggesting the inability of the family to transcend time and disorder, and the provisionality of everyone's life. Rather than the mounting feeling of inevitability to which we are accustomed in family narratives, Tyler's plots impart the feeling almost of random branching. She seems to need a minimum of three generations in her books, not to represent larger historical movements or stronger family definition, but to allow for the free play of interruption of a family's order by the unexpected people who embody the Perseus movement against the Medusa. Her plots reveal along the horizontal axis a continual questioning of the proper vertical boundary between family and not-family. The margin thus always threatens the center, even as it paradoxically also provides an escape valve that enables the family to persist, in a manner of speaking. Intriguingly, then, while Tyler would seem to be the last candidate for the ranks of the postmodernists, who are usually perceived as stylistically radical, her assault on the notion of what is a proper family makes her close in spirit to other postmodernists who regularly engage in what might be called category assassination, questioning just about every conventional distinction between one concept and another that we use to order our lives and thought.

Dinner at the Homesick Restaurant exhibits the features and principles just discussed. Family chronology seems to be respected in the linear movement of the characters' lives contained within the circle of Pearl's expiring life. Most of each chapter is told from the viewpoint of one member of the family—the first and the penultimate from Pearl's point of view and the others from the points of view of her children and her grandchild. In the final chapter the three generations are assembled at a meal to which the abandoning father has returned. Superficially, therefore, the form might seem to imply that families triumph, that we need the order they provide, that all the suffering and disappointment merely contributes to the family's growth. But the real story in *Homesick* does not confirm the family's heroism or even its lasting identity; it shows, rather, how the children have changed the signification of the family identity almost beyond recognition. The maturity of the members of the family is allied with successful disorder, a genuinely scattering movement in time. When Beck Tull left her, Pearl patterned her life on a model she had noted in her youthful diary: "Bristlecone pines, in times of stress, hoard all their life in a single streak and allow the rest to die." Pearl's child, Cody, also tries to adopt this posture, but his son, Luke, belies his success. Jenny and Ezra, in contrast, develop the capacity to drift—that is, to discard both Pearl's notions of daily order in their lives and the conceptual order of family definition. The significance of their lives develops through their turning away from agony over the Medusa points in family life toward the energizing and formative contact points with sundry persons outside the family. They allow the disorder—from the point of view of what is proper—to open new routes without necessarily abandoning the old routes entirely. They exhibit the truth of Morgan's rhetorical assertion: "Aren't we all sitting on stacks of past events? And not every level is neatly finished off, right? Sometimes a lower level bleeds into an upper level. Isn't that so?"

In *Homesick,* Ezra is the character who most fully embodies the narrative paradox of maintaining the outline of family relations while forming a mature identity through contact points outside the family. He lives his whole life at home, caring for Pearl, yet the center of his life is outside that home in the restaurant, in which at first he works for Mrs. Scarlatti and which he then inherits from her. The long intimacy between Ezra and Mrs. Scarlatti does not fit any of the usual categories. He never addresses her except as Mrs. Scarlatti,

yet he is her "significant other" in her final illness in the hospital. The nature of their interaction in the hospital shows that Tyler considers it important that peripheral but significant figures remain confirmed in their recalcitrant otherness. Ezra brings her some soup he has made, knowing that

> after he left someone would discard his soup. But this was his special gizzard soup that she had always loved. . . . He only brought the soup out of helplessness; he would have preferred to kneel by her bed and rest his head on her sheets, to take her hands in his and tell her, "Mrs. Scarlatti, come back." But she was such a no-nonsense woman; she would have looked shocked. All he could do was offer this soup. . . . He only sat, looking down at his pale, oversized hands, which lay loosely on his knees.

Mrs. Scarlatti, then, has her own rigidities, but they do not paralyze Ezra with guilt as his mother's did. In fact, even before she dies, he begins to alter her restaurant radically, changing the menu from fancy French to down-home cooking, tearing out walls, leaving the kitchen exposed to the dining room and so on. When she unexpectedly makes a sufficient temporary recovery to return home and finds what he has done, she cries: "'Oh, my God,' . . . She looked up into his eyes. Her face seemed stripped. 'You might at least have waited till I died,' she said. 'Oh!' said Ezra. 'No, you don't understand; you don't know. It wasn't what you think. It was just . . . I can't explain, I went wild somehow!'" Tyler shows here that a person's contact points with outsiders are still subject to betrayals and difficulties; differences are not erased in some blissful harmony with outsiders that cannot be attained with insiders. But the fact that relationships with outsiders occur makes the crucial difference in the characters' ability to grow and be themselves. Even though Mrs. Scarlatti is appalled at Ezra's changes, she does not revoke her decision to leave him the restaurant, and though he is grief-stricken, her death clearly releases new energies in him. He soon changes the name from "Scarlatti's" to "The Homesick Restaurant," and he thrives by arranging matters more in his own way.

Jenny, another character who, like Ezra, escapes the rigid patterns of her early life, makes her own disorderly way through three marriages. She becomes a pediatrician, exerting in her work the same strong will as her mother, but each of her marriages represents a move away from rigidity to disorder. Her final marriage is to Joe, a man whose wife has left him with six children. He says he married Jenny because he "could see she wasn't a skimpy woman. . . . Not rigid. Not constricted. Not that super-serious kind." But of course she had been more so in her younger days when she was closer to Pearl's influence. It may be implausible to us that she could run a household of nine and still not stint on a demanding career, but that seems beside the point that Tyler wishes to make. Jenny is shown to have moved through the nervous-breakdown stage into an impressive equanimity gained from learning to drift through demands upon her. She is perhaps at risk for turning everything into a joke; nevertheless, she is a compelling example of a character's ability to outgrow a destructive background. And not only does she show greater tolerance for the literal physical disorder of her new household, but in her way she accomplishes in her final marriage what Ezra accomplishes in his relationship with Mrs. Scarlatti; with her third marriage she breaks the purity of the family line decisively by blurring the boundary between who is real family and who is not. By the end, most of her immediate family is not even her own, but consists of stepchildren she has accepted the responsibility of nurturing.

Ezra and Jenny's brother, Cody, in **Homesick,** does not manage to form a flexible and freely determined personality as his siblings do. He is the classic example of the child who unwittingly replicates the very childhood condition he tries to flee. He considers Ezra his oldest enemy because Ezra was always liked more than he, and he keeps a distance from his mother and siblings most of his adult life. Yet Cody's hate is just the outer skin that hides his eternal longing to be like Ezra. For much of the book the reader feels that Cody is a villain. The reader would like to roast him over hot coals when, a Cain to Ezra's Abel, in a calculated way he woos Ezra's fiancée, Ruth, away from his lovable brother. Ruth and Ezra had seemed destined only for each other, since they are both eccentric in the same way. The defection of Ruth to Cody is an interesting example of those implausible turns in Tyler's narrative design for which a higher logic must be sought than character psychology alone would provide. It is difficult to credit that Cody, the rich city slicker, would fall in love with this barefoot country girl and even more difficult to believe that she would go with him. True, the episode does teach us something profound about the dialectics of longing, but Tyler wishes above all to use the implausibility to make a narrative argument that people will often choose strangeness over similarity for their own self-preservation. Her narrative ethos, borne out in the other novels too, seems to say that such a choice is somehow right, as if Ezra and Ruth are too much alike for their own good. Tyler does not seem to allow relationships between like and like to flourish. While Cody and Ruth's marriage is not especially happy, it is loyal, and we do not, as we expect, hear Ruth complaining later that she should have married Ezra. She seems to have known she needed something different in life from living with her soul twin. And, through Ruth, Cody is able in part to incorporate that lost part of himself—the brother whom he so wished to be like. Thus, Cody too is a character affected beneficially by disorder and strangeness.

Cody's son, Luke, is the only third-generation member of the family to have a viewpoint chapter of his own. What emerges is the likeness, much to Cody's overt disgust, between Luke

and Ezra. Cody rails at it and probably damages the boy somewhat by absurdly and jealously accusing Ruth of having had Ezra's son rather than his own. Cody feels that the resemblance is the vengeance of fate, but we see it as a kind of fortunate prevention of a too-pure family identity, for Cody has tried to seal off his own family just as Pearl had. Cody's rigidity is reflected in his profession, that of efficiency expert, doing time-and-motion studies for industry. He tells us: "Time is my favorite thing of all. . . . Time is my obsession: not to waste it, not to lose it. It's like . . . I don't know, an object to me; something you can almost take hold of. If I could just collect enough of it in one clump, I always think. If I could pass it back and forth and sideways, you know? If only Einstein were right and time were a place or river you could choose to step into at any place along the shore." This insight is the opposite of Virgie's perception about time in *The Golden Apples* or Pearl's drift. Cody dreams of killing the Medusa in one final stroke, but he is forced through Luke and Ezra to submit to time, like everyone else, as the repetition of ceaseless conflict. Cody might fight disorder, but it is always there to exert a pressure on him to be more flexible than he might otherwise be.

Running through **Homesick** like a bolt through a door hinge is a series of six family dinners he has tried to make "just like home" that Ezra plans at the restaurant. The inability of the family ever to complete a meal eventually becomes comical in spite of our sympathy for Ezra's disappointments. Yet this unfinished-dinner pattern is the book's strongest narrative emblem for Tyler's complex vision of order, disorder, and the family. Ezra is the "feeder," unlike his mother, who, Cody reflects, was a "non-feeder if there ever was one . . . neediness: she disapproved of neediness in people. Whenever there was a family argument, she most often chose to start it over dinner." Tyler never uses gender stereotypes; men can be nurturing as well as women, and women can exhibit patriarchal attitudes. Indeed, Pearl is at first the reason Ezra's dinners are never finished before someone walks out. In being stalled by someone's bitterness the dinners are emblems of the Medusa syndrome, but in going on anyhow, eventually by including more outsiders, they are also emblems of Perseus' slaying of the Medusa through the fruitful disorder of contact points. The first four breakdowns during meals occur because Pearl thinks that one character or another is insufficiently concerned about the family's integrity: Ezra's business partnership will dissolve the family; Jenny is too familiar with Ezra's eccentric friend, Josiah; Jenny does not heed her mother's opinion; Cody has "set up shop too far from home." The fifth breakdown occurs because Cody reacts jealously when his wife talks to Ezra; his jealousy often cuts his family off entirely from innocent interchanges with others. Through the failure of meals, which are usually the classic expression of family order, Tyler shows symbolically the family's inability to thrive when its ideals are hermetic.

Ezra occupies an ambiguous position in this narrative pattern, and eventually his actions prevent the total petrification of the family. No one wishes more than he that the family care about one another, and, he cries, "I wish just once we could eat a meal from start to finish." Yet he is not annihilated when things fall apart; he does not give up but placidly and resiliently keeps the institution going, even in apparent defeat. Significantly, however, in keeping the tradition going, Ezra does not follow an orthodox plan for family meals. They occur in a public place, the restaurant, where the members of the family are always in marginal relation to others, such as Mrs. Scarlatti, the kitchen crew, the friend, Josiah (whom Pearl had made unwelcome in her house), and the other customers. That is, Ezra upholds the tradition of the family meal in one way, yet he revises it, loosens its joints, forces it to articulate with outsiders who remain outsiders. Though it is true that the family never stops arguing and never finishes the meals, even its minimal survival as a unit thus "depends on total strangers" in order to keep it from being turned into stone altogether.

With the last dinner, not only has Ezra's more public sphere replaced Pearl's tightly guarded kitchen as the family meeting place, but the composition of the family has become less pure. The direct descendents among the grandchildren, Cody's Luke and Jenny's Becky, are vastly outnumbered by Joe's gaggle of children, who are technically outsiders. Beck starts to swell with grandfatherly pride when he looks around the table, but Cody says, "It's not really that way at all. . . . Don't let them mislead you. It's not the way it appears. Why, not more than two or three of these kids are even related to you. The rest are Joe's by a previous wife." Furthermore, Beck's unexpected presence conveys no sense of the missing piece that triumphantly closes the circle in an image of final reconciliation and unity. On the contrary, it is clear that he returns as a stranger and will always be a stranger, like a bird alighted on a branch, about to depart at any moment. When Joe's baby chokes on a mushroom, distracting everyone, Beck slips out before the meal is over. Ezra, beside himself at another unfinished dinner, organizes the whole party to run out in different directions to find Beck. Cody is the one to do so and brings him back after finally hearing his father's side of the story of the abandonment. There is a hint that Cody will be somewhat liberated from his constricting beliefs after receiving this information, but, if so, only because Beck makes real for Cody his father's separate existence, forces Cody to see him not as Cody's projection but as a person with his own needs and rights. Beck agrees to go back to the meal for "one last course," but says, "I warn you, I plan to leave before the dessert wine's poured." The reason he must leave is that he feels obliged to return to a woman he is dating and will marry now that Pearl is dead. The progenitor does not finally offer an image of reunion, wholeness; he too, in fact, moves in the direction of another connection peripheral to the original family. The meal is more nearly finished than any of the previous ones, but it is not finished with everyone who would symbolically confirm the intactness of the Tull family present. Thus "Homesick" in the name of the restaurant is a pun: people go there who yearn for the nurturing of home, but the restaurant stands equally as an alternative to the home which, if too much ingrown, or if conceived of as the place of a golden age, is sick. The Tull family is finally like this restaurant itself: the shell of the original still stands, but the interior has been demolished and refashioned through the beneficial agency of significant outsiders. The tones and meanings are now quite as different as Ezra's food is from French cuisine. Thus the overall narrative shape that might have signified that the family is a real sign of order and growth is so heavily qualified by the actual patterns of meaning and growth as to be voided as a narrative and thematic signifying system.

Space does not permit detailed documentation of the way *Morgan's Passing* and *Earthly Possessions* exhibit a similar narrative semiosis questioning the traditional family as a sign of order, but it is important to recognize that such narrative semiosis exists in each novel, in which plot and character patterns show meanings independent of their special content. The charming Morgan himself, a Hermes-like figure lurking at boundaries, provides a vehicle to show that energy comes from the disorderly transactions both within and between families. Just as Morgan is the character who shakes up the Merediths' lives for the better, so, in *Earthly Possessions,* Jake, the bank robber, pulls Charlotte roughly out of her trancelike life and forces her to recognize that the Medusa is not so much in her husband's domestic style as it is in her own inner, unspoken dream of perfect order for herself. She finally perceives that there is no need to unload those she had thought responsible for her unhappiness.

Tyler also has a suitably wry sense that the most disorderly characters themselves have a fascination with or craving for order. Morgan says comically as he shakes out Emily's purse,

> "Look at that! You're so orderly." Emily retrieved her belongings and put them back in her purse. Morgan watched, with his head cocked. "I too am orderly," he told her. "You are?" "Well, at least I have an interest in order. I mean order has always intrigued me. When I was a child, I thought order might come when my voice changed. Then I thought, no, maybe when I'm educated. At one point I thought I would be orderly if I could just once sleep with a woman." . . . Emily said, "Well?" "Well what?" "Did sleeping with a woman make you orderly?" "How can you ask?" he said. He sighed.

Similarly, Jake the robber detests the irregularity of his life on the lam, and his conscience causes him to head the stolen car for the home of a girl he had made pregnant. This dangerous adventure thus soon bogs down in domestic problems such as the girl's nausea and the care of the cat she has brought with her.

In *Homesick,* the narrative pattern of family dinners is symbolic of disorderly movement within an apparently fixed figure; in *Morgan,* Tyler makes the same point, that nothing in our lives can or should stay rigid, through the symbolism of both Emily's puppets and the leotards she always wears. Leon Meredith explains in a condescending manner that, whereas he can improvise in his management of the puppet shows which are their livelihood, "Emily makes them according to a fixed pattern. *They're* not improvised." Emily thinks to herself, however, "This was true, in a way, and yet it wasn't. Emily did have a homemade brown-paper pattern for the puppets' outlines, but the outlines were the least of it. What was important was the faces, the dips and hills of their own expressions, which tended to develop unexpected twists of their own no matter how closely she guided the fabric through the sewing machine."

Later, when Morgan has become her new husband and is characteristically chafing at the very disorder he brings with him, he complains,

> We don't have any chance to be alone. . . . Mother, Brindle, the baby . . . it's like a transplant. I transplanted all the mess from home. It's like some crazy practical joke." . . . "I don't mind it," Emily said. "I kind of enjoy it." "That's easy for you to say," he told her. "It's not your problem, really. You stay unencumbered no matter what, like those people who can eat and eat and not gain weight. You're still in your same wrap skirt. Same leotard." Little did he know how many replacement leotards she had had to buy over the years. Evidently, he imagined they lasted forever.

In *Earthly Possessions,* Charlotte's found trinket saying "keep on truckin'" is the symbol equivalent to the dinners of *Homesick* and Emily's puppets and leotards in *Morgan.* When she finds it, Charlotte takes it as a sign that now is the time to leave Saul. After her abduction, however, she returns to Saul with a different sense of the phrase; now the phrase suggests endurance, and the novel finishes this way: "Maybe we ought to take a trip, he says. Didn't I use to want to? But I tell him no. I don't see the need, I say. We have been traveling for years, traveled all our lives, we are traveling still. We couldn't stay in one place if we tried. Go to sleep, I say. And he does." Yet Tyler is no Hegelian of domesticity, portraying disorder merely as an antithetical way station to greater order, recapturing drift for the greater benefit of the concept of the private family. Charlotte does go back to Saul, but Jenny and Emily both rightly obtain divorces. Tyler designs narratives in which there is constant oscillation between shedding and

incorporation without any suggestion of some final resting place, either totally within the family or totally outside it.

While freedom from suffocation of family life is a favorite theme of feminist writers, Tyler's prescription about means differs notably from those writers, such as Tillie Olsen, to whom *drift* is a red-flag word signaling loss of coherent identity and personal purpose. Olsen's Eva in "Tell Me a Riddle" is a famous example of a character who evinces this sense of loss. While raising her family, Eva had to abide by the idea that "empty things float," but the story represents such drift as a tragic forfeiture of her own identity, which she can only recover bitterly as she is dying. Ruth, in Marilynne Robinson's *Housekeeping* might seem closer to Tyler, since she asserts the value of drift and sheds domestic encumbrances by choosing the equivalent of Huck Finn's "lighting out for the territory" and leaving with her eccentric Aunt Sylvie for a vagrant life on the railroad boxcars. Yet that pattern obviously perpetuates the old either-or dilemma for those stifled by family closeness. Sylvie and Ruth become pariahs. For Tyler, the negative freedom of merely shedding is undesirable. In her novels, drift signifies not only such emptiness of infinite potential, but also a movement toward a positive condition of greater fullness accomplished through commitments in exogeneous exchanges. For Tyler, drift must include the second phase of incorporation, taking into one's life, however temporarily, others who do not merge with oneself but remain different; otherwise one merely reproduces within oneself the Medusa influence of family life.

In Tyler's narratives that represent this oscillation between shedding and incorporation, metonymies of household effects are abundant. They might remind the reader of Kafka's *Metamorphosis,* but the difference from Kafka is instructive. In Kafka's story both the emptying and refilling of Gregor's room are symptoms of alienation. In *Homesick* Ezra's demolition of Scarlatti's restaurant is a sign of his rejection of Mrs. Scarlatti's dominance, a temporary alienation perhaps, but the demolition also allows for the constructive substitution of his own adult identity, which is being formed through his life outside his family. He does go nearly bankrupt at first, but when the restaurant fills up again, it does not parallel Gregor's trash-filled room, which is a sign that Gregor no longer matters. On the contrary, the crowded restaurant testifies to Ezra's significance. The same is true of the overstuffed households of Emily and Morgan and Charlotte and Saul. Both women realize there is no exit from the disorder of claims upon them by people who are technically outsiders to their own families, but it does not feel like hell to them because they have learned to respect true difference as nourishing. Tyler's stories might be seen as affirmative complements to Kafka's fable about the damaging effects on personality of a rigid family identity.

The bountiful environments portrayed in Tyler's conclusions

suggest that Updike is right to contrast Tyler with Beattie and Didion, whose "spareness" is a result of their vision of alienation. A critic who believes that alienation is still the only authentic response to the world will not like Tyler. Her work makes room for the alienated moment, but it finally makes one wonder whether the alienated attitude does not rest on a secret, stingy resentment that the world and its many people are different from oneself.

Even Tyler's physical settings underscore her rejection of alienation and her theme that disorder is a remedy for excessive family order. In each novel a building structure symbolizes the paradox that one can best be oneself if one is connected in some significant way with those in the public who are different from oneself. Charlotte's house has a room with an outside door which serves as a photography studio that is open to the public. Ezra's "homesick" restaurant similarly connotes both the public and the private life. The Merediths' apartment, into which Morgan eventually moves with Emily, is located above a public crafts shop with a common hallway. Further suggesting connectedness of the private to the public scene, Tyler's novels are emphatically urban rather than suburban. Charlotte's neighborhood changes from strictly residential to partly commercial when Amoco buys the property next door for a filling station. Ezra's is a city restaurant in Baltimore, and Morgan's people reside in Baltimore too. Morgan says, "We're city people. . . . We have our city patterns, things to keep us busy." The city is of course the place where one is maximally involved with the difference of other people in one's daily affairs.

Tyler's insistence on the public and urbane quality even of family life calls to mind the argument of an urban theorist, Richard Sennett, whose ideas seem remarkably apposite to Tyler's vision. In *The Uses of Disorder,* Sennett argues that our contemporary society, with its preference for sequestered suburban life or for the highly rationalized city of city planners, instantiates an adolescent mode of personality development in our public life. According to Sennett, adolescence is marked by a rigid drive for a "purified identity," which enables the powerless youth to mediate his self-image and his image of the outside world. Beneficial as it is at that stage, this drive is "extremely dangerous if it remains fixed in a person's life, if it meets no challenge and becomes a permanent modality. . . . It can lead to a language that similarly does away with the 'factness' of new people or new experiences . . . and assumes that one has had the meanings of experience without the threat of actively experiencing." Suburbs and rationalized cities, by restricting the number of contact points for citizens, lock our public life into such a defensive, closed-off mode that we never learn the essential lesson of adulthood, which the real city teaches us—how to live with the "unachieved situations" that the radical differences of others impose on us. Sennett says that this *"intense family life is the agent, the middleman for the infusion of adolescent fear into the social life of modern cities.* . . . It is exactly the character of intense families to diminish the diversity of contact points that have marked out a community life in the teeming cities at the turn of the century."

Whatever we might feel about certain corollary arguments in Sennett's book, which, if followed, could produce municipal anarchy, his diagnosis seems cogent, and Tyler's novels echo it. They enact thematically the growth from adolescent notions of identity to the adult willingness to live with unachieved situations of involvement with people's otherness. In her quiet way, Tyler stakes out a position against the whole existentialist nausea over "otherness" and makes it seem puerile. Emily reflects toward the end of *Morgan's Passing,* "You could draw vitality from mere objects, evidently—from these seething souvenirs of dozens of lives raced through at full throttle. Morgan's mother and sister (both in their ways annoying, demanding, querulous women) troubled her not a bit, because they weren't hers. They were too foreign to be hers. Foreign: that was the word. . . . She drew in a deep breath, as if trying to taste the difference in the air. She was fascinated by her son, who did not seem really, truly her own, though she loved him immeasurably." Tyler's typical narrative patterns mirror this theme by refusing the kind of unswerving focus on members of a family as the repository of meaning that we expect in a family novel and by spinning the plots off at tangents that are not just detours from which we return. Likewise, her endings are not merely inconclusive and ambiguous as so many modernist fictional endings are, but instead convey more aggressive images of continuing flux, of the unachieved situation, understood and welcomed as such, like that we saw in *Homesick's* final dinner, or in Morgan and Emily's improvisational spirit at the end of *Morgan,* or in Charlotte's thoughts as she returns to Saul in *Earthly Possessions.*

Tyler's emphasis on continuing flux, moreover, bears upon a serious problem with which feminist writers struggle: the difficulty of depicting feminist men and women using their knowledge in plausible ways in actual society. A careful reader can see that Tyler has to a great extent come to terms with that problem. A main ingredient, if not the essence, of the patriarchal attitude is a hypostatization of category differences—family/outsiders, for example—that makes it possible to transcend the disorderly flux of real relations among members of different classes. It might plausibly be argued that the whole notion of "proper" family is patriarchal; it was surely not the mothers who cared whether their children were bastards or whether blood relatives were treated better than outsiders. The nature of patriarchal thought, as of all ideologies, is Medusa-like in its reifications. The feminine personality has traditionally been allowed a dispensation from this way of thinking, but only at the price of being segregated from the world of significant action, which seems to require firm categories, and of being marked as amorphous—thus the fear of drift as regressive by many feminists. It seems difficult to dramatize people who are both taken seriously by society and consistently question prevailing conceptual boundaries, precisely for the reason that actual society does not take them seriously; indeed, they are marginalized as implausible, unrealistic, or irresponsible. Delightful or not, for example, Gower Morgan is probably perceived by many readers as little more than a humorous, self-indulgent stunt man and Ezra, Jenny, and Emily as memorable for their weirdness. If taken seriously as possible types of real people, they threaten the system that depends on ideological purities of various sorts. A reader who indulges in Tyler's novels for their "zaniness," however, does himself or herself a disservice. Tyler is rare in her ability to portray practical and constructive ways in which impatience with the "drive for purification" can translate into concrete, constructive action. Here these boundary-doubters are actually seen acting in a recognizable world. None of what might seem at first implausible in Tyler is really so unrealistic. It is not even so farfetched these days that one might be taken hostage, and a person who was might have gained from *Earthly Possessions* some realistic instruction, not only in the psychology of the outlaw, but in the real horizons of his or her ordinary life, which had conveniently gone unnoticed. Likewise, the implausible semifriendship that develops between Morgan's first wife and Emily, once Bonny's anger at Morgan's leaving has cooled, is not really so uncommon these days among divorced families. *Time* magazine and the U.S. Census tell us that the typical nuclear family is much in the minority now, but ideologically the model still has a grip on us. Thus Tyler's idea that a respect for the difference of "significant others" in such disorderly family structures can liberate us is valuable in a practical way.

Indeed, Tyler's narrative vision of family disorder seems to have been derived directly from her sense of her own life's problems and patterns. The fact that she is married to an Iranian is bound to have had some influence on Tyler's theme of difference. Her essay **"Still Just Writing"** shows that as a writer and mother her personal anxiety is with the problem of interruption of her work and, by extension, the threat of "disorderly" deviations from her path as a writer. She seems to have learned the coping mechanism of drift from her father rather than from her mother. She explains that whenever his schedule was interrupted, even to the extent of having to cancel a long-awaited foreign sojourn at the last minute, he just whistled Mozart and occupied himself with whatever was available to him at the time. She claims to have found that the threatening detours actually enrich her work. This equanimity, however, is not without recognition of the dangers. Clear-eyed she says, "What this takes, of course, is a sense of limitless time, but I'm getting that. My life is beginning to seem unusually long. And there's a danger to it: I could wind up as passive as a piece of wood on a wave. But I try to walk a middle line." This sense of limitless time should not be read, I think, as the classic feminine suspension above a real-

world sense of deadlines and irrevocable actions. It is more like Virgie Rainey's "beat of time." A musical beat is a concrete commitment, a movement from the virtual to the actual, just as the productive interruption in Tyler's novels is. Virgie's phrase is also a way of recognizing that our shortsighted desire for finalities is often blind to time's amplitude and to the way unexpected turns taken by the beat can make life more interesting and fulfilling.

Although she lacks his stylistic genius, Faulkner is in a way the American author to whom Tyler seems closest. He too depicted the way a "drive toward purification" could ruin personalities and the whole culture of the South. Just as he saw at the center of the ideal of white supremacy the taboo against miscegenation as the chief means of sapping the vital energy of the South, so Tyler shows that the desire for family purity leads to entropy. The social critic might respect Tyler's family novels about private existence as significant for public life. If, as Sennett says, the family is the "middleman" institution between our psychological fears and our public life, then a novelist who alters the narrative line of the family novel to open it up to the radical disorder of outside influences that are not merely contingent does her part to suggest a new possibility for our actual history. She also does her part in altering the very idea of history, which, in the guise of recording events in time, more often artificially kills time, the beat of time, through concepts, such as the family, that deny history's real randomness and disorder.

Bradley R. Bowers (essay date Winter 1988)

SOURCE: "Anne Tyler's Insiders," in *Mississippi Quarterly,* Vol. 42, No. 1, Winter, 1988, pp. 47-56.

[*In the following essay, Bowers discusses the inside knowledge that Tyler shares with the readers of her novels.*]

In her most successful novel, *Dinner at the Homesick Restaurant,* Anne Tyler's central character, Pearl, reacts to her husband Beck's abrupt announcement that he "didn't want to stay married":

> "I don't understand you," she said. There ought to be a whole separate language, she thought, for words that are truer than other words—for perfect, absolute truth.

Tyler does not create the language of pure truth, but she succeeds in pushing through the limitations of traditional narrative by collusion with the reader, in essence, by sharing a joke. She allows the reader to share inside knowledge, not only family secrets but self-delusions, true motives, quirks of perception. When Pearl reckons with Beck's leaving and debates how to tell the children, the reader is let in on the plotting:

> She planned how she would do it: she would gather them around her on the sofa, in the lamplight, some evening after supper. "Children. Dear ones," she would say. "There's something you should know."

Even before she echoes the chapter title in her final words, the reader knows much more of the truth in Pearl's thoughts than she herself. She has not been able—for four years—to tell the children that their father has abandoned them. She tries to carry out her plan but the children are discussing Cody's plans to work during college:

> "It's about your father," Pearl said.
>
> Jenny said, "I'd choose the cafeteria."
>
> "You know, my darlings," Pearl told them, "how I always say your father's away on business."
>
> "But off-campus they might pay more," said Cody, "and every penny counts. . . ."
>
> "There's something I want to explain about your father," Pearl told them.
>
> "Choose the cafeteria," Ezra said.
>
> "Children?"
>
> "The cafeteria," they said.
>
> And all three gazed at her coolly, out of gray, unblinking, level eyes exactly like her own.

Only the reader shares the knowledge of Pearl's plight and her failure to connect with her children. By creating this conspiracy, Tyler shares a laugh at the expense of her characters. We become "insiders" who understand the implication of a particular phrase, who watch the characters verbally run toward each other with loving and open arms, sometimes connecting but all too often running past. In *The Accidental Tourist,* Tyler describes the deteriorating marriage of Macon and Sarah Leary with that comic image: "They were like people who run to meet, holding out their arms, but their aim is wrong; they pass each other and keep running." Thus her characters, usually family members, usually Southern, are intimately portrayed but examined at a distance, a comic distance so that we might laugh along with the author. But she creates a unique kind of perspective, one which includes not only certain family members but the narrator and the reader as well, all of whom form the group of insiders; the obvious outsiders are those family members whose "aim is wrong,"

who pass closely by but fail to understand the true meanings, the inside jokes.

One technique of Tyler's is to use language to create nonce forms which hold meaning for insiders, and only for insiders; we share a knowledge derived entirely from the context of the family and share with them a point of contact. In addition, Tyler repeatedly reveals missed connections, verbal interchanges which seem to some readers to be unrealistic, but which the insider—character or reader—understands to be a connection that *should* have been made, but is not because of the uncareful aim of the people involved. Tyler therefore creates an extended family; she seems to approach her "children"—characters and readers—in much the same manner as her own offspring: "Who else in the world do you *have* to love, no matter what? Who else can you absolutely not give up on?" She lets the reader share a sort of parental knowledge, her characters all considered her offspring who attempt to communicate, who run lovingly toward each other's arms, failing to connect while we watch through Tyler's "mist of irony."

Tyler's characters are forced to deal with each other within their family structure, much like the characters who populate Eudora Welty's families, an influence Tyler readily acknowledges. In Tyler's earlier *Searching for Caleb,* the Peck family's unifying force evolves out of the search for the lost member. In a typical Welty story, such as when Sister leaves home to live at the P.O., the family tie is severed. But Tyler's characters try to preserve the family unit at all cost. This forced situation allows Tyler to focus on her characters' intentions, often hidden in their speech; it allows her characters to reveal themselves to the reader, while not necessarily doing the same with each other. When a character articulates his true feelings, we see how he fits his perception of the world around him into the structure he must live in, his family. The words he forms reflect those patterns. A phrase may intimate a knowledge of a situation, defined for those "on the inside," spoken as if a code: "This Really Happened," a chapter title in *Dinner at the Homesick Restaurant,* is also the signal shared by the narrator, the reader, and in this case, Luke, Cody's son, when Cody begins describing an episode in his life as Pearl's child:

> "Let me give you an example," he said. "Listen now. This really happened." That was the way he always introduced his childhood. "This really happened," he would say, as if it were unthinkable, beyond belief, but then what followed never seemed so terrible to Luke.

Tyler's creation of a nonce phrase creates in turn an inside joke. Often it works simply as an indication of a shared misperception, having only one possible meaning to a certain group of people in a certain and unique situation. The technique is not uncommon to modern writers, but few handle it as conspiratorially as Tyler. John Irving provides an archetype of the method in *The World According to Garp.* T.S. Garp's children are warned repeatedly, during summers at the beach, to watch for the dangerous undertow, which, over the blur of the pounding waves, becomes "the dangerous Undertoad." The misperception evolves into a family joke. But in Tyler's work, these nonce phrases become inside jokes, signalling the reader as well as the character to look beyond the surface of a situation, to interpret it as a person with shared knowledge of all that the phrase brings to bear on the situation and the character involved. Tyler acknowledges the value of making these connections, of having shared, secret knowledge, even in her first novel, *If Morning Ever Comes.* Shelley Jane Domer and Ben Joe Hawkes go beyond mere language; Shelley's "sudden outspokenness, like her secret fantasy about Ben Joe . . . serves to isolate her from those around her, to shock her family, and to give her at once both a secret power and knowledge." The "power" is that of communication, of making connections with other insiders.

In her early works, the intent is not always comic, but more to suggest meaning or innuendo. Tyler shares a technique that Welty often uses to signal her readers. Because it is "A Worn Path," both the persistence and the perceptions of Phoenix are interpreted in light of that knowledge, despite her outward appearance of confusion.

The third chapter title in *Homesick Restaurant,* "Destroyed by Love," rings with the melancholy and melodrama of a country song title, and the joke it creates for the reader is the same shared by listeners of those ballads of lost love. When Jenny asks if she should marry Harley Gaines, Mrs. Parker, the palm reader, remains an outsider, "scrutinizing Jenny's hand" and telling her "If you don't, see . . . you'll run into a lot of heartbreak. Lot of trouble in your romantic life. . . . What I mean to say . . . if you don't go and get married, you'll be destroyed by love." Jenny reacts only with "Oh," undercutting the gravity of the jaded pronouncement, suggesting at that point the same observation made later that—had she been an insider like the rest of us—Mrs. Parker would have "guessed from the very first instant, from the briefest, most cursory glance, that Jenny was not capable of being destroyed by love." We understand what the palm reader could not. Judging her from appearances, she saw Jenny as the typical victim of circumstance, not knowing she was Pearl Tull's daughter, not knowing she was governed by the same resiliency and single-mindedness.

Flannery O'Connor cites the aphorism "A Good Man is Hard to Find" and plays upon the phrase in the grandmother's confrontation with the Misfit:

> "I just know you're a good man," she said desperately. "You're not a bit common!"

> "Nome, I ain't a good man," The Misfit said after a second as if he had considered her statement carefully, "but I ain't the worst in the world neither."

The Misfit interprets her statement literally, as a joke among his boys, Hiram and Bobby Lee, and himself, perhaps with Bailey Boy (were he still alive), certainly with the reader, but certainly *not* the grandmother. Luke, Jenny, The Misfit—and the reader—share an inside perspective, a knowledge which runs deeper than outside appearances or what might naively be expected. O'Connor's Grandmother always has been, always will be an outsider, unless, of course, "if it had been somebody there to shoot her every minute of her life."

But occasionally, for the reader, the outward appearance appears implausible when tempered by the inside perspective. Tyler's second technique, rather than making the inside connection, leaves the expectation of fulfillment unresolved. John Updike notes that Tyler "is sometimes charged with the basic literary sin of implausibility," but he defends "the delayed illuminations that prick out her tableaux." Others may have supposed that she *wanted* to fulfill the reader's expectations along with the character's, neither of which she does consistently. Mary F. Robertson dubs these disruptions "Medusa points":

> . . . such failures of communication . . . are best not read as individuals' character problems but as a narrative pattern drawn by Tyler to make a point about family relations in general. These points in the narrative assume a significance that stands apart from their particular content. Through them Tyler shows that situations calling for responses considered proper in certain spousal and filial roles petrify people. . . .

In *The Accidental Tourist,* Tyler remarks directly on the idea, describing the progress toward divorce by Macon and Sarah as "those months when anything either of them said was wrong, toward that sense of narrowly missed connections." And in *Homesick Restaurant,* when Ezra is afraid to make a small gesture to comfort a child, he laments that "he had missed an opportunity, something that would never come again." Welty's influence perhaps extends beyond Tyler to her critics, as Robertson's explanation reflects the dominant image of Welty's "Petrified Man," a story which deals more brutally with missed connections among family members. But the characters of Tyler's families are distinctly unlike Welty's Mrs. Fletcher, who says her husband "can't do a thing with me" because "he knows good and well I'll have one of my sick headaches, and then I'm just not fit to live with." Tyler's readers get the feeling, as Welty's Leota would say, that the characters are not "funny-haha" as much as they are "funny-peculiar."

The wry observer, armed with the secret knowledge, may notice that, as Robertson points out, "a certain pattern obtains in the dialogues and interchanges" of the family. Updike calls it the "daily communication that masks silence." Those on the inside, actually those who *should* be on the inside, repeatedly fail to connect; thus, the reader becomes privy to deeper insight and more of the near-misses than even the rest of the family. These episodes are tragedy to the characters' lives but create a series of comic exchanges accessible—for the most part—only by the reader, with an implied smile and knowing look from Tyler.

The comic effect is subdued in Tyler's earlier novels, perhaps indicating that her confidence in later works grew to create more brutal, more slapstick characterizations. In the relatively early *Earthly Possessions,* she introduces the idea of an insider who shares knowledge directly with the reader (this novel is Tyler's first to be told from a single, first-person point of view). Charlotte Emory is attuned to "God's little jokes" and holds foremost among them her home life with two unfeeling parents: "Horrible things . . . happened at our house that would have been very embarrassing if witnessed by an outsider." Charlotte speaks of the two overriding concerns of her childhood in terms which are stoic and ironic, but most of all funny:

> One was that I was not their [her parents'] true daughter, and would be sent away. The other was that I *was* their true daughter and would never, ever manage to escape to the outside world.

In her subsequent novel, *Morgan's Passing,* Tyler brings the missed connection more concretely into play for comic purposes. Gower Morgan, though a compulsive impersonator, nonetheless fails to deal with his wife, Bonny, when the truth of their lives intrudes. Bonny asks his advice regarding their daughter Amy's impending marriage:

> "Morgan, in this day and age, do you believe the bride's mother would still give the bride a little talk?"
>
> "Hmm?"
>
> "What I want to know is, am I expected to give Amy a talk about sex or am I not?"
>
> "Bonny, do you have to call it sex?"
>
> "What else would I call it?"
>
> "Well . . ."
>
> "I mean, sex is what it is, isn't it?"
>
> "Yes, but, I don't know . . ."

> "I mean, what would you say? Is it sex, or isn't it?"
>
> "Bonny, will you just stop *hammering* at me?"

The next novel, *Homesick Restaurant,* develops this comedy furthest, among and between every family member. Ezra pushes hardest to connect. He and his mother, Pearl, debate whether Jenny has separated from her husband, Harley, though she still wears a wedding ring, perhaps to fool the family. Ezra argues the side of honesty:

> "She wouldn't wear a ring if she and Harley were separated, would she?"
>
> "She would if she wanted to fool us."
>
> "Well, I don't know, if she wants to fool us maybe we ought to *act* fooled. I don't know."
>
> "All my life," his mother said, "people have been trying to shut me out. Even my children. Especially my children. If I so much as ask that girl how she's been, she shies away like I'd inquired into the deepest, darkest part of her. Now, why should she be so standoffish?"
>
> Ezra said, "Maybe she cares more about what *you* think than what outsiders think."

Though the reader unfamiliar with Tyler's style may anticipate a resolution, a connection of two family members, or a reconciliation of all three, Tyler again introduces the comic incongruity of Pearl's response to Ezra's dilemma:

> "I'm worried if I come too close, they'll say I'm overstepping. They'll say I'm pushy, or . . . emotional, you know. But if I back off, they might think I don't care. I really, honestly believe I missed some rule that everyone else takes for granted: I must have been absent from school that day. There's this narrow little dividing line I somehow never located."
>
> "Nonsense; I don't know what you're talking about," said his mother, and then she held up an egg. "Will you look at this? Out of one dozen eggs, four are cracked. Two are *smushed.*"

Tyler's work has developed, as Doris Betts points out, toward "experimenting with intense individual portraits, almost to the point of caricature." This focus on characterization means that her writing cannot "become Faulkner's historical South" because among other things "there are subjects she passes over with minimal treatment—sex and philosophy." But this is not so much a shortcoming as a constraint adhered to by Tyler herself. The further distinction might be drawn between the humor of Welty, Faulkner, and earlier male Southern writers, and that of modern Southern writers such as Tyler, so much now a feminine trade. As early as 1935, John Wade pointed out in his attempt to define "Southern" humor that "we cannot laugh ever again with a free heart at physical deformity or at madness as people—and very good people, too—did everywhere until very recently." As suggested earlier, Tyler treats everyone—character and reader alike—as family, as those who have been "born into situations," into the human situation, not by choice but as victims, each an "accidental tourist" on the planet. Her humor, while perhaps at the expense of her characters, is not at the expense of their essential humanness, their "good intentions." Brutal humor gives way to (supposedly) less brutal attacks by innuendo; the mode of interaction is familial humor, which provides a connection among even disparate family members, vicious though it may be, as Wade suggests in his account of rules for a family dinner, Southern-style, beginning with the "fundamental admonition—keep, oh, whatever you do keep the occasion moving—a conversation that man-carrying Uncle Jack and Proust-teaching Cousin Julius will both think pointed, that knit-bed-spread-knitter Aunt Susan can endure without fainting, that Rabelaisian Uncle Rob can endure without nodding." The answer is humor, not brutal in the sense of Tyler's predecessors in Southern humor, but less overtly brutal attacks by innuendo:

> Slash in where you can, echoing that word of Aunt Susie's, giving it an emphasis that she did not mean to give it, making her disclose more than she meant to, covering her with confusion, while the table roars.

Tyler, of course, adopts this idea of the family dinner as a dominant motif in *Homesick Restaurant,* creating a recurrent point of tension for the characters, loving and hating, consoling and destroying each other over dinner. At the final dinner, when the abandoning father, Beck, returns for Pearl's funeral, her "last supper" becomes instead a battle royal of a Southern family gathering, beginning when Beck gushingly observes that "it looks like this is one of those great big, jolly, noisy, rambling. . .why, *families!*" Beck is making what Tyler calls in her own life "deliberate conversation," the product of people brought together ostensibly by mutual care and interest and thus forced to articulate, or fail to articulate, their perceptions of the situation. And Beck fails to connect. His opportunity was missed long ago, and his late attempt to connect with family members only labels him the outsider that he has always been.

Humor, in a novel or across a dinner table, ultimately brings together and bonds those on the "inside" into a fraternity of humanness, beyond family lines, and creates a family of "insiders" who share a perspective, an ability to laugh and acknowledge that they are all a bit "funny and strange." The reader of Tyler's novels is an insider, more so than Beck or

even Cody, able to share the uneasiness of the dinner-table tension, able to imagine, even wish to speak to the rest of the family, to initiate a story about Pearl which might "disclose more than she meant to," to help make the sadly missed connections.

Tyler treats the same subject matter as Southern writers have often before: when Faulkner's idiot Snopes in *The Hamlet* falls in love with a cow, the cow is romantically idealized through the author's language very much as the "country cook" Ruth—"a weasel-faced little redhead"—is idealized in the eyes and mind of Cody Tull. But where Faulkner brutally examines a male's manifestation of desire, Tyler addresses the same desire by focusing on Cody above the belt rather than below. Seated at the dinner table, her characters must in all respects become more genteel in their interactions: indiscretions, lapses of conformity, missed connections of the past must all be treated with at least a forced smile to make them palatable. Tyler portrays the same minor and major aberrations that earlier writers, largely male, were allowed to portray by conventions of the time. And by making the tragic action now fit into words, especially words over dinner, she forces onto the situation an incongruity. Her characters have been "born into situations"; now their thoughts, feelings, and desires must be "born into words." When they connect, we share the joke; when they do not, we share the joke only with the other insiders. Tyler allows the reader to pull up to the table, as knowledgeable as any family member about the true goings-on, to take part in the ritual, to laugh at her family, her fellow human beings and their "funny and strange" behavior, and to do it, importantly, as an insider. She allows the reader to connect where her characters do not, and to connect with her as she shares her—our—family secrets. She has said that she writes because she wants "more than one life." Perhaps the complexity she confronted as she emerged from an experimental Quaker commune at age eleven "into the outside world" lets her favor so much the insider. Perhaps Tyler found great comfort and humor in becoming an insider, and found that sharing her perception of the world answers the question of what makes life worth living, or in Tyler's case, what might make life so much worth living that she wishes for many more.

Paula Gallant Eckard (essay date Spring 1990)

SOURCE: "Family and Community in Anne Tyler's *Dinner at the Homesick Restaurant,*" in *The Southern Literary Journal,* Vol. XXII, No. 2, Spring, 1990, pp. 33-44.

[*In the following essay, Eckard compares Tyler's* Dinner at the Homesick Restaurant *to William Faulkner's* As I Lay Dying *and Carson McCullers's* The Ballad of the Sad Cafe.]

At eighty-five, Pearl Tull is blind and dying. She drifts through dreams and recollections, sliding back and forth through time as she remembers the grandfather who smelled like moth-balls, the aunts scented with pomade and lavender water. Pearl even recalls her cousin Bertha, who carried a bottle of crystals to ward off fainting spells. But most of all, Pearl remembers her children. She recalls Cody, her eldest, as always being a troublemaker, a "difficult baby." Ezra, her second child, was "so sweet and clumsy it could break your heart." And Jenny, "the girl," in Pearl's mind was a kind of luxury. Also, Pearl realizes that she was "an angry sort of mother." Deserted by her husband, Pearl had always felt "continually on edge . . . too burdened . . . too alone" in raising her children. She considered her children to be inept in handling everyday concerns, and she regarded their incompetence with indulgent scorn. Even now on her deathbed she calls them "duckers and dodgers." However, as the dying Pearl slips in and out of consciousness, she dreams of her three young children at the beach, laughing and running towards her across sunlit sand. The pain and anger of their troubled relationships are all but forgotten.

Pearl's recollections in Anne Tyler's *Dinner at the Homesick Restaurant* mirror the ambivalence of feeling that comes with the birth of children and follows a mother even unto death. They suggest emotions common to many women as they grapple with maternal roles and struggle to give their children earnest measures of love and acceptance. However, Pearl's recollections represent just one perspective, a singular look at a fragmented and troubled family. In *Dinner at the Homesick Restaurant,* Tyler examines many facets of family relationships, particularly as they evolve between mother and child, fester between siblings, and extend into the world beyond. In life, as in Tyler's novel, the family is the base from which the individual moves into society and acquires a sense of community. The community serves in turn as an enlarged version of the family, a larger arena for each person to act out the same conflicts, struggles, hopes, and dreams as he did in his family of origin. However troubled and strained relationships may be, family and community represent "home," and, for better or worse, the individual must come to terms with this. In Tyler's novel these things are no less true. Depicting the dynamics of the Tull family with a shrewd and keen insight, Tyler carefully explores its members' connections to the past, to the community, and with each other.

In creating the eccentric Tulls, Tyler establishes her own connections while writing out of a literary tradition that leaves few Southern writers unaffected. In particular, *Dinner at the Homesick Restaurant* shares marked similarities in the portrayal of family and community with William Faulkner's *As I Lay Dying* and, to a lesser extent, Carson McCullers' *The Ballad of the Sad Cafe. As I Lay Dying* opens with the impending death of Addie Bundren and incorporates several points of view into the telling of the story. Chapters of the novel are told by Addie, her children, her husband, and members of the community, as they recount their relationships with her. While Addie's family embarks on a funeral journey of grotesque proportions, each member also travels on a disquieting inner journey, one that reveals the utter loneliness at the heart of the Bundren family.

Similarly, *Dinner at the Homesick Restaurant* opens at the bedside of the dying Pearl Tull as she recalls her memories as a young wife and mother. Succeeding chapters are told from different points of view as Pearl's children explore their troubled relationships with their mother and with each other. Years before, Pearl and her children had been abandoned by her husband, Beck Tull. This event had plunged the family into a quiet, swirling darkness that was frequently punctuated by hatred and violence. In journeying through their shared pasts and individual psyches, Cody, Ezra, and Jenny Tull struggle to "understand their father's desertion, their mother's love and anger, and their own responsibility for themselves." In their doing so, past and present alternate throughout the book as the characters search for an understanding of these events and relationships. Like the Bundrens, the Tull family also experiences isolation and alienation from within, producing conditions which Tyler subjects to careful scrutiny, painful exploration, and, finally, a cautious resolution.

While such commonalities in plot and structure can be found in *As I Lay Dying* and *Dinner at the Homesick Restaurant,* characterization provides the richest material for examining family dynamics. As dying matriarchs, Addie Bundren and Pearl Tull are much alike. From her deathbed Addie watches Cash build her coffin. Aware of her wasted potential and her seething ambivalence as a mother, Addie seems to die willfully at a rather young age. In a similar manner, Pearl helps Ezra plan the guest list for her funeral, noting with detached dismay that most of her friends are already dead. Like Addie, Pearl knows that her relationships with her children are far from satisfactory; however, she dutifully holds onto life until age eighty-five. Once as a young mother, Pearl almost died from a penicillin reaction, but to her that was "nonsense." Unlike Addie, Pearl "wouldn't have died; she had children"; and according to Pearl, "When you have children, you're obligated to live."

Pearl's sense of responsibility toward her children is indeed the main theme of her life. All of her life she has suffered a kind of maternal angst in her duty towards them. Although she never trusted others to care for her children, Pearl worried about her ability to single-handedly carry out her maternal obligations. For so long, Pearl felt like the "only one, the sole support, the lone tall tree in the pasture just waiting for lightning to strike." And now that she is dying, Pearl tells Jenny, "You should have got an extra," a "second-string mother" to take over, much as Pearl had "started extra children" after Cody had fallen seriously ill as an infant. What would she have had left if Cody had died, Pearl had wondered. To relieve this anxiety, she had Ezra and Jenny, but ended up feeling "more endangered than ever." Pearl then had to worry about the potential loss of three children and not just one.

Addie Bundren does not possess the same maternal angst and sense of responsibility towards her children as does Pearl towards hers. Addie is described as "not a true mother," and, indeed, she seems only to be going through the motions of motherhood. Addie is archetypally aligned with the darker aspects of the female principle. She regards motherhood with an almost vicious intensity, seeing thematic connections between sin, birth, and death. In regard to begetting her children, Addie speaks of lying beside Anse Bundren in the dark, hearing "the dark land talking of God's love and His beauty and His sin." In regard to bearing her children she speaks of "the terrible blood, the red bitter flood boiling through the land." To Addie her children were "of the wild blood boiling along the earth, of me and of all that lived, of none and of all." Through these words Addie establishes almost mythic connections to motherhood, reflecting a universality of experience shared by the female collective unconscious. However, Addie's view is a perversion of the procreative experience. After the bearing of her children, Addie felt her aloneness "violated over and over each day."

While Pearl Tull's "extra children" are conceived out of a gripping maternal angst and fear of loss, Addie's are conceived and born out of a cold, detached rage. She dispassionately and cryptically tells how she "gave Anse Dewey Dell to negative Jewel" and how she "gave him Vardaman to *replace* the child I had robbed him of." As Addie interprets it, to give birth is to die. With the bearing of her children, Addie finally perceives the ironic truth in her father's belief "that the reason for living is getting ready to stay dead." After the birth of Vardaman, her youngest child, Addie says she then "could get ready to die." With motherhood Addie indeed experiences a symbolic death, one which culminates much later in her physical death. In the intervening years, she professes to love Cash and Jewel, but Addie rejects her other children with a harsh and violent cruelty.

Although she is not cast with the same vigor, Pearl Tull shares many of Addie's Terrible Mother characteristics. Pearl favors Ezra over Cody and Jenny, but all three children suffer her anger and rage. Pearl admits that she was not a "tranquil woman" and that often she "lost her temper, snapped, slapped the nearest cheek, said things she later regretted." She perceives herself as a mother as "difficult," that she sometimes carried on "like a shrew." Pearl believed that in struggling to raise three children alone she acted out of helplessness and fear, overwhelmed by the responsibilities of motherhood. For as she once told Cody, "How scary it is to know that everyone I love depends on me! I'm afraid I'll do something

wrong." However, the perceptions of Pearl's children are not so forgiving. Cody recalls how as a child, he saw Pearl for what she was *not*. He wanted a mother who "acted like other mothers," who talked on the telephone and gossiped in the kitchen with other women. He wanted her to have "some outside connection, something beyond that suffocating house." Ezra, on the other hand, "trusted his mother to be everything for him." Once when Pearl cut her finger with a paring knife, he felt "defenseless" and "defeated by her incompetence." Ezra found himself asking, "How could he depend on such a person? Why had she let him down so?" In contrast, Jenny perceived her mother as something dangerous and unpredictable, something more in keeping with Addie Bundren's persona. To Jenny, Pearl was a shrieking witch whose "pale hair could crackle electrically from its bun" and whose "eyes could get small as hatpins." More than once Pearl had slammed Jenny against a wall and called her "serpent," "cockroach," and "hideous little sniveling guttersnipe." Also, Jenny is given to dreams about her mother, including one in which Pearl, with an "informative and considerate tone of voice," revealed that "she was raising Jenny to eat her."

Besides these disturbing maternal similarities, Addie and Pearl have other aspects of life in common, tamer and more mundane perhaps, but significant in what they reveal about family and community. Addie and Pearl both had been "orphaned" spinsters with no immediate family. While Addie's family lay buried in the Jefferson cemetery, Pearl's consisted of a loosely-knit conglomeration of aunts, uncles, and cousins with whom she eventually lost touch. Relatively late in life, both women had married men somewhat beneath themselves. Addie married farmer Anse Bundren, while Pearl married Beck Tull, a farm equipment salesman. Pearl's married name, Tull, is suggestive of Addie's neighbor, Cora Tull. Marriage for both Addie and Pearl was an escape from spinsterhood and from bleak futures in tiresome jobs. As a rural school teacher Addie loathed her students, looking forward to the times when they "faulted" so she could whip them. Addie's anger and hatred was also inner-directed, making the whippings a kind of self-flagellation that enjoined her flesh with theirs. With each blow of the switch Addie could feel "it upon [her] flesh," and when their flesh "welted and ridged it was [her] blood that ran." She would think, "Now you are aware of me!" Perhaps to escape from her own raging desperation, Addie tells how she then "took" Anse, a simple man with "a little property" and "a good honest name." However, her life with Anse was equally dismal, and after the birth of Cash she found "that the living was terrible." For Addie, marriage and motherhood initiated a slow, downward spiral to death.

Pearl's marriage at age thirty to Beck Tull represented a welcomed release from an inevitable future as an "orphaned spinster niece" tying up her uncle's spare bedroom. She had scorned a college education for fear it would be an admission of defeat, and before following her Uncle Seward's suggestion about a secretarial course, Pearl met Beck Tull. He courted her with chocolates and flowers and told her what a "cultured and refined little lady" she was. However, marriage for Pearl also proved to be a disappointment. After they were married, Pearl and Beck set off on a series of moves that took her away from what family she had. In each new community Pearl kept to herself. She "didn't hold with depending," and once, rather than leave her children with neighbors so she could seek help for a broken arm, Pearl waited nearly two days for Beck to return from a business trip.

After Beck Tull's eventual desertion, Pearl staunchly carried on as if nothing had happened. She took a job at Sweeney's grocery but acted cool and crisp towards any neighbors who dropped in to shop. In her Baltimore neighborhood she was thought to be "unfriendly, even spooky—the witch of Calvert Street." Unperturbed by her neighbors' speculations and criticisms, Pearl remained aloof and detached from her community in much the same way that Addie held herself apart from Cora Tull and her other Mississippi neighbors. Pearl simply wanted to get on with the practical, everyday things that mattered, such as caulking the windows and weatherstripping the doors. By keeping the house maintained and repaired Pearl could more confidently hold her own world together. With tools she felt like "her true self, capable and strong," perhaps much like the dull and steady Cash Bundren with his saw and adze.

Despite the difficulties that marriage and motherhood brought, Pearl Tull didn't give up. Unlike Addie, she continued to plod steadily through life with a blind and numb tenacity, experiencing an occasional, poignant awareness about her children and life itself. Unable to hold back time, Pearl equated her children's growing up with the "gradual dimming of light at her bedroom door, as if they took some radiance with them as they moved away from her." In her later years, with a growing preoccupation with death, Pearl realized that with dying "you don't get to see how it all turns out" and "questions you have asked will go forever unanswered." As a result, she was left wondering, "Will this one of my children settle down? Will that one learn to be happier? Will I ever discover what was meant by such-and-such?"

In certain respects, Pearl's sensibilities are similar to Addie Bundren's, only gentler and more embracing of life and motherhood. With a restless longing, Addie recalls the early spring with "the wild geese going north and their honking coming faint and high and wild out of the wild darkness." In a similar manner, Pearl listens as traffic sounds of "horns and bells and rags of music" mingle with her memories of "the feel of wind on summer nights—how it billows through the house and wafts the curtains and smells of tar and roses." In her reverie, Pearl remembers the wondrous feeling of "how a sleeping baby weighs so heavily on your shoulder, like ripe fruit." She recalls the delicious privacy of walking in the rain "beneath the drip and crackle of your own umbrella." Pearl's words reveal a quiet, buoying affirmation of life. In contrast to the nihilistic Addie who angrily rejects life and motherhood, Pearl accepts the totality of pain, disappointment, and joy that love and family often bring. For better or worse, she bears these things dutifully and simply carries on. Pearl is no martyr, but neither is she consumed with anger or bitterness. In her dying reveries she takes a final, matter-of-fact look backwards at children, husband, and family and then brings a not unhappy closure on her life. Having done this, Pearl no longer feels obligated to live.

While parallels can be drawn between Addie Bundren and Pearl Tull, similarities extend into their families as well. In both novels, the children must deal with the familial upheaval created by a dying mother, and to some extent they must come to terms with themselves and each other. Noteworthy similarities between Addie's and Pearl's children evolve in this process and cannot go unmentioned. In characterization, Jenny Tull is a modern inversion of Addie's daughter, Dewey Dell, who is a not-so-bright, fecund Earth Mother. Dewey Dell is in her actions the real mother in *As I Lay Dying,* as she displays a caring, nurturing love towards Vardaman and tirelessly fans Addie on her deathbed. Her name is suggestive of nature and the earth with its moist, rich female fertility. Dewey Dell appears to be a sexually-duped country girl, while Jenny Tull on the other hand is intelligent and well-educated. Jenny is not fertile in the traditional sense, as she has only one child of her own. However, from her third marriage Jenny acquires six step-children who have been deserted by their natural mother. She generously mothers them all, much as Dewey Dell kind-heartedly treats her younger brother, Vardaman. With grace and ease, Jenny raises her step-children without the torment and ambivalence that she experienced at the hands of her own mother. Jenny is also a pediatrician, a fact that enhances this contemporary Earth Mother image. She good-naturedly endures the "scrapes and bruises that [she] gathered daily in her raucous games with her patients." In her role as a physician, Jenny is a kind of surrogate parent who conscientiously labors for the well-being of her community. Unlike her mother, she is much involved with the concerns of other people. Whether in caring for her patients or her step-children, Jenny has an acute sense of family and community which underlies her actions.

However, neither Jenny nor Dewey Dell is wholly cast in the image of the Good Mother; paradoxes exist within both. After all, Dewey Dell has embarked on the funeral journey not so much to bury Addie but rather in hopes of finding an abortifacient to end her unwanted pregnancy. She shares many of Addie's Terrible Mother characteristics. Like Addie, Dewey Dell also feels the pull of the earth's darkness, stating that the earth "lies dead and warm upon me, touching me naked through my clothes." Dewey Dell also describes how she feels like "a wet seed wild in the hot blind earth." These dark, negative images foreshadow the vehemence which she later turns on Darl after he burns Gillespie's barn. When Darl's arrest is imminent, Dewey Dell jumps on him "like a wild cat. . . . scratching and clawing," her rejection and hatred of Darl paralleling Addie's.

Jenny Tull contains a similar propensity for love and violence, one which emerges early in her relationship with her daughter Becky. As a single mother and struggling intern, Jenny was often irritable and overwhelmed. Once she "hauled off and slapped [Becky] hard across the mouth, then shook her till her head lolled"; and at another time Jenny "slammed Becky's face into her Peter Rabbit dinner plate and gave her a bloody nose." After these events occur, Jenny recalls childhood memories of "her mother's blows and slaps and curses, her mother's pointed fingernails digging into Jenny's arm." Jenny realizes she is reenacting her mother's pattern of violence, and through a total, desperate collapse, she is able to end it. Ironically, it is Pearl who cares for Jenny and Becky during Jenny's breakdown and puts their "world in order again." Pearl reads to Becky and takes her to the playground. She "smoothed clean sheets on Jenny's bed, brought her tea and bracing broths, shampooed her hair, placed flowers on her bureau." Through Pearl's renurturance, Jenny breaks this cycle of destructive ambivalence and is able to love her daughter again without any violence threatening their relationship. At the same time, Pearl herself is redeemed. Jenny goes on to love other people's children as her own, something she exhibits in her work as a pediatrician and with her six, very needful step-children. Thus she transcends the violence she suffered as a child and conquers the same frightening tendencies within herself. In Jenny's character Tyler deals most deftly with the archetypal aspects of both the Good Mother and the Terrible Mother, and in doing so she creates a very real and human mother.

Parallels also can be found in the characters of Cody Tull and Darl Bundren. Compared to their siblings, Cody and Darl have the most difficulty resolving troubling conflicts with their families. Cody bears a hostile resentment towards his brother Ezra in much the same manner that Darl resents Jewel. Ezra is Pearl's favorite child much as Jewel is Addie's, and neither Cody nor Darl can accept a secondary position in his mother's affection. As a result, Cody lashes out at Ezra with much the same anger that Darl directs towards Jewel. As children, Cody teased Ezra, tormented him, and falsely implicated him in "crimes" not of his doing. As adults, Cody still grudgingly blames Ezra for the pain in his life, and he half-consciously seeks revenge.

Structurally, *Dinner at the Homesick Restaurant* and *As I Lay Dying* belong mostly to Cody and Darl. This is evident by the number of chapters Cody and Darl have in proportion to other characters in the two novels. With nineteen chapters, Darl claims at least thirty percent of the novel's fifty-nine

chapters. The remaining forty chapters are divided among fourteen other characters. Similarly, Tyler devotes four out of ten chapters, forty percent, to Cody's point of view. Pearl, Ezra, and Jenny receive two chapters each. Even with multiple points of view, these numbers suggest that Tyler and Faulkner are speaking through the characters of Cody and Darl and that the true consciousness of each of the novels lies in these characters. Indeed, Cody and Darl are the ones most affected by the events in the novels. Darl's exposition of truth throughout the course of his narratives leads to a slow but total disintegration of self by the end of the novel. Warped and twisted by his mother's rejection, Darl tumbles down a fragmentary spiral into a state of madness and final alienation. Cody Tull has been similarly hurt by his mother's rejection and his father's abandonment. However, despite his confusion, anger, and jealousy, Cody experiences a growth towards light and not madness. At Pearl's funeral supper, through an epiphany of sorts, Cody comes to understand and accept the hurt, the anger, and the injuries of the past. Through his actions, Cody is redeemed, his father is forgiven, and his mother is remembered for the goodness that she possessed. In a sense then, Cody is responsible for the unity that his family finally achieves.

While the dynamics of the Tull family parallel the Bundrens', *Dinner at the Homesick Restaurant* is also suggestive of McCullers' *The Ballad of the Sad Cafe,* particularly in what it says about community. The titles of the two novels seem to echo each other, and the similarities extend into their texts as well. In each novel a restaurant serves as a focal point that represents a gathering of community. McCullers' cafe becomes a "joyous place" where people trapped in the monotony of mill town life can see themselves as individuals of worth. They come to the Sad Cafe for food, drink, and fellowship. Customers come to the Homesick Restaurant for similar reasons. Most are neighborhood residents who are seeking the family connections that have been lost to modern life. At the Homesick Restaurant customers can get those foods for which they are "homesick." They can be nourished in body and spirit much as they would be at home.

The restaurant in each novel is operated by an eccentric proprietor. The Sad Cafe is owned by Miss Amelia, "a dark, tall woman with bones and muscles like a man." She is a solitary individual who lacks any genuine basis for communication with either men or women. Since Miss Amelia claims kin with no one, relatives never crowd her restaurant, and she invariably eats alone. Ezra Tull, owner of the Homesick Restaurant, appears to contrast with Miss Amelia, and yet there are similarities. Slightly overweight, Ezra is soft, sensitive, and lovable. He does have family to claim, but there is so much tension and conflict between family members that Ezra seems as isolated as Miss Amelia. Throughout the novel Ezra struggles to organize family dinners at his restaurant, but fights erupt whenever he tries to bring his mother, brother, and sister together for a meal. Like Miss Amelia, Ezra too ends up dining alone. However, unlike Miss Amelia, Ezra is not isolated from his community. Unable to unite his family, Ezra finds a sense of family and belonging in his community. He has genuine affection and concern for his neighbors and co-workers. He lovingly cares for Mrs. Scarlatti, his business partner, when she is dying from cancer. He fixes meals and hot cocoa for the Payson family and comforts them when Mr. Payson dies. Ezra generously gives to his community, and the love and concern are reciprocated.

Both Ezra and Miss Amelia create concoctions purported to have powers that go beyond the ordinary. Miss Amelia brews a potent liquor that has the power to heal, kill pain, and produce sexual potency. Early in the novel Miss Amelia offers a weeping and distraught Cousin Lymon some of her brew, saying, "Drink . . . It will liven your gizzard." Similarly, Ezra Tull is noted for his hot and garlicky gizzard soup. While Miss Amelia's brew seems to have almost magical powers, Ezra's gizzard soup is simply "made with love." Ezra seeks to nourish and heal with such foods. He imagines examining a customer and saying, "You look a little tired. I'll bring you an oxtail stew." Indeed, he develops his gizzard soup for just this purpose. Ezra even replaces his "somber-suited waiters" with "cheery, motherly waitresses," who have more success in getting people to eat his gizzard soup.

The meals that are served in the Sad Cafe and the Homesick Restaurant are substitutes for familial love, but they also represent a celebration and a coming together of community. The foods in both novels reflect a regional emphasis, one specific to the South. In *The Ballad of the Sad Cafe* whenever a meal is eaten, the narrator lists the menu, "fried chicken . . . mashed rootabeggars, collard greens, and hot, pale golden sweet potatoes." In *Dinner at the Homesick Restaurant* food is given similar treatment. Ezra's menus list foods which might appear on a Southern family table, including "pan-fried potatoes, black-eyed peas, beaten biscuits genuinely beat on a stump with the back of an ax." Ezra sometimes lists several selections of entrees on a blackboard, while at other times he offers only one choice. More strangely, customers might order Smithfield ham and are served okra stew instead, along with Ezra's solicitous comment, "with that cough of yours, I know this would suit you better." Like a concerned mother, Ezra serves his customers those foods he thinks are for their own good and not necessarily what they want.

Another point of comparison between *The Ballad of the Sad Cafe* and *Dinner at the Homesick Restaurant* deals not with food but with love. In both novels a three-sided love affair develops among the main characters and reveals "the destructive nature of Eros." McCullers' theme of the "isolated individual seeking escape from loneliness through love" is apparent in *The Ballad of the Sad Cafe* and is reflected in the lives of Miss Amelia, Cousin Lymon, and Marvin Macy. Af-

ter two years with Miss Amelia, Cousin Lymon falls in love and elopes with Marvin Macy, Miss Amelia's ex-husband. Love in this novel is the "dreadful result of an individual's isolation and its intensifier, rather than its cure." Furthermore, it is a force that drives the lover inward into deeper isolation and self-pity. In *Dinner at the Homesick Restaurant* Ezra is similarly betrayed in affairs of the heart, but his response does not lead to self-pity or worsening isolation. His brother Cody, jealous over anything that Ezra has, plots to lure Ruth, Ezra's fiancee and chief cook, away from the Homesick Restaurant. Cody succeeds in marrying Ruth, leaving Ezra confused and bewildered. However, Ezra bears no anger or resentment towards them, and he continues to cook and serve and nurture. Ezra persists in his struggle to unite his alienated family for at least one successful dinner, and ironically, with Cody's intervention, he finally succeeds.

Thus, in veins of Faulkner and McCullers, Tyler tells the story of the Tull family and how they finally come together in a delicate but perhaps lasting harmony. By focusing on different pieces of the past Tyler enables her characters to perceive different realities of themselves and each other. By showing these different perspectives, she illustrates a fundamental truth inherent in most families: although children grow up together in the same household, they have very different experiences within the family. Although they are exposed to much of the same family history, dynamics, and conflicts, they are shaped differently by these influences. Cody, Ezra, and Jenny Tull certainly prove this to be true. The pieces of the past they choose to remember are like parts of a torn photograph. Individually, the pieces reflect each one's perception of his or her experience within the family. However, Tyler fits these pieces together to create a unified but complex portrait of individuals who are torn apart by the past and alienated by conflict, but who are a family nevertheless. Through the Tulls, Tyler shows that while families can be a source of anguish and pain, they also can provide a touchstone for remembering common pasts and for finding a sense of place, belonging, and, ultimately, oneself.

Like Faulkner and McCullers, Tyler demonstrates how the past is inextricably linked to the present and how family and community, as a natural extension of the family, are centers for the ironies of life—love and rejection, growth and entrapment, stability and conflict. Tyler resists the temptation to indict parents, particularly mothers, for the transgression of the past and for the ultimate shaping of offspring. Maternal ambivalence is a not uncommon thread in the fabric of human experience. However, as Tyler knows, it is just one factor in the development of the individual. Family and community also exert important influences that shape, direct, and complicate human existence. Tyler portrays this process in the Tull family, and in the end she renders a contemporary and enduring message about the nature of families, one that speaks with some measure of truth about all of our lives.

Susan Gilbert (essay date 1990)

SOURCE: "Anne Tyler," in *Southern Women Writers: The New Generation,* The University of Alabama Press, 1990, pp. 251-78.

[*In the following essay, Gilbert presents an overview of Tyler's work and major themes.*]

Anne Tyler, with ten novels, the last the winner of the National Book Critics' Circle Award, has a secure critical reputation and a large and faithful audience. Her fictional world is well defined. It is a personal world. The concerns of her characters are the persistent and primary psychological anxieties of life. Children hunger for their mothers' approval. They feel grief and guilt at the death or disappearance of a parent. Siblings' rivalries and dependencies, loves and angers, last for lifetimes. Sons and daughters spend decades running away from, or back to, their homes.

On these private lives, the great world impinges little. Except to her artist characters, envied in their absorptions, neither work nor politics, social status nor religious devotion matters much. Familial relationships consume the reader's attention as well, for her families are for the most part unhistorical and unchanging, groups wherein types persist unaffected by changes in social patterns in the towns where they live.

Time passes; things change; the characters live on streets in changing neighborhoods without noticing the changes. Pearl Tull of *Dinner at the Homesick Restaurant* wonders where the years have gone and what has become of the aunts to whom she used to write, but the reader has little sense of the changing South in her long life. In *Earthly Possessions,* Charlotte Emory, married seventeen years and living still in her parents' house, looks out "at the crumbling buildings across the street: the Thrift Shop, newsstand, liquor store, Pei Wing the tailor . . . not a single home in the lot, come to think of it. Everyone else had moved on, and left us stranded here between the Amoco and the Texaco."

It is a telling passage. The want of a historical dimension is what makes many of Tyler's characters seem anachronisms: Pearl Tull, wearing her hats to work as a checkout clerk; Emily of *Morgan's Passing,* in her long skirts and leotards, out of place on the city streets of Baltimore. The families are close, insular, isolated. The Pecks of *Searching for Caleb* are "very close knit, a *fine* family" who have always "stuck together" in a snobbish clannishness from which a few in every generation flee. Pearl Tull, with her three children, lives all alone barely making ends meet after her husband deserts them. They do not relate well to others. Once, waiting for Beck, Pearl "walked around with a broken arm for a day and a half. . . . She was a stranger in town and had no one to turn to." These

families lack not only neighborliness; they lack any sense of belonging to a larger social order.

In twenty years, Tyler's focus has not broadened. Her books run deeper but not wider. Her concerns are at opposite poles from the historical novelists in this collection. One does not look here for Mary Lee Settle's tracing of political ideas across countries and generations, for Harper Lee's examination of racial conflict, for Lee Smith's evocation of a place where a whole culture vanishes in a generation. Nor, looking outside the South, does one see likeness to Joan Didion's habit of working very close to the headlines of the news or to Joyce Carol Oate's attempts to bring her characters' lives into focus against the panorama of historical crises. In the all-Southern settings of Tyler's novels, children trundle off to schools never touched by *Brown v. the Board of Education*; her young men never receive or burn their draft cards; their parents never keep vigil on courthouse steps in protest against a war; no women parade with placards for, or against, the ERA.

Agoraphobics such as Jeremy Pauling of *Celestial Navigation,* who cannot venture off his block; Pearl Tull of *Dinner at the Homesick Restaurant,* who for decades does not go beyond the grocery where she is checkout clerk by day and the house where she hammers and putters in the evenings; Charlotte Emory's mother in *Earthly Possessions,* confined first to one big lawn chair and then to bed; and Morgan's mother in her wing chair by the hearth are just the most extreme cases of the class to which they all belong, characters living in oblivion of sexual or political revolutions, characters whose problems are described in psychology texts, not news clippings.

Thus Tyler's work and characters occupy a timeless world of fiction, and the plots move back as often as they go forward. The pattern of the novels is, repeatedly, circular. Characters who feel themselves imprisoned within the routines and encumbering possessions of their own and others' lives seek to break away. They flee or dream of flight. Then most of them return, or they find that the bonds and the stuff that they sought to leave behind have followed them, to make another place, envisioned as spare and stripped, become moldy, cluttered, heavy with earthly freight, buried under layers of the past.

Tyler's first novel, *If Morning Ever Comes,* begins with the hero's coming home and ends with his leaving. His sister leaves her husband and then goes home again. Tyler's stories are as likely to be about fleeing as returning, and whichever the case, the meaning seems to be the same.

The point of view is that of Ben Joe Hawkes, only son in a family of several sisters, a mother, and their "Gram." Theirs is a large Southern family in a big comfortable house with an ill-tended lawn. The father, now dead, was a doctor and an alcoholic and kept a mistress on the other side of town. Ben

Joe visits her and her child. Most of the rest of the time, he wanders about home, vaguely in the way.

Most of the themes of Tyler's mature work are to be found in this remarkably crafted first novel, published when she was twenty-three. There is the central character's ongoing sense of deep attachment to his family. He leaves law school to go home because he thinks they need him. But at home he feels neither needed nor close, but vaguely estranged. He elopes at the last without telling them and rides off on the train, wondering if he will always feel this separation, even from his wife and the child they may someday have: "One part of them was faraway and closed to him, as unreachable as his own sisters, and blankfaced as the white house he was born in. Even his wife and son were that way. Even Ben Joe Hawkes." In this sense of remoteness from his present life, he sets a type for many Tyler characters to come, a tribe "unable to realize a thing's happening or a moment's passing."

As in all later Tyler novels, there is the repeated emphasis on movement without change, on change without movement. The sister who left her husband did so for fear that "history was repeating itself." Her parents' marriage had been unhappy and hers was becoming so. But she tells Ben Joe, "It's not the same place I'm coming back to, really. Not even if I wanted it to be." At that stage, he does not see her point, but later, foreseeing her decision to return to her husband, he says, "I don't know that I would call it going backwards instead of forwards. Sometimes it's not the same place when a person goes back to it, or not . . . the same person." This realization of the hero's is all there is to forward movement of the plot, and he is left with the unresolved doubt of his ability to grasp the present.

The novel is fine in its depiction of families, their internal strifes and their physical features, and in its descriptions of house and furnishings and photographs and the ways these preserve the past. To all these themes, she will return.

The Tin Can Tree is a small masterpiece. Two characters run away and then return. A little girl, Janie Rose Pike has died. Her brother Simon runs away from home because those around him are grieving for her so much that he feels himself unnoticed. In the days before he goes, he says, time after time, when asked if he's had lunch or combed his hair, that his mother "won't care." When he is found and she comes to bring him home, he beams with a joy he cannot contain because she has come "specially" to get him: "You mean you're here on *account* of my going off?" he exclaims.

Interwoven with the family's loss and Simon's sense of loss of his own significance is the romance of his cousin Joan, who has been living with them, and James, one of two brothers living in the adjoining triple house. Joan runs away for much the same reason as Simon, not displaced in a mother's

eye by a dead sister, but in her lover's eye by his living brother, Ansel, an alcoholic hypochondriac who has claimed and will claim much of James's attention all his life. A third set of family breaks is the brothers' with their family. This break remains unhealed, though their father tells James they still have his old bed.

Two significant technical achievements and one major thematic advance stand out in *The Tin Can Tree*. Tyler uses the house to anchor a larger set of unrelated characters and to make of them Simon's and Joan's real family. She makes much of photography to point the significance of life's fleeting moments. Thematically, she introduces, in polished form, the needs of the two characters, Joan and Simon, to be seen and loved for themselves alone. Simon is satisfied. His mother has been jolted from her daze of grief to be grateful to have him home. For him, the plot has moved forward.

For Joan, the advance is only in her perception. In the excitement of Simon's running away, her own leaving goes unnoticed. Her return is to the same relationship. In looking for Simon, James neglects his brother's supper. He will cook him a steak tomorrow; Joan will never hold all his attention. And she knows this as, in the last scene, she is photographing Simon's homecoming party. Though all the characters are moving, looking into the camera, she foresees the image in which they will be still, forever: "they could leave and return, they could marry or live out their separate lives alone, and nothing in this finder would change. They were going to stay this way, she and all the rest of them, not because of anyone else but because it was what they had chosen, what they would keep a strong tight hold of. James bent over Ansel; Mrs. Pike touched the top of Simon's head. . . ." Though Joan will not have her love all to herself, this is one of the happiest endings in Tyler's fiction, for she sees life as choice, not fatality, and she too has chosen to be where she is, and she knows it.

A Slipping-Down Life presents the most bizarre of her characters' ploys to gain attention. A homely, fat high school girl, Evie Decker, carves, with fingernail scissors, a rock singer's name in her forehead. They do marry and very briefly find a quiet haven. He puts up household gadgets. Her old friend envies her that she is an outsider no longer but one of those married people "so cozy with someone they belong to."

Their barely broken loneliness soon returns. He loses his job. She quits going to school. In their worry, she neglects to tell him she is pregnant. Suddenly, in the midst of a wild escapade to gain him publicity, Evie's father dies; she finds her husband in bed with his "kidnapper." Within a year from the start, Evie is home again in her father's empty house, to await the birth of her baby.

Evie's is the smallest of the families Tyler draws. Without a mother, she has had only a distant relationship to her father. At the end, she is in the house with photographs, one in her father's room: "An ancestor, maybe; no one could tell her anymore," and another in the living room, a picture of her mother, "remembered now by no living person."

In its characters and in its humor, *A Slipping-Down Life* differs markedly from the earlier two works, filled with the most ordinary people. Tyler insisted that such as the alcoholic father of the first and brother in the second were part of normal families. But Evie, with her grotesque scar, her friend Violet, enormously fat and dressed always in purple or chartreuse, and Drumstrings Casey, the would-be rock star, dark and mesmerizing as he sings, apparently to no one present—these are oddities indeed, more strange as a complete cast than those of any books to follow, but introducing Tyler's large company of weird characters. They are types, especially the serious, brooding singer, much like Flannery O'Connor's creations.

The humor of Tyler's first two novels derives from close observation of the incongruities in daily family life, a homey humor, much of it in the careful rendering of the folk speech of small-town Southerners. *A Slipping-Down Life* has scenes with as violent mixture of humor and horror as John Irving's *The World According to Garp*: the commotion when Evie brands herself; Evie's carving the letters backward, in a mirror image; the disruption of a revivalist's preaching coupled with the deep wound of Casey's insult to Evie; the juxtaposition of a hospital, an empty house, and Evie's finding Casey on top of "Fay-Jean Lindsay, in her orange lace slip." That Tyler describes the macabre externals at these moments of unexpressed hurt and grief gives the humor a dark, dark tone.

The first three works employ love stories for plots—Ben Joe's courtship and elopement, Joan and James's romance, Evie's marriage—without ever describing sex. In a short story about a rape, Tyler tells only that the feel of the rapist's hand on the girl's mouth differs little from the feel of her boyfriend's; at the scratchy sound of a zipper unzipping, she interrupts the scene. She does not go beyond this in the description of sexual feeling or experience.

In the next two novels, *The Clock Winder* and *Celestial Navigation,* Tyler draws a pair of heroines competent to all the exigencies of daily life, managing households of inept, dreamy men, old people, or children. Both Elizabeth Abbott and Mary Tell have run away from their first families only to have families accrue to their solitary strengths. They are capable and inexpressive, loved and loving, but shying from examination of deep emotion.

The Clock Winder is the story of the Emersons, a widow and her seven grown children, and Elizabeth Abbott, who comes to live with Mrs. Emerson as her house handy-woman. Eliza-beth is courted by two of the sons, Matthew and Timothy, leaves when Timothy commits suicide, returns to nurse Mrs. Emerson after a stroke, is shot by Timothy's twin, Andrew, stays, marries Matthew, and lives, as happily ever after as folk do in Tyler's world, with Matthew, their children, Andrew, and Mrs. Emerson, and with the other brother and the sister returning from time to time.

Not one of Tyler's best books, *The Clock Winder* is yet important, presaging in technique and theme what she will add in the next ten years to what she carries over from her first ten years as a novelist.

She handles more time than she has before, 1960 to 1972, and employs multiple points of view, including letters at one point. She continues to draw insular families. The turbulence of America in the sixties touches none of the young Emersons. Though the youngest son is in Vietnam, no one else in the work notices that a war is going on; his mother writes to ask if he is visiting any tourist sights, and only he seems to feel reproach that she lives in a "sealed weightless bubble floating through time."

Fathers in Tyler's work play insignificant roles as heads of households; Dr. Hawkes of the first leaves permanent scars and gaps in his family by his absence, not his presence; Mr. Pike of *The Tin Can Tree* is colorless; Evie's father is colorless, kind, and uncommunicative; Mr. Emerson, who has died just before the novel opens, is dimly remembered.

A distinct mark of Southern life, if not of Southern literature, prominent in Tyler's works is the degree to which families are female affairs. Men go off to work; some of them make money; and some have a bit of public reputation. These things matter not at all "at home," the locus of all the life that concerns Anne Tyler. It is surprising, faintly amusing to one of Mr. Emerson's sons to remember that as a real estate tycoon the father had a name some thought worth dropping. Elizabeth Abbott is surprised that some of her preacher father's congregation lean on him. Indeed, here and in *Earthly Possessions,* Tyler makes humorous swipes at the stereotype of the Southern patriarch, the Protestant preacher. They are humored by their wives and families. Elizabeth Abbott's mother makes her funeral casseroles by the dozen; her husband wishes she did not act as though she were playing tea party when she does it. Neither wife is a believer; no one at home accords these men the pontifical importance they think they should have.

Nor does money count in Tyler's world, a strikingly immaterial mid-twentieth-century America in which concern for finances or status is a permanent foible only of humorous characters, rarely directing the lives of the central ones. Mrs. Emerson, a rich woman, is stingy in small affairs and disappointed that her children are not successes. Elizabeth, like most of Tyler's heroes and heroines, is oblivious to worldly success. Rarely and briefly does money seriously affect her characters' lives: their poverty affected the teenagers' marriage in *A Slipping-Down Life;* in *Celestial Navigation,* the heroine hates to interrupt her artist husband with the bother of finances; several well-off youngsters turn their backs on respectable careers. But it is personal, not economic, forces that shape all their lives. Real need or desire for money is more rare in Tyler's world than it would be in a monastery or commune; few of her characters bother enough with it to renounce it.

In family motifs and themes, *The Clock Winder* outlines Tyler's ongoing concerns: family dinners interrupted by quarrels, brothers courting one girl, and the influence of one generation on the next. There are two disparate views on the awful responsibility of parents, that of the anxious Mrs. Emerson, whose children flee her, and that of Elizabeth at the end, humorous, all accepting, calmly nursing one baby while her son plays with bugs on the kitchen floor. Of Mrs. Emerson's sons, one is a mental patient, one a suicide; her daughters' loves and marriages do not suit her. She laments: "'They say it's the parents to blame, but what did we do? I'm asking you, I really want to know. What did *we* do? . . . Just loved you and raised you, the best we knew how. . . . Made mistakes, but none of them on purpose. What else did you want? I go over and over it all, in my mind. Was it something I did? Something I didn't do?'" Elizabeth tells her of watching a parade and thinking of an unending line, stretching back beyond history, of human beings caring for their children, all the years of feeding, protecting, and teaching that a human child must have from at least one adult simply to survive: "People you wouldn't trust your purse with five minutes, maybe, but still they put in years and years of time tending their children along and they don't even make a fuss about it. Even if it's a criminal they turn out, or some other kind of failure—still, he managed to get grown, didn't he? Isn't that something?" In a richer characterization in Pearl Tull of *Dinner at the Homesick Restaurant,* Tyler will bring the two points of view together.

Unlike the meddlesome Mrs. Emerson, Elizabeth is passive, and her passivity reveals a constant feature of Tyler's work more clearly than any of her other characters do. She can fix anything with a screwdriver, caulking gun, or drill, but she exerts energy and initiative only on things that can be literally manipulated, never on people. At the outset, she says she accepts all invitations. She seeks nothing and makes no choices. But the awful blame for what people do and do not do in others' lives seems to catch her. She is haunted for years with guilt that she should have done, or not done, something to prevent Timothy's suicide. In this state, she moves to refusing all invitations, all connections. She can only go along or flee. Serious as Tyler is, she seizes the chance for humor this affords for a bride at the altar to say "I don't."

It is a sine qua non of the characters for whom Tyler shows affection that they rarely, and only ineptly, pursue or seek to hold those they love. They drift. They watch. Weeping alone, they express little emotion; for loud complainers, Tyler has a caustic wit.

Elizabeth refuses Matthew's suit until she is shot by Andrew. Only then does she realize, and is she sure all the Emersons realize, that nothing she did or did not do either time could prevent the shooting. Thus absolved of guilt for the way human lives turn out, she can stay and join the parade of people raising children. *The Clock Winder* ends in forgiveness and in healing, with Elizabeth at the center of a home the large family will return to as inevitably as the locusts that are featured in the coda.

Celestial Navigation covers ten years in a run-down boarding-house in Baltimore, during which separate, lonely people come together, become part of a family of noisy children, and sink back at last to loneliness. Mary Tell, a young runaway wife with a small baby, takes up with Jeremy Pauling, an eccentric artist, lives with him, bears five children, and runs away again at the end. Of this Tyler makes a dense jewel of a work, informed by the image of Pauling's creations, collages of miniatures, scraps rendered in perfectly focused detail to suggest a life of infinite variety and wonder.

The house and its inhabitants are cut off in space and time, all of them anachronisms. Pauling, an agoraphobic, does not leave the block for decades. Before him, his mother was "a *stagnant* kind of person" who "didn't even notice what the neighborhood had turned into" and who "hardly ever left the house." This is a world seen, as Thoreau saw the universe in Walden Pond, by looking in, not out.

The novel is packed with description, of things and people's feelings, in a style different from the spareness of Tyler's earlier works. At rendering detail, she is here in full mastery. They all complain of clutter, of the house and its "clutter of leaded panes and straggly ivy and grayish lace curtains dragging their bottoms behind black screens," and junk inside, "circus paintings and laughing dolls and plastic horses and coffee cans overflowing with broken crayons," "tattered construction paper Valentines glued to the upstairs panes and the dead Christmas tree on its side in front, dripping tinsel." Packing for her escape, Mary Tell wishes to get away, but the stuff of life sticks to her, "children, grocery bags, stuffed animals . . . Dramamine tablets." When Jeremy the artist drives his children away for interrupting him in his study, he is left lonely and guilty: "How could he have scolded them like that. He knew them so little. . . . He looked around the hall and saw the traces they had left behind—one roller skate, a homemade doll, a chalky hand-print on the newel post."

All the characters wish at times to escape from clutter to spareness, to purity. Mary and Jeremy, like the heroes and heroines of Tyler's earlier works, feel unable to realize the import of life in the present. Mary laments: all of life "can be reduced to a heap of trivia in the end. When I die I expect I will be noticing a water ring someone left on the coffee table, or a spiral of steam rising from a whistling teapot. I will be sure to miss the moment of my passing." Here, if anywhere in Tyler's work, one sees that life is clutter. Its only spareness is in the "great towering beautiful sculptures" that Jeremy makes at the end of his life, alone in a quiet, darkening house.

The narrative technique of *Celestial Navigation,* ten chapters titled by season, year (1960-73), and name of the character whose perspective rules in each one, serves well and is one Tyler will repeat. In their monologues, the central characters articulate their understanding more fully than do the people in any of her other works. The shifting perspective shows starkly the gaps between their feelings and what they can tell others. Whatever Mary or Jeremy understands of their need and love for each other avails nothing toward holding their lives together. For Mary, indeed, it is the urgency to have spoken things that neither of them is capable of saying that makes her pull their life apart. All the pain and perception will go into his art, but it cannot mend their lives.

The humor in these voices, especially in the brilliant opening monologue of Amanda, is Tyler at the peak of her form. It is as captivating as Lee Smith's *Oral History*. The disjunctions of life are portrayed deftly, in small things, not in the violent, macabre pairings of *A Slipping-Down Life.*

Three of Tyler's works stand out from the rest—this one for its intensity and immediacy. From the opening voice of Amanda to the closing one of Miss Vinton, the characters are at much closer range than they have been before, palpably near. In its density, the novel is not like any of Tyler's other works. The style is a piling on, crowded listing in places and in much fuller characterization with not a single strain, but many threads to each life. The siblings' rivalry is just one example. Amanda is resentful that Jeremy absorbed all their mother's attention; he remembers only being never quite able to please her. A small thread in the dense fabric of this novel, this will be the main theme in *Dinner at the Homesick Restaurant.* For its shimmering surface over more detail than one's senses can absorb, *Celestial Navigation* is a great advance and a different direction from earlier works.

The family in *Searching for Caleb* covers several generations of the descendants of a Baltimore merchant, Justin Peck. In this novel of broken relationships and unbreakable love, Daniel Peck goes looking, with the help of his granddaughter, Justine, for the half-brother he hasn't seen in more than half a century. Caleb is found and leaves again. Justine is married to her first cousin Duncan Peck, in their generation

the chief runaway. At the last, they are seen making one more remove, to live in a trailer and travel with a circus.

Like all Tyler's families, the Pecks live to themselves: "you couldn't say that the Pecks had *friends,* exactly. They kept to themselves. They were suspicious of outsiders." For years, the first Peck is shut up inside, immobilized by a stroke. When his wife arranges mirrors so he can see the street scene below, because she thinks "he might like to keep in touch with things," he sees only his son, descending the steps, and orders the mirrors taken away. Succeeding generations, those who stay in their houses where furniture sits in the same spot for decades and those who live like vagabonds, are out of the currents of history, a family whom history washes over without touching them, unaware of wars or social changes, stranded in time, anachronisms like their predecessors.

The time that does matter in the book is internal family time. The characters divide between those who hold onto stuff and those who do not. Things, Justine notices when she comes home for her parents' funeral, are never simply things: "There was no such thing as a simple, meaningless teacup, even. It was always given by someone dear, commemorating some happy occasion, chipped during some moment of shock, the roses worn transparent by Sulie's scrubbing, a blond stain inside from tea that Sam Mayhew had once drunk, a crack where Caroline, trembling with headache, had set it down too hard upon the saucer." Such are the outward and visible signs of the connections by which individual lives remain part of a longer family life. To throw away such is to cast off memory, as does Duncan, the youngest runaway, who is said to live, "forever in the present!" Preparing for their last departure, Justine looks forward to the escape from clutter, to living in a trailer where everything will be built-in, but she is defeated by things pushed on her as she prepares to drive away, a pot of ivy, a rubber plant, things that serve memory, ties to her former self and to people from her past.

Despite the disruptions of place and the silence between brothers for decades, this novel shows not the impossibility of human expression of love, but its possibilities and endurance, in gestures as ritualized as the Pecks' bread-and-butter letters on monogrammed paper or as spontaneous as a toy. Though they unquestionably belong to Tyler's tribe, who find it impossible to articulate love, the Pecks manage to convey their deepest feelings. Duncan cannot plead with Justine to come with him and leave the old aunts. He makes a little stick figure of twisted wire, looking like her, "looking so straight-backed and light-hearted that even a tribesman in darkest Africa could tell that someone cared for her." Without more said, she leaves with him. Though the main characters in *Searching for Caleb* take off at the last, and Jeremy Pauling of *Celestial Navigation* stays home, this novel points at the thread of continuity even in departures; the earlier one showed the terrible gaps left by severed human ties.

In this novel of four generations, the longest span she has yet treated, Tyler develops for the first time the idea of heredity as fate, a slight motif in several earlier works. In the first novel, characters bear the indelible marks of physical inheritance, the Dower nose, the Hawkes nose. A daughter feels that in her generation history is repeating itself. In *Searching for Caleb,* personality types as well as physical features are handed down, the Pecks' stolid conformity and a forgotten foreign grandfather's wildness. Tyler describes the wandering Caleb: "blond like his half-brother, but his tilted brown eyes must have snuck in from the Baum side of the family, and he had his Grandpa Baum's delight in noise and crowds." However often Justine and Duncan Peck run away, as they age, they become more visibly Pecks. Heredity, upbringing, the early childhood years—characters may wish to escape these, to become themselves alone, unique individuals; they never do. Later, in *Dinner at the Homesick Restaurant,* Tyler will paint in darker tones the effects of generations' repeating their parents' failures.

The Pecks are more well-to-do than most Tyler families but are no more social or stylish. Their house is "bristling with chimneys and lined with dark, oily wood . . . filled with golden oak furniture and Oriental screens, chandeliers dripping crystal, wine velvet love-seats with buttons and more buttons up and down their backs . . . curlicued urns, doilies, statuary . . . great globular lamps centered on tasseled scarves, and Persian rugs laid catty-corner and overlapping." Tyler will draw a house of wealth but not one of fashion. Here and always she paints folkways with more affection, Justine Peck in country clothes peddling goat cheeses, a city-bred girl from this Peck domicile coming to like the smells of kerosene and fatback. This country domesticity may have added to Tyler's appeal for some readers in the last two decades, with their flourishing fads of healthful, simple country-ness.

Artistic sophistication is the only sophistication presented in Tyler's world, and this artistry is only in nonverbal plastic arts, such as collages or statues, or in highly stylized simple forms, such as puppetry. Tyler herself desired a career in painting before writing; she says she sketches her characters before she describes them in words. But the artworks in the novels, except for Pauling's barely mentioned late towering sculpture, are homey stuff. Tyler's own work is highbrow, the critical organs for it are the *New Yorker* and the *New York Times.* Educated and cosmopolitan, a writer married to a psychiatrist, she writes almost entirely of uneducated folk. When she draws an artist, he is never in an artistic or—god forbid—an artsy milieu. She describes no fashionable interiors, stylish dress, or bons mots of up-to-date wits. And never does she draw characters broadly able to think and speak in abstract terms of the human condition. The only trenchant and comprehensive intelligence she permits within the pages of her books is her own.

Earthly Possessions is titled for Tyler's message that the cluttered minutiae of life, though they seem to obscure one's vision of some life of grander import, are what life is. The title may imply that if there are "earthly" possessions, then there may be also unearthly ones, accruing in some heavenly mansion, waiting for the individual in some fairer, faraway place; it isn't so. Her fortunate characters learn this in time to return and, in learning this, realize what the hero of Tyler's first novel said, that going forward can look a lot like going backward: "Sometimes it's not the same place when a person goes back to it, or not . . . the same person."

Charlotte Emory, the heroine of *Earthly Possessions,* is one of the lucky ones. At the novel's opening, she is taking money from the bank to run away from her husband, family, and home. She feels encumbered, buried, unnoticed, and unappreciated. Her parents' home, which she has never left, is crowded with people, with several children, with her husband's brothers, and with the stuff his mother left. At the bank, she is kidnapped by a robber and taken as his hostage on a long drive to Florida, farther from home than she has ever been before. At the last, she is home again, content to stay.

Like Justine Peck and Mary Tell, Charlotte is trying to escape clutter for the "bare essentials." "My life," she says, "has been a history of casting off encumbrances, paring down to the bare essentials, stripping for the journey." In book after book, Tyler's metaphors of weight and freight convey Wordsworthian echoes of mortality: "Full soon thy Soul shall have her earthly freight, / And custom lie upon thee with a weight, / Heavy as frost, and deep almost as life!" In her first novel, the young hero on his first evening home "was beginning to feel the weight of home settling back on him, making him feel heavy and old and tired." Here Charlotte says, "I have been trying to get rid of all belongings that would weigh me down on a long foot-march." For Tyler, the weight is no intimation of immortality but the inevitable yoke of the only life there is.

Things conveying memory of a human past fill Tyler's characters' houses in "layers" and in "webs." Both figures recur, the first suggesting the connection of the present to the past, and the other that of the individual to his family or surrogate family. In Tyler's first novel, the hero's room seemed to him to be "made up of layers, the more recent layers never completely obliterating the earlier ones." For him and for Charlotte the layers of the past are clear and bright, the present hard to discern. About to run away, Charlotte fingers bits of past and present, "rolled socks, crumpled homework papers" and the "worn, smudged woodwork, listening to absent voices, inhaling the smell of school paste and hymnals." But deluded, she flees because, as she says of herself, she had not "the knack of knowing I was happy right while the happiness was going on."

These two failures of vision have impelled all of Tyler's characters on their flights, the inability to see the beauty of the present, its outlines obscured in layers of the past, and the inability to see themselves at all, the fear that they are invisible as individuals in the webs of others' lives. Photographs, moments frozen in time, individuals centered in the lens's focus, are a prominent motif in all of Tyler's works. Here Charlotte has taken over, without, it seems, a conscious decision to do so, her father's profession of photographer. She makes portraits in which ordinary folk of their small town seem to stand out as people from another age.

Although the exclusively first-person narration of *Earthly Possessions* should afford Charlotte chance to explain fully the reasons for her return, these remain scantily articulated. She is less revealing of self-understanding than are Mary Tell and Jeremy Pauling in *Celestial Navigation.* In the flashbacks to her past, interspersed with the forward movement of her days with her captor, she does not spell out the lessons she learns in the journey of her soul. In a brief coda, she is back home with her husband, taking pictures of plain people in exotic costumes, and sure to stay. She is no more communicative with her husband or the reader than she has ever been. He lies awake, vaguely disturbed by slight misunderstandings of daily life, questioning whether they are "happy," whether they ought to take a trip. Charlotte is past questioning or seeking afield: "I tell him no. I don't see the need, I say. We have been traveling for years, traveled all our lives, we are traveling still. We couldn't stay in one place if we tried. Go to sleep, I say. And he does."

Without adding much particularly new in characterization or technique, *Earthly Possessions* consolidates several of Tyler's most important themes: the contrast between a muddled web of daily life and a dream life, spare and solitary; the characters' inabilities to feel themselves alive in the present; their desire to be seen for special, individual significance; and the barely articulated return to place.

Earthly Possessions closes with Charlotte Emory's wordless contentment with ordinary life. *Morgan's Passing* ends with its hero, Morgan Gower, smiling and humming: "Everything he looked at seemed luminous and beautiful, and rich with possibilities." "Passing" is the Southern country euphemism for dying; people "pass" to a greater life. Morgan's passing is from a divided life, in which his earthly situation of dismaying ordinariness is disjoint from his fantasy life, to another in which, though its outline shows little difference, he sees wonder in the commonplace. At the beginning of the novel he is a hardware store manager, filling an unnecessary role in one of the stores his wife has inherited, insignificant at work and at home, where all affairs social and practical are managed by his competent wife. Morgan misses the days when infants ran to greet him. Now they barely notice him. Somehow they have neglected to tell him one of his daugh-

ters is to be married. Seeking another identity, he roams Baltimore in costume and so becomes entangled with Emily and Leon Meredith, the other principals of the novel, a pair of young puppeteers whose exotic life fascinates him. They, like Justine and Duncan Peck, are runaways from respectability.

At the end, Morgan has replaced Leon as Emily's husband. He has fled one household, where he felt lost in a clutter of tennis shoes, Triscuit boxes, and pets' feeding bowls, to a life with Emily, which he envisaged as spare, the bare essentials. But he finds, as other of Tyler's characters have, that clutter is life's inescapable condition. Their baby will require a crib and changing table and potty seat, like all others. Though he is not far from where he began, Morgan is content, for the time being at least, looking out at the wonder of his life, freed from the foolish, frantic pursuit of his own identity.

Morgan Gower, dashing about Baltimore in his strange garbs, butting into other people's lives, is the most extroverted character in Tyler's long collection of introverts, but since his interventions are a series of charades, he has no more real links to a historical community than the rest. And for all that he pops in and out of strangers' lives, he is as self-absorbed as his predecessors. Certainly, he and Leon and Emily make a cast that is more exotic than any since *A Slipping-Down Life.* Tyler has remarked that she is pained when people ask about the oddity of her characterizations and insists that all people, looked at closely enough, become odd in their peculiarities, in their uniqueness.

Feeling that they are missing the present, feeling themselves lost and unseen in the layers of past, present, and future, and obscured in the webs of their myriad daily doings with others, Tyler's characters go to extraordinary lengths to break out and be seen. To be seen as an individual, alive in the present, to have focused upon oneself the full, attentive gaze of another, is time after time what lures her characters to their escapes and to drastic measures, momentary or stretching over lifetimes. In the first novel, Ben Joe's sister wears red dresses and jangling bracelets to secure the boys' attention; later she does not know how to live with her husband, or with anyone, after the attention of the first date wears off. More desperate for attention, Evie carves the singer's name in her face. Simon and Joan of *A Tin Can Tree* run from the mother and lover who fail to notice them. Mary Tell of *Celestial Navigation,* taken for granted and unnoticed by Jeremy, succumbs to the gaze of their good friend Brian. Charlotte Emory, feeling herself invisible, falls into a brief affair with her husband's brother because he alone sees her, notices her, as she bakes the cakes, washes the clothes, feeds the dog. Morgan looks for a new life because he is unregarded at home, and Emily, in a marriage where her husband is star and her contribution and creativity are unseen, is irresistibly drawn to Morgan because he watches her. In *Dinner at the Homesick Restau-*

rant, a girl is again stolen, from one brother by another, because she cannot resist the attention, the notice lavished on her. These characters—imagining themselves unseen in their families, in meshes of domestic chores; angry, with a parent or spouse or lover, feeling, usually with reason, that they are so taken for granted as to be not merely unregarded but invisible in their roles—respond to the inherently sexual appeal of someone else who, looking at them, sees them. The desire to be seen "for oneself alone" is to Tyler romantic delusion.

Usually for Tyler's characters, the sight lasts just a moment, like an expression caught in a snapshot. The photographs that figure prominently in all her books are a foil to the characters' uneasiness that the present is escaping them, their being "unable to realize a thing's happening or a moment's passing." Pictures freeze the moment.

In Tyler's first novel, the hero finds among the "layers" of his room an old snapshot of himself and his sister on tricycles, their mother standing between them. Of this frozen moment and the relationships pictured in it, he is sure; of the present and their relationship, he is uncertain. In the second novel, the face of Janie Rose appears unexpectedly in a picture taken just a few days before her death, her image hard to pick out among little patches of Queen Anne's lace that dot a field. The work closes with a camera's reducing change to permanence; in the lens, Simon's mother bends over him eternally, James leans to his brother. In the third novel, Evie, the expectant mother is alone with pictures of an unknown ancestor and of her own mother, no one in the world left to remember either of them. Charlotte Emory in *Earthly Possessions* resists taking up her father's profession of photographer because she dislikes the way "photos froze a person, pinned him to cardboard like a butterfly." A photograph of a little girl, smiling and dimpled, focuses Charlotte's tortured relationship with her mother. Neither had pleased the other; Charlotte never felt she was her mother's daughter. Finding this photo hidden in her dying mother's drawer, she demands to know who it is, this one she feels is her mother's longed-for daughter, only to be told it is the mother herself.

In *Morgan's Passing* too, pictures trigger several revelations. It takes a picture in the newspaper to make Emily see that her husband is not a young boy any more. Morgan's sister is at last married to the suitor who jilted her decades ago, but she runs out on him because he spends his days mooning over her old graduation photo, jealous, she says, "of my own self . . . of my photograph." However muddled peoples' daily relationships are, in photographs they look out "steadily," with "trust" and with "concentration." It is in looking at Emily's photograph that Morgan sees her most clearly and imagines her seeing him: "Emily herself, marble-pale in folds of black, met his scrutiny with eyes so clear that he imagined he could see through them and behind them; he could see

what she must see, how his world must look to her." This vision of himself as seen by another makes him "a man in love."

In photographs, insignificance, ordinariness, transience are lost. Pictures of people taken long ago, or days or hours before, seem, even to those who take the pictures and see their living models, "lost and long ago." For pictures show individuals, and individuals seem always odd.

Tyler's books are full of oddities, alcoholics, hypochondriacs, neurotics, obesities, suicides. These are most understandable seen in the context of their families. In small towns where a person's family place is known, they stand out less than when they are cut off, alone in cities. Emily of *Morgan's Passing,* an orphan married to a runaway, appears like a gypsy in leotards and long skirts on the streets of Baltimore. She, or Justine Peck, a circus fortune-teller, would have been, had either stayed home, one of the Merediths, one of the Pecks, far less strange and far less visible. Human eccentricities thus stand out in sharper focus as characters move toward individuality. Some readers have remarked that individuals in Tyler's large families blur, that the characterization is halting. It is an intended effect; what she draws are families seen as they are seen by older residents of closed communities, in relation to their parents, aunts, or siblings.

They go to great lengths to break out of this ego-deflating invisibility, and they are quickly stirred to love by being seen all alone. Romance is not the only way characters seek to be seen. Sickness is a more effective way to hold the attention of others. The absorption of sexual passion is fleeting in Tyler's world. But malaise, malingering, and mental instability last longer than lifetimes; they affect generations. Alcoholics, invalids, the mentally frail maintain the central position in the vision of the ones who consume their lives caring for them. Some try this game, fail, and therefore flee. Morgan's wife refuses to let his eccentricities become the exclusive concern of the household. Beck, the errant husband of *Restaurant,* has wandered off from his wife and family, and from dozens of women later, it turns out.

It is a war first and last of "normal" families against "odd" individuals. In her first work, the son complains of the "*amazing*" things that go on in their family; his mother insists, "This family's just like any other family." Morgan says he has a "very ordinary family . . . *determined* to be ordinary." In Tyler's fiction, all families are normal, all are recognizable in their tensions and routines. The works teach not merely that all families have eccentric members but that seen individually all people are odd. Only in the ego-threatening place where one is of the Dower boys or one of the Gower girls are people ordinary.

Seen alone and still, as in photographs that catch one's expression for a second, her people are stranger than they are familiar, but such a sight lasts just a moment. It flickers; then family life resumes. In a tone more affirmative than resigned, Tyler returns her characters to old relationships or dissolves them in new ones barely distinguishable from those they had known before. The dazzling sight of an individual is, like the flush of first love, merely an illusion. It is a momentary glimpse of a young person's features before they become a "Dower nose," the "Peck eyes," the persistent marks of family, an organism more lasting than any of its members.

Thus the Tulls of *Dinner at the Homesick Restaurant* are a family in spite of themselves, one generation indelibly marked by the hurts and mistakes of the last. They are a small family living to themselves in a Baltimore row house, cut off from their ancestors and their neighbors. Pearl, an old-maidish woman, married Beck Tull, a bounder. She moved with him half a dozen times, lost track of her past, bore three children, Ezra, Cody, and Jenny, and, after Beck walked out on them, reared them, in rage, frustration, and poverty. Dying, Pearl muses with regret that "something was wrong with all of her children," and she wishes to be excused of blame for the hurt and anger she has passed on to them. She thinks of Cody: "Honestly . . . wasn't there some statute of limitations here? When was he going to absolve her? He was middle-aged. He had no business holding her responsible any more." There is in Tyler's world no statute of limitations; the sins and hurts of the fathers and mothers are visited upon the sons and daughters for countless generations.

Like *Earthly Possessions* and *Searching for Caleb,* this family's story is told in flashbacks, from a present in which the mother is old and dying, the children grown. Like *The Clock Winder* and *Celestial Navigation,* it is told from different points of view, which show the gaps in the Tulls' understanding of their single, shared past.

They have weathered it with few external scars. Pearl as a grandmother has a peace and gentleness she never had as a mother. Ezra, if somewhat dreamy and distant, manages a restaurant where he seeks to dispense to the world the warm nourishment his childhood missed. Jenny, competent and cool, is a pediatrician and mother to a brood of children, her own and those she has acquired in her third marriage. She seems fully recovered from a nervous breakdown when she, as a young medical student, was abusing her daughter as her mother had her. And Cody is a financial success, something of a wizard as a time efficiency consultant. But in Jenny's distant cheerfulness is the defensive armor by which the hurt child learned to cope. And in all his inner life, Cody is the angry sibling, jealous of his mother's preference for his brother, guilty over his father's desertion, unable ever to trust, however desperately he clings to them, the wife he stole from his brother and the son he fantasizes is not his own.

Year after year, decade after decade, they come "home" to family dinners interrupted by quarrels that wait, never settled, to trip them up each time. Pearl has carefully instructed Ezra to "invite" everyone in her address book to her funeral. At the last dinner after the funeral, the absent father is with them, just as, in a sense, he has always been part of all they have suffered and become. He looks around and remarks, "'Haven't you all turned out fine—leading good lives, the three of you?'" He has been coaxed back to the table after one quarrel but will not stay long, warning them he will leave before the dessert wine is poured.

Dinner at the Homesick Restaurant has been much praised for the qualities Tyler has long been noted for—her wit, her rendering of detail, her compassion—and it has been praised beyond these for its intensity and darkness. John Updike, who has long championed her work, says it shows a "new level of power." Benjamin DeMott says that its truths are "deeper than many living novelists of serious reputation have penetrated, deeper than Miss Tyler herself has gone before. It is a border crossing."

The border is of anger and pain. The depth and power of the book derive from Pearl's barely contained rage that now consumes her son and is clearly marking her grandson Luke. And the work articulates less of tragic insight than Tyler has allowed before. No characters see through mistakes and pain to another vision of the wonder of common life. Less, not more, is articulated of what the Tulls have learned from pounding down life's ruts.

Brief moments of vision do come. The old blind Pearl is humored by Ezra's reading pages of her old diaries and scrapbooks to her. Among these, at the last, they discover an entry from her girlhood, of herself kneeling in a garden, dirty and perspiring, hearing someone play the piano, seeing a fly buzz: "I saw that I was kneeling on such a beautiful green little planet. I don't care what else might come about, I have had this moment. It belongs to me." The book closes with Cody's recollection of a frozen moment from a long-ago family outing that ended disastrously with his shooting his mother with an arrow: "He remembered his mother's upright form along the grasses, her hair lit gold, her small hands smoothing her bouquet while the arrow journeyed on. And high above, he seemed to recall, there had been a little brown airplane, almost motionless, droning through the sunshine like a bumblebee."

Like Virginia Woolf's "Moments of Being," these are occasions when life seems to break through the shell of the characters' consciousness. They are as fine and shining as any Tyler has drawn. It is only the placement of them in the characters' lives that makes this work darker than its predecessors. They are remembrances for Pearl even a "forgotten" memory, triggered by the diary, for Cody a day long ago in his childhood. The life that is un-being has gathered round and darkened Pearl; there is no hope that this vision will effect any change in Cody's way of seeing himself, his brother, or his wife and son.

In the shifting points of view of *Dinner at the Homesick Restaurant,* none of the characters reveal self-understanding. What in earlier works were much-understated pronouncements, outspoken only in the case of Morgan Gower, of what they had learned of the wonder of everyday life lived piecemeal is here only for the reader to see. Over and over in Tyler's world—she says she has been populating a town—rings the question of *Our Town,* "Do any human beings ever realize life while they live it, every, every minute?" The answer of *Restaurant* is no, not every minute, not any minutes at all.

Reviewing the book, DeMott says that Tyler has taken the reader beyond the "truism" that adversity teaches: "the important lessons taught by adversity never quite make themselves known to the consciousness of the learners—remain hidden, inexpressible." He finds in the book an Emersonian kind of compensation, a psychic ability to endure, which is like a physical attribute, the strength derived from stress. Bruised psyches, like broken bones and scarred skin, heal tougher. What is best in these characters, DeMott says, Ezra's wordless nurturing and Jenny's determined cheerfulness, results from their deprivation.

With her tenth novel, *The Accidental Tourist,* Tyler received the National Book Critics' Circle Award, critical America's recognition of the importance of her rendering of family life and characters in a perpetual pull between returning home and running away. Some, in Tyler's books and in her audience, where most Americans move at least once in five years and half of all marriages end in divorce, dream of a glamour that recedes forever in the distance. Not so is Macon Leary, the "accidental tourist," author of books for people who prefer to go nowhere, guides to tell the business traveler where he can find, in Madrid "king-sized Beautyrest Mattresses," in Tokyo "Sweet'n Low," in Stockholm "Kentucky Fried Chicken."

It is a story that begins in grief and ends in joy. The catalyst to the action has occurred. Leary's only son, Ethan, has been murdered in one of the bizarre phenomena that fill the news, in a shoot-out at a fast-food restaurant. The routine of their lives disrupted, its meaning unclear to her, his wife, Sarah, leaves him. Leary's journey is from solitude in their empty house, back to his childhood home, inhabited by his siblings, to an affair with Muriel, a not-at-all-routine young dog trainer, back to his wife, and finally to Paris, whither both women pursue him, the old and the new claiming his life. The seesaw on which the passive Macon teeters between them is so carefully balanced that the novel feels as if written to go ei-

ther way. Like reviewers of mystery tales, one hates to tell the end and spoil the reader's fun.

Tyler's novels alternate between those interrupted at the high or the low of her circles of return and departure, between those that suggest the inevitability of the past's wounds and those that proclaim the persistent possibility of happy accident in life. Some, like *The Clock Winder,* end in scenes of homey—"cozy" is a favorite word of hers—family life; there the gathered clan, several generations, a new baby, a new bride, and the seventeen-year locusts symbolize the cyclical rise and fall of the welfare and troubles of the tribe. *Dinner at the Homesick Restaurant* ends with the dinner that is but a momentary interlude in the Tulls' lives of separation. *A Slipping-Down Life* and *Celestial Navigation* close in loneliness. *Earthly Possessions* and *The Tin Can Tree* end in returns, in new visions of people in old settings; *If Morning Ever Comes, Searching for Caleb, Morgan's Passing,* and *The Accidental Tourist* end with departures. Her first novel and her latest end in new marriages.

A corollary to the theme of staying in place and moving on, that of belonging and estrangement, has also a happy twist in this work. The characters, while no less caught up in personal turmoil and no more political than their predecessors, live in less bleak isolation. Though the hero wanders in limbo for most of the book, his sister looks out for her elderly neighbors on the block where she has always lived. Muriel, his girlfriend, has weathered the hurt of a husband's desertion to live on easy terms with neighbors who make themselves at home in her kitchen. When pipes freeze at Leary's home and it floods, neighbors notice, though, like a typical Tyler hero, he has gone off without telling anyone where he is going.

Though the protagonist returns to his family home and to spending evenings playing an old game intelligible only to his siblings, the book holds more of adult struggles and of sexual lure and less of the griefs of children than earlier novels. *Dinner at the Homesick Restaurant* provoked at least one strong attack that Tyler's insistence on the primacy of childhood hurts and rivalries was a case of "arrested development." Here Tyler is closer to such writers as Updike, Oates, Beattie, Didion, who treat frequently the insubstantiality of connections, the breakups of loves and marriages. Still her voice is distinct. To most of her characters, as to Leary's grandfather in this novel, relatives acquired by marriage, even spouses, hardly count.

The third tension in Tyler's work, finally the most important, is between the view of life as a still, bright, timeless present and the dull routine of years, which films sight and blurs the outlines of self, of others, and of earth itself to a smudge of dust and clutter. Leary and the two women form a triangle in what and how they see. He is not surprised by life but has all along, before tragedy struck, seen its capacity for violence.

Long before Ethan's murder, he watched helplessly as the child ran into a street before a truck and in "one split second" saw through life's terror and its caprice, "adjusted to a future that held no Ethan—an immeasurably bleaker place but also, by way of compensation, plainer and simpler. . . ."

The wife, Sarah, startled by the tragedy, is awakened to bitterness and is resentful of her husband's impassive surface, a trait he shares with most Tyler heroes of being distant and uncommunicative. Hers is a vision of the evil in a world of human atrocity. As one of Tyler's uninitiated, she seeks expression of their grief and complains of his "muffled quality." Like a Tyler hero, reticent and as wary of words as of commitment, he can answer her cries that life has lost its point only with, "Honey, to tell the truth, it never seemed to me there was all that much point to begin with."

Muriel is tough where Sarah was sheltered but has through her suffering acquired a different vision. At the birth of her child, premature and sickly, her husband bolted; she worked for months as a hospital maid. Vision came to her as she stared out a window at ambulances arriving and attendants scurrying. A Martian visitor surprising Earth at such a moment would, she muses, observe "what a helpful planet, what kind and helpful creatures" and would not guess this was not "natural" human behavior.

Flashes of vision can be of terror or of loveliness. Another window in the novel is the lens through which Leary sees life as separation. As a dutiful author of guides he visits a round glass restaurant of the sort, the tops of something or other, that dot American cities. Looking out, he observes "the planet curving away at the edges, the sky a purple hollow extending to infinity." He is terrified at the "vast lonely distance from everyone who mattered. . . . He was too far gone to return. He would never, ever get back. He had somehow traveled to a point completely isolated from everyone else in the universe, and nothing was real but his own angular hand clenched around the sherry glass."

In Tyler's writing, the direct point of a plot is to bring people to a still moment of vision. But moments of epiphany seem to come unpredictably, by "accident," and to have little to do with process or progress, to be timeless, disconnected from the daily order.

Most of her characters, caught in the routines of life, travel the same streets for years without seeing them. Caught in the webs of old relationships, they go for decades without acute sense of closeness or distance. Lives fall into patterns that people do not devise, that they perpetuate but do not desire. Over and over, they play the same games, fight the same no-win wars with their kin, living and dead. Patterns triumph over all will to break out, as in the clan of Pecks: "Everything was leveled, there were no extremes of joy or sorrow

any more but only habit, routine, ancient family names and rites and customs, slow careful old people moving cautiously around furniture that had sat in the same positions for fifty years."

Routine is comforting to some, terrifying to others for the same reason, that it blinds them to the significance of life or to the sense of self. These come only in momentary flashes, epiphanies stark or tender, always unsettling. At these rare moments, by an altered angle of vision, characters see life's possibilities, not merely its worn outlines. Mary Tell of *Celestial Navigation,* one of the most articulate of Tyler's heroines, reflecting over her life with Jeremy, says, "We have such an ability to adjust to change! We are like amoebas, encompassing and ingesting and adapting and moving on, until enormous events become barely perceptible jogs in our life histories." *Morgan's Passing* closed with its hero's vision of a world aglow: "Everything . . . luminous and beautiful, and rich with possibilities." And Leary, the accidental tourist, rides off to a new life, the dirty windows of a taxi the prism through which he views a bright future: "A sudden flash of sunlight hit the windshield, the spangles flew across the glass. The spangles were old water spots, or maybe the markings of leaves, but for a moment Macon thought they were something else. They were so bright and festive, for a moment he thought they were confetti."

Tyler cannot take her heroes very far into a new life, for soon wonder subsides to dullness. Tourists may see things afresh, but the human eye seems able to see, really see, things only once. Then routine films the vision; habit and clutter fill the days; nothing will have changed very much.

But the moments of detachment from time matter as much in her world as the patterns of years that she records so well. They are the moments when time meets eternity. The tension in her work is finally not only between going and staying but also between living and seeing. In attachment, they live; in detachment, they see.

What do her works then teach, with their passive, unchanging heroes, their circular plots? Certainly not the efficacy of human moral resolve, nothing of the energy of a Protestant work ethic, and nothing either of caution against heedless rapidity, headlong careening toward tragedy. Mostly it is a lesson of mundane quietism. It is through contemplation, not action, not even the articulation of the lessons of insight, that some of Tyler's characters move from feeling that life has them trapped in patterns too old and strong for them to break, to the vision of Morgan Gower, one of her least popular but happiest heroes, that there is "virtue in the trivial, the commonplace."

Tyler is still a young writer, celebrating her forty-seventh birthday in October 1988. Tyler is her maiden name; she was born to Phyllis and Lloyd Tyler in Minneapolis, Minnesota, in 1941. The features of her childhood that may have mattered most to her writing are that the family lived for some years in communes and that she felt herself something of an outsider when they moved to Raleigh, North Carolina, very much a small Southern town in her day. As a student, she was bright and precocious, graduating Phi Beta Kappa from Duke University at age nineteen. She has been married since 1963 to Taghi Modaressi, a psychiatrist. They have two daughters, Tezh and Mitra. After working briefly in the Duke University library and McGill University library, she has been "just writing," in her words, since 1965 and living with the family in Baltimore, Maryland, since 1967.

She has said that she spent her adolescence "as a semi-outsider—a Northerner, commune-reared, looking wistfully at large Southern families around me." The notes about the author printed in her books, however, say she "considers herself a Southerner." The primacy of family as her subject, the attention to time, the influence of the past on the present and future, the settings, the use of one setting over and over, the attention to manners and to folk speech, the range of characters from the quaintly anachronistic to the eccentric to the grotesque, the writer's sense of being outside are all qualities for which she and other writers are tagged as Southern.

While these features are wholly true of her work, they do not mark her as exclusively a regional writer; some qualifications may be in order. John Updike has written that her belief "that families are absolutely, intrinsically interesting" is "extinct save in the South." If so, it wasn't always so; Tyler has Jane Austen and Henry James for predecessors here. Novelists of all great traditions draw the locale and the speech patterns they know, but it is true that Tyler has concentrated on her Southern experience. She has exploited only briefly in short pieces the subject of international difference that her marriage to an Iranian might have permitted. Tyler speaks often of the influence of Eudora Welty on her becoming a writer. In her education and reading, her teachers having been Phyllis Peacock in high school and Reynolds Price at Duke, she was also under Southern influence.

On the question of eccentrics, Tyler is as defensive as Flannery O'Connor but for a different reason, individuality itself being the source of peculiarity for Tyler. Her self-absorbed grotesques certainly have their counterparts in Southern fiction, but as some critics of her work have noted, all modern literature is full of pathologically self-absorbed characters. And the posture of the artist as self-conscious outsider knows no regional boundaries.

But putting the locus of value in the private life alone sets Tyler apart from the broad historical concerns of the main current of Southern writing. Like her insular families and anachronistic individuals, Tyler lacks the perspective of those writers—Simms, Page, Cable, Glasgow, Faulkner, Wolfe, Porter, Agee, Warren, Tate, Williams, Settle, Capote, Lee, Betts, Walker, Smith—who have examined Southern American life for the shaping force of cultural habits and beliefs on individual lives. If Tyler has her eyes always to the timeless, as does Flannery O'Connor, she has not O'Connor's attention to the historical versions of her creed. Tyler's characters, whether they find their way or lose it, do so with little effect from any religious or social dogma that they share with any identifiable class or segment in their communities.

Without concern for placing her characters in large social or historical context, Tyler treats them in families, not as lone individuals seeking self-expression or self-identity. She is thus doubly distant from much twentieth-century feminist writing, which frequently does one or the other.

Like Anne Bradstreet, Anne Tyler writes of "thyme and parsley" wreaths, not "bays," nor "wars," "captains," "kings," "cities founded, commonwealths begun." Whether this makes her a pacesetting female writer, taking the subjects of women's lives, marriage, child rearing, housekeeping, and tending the aged as life's most important business, or whether it puts her to the right of Phyllis Schlafly, relegating women and her own art to the backwaters, depends on the critic's bias. Some have sneered that her work falls between high art and stuff for women's magazines. Tyler continues to write for women's magazines, as well as for the *New Yorker*. Her insistence on the primacy of roles of mother, spouse, and tender of the hearth is certainly old-fashioned, if not anti-feminist.

Tyler's work shares the subject matter of the feminist revolution but not its attitudes. In her novels and stories, fathers are often absent, dead or run away. Her heroines live interruptible lives. Her happiest visions of human life as well as her stiffest are of extended families. Rarely she exploits the pathos of children. In one short story, a small boy carries from house to house photographs of foster families he has stayed with. In another, a young single mother of a teenage marriage that failed leaves her retarded son at an asylum.

Tyler regularly makes women the strong centers of the home, but strength is not always benevolent, and she never presents women "achievers," the strong hero models some ardent feminists have called for. Though Tyler's women manage domestic details with ease, when they attempt to exert influence on people, they often become meddlesome, half-humorous harridans, half-terrifying vixens, driving their husbands and children from them. These clean-house busybodies, like Mrs. Emerson and Pearl Tull, are cold and sexless, equaling Eliza Gant in their destructive force. The strong women portrayed with affection are easygoing, passive. They are unaffected by a baby on their hip, milk dribbled or spilt down their clothes; best of all they can nurse the baby, get locusts out of the parlor, branches out of the gutters, and receive unexpected in-laws for dinner with a nary a flap.

Many have used the word "private" about Anne Tyler's life, as she so often describes herself. Her life is centered on her family and her work; anything else, she says, just "fritters" her away. And as she describes it, it is an old-fashioned life of a woman, in which she tends children first and does what she pleases—writing—last. For years, Tyler says, she worked when her children were in school and put aside her writing during vacations or when someone was ill, or when company came, or when the dog had to go to the vet. Still, she has argued against the idea that this interruptible life has been less beneficial to her work, not to mention to her emotional life, than that of her husband, also a writer, who has had to go off to the hospital every day. To such constraint, Tyler has asked for no "liberation." Certainly her production of ten novels and at least one volume's worth of uncollected short stories shows that she has not been "silenced," in Tillie Olsen's word, by her woman's lot, And she has found in her family the richest emotional lode for her work.

The chief features of Tyler's life are echoed in the critical reception of her work. She has given her own family the central position; she was a precocious young person; she has led an apparently stable adult life. Critics have dwelt on related issues, some praising her examination of the inner life, some complaining that her range is too narrow. Her early work was declared astonishingly good for one so young. The most frequently expressed reservation against her work has been that she has not developed the potential she first promised. Like her adult life, Tyler's development as a writer has been without sudden shifts of direction.

Disagreement about Tyler's work comes not in descriptions of it, where the agreement is fairly widespread, but in estimates of the value of what she does. Her admirers praise her wit, her humor, which by contemporary measure is a kindly, not a sardonic, humor, her sense of detail, her characterization, her emotional power, her compassion, her wisdom, and the understanding she has for inner pain and joy in outwardly unremarkable lives.

Sometimes even her admirers complain that her writing is too literary, that she strains for effect. They may balk at her odd juxtapositions, her wry observations, her method of piling on detail. At worst she has been called "arch," "coy," and "glib."

The place Tyler occupies in American letters seems to have much to do with the fact that she is not in step with the waves of fiction in the last two decades. The absence of a moral dimension, the fact that her characters are often mistaken but are not "evil" or "good," makes them seem without excitement or importance to some. To others, attuned to the newer

vogues of a hard-boiled age, she is tender, almost soft. In years when many artists employ violent projection and subdued response, Tyler depicts deeply resonant perception and memory. Although she is of this century, she has been ever more distant from a literary current moving away from her. Her adoption of Eudora Welty as a model was old-fashioned thirty years ago. It is now antique, fine and good to those who appreciate it, not likely to be imitated by a younger generation. Tyler's ardent admirers include those not delighted with the newest modes of American writing, for whom she is a model of timeless worth.

Her last works show greater control over her characterization, a surer sense of balance in descriptive detail, and the writer comfortable at a fairly great distance from her characters, relying less on their explaining themselves and more on dramatic scene. Anne Tyler has never been voguish; she is unlikely to become so even if the movie of *The Accidental Tourist* becomes all the rage with the young set. Her distance may continue to limit her reputation somewhat. With the audience she has, she is probably content.

Jay Parini (review date 25 August 1991)

SOURCE: "The Accidental Convert," in *The New York Times Book Review*, August 25, 1991, pp. 1, 26.

[*In the following review, Parini states that Tyler's* Saint Maybe *is "a realistic chronicle that celebrates family life without erasing the pain and boredom that families almost necessarily inflict upon their members."*]

Anne Tyler likes to break America's heart, and she will do it again in *Saint Maybe.* Her subject, as ever, is family life, with the family pictured as a kind of leaky but durable vessel that ferries her motley characters down the tortuous river of time. Ms. Tyler is fascinated by the unexpected ways that people affect one another, for good and ill, and this fascination has given her shelf of books an impressive unity. *Saint Maybe,* her 12th novel, is vintage Tyler, delicately stamped, like a watermark, with her intimate and unmistakable voice.

One is used by now to Ms. Tyler's oddball families, which any self-respecting therapist would call "dysfunctional" but which Ms. Tyler's readers find endearing. There are, for instance, the Pecks of *Searching for Caleb,* the Tulls of *Dinner at the Homesick Restaurant,* the Learys of *The Accidental Tourist.* An inexplicable centripetal force hurls these relatives upon one another, catches them in a dizzying inward spiral of obligation, affection and old-fashioned guilt—as well as an inexpressible longing for some perfect or "normal" family in a distant past that never really was.

Almost every novel by Anne Tyler begins with a loss or absence that reactivates in the family some primordial sense of itself, and *Saint Maybe* is no exception. The novel rocks on the fulcrum of its hero, Ian Bedloe, who believes himself responsible for the death of his older brother, Danny, killed in a late-night car crash after an angry confrontation with Ian. Danny's wife, grief-stricken and unstable, soon commits suicide, leaving behind three children (two from her previous marriage, to a man who has vanished). Overwhelmed by guilt, Ian takes unusual measures to redeem himself. Inspired by a weird but engaging little Protestant splinter group called the Church of the Second Chance, he drops out of college after only one semester to help his parents care for the orphaned children.

Ian, the Saint Maybe of the title, sponges up our emotions as Ms. Tyler tracks him fondly through several decades. At 17, he has "the Bedloe golden-brown hair, golden skin, and sleepy-looking brown eyes." His fairy-tale good looks are somehow enhanced by his off-hand way of dressing, and when he becomes a cabinetmaker (as Jesus was a carpenter?), specializing in fine furniture built without nails according to ancient principles, he has every opportunity to dress down. We rarely see him—even at church—in anything but jeans and a T-shirt. Two decades later, he is described excitedly by Rita diCarlo—a zany mansaver perhaps too reminiscent of Muriel Pritchett in *The Accidental Tourist*: "The clothes in his closet smell of nutmeg. . . . He has this really fine face; it's all straight lines. I thought at first his eyes were brown but then I saw they had a clear yellow light to them like some kind of drink; like cider." Rita, as one might expect, comes vividly into Ian's life before the novel closes.

Ms. Tyler charges Ian Bedloe with a wonderfully subtle sexual presence. She does this, cannily, by making his avoidance of sexuality a defining characteristic. His sexual life begins predictably, with a pretty girlfriend called Cicely, with whom he sleeps on the weekends while at college. Once he joins the Church of the Second Chance, the sex stops, and Cicely, alas, falls away. Ms. Tyler peeps into Ian's fantasy life: "In his daydreams, he walked into services one morning and found a lovely, golden-haired girl sitting in the row just ahead. She would be so intent on the sermon that she wouldn't even look his way: she had grown up in a religion very much like this one, it turned out, and believed with all her heart. After the Benediction Ian introduced himself, and she looked shy and pleased." And so forth, onward and heavenly upward.

Only Anne Tyler could make an arresting novel out of material like this. She does so, I think, by placing Ian at a series of perilous crossroads, as when he becomes frustrated with unclehood and hires a detective called Eli Everjohn (who also appears in *Searching for Caleb*) to find his sister-in-law's first husband. Meanwhile the reader bites off a few nails,

waiting to see if Ian will do the proverbial "right thing"—not for himself, so much, as for the children.

Ms. Tyler is one of the few contemporary writers who can really "do" children, and her brood steals the reader's heart. There is homely Agatha, whose wry confidence anticipates a moving turn at the story's end. There is Thomas, her self-contained younger brother, who remains firmly in the shadows throughout the novel. And there is Daphne, the youngest, who has everybody's number; sassy but lovable, she teeters on the brink of waywardness, always retreating at the last moment into a kind of idiosyncratic goodness. It is she who, in a moment of gentle derision, refers to her Uncle Ian as "King Careful. Mr. Look-Both-Ways. Saint Maybe."

The Church of the Second Chance is never far from the center of this novel, and Ms. Tyler mines its comic potential with ruthless affection. This genial flock of fundamentalist misfits has a kindly but firm shepherd in its founder, Reverend Emmett. (Emmett is his first name, since last names are scorned by Second Chancers; they remind one too much "of the superficial—the world of wealth and connections and who came over on the *Mayflower*.") What binds the members of this distinctly downscale congregation is their adamant belief in the need for "amending"—for showing God they are serious about making up for past sins by doing good deeds. Ian, for instance, makes amends for his part in his brother's death by helping to raise Agatha, Thomas and Daphne.

For all his noble self-sacrifice, Ian is hardly alone in raising the children. Ms. Tyler is intrigued by family circles, and she draws a wide one in *Saint Maybe*. Ian's parents, Bee and Doug, are the sort of people who can be found in any McDonald's on a Saturday afternoon with a gang of grandchildren. They say things like "hot dog" and exude good will. Their tumbledown house on Waverly Street in Baltimore is a world unto itself; indeed, as the "real" world grows steadily less tolerable down the decades, the Bedloes rely increasingly on one another for the little decencies, the graceful touches, that make life bearable.

Saint Maybe is not without flaws (I'm reminded of Randall Jarrell's definition of a novel as a long narrative that has something wrong with it). Ian's abrupt decision to drop everything, including his sex life, to assuage his guilt is not foreshadowed: Ms. Tyler doesn't sketch Ian's adolescence with sufficient particularity to make his decision plausible. And a fair number of the peripheral characters—like the continuously changing group of "foreigners," students who live nearby and who attend the Bedloes' annual Christmas fest—seem astonishingly caricatured.

Nonetheless, I adored *Saint Maybe*. It's not as complex a narrative as either *The Accidental Tourist* or *Dinner at the Homesick Restaurant*. Nor is it a whimsical tour de force like ***Breathing Lessons,*** which won a Pulitzer Prize. But in many ways it is Anne Tyler's most sophisticated work, a realistic chronicle that celebrates family life without erasing the pain and boredom that families almost necessarily inflict upon their members. Ian Bedloe, for his part, sits near the top of Ms. Tyler's fine list of heroes. Exactly how she makes us care so much about him remains a mystery to me. That is, perhaps, the mystery of art.

Gene Koppel (essay date Fall 1991)

SOURCE: "Maggie Moran, Anne Tyler's Madcap Heroine: A Game-Approach to *Breathing Lessons,*" in *Essays in Literature,* Vol. XVIII, No. 2, Fall, 1991, pp. 276-87.

[*In the following essay, Koppel discusses the game playing in Tyler's* Breathing Lessons *and the assertion that a balance between game playing and responsibility is necessary to live successfully.*]

When Maggie Moran, a nursing assistant in a home for the elderly and the central character of Anne Tyler's novel ***Breathing Lessons,*** tries to locate a favorite patient during a fire drill, the resulting fiasco bears more than a coincidental resemblance to a slapstick scene from an *I Love Lucy* episode. Maggie ends up in a part of the home off-limits to her and leaps into a laundry cart to conceal herself when she thinks she detects the approach of a supervisor:

> Absurd, she knew it instantly. She was cursing herself even as she sank among the crumpled linens. She might have got away with it, though, except that she'd set the cart to rolling. Somebody grabbed it and drew it to a halt. A growly voice said, "What in the world?"

It is not a supervisor, but a fellow employee. The latter, however, having discovered Maggie inside the cart, mischievously calls over another attendant standing nearby and together the two noisily and rapidly push the cart down the corridor. At the end of Maggie's ride stand, of course, the two people who can embarrass her the most, Mrs. Inman, "the director of nursing for the entire home," and the man Maggie was seeking, Mr. Gabriel. The latter is a dignified gentleman whom Maggie admires and who (she believes) had admired Maggie for her competence and self-command. He will think of her this way no longer.

That Anne Tyler expects the reader to compare Maggie Moran's laundry-cart episode to television situation comedy is clearly indicated one page later:

> Maybe [Mr. Gabriel] could view her as a sort of *I*

Love Lucy type—madcap, fun-loving, full of irrepressible high spirits. That was one way to look at it. Actually, Maggie had never liked *I Love Lucy.* She thought the plots were so engineered—that dizzy woman's failures just built-in, just guaranteed. But maybe Mr. Gabriel felt differently.

But Mr. Gabriel is not amused by his real-life Lucy; his idealization of Maggie ends with this incident. The reader's interest in Maggie, however, continues. Unlike Mr. Gabriel, the reader has never had illusions about Maggie. That aspects of her character are similar to Lucy Ricardo's has probably occurred to him before. For example, in the opening scene of the novel Maggie calls for the family car at the body shop; the moment she pulls into the street she collides with a truck [she had turned on her radio to a local talk show and mistakenly thought she heard the voice of her former daughter-in-law announcing an approaching second marriage]. Hearing the crash, the manager of the body shop rushes out; when he yells,

> "What the. . . ? Are you all right?" she stared straight ahead in a dignified way and told him, "Certainly. Why do you ask?" and drove on before the Pepsi driver could climb out of his truck, which was probably just as well considering the look on his face.

Maggie's resemblance to Lucy has been implicit since the beginning of the novel.

If a reader wishes, it would be easy to argue that the above Lucy-passages work to undercut the positive elements in Maggie's character; some of the early reviewers of ***Breathing Lessons*** disapproved of Tyler's associating her heroine with a popular television character. Still, I do not believe that most readers will respond to Maggie's failures with the easy, condescending laughter that they give to the shallow farce of a typical television comedy. For both Maggie's games and the textual world which contains them are related to actual life in complex ways which Lucy's games are not.

While many of the pursuits and activities of our everyday world are often casually referred to as "games," most people (not only book reviewers) look askance at those, like Maggie, who seem to have difficulty distinguishing "real life" from actual games. Ira Moran clearly disapproves of Maggie's confusion of life and play:

> And his wife! He loved her, but he couldn't stand how she refused to take her own life seriously. She seemed to believe it was a sort of practice life, something she could afford to play around with as if they offered second and third chances to get it right. She was always making clumsy, impetuous rushes toward nowhere in particular—side trips, random detours.

The truth is—if we judge him by our society's standards of financial and social success—Ira Moran has fared no better than Maggie in the real world. Both were highly intelligent, promising high-school students. After high school, however, Ira reluctantly took over his family's picture-framing shop to support his hypochondriac father and two agoraphobic sisters instead of pursuing his plan to become a doctor. Maggie more willingly gave up her chance to go to Goucher College, becoming instead a nurse's aid in a retirement home. Both are quite aware that they are, in the usual sense of the word, failures. Ira laments that he "was fifty years old and had never accomplished one single act of consequence." And, during a depressed moment, Maggie makes an assessment of their lives that is even more depressing than Ira's:

> What Maggie's mother said was true: The genera-
> tions were sliding downhill in this family. They were
> descending in every respect, not just in their profes-
> sions and educations but in the way they reared their
> children and the way they ran their households.

Thus the Morans realize that the great majority of their con-temporaries must consider them to be almost completely in-ept at the game of success—a game which many believe is the most serious thing in life.

On the other hand, Maggie and Ira are also aware that the game of material success is not "the only game in town." During a rare family outing to the Baltimore harbor, when he seriously considers the value of the commitments he has made, Ira's regrets disappear:

> He hugged [his sister Dorrie's] bony little body close
> and gazed over her head at the *Constellation* float-
> ing in the fog. . . . And Junie had pressed close to
> his other side and Maggie and [his father] Sam had
> watched steadfastly, waiting for him to say what to
> do next. He had known then what the true waste was:
> Lord, yes. It was not his having to support these
> people but his failure to notice how he loved them.

Ira is only human and thus cannot sustain this intense aware-ness of his love for these helpless, difficult people for more than an "instant," but there is no doubt that this love plays an important role in authenticating his existence. And the reader also does not doubt that Maggie finds in her work and in her efforts (wise and otherwise) to love and help her family what she needs to consider her life worthwhile.

Ira's disapproval of Maggie's less-than-serious approach to life might lead the reader to suppose that Ira himself has little room in his life for playing games, but this would not be true. There are two pastimes that Ira holds dear. The first is an elaborate form of solitaire in which he indulges as often as possible; the second is losing himself in books which center on the adventures of lonely explorers: "It struck [Maggie] as very significant that Ira's idea of entertainment was those interminable books about men who sailed the Atlantic abso-lutely alone." These books obviously provide Ira with vi-carious adventures which give him relief from his daily routines and responsibilities, but Maggie is correct about the significance of his preference for solitary heroes. Earlier we learned that "Ira didn't have any friends. It was one of the things Maggie minded about him." And we also learn that Ira cannot cope with life's grimmer contingencies (which is rather ironic, when one remembers that he had longed to be a doc-tor):

> How peculiar [Ira] was about death! He couldn't
> handle even minor illness and had found reasons to
> stay away from the hospital the time she had her
> appendix out. . . . Whenever one of the children fell
> sick, he'd pretended it wasn't happening. . . . Any
> hint that he wouldn't live forever—when he had to
> deal with life insurance, for instance—made him
> grow set-faced and stubborn and resentful.

Perhaps, then, Ira's favorite game of solitaire, which he plays with a deck of cards he keeps in his pocket (he even carries it on the funeral journey that takes up the first section of the novel), provides him with a framework within which he can cope with and even enjoy the element of contingency which terrifies him in the actual world. And as there is nothing in our lives that is either more important or more undependable than our fellow human beings, it is clear why Ira's imaginings are most comfortable when they center on vicarious voyag-ing with men whose isolation makes them impervious to the unreliability of any other person. The books about solitary explorers and the games of solitaire provide him with frame-works within which he can confidently face the unpredict-able element in life—as his making and selling of picture frames provide him and his family another kind of "frame-work" to order life in a way they find tolerable. (There is a roughly parallel situation in *The Accidental Tourist* with Macon Leary and his family; the latter are also more terrified of the unpredictable world and even more irrationally com-pulsive in their routines than Macon himself.)

The readers of *Breathing Lessons,* like the viewers of *I Love Lucy,* know that the heroine's game-strategies are comically doomed from the beginning. And Maggie—as Lucy would be in her place—is pathetically sincere about her devious, far-fetched scheme of reuniting her terminally immature son, Jesse, with his former wife, Fiona, and his daughter (and Maggie's only grandchild), Leroy. First, on their way back from the funeral, Maggie persuades Ira to detour to the small town where Fiona is living with her mother. Next, she ma-nipulates Fiona and Leroy into riding back with her and Ira to their home in Baltimore where (through a surreptitious telephone call from Fiona's home) she has arranged for Jesse to appear at dinner.

The reunion dinner proves to be a fiasco. Jesse, fearful that his ex-wife and his family view him as a "loser" (the word that game-players dread hearing above any other), is too tense and defensive to control his childish ego and his temper long enough to establish any kind of meaningful communication with his wife and daughter. But it is Ira who brings the dinner to a sudden end with a brutally frank condemnation of his son. He reveals to Fiona that Jesse is living with another woman and then describes what he believes is his son's permanent inability to overcome his inadequacies:

> This is the way things *are* . . . [Jesse] never was fit husband material! He passes from girlfriend to girlfriend and he can't seem to hold the same job for longer than a few months; and every job he loses, it's somebody else's fault.

As a result of this speech, Jesse (rapidly followed by Fiona and Leroy) walks out on Maggie's reconciliation dinner.

What conclusion is the reader supposed to draw from this incident—that Ira sees Jesse and others as they really are and Maggie sees them as she would like them to be? As Ira had explained to Fiona earlier, "It's Maggie's weakness: She believes it's all right to alter people's lives. She thinks the people she loves are better than they really are, and so then she starts changing things around to suit her view of them."

Is the reader, then, to conclude that Maggie views life as a game she can play according to her own rules and for her own amusement, in the course of which she is free to manipulate others? And, of course, to treat people as objects to be manipulated is unKantian, unChristian, and generally inhumane. This is certainly a possible interpretation of Maggie, but other factors are present in the text to qualify or even to reverse these conclusions. Maggie's rose-tinted glasses can be seen partly as weakness, partly as charity towards others. Similarly to Miss Bates in *Emma,* Maggie actually *sees* those she loves as better than they are: she is convinced that Jesse is *nearly* the young man she wants him badly to be and that he *could* be happily reunited with his family:

> She was in trouble with everybody in this house, and she deserved to be; as usual she had acted pushy and meddlesome. And yet it hadn't seemed like meddling while she was doing it. She had simply felt as if the world were the tiniest bit out of focus, the colors not quite within the lines—something like a poorly printed newspaper ad—and if she made the smallest adjustment then everything would settle perfectly into place.

If Maggie's inability to see life in all its grim reality can be considered, at least in part, a positive side to her character, Ira's clear-headed realism has its negative aspect. Ira has a deep fear, it will be recalled, of life's contingencies. Since his mother's death when he was fourteen, he has tried to avoid all thoughts of sickness or death or any other of life's unpleasant surprises. He refuses to make friends, obviously because friends, more often than family, disappoint one or prove unreliable. Thus there is a distinct possibility that his unchanging, bleak view of his son owes as much to his fear that hope will lead to disappointment as it does to the presence of an inner strength which always leads him to see things realistically. When Maggie interferes in the lives of Jesse and Fiona, it is to reunite them. When Ira interferes, it is to end the suspense associated with the shaky relationship of his son and Fiona. In this way Ira brings about the sad but secure state of a defeated relationship; Ira need no longer be disturbed by the insecure hope that his son will make a success of his marriage. It is a fear of life as much as the courage to face reality that underlies Ira's refusal to entertain illusions. On the other hand, Maggie is open to life in all its unpredictabilities: "Oh, Ira, you just don't give enough credit to luck," she says at one point. "Good luck or bad luck, either one." But giving credit to luck, to the unpredictability of life, is what Ira fears most.

Since Ira and Maggie are so different in their attitudes toward the contingencies of life, it might appear at first glance that the success of their marriage is either poorly conceived fiction or outright miracle. How somber, defensive Ira, with his rigidly ordered approach to life can tolerate, much less love his outgoing, recklessly playful wife is not an easy problem to resolve. There is no doubt, however, that Ira does love Maggie: "Well, face it, there were worse careers than cutting forty-five-degree angles in strips of gilded molding. And he did have Maggie, eventually—dropping into his lap like a wonderful gift out of nowhere." This unexpected development in his life Ira accepts without regret! I believe that the insight of Tony Tanner into the happy relationship of Jane Austen's stuffy hero, Fitzwilliam Darcy, and her light-hearted heroine, Elizabeth Bennet, in *Pride and Prejudice* will also serve for Anne Tyler's contrasting couple:

> . . . in their gradual coming together and Darcy's persistent desire for Elizabeth we do witness the perennial yearning of perfect symmetry for the asymmetrical, the appeal which 'playfulness' has for 'regulation', the irresistible attraction of the freely rambling individual for the rigidified upholder of the group. Indeed it could be said that it is on the tension between playfulness and regulation that society depends, and it is the fact that they are so happily 'united' by the end of the book which generates the satisfaction produced by the match.

The insight that successful relationships and successful societies need both the spirit of the game and the spirit of discipline not only explains Maggie and Ira Moran's satisfying marriage, it also explains why their son Jesse, who as a child loved to make up stories that "had in common the theme of joyousness, of the triumph of sheer fun over practicality," fails at every relationship and every task he attempts. What Jesse does not have, as Ira pointed out above, is perseverance, a sense of duty or responsibility which is necessary to sustain any relationship. Without this even Jesse's potential for love, which is very real, is largely wasted. As important as love is in Anne Tyler's fictional world, it cannot survive unless those who love are willing to adjust to and often simply to endure the complexities and strains which are always present in adult relationships. Ira's love for his emotionally maimed father and sisters is an obvious example of how much strength and sustained sacrifice can be demanded by those whom one loves. And in the central relationship in the novel, Ira and Maggie had to make drastic changes in their romantic expectations of each other. In the bedroom of Serena's house after the funeral Maggie discovers Ira alone, playing his game of solitaire, and reminisces with him about the early days of their marriage:

> He pondered a king, while Maggie laid her cheek on the top of his head. She seemed to have fallen in love again. In love with her own husband! The convenience of it pleased her—like finding right in her pantry all the fixings she needed for a new recipe.
>
> "Remember the first year we were married?" she asked him. "It was awful. We fought every minute."
>
> "Worst year of my life," he agreed, and when she moved around to the front he sat back slightly so she could settle on his lap. His thighs beneath her were long and bony—two planks of lumber. "Careful of my cards," he told her, but she could feel he was getting interested.

Of course, Maggie and Ira both have their moments of regretting the lost dreams of youth, the dreams of the perfect mate. Maggie realizes that her nursing-home friendship with Mr. Gabriel (before the Lucy-side of her emerged and destroyed his image of her) was a subconscious attempt to revive her (and Ira's) youthful romantic fantasies: "All Mr. Gabriel was, in fact, was Maggie's attempt to find an earlier version of Ira. She'd wanted the version she had known at the start of their marriage, before she'd begun disappointing him." But Maggie and Ira's love has survived the rough journey into reality. Jesse's love for his wife, Fiona, is capable of little more than beginning the trip.

Thus *Breathing Lessons* makes an unambiguous point about the need for the game-spirit to be accompanied by a sense of

responsibility and by the ability to endure through adversity. Without this "rule" of an underlying stable commitment the marriage-game has little chance of lasting long enough to bring fulfillment to the players. But there is also no doubt that the main emphasis of the novel is on the need of a spirit of play if a person is to be truly fulfilled.

The very form of the work itself attests to this. Ira Moran, it will be recalled, is frequently exasperated by Maggie's refusal to recognize that life is a deadly serious business; instead of living in dread of making wasteful errors, "She was always making clumsy, impetuous rushes toward nowhere in particular—side trips, random detours." And at the center (both literally and figuratively) of Anne Tyler's plot there is such a side trip, a seemingly random—and quite lengthy—detour with no apparent purpose. It comes about on the Morans' return trip from the funeral. Irritated by the erratic driving of an elderly African-American in front of them, Maggie shouts at the driver as Ira finally manages to pass him that his wheel is coming off. Then, guilt stricken, Maggie forces Ira to return to where the old man has stopped and gotten out of his car to contemplate his (falsely) suspect wheel. After some consideration, Mr. Otis (the name of the old man) gets into the Moran Dodge and Ira detours off the main highway and drives him to a Texaco station managed by his nephew, Lamont. There, while waiting for Lamont to return from a service call, Mr. Otis describes how his wife threw him out of the house because she had dreamed that he stood on her needlepoint chair and trampled on some of her embroidery. After Lamont arrives and learns what has happened, he castigates his old uncle both for his erratic driving and his childlike marital conduct (although ironically Lamont, like Jesse Moran, is divorced). Mr. Otis's reply to Lamont, which comes at the approximate center of the novel, is so important that both men's speeches are worth quoting at length:

> "You two act like quarrelsome children," Lamont told him.
>
> "Well, at least I'm still married, you notice!" Mr. Otis said. "At least I'm still married, unlike certain others I could name!"
>
> Ira said, "Well, at any rate—"
>
> "Even worse than children," Lamont went on, as if he hadn't heard. "Children at least got the time to spare, but you two are old and coming to the end of your lives. Pretty soon one or the other of you going to die and the one that's left behind will say, 'Why did I act so ugly? That was who it *was*; that person was who I was with; and here we threw ourselves away on spitefulness,' you'll say."
>
> "Well, it's probably going to be me that dies first,"

Mr. Otis said, "so I just ain't going to worry about that."

"I'm serious, Uncle."

"*I'm* serious. Could be what you throw away is all that really counts; could be that's the whole point of things, wouldn't that be something? Spill it! Spill it all, I say! No way *not* to spill it. And anyhow, just look at the times we had. Maybe that's what I'll end up thinking. 'My, we surely did have us a time. We were a real knock-down, drag-out, heart-and-soul type of couple,' I'll say. Something to reflect on in the nursing home."

Lamont rolled his eyes heavenward.

Lamont doesn't understand his uncle's musings on the essential importance of appreciating the non-essential, apparently foolish or wasteful aspects of life, and during a first reading perhaps the reader also doesn't understand why Anne Tyler has "thrown away" the central portion of her novel on an episode apparently unrelated to the main plot and characters. (Random House's recent cassette-recording condensation of *Breathing Lessons,* read by Jill Eikenberry, omits the entire Mr. Otis episode.)

But the detour to Lamont's station is no more wasted than the "unsuccessful" lives of Maggie and Ira Moran. *Breathing Lessons'* irregular form, as well as its characters and events, is a warning against taking the games of life and of art too seriously, or more accurately, against trying to make all women and men and all artists play the same kind of game, devoted to achieving the same kind of goal. At the same time, of course, Anne Tyler is providing us with a game; she eschews the obvious tight plot or transparently coherent form in which important, organic developments neatly fall into place without too much effort from the reader, and provides us instead with an eccentric, episodic plot which invites us to experience and evaluate the chain of events not in the spirit of a tight artistic logic but of adventure, of creativity.

Thus the psychology and spirit of game-playing permeate *Breathing Lessons,* shaping its characters, events, themes, and basic form. And in its central concern with game-playing the novel explores the nature of art itself. Hans-Georg Gadamer has based a large part of his philosophy on the assumption that art is a kind of game; thus a literary work such as *Breathing Lessons* accomplishes its purposes by stimulating us to enter the playing field of its textual world. We become players, responding to fictional events as though they were real. At the same time we are aware that the world of the novel is not real. Thus our experiences as readers both insulate us from the real world and its dangers and yet constantly draw on our experiences in that real world. Gadamer

forcefully argues that we must never let the game-like apartness of a work of art, the discontinuity of our experiences of art from our everyday existences, tempt us to consider those experiences as purely aesthetic, unrelated to our understanding of the rest of our lives, or to the understanding of the culture that has shaped us.

In all of his discussions of the arts, Gadamer holds to both sides of the paradox that art, as a kind of game, is set apart from real life and at the same time vitally and necessarily related to actual existence. Concerning the first part of the paradox, he states: "Beautiful things are those whose value is of itself apparent. You cannot ask what purpose they serve. They are desirable for their own sake . . . and not, like the useful, for the sake of something else." But, again, there is always the emphasis that when one enters upon the playing-field of a work of art and gives oneself up to its game—"Play fulfills its purpose only if the player loses himself in his play"—the world of that work of art will reveal its structure to the participant. The result is an increase of knowledge, an Aristotelian "recognition" which has significant relationships to the reader's life:

> The being of all play is always realisation, sheer fulfillment, energeia which has its telos within itself. The world of the work of art, in which play expresses itself fully in the unity of its course, is in fact a wholly transformed world. By means of it everyone recognises that that is how things are.

This paradox that the game of art is at the same time separated from real life and yet meaningfully related to our actual lives is obviously at work in the form of *Breathing Lessons* and in the fictional world revealed through that form. And as neither the novel's world nor ours is simple and unambiguous, the insight that we gain from the novel that "that is how things are" can not be reduced to a tidy little moral about the nature of happiness—or, for that matter, about the nature of Maggie Moran.

Near the end of the novel Maggie has severe doubts about her own basic character: perhaps her lack of practical sense has prevented her from accomplishing anything for those she loves. Immediately after her Fiona-and-Jesse reunion plot collapses, she has "a sudden view of her life as circular. It forever repeated itself, and it was entirely lacking in hope." And later that night, after describing to Ira another of her dreadful miscalculations which years before had badly embarrassed her friend Serena and Serena's ill, aged mother, Maggie comments, "I don't know why I kid myself that I'm going to heaven." At this point the reader might conclude that the textual world in which Maggie lives has thoroughly discredited any pretensions that either she or the reader has held that her character and her life should be viewed positively.

But another interpretation is possible. When Maggie contemplates her poor chances of getting into heaven, the reader might recall that during a Moran family trip to the Pimlico race track Maggie had advised (with what success isn't certain) the women of the family to bet on a horse named Infinite Mercy. Infinite mercy is, of course, what we all need from God if we are to get to heaven, and as much of it as possible from our fellow human beings, if we are to get through life. Further, Maggie's depressed mood clears away by the time she is ready for bed. She becomes quite cheerful again as she begins to generate another plot—which will be immediately shot down by Ira—to convince Fiona to send Leroy to live with them for the sake of Leroy's education, and she watches Ira enjoying his favorite game of solitaire:

> He had passed that early, superficial stage when any number of moves seemed possible, and now his choices were narrower and he had to show real skill and judgment.

Similar to Ira's game, Ira's and Maggie's lives are now at a mature stage, and to play them out satisfactorily will demand their best efforts. Maggie's best efforts will involve her adapting her spirit of play, her vivid imagination, to human relationships as they really exist—to realize that her grown son and her almost grown daughter (not to mention her separated daughter-in-law and granddaughter) will be playing their own games, on their own fields, all unrelated to Maggie's own fantasies and desires. As part of this realization, Maggie must also more fully grasp what the author who created her has always (from her first novel, as a matter of fact) known: loving, understanding relationships between men and women are difficult to achieve, but they are possible; romance, however, is always an illusion. Occasionally, Maggie has realized this:

> Why did popular songs always focus on romantic love? Why this preoccupation with first meetings, sad partings, honeyed kisses, heartbreak, when life was also full of children's births and trips to the shore and longtime jokes with friends? . . . It struck Maggie as disproportionate. Misleading, in fact.

But this kind of hard look at the shallowness of the rules and roles demanded of those who play at romance has been too unpleasant for Maggie to sustain. It is more typical of her to give way to the kind of sentimental, gushing emotions that caused her to sentimentalize Mr. Gabriel or to believe that even where Jesse and Fiona were concerned, love would conquer all:

> Then Jesse wrapped his arms around [Fiona] and dropped his head to her shoulder, and something about that picture—his dark head next to her blond one—reminded Maggie of the way she used to en-

vision marriage before she was married herself. . . . She had supposed that when she was married all her old problems would fall away. . . . And of course, she had been wrong. But watching Jesse and Fiona, she could almost believe that that early vision was the right one. She slipped into the house, shutting the screen door very softly behind her, and she decided everything was going to work out after all.

But, of course, it didn't.

This growing, painful realization of the futility of the sentimental aspects of her vision of life causes Maggie to exclaim despairingly, "Oh, Ira . . . what are we two going to live for, all the rest of our lives?" Ira embraces her, giving her the loving, supportive response that she needs:

> "There, now, sweetheart," he said, and he settled her next to him. Still holding her close, he transferred a four of spades to a five, and Maggie rested her head against his chest and watched. He had arrived at the interesting part of the game by now, she saw. He had passed that early, superficial stage when any number of moves seemed possible, and now his choices were narrower and he had to show real skill and judgment. She felt a little stir of something that came over her like a flush, a sort of inner buoyancy, and she lifted her face to kiss the warm blade of his cheekbone. Then she slipped free and moved to her side of the bed, because tomorrow they had a long car trip to make and she knew she would need a good night's sleep before they started.

On this positive note the novel ends, and it is up to the reader to decide whether it is ironic (as I believe the optimistic final paragraph of *Morgan's Passing* is) or whether the text as a whole encourages us to believe that Maggie has gained enough insight, and that she and Ira share enough love, to continue their lives successfully. Of course, any growth Maggie experiences will certainly not involve her losing the spirit of play that lies at the core of her personality. For those like Maggie Moran and (as Tony Tanner pointed out) Elizabeth Bennet view life in much the way that the rest of us think of a game: it is there to be enjoyed. After all, one chooses to play a game; if one "plays" mainly out of a sense of duty or obligation then one's participation becomes mechanical and the essence of the game is destroyed. Of course, all aspects of life cannot be approached in the spirit of play. Jesse Moran and (again in *Pride and Prejudice*) Lydia Bennet do themselves and others a great deal of harm by not realizing this. And at times Maggie Moran also goes too far in "playing with" people's lives without their consent or knowledge. Most of the time, however, Maggie understands and honors the central relationships of life and the duties that belong to them. And when she does blunder and end up looking like a fool, her resulting fits of futility and self-loathing are soon swept away by her innate love of living, her underlying certainty that life is basically good and that the games *she* chooses to play are worth playing for their own sakes—not for the social and financial prizes that our popular materialistic culture awards to the winners of *its* favorite games. Maggie's wisdom clearly reveals to her (and to us) that the most important goals of life, loving relationships, are certainly not damaged or lost by one's possessing a joyful spirit.

What all of this amounts to, this peculiar mixture of optimism, futility, charity and irony which **Breathing Lessons** brings to a reader, will depend upon the total response to the text (and to his own life) of each reader. In spite of the apparently light, breezy nature of this novel, each reader will become aware, as he experiences his day with the Morans, that he, like Ira during that final game of solitaire, is being challenged, and as he advances in his solitary pursuit of the text his interpretive skill is increasingly important. For playing games of life and art to human beings is like friendship or marriage or even breathing. These activities come naturally to us, yet at times, as Maggie tries to convince the pregnant Fiona when they discuss childbirth classes, they demand all of our effort, all of our skill if we are going to successfully play our "natural" roles. As Maggie does with Fiona and Jesse, Anne Tyler can lure us into the game, and keep us playing until the end. However, Tyler, unlike Maggie, knows that when each reader decides, "That's how things are," the exact nature of "that" must be decided by the reader. In determining the final effect of a work of art, in contrast to the outcome of a competitive game, or one of Maggie's elaborate schemes, Anne Tyler knows that relinquishing ultimate control is the way in which an artist wins.

John Sutherland (review date 12 March 1992)

SOURCE: "Lucky Brrm," in *London Review of Books,* Vol. 14, No. 5, March 12, 1992, pp. 23-4.

[*In the following excerpt, Sutherland discusses the humility of Ian, the main character of Tyler's* Saint Maybe, *and calls him "the accidental hero" of the novel.*]

Anne Tyler's stories are set in Baltimore, a city which many readers will neither know nor feel guilty about not knowing. That there will be many readers of *Saint Maybe,* however, is a certainty. It is Anne Tyler's 12th novel, and she has a loyal and growing band of admirers. Her last effort, **Breathing Lessons,** won a Pulitzer and the title before that, **The Accidental Tourist,** was made into an Oscar-nominated film in 1988. Flattering comparisons with Eudora Welty are now routine.

On the face of it, Tyler's subject in **Saint Maybe**—what is a good life?—is as unprepossessing for a novelist as her favorite Maryland setting. Novels about inconspicuously good men—Dr Primrose, the Rev. Robert Elsmere, Sorrell Sr— are not much imitated by today's fashionable writers. But **Saint Maybe** is told in an artfully off-hand way which teases the reader into close engagement while suggesting that Tyler herself is only just this side of sarcasm. (One of the few facts she has released about her life is that she was brought up in a Quaker commune and didn't much like enforced sanctity.) The control of tone in **Saint Maybe** is masterly, and apparently effortless. So, too, is the control of a difficult chronology. The novel covers twenty-five years in a self-consciously spotty way. Unlike most contemporary novelists, Anne Tyler likes titled chapters which could stand if they had to as independent stories. The technique gives the impression of a narrator dipping into the primary narrative pudding, almost absentmindedly, yet always coming up with a plum.

In 1965, as **Saint Maybe** opens, the Bedloes of Waverly Street, Baltimore, have 'an ideal apple-pie household: two amiable parents, three good-looking children, a dog, a cat, a scattering of goldfish'. American Eden. But the younger son, Ian, makes a spiteful remark to his brother Danny, suggesting that Danny's wife has been unfaithful. Two suicides and the disorder of the apple-pie family result. Paradise lost. The older Bedloes get sick and cranky. The children are disturbed. We are not told, but presumably the pets also have a bad time of it. Inspired by a chance visit to the Church of the Second Chance, Ian resolves to atone by works with the aim of achieving complete forgiveness. Just 19, he drops out of college to work as a carpenter, takes over the charge of his orphaned nephews and nieces, and generally fights the good fight. Finally, having re-established the Bedloes as a happy American family, the 42-year-old Ian marries blissfully and makes some children of his own. Paradise regained.

Ian is, as the title proclaims, a modern saint (perhaps). His is the good life. But as he thinks when someone congratulates him: 'There was no call to make such a fuss about it.' These are the novel's last words and one has to ask if it's worth making the fuss that a 337-page work of fiction represents. Does Ian merit this kind of attention? He has no obvious charm, no noteworthy characteristics of any kind. He never says anything interesting or thinks anything profound. He owns six books, all on self-improvement. He is not even a particularly competent carpenter (but then he wonders if Christ was—all that talking he did). As his fiancée tells a friend, he has only slept with two women in his life, 'his high-school girlfriend before he joined the church and then a woman he dated a few years ago, but he felt terrible about that and vowed he wouldn't do it again.' Ian himself does not want to be noticed—or at least not by the kind of woman Anne Tyler is, a smart writer of books. *The Accidental Tourist* is built round an analogous idea—a travel writer who hates travelling, and whose guides supply a kind of damage control system for those forced into it against their wishes. Ian, we may say, is the accidental hero of a novel—a character who implicitly upbraids his creator for making so much fuss about him.

Patricia Rowe Willrich (essay date Summer 1992)

SOURCE: "Watching Through Windows: A Perspective on Anne Tyler," in *The Virginia Quarterly Review*, Vol. 68, No. 3, Summer, 1992, pp. 497-516.

[*In the following essay, Willrich presents an overview of Tyler's life, career, and approach to writing.*]

Novelist Anne Tyler has spent most of her 50 years observing from a distance, using her imagination to satisfy her curiosity. In an essay published in 1976—"Because I Want More Than One Life," Tyler commented:

> "It seems to me often that I'm sort of looking from a window at something at a great distance and wondering what it is. But I'm not willing to actually go into it. I would rather sit behind the window sill and write about it. So all my curiosity has to be answered within myself. . . ."

Tyler avoids our contemporary literary marketplace. As Reynolds Price, her writing teacher at Duke University, says, she doesn't go out on the "good-looking-lady-star circuit," making public appearances, granting interviews. Tyler stays home and writes and lets her books promote themselves. Publicity seems "artificial" to Tyler. She says, "None of it seems to have any purpose or value. And it has nothing to do with writing."

Indeed, only a few photographs have been published of this tall, slender, attractive blue-gray-eyed woman who wears her dark hair pulled back in a bun and cuts her straight bangs herself.

Tyler's lifestyle has led one critic to label her the "Greta Garbo of the literary world." Nevertheless, Anne Tyler emerged as one of America's leading fiction writers during the 1980's. Her novels are published in many languages around the world. *Accidental Tourist,* published in 1985, and *Breathing Lessons,* in 1989, received wide critical acclaim and earned her prestigious literary prizes—the National Book Critics Circle Award and the Pulitzer Prize. Tyler reached another large audience when *Accidental Tourist* was produced as a highly successful motion picture. Many of her other novels have been optioned for the movies as well. Tyler's 12th novel, *Saint Maybe,* published in the fall of 1991, was a Book-of-the-Month Club main selection. A play adapted from Tyler's 1977 novel, *Earthly Possessions,* was performed at Chicago's Steppenwolf Theatre in the summer and fall of 1991.

Anne Tyler didn't plan on the acclaim her writing has brought her. She says, "I pictured fame as my entering other peoples' lives, not their entering mine." Tyler wrote in an essay in 1980, "Still Just Writing:"

> "Why do people imagine that writers, having chosen the most private of professions, should be any good at performing in public or should have the slightest desire to tell their secrets to interviewers from ladies' magazines. I feel I am only holding myself together by being extremely firm and decisive about what I will do and what I will not do. I will write my books. . . . Anything else just fritters me away."

Several years ago, as a literary lecturer and teacher, I wrote to Anne Tyler. Thus began a correspondence and literary friendship.

II

Anne Tyler is reluctant to talk about her childhood. She writes: "for some reason the thought of going back to childhood—even long enough to think of brief information about it—depresses me."

Tyler was born in Minneapolis, Minnesota, on Oct. 25, 1941. Her father was an industrial chemist and her mother a social worker and sometime journalist. Both her parents are members of the Society of Friends, and they have been long-time activists in liberal causes: pro-human rights, antinuclear, antiwar. With her parents and three younger brothers, she spent her childhood living in various rural Quaker communes in the Midwest and South. From the age of six until she was eleven, she and her family lived with a community of conscientious objectors northeast of Asheville, North Carolina.

Tyler's parents, along with other members of the commune, provided the children much of their early education outside any formal school. This was supplemented with the Calvert School Correspondence System. Later she attended public schools outside the commune, graduating from Broughton High School in Raleigh, North Carolina.

Tyler spent her childhood behind a book, waiting for adulthood to arrive. She read "anything I could get my hands on" and often had to reread books because there weren't many children's books available.

Tyler traces the origin of her craft to age three. When sent to bed early, she was faced with having to amuse herself. She told an interviewer: "I pulled my knees up under the blanket and pretended I was a doctor and patients were coming to me with broken legs and arms and they had to tell me how they'd gotten them." Tyler realizes she's really doing no more now than she did at age three—"telling myself stories in order to get to sleep at night. Except that now I tell stories in the daytime as well: they've taken over my life."

Tyler wrote her first book when she was seven. It was in notebook form with drawings, "Written and Illustrated by Anne Tyler," and it was followed by dozens of others in a similar form. She says these were "wishful thinking books—all about girls I wished I were like who got to go west in covered wagons."

At that point in her life, Tyler thought she would be an artist, but she decided she was not good enough. She still finds drawing helpful as she thinks up characters. She doodles to see what faces emerge that seem to interest her and tries to understand "what's inside them so I can know more about them."

The experience of living in a commune made Tyler look at the normal world with a certain amount of distance which she feels is helpful to a writer. From the essay, **"Still Just Writing":**

> "I know a poet who says that in order to be a writer, you have to have had rheumatic fever in your childhood. I've never had rheumatic fever, but I believe that any kind of setting-apart situation will do as well. In my case, it was emerging from the commune . . . and trying to fit into the outside world."

Tyler was eleven when she and her family left the commune. She had never used a telephone and could strike a match on the sole of her bare foot. Tyler has retained throughout her life the sense of surprise and distance she felt as a child. From the same essay:

> "I have given up hope, by now, of ever losing my sense of distance; in fact, I seem to have come to cherish it. Neither I nor any of my brothers can stand being out among a crowd of people for any length of time."

When Anne Tyler was 14, she discovered Eudora Welty's books in the school library, and this was a turning point. Welty's story, "The Wide Net," influenced Tyler more than any other piece of literature. She told an interviewer:

> "I can even name the line. It's the one where she says Edna Earle is so dim she could spend all day pondering on how the little tail on the 'C' got through the 'L' in a Coca-Cola sign. I knew many Edna Earles. I didn't know you could write about them."

Tyler says that hitherto she thought books had to be about major events and none had ever happened to her. Eudora Welty has been a role model for Anne Tyler ever since.

Phyllis Peacock, Tyler's English teacher at Broughton High School, also had a large impact on her early development. In a letter, Tyler recalled: "I showed my writing to my parents and my mother, especially, was supportive but Mrs. Peacock got really excited and that made a huge difference. . . . Mrs. Peacock just had something about her that encouraged imagination and experimentation; I can't explain what."

Tyler wanted to go north to Swarthmore College. Her parents felt, however, she should go to Duke University, where she had been awarded the Angier Biddle Duke scholarship, because she had three brothers coming along behind her and it was more important for boys than girls to get a good education. That was the only time Tyler remembers being treated unfairly as a female in her family. "I still don't think it was just, but I can't say it ruined my life. After all, Duke had Reynolds Price who turned out to be the only person I ever knew who could actually teach writing. It all worked out in the end."

Tyler entered Duke University at 16 and graduated in three years with a degree in Russian and a Phi Beta Kappa key. Something of a maverick in college, she majored in Russian language and literature because she wanted to "embark on something new and different and slightly startling." Now, she says, "To my great shame, I have forgotten every last bit of my Russian. Now I couldn't manage so much as a Dick-and-Jane book."

At Duke, Tyler took several writing courses, including freshman composition and an advanced short story writing course her sophomore year from Reynolds Price. Tyler was in the first class Price taught at Duke (when he was 25 and she 16). He acknowledges the encounter spoiled him. "I thought the students were all going to be like that!" Price told an interviewer in 1983, "Anne Tyler was almost as good a writer at age sixteen as she is now; and she's now one of the best novelists alive in the world."

When Price gave his students an assignment to write about their earliest childhood memory, Tyler could remember back the farthest—to a memory of her mother putting a certain jacket on her and her feelings about it. She later recalled: "My feelings . . . were of frustration, because I thought I was explaining very lucidly to my mother that I didn't like that coat because it was padded and it didn't allow me to bend my arms. Actually, as I see now, I couldn't possibly have been understood because I was somewhere between seven and ten months old and didn't talk yet; I only thought I could talk."

Price treated Tyler differently from the other students in his composition class because of her obvious talent. He told me in an interview in May 1990:

> "She started out very quickly writing highly finished, skillful prose sketches about the Quaker community she lived in up in the mountains as a very young child. And so I pretty well set her free at that point to write whatever she wanted and not necessarily to write the critical papers that most of the others were writing . . . Tyler's pieces were basically about this wide-eyed extremely watchful girl child, who was not so much watching the community itself as watching the mountain people who lived around the community, with whom they would go mountain climbing, or flower picking. My memory [of the writing pieces] is of this outsider child, this very watchful child recording, recording, recording the world."

During her sophomore year, Tyler wrote a story called **"The Saints in Caesar's Household."** Price says the story, about returning home to see a friend from childhood who has had a psychotic breakdown, "is the most finished, most accomplished short story I've ever received from an undergraduate in all my thirty years of teaching."

Price sent the story to his agent, Diarmuid Russell, who was also Eudora Welty's agent, and soon Russell became Tyler's agent as well. **"The Saints in Caesar's Household"** became her first published short story. Two other stories Tyler wrote at Duke were published in literary journals: **"I Never Saw Morning"** (*Archive*, April 1961) and **"Nobody Answers the Door"** (*Antioch Review*, Fall 1964). Anne Tyler twice won the Anne Flexner Award for creative writing at Duke University.

While at Duke, she also acted with the Westley Players, playing Laura in *The Glass Menagerie,* Mrs. Gibson in *Our Town,* and the female lead in an original play by a fellow student.

After graduating from Duke, Tyler, went to New York City for a year to study Russian at Columbia University. While there she became "addicted" to riding any kind of train or subway.

> ". . .While I rode I often felt I was . . . an enormous eye, taking things in and turning them over and sorting them out. But, who would I tell them to. . . ? I have never had more than three or four close friends at any period of my life; and anyway, I don't talk well . . . for me, writing down was the only way out."

Returning to Duke in 1962, Tyler worked as the Russian bibliographer at the Duke Library. At that time she was "vague" about what she wanted to do. She now admits, "Writing was something that crept in around the edges."

Tyler met and married Iranian-born Taghi Mohammed Modaressi in 1963. His study visa expired in 1964, and they moved to Montreal, where Modaressi continued his medical studies at McGill University.

III

During her first six months of marriage, to keep occupied while she was looking for a job, Tyler wrote her first novel, *If Morning Ever Comes.* She left the first half of her only draft of the manuscript at the Montreal airport.

> "When I realized later I said oh, well, no great loss, and didn't bother going all the way out to the airport to get it. I think it was a month or so before Taghi picked it up on his own initiative while he was out at the airport on some other errand. I didn't have any particular feelings about it then, but I was glad to have it later when it took so long to find work and I needed something to do with my time. Now I wish we'd left it at the airport."

With the publication of this novel in 1964, Anne Tyler, at age 22 began her literary career. The themes in *If Morning Ever Comes* are those she continues to focus on in her later novels: family relationships, love, old age, and death. In this book, Ben Joe Hawkes returns home to Sandhill, North Carolina, from law school to help his family during a crisis—as well as to find himself. After a week with his mother, grandmother, and six sisters, he returns to New York with the insight "that sometimes it's not the same place when a person goes back to it, or not the same . . . person."

Tyler and her husband had been planning to return to Iran to live, but after he found that Iran didn't have any fulfilling professional jobs, they moved to Baltimore in 1965. There Modaressi started his child psychiatry practice and Tyler continued writing. [Modaressi also writes and has published two novels in English.] Her career was unexpected:

> "I never really planned to be a writer; I just didn't know what else to do. And writing full-time wasn't actually a decision at all—I had quit my library job to have a baby, and never went back to it but did go on writing. So you can see it didn't take much courage."

Tyler's second novel, *The Tin Can Tree,* was published in 1965. Again, this novel centers around a family—each member trying to recover from the death of six-year-old Janie Rose. A brother runs off to regain his mother's attention and to explore new worlds. Janie Rose had strung together tin cans which she hung from the tin can tree and these cans, rattling in the wind, make her a continuing, powerful presence throughout the story.

In the 1960's, Tyler's short stories began appearing in *The New Yorker, The Saturday Evening Post,* and *Harpers.* In the more than 40 stories she published, Tyler frequently focused on a single character, writing from an understated third-person voice, presenting a single incident or a single day in a way that symbolizes a whole life. The settings were usually Southern, and the themes—as in her novels—were family relationships, alienation or loneliness, the failure of communication between individuals, and the search for meaning in life. Tyler says there will never be a published collection of her short stories because she only likes about five of them.

In the introduction to *The Best American Short Stories* of 1983, which she edited, Tyler explored the question—"What are the qualities that separate a wonderful short story from a merely good one?"—and she concluded: ". . . almost every really lasting story . . . contains at least one moment of stillness that serves as a kind of pivot." To Tyler, the short story writer should be a "wastral. He neither hoards his best ideas for something 'more important' (a novel) nor skimps on his material because this is 'only' a short story."

There were five years during the late 1960's when Tyler did not publish, when she was preoccupied with caring for her two infant daughters. It was a difficult time.

"Everything I wanted to write was somehow coagulating in my veins and making me fidgety and slow," she later noted. Her life during that period was like "living in a very small commune . . . one member was the liaison with the outside world, bringing in money; another was the caretaker, reading the Little Bear books to the children and repairing the electrical switches. . . . I was trying to convince myself that I really did pull my own weight."

In summing up that period, Tyler wrote in the 1980 essay: "Since I've had children, I've grown richer and deeper. They may have slowed down my writing for awhile, but when I did write, I had more of a self to speak from."

Tyler based the story in her third novel, *A Slipping Down Life,* published in 1970, on an actual incident involving an Elvis Presley fan who etched Presley's name across her forehead with a razor blade. She thinks this work is "flawed, but represented, for me, a certain brave step forward."

In 1972, Tyler published *The Clock Winder.* In this novel, the newly-widowed Mrs. Emerson finds her life changed when Elizabeth, the "handyman-girl," appears seemingly from out of nowhere and stays for ten years, involving herself in the Emerson family and its affairs.

From this book on, the setting of Tyler's work is Baltimore. Tyler told an interviewer: "Baltimore has a lot of gritty character to it that's good for a novel to have."

Tyler doesn't like to claim any books written before *Celestial Navigation,* published in 1974. By then both of her children were in school. She says, while writing this novel, she learned to rework and rework the drafts to find out more about what her characters "really meant." Although she says this was the hardest novel to write up to that time, it is her own favorite.

Celestial Navigation is the story of Jeremy, an artist living in a boarding house in Baltimore, who doesn't like to leave home. While Tyler doesn't have agoraphobia as Jeremy does, she can identify with him. She says, "Creating Jeremy was a way of investigating my own tendency to turn more and more inward [as I write.]" In the book, Tyler also described another facet of herself through the character of Miss Vinton, a spinster who works in a bookstore and whose favorite daydream is: "I would be reading a book alone in my room, and no one would ever, ever interrupt me."

Searching for Caleb, appearing in 1976, concerned a Baltimore family's hunt for a long-missing relative. Tyler told an interviewer: "It's not my best book but it was the most fun to write. Each morning was like going to a party . . . if I could somehow arrange it so that for the rest of my life all I was doing was writing that book, I'd be delighted to do it."

Earthly Possessions, published in 1977, is a story about Charlotte, a passive woman who is kidnapped by a bank robber as she is preparing to leave her family. She finds she can only think of the possessions she left behind. Tyler considers *Earthly Possessions* "the work of somebody entering middle age, beginning to notice how the bags and baggage of the past are weighing her down and how much she values them." For *Earthly Possessions,* Tyler received a citation from the American Academy and Institute of Arts and Letters (1977)— "for literary excellence and promise of important work to come."

Morgan's Passing, out in 1980, is about a 43-year-old bearded, overweight man who is always pretending to be someone else. His closet is full of costumes and hats "stacked six deep on the shelf." Tyler deems *Morgan's Passing* as "a story that deals with a situation I've been fascinated by for most of my life, and one which probably is not unrelated to being a writer: the inveterate imposter, who is unable to stop himself from stepping into other people's worlds."

Again, Tyler seems to be writing about facets of her own character in this novel. Like Morgan, she is not a saver. Her old stone home in Baltimore is organized and spare. The living room and dining room, with oriental rugs and a few pieces of furniture, are uncluttered. Floor to ceiling bookcases are full, but neatly organized. When someone gives Tyler a new book, she gives one away. This is like Morgan who urges his newly-wed daughter, Amy, to:

> "Take a cardboard box, carry it through the rooms, load into it everyone's toys and dirty clothes and such, and hide it all in a closet. If people ask for some missing object, you'll be able to tell them where it is . . . if a week goes by and they don't notice the object is gone, then you can be sure it's non-essential, and you throw it away. You would be surprised at how many things are non-essential. Throw everything away. All of it! Simplify!"

Morgan's Passing was nominated for the 1980 National Book Critics Circle Award.

IV

Dinner at the Homesick Restaurant, published in 1982, was the book that made Anne Tyler famous, and it remains one of her best. The story traces 50 years in the life of Pearl Tull, who after being deserted by her husband, raises her three children. It is a story about relationships within a family, pain, attempts at survival, nourishment, and love. This is how Tyler views the novel:

> "With *Dinner at the Homesick Restaurant,* I just wanted to show both sides of family life—that it can be horrific at times, but that it is the one situation that we are generally forced to go on with, even so, picking ourselves up and trying again in the morning. And that is valuable in itself."

Dinner at the Homesick Restaurant was nominated for the National Book Critics Circle Award in 1982. The following year Tyler was elected to the American Academy and Institute of Arts and Letters and nominated for the PEN/Faulkner Award as well.

Accidental Tourist, published in 1985, brought Anne Tyler the National Book Critics Circle Award, after her two previous nominations. This novel concerns Macon Leary, who writes travel books for the business man who doesn't like to travel. His wife, Sarah, leaves him in the first chapter, in part because of their inability to connect, to help each other. It has been one year since their only child, 12-year-old Ethan, was shot to death in a random killing. Tyler says of *Tourist:*

> "It's hard to think what I had in mind for this book when I started—it has gone through so many changes. It was unusually difficult to write, maybe in part because I hated to handle even the thought of a child's dying. In fact I superstitiously made Ethan

younger than either of my own children so that I could take comfort that they were already past that danger."

Accidental Tourist is also about families and about relationships. The most vivid character is Muriel, the dog trainer, who steps into the picture when Macon's dog, Edward (a Corgi like one Tyler had at the time), seems to have a nervous breakdown. Tyler worried that the brassy, assertive Muriel would put people off or bore readers with her monologues: "Although she was very foreign to me at first I did grow fond of her as I came to know her and I wanted people to see her in the best light."

The novel is hopeful, full of humor as well as pathos. Tyler leaves the reader with this thought from Macon: "It's kind of heartening, isn't it. How most human beings do try. How they try to be as responsible and kind as they can manage."

While some critics have contended that Tyler's women are stronger characters than the men in her books, the Baltimore novelist demurs: "I'm not interested in generalizations about the sexes. Men and women can do anything the other sex can do. Macon isn't passive because he's a man."

Watching the Warner Brothers filming of the movie adaptation of *Accidental Tourist* in Baltimore fascinated Anne Tyler. She confesses, "I never knew movies required so much patience and such attention to detail." Although she didn't write the screenplay, she believes that the movie is "very true to the book."

Tyler worked for three years on her eleventh novel, *Breathing Lessons,* released in 1989 and awarded the Pulitzer Prize in 1990. It involves one day in the life of a marriage but in actuality describes 30 years of ups and downs in the lives of a middle-aged couple, the Morans, Maggie (48) and Ira (50). The Morans spend the day in their car driving from Baltimore to a funeral of a high school friend 90 miles away. One of the moving scenes in the novel occurs when an old man in the nursing home where Maggie works tells her he believes that once he reaches heaven, all he had lost in his lifetime would be given back to him. Maggie thinks of what she might find in her own gunnysack—misplaced earrings and umbrellas, the 1950's skirts and her cat, Thistledown, and the mongrel dogs on Mulraney Street whose howls barked her to sleep in her childhood.

> "And the summer evening as well, why not—the children smelling of sweat and fireflies, the warm porch floorboards sticking slightly to your chair rockers, the voices ringing from the alley. . . . She pictured Saint Peter's astonishment as he watched what spilled forth: a bottle of wind, a box of fresh snow, and one of those looming moonlit clouds that used

to float overhead like dirigibles as Ira walked her home from choir practice."

Tyler's most recent novel, *Saint Maybe,* a fall 1991 publication, traces the Baltimore "apple pie household" of the Bedloe family from 1965 to 1988. Reminiscent of *Dinner at the Homesick Restaurant,* with its longer, more leisurely time span, *Saint Maybe* draws the reader in deeper, demanding an emotional attachment that brings both laughter and tears. Ian Bedloe is only a 17-year-old as the story begins, a "medium kind of guy," whose life changes when he accepts the self-imposed blame for the accidental death of his older brother and becomes a born-again Christian. Ian stumbles into the brotherhood of the Church of the Second Chance and, believing that he must earn forgiveness, he takes on the responsibility for raising his brother's stepchildren.

"As for the germ of the new book, and of Ian—it was as usual all a matter of daydreams," Tyler later commented. "Nothing more concrete than that. All I knew at the start was that I wondered what it must feel like to be a born-again Christian, since that is a kind of life very different from mine." According to its author, *Saint Maybe* almost wrote itself. "It was one of those occasions when the characters' voices were almost literally audible, so that they would chatter on and I would write it down, wondering meanwhile where it came from." In Tyler's sensitive, amusing, touching way, the reader watches the growth to maturity of the three children. Her touch adds a universality to the commonplace, not allowing the reader to escape without an enlargement of his own sense of humanity.

V

Anne Tyler's main interest is character. She wants her characters to "shine through." She says, "As far as I'm concerned, character is everything. I never did see why I have to throw in a plot, too." She commented in a 1977 interview:

> "The real joy of writing is how people can surprise one. My people wander around my study until the novel is done. It's one reason I'm very careful not to write about people I don't like. If I find somebody creeping in that I'm not really fond of, I usually take him out. I end a book at the point where I feel that I'm going to know forever what their lives are like."

Tyler finds her characters almost entirely in her own mind, or in her own words, "Sometimes a news item or the sight of someone standing at a bus stop will set me to thinking, and maybe years later a character will come out of that." Some of her more important characters are, quite clearly, facets of herself. Tyler knows she's on the right track with her writing when her characters take on a life of their own and start informing her:

> "What's hard is that there are times when your characters simply won't obey you. I'll have in mind an event for them—a departure, a wedding, a happy ending. I write steadily toward that event, but when I reach it, everything stops. I can't go on. Sentences come out stilted, dialogue doesn't sound real. Every new attempt ends up in the wastebasket. I try again from another angle, and then another, until I'm forced to admit it. The characters just won't allow this. I'll have to let the plot go their way. And when I do, everything falls into place."

Tyler thinks about her characters for awhile once she finishes a book. She worried about Jeremy, in *Celestial Navigation,* who feared leaving home, having a hard time going by himself in her manuscript to her publisher in New York. She also realizes after she finishes a book "that the day dreams I have been weaving are no longer my private property."

The novelist regards her characters as populating a town where they would know each other and would become friends. As she wrote in an essay: "Sometimes I imagine retiring to a peaceful little town where everyone I've invented is living in houses on Main Street. There are worse retirement plans. After all, they are people I've loved, or I never would have bothered writing about them." Tyler also says she knows that "there are some central preoccupations that keep popping up over and over in my books. I'm very interested in space around people. The real heroes to me in my books are first the ones who manage to endure and second the ones who somehow are able to grant other people privacy . . . and yet still produce some warmth."

Tyler doesn't consciously write a novel to fit a theme:

> "Any 'large questions of life' that emerge in my novels are accidental—not a reason for writing the novel in the first place but either (1) questions that absorb my characters, quite apart from me, or (2) on occasion, questions that may be thematic to my own life at the moment, even if I'm not entirely aware of them. Answers, if they come, come from the characters' experiences, not from mine, and I often find myself viewing those answers with a sort of distant, bemused surprise."

Writing novels is, for her, mostly telling lies. "You set out to tell an untrue story and you try to make it believable, even to yourself," she says, "which calls for details; any good lie does. I'm quicker to believe I was once a circus aerialist if I remember that just before every performance, I used to dip my hands in a box of chalk powder that smelled like clean, dry cloth being torn."

Anne Tyler's working habits are precise and productive. There is only one room in her home where she can work—a small corner room on the second floor where she "can hear children playing outside and birds." One wall of this spare and orderly room has a few family photographs and an inscription by Richard Wilbur, the former Poet Laureate of the United States:

"Source"

As a queen sits down
knowing a chair will be there
or a general raises his hands
And is given the field glasses—
Step off assuredly
into the blank of your mind
Something will come to you.

A bright blue quilt covers the hard couch where Tyler sits cross-legged and writes with a black pen her first drafts in longhand on an antique writing box, a gift from her husband. An antique oak roll-top desk sits against the opposite wall. The bookcases are filled with almanacs that date back to 1948, *Time-Life* history books, decade by decade back to 1870, and several photography books, as Tyler puts it, "just to sink into, to fill up on when I feel empty." She also has dictionaries of slang expressions, lined up by year, so that her characters will have an authentic voice.

Tyler works in this room Monday through Friday from early in the morning until about two in the afternoon, unless she breaks earlier to have lunch with a friend. While she is writing, Tyler doesn't like to think about her audience. She doesn't read reviews about her work because she says that would remind her that she has readers. But she does care about the connection she makes with her audience. She hopes for "empathetic readers. . . . They in their solitude and I in mine, have somehow managed to touch, without either of us feeling intruded upon . . . We've spent some time on neutral territory, sharing a life that belongs to neither of us."

It is not easy for her to start her writing day, for she feels that "I'd rather do almost anything than go into my study. The door is so tall and dark; it looms. The whole room smells like a carpenter's shop because of the wooden bookcases. Ordinarily it's a pleasant smell, but mornings it makes me feel sick. I have to walk in as if by accident, with my mind on something else. Otherwise, I'd never make it."

Tyler says it took her years to develop the discipline she requires to write. "I've learned to be narrow in what I am willing to do and what I'm not willing to do. Often my books come out of my own confinement." Reynolds Price says, "Tyler could maintain her lifestyle in a tornado. I've never known anyone in better control of her professional life." She no longer accepts the occasional invitations to be a guest teacher in writing classes. Because, "If I talk about the process I'm working by, I can't use the process for a while." This writer says that she is not "driven" to write. Rather, she adds,

"I am driven to get things written down before I forget them. My work goes in two parts. The first part is the story, with my characters talking and surprising. But I still don't know what it's about, or what it means. The second part comes when I read it back, and suddenly it seems as if someone else is telling me the story and I say, 'now I see' and then I go all the way back and drop references to what it means. I keep telling my husband to burn any manuscript if I die before I get to part two. It isn't mine until I see what my subconscious is up to."

Tyler doesn't wait for an inspiration before she begins writing. She makes writing a routine, reviewing a bit of her previous day's work and then starting again, following the characters through the plots. "It's like playing dolls," she believes. "Writing is a sort of way of disobeying two major rules I heard as a child: stop daydreaming and stop staring into space." To Tyler, tapping her imagination "is really an extension of day dreaming. I just sit around thinking 'What if?' about things." The process of writing for Tyler is one of continual discovery.

Tyler has been writing thoughts and observations on white, unlined index cards since high school. The cards are eventually filed in a small metal box; divided by chapter number, the box also has "extra," "general," "look up," and "revise" sections.

When starting a novel, Tyler reads through her file of cards and selects ones that bring to mind interesting associations, looking for a story that will tie them together. As characters emerge and develop in her imagination, she explores their personalities. Before she begins writing, she insists on knowing her characters intimately so that she will understand each person's reaction to the events that occur. Only after this preparatory period is over will she be able to outline the novel, using a single sheet of paper and one or two sentences per chapter.

While she sleeps, she told an interviewer, "some sort of automatic pilot works then to solve problems in my plots; I go to bed trustful that they'll be taken care of by morning. And toward dawn I often wake up and notice, as if from a distance, that my mind is still churning out stories without any help from me at all."

Tyler frequently suffers from insomnia from two to four in the morning, a malady she believes she inherited from her family. She says that half of her family "fights" this condition; the other half gets something done. Tyler uses those wakeful hours to write on index cards.

Tyler dislikes doing research. In a recent letter, she observed, "I wanted to do a fortune teller—Justice—in *Searching for Caleb.* Haven't you ever been tempted to have your fortune told? It would have killed it off instantly if I'd ever gone to see one. Instead, I bought a little dime-store Dell book—just to pick up the names of the card formations. It's a lot more fun to make things up." But she didn't do any research for her last novel, *Saint Maybe.* "I think research of that sort cramps and stunts a novel—and also, with a view to avoid offending any particular religion, I figured it was best to just think up my own imaginary one."

Reynolds Price mentioned in an interview in 1986 that "Anne Tyler has always spoken of a voice that she hears just above her right or left ear." Tyler writes:

> "The voice I 'hear' is that sort of neutral, neuter voice that your mind employs when it's thinking in actual words; it seems that when I'm really inside what I'm working on, my mind's voice sometimes begins rolling ahead of its own accord. Most often this occurs with dialogue, or with a character's internal monologue. I don't think it's in any way mystical or even, strictly speaking, a matter of 'inspiration'—just momentum."

To Anne Tyler, "a serious book is one that removes me to another life as I am reading it. It has to have layers and layers and layers, like life does." Judged by her own definition, she is a serious writer. As she continues to put her thoughts into books, her characters will continue to "shine through," giving her readers, as well as herself, chances to lead other lives.

Alice Hall Petry (essay date Fall 1992)

SOURCE: "Bright Books of Life: The Black Norm in Anne Tyler's Novels," in *The Southern Quarterly,* Vol. 31, No. 1, Fall, 1992, pp. 7-13.

[In the following essay, Petry discusses how Tyler uses black characters as repositories of wisdom and knowledge in her novels.]

To be frank, black characters do not loom large in the twelve novels of contemporary Baltimore novelist Anne Tyler. Most of them function as domestics, such as the housekeeper Clotelia of *A Slipping-Down Life* or Richard the gardener in *The Clock Winder;* others are barely-delineated background figures, like the superstitious clients of the fortune-teller Madame Olita in *Searching for Caleb* or the silent, shifty-eyed gamblers frequenting the No Jive Cafe in *Morgan's Passing.* But even as one makes these sweeping observations, one must counter them. For if there is one insistent quality about Tyler's fictional vision, it is her humanity—a humanity that prevents her from resorting to stereotypes or sentimentality, from using black characters either as comic "stage darkies" or as their late twentieth-century counterparts in the white popular imagination: ne'er-do-wells whose lives revolve around drugs and sex and numbers and welfare checks. For from the dawn of her career, Anne Tyler chose to go against the grain, not only to depict blacks more positively than American society has been wont to do, but more importantly, to empower them to articulate her most salient themes. Often the most clear-eyed and admirable characters in her novels, they do more than "endure," like Faulkner's Dilsey Gibson. They live; they thrive; they derive happiness from the very fact of existence. Though there are some exceptions, for the most part Anne Tyler's black characters are splashes of brightness in novels striated with the "grayness" that drove Beck Tull to abandon his family in *Dinner at the Homesick Restaurant.*

The special status of blacks is evident even in Tyler's first novel, *If Morning Ever Comes.* As young Ben Joe Hawkes dashes home to Sandhill, North Carolina, from law school in New York, he shares his train car with several black families, including fellow Sandhill residents Matilda and Brandon Hayes, and their baby Clara Sue. To us consciousness-raised readers of the 1990s, there's plenty to offend in Tyler's depiction of these blacks: the children's hands are like "four little black spiders"; the men sit in the back of the train, "tipping hip flasks"; the women eat fried chicken and wax eloquent over collard greens and okra; they say things like "Law, law"; and they subscribe to folk tales: Matilda knew her baby would be a girl because "I got fatter and fatter in the behind all the time I [was] carrying her." But however offensive these stereotypes may be, one must look beyond them to the spirit underlying them. Matilda's folk wisdom, for example, was accurate: she did indeed have a daughter. And in fact these blacks are depicted as repositories of the kinds of knowledge, and attitudes, and values that Ben Joe and others in his white circle *should* possess. Black Matilda is shocked that Ben Joe's "coldhearted" mother Ellen, who drove her physician-husband into an affair with a factory worker, did not even travel to Kansas when her daughter gave birth. It is clear that Matilda could not imagine a black grandmother-to-be acting in such an unfeeling fashion. But with her innate dignity, Matilda refuses to condemn Ellen, excusing her on the grounds that she probably was prevented from being with Joanne due to family responsibilities in Sandhill. Likewise, Matilda tries to comfort Ben Joe about his father's death by asserting that it probably was "a dignified passing." When Ben Joe's embarrassed silence indicates otherwise, Matilda's husband Brandon says—"soothingly"—"Oh, I sure it was *very* dignified." So complete is the innate good breeding of these black characters that even though Brandon is so drunk that he inadvertently sits down on another passenger, he is able to apologize profusely and sincerely. No wonder these black characters unsettle Ben Joe, the "yellow-haired gentleman" whose family has been racked by infidelity, who is just starting Columbia Law School at the ripe age of twenty-five because he doesn't know what else to do, who like a child wraps himself in his crazy quilt from home and who reads literally upside-down—the perfect emblem of his messy white world. Both Ben Joe and his elderly white double from the train—eighty-four-year-old "Jamie" Dower, who has come home to Sandhill to die—scarcely conceal their envy of their black fellow passengers, who appreciate the importance, and indeed the necessity, of warm family ties and the food which is as symbolic of love as it is nutritive:

> [Y]ou know them colored folks off the same train as us? [asks Jamie]. Know what they're doing now? Setting down to the table with their relations, partaking of buckwheat cakes and hot buttered syrup and them little link sausages. Makes me hungry just thinking of it.

Ben Joe even knows "almost for a certainty" what the homes of these blacks are like; but "Who could be that definite about where *he* came from?" Appropriately, there is no one to greet either Ben Joe or Jamie at the train station; "pale and plain" Ben Joe must walk back to the "big pale frame house" in which he was raised, and where still reside the mother and sisters who neither need nor want him around, while the black Hayes family is welcomed home by "a dusty black Chevrolet . . . stuffed with laughing brown faces, piled three deep." That "whole wealth of brightly dressed Negroes" underscores how spiritually poor Ben Joe truly is.

Tyler's use of blacks as repositories of good sense and emotional stability is likewise evident in her second novel, *The Tin Can Tree.* A story about the response of a family and its friends to the death of six-year-old Janie Rose Pike in a tractor accident, this novel presents Tyler's ideas primarily through what Joseph C. Voelker identifies as a "choral" character, a "huge and black" woman named Missouri. Rendered with less sentimentality than the blacks in *If Morning Ever Comes,* Missouri displays annoyance and even anger when her fellow tobacco workers don't work fast enough, and is blunt enough to deem "silly" a co-worker's well-intended but ill-considered plan to ease Janie Rose's mother out of her grief. Missouri speaks her mind, and yet she is sensitive to human psychology: she can criticize Mrs. Hall's plan while yet acknowledging that renewed contact with her sewing customers is necessary for Mrs. Pike's recovery. She is also more effective than the males around her, activating a recalcitrant mule by pulling on its ears; is feminist enough to declare, "In the end, it's the women that work"; and is secure enough in her racial identity to joke that white photographer James

Green is "going to change races" if he stays in the sun much longer. Physically and spiritually strong, Missouri states the novel's main theme: "Bravest thing about people . . . is how they go on loving mortal beings after finding out there's such a thing as dying."

Beginning with her third novel, *A Slipping-Down Life,* Tyler integrates black characters more fully into her white family circles by having them serve as domestics, but they still retain their choral function, often possessing knowledge that is inaccessible to their white employers. In *A Slipping-Down Life,* the housekeeper Clotelia seems to be a peculiar cross between Hazel and Angela Davis, sporting an Afro and an African cape, kicking dust bunnies with her "cream suede high-heeled boot," and steadfastly refusing to be a mammy figure: after four years of employment "other people would have turned into members of the family" grouses Evie, the motherless teenage daughter of the Decker family. But Clotelia has ample reason to hold herself emotionally aloof from her white employers, a family even more dysfunctional than the Hawkeses of *If Morning Ever Comes.* Clotelia, after all, deals with reality. To be sure, she talks about soap opera characters "as if they were relatives," but Clotelia knows they are not—and more to the point, she knows the false images of love and marriage, the "sweet-talk" that soaps and other aspects of popular culture convey, are distortive and unreal. Clotelia would never do what white Evie did—carve the name of a local would-be rock star in her forehead with fingernail scissors—because she would never buy into sentimental notions of romance. Clotelia does not share Evie's surprise that the object of Evie's ardor ignores her: "Ha. Thought that Casey boy would come riding up and spirit her away, once he heard what she done. . . . I don't see him beating down no doors. Do you?" Ultimately Evie *will* come to see the emotional healthiness underlying Clotelia's bluntly realistic ideas about man/woman relations, but it will take a failed marriage to "that Casey boy," a baby and the death of her father to achieve it.

There are two black domestics in Tyler's next novel, *The Clock Winder,* and although they are even less prominent than Clotelia, they nonetheless serve important functions. Alvareen the housekeeper seems at first glance to be a comic black domestic, a "black hulk" unable even to "warm up a brown-and-serve pie." But as Alvareen points out, her mistress, Mrs. Pamela Emerson, is even less capable of cooking than she—an important shortcoming for a novelist who (witness *Dinner at the Homesick Restaurant*) regards feeding as a vital expression of familial love. Not surprisingly, the Emersons are yet another white Tyler family running amok, what with elopements, failed marriages, mental instability and suicide. Significantly, in the epistolary sequence at the center of *The Clock Winder,* only the letters of Alvareen the black maid are clear, direct and astute. Those of the white Emersons and their circle may be more grammatically correct, but they nevertheless are masterpieces of evasion and incoherence written, we are told, at the level of "a fifth-grader." The other black domestic in this novel, Richard the gardener, opens *The Clock Winder* by urinating on Mrs. Emerson's rosebush, for which she promptly fires him. But as he warns her, she cannot function alone, and he is right, as her prim spiked heels literally sink into her well-trimmed lawn. He articulates on behalf of Tyler that we do not, and cannot, function in isolation. Her surname notwithstanding, Mrs. Emerson can never achieve complete self-reliance, nor can anyone else. That we need one another for survival renders the breakdown of Tyler's many white fictional families all the more tragic.

Looming even less largely in Tyler's sixth novel, *Searching for Caleb,* are black husband-and-wife domestics, Lafleur and Sulie Boudrault, but their significance is in inverse proportion to their importance in the story. It is Lafleur who introduces young Caleb Peck to ragtime, "a disreputable, *colored* kind of music"—and a kind he loves so much that he runs away from his luxurious home in Baltimore to be a street musician in the black districts of New Orleans. With his honorary black name of "Stringtail Man," Caleb earns his keep as a fiddler, composer and guide to an old black guitarist named "White-Eye." Caleb is supremely happy in that black world, but his horrified family vows to find him and return him to the fold. Significantly, the Pecks had no idea where Caleb had run off to and did not think to hire a detective to find him until a bit later—sixty years later, in fact. But all the while, Lefleur's wife Sulie had known where Caleb had gone; the only problem, as her husband points out, is that no one thought to ask her: "Them [white] folks don't think you know *nothing.*" Once again, it is blacks who have specialized and quite *practical* knowledge—Sulie even knew Caleb's New Orleans address—which whites unfortunately choose not to use.

That status is perhaps most dramatic in Tyler's eleventh novel, the Pulitzer Prize-winning *Breathing Lessons.* In part 2, Tyler describes the encounter between Maggie and Ira Moran and Mr. Daniel Otis, a "stoop-shouldered man the color of a rolltop desk." Neither a domestic nor a musician, Mr. Otis had been a roofer in North Carolina until debilitated by arthritis. He meets Maggie and Ira on the road as they confront such dramatic changes as the breakdown of their son's marriage, their daughter's departure for college and the early death of a high school friend. They meet Mr. Otis in a moment of anger: his dangerously slow driving leads them to go off the highway, and they retaliate against him by lying that his car's front wheel is loose. The lie brings out Maggie's guilt: "Not only was he old. . . . He was black." Fearing that he thought them members of the Ku Klux Klan, they compensate for their insensitivity by befriending him and taking him to the service station for help. Significantly, Maggie and Ira are never sure if Mr. Otis is as mild-mannered and grateful as he seems: the

"haughty, hooded expression" caused by his lowered eyelids may indeed have meant he realized Maggie had lied about the wheel, and Ira even wonders if his inconvenient request to be driven to the Texaco station "might be Mr. Otis's particularly passive, devilish way of getting even." Tyler never says outright. But in that very reticence she is making a statement: Mr. Otis embodies all that is unknown and uncertain in this world—and yet he articulates the central theme of the novel. As both Morans chafe at the sense of time passing—and, more importantly, at the sense of personal potential left unrealized—Mr. Otis explains that loss need not be debilitating: "Could be what you throw away is all that really counts; could be that's the whole point of things, wouldn't that be something? Spill it! Spill it all, I say! No way *not* to spill it." That loss is inevitable is a harsh truth softened by the anecdote of Bessie, the dog who assumed her ball was lost forever simply because it was blocked by a chairback: a lot of us, muses Mr. Otis, have "blind spots" which make us fail to appreciate what we have *not* lost. Neither truth changes the harshness of reality; they simply shift perspectives a bit. It took an old black man living in a car, "his eyes so yellow . . . they were almost brown," to convey these simple truths to this comparatively well-off, healthy white couple.

Perhaps Mr. Otis, that angel bearing a message of survival, could ascertain these truths precisely because he, as an elderly black man, had always been an outsider. As someone excluded from the mainstream of southern white society for decades, he did not have the luxury of falling into the counterproductive lifestyle of those with more opportunities, more education, more money. He *had* to learn to see things aright in order to survive, just as the Hayes family of *If Morning Ever Comes* had to find their happiness and stability in a strong family unit, in a secure (albeit modest) home and in the simple pleasures of food lovingly prepared. That stable foundation enables them to weather the shock of sudden change, or of gradual change (witness the words "White" and "Colored" fading slowly from the wall of the once segregated railroad station waiting room), or indeed of no change at all. When Brandon Hayes casts an eye on the Sandhill cityscape and remarks, "See they ain't fixed the clock on the Sand-Bottom Baptists' steeple tower yet," he evinces no particular emotion. Why rail against what he, as a southern black, cannot control? Better to invest one's energies in the things that matter, such as the family, and to cultivate the values and acquire the kinds of practical knowledge needed to survive and to be happy. One may go "bumbling along" like Mr. Otis, but the destination will be reached eventually.

To be sure, various critics have noted that Tyler rarely uses black characters in her fiction and that she skates handily around anything that smacks of racism. Edward Hoagland, in a 1988 review of *Breathing Lessons,* for example, remarks that Tyler "is not unblinking. Her books contain scarcely a hint of the abscesses of racial friction that cat at the very neighborhoods she is devoting her working life to picturing. Her people are eerily virtuous, Quakerishly tolerant of all strangers, all races." Similarly, Voelker points to those fading letters on the waiting-room wall as an emblem of "the persistence of racism"—but notes further that the novel "moves swiftly inward, toward domestic matters, and never addresses the intriguing questions it raises." But even as one acknowledges that Tyler avoids facing the complexities of southern racism, it cannot be gainsaid that she has come a long way from her earliest attitude toward blacks, as expressed in a 1965 interview in a Baton Rouge newspaper: "And I love the average Southern Negro—they speak a language all their own." As her career has progressed—and as she herself has matured—Tyler has evinced increasingly less interest in such "picturesque" aspects of black life as colorful dialect, and increasingly more concern with the capacity of blacks to survive and thrive in a hostile world. Tyler once wrote to this author that "I would feel presumptuous writing about black life as if I really knew what it was like," but that is not to deny that she sees blacks as possessing qualities that whites would do well to acquire. Thanks to the wisdom and dignity of her black characters, Anne Tyler's novels—striated though they are with sudden death, dysfunctional families and disappointment—are indeed ultimately bright books of life.

Barbara A. Bennett (essay date January 1995)

SOURCE: "Attempting to Connect: Verbal Humor in the Novels of Anne Tyler," in *South Atlantic Review,* Vol. 60, No. 1, January, 1995, pp. 57-75.

[*In the following essay, Bennett outlines the various types of verbal humor Tyler employs in her novels.*]

In the essay **"Still Just Writing,"** Anne Tyler comments on her unusual characters: "People have always seemed funny and strange to me"; in a letter to me dated November 24, 1991, she clarified what she means in describing people that way: "I think of 'funny and strange' as wonderful traits, which always make me feel hopeful when I spot them." Some reviewers have faulted Tyler, however, for exaggerating her characters to bizarre or eccentric proportions. Marita Golden, for example, reviewing **Breathing Lessons,** writes that Maggie Moran "has a Lucy Ricardo quality that undermines our empathy." However, other critics, Robert Towers, Joseph Mathewson, Wallace Stegner, and Alice Hall Petry specifically, have compared her characterization to that of Charles Dickens. Stegner writes that Tyler's characters, "a Dickensian gallery of oddballs, innocents, obsessives, erratics, incompetents and plain Joes and Janes, all see the world a little skewed, but their author sees them with such precision and presents them with such amusement and lack of malice that they come off the page as exhilaratingly human." Tyler her-

self has responded to such criticism by saying, "I write about those off-beat characters and that blend of laughter and tears because in my experience, that's what real life consists of."

Ordinary life. Ordinary people. Tyler has a way of portraying them at their best—and worst. She shows people with basic human faults, struggling to endure in a sometimes unfair, sometimes insane world, attempting to work out the problems in relationships and communication. In her twelve novels, published between 1964 and 1991, Tyler has created a cast of memorable characters rife with weaknesses common to the human race. But she is not just a weaver of tales full of quirky characters. Her novels transcend the ordinary plots and characters found in so many popular writers' works, and in her humor we see more than comic situations designed merely to make us laugh. Tyler's humor accomplishes what George Meredith specifies as the goal of true comedy: it awakens "thoughtful laughter," forcing us to take a closer look at ourselves and our relationships with others.

Tyler's own description of her writing as a "blend of laughter and tears" seems especially appropriate, as tragedy and comedy are indisputably linked in her stories. She also comments: "I can't think of any tragic situation in real life that hasn't shown a glimmer of comedy too," and Louis D. Rubin, Jr. remarks in his study, *The Comic Imagination in American Literature,* that the "American literary imagination has from its earliest days been at least as much comic in nature as tragic." Several critics have recognized the significance of the juxtaposition of tragedy and comedy in Tyler's work, yet another similarity to Dickens: Peter S. Prescott describes *The Accidental Tourist* as a "delicate balance of comedy and pathos"; Jonathan Yardley comments that the same novel "leaves one aching with pleasure and pain"; and Benjamin DeMott compliments Tyler's "mastery of grave as well as comic tones." Certainly, human relationships hold the potential for both comedy and tragedy, and Tyler often places her readers on that thin line between the two. As Regina Barreca points out in her book on women's strategic use of humor, "Often women's humor deals with those subjects traditionally reserved for tragedy: life and death, love and hate, connection and abandonment."

Rubin remarks that "it is remarkable how comparatively little attention has been paid to American humor, and to the comic imagination in general, by those who have chronicled and interpreted American literature," and this is certainly true of Tyler's canon. Although Tyler's humor has been praised briefly in reviews and essays on her work, its full significance has been virtually ignored. In the introduction to his book of essays, *The Fiction of Anne Tyler,* C. Ralph Stephens remarks: "Tyler's comic sensibility and the important roles humor and irony play in her fiction . . . have only begun to be investigated critically; the sources of her humor and its thematic and structuring functions in her work clearly merit fuller attention." Alice Hall Petry concurs in the introduction to her book of essays, commenting that "an astute appreciation of Tyler's subtle, ironic humor . . . too often is lacking in commentaries on her work."

To understand fully many of Tyler's ideas, it is necessary to examine how and why she uses humor. Humor is especially key in analyzing one of Tyler's major themes: missed connections. The idea of "connecting" is crucial to Tyler's canon and one that is potentially either tragic or comic. In commenting on the similarity of Tyler to another Southern writer, Carson McCullers, Petry explains, "Tyler seems receptive to McCullers' dictum that we must learn to 'connect' with one another, that love is one of the few defenses we have against a world that seems antagonistic towards a strong sense of both selfhood and freedom."

It is communicating that makes us human, that sets us apart from other living creatures. It is communication that brings people together, and ironically and tragically, it is what often drives people apart. Very often Tyler uses humor to illustrate the lack of communication that is the source of much of this tragedy/comedy in her novels and in modern society. Tyler herself comments: "[M]iscommunication is one of the situations that most often lets characters say something funny," forcing us to laugh at our clumsy attempts to connect with each other. Since much of human communication is verbal, words themselves—mis-spoken, misunderstood, and mis-analyzed—from the basis for a great deal of the humor of miscommunication.

Such verbal humor falls into various categories, each of which serves a specific purpose in extending the theme of miscommunication. Although these categories overlap in some instances, it will be easier to analyze them by separating them as clearly as possible. These categories include: (1) Linguistic errors that characters make either consciously or subconsciously; (2) The psychological shift or attempt to divert attention away from the real issue; (3) Inadequate words in communication; and (4) Non-traditional means of communication.

Linguistic Errors

According to Freud, when people joke, they "are in a position to conceal not only what they have to say but also the fact that they have something—forbidden—to say." Perhaps the humor, however unintentional it may seem, sends a message—of defiance, anger, frustration, jealousy. For example, Maggie Moran in *Breathing Lessons* comments on her ex-daughter-in-law Fiona's thinness: "Just a twig, she was going to say; or just a stick. But she got mixed up and combined the two words: 'You're just a twick!'" Known as a spoonerism, an unintentional and spontaneous transposition or combination of sounds, this type of slip of the tongue often reveals

something significant about the speaker. In this case, Maggie's true feelings for Fiona—perhaps resentment, jealousy, or anger—are suggested through this nebulous term "twick" that sounds, at once, like a compliment *and* an insult.

In *Saint Maybe,* linguistic confusion is taken to the extreme in the character of Ian Bedloe's neighbor, a foreigner who, with his limited knowledge of English, attempts to express sympathy about the death of Ian's brother. He says, "'Woe betide you' and 'O lud lud! Please to accept my lamentations.'" Again, there is more here than a simple linguistic mistake. The foreigner's inability to communicate his feelings of sadness because he lacks the appropriate words parallels the inadequacy of all people in their attempts to console someone in anguish over the death of a loved one. This is an excellent example of Tyler's ability to combine tragedy and comedy in the same scene to make a point. Readers laugh at the character's absurd chatter but also realize the serious statement behind the humor: in tragic situations, most people find themselves helplessly muttering words as awkward and meaningless as those spoken by the foreigner.

As with this character, Tyler usually makes her characters seem unaware of their linguistic errors, which her readers see clearly. In *The Clock Winder,* Mrs. Emerson describes her husband's fondness for Christmas and his favorite reindeer: "Always so fond of Randolph." Mrs. Emerson's error suggests ignorance on her part, a lack of understanding not only of her husband, but also of the customs and norms of society. Her inability to communicate with her family is only an indication of her inability to survive in and relate to the outside world without help from someone, someone to "wind the clocks" in the house and maintain order. And, in an ironic twist, Tyler gives her the last name of the philosopher most closely associated with self-reliance.

Tyler creates a similar misunderstanding in *A Slipping-Down Life.* A fan misreads the name "CASEY" that Evie Decker has carved into her forehead and tells a friend that the singer "YEZAC" will be performing that night. Although Evie initially intends to draw the attention of the community to Drumstrings Casey and Casey's attention to herself, her plans backfire. Much like the fan who misreads the name on Evie's forehead, intentions and results get twisted around while events turn out to be more tragic than Evie imagines. When Casey comes to see her in the hospital, he complains that she used "CASEY" instead of his first name, and Evie responds:

> "What, *Drumstrings*? I don't have that big of a forehead."
>
> "Drum," he said. "Nobody said the whole thing for Lord's sake."
>
> "They call you Drum?" asked Evie.

"That's right."

"Well, I certainly wish I'd of known."

"Yeah, I suppose it's too late now," he said.

Acting before communicating, Tyler suggests, may be worse than not acting at all, as can be seen later in the novel after the incident is reported in the newspaper. Evie receives a note in the mail with the following message: "Congratulations on your recent achievement. And when it's the *tops* in achievement you want, just think of Sonny Martin, Pulqua County's Biggest Real Estate Agent." Obviously, Sonny also needed more information before sending the note. His rash actions exemplify a sharp criticism Tyler makes about contemporary society: people are so intent on making a profit, they fail to take the time to find out the facts before acting, and instead of achieving their true purpose, these efforts to communicate appear absurd and inappropriate.

Another type of linguistic error is the malapropism, the inadvertent replacement of one word with another similarly pronounced, as when Janie Rose, a small girl, runs through her nightly prayers, saying, "'Deliver us from measles.'" As Henri Bergson points out: "Inadvertently to say or do what we have no intention of saying or doing . . . is, as we are aware, one of the main sources of the comic." Although this explanation is applicable to many situations, it is especially significant in regard to malapropisms because in such cases speakers are never aware of their errors, a further development of the theme that people often do not successfully communicate simply out of ignorance. In *Dinner at the Homesick Restaurant,* Ezra Tull is told that a patient down the hall from Mrs. Scarlatti has a "'heart rumor'"; and in *Saint Maybe,* the Church of the Second Chance is called the "Church of the Second Rate." These malapropisms explain much about how we communicate. Perhaps the sterile atmosphere of a hospital has so dehumanized dying that identities and feelings become merely rumors, while the dying are treated impersonally. The comment in *Saint Maybe* is uttered by a disgruntled father who disapproves of his daughter's church membership. Both remarks, made in ignorance, force the reader to see past the humor to deeper meanings—with perhaps tragic implications. These characters are unable to express their true feelings, which are revealed instead through subconscious jokes.

Taking confusion of words one step further, Tyler even pokes fun at the limited comprehension of the partially deaf or mentally incompetent, character types not normally the target of jokes. In *Searching for Caleb,* for example, Justine's grandfather communicates with difficulty because he is nearly deaf. In the following dialogue between the two, Justine, who begins the conversation, appears to ignore her grandfather's misunderstanding:

"Tell her we're just about to leave."

"Knees?"

"And don't forget your hearing aid."

"They don't get better *that* fast, the cold has sunk into the sockets," her grandfather said. "Ask me again tomorrow. Thank you very much."

In a later encounter, Justine again ignores her grandfather's difficulty. Her husband Duncan begins the conversation:

"So you're going to take their side."

"I didn't know there were sides."

"How's that?" asked her grandfather.

"Duncan thinks I'm defecting."

"Hmm?"

"*Defecting.*"

"Nonsense," said her grandfather. "You're as smart as anybody."

Similarly, Elizabeth, in *The Clock Winder,* takes care of an elderly man, Mr. Cunningham, who moves in and out of mental competency. In one scene, she introduces him to her friend, Matthew:

"Here I am. Come in Matthew. This is Mr. Cunningham."

"How do, Mr. Cunningham," the old man said.

"No, this is Matthew Emerson. *You're* Mr. Cunningham."

"Well, I knew that." He raised his chin sharply.

Beneath the surface humor, Tyler makes a serious point about the tragedy of aging. Growing older, Mr. Cunningham has lost the ability to communicate because he has lost the power of words. In effect, this loss of power is a loss of identity, evidenced by his inability to recognize his own name. His final words and gesture are defensive, a last attempt to maintain dignity. Similarly, Justine's grandfather continues to respond to conversations as if he understands them entirely, while those around him, recognizing his need for dignity, refrain from correcting his errors.

One final type of linguistic misunderstanding occurs when a

character misinterprets the *intent* behind words, what Freud describes as a "contrast of ideas" or "a contrast between the words and what they mean." Among Tyler's novels, ***Dinner at the Homesick Restaurant*** offers the best examples of such confusion. When Ezra shoots a bullseye by splitting an arrow that had previously hit the mark, his sister Jenny cries, "'Ezra, look what you did! What you went and did to that arrow!' Ezra took the straw from his mouth. 'I'm sorry,' he told Beck. (He was so used to breaking things)." This archery incident functions as a microcosm of the novel, illustrating this dysfunctional family's difficulty in connecting through words. Cody, often jealous and resentful, remains silent, refusing to congratulate or acknowledge his brother's achievement; Jenny misunderstands the act, frantically calling attention to possible blame; while Ezra, so often victimized by his own lack of confidence, immediately becomes humble and ashamed. All of the characters replay these defective roles over and over because of their poor communication skills.

Freud tells us that words "are a plastic material with which one can do all kinds of things." Whether motives are subconscious or conscious is not as important as the effect words produce. Linguistic errors may confuse characters and readers alike, eliciting their laughter and pity, but significantly this confusion is a "bewilderment succeeded by illumination."

Another kind of verbal humor develops when characters make incongruous remarks or respond inappropriately to others' remarks in order to shift attention away from sensitive issues, usually intending to avoid awkward, rude, or unpleasant conversations. Aunt Hattie, the elderly matriarch in ***If Morning Ever Comes,*** says of a pushy niece who has just exited, "'She's putting on weight, don't you think?'" when she is not actually concerned with her niece's weight. By making this comment, she belittles her niece, minimizing the woman's presence and influence, and thereby increasing her own importance and power. Tyler uses a similar tactic in ***Dinner at the Homesick Restaurant*** when Cody Tull's estranged father, Beck, returns for his wife's funeral. After Beck tells Cody, "'I often thought about you after I went away,'" Cody responds, "'Oh? . . . Have you been away?'" Cody's sarcasm minimizes not only the significance of his father's desertion, but also his reappearance.

Searching for Caleb offers several examples of this kind of unexpected retort, the first developing from Duncan's frustration at the lack of meaningful conversation around the family dinner table. Duncan's mother meets this criticism with a trivial reply, avoiding the confrontation:

> "Can't you say something that means something?" Duncan asked.

> "About what?" said his mother.

> "I don't care. Anything. . . . Don't you want to get to the bottom of things? Talk about whether there's a God or not?"

> "But we already know," said his mother.

Later in the novel, Duncan clearly imitates his mother's avoidance technique in an argument with Justine about visiting their newly-married daughter, Meg. Justine tries to make Duncan admit that he loves and misses Meg:

> "You used to take her to the circus when she was too little to hold down a spring-up seat. For three straight hours you leaned on it for her so she wouldn't pop right up again."

> "There was an intermission."

In this way, Duncan draws attention away from a sensitive issue, that he misses and loves his daughter, by focusing on an incidental detail that disavows his attention and affection, making his sacrifice inconsequential and his confession of love unnecessary. Freud terms this kind of humor a "displacement joke," defined as redirecting the topic of conversation, and he comments that "diverting . . . the reply" causes a "shifting of the psychical emphasis" away from something unpleasant.

The Clock Winder offers several examples of displacement jokes, such as the scene in which Mrs. Emerson attempts to speak to Elizabeth about her disheveled appearance. Elizabeth evades the criticism by humorously focusing on an unimportant detail:

> "'Above all else, be feminine,' I used to tell my daughters, and here you are in those eternal blue jeans, but every time I look out the window some new boy is helping you rake leaves."

> "Oh, well, the leaves are nearly gone by now," Elizabeth said.

A similar instance occurs in a conversation between Bee Bedloe and her husband in ***Saint Maybe.*** He laments his daughter's growing older and scolding him the way he once scolded her. He declares, "'[T]here was some stage when we were equals. I mean while she was on the rise and we were on the downslide. A stage when we were level with each other.'" Bee answers, "'Well, I must have been on the phone at the time,'" thereby absolving herself of responsibility for any miscommunication between parents and child by diverting attention away from the real issue.

While much of this humor is unconscious, sometimes characters consciously say something amusing to mitigate an uncomfortable situation or make a serious point in a subtle, non-threatening way. In *Dinner at the Homesick Restaurant,* for example, Cody writes letters to Ruth on samples sent to him by a stationery company that are imprinted with the names of imaginary people. Rather than having Cody tell Ruth he loves her and does not want her to marry his brother, Tyler has him send notes signed with invented names, warning her against becoming involved with "those pale blond thoughtful kind of men" who are "a real disappointment" and encouraging her to see "someone tall, [with] black hair and gray eyes" who is "really a good man at heart and has been misjudged for years by people." Cody is somewhat protected by the charade, and while we laugh at the subtlety of such strategy to steal his brother's fiancee, Tyler makes a more serious point as well: we communicate better with complete strangers than we do with those who supposedly are closest to us. Ironically and unfortunately, anonymity is less threatening; strangers are less apt to respond negatively and abusively than those who love us. Robert McPhillips describes this subtlety in Tyler's work as "gently comic." Approaching many serious subjects, Tyler is able to make her point clear without resorting to bitterness or accusation about the tragedy of family members who feel justified in verbally abusing each other.

Another example of this "gently comic" style that awakens "thoughtful laughter" is found in the conversation between Charlotte and Jake about staying cooped up in their getaway car in *Earthly Possessions:*

> "If you like," he said, "you can sleep in the back tonight. I ain't sleeping anyhow. I plan to just sit here and go crazy."
>
> "Okay."
>
> "I don't see how you stand this," he said.
>
> "You forget," I told him, "I've been married."

Making light of an unhappy situation, such as a marriage that feels more like a prison, enables Tyler to express serious concerns about relationships without calling for pity for the characters. Tragedy shifts to comedy simply through Tyler's tone.

The children Tyler creates are not so subtle, as *Saint Maybe* exemplifies. In an attempt to marry her Uncle Ian to the "right" woman and scare away the "wrong" one, Daphne tells the entire dinner party:

> "I just can't help thinking about this dream I had a couple of nights ago. . . . God was speaking to me from a thundercloud. . . . 'Daphne Bedloe, beware of strangers! . . . Daphne Bedloe, a stranger is going to start hanging around your uncle . . . somebody

fat, not from Baltimore, chasing after your uncle Ian.'"

The message is painfully clear to the reader and all the characters present at the dinner: Daphne's technique is somewhat unpolished, therefore realistically childlike. More often, Tyler's adult characters use humor to smooth over unpleasant scenes, rather than worsening them as Daphne does, often by this shifting of attention away from something painful. Regina Barreca explains how humor is able to achieve this:

> [Humor is] a way of making our feelings and responses available to others without terrifying our listeners. When we can frame a difficult matter with humor, we can often reach someone who would otherwise withdraw. Humor is a show of both strength and vulnerability—you are willing to make the first move but you are trusting in the response of your listener.

In one such situation, Jenny Tull, a character in *Dinner at the Homesick Restaurant,* uses humor to defuse tense situations with her struggling step-son, Slevin, by shifting the emphasis from what he does to the absurdity suggested by his motives. Rather than confront him about his reasons for stealing a vacuum cleaner that reminds him of his mother's, Jenny says: "'What's next, I wonder,' Jenny said. She mused for a moment. 'Picture it! Grand pianos. Kitchen sinks. Why, we'll have his mother's whole household,' she said, 'her photo albums and her grade-school yearbooks, her college roommate asleep on our bed and her high school boyfriends in our living room.'" Jenny's technique influences Slevin's approach with his teacher, who repeats a conversation to Jenny:

> "He's had so many absences, I finally asked if he'd been cutting school. 'Yes, ma'am,' he said—came right out with it. 'What did you cut?' I asked him. 'February,' he said."

Tyler knows it is difficult to feel anger and amusement simultaneously toward the same person, and in such characters as these, we see that humor can achieve the same purpose as a lecture or argument, with minimal damage to a relationship. Barreca further explains: "Making a generously funny comment, pointing to the absurdity of a situation, turning embarrassment or unease into something to be shared instead of repressed is risky, but it is also often exactly what is needed."

Another category of miscommunication includes meaningless or inadequate words uttered because any communication, even inane, is more satisfactory than none at all. This effect is mainly accomplished through Tyler's near perfect creation of dialogue. In all her novels, Tyler uses conversations to convey the inadequacy of words to express feelings.

Joseph C. Voelker explains that her dialogue is "musically rendered, inconclusive, and comic in its apparent insufficiency as a mode of human communication. . . . More is heard in its silences, gaps, misunderstandings, and failures to listen than in the words themselves."

Voelker terms her particular style "pointillistic," referring to the practice in art of applying small strokes or dots of paint to a surface so that, from a distance, they blend together to create an image. In short, individual words may seem unimportant, but when viewed from a literary distance, they mean much more. Voelker further clarifies: "Several words or phrases, always at the beginnings of sentences that never get spoken, form the actual dots of Tyler's pointillism. Characters say 'Oh,' 'Well,' 'Oh, now' and then stop. The consequence is anxious, even rueful comedy."

Macon's agent, Julian, in *The Accidental Tourist,* for example, continually makes valiant efforts to get to know Macon's family, while Macon makes every effort to keep him distant. In one of his first encounters with one brother, Charles, Julian politely inquires about Charles's job:

> Julian said, "What do you do for a living, Charles?"
>
> "I make bottle caps."
>
> "Bottle caps! Is that a fact!"
>
> "Oh, well, it's no big thing," Charles said. "I mean it's not half as exciting as it sounds, really."

Note the inanity of Charles' final remark. Exaggerated interest and false enthusiasm from Julian have left Charles in an uncomfortable position, and he feels pushed into uttering ridiculous words in response to Julian's obsequious comments.

Julian doggedly pursues his relationship with the Learys, whose name aptly fits their "leeriness" in accepting any outsiders into their tight family unit. While Julian visits Macon and Muriel, Muriel tries to write country and western song lyrics for a contest, and Julian again does his best to connect by helping her find a line to replace "When we shared every pain." As Macon forces him out the door, Julian tenaciously contributes, "When our lives were more sane," "When we used to raise Cain," "When I hadn't met Jane," "When she didn't know Wayne," "When she wasn't inane," "When we guzzled champagne," and "When we stuffed on chow mein." In addition to creating a very funny scene, Tyler dramatizes our frantic and futile efforts to use words to express our need for one another. We see that by accepting one of Julian's ridiculous lines, Muriel would be accepting Julian himself, and that is the true goal: a significant connection to another human being.

Similarly, Drumstrings Casey has a habit of speaking out during his songs; most of his thoughts, his manager admits, are "'not even connected.'" Symbolically, Drum represents the disjointed way we often talk, not conversing, just speaking.

> "She left you, you say?"
>
> He hit one note several times over.
>
> "Where were you? Did you see her go?
>
> "The meter man's coming.
>
> "Buy the tickets. Wait in the lobby.
>
> "Have you noticed all the prices going up?"

His words are clearly not as important as his need, shared by all people, to connect.

Speaking without communicating—or talking without listening—is one of the major problems in relationships in Tyler's novels. Many times characters converse on different planes with each one carrying on his or her own monologue. With Ansel Green, in *The Tin Can Tree,* this occurs regularly, mainly because everyone is tired of listening to him complain. He tells his brother: "'I've noticed more and more . . . that no one listens when I talk. I don't know why. Usually I think about a thing before I say it, making sure it's worthwhile. I plan it in my mind, like.'" Ironically, his brother is not paying much attention to Ansel's words; he is reading the newspaper.

Such disjointed conversation is used most successfully in *Dinner at the Homesick Restaurant* and *The Accidental Tourist.* The former novel offers the Tull family, whose members lack the necessary skills to communicate with others. For example, Pearl initially decides not to tell her children their father has deserted them, hoping they will not notice, but she finally tries to tell them in a disjointed conversation that is at once humorous and tragic:

> "Children," she had said. . . . "Children, there's something I want to discuss with you."
>
> Cody was talking about a job. He had to find one in order to help with tuition fees. "I could work in the cafeteria," he was saying, "or maybe off-campus. I don't know which." Then he heard his mother and looked over at her.
>
> "It's about your father," Pearl said.
>
> Jenny said, "I'd choose the cafeteria."

"You know, my darlings," Pearl told them, "how I always say your father's away on business."

"But off-campus they might pay more," said Cody, "and every cent counts."

"At the cafeteria you'd be with your classmates, though," Ezra said.

"Yes, I thought of that."

"All those coeds," Jenny said. "Cheerleaders. Girls in their little white bobby sox."

"Sweater girls," Cody said.

"There's something I want to explain about your father," Pearl told them.

"Choose the cafeteria," Ezra said.

"Children?"

"The cafeteria," they said.

This conversation also illustrates that Beck's desertion has been the central focus of Pearl's existence but her children have moved on to deal with other issues.

The three children in this novel have their own problems in communicating. Ezra laments his inability to "get in touch with people," confronting his mother with his fear:

> "I'm worried if I come too close, they'll say I'm overstepping. They'll say I'm pushy, or . . . emotional, you know. But if I back off, they might think I don't care. I really, honestly believe I missed some rule that everyone else takes for granted; I must have been absent from school that day. There's this narrow little dividing line I somehow never located."

Pearl responds, "'Nonsense; I don't know what you're talking about,'" ironically illustrating Ezra's point. In fact, he cannot even get his mother to admit he has a communication problem. She refuses to do more than hear his words, never listening to their implicit plea for understanding.

Cody also has trouble making himself understood. In one scene, he brings Ruth copper-colored roses to go with her hair, but clearly she does not understand his intentions and therefore pays minimal attention to the gesture:

> "Greenhouse roses. I especially ordered copper, to go with your hair."

"You leave my hair out of this," she said.

"Honey, he meant it as a compliment," Ezra told her.

"Oh."

"Certainly," said Cody. "See, it's my way of saying welcome. Welcome to our family, Ruth."

"Oh. Well, thanks."

"Cody, that was awfully nice of you," Ezra said.

"Gin," said Ruth.

The sharp last line, another example of Tyler's pointillism, emphasizes not only how listeners pay little attention, but also how people make inappropriate remarks to cover their inability to communicate effectively.

Similar communication problems haunt the Leary family in *The Accidental Tourist.* Ironically, the Leary brothers and their sister are most indignant about the decline of the English language: "[H]ow sloppy everyday speech had become. . . . [how] words are getting devalued." The Learys seem sure that if people would only clean up their usage, there would be no communication problems—as if words were the only thing to consider.

It is Macon who is most obsessed with policing proper usage, often at the expense of alienating those around him. He consistently ignores the message, focusing on the words: when Sarah tells him she has been dating a physician, he remarks, "Why not just call him a doctor"; when she comments that Rose has been "[c]ruising hardware stores like other people cruise boutiques," he corrects her with "As other people cruise boutiques"; when she remarks that she is sending him a letter through her attorney, he says, "I guess you mean a lawyer"; he corrects Muriel when she says, "My speciality is dogs that bite" by saying "Webster prefers specialty"; and he corrects Julian, who says "momentarily" instead of "any moment." It is not surprising that "communicate" is Macon's "least favorite word," considering how little he understands about the complexity of the process. In each of the conversations quoted above, Macon is afforded the opportunity to exchange feelings and insights with another character, yet he refuses such possibilities by focusing on words. Even when the words are grammatically correct, Macon cannot communicate effectively. After telling a neighbor he is staying at his family's home until his broken leg is healed, Macon has difficulty in maintaining an ordinary conversation:

> "We didn't see no ambulance though or nothing."

"Well, I called my sister."

"Sister's a doctor?"

"Just to come take me to the emergency room."

"When Brenda broke her hip on the missing step," Garner said, "she called an ambulance."

"Well, I called my sister."

"Brenda called the ambulance."

They seemed to be stuck.

They *are* stuck, and neither character is skilled enough to break the cycle of their circuitous conversation. Instead of communicating effectively, they take part in an absurd dialogue that makes Tyler's point clear: most of us lack effective communication skills, using words which inadequately express how we feel.

Non-traditional Communication

Tyler's characters often turn to non-traditional forms of communication, refusing to use words at all. For example, Ira Moran whistles songs with titles that suggest how he is feeling at the moment, while Ansel's mother in *The Tin Can Tree* acts out her opposition to the father's desire to eat the pet goats, as Ansel describes: "When my mother brought a roasted kid in, or any part of it, holding it high on a wooden platter with potatoes around it, she always dropped it just in the doorway between the kitchen and the dining room. It never failed."

The Leary family also engages in such refusals. Rather than deal with an unpleasant telephone confrontation, they simply refuse to answer the phone, thereby avoiding communication completely. Their own conversations are often forced and uncomfortable until they adopt the same simple method Muriel uses to train Edward the dog—clucking: "By suppertime, a cluck was part of the family language. Charles clucked over Rose's pork chops. Porter clucked when Macon dealt him a good hand of cards." The tragedy of their situation is alleviated only by its humorous absurdity. Having cut themselves off from the world by living together in their family house, not answering the phone, and only emerging from their cocoon when absolutely necessary, the Learys short circuit their only means of communication—words— by replacing them with mere sounds. Thus, even their communication with one another becomes minimal.

Of all Tyler's characters who find difficulty in dealing with others, however, the most psychologically aberrant communicator is Jeremy Pauling in *Celestial Navigation.* Agoraphobic Jeremy has cut himself off from the world, refusing to answer the phone, open mail, talk to strangers, or leave his house. Even when he needs to tell the family about something important, such as the impending delivery of a new refrigerator, Jeremy remains silent. His infrequent attempts to connect with the outside world humorously misfire because he lacks the proper experience. One time he brings Mary flowers, but says, "'These are for, I brought these for the room. . . . I found them by the trashcans.'" Jeremy successfully communicates with society only through his art—a uniquely cryptic representation of ordinary life pieced together in collages, expressing feelings and thoughts his words cannot relay.

Tyler's novels teem with characters less extreme than Jeremy who prefer not to communicate in order to avoid difficult situations, such as the Pecks in *Searching for Caleb,* who fear telling Caroline about the death of her husband, wishing, "Oh, if only we could just never tell her and this would all blow over!" Elizabeth, in *The Clock Winder,* cannot bear to tell her employer she is unable to kill the Thanksgiving turkey and so buys a second turkey at the supermarket, while Peter, in the same novel, avoids telling his family he is married until they naively ask his wife, "[W]hat's your last name, anyway?" In *Earthly Possessions,* Charlotte Emory's mother, although she believes she has been given the wrong baby at the hospital, does not tell anyone, saying: "But I was still so surprised, you see, and besides didn't want to make trouble. I took what they gave me." Duncan Peck "speaks" to his family with humorous messages cut out of magazines, such as "Have you ever had a bad time in Levi's?" and "You are far, far from home . . . in unfamiliar territory," while Mrs. Emerson records messages to her children on her dictaphone so they cannot interrupt her and cannot talk back. Reducing conversation to the minimum lessens the threat of miscommunication, a trade-off many of Tyler's characters eagerly make.

Petry says that Tyler's first two novels are "implied commentaries on the lack of thought or feeling underlying what generally passes for communication." This description, in fact, fits her entire canon. Lack of communication in relationships is a common yet grim problem, but Tyler provokes our laughter at this human failing. Tyler, however, claims that such humor is unplanned in her work rather than a consciously developed theme:

> I never plan humor in my writing (and would be suspicious of any I *did* plan). What usually happens is, I get a patch of dialogue rolling to the point where the characters seem to take over, and then one of them will say something that catches me completely by surprise and makes me smile.

If George Meredith is right that "the test of true comedy is that it shall awaken thoughtful laughter," surely Anne Tyler is a truly comic novelist who opens our eyes to the tragic yet comic truth of our persistent but unsuccessful attempts to communicate with each other. Regina Barreca writes that "[l]aughing together is as close as you can get to a hug without touching," so perhaps even if words fail, laughter can provide the needed connection.

Roberta Rubenstein (review date 30 April 1995)

SOURCE: "The Woman Who Went Away," in *Chicago Tribune Books,* April 30, 1995, p. 1.

[*In the following review, Rubenstein praises Tyler's* Ladder of Years *as "virtually flawless."*]

Anne Tyler's wonderfully satisfying 13th novel begins with a newspaper headline: "BALTIMORE WOMAN DISAPPEARS DURING FAMILY VACATION." The accompanying news item includes the few facts related to the sudden disappearance of Cordelia Grinstead, whose eyes are "blue or gray or perhaps green. . . ." Then Tyler circles back to let us see the circumstances that trigger Delia's unpremeditated decision to vacate her current life—without even saying goodbye—to assume a new one.

The wife of a successful doctor (a family practitioner 17 years older than she) and the mother of three adolescent children, Delia still lives in the same house in which she grew up as the youngest of three daughters. Her father, also a doctor (recently deceased) left his practice to his younger partner, Delia's no-nonsense husband, Sam. Working informally as Sam's secretary and receptionist and reading romance novels in her spare time, Delia has begun to wonder whether her husband married her only to secure a future in her father's established medical practice. Turning 40 as her children begin to drift away into lives of their own, she feels both expendable and utterly taken for granted by her family.

The event that propels Delia from one life into another is her chance encounter in a grocery store with a young man whose own wife has recently left him. Having spotted his wife and her current partner in a nearby aisle, the stranger impulsively asks Delia to pretend she's with him. *Ladder of Years* is full of such chance moments and full of dissatisfied wives (and husbands) and of women who have left their marriages either literally or emotionally, temporarily or permanently.

Some weeks later, during a family vacation at the Delaware seashore, Delia starts to walk away from the beach and— wearing only her swimsuit and her husband's robe—keeps traveling until she finds herself miles away, in a small town in Maryland. Much of the narrative traces her efforts to shed her former life and start over again at a new location, not only on the map but also within herself.

That process, recounted detail by fascinating detail, is utterly compelling in Tyler's hands—more so because Delia's story taps a fantasy that many people, if they are honest with themselves, will admit to harboring on occasion: the wish to escape, to shed one's responsibilities, to jettison the complexities of one's current life and establish a new life somewhere else on simpler terms.

Taking a room in a boarding house and locating a job as a secretary, Delia establishes new routines and savors her spartan new life as "Miss Grinstead": only two changes of clothes; a room so bereft of personal possessions that she can look around and "detect not the slightest hint that anybody lived there"; a town so small that, before long, everyone from cooks at the local diner to young mothers with their toddlers at the park recognizes and welcomes her.

But can anyone become "a person without a past?" Inevitably, members of Delia's family discover her whereabouts, write to her and even visit, trying to fathom the reasons for her abrupt departure. Delia stubbornly clings to the new life and self she has begun to create, feeling as if she is "clearing out her mind to see what was left. Maybe there would be nothing." Instead, she discovers that her new life begins to resemble the one she thought she'd shed. She even acquires a stray kitten whose ingratiating habits recall those of the cat she left behind.

Other responsibilities follow. Delia's shift to a second job as a "live-in woman" for a man whose wife has left him and their pre-adolescent son may seem almost too obvious a plot twist, a variation on Delia's abdication of her own marriage. But through it, Tyler shows us Delia's further self-discovery in a position once-removed from her habitual roles.

Both her employer—a high school principal whose pet peeve is creeping slang—and his son cherish Delia rather than taking her for granted, while she enjoys occupying a position that is less than but akin to a wife and mother. Through their regard, she finds herself becoming a more capable and necessary person than she had felt with her own family, "a woman people looked to automatically for sustenance."

Delia's new life in a small town introduces her (and us) to a group of unforgettable characters, including Belle Flint, Delia's flamboyant landlady, who longs for precisely the kind of life Delia has discarded: husband, family, commitments. Unfortunately, Belle is mostly attracted to ineligible men. As she reflects, ". . .it's kind of like I lack imagination. I mean, I can't seem to picture marrying a man till I see him married to someone else. Then I say, 'Why! He'd make a good husband for me!'"

Another wonderful creation is Nat, grandfather of Delia's surrogate son, who lives in a retirement home but possesses the spirit of a much younger man. During the course of the narrative, the widowed Nat marries a lively divorcee half his age and (rather bemusedly) fathers a child, thus unsettling the "ladder of years" that structures the living arrangements—and age-based assumptions—of Senior City's residents.

Inevitably, Delia's two lives begin to collide in ways I won't spoil by revealing here. Suffice it to say that eventually one realizes her story is not only about the peaks and troughs of relationships but also about their intersections with time. Delia wonders "how humans could bear to live in a world where the passage of time held so much power"—and her midlife crisis allows Tyler to explore a real-world form of time-travel. Who, after all, wouldn't like to return to certain moments in the past and play out the choices differently? Then there is the fear of being trapped in time-in routines and relationships that leave the self calcified.

It is to reclaim her true/lost self that Delia vacates her life. But in this spellbinding story, she also comes to confront the inevitable grievances and losses that accumulate as people age, parents die, marriages evolve, children grow up.

Perhaps Tyler permits Delia too few dark moments or backward glances. (Wouldn't a mother who abandons her children feel more than a few qualms?) Otherwise, though, *Ladder of Years* is virtually flawless, a book that leaves one unsure until virtually the final page which of Delia Grinstead's two lives will claim her.

Richard Eder (review date 7 May 1995)

SOURCE: "Trying on a New Life," in *The Los Angeles Times Book Review,* May 7, 1995, p. 3.

[*In the following review, Eder complains that Tyler's* Ladder of Years *fails to sustain its momentum.*]

Why does Delia Grinstead run away from her overbearing physician husband, her three sulky children and her depressive suburban life? With any of our realistic chroniclers of American middle-class life the answer would lie in the question. With Anne Tyler it lies there too, but the really interesting answer is: because her cat's name is Vernon.

Tyler only seems to be a realist. It is true that in such novels as *The Accidental Tourist, Dinner at the Homesick Restaurant* and *Breathing Lessons,* her characters stumble out of the pages of the book, hang around, have supper with us, stay the night and never quite leave. Their lives are set on a prosaic chessboard: families, marriages, growing up and growing older, relinquishing choices and acquiring fantasies, and relinquishing the fantasies.

They move, though, not by straight lines but by a crookback hop and swivel, like tipsy chess knights. They move not by causes, effects and purposes but by accidents—accidents that in some hidden and exhilarating way they are prepared to incur, as one seemingly humdrum species of corn kernel is prepared to turn inside out and bloom white.

Thus in one sense, Delia Grinstead's flight is entirely foreseeable. Tyler even announces it at the start, in the form of a small news clipping. It reports the disappearance, during a family beach holiday, of a Baltimore housewife, age 40, whose eyes are "blue or gray or possibly green," and who "stands 5'2" or possibly 5'5" and weighs either 90 or 110 pounds" and who was wearing, her husband reports, "something pink or blue, either frilled or lacy or looking kind of baby-doll."

So her family has only a hazy idea of what she looks like. For that matter, Delia hasn't much idea herself. Sam, her husband, is bossy and matter-of-fact; her children, aged 15, 19 and 21, are oblivious unless dinner is late; her beloved father has recently died; and she has moved into and out of a comically embarrassing flirtation with a younger man. She picks up her answering-machine messages: Neighbors have invited them to dinner. She calls to accept but it turns out that the message is an old one and they'd gone there the previous week. "What kind of life was she living if every one of last week's telephone calls could just as easily be this week's?" she wonders.

Then one day, at the annual beach holiday—in a leaky cabin and with relatives packed grouchily together—Delia leaves the beach early and comes back to the cabin. When she calls the cat, a young man who is fixing the roof pops down; his name is Vernon, too. She has noticed his gleaming recreation vehicle parked outside, and she covets it as avidly as Toad coveted the painted caravan in *Wind in the Willows:* It means the open road.

Not quite deciding to, she cadges a ride. Before long they are driving down the Maryland shore and Vernon is nattering on about his family troubles. Young Lochinvar has turned kvetch, and Delia's impulsive gesture dissolves into one more domestic assignment as sympathetic ear.

She hops off at a little town named Bay Borough. In the square she contemplates the comfortably seated statue of the town's founder. "On this spot in August 1863," the inscription reads, "George Pendle Bay, a Union soldier encamped overnight with this company, dreamed that a mighty angel appeared to him and said, 'Ye are sitting in the barber's chair of infinity,' which he interpreted as instruction to absent himself from the remainder of the war."

And so, still in her beach robe and with the week's grocery money in her purse, Delia joins George in his absenting. She finds a rented room, buys some deliberately dowdy clothes and talks the town lawyer into hiring her as his secretary. She had worked for a Baltimore doctor, she explains, but—killing off Sam—he died. She settles down in the guise of a spinster seeking a new life; she makes friends and joins in such town traditions as watching the annual Bay Day softball game. Tyler, of course, does not provide a standard game. She sets it in an impenetrable fog through which Delia and her friends catch muffled shouts:

"Batter's out." "He's what?" "He's out." "Where is the batter?" And, a beat or two later: "Who is the batter?"

Ladder of Years is the story of a fugue to change one's life. It is told in Tyler's characteristic manner, one that no other American writer approaches. Just as she subverts the domestic with fantasy—her situations are earthbound until you notice that they are gliding along two inches above the earth—she subverts fantasy with the domestic.

Delia's new life is, in many ways, as dreamy and comically cluttered with tiny concerns as her old one. And the emotional clatter she had expected to get from her family amounts to an occasional irascible and oddly spaced burp. Her sister turns up after a week or two, talks vaguely about "stress" and leaves. The children are virtually silent. Sam fails to appear—Delia had been rehearsing her postures for the moment he should arrive—and finally sends a stiff note. It offers to discuss any complaints she may have but assures her that he "will not invade your privacy."

The stiffness is undermined by two heavily inked outlines. Delia's desire to flee across the border is undermined by the news that Sam will not invade. The arc of her escape is undermined by the gravitational force of her nature. Fugue turns to round. She quits the law office for a job as live-in homemaker to the local school principal, whose wife has walked out on him and their 12-year-old son. Delia replaces Delia; one set of family responsibilities replaces the other. The need to mother and to love is not easy to extirpate; a comically and tenderly drawn attraction trickles up between her and her employer.

In short, it has become a Tylerean logjam of decisions that add up to indecision and doors that slam latchlessly and bang open again. A number of loopy characters and situations zigzag their way through by the time a year has gone by, and Delia is summoned home to deal with her daughter's wedding, gone chaotically askew. (Weddings are Tyler's moments of truth, equivalent to Hemingway's hunting and fishing exploits, though funnier.) It will force her to choose between Delia and Delia, between her new life and her old.

Tyler does not condemn her characters to stasis. She lets them move, though never as much as they think they are moving.

She teaches them to blunder into the art of letting life subvert them.

Subversion—the parade that brings clowns, the clowns that bring a parade—is her art too, and the risk that goes with it. Pick up too many outriders, particularly if they are dedicated to slipping spokes in the wheel, and your vehicle slows. Momentum is Tyler's difficulty; even in her best novels there are moments when vitality flags and things bog down. In *Ladder,* the bogging down can become especially onerous in the time between Delia's flight and her return. A year is perhaps too long for what may or may not be—we only learn at the end—a round trip.

Cathleen Schine (review date 7 May 1995)

SOURCE: "New Life for Old," in *The New York Times Book Review,* May 7, 1995, p. 12.

[*In the following review, Schine praises Tyler's* Ladder of Years.]

The French have said that William Wyler, the great director of movies like *Dodsworth* and *The Best Years of Our Lives,* had a "*style sans* style." Anne Tyler has this same deceptive "style without a style." Opening one of her books in the middle and picking a page at random, a reader might not immediately recognize her individual rhythm or idiosyncratic temperament. She does nothing fancy, nothing tricky. But so rigorous and artful is the style without a style, so measured and delicate is each observation, so complex is the structure and so astute and open the language, that the reader can relax, feel secure in the narrative and experience the work as something real and natural—even inevitable.

In *Ladder of Years,* Ms. Tyler's 13th novel, the story that appears to unfold of its own accord is a fairy tale of sorts, a fairy tale with echoes of both the tragedy of *King Lear* and the absurdity of the modern romance novel.

Delia (short for Cordelia) is the youngest of three sisters. At 40, she has long been married to a kindly doctor who still makes house calls. They live in the large old Baltimore house in which she grew up. Delia's father was also a doctor. When she was 17, Sam Grinstead came to be his assistant and to choose one of the three princesses. "Like the king's three daughters in a fairy tale, he said, they'd been lined up according to age, the oldest farthest left, and like the woodcutter's honest son, he had chosen the youngest and prettiest, the shy little one on the right who didn't think she stood a chance."

And, Delia thinks, it certainly ended like a fairy tale, with the two of them getting married, "except that real life continues past the end." *Ladder of Years* is the story of what happens past the end, now that her beloved father is dead, her three children are grown (the youngest is a hulking, sullen 15-year-old who sneers at her), and her house has been invaded by workmen invited there by a husband suddenly obsessed with renovation. "She fancied she could hear the house groaning in distress—such a modest, mild house, so unprepared for change."

Delia is herself unprepared for change, yet it waits for her around every corner. Her response is to turn and simply walk away. On her yearly holiday at the beach with her husband and children, her sister Eliza (a committed aromatherapist in a pith helmet) and her divorced sister, Linda (an adamant Francophile who's brought along her twin daughters, Marie-Claire and Thérèse), Delia sits on the sand feeling more and more distant. Her husband irritates her, the way he pats water "so fastidiously on his chest and upper arms before ducking under," then checks his watch as he rises from the waves.

She also thinks of the younger man she met at the supermarket, who asked her to pretend to be his girlfriend because he'd just spotted his ex-wife in the next aisle. They see each other after that, though the relationship doesn't advance very far. Still, for Delia it is an awakening. "Whenever she imagined running into Adrian, she was conscious all at once of the light, quick way she naturally moved, and the outline of her body within the folds of her dress. She couldn't remember when she had last been so aware of herself from outside, from a distance."

But this consciousness of herself, of a body and a soul with outlines not defined by her pretty, pastel clothes, is not entirely new for Delia. There is a wonderful awareness in this book of how women, even little girls, self-consciously act out their roles, watching themselves as they serve tea, as they play picturesquely with their dolls. Delia now watches herself get up from the beach and walk away. She watches herself leave her family without a word, hitch a ride to a new town, buy a new dress in a new style, find a job and a room in a boardinghouse. "She climbed the stairs, thinking. *Here comes the executive secretary, returning from her lone meal to the solitude of her room.* It wasn't a complaint, though. It was a boast. An exultation."

If the reader is never quite sure why Delia deserts her life, neither is Delia herself. All she can say to explain herself when her family finally tracks her down is, "I'm here because I just like the thought of beginning again from scratch." This Cordelia is not asked for a declaration of her love in order to prove herself to anyone. No one casts her out to wander on the moors like Lear, either. But she casts herself out, strips herself bare and exiles herself in the scrappy little

town of Bay Borough, and it is she who tests the love of her family, she who waits for a declaration.

Ms. Tyler's style of small, perfect observation mirrors Delia's attentiveness to detail, which only very gradually allows her to see what's really around her. But for Delia, and for us, the discreet observations are almost physically satisfying. "For her walk," Ms. Tyler writes, "she wore her Miss Grinstead cardigan, which clung gently to her arms and made her feel like a cherished child." And that reassurance extends to readers, allowing us to enjoy the walk even when, like Delia, we're not sure where we're going.

In Bay Borough, the new, ascetic Miss Grinstead, who has left behind the complications of her life, finds new complications—in other words, she finds a new life. At first, she is "alone, utterly alone, without the conversational padding of father, sisters, husband, children." But soon her isolation is compromised. The people she meets, so different in manners and background from those in her usual milieu, appeal to her, and they like her. Looking for a job, she is interviewed by a divorced man seeking a housekeeper; he and his young son want her, and insist that she join their family. There is even a stray cat whom she valiantly resists, but he insists on becoming *her* cat. Delia has walked away from one fairy tale right into another.

Anne Tyler's dissociated characters have always been in danger of becoming annoying and a little boring, just like real unresponsive people. One sometimes has an urge to poke them—hard. In *Ladder of Years,* Ms. Tyler herself gives a playful poke, seeing Delia's defection from life partly as farce. Cordelia Grinstead tests her family's love, wandering into the wilderness stripped of everything—except a ruffled bathing suit. And then the family's reaction is just as laconic and dissociated as Delia's decision to disappear. Baffled, hurt and passive, her various relatives decide not to invade her privacy. "Just sit back and give up on her," Delia thinks, "as if she were a missing pet or mitten or dropped penny!" When, after a year and a half, she does return home for a visit, as a guest at a wedding at her own house, she discovers many changes, but few discussions. "Mom," her younger son says, "could we just eat?" The woman with the doomed Shakespearean name throws a tragedy and nobody comes, for *Ladder of Years* is a comedy, generous and humane.

The novel examines marriage—there are all sorts of marriages Delia comes across in her adventures, good and bad—as well as aging and independence, but finally it is a book about choice. All those years ago, Sam chose Delia, the youngest sister, the one on the right. But whom did Delia choose? Pulled yet repelled by her past, by her complicated and idiosyncratic family, and lured by a new town with a new complicated and idiosyncratic family, what will Delia choose now?

Like the cats Ms. Tyler describes throughout the novel, Delia Grinstead circles and sidles. "He ducked beneath the bureau and returned with linty whiskers," Ms. Tyler writes of the stray Delia has brought home. "He approached the bed obliquely, gazing elsewhere. Delia turned her head away. A moment later she felt the delicate denting of the mattress as he landed on it. He passed behind her, lightly brushing the length of his body against her back as if by chance. Delia didn't move a muscle. She felt they were performing a dance together, something courtly and elaborate and dignified." It is this dance, subtle, passionate and oddly passive, that Anne Tyler creates with such ease and grace.

FURTHER READING

Criticism

Binding, Paul. "Anne Tyler." In his *Separate Country: A Literary Journey through the American South,* pp. 171-81. Jackson: University Press of Mississippi, 1988.

> Analyzes the South in Tyler's novels and asserts that she carries on the tradition of the great southern writers.

Brown, Laurie L. "Interviews with Seven Contemporary Writers." In *Women Writers of the Contemporary South,* edited by Peggy Whitman Prenshaw, pp. 4-22. Jackson: University Press of Mississippi, 1984.

> Contains a collection of interviews with Anne Tyler, Lisa Alther, Ellen Douglas, Gail Godwin, Shirley Ann Grau, Mary Lee Settle, and Elizabeth Spencer in which the authors discuss writing as a vocation.

Jones, L. Gregory. "The Craft of Forgiveness." *Theology Today* L, No. 3 (October 1993): 345-57.

> Discusses the place of confession and forgiveness in Tyler's *Saint Maybe* and in Christianity.

Persing Papadimas, Julie. "America Tyler Style: Surrogate Families and Transiency." *Journal of American Culture* 15, No. 3 (Fall 1992): 45-51.

> Discusses how Tyler has redefined the family in American terms in her novels.

Shafer, Aileen Chris. "Anne Tyler's 'The Geologist's Maid': 'Till Human Voices Wake Us and We Drown.'" *Studies in Short Fiction* 27, No. 1 (Winter 1990): 65-71.

> Asserts that in "The Geologist's Maid" Tyler is "playing with and against the tone, language, and structure of [T.S. Eliot's] 'The Love Song of J. Alfred Prufrock,'" adding depth to her characterization of the main character.

Additional coverage of Tyler's life and career is contained in the following sources published by Gale: *Authors and Artists for Young Adults,* Vol. 18; *Bestsellers,* Vol. 89:1; *Contemporary Authors,* Vols. 9-12R; *Contemporary Authors New Revision Series,* Vols. 11, 33, and 53; *DISCovering Authors Modules: Novelists* and *Popular Fiction and Genre Authors; Dictionary of Literary Biography,* Vols. 6 and 143; *Dictionary of Literary Biography Yearbook,* Vol. 82; *Major Twentieth Century Writers;* and *Something About the Author,* Vols. 7 and 90.

Gerald Vizenor

1934-

(Full name Gerald Robert Vizenor) American novelist, short story writer, poet, essayist, nonfiction writer, scriptwriter, editor, and educator.

The following entry presents an overview of Vizenor's career through 1995.

INTRODUCTION

Vizenor is considered one of the leading voices on Native American experience, culture, and literature. As a novelist, poet, and essayist, he has published extensively. His writings, while varied in format, center on discussions about control of Anishinabe (Chippewa) culture and the role of the trickster in Native American literature. He has also written about the role of the mixed blood—half Native American and half European—in Native American society.

Biographical Information

Vizenor was born in Minneapolis, Minnesota, on October 22, 1934, the son of Clement William, a mixed-blood Anishinabe from the White Earth Reservation, and La Verne Peterson. Vizenor's father worked in Minneapolis as a painter and paperhanger; he was killed by a mugger when Vizenor was 20 months old. Vizenor was shuttled among his mother, his paternal grandmother, and foster homes until he was eight years old. His mother married Elmer Petesch, a mill engineer, with whom Vizenor lived until Petesch's death about nine years later. In 1950 Vizenor joined the Minnesota National Guard, and from 1952 to 1955 he served with the U.S. Army in Japan. Vizenor attended New York University from 1955 to 1956 and acquired his bachelor of arts degree from the University of Minnesota in 1960, where he did graduate work from 1962 through 1965. He later studied at Harvard University. Since then, he has been a social worker, civil rights activist, journalist, and community advocate for Native people living in urban centers. Vizenor organized the Indian Studies program at Bemidji State University and has taught literature and tribal history at Lake Forest College, the University of Minnesota, the University of California at Berkeley, and Macalester College.

Major Works

Vizenor's first forays into literature were as a poet. He was introduced to haiku while serving with the U.S. Army in Japan. His collections of haiku include *Raising the Moon Vines* and *Seventeen Chirps* (both 1964) and *Empty Swings* (1967).

In 1984 he published another volume of poetry entitled *Matsushima: Pine Islands*. Vizenor's first published novel, *Darkness in Saint Louis Bearheart*, appeared in 1973. *Darkness in Saint Louis Bearheart* revealed Vizenor's mastery of Anishinabe myth and storytelling and featured a trickster, a character important in Anishinabean literature and pervasive in Vizenor's writing. The catalyst for Vizenor's 1987 novel *Griever: An American Monkey King in China* came from a visit to China, where he taught for a short time. The novel explores the relation between the trickster in Native American literature and its counterpart in Chinese literature. Some of Vizenor's most noted other works include *Wordarrows* (1978), a collection of stories about language and culture, *Earthdivers* (1981), a short story collection, and *The People Named the Chippewa* (1984), a nonfiction account of the Chippewa people. Both of the latter works examine the experiences of the Anishinabe in relation to American society as a whole.

Critical Reception

Critics agree that one of the most distinctive aspects of

Vizenor's writing is his use of post-modern techniques. He experiments widely with narrative and plot development while fantastic events and mystical characters are common in his works. Commentators disagree, however, on the effectiveness of these techniques. Ward Churchill, for instance, states that *Manifest Manners* (1994) "combines the very worst of postmodernism's vernacular-driven plunge into cliquish obscurantism. . . . The result is largely sterile where it is not opaque to the point of sheer meaninglessness." While many critics applaud Vizenor's postmodern style, they agree that his writing is difficult to read. Elizabeth Cook-Lynn, reviewing *The Heirs of Columbus* (1992), writes that Vizenor's writing "requires more intellectual investment than the quickly distracted readers of today are willing to render." Despite these difficulties, reviewers praise Vizenor's writing as original, humorous, and imaginative. They also credit him for raising the general public's awareness of Native American cultural issues and for relating traditional American experiences and history from a Native American viewpoint.

PRINCIPAL WORKS

Born in the Wind (poetry) 1960
The Old Park Sleepers (poetry) 1961
Two Wings the Butterfly (haiku) 1962
South of the Painted Stone (poetry) 1963
Raising the Moon Vines (haiku) 1964
Seventeen Chirps (haiku) 1964
Summer in the Spring: Lyric Poems of the Ojibway (poetry) 1965
Empty Swings (haiku) 1967
Thomas James White Hawk (nonfiction) 1968
The Everlasting Sky (essays) 1972
**Darkness in Saint Louis Bearheart* (novel) 1973
***Anishinabe Nagomon: Songs of the Ojibwa* (poetry) 1974
***Anishinabe Adisokan: Stories of the Ojibwa* (short stories) 1974
Tribal Scenes and Ceremonies (essays) 1976
Wordarrows: Indians and Whites in the New Fur Trade (short stories) 1978
Earthdivers: Tribal Narratives on Mixed Descent (short stories) 1981
Harold of Orange (screenplay) 1983
Matsushima: Pine Islands (haiku) 1984
The People Named the Chippewa: Narrative Histories (nonfiction) 1984
Griever: An American Monkey King in China (novel) 1987
The Trickster of Liberty (novel) 1988
Crossbloods: Bone Courts, Bingo, and Other Reports (essays) 1990
Interior Landscapes: Autobiographical Myths and Metaphors (autobiography) 1990
Landfill Meditation (short stories) 1991

The Heirs of Columbus (novel) 1992
Dead Voices: Natural Agonies in the New World (novel) 1992
Manifest Manners: Postindian Warriors of Survivance (essays) 1994
Shadow Distance: Gerald Vizenor Reader (fiction and essays) 1994

*This novel has also been published as *Bearheart: The Heirship Chronicles.*
**These works were reprinted in 1981 as *Summer in the Spring: Ojibwa Songs and Stories.* A revised edition was published in 1993.

CRITICISM

Alan R. Velie (essay date 1982)

SOURCE: "Beyond the Novel Chippewa-style: Gerald Vizenor's Post-Modern Fiction," in *Four American Indian Literary Masters: N. Scott Momaday, James Welch, Leslie Marmon Silko, and Gerald Vizenor,* University of Oklahoma Press, 1982, pp. 124-48.

[*In the following excerpt, Velie provides an overview of Vizenor's works and argues that Vizenor's writing can be best understood through a consideration of Anishinabe beliefs, his life experiences, and the nature of the postmodern novel.*]

Gerald Vizenor is a mixed-blood Chippewa or, as the Chippewas prefer to call themselves, Anishinabe. His father's family was from the White Earth Reservation in northern Minnesota. Vizenor's father, Clement, who was half Anishinabe and half white, left the reservation for Minneapolis, where he worked as a painter and paperhanger for three years before he was murdered by a mugger, who nearly severed his head while cutting his throat. The chief suspect, a large black man, was apprehended but was released without being prosecuted. During the same month Clement's brother died in a mysterious fall from a railroad bridge over the Mississippi.

Gerald was twenty months old at the time of his father's murder, too young to remember him. Twenty-five years later, however, he questioned the officer in charge of investigating the crime. The detective defended his shoddy investigation by saying, "We never spent much time on winos and derelicts in those days . . . who knows, one Indian vagrant kills another."

While Vizenor's mother battled poverty in Minneapolis, she sometimes kept Gerald with her and sometimes left him with his Anishinabe grandmother; sometimes she allowed him to be taken to foster families. When Vizenor was eight, his mother married a hard-drinking, taciturn mill engineer named Elmer Petesch, and this brought some stability if not joy into Vizenor's life. After eight years, however, Vizenor's mother deserted Petesch, leaving Gerald behind. After several months Vizenor also moved out, but Petesch broke his dour reserve and pleaded with Vizenor to return, and for a brief period the two lived together as close friends. After five months, however, Petesch died in a fall down an elevator shaft, and Vizenor was alone again.

Given this childhood, filled with desertion and violent deaths, it is not surprising that Vizenor developed a bizarre and bloody view of the universe. Rather than reacting with despair, however, Vizenor has joined the fight against absurdity and injustice with the elan of the Anishinable trickster Wenebojo.

Vizenor has had a varied professional career. He has served as director of the American Indian Employment and Guidance Center in Minneapolis and worked as an editorial writer for the Minneapolis *Tribune.* Currently he teaches in both the Department of Native American Studies in the University of California at Berkeley and the English Department of the University of Minnesota.

Like Momaday, Welch, and Silko, Vizenor writes both poetry and fiction. He published thirteen poems in Kenneth Rosen's *Voices of the Rainbow,* for the most part mordant glimpses of Indian life in America today. He has also published a collection of haiku, the result of his experiences—as a private first-class in the army—on the Japanese island of Matsushima.

Vizenor has published a memoir of his early life entitled **"I Know What You Mean, Erdupps MacChurbbs: Autobiographical Myths and Metaphors."** In it Vizenor not only relates the violent and bizarre story of his childhood but also tells about his fantasy life. Erdupps MacChurbbs is one of the "benign demons and little woodland people of love" who people his fantasies. These little people provide a rich inner life for Vizenor and help him keep his sanity in a mad world.

> They are the little people who raise the banners of imagination on assembly lines and at cold bus stops in winter. They marched with me in the service and kept me awake with humor on duty as a military guard. The little people sat with me in baronial ornamental classrooms and kept me alive and believable under the death blows of important languages.

Chippewa mythology is full of stories about benign demons and little woodland people, and stories about Vizenor's Anishinabe grandmother are probably the chief source for MacChurbbs and his friends. However, as the name

MacChurbbs suggests, Vizenor, like most other Americans, probably picked up some Irish fairy lore as well.

In 1978, Vizenor published a series of sketches entitled *Wordarrows: Indians and Whites in the New Fur Trade.* The book is a series of sketches, principally about Anishinabe whom Vizenor met as Director of the Employment and Guidance Center. In these sketches Vizenor appears to be the Isaac Bashevis Singer of the Chippewa: he combines an extremely keen eye for detail and an appreciation for an interesting story with a scrupulous sense of honesty. The result, like that of Singer's works, is a highly revealing picture of a ghetto people—their power and dignity, flaws and foibles, and, above all, their essential humanity.

Wordarrows is an important key to understanding Vizenor's poetry. The poems, although they often deal with the same characters and subjects as the essays, are cryptic and allusive, and the reader can understand them more fully after reading Vizenor's prose pieces. For example, the nameless heroine of the poem **"Raising the Flag"** is described more fully in the sketch **"Marlene American Horse"** in *Wordarrows,* and the "wounded Indian" in the poem **"Indians at the Guthrie"** is the Rattling Hail of **"Rattling Hail's Ceremonial"** in *Wordarrows.*

Wordarrows also provides valuable background information for understanding *Darkness in Saint Louis Bearheart,* Vizenor's major work. The fictional framework of the book is as follows: Saint Louis Bearheart, an old man who works in the Heirship Office of the Bureau of Indian Affairs, has spent ten years at his desk in the Bureau secretly writing a manuscript entitled "Cedarfair Circus: Grave Reports from the Cultural Word Wars." When members of the American Indian Movement break into the offices of the BIA, one of them, a young Indian girl, encounters Bearheart sitting in the dark, and, after having sex with him, goes off to read the book. What she reads is what we read.

"Cedarfair Circus" is the story of a strange group of Indian pilgrims who wend their way from Minnesota to New Mexico at some future time when, because of insufficient oil supplies, American civilization has collapsed into bloody anarchy. Murderous and perverted figures hold power, among them the Evil Gambler, the fast-food fascists, and the pentarchical pensioners. The wanderers do battle with these forces of evil, sustaining heavy losses, but eventually a few of them make it to freedom.

The leader of the pilgrims is Proude Cedarfair, the last in the line of the Cedarfairs who refused to leave their ancestral home in northern Minnesota to go to the Red Cedar Reservation, the fictional name of the White Earth Reservation where Vizenor's forebears lived. Proude lives in the midst of a large circle of cedar trees named by his family the Cedar Circus (the Cedarfairs have lived as clowns and tricksters for generations, battling the evil incursions of the whites and hostile Indians with their wit).

When there is no more oil available, the government commandeers trees, and Jordan Coward, the corrupt, drunken president of the Red Cedar Reservation government, attacks the trees of the Cedar Circus. Proude decides not to confront the evil chief and the federal agents, however, and with his wife, Rosina, he sets out on his cross-country odyssey. Others join them in their wanderings, until they have assembled quite a ragtag army.

The first to join Proude and Rosina is Benito Saint Plumero, who calls himself "Bigfoot." He is a "little person, but his feet and the measure of his footsteps were twice his visual size." Bigfoot received his cognomen in prison while serving time for stealing from a park the bronze statue he is in love with. The Cedarfairs meet Plumero at the "scapehouse of weirds and sensitives," a survival center established (with federal funds) on the Red Cedar Reservation by thirteen "women poets" from the cities. Bigfoot has been staying at the scapehouse to provide sexual services to the weirds and sensitives with his remarkable penis, President Jackson. The most interesting of the weirds and sensitives are Sister Eternal Flame, whose "face was distorted with comical stretchmarks from her constant expressions of happiness"; Sister Willabelle, whose body is marred by horrible scars from worms and piranhas which attacked her when her plane crashed in the Amazon jungle; and Sister Talullah, the "law school graduate [who] could not face men in a courtroom without giggling like a little girl so she concentrated on interior litigation and the ideologies of feminism and fell in love with women."

The Cedarfairs take Bigfoot with them and soon are joined by Zebulon Matchi Makwa, a "talking writer and drunken urban shaman"; Belladonna Darwin-Winter Catcher, the daughter of a white reporter named Charlotte Darwin and Old John Winter Catcher, a Lakota holy man Charlotte met while she was covering the Wounded Knee episode of 1973; Scintilla Shruggles, a "new model pioneer woman" and keeper of the Charles Lindbergh house for the Minnesota Division of Historic Sites; Iniwa Biwide, a sixteen-year-old youth who "resembles a stranger"; Bishop Omax Parasimo, a religious master who wears a metamask with the same features as Scintilla Shruggles; Justice Pardone Cozener, "the tribal lawyer and one of the new prairie big bellies"; Cozener's homosexual lover, Doctor Wilde Coxswain, "the arm wagging tribal historian"; Sun Bear Sun, "the 300 pound, seven foot son of utopian tribal organizer Sun Bear"; Little Big Mouse, "a small white woman with fresh water blue eyes," whom Sun Bear Sun carries in a holster at his belt; Lilith Mae Farrier, the "horsewoman of passionless contradictions," a child-hating school teacher who is the mistress (literally) of two massive

boxer dogs; and Pio Wissakodewinini, the "parawoman mixedblood mammoth clown," a man who was sentenced to a sex change operation for committing two rapes.

On their travels the pilgrims face and overcome a succession of enemies. First is the Evil Gambler, Sir Cecil Staples, the "monarch of unleaded gasoline," who wagers five gallons of gasoline against a bettor's life in a strange game of chance. Sir Cecil always wins, then allows losers to choose their form of death. Sir Cecil was reared on interstates by a truck-driving mother. Because Ms. Staples had been sterilized by the government (for having illegitimate children while on welfare), she took to kidnapping children from shopping malls. She stole thirteen in all, bringing them up in her truck as she drove back and forth across the country and finally turning them out at rest stops when they were grown. Staples told her children that they "should feel no guilt, ignore the expectations of others, and practice to perfection whatever [they did] in the world." Sir Cecil decided to practice the art of killing people.

Needing gasoline for the postal truck they have obtained, the pilgrims choose lots for who will gamble with Sir Cecil. Lilith Mae Farrier, the lady of the boxers, is selected. When she loses, Proude also gambles with Sir Cecil, with the understanding that, if he should win, Lilith lives and Sir Cecil dies. Proude wins, and kills Sir Cecil by strangling him with a "mechanical neckband death instrument," but Lilith, depressed by her loss, immolates herself and her boxers.

Back on the road, the pilgrims meet a procession of cripples: "The blind, the deaf, disfigured giants, the fingerless, earless, noseless, breastless, and legless people stumbling, shuffling and hobbling in families down the road." Belladonna Darwin-Winter Catcher warns the pilgrims: "Never let the cripple catch your eye. These cripples are incomplete animals lusting for our whole bodies." Little Big Mouse ignores Belladonna's advice and performs a nude dance for the cripples, who become so excited that they pull her into hundreds of pieces.

When they reach Oklahoma, the pilgrims meet the "food fascists" who have hung three witches from the rafters of the Ponca Witch Hunt Restaurant and Fast Foods to season them before cutting them into pieces for takeout orders. The pilgrims decide to save the witches and, sneaking back at night, rescue two of them, but Zebulon Matchi Makwa, the smelly drunken urban shaman and talking writer, is overcome by desire and has intercourse with his witch in the restaurant, where they are discovered and killed by the fascists.

Belladonna Darwin-Winter Catcher is killed by a colony of "descendants of famous hunters and bucking horse breeders," who put to death anyone they catch espousing a "terminal creed," that is, the belief that there is only one true way.

Vizenor borrows the idea of terminal creeds from Eric Hoffer's remarks about "true believers." Ridiculing terminal beliefs is a major theme in Vizenor's work, since he detests zealots, whatever their views, and particularly those who are humorless as well as narrow-minded. Belladonna's terminal beliefs, which concern the superiority of the tribal way of life, are views Vizenor finds congenial in many respects, and the people who kill her are unlovable, rigid rednecks, so the story of the death is told with a good deal of ambiguity and irony.

Many other curious events follow. Bishop Omax Parasimo is killed by lightning, and Justice Pardone Cozener and Doctor Wilde Coxswain, the homosexual lovers, decide to stay at the Bioavaricious Regional Word Hospital, a facility established by the government to investigate public damage to the language. Sister Eternal Flame catches Proude's wife Rosina and Bigfoot at fellatio and murders Bigfoot. Proude and Iniwa Biwide travel by magic flight to Pueblo Bonito where a vision bear tells them to enter the fourth world—as bears—through a vision window in the pueblo. The novel ends with Rosina arriving at the pueblo and finding beartracks in the snow.

Clearly this is a strange book. . . . We can better understand it by examining the Anishinabe and other Indian influences of Vizenor's, by taking a look at what he has written about his personal experiences, and by examining the "post-modern" novel, the tradition in which Vizenor is writing.

Tricksters and clowns are common in Indian cultures. Among the Indians the trickster, under various names and guises, is usually the principal culture hero of the tribe, a figure second in importance only to the supreme god. But he is a highly ambiguous figure. As his name implies, he is primarily one who plays tricks. He is also the butt of tricks, and how often he is the tricker rather than the trickee seems to depend in part on how the tribe views itself. Some tricksters are usually successful; others are almost always the victim of tricks. Although the trickster is generally a benefactor—who in some cases creates man, brings him fire, and rescues him from enemies—he can also be a menace, because he is generally amoral and has prodigious appetites for food, sex, and adventure. He is capable of raping women, murdering men, eating children, and slaughtering animals. In fact, the trickster violates all tribal laws with impunity, to the amusement of the listeners of the tales, for whom he acts as a saturnalian surrogate.

The Chippewa trickster is called Wenebojo, Manabozho, or Nanabush, depending on how anthropologists recorded the Anishinabe word. According to the myths, Nanabush is the son of a spirit named Epingishmook and Winonah, a human. His mother dies shortly after he is born, and Nanabush is reared by his grandmother Nokomis. He has miraculous pow-

ers, particularly the ability to transform himself into whatever shape he wants. In his metamorphosis as a rabbit he acts as a benefactor, bringing the Chippewas fire. He saves mankind and the animals by taking them on his raft in a flood, and he teaches the Chippewa the Mide ceremonies, their most important religious rituals.

Like most tricksters, however, Nanabush is also a dangerous figure, and in one tale he murders most of his family before he realizes what he is doing. In another, he marries his sister, bringing shame on himself and his family.

Vizenor's conception of the trickster seems to be in line with Chippewa tradition—tricksters are benevolent but amoral, lustful, irresponsible, and given to fighting evil with trickery. Trickster tales often combine violence with humor. Tricksters are peripatetic, and trickster tales usually start, "Trickster was going along. . . ." Vizenor's pilgrims, and the structure of his book, reflect this.

Sacred clowns are important in Indian religion. Although they appear to have played little part among the Chippewas, Vizenor would have heard of them from members of other tribes. Among the Sioux, Cahuilla, and Maidu, for instance, clowns performed absurd acts at the most important religious ceremonies, mocking shamans and religious leaders, pestering participants by throwing water or hot coals, dancing and cavorting, and trying to swim in shallow puddles. Among the Cheyenne, clowns acted as "contraries" who did everything backwards, saying "goodbye" when they met someone and "hello" when they left, and walking or sitting on their horses backwards. Among Pueblo tribes clowns ate feces and drank urine, pretending that they were delicious.

Anthropologist Barbara Tedlock claims that the purpose of the clowns was to cause laughter, thus "opening up" spectators emotionally to spiritual forces. She also argues that the mockery of sacred objects and rituals by the clowns served to show spectators that terrestrial rituals were not important. It was the meaning behind them, the higher world of the spirits, that was important.

What Tedlock says may be so, but I think that she overlooks the most important function of clowns, a function similar to the clowning at the medieval European Feast of Fools, in which once a year subdeacons sang filthy songs in church, mocked the sacrament, and threw the bishop in the river. These ceremonies allowed a saturnalian release to people whose religious and moral codes were very demanding. In a way the clowns are the reification in the tribe itself of the trickster figure of mythology; that is, they are figures who can ridicule customs, rituals, and taboos with impunity to the delight of spectators who are forced to obey them.

The Evil Gambler is a familiar figure in Indian mythology,

although I could not find a reference to him in the collections of Chippewa tales that I read. Silko has a version of the story in the Laguna myths that she intersperses in *Ceremony.* In it *Kaup'a'ta,* or the Gambler, who lives high in the Zuni Mountains, plays a stick game with people, gambling with them for their beads and clothes. By feeding his victims a combination of cornmeal and human blood the Gambler gains control over them, and they cannot stop gambling until they lose everything they own. When the victims are naked, the Gambler gives them one more play, to recoup their losses or lose their life. The Gambler has killed many victims before Sun Man, using the knowledge that his grandmother Spiderwoman gives him, is able to outwit the Gambler and kill him. Vizenor's episode of Sir Cecil Staples puts the same story into a different context.

As bizarre as *Darkness in Saint Louis Bearheart* seems, Vizenor derives much of his material from people he actually knows. Lilith Mae Farrier, for instance, the zoophilic boxer lover in *Bearheart,* was an acquaintance of Vizenor's, to whom he devotes a chapter in *Wordarrows.* Like the fictional Lilith, the real Lilith was molested by her step-father on a camping trip, made a point of feeding reservation mongrels, and was thrown off the reservation by the outraged wives of the reservation officials by whom she had been propositioned. When she left the reservation, the dogs followed her van. All of them eventually dropped out in exhaustion except for two boxers that she had refused to feed (they had reminded her of her stepfather). She fed the boxers, and "In time they learned to take care of me, you know what I mean." The real Lilith Mae did not immolate herself, although she did have the boxers chloroformed. So, in this case, if the book is kinky, it is because the truth can be as bizarre as fiction.

The combination of humor, fantasy, violence, and explicit sex that characterizes *Bearheart* is nothing new in literature: Petronius's *Satyricon,* Rabelais's *Gargantua* and *Pantagruel,* and Gascoigne's *Adventures of Master F.J.* are three of many older works one could cite that mix sex and violence with fantasy in comic fictions. But with Cervantes, and writers like Defoe and Richardson in England, the European novel turned away from fantasy, toward realism and the complexities of experience for the rising middle class. This trend reached its pinnacle with Henry James, who said, "The only reason for the existence of a novel is that it does attempt to represent life . . . the air of reality (solidity of specification) seems to me to be the supreme virtue of a novel." This is not to say that nonrealistic fiction disappeared after the mid-eighteenth century, of course, but merely that it was not in the mainstream of the novelistic tradition, and often, as with science fiction, it was dismissed as subliterary.

In recent years, however, nonrealistic writers like Jorge Borges, Alain Robbe-Grillet, and Italo Calvino have emerged as major literary figures abroad, and in America in the 1970s much of the best, and even best-selling, writing has been utterly nonrealistic. Writers like Kurt Vonnegut, Richard Brautigan, Tom Robbins, Robert Coover, Stanley Elkin, Ishmael Reed, Donald Barthelme, and Alvin Greenberg now dominate American fiction, and *Bearheart* puts Vizenor squarely in their tradition.

There has been a great deal written on the "post-modern novel" or "new fiction" as it is variously called, but in my opinion the best analysis and description is in Phillip Stevick's "Scherezade runs out of plots, goes on talking; the king puzzled, listens: an essay on the new fiction." At the end of the essay Stevick proposes some "axioms" as a step toward establishing an aesthetic of the new fiction. Essentially Stevick argues that the new fiction ignores established fictional traditions to an extraordinary extent, purposely establishes a limited audience, departs from the illusionist tradition, and represents writing as play.

These things are certainly true of *Bearheart,* which is clearly a fair specimen of the post-modern novel. To expand on Stevick's points: first of all, whereas most fiction of the past centuries has reacted against some aspect of previous fiction, the new fiction simply ignores the tradition of the modern novel. Cervantes, Defoe, Fielding, Hawthorne, James, Hemingway—to name just the first novelists that come to mind—reacted against, borrowed from, parodied the writers of previous generations. Scott Momaday, the Kiowa novelist, reveals the influence of Melville, Faulkner, and Hemingway in *House Made of Dawn.* But Vizenor, like most of the post-modernists, simply ignores American writers of previous generations. He owes more of a debt to his Anishinabe grandmother than to Hemingway or Faulkner.

Second, we should note that, however much most European and American writers have railed against the philistinism of the bourgeoisie, western literature since Homer has aimed nonetheless at what Dr. Johnson called the "common reader." The new novel decidedly is not for that good soul. It is too raunchy, too crazy, too strange. Scenes like that in which the Scapehouse sisters eat stuffed kitten while Bigfoot crouches under the table performing cunnilingus on them, or in which Bigfoot decapitates the man who has stolen the bronze statue he is in love with, or in which the cripples tear Little Big Mouse limb from limb, are too bizarre and painful for the "common reader." Post-modern fiction, as Stevick puts it, "willingly acknowledges the partiality of its truth, the oddity of its vision, and the limits of its audience."

Third, *Bearheart,* like other post-modern novels, incorporates generous amounts of bad art. It is an irony that new fiction, caviar to the general, borrows much from the art of the masses. This is not new to literature: a New York Irish barroom song is at the heart of *Finnegan's Wake,* and Ionesco, when asked about the major influence on his work, named Groucho, Chico, and Harpo Marx. But if this tendency predates the new fiction, it is carried to new highs—or lows—there. Ishmael Reed works Minnie the Moocher and Amos and Andy into *The Last Days of Louisiana Red,* and Alvin Greenberg's *Invention of the West* is based on the schlock Western novel and horse opera. Although greatly transcending them, *Bearheart* has certain similarities in tone, subject, and approach to *Mad* and *Penthouse* magazines and to Andy Warhol movies like *Frankenstein.*

Stevick points out that, although we are oblivious to and therefore unoffended by the Irish popular culture in Joyce's work, the popular art in the new fiction is our own bad art, and we recognize and deplore it. As Stevick puts it, new fiction seems more "audacious and abrasive than it really is because it occupies a place at what William Gass, following Barthelme, calls the 'leading edge of the trash phenomenon.'"

> **What Vizenor is doing is creating a caricature by exaggerating tendencies already present in American culture, so that even if the picture he paints is grotesque or not at all true to life, it is recognizable, like a newspaper cartoon of Jimmy Carter or Ronald Reagan.**
> —*Alan R. Velie*

As for philosophical and aesthetic depth, *Bearheart* is as devoid of it as are the works of Barthelme, Reed, and Elkin. In contrast to writers like Momaday, who makes heavy use of symbolism, novelists like Vizenor eschew it completely. For them the surface is the meaning; there is nothing between the lines but white space, as Barthelme says.

I hardly need to belabor Stevick's point that new fiction departs from the illusionist tradition. Obviously *Bearheart* is a radical departure from the air of reality that James admires in novels. What Vizenor is doing is creating a caricature by exaggerating tendencies already present in American culture, so that even if the picture he paints is grotesque or not at all true to life, it is recognizable, like a newspaper cartoon of Jimmy Carter or Ronald Reagan.

Finally, the post-modern novel is writing as play. There are precedents for this, of course: Laurence Sterne's *Tristram Shandy* comes to mind, and undoubtedly Joyce was playing in *Finnegan's Wake,* though the joke seems to be on the reader. The tone of *Bearheart* may be at times savage, bitter, or violent, but at the heart of the book is an ever-present and peculiarly Indian sense of humor.

Whites may wonder just what it is that Indians have to laugh

about today, or they may psychologize about the Indians' need for laughter, but this is unfair to Indians, who, despite the dour image of the cigar-store mannikin, have always cherished humor for its own sake. Vizenor has a story in **Wordarrows** about how the U.S. Communist Party's secretary general, Gus Hall, asked protesting Indians in Minneapolis to write about their grievances for communist newspapers. Vizenor states: "The tribal protest committee refused to write for the communists because—in addition to political reasons—there was too little humor in communist speech, making it impossible to know the heart of the speakers."

Bearheart shocks and puzzles many readers, but once it is understood that Vizenor's fiction is shaped by Anishinabe folklore and the post-modern tradition, the book is not so puzzling after all.

Earthdivers, Vizenor's latest book, is about mixed-bloods. In this work Vizenor (who, like Silko, is keenly aware of being half-white and half-Indian) tries to celebrate the unique status of the mixed-bloods—to reverse the prejudice that has plagued them, to make a hero of the half-breed. To appreciate what Vizenor does, it is useful to review racial attitudes toward Indians and mixed-bloods in America.

The word *half-breed* has always had a negative connotation in American English, like *half-blood,* it seems to connote bastardy. Mixed descent is not necessarily bad; Oklahoma politicians, and most other Oklahomans, for that matter, are eager enough to claim Indian blood. But the figure of the half-blood in the racist mythology of the Old West often represented an illicit mixture of the worst of both races, the hateful, untrustworthy spawn of renegades and barmaids.

According to Harold Beaver, John Rolfe was the first British colonist to marry an Indian, a woman named Motsoaks'ats. Their son, Thomas Rolfe, would appear to have the distinction of being the first American mixed-blood. Although the colonists were aware of the Biblical prohibition about marrying "strange wives" and passed laws against intermarriage between whites and Indians, the practice was widespread, and mixed-bloods like Sequoyah, Osceola, Stand Watie, and Jesse Chisholm were famous—or infamous, depending on one's politics—in the nineteenth century.

Mixed-blood characters in American fiction are generally negative, or at best ambiguous; Injun Joe of *Tom Sawyer,* for instance, is a "half breed devil." Twain, who was so compassionate to blacks, revealed a great deal of intolerance in his depictions of Indians, not only in *Tom Sawyer* but also in his account of the "Goshoot Indians" in *Roughing It.* His hideous portrait of Injun Joe seems to indicate a belief that, if full bloods were backwards, half-breeds were bestial.

Beaver lists other literary mixed-bloods who appear in major American literary works—Poe's Dirk Peters (*The Narrative of Arthur Gordon Pym*), Hemingway's Dick Boulton (*In Our Time*), and Faulkner's Boon Hogganbeck and Sam Fathers (*Go Down Moses*)—and states that "all are pariahs in some sense—quick-witted, tough, valiant even—who are revealed as the ambiguous saviors of white men." To this list we might add Ken Kesey's Broom Bronden of *One Flew over the Cuckoo's Nest,* who, though certainly not quick-witted, is a pariah and who, in a highly ambiguous sense, saves Randle Patrick McMurphy from what he perceives as a fate worse than death, life as a vegetable.

Racial attitudes change quickly, and today white Americans' ideas about mixed-bloods are a subset of their ideas about Indians, and these need to be briefly reviewed, and in particular contrasted to, their ideas about other minorities, especially blacks. In the chapter "The Red and the Black" in *Custer Died for Your Sins,* Vine Deloria points out that Indians and blacks were treated not only differently, but with an opposite emphasis: blacks were systematically excluded from white American life, while Indians were forced into it:

> It is well to keep these distinctions clearly in mind when talking about Indians and blacks. When liberals equate the two they are overlooking obvious historical facts. Never did the white man systematically exclude Indians from his schools and meeting places. Nor did the government ever kidnap black children from their homes and take them off to a government boarding school to be educated as whites. . . . The white man systematically destroyed Indian culture where it existed, but separated blacks from his midst so that they were forced to attempt the creation of their own culture. . . . The white man forbade the black to enter his own social and economic system, and at the same time force-fed the Indian what he was denying the black.

Whatever progress in integration of blacks has been made in the past decade, the legacy of segregation remains, and the point is still valid.

Perceptive as his essay is, Deloria omits two points that have an important bearing on our perception of mixed-bloods. The first is that you can be half Indian, but you cannot be half black; if you are discernibly black, you are black, period. During slavery, when blacks were sold, distinctions were made between *mulattos, quadroons,* and *octaroons,* and the term *mulatto* was current in American speech in my youth. Whether because of black pride or some other factor, there is no such word any more: *mulatto* is a signifier without a signified. The coffee-colored O.J. Simpson is a black, or an Afro-American perhaps, but he is definitely not a mulatto.

Contrarily, a mixed-blood with one full-blood grandparent, with one-quarter Indian "blood," is considered presumptuous, mendacious in fact, if he claims that he is simply Indian. Whereas light-skinned products of black-white marriages are accorded the same sort of treatment as their darker brothers, the lighter progeny of Indian-white marriages are often derided by whites if they try to claim tribal identity. "You are not an Indian; you're one of us" is what mixed-bloods are told, even in cases in which they have an Indian name.

The rules for ethnic identity vary with the group. You are a Jew only if your mother is a Jew or if you convert, and among the orthodox your gentile mother must convert, too (a hangover from the days when men were more suspicious of their wives and when Cossacks raped Jewish girls). The mainstream American attitude toward ethnicity is that you are what your father is, that is, what your name is. If your name is Kowalski, you are Polish, even if your mother's name is O'Brien or Goldberg. Nor are you asked to prove that you are Polish. Finally, Indians are the only racial group, with the exception of WASPs, that anyone ever tries to sneak into. I have never heard of anyone who tried to pass for black, or Jewish, or Italian, but I know a number of cases in which whites have tried to pass for Indians.

> White attitudes toward Indian mixed-bloods are more hostile in literature and film than they are in life. In Oklahoma, for instance, the Cherokee Indian blood of Will Rogers and W.W. Keeler (former president and chairman of the board of Phillips Petroleum Company) was regarded as a positive, romantic, and colorful attribute. Keeler, who was elected principal chief of the Cherokees, was proud of his Indian blood and received a great deal of publicity as a result of it.

Vizenor comes from a corner of the country where mixed-bloods have a sense of identity of their own. He is a Minnesota Métis. *Métis* is a French word (cognate with Spanish *mestizo*) for a person of mixed Indian and French-Canadian ancestry. Whether it was because these whites were Gallic rather than English, Catholic rather than Protestant, or nomadic trappers rather than sedentary, land-hungry farmers, the French Canadians were more tolerant of the Indians than were the Anglo-Americans, and married with them more frequently. The result was the Métis, a mixed-blood people with a definite cultural identity. Vizenor quotes historian Jacqueline Peterson: "Intermarriage went hand in glove with the trade in skins and furs from the first decades of discovery. . . . The core denominator of Métis identity was not participation in the fur-trading network per se, but the mixed-blood middleman stance between Indian and European societies." Because Vizenor's family were Anishinabes from the White Earth Reservation, and his mother was a Beaulieu, he is Métis in the narrow as well as the extended sense of the term, which now simply means mixed-blood.

Vizenor's central metaphor for mixed-bloods is the earthdiver of the Anishinabe creation myth. This myth, which appears in many cultures throughout the world, has four invariable traits: a world covered with water, a creator, a diver, and the creation of land. The Anishinabe version, in which the trickster Wenebojo is the diver, goes as follows: Wenebojo is on top of a tree that is protruding from the water. He defecates, and his excrement floats to the top. He asks Otter to dive to the bottom and bring up some dirt out of which to construct the earth. Otter tries but drowns. Wenebojo revives him and asks him if he saw any dirt, but Otter says "no." Next Wenebojo asks Beaver, who also drowns. When revived, Beaver says that he saw some dirt, but could not get to it. Then Muskrat tries. He too floats to the surface, senseless, but clenched in his paws and in his mouth are five grains of sand. Wenebojo revives Muskrat and throws the sand into the water, forming a small island. Wenebojo gets more dirt, enlarging the island, and lives there with the animals.

Psychologizing anthropologists explain this tale as a cloacal myth, that is, as one that reflects male envy of female pregnancy in its excremental theory of creation. It is typical of Vizenor's sense of irony that he both presents and ridicules the theory of excremental creation. It is always hard to pin Vizenor down. He seems to give credence to the idea, which he finds amusing, but deplores the "secular seriousness" of the scholars who propose it: "The academic intensities of career-bound anthropologists approach diarrhetic levels of terminal theoretical creeds."

The earthdiver is Vizenor's central metaphor for the mixed-blood. The vehicle *earthdiver* has two elements, the earth and the diver. As a diver the mixed-blood cuts through the polluted sea we live in to the rich floor below, and brings back some earth to create a new land:

> White settlers are summoned to dive with mixed-blood survivors into the unknown, into the legal morass of treaties and bureaucratic evils, and to swim deep down and around through federal exclaves and colonial economic enterprises in search of a few honest words upon which to build a new urban turtle island.

The earth, the other part of the vehicle, not only signifies nature, the sacred earth, but also federal funds, the rich muck that acts like manure on tribal projects:

> When the mixed-blood earthdiver summons the white world to dive like the otter and beaver and muskrat in search of the earth, and federal funds, he is both animal and trickster, both white and tribal, the uncertain creator in an urban metaphor based on a creation myth that preceded him in two world views and oral tradition.

And, as a metaphor yokes two different things in one comparison, mixed-bloods are linked between white and tribal cultures: "Métis earthdivers are the new metaphors between communal tribal cultures and those cultures which oppose traditional connections, the cultures which would market the earth." All of Vizenor's mixed-bloods are earthdivers of one kind or another, but the story of Martin Bear Charme corresponds best to the earthdiver myth as a cloacal creation story. A founder of the Landfill Meditation Reservation, Bear Charme pops up in a number of Vizenor's works.

Bear Charme left his reservation in North Dakota and hitchhiked to San Francisco when he was sixteen. He tried welding in a federal relocation program but soon turned to garbage, out of which he built his fortune, "hauling trash and filling wet lands with solid waste and urban swill" in the South Bay area. Having made his life out of refuse, Bear Charme, unlike other scraplords who went from dumps to mansions, made garbage his life, meditating in his dump, and seeing garbage as a metaphor for the worthwhile things in life—contact with the earth, and the process of recycling and renewal.

With Bear Charme, Vizenor stands a cliché on its head. We normally think of filling the Bay as despoiling nature—that is certainly the way conservation-oriented newspapers like the *Bay Guardian* portray it—but Vizenor, with his characteristic irony, shows that making land from garbage is a reverential act to nature:

> The status of a trash hauler is one of the best measures of how separated a culture is from the earth, from the smell of its own waste. Bear Charme teaches that we should turn our minds back to the earth, the rich smell of the titled earth. We are the garbage he [once said]. We are the real waste, and cannot separate ourselves like machines, clean and dumped, trashed out back into the river. We are the earthdiver and dreamers, and the holistic waste.

Bear Charme makes his dump a "meditation reservation," a place to renew one's link to the earth:

> Charme chanted "*come to the landfill and focus on real waste,*" shaman crow crowed backward on her perch in the sumac. "*Mandala mulch, and transcend the grammatical word rivers, clean talk and terminal creeds,* and put mind back to earth. Dive back to the earth, *come backward to meditate on trash, and swill and real* waste that binds us to our bodies and the earth.

One of the appealing things about Vizenor's works is that they appear to be one huge moebius strip. Never mind that there are poems, essays, stories, and novels. They seem to be parts of a unified whole because the same characters scuttle in and out, often telling the same stories. Rattling Hail appears in a poem and then an essay; Lilith Mae Farrier is in an essay and then a novel; Clement Beaulieu appears everywhere. Bear Charme first appeared in a story entitled **"Land Fill Meditation,"** which was published in the *Minneapolis Star Saturday Magazine* in February, 1979. In the story, Beaulieu/Vizenor introduced Bear Charme as the narrator who tells the story of Belladonna Darwin-Winter Catcher, the mixed-blood killed for her terminal views. Vizenor lifts the tale, without Bear Charme, and puts it in *Darkness in Saint Louis Bearheart*. The story appears a third time in **"Windmills of Dwinelle Hall,"** an episode in *Fourskin,* Vizenor's unpublished novel about life in the Native American Studies Department at Berkeley. The story is narrated by Bear Charme, a character in "Landfill Meditation," a collection of stories by Clement Beaulieu, alias Gerald Vizenor. These stories are the subject of a seminar conducted by Pink Stallion, a key *schlussel* in this *roman à clef,* a mixed-blood Valentino known for picking the lock of every blonde in Berkeley.

The narrative technique of **"Windmills"** is marvelous, a *mise en abime* in which Vizenor is the oat box Quaker holding up a box on which Pink Stallion is seen holding up a box on which Beaulieu/Vizenor is seen holding up a box on which Bear Charme is seen telling the story of Belladonna Darwin-Winter Catcher. This story, slightly revised, appears as **"Classroom Windmills"** in *Earthdivers*.

In the Anishinabe myth the earthdiver is the trickster Wenebojo. As the product of the marriage between a spirit and a man, Wenebojo is a sort of mixed-blood himself. In Anishinabe mythology, and indeed, all Indian mythology, the trickster is mediator between man and god, a hero sent by God (Manito, Earthmaker, Wakan Tanka) to help man on earth. In a way the mixed-blood is a mediator as well: most Indian Studies programs are staffed by mixed-bloods, who become interpreters who define tribal culture to the white community.

The trickster in Vizenor's work who best captures the spirit of Anishinabe mythology is one who operates in the academic arena, Captain Shammer, the short-term chairman of American Indian Studies at Berkeley in *Earthdivers*. Shammer, called Captain because he is a trickster of martial masks who parades around campus as a military man, was selected as the seventh chairman of American Indian Studies because he had the fewest credentials and was lowest on the list of applicants. The search committee reasoned that the past six chairs, who had failed miserably, were experts, and that it was time to pick someone without qualifications. Shammer, true to his military nature, "took hold of the well-worn pink plastic mixed-blood reins and rode the old red wagon constellations proud as a tribal trickster through the ancient word wars, with mule skinners and ruminant mammals, behind academic lines."

Shammer's term lasts three weeks—tricksters, as I said, are traditionally peripatetic—but during those weeks he has an enormous impact. His first move is to put the Department of American Indian Studies up for sale to the highest bidder. This may seem outrageous, but as Dean Colin Defender puts it, "Higher education has always been for sale on both ends, research and instruction; the difference here is that this new Chair, part cracker I might add, is seeking the highest, not the lowest, bids." The winner of the bidding is the Committee on Tribal Indecision, which changes the name of the department to Undecided Studies.

Another service that Captain Shammer performs for his department is to bring in Old Darkhorse, proprietor of the *Half Moon Bay Skin Dip,* whose specialty is coloring skin. Now America's attitude about skin color is not simple. On the one hand, light skin is better than dark when it serves to identify a person as Caucasian rather than Indian or black. Being pale, however, is inferior to being tan the color of the leisure class of Aspen and Acapulco. As long as one is easily identifiable as a Caucasian, it is good to be as dark as possible. Lightness is also a disadvantage for mixed-bloods, both among tribal people and among members of the white community (who can feel more liberal if they are dealing with dark dark people and not wasting their liberalism on light dark people). Accordingly, Old Darkhorse performs a real service by darkening mixed-bloods through dunking. In his early experiments the technology was not very sophisticated, and the dunkees would emerge "marbled. . . like the end papers on old books." Soon, however, Darkhorse perfects his process and is able to help light mixed-bloods "when the darkest mixed-bloods were much too critical of the light inventions, the pale skins varieties needed darker flesh to disburden their lack of confidence around white liberals."

One of the main thrusts of the "satirical contradance" Shammer performs is Vizenor's spoof of Americans' reactions to skin color—not only the prejudices of whites but those of mixed-bloods and full bloods as well. Vizenor is well aware that no race has a monopoly on prejudice, and he has no reluctance to satirize the color consciousness of Indians. To this end he has Captain Shammer introduce his colorwheel, a register of skin tones ranging from white through pink and tan to dark brown. The colors are numbered and refer to explanations in a manual on tribal skin tones and identities. Shammer, for instance, was a four, about which the manual reads:

> Mixedbloods with the skin tone color wheel code four are too mixed to choose absolute breeds or terminal creeds. Fours are too light to dance in the traditional tribal world and too dark to escape their flesh in the white world. . . . Fours bear the potential to be four flushers, too much white in the hand and not enough in the tribal bush.

Having darkened the pale mixed-bloods and sold the department, Shammer moves on, trickster fashion.

In all his works, but most of all in *Earthdivers*, Vizenor deals with the delicate subjects of race relations, color, and ethnic identity. But he does not deal with them delicately. He slashes away at prejudices and "terminal beliefs" with merciless satire, exposing and ridiculing whites, full bloods, and mixed-bloods. His friends are no safer than his enemies, and being on his side does not guarantee immunity from being lampooned. That is the way it should be, of course, and, as much as anyone, Gerald Vizenor deserves a place in the Half-Breed Hall of Fame.

Linda Ainsworth (review date Winter 1985)

SOURCE: "History and the Imagination: Gerald Vizenor's *The People Named the Chippewa*," in *American Indian Quarterly,* Vol. IX, No. 1, Winter, 1985, pp. 49-54.

[*In the following review, Ainsworth argues that in* The People Named the Chippewa, *Vizenor challenges contemporary beliefs about Native American culture.*]

It is perhaps a truism of modern history that they who control the past control the future. According to this maxim, those in control have the power to shape memory to suit their own requirements of the future, naively or uncaringly expecting those without control to pay homage to this vision. Official history is most credible then when all those people who remember a different story have been robbed of their memories.

Thinking that in large part the Native American population had been robbed of its memories, nineteenth-century ethnographers hurried into the field to document what were generally acknowledged to be dying cultures. Many of these ethnographies record in gruesome detail the condition of peoples stripped of their land, stripped of their language, without many of the implements of their material culture, and without any memory, or only vague memory, of the past. Kindly intentioned as they were, these documents nevertheless offer testimony to the accuracy of the official history, which depicts the "redman" as the loser in a battle for land.

Because the most telling yardstick was control of the material wealth of this country, it was widely held that Native American culture could not survive. Moreover, there was a tendency to eulogize the passing of a largely unknown but uncorrupted culture and to lament, if it were to survive at all, the coming of an acculturated and assimilated Native American. There has been a tendency to view most cultures in such

either/or terms. One either "clings to" an unworkable past or gets swept away by the tidal wave of modern life.

The ability to view the Native American fairly and honestly has been hampered, therefore, by the role he has been assigned in American history, as well as by the definitions of culture. Gerald Vizenor's *The People Named the Chippewa* challenges on two fronts, first that his own Chippewa are to be identified with the Indians who populate American history textbooks, and second that the continuance of Chippewa culture rests on adherence to a set of inflexible rules governing behavior.

To do so, Vizenor turns to what has been most long-lived among his own Chippewa: he looks to the oral storytelling tradition. There he finds not the repository of tribal traditions that can be reconstituted whole, without change, in the present, but evidence that something vital has never been lost. The figure that best represents this vitality is Naanabozho, the "compassionate woodland trickster."

In the "Prologue" to *The People Named the Chippewa*, Vizenor tells the story of the creation of the first earth. Naanabozho travels the earth searching for his mother who has been abducted by evil spirits. After traveling great distances, Naanabozho comes upon the wigwam of the great gambler. The gambler challenges Naanabozho to a game; if the trickster loses the tribal people will lose their lives and their spirits will be consigned to the flesh eaters in the land of darkness. The great gambler misjudges his opponent, however, and Naanabozho, using some deception of his own, wins the game.

The trickster is such a compelling figure for Vizenor because he is an embodiment of "the realities of human imperfections":

> More than a magnanimous teacher and transformer, the trickster is capable of violence, deceptions, and cruelties. . . . The trickster is comic in the sense that he does not reclaim idealistic ethics, but survives as a part of the natural world; he represents a spiritual balance in a comic drama rather than the romantic elimination of human contradictions and evil.

It would be wrong then to reduce the Chippewa story of Naanabozho's meeting with the great gambler to its simplest terms: good triumphs over evil. Indeed, the story ends as Naanabozho takes one last turn; if he wins the great gambler loses *his* life. Turning again and again to the idiom of comedy rather than to that of tragedy, Vizenor disallows such a simplistic view of history as well.

Along these lines, Vizenor tells us that the Chippewa themselves can accommodate several different versions of their own beginnings. Nineteenth-century anthropologists tended to see variations as evidence of the corruption of a "pure" culture that existed some time in the past. Vizenor quotes from the recent work of Krocber, Tedlock and Ong to argue differently. They, along with Vizenor, challenge some of the assumptions inherent in discussions of so-called "corrupted" variants. They question whether such assumptions apply to works from primarily oral traditions. They tend to emphasize the artistry of the storyteller, rather than quibble about the authenticity or accuracy of the text. Vizenor says:

> The teller of stories is an artist, a person of wit and imagination, who relumes the diverse memories of the visual past into the experiences and metaphors of the present. . . . The tribal creation takes place at the time of the telling in the oral tradition; the variations in mythic stories are the imaginative desires of tribal artists.

Notice that Vizenor does not say that the storyteller retrieves or recaptures or testifies to historical facts; instead he relumes, rekindles, re-illuminates.

And thus we come to one of the key terms for Vizenor: imagination. If we can concede that colonial America won the political struggle over land rights, Vizenor cautions us against such a concession regarding the tribal identity. In the stories the Chippewa tell about themselves he finds the true strength of his people. They did not relinquish the ability or freedom to imagine themselves when they relinquished their lands, Nor do their imagined selves conform to the "official" view. Speaking of the differences between tribal views and those of anthropologists and historians, Vizenor says:

> Traditional tribal people imagine their social patterns and places on the earth, whereas anthropologists and historians invent tribal cultures and end mythic time. The differences between tribal imagination and social scientific invention are determined in world views: imagination is a state of being, a measure of personal courage; the invention of cultures is a material achievement through objective methodologies. To imagine the world is to be in the world; to invent the world with academic predications is to separate human experiences from the world, a secular transcendence and denial of chance and mortalities.

The term "culture" itself imposes boundaries, restricts freedom and is the ideological equivalent of the reservation. Liberated from theoretical categories, the Chippewa can get out from under the weight of either "preserving" the past or "adopting" the ways of the white man.

Having said as much, we can confront the irony imbedded in the title to this book. "Chippewa" and "Ojibway" are the names given to the people of the central woodlands by the colonists. The word that tribal people used to refer to themselves was Anishinaabeg. For Vizenor, the distinction between Anishinaabeg and Chippewa is not one of mere semantics. The "collective name [Anishinaabeg] was not an abstract concept of personal identities or national ideologies." The "family" and not the "nation" was the "first source" of personal identity. The collective identity came through sharing a language with other families and by sharing the dreams and visions expressed in the myths and stories.

The identity of these tribal communities was, therefore, more fluid than we can perhaps understand. Without the restrictions imposed by a "scriptural" past, the Chippewa's identity was fixed and constrained by nothing but the circumstances governing the present of individual lives. It is in the present, after all, that the stories are told and for the present that they have meaning. Tribal traditions may help to reinforce tribal identity but they do not necessarily add up to circumscribed culture and history.

In writing the history of the people *named* the Chippewa, Vizenor must take pains to clarify such distinctions between history and identity. The history of the Chippewa is one of resistance *and* capitulation to the "historical identity" invented and imposed by the invading whites. The people named the Chippewa about whom anthropologists and historians have written are not to be confused with the Anishinaabeg of the woodlands nor should they be equated with the people who live on the reservations of Minnesota, Wisconsin, and Canada. The woodland tribes did not bear many of the allegiances attributed to them, and the present-day Chippewa, long separated from the woodland, can not live out but only "express romantic instincts, dreams and visions of the wilderness."

Vizenor would seem to be arguing that unless and until the people named the Chippewa can accept that they can not be the Chippewa *and* the Anishinaabeg at the same time, they will not be able to exercise the control over the past that will allow for a vision of the future. The Chippewa can not hold onto romantic dreams about the past without continuing to conspire in the victimization of traditional cultures.

There is in all of this a fierce honesty that comes from living on the edge, perched somewhere between despair over how well the Chippewa have learned the lessons of the dominant culture's history and a kind of free-spirited zaniness over having reasoned out for oneself that none of the rules apply. Freed of invented cultural restraints, he can take a critical look at the histories written by cultural conspirators William Whipple Warren, George Copway (Kahgegagahbowh), and Peter Jones (Kahkewaquonaby). He can also assess the aims of the American Indian Movement in less than favorable terms:

The poses of tribal radicals seem to mimic the romantic pictorial images in old photographs taken by Edward Curtis for a white audience. The radicals never seem to smile, an incautious throwback to the stoical tribal visage of slower camera shutters and film speeds. The new radicals frown, even grimace at cameras, and claim the atrocities endured by all tribal cultures in first person personal pronouns.

Some militants decorate themselves in pastiche pantribal vestments, pose at times as traditionalists, and speak a language of confrontation and urban politics. The radical figures were not elected to speak for tribal reservation people, nor were they appointed to represent the interests and political views of elected tribal officials.

Such self-appointed saviors as Dennis Banks would seem to pose as big a threat to the survival of the Anishinaabeg as do the racist policies of the U.S. government.

The vast majority of the Chippewa get lost in the cracks and crevices created by these ideological word wars. These are the ones for whom Vizenor may well have written this book. They include the students at a private college who "were asked to define the word *Indian* during a special program on tribal cultures." Among their definitions we find the following:

> Indian is a cultural nationality.
> Real Americans.
> A member of the mongolian race.
> A human being.
> A wild savage.
> Indian means man.

They would include, too, the estimated half of the tribal population that is chemically dependent on alcohol. There is, as well, Cora Katherine Sheppo, who "smothered her grandchild because he had been 'spawned by the devil'." Trapped between some vague knowledge of tribal religion and Christianity and a psychiatric diagnosis of paranoid schizophrenia, Cora Sheppo will live out what remains of her life in a state mental hospital.

Neither pan-Indianism nor radical politics will do much to help the Cora Sheppo's of this world. These factional ideologies depend in their own ways upon the acceptance of the historical identity imposed from without. Traditionally, the Anishinaabeg did not predicate the present reality on a past reality. Survival then depends in large part on their willingness to forego a historical identity. Ironically, those who seek a historical identity gamble away all claims to an Anishinaabeg identity.

Vizenor is, of course, less polemical than this review makes him sound. Identified as he often is with the "compassionate woodland trickster," he does nevertheless prefer to live in the realm of the possible. Freed of the trappings of an imposed identity, either from within or without the tribal community, he is free to imagine himself and the world of which he is a part.

In the "Epilogue" to *The People Named the Chippewa*, Vizenor includes a narrative, originally translated by Peter Jones, an anthropologist killed by tribal people while doing research in the Philippines.

> Something else I will relate concerning what the people of old have said. Whenever any one died, it was common for him to rise from the dead; and so he would give an account of what it was like at the place where the dead go. A very large road leads to the place where go those who have died. A great many one saw walking straight west where leads the road. . . .
>
> In various forms appeared they who danced, even upon their heads they stood when they danced. And this was why the people of old used to say whenever anybody died: "Don't ask anybody to accompany you." They pointed out to one the way straight towards the west. . . .
>
> And then there at the grave they sometimes kindled a fire and cooked food, when they were mindful of one that had died. Food, tobacco, and fire they placed there. And then over there at the place where the ghosts were arrived the food.
>
> There was one great ghostly person who watched over the ghosts, for such as what I have heard people of old say. Sometimes the great ghostly man sent one back to the earth. "Not yet is your time up to come to this place." And this was the occasion when one sometimes came back to life.

Having read Vizenor's book, we may well agree that it is not yet time for the Chippewa to die.

Throughout his career, Gerald Vizenor has exhibited a willingness to experiment with and to work in a variety of forms—he was a reporter, he has written poetry, a novel, and a filmscript. It should come as no surprise then that he has ventured into another arena. *The People Named the Chippewa* is not just "revisionist" history though. Instead it poses some serious historiographical questions. The "Indian" of American history, largely a creation of the colonist, has had such a damaging effect on the Native population itself that we can only wait to see if its influence can be eradicated.

Franchot Ballinger (essay date Winter 1985)

SOURCE: "History and the Imagination: Gerald Vizenor's *The People Named the Chippewa*," *American Indian Quarterly*, Vol. IX, No. 1, Winter, 1985, pp. 55-59.

[*In the essay below, Ballinger discusses the vehicle for the "imaginative metaphor" presented in* Earthdivers.]

"Earthdivers," says Gerald Vizenor at the beginning of ***Earthdivers: Tribal Narratives on Mixed Descent*** (1981), is "an imaginative metaphor." The vehicle for this metaphor is a culture hero (sometimes trickster, like Wenebojo in the Ojibwe story Vizenor cites in his preface) found extensively in native American myth. This figure directs animals to dive into the great flood until one finally returns with grains of dirt from which the hero magically creates the present earth mass. The tenor of the metaphor is Vizenor's protagonists, the "mixedbloods, or Métis, tribal tricksters and recast culture heroes, the mournful heirs and survivors from that premier union between the daughters of the woodland shamans and white fur traders. The Métis or mixedblood earthdivers in these stories dive into unknown urban places now, into the racial darkness in the cities, to create a new consciousness of coexistence." Traditionally standing between two cultures, the Métis earthdiver will integrate America's divided anima. Furthermore, "in the metaphor of the Métis earthdiver, white settlers are summoned to dive with mixedblood survivors into the unknown . . . to swim deep down . . . in search of a few honest words upon which to build a new urban turtle island."

To lead us to such creative realization, the Métis earthdiver must also be a trickster, for "the world must be realized through inversions and opposites, sacred and secular reversals" of the sort associated with tricksters. Because Vizenor refers frequently to his characters as tricksters and to their reversals and "contradances," the trickster element is apparent throughout the twenty-one mainly satirical narratives of ***Earthdivers***. Because the association of the blood with the earthdiver-trickster is Vizenor's own, rather than one found in the oral traditions, what might be less apparent is that Vizenor's tricksters are very much those of native American oral traditions, even if their trickery is in the contemporary world.

Whether Vizenor's rendering or that of the oral tradition, trickster is an elusive figure. Like a subatomic particle, he defies final definition of time, place and character. (Perhaps the Dakotas were suggesting as much when they ended stories about the trickster Ikto with "and from then on, who knows where Ikto went next.") Vizenor acknowledges this elusiveness by rejecting the trickster of categorized and defined properties: that is, the trickster who is gluttonous, lascivious, greedy, deceptive, creative, destructive. He demonstrates that ultimately trickster is best experienced as a dramatization of

event and process, not fixed in the amber of description. Trickster is, after all, always travelling, and we might add, almost in apposition, *transgressing, becoming, transforming, making*. In Vizenor, we can see that an authoritative discussion of trickster would be carried on in verbal, not in terminal adjectives. No doubt, this trickster is no less elusive, but we can better comprehend the nature of his power.

To begin with, we must consider a major source of trickster's power—his ambiguous marginality. Vizenor treats this theme in terms of the dynamic. Trickster is a transgression of the "purities" of society's accepted strata and conventions. To be sure, Vizenor's tricksters are marginal first of all because they are mixed-bloods and thus act between two worlds, while the traditional trickster is marginal because he violates established rules and values; nevertheless, marginality is fundamental to the powers of both. From the reversals and transgressions of Coyote and Wenebojo often come creativity, magic power and other special benefits. From the mixed-blood marginality of Vizenor's tricksters can come the realization of a new turtle island. The world regards such figures ambivalently because mixed blood and the concomitance of rule-breaking and creation are themselves ambiguities. But by quoting Donald Davidson on metaphor, Vizenor suggests that ambiguity is itself a force: "perhaps, then, we can explain metaphor as a kind of ambiguity; in the context of a metaphor, certain words have either a new or an original meaning; and the force of the metaphor depends on our uncertainty as we waver between the two meanings. . . . " Similarly ambiguous, Vizenor's Métis tricksters, as they "waver and forbear extinction in two world's . . . are the force in the blood and the uncertain word. . . . " The ambiguous marginal trickster brings new meaning and force to the language of experience, liberating us in the process from conventional notions, just as the ambiguity of metaphor infuses perception with creative meaning and reveals the limitations of stereotyped seeing.

Metaphor also figures significantly in Vizenor's treatment of tricksters' defiance of accepted categories and norms. Vizenor quotes Susan Stewart's *Nonsense:* "The systematic violation of categories and norms of behavior that the trickster presents appears as a negation, a reversal, an inversion of those cultural categories and behavior norms that make up common sense . . . . As the embodiment of disparate domains, trickster is analogous to the process of metaphor, the incorporation of opposites into a new configuration." Thus in the Ojibwe earthdiver myth the creative joins the scatological as Wenebojo creates earth to escape his own feces floating in the Deluge. In other stories, some capricious act of Coyote's brings permanent death to humans, but he gets himself out of trouble with them by rationalizing that without death the world would become too crowded: a caprice rationalized becomes a sensible part of the scheme of things. In their contrary behavior, Vizenor's tricksters, like traditional tricksters, repeatedly stand akimbo the established categories and codes, freeing us from spiritual and imaginative enslavement to what Vizenor calls "terminal creeds." Captain Shammer says in **"The Chair of Tears"**, "The trickster seeks the balance in contraries and the contraries in balance," and "in the white face of the obvious, the opposite must be done." In **"Blue Boom Ceremonial,"** a Lumbee economist shows through his satirical inversions (for example, his insistence that laughter is a dance) that Indianness is a "*way* of doing and being that is 'Indian,' not what is done or the blood quantum of the doer." Similarly, Pink Stallion teaches his students, (who are "invented" Indians, that is, living the image of Indians invented by whites) more authentic tribal ways of seeing. For example, he negates his students' affected solemnity about their Indianness when to Token White's protest that "satire is not sacred" he responds, "Mother Earth is satire" (and, incidentally, legitimizes the satirical mode of Vizenor's book as a sacred reversal or opposition).

The new "configuration" that the traditional trickster's contrary behavior brings about realizes our, and the world's, creativity. This makes trickster a literary representation of the forces dramatized ceremonially in native American sacred clowns. In their trickster-like buffoonery, Navajo and Pueblo clowns topple the conventional and defy the formal outlines of ritualism to contribute to the creative power of ceremony. We should also note that their ugly, poor, bedraggled appearance belies the power they possess. Similarly, the contrary behavior of the Heyoka, behavior which violates all definitions of "common sense," conceals the power they possess. Like trickster, the clowns do not *appear* suited for the creative powers they in fact exercise.

In **"Natural Tilts,"** Vizenor reveals the powers of his shaman-trickster-clowns: "Some shaman sprites and tricksters are spiritual healers, with warm hands and small medicine bundles loaded with secret remedies, and some shaman spirits are clowns who can tell and reveal the opposites of the world in sacred reversals, natural tilts in double visions, interior glories. The shaman clowns and tricksters are transformed in familiar places and spaces from common grammars, the past and the present in the shape of animals and birds." While there are few transformations of the latter sort in *Earthdivers*, reversals are clearly part of the shamanic powers of Vizenor's trickster-clowns. In **"The Chair of Tears,"** a title whose tragic allusion is the contrary of the story's satirical content, Captain Shammer appears on campus the first time "dressed in the uniform of a general, ritual clowns bearing the estranged mask of General George Custer." Appointed chairman of the Department of American Indian Studies, he proposes to save the department by selling it to the highest bidder. In the middle of a comic exchange with Ramon, the mixed-blood black departmental secretary, Shammer quotes one of Black Elk's more elegiac pronouncements. All of this is a sign that Shammer, like a sacred clown, is a contrary and a "person of

magical ethos, [revealing a] connection of satire with magical power."

Father Bearald One (**"The Sociodowser"**) is another trickster-shaman-clown. Dressed in the clothes of a cleric (his father was rumoured to be a Roman Catholic Priest), Bearald One also wears in the summer one conventional shoe and one "plain black rubber zipper overshoe." When an Indian Center board member asks to see his foot, Bearald One refuses, but Heyoka-like his "no" briefly seems to become "yes," for almost immediately he moves to comply. "But rather than showing his foot in the overshoe, he remove[s] the shoe on his other foot, his normal foot, because no one specified which foot [although which foot is intended is clear]. Then he remove[s] his sock and stretche[s] and wriggle[s] his angular toes in the direction of the board members." Yet this apparently doddering, foolish man is himself a reversal, for he possesses sacred power. Father Bearald One moves with *jiibayag,* tribal spirits, "on the wind from dark woods," hears voices and visits "distant places in his dreams." He also engages his powers in somewhat more secular activities: divining the whereabouts of the Indian Center vans after their confiscation by the government and mysteriously fixing Center bingo games in favor of the most needy. First his strangeness and then his powers make corrupt members of the Center board uneasy, but Bearald One is quite comfortable enough; for this trickster, the Center is "an appropriate place in the world to chance to outwit evil and balance the universe."

Native American oral traditions have proved very resilient in the face of their world's imbalance caused by white incursions. This is obvious in their adapting traditional themes to contemporary circumstances. (Witness, for example, stories of trickster and the WPA or anthropologists.) Vizenor's placing mixed-blood earthdiver-tricksters in the contemporary urban world is, then, within the tradition. And like the Navajo Ma'i, who, Yellowman told Barre Toelken, reveals what is possible, Vizenor's tricksters too reveal the possible. Standing at the brink between tribal tradition and modern colonial America, seeing all of its imbalance, they challenge us to dive. The challenge accepted, we discover that the inspiration and power of life are in the world of contraries, the trickster's world. We discover, as Vizenor says in another context, that "respiration and transpiration are possible under water."

Maureen Keady (essay date Winter 1985)

SOURCE: "Walking Backwards into the Fourth World: Survival of the Fittest in *Bearheart,*" in *American Indian Quarterly,* Vol. IX, No. 1, Winter, 1985, pp. 61-5.

[*In the essay below, Keady discusses Vizenor's use of lan-*

guage in The Darkness in Saint Louis Bearheart, *and how his technique emphasizes the importance of a strength of spirit over belief in empty words.*]

Gerald Vizenor's book, *The Darkness in St. Louis Bearheart*, is a comic and brutal satire on all of us who cling to "Terminal Creeds," whose values, and very identities, amount to no more than bundles of words, bereft of meaning. Just as the characters in *Bearheart* suffer because of their vanities, their attachment to words and "sacred" idiosyncrasies, we too are challenged, and even assaulted by Vizenor's ruthless depictions of bizarre sex and violence, and his consistently crude language. Throughout the book, our expectations are thwarted, our notions of morality are violated, and our desire for resolution (or a little compassion) is overruled again and again. Perhaps as disturbing as the actual events of the book is the offhand and comic manner in which Vizenor presents them. Much of *Bearheart* is hard to stomach, but Vizenor's fiction is only slightly stranger than truth. His own early life was wrought with violence and under "Acknowledgments," Vizenor writes. "Most of the characters . . . are real people with fictional names. . . . " In effect, Vizenor's book is hyper-real—or reality condensed, and the pilgrims' journey across America is an accelerated tour through modern life. Vizenor sets his story in a probable future, taking modern values one step further to reveal their emptiness and the bleakness of the path we are now on. Vizenor's concern with words, the bizarre content of his book and its irreverent telling may mark *Bearheart* as a distinctly "modern" novel. But at its core, Vizenor's book is more Indian than western, and more saturnalian than satirical with Vizenor as the ultimate clown and trickster.

Like many modern writers, Vizenor is obsessed with words, but unlike them, he is not concerned with the "inadequacy" of words themselves. On the contrary, Vizenor has faith in the power of words to evoke emotion and convey real meaning.
—*Maureen Keady*

That Vizenor so often condemns words, that he creates a hero who rarely speaks, and goes on to make a book of words, may seem like a series of contradictions. Like many modern writers, Vizenor is obsessed with words, but unlike them, he is not concerned with the "inadequacy" of words themselves. On the contrary, Vizenor has faith in the power of words to evoke emotion and convey real meaning. The opening chapter of the novel, entitled "The Darkness in Saint Louis Bearheart" is chant-like and poetic. Aside from serving as the story's frame, this chapter works as ceremonial prayer; though truly dark itself, the rhythm and poetry of the language is emotional preparation for the ensuing chaos of the

novel. All in all, Vizenor seems more concerned with truth than with words, and the rest of the novel shows the folly of those who hold words up like shields to protect them from reality. He goes out of the way, (via the Bioavaricious Word Hospital) to point out the absurdity of those who would dissect the language and discard its meaning. Through *Bearheart*, Vizenor acts as a trickster/teacher, degrading words and using them to violate and degrade. By desecrating the "sacred" through words, he restores the value of words, and more importantly, the values which words express.

As strange as the events of *Bearheart* may be, Vizenor's novel is really a teaching tale about truth and choice, about those who are willing to sacrifice their "Terminal Creeds" for real meaning, and those who will not. In the first chapters of the novel, Proude Cedarfair and Rosina Parent adopt a growing number of pilgrims in their journey across America. Each of the pilgrims has his own story, his own bizarre and often violent personal history to which Vizenor devotes many pages. Though comic, or rather, blackly humorous, their stories are all tragic, and certainly many of the pilgrims can be seen as "victims of circumstance." Because the pilgrims are "seekers" and because they have sense enough to recognize Proude as their leader, the pilgrims do seem "better" than the other survivors they meet. But for all their good intentions, only one is willing to give up his sad story for a better life. Instead, the pilgrims cling to words as identities; their personal pasts become self-serving postures, and their sad stories of victimization become excuses for all their actions.

What is perhaps most confusing about Vizenor's novel is that good and evil are so often blurred—that truths and falsehoods are so often spoken from the same mouths and within the same sentences. But such complexity is accurate and realistic. Like Milton, Vizenor shows that evil is not the absence of good, but the perversion of it. Thus, the pilgrims' stories contain much truth and insight, but their distortion of these truths become the "Terminal Creeds" they live by and die by. Likewise, words of wisdom often come from the most despicable characters in the book. On the whole, the Gambler's philosophy is utterly perverse, but within it there are kernels of truth; "biological families are not the center of meaning and identities," and "the government tortured people and sanctioned killing." Though the Gambler mocks the pilgrims as "Terminal believers in their own goodness," his nihilism is itself a "Terminal Creed" and he is a devout believer in it.

Like the pilgrims, the Evil Gambler indulges himself in his personal history. He rejects "biological families" as a source of identity but draws his own identity from the "family" which adopted—or rather, abducted him. His sentimentality is cloying as he quotes his mother's poetry, has her pictures on the wall, and glorifies her and his childhood before the captive audience of pilgrims. Though powerful as he has proven to be, the Evil Gambler is entirely enmeshed in his past and in the material world. His arrogance and materialism are his weakness and his downfall. Unlike Proude, he is not willing "to risk everything"—even to achieve his own evil purpose. Thoroughly cruel and grotesque, the Gambler is "evil incarnate." But his evil, too, has words and "Terminal Creeds" at its source; the evil he demonstrates is the same spiritual weakness that to some degree, each of the pilgrims will succumb to.

When confronted by the Evil Gambler, the pilgrims substitute piles of words for personal strength. The lists of "words that please them" that each pilgrim composes is like a condensed version of their personal stories; a naming of passions and pet-peeves. Lilith Mae lists "cocker, boxer, springer . . . " while Bigfoot, with his "president Jackson" produces a list of American presidents. That Proude, in contrast, lists the names of the pilgrims themselves demonstrates his more immediate connection to the present reality and suggests his willingness to risk everything in order to conquer evil. In his encounter with Sir Cecil, Proude, both literally and symbolically, saves the lives of all the pilgrims, but he cannot change their wills, or save them from themselves. Thus, as the chapters which precede the "Evil Gambler" section show the accumulation of the pilgrims, the chapters which follow this encounter show the demise and disintegration of the group. One by one, the pilgrims fall victim to their own vanities and those who hold hardest to "Terminal Creeds" are the first to go.

When Proude saves the life of Lilith Mae, her response is to commit suicide. Her death is literally the working of her own will, but also, the manifestation of her "Terminal Creed." In *Bearheart,* Vizenor twice tells the legend of a child-woman who takes animals as lovers, and these stories work to evoke some sympathy for Lilith Mae. But, as Proude says, "We become our memories and what we believe," and we see Lilith Mae as a firm believer in her "Terminal Creed" long before her suicide. Lilith Mae believes the stories she has been told about herself and acts out of them. Having been mocked by the Anishinaabe women as a "lover of dogs" Lilith Mae goes on to become a lover of dogs. She tells of victimization by her incestuous father, but offers herself as a victim to the Anishinaabe men, and then to the Evil Gambler. Her optimism is superficial, and lacking spiritual strength, she places her faith in words and Vizenor writes "She had known evil in her past and was pushing her thoughts with words of confidence." According to her own "Terminal Creed" when Lilith Mae is not victimized by the Gambler, she must take her own life.

In the chapters that follow, the pilgrims suffer a variety of strange deaths and disappearances as they prove, like Lilith Mae, to be believers in "Terminal Creeds." Vizenor's treatment of his characters may seem cold-hearted, but if the pilgrims' deaths are pointless, they are also appropriate. After

the "Evil Gambler" chapter, Vizenor, as trickster, throws up the pieces of his characters' lives, and they fall, neither by chance, nor fate, but exactly where they fit.

When Belladonna Darwin Winter-Catcher expresses her "Terminal Creed' that "An Indian is a member of a recognized tribe and a person who has Indian blood," (the federal definition) she falls victim to the band of "descendants of famous hunters and bucking horse breeders" at Orion. The cookie that kills her is, in effect, the poison of her own false-pride and superiority. In contrast, Little Big Mouse's "Terminal Creed" proves to be a grotesque and patronizing liberality. She tells the cripples they meet on the interstate that "Parts of bodies do not make the person whole," but becomes blinded by her own big-heartedness. The nude dance she performs for the cripples is pathetically vain and egocentric. Before they tear Little Big Mouse to pieces, the cripples tell her, "You are perfect and now you want our imagination and visions for your own."

Although Judge Pardone Cozener and Doctor Wilde Cozwaine escape violent deaths, and though each seems to have found their niches at the Bioavaricious Word Hospital, the decision to stay there is clearly a choice of nihilism. The fate of Sun Bear Sun is thus unfair in comparison, but it is similarly a direct result of a terminal belief in words. Though truly good-hearted, Sun Bear Sun is "locked in the part without visions." In his effort to explain himself to the soldiers, the tribal leader plays their game and demonstrates his misplaced faith. Sun Bear Sun is trapped by words, and so remains a prisoner as "the honest fool answering unanswerable questions."

In light of this, it is perhaps appropriate that as the novel ends, Vizenor answers few of our questions. It may be Rosina's role as "earth mother" that keeps her bound in the third world, and unlike the pilgrims, she espouses no "Terminal Creed." But in the end of *Bearheart,* Rosina does seem to share the pilgrims' spiritual weakness and it is appropriate that her mistake takes the physical, rather than verbal form. When she has sex with Bigfoot, it is because he forces her to, but she also allows him to break her will, and it is his aspect of their encounter which makes it particularly repugnant. In her utter submission to Bigfoot, Rosina surrenders her will and undergoes a sort of "death of spirit" which seems to bar her entry into the fourth world. Vizenor writes: "She had traveled with death during the night." Though Rosina's plight is ambiguous, it does seem hopeful. Proude's note suggests his faith in her and the tracks she finds in the snow may very well lead her to join him in the fourth world.

In as much as *Bearheart* is a tale of the world's end, it is also about the beginning of a new world. The corrupt society has done itself in, but Vizenor tells us that "Myths became the center of meaning again," and that "Oral traditions were honored" by the survivors on the interstate. As Proude says, " . . . all is not lost. Our world has turned again to hunting and the hunter." The journey of the pilgrims in *Bearheart* is, in essence, a walking backwards, to beginnings to New Mexico and to the fourth world. But those who cling to words as evidence of their existence will be unable to enter. In the wasted and poisoned America, "survival of the fittest" prevails, but Vizenor points out that, here, as always, it is spiritual strength which makes one fit.

A. LaVonne Brown Ruoff (essay date Winter 1985)

SOURCE: "Gerald Vizenor: Compassionate Trickster," in *American Indian Quarterly,* Vol. IX, No. 1, Winter, 1985, pp. 67-73.

[*In the following essay, Ruoff discusses the major thrust of all of Vizenor's work, whether poetry, drama, or prose, as being an examination of relationships between tribal and non-tribal worlds.*]

Gerald Vizenor (Ojibwe) is one of the most prolific Indian authors writing today. To have published so extensively in so many genres is a remarkable achievement for any author, Indian or non-Indian. Now primarily known as a prose writer, Vizenor began as a poet, publishing early in his career such volumes as *Raising the Moon Vines* (1964), *Summer in the Spring* (1965), *Empty Swings* (1967), *Slight Abrasions* (1966; with Jerome Downes). His *Seventeen Chirps* (1965; unpaged) has rightly been praised by Louis Untermeyer as Haiku "in the best tradition" (book cover). Divided into poems on the four seasons, this collection contains such strikingly beautiful images as "Spider threads / held the red sumac still / Autumn wind" or "The quick wind / Drags the leaves like sled runners / Down the tin roof."

The major thrust of Vizenor's work—whether poetry, prose, or drama—is the examination of the interrelationships between the tribal and non-tribal worlds. His commitment to the traditional origins of his own Ojibwe heritage is reflected in two books: *anishinabe nagamon* (1965) and *anishinabe adisokan* (1970). The former is a collection of traditional Ojibwe songs that Vizenor reinterpreted, using Francis Densmore's literal translations and incorporating Ojibwe words. His delicate rephrasing is exemplified in these lines from a dream song: "sound of thunder / sometimes / i pity myself / while the wind carries me / across the sky, across the earth / everywhere / making my voice heard." Vizenor focuses the reader's attention on the beauty of individual lines by placing each stanza on a separate page. Both *anishinabe nagamon* and *anishinabe adisokan*, reprinted in 1981 as *Summer in the Spring: Ojibwe Lyric Poems and Tribal Sto-*

ries, are accompanied by notes, Ojibwe pictographs, and vocabulary.

anishinabe adisokan is a collection of traditional stories about Ojibwe life, customs, and religion originally published in the White Earth reservation newspaper *The Progress* (1887-1888), edited by Theodore Beaulieu, Vizenor's great uncle. A valuable collection in itself, *anishinabe adisokan* is also important because it introduces several myths Vizenor incorporates into his own creative work. Among these is the myth about the origin of the most sacred Ojibwe rite, the midewiwin ceremony, that elucidates Vizenor's frequent references to the bear, cedar, and task of the culture hero. Another myth Vizenor uses in his later work is "Manabozho (The Ojibwe culture hero) and the Gambler."

Much of Vizenor's work deals with the struggles of the Ojibwe and other tribal peoples to cope with the dominant society. His poems published in *Voices from the Rainbow* (1975) and *Songs from This Earth on Turtle's Back* (1983; hereafter *Songs*) voice themes that dominate his prose. In **"Indians at the Guthrie,"** Vizenor vividly portrays the lives of contemporary urban Indians: "Once more at wounded knee / sniffing glue in gallop / sterno in bemidji / cultural suicides / downtown on the reservation" (*Voices from the Rainbow; Songs*). As **"Tribal Stumps"** reveals, Vizenor's own father was destined to become one of these cultural suicides: "My father returns / with all the mixed bloods / tribal stumps / from the blood soaked beams of the city" (*Voices from the Rainbow*).

Vizenor vividly describes these struggles in four collections containing his news articles, essays, and stories: *The Everlasting Sky* (1972), *Tribal Scenes and Ceremonies* (1976), *Wordarrows* (1978), and *Earthdivers* (1981). The first two books consist primarily of Vizenor's news articles about contemporary Indian life on the reservation and in the city. The last two are fictional accounts of Indian-white relations organized around specific themes. In *Wordarrows,* Vizenor describes the "cultural word wars" in which "the arrowmakers and wordmakers survive the word wars with sacred memories while the factors in the new fur trade separate themselves in wordless and eventless social and political categories." In *Earthdivers,* he focuses on the modern earthdivers, descendants of the mythic earthdivers who dove below the waters to find a bit of earth to place on turtle's back. By blowing on the earth and casting it about, the Ojibwe culture hero created the world. For Vizenor these modern earthdivers are mixedbloods, "tribal tricksters and recast cultural heroes, the mournful and whimsical heirs and survivors of that premier union between the daughters of the woodland shamans and white fur traders." These earthdivers "dive into unknown urban places now, into the racial darkness in the cities, to create a new consciousness of coexistence."

These four books contain memorable portraits of real people who defied yet finally were overcome by the dominant society. In **"Buried in a Blue Suit,"** from *The Everlasting Sky* (reprinted in *Tribal Scenes and Ceremonies*), Vizenor pays tribute to John Ka Ka Geesick, traditional Ojibwe trapper who was both humiliated and immortalized by a white society that dressed him in a blue suit, turkey feather headdress, and green blanket for an official souvenir postcard photograph and, after his death at age 124, insisted that he be buried in the same suit and given a Christian funeral service.

Especially moving is **"Sand Creek Survivors"** from *Earthdivers,* which describes the circumstances surrounding the death of 13-year-old Dane Michael White (Sioux), who hanged himself in a Minnesota jail. White had been jailed as a runaway for 41 days because the courts denied his request to live with his grandmother and could not decide where to put him. To emphasize the continuing assaults on tribal people by the dominant society, Vizenor intersperses his account with passages describing the massacres of the Cheyenne at Sand Creek and the Blackfeet at the Marias River and Black Elk's vision of destruction.

The case that fascinates Vizenor most is that of Thomas White Hawk, a Sioux premedical student originally condemned to death and then sentenced to life imprisonment for murdering an elderly white man and raping his wife. Vizenor suggests that White Hawk was driven to violence by cultural schizophrenia. White Hawk, neglected by his Indian parents and orphaned at 12, became the foster son of a rigid white guardian who set high goals for the young Sioux and abandoned him after his arrest. In *Thomas White Hawk* (1968) and *Tribal Scenes and Ceremonies,* Vizenor reprints his news articles on the case. In the "White Hawk and the Prairie Fun Dancers" section of *Wordarrows,* he recreates his investigation, providing vivid portraits of White Hawk, haunted by his crimes; the sheriff, determined to protect his prisoner from mob violence and his country from such communist-front organizations as the Civil Liberties Union; and the minister's wife infatuated with the imprisoned White Hawk. These portraits are some of Vizenor's best work.

Satire, however, is the genre Vizenor most frequently uses to convey the conflicts between tribal and non-tribal worlds. (Vizenor uses the word *tribal* rather than *Indian* because it suggests a "celebration of communal values which connect the *tribal celebrants* to the earth" (*Earthdivers*). The closer Vizenor's satire is to reality the more effective it is. His stories in the "Downtown on the Reservation" section of *Wordarrows* effectively chronicle the word wars between tribal people and the dominant society, wars Vizenor understands as a mixed-blood Ojibwe who was raised both in Minneapolis and on his father's White Earth Reservation, and as a former director of a Minneapolis Indian Employment and Guidance Program. **"Laurel Hole in the Day"** vividly de-

picts the futility of such programs. The well-meaning director, presumably Vizenor, finds jobs and an apartment for an Ojibwe family newly arrived from White Earth, only to realize that his action has started them on the road to failure in the big city. Realizing that their tribal friends and neighbors are eating them into the poorhouse, the couple moves to a white neighborhood, where loneliness drives them to the tribal bar for companionship. The wife, abandoned by her husband who has been fired for absenteeism, returns to her tar-paper shack on the reservation, where she is reunited with her husband and gives up her dream of urban paradise.

Vizenor's descriptions of the cultural wars ring true because he accurately depicts both the underlying causes of these wars and the nature of the wounds suffered by tribal people. Many of these wounds are self inflicted, as Vizenor makes clear. In **"Sociodowser"** from *Earthdivers,* Vizenor describes the efforts of an Indian Center to locate its vans, purchased with federal funds to transport Indians to industrial education classes but impounded by the state because they were used by Center staff and clients for travelling to bingo games and other businesses. Rallying to the cry of "Give us back our land and our vans," the Center board hires a shaman to help in the search. For Vizenor the center has become "more like a colonial fort dependent on federal funds, than a place for visions and dreams in the new tribal urban world."

Such self destructiveness is not limited to tribal centers, as Vizenor demonstrates in his stories about the fate of tribal studies programs in academe. One of Vizenor's best stories in *Earthdivers* is **"The Chair of Tears,"** which describes the efforts of Captain Shammer to auction the Department of Tribal Studies for sale to the highest bidder. Hired without interview, application, or academic credentials because the department wanted an unknown mixed blood, Shammer is renowned as the founder of the Half-Breed Hall of Fame. Vizenor deftly satirizes the blood-quantum issue in such departments by describing Shammer's plan to hire Old Darkhorse as skin-color consultant. Founder of the *California Half Moon Bay Skin Dip,* Darkhorse darkens light-skinned mixed bloods by dunking them in his Skin Dip.

Shammer is first to realize that rumors "about tribal troubles in higher education are the structural substitutes for adventures on the mythical frontier." The character types who mount the assault are those who led the radical movements of the 1960s and 1970s: Sarah Blue Welcome, a self-named white feminist and the first uninvited guest speaker at student protests for control of the tribal studies department; Four Skin, her full-blood Indian male hand puppet; Bad Mouth; Touch Tone, famous for long-distance calls to reservations; Fine Print; and Token White. Vizenor all too accurately depicts the administrative and student pressures that have led to the destruction of many such departments.

Entrepreneurship is not limited to tribal studies programs. Ingenious mixed bloods establish business empires in the city and on the reservation. One such entrepreneur is Martin Bear Charme, a Turtle Mountain Ojibwe from North Dakota, who hitchhiked to San Francisco to study welding under a federal relocation program. After he abandoned welding, he hauled refuse to a worthless mudflat, where he established his own Landfill Meditation Reservation, now worth millions. A philosopher as well as businessman, Martin also teaches a seminar on Landfill Meditation.

In Vizenor's unpublished screenplay *Harold of Orange*, Harold Sinseer exhibits similar enterprise. Previously successful in persuading a foundation to finance his miniature orange grove (a potted orange tree), Harold now seeks $200,000 to grow a coffee grove (a potted coffee tree). Harold predicts that coffee will revolutionize the tribal world. He persuades his warriors that reservation coffee beans will saturate the world market and disrupt international coffee markets, and he convinces foundation board directors that coffee will both block the temptation of tribesmen to drink alcohol and foster radical political discussions in reservation coffee houses. Harold has cast off the role of street radical and speaker in church basements: "The money was good then, but the guilt has changed, so here we are dressed in neckties . . . The new tribal entrepreneurs of the oranges and pinch beans, . . ." Harold asks only that the foundation give him funds to "market pinch beans in peace."

As one of the foundation directors realizes by the end of the play, Harold, with his fry bread, oranges, and coffee, is really in the traditional breakfast business. Vizenor's screenplay won the Minnesota Film-in-the-Cities award and has been made into a 30-minute film starring Oneida comedian Charlie Hill in the title role.

The most complex of Vizenor's works is *Darkness in Saint Louis Bearheart* (1978), a satirical and allegorical epic cycle that combines elements of classical and Western European epics and American Indian oral narratives. The protagonist is the culture hero/shaman Proude Cedarfair. In his quest for ritual knowledge, Cedarfair journeys across the United States, whose culture has been destroyed by the disappearance of energy resources. Cedarfair moves backward in time to achieve harmony with nature. Vizenor's descriptions of the four worlds of Indian people combine the emergence and migration myths of Southwestern tribes with the flood myths of the Algonkin-speaking tribes. Cedarfair begins his journey in the third world, which evil spirits have filled with contempt for the living and fear of death. He must reach the fourth world, in which these spirits will be outwitted through using the secret languages of animals and birds. Accompanying Cedarfair on his journey is a bizarre collection of followers that represent various figures from Indian mythology as well as human vices and virtues. Episodes in the novel denote

stages of the ritual quest and incidents occur without explanation, as they do in American Indian hero cycles.

In his books and in his screenplay, Vizenor uses many other aspects of American Indian oral tradition. He embeds traditional myths in his novel and his stories. For example in *Darkness in Saint Louis Bearheart*, the epic battle for life waged between Belladonna Winter Catcher and Cedarfair and the evil gambler Sir Cecil Staples, monarch of unleaded gasoline, is an updated version of the Ojibwe myth "Manabozho and the Gambler" that Vizenor includes in *anishinabe adisokan*. Vizenor uses an animal-husband myth in his stories of Lilith Mae Farrier's sexual relationship with her boxers included in both *Wordarrows* and *Darkness in Saint Louis Bearheart*.

Vizenor also uses the traditional Indian motif of transformation; this is exemplified in his novel by Bishop Omas Parasimo's penchant for wearing "metamasks" of other pilgrims' faces. Animal, especially bear, transformation appears more frequently than any other form. Vizenor makes clear the significance of this to his work by citing *Bear Ceremonialism in the Northern Hemisphere,* in which A. Irving Hallowell states that animals are believed to have essentially the same sort of animating agency as man: "They have a language of their own, can understand what human beings say and do, have forms of social or tribal organization, and live a life which is parallel in other respects to that of human societies'" (Quoted in **"Sociodowser,"** *Earthdivers*). Vizenor's emphasis on bear transformation is explained by that animal's role as the renewer of Ojibwe life in their mide ceremony. In *Darkness in Saint Louis Bearheart,* two characters possess bear power: Cedarfair, who speaks with the voice of the bear and takes on bear form permanently after he reaches the fourth world, and Zebulon Matchi Makwa (Wicked Bear), a talking writer and drunken urban shaman who offends everyone with his foul stench. In *Earthdivers,* those with this power are Martin Bear Charme and Father Berald One, the shaman who dreams of blue birds and bears, dresses as a priest, and wears an overshoe on one foot.

The trickster/transformer figure from Indian oral literature pervades Vizenor's recent work. Although the trickster as mixed-blood entrepreneur is one of Vizenor's favorite subjects, Vizenor also creates characters that reflect other aspects of the trickster. For example, in *Darkness in Saint Louis Bearheart,* Beneto Saint Plumero (also known as Bigfoot) possesses the enormous genitals and sexual appetite of the traditional trickster. Vizenor even portrays himself as a compassionate trickster. In both *Earthdivers* and *Wordarrows,* the author often appears as Clement Beaulieu, wise fool, truth speaker, and story teller, or as Erdupps MacChurbbs, "Shaman sprite from the tribal world of woodland dreams and visions."

Vizenor prefers to appear in his work as an observer rather than as central character. An exception to this is one of Vizenor's best works: **"I Know What You Mean, Erdupps MacChurbbs: Autobiographical Myths and Metaphors"** in *Growing Up in Minnesota: Ten Writers Remember Their Childhoods,* edited by Chester Anderson (1976). Vizenor reveals episodes from his childhood and adolescence that provide insights into his sensitivity to the plight of urban Indians who suffer and sometimes die (as did his father) in the back alleys of Minneapolis-St. Paul. Because so little has been written about the problems of Indian children in the city, the essay is an important contribution to our understanding of how an urban mixed-blood survives youthful traumas. The essay also reveals Vizenor's early ability to create characters to act out his fantasies. The advice to Vizenor from his imaginary companion MacChurbbs captures the author's stance in much of his prose: "You have given too much thought in your life to the violence of terminal believers! Show more humor and give your self more time for the little people and compassionate trickery."

Vizenor's work demonstrates considerable range. The strength of his work is his ability to depict with accuracy and humor the contrarieties in Indian-white relations. In Vizenor's view, whites invented "Indian" as a new identity for tribal people in order to separate them from their ancient tribal traditions. To survive this cultural genocide, tribal people responded by inventing new pan-Indian creeds, ceremonies, and customs that have blinded them and whites to their true tribal heritages. Only through the visions and dreams of tricksters and shamans can both tribal people and whites be led to truth. As a compassionate trickster, Vizenor sees his literary role as that of illuminating both the sham of contemporary "Indianness" and the power of vision and dream to restore tribal values.

Michael Loudon (review date Winter 1986)

SOURCE: Review of *The People Named Chippewa: Narrative Histories,* in *World Literature Today,* Vol. 60, No. 1, Winter, 1986, p. 160.

[*In the review below, Loudon praises* The People Named Chippewa *as a witty and imaginative discussion of current Native American culture.*]

Gerald Vizenor's writing began in a boldly experimental mode and has moved steadily toward more conventional prose, but even in his most recent nonfiction, he has never once left the battlefield of his "word wars." In the prologue to the "narrative histories" of *The People Named Chippewa* he deconstructs the unconscious conspiracy of the either-or fallacy that dominates the view which many Native Americans

have of themselves and with which they are frequently viewed by others. Nineteenth-century ethnologists and revisionist historians unwittingly fashioned an academic attitude, eventually popular, that tribal peoples must either assimilate or, suffering the loss of a "pure" culture, die. Vizenor, referring to the work of Kroeber, Tedlock, Ong, and others, shatters the romantic stereotype, however well-intentioned, of an uncorrupted, pristine "culture" that existed before the invasion of the whites. The consequent "historical identity" that results from theoretical categories of culture casts the "Indian" as an eternal loser. Thus the irony of Vizenor's title: the passive reception of a cultural designation bestowed from without and accepted from within. The Chippewa or the Ojibway were never such; they were the Anishinaabeg.

To rekindle and renew the spirit—not to retrieve the facts—of the past lives of the Anishinaabeg, Vizenor turns to the present "Chippewa" and begins with Naanabozho (not Nanabush), "the compassionate woodland trickster." To liberate the Chippewa from the ideologies of culture and history, Naanabozho represents the immediacy of storytelling to the present circumstances of individuals and their first source of identity, the family. Naanabozho affirms not a rigid set of rules for behavior (or even kinship), but flexible, nurturing principles of change that address the present in order to sustain the future. Wit and tribal imagination survive longer than a colonially inspired yearning for a conquered wilderness.

Although Vizenor's polemic is clear, it also displays the same wit and imagination he attributes to Naanabozho. His critique of the American Indian Movement is a satirical attack mounted precisely on the ground that the movement lacks humor and postures a false collective identity: the archetypal victim, colonial in its origin. Only a trickster could see Dennis Banks and Ronald Reagan in the same face. Through some very funny moments, Vizenor raises serious questions for the pan-Indian movements and "radical" academics. (His bibliography will direct scholars to further, similar points of view.) A teacher and scholar wishing to avoid and to correct the mistakes of twentieth-century scholarship in discussing "Indians," "Native Americans" or "Amerindians" would do well to begin with these stories; they are the strength of the Anishinaabeg.

Anthony C. Yu (review date 11 October 1987)

SOURCE: "Fulbright Monkey in China," in *The Los Angeles Times Book Review,* October 11, 1987, p. 8.

[*In the following review, Yu compares the trickster in Vizenor's* Griever *with the Mind Monkey in Chinese literature.*]

In religion and folklore of Africa and of North and South America, the trickster is a familiar figure often distinguished by his cunning, skill, penchant for adventure and mischief, sexual energy, and frequently exaggerated body parts. True to his name, this mythic figure, which unites in his (or her) person traits of the divine, the human, and the animal, would exploit deceit and trickery to overcome all obstacles or opponents. In the struggle for survival, the trickster is both iconoclast and tribal/cultural hero; he destroys in order to transform and re-create.

As conceived by its author, the trickster of this tale [*Griever: An American Monkey King in China*] is first and foremost a person of the capable imagination, and the reader is never quite certain whether many of his whimsical and outrageous acts are real or merely mental. Griever de Hocus, an irreverent exchange-program teacher at Zhou Enlai University in Tianjin, "is a mixed-blood tribal trickster, a close relative to the old mind monkeys; he holds cold reason on a lunge line while he imagines the world. With colored pens, he thinks backward, stops time like a shaman, and reverses intersections, interior landscapes. The lines and curves in his pictures are dance, meditation moves, those silent gestures in an opera scene."

Griever liberates a flock of chickens from the knife of an open market butcher, winning for himself the abiding companionship of Matteo Ricci, a spirited rooster. On a crowded bus of the Chinese city, he demands from unresponding Communist cadres a seat for an old lady. "'Confucius would give his seat to an old woman,' he insists. 'Communist cadres, on the other hand, took the best seats and called it a cultural revolution.'"

The story's constant reference to traditional Peking opera is etched in the names of the Chinese characters: Wu Chou (martial clown), a gatekeeper; Hua Lian (painted face), a blind caretaker of a park; Hester Hua Dan (flower maiden), a translator who had an affair with the hero. In specific echo to "The Journey to the West," the classic Chinese novel of pilgrimage which in turn has inspired several popular operas still in the repertoire, Griever is named the Monkey King, while a displaced hog-trader and a wanderer appear as Pigsie and Sandie.

When Griever intervened on the bus for the woman, "people watched him from a cultural distance, but their laughter was not unkind. Several children stared at his outsized nose." Cultural distance is indeed a prominent theme of the book: the chasms of language, appearance, behavior, history and world perception. It is a distance that separates the Americans from the Native Americans, the Americans from the Chinese, the contemporary Chinese from their ancestors and from their liminal counterparts—the sociopolitical or miscegenatic pariahs.

For the People's Republic, American educators, advisers, and traders seem to represent a new breed of secular missionaries—strident in their gospel of commerce, technology, and freedom, insistent in the gratification of their own inquisitiveness, and indifferent in the face of indigenous fears or desires. "Gloome wanted to know more about plastic surgeons; Jack and Sugar Dee continued their search for information about lesbianism in socialist states; Carnegie, on the other hand, proposed a heterosexual union with the translator." To such queries the obligatory reply of a cautious but not wholly uncomprehending proletariat must be: "Our new leaders have studied these problems and will report on them soon."

Much of the American experience of the New Post-Cultural Revolution China is related with devastating comic irony. The sights, sounds and smells of the land are often unerringly captured by the author's lean, laconic prose. Griever's ordeal of using a public toilet on the train should elicit the smiles and tears of recognition by all non-native travelers of China. The translated inanities of the Tianjin mayor's speech on national day are rendered flawlessly.

The adventures or misadventures of the hero continue to poke fun at both the ridiculous rigidities of socialist conventions and the romantic myopia of the visitor. Encountering a truckload of criminals (condemned rapists, murderers, and dope dealers), Griever, calling himself Sun Wukong, White Earth Monkey King, demands their release in the name of Wei Jingsheng, the celebrated editor still jailed (in real life) for his outspoken advocacy of freedom and human rights. When the authorities refuse, Griever hijacks the truck and frees the prisoners, only to have most of them shot by the pursuing soldiers.

In the antecedent Chinese classic, the human pilgrim's disciple was called Mind Monkey (*xinyuan*) not only because he was daring and imaginative, but also because restless intelligence, according to Buddhist wisdom, must be constructively harnessed. The obstreperous ape's good works did serve the human community. The American Version here seems useful only for creative parody, and one wonders whether these two notions of the trickster also betoken "cultural distance."

Gerald Vizenor with Joseph Bruchac (interview date 1987)

SOURCE: "Follow the Trickroutes: An Interview with Gerald Vizenor," in *Survival This Way: Interviews with American Indian Poets,* Sun Tracks and the University of Arizona Press, 1987, pp. 287-310.

[*In the interview below, Vizenor discusses his ideas on language, the role of storytelling in Native American culture, and the role of the trickster in Native American literature.*]

Since his first publications, Gerald Vizenor has been recognized as a multifaceted writer. His books include collections of haiku poetry, short stories, a novel, reworkings of Anishinabe traditional tales, and several nonfiction works. A member of the White Earth Reservation, his teaching has taken him to the University of Minnesota, the University of California at Berkeley, the Southwest and, just prior to this interview, China.

The interview with Gerald Vizenor took place on one of those cool but sunny days which characterize Berkeley, California. There Vizenor and his wife, Laura Hall, were living while he taught for a semester at the University of California. Just back from mainland China, Vizenor and his wife were staying in a small apartment piled high with books—some on shelves, some as yet unpacked. As we drank tea and talked, I thought how much Vizenor is like his trickster heroes, a man always in motion, rooted and rootless, his eyes flashing with wry humor as he speaks.

"Auras on the Interstate"

follow the trickroutes
homewardbound in darkness

noise tired
from the interstates

trucks whine through our families
places of conception

governments raze
half the corners we have known

houses uprooted
sacred trees deposed
municipal machines
plow down our generation vines
tribal doorsteps

condominium cultures
foam low
stain the rivers overnight

thin auras
hold our space in dreams
cut the interstates
from the stoop
bedroom window ruins

noise tired

we are laced in dark arms
until morning

—Gerald Vizenor

[*Bruchac:*] *I'm pleased you began with that poem. It leads into a question I feel is central to your work—migration and the sense of movement. There are references to motion, roads, travels, and even pilgrimages throughout your writing. Why is this so and what do those motions and migrations mean to you?*

[Vizenor:] Life is not static. Philosophically, I think we should break out of all the routes, all the boxes, break down the sides. A comic spirit demands that we break from formula, break out of program, and there are some familiar ways to do it and then some radical or unknown ways. I suppose I am preoccupied with this theme because the characters I admire in my own imagination and the characters I would like to make myself be break out of things. They break out of all restrictions. They even break out of their blood. They break out of the mixture in their blood. They break out of invented cultures and repression. I think it's a spiritual quest in a way. I don't feel that it's transcendence—or escape as transcendence. That's not the theme I'm after, but I'm after an idea of the comic, that the adventures of living and the strategies of survival are chances. They're mysteries because they're left to chance. Life is a chance, all life is a chance. And that's a comic spirit. A tragic spirit is to trudge down the same trial, try to build a better path, make another fortune, build another monument and contribute it to a museum and establish more institutions to disguise our mortality. I consider all of that a formula to control and oppress—not evil, not in an evil manner, but it does control. So, I feel this need to break out of the measures that people make.

That's interesting to me because, when we were talking earlier, you mentioned the importance of a sense of place. A sense of place is still meaningful despite the motion?

Well, the place is in imagination, an imaginative landscape. The place isn't really on the earth because it'll change. But I think you need a place to attach to in moments of fear and detachment and confusion, a place that's familiar, a dream place. I think it's an *oral traditional* place, which means that it's greater than reality and it's greater than a material place you would find on the earth—this is more than just an intersection. It's a universal place. If you turn your back on the earthbound place, it will change. The seasons will change it. And surely human beings are going to alter anything you ever want to remember as a sacred place. So we take it into imagination, and I don't ever expect any place I've ever been in a spiritual way will ever be the same except in my imagination. So I see the permanence of things in a kind of oral traditional visual place. Now, there is, I think, a spiritual and a political risk in this. It is very impractical. The bulldozers can come and if you're off imagining, you can ignore it. I don't carry this as a life philosophy, but in response to your question.

You have to strike a balance between an actual physical connection to a physical life on this physical earth and the imaginative connection which, in some ways, sustains you even when the physical reality changes or breaks down—or is taken away by the bulldozer. What is the physical and emotional reality you proceed from and what is the place on earth you carry about with you now in your imagination?

That's very nice. Let me get there slightly indirectly. My father moved from the reservation to Minneapolis. I went around to hang out for a few minutes at all the places I had ever lived in the city. When I went to do this, less than ten years ago, I found that the places I had lived up until I went to college at the University of Minnesota, more than half were under cement. They were interstates, they had been razed. I thought, "My God, my past doesn't exist." I don't exist with respect to a geographical place. I saw this in myself and I've also written about in other people. Marleen American Horse, for example, a fictional name but a real person who comes from North Dakota. Her place is under the reservoir. She doesn't have a home place anymore. But they exist, our past intersections, in my imagination. And anyway, I say to myself, everything out there is like television. They'll change the channel and it will be a different place, they'll redesign it. I have to separate what is mine by way of connections to the earth and what is "television." Most of what I've seen in the world is television—I mean, the world is television.

In the most romantic sense, there's a small grove of cedar in the Chippewa National Forest in northern Minnesota that is a very special place. I can't tell you why. There's no particular genealogical or geographical significance to it other than the fact that cedar is significant to religion in the tribal sense. But I found that cedar on a walk, a lovely place. I think of it often and I am connected to it. Somebody may have cut it down, conceivably, but it may still be there. *Physically,* I haven't been there for two years. There's another place at White Earth Reservation. It's on a hill right outside of White Earth, the St. Benedict Catholic Cemetery. That's a genealogical connection, historical, tribal-historical, a family place. There are family members buried there, Vizenors and Beaulieus, and right at the top of the hill there's a plot with several Beaulieus. It's the end of rolling woodlands and the beginning of the plains. From that hill you can see infinity. That's special place; it represents, obviously, the Catholic Church Mission, conflicts of culture, religion, blood, geographies, everything, and that tension is not debilitating. That kind of tension in blood and in history is a stimulation, a chance to survive and prevail in good humor. I'm not oppressed by that. I'm stimulated. And that's special place. And

most bodies of water, being on most bodies of water is a stimulation.

Some questions have come to me as a result of reading your work and thinking about it for a number of years. The first has to do with certain words or phrases you've coined. I think of these as they show up in the titles of some of your books: "Tribal Histories," "Wordarrows." What do you mean by terms such as these. Why do you coin them and how do they work?

I like to imagine words, imagine metaphors not theories, so that the ideas and images are not stereotyped. The word *"indian,"* for example: I try to avoid it in almost all of my writing. Where I've used *indian,* I've identified it as a problem word in some writing or italicized it in others. I think it ought to be lower-case italicized everywhere. It is one of those troublesome words. It doesn't mean anything, it is a historical blunder, and has negative associations. So I try to avoid the word in writing by referring the reader to the tribal people or "tribal histories" rather than *indian* histories to try to avoid some of the problems. So, some of the words I imagine or invent or combine are ways to avoid the traps, the historical traps. "Wordarrows" is an obvious metaphor for the cultural and racial tensions between tribal and European cultures and it's a verbal device. "Socioacupuncture" is another one of my words, or neologisms, as the critics might say. I'm rather pleased with that, borrowing an Asian theme. That's the right pressure at the right place at the right time and tricksters are marvelous at that, especially tribal tricksters. You apply just the right humor and the right pressure at the right moment to convince or persuade or to achieve something. I used that as a theme in my filmscript *Harold of Orange*. He actually has a school of socioacupuncture. What they learn in that school is how to raise foundation money and how to play it right to the foundations. The problem is that, while I may be able to write about this, I've been an absolute failure at getting any foundation money myself. Perhaps what I've done is so advanced that foundation people don't trust me and say, "Oh no, we're on to his game." That's a good question. I like playing with words and I think part of it is a mixed blood tribal effort at "deconstruction." I want to break the language down, I want to re-imagine the language. It's the same as breaking out of boxes. I still haven't broken very far out of grammar. I've broken out of the philosophies of grammar, English language grammar, but I haven't broken out of the standard grammatical structure. I guess I don't feel a powerful need to do that and I also think that if I broke that far I just wouldn't have any reading audience at all. I don't have much as it is! The more unfamiliar it becomes, the less possibility of finding a reader. But I do break out of the philosophy of the grammar by trying to avoid most modifiers. If the noun or action is not clear in itself I won't modify it with "l-y's." I also like to run on images when pursuing an idea with mythic associations. When there is action, most of my sentences are short and direct. When a scene is associated with dream and with transcendence, with a shift in time, something magical, or mysterious, or mythic, or when I'm drawing upon traditional sources, the sentences are compound, they're run on. I try to dissolve all grammar, any interruptions in the imagistic flow.

I had a sense of that in your work but I hadn't seen it as clearly as you've just expressed it. The idea of the shaman, the trickster, the medicine person, appears to be central to your work. What is the place of the shaman-trickster-medicine man in your writing and how does that character work as a symbol of the writer?

I think a number of people have pointed out before that the writer can be a shaman and trickster. I think that writers in general are tricksters in the broadest sense of disruption. I don't think it's worth writing, for myself, unless you can break up a little bit. I don't think it's worth the energy unless the formulas can be broken down, unless the expectations of the reader are disrupted, because I think writing is revolutionary, radical in behavior. It's radical in action, it's disruptive in the social and cultural values. That's trickster's business. The tragic risks all humans run are associated with their terminal creeds. They focus too narrowly, they derive too much pleasure and comfort from simple verbal formulas, simple rituals of transportation and movement and direction. So, as a result, I believe people who control their lives in such terminal ways are vulnerable, highly vulnerable to oppression, to violence, to totalitarian and authoritarian systems, colonial administration, the Bureau of Indian Affairs. So, the tricksters in all my work, everywhere, and, in one character or another, disrupt the ambitions of people, contradict, unsettle, and unglue the creeds. No trickster I have ever written about is evil, no trickster I've written about has ever taken advantage of weakness; my imagined tricksters are compassionate and comic.

When the Trickster confronts the Gambler, for example, and defeats him, it is not through becoming like him?

No, he doesn't take anything from him, doesn't gain anything. It's not a competitive act. And I have tricksters who make fun of themselves. Now that's a little more complicated because that's a form of masturbation. How can you be controlled by something and then break it down yourself? That's probably the highest development of humans, when individuals see their own folly.

Having just been in the Southwest, I think of the way sacred clowns make fun of themselves even as they act out an important role. I see that in your trickster characters—the clown crows, other central actors in the journeys which take place in your poems and stories.

Let me borrow two ideas: in a tragic worldview people are

rising above everything. And you can characterize Western patriarchal monotheistic manifest-destiny civilizations as tragic. It doesn't mean they're bad, but they're tragic because of acts of isolation, their heroic acts of conquering something, always overcoming adversity, doing *better than* whatever, proving something, being rewarded for it, facing the risks to do this and usually doing it alone and almost always at odds with nature. Part of that, of course, is the idea of the human being's divine creation as superior. The comic spirit is not an opposite, but it might as well be. You can't act in a comic way in isolation. You have to be included. There has to be a collective of some kind. You're never striving at anything that is greater than life itself. There's an acceptance of chance. Sometimes things *just happen* and when they happen, even though they may be dangerous or even life-threatening, there is some humor. Maybe not at the instant of the high risk, but there is some humor in it. And it's a positive, compassionate act of survival, it's getting along. Now there's good and bad philosophical and economic considerations to both points of view, but tribal cultures are *comic* or mostly comic. Yet they have been interpreted as tragic by social scientists; tribal cultures have been viewed as tragic cultures. Not tragic because they're "vanishing" or something like that, but tragic in their worldview—and they're *not* tragic in their worldview. Only a few writers among the social scientists have seen this, say Karl Kroeber and Denis Tedlock, people who understand stories real well, who understand the comedy, the play, the chance, the ritual and festive connections to things universally. So I make that distinction, that the trickster is in a comic world, surviving by his wits, prevailing in good humor. He's in a collective, hardly ever in isolation. When he is in isolation, he's almost always in trouble, in a life-threatening situation he has to get out of through ritual or symbolic acts. Through reversals he has to get back to connections to imagination, to people, to places.

For example in the Anishinabe story when Manabozho is swallowed by the great fish and then helped by Chipmunk who chews the way out?

Yes, you have to restore some connection. You can't just rise above that by yourself like the tragic hero would without any help.

These days the tragic hero dies in the whale's belly after giving a great speech.

That's it! (laughs)

I like the way this conversation is flowing.

It almost makes sense. We are at some risk here of actually making sense!

What about the various animals which appear in your writ-

ing? It seems that in your poems and stories animals and people not only intercept each other and interact, but in some ways they are almost interchangeable.

Yes. It is the obvious tribal connection. That animals are not lower in evolutionary status. In all the woodland stories animals are significant beings. A language is shared, some humans remember the language, especially shamans, and there are many stories about intermarriage or relationships between humans and animals. Notice what happens to the language: children, contemporary children, use metaphors about animals in a very affectionate and humanistic way. They're in the family, all kinds of animals, even imaginary ones. But as soon as they become *rational,* in school, when they're obligated in their intellectual growth and the emphasis upon a philosophy of grammar, cause and effect, time, logical and rational, they start using negative metaphors for animals. We all do that. "Bird-brain" and so on. Almost all the references to animals we have make it appear as if we must be incredibly self-conscious and insecure about our status as humans, that we must deride all other life. "Like a snake," "like a chicken," "like a pig," all these negative references.

The thing I'm getting at, in **Bearheart,** to choose an example, is seen in the woman who has sex with two boxers. Now some readers find that pornographic, extremely obscene and disgusting. Bestiality. Well, it is none of those. What I am doing is simply saying—though there is nothing simple about it—that there isn't anything wrong, is there, with a human being expressing some love of a physical and emotional kind for animals. There are tribal stories everywhere and I use some variations of those stories. Characters tell those stories within my writing about those relationships with animals.

Animals that are very important to me are bear, squirrel, dog, and several birds. Crow. Cedar Waxwing is a very special kind of totem. I have felt in my life a kind of communication with Cedar Waxwing and Crow and Squirrel and Bear and Dog. These are either animals that I have felt tremendous fear or tremendous love for an emotional attachment, involvement, conversation, at one time or another. In all of my writing you'll see that Bear appears.

What does the bear mean to you? Does the bear fit into your work as a metaphor, or perhaps not as a metaphor but as the protean character of the person at the center of your vision, your imagination, as a sort of shape-shifter?

Oh yes, it is the great interior darkness of everything. It is the greatest power. We must all want to be bears. If we could be anything it should be bears. I say that, too, intellectually, knowing as most tribal people did that bears are skeletally and in muscular structure more like humans. And they play like humans. They chatter and talk. They're unpredictable and quick-witted. They even masturbate. They're like us and

they're in us *and we're in them.* We're in the bear. We're in the bear's maw. Galway Kinnell has this fantastic poem, "The Bear," where the persona crawls inside the bear to sleep and be warm as it freezes overnight.

Certain other things turn up frequently in your work. One of those is cedar itself. What is the role of cedar for you? Why is it so important?

It's a ceremonial, burning cedar. The center of the idea of cedar is that it purifies and protects, and the smoke will restore a balance. My experience with it comes through culture, linguistics, and practice. I can't answer scientifically about cedar smoke, but I have heard someone say that it has something to do with ionization, rather like standing near a waterfall where there is higher negative ionization so it is more relaxing. So there may be properties in the environment which are altered by it, but it has drawn us all to it. There's a power in the word and it's good word. It works everywhere and I draw people together with it, use it as a sacred reference. It doesn't require any iconography. It requires no symbols. It requires nothing. You don't even have to say anything. You just burn a little of it and it'll do the rest. To be truly comical about it, it's the ultimate in deconstruction. (laughs) It's a little puff of smoke. You don't need any language about it. So, if I draw upon it between characters, you can explain a lot of things about people in the way they use it or abuse it. In Cedarfaire, for example, people have made a business out of it. But it doesn't make any difference. You can sell it as they do. They don't understand anything about it, but it still works. Unlike icons. Do you suppose it could be the same as a plastic crucifix, or a figure of Mary has equal power? These are symbols, they don't have any aromatic power. But it's close. You can market all that stuff and make a lot of money about it, even have it glow in the dark. But if you believe in it, it still works. It's irresistible. But the powerful part of it for me is that it can be a ceremonial without icons and language. There isn't very much else you can do. You can bleed yourself, you can have a vision. It's possible to sing without ceremony and words. Sound things, you can sound as animals. But there isn't very much else we can do that has such a powerful ceremonial connection to so many people in this country, tribal people. So you can't abuse it. It works without the language and the ritual and the icons.

Lance Henson told me that burning cedar as the sun rises is the first ceremony a Cheyenne child is taught.

Is that so? I was told a wonderful story by a woman while I was teaching classes at the John F. Kennedy University. They were very earnest and eager to be saved by somebody. One woman got very angry and told a story about Rolling Thunder organizing a sunrise ceremony in the Santa Cruz mountains. They all paid about fifteen or twenty bucks to go to this ceremony—in advance. They all got there before dawn in the dark and climbed up the mountain in the fog and the cold. They waited and waited and Rolling Thunder didn't show. And that was the end of her story. She had finally unburdened herself of this terrible thing that was done to them and she felt cheated. I said, "So?" She said, "He didn't show!" I said, "Well, did the sun rise?" She said, "Well, of course." And I said, "Well, it just goes to show that you didn't need him."

The same thing goes with cedar.

That's a great trickster story. (laughter) Can you tell me a bit about your own Chippewa background, how your knowledge of Chippewa practices and beliefs has come into your writing?

Mostly through stories. I've never, in any way, lived anything like a traditional life, whatever that might have been. My contact with that is through elders. The closest would be my great-uncle Clement Beaulieu, John Clement Beaulieu, and my grandmother who is a good storyteller. I wouldn't characterize her as being traditional, but she's a wonderful storyteller. Clem, or John Clement, was not only a fine storyteller with a trickster's imagination, but there was a calmness and a great generosity about him. He lived at many places, White Earth and Cass Lake, and he lived at Red Lake for a time. He had several little shacks at Bena. He would buy one, fix it up, and give it away—and go get another one. He would do this because people around him had greater need. He never talked about it. These are stories I heard around him. He didn't boast about it. Part of the way he looked at it was that he was getting bored with the place anyway. So it was just as well to give it away. He had more interesting things to do. Clem was an introduction to language, to an imaginative resolution between mixed blood. A rich imagination about everything—women, animals, conflict, governments. He served in the First World War in Europe. I would say that of any one person, I was more stimulated by the possibilities of imagining things in a certain way because of Clem. He directed me . . . no, I shouldn't say he directed me. I was directed by things he said to pursue some loose ends of things that he understood pretty well. As a result I met a lot of people and found out things. I found out things about shamanism—I'm not a shaman, but I understood the energy. I wasn't afraid of people and I think that was helpful because practically every healer I talked with was pleased that I wasn't. Although I am sure they also had great fun playing with people who were afraid, too. Those were ways in which I found things out. I must say I found out a tremendous amount of things about this tension from non-Indians who have lived with, been around, admired, hated, married, divorced, been with, about, and engaged directly with Indians. I don't know how to say how much I learned, but the picture would *never* be complete for me without their view.

I had another insight into that in reading some stories about a woman who is Rumanian, becomes an American citizen, a Yale Ph.D. in Chinese. She's one of the first scholars to be in China in the late '70s. She was talking about the indirect way you have to learn about China. You can't learn about it directly. You have to learn about it *partly* through the way non-Chinese respond to the Chinese. I see that has been an insight for me, too. I have learned a lot from the way people have responded to me. I still do. I think I may have tremendous insight into that. I think that part of my insight is a bit cruel because I turn it into kind of a counter ideology.

What is storytelling itself?

Well, there is storytelling without the pen, the book. That is probably easier to explain than storytelling. My own feeling is that sometimes it works and sometimes it doesn't. When it does, I notice that teller and listener-participant are either willing to be surprised—they have subscribed to a surprise, they are present and loyal participants ready to be surprised—or, knowing that the story will lead them nowhere, they accept it. They're not audience and that's important. The story doesn't work without a participant. There are a lot of people who walk around Berkeley and they're crazy. They haven't found a listener in ten or twenty years. And it's sad because there *are* stories, but those stories are now just floating loose. You bump into everybody and try to shed yourself of the stories because they're really burden stories. The humor is gone from them—they're desperate stories and you don't want to listen to that any more. So there has to be a participant and someone has to listen. I don't mean listening in the passive sense. You can even listen by contradiction. You can even listen by saying "Bullshit!" if that's in good humor and not in a negative sense. So that's really critical in storytelling. The storyteller's properties have to tie in metaphorically to some kind of experience. And now I have to borrow from Hymes and Tedlock in observing Zuni storytellers, and I really celebrate their work so much and praise them so highly for making the simple observation that the storyteller *is an artist*. Right? Not, as Tedlock says, just a conduit of tradition. And the stories vary—now who would have though that? Of course all stories vary! There's not two stories alike and that's the tragic thing which has happened to stories. They have been published and appear standardized. So young people come to these stories, especially in tribal areas where there's not a rich and centered traditional life as there is in the Southwest. In most of the woodlands states there's little traditional connection and oral tradition left and there's a lot of mixed bloods. There a lot of young people are offered these published stories in classrooms through well-meaning teachers who want to do a good curriculum on Indians and to help their Indian students discover themselves and their traditions. But they do it through a kind of standardized liturgy, as if it were scripture.

Static?

Yes, there's no life in it. It's just memorization, it's no story at all—and I think that stuff kills imagination because it's leading to people believing if you depart from the stories you depart from the scripture. So they don't listen to you anymore, and they believe you're cheating them or you're dishonest or you have some ulterior motive or purpose that's not honorable. That's shame because imagination is so rich there shouldn't be any story that's limited by the text. And even a published text is not a limited story. The healthiest way to read is to look upon this as a possibility of the story.

You've pointed out something very interesting here—the spiritual nature of the story itself. By "spiritual" I mean a carrying of a kind of power so that a person can be burdened by a story when that story can't be told because the participant audience has disappeared. I think that's a very crucial point.

I don't know where we find the audience now. Once in a while I find it as a teacher. When I'm around nonstudents, people I trust and I'm familiar with, we always exchange stories. You're just ready for it. And I say, give me your best story! You know that. People call *you* long-distance late at night just to tell you a story. You're a wonderful participant.

Can you remember any particular stories your Uncle Clement told which were particularly significant to you?

He had a lot of stories about priests and the way people responded to priests, the tricks they pulled on them. Feeding them wild game they wouldn't eat themselves. I'm a little reluctant to . . .

I'm not asking you to retell a story here and now. Just asking about the sort of content and the context.

Oh, I see! I was getting a little nervous about repeating one.

I get nervous about such things, too. I should have asked the question a bit better.

No, no, I understand it. Two general contents. One is the stories of magic and faith healing and how things just mysteriously happened, how people appeared and disappeared. He'd have lots of those. Stories about people going hunting who would disappear and reappear. There would be mythic events taking place in unusual circumstances. Severe weather, for example. Somehow people would do remarkable things in this. They would come through or appear in half the normal time and show no physical wear and tear.

A seven-days' journey in a day or something like that?

Exactly. Time would be dissolved. The dissolution of time

and out-of-body possibilities. He didn't tell these, though, in emphasis of this being unusual. This was just built in as ordinary circumstance. It was just after the story you would have to ask a few questions. The other category was stories of resolution of tensions and the play between the colonists—and I would include the government and the Church—and Indians. Then, the tension also between fullbloods and mixed bloods. Though that tension was different. There was much more play, much harder play in the best sense of the word between mixed bloods and fullbloods.

That rough sort of teasing?

Tease and put down—which I would characterize as more affectionate. Whereas the tension between colonists and Indians, mixed blood or fullblood, didn't lack compassion, but it was manipulative. You wanted to outwit. That was the motivation in imagination. You wanted to outwit either restrictions and bureaucracies or impositions. Whereas with mixed blood and fullblood, it was a duel and had a different character. It was a duel in the tribal sense, a compassionate duel. It wasn't competitive to win or outwit, but it was duel. Actually it was a leveler in a sense.

The competition was as important as who came out on top.

Um-hmm. For example, there's a story—one of my favorites, which I recently retold in a different sense—about the young priest who would thrust his head into a rain barrel. People wondered about that. But some people understood that. You put you head under water and thump the sides and there's a tremendous sense of distance. You could stand up and look across the prairie, but you put your head in a rain barrel and you can go farther. You can thump your way all the way to Asia in a rain barrel. So some people were taking bets on how long the priest could hold his head under. It was related apparently to the priest's imagination and what he was thinking at the time. The point was that, if the priest was concentrating on some imaginative event while his head was under water, he didn't need as much oxygen. So they timed him and took bets, spread it out over a few days and got an average and then took bets on him.

I think one of the reasons I wanted to have you describe the kinds of stories your Uncle Clem used was to get a description of the kind of stories you use. I see a very direct connection between his categories and yours. Miraculous journeys, conflicts between white and native, mixed blood and fullblood.

That's true. That's true. I have to say something else, though. Sometimes the interactions and the connections between people tell their own stories. I'm thinking of a little community named Bena. It's a mixed community, Indian and white. It's on Lake Winnebigoshis. Clem lived there, and I spent a fair amount of time visiting him and made some other friends there. The most incredible things went on in that place. Even if you weren't a storyteller you would be made one if you paid attention. You would have to be an absolute idiot not to—if you weren't arrogant and just holding yourself above them. Crazy things that went on there. There was a deputy sheriff, for example, who lived in a house trailer. He was the only law enforcement person in this village and he wasn't Indian. When I visited him he had dogs around the place and a dozen broken-down machines from snowmobiles to tractors. I knocked on the door and he opened it and dogs rushed out. None of them were angry, they were all friendly lap dogs of various sizes. So I felt pretty good about this sheriff. I knew this was going to be an unusual sheriff. Nice looking, balding man with a half-ass smile as if he wasn't really there, as if he was already ready to tell you it was a joke. He invited me in and I swear to god there were hundreds of pounds of chicken bones everywhere. I crunched on them as I walked across the floor. That was his primary diet. I'm just leading up to one sentence which focuses on this man. I said, "Well, didn't they call you that I was coming?" And he said, "I don't have a phone." And I said, "But you're the sheriff, the law enforcement officer here, and you don't have a phone?" He said, "Naw, I tried one for a while. But I had all these people calling me up with domestic problems, and I couldn't do anything about people's personal problems. So I figured if I took the phone out I wouldn't be bothered. If somebody wants to drive way back here, crawl through the dogs and the chicken bones to talk to me about it, it's probably serious." He also said, "I don't make many arrests around here." Now you have to understand this area has the highest arrest rate in the state. They called it the "Little Chicago" of Minnesota. But he said, "I don't like to arrest people. Most of the people I'd have to arrest around here are drunk." He wasn't just referring to Indian, he meant Indian and white. And he said, "If I have to arrest them, I have to put them in the back of my car and then I have to drive them twenty miles to Cass Lake and half the time they throw up in the back seat and the county won't pay me anything to clean up my back seat. So I won't arrest anybody." My point is that the sheriff was a wonderful human being who had worked out his own comic trickster resolutions to life. He was a living story. You'd have to be totally blind not to see some of these stories.

I like the term "living story." It relates strongly to what you do with your characters. There's a direct connection, in many cases, between your characters and real-life people. You draw people you know—people I know—into your stories. How did you come to that?

Part of that is just the way I tell stories. You put each other down in that playful trickster way and that's mutual. The difference is that I'm a writer and most of my friends aren't. So I have a slight advantage. We exchange the same kind of subtle trickster put-downs, but I figure out a way to put it into print.

Yes, there's satire, of course, name a work that doesn't have satire. Any work that's worth a shit has got to have some satire. If I was just getting even with somebody, I already was even in play. And *even* is a good thing. That's a problem, because people suggest getting even is not a good thing. But it's just part of the give and take in the play. It's part of breaking down the terminal beliefs, so I don't look upon "getting even" as a negative thing. I know the term has negative associations and I don't like to use it much, but "getting even" is really positive energy. It's an honest, direct, playful engagement. You can go ahead and get into print and knock me down if you want—but that's not what I'm about. I really celebrate people I love in what I write. I don't have enemies that I get even with in my work. Not in my imaginative work.

I sense a lot of objectivity in your journalistic pieces. People are allowed to speak with their own voices, events are allowed to unfold without a lot of editorializing.

Yes, I've done that with the AIM leaders, for example. Even though I've been very critical of some of them and been uneasy about a number of things, I let them speak for themselves and don't try to snooker it or hoodwink or trick in the worst sense of the word—manipulate things so I have the power and control.

I think it's difficult to write with the sort of clarity you use. I notice, too, you have a way of layering images and experiences. Things keep building up, almost by accretion, like sediment. How did you come to that particular form?

Hmm, let me think out loud about that. I think in writing, when I come to say it directly, usually the first noun or verb in this layered scene or image, the first reference to action or description, is usually the obvious or categorical one. Then, I think, I break it down by additions or expand on it. I make it broader, expand the possibilities of it or even contradict it, which, I believe, expands it. Rather than simply modifying it. I think then you reduce it. Ah, here I'm close—if I write something which is categorical there's clarity in that on the printed page. There's clarity in that as a sentence, but it isn't clear, there's more to it. Now you could say in expository writing, "for example" or "on the other hand" there are exceptions. You could quote someone, you could line up other points of view. But in imaginative prose I think I want the mind to go visually, so there's a category, comma, then even a few phrases or words which are variations, contradictions, or expansions of the category. So that the image, the event, the action, or description is broader than what is grammatically allowed.

I think it's exemplary of some of your best work. I also wonder, too, how much effect the writing of the Far East has had on you. I know you have written haiku and been published in major anthologies of haiku. I know some people think of you as one of the better haiku writers in the United States.

Really? I'm pleased to hear that.

How does haiku affect your sort of image?

Oh, I see! The haiku is the subtlest image. No need to break down the doors here because the house is open to dreamscapes. I have a new book of haiku, *Matsushima*. I think it is some of my best in a long while, a few of the images there are the best I've ever done. In it, for the first time, I've written an introduction on what I think haiku is. It's the first time I've ever done that, because I don't think we ought to get critically involved in explaining haiku. Either it works or it don't! But I've gone against that and decided to make my own statement because I don't think I want to come back to think like that again. In it I fool around with ideas from some deconstruction critics and structuralists. I say that haiku may be an unusual form of deconstruction. You reduce it to the briefest brush stroke and you don't conclude anything. Everything is open. What happens, if it happens, is that the reader takes it in and the words disappear. It becomes a visual event, which of course is the heart of a storyteller. The power of a storyteller—the words disappear in visual memory through metaphor, gestures, animals, birds, seasons, tropisms trip the visual memory and your own imagination. The haiku does that, if the haiku does that in one image and the listener-participant makes that a personal experience-event from his or her own experience, it's deconstructed. The words disappear.

I think you've already answered the question I was going to ask about why you came to haiku and what relation the haiku has to your consciousness as a Native American poet.

Yes. Well, I came to it physically in Japan when I was in the Army. I was delighted with haiku. It wasn't until I got back and was in the University of Minnesota that I studied Asian Civilization and ultimately ended up in graduate school in Asian Studies. I had a wonderful teacher, Edward Copeland, at the University of Minnesota. I want to tell this story because it is very brief and it was a remarkable experience with a teacher. I'm sure everyone has had one lesson, one sensitive profound experience with a teacher. I took his class on Japanese Literature in translation. It was in the spring term and the trees were budding outside the window. Obviously, the trees and birds were more interesting than the subject, much as I liked the subject. Copeland, about the third or fourth week of class—a very sensitive and gentle scholar—wrote a note and left it on my desk as he concluded class and walked out. I opened it up and he'd written: "The past month during class period you've been looking out the window. What do you see?" I read this as a real criticism; obviously, he'd caught me daydreaming and we're in this business for grades and I

liked the subject and I liked him and I'd disappointed him. So I wrote him a haiku, a very risky thing to do, though I didn't think of it as that at first. But when I left it on his desk and walked out the door and was halfway down the stairs, I was in terror. I was totally vulnerable. I'd made a stupid error. Can you imagine trusting a university teacher with a subtle poem? Aggh! I was so disgusted with myself that I had done such a dumb thing. I was embarrassed and humiliated and I wanted to grab it back, but I didn't. I suffered through the weekend and next Monday tried to be an attentive student to overcome this vulnerability. He left a note on my desk and answered my poem *in a linking haiku!* It brought tears to my eyes, this wonderful sensitive man. I still love him and speak of him and see him. That trust and loving relationship led not only to A's in class, but we put a book together, my first publication in haiku. It had a preface of seasonal Japanese poems translated by Copeland, and then my original haiku. *Raising The Moon Vines* was the title of the book.

Was that your first book?

No, just a few months before that I had worked as a social worker at the state reformatory and I published—they had a print shop—for about $35 two hundred copies of a small saddle-stitched haiku book, *Two Wings The Butterfly*. But *Raising The Moon Vines* was the first serious book from a publisher, and it was reissued a couple of times.

What do you see going on now in Native American writing?

In prose writing, I see there's much more sophistication in reference to traditional events and experiences. By that I mean it's not drawn ideologically any more—although that was not so in Momaday and Silko. I think now any theme is open, any theme, any structure, any style, and it can still be seen and felt as Indian literature. I've been developing some other ideas and critical thinking about Indian literature. What is Indian literature? How can you tell the difference? So what's the difference that you can perceive with a critical theory and write about in some way that is Indian literature and that would suggest it is different from other literature? I'm calling it "mythic verism." Mythic truth. Not just myths. There are myths everywhere. But mythic verism. Here I'm talking about my own work, also. There is something alive in the work which gives it a truth. Now that is something which comes from a metaphorical use of traditional energy and references. Momaday has it. Silko has it. You can do it through symbols, you can do it allegorically, you can do it through dialogue, you can do it in all kinds of ways. There's no limit to the ways you can make reference to traditional events, tribal events. That doesn't make it, though. It is the attitude of the characters which gives it the mythic verism and that attitude is comic. That's my theme. It is something that is alive and that is what makes the myth a truth, the way time is handled and resolved, the tension in time, and the sense of comedy or comic spirit through imagination and a collective sense that people prevail and survive, get along, get by. They're not at war with the environment, they're not rising above, and there are no subtle references to manifest destiny, monotheistic superiority. All of that's very subtle, but it's there and I think you can find it and I think we can focus on it and I think we can make a theory of it. There are people who appear to be white but they aren't. You can see in their language and their own conflicts, the way they resolve their conflicts or *avoid* resolving them that there is a comic spirit. You won't find that in much other writing. You can find a comic spirit in other non-Indian literature, but it won't have the same characteristics.

Where are you going with your own writing now?

I'm just about finished with a novel bringing together the Woodland trickster whom I think I understand very well and the Chinese Monkey King whom we met in China. So I have a mixed-blood trickster character who's teaching in China and the only way the Chinese can understand him—because he is in conflict with the bureaucracy and everything—is that he is the Monkey King and they really celebrate this Monkey King who disrupts everything. They love this character. The title is *Griever: An American Monkey King in China*.

The Monkey is also one of the most effective of the styles in the martial arts.

That's right! It's a trickster style. That's very good. I hadn't thought about that. So I draw together the ideas from Chinese opera in it and my character is in conflict and a number of good things come from this—but only because the Chinese can understand him in their own cultural terms as the Monkey King. So what it suggests is the universality of the trickster character. In the future I hope to work on more stories out of Minnesota, trickster things, a collection of stories. One will be in *New America* and one will be in the *North Dakota Quarterly*—the same issue you're going to be in?

Yes.

The character in the story in *New America* is a much wilder trickster. **"Monsignor Missalwait's Interstate."** The main character has bought up a section of an interstate on the reservation and he sets up toll booths.

Roads—and again you're going forward by going backward.

Yes. It begins with a quote. I was horrified when I read that Hawthorn Dairy near Chicago is printing photographs of lost and stolen children on their milk cartons. Now several are doing that, but I was just horrified at the whole idea. A civilization in which children are stolen, what awful energies. These people are so vacant in their connections to other human be-

ings that they have to steal it! They're carrion crow, they're vultures, they don't have any connections left. It has to be the leading worst primary response to the worst experiences of materialism and capitalism. Anyway, I quote that and my Monsignor, a pretend Monsignor—the Tribe gave him that name because he has a vision and consecrated himself— Monsignor Missalwait says in response to this stolen children Hawthorn Dairy thing, "Listen, when milk cartons bear the pictures of stolen children, then civilization needs a better Trickster. Look, white people drink too much milk before they come out to play anyway." Listen and Look reversed.

Stanley Trachtenberg (review date 10 January 1988)

SOURCE: "A Trickster in Tianjin," *New York Times Book Review*, January 10, 1988, p. 18.

[*In the his review of* Griever: An American Monkey King in China, *Trachtenberg states that the novel is strengthened by Vizenor's use of language.*]

"Imagination is the real world," claims the mournful clown Griever de Hocus, "all the rest is bad television." Griever, hero of Gerald Vizenor's second novel [*Griever: An American Monkey King in China*], is a Native American of mixed blood who abruptly appears as one of an ill-assorted group of American teachers at a Chinese university in Tianjin. Here his trickster heritage of tribal folklore and myth, not to mention his readiness to dream, helps him to cope with a socialist cadre and the closed society it monitors. For despite the repudiation of the Cultural Revolution, China remains suspicious of foreign devils. At the same time, it struggles with population control and welcomes modernization in the form of plastics, dermabrasion and Western venture capitalism.

Griever screams his rage at these responses into what he calls "panic holes" or turns it into playful wisdom in the manner of the monkey kings that populate China's myths of the poor and oppressed. Like the monkey kings, other animals—bears, bats, spiders, even mosquitoes—are also seen by Griever to help shape human conduct. And so, with a pet rooster for a companion, he follows their lead, playing basketball with hogs and liberating both chickens and political prisoners. Later, he disrupts the opening of an extravagant French restaurant and begins a brief affair with a local translator, a dalliance that leads to tragic consequences when it is discovered by her sinister father, a chain-smoking bureaucrat who conceals his contempt for Westerners behind a snakelike smile. Among the other figures Griever encounters are an enigmatic Russian painter who protects his hands with white mittens while serving a prison sentence hauling coal and an actor-sage who preserves Griever's history on a picture scroll that introduces his adventures with a cloudy but comic shrewdness that sets the tone for much of the novel.

Like his hero, Mr. Vizenor attempts to overcome the stale political realities of a Communist state through the renewal of language. For the characters as well as the reader, his world is laid out like-brush strokes in an ink painting.

It is technology, however, rather than metaphor that finally determines the outcome of the novel. And after a climactic carnival, the story's magical disregard for time and space collapses under the weight of a high-tech escape from the mainland. Griever's often burlesque encounters, like his visionary impulses, reflect his desire to escape rather than confront China's dusty streets and oppressive social conditions. Thus his opposition to injustice eventually dissolves into a mere expression of personal vexation. The real arena for Griever's wild history is poetic dreamscape.

Though grounded in the author's experience as a teacher in China and in extensive historical references that are scrupulously identified in an epilogue, the novel gains its strength more from associations of color and from the play of words than from bare facts. Beyond our need for them, words, as Griever realizes, need us to hold down a sense of place. They also need to take off on their own. When they do, this modestly experimental, often luminous novel, which won the 1986 Illinois State University/Fiction Collective Award, evokes a world that does not mirror but parallels our own.

Dexter Westrum (review date Summer 1988)

SOURCE: Review of *Griever: An American Monkey King in China,* in *Western American Literature,* Vol. XXIII, No. 2, Summer, 1988, p. 160.

[*In the review below, Westrum remarks that Vizenor attempts to keep his readers off balance.*]

Reading Gerald Vizenor one begins to feel the fun of ambivalence. In *Earthdivers,* his finest book, *Darkness in St. Louis Bearheart,* and now *Griever,* Vizenor specializes in the difference between what appears to be and what is; he persists in pointing out that the world is not what we see, nor does it have to be left the way we find it. If authority is out for its own good—as it often is—authority should be tickled into laughing at itself.

If we are confused by his work, our mistake is that we bring our own cultural assumptions about the truth of the established order into Vizenor's world. But Vizenor will not limit himself to our imaginations. His earthdivers, frantic contemporary trickster figures, simply re-imagine the world. They

turn established orders inside out and deconstruct foundations. His Griever is an earthdiver who seeks liberation by dismantling the established order of the Republic of China.

Even though Griever isn't entirely successful, he is not defeated. As he puts it: "We were lost and asked [the Chinese] to make a map in their heads to tell us where they were so we could find out where we were. They know where they are, but we are in the air." And that is the joy of Vizenor's work. The important thing is not to subdue the people who think they know where they are, but to keep them off balance by not taking them as seriously as they take themselves. Griever will not be overcome by reality, but will stay up in the air away from the foundations, savoring delicious ironies where nothing is sacred.

All who would not be defeated can take heart from Vizenor, the work and the man. A blue-eyed Chippewa mixedblood, a tribal person with a strong belief in his own individualism, he knows that the ultimate truth may be made up of so many conflicting truths that the ultimate truth may indeed be false. But that of course is not a reason to keep from believing. His message is simple: "Imagination liberates the mind."

San Francisco Review of Books (review date Winter 1990)

SOURCE: "The American Monkey King at Home," in *San Francisco Review of Books,* Vol. XV, No. 3, Winter, 1990, p. 23.

[*In the following review, the critic provides an overview of Vizenor's works, commenting on the author's varied forms.*]

Complaining about those "wily, more competent Indians" who could use their knowledge of the White Man to make him appear in a bad light, the former head of the Bureau of Indian Affairs Dillon S. Myer wrote to Interior Secretary Douglas McKay in 1953: "[They] are capable of making the Bureau . . . appear as a group of paternalistic bureaucrats who will not allow them to handle their own internal affairs . . . "

Indians are expected to use education as the way out of the misery of poverty and discrimination, and join ranks with those who have helped them. This makes a "good Indian." A "bad Indian" either rejects the offer or uses it to his own ends, which means bucking the status quo.

So what do you do with an Indian who masters the system and then tries to subvert it, using every trick he knows? Rather than run and hide behind the safety of academia (he was professor of literature at the University of Oklahoma last year, following several years at Santa Cruz), Gerald Vizenor has laid himself out in his 1990 autobiographical work *Interior Landscapes*. Vizenor has stirred the literary world, not only with his range but with the excellence of his thought and the dry cutting edge of his insight. He has been praised by Indians and non-Indians alike.

The trail of books behind him ranges from wild magical fantasy (*Bearheart—the Heirship Chronicles*) to gut-wrenching documentary (*Crossbloods*) and from introspective sojourns (*Interior Landscapes*) to near ethnographic documentation (*The People Named Chippewa*). Such variety in writing forms seems at once prolific and insecure. It might appear that Vizenor is trying to fill the library all by himself. Apparently Vizenor has used the art of writing to express as many facets of himself as possible, with a type of creative artistry usually reserved for actors—cowboy in one script, sailor in the next, and so on. Whereas writers are generally supposed to settle on a format and stay put, what Gerald Vizenor has accomplished is a complete documentation of the concerns and hopes of a 20th Century Indian. His desire to convey the twists and turns of Indian mythos is demonstrated in the novels, where his creatures play our the dramas of human desires, foolishness and visions. In *Bearheart* he uses the English language in ways that American writers might never have dreamed. With characters' names like Proude Cedarfair, Perfect Crow, Little Big Mouse, Scintilla Shruggles, Sister Caprice, and Jordan Coward, any presumptions are immediately scrambled. Interactions among these folks range from sensitive encounters to almost pornographically described sexual forays, to outright battles. Underlying this confusion are the themes of Indian intellectual life. The overall effect is to cause one to wonder at the true nature of reality.

This may dislodge the unwary reader from his or her own mythology, and allow alien thoughts to enter. Unchecked, it can lead to a rethinking of morals and values. One might even find an alternative right and wrong. Yet these results can easily be blocked by dismissing them all as mere fiction. History, however, is harder to ignore. As a reporter on the *Minneapolis Tribune*, Gerald Vizenor interviewed Indian leaders of the day as well as politicians and common folk involved in the opposing struggles to control and liberate Indians. *Crossbloods* documents stories, essays, and editorials he produced to give insight into the forces at work within and upon American Indians today. Reporters can be attacked for slanting their stories or coloring the history they record, but it is much harder to argue with the spoken word of oral history.

In *A People Named Chippewa*, Vizenor has brought the truth of the Chippewa to America in their own words. His interviews with tribal members bring their truth to public record, at a time when ethnology and anthropology are denigrated sciences. Entertainment is king today, not fieldwork; yet

Vizenor has used his success to force the issue. His ability to gain acceptance as a noted writer brings a latitude to what his publishers will accept; but when does all of this start to smack of "wily" old Indian? Despite all the finer exposition, the true Gerald Vizenor still seems to be tucked away somewhere, hiding. What he has presented us with are his insights into Indians, non-Indians and the process of cultural warfare. So which kind of Indian is Gerald Vizenor? Whatever kind of Indians there are, perhaps.

Ron Carlson (review date 23 September 1990)

SOURCE: "Tribal Tribulations," in *New York Times Book Review*, September 23, 1990, p. 52.

[*In the following review, Carlson argues that* Crossbloods *is an eclectic but revealing look at contemporary Native American culture.*]

Gerald Vizenor's *Crossbloods: Bone Courts, Bingo, and Other Reports* is, as the title suggests, an eclectic collection of essays and articles written over the last two decades by this prolific author, whose subject matter is Native American life and culture. Mr. Vizenor, a mixed-blood member of the Minnesota Chippewa tribe, has been a reporter and editorial writer for The Minneapolis Tribune and now teaches literature at the University of California, Santa Cruz. He has also written two novels, *Bearheart: The Heirship Chronicles* and *Griever: An American Monkey King in China*, the latter of which won an American Book Award from the Before Columbus Foundation in 1988; beautiful new paperback editions of these books are being published by the University of Minnesota Press along with this new collection.

This is a collection of picked-up pieces. The introduction and the first set of essays, "Crossblood Survivance," are free-flowing polemics that touch on the major issues confronting Native Americans in the United States. "Crossbloods," he says, "are a postmodern tribal bloodline" of part-Indian, part-white individuals, and their economic survival has become interwoven with the development of high-stakes gambling on reservations; the redefinition of treaties and land allotments; fishing and hunting rights; new concepts of entrepreneurship, and other concerns. Bingo, which generates an estimated $3 million to $4 million a year on one reservation alone, is both boon and bane. On the one hand there is all that money; on the other, there are all the problems of gambling and the strong feeling in some corners that bingo runs counter to any sense of tribal heritage.

The longest sustained narrative is the story of Thomas White Hawk, who murdered a jeweler in Vermillion, S.D., in March 1967. This section, **"Capital Punishment,"** shows Mr.

Vizenor's true skill as a reporter as he recounts the crime, the trial and the aftermath in magazine articles he wrote in 1968 and 1970. It would have been better still if there had also been a more complete update on Mr. White Hawk (whose sentence was commuted) and the community of Vermillion.

In fact, the entire second half of the book, composed mainly of short newspaper articles written in the early 70's about tribal matters, would have benefited from current news or updates, especially on the issues of education, the phenomenon of "stolen children" (children who are placed in foster care and adoptive homes in white society), the movement back to the reservation, ideas of natural tribal rights and the American Indian Bank, which was established in Washington almost 20 years ago.

Mr. Vizenor's intriguing essay **"Bone Courts: The Natural Rights of Tribal Bones"** confronts the issue of the hundreds of thousands of tribal bones that now reside in museums and research institutions. He proposes a "Bone Court," in which the bones would be "mediators and narrators" and have the legal right to be represented. He quotes Walter Echo-Hawk, an attorney for the Native American Rights Fund, who said, "If you desecrate a white grave, you wind up sitting in prison. But desecrate an Indian grave, and you get a Ph.D." Mr. Vizenor doesn't offer a way to implement his very moral plan, but his essay is a telling glimpse at a huge injustice.

This collection is confusing at first, because Mr. Vizenor spans so many years on such an array of issues (even using completely different prose styles—from reportorial to academic), but he does offer an unvarnished view of aspects of contemporary tribal culture. "Thirty years ago," he notes, "it was not uncommon to read about tribal people as if they were somnolent cultural artifacts or uncivilized pagans living on wilderness reservations." *Crossbloods*, scattered as it may be, is another step toward rectifying that notion.

Gerald Vizenor with Larry McCaffery and Tom Marshall (interview date January 1992)

SOURCE: "Head Water: An Interview with Gerald Vizenor," in *Chicago Review*, Vol. 39, Nos. 3-4, 1993, pp. 50-4.

[*In the following interview, Vizenor discusses the impact of his experiences in Asia on his writing.*]

As Gerald Vizenor explains in the following interview, the act of going away has allowed him to return home richer as an individual and as a writer. Asia has been especially important in this regard: it was in Japan just after the Korean War that Vizenor experienced his first major literary discovery—haiku. Then, over twenty years later, after having pub-lished numerous books of poetry (including several books of haiku) and journalism, a year teaching in Tianjin, China resulted in Vizenor's second novel, *Griever: An American Monkey King in China.*

We talked with Gerald Vizenor in his office at UC-Berkeley in early January 1992, just a few months after the publication of *The Heirs of Columbus,* a work which, appearing as it did in the face of the quincentennial, announced in no uncertain terms, "I'm not a victim of Columbus." For a mixed-blood Native American, that was quite an assertion. Looking at his own life and that around him, Vizenor continues reshaping it, joined by the trickster who assists him in remembering "how to turn pain and horror into humor."

[*McCaffery:*] *In your novel,* **The Heirs of Columbus,** *you describe Nanabozho, the first trickster and the brother of a stone. Wasn't the Chinese Monkey King also born from a stone?*

[Vizenor:] Indeed he was. In fact, you may remember that in *Griever* I specifically mentioned that the Monkey King, the first version of the Chinese trickster, was born from a stone. I was trying to show how the beginning of life comes from something substantial, like a rock. *Dead Voices* actually opens with the trickster story and goes on for some time about this. You have the trickster brother of the stone that can't move any more, so trickster has to come back all the time and tell him what he has been doing. Eventually he gets more or less pissed off and wants to do his brother in. So he says to the stone, I'm getting sick of this! I mean, I hit you, I try to break you, but I can't do it. How can I kill you? The stone replies, that's easy—just heat me up and then throw cold water on me; I'll break into a thousand pieces. Well, the brother does that and, sure enough, in the early tellings, the trickster-stone bursts into millions of pieces and covers the earth—and today every stone from anywhere on this world is metaphorically from that first break-up of the trickster. So the character in *Dead Voices* collects stones, which represent the metaphors of the stories. They fit the stories, allow her to tell and imagine stories, and give her presence and existence in a story. That's everywhere, always.

Had you already researched the Chinese version of the trickster—that is, the Monkey King—before you went to China? I'm interested, for example, in what connections and differences you found in the presentations of the Chinese and Native American versions of the trickster. It's certainly significant that this figure appears in both cultural stories.

I studied Chinese and Japanese literature in graduate school. I read Arthur Waley's translation of the Monkey King. I have to say, though, that the way it was presented in class as a cultural document made it difficult for me to relate this stuff to my own world. I make this very same argument today about the way tribal stories are represented by anthropologists. The Monkey King that I studied in graduate school didn't connect with me as a trickster until I arrived in China. Up until then it was just this cultural document to me, a folk story.

Obviously, then, learning more about this Chinese Monkey King-Trickster figure wasn't specifically involved in your trip to China. . . .

Not at all. I went because it was a chance. I gave up my tenured position at the University of Minnesota. Then this position in China was open. I had some interests in writing a few situational journalistic pieces about my experiences there for a newspaper. I'd just have to see what would come of this. Maybe nothing would, but depending on what happened, I thought I might be able to do one of these journalistic pieces a month—not travel stuff or magazine writing, but if something interesting was happening, I knew I could make a story out of it.

[Marshall:] Something obviously happened over there to change your mind, because you didn't appear to do anything like that.

No. What happened instead was that in the fall, a month into teaching over there, I was invited to see a production of some of the scenes from the Monkey King opera. That experience changed everything for me. The theater was overflowing with Chinese, of course, and at first I was overwhelmed by the audience—not simply because the place was so jammed but because the audience was dynamic, so completely engaged in the production even though there's no applause. I'm sure everyone in the audience must have changed seats at least twice, maybe more (we, of course, were the only people in the whole place who stayed in the same seats!); people would go out to the lobby to gossip, come back in when their favorite scene was about to be performed, and then rush right up to the stage. Then they'd leave again, and nobody would applaud. At first I was distracted by this rich and powerful dynamic between what was happening on the stage and the audience—and also by the smell of garlic and all these other good things. Of course, what's going on is also revolutionary, but not in this case revisionist or social realism, the way most theatrical productions were in China. In other words, this Monkey King material hadn't been converted to serve the state. The revolutionary state accepted these not as bourgeois spiritual pollution, but as folk culture, original literature that represented the Chinese consciousness. They accepted it for what it was because it was in their soul—and the soul in this case was not dangerous to the Communist Party. This was on-the-street stuff, a bit like puppet theater, not an elitist-Communist Party performance. So there it is. This probably sounds naive on my part, but it's true. And these wonderful distractions with the audience—I started paying attention to the play, and of course it was only then that I

began to recognize all the stuff I had read about the Monkey King. Then, in one of those occasional strokes of insight you get, I suddenly saw the trickster figure. When I saw this stuff performed in this other context, there it was, suddenly alive, and I was thrilled. I knew immediately that I had a book. I didn't know what it was going to be exactly, but I knew I had a book somewhere. When I got back, I still didn't have a book, although I did have a powerful theme—the idea that the only figure in a story who could confront the oppressive bureaucracy and contradictions existing in the People's Republic of China would have to be a mind monkey or trickster. The trickster Griever bashed at habits and rules in an established historical context.

[McCaffery:] You've recently presented a number of discussions concerning the "postmodern" features of Native American literature. Interestingly enough, your analysis runs somewhat along the same lines as what Japanologist Maseo Miyoshi has said about very early literature in Japan—namely, that the Japanese literature exhibits many of the stylistic tendencies associated with postmodernism long before even "modernism" came along in the West. Obviously a lot of issues related to this topic come down mainly to a matter of definition and perspective—the problem being that in the West we always wish to see artistic "evolution" and development in terms of our own cultural paradigms and history.

I can see the angle you're taking there, as well as what Miyoshi is driving at. It's closely connected to my argument that Native American storytellers were the first postmodernists. Making that assertion stick is tricky because of course this implies you could have a narrative tradition that's postmodern before it's ever gone through a "modern" phase. Premodern postmodernist.

What's the theoretical basis of your claim for Native American literature as a postmodernist form? Or in making these claims, are you mainly just adopting the trickster position of playing with terms to reveal their limitations?

First of all, I don't approach this topic theoretically because that would mean I'd have to carry back a formula for discovery. Instead I use the idea of postmodern *conditions,* which is Lyotard's notion. So I don't impose a theory—in fact, I'm very careful about not doing this because I am arguing against that.

[Marshall:] How would the "conditions" you're referring to here relate to Native American Writing?

The conditions are that, first, no story is the same. The conditions are postmodern because of their connection to oral expression which is usually a kind of a free-floating signifier or a collection of signifiers, depending on who's present. The meaning of such stories that are orally presented depends on a number of interesting, lively, immediate, temporal, and dangerous, dangerous natural conditions.

[McCaffery:] What do you mean here by "dangerous"? A linguistic or conventional danger—the danger of a speaker upsetting the expectations?

Something like that. Dangerous not specifically in the sense of life-threatening but dangerous in nature and *in language*. Telling a story is as "dangerous" as hunting—dangerous because your life depends on seeing and catching something. It's dangerous because it's an encounter with the unknown—something generally understood, but specifically unknown that may come together, alive or present in the telling or the hunting. To hunt, to tell stories, to write is dangerous. It's also survivance.

[Marshall:] I take it that "survivance" is an invented word that has additional meanings other than its French equivalence of "survival"?

Yes. I wanted a term that would have a broader meaning than survival—that is, as a conditional experience rather than a mere response to domination or victimization. "Survivance" is not just carrying this burden and surviving—showing that I'm a survivor of victimization, for example—but also inventing a world view. It's an attitude of play—play in a very serious sense. Survivance is the end of domination in literature. It's also a new kind of existentialism, a source of identity—not the French atheistic existentialism but tribal existentialism or spiritual existentialism (I'm a little hesitant using the word "spiritual" here because I have to qualify it too much, whereas saying "tribal" leaves it open). The discovery of self through action, through being present, is the part of existentialism I borrow from Jean-Paul Sartre, but when I add to this the dream, the presence of previous experience, I get more mystical than Sartre and the others ever allowed. I argue that life is a chance, a story is a chance. That I am here is a chance. This interview is a dangerous, chance survivance. The advantages to survivance are that it provides a way to accept this condition, reverse what's been imposed upon us—and play with that!

Alan R. Velie (essay date Spring 1991-92)

SOURCE: "Gerald Vizenor's Indian Gothic," in *MELUS*, Vol. 17, No. 1, Spring, 1991-92, pp. 75-85.

[In the following essay, Velie argues that Vizenor has adapted the traditional "frontier gothic" into an "Indian gothic" which portrays changes in the West from the Native American perspective.]

Much of American literature is concerned with conquering the hostile wilderness and "winning the West." For a long time Americans read little Indian literature, and so we learned almost nothing from the people who "lost" the West, and who considered the wilderness not hostile, but home.

In the past fifteen years, however, there has been an efflorescence of Indian literature. The best known of the Indian writers not only have strong tribal identities, but as they are or have been English professors (Scott Momaday at Berkeley, Stanford, and Arizona, James Welch at Montana, Leslie Silko at New Mexico and Arizona, Paula Gunn Allen at Berkeley, and Gerald Vizenor at Berkeley, Minnesota and Santa Cruz), they have a thorough grounding in American literature. It is not surprising that these writers have been reexamining traditional American genres, myths, and themes from a different perspective, the Indian point of view.

In *Darkness in Saint Louis Bearheart* Gerald Vizenor takes the tradition of what has been called "frontier gothic" and stands it on its head. If the frontier gothic is a romantic novel of terror set in the western wilderness with Indians playing the role of satanic villains, *Darkness in Saint Louis Bearheart* is the obverse: it is a novel of horror written from an Indian point of view about a group of Indians forced from the security of their woodland reservation and driven into the civilized West where cowboys, fascists, and other enemies attempt to exterminate them.

A futuristic fantasy, *Bearheart* takes place in the United States after the country has run out of oil. In its desperation for fuel, the government turns to lumber, commandeering the trees on the White Earth reservation of the Anishinaabes (or Chippewas or Ojibways, as the whites refer to them) where the protagonist Proude Cedarfair lives. Realizing the futility of fighting the government, Proude and his wife Rosina set out on a cross-country odyssey attracting a bizarre crew of displaced persons, mostly mixedblood Indians, as they go. These pilgrims include Sun Bear Sun, a 300 pounder who carries a small white woman, Little Big Mouse, in a holster at his belt; Benito Saint Plumero, an Anishinaabe clown who has done time in jail for murdering his rival for the favors of a bronze statue; Belladonna Darwin Winter Catcher, the daughter of a white reporter and Lakota holy man who met at the occupation of Wounded Knee; and Lilith Mae Farrier, a white woman who worked as a teacher on a reservation until the tribal elders raped her and their wives ran her off in disgust. To console herself she took two boxers—dogs, not athletes—as lovers.

The gothic novel, as Leslie Fiedler puts it, substitutes "terror for love as a central theme of fiction." In this regard, Vizenor's book far outstrips most of Fiedler's examples: the horror of "Rip Van Winkle," *Huckleberry Finn, The Leatherstocking Tales, Moby Dick* or "Young Goodman Brown" is tame next to the horror of **Bearheart**, where Little Big Mouse is torn limb from limb by lepers and cripples, Lilith Mae Farrier immolates herself and her boxers; and Benito Saint Plumero castrates his rival and suffocates him by stuffing his penis and testicles down his throat, and then is himself strangled by a nun. There is an element of grisly humor to be sure, but beneath the humor is a horror deeper than anything in Fiedler's examples, with the possible exception of Poe's stories.

Gothic fiction is essentially melodramatic, typified by polarized characterization: there are two sets of characters, good guys and bad guys. The heroes and villains fight to the death—the death of the villains—and the tone is one of extreme tension. As Northrop Frye puts it, at the climax of the work, the mood of the audience is that of a lynch mob.

In melodrama the differences between good guys and bad guys are essentially political, although the conflict may take the form of a racial or religious struggle. Cowboys v. Indians, Marines v. Japanese, Crusaders v. Saracens, whoever the specific combatants, there is a Manichaean polarization based on social and economic factors which indicate that however groups choose to describe their differences, they are really political—that is, concerned with who will have the power to run things. Comedy ends in marriage, tragedy in death, and melodrama in revenge. It isn't hard to figure out why Vizenor inverts the frontier gothic tradition, in which white makes right, and dark skin indicates dark purposes: even if the Civil Rights Movement has caused the demise of simplistic horse operas with the Indians cast as villains, and alleviated much of the prejudice that Indians and other minority groups face, bigotry is far from dead. Indians feel the need to tell their side of the story.

The legacy of anti-Indian bigotry goes back to Columbus: from the very first contact between the races, whites depicted Indians as superstitious at best, and evil, even satanic, at worst. Columbus describes the Indians he met on Hispaniola as naked and credulous: they had rings in their noses, and believed that the Spanish were men from heaven. Columbus apparently found this superstition more amusing than vicious, but Gonzalo de Oviedo, who followed Columbus to the New World a quarter century later, believed that the Indian religious rituals were Devil worship. In his *General Historie of the Indies,* Oviedo speaks of "the familiaritie which certain of the Indians have with the Devill," identifying their deity Tuyra as Satan.

The English, like the Spanish, believed that Indians who were not converted to Christianity were Devil worshippers. Alexander Whitaker, Minister of the Virginia Colony, wrote in 1613 of the contrast between the Christian Pocohantas and her fellow tribesman Tomocomo, whom Whitaker describes as a

blasphemer of what he knew not . . . preferring his God to ours, because he taught them (by his own so appearing) to weare their Devill-lock at the left eare; hee acquainted mee with the manner of that his appearance, and beeleeved that this Okee or Devil had taught them their husbandry, &c.

In New England the Puritans believed that the battles between whites and Indians were merely the latest skirmish in a holy war between the forces of God and the Devil, a "quarrell . . . as ancient as Adams time, propagated from that old enmity between the Seede of the Woman, and the Seede of the Serpent, who was the grand signior of this war."

As American literature developed, the Indian became the shadow who opposed the white persona not only in shoddy dime novels, but in the works of authors of the caliber of Twain and Hawthorne. In "Young Goodman Brown," Deacon Gookin, on his way to the Devil's ceremonies in the forest, speaks of "Indian powwows, who after their fashion, know almost as much deviltry as the best of us." In *Tom Sawyer,* Injun Joe is a "murderin' halfbreed" who Tom fears worse than devils. As he murders Dr. Robinson, Joe says, "The Injun blood ain't in me for nothing."

Writers of dime novels knew that to sell their wares they had to slaughter Indians on their pages. This they believed to be morally justified because of the heinous excesses of the "red devils." For instance, in *Corduroy Charlie, The Boy Bravo,* or *Deadwood Dick's Last Act,* the Indians worshipped a Sun God who demanded human sacrifice.

> **Although by the time Vizenor started to write . . . the worst of the stereotyping was over, it is not surprising that he was anxious to even the balance.**
> **—Alan R. Velie**

The films of the first two-thirds of the twentieth century were no better. Anyone over thirty can remember Saturday matinees of bloodthirsty Indians attacking wagon trains, and John Wayne in pursuit of the "Commanch." Indians not only provided the villains in scores of grade B films, but were also treated harshly in the films of the major directors. In "The Battle of Elderbush Gulch," D.W. Griffith depicts the Indians as warlike barbarians who feast on dogs. Cecil B. DeMille in "The Unconquered" shows Indians torturing a white woman and massacring settlers. John Price sums up Hollywood's approach:

> The movie story was told by white American producers and directors to a white North American audience, assuming and building a plot from anti-Indian

attitudes and prejudices. Indian life was seen as savage, one at an earlier stage of development, and therefore rightly vanishing as Indians are exterminated or assimilated into white society.

Although by the time Vizenor started to write (he published his first book in 1978) the worst of the stereotyping was over, it is not surprising that he was anxious to even the balance. In *Bearheart* his choice of the frontier gothic mode, with its melodramatic separation of characters into good guys and bad guys on the basis of race, and its emphasis on the division of America into civilization and wilderness, lends itself to his purposes. All that remains is to substitute traditional Indian values for those of Christianity.

Of course, strictly speaking there is no such thing as "Indian values." Traditionally Indians think of themselves as members of one tribe in particular rather than as Indians in general. In fact, in *Bearheart* itself, a group of redneck cowboys make some telling points in arguing with Belladonna Darwin Winter Catcher on this question when she attempts ineffectually to explain what Indian values are. Nonetheless, Vizenor does not present the values of one tribe, the Anishinaabe, but draws myths and customs from many. Vizenor does not specify the tribal affiliation of all his characters; some he designates by a general label like "tribal historian."

Tribes often shared myths, rituals and customs, even if they were not related ethnically. Today, by and large, most Indians who are religious belong to some sect or other of Christianity, but traditionally their religions were part of their tribal culture. The most important figure in the mythology of virtually all North American tribes was—and still is—the Trickster, the quintessential culture hero. The Anishinaabe trickster, Nanabozho, is actually the basis for two characters in *Darkness in Saint Louis Bearheart,* Proude Cedarfair, and Benito Saint Plumero. To understand these characters, and to see how they fit the melodramatic gothic pattern, it is necessary to describe the trickster briefly.

The Trickster

Nanabozho—or Wenebojo, Manabozo or Nanabush, depending on how anthropologists recorded the Anishinaabe word—was the chief culture hero of the Anishinaabe, and a very complex figure, a combination of savior and rogue not unlike tricksters who have served as the heroes in western literature. According to Anishinaabe tradition, he was the son of Epingshmook, a spirit, and Winonah, a mortal woman. Nanabozho combines the traits of *manidos,* or spirits, with the traits of animals and humans.

Nanabozho, like all tricksters, is constantly on the move. Trickster tales of all tribes inevitably begin with a variation of the formula, "Trickster was going along when . . . " The trickster is a figure of insatiable appetites, and no moral constraints when it comes to filling them. He is fond of playing tricks, but more often than not he is a buffoon who ends up as the butt of the joke.

Nanabozho violates the most sacred Anishinaabe taboos, murdering most of his family and marrying his sister. He is so ashamed of himself that he disguises himself and goes into exile. But Nanabozho is also the culture hero of the Anishinaabe, who in his manifestation as a rabbit steals fire in one tale, and in another saves man and the animals by putting them on his raft in the great flood.

Nanabozho is obviously related to the trickster archetype as it exists in western literature. He is a brother to Odysseus, Til Eulenspiegel, Huck Finn, and Randle Patrick McMurphy, to name just a few. Often the trickster figure is split into two opposite but complementary figures, like Prometheus and Epimetheus, the "forethinker" and "afterthinker" of Greek mythology. In *Bearheart,* Proude is the avatar of the culture hero, and Benito plays the irresponsible trickster and buffoon. Both are based on Nanabozho, whose adventures Vizenor heard from his Anishinaabe grandmother.

Vizenor's Tricksters

Like Nanabozho, Proude is always on the move in *Bearheart.* It is true that he was originally reluctant to leave his home in Minnesota: he is driven from the reservation by Jordan Coward, the corrupt chief of the Anishinaabe, who acts as an agent of the federal government which covets the reservation's trees. Whatever the impetus, however, once Proude starts his travels he doesn't stop, traversing western America until he finally passes from this world into the next. Like Nanabozho, Proude is committed to surviving by his wits rather than by force. His creed is:

> Outwit but never kill evil . . . evil revenge is blind
> and cannot be appeased by the living. The tricksters
> and warrior clowns have stopped more violence with
> their wit than have lovers with their lust and fools
> with their power and rage.

Proude departs from this credo in defeating the Evil Gambler and watching as the Gambler kills himself, but inconsistency is part of the trickster's nature, and it is traditional in Anishinaabe mythology for the trickster to kill the Evil Gambler. Like Nanabozho, Proude has the ability to change shapes. Rather than becoming a rabbit however, Proude becomes a bear, and in that form escapes from the third world to the fourth world.

The biggest difference between Proude and Nanabozho is that Proude seems very decorous and moderate in his appetites for a trickster. He is neither the pest nor buffoon of

Chippewa tradition; instead he seems to be a highly sensible leader who possesses extraordinary powers, but is somewhat chary of using them. Proude is Nanabozho in his role of leader and culture hero—the Nanabozho who kills the evil giant who eats Chippewas, Windigo, the Nanabozho who brings fire and saves mankind on his raft. In his role as savior Proude kills the Evil Gambler and frees the pilgrims from imprisonment at the hands of the Pentarchical Pensioners, a paramilitary group which has taken over New Mexico.

The other face of Nanabozho—Nanabozho the menace who kills his brother and marries his sister, Nanabozho the buffoon who tries to share his meal with the trees and gets stuck in a branch, who tries to fly like a bird but falls to the ground—that Nanabozho is portrayed in Benito Saint Plumero, alias Bigfoot. Bigfoot is a small mixedblood with the "guileless face of a clown," outsize feet which "moved in the grass like huge rodents," and a huge penis, which he calls "President Jackson," and uses to service the thirteen women of the Scapehouse of Weirds and Sensitives, a refuge for women poets who are avoiding the crass masculine world. The Sensitives insist that no man may enter the scapehouse as the sex object of one woman: any man allowed to stay must be shared. The women first reject Bigfoot because of his outlandish appearance ("He must have been put together from broken clowns," says one sister), but when they learn of his sexual prowess, they allow him to remain. Although most trickster stories in print today have been cleaned up either by the collectors who first recorded them, or by publishers who printed them as tales for children, traditionally the trickster was known for his uncontrollable sexual appetite. Nanabozho, as mentioned above, commits incest; Wakdjunkaga, the Winnebago trickster, sends his penis across a lake to rape the chief's daughter, and then transforms himself into a woman to marry the chief's son; and Sendeh, the Kiowa trickster, injures himself trying to have sex with the whirlwind. Bigfoot is solidly in this tradition. Having eaten some hallucinogenic vine leaves, he falls in love with a statue in the park, and steals her, taking her to the reservation. Bigfoot's most outrageous sexual act, however, is the seduction of Proude's wife, Rosina. Bigfoot forces Rosina to commit fellatio, but it soon becomes clear that what may have started involuntarily for Rosina has become pleasurable. While Bigfoot and Rosina are occupied, one of the Sensitives, Sister Eternal Flame, strangles Bigfoot.

Proude and Bigfoot are clowns as well as tricksters. Before he moves from the reservation Proude lives in a grove of trees called "Cedarfair Circus" with his fellow clowns, seven crows. Bigfoot describes himself as a "trickster clown, sort of a new contrarion."

Because clowns in the American tradition of western melodrama are confined to the role of sidekick—the Gabby Hayes, Slim Pickens sort of figure—it seems odd that they could serve as central figures in *Bearheart*. But it is not surprising if one is familiar with the role of the clown in tribal culture, and if one knows Vizenor's ideas about humor as a weapon.

Clowns were an important part of tribal religious life: they were ridiculous figures who interrupted serious ceremonies with their horseplay, diving into puddles, drinking urine, throwing feces at celebrants. Contrarions were clowns who did everything backwards: they walked backwards, rode their horses facing the tail, and said "good-bye" when they entered and "hello" when they left.

There are numerous explanations for the behavior of clowns, but essentially they are reifications of the mythical trickster in the everyday life of the tribe. That is, the trickster is a saturnalian figure, whose disregard for the laws and customs of the tribe make him a surrogate whom the tribal members can identify with and so feel freed from the trammels of tribal restrictions.

Any society that has oppressive rules of moral and ceremonial behavior needs mythic and ritual sources of rebellion which allow tribal members to flout the rules through surrogates. The surrogates were irresponsible, amoral figures who mocked everything sacred with impunity to the delight of the rest of the community which remained obedient and orderly.

To Vizenor, humor is the supreme virtue, the thing that keeps man from taking himself too seriously, and allows him to retain his perspective and honesty. This is in part a political question, for, Vizenor resembles Umberto Eco, who makes the point in *The Name of the Rose* that laughter is the most effective weapon against tyranny and intolerance.

Indian religion has demonic figures, and Vizenor adopts one of these, the Evil Gambler, as his chief melodramatic villain. Versions of the Gambler myth are told by many tribes. In the Anishinaabe version a foolish tribesman bets recklessly at some game with the Gambler, losing his possessions, then his clothes, until finally he has nothing left to lose but his life (Vizenor, *People*). He wagers this in the hope of regaining all that he has lost, but loses again, and the Gambler puts him to death.

Vizenor's Evil Gambler is Sir Cecil Staples, a demonic figure who practices his life's calling, murder, in the ruins of a trailer park at the edge of What Cheer, Iowa. Sir Cecil claims to be the monarch of unleaded gasoline, and offers to gamble with desperate motorists, five gallons against their lives. When they lose, as they inevitably do, he allows them to choose their method of death. The intertwined skeletons of two lovers who asked to be strangled as they copulated hang in Sir Cecil's office. Vizenor portrays Sir Cecil as the personification of evil:

"I seek no one to come and gamble with me but those who would gamble for their lives," the monarch of unleaded gasoline explained. His soothing voice had overtones of hissing and echoes of fiendish groans. "I demand nothing but the lives of those who gamble with me for gasoline and lose."

Sir Cecil was raised on interstate highways by a truck-driving mother. Because Ms. Staples had been sterilized by the government for having illegitimate children while on welfare, she took to kidnapping children at shopping malls. She stole thirteen in all, bringing them up in her truck as she drove back and forth across the country, finally turning them out at reststops when they were grown. Ms. Staples told her children that they should "feel no guilt, ignore the expectations of others, and practice to perfection whatever [they did] in the world." Sir Cecil decided to practice the art of killing people. In the confrontation between the Indians and the evil white Sir Cecil, the Gambler wins the first round. Lilith Mae Farrier, the boxer lover, is selected to gamble against Sir Cecil. She loses, and the Evil Gambler allows her to choose her method of death. She soaks herself in gasoline, and sets herself afire. The boxers choose to be immolated with her.

Although Sir Cecil wins initially, Proude defeats him at his own game, and the Evil Gambler chooses to die by strangulation, using a "chronometric neckscrew," one of the infernal machines he designed to kill his victims.

Proude's conquest of Sir Cecil—the trickster's defeat of the Evil Gambler—is not only an incorporation of an Indian myth into the modern novel, but a classical example of the melodramatic showdown. The hero, exemplar of the author's values, faces the villain, the personification of absolute evil in terms of those values, in a climactic showdown. In epic and romance the showdown takes place on the battlefield; in the traditional gothic it occurs in the bowels of the crumbling castle or monastery, and in the frontier gothic novel in the forest. In Vizenor's Indian gothic, the showdown takes place in a trailer park, one of the seedier venues of modern American civilization. What Cheer isn't big enough for both of them, so Proude must kill Sir Cecil, allowing virtue to triumph once again.

Another reversal of the ethos of the traditional gothic in *Bearheart* is that witches are good, not evil. To the Puritans, Indian religion was a form of witchcraft, and witches and Indians were leagued in evil. Witchcraft is more often the obverse of a religion than a faith in its own right—witches in Europe and America celebrate a Black Mass, recite the Lord's Prayer backwards, and hang crucifixes upside down, for instance—and Indian religions have their own naysayers and witches, whom the Indians have fought themselves. Vizenor however, depicts witches solely as victims.

In *Bearheart*, two eastern families invade Oklahoma and set up the Ponca Witch Hunt Restaurant and Fast Foods, where three witches, or women the Fast Food Fascists suspect of being witches (they use luminescent makeup as their test) have been hung from the ceiling to season. The pilgrims liberate two of the witches, but a pilgrim and a witch die when they stop to have sex before leaving the restaurant.

Another of Vizenor's changes has to do with pastoralism. The frontier gothic tradition is anti-pastoral. The forest replaces the European castle as the place of evil, and the Indian replaces the monk as the devil figure. As D.H. Lawrence puts it in his chapter on Fenimore Cooper, "When you are actually IN America, America hurts, because it has a powerful disintegrative influence upon the white psyche. It is full of grinning, unappeased aboriginal demons, too, ghosts, and it persecutes the white men like some Eumenides." The unappeased aboriginal demons, of course, are the spirits of the slaughtered Indians, and the disintegrative influence on the white psyche is a combination of guilt and the uneasiness of being in the wilderness.

Although Cooper presents a highly romanticized view of life in the American forest ["Too romantic" says Lawrence. "Fenimore puts in only the glamour"], even he gives a sense of Indian as devil. The most dramatic example is the death of Magua in *The Last of the Mohicans*. When Natty Bumppo shoots Magua, the beautiful, evil Iroquois falls to his death in a scene reminiscent of Lucifer's fall from heaven. The feeling of the woods as evil and the Indian as devil figure is even stronger in novelists like Charles Brockden Brown and Hawthorne. As Leslie Fiedler says:

> It should be noticed that the shift from the ruined castle of the European prototypes to the forest and cave of Brown involves a shift not just in the manner of saying what the author is after. THE CHANGE OF MYTH INVOLVES A PROFOUND CHANGE OF MEANING. In the American gothic, that is to say, the heathen, unredeemed wilderness and not the decaying monuments of a dying class, nature not society becomes the symbol of evil.

Vizenor's Indian gothic, reversing the values of frontier gothic, in which the forest is evil and civilization is good, falls into the pastoral tradition. In the world of *Bearheart* the forest is good, a source of strength, and civilization is evil, a corruptive influence on man. For generations Proude's forebears lived among cedar trees which they considered sacred. In fact, in a mystical way the Cedarfairs become one with the trees. Vizenor says of the first Proude:

> The cedar became the source of personal power. He dreamed trees and leaned in the wind with the cedar ... He spoke with the trees. He became the cedar

wood. "We are the cedar," he told his sons. "We cannot leave ourselves."

Proude is spiritually strong as long as he lives among the cedars. In stark contrast to him are the "capitalist treekillers," evil not only because they destroy trees, but also because they believe trees are possessions which can be bought and sold. To Proude this is almost as unnatural as buying and selling people. Unfortunately, history is on the side of the treekillers:

> Nineteenth century frontier politics favored the interests of the railroads and treekillers and agrarian settlers who were promised the ownership of the earth . . . Whitemen possessed trees and women and words. Violence eclipsed the solemn promises of woodland tribal celebrants.

Lawrence predicted that one day white Americans would tame the land, and remove the "menace" from the landscape. And so they did; a continent of forests and plains became a land of lawns and freeways, slums and suburbs. That America is a place of menace to Vizenor and the Indians he depicts. In *Bearheart* the sites of horror are a trailer park and a fast food restaurant.

The expulsion of Proude and Rosina from the cedar forests of their reservation is reminiscent of the exile of Adam and Eve from Eden in *Paradise Lost*. Proude and Rosina have the whole world before them, but it seems a desolate wasteland.

In that *Bearheart* describes the end of an era, it recalls "The Bear," Faulkner's allegorical treatment of the end of the frontier in Mississippi. But whereas Faulkner is elegiac, Vizenor is sardonic.

Nonetheless, this being melodrama, there must be a happy ending. Since the Indians can hardly throw the whites off the continent, Vizenor makes Proude's triumph spiritual and mystical. Along with his last remaining companion, Iniwa Biwide, Proude follows the vision of a giant bear to the ruins of Pueblo Bonito in western New Mexico. On the morning of the winter solstice, when the sun rises in the center of the vision window of the pueblo, the pilgrims change shape and float out towards the sun and into the perfect light of the fourth world. Rosina, who has betrayed Proude, is left behind, gazing at the bear tracks in the snow, the last sign of her husband in this world.

The significance of the ending appears to be that the Indians' best alternative is to retain their spiritual heritage, and transcend the horrors of the white domestication and suburbanization of America. Although there can be no literal escape—Indians must in fact live here, and have commerce with their fellow Americans—they can preserve their cultural integrity to transcend the white way. Living spiritually is the best revenge.

Robert Allen Warrior (review date Spring 1992)

SOURCE: A review of *The Heirs of Columbus*, in *World Literature Today*, Vol. 66, No. 2, Spring, 1992, p. 387.

[*In the following brief review, Warrior asserts that in Vizenor's novel* The Heirs of Columbus, *the author takes shreds of a "tragic history and claims them as property of the liberating liberal trickster."*]

The Heirs of Columbus, Gerald Vizenor's fourth novel, is a compelling and rewarding contribution to the cacophonous chorus of voices in this quincentenary year. The wild fable [de]centers on the exploits of a group of this continent's Natives who claim to be direct descendants of the famed Genoan explorer. Columbus, in Vizenor's telling, was actually the son of Mayans who traveled from the New World to the Old. Christopher raised money from the crown of Spain to make his way back home. His heirs now live at the headwaters of the Mississippi and are looking for a way to bring the bones of their ancestor to find final rest among family.

With this narrative Vizenor takes what he sees as the tragic shreds of a tragic history and claims them as property of the liberating tribal trickster, who is able to take even the most deadly stories and gain from them healing and liberation. In place of the already worn-thin clichés of quincentennial revisionism, Vizenor offers a comic path of imagination and survival. On that path the story's unlikely heirs manage to spirit the bones of Columbus away from the Brotherhood of American Explorers (a veiled reference to the American Bureau of Ethnology). Doric Michéd, a self-proclaimed Native and member of the elite group of grave robbers, is the villain of the novel.

Michéd, ashamed when he brings dishonor to his fellow grave robbers, masks his identity and induces Felipa Flowers, one of the heirs, to London. There, he promises, he will give over the bones of Pocahontas for a proper reburial alongside the Mayan Columbus at the headwaters of the Mississippi. In her desire to repatriate another set of bones and stories, Felipa does not realize that she is walking into peril.

Through the various twists and turns, Vizenor, in vintage form, uses digressions and other devices to comment on a wide variety of issues that affect the lives of American Indian people and communities. Native Americanist Arnold Krupat, Métis rebel Louis Riel, Antonín Dvorák's *New World Symphony*, some separatist feminists, Shakespeare's Caliban, and lots of others also make appearances. Such digressions and veiled references require quite a bit of knowledge about contemporary American Indian, Native Americanist, and other letters and may tax those without background, but they yield rich rewards for those who keep up with such currents.

Even those uninitiated in the imaginary landscapes of Vizenor's universe, though, will feel the real power of *Heirs of Columbus* in its final section. There the heirs discover that the genetic code they carry from their Mayan explorer ancestor holds the secret of healing the wounds from these last five centuries of oppression and tragedy. After withdrawing from the corruption-ridden realms and terminal creeds of tribal governments, they declare sovereignty and set about the task of building a community.

Amid a fantastic and apocalyptic narrative, Vizenor reminds his readers of what is really at stake in Indian America: the lives and futures of Indian children and grandchildren. In doing so, the trickster is never far from view (or at least earshot), waiting to overturn our expectations and forcing us to look for liberation in places we had not thought to look.

Los Angeles Times Book Review (review date 11 October 1992)

SOURCE: Review of *Dead Voices,* in *Los Angeles Times Book Review,* October 11, 1992, p. 6.

[*In the review below, the critic states that* Dead Voices *is a difficult but original work.*]

A dirty, toothless, malodorous American Indian woman lives in an apartment near Lake Merritt in Oakland. People who wait at a nearby bus stop call her "the crazy bear." This isn't just an insult; it's a remnant of the intuitive animal knowledge that white city-dwellers have almost lost. For the woman, playing the "wanaki game" with cards and mirrors, can indeed transform herself into a bear—or into a stone, a flea, a squirrel, a praying mantis, a crow, a beaver or that staple of Indian folklore, a "trickster."

Then along comes a young academic—much like author Gerald Vizenor, a professor of ethnic studies at UC Berkeley. He persuades the woman, Bagese, to tell him her animal stories, which are linked to Indian creation myths. She forbids him to write them down, saying "wordies"—white people and their imitators—have already done enough to destroy an oral tradition and reduce knowledge to mere science. But he writes them down anyway.

The result is *Dead Voices,* subtitled "Natural Agonies in the New World." It's an uncompromisingly original book. For the non-Indian reader, accepting the idea of transformation is the easy part. More difficult is linking the story cycle, as Vizenor intends, with the idea that Indians should struggle to affirm themselves as "crossbloods" in the cities rather than cling to a sterile purity on reservations. The human-animal synthesis is a metaphor for how this struggle should be waged, but Vizenor's animals are more real than his people, and the battlefield—in this case, quotidian Oakland—is foggy.

Robert Crum (review date 8 November 1992)

SOURCE: "Big Bad Wordies," in *New York Times Book Review,* November 8, 1992, p. 18.

[*In the following review of* Dead Voices, *Crum commends Vizenor's efforts to retell traditional Native American myths but finds the work unconvincing.*]

Those wild animals that hold center stage in the traditional stories and dreams of American Indians, those beings that are mythically empowered with magical talents—what do they think about this crazy century of ours? In his latest novel, Gerald Vizenor gives them voice, and it turns out that they easily fit the post-modernist mode.

The governing condition of the animals in *Dead Voices: Natural Agonies in the New World* is dislocation. These creatures—bears, fleas, praying mantises, crows, beavers and others—have lost some of their power. Or they have power and don't always know what to do with it. They are urban animals now, and they display a discomforting urban energy. They're still capable of transformation and trickery, but these days they perform feats in order to heal new sorts of spiritual wounds, those caused by the separation of modern civilization from the natural world.

But the biggest obstacle these animals face in getting their message across is the author's own penchant for verbal tricksterism. Mr. Vizenor, a professor of ethnic studies at the University of California, Berkeley, who is himself part Indian, seems intent on using his novel to out-Coyote Coyote, the trickster of Indian lore. It would seem a dubious enterprise.

Mr. Vizenor's book (the second volume in the University of Oklahoma Press's American Indian Literature and Critical Studies Series, for which he serves as general editor) takes its structure from an Indian card game called wanaki, which is a little like tarot—except that the player is temporarily transformed into the animal pictured on the turned-up card. The player in this case is an old Indian woman named Bagese, a shaman whom the narrator meets on the streets of Oakland, Calif. Fascinated by the way Bagese seems to converse with the birds in a local park, he follows her back to her apartment. There, in encounters that stretch over the next two years, she teaches him "how to hear and see the animals in stories."

Each chapter begins with a turn of a card and a different animal. And each story progresses by means of ritual, symbol and philosophical debate, by repetition and transformation, by jokes and puns, even by traditional narrative forms. Characters hide in mirrors and shadows. They easily exchange identities. Surprisingly enough, they face only a few antagonists, notably the "wordies"—people too slow and literal-minded to follow along. (Anthropologists appear to be archetypal wordies.)

But uninitiated readers may find that the going can get pretty slippery. After struggling through the following paragraph (and this is one example out of many), I resigned myself to the fact that I too may well be a wordy:

> "The praying mantis wear chance on their sleeves, a chance to hear the comic side of their survival. Mantis pray that sex is a chance, and comic survival is on their side. The mantis are slow but not stupid, and everyone knows sex can be a trickster at the right moment, even the word ies. Sex can turn the best minds to comedies, but how do the mantis survive sex with a chance?"

As presented in many Indian tales, tricksters often work wonders by mistake. Hurling the stars into the sky in a fit of rage, for instance, Coyote accidentally created the constellations. Such luck does not always hold for Mr. Vizenor, who appears to be wearing the trickster spirit on his sleeve.

The attempt to resurrect traditional myths and set them loose in the modern world is a creditable one. The magical powers of animals—their particular ways of knowing; their talents for surviving; their reluctance, in Walt Whitman's phrase, to "sweat and whine about their condition"—should be recognized as complements to human experience. We ignore these creatures (or exterminate them) at our own peril.

Unfortunately, the characters in this book are less animals than puppets. We cannot believe in them; we can only remark on the artfulness of Mr. Vizenor's presentation.

Louis Owens (essay date 1992)

SOURCE: "'Ecstatic Strategies': Gerald Vizenor's Trickster Narratives," in *Other Destinies: Understanding the American Indian Novel*, University of Oklahoma Press, 1992, pp. 225-54.

[*In the following essay, Owens considers the role of the trickster in Vizenor's work.*]

Born in 1934, Gerald Vizenor has devoted an incredibly prolific career to exploring the place and meaning of the mixedblood in modern America. With more than twenty-five books and scores of essays, poems, and stories published, in addition to a movie (*Harold of Orange*, 1983), Vizenor is one of the most productive as well as one of the most radically imaginative of contemporary American writers. At the heart of Vizenor's fiction lies a fascination with what it means to be of mixed Indian and European heritage in the contemporary world—in Vizenor's terminology, a "crossblood." And out of this fascination arises the central and unifying figure in Vizenor's art: the trickster. In Vizenor's work the mixedblood and the trickster become metaphors that seek to balance contradictions and shatter static certainties. The mixedblood, that tortured Ishmael of the majority of novels by both Indian and non-Indian authors, becomes in Vizenor's fiction not a pained victim but a "holotropic" and celebrated shape shifter, an incarnation of trickster who mediates between worlds. In Vizenor's fictional world—a coherent and fully realized topography as complete as Faulkner's South or Garcia Marquez's Macondo—the tortured and torturing mixedblood represented so unforgettably in Mark Twain's "Injun Joe" and Faulkner's "Chief Doom" simply refuses to perish in the dark cave of the American psyche but instead soars to freedom in avian dreams and acrobatic outrage.

Harsh laughter is the matrix out of which Vizenor's fiction arises, the kind of laughter Mikhail Bakhtin finds at the roots of the modern novel. "As a distanced image a subject cannot be comical," Bakhtin writes; "to be made comical, it must be brought close." And he continues:

> Everything that makes us laugh is close at hand, all comical creativity works in a zone of maximal proximity. Laughter has the remarkable power of making an object come up close, of drawing it into a zone of crude contact where one can finger it familiarly on all sides, turn it upside down, inside out, peer at it from above and below, break open its external shell, look into its center, doubt it, take it apart, dismember it, lay it bare and expose it, examine it freely and experiment with it. Laughter demolishes fear and piety before an object, before a world, making of it an object of familiar contact and thus clearing the ground for an absolutely free investigation of it.

In Bakhtin's words—a remarkably accurate description of a raven examining and dissecting an object of interest—we find a precise definition of the humor and method of the Native American trickster, he/she who brings the world close and directs this "comical operation of dismemberment," laying bare the hypocrisies, false fears and pieties, and clearing the ground "for an absolutely free investigation" of worldy fact. This is the trickster Vizenor has taken to heart and to the heart of his fiction. Bakhtin's explanation of the effects of these parodic forms in ancient art applies equally well to Vizenor: "These parodic-travestying forms . . . liberated the object from the power of language in which it had become entangled as if in a net; they destroyed the homogenizing power of myth over language; they freed consciousness from the power of the direct word, destroyed the thick walls that had imprisoned consciousness within its own discourse, within its own language." The liberation of language and consciousness is Vizenor/trickster's aim, particularly the liberation of the signifier "Indian" from the entropic myth surrounding it.

Vizenor's consistent contribution has been the way he shows us a way to avoid cynicism; and while he indulges extravagantly in irony, he does so in a manner that finally returns ideals to a purity that leaves no further need for irony.
—Elaine Jahner

The trickster discourse of Vizenor's fiction resembles Bakhtin's definition of Minippean satire:

> The familiarizing role of laughter is here considerably more powerful, sharper and coarser. The liberty to crudely degrade, to turn inside out the lofty aspects of the world and world views, might sometimes seem shocking. But to this exclusive and comic familiarity must be added *an intense spirit of inquiry and utopian fantasy*. In Minippean satire the unfettered and fantastic plots and situations all serve one goal—to put to the test and to expose ideas and idealogues. . . . Minippean satire is dialogic, full of parodies and travesties, multi-styled, and does not fear elements of bilingualism.

Vizenor's "parodia sacra" is often shocking, his plots "unfettered and fantastic," "full of parodies and travesties," and designed to serve the one goal Bakhtin defines: to test and expose ideas and idealogues. The result is never nihilistic, a point Elaine Jahner has made well: "Vizenor's consistent contribution has been the way he shows us a way to avoid cynicism; and while he indulges extravagantly in irony, he does so in a manner that finally returns ideals to a purity that leaves no further need for irony." It is the utopian impulse that guides Vizenor's mythic parodies, a quest for liberation from the entropic forces that attempt to deny full realization of human possibilities. Vizenor discovers such utopian potential in American Indian mythologies; and in trickster—

who overturns all laws, governments, social conventions— Vizenor finds his imaginative weapon. Simultaneously, his profound identification with the mythic trickster enables Vizenor—who writes even autobiography in the third person—to repudiate that "privileged moment of *individualization*" Foucault identifies with the "coming into being of the notion of 'author,'" and to write multivocal narratives that deconstruct the egocentric authorial presence conventional in the genre of the novel in favor of an ecocentric voice that springs from liminal thresholds.

Vizenor was born in Minneapolis, the son of a half-Ojibwe father (or Chippewa or, as the tribal people call themselves, *anishinaabeg*). Vizenor's grandmother, Alice Mary Beaulieu, was born into the crane totem on the White Earth Reservation, a totemic identification that manifests itself throughout Vizenor's work in avian visions and trickster flights. Vizenor has written, "My tribal grandmother and my father were related to the leaders of the crane; that succession, over a wild background of cedar and concrete, shamans and colonial assassins, is celebrated here in the autobiographical myths and metaphors of my imagination; my crossblood remembrance. We are cranes on the rise in new tribal narratives." Moved from the White Earth Reservation to the city as a result of the federal government's ill-conceived Relocation Program, Vizenor's twenty-six-year-old-father, Clement Vizenor, was found with his throat cut, the victim of a still unsolved murder. (Years later while a professional journalist, Vizenor attempted to investigate his father's murder but was told by a police official that nothing was known because no one paid much attention to the murder of an Indian in those days.) Not quite two years old at the time of his father's death, Gerald Vizenor grew up in a series of foster homes in the Minneapolis area close to the White Earth Reservation where his father's *anishinaabe* relatives lived. It was a peripatetic childhood that would echo the beginning of almost all trickster narratives in Native American tradition: "Trickster was going along." And as he was going along, Vizenor served in the U.S. Navy in Japan, where he became interested in both drama and haiku, studied at New York University, received a degree from the University of Minnesota, did graduate work briefly at Harvard, and carved out a successful career as a journalist and mixedblood provocateur with the *Minneapolis Tribune*. Always active in Native American concerns, Vizenor headed the American Indian Employment and Guidance Center in Minneapolis, organized protests, and wrote troubling articles and essays about injustices directed at Native Americans. All of this before he began his career as an academic culminating in his acceptance of an endowed chair at the University of Oklahoma.

Mixedbloods, Vizenor has written, "loosen the seams in the shrouds of identities." The mixedblood, he adds, "is a new metaphor . . . a transitive contradancer between communal tribal cultures and those material and urban pretensions that counter conservative traditions. The mixedblood wavers in autobiographies; he moves between mythic reservations where tricksters roamed and the cities where his father was murdered." Vizenor's poetry, fiction, and essays, and his novels in particular, are surely the products of such a coming of age, the creations of a "transitive contradancer" defining the places of the mixedblood in the modern world. The vision and voice are those of the trickster; the terrain begins with a baronage on the White Earth Reservation and a dynasty of mixedblood tricksters and expands around the globe. In the process, Vizenor shifts American Indian fiction into urban cities as well as reservation woodlands, invading the privileged metropolitan center with mixedblood clowns, detectives, and "landfill reservations" that constitute a kind of Indian reinhabitation of stolen America.

Vizenor's first novel, *Darkness in Saint Louis Bearheart*, is a tale of agonistic celebration that charts a new course for American Indian fiction and American literature. Alan Velie was the first critic to recognize Vizenor's post-structuralist methodology and to point out the central thread in Vizenor's writing: "In this work, Vizenor . . . tries to celebrate the unique status of the mixed-bloods—to reverse the prejudice that has plagued them, to make a hero of the half-breed." *Bearheart* is a postapocalyptic allegory of mixedblood pilgrim clowns afoot in a world gone predictably mad. This post-modern pilgrimage begins when Proude Cedarfair—mixedblood *anishinaabe* shaman and the fourth in a line of Proude Cedarfairs—and his wife Rosina flee their Cedar Circus reservation accompanied by seven clown crows as the reservation is about to be ravaged for its timber by corrupt tribal officials. The nation's economy has collapsed because of the depletion of fossil fuels, and the government and tribal "bigbellies" lust after the Circus cedar.

As the pilgrims move westward toward the vision window at Pueblo Bonito, place of passage into the fourth world, their journey takes on ironic overtones in a parody not merely of the familiar allegorical pilgrimage à la *Canterbury Tales* but also more pointedly of the westering pattern of American "discovery" and settlement. Very early in their journey, Proude and Rosina are joined by an intense collection of misfits, both mixedblood and white. Benito Saint Plumero, or Bigfoot, is a mixedblood clown and "new contrarion," a "phallophor" descended from "the hotheaded political exile and bigfooted explorer, Giacomo Constantino Beltrami." Like James Welch in *Fools Crow,* Vizenor's fictional names often echo history and mythology, both Indian and non-Indian. Bigfoot, for example, is the translated name of the celebrated Ojibwa war chief, Ma-mong-e-se-da. This fictional Bigfoot's pride, in addition to his huge feet, is an enormous and exuberantly active penis, named President Jackson by the appreciative sisters in the "scapehouse of weirds and sensitives," a retreat founded with federal funds by thirteen women poets from the cities. Another pilgrim, Pio Wissakodewinini, "the

parawoman mixedblood mammoth clown," has been falsely charged with rape and sentenced to a not-quite-successful sex change. Inawa Biwide, "the one who resembles a stranger," is sixteen, "an orphan rescued by the church from the state and the spiritless depths of a federal reservation housing commune." Inawa Biwide will quickly become the novel's apprentice shaman, eventually following Proude Cedarfair into the fourth world. Rescuer of Inawa Biwide from the state is Bishop Omax Parasimo, wearer of metamasks which allow him to pass from Bishop to Sister Eternal Flame and other transsexual metamorphoses. Justice Pardone Cozener, a minor figure in this oddly Chaucerian pilgrimage of the outraged and outrageous, is an "illiterate law school graduate and tribal justice . . . one of the new tribal bigbellies . . . who fattened themselves overeating on expense accounts from conference to conference." Justice Pardone is in love with Doctor Wilde Coxwaine, the bisexual tribal historian also along on this journey westward.

One of four consistently female characters journeying with Proude is Belladonna Darwin-Winter Catcher, the daughter of Old John Winter Catcher, Lakota shaman, and Charlotte Darwin, a white anthropologist. Conceived and born at Wounded Knee, Belladonna is a victim of rigid world views. Other female pilgrims include Little Big Mouse, "a small whitewoman with fresh water blue eyes" who rides in foot holsters at the waist of the giant Sun Bear Sun, "the three hundred pound seven foot son of the utopian tribal organizer Sun Bear," and Lillith Mae Farrier, the white woman who began her sexual menage with two canines while teaching on an Indian reservation.

Unarguably the most radical and startling of American Indian novels, *Darkness in Saint Louis Bearheart* is paradoxically also among the most traditional of novels by Indian authors, a narrative deeply in the trickster tradition, insisting upon values of community versus individuality, upon syncretic and dynamic values versus the cultural suicide inherent in stasis, upon the most delicate of harmonies between humanity and the world we inhabit, and upon our ultimate responsibility for that world. At the same time, through the eclectic lenses of his caricatured pilgrims, Vizenor demonstrates repeatedly the truth of Paul Watzlawick's declaration that the real world "is an invention whose inventor is unaware of his act of invention . . . the invention then becomes the basis of his world views and actions.

The fictional author of this novel-within-a-novel is old Bearheart, the mixedblood shaman ensconced in the BIA offices being ransacked by American Indian Movement radicals as the book begins. Bearheart, who as a child achieved his vision of the bear while imprisoned in a BIA school closet, has written the book we will read. According to William Warren, writing in 1885, "The No-ka or Bear family are more numerous than any of the other clans of the Ojibways, forming fully one-sixth of the entire tribe.... It is a general saying, and an observable fact, amongst their fellows, that the Bear clan resemble the animal that forms their Totem in disposition. They are ill-tempered and fond of fighting, and consequently they are noted as ever having kept the tribe in difficulty and war with other tribes.... " Bearheart, whose totem is the bear, is somewhat ill-tempered in his response to the AIM radicals and, through his novel, to American culture, but, like Proude, he assumes the role of trickster and uses laughter as his weapon in his war against hypocrisy and "terminal creeds." "When we are not victims to the white man then we become victims to ourselves," Bearheart tells a female AIM radical with her chicken feathers and plastic beads, underscoring Indians' inclination to embrace their own invention from "traditional static standards" as "artifacts." He directs her to the novel locked in a file cabinet, the "book about tribal futures, futures without oil and governments to blame for personal failures." To her question, "What is the book about?" Bearheart answers first, "Sex and violence," before adding, "Travels through terminal creeds and social deeds escaping from evil into the fourth world where bears speak the secret languages of saints."

"Terminal creeds" in *Bearheart* are beliefs which seek to fix, to impose static definitions upon the world. Whether those static definitions arise out of supposedly "traditional" Indian beliefs or out of the language of privileged Euramerica, they represent what Bakhtin terms "authoritative discourse," language "indissolubly fused with its authority—with political power" as a prior utterance. Such attempts to fix meaning according to what Vizenor terms "static standards" are destructive, suicidal, even when the definitions appear to arise out of revered tradition. Third Proude Cedarfair expresses Vizenor's message when he says very early in the novel, "Beliefs and traditions are not greater than the love of living," a declaration repeated near the end of the novel in Fourth Proude's insistence that "the power of the human spirit is carried in the heart not in histories and materials."

Within the idea of trickster that has evolved through Native American oral literatures, Vizenor finds an approach to both the phenomenal and noumenal that is distinctly "Indian." "In trickster narratives," Vizenor has written, "the listeners and readers imagine their liberation; the trickster is a sign, and the world is 'deconstructed' in a discourse." *Bearheart* is such a liberation, an attempt to free us from romantic entrapments, to liberate the imagination. The principal target of this fiction is precisely the sign "Indian," with its predetermined and well-worn path between signifier and signified. Vizenor's aim is to free the play between these two elements, to liberate "Indianness," and in so doing to free Indian identity from the epic, absolute past that insists upon stasis and tragedy for Native Americans.

While the authorial voice explains that Rosina "did not see

herself in the abstract as a series of changing ideologies," most of the pilgrims in this narrative, to varying degrees, do indeed suffer from the illness of terminal creeds. Bishop Omax Parasimo is "obsessed with the romantic and spiritual power of tribal people," a believer in the Hollywood version of Indianness. Matchi Makwa, another pilgrim, chants a lament of lost racial purity, "Our women were poisoned part white," leading Fourth Proude to explain, "Matchi Makwa was taken with evil word sorcerers."

Belladonna Darwin-Winter Catcher, the most obvious victim of terminal creeds, attempts to define herself as "Indian" to the exclusion of her mixedblood ancestry and, more fatally, to the exclusion of change. "Three whitemen raped me," she tells Proude, "three evil whitesavages." Upon learning she is pregnant, Proude replies, "Evil does not give life." Belladonna does not heed the warning Proude offers when he underscores the power of language to determine reality, saying, "We become the terminal creeds we speak."

When the pilgrims come to Orion, a walled town inhabited by the descendants of famous hunters and western bucking horse breeders, Belladonna is asked to define "tribal values." Belladonna replies with a string of clichés out of the "Hiawatha" vein of romantic literature, stating, "We are tribal and that means that we are children of dreams and visions.... Our bodies are connected to mother earth and our minds are part of the clouds.... Our voices are the living breath of the wilderness.... " A hunter replies, "My father and grandfathers three generations back were hunters.... They said the same things about the hunt that you said is tribal.... Are you telling me that what you are saying is exclusive to your mixedblood race?" Belladonna snaps, "Yes!" adding "I am different than a whiteman because of my values and my blood is different ... I would not be white." She blithers on, contradicting much of what we have witnessed thus far in the novel: "Tribal people seldom touch each other.... We do not invade the personal bodies of others and we do not stare at people when we are talking.... Indians have more magic in their lives than whitepeople."

A hunter responds: "Tell me about this Indian word you use, tell me which Indians are you talking about, or are you talking for all Indians." Finally, after trapping Belladonna in a series of inconsistencies and logical culs-de-sac, he asks the question which cuts through the heart of the novel: "What does Indian mean?" When Belladonna replies with more clichéd phrases, the hunter says flatly, "Indians are an invention.... You tell me that the invention is different than the rest of the world when it was the rest of the world that invented the Indian.... Are you speaking as an invention?" Speaking as a romantic invention indeed, a reductionist definition of being that would deny possibilities of the life-giving change and adaptation at the center of traditional tribal identity, Belladonna is further caught up in contradictions and dead ends. The hunters and breeders applaud and then deconstruct the invention, giving the young mixedblood her "just desserts": a cookie sprinkled with a time-release alkaloid poison. They have recognized their guest's exploitation of language as "the medium through which a hierarchical structure of power is perpetuated," the only difference from the usual colonial impulse being that Belladonna inverts the hierarchy by placing the static "Indian" at the top. "Your mixedblood friend is a terminal believer and a victim of her own narcisism," a breeder says to the pilgrims.

Belladonna Darwin-Winter Catcher is a clear example of what Vizenor has described in an interview as the "invented Indian." In the interview, Vizenor confesses his satirical, didactic purpose:

> I'm still educating an audience. For example, about Indian identity I have a revolutionary fervor. The hardest part of it is I believe we're all invented as Indians. . . . So what I'm pursuing now in much of my writing is the idea of the invented Indian. The inventions have become disguises. Much of the power we have is universal, generative in life itself and specific to our consciousness here. In my case there's even the balance of white and Indian, French and Indian, so the balance and contradiction is within me genetically. . . . There's another idea that I have worked into the stories, about terminal creeds. I worked that into the novel *Bearheart.* It occurs, obviously, in written literature and in totalitarian systems. It's a contradiction, again, to balance because it's out of balance if one is in the terminal condition. This occurs in invented Indians because we're invented and we're invented from traditional static standards and we are stuck in coins and words like artifacts. So we take up a belief and settle with it, stuck, static. Some upsetting is necessary.

Belladonna is obviously inventing herself from "traditional static standards." In its association with both beauty and deadly nightshade, Belladonna's very name hints at her narcissistic dead end. That the belladonna, or nightshade, plant is also associated historically with witchcraft implies the nature of evil witchery according to Native American traditions: the misuse of knowledge for the benefit of the individual alone rather than for the community as a whole. Her mixedblood surname, "Darwin," calls to mind also the scientist most responsible in the popular consciousness for the substitution of random event, or evolutionary chance, in place of a world of imagined structure and order. In the wake of Darwinian evolution, we were made capable of imagining ourselves as victims—pawns of chance—instead of creators of order from chaos in the tradition of storytellers. According to the Darwinian origin myth, as conveyed to the modern mind through the vehicle of naturalism, powerless humanity inhabits a world

antithetical to that evoked in the Native American origin myths in which men and women share responsibility for the creation and care of the world. In her attempt to define herself and all Indians according to predetermined, authority-laden values, Belladonna has forsaken such responsibility. She is a victim of her own words. As Proude explains, "We become our memories and what we believe. . . . We become the terminal creeds we speak."

Bearheart seems to embody dialectically opposed conceptions of chance, or random event. On one hand, a deconstruction of "terminal creeds," in trickster fashion, represents an insistence upon the infinite proliferation of possibility, including the polysemous text. This is the kind of celebration so common to postmodern literature and theory, an insistence that "coherent representation and action are either repressive or illusionary," and a reveling in what we might call chance. On the other hand, a mere capitulation to chance, or random event, would deny the emphasis upon our ultimate responsibility for ordering and sustaining the world we inhabit that is central to Native American ecosystemic cultures. For example, when Vizenor's pilgrims arrive at What Cheer, Iowa, to gamble for fuel with Sir Cecil Staples, the "monarch of unleaded gasoline," Proude declares flatly that "nothing is chance. . . . There is no chance in chance . . . Chances are terminal creeds." With chance, responsibility diminishes, a criticism the novel's author voices early in the novel:

> Tribal religions were becoming more ritualistic but without visions. The crazed and alienated were desperate for terminal creeds to give their vacuous lives meaning. Hundreds of urban tribal people came to the cedar nation for spiritual guidance. They camped for a few days, lusted after their women in the cedar, and then, *lacking inner discipline, dreams, and personal responsibilities,* moved on to find new word wars and new ideas to fill their pantribal urban emptiness. (emphasis mine)

The key to reconciling, or at least containing, this apparent dialectic lies once again in Vizenor's trickster pose. Embodying contradictions, all possibilities, trickster ceaselessly dismantles those imaginative constructions that limit human possibility and freedom, allowing signifier and signified to participate in a process of "continually breaking apart and re-attaching in new combinations." In **"Trickster Discourse"** Vizenor quotes Jacques Lacan, who warns us not to "cling to the illusion that the signifier answers to the function of representing the signified, or better, that the signifier has to answer for its existence in the name of any signification whatever." At the same time, however, trickster shows by negative example the necessity for humanity to control and order our world. Within the straitjacket of a fixed, authoritative discourse the self is made lifeless, like Belladonna, by stasis; within the unordered infinitude of pure possibility, the self deconstructs schizophrenically, the way trickster's body is continually coming apart in the traditional stories. Through language, stories that assert orders rather than order upon the chaos of experience, a coherent, adaptive, and syncretic human identity is possible without the "terminal" state of stasis. Every such utterance then becomes not "the telling of a story" but "the story of a telling," with responsibility falling upon the teller.

At the What Cheer Trailer Ruins, the pilgrims encounter not only the chances of chance, but also additional victims of terminal creeds, the Evil Gambler's mixedblood horde: "The three mixedbloods, dressed in diverse combinations of tribal vestments and martial uniforms, bangles and ideological power patches and armbands. . . . Deep furrows of ignorance and intolerance stretched across their unwashed foreheads." In an experience common to Native Americans, the three killers feel themselves, with some accuracy, to be the victims of white America. Cree Casket, the "mixedblood tribal trained cabinet maker with the blue chicken feather vestments," tells the pilgrims, "I was trained in the government schools to be a cabinet maker, but all the cabinets were machine made so making little wooden caskets made more sense." Cree Casket, we discover, is also a necrophiliac, a literal lover of the dead past. Carmine Cutthroat, described by Justice Pardone as "the red remount . . . with the green and pink stained chicken feathers," cannot speak, the Papago and Mescalero mixedblood having had hot lead poured down his throat by "seven whitechildren" while he slept. Willie Burke, the "Tliingit and Russian mixedblood" with a "compulsive need to kill plants and animals and trees," is rendered unconscious by Pio before he has a chance to tell his story of victimage. Doctor Wilde Coxwaine, examining the three mixedbloods, labels them "breathing plastic artifacts from reservation main street," declaring, "Here stand the classic hobbycraft mannikins dressed in throwaway pantribal vestments, promotional hierograms of cultural suicide."

Even the Evil Gambler himself is a victim of modern America, having been kidnapped from a shopping mall and raised in a bigrig trailer on the road, his upbringing a distillation of the peripatetic American experience. Being raised outside of any community, Sir Cecil has no tribal or communal identity; he exists only for himself, the destructive essence of evil witchery. From being doused repeatedly with pesticides, he has become pale and hairless, a malignant Moby-Dick of the heartland. He explains, "I learned about slow torture from the government and private business. . . . Thousands of people have died the slow death from disfiguring cancers because the government failed to protect the public." Sir Cecil, the Evil Gambler, is the product of a general failure of responsibility to the communal or tribal whole.

Among the trailer ruins, Lillith Mae Farrier is selected to gamble for fuel with Sir Cecil, the Evil Gambler reminiscent of the traditional Evil Gambler in American Indian mythologies. Because she "did not know the rituals of balance and power," because she has not been properly prepared according to tradition for her contest with the Evil Gambler, Lillith loses and destroys herself. Proude then tosses the four directions in competition with Sir Cecil and, because chance plays no part in Proude's vision, the Gambler loses and is condemned to death by Saint Plumero. Sir Cecil complains to Proude: "The pilgrims wanted gasoline which is part of the game, but you want to balance the world between good and evil. . . . Your game is not a simple game of death. You would change minds and histories and reverse the unusual control of evil power."

From the Trailer Ruins, the pilgrims, whose postal truck soon runs out of gas, travel westward on foot, encountering hordes of deformed stragglers on the broken highways. This host of cripples and monsters are, in the words of Doctor Wilde Coxwain, "Simple cases of poisoned genes," all ravaged by pesticides, poisoned rain, the horrors of the modern technological world. The authorial voice describes this national suicide: "First the fish died, the oceans turned sour, and then birds dropped in flight over cities, but it was not until thousands of children were born in the distorted shapes of evil animals that the government cautioned the chemical manufacturers. Millions of people had lost parts of their bodies to malignant neoplasms from cosmetics and chemical poisons in the air and food." Insisting blindly on identifying the cripples as romantic figures, Little Big Mouse is attacked and torn to pieces by a mob of technology's victims.

Following the canonization of Saint Plumero, a ceremony making Bigfoot a "double saint," the pilgrims arrive at Bioavaricious, Kansas and the Bioavaricious Regional Word Hospital, where terminal creeds—language whose meaning is fixed, language without creative play—are the goal of the hospital staff. In an attempt to rectify what is perceived as a national breakdown in language, the scientists at the word hospital are using a "dianoetic chromatic encoder" to "code and then reassemble the unit values of meaning in a spoken sentence." We are told that with "regenerated bioelectrical energies and electromagnetic fields, conversations were stimulated and modulated for predetermined values. Certain words and ideas were valued and reinforced with bioelectric stimulation." The endeavor at the word hospital suggests what Foucault has labeled an intention "to programme . . . to impose on people a framework in which to interpret the present." The "Bioavaricious Word Hospital" seems suspiciously like a metaphor for the Euramerican colonial endeavor seen from the point of view of the American Indian. Certainly the entire westering impulse of American manifest destiny is indisputably bioavaricious, devouring the continent—and now the third world—as it attempts to re-form the world in its own image. Part of this avaricious attempt to subsume all of creation into its own destiny has involved—particularly from an Indian point of view—an assertion of the absolute privilege of English; "fused with authority" and monologically predetermined. In such a "hospital" the life of language is consumed and destroyed.

Such an endeavor stands in sharp contrast to the oral tradition defined in a description of life among *Bearheart*'s displaced just a few pages earlier:

> Oral traditions were honored. Families welcomed the good tellers of stories, the wandering historians of follies and tragedies. Readers and writers were seldom praised but the travelling raconteurs were one form of the new shamans on the interstates. Facts and the need for facts had died with newspapers and politics. Nonfacts were more believable. The listeners traveled with the tellers through the same frames of time and place. The telling was in the listening. . . . Myths became the center of meaning again.

In the oral tradition a people define themselves and their place within an imagined order, a definition necessarily dynamic and requiring constantly changing stories. The listeners are coparticipants in the "behavioral utterance" of the story; as Vizenor himself has written elsewhere, "Creation myths are not time bound, the creation takes place in the telling, in present-tense metaphors." Predetermined values represent stasis and cultural suicide. Roland Barthes says simply, "the meaning of a work (or of a text) cannot be created by the work alone."

Impressed by the word hospital, Justice Pardoner and Doctor Wilde Coxwaine remain at Bioavaricious while the remaining pilgrims journey onward toward New Mexico. As they move westward, the pilgrims and sacred clowns meet fewer deformed victims of cultural genocide until finally they encounter the modern pueblos of the Southwest and a people living as they have always lived. At the Jemez Pueblo, the Walatowa Pueblo of N. Scott Momaday's *House Made of Dawn,* the pilgrims encounter two Pueblo clowns who outclown with their traditional wooden phalluses even Saint Plumero himself. The clowns direct Proude and the others toward Chaco Canyon and the vision window where, finally, Proude and Inawa Biwide soar into the fourth world as bears at the winter solstice.

A great deal is happening in *Bearheart,* but central to the entire thrust of the novel is the identification by the author's author, Vizenor, with trickster, the figure which mediates between oppositions, and in the words of Warwick Wadlington, "embodies two antithetical, nonrational experiences of man with the natural world, his society, and his own psyche." Citing Wadlington, Vizenor stresses the duality of trickster's role as on the one hand "a force of treacherous

disorder that outrages and disrupts, and on the other hand, an unanticipated, usually unintentional benevolence in which trickery is at the expense of inimical forces and for the benefit of mankind."

In one of the epigraphs to *Earthdivers,* Vizenor quotes Vine Deloria, Jr.'s, declaration that life for an Indian in today's world "becomes a schizophrenic balancing act wherein one holds that the creation, migration, and ceremonial stories of the tribe are true and that the Western European view of the world is also true. . . . [T]he trick is somehow to relate what one feels to what one is taught to think." About this balancing act, Vizenor himself says in the preface to this same collection of trickster narratives:

> The earthdivers in these twenty-one narratives are mixedbloods, or Métis, tribal tricksters and recast cultural heroes, the mournful and whimsical heirs and survivors from that premier union between the daughters of the woodland shamans and white fur traders. The Métis, or mixedblood, earthdivers in these stories dive into unknown urban places now, into the racial darkness in the cities, to create a new consciousness of coexistence.

For Vizenor, trickster is wenebojo (or manibozho, nanibozhu, and so on), "the compassionate tribal trickster of the woodland anishinaabeg, the people named the Chippewa, Ojibway." This is not, according to Vizenor, the "trickster in the word constructions of Paul Radin, the one who 'possesses no values, moral or social . . . knows neither good nor evil yet is responsible for both,' but the imaginative trickster, the one who cares to balance the world between terminal creeds and humor with unusual manners and ecstatic strategies." Vizenor says in the same interview: "When I was seeking some meaning in literature for myself, some identity for myself as a writer, I found it easily in the mythic connections." Central to these mythic connections is trickster, the shapeshifter who mediates between humanity and nature, humanity and deity, who challenges us to reimagine who we are, who balances the world with laughter.

Near the end of *Darkness in Saint Louis Bearheart,* Rosina and Sister Eternal Flame (Pio in the late bishop's metamask) encounter three tribal holy men "who had been singing in a ritual hogan. It was the last morning of a ceremonial chant to balance the world with humor and spiritual harmonies. . . . The men laughed and laughed knowing the power of their voices had restored good humor to the suffering tribes. Changing woman was coming over the desert with the sun." Changing Woman is perhaps the most revered of the Navajo Holy People, the mother of the Hero Twins and one of the creators of humankind. Marked by a somewhat fluid identity and eternal youth, she taught humanity the ceremonial ways to keep the natural forces of wind, lightning, storms, and animals in harmony—to balance the world.

Coming over the desert with the sun, from east to west, is Rosina herself, who, like Proude, has achieved mythic existence here near the end. "During the winter," we are told in the novel's final line, "the old men laughed and told stories about changing woman and vision bears." Translated through trickster's laughter into myth, Proude and Inawa Biwide and Rosina have a new existence within the ever-changing stories, the oral tradition. For all peoples, Vizenor argues, but for the mixedblood in particular, adaptation and new self-imaginings are synonymous with psychic survival. Those who would live as inventions, who, like Belladonna, would define themselves according to the predetermined values of the sign "Indian," are victims of their own terminal vision. Bearheart's mocking laughter is their warning.

If *Bearheart* takes an original path in the thickets of Native American fiction, eschewing the conventional agonies of the mixedblood trapped between cultures, Vizenor's next novel is more radical yet. In *Griever: An American Monkey King in China* (1987), Vizenor takes the trickster to Tianjin and forges a new fiction of nonmimetic monkeyshines that departs still further from the recognizable traditions of Native American literature while forging even deeper ties between the archetypal trickster figures that populate the literatures of divergent cultures.

In 1983 Vizenor and his wife, Laura Hall, traveled to China, where they served as exchange teachers at Tianjin University. In 1986, *Griever*, a product of that experience, won the 1986 Fiction Collective Award and was subsequently published in 1987 by Illinois State University and the Fiction Collective. In 1988 *Griever* won an American Book Award and was described by the *New York Times* as "experimental and . . . luminous." Somewhat paradoxically autobiographical while at the same time determinedly nonrepresentational, *Griever* draws upon Vizenor's experiences within the rigid structures of the Communist state, where, as in *Bearheart*, it seems that "some upsetting is necessary." To accomplish this upsetting and liberation, Vizenor creates a mixedblood Native American trickster-teacher, Griever de Hocus, from the White Earth Reservation. Merging through dreams with the classical trickster of China, the Monkey King, Griever reimagines the world, attacking the hypocrisies and empty dogma of his host country as well as the foibles of his fellow American exchange teachers and, in trickster tradition, all of humanity.

With Griever, Vizenor participates in reimagining spatial and temporal relations. If, as Foucault implies, the human body is ultimately the one irreducible element in the social scheme, and the body "exists in space and must either submit to authority . . . or carve out particular spaces of resistance and freedom—'heterotopias'—from an otherwise repressive world," in the figure of Griever de Hocus, an animated hybridization, Vizenor demonstrates the trickster's ability to transcend both spatial and temporal repressions. Soaring through dream-visions, Griever escapes temporal and spatial categories, destroys the "chronological net" and finds his "heterotopia"—or particular space of resistance and freedom—to be the world without map or chronology.

Whereas the allegory of *Bearheart* is often intentionally obscure, in *Griever* the author is careful to provide signposts to direct us in our reading of another difficult fiction. The first of these hints comes in the novel's epigraphs. The first epigraph quotes Octavio Paz's *The Monkey Grammarian* "Writing is a search for the meaning that writing itself violently expels. At the end of the search meaning evaporates and reveals to us a reality that literally is meaningless. . . . The word is a disincarnation of the world in search of its meaning; and an incarnation: a destruction of meaning, a return to body." And Vizenor follows with a second epigraph taken from James J.Y. Liu's *Essentials of Chinese Literary Art:* "Chinese drama is largely nonrepresentational or nonmimetic: its main purpose is expression of emotion and thought, rather than representation or imitation of life. In other words, it does not seek to create an illusion of reality, but rather seeks to express human experience in terms of imaginary characters and situations."

Together, these quotations should alert us to the way *Griever* must be approached: as nonrepresentational, nonmimetic. Despite the temptation to read the novel as a stylized rendering of the author's experience in China—that is, as an imitation of that autobiographical reality—Vizenor wants us to read his trickster's antics as we would approach the mythic: as expressions of "human experience in terms of imaginary characters and situations." Furthermore, the epigraphs serve as a warning to readers not to seek a "meaning" from this novel, the implication being that there are infinite and contradictory meanings coexisting and multiplying toward ultimate liberation in the polysemous text. Vizenor resists closure in his fiction with a determination resembling that of the Mind Monkey himself, of whom Vizenor writes, "He was driven to be immortal because nothing bored him more than the idea of an end; narrative conclusions were unnatural." Lest we be tricked into merely embracing the ephemerality and fragmentation of the text as its sole significance, however, we should bear in mind that it is precisely the resistance to structure, to "meaning" and closure, in the novel that conveys the sharpest political message: the fragmentation of the novel is meant to illuminate the necessity for resistance to the oppressive hegemony of the society depicted in the novel. Bakhtin has written, "A particular language in a novel is always a particular way of viewing the world, one that strives for social significance." In this novel, the language of the text itself asserts its privileged authority—its social significance—over the subjects of the text. In short, *Griever* is a very political work aimed like an explosive mine at the great walls of totalitarian China as well as the strictures/structures of modernist literature. And, as always, Vizenor finds the source of his explosive force in the "holotropic" trickster of Native American myth.

To further direct us in our fictional exploration, Vizenor—a kind of Indian guide in this textual wilderness—provides an epilogue that informs the reader that the author and his wife indeed served as exchange teachers in Tianjin and did in fact invade Maxim's de Beijing in the guise of interior reproduction inspectors. However, just in case this confession causes us to read *Griever* as a kind of confessional-qua-trickster novel, Vizenor adds a list of works "the author has considered in the imaginative conception of this novel," including especially *The Journey to the West,* translated by Anthony C. Yu, and *Monkey,* translated by Arthur Waley.

Both *The Journey to the West* and *Monkey* are translations of Wu Ch'êng-ên's epic story of Tripitaka's pilgrimage to India to bring the True Scriptures of Buddha back to China. Highly featured in the tales is Monkey, the immortal trickster of Chinese mythology who wars against stasis and rigid order on earth and in Heaven. Like his brethren the world over, Monkey is a creature of insatiable appetite and whim, an incorrigible shapeshifter for whom rules exist only as challenges. Powerful and wise enough to challenge the Jade Emperor himself, Monkey nonetheless finds himself repeatedly in trouble brought on by sheer impulse, so that he exclaims, "Bad! Bad! This escapade of mine is even more unfortunate than the last. If the Jade Emperor gets to hear of it, I am lost. Run! Run! Run!" Arthur Waley's description of *Monkey* might well serve as an introduction to all of Vizenor's fiction: "*Monkey* is unique in its combination of beauty with absurdity, of profundity with nonsense. Folk-lore, allegory, religion, history, anti-bureaucratic satire and pure poetry—such are the singularly diverse elements out of which the book is compounded." Like Vizenor's American Indian trickster, however, Monkey is at core a satirical litmus test for hypocrisy and false value.

Griever is dedicated "to Mixedbloods and Compassionate Tricksters," an announcement that underscores Vizenor's merging of the two figures that dominate his fiction. For Vizenor the mixing of bloods, cultures, and identities leads to liberation, a freeing of the individual from the masks of a fixed cultural identity. The mixedblood becomes the essential trickster, a transformationist between the icons of identity that limit the imagination. Neither "white" nor "Indian," neither Chinese nor English, the mixedblood is his/her own person, a "socioacupuncturist," to use Vizenor's term, a prick capable of puncturing facades and stereotypes, administering needles to free the flow of energy and balance the whole.

Trickster/mixedblood is, therefore, the perfect adversary of a totalitarian state that finds its lifeblood in "terminal creeds."

Like other Native American authors, Vizenor divides his novel into four parts, a number especially powerful in Indian tradition. For Native Americans a four-part structure, paralleling the seasonal cycles, suggests completeness and wholeness as well as closure. Barre Toelken and Tacheeni Scott write that for a Navajo audience the sequence of four parts suggests "an automatic progression ending on something important at the fourth step." From a different perspective, David Harvey notes that "cyclical and repetitive motions . . . provide a sense of security in a world where the general thrust of progress appears to be ever onwards and upwards into the firmament of the unknown."

Vizenor frames his novel with letters from Griever de Hocus to China Browne, a child of Luster Browne's mixedblood dynasty. China has come to China "to interview a warrior clown about Griever de Hocus, the trickster teacher who liberated hundreds of chickens at a local street market and then vanished last summer on an ultralight airplane built by her brother." A fair-skinned mixedblood from the White Earth Reservation, like Vizenor himself, Griever is the son of a Gypsy who passed through the reservation with a caravan named "the Universal Hocus Crown" which sold "plastic icons with grievous expressions, miniature grails, veronicas, and a thin instruction book entitled, 'How To Be Sad And Downcast And Still Live In Better Health Than People Who Pretend To Be So Happy'." From his itinerant father Griever inherits his name and his practice of "Griever Meditation." From his mother he inherits his identity as a mixedblood Native American.

As a mixedblood trickster, Griever has never fit conveniently into any niche. His tribal grandmother at home on the reservation pretends that she cannot understand him: "His urban mixedblood tongue, she snorted when he graduated from college, 'wags like a mongrel, he's a wild outsider.' Even at home on the reservation he was a foreigner." "Griever has an unusual imaginative mind," a teacher writes of the child, "and he could change the world if he is not first taken to be a total fool." Still another teacher declares, "The cause of his behavior, without a doubt, is racial. Indians never had it easier than now, the evil fires of settlement are out, but this troubled mixedblood child is given to the racial confusion of two identities, neither of which can be secured in one culture. These disruptions of the soul . . . become manifest as character disorders. He is not aware of his whole race, not even his own name." Griever illustrates the radical dismemberment typical of both trickster and traditional satire. The teachers' words are a satirical echo of the standard lament for the poor mixedblood caught between cultures and identities. Ironically, this is in one form or another the lament of many Native American writers such as Mourning Dove, Mathews,

McNickle, and even, to lesser degrees, Momaday, Silko, and Welch. In spite of the fact that Vizenor makes Griever, like Momaday's Abel and Benally, a victim of the federal government's misguided relocation policy, in satirizing the white teachers' words Vizenor once again makes it clear that he will have none of the sentimental posture that mourns the entrapment of the mixedblood.

An actor before the revolution, Wu Chou, whose name means "warrior clown," "is remembered for his performances as the Monkey King in the opera *Havoc of Heaven*. When he was too old to tumble as an acrobat, he studied the stories of tricksters and shamans in several countries around the world." At the time the novel takes place, Wu Chou is the "overseer of the electronic portal at the main entrance to Zhou Enlai University." The actor/trickster/scholar and keeper of the gateway to knowledge is the perfect character to recognize Griever's own acting out of the role of Monkey King.

"Griever was holosexual," the warrior clown tells China Browne, adding, "Griever was a mind monkey. . . . a holosexual mind monkey." Griever carried a holster "To shoot clocks," Wu Chou explains, a holster containing "pictures from wild histories." When the warrior clown shows the scroll from the holster to China, the pictures she sees on the scroll illustrate the events of the novel we are about to read. Filling out Wu Chou's definition of the trickster teacher, the narrator of the novel explains: "Griever is a mixedblood tribal trickster, a close relative of the old mind monkeys; he holds cold reason on a lunge line while he imagines the world. With colored pens he thinks backward, stops time like a shaman, and reverses intersections, interior landscapes." Through stories, we escape from the tyranny of chronology, history: "The listeners traveled with the tellers through the same frames of time and place," Vizenor wrote of the oral tradition in *Bearheart*. "The telling was in the listening."

As Wu Chou reconstructs Griever for China Browne, Vizenor adds casually, "Two spiders waited near the narrow crack in the pane." Watching and waiting is the creative presence of Spider, from whom the stories are spun by which, like Momaday's man made of words and Silko's Ts'its'tsi'nako, we comprehend the world. With the incidental touch of Spider's presence, Vizenor underscores the mythic dimension and the underpinnings of the oral tradition.

In the opening letter to China, Griever declares that his fellow exchange teachers are "the decadent missionaries of this generation" and that postrevolutionary China is made up (like Belladonna's Indian identity) of "invented traditions, broken rituals." In Vizenor's fiction invented traditions are trickster's targets, and Griever assaults these inventions with the antic fury of the Monkey King disrupting Heaven. One of the trickster's first acts is to free chickens waiting for slaughter in the free market, a radical performance that the Chinese

understand in the context of myth: "Chicken liberation, then, was better understood as a comic opera. The audience was drawn to the trickster and his imaginative acts, not the high cost of chicken breasts. Mind monkeys, from practiced stories, would have done no less than emancipate the birds in a free market. Those who liberate, in traditional stories, are the heroes of the culture." And as they watch Griever's liberation, the people "whispered about scenes in the other mind monkey stories." Implicit in this line is the fact that we are witnessing another in the tradition of mind monkey stories, that the novel we are reading has no more commitment to "realism" than do the traditional stories of mythic heroics.

Like the trickster of Native American stories, Griever is an imaginative shapeshifter and "holosexual." In his imagination, Griever invades the voluptuous Sugar Dee: "He became a woman there beneath her hair, and with thunder in her ears, she peeled the blossoms; she pulled her head down in the lambent heat, down on her breasts, dibbled and sheared her high nipples with the point of her tongue. She towed her flesh back from the cold and heard the cocks and animals on her breath." Becoming Sugar Dee, trickster engages in erotic union with him/herself, an act fully in the tradition of Native American tricksters. And from the moment of his chicken liberation early in the novel, Griever is accompanied by Matteo Ricci, a cock named for an Italian Jesuit missionary. Perched on Griever's shoulder throughout the novel, Matteo Ricci allows Vizenor to pun unceasingly upon the liberated cock that distresses everyone with its refusal to conform to codes. Adding a disturbing element of energy and uncertainty, Griever's outrageous cock—just like that of the trickster in traditional stories—causes every situation to be unstable, unpredictable, fertile with potential. In one scene a female teacher, Gingerie, "brushed her hair back and watched the trickster and his cock circle back to the guest house. She waited at the window and waved to him when he passed. Matteo Ricci spread his sickle feathers and shook his wattles." Hilariously, Gingerie and the trickster's cock appear to respond to one another in the author's word-play.

Surrounding Griever is a cast of nearly allegorical figures, whom the author terms "eight uncommon teachers from east to west":

> Luther Holes, the valetudinarian and guest house sycophant; Hannah Dustan, the computer separatist; Carnegie Morgan, also known as Carnie, the tallest teacher with the widest mouth and a rich name; Gingerie Anderson-Peterson, place name consumer with a peculiar accent; Jack and Sugar Dee, the inseparable industrial management consultants; and Colin Marplot Gloome, the retired time and motion scholar.

Hannah Dustan, the "computer separatist," is a "hereditist"

who "withstands miscegenation, and neither speaks nor listens to people that she determines are mixedbloods." Hannah explains that "when people can be recognized for what they are, then they do better in the world. Jews, like the Chinese and other races, achieve more and earn more in those countries where there is discrimination, but not mixedbloods because no one knows who they are. Mixedbloods are neither here nor there, not like real bloods." A true believer in terminal creeds, Hannah is not aware of Griever's own mixedblood and thus tolerates the trickster. Hannah's dreams are racially disturbed: "In the first she is haunted by dark children who claim she is their mother; in the second, columns of silent immigrants stand in public welfare lines around her house. . . . In both dreams the children and immigrants are mixedbloods, their hands soiled and covered with mold."

Like Hannah, Griever has a troubling dream, in the first part of which he hears slogans chanted by men and women who march in circles:

> "Remember our national policies, our proud new policies," the voices intoned, "we strive to better our lives, death to cats and dogs, one child, death to criminals, one child, death to venereal diseases, one child, death to capitalist roaders, one child, death to spiritual pollution, one child, no spitting, one child, no ice cream with barbarians, one child, no sex on the road, one child, no bright colors, one child, no decadent music, one child, no telephone directories, one child, the east is red."

An unmistakable indictment, this aspect of Griever's dream underscores the terminal condition of the totalitarian mentality, the state that opposes creation with death. And immediately after this litany in the dream a mute child (one child) appears and follows the trickster through the streets like a shadow, the child's reflection rippling back at Griever from all surfaces. The trickster gives the mute child a pencil and the child draws pictures on the concrete: "First he outlined a prairie schooner pulled by a small horse, then a lake with an island and brick houses surrounded by several oversized swine. Near the screen door he made a man who wore a round mask with a wide evil smile. The man held bones in his hands." The child is surrounded by a pale blue light, and as the dream ends the light shoots from the mute child to the trickster and to the telephone, and Griever explains in his letter to China Browne, "When the light passed through me, I became the child, we became each other, and then we raised the receiver to our ear." A voice on the telephone then asks the awakened Griever if he is alone in his room, protesting that visitors are required to register before entering the guest house. When Griever describes the dream child to Egas Zhang, the corrupt director of the foreign affairs bureau at the university, Egas explains that the child is "Yaba Gezi, the mute pigeon. . . . Child from old stories, no one sees the mute, from stories

before liberation." Later, Griever finds the child's drawings on the concrete balcony.

Ironically, of course, the old stories—like all traditional trickster tales—are stories of liberation, of imaginative freedom opposed by the new "liberation" of Egas Zhang's postrevolutionary China. And as the repeated reflection and mirroring of the child's face suggests, Yaba Gezi springs from within Griever, the child of imagination and creation silenced by the totalitarian state. The mute child's drawings depict key elements in the story we are about to read. The prairie schooner is the cart of the mixedblood, Kangmei, in which Griever will be smuggled to safety. It is also Kangmei who will soar to final freedom with Griever at the novel's end. The island drawn by Yaba Gezi will appear in the novel as Obo Island in the midst of Shuishang Water Park, "a tribal place where shamans gather and dream" and home to those who have escaped the terminal creeds of totalitarianism.

When Griever is welcomed to Obo Island, he discovers one of the inhabitants is the "mute pigeon," Yaba Gezi. In keeping with Native American cosmology, the dream world and the waking world once again are one, without boundaries. Dreams arise from the self defined in dreams. Also living on the island are Kangmei; Shitou, the "stone man"; Pigsie, who teaches his swine to play basketball; and Sandie, the government rat hunter. Both Sandie and Pigsie bear names drawn from the "comic opera" stories of the mind monkey. Sandie had studied at the University of California at Berkeley before falling afoul of the revolution and being demoted to rat hunter. Pigsie had gone to the United States to study the operation of ultralight airplanes and play basketball, but his lasciviousness had caused his downfall to swine herder. In the classic stories of the Monkey King, both Sandie and Pigsie are monsters fallen from grace and redeemed to accompany the monk, Tripitaka, on his journey to bring the holy scriptures to China. Sandie, like the rat hunter, is rather colorless and sincere in the mythic tale, while Pigsie, like his swine-herding namesake, is beset by appetites and a fondness for buxom young women. Like Griever, the inhabitants of the island are too liberated to exist easily in a terminal state.

Kangmei is the daughter of Egas Zhang's wife and "Battle Wilson, Oklahoma-born Sinophile, poet, idealist, and petroleum engineer." Like Tripitaka in the Monkey King stories, Battle Wilson comes to China with sacred scriptures. Wilson, however, has stolen his scrolls from the British Museum to return them to their rightful home in China, and Battle Wilson's scrolls will, at the novel's end, turn out to contain not terminal truths but a recipe for blue chicken.

Griever de Hocus overturns the terminal creeds of his hosts, liberating not only chickens in the marketplace but also a caravan of condemned prisoners en route to execution. In a moment of surprisingly undisguised rhetoric for this trickster novel, Griever shouts at the convoy: "I would sooner be dead than submit to tyranny. A legal system that can try thirty people in half a day, and commit them all to their graves as a result of that trial, is a tryannical system."

With his face painted like that of the Monkey King in the comic opera, Griever identifies himself first as "White Earth Monkey King" and then successively as Wei Jingsheng and Fu Yuehua, both actual, historical political prisoners in China, before leaping aboard a truck and racing to freedom with three rapists, a heroin dealer, a murderer, a prostitute, a robber, and an art historian who "exported stolen cultural relics"—a crime familiar to American Indians. Though the prostitute turns out to be simply an organizer of a homework business for nannies, trickster's prisoners prove to be a sordid lot. Only the rapists make a serious attempt to escape, and they are shot by the pursuing soldiers. The others wait tamely to be recaptured. As is often the case with trickster, Griever's heroic gesture results in anticlimax.

When his affair with Hester Hua Dan results in pregnancy, Griever rejoices, giving the unborn child the name of Kuan Yin, the Efficacious Bodhisattva from the Monkey King stories. However, while Griever is delivering mooncakes to the mixedblood Lindbergh Wang during the Marxmass Carnival, Hester drowns herself in the guest-house pond to escape the wrath of her father, Egas Zhang. A typical trickster, Griever in disguise has been fondling the breasts of Gingerie a few minutes earlier, but now he rages with loss and despair over the deaths of Hester and their unborn daughter. Finally he escapes from the terminal state in an ultralight airplane bound for Macao.

Just as the novel began with a letter to China Browne, it ends with a letter to China that concludes the book on a lyrical note of despondency surprising for a trickster narrative. "China opened in pale blue smoke on the night he arrived and closed now in dead water," the author writes. And Griever tells China: "The Marxmass Carnival was horrible this year, no more carnivals like that for me. No panic holes are deep enough to hold my rage over what happened that night." Redeeming the narrative from despair, however, are both Griever's final words, "This is a marvelous world of tricksters. Love, Griever de Lindbergh," and the fact that Griever and Kangmei soar in ultralight avian dreams toward ultimate liberation. That they have apparently never reached their proposed destination—Macao—underscores the story's refusal to end, Griever's resistance to narrative closure. Trickster is still "going along."

Griever is an intensely political text, both as an incomplete attempt to escape from the "readerly" novel and as a bitter indictment of the totalitarian state. Though he/she may assume the guise of hypocrisy and even repression in comic roles, as a trope, trickster abhors repression and hypocrisy

and challenges us to reimagine the world and liberate ourselves in the process. In his epilogue, Vizenor notes that "President Li Xiannian was in the United States to sign an agreement with President Ronald Reagan that allows the People's Republic of China to buy American reactors and other nuclear technology 'designed for the peaceful use, and only the peaceful use of nuclear materials.'" These are the book's final words, another skirmish in what Gerald Vizenor has called the "wordwars." Given the contents of the novel they conclude, their irony is devastating. In this novel, American Indian fiction soars free of rural reservation America, past the privileged metropolitan center, to the other side of the earth.

Vizenor's third novel, *The Trickster of Liberty* (1988), might be considered a prequel to *Bearheart* and *Griever*. In this brief and highly episodic work, Vizenor takes his readers back to the origins of the Patronia Baronage on the White Earth Reservation and introduces Luster Browne and Novena Mae Ironmoccasin, the founders of a mixedblood trickster dynasty that spawns Shadow Box Browne and his nine siblings. Shadow Box in turn marries Wink Martin and the two continue the trickster line with their own swarm of mixedbloods: China Browne, Tulip Browne, Tune Browne, Garlic Browne, Ginseng Browne, Eternal Flame Browne, Father Mother Browne, Mime Browne, and Slyboots Browne. Part of the extended family through marriage or adoption are Mouse Proof Martin and Griever de Hocus.

Vizenor opens *The Trickster of Liberty* with a prologue entitled "Tricksters and Transvaluation," in which mixedblood trickster Sergeant Alex Hobraiser debates the nature of tricksters with cultural anthropologist Eastman Schicer while an implied author provides informative declarations and pertinent quotations from poststructuralists such as Barthes and Lacan as well as various authorities on Indians and tricksters. While the alien anthropologist attempts in the best modernist tradition to discover a "trickster code" in the sergeant's words—that is, to decode the text—the reader is provided with Vizenor's most direct clues to the nature of the (inherently indefinable) trickster presence in his fiction. "The Woodland trickster is a comic trope; a universal language game," the third-person voice of the prologue explains. "The trickster narrative arises in agonistic imagination; a wild venture in a communal discourse, an uncertain humor that denies aestheticism, translation, and imposed representations. . . . The tribal trickster is a comic *holotrope,* the whole figuration; an unbroken interior landscape that beams various points of view in temporaral reveries." Perhaps most to the point for Vizenor's trickster narratives, we are told that "the trickster is comic nature in a language game, not a real person or 'being' in the ontological sense. Tribal tricksters are embodied in imagination and liberate the mind; an androgyny, she would repudiate translations and imposed representations, as he would bare the contradictions of the striptease." Quoting Lacan, the narrator points out that "every word always has a beyond, sustains several meanings." The narrator goes on to add succinctly, "The trick, in seven words, is to *elude historicism, racial representations, and remain historical.*"

Though it may strike some as merely ducking a tough issue, it seems readily apparent that any attempt to explain with certainty Vizenor's conception of trickster would foolishly resemble Eastman Schicer's yearning to "decode" a trickster monologue. However, the prologue underscores the essence of the author's identification as trickster "crossblood": the trickster "holotrope" defies terminal creeds, demands a transcendent freedom that negates such reductionist historicisms as the concept labeled "Indian," a codified image that attempts to enforce conformity to preconceived and static concepts, or "racial representations." The "Indian" in the terminal Euramerican imagination becomes an aesthetic artifact frozen on coins, "a designer brave engraved in a cultural striptease," as Sergeant Alex Hobraiser puts it. Tune Browne, an "intuitive scholar" and political candidate posing ironically in braids, ribbons, bones, and fur, explains this terminal state differently, pointing to a staged photograph by Edward Curtis and declaring, "Curtis has removed the clock, colonized our cultures, and denied us our time in the world." Curtis, we might add, aestheticized the Indian, decontextualizing his living models the way sacred fetishes have been routinely decontextualized into iconic "art" in the world's museums—like the Feather Boy bundle in McNickle's *Wind from an Enemy Sky.* Griever de Hocus, avian trickster and "an adopted heir to the baronage," demands this "time in the world," explaining in *The Trickster of Liberty* that "we wear the agonistic moment, not the burdens of the past."

Quoting Joseph Meeker's *The Comedy of Survival,* Vizenor's prologue further asserts that "the comic mode of human behavior represented in literature is the closest art has come to describing man as an adaptive animal." This is the comic mode described by Bakhtin, that which "works in a zone of maximal proximity," drawing the subject "into a zone of crude contact where one can finger it familiarly on all sides . . . dismember it. . . . making it an object of familiar contact and thus clearing the ground for an absolutely free investigation of it." Vizenor's darkly comic art asserts precisely that syncretic, adaptive, investigative nature, a liberation for the "Native American" from artifact and fact. Characteristically illustrative of this metaphor is Slyboots Browne, "the most devious, clever, and artful of the tricksters at the baronage . . . a wild avian dreamer who assumes, surmises, and imagines a world with no halters." It is Slyboots who develops a microlight industry on the reservation baronage and who ships two of the microlights to Griever in Vizenor's previous novel, one to facilitate Griever's escape and one to bribe the Chinese cadres.

Moving out from the reservation, Luster Browne's progeny populate the world with tricksters who challenge, moment by moment, the values and creeds of the worlds they invade. Griever, as Vizenor illustrated in his previous novel, goes to China. China Browne goes to China after Griever, and her adventure is recorded in both *Griever: An American Monkey King in China* and *The Trickster of Liberty.* Tune Browne graduates from the University of California along with Ishi, the captive, aestheticized "Indian" housed in the Berkeley museum, last of the Yahi and, in phrases Vizenor quotes in *Trickster,* the "ideal museum specimen" sought by anthropologists. As Vizenor views him, Ishi is the perfect Indian, a modernist icon, the "primitive" decontextualized and thus made an autonomous and collectible artifact. In the museum, Ishi becomes an illustration of the insidious Western impulse James Clifford has described: "We need to be suspicious of an almost-automatic tendency to relegate non-Western peoples and objects to the pasts of an increasingly homogeneous humanity."

Tune founds the New School of Socioacupuncture on the Berkeley campus and liberates dogs from the medical laboratories. Tulip Browne makes windmills and practices her profession as a private detective in Berkeley, where in a Vizenoresque roman à clef she solves the mysterious disappearance of a computer from the Native American Studies offices. Eternal Flame, who also figures prominently in *Bearheart,* founds a "scapehouse for wounded reservation women," and in a scene from *Trickster,* Sister Eternal Flame listens as Griever tells the story of the "scapehouse of weirds and sensitives" from *Bearheart,* to which Sister Eternal Flame responds, "You are the weird one."

One by one, Vizenor chronicles the trickster adventures of each of Shadow Box and Wink Browne's children as they travel their peripatetic paths. The harshest satire of the book is reserved for self-deluding Indians and would-be Indians in a chapter describing the Last Lecture, a "tavern and sermon center" opened by Father Mother. In the tavern, tribal people listen as individuals are allowed to give a final lecture before dropping over a short precipice named the "Edge of the White Earth" into new names and identities with legal papers provided by Father Mother. In the most pointed lecture, one uncomfortably pertinent to all of us who identify as mixedbloods and educators, Marie Gee Hailme, an urban mixedblood, confesses her sins:

> We were all mixedbloods, some light and some dark, and married to whites, and most of us had never really lived in reservation communities. Yes, we suffered some in college, but not in the same way as the Indian kids we were trying to reach, the ones we were trying to keep in school when school was the real problem. But there we were, the first generation of Indian education experts, forcing our invented

curriculum units, our idea of Indians, on the next generation, forcing Indian kids to accept our biased views.

In addition to chiding Indian educators (and everyone else), Vizenor launches another of his many attacks upon those he sees as hypocritical activists pandering to whites' conceptions of invented Indians, introducing Coke de Fountain, "an urban pantribal radical and dealer in cocaine." De Fountain is a paroled felon whose "tribal career unfolded in prison, where he studied tribal philosophies and blossomed when he was paroled in braids and a bone choker. He bore a dark cultural frown, posed as a new colonial victim, and learned his racial diatribes in church basements." Sharply reminiscent of his published criticisms of American Indian Movement radical Dennis Banks, Vizenor's sketch of De Fountain is the most blunt and effectively uncomfortable moment in *The Trickster of Liberty*. Comparatively mild is Vizenor's satire directed at Homer Yellow Snow, who gets up to confess in his Last Lecture that he is, in fact, a pretend Indian. Pointedly calling to mind published doubts concerning the authenticity of author Jamake Highwater's claim to an Indian identity, Homer Yellow Snow's confession lays bare the essense of such controversy when he says to his tribal audience: "If you knew who you were, why did you find it so easy to believe in me? . . . because you too want to be white, and no matter what you say in public, you trust whites more than you trust Indians, which is to say, you trust pretend Indians more than real ones."

Shapeshifting across the middle ground long reserved for displaced and distraught mixedbloods, Vizenor is the first American Indian author to find "crossbloods" a cause for joyous celebration.
—Louis Owens

In *The Trickster of Liberty*, as in all of Vizenor's fiction, it is obvious that "some upsetting is necessary" and that the author/trickster is again intent upon attacking terminal creeds and loosening the shrouds of identities. Shapeshifting across the middle ground long reserved for displaced and distraught mixedbloods, Vizenor is the first American Indian author to find "crossbloods" a cause for joyous celebration. The most ambitious and radically intellectual of American Indian writers, Vizenor has taken Indian fiction—and the figure of the mixedblood in particular—into the future. In the irresistible penetration of his satires, Vizenor insists upon ethics beyond aesthetics, upon the immutable values of spirit and heart articulated by Proude Cedarfair, and though he celebrates the liberated play of postmodernism, he nonetheless goes well beyond the "contrived depthlessness" that has been defined as "*the* overwhelming motif in postmodernism." In so doing,

Vizenor has produced one of America's most distinctive literary voices.

Robert Allen Warrior (review date Spring 1993)

SOURCE: Review of *Dead Voices: Natural Agonies in the New World*, in *World Literature Today*, Vol. 67, No. 2, Spring, 1993, pp. 423-24.

[*In the following review, Warrior argues that while retaining many aspects characteristic of Vizenor's previous work,* Dead Voices *is more mature and confident.*]

Gerald Vizenor's new novel is an ideal followup to his *Heirs of Columbus* (1991) and other recent books. *Dead Voices* tells a ceremonial story of urban dwellers who play a tribal card game in which they become various animals, objects, and insects who face various urban challenges and dysfunctions. The elusive and allusive guide through the game is Bagese, a scatological urban trickster who has become a bear. Through this tribal card game, Vizenor's urban characters become fleas who fight against an exterminator ready to spray them into oblivion, squirrels chased by a heartless hunter who comes to be haunted by his wanton killing, praying mantises who raid a fruit truck, and others. Throughout, various bears lurk behind and in front of the text.

Though many of these eccentric themes will be familiar to readers of Vizenor's work, much here is innovative. Perhaps most important, Vizenor writes here with more of a sense of mature and consistent calm than in any of his earlier work. His usual aggressiveness remains, but the overall tone is one of full and rich confidence. This is most evident in the way that each chapter begins with the same evocative litany, giving a ceremonial aspect to the stories that follow. This new form allows Vizenor to present a rich and various description of his environs. The city he describes and the people and animals that inhabit it come across as desperately hollow, with their faint whispers of hope and healing ringing into the night. Throughout, the great enforcers of the hollow darkness are the "wordies," those who would ossify tribal stories and human existence into predictable patterns and banal behaviors.

Along with exploring the tragically mundane contours of contemporary existence and the power of stories in overcoming that, *Dead Voices* also travels along the edges of the question of whether or not stories, when recorded on the page, can retain their healing power. Vizenor, finally, hopes they do, even if he shares the reservations of Bagese that writing down the secrets of tribal games might devalue them of their liberative potential.

Kathy Whitson (review date Winter 1994)

SOURCE: Review of *Dead Voices: Natural Agonies in the New World* and *Summer in the Spring: Anishinaabe Lyric Poems and Stories,* in *Studies in Short Fiction,* Vol. 31, No. 1, Winter, 1994, pp. 130-32.

[*In the review below, Whitson states the two works under review expand the readers exposure to Anishinaabe culture and literature.*]

Gerald Vizenor, a Professor of Native American Studies at the University of California, Berkeley, and a member of the Minnesota Chippewa Tribe, has already contributed significantly to the body of Native American literature. Now we have two more volumes from him—*Dead Voices*, a novel, and *Summer in the Spring*, a volume of Anishinaabe lyric poems and stories that he has edited and interpreted. Like much of Vizenor's earlier work, these volumes find their energy in the retelling and reshaping of trickster tales. In his introduction to *Summer in the Spring*, Vizenor suggests that the stories constitute a "new tribal hermeneutics." That Vizenor continues to rework the trickster tales is testament to both the richness of the tribal tales and to his abundant imaginative and hermeneutic powers.

Subtitled "Natural Agonies in the New World," *Dead Voices* establishes polarities between the aboriginal cultures and their values and the "values" of the New World. Vizenor draws contrasts between the "treeline" and the city, between the eye and the car, between the oral and the written, between the "wordies" and the non-wordies, between the clean of soap and natural body odors, and, of course, between "dead voices" and live voices—those voices that still have their stories. He also contrasts the community of the tribal world where the protagonist, Bagese, always speaks with the plural pronoun "we," with the isolation of the frame narrator who uses the singular pronoun, "I."

The novel uses a framing device that echoes the thematic polarities. The first and last chapters are narrated by an academic, Vizenor-like character, and the heart of the novel is given over to the voice(s) of Bagese, an ancient tribal woman. Within the frame, the novel is developed around the convention of a seven-day, seven-card wanaki game (the narrator says "the word 'wanaki' means to live somewhere in peace, a chance at peace") wherein the protagonist moves from experience to experience in the shape-shifted forms of a bear, a flea, a squirrel, a mantis, a crow, a beaver, and a trickster. Vizenor's use of a shape-shifting narrator allows him to explore any number of issues, each time with a startlingly fresh perspective. The shape-shifting Bagese grieves over several "natural agonies in the new world," including the pollution of the environment by a chemical civilization, the educational system, the imprisoning childcare system, the fur trade, and the diminution of the animal kingdom by civilization. The chapter on the fleas is rich indeed. The attitudes of the fleas mirror the different tribal attitudes toward the European invasion of the continent and surely comments as well on those who allowed themselves to be put on exhibit in shows such as the Wild West Show. One suspects that the allegory runs deeper than the casual reader might recognize. There is a price to be paid, however, for the use of multiple, shape-shifted narrators: the novel loses its narrative impulse and fictive appeal and reads more like a moral allegory.

One of the triumphant ironics of the book is that the tribal woman warns all along of the dead voices of the wordies, that once the eye is privileged over the ear, once the oral tradition yields to a literate tradition, then the stories cease to have life and the voices become dead. But Vizenor and his frame narrator affirm that the publication of the stories invests them with another life, one that arcs out in a pattern that the merely oral word could never achieve, and thus that the medium of the wordies, publication, is subverted and pressed into service by the tribal people who have live voices and live stories. In the same way, the novel shows that the animals of the wild who have been hunted and shunted off their land have found a way to accommodate themselves and adapt to the cities. Whereas they were once able to survive only in and beyond the treelines, they now arc thriving in the cities. This plot parallels the encroachment into the world of the published word by the tribal people.

At the heart of the novel is the ability to transform, to shape-shift, and that seems to be the moral of the tale as well. In order to survive, crossbloods and tribal people must shape-shift to ward off the deadening magic of those wordies who would turn tribal culture into nothing more than artifact, something to be recorded quickly before it disappears completely.

Dead Voices is a powerful book that warns all cultures of the dangers of abandoning tribal and natural values. Above all, *Dead Voices* celebrates survival. The last utterance of the tribal woman, Bagese, and of the frame narrator, is "We must go on."

In *Dead Voices*, Vizenor reworks Anishinaabe tales by placing them in a Western genre—the novel. But in *Summer in the Spring*, he edits and interprets many of the same narrative kernels in the tribal art forms of a century or more ago—the lyric poem, the pictomyth, and the story.

The lyric poems are lovely, often cryptic—with deeper meaning hidden within the cultural context of the poems. For example, the following short lyric embeds the wonderful trickster story of the dancing ducks:

    naanabozho song

dance and sing
across the water
if you open your eyes
they will turn red.

But unless the reader knows the story of the dancing ducks, the poem seems oblique and without a narrative thread. The spareness of the lyric poems reflects their orality and the necessity of a culturally tuned audience which, given the bare bones of the narrative, will supply the meat. The hearer reconstructs the tale through synecdoche and generates a meaning both communal and personal. The strongly narrative pictomyths require the same kind of audience participation in order to generate meaning. It remains unclear why Vizenor pairs certain pictomyths with certain poems, but their presence is significant—if only because no other modern edition that I know of includes them.

Vizenor incorporates two kinds of stories in his collection, informational and mythic. The informational stories transmit cultural practices, such as naming ceremonies, female and male puberty rites, marriage, and initiation into the grand medicine lodge—the midewiwin. The mythic stories celebrate the Anishinaabe culture hero, Naanabozho.

In his introduction, Vizenor explains the publishing history of the contents of the present volume. *Summer in the Spring* represents the third publication of the stories and the fourth publication of the lyric poems. While I am impressed with the quality of the lyric poems, especially, and while any and every version of the trickster stories adds breadth and dimension to the larger trickster canon, I am a little disappointed that this material receives yet another audience while there are manifold Native American texts that deserve a first chance at publication and may have been passed over for inclusion in the American Indian Literature and Critical Studies Series, edited by Vizenor himself. In addition, though Vizenor acknowledges that he is the editor and interpreter of the selections in the volume, the extent of his role as interpreter is not completely clear. Perhaps the inclusion of a text before and after interpretation would have been helpful to allow the reader to see the nature of Vizenor's contribution.

Beyond these few misgivings, I find both of Vizenor's volumes to be significant additions to the canon of American Indian literature. Read in tandem or alone, each volume confirms the strength of the Anishinaabe oral and written traditions, and both sound the call of survival, "We must go on."

David Mogen (review date Winter 1994)

SOURCE: Review of *Dead Voices: Natural Agonies in the*

New World, in *Western American Literature,* Vol. XXVIII, No. 4, Winter, 1994, pp. 361-62.

[*In the following review, Mogen contends that while* Dead Voices *is difficult to read, it is an eloquent and original work.*]

Like Vizenor's earlier work, **Dead Voices** dramatizes the complex "word wars" waged between tribal peoples and mainstream culture. Indeed, this strange "novel" creates a living trickster voice—at once profane, lyrical and wondrously bizarre—through which to dramatize a radical perspective on the Western tradition of written culture, embodying "dead voices" that suppress the "natural agonies" of tribal peoples and the natural world. By giving written "voice" to the internal narrator Bageese, a reclusive tribal woman who is at once a bear and the vehicle through which we hear the agonies of animal beings surviving in the urban landscape, Vizenor paradoxically translates unspeakable realities into a written medium that historically has obliterated them in wars of words. Because the very voice of the novel embodies a paradox of articulation, this is a difficult book to read, one in which meaning and narrative alike seem to hover just beyond the reach of written language. Like the mirrors in Bageese's home that provide glimpses of her bear identity, the language here presents tantalizing refractions from realms of experience that never entirely come into focus. But this effect of suspension between worlds of discourse creates a curious poetry as well, in which conventional images of tribal cultures, nature, and reality itself are radically transposed.

The novel's messages are implicit in its paradoxical point of view, which integrates "voices" that are inherently untranslatable, so that decoding the perspectives of the various voices telling the narrative becomes part of the process of "reading." The three major categories of "voice" are suggested in the opening chapter, "Shadows," which serves as a fictional author's preface to the tales that follow. Here the tribal storyteller Bageese warns the scholarly narrator of the dangers of translating her stories into the "dead voices" of lectures and printed words. This introductory warning about the difficulty of translating oral into written "hearing" is later compounded by the nature of the stories themselves, which originate in the tribal "wanaki game," and which must be experienced and told from a first person plural point of view, in which the human narrator's voice is fused with those of the beings whose stories are being told. Bageese's education of the narrator also prepares the reader for the uniquely conceived voice of the stories that follow: "The secret, she told me, was not to pretend, but to see and hear the real stories behind the words, the voices of the animals in me, not the definitions of the words alone." Thus we are introduced to the wanaki game, in which the "we" of the stories become, in turn, the being designated in the story titles.

Despite the difficulties it presents to readers—or perhaps partially because of them—**Dead Voices** is a humorous, original, and curiously eloquent contribution to contemporary Native American fiction, which translates onto the page living voices that finally can be heard.

Robert L. Berner (review date Summer 1994)

SOURCE: Review of *Manifest Manners: Postindian Warriors of Survivance,* in *World Literature Today,* Vol. 68, No. 3, Summer, 1994, p. 616.

[*In the following review, Berner states that while Vizenor makes astute points in* Manifest Manners, *the writing is muddled and infused with jargon.*]

Those readers who may wonder what the terms in Vizenor's title mean will have to read the book. "Manifest manners" plays on "manifest destiny" to suggest a variety of cultural realities which falsify the experience of American Indians and exploit their culture for commercial, political, and other inappropriate purposes. "Postindian warriors" are the present generation of Indian writers who counter these "manifest manners" with representations of authentic Indian experience. (*Survivance* means "survival.")

In a discussion of traditional tribal storytelling, Vizenor contrasts it with "the classical notion that thoughts were representations of content, or the coherent meaning of words." Maybe he's right about these storytellers, but no matter how bemused he might be by odd notions justified as "postmodern," the cultural or social critic who wants to tell readers exactly what he means ought to remember that the "classical notion" here dismissed so casually remains a sensible assumption. It is also worth nothing that the above claim is embedded in almost two pages of quotations strung together with little comment to leave the addled reader suspecting that in spite of modish allegiance to supposedly advanced ideas, the academy today is grinding out as much muddled writing as it ever did. Indeed, Vizenor's citation of one Richard Wolin's explanation of Foucault's comment on Derrida's "[leading] us into the text from which . . . we never emerge" suggests that he expects his readers to wander around in his linguistic maze and never return to a world where most people—some of them even professing English in universities—try to say clearly what they mean.

If this judgment seems harsh to reviewers who have admired Vizenor's fictional writings—I am one of them, by the way—they can tell me what is meant by the following: "The postindian turns in literature, the later indication of new narratives, are an invitation to the closure of dominance in the ruins of representation. The invitation uncovers traces of tribal survivance, trickster hermeneutics, and the remanence of intransitive shadows."

What is most unfortunate about the publication of **Manifest Manners** is that Vizenor's complaints point in the right direction. Reservation casinos probably will lead to disappointment, the Indian "activists" he condemns do deserve it, mainstream American culture does falsify Indian experience, and so on. Still, those who need to be told this—and even those who don't—will finish the book, if they do finish it, feeling they have fallen into a mudbath of jargon, much of it invented by the author, the rest of it already proving a great bore in our graduate schools. Come to think of it, however, Vizenor's contention that the true Indian vision is comic might make us wonder. Could he have intended his book as a joke, a spoof of the worst excesses of academic self-indulgence? If so, the joke is less on defenders of clear prose than on those of us who really do believe that it matters whether Indian tribes maintain their social and cultural integrity.

Kenneth M. Roemer (review date December 1994)

SOURCE: Review of *Manifest Manners: Postindian Warriors of Survivance,* in *American Literature,* Vol. 66, No. 4, December, 1994, pp. 871-72.

[*In the review below, Roemer argues that while* Manifest Manners *is at times repetitive, it is nonetheless a powerful book.*]

Manifest Manners comes to us with particular authority. Gerald Vizenor is a literary-cultural critic who is an insider literarily and culturally: he is a respected novelist, an Anishinaabe, and a member of the White Earth Reservation in Minnesota. Vizenor is also a master creator of tricksters in film and fiction.

All this makes for tricky reviewing. Should **Manifest Manners** be evaluated as a Whitmanesque self-analysis/promotion (his comments on trickster hermeneutics illuminate and privilege his protagonists) or as provocative announcements of Native American viewpoints or as a trickster narrative (including a fictional dialogue with a salamander man) or as a wide-ranging series of literary-cultural meditations and vignettes? Though all four approaches are justifiable, for an *American Literature* review the latter seems most appropriate, especially since *Manifest Means* analyzes the creation and implications of representations of Native Americans in fiction and nonfiction.

Vizenor examines these representations in two types of chapters: those that emphasize his basic concepts of oppositional discourses of simulation (chapters one through three and the epilogue) and those that focus on specific simulations (Columbus/discovery [chapter four], Ishi [chapter five], images of casinos [chapter six], and media-created panindian leaders [chapter seven]). Drawing upon Jean Baudrillard, Larzer Ziff, and other critics, the first three chapters define the "manifest manners" (greed, "perverse determinism," racialism) that cause a "literature of domination"—simulations that close and annihilate Native oral histories and stories. Beginning in the late nineteenth century (Luther Standing Bear and Charles Eastman) and continuing through today, the literature of dominance has been opposed by "simulations of survivance": shadows and "natural traces of liberation and survivance in the ruins of representation." Vizenor especially champions "an aesthetic restoration of trickster hermeneutics, the stories of liberation and survivance without the dominance of closure": they emphasize "wonder, chance, coincidence."

To illuminate his concepts, in the early chapters Vizenor offers catalogues of brief excerpts and comments: for example, Jefferson, Parkman, Lynn Andrews, John Bly, Jamake Highwater (dominance); Standing Bear, Eastman, Momaday (survivance). In Chapters four through seven he offers extended illustrations, primarily of simulations of dominance: for instance, the legacies of discovery and naming associated with Columbus and the creation of nostalgic "anti[twentieth-century]-selves" derived from Ishi. In his final extended illustration he examines the "tried simulation[s]" of media-discovered panindian leaders; they are the "kitschymen"—"the resistance enterprises of consumer sun dances."

Occasionally the impact of Vizenor's creative language and mixings of critical models is undercut by a tendency to repeat key phrases like manifest manners too often and to turn his arguments into catalogues of brief excerpts and comments. I also wish that Vizenor had devoted more space to the "warriors of survivance" announced in the book's subtitle. Instead the focus is on examples of the simulations of dominance. Vizenor's rapid-fire collages can, nonetheless, build to powerful summations that bring together apparently disparate elements in illuminating ways. Witness his image of Columbus: he "pursued the marvelous other in the narratives of his time, searched for an eternal haven, landed in the simulations of mother earth, and was discovered, at last, in a constitutional democracy." Many of the summations and collages are in themselves engaging performances of the literature of survivance.

Ward Churchill (review date 1994)

SOURCE: Review of *Manifest Manners: Postindian Warriors of Survivance,* in *American Indian Culture and Research Journal,* Vol. 18, No. 3, 1994, pp. 313-18.

[In the following review below, Churchill argues that when Vizenor relies on his journalistic talents, Manifest Manners *provides useful insights but Vizenor's use of postmodern vernacular creates a sterile, unsuccessful work.]*

Gerald Vizenor's **Manifest Manners** is a book one can love to hate. It combines the very worst of postmodernism's vernacular-driven plunge into cliquish obscurantism with its author's already hyperinflated sense of self-importance. The result is largely sterile where it is not opaque to the point of sheer meaninglessness.

I mean, really. What, exactly, is *survivance?* How does it differ in substance from preexisting terms like *survival?* If it does not, where then may we find the necessity—or even the propriety—of Vizenor's having cloned yet another buzzword with which to encumber the long-since overloaded (but underclarifying) language of literary / cultural criticism?

Or, to take another tack, what does the author actually mean when he classifies the contemporary indigenous population of North America as "postindians?" In his first chapter, Vizenor offers the notion that the term is appropriate insofar as we have all, in his opinion, been reduced to acting out charades of our tribal past, mostly for the edification of the dominating Euro-American culture that has come to overwhelm and negate it.

This is an intriguing concept, to be sure. But it is one that opens up at least as many questions as it can purport to answer. How, for example, is our situation today dissimilar in principle from that of Pocahontas during her stint at the Court of St. James? Or Squanto or Joseph Brant or John Ross? Or how about those of our ancestors who were among the initial batch of *In Dios Columbus* spirited away to Iberia at the end of his first voyage?

Were the Great Navigator's Taino captives of 1493 somehow converted into "postindians" by the very fact that they were ripped bodily from their own setting and compelled to adapt themselves to a wholly alien one? Or did they remain "Indian" despite the grotesque deformity of circumstance imposed on them? And more or less so than the supposed postindians upon whom Vizenor focuses five centuries later, amidst the sociocultural environment of 1993?

Are the distinctions between those of us alive today and those who have gone before quantitative, qualitative, or both? How are such differentiations to be drawn? By whom? For what purpose and to what extent? These would seem fairly obvious concerns, matters requiring a fullness of consideration and response if Vizenor's analysis of topical phenomena were to be more than superficial. Yet, in the end, he begs them all, consistently glossing over the inadequacy of his approach with a transparently deliberate resort to obfuscatory word play.

"Manifest manners," he says, "are the simulations of dominance; the notions and misnomers that are read as the authentic and sustained representations of Native American Indians. The postindian warriors are new indications of narrative creation, the simulations that overcome the manifest manners of dominance." Again,

> Native American Indians have endured the lies and wicked burdens of discoveries, the puritanical destinies of monotheism, manifest manners, and the simulated realities of dominance, with silence, traces of natural reason, trickster hermeneutics, and interpretation of tribal figurations, and the solace of heard stories. . . . The various translations, interpretations, and absence of tribal realities have been posed as the verities of certain cultural traditions. Moreover, the closure of heard stories in favor of scriptural simulations as authentic representations denied a common brush with a shimmer of humor, the sources of tribal visions, and tragic wisdom. . . . In other words, the postindian warriors of postmodern simulations would undermine and surmount, with imagination and the performance of new stories, the manifest manners of scriptural simulations and "authentic" representations of the tribes in the literature of dominance.

And again,

> The postindian warriors and posers are not the new shaman healers of the unreal. Simulations and the absence of the real are curative by chance; likewise, to hover over the traces of the presence in literature is not an ecstatic vision. The turns of postindian remembrance are a rush on natural reason. Some simulations are survivance, but postindian warriors are wounded by the real. The warriors of simulations are worried by the real more than other enemies of reference. Simulations are substitutes of the real, and those who pose with the absence of the real must fear the rush of the real in their stories.

Yeah, sure, you bet. The construction of such impenetrable prose is meant not to illuminate and explain but the precise opposite. Its function is mainly to cast an aura of profound importance over thoughts that are trivial at best or, more usually, utterly barren. It also serves to lend a shallow veneer of intellectual significance—"I've read this thing three times, still can't understand it, so I can only conclude that the author *must* be smarter than I!"—to those with little or nothing consequential to say.

One is tempted at this point to simply consign *Manifest Manners* to that ever-growing pile of tomes representing nothing so much as a vulgar genuflection to the more puerile

impulses of academic pretension. Still, a few elements of genuine utility do manage to peek from time to time through Vizenor's swirling clouds of otherwise irredeemable verbiage.

Perhaps predictable, these shining moments occur whenever he drops his guise as a deep thinker and reconnects to the solidity of his roots in journalism. More accurately, such moments come when Vizenor himself steps aside, allowing working journalists to do his job for him. Thus, he finally lays bare whatever kernel of honest outrage might have motivated his writing in the first place.

Here, Vizenor proceeds by concrete example to explore the sordid realities attending the activities of several individuals embraced by the dominant society as "radical Indian leaders." It is plain that he sees those discussed as no more than instruments used by the status quo for purposes of confusing and usurping the legitimate aspirations of native people to continuity and liberation. Notable in this connection is the author's reliance on the accounts of reporters Kim Ode, Joe Geshick, Kevin Diaz, and Randy Furst in dissecting the case of Clyde Bellecourt, self-ordained "National Director" of the American Indian Movement (AIM).

> Bellecourt was discovered by the media and established as a leader by foundations and government institutions. He could have been historical in the banal sense of time, causation, and aesthetic melancholy; instead, he became one of the kitschymen of resistance enterprises. . . . Bellecourt is a kitschyman, one of the most contumacious cross-blood radical simulations in the nation. He is a word warrior on commission, a man who has abused the honor of tribal communities to enhance his own simulations of pleasure. . . .

Vizenor then goes on to interweave the various journalists' work in elaborating how Bellecourt used his position as a famous AIM leader to profit from the peddling of drugs— LSD, cocaine, marijuana, angel dust—to the children attending his Heart of the Earth Survival School and/or living in his Little Earth Housing Project (both in Minneapolis), among other native groups.

Furst's writings indicate that this pattern of behavior eventually resulted in Bellecourt's arrest in March 1985 on nine counts of drug distribution. Ode, Furst, and Diaz point out that in April 1986 the defendant was allowed to negotiate a plea bargain in which he accepted a reduced sentence on a single felony. This was after a number of non-Indian community leaders testified as character witnesses, urging the court to show leniency because of Bellecourt's supposed "dedication to his people."

Meanwhile, Bellecourt himself meekly "pleaded guilty in the

courtroom" even as he loudly, publicly, and repeatedly "claimed entrapment outside it." Far from penalizing him for these active attempts to evade the sociopolitical onus of his confession, federal district judge Paul Magnuson capped things off by stressing his "great respect for what Bellecourt had done for the Indian community and society as a whole." Indeed, the convict was rewarded for his documented lack of contrition when the good judge deferred his punishment so that Bellecourt might desecrate the 1987 Big Mountain Sun Dance with his presence before entering his cell. This, at the height of the Reagan administration's "War on Drugs!"

Small wonder that Vizenor at one point ponders "why law enforcement agencies did not investigate and arrest [Bellecourt] sooner" and whether he could "have been protected [by the police or FBI] in his enterprise of resistance." Be that as it may, Joe Geshick next reveals that when Bellecourt was released from prison, having served less than two years of his five-year term, he quickly began to employ violence and intimidation against the Minneapolis Indian community in order to reassert his position of "centrality" within it. Quoting Ode in the *Minneapolis Star Tribune*, Vizenor notes that, since his incarceration,

> Bellecourt may have changed, but not everybody is buying it. Those who dislike him refuse to speak on the record, saying they fear reprisals. Word of [Ode's] newspaper article ignited the grapevine and the telephone rings with anonymous voices, all of whom identify themselves as American Indians, urging caution.

Taken as a whole, this is a devastatingly penetrating portrait of a man who is still hyped as a sort of benchmark "Indian militant" by an astonishingly broad sector of the Euro-American Left; a man who, despite his status as an admitted "drug kingpin," continues to receive—by his own estimate—federal funding in the neighborhood of $4.5 million per year and well over $3 million annually in major corporate dollars, with which to run his "community service" operations in Minnesota.

Unquestionably, some of the material incorporated in Vizenor's handling of Clyde Bellecourt and others he accuses of embodying the shabby phenomenon of postindianism is important and deserving of the widest possible reading. Thus his ineptitude in attempting to place such information within the trendy and culturally totalizing abstractions of postmodernism is not just unfortunate but tragic. What is most striking in this respect is how avoidable it all was. Had Vizenor opted to employ the readily available and relevant framework of anticolonialist analysis developed a generation ago by theorists Frantz Fanon (*Black Skins, White Masks*) and Albert Memmi (*Colonizer and Colonized*), *Manifest Manners* might have lived up to its potential as a coherent and

useful book. Instead, he chose to squander this prospect, indulging himself once again—as he has several times previously—in the glitzy pose of professional literati.

We are left with a paradox, an irony of the sort in which postmodernism delights. *Manifest Manners* is largely an empty husk, a miserably failed promise. Yet we can ill afford to ignore its relatively meager content. In that he may be said to have intentionally orchestrated this outcome, Gerald Vizenor himself should be seen as the very epitome of the type of trickster charlatan he claims to detest so vociferously. He is, by this standard, the most wretchedly postindian of us all.

Robert Allen Warrior (review date Autumn 1995)

SOURCE: Review of *Shadow Distance: A Gerald Vizenor Reader*, in *World Literature Today*, Vol. 69, No. 4, Autumn, 1995, pp. 845-46.

[*In the following review, Warrior states that* Shadow Distance *serves as an excellent introduction to Vizenor's extensive and varied oeuvre.*]

For those who teach the work of the Anishanaabe novelist, poet, essayist, and critic Gerald Vizenor but never know what to assign from his massive and growing oeuvre, an answer has arrived. *Shadow Distance*, a reader of Vizenor's work, follows the many twists and turns of his writing career and offers substantial pieces of his creative path. For readers who have never encountered Vizenor's work before, this is an outstanding introduction.

The reader employs five sections. The first offers autobiographical selections and draws mainly from Vizenor's 1990 memoir *Interior Landscapes*. It also includes, though, an autobiographical essay in which he makes links between his work in tribal literature and his early work as a leading North American haikuist. He includes in that essay a number of his difficult-to-find haiku. The second section covers his long fictional works, *The Heirs of Columbus* (1991), *Griever: An American Monkey King in China* (1986), *Dead Voices* (1992), and *Bearheart: The Heirship Chronicles* (1978, 1990). The selections are long enough to provide a long drink rather than just a few swallows of Vizenor's word games, shifting meanings, and agonistic point of view.

A section of stories follows, drawing on a number of collections Vizenor has written over more than a decade. These stories show how much Vizenor is able, using the short form, to make great impact. The longest section is a generous tour through his essays, including some from journals to which many people do not have easy access. Ishi, tribal casinos, the

Sand Creek Massacre, and Anishanaabe history are some of the issues the essays cover. In this section the critical, incisive mind that exists alongside the fiction's creative thrust and power most clearly reveals itself. Finally, and what is perhaps most welcome, the volume includes the full text of Vizenor's screenplay *Harold of Orange*.

A. Robert Lee of the University of Kent at Canterbury provides an able and informative introduction. The six-page selected bibliography at book's end is a reminder of just how much Gerald Vizenor has contributed to American letters over the past three decades. By the end, the major themes of Vizenor's writing career to date are all there: his groundbreaking approach to trickster figures, his critical playfulness with language, and his attempt to find new ways of telling the truth artistically, academically, and politically. *Shadow Distance* is sure to be a wonderful pedagogical tool. The sheer pleasure of the artistry will no doubt impress those who have not previously encountered the range and creativity of this most significant twentieth-century American Indian writer.

Elizabeth McNeil (essay date 1995)

SOURCE: "'The Game Never Ends': Gerald Vizenor's Gamble with Language and Structure in *Summer in the Spring*," in *American Indian Culture and Research Journal*, Vol. 19, No. 2, 1995, pp. 85-109.

[*In the following essay, McNeil argues that Vizenor continues the work of the original editor of the stories—Theodore Hudon Beaulieu—by bringing them to a general readership.*]

The trickster myths in Gerald Vizenor's *Summer in the Spring: Anishinaabe Lyric Poems and Stories* come nearly verbatim from a series of tales in *The Progress,* the first newspaper published on an Indian reservation in Minnesota. Appearing in the late 1880s, the series was originally edited by Theodore Hudon Beaulieu. From the standpoint of the contemporary literary scholar, the series might simply seem an historical collection of tribal lore and a useful collection from which to develop a source study for Vizenor's works, but for Beaulieu's Anishinaabe (Ojibwe/Chippewa) audience or Vizenor's interested non-Anishinaabe academic audience engaged in the study of the dynamic function of open-ended trickster discourse, these narratives offer insight concerning the function and enduring value of native texts.

A brief review of the publication history of the tales offers Vizenor's contemporary audience insight into their original intention. Twenty years before Beaulieu's publication of the narrative series in *The Progress,* Anishinaabe families had begun to experience another in a series of removals, this time from their homes in different parts of the state to the newly organized White Earth Reservation in northern Minnesota. One hundred years of the gradual stripping away of Anishinaabe land and natural resources, as well as the threat of further erosion of tribal sovereignty, compelled Gus and Theodore Beaulieu to establish *The Progress.*

With Gus as publisher and Theodore as editor, the Beaulieus initiated publication of *The Progress* because they believed the Anishinaabeg needed a forum in which to share vital news and to vent frustrations. The "Salutatory," written by Gus's brother, Reverend Clement H. Beaulieu, as the opening article of the first issue, states the Beaulieus' purpose: to advocate for the tribe's best interests. Beaulieu specifically notes that, while they do not wish to antagonize the government, they "may be called upon at times to criticise individuals and laws, but," Beaulieu qualifies, "we shall aim to do so in a spirit of kindness and justice. Believing that the 'freedom of the press,' will be guarded as sacredly by the Government, on this Reservation as elsewhere. . . . " The newspaper's masthead dedicates *The Progress* to "A higher Civilization: The Maintenance of Law and Order."

Despite this rather moderate statement of intentions and conservative motto, after publication of the first issue the U.S. Indian agent on the White Earth Reservation seized the press, charging the Beaulieus with voicing "incendiary and revolutionary sentiments." A jury trial and a subsequent hearing before the U.S. Senate Subcommittee of the Committee on Indian Affairs in Washington, D.C., cleared the Beaulieus of the charges, awarded damages, and restored them to their newspaper. After a nearly twenty-month hiatus for litigation, the Beaulieus published the second issue of *The Progress.*

The Progress continued to include criticism of the federal Indian Bureau, as well as current local, national, and international news. In the third weekly issue of the renewed publication, Theodore Beaulieu lets subscribers know that the paper will soon begin "a series of Indian stories, traditional and legendary . . . which will date away back when this country was one great reservation and no Indian agents but Winne-boo-zho," the trickster. However, the Beaulieus' publication of the text of the Dawes or General Allotment Act, which appears "by request" of their readership, temporarily held back presentation of the series. The Dawes Act was of monumental significance to the Anishinaabeg, because it served to break up the people's communally held land into individual family allotments which then, in concert with further legislation that followed almost immediately, allowed Anishinaabe land to be sold to white settlers or lost to speculators, especially those working for the timber industry. The Dawes Act proved divisive in certain Anishinaabe communities by inspiring competition and breaking down communal cohesiveness. By delaying the trickster stories to publish the General Allotment Act text, the Beaulieus served their readership by informing the people of the exact nature of the act, hence perhaps discouraging land sales in communities that resisted allotment.

The front-page series of cultural information and trickster stories finally begins in December 1887, with twelve installments appearing until May 1888. The Anishinaabe texts edited by Theodore Beaulieu were narrated by Saycosegay and Day Dodge, two leaders of the Midéwiwin, the Anishinaabe sacred society (*Summer*). Day Dodge, "Grand Sachem and Medicine Seer of the White Earth Ojibwas," was then about ninety years old, "which means he was born before the turn of the nineteenth century," Vizenor says, "when the *anishinaabeg* were not yet colonized and suppressed on federal exclaves or reservations" (*Summer*). In his introduction to the stories, Beaulieu insists that these men are the best living authorities and that the translation of their texts is as near verbatim as possible because, he later adds, it is in the readers' best interest to offer them "the exact language" of the Meda priests. The series includes "many interesting and useful lessons on the History, Customs, Traditions and Legends of the Ojibwas, not omitting the charming jocularity of the endless tales of the never dying WAIN-NAH-BOO-ZHO!" As the series unfolds over the months, Beaulieu lets his readers know that the never-ending "story of 'WAINAHBOOZHO' and his many adventures, will be continued as fast as the manuscript can be prepared."

In 1970, Vizenor published in *Anishinabe Adisokan* stories he had selected and edited from Beaulieu's *Progress* series. Along with the third edition of his collection of Anishinaabe lyric poems (1965, 1970), Vizenor republished the *Anishinabe Adisokan* stories in *Summer in the Spring: Ojibwe Lyric Poems and Tribal Stories* in 1981. The 1993 edition of *Summer in the Spring: Anishinaabe Lyric Poems and Stories* is a contribution to the American Indian Literature and Critical Studies Series.

The above brief history of the publication of the trickster tales demonstrates their complex publication context. Because the 1887-88 series came at a time when the Anishinaabeg were in need of renewed hope—removal to White Earth Reservation in many cases meant abandoning homes, possessions, and livelihoods to begin again in a new place—the myths served Beaulieu's audience as a kind of wide-reaching communal invocation of the people's enduring strength and humor. The central figure in the series is, appropriately, the humorous, "never dying" trickster Wainaboozho.

With Wainaboozho—or Naanabozho, as Vizenor calls him—anything is possible. In some Anishinaabe tales, he is stupid, greedy, lustful, incestuous, abusive. He engages in mean, thoughtless escapades, sometimes premeditating vengeful tricks; he even kills his own brothers. And yet, as the Anishinaabe culture-hero, Naanabozho also commits the self-

less creative acts that he was put on the earth to perform (*Summer*). In his introduction to *Summer in the Spring*, Vizenor describes Naanabozho in these Beaulieu-Vizenor narratives as the "compassionate tribal trickster" (*Summer*). As a culture-hero, Naanabozho recreates the world after the flood, brings fire, and offers "salvation" to the people. He is "reputed to possess not only the power to live but also the correlative power of renewing his own life and of quickening and therefore of creating life in others." Naanabozho has been sent by Giizis Manidoo, the Great Spirit, to teach the people what is essential for their existence.

In the "Naanabozho Obtains Fire" tale in *Summer in the Spring*, the trickster goes against the wishes of his grandmother (his *nookomis*) and sets out to steal a ray—a smile—from the sun spirit, Giizis Manidoo. Naanabozho, who was born of an earthly mother and the *manidoo* (spirit/god) who is the north wind, journeys to the sun's island home and then turns himself into a rabbit; the sun's daughters find him wet and bedraggled on the lake shore. They rescue the little bunny, and thus Naanabozho gains entrance into the sun's house. The rabbit revives and, "twitching his lips and nose in a most ridiculous fashion," is so comical that he makes the sun smile. Naanabozho catches the burning ray in a piece of punk he had tied onto his back for the purpose and exits before the sun can catch him. Because he paddles so quickly back to the earth and his grandmother's wigwam, the fire is fanned to a blaze that spreads to his rabbit fur.

> [B]efore he could extricate himself from his rabbit skin, the hair was afire, and matters looked serious sure enough. He was now nearing the shore from whence he came, and he at once commenced to howl and called loudly for *nookomis* to hurry up: *Come to me, I am afire, hi-hai, nookomis come quick!*

The humorous scene continues with the old woman "so excited . . . that she forgot all about her stick and a sprained ankle" in her haste to get to the canoe—although she does remember to grab a pot in which she plans to collect the fire. The undignified hero yells pathetically for his grandmother, who, probably because he is not always nice to her, takes her time attending to him. Only after she has the fire safely in the pot does she care for her smoldering grandson. As a result, "In many places the rabbit skin had burned through. And when at last *nookomis* pulled it off his back, great pieces of his own skin and flesh came off with it. Poor *naanabozho,* he was indeed a sorry-looking sight after he was relieved of his fiery jacket" (*Summer*). As this tale demonstrates, the trickster is a creator, a destroyer, a shapeshifter—an agent of transformation. At the same time, even in the same story, the culture-hero—as a raggedy rabbit or an angry grandchild—is a comical, risk-taking fool. Although anyone who reads the Beaulieu-Vizenor stories is likely to make choices more consciously than Naanabozho does, he or she is bound to be confronted at some point with the confusing double role of creator and destroyer that human beings must fulfill even in the "transformations" of everyday life.

After his brush with Giizis Manidoo, Naanabozho revives himself through sleep. Then he feasts on food Nookomis has prepared, afterward entertaining the two of them by making speeches. His heated discourse leads Nookomis to disclose the truth of the circumstances of Naanabozho's birth, which, in turn, launches Naanabozho into his next adventure. The demigod trickster always has another scheme hatching. If he were as careful and calculating as someone entirely mortal—like his grandmother or the Beaulieu-Vizenor reader—he would never set out on such risky journeys into the natural and supernatural worlds. But Naanabozho lives on the threshold between worlds, neither belonging fully nor living solely in just one, possessing neither human common sense nor the dignified omnipotence of the *manidoog* (spirits). Because he is both human and spirit, like any living creature Naanabozho can be hurt, but like the manidoog he cannot die. Since he belongs in part to each world, both affect him, but neither has full control over his person, spirit, or destiny, and, significantly, in neither is he in full control of himself.

After hearing the truth about the circumstances of his mother's death, the enraged Naanabozho is determined to take control of the situation by exacting vengeance. Impetuous as always, the trickster goes on the "war path" to destroy his manidoo father, who was indirectly responsible for his mortal mother's death in childbirth. However, in the next installment of the series, "Naanabozho and His Father," Naanabozho arrives at the "fourth fold of the skies," where his father talks him out of revenge. The manidoo of peace, Naanabozho's twin brother who died with their mother at their birth, further appeases Naanabozho by telling him that the council of manidoog are now "giving him the full control of the earth, as sovereign lord and master" (*Summer*). When they had seen Naanabozho coming, the council of manidoog hurriedly had decided on this action, because they knew Naanabozho was invincible to the manidoog as well as to human beings (*Summer*).

In the Beaulieu-Vizenor series, although he is given stewardship of the earth and now has the grave responsibilities of a mature, compassionate leader, Naanabozho is, in some respects, still the same obstinate risk-taker he has always been. As a steward who is sometimes heroic, sometimes selfish, he is a mediator who may intercede for good or to stir up trouble; in other words, he promotes all facets of life. Naanabozho intercedes between the people and their earthly environment, and between the Anishinaabeg and the evil spirits who threaten their lives. The culture-hero trickster in these tales is also a mediator between the late nineteenth-century Anishinaabeg and the U.S. government, in that he ultimately inspires the people to act on their own behalf. Most fundamentally, in the complex way that he is sometimes hero, sometimes villain,

and as that reflects the paradoxical human condition, for the Beaulieu-Vizenor storytelling audience the trickster is also a mediating force between active aspects of the self.

In "Naanabozho and His Father," after he has been given stewardship of the earth Naanabozho tells Nookomis he is planning to set out on an extended tour of his realm. She is alarmed and tells him that no one has been known to return who "got within" the power of the assorted evil spirits that "infest" the land (*Summer*): "They first charm their victims by the sweetness of their songs, then they strangle and devour them," she continues. "But your principal enemy will be the gichi nita ataaged, the great gambler, who has never been beaten and who lives beyond the realm of the niibaa giizis, darkness, and near the shores of the happy hunting-ground." Nookomis ends her warning by saying, "I would beseech you, therefore, not to undertake so dangerous a journey." But Naanabozho is feeling cocky after his recent confrontation with his father: "With the increasing laurels of conquest, *naanabozho* felt that he was brave and as such, should know no fear." He continues to prepare for his journey and the warning words of Nookomis seem to go unheeded (*Summer*).

One does begin to wonder how Nookomis, a mortal woman, has come to know so much that she can warn her grandson in specific terms about the dangers that lie ahead. She is, at the very least, a wise woman; we know earlier in the series that she is one who, in dream, receives information from the manidoog (*Summer*). Even though Naanabozho does not heed her warning to stay home (since the people are in need of his help, this may not have been what she had intended, anyway), he is forewarned and hence thoroughly readies himself for a successful journey by making "all necessary preparations" before setting out (*Summer*). Possibly because Nookomis—along with sympathetic animals and manidoog—have made him aware of what lies ahead, Naanabozho now knows "the place where the *great gambler* consigned the spirits of his many victims" (*Summer*). Based on this foreknowledge, his purpose becomes clear, and he vows "that if he ever destroyed the *gichi nita ataaged,* he would liberate the victims who were being tortured" (*Summer*).

In a brief introduction to this installment of the continuing trickster story in *The Progress,* Beaulieu says that "the great spirit gambler" is destiny. The gambler's prisoners, the Beaulieu-Vizenor text states, are the "victims of sin and shame" (*Summer*); they are Naanabozho's Anishinaabe relatives who have gambled with destiny by risking interaction with this overpoweringly evil creature (*Summer*) or, simply, have "gambled" by having faced their destiny fearfully. In Naanabozho's game with the great evil gambler, "one chance remained, upon which depended the destiny of *naanabozho* and the salvation of the *anishinaabe* people" (*Summer*).

Beaulieu's late nineteenth-century Anishinaabe readers were dealing with their own harsh fates, their worst fears repeatedly having been realized. But, judging from the Beaulieus' criticism of white manipulation of their lives, the Anishinaabeg were not placing themselves in the role of helpless victims—and the trickster story would have served to remind them of their cultural resources. Some Anishinaabeg, like Theodore Beaulieu, were helping the people help themselves, in much the same way as Naanabozho takes an active, dangerous role when he decides to face the gambler. One hundred years later, Vizenor's readers, too, face a risk-filled destiny (environmental pollution and general lack of respect for life in the seemingly unending race for material gain), and, like the readers of *The Progress,* are challenged to choose between apathy and action. Both native and nonnative audiences can relate to Naanabozho as culture-hero and can understand the idea of people caught in servitude or addiction to destruction.

In the gambler tale, the images are as grizzly as any that life might offer. The great gambler's front door is a mat of human scalps. Showing Naanabozho the hands of his "relatives who came here to gamble," the gambler tells Naanabozho, "They played and lost and their life was the forfeit. . . . Seek me and whoever enters my lodge must gamble" (*Summer*). Naanabozho the culture-hero has come not because he has an addictive, self-destructive urge to gamble with his destiny, as the previous Anishinaabe victims may have had. He is risking his destiny by using his power to resist and disable the gambler and hence to liberate/empower his human relations, including the reader—liberating simultaneously that angry human part of himself that the manidoog had hurried to try to appease by making him earth's steward.

Without his human relations, who provide him his role of liberator and teacher, Naanabozho's risk is pointless; only because of them is he a redemptive and instructive figure. For Beaulieu's Anishinaabe audience, Naanabozho's interposing as their never-dying agent is original, ancestral. For both Beaulieu's and Vizenor's readers, the model of risk for potential acquisition of power and restoration of a balance between good and evil is archetypal.

To reintegrate ancestral story/history—especially given the instructive elements of trickster texts—is, for the Anishinaabe reader, to reaffirm the roots of Anishinaabe purpose, liberating the socially oppressed reader from purposelessness and victimization. With varying degrees of personal apathy, the members of both Beaulieu's nineteenth-century and Vizenor's twentieth-century audiences come from spiritually splintered communities that face uncertain futures; for each the present, and hence the future, is set against a background of their own century of intensely violent and psychologically devastating past. For Beaulieu's and Vizenor's readers, strength of will bolstered by the trickster narrative may help to fortify the spirit in the face of community fragmentation. Confrontation in the story offers a model for action against the forces threatening to destroy. The message is that it is better to take a potentially fatal risk than to remain a passive victim.

The trickster's confrontation with the gambler is also significant in that this tale is set in the afterlife. For the Anishinaabeg, loss to the gambler means relegation to Anishinaabe hell. Winning means eternal salvation. The individual's preparation for entrance into either a peaceful or a troubled afterlife is a familiar spiritual dichotomy for both native and nonnative audiences. Vivifying clarification, or "salvation," of personal and communal sense of purpose—along with the reminder to replace one's fears with strength or faith—helps not only to ensure strength in living but to earn peace in the afterlife (or at least a more peaceful contemplation of one's mortality).

Status in the afterlife is generally seen as dependent on one's behavior in life. The variety of good and bad in any individual's behavior reflects the human-divine dichotomy of heaven and hell. Like the multiple aspects of the human personality, different parts of the trickster also exist at once, even within the same story. Naanabozho's father is "a powerful manidoo for good or evil," Nookomis tells her grandson (*Summer*). Similarly, Day Dodge explains in *The Progress* that when, at the onset of menses, a girl went into isolation and fasted for her life vision, she was a "strong . . . spirit for good or evil", she was on the brink of deciding the major course of her life's journey. Representing the individual's power which, over a lifetime or at a given moment, can work for both good and evil, Naanabozho and the great gambler are simply aspects of one being. Thus the model for choice is brought to an intensely personal level for the reader of this tale.

The Anishinaabe trickster is also known as the Great Hare or the moon, the Great Light, the Spirit of Light, or the Great White One. In "Naanabozho Obtains Fire," discussed above, the trickster changes himself into a rabbit in order to obtain fire from the sun spirit; his own body catches fire in the course of bringing this source of warmth and light into the dark of the earthly night. The trickster performs this feat by drawing the sun to himself, which, in a sense, is similar to the way the moon "steals" sunlight to send down to, or reflect onto, the earth at night. In "Naanabozho and the Gambler," the last tale included in the Beaulieu-Vizenor narrative series, the evil gambler is the polar opposite of the compassionate trickster, or compassionate human self. The gambler is "a curious looking being" who "seemed almost round in shape" (*Summer*); in his dwelling out beyond the vast darkness, the gambler is, in other words, the almost-full moon. The gambler is the trickster in his greediest, most evil mode. In a human being, such selfish, destructive behavior may be beyond the person's control, because it is an aspect of his/her behavior that the individual is "in the dark" about. However, the gambler story shows that the courageous part of oneself that seeks clarity can bring such negative behavior into the light, as the trickster does by confronting the gambler. In this story, neither aspect of the trickster—neither Naanabozho nor the gambler—possesses a full range of human physical or psychological characteristics; they complement one another in form, purpose, and behavior. Here the gambler, who is not human, pursues a completely selfish and evil intent, while Naanabozho operates in human form as an altruistic hero whose goal is the liberation of his people.

The story is not tragic, however; it is comical. Trickster absurdity is at work when the fate of an entire people rests on the outcome of a game of chance. Only someone as ridiculously overconfident as Naanabozho would calmly step in to gamble with others' lives, not to mention risking his own destiny in the bargain. Common sense—and a concerned grandmother's warning words—would be enough to convince most human beings not to undertake such a huge risk. But the trickster does not possess a human conscience, not in the ordinary sense of weighing proposed action against probable outcome.

After the gambler explains what has happened to Naanabozho's relatives who have come before him—a speech meant to terrify Naanabozho and thereby render him incapable of winning the game—Naanabozho "laughed long and heartily. This was unusual for those who came there to gamble and the great gambler felt very uneasy at the stolid indifference of his guest" (*Summer*). The gambler's discomfort offers comic relief in the midst of what has been, for the gambler's previous visitors, the most hopeless of situations. Encouraged by the trickster story, readers of the Beaulieu-Vizenor text thus may discover that laughter is possible even within what they had previously thought were impossible situations in their lives.

Naanabozho's humor and strength are possible only because he has properly prepared himself for the journey and has confronted and dismissed his fears. To fear the enemy or oppressors (in this story comically depicted as an Anishinaabe weakness for gambling) is to lose footing as one passes through a paralyzing limbo to make the final gamble with one's destiny. To be fearful, to lose one's command or sense of purpose while in this depressed/oppressed state, is to fall, to be already lost. On his way to confront the great evil gambler, Naanabozho walks through the darkness where the gambler has "consigned the spirits of his many victims." Naanabozho overcomes his fear because he has the power of the manidoog with him: "For the first time in his life he experienced the chilly breath of fear, and wished that he had listened to the counsel of *nookomis*. But just then a voice whispered in his ear saying: *I am with you. You should never*

fear. At this his fears were dispelled and he boldly walked on" (*Summer*).

In his typically obtuse way, which Nookomis had surely anticipated, Naanabozho had heeded his grandmother's counsel by consulting "friendly manidoog" and animals before undertaking his adventure (*Summer*). On his journey, he finds he has the power of the Anishinaabe spirits with him. He passes through the darkness, the owl his eyes and the firefly his light, until he arrives again in the daylight, where the great gambler's wigwam is visible in the distance. He overcomes that dangerous period of his fear and then, with his greatest challenge clearly illuminated before him, he can dismiss his helpers, their assistance no longer needed. Readers are being reminded that ancestral and animal spirit assistance, always available, can bring them strength of will and clarity of purpose.

The narrative continues, "When he was very near the *wiigiwaam,* he saw that there were numerous trails coming from different directions but all leading towards the *wiigiwaam*" (*Summer*). The other visitors to the gambler's wigwam may not have been so well prepared as Naanabozho. Because they had no spiritually bolstering assistance for the journey, when the imminent challenge came—that is, confrontation with the weakest part of oneself, which emerges at that lowest psychological point, the final gamble for one's survival—their fear and limited sense of communal and spiritual resources had already set them up to lose.

The risk theme works for both Beaulieu's and Vizenor's audiences in that, by identifying with the trickster—his ability to challenge destiny creatively, to exert his free will—readers are given a model of behavior that can help them overcome their propensities toward apathy. The consequences of white encroachment have put a pall over native lives for generations. Through his essential liminality and his comic ability to make the story audience laugh at itself, the trickster—always on the threshold between worlds, adventures, behaviors, and aspects of personality—reminds both Beaulieu's and Vizenor's readers that life requires choices, even if the only choice is whether to meet impossible situations with fear or with resolve.

Vizenor's series ends as Beaulieu's does, with Naanabozho ready to take his turn in the game after the gambler has tossed the bone figures and Naanabozho has called upon the wind to knock them down. Naanabozho is not frightened when he seizes the dish, telling the gambler, "It is now my turn, should I win, you must die" (*Summer*). In *The Progress,* Beaulieu adds that the tale is "to be continued," but, as in the Vizenor text, the narrative is left hanging.

The trickster story itself does not end, however; the reader must bring it to closure. The point of the open-ended story is to intimate that the risk goes on and on and on, just as the traditional—and archetypal—story itself is sure to be retold, in some form, as long as life exists. The game—Anishinaabe life and history/story—is not over. Beaulieu is reminding his audience not to give in or give up. "Open-ended" means open to change, able to adapt to the developing needs of a situation by permitting spontaneous and unguided responses. Beaulieu's readers were faced with tremendous change. For their own survival, they needed to be able to formulate wise and creative solutions to the difficult challenges of their situation.

Vizenor's intention for his audience may be a similar awakening to the possibility of human endurance, as well as an appreciation for the idea of free will in terms of active rather than passive responses to texts. He argues that "no critical closures, representations, or essential cultural conditions could hold" these trickster stories (*Summer*). Vizenor wants to assure scholars that the native story—with its balance of humor and struggle—is a tradition that has resisted colonization. Trickster tales and other Native American stories continue orally; in addition, as is evidenced by the Beaulieu and Vizenor texts, for more than a hundred years now they have taken to a wider intercultural life in print.

Alan Velie points to several interesting problems in the Beaulieu-Vizenor text as a written form of traditional, orally presented narrative. Velie implies that the "highly solemn and formal English" in which Beaulieu originally casts the texts—and that Vizenor retains—is somehow inappropriate to traditional performed narrative and that Beaulieu and Vizenor have taken further editorial liberties in their presentation of Saycosegay's and Day Dodge's texts.

Storytellers invariably cast their tales in language that they believe best suits the intended audience. Beaulieu's English was the educated English of the late 1800s—the same English, we can assume, used by his educated Anishinaabe audience. As an editor who decides how to present the material, what text to keep and what to excise—forming his own version of the stories—Beaulieu is operating in the role of storyteller, only this time telling the story through the medium of print and in English. The care that attended preparation of the narrative series and the overall mission of the newspaper to provide tribal members with critical discussion of pertinent issues—both intentions clearly stated in *The Progress*—indicate that Beaulieu's choice of vocabulary would have been just as carefully tended.

This formal turn-of-the-century English also works for Vizenor's academic audience, whose literary expectations are honed to appreciate the language of oral tradition as recorded in legend and folktale. Even though he makes minor editorial changes, Vizenor's text nearly duplicates the carefully prepared narrative in *The Progress*. As mentioned above,

Vizenor's changes include his renaming "Wainahboozho" as Naanabozho. Highly conscious of the semantic impact of language, Vizenor also italicizes the Anishinaabe words and makes them lower case in order to emphasize "the values of the oral language rather than a total imposition of the philosophies of grammar and translation" (*Summer*) and to call attention to "semantic blunders" (e.g., "indian"). In addition to these revisions, Vizenor does omit or change certain words and phrases in the text.

An example of one of the more significant and yet still subtle changes occurs in the translation of Day Dodge's comments on traditional Anishinaabe rites for a girl during her first menses, discussed briefly above. The *Progress* text reads, "My grandson, you cannot properly understand without an illustration, how strong a spirit for good or evil a girl is during this period." Vizenor changes the text in this segment to "My grandchild, you cannot properly understand without an illustration, how strong the *manidoog,* spirits, are during this period" (*Summer*). Assuming that the text he edited represents Beaulieu's point of view, even though Beaulieu may not have translated the narrative himself, Vizenor's version may indicate shifts in thought concerning this particular topic. In Beaulieu's text, the pubescent girl is the spirit ("how strong a spirit for good or evil a girl is") and therefore the active agent, whereas, in Vizenor's version, the spirits, existing seemingly both inside and outside the girl, are the agents of the action ("how strong the *manidoog,* spirits, are"). Also, Beaulieu describes the girl's spiritual power in terms white readers would be likely to respond to as signifying specific polar extremes—"good or evil"—while Vizenor withholds that opportunity for judgment by indicating only that the spirits become strong at this time. The personal example that Day Dodge goes on to relate in the *Progress* text, and that Vizenor retains, is an illustration of a menstruating girl's awesome power. As a young man, Day Dodge had gone to a girl's hut during her first menses in order that she cure the warts on his hands, which she/her power did accomplish.

Dropping the "good or evil" phrase that his largely non-Native American academic audience might perceive as dichotomous could mean that Vizenor simply wants readers to come to their own conclusions—based on Day Dodge's illustration—of what this female power indicates. Vizenor's omission of the phrase could also come from an awareness of his academic readers' cultural filter, which, in a discussion of women's power, might lead them, consciously or unconsciously, to associate evil with the biblical fall and woman's alleged part in it. Beaulieu's edition of Day Dodge's discussion of the first menses does not indicate that the girl herself may use her power toward a willful or evil end; the Beaulieu text simply explains that males had to be careful and conscious of heightened female metaphysical strength (equated with women's physical power to create new life) during this period. That Vizenor's changes may come from a feminist awareness can be supported by the fact that he also changes the "grandson" address of the Day Dodge-Beaulieu text to "grandchild"—the genderless term encouraging a wider readership that includes women. In his subtle editing of the cultural information and trickster tales from *The Progress* for a twentieth-century audience, Vizenor does not, however, seem to intend a radically different reading of the Beaulieu text.

Velie implies that both Beaulieu's and Vizenor's "re-expressions" of the Saycosegay and Day Dodge text are inappropriate—that the Midéwiwin teacher-storytellers' earlier versions of the mythic texts have been compromised in some way. But as Vizenor points out, there are as many versions of tribal stories as there are tellers, listeners, and readers. In fact, the text has proven its essential viability by its reemergence in the textual repertoire of those generations succeeding the Midéwiwin elders to which Beaulieu and Vizenor belong.

Velie's biggest point of contention in regard to Beaulieu's and Vizenor's series is that both end the trickster text in the middle of the narrative; he claims that this is not "traditional." Naanabozho has not yet acted and has not yet won—or lost—his battle with the gambler.

> He was not frightened, and when the great evil gambler prepared to make the final shake, *naanabozho* drew near and when the dish came down on the ground he made a whistle on the wind, as in surprise, and the figures fell. *Naanabozho* then seized the dish saying: *It is now my turn, should I win, you must die.*

Velie states that "the traditional ending in Anishinaabe myth, as well as the tales of other tribes, is for the trickster to win and the gambler to die." In other versions of the Anishinaabe trickster recreation cycle, after Naanabozho has finished recreating the land and has completed his task of killing the evil being, the stories end with his "roaming about." However, as nineteenth-century anthropologist Basil Johnston points out, Anishinaabe stories he recorded "are not to be interpreted literally; but freely, yet rationally according to the Ojibway views of life. Readers and listeners are expected to draw their own inferences, conclusions, and meanings according to their intellectual capacities." Even if the trickster completes a task and wanders off, the text is left up to each story participant/audience member to conclude and possibly later to retell as the particular version of the story that person has apprehended. Leaving the text in medias res may represent, to Velie, a lack of aesthetic and thematic sensitivity, but to an Anishinaabe reader (and to contemporary literary scholars accustomed to ambiguous endings), it may not be so jarring; in fact, it may elicit an entire body of cultural text—other versions and other tellings of this trickster story, as well as other related texts and events in the reader's life.

Jarold Ramsey says that "myth evokes a mood of self-conscious expectancy." Because he is a powerful trope or unit of cultural performance, the tribal trickster is particularly capable of conjuring up, within the culturally knowledgeable listener/reader, the entire traditional cultural "tapestry" or semiotic context. The mythic trickster and his stories then become much more than "merely functional instruments or mediating mechanisms" engaged in a symbolic process. Much more than a comforting symbol, Naanabozho, in his many aspects and adventures, is an active element in the Anishinaabe reader's life—as he can be even in the life of the culturally sensitive non-Anishinaabe reader.

Velie further suggests that Beaulieu's tagging of the last installment of the series, the confrontation between Naanabozho and the gambler, with "to be continued" may be the played-out limit of the series project for Beaulieu and his collaborators or simply a literary "trick." Actually, "to be continued" establishes an expectant, enjoyable tension. Even if the story is not continued—and even if the story continues and the trickster does die—the call to the greater continuing body of Anishinaabe oral literature has been made in the mind of Beaulieu's audience. Additionally, Beaulieu's Anishinaabe readers, and Vizenor's mainly nonnative academic audience familiar with the pan-Indian qualities of the trickster figure, know that Naanabozho does not die—or, if he does, he can always come back to life. Also, when the tale is told again in the future—in whatever version—the unending story of the trickster, and the people, continues.

The ambiguous ending may have been unintentional on Beaulieu's part, but the truncation of the series at this suspenseful point would ultimately not have mattered much for the tribal audience, who could construct their own outcomes and call up their own remembered texts. On the other hand, Vizenor clearly intends the ambiguous ending; he deliberately stops the action at a place where readers unfamiliar with the culture are forced to participate in the narrative—to learn more about Anishinaabe lives and texts (his informative and interpretive sections framing the narrative series indicate that this is what he wants) or at least to allow his readers the opportunity to engage actively enough with the text to produce their own conclusions. The courageous hero has at his command the power of the manidoog (Naanabozho whistles for the wind, which then knocks over the figures left standing after the gambler's loss [*Summer*]) and is on an altruistic mission to save his people. The trickster's demonstrated supernatural power and the righteousness of his mission are ingredients Vizenor's primarily non-Indian academic readers are likely to expect will lead to a "happy" ending.

However, the nonnative reader who is familiar with American Indian texts will realize that happily-ever-after is an oversimplification, that the trickster is not simply hero or villain but both, his actions akin to the ongoing struggle of human existence. In yet another version of the Beaulieu story in the prologue to his book *The People Named the Chippewa*, Vizenor the storyteller says that, even if Naanabozho does not win, "The trickster had stopped evil for a moment in a game", even if only for a moment, Naanabozho has successfully mediated between good and evil.

Similarly, the Beaulieus and then Vizenor have offered a mediating moment to their readers through their published versions of the trickster text. Participation in the storytelling moment offers the reader the opportunity to mediate events along with the trickster and to mediate between aspects of the trickster's complex self. The threshold inherent for the listener/reader in tribal texts, specifically here the never-ending trickster story, is a liminal stance, a rite of passage that transports the actively involved story participant/reader through what Victor Turner has dubbed a "moment in and out of time"; this moment homogenizes differences between the sacred and the secular, between individuals from different social levels, between past, present, and future, and between aspects of self. In the suspension of real time is a moment of breathing space or inspiration in which all things are possible.

Comedy, especially trickster humor that deals with human interactions ranging from the mundane to the taboo, is a vehicle for serious as well as light concerns that mediates and brings into balance contradictory aspects of human life. The storytelling moment that facilitates imaginative engagement in narrative choices could serve the listener/reader whose life surely involves choices—action considered and taken. To operate as an objective actor or intermediary in one's life is to retain freedom of choice in thought and action. Most importantly, an intermediary, by definition, is one who acts as an integrative force, bringing two seemingly opposed elements together in order to reconcile differences. Both the trickster and the storyteller, as the mythic and real-life agents of the stories, offer the reader models for reconciling and hence integrating oppositional forces.

The traditional multifaceted and multifaced trickster figure—a communal, many-voiced sign—and the open-ended narrative each offer what Vizenor calls "narrative chance." The unfinished nature of the Beaulieu-Vizenor text is appropriate to the trickster genre of tales, as it is, in fact, appropriate to oral literature, which relies on the quality and principle of open-endedness. "Sentiment and sensation and worldview of the Gambler story denies closure," Vizenor states. It is more about "balance," he suggests, "but it's not balance"—not really balance because that is a rigid delineation. "We're all good and evil," he says. The tug of war between the two aspects of being is, at the level of the individual or at the level of societies, a game of constant rebalancing. The game between the trickster and the gambler is also never-ending—the story can always be retold. "The game never ends,"

Vizenor says, and language, including storytelling, is a game, too.

Beaulieu and Vizenor, as storyteller-editors publishing their interpretations of these trickster tales, are cultural historians. Beaulieu offered his audience text that was already their own story and, through that publication, reminded his people of their strength, pride, and hope as Anishinaabeg. Vizenor intends the *Summer in the Spring* series of trickster texts to be a point of open-ended engagement with Anishinaabe culture, and the readers' structural interaction with textual open-endedness is an additional gift intended to remind them of the possibility of spontaneous engagement with life.

Jon Hauss (essay date 1995)

SOURCE: "Real Stories: Memory, Violence, and Enjoyment in Gerald Vizenor's *Bearheart*," in *Literature and Psychology*, Vol. XXXXI, No. 4, 1995, pp. 1-16.

[*In the following essay, Hauss discusses the role of violence and history in* Darkness in Saint Louis Bearheart.]

From the beginning, there is the violence. Critics have remarked on the shocking, often graphic and extended, depictions of physical violence in Vizenor's 1978 novel, *Darkness in Saint Louis Bearheart*. Louis Owens says he had a hard time getting students to read the novel, part of their objection being that it remained true to Vizenor's remark in the preface that it's just a book of "sex and violence"—and, one should add, a book whose violence is rendered in particularly unsettling ways: traumatic images abruptly emergent within the generally comic current of the narrative. By the third page of the novel's opening genealogy of the "Cedar Circus"—the mythical tribe whose forced exodus from their ancestral cedar grove the novel will follow—the unthinkable violence has already begun. Forced into defensive warfare against "federal forces and tree killers" intent on converting the sacred grove of cedar into lumber for urban construction, the Cedar Nation sustains a rapid series of losses. In the course of combat, the mixed-blood spouse of First Proude Cedarfair, ancient chief of the nation, is raped, tortured and killed:

> [She] was raped by whitemen. Her blue eyes were burned with hot coals. Her flesh was pinched and torn. The soft brown hair on her pubic arch was cut and stuffed into her broken mouth by officials of the federal government.

In the following paragraph, a white "surveyor," recently converted to the cause of the cedar circus against the government that had formerly employed him, is captured and bound by federal troops. That night, while his captors were sitting around a fire drinking near the border of the cedar circus, the surveyor loosened his bonds and ran through the stumps into the darkness of the cedar. He was shot nine times in the back, three in the head, and impaled on a cedar stake facing the circus.

Despite the protest of some readers, this is a violence we know is in the real history of North America and its indigenous peoples, a federally sponsored violence which Vizenor presents as having long produced, indeed as continuing to produce, a particularly excessive history of human and natural loss. The passages suddenly and shockingly render brief moments of this unthinkable, unthinkably routine and extended history, refusing familiar rhetorics of "Indian" melodrama or tragedy at the eruption of this barbaric "other side" of reigning historical texts.

Yet in its recovery of this violent history, the novel never claims to represent the past "the way it really was," the "real story," over against the falsehoods propagated by official historians. For Vizenor, the official histories are certainly false, but what makes them false is exactly such claims to have rendered the historical past, and present, objectively and conclusively. These claims—and the static representations of "Indians" they sustain—are, for Vizenor, the peculiar product of "cultures of death." Their operative discourses are "terminal creeds": ways of writing whose deadliness is directly attendant upon the positing of privileged terms and termini. Terminal creeds legitimize monopolies of coercive force: in this case, writing U.S. history in triumphally democratic terms—as the march of "Progress." Like recent American t.v.'s "real stories of cops," such "histories" insist the essential identities of their players, and the ordained outcome of their encounter, before action even begins. In the passages quoted above, Vizenor renders not only a suppressed violence, but also the discursive terms within which the expansionist culture enacting that violence renders itself. The visibly phallic character of federal violence, in these passages and others—the obscene foregrounding of the phallus in acts of mutilation and destruction—registers expansionist America's proclamation that it acts as bearer of a sacred totem—the final term of history as "Progress." A fantasy of wholeness is thus projected across both the trauma of violent antagonism— what Fredric Jameson calls "the Real of History"—and the signifying action that legitimates it: the "quilting" of a field of historical meanings around the strike of a new master-signifier.

For Vizenor, such rigidly designating symbolic orders not only delimit the possibilities of meaning, they also rechannel desire into superegoic cycles that hyperproduce loss and destruction. To use Slavoj Zizek's terms for the pleasures of superego, such orders—forcibly recruiting subjects whose former lifeways have been shattered—are "permeated by an obscene enjoyment." They channel desire away from inventive and transformative cultural practices into moralistic and punitive repetitions. These are historical conditions within which what Lacan calls the "real of desire" attains a paralyzed and paralyzing formation. The "real of desire" names, for Lacan, that surplus pulsation of "enjoyment" (*jouissance*) constituted within every social and symbolic order: an enjoyment whose fate may be either a relatively open-ended metonymy along the chains of the symbolic, or the saturation of a particular signifying formation organized around a single "point de capiton." Vizenor's *Bearheart* studies the deadlocks of enjoyment possible at moments of history when desire's metonymic movements and transformations are weakened or deadened, and enjoyment is overbalancingly channelled into superegoic functions of the objectification, judgment, and punishment of bodies. What such moments demand, what they in fact are inevitably destined for, regardless of interventionist intention, is renewed eruptions of enjoyment—the eruptive laugh of the bear in *Bearheart*—making possible new articulations of the socio-symbolic order.

Bearheart emphasizes the crucial functions of eruptive memory in this renewal. Here, the relation of *Bearheart* to Walter Benjamin's "Theses on the Philosophy of History" seems to me crucial. Benjamin's famous passage on the "memory [that] flashes up at a moment of danger" suggests, as does Vizenor in *Bearheart,* that the eruption of buried memory is a critical event in the reanimation of both desire and discourse. Memory's flashing return blows open contemporary intersubjective orders, large and small, making possible their general reconstitution—to articulate now channels of desire outraged or closed down in the violence of the past.

Bearheart offers a series of vignettes of the transformative interaction of memory and desire in the subjects of history. In Vizenor's novel, the regenerative power of memory has fundamentally two dimensions. First, memories of traumatic assault—often triggered, as in Benjamin, by the contemporary persistence of such assault—reanimate the channels of desire shut down, foreclosed, or destroyed in the original violence. Second, memories of alternative and subcultural forms—what Vizenor calls cultural "holotropes" of an American Indian past—provide alternative terms for the resymbolization of past and present. That is, precisely in the aftermath of the symbolic catastrophes, or "encounters with the Real," that traumatic memories induce, the memory of alternative cultural forms makes possible a rewriting of history itself—as well as of contemporary subjectivities, with their orders of enjoyment. Under pressure of a dominant culture that persistently fails to "account" for this enjoyment in its subaltern populations, memorial "holotropes" may provide the only means of overcoming that other danger Benjamin locates in the "moment of danger": a "conformist" reconsolidation of oppressive cultural formations after their momentary upheaval. It goes without saying that a specific practice of storytelling is itself one of the "holotropes" at issue here: a "comic" or "trickster" storytelling, alternately collapsing and recovering through all these eruptions of the traumatic and impossible—a storytelling that always reconfigures, in its recovery, new possibilities of relation to the real of enjoyment. In this sense, the most real of "real stories" are those that fail, that effectively break down in the face of trauma—beginning again only through a radical resymbolization of past and present.

In *Bearheart*, the maimed, the deformed, and the diseased— "survivors" of a multiply destructive "culture of death,"— march in refugee formations along the interstate highways of the U.S. All are scarred by a history of violence and destruction. Yet their recovery and reinvigoration, their capacity to both feel and desire again, is predicated upon their return, in memory, to precisely the violence that has scarred them. The "Scapehouse of Weirds and Sensitives" on "Callus Road," in the novel's sixth chapter, is the site of a protected counter-culture of "survivors," female victims of unspecified violences who, within the protecting walls of the scapehouse, set out to reconstitute, through poetry, the world around them. But the suggestion of the chapter is that this poetic project cannot recover and reconstitute "enjoyment" itself until the violent traumas survived are themselves revisited. Sister Willabelle considers the scapehouse a place of "survivors protecting ourselves from our fears and past memories." But her own ordeal in the chapter makes clear that precisely this symbolically "protective" dimension of scapehouse culture must be surrendered. Willabelle is the sole survivor of a commercial jetliner crash, witnessing the death of her mother amid the general carnage. Willabelle's own body is now a flesh made entirely of scars, "the skin so tight in places that it turned white when she moved her arms and neck." She invites Rosina Cedarfair to test her "instincts for survival" by joining Willabelle in a storytelling return to the horrors of the crash. They are sharing a bath, Rosina caressing the scarsurfaces of Willabelle's body. "Instincts for survival" are at stake here because the self-protective anxieties they induce mitigate against psychic encounters with traumatic memory. Rosina's characteristic emotional courage is, however, equal to the moment, and she accompanies Willabelle in her terrible descent into memories of death and loss, a descent that ends in a tremulous resurgence of affect and desire. Willabelle's storytelling approach, and surrender, to trauma ends with the two women sinking, in sensuous embraces, beneath the waters of the bath.

The adventure of Benito Saint Plumero, in the same chapter, is analogous. This little-man clown and trickster, whose over-sized penis the sisters call his "superlative president jackson," is also a character broken by his past—the loss of the bronze statue/woman of his dreams. This "lifeless" other in whom his desire seemed to find its safety, was taken from him,

"drowned" in a river by people who think he's crazy. He seems to the sisters, on his arrival, a clown "put together from broken clowns." His recovery is a tale of accession to a desire that does not give way through fears of loss, death, otherness and change. That is, in Lacanian terms, the point of Saint Plumero's recovery is "not to cede his desire": to recover desire in its most radical dimension, as a "being toward death." Saint Plumero, beating the ground in his grief, recovers this desire the moment he passes through mourning to discover a new materialization of desire in Pure Gumption—the dog who, in a kind of pure and comic accident, occupies the space within which Saint Plumero's desire reawakens; the space where he literally "look[s] up" from his mourning. In the next paragraph, we find Saint Plumero responding to the multiplying erotic demands of the scapehouse sisters. In this new fluency of a desire that had been baffled by the losses of the past, Saint Plumero is

> so overwhelmed with love and pleasure . . . that during the first weeks there he could for the first time in his life accept death. Because of his intense survival instincts he responded with selfish panic whenever he faced thoughts of death, but in the orgiastic arms and legs of the weirds and sensitives he sighed that death, waiting in the space between lips and legs, could take him whenever she found him a place to ride high.

As in the story of Willabelle, "survival" is accomplished through the repression of trauma; contemporary transformation, however—what Vizenor calls "survivance"—is accomplished only through the repressed's traumatic return. The contemporary repetition of trauma recovers a desire that does not fear death, which reckons itself as "death drive" even in the space "between lips and legs."

These examples involve a crucial dimension of what Lacan called "symbolic suicide": a surrender of formerly stable articulations of identity and history that is simultaneously a surrender to the real of traumatic enjoyment. These examples also render the explosive affect attending such surrender. What *Bearheart*'s passages of violence might be said most persistently to gamble for, against a particular range of ideological odds in the U.S. today, is an intensity of affect in the reader—of fear, grief, rage over these unspeakable losses—an intensity that keeps obliterating the simple progress of the sentences themselves, schooling the reader in precisely the unnarratability of what nonetheless will here be narrated. While the sentences persist unbroken, they invoke a repeated caesura of affect. In this sense, it is a novel which keeps obliterating its own narrative progress—a novel that repeatedly demands to be removed from sight: set down, closed, taken up again only after traumatic interruption; but one which at the same time insists on its own continuation, right through the "ending" that is not an ending but an opening to imaginative and interpretive extensions.

Which is to say that the novel's concerns do not end with memory's disruption of reigning texts of the past. The other crucial dimension of memory in *Bearheart* is its recovery of cultural "holotropes" to be re-imagined, reconfigured, within the particular chance games of the contemporary world. It goes without saying that such reconstitution of contemporary intersubjective orders retroactively rewrites history, and that, in its most fundamental dimension, such cultural rewriting means a reconfiguration of the contemporary orders of enjoyment. Here, *Bearheart* may be seen as elaborating Benjamin's suggestion that the memory flashing up at a "moment of danger" is not only traumatic, but also potentially reconstitutive. *Bearheart* suggests, on the one hand, that the memory of violence, as a memory of a former *order* of enjoyment outraged, makes available to consciousness, in its emergence, the abandoned holotrope of that order itself. On the other, it suggests that the associative chains of discourse attendant upon encounters with trauma can "chance" upon holotropic exigencies.

The story of Lilith Mae, in the chapter "Abita Animosh," may be said to exhibit both these aspects of holotropic recovery. At the end of the story she tells Inawa Biwide—the story of forced sex with her stepfather in childhood—she both recovers the curious, trustful, tentatively exploratory sensuality of childhood, and is guided in this recovery by Inawa Biwide's responsive tale of sacred dogs-become-dream-lovers. Like Benito Saint Plumero and Sister Willabelle, Lilith Mae's desire has been broken by her past. But she is a much purer instance of the re-channelling of enjoyment from play into a routinized superego severity: in her case, a "terminal creed" that locates "evil" in men, penises, and sexuality. The chief symptom is her relationship to her two boxers: attentive, slobbering, sexually frisky males she at one moment distractedly fondles, at the next, rejects with furious contempt. Sexuality, traumatized for Lilith Mae by her stepfather's violence, is cathected now entirely to the controllable relationship with the boxers: "I hate you father fuckers, how I hate you and love you at the same time."

Through storytelling, Lilith Mae returns to the violence of the past:

> When I was eight years old, [my stepfather] took me
> on a camping trip and told me that all fathers and
> daughters share a secret and then made me suck the
> head of his fat purple penis until it spit all over me.

Again the crucial memory is one of a destructive phallic prerogative. Lilith Mae's narration of the event is at first rigidly guarded against the traumatic force of memory. Explosive affects of resistance and outraged desire are held at bay by a

distancing shame in which the original event has schooled her: "all fathers and daughters share secrets," secrets surrounding which the father soon enacts a ferocious disavowal. The shame internalized in response to her stepfather's abuse locks the adult Lilith in a rigid, humorless relation to sexual enjoyment. The real conflict of this chapter is thus not only between free explorations of desire and their violent foreclosure by others with a monopoly of force, but also between a liberating humor and the shame-binds of a rigidly moralistic culture: shame with its ritual cycles of secret pleasure and disavowal; humor with its releases, transgressions, and pleasures in the unexpected. It is Lilith Mae's "smile" that signals her symbolic transformation, her passage through traumatic memory into a radical reconstitution of her life-history. Accepting the holotropic terms offered by Inawa Biwide's traditional story of human-animal erotic combinations, Lilith, at the chapter's close, surrenders without shame to sexual explorations and strivings with her boxers: a rediscovery of enjoyment that is one of the novel's great little redemptions.

The plot structure of *Bearheart* underscores the need to recover traditional, visionary materials for contemporary change. The "cedarnation" carries with it everywhere, in its very name, its past: its point of embarcation, both geographic and cultural. Throughout the nation's travels, Fourth Proude Cedarfair returns in visions to the old cedar grove itself, visiting there the bones and still-hovering spirits of his ancestors. In an act of imaginative exploration akin to the novel's own reconstitution of a widening range of past and present experiences, Proude "enters into [his ancestors'] frames of time and place." He returns from these journeys back reinvigorated for the journey forward. Rosina Cedarfair says of their pilgrimage, "We are seeking nothing more than a place to dream again." Any future places must be places still dreaming the past. But of course, every place along the way is a place in which to dream too. The microsociety of pilgrims manifests this insistence on sustaining traditional-tribal "balancing" relations among themselves, between themselves and the animals that travel with them, and between all of these and the natural environments they pass through. A larger American social world of balance is made imaginable through this microsociety's example, and the vision which makes this possible is one actively sustained by the cedarnation from its cedar-grove past.

It should be more than clear, then, that no escapism or defeatism informs this insistence on re-visioning the past. These are visions called up within a consciousness of the contingencies and limitations of contemporary history. The point is not to return to the past in order to remain there, but to return for the symbolic tools with which to reconfigure present and future. Under interrogation at the federal "Word Wards," the pilgrims say, "we are . . . working out the models and paradigms and experiments on our language to learn where we are and where we will be." The "models and paradigms" that the pilgrims recover from past generations are less structured traditions than traditions of structural upheaval and rebalancing. This is clear in the gambling scene at the narrative center of *Bearheart*: It is a scene of trickster against gambler with a long traditional background in Chippewa culture. Fourth Proude undertakes the gamble with Sir Cecil Staples, the "tycoon of gasoline," who after years of human and natural depredation in the accumulation of his fortune, hoards the last of the commodity and gambles with those who need it. When the gambler remarks, during play, on the abstract equivalence between himself and his final opponent, Fourth Proude, both gamblers after all in dangerous games of chance where the stakes are, in part, a shared social future, Proude responds:

> But we are not equals . . . we do not share a common vision. Your values and language come from evil. Your power is adverse to living. Your culture is death.

Proude's emphasis on a fundamental difference of "vision" between himself and Staples should not be understood in terms of a simple opposition of "world-views"—of two equally stable and articulated symbolic structures. Staples's "culture" is certainly stable; indeed, it is monotonously repetitive, risking few departures from the familiar routine. Just as Staples risks little materially in the games, offering a few gallons of gasoline to would-be winners, so he risks little symbolically, merely reconfirming his "tycoon"-status with each repetition of play. His opponents, on the other hand, must stake their own lives—the consequent fear paralyzing their play and producing repeated losses. Fourth Proude, however, is ready to risk all—both actual and "symbolic death"—and it is here that the crucial difference of "culture" between Proude and Staples must be located. What Proude sustains in play is not stable cultural gridwork but an openness to radical cultural transformation: his "vision" is a commitment to revision at every eruption of the real. This is why the gambling scene's emphasis must finally fall on Proude's attunement to disruptive powers beyond the comprehension of his adversary, and on his readiness to pass through the abyss of symbolic collapse to new spaces of symbolic configuration. Proude's "low whistle," at the game's crisis, invokes imperceptible winds of chance, in whose path his playing-pieces first catastrophically collapse, before rising to new balance on the gameboard.

Though the evil gambler loses to Fourth Proude—is in fact killed by the pilgrims, in an extended and torturing act of counterviolence—the game is not, nor is it ever over. As the evil gambler himself says to Proude in the course of their game:

> . . . at the end, the end of all games, when we both have the power to balance the world . . . , we will

find a new game, because we are after all bound to chance.

The larger context within which such games are played are, of course, particular contemporary moments of balance or imbalance between "the forces of life and death." In this case, imbalance has been created by precisely the graphic brutalities of a dominant Euroamerican culture intent on seizing, controlling, or destroying anything—sex, nurturance, amusement, mythic identities—desired by those with a monopoly of force from those unwilling or unequipped to resist.

For Vizenor, visions of revision must be redeployed within every "new game." The novel insists on the "necessity of existential engagement," as against all forms of disengaged aestheticism, all "terminal creeds" that let the living die, or indeed actively destroy them, in fetishistic devotion to fantasy-visions of wholeness. This is perhaps the chief reason why the narrative of *Bearheart* itself always turns over again and faces the future, even amid all this work it must do with the past. It is why, as in the novel's powerful close on the threshold of a renewable social world, Vizenor's text always demands that we imagine a future with the aid of reconfigured visions of balance out of a sustained American Indian past. It is a past virtually, but never entirely, obliterated, in part exactly because of storytelling's ability to recover and reconfigure its urgent cultural visions in the present.

It seems to me possible to talk about a particular range of novels being written in the U.S. today which share the commitment to negotiate the historical traumas of both past and present in contemporary reconstitutions of enjoyment. A brief list of these novels would include Morrison's *Beloved*, Silko's *Almanac of the Dead*, Kathy Acker's *Childlike Life of the Black Tarantula*, Kingston's *China Men*, Paul Auster's *Music of Chance*, and Julia Alvarez's *In the Time of the Butterflies*. Working in the tradition of the novel overhastily dismissed by Benjamin, these writers might be seen as now producing, in a kind of loose, sometimes unconscious, alliance, a multiplied series of subcultural narratives that counter, from their varying positions within the race, class and sex hierarchies of our nation, those still dominant narratives of a triumphally democratic "American History." These novels offer a privileged site within which to study both the partially failed interpellations of a strategically shifting dominant American culture, and the elaboration of a whole series of counterhegemonic cultures which begin imaginatively to limn—to "blueprint with words" as Vizenor says—a radically democratic connective culture: one which refuses to simplify or reduce the specific and real experiences of loss and violent repression out of which different contemporary lives emerge.

There is, I think, a specific quality in these narratives which results in precisely the possibility of this nondominative, connective, and democratic imagination: the sense of a traumatic core of human experience which radically refuses symbolization. Contemporary theorists of "radical democracy," Chantal Mouffe, Ernesto Laclau, and Slavoj Zizek among others, discuss the unwriteable "traumatic core" around which every social and symbolic order is structured, and across which most dominating cultural visions project fantasies of social wholeness and completion, denying the inescapability of trauma, desire, and change in the subjects of history. There is an honoring of the unwriteable in both this theoretical work and the contemporaneous novels I've alluded to—a deeply felt awareness of the ultimate unwriteability of all our subjectivities and histories. From this perspective, only racial and sexual essentialisms take the road of confidently and conclusively writing such lives; only a "terminal" historicism claims to have located and catalogued the enormous losses produced in U.S. history, to have "put them to rest," in the dominant-cultural sense of a "past" now "behind us."

But while the traumatic kernel of every history is thus ultimately unsymbolizable for these writers, it is also inescapable: like the Lacanian "real," it "always returns to the same place." For Vizenor, the eruptive return of memories excised from dominant accounts not only disruptively announces the reality of social antagonism, it also opens the spaces for genuine socio-symbolic reconstitutions—what Benjamin calls the "redemption" of outraged desire. Memories of violence—unintegrated within, but repeatedly triggered by, contemporary orders of discourse—summon up in their advent a baffled but resurgent real of desire, with all the intense affect of its bafflement. In such moments, the subject experiences what Lacan called "a parenthesis of time"—Benjamin's "time of the now"—a return of the subject to that moment of possibility in which, this time, violent suppression may be outwitted if not overtly defied. Such resistance involves ultimately nothing less than the radical reconstitution of intersubjective orders of enjoyment, a refusal of desire's foreclosure in rigidly demarcated regions of the social network.

FURTHER READING

Criticism

Haseltine, Patricia. "The Voices of Gerald Vizenor: Survival through Transformation." *American Indian Quarterly* (Winter 1985): 31-47.
> Considers Vizenor's use of the trickster in his novel *Earthdivers.*

Jahner, Elaine. "Cultural Shrines Revisited." *American Indian Quarterly* (Winter 1985): 23-9.
> Describes Vizenor's use of metaphor to discuss the power of language.

Olsen, Lance. "Third Generation Post-Modernists." *American Book Review* 9, No. 6 (January/February 1988): 12-13, 20.
> Reviews Vizenor's novel *Griever* as well as works by other authors.

Ross, John. "A Funny Thing Happened to Columbus on His Way to Japan." *San Francisco Review of Books* 16, No. 3 (1991): 11-12.
> Reviews *The Heirs of Columbus* and compares it to other works about Columbus.

Sale, Kirkpatrick. "Roll on, Columbus, Roll on." *The Nation* (New York) 253, No. 13 (21 October 1991): 465, 486-90.
> Argues that although *The Heirs of Columbus* is not a novel in the traditional sense, it is nonetheless a successful work of Native American literature.

Silberman, Robert. "Gerald Vizenor and *Harold of Orange:* From Word Cinemas to Real Cinema." *American Indian Quarterly* (Winter 1985): 5-21.
> Discusses the relationship between the screenplay *Harold of Orange* and Vizenor's career as a writer.

Vizenor, Gerald. "The Envoy to Haiku." *Chicago Review* 39, Nos. 3-4 (1993): 55-62.
> Discusses how exposure to haiku while stationed in Japan brought him closer to Native American literature.

Alice Walker
1944-

American novelist, short story writer, essayist, poet, critic, and author of children's books.

The following entry presents criticism of Walker's work through 1996. For further information on her life and career, see *CLC*, Volumes 5, 6, 9, 19, 27, 46, and 58.

INTRODUCTION

The acclaimed writer of the Pulitzer Prize-winning novel *The Color Purple* (1982), Walker sees writing as a way to correct wrongs that she observes in the world, and has dedicated herself to delineating the unique dual oppression from which black women suffer: racism and sexism. Her work is an exploration of the individual identity of the black woman and how embracing her identity and bonding with other women affects the health of her community at large. Walker describes this kinship among women as "womanism," as opposed to feminism.

Biographical Information

Walker was born and raised in Eatonton, Georgia, where her father was a sharecropper. When she was eight years old her brother shot her with his BB gun, leaving her scarred and blind in one eye. The disfigurement made Walker shy and self-conscious, leading her to try writing to express herself. The accident also had a permanent impact on her relationship with her father: his inability to obtain proper medical treatment for her forever colored her relationship with him, and they remained estranged for the rest of his life. In contrast, Walker notes that she respected her mother's strength and perseverance in the face of poverty, recalling how hard her mother worked in her garden to create beauty in even the shabbiest of conditions. Despite her disadvantaged childhood, Walker won the opportunity to continue her education with a scholarship to Spelman College. She attended Spelman for two years, but became disenchanted with what she considered a puritanical atmosphere there and transferred to Sarah Lawrence College in Bronxville, New York, to complete her education. It was while at Sarah Lawrence that Walker wrote her first collection of poetry, *Once* (1968), in reaction to a traumatic abortion. Walker shared the poems with one of her teachers, the poet Muriel Rukeyser, whose agent found a publisher for them. After college, Walker moved to Mississippi to work as a teacher and a civil rights advocate. In 1967, she married Melvyn Leventhal, a Jewish civil rights attorney; they became the first legally married interracial couple to reside in Jackson, Mississippi. She and Leventhal had a

daughter, Rebecca; they divorced some years later. While working in Mississippi, Walker discovered the writings of Zora Neale Hurston, an author who would have a great influence on Walker's later work. Walker eventually edited a collection of Hurston's fiction called *I Love Myself When I Am Laughing . . . and Then Again When I Am Looking Mean and Impressive: A Zora Neale Hurston Reader* (1979). In addition to poetry, Walker has written short stories, collected in *In Love and Trouble* (1973) and *You Can't Keep a Good Woman Down* (1981), and several novels, most notably *The Color Purple,* which received both the Pulitzer Prize and the American Book Award.

Major Works

Walker's work is occupied with the task of what Alma Freeman calls "unveiling the soul of the black woman," as Hurston endeavored before her. Walker's first novel, *The Third Life of Grange Copeland* (1970), introduces many of the themes that would become prevalent in her work, particularly the domination of powerless women by equally powerless men. The novel follows three generations of a black southern family of sharecroppers and its patriarch, Grange Copeland, as they struggle with racism and poverty. In Grange's "first life" he tortures his wife until she commits suicide. His son Brownfield inherits his sense of helplessness and hatred, and eventually murders his own wife. In Grange's "second life" he attempts to escape to the industrial North. Walker does not present industrial labor as a viable solution to the poverty of the South, however, and in his "third life" Grange returns to his southern home. At the end of the novel, Grange has become a compassionate man who longs to atone for the legacy of hate he has left his family, attempting to help his granddaughter Ruth escape from her father (Brownfield) and the South as a gesture of his remorse. Another theme in Walker's fiction is the way in which the black woman's attempt to be whole relates to the health of her community. The attempt at wholeness comes from remaining true to herself and fighting against the constraints of society, as in the stories from Walker's collection *In Love and Trouble*. *Meridian* (1976) is considered an autobiographical work. The title character was born in the rural South, like Walker, and uses education as a means of escape. Pregnant and married to a high school dropout, Meridian struggles with thoughts of suicide or killing her child, but eventually decides to give the child up and attend college. After graduating she enters an organization of black militants in Mississippi, but realizes that she is not willing to kill for the cause. With this knowledge she resolves to return to rural Mississippi to help its residents struggle against oppression. In *The Color Purple*, Walker uses the form of letters in creating a woman-centered focus for her novel. The letters span thirty years in the life of Celie, a poor southern black woman who is victimized physically and emotionally by her stepfather, who repeatedly rapes her and then takes her children away from her, and by her husband, an older widower who sees her more as a mule than as a wife. The letters are written to God and Celie's sister, Nettie, who escaped a similar life by becoming a missionary in Africa. Celie overcomes her oppression with the intervention of an unlikely ally, her husband's mistress, Shug Avery. Shug helps Celie to find self-esteem and the courage to leave her marriage. By the end of the novel, Celie is reunited with her children and her sister. *The Temple of My Familiar* (1989) is an ambitious novel recording 500,000 years of human history. The novel's central character, Miss Lissie, is a goddess from primeval Africa who has been incarnated hundreds of times throughout history. She befriends Suwelo, a narcissistic university professor whose marriage is threatened by his need to dominate and sexually exploit his wife. Through a series of conversations with Miss Lissie and her friend Hal, Suwelo learns of Miss Lissie's innumerable lives and experiences—from the prehistoric world in which humans and animals lived in harmony under a matriarchal society to slavery in the United States—and regains his capability to love, nurture, and respect himself and others. In *Possessing the Secret of Joy*, (1992) Walker examines the practice of female genital mutilation. The novel focuses on Tashi, a woman who willingly requests the ritual, in part because she is unaware of what the ceremony involves. Since discussion of the ritual is taboo in her culture, Tashi is ignorant of the profound impact the procedure will have on her life. The ritual is further examined in *Warrior Marks*, (1994), a nonfiction account of this ceremony still practiced throughout the world. Walker also collaborated with Indian filmmaker Pratibha Parmar to produce a film with the same title. The book covers the making of the film as well as bringing to light the consequences of this practice.

Critical Reception

Walker earned high praise for *The Color Purple*, especially for her accurate rendering of black folk idioms and her characterization of Celie. Peter S. Prescott echoed the opinion of most reviewers when he called Walker's work "an American novel of permanent importance, that rare sort of book which (in Norman Mailer's felicitous phrase) amounts to 'a diversion in the fields of dread'." Despite the nearly unanimous praise, there are several widely debated aspects of Walker's writing. One such aspect is her portrayal of black male characters as archetypes of black men in modern society. Many reviewers condemn her portrayals of black men as unnecessarily negative, pointing to the vile characters in some of her work and to her own comments about black men as evidence of enmity on her part. Other critics assert that the author, in presenting flawed characters, reveals typical shortcomings in the hope that real people burdened with these flaws will recognize themselves in her stories and strive to improve. Some reviewers also assert that Walker's work contains positive images of black men that are often ignored by critics. Beyond her portrayal of black men, some reviewers have found fault with Walker's characterization in general, opposing her tendency to refer to characters only with pronouns, thereby encouraging readers to consider the characters exemplary of anyone to whom that pronoun could apply. Finally, much of Walker's work is viewed as political in intent, at times to the detriment of its literary value. In contrast, reviewers praise works such as *In Love and Trouble* for balancing the art of storytelling with political concerns. Reviewers often praise Walker in her use of oral storytelling tradition, finding her work most convincing when she employs anecdotal narrative. Overall, critics commend her ability to incorporate a message within her narratives. In commenting on *Possessing the Secret of Joy*, Alyson R. Buckman states that [Walker's] "text acts as a revolutionary manifesto for dismantling systems of domination," echoing the sentiments of many reviewers. Critics have also lauded the nonfictional *Warrior Marks* for its exposure of the practice of female genital mutilation. Walker's work consistently reflects her concern with racial, sexual, and political issues—particularly with the black woman's struggle for spiritual survival. Addressing detractors who fault her "unabashedly feminist viewpoint," Walker explained: "The black woman is one of America's greatest heroes. . . . Not enough credit has been given to the black woman who has been oppressed beyond recognition."

PRINCIPAL WORKS

Once (poetry) 1968
The Third Life of Grange Copeland (novel) 1970
Five Poems (poetry) 1972
In Love and Trouble (short stories) 1973
Revolutionary Petunias and Other Poems (poetry) 1973
Langston Hughes, American Poet (biography for children) 1974
Meridian (novel) 1976
Good Night, Willie Lee, I'll See You in the Morning (poetry) 1979
I Love Myself When I Am Laughing . . . and Then Again When I Am Looking Mean and Impressive: A Zora Neale Hurston Reader [editor] (fiction) 1979
You Can't Keep a Good Woman Down (short stories) 1981
The Color Purple (novel) 1982
In Search of Our Mothers' Gardens: Womanist Prose (essays) 1983
Horses Make a Landscape Look More Beautiful (poetry) 1984
Living by the Word: Selected Writings 1973-1987 (essays) 1988
To Hell with Dying (juvenile) 1988
The Temple of My Familiar (novel) 1989
Finding the Green Stone [with Catherine Deeter] (juvenile) 1991
Her Blue Body Everything We Know: Earthling Poems 1965-1990 (poetry) 1991
Possessing the Secret of Joy (novel) 1992
Warrior Marks [with Pratibha Parmar] (nonfiction) 1994
The Same River Twice (essays) 1996

CRITICISM

Barbara Christian (essay date March/April 1981)

SOURCE: "The Contrary Women of Alice Walker," in *The Black Scholar,* Vol. 12, No. 2, March/April 1982, pp. 21-30, 70-1.

[*In the following essay, Christian discusses how the women of Walker's* In Love and Trouble *fight to embrace their individual spirits and to overcome convention.*]

In Love and Trouble, Alice Walker's collection of short stories, is introduced by two seemingly unrelated excerpts, one from *The Concubine* by the contemporary West African writer, Elechi Amadi, the other from *Letters to a Young Poet* by the early 20th century German poet, Rainer Maria Rilke. In the first excerpt, Amadi describes the emotional state of the young girl, Ahurole, who is about to be engaged. She is contrary, boisterous at one time, sobbing violently at another. Her parents conclude that she is "unduly influenced by *agwu,* her personal spirit," a particularly troublesome one. Though the excerpt Walker chose primarily describes Ahurole's *agwu,* it ends with this observation: "Ahurole was engaged to Ekwueme when she was 8 days old."

The excerpt from Rilke beautifully summarizes a view of the living, setting up a dichotomy between the natural and the social order:

> . . . people have (with the help of conventions) oriented all their solutions toward the easy and toward the easiest side of the easy; but it is clear that we must hold to what is difficult; everything in nature grows and defends itself in its own way, and is characteristically and spontaneously itself, seeks at all costs to be so against all opposition.

How are these two excerpts from strikingly different traditions related and why are they the preludes, the tone-setters to a volume of short stories about black women?

I am coordinating a seminar on the works of Alice Walker. We have read and discussed *Once,* Walker's first volume of poetry, and the *The Third Life of Grange Copeland,* her powerful first novel. The tension in the class has steadily risen. Now we are approaching *In Love and Trouble.* There is a moment of silence as class starts. Then one of the black women, as if bursting from an inexplicable anger says: "Why is there so much pain in these books, especially in this book?" I know this student; her life has much pain in it. She is going to school against all odds, in opposition to everything and everyone, it would seem. She is conscious of being black; she is struggling, trying to figure out why her relationships as a woman are so confused, often painful. She repeats her question adding a comment—"What kind of images are these to expose to—(pause)?" To whom, she will not say. "I don't want to see this, know this." There is more anger, then silence. But she is riveted on the stories in this and other class sessions, and insists on staying in this class. She seems to all appearances, to be together, well-dressed, even stylish, a strong voice and body, an almost arrogant, usually composed face. But now she is angry, resistant, yet obsessed by these stories.

Alice Walker has produced a significant body of work since 1968, when *Once,* her first volume of poetry, was published.

Since then she has published two other volumes of poetry, *Revolutionary Petunias,* 1973, and *Goodnight Willie Lee, I'll See You in the Morning,* in 1979; in addition to *In Love and Trouble* she has published two novels, *The Third Life of Grange Copeland,* 1970, and *Meridian,* 1976; *A Children's Biography of Langston Hughes,* 1974. She has also edited an anthology of the work of Zora Neale Hurston, *I Love Myself . . .* in 1979, and has written any number of articles among which **"In Search Of Our Mother's Gardens"** (1974) and **"One Child of One's Own"** (1978); stand out as significant essays written by a black woman. Another collection of short stories *You Can't Keep A Good Woman Down* has just been published. Walker, has been a consistently prolific writer of poetry, essays and fiction. A young writer, she is already acclaimed by many as one of America's finest novelists.

Walker's already substantial body of writing, though varied, is characterized by specific recurrent motifs. Most obvious is her attention to the black woman as creator and how her attempt to be whole relates to the health of her community. This theme is certainly focal to Walker's first collection of stories *In Love and Trouble.*

Who are the characters in these stories? What happens to them? More to the point, what do they do that should cause this young black woman, and many others like her to be so affected? What have they or she to do with *agwu* or with Rilke's words?

In these 11 stories, Walker's protagonists share certain external characteristics that at first might seem primarily descriptive. All are female; all are black; most are Southern; all are involved in some critical relationship—to lover, mother, father, daughter, husband, woman, tradition, God, nature—that causes them some discomfit. But the external characteristics so easily discerned, are not emblems. They are far more complex and varied. The words, *Southern black woman,* as if they were a sort of verbal enchantment, evoke clusters of contradictory myths, images, stories, meanings according to different points of view. Who is a Southern black woman? To a white man, those words might connote a mammy, a good looking wench, or Dilsey, as it did to Faulkner. To a white woman it might connote a servant, a rival, or a wise indefatigable adviser, as it did to Lillian Hellman. To a black man, it might connote a charming, soft-spoken, perhaps backward woman, or a religious fanatic and a vale of suffering as it did to Richard Wright. But what does *being* a Southern black woman mean to her, or to the many that are her?

Focal to Walker's presentation is the point of view of individual black Southern girls or women who must act out their lives in the web of conventions that is the South—conventions that they may or may not believe in, may or may not feel at ease in, conventions that may or may not help them to grow. And because societal conventions in the South have much to do with the conduct of relationships—man and woman, young and old, black and white, our female protagonists, by their very existence, must experience and assess them. So naturally, Walker's women are in love and trouble. However, unlike Toomer's women in *Cane,* who too are restricted by their race, sex, and origins, Walker's women are not silent. Her women are not presented through a perceptive male narrator, but through the private voices of *their* imaginations or through their dearly paid for words or acts.

The way in which Walker uses point of view, character is not mere technique, but an indication of how free her protagonists are to be themselves within the constraints of convention. If they cannot act, they speak. If they cannot speak, they can at least imagine, their interiority being inviolate, a place where they can exercise autonomy, be who they are. Through act, word or dream, they naturally seek to be "characteristically and spontaneously" themselves. In order to defend the selves they know they are, they must hold to what is difficult, often wishing, however that they were not so compelled. As all natural things, they must have themselves—even in conflict. So their *agwu,* their personal spirits are troubled, as they strain against their restraints. And their acts, words, dreams take on the appearance, if not of madness, of contrariness.

What specifically are some of the conventions that so restrict them, causing their spirits to be troubled even as they seek love? It is interesting to me that the stories from this volume my students found most disturbing take place within the imagination of the character. And that often that character mentally sees herself as different from her external self. She sees a different self—a dangerous self, as if a reflection in a mirror.

Roselily is such a character. The form of her story, itself a marriage ceremony, is a replica of the convention, the easy solution to which she has been oriented. As a poor black woman with four illegitimate children, she is, it seems, beyond redemption. Thus, her wedding day, attended as it is by satin voile, and lily of the valley, is from any number of viewpoints a day of triumph. But *she,* how does she see it? Walker does not use "I," the first person point of view, but the pronoun "She" throughout this marriage ceremony, as if Roselily is being seen from an external point of view. Yet what she does is dream: "She dreams; dragging herself across the world." It is as if even in Roselily's mind, the being who wonders about, questions this day of triumph, is both herself, and yet not herself.

Troubled, though feeling she should not be troubled, Roselily's meditation on the words of the ceremony is intensely focussed, almost fixated on images of entrapment. "She feels old. Yoked." "Something strained upward behind her eyes. She thinks of the something as a rat trapped, cornered, scurrying to and fro in her head peering through the window of her eyes." Even the flowers in her hand, flowers associated with the sweet South, seem "to choke off three and four and five years of breath." Yet because of her condition, she feels she should not feel this way. She should want: "Respect, a chance to build. Her children at last from underneath the detrimental wheel." What she feels is—trapped in her condition—trapped in her deliver from that condition.

As Roselily struggles with her *agwu,* as she resists the urge to rip off satin voile, to toss away lily of the valley, her dreaming also gives us insight into the complexity, sheer weight of the conventions that have trapped her. Different sets of values are affecting her life. They are as different, as they are black, in the way they restrict her or allow her to grow. One set of values seems to be giving way to another, satin voile to black veil. Tradition is undergoing change, affecting the society's definition of her role as a woman, intensifying the conflict within herself.

She comes from a Southern black community, poor, Christian, rural, its tradition held together by "cemeteries and the long sleep of grandparents mingling in the dirt." Here she can be "bare to the sun." But she must be poor; she must work in a sewing plant—work from which no growth will occur, work only for the purpose of survival. Here she must be a mother, preferably within the confines of marriage, where her sensuality will be legitimatized and curbed. But even without marriage she must be a mother. Tradition decrees it. Here the responsibility of her children's fathers are minimized, their condition as restricted as hers except they have mobility, can drive by "waving or not waving." Here the quality of suffering is legitimatized by Christianity, as rooted in sorrow as the graves of her grandparents. Here there is nothing new, as the cars on the highway whiz by, leaving behind a lifestyle as rooted in the past as the faces at this country wedding.

What is new comes from the North, challenging this traditional way of life. New gods arise, affecting the quality of Roselily's life. What freedoms do these new conventions afford her? The nameless New England father of her fourth child, brings the god of social justice. Though he exalts common black people, he cannot "abide TV in the living room, 5 beds in 3 rooms, no Bach except from 4-6 on Sunday afternoons." He cannot abide the backward ways of the people that in the abstract he wants to save.

To the man she is marrying, God is Allah, the devil is the white man, and work is building a black nation. But he cannot abide the incorrect ways of Roselily's community, their faith in a white Christian God and their tolerance of sensuality. Just as the old women in the church feel that he is "like one of their sons except that he had somehow got away from them," he feels that this community is black except that it has

gotten away from its blackness. For him, a veiled black woman in his home is a sign of his righteousness, and in marrying Roselily he is redeeming her from her backward values. With him, she will have black babies to people the nation.

Whether Southern or Northern, traditional or modern, rural or urban, convention confines Roselily to a role, a specific manifestation of some dearly held principle. As a result, her *agwu* though expressed only in her dreaming, is even more troubled by change. For even as she glimpses possibilities, she is left with the same vision of confinement. She can only dream that "she wants to live for once. But doesn't quite know what that means. Wonders if she has ever done it. If she ever will." Not even the *I do* that she must speak in order to accept the delivery from her condition is allowed, in this story, to interrupt the dreaming. She does not speak aloud. Her dreaming is as separate from her external behavior, as this Mississippi country church is from her future home, cinder-filled Chicago. But at least she can, in her imagination, know her confinement to be troublesome and recognize in a part of herself that this change is not the attainment of *her* fulfillment.

As the first story in this volume, Roselily's meditation on her condition touches major themes that will be explored in most of the others. Distinctions between the shells of convention, to which people are usually oriented, and the marrow of a living, functional black tradition is examined in most of these stories in terms of the span and degree of freedom afforded the black woman. Like **"Roselily," "Really, Doesn't Crime Pay,"** focusses on the limited image of black femaleness within Southern tradition. Only now the image is no longer a "peasant" one but a black and middle class one as modified by the sweet smelling idealizations of the Southern Lady.

Both Roselily and Myrna's stories are couched in the images of sweet smelling flowers. But while Roselily's name emphasizes the natural quality of her Southern environment, Myrna buys her artificial scents from the shopping mall. Her creamed, perfumed body proclaims her a well kept lady and evoked images of the delicate, decorative Southern belle. But the South's mystique, as evoked through Roselily's name and Myrna's perfumes chokes rather than pleases both these women. Natural or artificial, peasant or lady, they are trapped by myth.

To all appearances, for that is what counts, Myrna has succeeded in ways that Roselily had not. Myrna, after all is married to Reul (Rule), an ambitious Southern black man, who wants her to have babies that he will support, and who insists on keeping her expensively dressed and scented. But, although Reul and Roselily's new husband are worlds apart, they agree on basic tenets: that the appearance and behavior of their wives mirror the male's values, and that their women stay at home and have babies. Both women must, in their physical make-up, be the part. Roselily must be clearly black; Myrna must look non-black, like a Frenchwoman or an Oriental. Both must wear appropriate uniforms: Roselily's black veil, Myrna's frilly dresses. Both must withdraw from the impure outer world, providing a refuge for their husband and children. But while Roselily does not know what she *wants* to do, when she is rested, Myrna knows that she wants to write, must write.

As in **"Roselily," "Really, Doesn't Crime Pay"** takes place within the imagination of the character. But while Roselily dreams during her wedding, Myrna's imagination is presented through her entries in her writing notebook. Unlike Roselily then, whose critical musings never move beyond her interior, Myrna's break for freedom lies in trying to express herself in words. However, like Roselily, as Myrna confronts the conventions she is expected to adhere to, she also experiences discomfit within her *agwu.*

As is often true with Walker's stories, the first few sentences succinctly embodies the whole:

> September 1961
> page 118
> I sit here by the window in a house with a 30 year mortgage looking down at my Helena Rubenstein hands.... And why not? Since I am not a serious writer, my nails need not be bitten off. My cuticles need not have jagged edges.

These first lines not only tell us that Myrna's story will be told through her entries in her writing notebook, we also begin to realize that she knows her value is perceived to be in her appearance and social position, not in her creativity. And because she has no external acknowledgement of her value as a writer, she, with some irony, doubts her own ability. Her husband's words to her, written as an entry, clearly summarizes society's view:

> Everytime he tells me how peculiar I am for wanting to write stories, he brings up having a baby or going shopping, as if these things are the same. Just something to occupy my time.

As a result of her own doubts, constantly reinforced by her husband, magazines, billboards, other women, doctors, Myrna is open, both sexually and artistically to Mordecai, an artiste. He rips her off on both counts precipitating the mental breakdown and her aborted murder of her husband that we see developing in her entries.

The presentation of entries, which begin with September 1961, go back in time and finally move beyond that date, is crucial to Myrna's story. For when we meet her, she has already tried to write and been rebuffed by her husband. She has been ripped off by Mordecai, has attempted murder, has been confined to a mental institution and has eventually been returned to her husband. Like Caroline Gilman's *The Yellow Wallpaper,* the entries that make up the substance of this story express the anger and rage, in madly logical terms, which drive the house-prisoned woman writer crazy.

But the story goes beyond that impotent rage. Having tried the madness of murder and failed, Myrna concocts a far more subtle way, contrariness rather than madness, to secure her freedom. Now she says yes to everything, the smiles, the clothes, sex, the house, until she has yessed her husband to fatigue. She triumphantly tells us that "the women of the community feel sorry for him to be married to such a fluff of nothing," and she confides that "he knows now that I intend to do nothing but say *yes* until he is completely exhausted." Cunningly, she secretly takes "the Pill," insuring her eventual triumph over him. But it is her discovery of the magnificence of the manipulation of words that brings her to a possible resolution of her troubled *agwu.* Like Ralph Ellison's nameless narrator's grandfather in *Invisible Man,* she yesses them to death, though in a peculiarly female way.

In saying *yes* to mean *no* Myrna uses the manipulative power of the word and secures some small victory. But it is a victory achieved from the position of weakness, for she has no alternative. Like countless Southern belles, she has found that directness based on self-autonomy is ineffectual and that successful strategies must be covert. Such strategies demand patience, self-abnegation, falsehood. Thus at the end of this story, Myrna has yet to act: "When I am quite, quite tired of the sweet, sweet smell of my body, and the softness of these Helena Rubenstein hands, I will leave him and this house."

What happens then when a black woman goes against convention, transgresses a deeply felt taboo, and says *No* directly and aloud? In perhaps the most powerful, certainly the most violent story of this volume, the woman in **"The Child Who Favored Daughter,"** speaks practically one word in the entire story, "No." By saying "No" with such firmness she resists convention, insisting on the inviolability of her *agwu.*

This story is as important in the light it sheds on the black men in other stories, Reul, and Roselily's Muslim husband, as it is in its own right. Moving back and forth between the imaginations of the woman and her father, it presents in almost cinematic rhythm, a black male and female point of view. In committing the most damnable act for a black woman, falling in love with a white man, the Child who favored Daughter sorely touches the vulnerability of the black man who has felt the whips of racism. To a compelling degree, Reul's desire that Myrna be feminine and Roselily's husband's insistence that she be pure and sheltered are related to these men's need to be on par with the white man. To have a wife who is a visual representation of one's financial achievement, or to protect and keep pure the black woman, despite the white man's often successful attempts to drag down the race, are goals essential to their view of themselves as men. Racism then has the effect, not only of physically and economically restricting these men, but also of reinforcing their need to imitate the oppressor's conventions in order to match his worth.

But **"The Child Who Favored Daughter,"** though encompassing the sexist results of racism, goes beyond them. For it is based on an apparently universal ambivalence men have toward the sexuality of their female kin, especially their daughters. Thus, it begins with an epigraph, the equivalent of which is found in every culture:

> That my daughter should
> fancy herself in love
> with *any* man
> How can this be?
> > Anonymous

And only a few words later, Walker underlines the result of such a sentiment. Succinctly defining *patriarch*, while exposing its absurdity, she introduces the father in this story in conceptual terms: "*Father, judge, giver of life.*"

Walker juxtaposes points of view of the Child and her Father by using the parts of this definition, *judge, giver of life*, as pivotal areas of contrast. As Father, the man judges his daughter based on one piece of evidence, a letter she has written to her white lover. As in **"Really, Doesn't Crime Pay,"** the written word takes on immense significance as proof of the woman's autonomy outside the realm of the man's kingdom. In an indelible way, the Child's written words are proof not only of her crime against her Father and societal conventions, but also of her consciousness in committing it. Thus we are introduced to her: "She knows he has read the letter," as she prepares herself for his inevitably harsh judgment. Her Father, too, is mesmerized by the letter itself, for it is both a proclamation of her separateness from him, and, ironically, a judgment on his life. The words he selects to remember from the letter heighten our sense of his vulnerability: "'Jealousy is being nervous about something that has never, and probably won't ever, belong to you.'"

Again, as in **"Roselily,"** although we are inside the characters' psyches, Walker uses the third person "She" and "He" rather than the first person "I." But here, its usage has a different effect; for unlike Roselily, neither the Child nor her Father are presenting a different self to the world. Rather the "She" and "He" used in the absence of personalized names give the characters, an archetypal quality, as if the Child stands not only for this individual black woman, but for all daughters who have transgressed against their father's law; and the Father stands not only for this bitter black man, but for all fathers who have been sinned against by their daughters.

That particular interpretation of the Child's act is organic to the story since the Father, not the Child defines himself as a patriarch. The Child does not see him as Father but as *her* father. There are other men who exist besides him; other laws that also govern. Her act proclaims this. Her words in the letter make it clear that she cannot be owned. It is precisely this difference in their interpretation of their roles that causes his *agwu* to be so agonized that it inflicts trouble on hers.

To the man in this story, he is Father, she is Daughter, a possessive relationship that admits no knowledge of any individual histories or desires. It is true that he clings to an individual history, his sense of his first betrayal by a woman who he loves. But that apparently individual story leads us back to the archetypal, for this woman is his sister, is called "Daughter," the original Daughter, rather than a particular name. Her image blots out all individualized details in other women, until all women, especially those who are "fragmented bits of himself," are destined to betray him. Sister, Daughter, he perceives them and their actions as a judgment of his own worth and capacity to be loved. From his perspective, because they have such power over him, they cannot exist apart from him. They must exist for him; because of him. Thus he must control them: "If he cannot frighten her into chastity with his voice he will threaten her with the gun." That he feels is his right as Father, as "*judge.*"

The authority vested in him as Father implies then not only that he has the power to enforce obedience, but that he has a right to this power precisely because he is the "*giver of life.*" Walker intensifies the archetypal tone of this tale by repeating two sets of poetic motifs in a relationship of tension between nature and time. One motif, "Lure of flower smells / The sun" emphasizes the sensuality of nature. The other "Memories of Once / Like a mirror reflecting" transforms the temporal into an eternal moment, obliterating the possibility of redemption. The Father's perception of himself as the "*giver of life*" is juxtaposed in the story to the keen awareness of his sister and daughter's sexuality, vital and beyond his control. He is affected by their sensual bodies, naturally capable of giving life, his daughter's "slight, roundly curved body," his sister, "honey, tawny, wild and sweet." His ambivalence toward that part of them that he can never have, that part of them that will naturally take them away from him, intensifies the physical feeling of betrayal he imagines has been dealt him by women.

"*Father, judge, giver of life,*" yet he cannot control it. Has he created it? Walker uses, throughout this story, images of Nature which overwhelm his senses: "the lure of flower smells," the busy wasps building their paper houses, the flower body of the Child. All around the Father life escapes his control, in much the same way that his daughter's body and her will overpowers him. Like Nature, his sister, and daughter, are "flowers who pledge no allegiance to banners of any man." As he will burn the wasps' paper houses down "singeing the wings of the young wasps before they get a chance to fly or to sting him," he must protect himself from "the agony of unnameable desire" caused by his sensuous wayward daughter.

If he cannot control the life he has given, then he must take it back. The violence the Father inflicts on his Daughter, for he literally cuts off her sexual organs in biblical fashion. ("If their right hand offend thee, cut it off") confirms his own sexual desire for her. It also underscores his fear of her proclaimed autonomy, her independence from him, which is based on her sexuality. In destroying her sexually, he is destroying that unknowable part of himself that he feels is slipping out of his control:

> . . . he draws the girl away from him *as one pulling off his own arm* and with quick slashes of his knife leaves two bleeding craters the size of grapefruit on her bronze chest (emphasis mine).

This Father kills *his* Daughter, not with the phallic gun, but with a knife, the instrument used in sacrificial blood ritual. He sacrifices her, to his definition of himself, what he and therefore she should be. And the brutality of his act also suggests that he must doubly kill her since he cannot attack the other object of his rage, her white lover. He kills in one blow, his desire for her and his long-frustrated rage at the white man. No longer can the white man despoil his sister or his daughter, for they no longer exist; no longer must he love what he cannot control. Now he is left with "the perfection of an ancient dream, his nightmare" and the gun, the child he now cradles, which he can completely control.

The Father's troubled *agwu* stands in contrast to the child's throughout this ballad of a tale. Her *agwu* is threatened from without; but it is not troubled within. Like Nature, she must be herself, grow and defend herself in her own way, not as defined by her father nor society. She must have herself even though she has learned that "it is the fallen flower most earnestly hated, most easily bruised," and that she has been that fallen flower the moment her father presumed to give her life. So, she cannot "abandon her simple way of looking at simple flowers." So she accepts her father's beating, rising from it strong-willed and resolved, and she cannot, will not deny that she loves whom she loves. It is her composure, paradoxically her contrariness, and her lack of torment which echoes for the father the original daughter's preference for the Other, worse—her complete indifference to his pained love. Thus, her ability to be so surely herself results in her destruction. Her inner spirit and her outer actions are as one, she is a woman. To her Father though, she must act and speak as a Child, though she may think as a woman, for then her sexuality will not be a danger to him.

"The Child Who Favored Daughter" lyrically analyzes two constraints of convention which, when fused, are uniquely opposed to the growth of black women. For it merges the impact of racism, not only on society but on the person, with the threat woman's sexuality represents to patriarchal man. One feeds the other, resulting in dire consequences for the black woman who insists on her own autonomy, and for whom love, the giver of life, knows "nothing of master and slave." For such a woman strikes at the heart of hierarchy, which is central to racism and sexism, two variants of the patriarchal view of life.

The young protagonists of **"Roselily," "Really, Doesn't Crime Pay,"** and **"The Child Who Favored Daughter,"** develop from one story to the next in their awareness of the conventions imposed upon them, and in their insistence on growing and defending themselves in their own way. Associated with the flowers of the South, their relationship to sweet-smelling nature mirror their consciousness. Thus, Walker presents Roselily as one who clutches lily of the valley, the symbol of her new condition, even as she questions her deliverance, though only in one part of her mind. Myrna does more than dream. Although she douses herself with gardenia perfume, the symbol of her comfortable prison, she writes of her intention to free herself, and has learned the difficult strategy of saying *yes* to mean *no*. The Child Who Favors Daughter goes even one step further. She will not give up "her simple way of looking at simple flowers," and her spoken word, "No" is a declaration of her internal freedom of mind. She is destroyed by her father and by convention, however, precisely because she tries to grow in her own way.

She is very much like most of Walker's elder protagonists in that their *agwu*'s too, are not troubled from within so much as they are from without. A major difference between the Child and these elders, Hannah Kemhoff, Mama in **"Everyday Use,"** the old woman in **"The Welcome Table"** is that they have survived. Perhaps they too had walked the paths of a Roselily or Myrna until they came to the realization that there is nothing more precious than being characteristically and spontaneously themselves. Too, they have become the repositories of a living tradition, which they know not only in conventional forms but more importantly in its spirit.

The old woman in **"The Welcome Table"** exemplifies the *agwu* that, though troubled from without, is aware of what is necessary for its fullness and tranquility. Her story is about her relationship to God which, for her, is above and beyond any conventions to which people have oriented their solutions. In contrast to the young flower heroines of this volume, she is described in nature imagery that expresses endurance rather than sensuality: "She was angular and lean as the color of poor gray Georgia earth, beaten by king cotton and the extreme weather." Rather than smelling of flowers, she smells of "decay and musk—the fermenting scent of onionskins and rotting greens."

Again, Walker uses the third person, "She" and "They," rather than the first person "I." This time she uses it so that we can hear both the old woman's mind and those opposed to her *agwu,* so that we can experience the contrast in spirit. For what she must do is prepare herself to be welcomed into the arms of her Jesus. For that overwhelming reason, she goes to the big white church without any regard for the breach of Southern convention she is committing. All that she is concerned with is the "singing in her head." In contrast they see her act as contrariness. For *they* see *her* as black and old, doubly terrifying to them because one state awaits them all, and the other frightens them. So they are able to throw her out of *their* church even as they beseech their God, according to convention, for protection and love.

Walker contrasts the two points of view in **"The Welcome Table"** in much the same way as she does the Child and the Father in **"The Child Who Favored Daughter."** Neither the old black woman nor the white congregation has names or specific identifying characteristics, except that each lives in Georgia. This absence of personalized detail gives the characters a quality that is both archetypal and Southern while it emphasizes the contrast in the way the old woman and the white congregation relate to Southern convention.

On one hand the white congregation does not see the old woman as worthy enough to enter their church, precisely because she is black and old, yet, they relate to her in familial terms for exactly the same reasons. Their confusion about how they are to react to her unconventional act is expressed in their uncertainty about whether they addressed her in the traditional familiar terms, "Auntie," or "Grandma." Their emphasis on this point is characteristic of the contradictions inherent in the white South's relation to its black folk. The old woman on the other hand is clear about her actions. She ignores them, is clearly *bothered* by these people who claim familial ties with her, yet know her or care about her not at all. In ignoring the conventions, she exposes the tradition of black and white familial ties as nothing more than form. All the sacred words of this tradition are brought into question by her simple act: "God, mother, country, earth, church. . . . It involved all that and well they knew it."

It is significant too, that the white men, all of whom seem younger than the old black woman, are the ones who express this confusion. It is the white women who are clear about their true relationship to this old black woman, for they do not idealize it. From their point of view, in her coming to their church, this old black woman challenges the very thing that gives them privilege. Both they and she are women—but

they are white, their only claim to the pedestal on which they so uneasily stand. They know they can only hold their position if that pedestal is identified with the very essence of Southern convention, and that this old woman, and others like her, are literally and symbolically the bodies upon which that pedestal rests. Just as sexism is reinforced by racism in **"The Child Who Favored Daughter,"** so in **"The Welcome Table"** racism distorts the natural relationship that should exist between woman and woman, and mutes the respect, according to convention and nature, that the young should have for the old.

According to white Southern thought, Christianity is the system upon which its culture and definition of woman and man is based. At the center of that system is the image of a white Jesus. Ironically Jesus' picture, which she has stolen from a white woman she worked for, is the old black woman's source of solace. But Walker does not present the old woman's white Jesus as an affront to her blackness; rather through the dynamics of her imagination and her culture, the old woman transforms this image into her own. For instead of being the meek and mild Jesus, her image of him is one of righteousness and justice. The words of the old spiritual, the epigraph of this story, embodies this old black woman's relationship to *her* Jesus:

> I'm going to sit at the welcome table
> shout my troubles over
> Walk and talk with Jesus
> Tell God how you treat me
> One of these days
> —Spiritual

One stereotypical image of the Southern black woman is that of the fanatically religious old mammy so in love with a white Jesus that she becomes the white man's pawn. **"The Welcome Table"** obliterates that image as it probes the depth of black Southern tradition. For this old woman cracks the conventional shell of white Southern Christianity, and penetrates the whiteness of Jesus' face to "the candle . . . glowing behind it," for she insists on the validity of her own faith and tradition, and on the integrity of her relationship with her God. Walker further reinforces the integrity of a black Christian tradition, of which Southern black women were the heralds, by dedicating her composition of her spiritual in prose form to Clara Ward, the great black gospel singer. For, like the slaves in their spirituals, the old black woman in **"The Welcome Table"** makes Christianity her own, going beyond its European images to its truth as it applies to her. It is her spirit that "walked without stopping."

This old woman's act, and the acts, words, even dreams of so many of Walker's protagonists in this volume appear to others, sometimes even to themselves, as manifestations of the innate contrariness of black women. The term, *contrary,* is used more often and with greater emphasis in Afro-American culture than it is in white culture. In fact, blacks often use it as if they all suffer from it. Yet behind their use of the word itself is a grudging respect for, sometimes even a gleeful identification with, a resistance to authority.

However, Walker's analysis of the contrariness of her main characters goes beyond the concept of unfocussed rebellion. Her women behave as if they are contrary, even mad, in response to a specific convention that restricts them, and they pay a price for their insistence on retaining their integrity. Even when they triumph, their stories are rooted in the pain . . . . Walker insists on probing *both* the white society and the black community's definition of black women. For in both worlds, words such as *contrariness* or a troublesome *agwu* are used to explain away many seemingly irrational acts of women; without having to understand them as appropriate responses. Her protagonists often discover that since they are black they are perceived by whites as "the other," or since they are women they are perceived by men as "the other." In either world they are not the norm. Their deviant behavior, then, is expected and therefore need not be understood.

That is why the excerpt from Amadi's *The Concubine* sets the tone so precisely for this volume, for Ahurole's contrariness, even in a black culture not yet affected by racism, is explained away as natural. Her life as an African woman is planned for her, regardless of her personality, desires, or development. And such a plan is so rooted in tradition, that Ahurole is allowed in her society to have this one outlet, which will neither change her situation or cause others to question it.

Yet Ahurole's story is not the story of Roselily, Myrna, The Child or the Old Woman. For these black women must not only bear the traditional definitions of women in their culture, they must confront, as well, the sexist myths of another race which oppresses them. The conventions that they are expected to hold to, are not even the conventions of their own communities, but ones imposed on them. It is no wonder then that these women seem mad whenever they insist on being "spontaneously and characteristically" themselves.

The stories in *In Love and Trouble,* provoke readers, especially black women, the audience to which they are clearly addressed, not only because of the pain or violence in them, but because Walker subversively admits to the contrariness of her black female protagonists. It is as if she says we do think as they suspect we do; we do speak and act as they say we do. What she does is to interpret that contrariness as healthy, as an attempt to be whole rather than as a defect of nature or as nonexistent. And in exposing the contrariness, in demonstrating its appropriateness, she assesses the false paths of escape from psychic violence that so many of us are wont to believe in or follow—those easy conventions that we would

like to see as solutions. These stories act out Rilke's words, for they show that there is no possibility for any living being to be whole unless she can be who she is. More disturbing they show that no matter how she might want to appear, no matter what conventions are imposed on her, no matter how much she resists herself, she will oppose those who inflict trouble on her. In the final analysis then, these stories are about the most natural law of all, that all living beings must love themselves, must try to be free—that spirit will eventually triumph over convention, no matter what the cost.

David Bradley (essay date 8 January 1984)

SOURCE: "Novelist Alice Walker Telling the Black Woman's Story," in *The New York Times Magazine,* January 8, 1984, pp. 25-37.

[*In the following essay, Bradley traces the devlopment of Walker's career and discusses the strengths and weaknesses of her writing.*]

I first met Alice Walker the way people used to: Someone I liked and respected pressed a dogeared copy of one of her books into my hands and said, "You've *got* to read this." The book was *In Love & Trouble,* a collection of stories written between 1967 and 1973. Some of them had been published previously in periodicals directed at a primarily black readership, in the feminist standard, *Ms.,* and in mainstream magazines like *Harper's,* a spectrum that hinted at the range of Alice Walker's appeal, just as the book's eventual winning of the American Academy and Institute of Arts and Letters' Rosenthal Award was a harbinger of honors to come, including the Pulitzer Prize for fiction.

My reaction to the book was complicated. Some of the stories I judged professionally. **"The Revenge of Hannah Kemhuff,"** the story of an old black woman who comes to a conjurer seeking revenge against a white woman who had humiliated her long ago, does not really work; the use of an educated apprentice to tell the tale seems intrusive and false. On the same professional basis, I liked **"Roselily,"** a stark tableau of a wedding between a Northern Muslim and a black Southern woman.

But my reaction to other stories forced me out of the shelter of professional detachment. I was moved deeply by **"The Welcome Table,"** in which an old, dying black woman is expelled bodily from a white church, but meets up with Jesus on the highway. I was horrified yet mesmerized by **"The Child Who Favored Daughter,"** in which a bitter, sullen, Bible-thumping sharecropper, full of confusion and guilt over the wanton life and eventual suicide of his sister, imprisons, tortures and eventually kills (by hacking off her breasts) his own daughter, who has shown an interest in boys. My response, in the end, was overwhelming admiration. For I was, at the time, trying to figure out how a writer should balance the demands of technique with the demands of emotion, of honest plotting and storytelling with larger political concerns. Alice Walker seemed to have found some kind of answer. Her technique was flawless—her plots inexorable, her images perfect, her control, even of the roiling Freudian undercurrents in **"The Child Who Favored Daughter,"** unwavering. Yet there was in every story, even the ones that did not seem to work, a sense of someone writing not simply to be writing, but because she wanted to make people see things.

I did not resolve to imitate her—I had enough sense to know that her way was not precisely mine—but I did decide to emulate her. I also decided to read everything she ever wrote (which now includes 10 books, the latest being *In Search of Our Mothers' Gardens: Womanist Prose*).

I first met Alice Walker in person in the summer of 1975, when she accepted my invitation to lunch. Alice Walker, who is now 39, was then 31; I was only 24. By that time, I had gone a long way toward reading everything she had ever published. I had only skimmed her first book of poems, *Once,* which was published in 1968 when she was 24, but completed by the time she was 21. But I had studied her second volume of poems, *Revolutionary Petunias & Other Poems,* which came out in 1973.

I was no lover of contemporary poetry, particularly the "radical" poetry of the 1960's and early 1970's. Some of it had moral force and authenticity, and some of the poets had a sense of craft. But the sentiments of nonjudgmental liberalism that characterized the movements of the period had made it possible for every idiot with a Bic pen and a Big Chief pencil tablet to claim to be a poet, so long as he or she was a member of some oppressed group, imitated Orwell's use of pigs as the symbol of the oppressor and occasionally stapled together a rudimentary chapbook of poems that seemed unified only because they were repetitious.

But Alice Walker's *Revolutionary Petunias* was about as far from that airheaded tradition as Leonardo da Vinci is from Andy Warhol. Her sense of line was precise, her images clear, simple, bitingly ironic, the book unified by the symbol of flowers. "These poems," Alice Walker writes, "are about . . . (and for) those few embattled souls who remain painfully committed to beauty and to love even while facing the firing squad."

Those "embattled souls" included members of her own large (eight children) family: a sister who escaped, through education, the narrow and impoverished world of Alice Walker's native Eatonton, Ga. ("Who saw me grow through letters / The words misspelled But not / The longing"); her uncles visiting from the North ("They were uncles. . . . / Who noticed how / Much / They drank / And acted womanish / With they do-rags"); her grandfather, seen at the funeral of her grandmother, Rachel Walker:

> My grandfather turns his creaking head
> away from the lavender box.
> He does not cry. But looks afraid.
> For years he called her "Woman";
> shortened over the decades to
> "Oman."
> On the cut stone for "Oman's" grave
> he did not notice
> they had misspelled her name.

They also included the women and the old men of Eatonton, and they also included figures from the larger world of political struggle. She mourned:

> The quietly pacifist peaceful
> always die
> to make room for men
> Who shout. Who tell lies to
> children, and crush the corners
> off of old men's dreams.

And she attacked on their behalf the con men of the revolution who: " . . . said come / Let me exploit you; / Somebody must do it / And wouldn't you / Prefer a brother?"

Those embattled souls included Alice Walker herself. She writes with sadness and defiance of the price she had paid for loving and marrying a white man, a civil-rights lawyer named Mel Leventhal. In **"While Love Is Unfashionable,"** she writes:

> While love is dangerous
> let us walk bareheaded
> beside the Great River.
> Let us gather blossoms
> under fire.

She made clear her love of peacefulness, but left no doubt as to her determination to ignore the standards of society and appeal to higher judges: "Be nobody's darling; / Be an outcast. / Qualified to live / Among your dead."

It took no unique perception to be enthralled by *Revolutionary Petunias,* which had already been enthusiastically reviewed, nominated for the National Book Award and given the Lillian Smith Award. However, unlike a number of reviewers, I was even more taken with Alice Walker's first novel, *The Third Life of Grange Copeland,* published in 1970, in which a black sharecropper, enslaved by circumstances and eternal debt, breaks free of the destructive cycle at the point where he would have slain his wife, who has betrayed him with the white landowner. Instead, he abandons her and his son, Brownfield, and heads north. Consumed with hatred for Grange, Brownfield nevertheless echoes his father's sins in more sinister harmonic; he destroys his wife's intellect, batters her and their three daughters and eventually kills her. The youngest daughter, Ruth, is taken in by Grange, now returned and transformed by time and experience into a wise and saintly old man. He nurtures and protects Ruth, in the end to the point of killing his own son and sacrificing his own life.

There is, to be fair to its critics, a lot not to like about the novel. Its structure is weak; despite the basic three-part plot implied by the title, the book is chopped up into 11 "parts" and 48 short chapters. The plot itself is both episodic and elliptical; the crucial "second life," which would have shown Grange Copeland's transformation, is largely missing.

But there is much to admire, especially in the "third life," in which Grange Copeland emerges as one of the richest, wisest and most moving old men in fiction. His speeches, never preachy, always set perfectly in context, ring with complex truth. Speaking of the difference between himself and his son:

> "But when he become a man himself, with his own opportunity to righten the wrong I done him by being good to his own children, he had a chance to become a real man, a daddy in his own right. That was the time he should have just forgot about what I done to him—and to his ma. But he messed up with his children, his wife and his home, and never yet blamed hisself. And never blaming hisself done made him *weak* . . . By George, I *know* the danger of putting all the blame on somebody else . . . And I'm bound to believe that that's the way the white folks can corrupt you even when you done held up before. 'Cause when they got you thinking that they're to blame for *every*thing they have you thinking they's some kind of gods!"

Much of Grange's humanity comes out in his interactions with Ruth, a sweet, sassy, feisty, precocious child ("I never in my life seen a more womanish gal," says Grange). Their dialogues are dramatic expressions of an unabashedly universalist philosophy.

But much as I admired *Revolutionary Petunias* and *The Third Life of Grange Copeland,* it was one of Alice Walker's essays, **"The Unglamorous but Worthwhile Duties of the Black Revolutionary Artist,"** that compelled me to meet her. At the time, I was awaiting the publication of my first novel and trying to figure out how I would deal with the political nonsense that seems to always attend the appearance of even the most nonpolitical book by a black.

Alice Walker "told" me: "The truest and most enduring impulse I have is simply to write. It seems necessary for me to forget all the titles, all the labels and all the hours of talk, and to concentrate on the mountain of work I find before me. My major advice to young black artists would be that they shut themselves up somewhere away from all the debates about who they are and what color they are and just turn out paintings and poems and short stories and novels."

I wanted to meet Alice Walker, I realized, because there were things I needed to learn from her.

We ate in a deli on Lexington Avenue in Manhattan and talked of many things—of the 1930's anthropologist and novelist Zora Neale Hurston, whose work Alice Walker had discovered while doing research "in order to write a story that used *authentic* black witchcraft." The results had been **"The Revenge of Hannah Kemhuff,"** and something less purely professional. Alice Walker fell in love with Hurston. "What I had discovered," she had told the Modern Language Association a few months before our lunch, "was a model. A model who, as it happened, had provided . . . as if she knew someday I would come along wandering in the wilderness, a nearly complete record of her life."

We talked of my own model, Jean Toomer, one of Hurston's forerunners of whose major work, *Cane,* Alice Walker had written, "*I love it passionately;* could not possibly exist without it."

She spoke of her years in the South, her impoverished childhood in Eatonton, the two years she had spent at Atlanta's elite black women's college, Spelman, before she found a way to escape from what she felt to be its puritanical atmosphere to an elite white women's college, Sarah Lawrence; her years in Mississippi as a civil-rights worker and teacher, a vulnerable position made more so because of her marriage to Leventhal. She spoke, too, of her turning away from formal religion. "I just need a wider recognition of the universe," she would explain years later.

She had little to say about publishing. Breaking into the business had not required the usual years of frustration. She had written most of the poems in *Once* during a short, frenzied week following a traumatic abortion while at Sarah Lawrence. One of her teachers, the poet Muriel Rukeyser, gave them to her own agent, who showed them to Hiram Haydn, then an editor at Harcourt Brace Jovanovich, who almost immediately accepted them.

Alice Walker in person was as many faceted as Alice Walker in print. She was a scholar of impressive range, from African literature to Oscar Lewis, the noted anthropologist. She was an earthy Southern "gal"—as opposed to lady. Her speech was salted with down-home expressions, but peppered with rarified literary allusions. She was an uncompromising feminist, capable of hard-nosed, clear-eyed analysis; she was also given to artless touching and innocent flirtation. She had a sneaky laugh that started as a chuckle and exploded like a bomb. Her eyes sparkled—I did not know then, and surely could not tell, that one of them had been blinded in a childhood accident.

I left Alice Walker in the lobby of the building that housed *Ms.* magazine, of which she was then a contributing editor, feeling both elated and uneasy—elated because I had liked her every bit as much as I had liked her books, and uneasy because I thought, as I had watched her walk toward the elevators, that the world into which she was moving was a steam-driven meat grinder, and she the tenderest of meat. The black movement, with which she still identified, was split on questions of anti-Semitism, integration, class, region, religion and, increasingly, sex. The women's movement, of which she was perhaps the most artistic and evocative contemporary spokesperson, was increasingly being accused of racism, and had factions of its own.

Alice Walker was black, a pacifist but a rejector of the organized religions to which that tradition belonged. She was married to a white, indeed, a Jew. She was a rejector of black middle-class education and pretensions, and an acceptor of white upper-class education—but not pretensions. She was a Southerner in the "liberal" North, a feminist who was also a wife and a mother. She was also sensitive enough to be hurt by criticism.

I worried for her. I watched her go. I wished her well.

I saw Alice Walker only twice in the next seven years: once, in 1976 at a party celebrating the publication of her second novel, *Meridian*; again, in 1983, at the ceremony where she accepted the American Book Award for her third novel, *The Color Purple,* which would, a few days later, be announced as the winner of the Pulitzer Prize. Between those occasions, I had no real conversations with her; I had even allowed our real acquaintance, based on her work, to lapse.

That was, in part, because I had become busy with my own writing and teaching. But I had also been terribly disappointed by *Meridian* and the collection of short stories that followed in 1981, *You Can't Keep a Good Woman Down.*

In this I was, to all appearances, alone. *Meridian* had been touted by *Newsweek* as "ruthless and tender," by *Ms.* as "a classic novel of both feminism and the civil-rights movement," and by *The New York Times Book Review* as "a fine, taut novel that . . . goes down like clear water." But to me it seemed far more elliptical and episodic (three parts, 34 chapters) than her first novel, without having that novel's warmth and simplicity. The title character, an itinerant civil-rights worker,

seems less pacifist than passive. She suffers from an intermittent paralysis of vague origins that, by the end of the book, she has managed to pass off to a weak skunk of a man, named Truman Held, a former lover who repeatedly betrayed her in order to be with white women. He seems to redeem himself years later by mothering her, accepting her illness and ignoring her sexuality.

The dialogue between Meridian and Truman Held, especially when compared to the easy conversation of Grange Copeland and Ruth, is just plain awful. ("Hah," he said bitterly, "why don't you admit you learned to hate me, to disrespect me, to wish I were dead. It was your contempt for me that made it impossible for me to forget.") The symbolic unity, so powerful in *Revolutionary Petunias,* is missing.

Many of the stories in *You Can't Keep a Good Woman Down* show the complexity and artistry of *In Love & Trouble.* There is **"A Sudden Trip Home in the Spring,"** in which a young, Southern black girl, a student at a Northern women's college, returns home for the funeral of her father, whom she has never understood, and discovers new sources of strength in her older brother and her grandfather. And there is **"Fame,"** a day in the life of Andrea Clement White, an aging and proper black woman of letters, who goes to a literary-awards luncheon uttering acerbic comments: ". . . white liberals told you they considered what you said or wrote to be new in the world (and one was expected to fall for this flattery); one never expected them to know one's history well enough to recognize an evolution, a variation, when they saw it; they meant new to *them.*"

But many of the stories are flawed by unassimilated rhetoric, simplistic politics and a total lack of plot and characterization. Some are hardly stories. One unsatisfying piece, **"Coming Apart,"** through its complex publication history, hinted at what was going wrong. Commissioned as an introduction to a chapter on third-world women in a feminist collection of essays on pornography, the "story" had been published in *Ms.,* entitled **"A Fable,"** then republished in *You Can't Keep a Good Woman Down,* retitled and with a polemical, confusing and somewhat inaccurate introduction: ". . . the more ancient roots of modern pornography are to be found in the almost always pornographic treatment of black women who, from the moment they entered slavery, even in their own homelands, were subjected to rape as the 'logical' convergence of sex and violence."

Meridian and *You Can't Keep a Good Woman Down* upset me. Alice Walker seemed to have lost the balance of form and content that had made her earlier work so forceful. She had ignored the human power of situations in favor of polemical symbolism. Worse, she appeared to have got caught up in the business she had advised young writers to avoid—

advice I had taken to the heart of my own existence. I was furious at Alice Walker. I felt . . . misled.

By the time I watched her receive the American Book Award, my anger had faded. By then, I had had some taste of what it is like to scribble in obscurity and then suddenly have people ripping manuscripts out of your hands before you have satisfied yourself and publishing them for reasons and standards far removed from yours. I no longer felt that Alice Walker had misled me; I believed she had been misled, and pressured in ways she could not possibly ignore. When Gloria Naylor, the black woman who won the American Book Award for first novels in 1983, acknowledged the debt that she and other black female writers owed Alice Walker, I could only think, what a heavy burden that tribute must be.

When Alice Walker rose to make her own acceptance speech, I could not help thinking of Andrea Clement White, who tells an interviewer, "In order to *see* anything, and therefore to create . . . one must not be famous" and could only summon up the energy to accept her "one hundred and eleventh major award" after hearing a small, dark-skinned girl sing an old slave song. I wondered who, if anybody, was singing for Alice Walker. I had not then, you see, read *The Color Purple.*

I rediscovered Alice Walker through reading *The Color Purple.* In my case, though, the rediscovery almost did not happen. I had read enough about the book to want to avoid it like the plague.

I had read that it was an epistolary novel, with most of the letters written by Celie, a black Southern woman, the victim of every virulent form of male oppression short of actual femicide, who eventually finds true love and orgasm in the arms of another woman. The description made me fear the book would be as disjointed as *Meridian* and as polemical as most of *You Can't Keep a Good Woman Down.*

I also sensed that *The Color Purple* was going to be ground zero at a Hiroshima of controversy. In June 1982, Gloria Steinem, in a profile of Alice Walker published in *Ms.,* had written about an "angry young novelist," male and implicitly black, who had been miraculously tamed by Alice Walker's writing. This, Miss Steinem said, was "a frequent reaction of her readers who are black men." But she then went on to question the thoroughness, integrity and motivation of all Alice Walker's reviewers, especially those black and male. "It's true," she wrote, "that a disproportionate number of her hurtful, negative reviews have been by black men. But those few seem to be reviewing their own conviction that black men should have everything white men have had, including dominance over women. . . ." That position would make expressing any reservations about *The Color Purple* risky business for a black man, and indeed, I had heard rumblings about

the review Mel Watkins, a black man, had written in *The New York Times,* because he had criticized the male portraits as "pallid" and the letters not written by Celie as "lackluster and intrusive" even though he termed the book "striking and consummately well written."

At the same time, I had heard some people—not all of them white and/or male—expressing some misgivings about the book. One black poet, Sonia Sanchez, criticized Alice Walker's theme of black male brutality as an overemphasis. Another black woman told me *The Color Purple* was "a begging kind of piece" and she was "getting tired of being beat over the head with this women's lib stuff, and this whole black woman/black man, 'Lord have mercy on us po' sisters,' kind of thing" in Alice Walker's work.

On the other hand, one white woman told me that once she had gotten through the first few depressing letters, "The rest was so uplifting and *true,* it made me cry."

All this considered, *The Color Purple* seemed a good book to stay away from. But then someone I liked and respected pressed a dogeared copy of *The Color Purple* into my hands and said, "You've got to read this."

I did and discovered a novel that seems a perfect expression of what, in my mind, makes Alice Walker Alice Walker. The epistolary form is perfectly suited to her experience and expertise with short forms—what in another book would have been choppiness is short and sweet. There is plenty of political consciousness, but it emerges naturally from the characters, instead of being thrust upon them. That Celie—after being repeatedly raped and beaten by a man she thinks of as her father, having him take the children she bears him away, and then, knowing that his brutality has rendered her sterile, hearing him tell her future husband, "And God done fixed her. You can do everything just like you want to and she ain't gonna make you feed it or clothe it"—should find herself uninspired by the thought of sex with men, and be drawn to a woman who shows her love and introduces her to ecstasy seems less a "message" of radical feminist politics and more an examination of human motivation. That the other woman, Shug Avery, should fall in love with a man gives any such message a counterpoint.

No matter what polemical byways Alice Walker might have strayed into, she had, in the process of creating *The Color Purple,* become a writer far more powerful than she had been. Before she had touched me and inspired me. This time, along about page 75, she made me cry.

On an airplane at 35,000 feet, I was suddenly scared to death. I was on my way to talk to Alice Walker, preparatory to writing about her, and I was reading my homework: galley proofs of Alice Walker's newest book, *In Search of Our Mothers'*

Gardens: Womanist Prose, essays, speeches and reviews written over 17 years—nearly her entire adult life.

The book made me see an error in my thinking about Alice Walker. I had allowed myself to become so mesmerized by *The Color Purple* and the fond recollections it inspired of *Revolutionary Petunias* and *The Third Life of Grange Copeland* that I had forgotten the works that came between. I had, therefore, set out to write about Alice Walker confident I would not be doing anything "hurtful," but rather testifying that she has a miraculous ability to transubstantiate the crackers and grape juice of political cant into the body and blood of human experience.

Yet Alice Walker, in her time, has produced some crackers and some grape juice, and that surely must show up in a collection such as *In Search of Our Mothers' Gardens.* Reading it, I realized I had more or less refused to really *see* Alice Walker. I had picked and chosen aspects of her, deciding which I would respond to, which I would not.

In Search of Our Mother's Gardens forced me to look at all of her. As it turned out, much in the book is not only pleasing, but impressive and moving. Alice Walker, the award-winning poet, novelist and short-story writer, proves herself the master of yet another form. Her descriptions are elegant. Her sarcasm is biting, her humor pointed.

Nor is her artistry merely a matter of rhetorical form. The content of much of her statements places so many troublesome controversies in proportion and perspective. Her 1976 speech, **"Saving the Life That Is Your Own,"** deposits the question of differences between literature written by blacks and whites into the appropriate circular file.

But there is also much that dismays me. Some of those things can be written off to polemical excess, such as her discounting of the ability of literature to reach across racial lines or her proclamation that she had once attempted to "suppress" statements made by another black female writer.

But other excesses are more troubling because they form, it seems, a pattern indicating Alice Walker has a high level of enmity toward black men. Her early praise of individual male writers seems to have been transformed over time to dismissal and disdain: Richard Wright's exile from Mississippi she no longer finds "offensive" but proof of his place of favor; Toomer is no longer a genius not to be thrown away but a disposable commodity ("*Cane* . . . is a parting gift . . . I think Jean Toomer would want us to keep its beauty but let him go"). Black male writers, in general, are possibly less insightful than their white male counterparts who, "It is possible . . . are more conscious of their own evil," and are guilty of "usually presenting black females as witches and warlocks."

Her acidity flows beyond black male writers. It pours over men who are attracted to light-skinned women—including, apparently, the Rev. Dr. Martin Luther King Jr. ("Only Malcolm X, among our recent male leaders, chose to affirm, by publicly loving and marrying her, a black woman.") It spatters, in general, men she considers fundamentally illiterate: "And look at the ignorance of black men about black women. Though black women have religiously read every black male writer who came down the pike . . . few black men have thought it of any interest at all to read black women."

The pattern makes me see that some of the "hurtful" criticism is demonstrably true: Black men in Alice Walker's fiction and poetry seem capable of goodness only when they become old like Grange Copeland, or paralyzed and feminized, like Truman Held. If they are not thus rendered symbolically impotent, they are figures of malevolence, like Ruth's murderous father, Brownfield, or the black "brothers" in Revolutionary Petunias ("and the word / 'sister' / hissed by snakes / belly-low, / poisonous, / in the grass. / Waiting with sex / or tongue / to strike. / Behold the brothers!").

Yet *In Search of Our Mothers' Gardens* has a wealth of honest self-revelation, enough to help me understand where some of that pattern—as well as some of Alice Walker's brilliance—came from. She writes of the aftermath of an accident that befell her at age 8, when her brother accidentally shot her with a BB gun, blinding an eye and filling her with a dread of total blindness as well as leaving her with a disfiguring scar.

After that accident, she felt her family had failed her, especially her father. She felt he had ceased to favor her, and, as a child, blamed him for the poverty that kept her from receiving adequate medical care. He also, she implies, whipped and imprisoned her sister, who had shown too much of an interest in boys, as had the farmer in **"The Child Who Favored Daughter."** In company with her brothers, her father had failed to "give me male models I could respect."

The picture that emerged is of a very unhappy existence, but, ironically, the loss of her sight enabled her to see those truths that imbue her writing: "For a long time, I thought I was ugly and disfigured. This made me shy and timid, and I often reacted to insults that were not intended . . . I believe, though, that it was from this period . . . that I really began to see people and things. . . ."

Five years ago, Alice Walker sold her small house in Brooklyn and flew to San Francisco in search of a place she had dreamed of without ever seeing, "a place that had mountains and the ocean." In time, she and her companion, Robert Allen, a writer and editor of the journal Black Scholar (she is now divorced from Leventhal), found a small, affordable house in Mendocino County, north of the city, in a locale that looked, to Alice Walker, like Georgia. She planted a hundred fruit trees around the house, just as her mother had "routinely adorned with flowers whatever shabby house we were forced to live in."

In San Francisco itself, Alice Walker also found an apartment, which she decorated to her taste—wood, clay, earth tones and, of course, several shades of purple. The apartment, a four-room, third-floor walkup, is in close proximity to Divisadero Street, the main thoroughfare in the black ghetto many San Franciscans maintain does not exist. Alice Walker has traveled far, but has not removed herself from anything. As I settle down in her apartment to talk to her for the first time in the better part of a decade, I wish she had; fatigue is obvious in her features and the tone of her voice. Once she had reminded me of Ruth; now, she reminds me of Meridian.

But unlike Meridian, Alice Walker is not paralyzed. She sits in a comfortable wooden rocker, in constant, rhythmic motion, and talks of the fight she has put up to keep the term "womanist" in the subtitle of *In Search of Our Mothers' Gardens.*

"I just like to have words," she explains, "that describe things *correctly.* Now to me, 'black feminist' does not do that. I need a word that is organic, that really comes out of the culture, that really expresses the spirit that we see in black women. And it's just . . . *womanish.*" Her voice slips into a down-home accent. "You know, the posture with the hand on the hip, 'Honey, don't you get in my way.'" She laughs. It is almost the same laugh that she used in the Lexington Avenue deli, but now it is deeper, fuller, more certain.

She goes on, expounding on a theme that had grown through *You Can't Keep a Good Woman Down* and her later essays: her dissatisfaction with white feminists.

"You see," she says, "one of the problems with white feminism is that it is not a tradition that teaches white women that they are capable. Whereas my tradition *assumes* I'm capable. I have a tradition of people not letting me get the skills, but I have cleared fields, I have lifted whatever, I have *done* it. It ain't not a tradition of wondering whether or not I could do it because I'm a woman."

But womanism, in Alice Walker's definition, is not just different from feminism; it is better. "Part of our tradition as black women is that we are universalists. Black children, yellow children, red children, brown children, that is the black woman's normal, day-to-day relationship. In my family alone, we are about four different colors. When a black woman looks at the world, it is so different . . . when I look at the people in Iran they look like kinfolk. When I look at the people in Cuba, they look like my uncles and nieces."

One of them looked like her father. The resemblance was part of the inspiration for one of her most moving essays, **"My Father's Country Is the Poor."**

I ask her about her father.

"He died in '73," she says sadly. "He was racked with every poor man's disease—diabetes, heart trouble. You know, his death was harder than I had thought at the time. We were so estranged that when I heard—I was in an airport somewhere—I didn't think I felt anything. It was years later that I really felt it. We had a wonderful reconciliation after he died."

I laugh, thinking that she is alluding to something she had written in the essay, that it is "much easier . . . to approve of dead people than of live ones." But she is serious: "I didn't cry when he died, but that summer I was in terrible shape. And I went to Georgia and I went to the cemetery and I laid down on top of his grave. I wanted to see what he could see, if he could look up. And I started to cry. And all of the knottedness that had been in our relationship dissolved. And we're fine now."

That year was the epicenter of some general upheaval in her life. In 1973, she wrote the answers to questions published in a collection called *Interviews with Black Writers,* and later in *In Search of Our Mothers' Gardens.* "Writing poems," she writes, "is my way of celebrating with the world that I have not committed suicide the evening before."

"I don't even remember," she says at first, when I ask if 1973 had been a particularly difficult year, but then she goes on to recall that it marked, besides the death of her father, her escape from Mississippi, which had "just about driven me around the bend," a period of physical separation from her husband, who had stayed behind to work, while she and her daughter, Rebecca, went to Cambridge, Mass. There she had discovered that "when I am ill and feel pain, things take on a certain extra clarity . . . something opens up and you begin to see things that you just wouldn't if you were surrounded by happy-go-lucky folk."

I remind her of another time of trauma she had written in that interview, when she, young, alone, pregnant and suicidal, "allowed myself exactly two self-pitying tears. . . . But I hated myself for crying, so I stopped."

Alice Walker laughs about that now. "Well, you know, I cry so much less than I used to. I used to be one of the most teary people. But I've been really happy here."

But writing is also a part of the reason she cries less. "I think," she says, "writing really helps you heal yourself. I think if you write long enough, you will be a healthy person. That is, if you write what you need to write, as opposed to what will make money, or what will make fame."

As when we talked before, and as when I have read Alice Walker at her best, I find myself being enchanted by her vision of things. She sees the writing process as a kind of visitation of spirits. She eschews the outline and other organizing techniques, and believes that big books are somehow antithetical to the female consciousness ("the books women write can be more like us—much thinner, much leaner, much cleaner"). Later, I will realize that her methods would make it well nigh impossible for her to write a long, sustained narrative and suspect the belief is something of a rationalization—and the kind of sexist comment a male critic would be pilloried for making. Yet when she says it, it seems a wonderful, magical way to write a book. But there is nothing mystical about what she sees as her role in life.

"I was brought up to try to see what was wrong and right it. Since I am a writer, writing is how I right it. I was brought up to look at things that are out of joint, out of balance, and to try to bring them into balance. And as a writer that's what I do. I just always expected people to understand. Black men, because of their oppression, I always thought, would understand. So the criticism that I have had from black men, especially, who don't want me to write about these things, I'm just amazed."

"You come down very heavy on the men," I say. "How about the black women?"

"Oh, I get to them. But I am really aware that they are under two layers of oppression and that even though everybody, the men and the women, get twisted terribly, the women have less choice than the men. And the things that they do, the bad choices that they make, are not done out of meanness, out of a need to take stuff out on people. . . ."

Her statement seems contradictory.

"In your writing," I suggest, "it's clear that you love old men. But they don't make out too well when they're young. None of them do."

"Well," she says, "one theory is that men don't start to mature until they're 40." She laughs, and I start to laugh, too. But then I realize her voice has taken on a certain rhetorical tone, and it makes me angry—because she herself is not yet 40. Then she slips out of the rhetorical tone, begins to explain, as she often does, how her perception of the general comes from intense feelings about the personal: "I knew both my grandfathers, and they were just doting, indulgent, sweet old men. I just loved them both and they were crazy about me. However, as young men, middle-aged men, they were . . . brutal. One grandfather knocked my grandmother out of

a window. He beat one of his children so severely that the child had epilepsy. Just a horrible, horrible man. But when I knew him, he was a sensitive, wonderful man."

"Do you think your father would have eventually gotten to be like your grandfather?" I asked her.

"Oh," she says wistfully, "he had it in him to be."

I ask her how her political involvements have affected her writing; if she has ever become aware of how the "brotherhood" or the "sisterhood" might see a particular piece, and thought about changing it.

"I often think about how they will see it, some of them," she says. "I always know that there will be many who will see it negatively, but I always know there will be one or two who will really understand. I've been so out of favor with black people, I figure if I can take that, I can be out of favor with anybody. In some ways, I'm just now becoming a writer who is directed toward 'my' people. My audience is really more my spirit helpers." She explains what a spirit helper does by describing a dream she had recently about one of them, Langston Hughes: "It was as if we were lovers, but we were not sexual lovers, we were just . . . loving lovers. Knowing it was a dream made me so unhappy. But then Langston, in his role of spirit helper, sort of said, 'But you know, the dream is real. And that is where we will always have a place.' I feel like that with all of them. They're as real to me as most people. More real."

Later, alone in my hotel room, I try to make sense of Alice Walker or, more correctly, of my feelings about her. I am not sure that I like her as much as I once did, that she sees as deeply and as clearly as I once thought. Yet I am sure that there is no one I like more as a writer, or who is possessed of more wisdom—that there is no writer in this country more worthy of the term seer. I would like to forget about 30 percent of what she has written and said. And yet the remaining 70 percent is so powerful that, even in this quandary, I am listening to the tapes of our conversation, and thumbing through her books, looking for an answer.

And it is there. On the tape, I hear her talking of her own reaction to her beloved Zora Neale Hurston: "I can't remember all the times that I would be appalled by some of the views that she held. But it wasn't her fault that she had to report things a certain way. That was what *she* found." And in the final essay in *In Search of Our Mothers' Gardens,* Alice Walker writes of how her daughter had finally liberated her from her sense that she is disfigured, and her fear that her own child will be alienated by her artificial eye. "Mommy," Rebecca tells her, "there's a *world* in your eye."

Yes indeed, I think, there *is* a world in Alice Walker's eye. It is etched there by pain and sacrifice, and it is probably too much to expect that anything so violently created would be free of some distortion. But it is nevertheless a real world, full of imaginary people capable of teaching real lessons, of imparting real wisdom capable of teaching real lessons.

Alma S. Freeman (essay date Spring 1985)

SOURCE: "Zora Neale Hurston and Alice Walker: A Spiritual Kinship," in *Sage,* Vol. II, No. 1, Spring, 1985, pp. 37-40.

[*In the following essay, Freeman compares the journeys of the main characters of several of Walker's works, including* Meridian, *to the protagonist of Zora Neale Hurston's* Their Eyes Were Watching God.]

Zora Neale Hurston, born in Florida near the turn of the twentieth century, was, for thirty years, the most prolific Black woman writer in the United States. Alice Walker, born in Georgia some forty years later, is one of the most prolific Black women writers in America today. Not only do both women stand as exemplary representatives of the achievement of the American Black woman as writer, but their fiction reveals a strong spiritual kinship. Though separated by place and by time, these two Black women writers, inevitably it seems, were drawn together, and Zora Hurston became an important influence in Alice Walker's life.

Zora Neale Hurston died in 1960. Alice Walker was not to encounter Zora Hurston and her work until the late 1960's. At this time, Alice was working with the Civil Rights Movement and collecting folklore stories in Mississippi. She was also "writing a story that required accurate material on voodoo practices among rural southern Blacks of the thirties," and she was finding the available resources, written primarily by "white, racist anthropologists and folklorists of the period," disappointing and insulting. Then she discovered *Mules and Men,* Zora Hurston's book recounting her folklore expeditions in the South and relating the stories she had found there. Direct influences from *Mules and Men* can be seen in Alice Walker's short story **"The Revenge of Hannah Kemhuss,"** a story obviously based on an incident that happened to Alice's mother in the thirties during the Depression. Like Alice's mother, Hannah in the story receives a box of clothes from a relative who lives in the North. She wears one of the dresses from the box into town to get food which is being distributed by the Red Cross. When Hannah presents her voucher, she is shamed and humiliated by a young white woman who refuses to give her food because she is so finely dressed. Unlike Alice's mother, who got the food she needed from a neighbor, Hannah endures extreme suffering as a result of the incident. Her husband deserts her, one by one her

children starve to death, and she gradually becomes a broken woman, mutilated both in spirit and body. Finally, when she is awaiting death, Hannah, driven by years of pain and remorse, visits the local rootworker to seek revenge on "the little moppet." Into this story-line, Alice Walker weaves material on voodoo practices from Zora Hurston's book of folklore. For instance, the central character of the story, an apprentice in the rootworking trade, quotes a "curse prayer" used and taught by rootworkers, and she indicates that she "recited it straight from Zora Neale Hurston's book, *Mules and Men,*" while engaging in a voodoo ritual with Hannah Kemhuss. Moreover, Alice Walker dedicates the story "In grateful memory of Zora Neale Hurston."

In *Mules and Men,* Alice Walker not only found the authentic folklore material that she needed for her own writing, but she also perceived a spiritual sister to whom she became intensely devoted. The following statements recorded in the Foreword of Robert Hemenway's biography of Zora Neale Hurston reflect the essence of Alice's commitment to Zora Hurston and her work:

> Condemned to a deserted island for life, with an allotment of ten books to see me through, I would choose, unhesitatingly, two of Zora's: *Mules and Men,* because I would need to be able to pass on to younger generations the life of American blacks as legend and myth, and *Their Eyes Were Watching God,* because I would want to enjoy myself while identifying with the black heroine, Janie Crawford, as she acted out many roles in a variety of settings, and functioned (with spectacular results!) in romantic and sensual love. There is no other book more important to me than this one.

By 1979, Alice Walker had read *Their Eyes Were Watching God* about eleven times, and she declared, "It speaks to me as no other novel, past or present, has ever done . . . There is enough self-love in that one book—love of community, culture, traditions—to restore a world. Or create a new one. Alice Walker was so inspired by Hurston's *Their Eyes Were Watching God* that she wrote the following poem entitled **"Janie Crawford"** which appears in her book of poems *Good Night Willie Lee, I'll See You in the Morning*:

> I love the way Janie Crawford
> left her husbands the one who wanted
> to change her into a mule
> and the other who tried to interest her
> in becoming a queen
> a woman unless she submits is neither a mule
> nor a queen
> though like a mule she may suffer
> and like a queen pace
> the floor

Zora Neale Hurston exerted such a strong influence in Alice Walker's life that Alice set out to bring back into public attention the work, for many years out of print, of the woman whom she had grown to admire, respect, and revere—a sister artist who "followed her own road, believed in her gods, pursued her own dreams, and refused to separate herself from the 'common' people." Feeling a strong spiritual kinship with her sister writer, Alice Walker, posing as a niece, traveled to Fort Pierce, Florida, found the segregated cemetery there, and placed a tombstone, proclaiming "a genius of the South," to honor Zora Hurston's unmarked grave. Another of Alice Walker's lasting tributes to Zora Neale Hurston is embodied in *I Love Myself When I Am Laughing. . . : A Zora Neale Hurston Reader* which Alice edited and dedicated to "Zora Neale Hurston . . . wherever she is now in the universe with the good wishes and love of all those who have glimpsed her heart through her work." Alice Walker is one who has truly glimpsed the heart of Zora Neale Hurston. From her first short story collection *In Love and Trouble: Stories of Black Women* to her latest novel *The Color Purple,* Ms. Walker, in her own fiction, is keeping alive, extending, and expanding the vital literary tradition that Zora Neale Hurston established in *Their Eyes Were Watching God*—a tradition which embodies a strong dedication to unveiling the *soul* of the Black woman.

A comparison of three of Alice Walker's Black women characters with Zora Neale Hurston's Janie Crawford underscores the bond of kinship that exists between Zora's and Alice's exploration of the experiences of the Black woman in the United States. Such a comparison also reveals the author's powerful and poignant portrayal of what it feels like, inside, to be a Black woman struggling to become an autonomous, well-integrated "self" in a society in which her options are severely limited. These four women begin their lives imprisoned by roles and by images and notions of womanhood that conflict directly with their history and with their own vigorous concept of themselves as Black women. Initially, for instance, they find themselves locked in loveless, unfulfilling marriages from which they appear to have no escape and which stifle their dreams, their creativity, and their desire for growth and freedom. Such a situation engenders in these characters a tension that forces them to make personal choices concerning their development as whole human beings. Fighting against both racial and sexual oppression, they choose either a life of continued subservience, anguish, and pain, or they opt to become growing, emergent women who seek to take control of their own lives.

In Hurston's *Their Eyes Were Watching God,* the sixteen-year-old Janie Crawford, against her own adamant protests, is forced, by her relentless grandmother, to marry Logan Killicks, a hard-working man who is much older than Janie but who owns property and has a degree of status in the community. The grandmother's motivation is clear. She wants to protect Janie from being sexually exploited, as she and Janie's mother have been, by men both Black and white. She also wants to see the dreams she had for herself and for her own daughter realized. Janie's grandmother has internalized the values of white society, which define "what a woman oughta be and do." Denied the opportunity to fulfill the woman's traditional role, she wants this for Janie—the security, protection, respectability, and the material possessions that a good provider like Logan Killicks can give. Dependent on whites all of her life for mere survival, the grandmother wishes to break this dependency for Janie. But she simply transfers it to the man she forces Janie to marry and sets in motion another cycle of dependency for Janie. Janie soon becomes convinced that Logan cannot give her the sweetness, beauty, and adventure she desires in marriage. And she leaves him for Jody Starks, a fast-talking, ambitious man who promises her love and excitement. Jody carries Janie to a newly founded all-Black community in Florida where he becomes a "big voice" and where he places her on a "pedestal," and, like Logan, treats her as property. Janie finds fulfillment only when Jody dies and she leaves the town with Tea Cake, a younger man and a free spirit, who loves and respects her for the person that she is.

Roselily, the central character of the first story in Alice Walker's collection *In Love and Trouble,* faces a kind of entrapment similar to Janie's. Young, Black, and poor, living in the rural South, the mother of four children, all by a different man, Roselily marries a Muslim man in order to escape a brutal life of labor in a sewing plant. She stands during her marriage ceremony weighed down with images of quicksand, ropes, chains, and handcuffs. As Janie sees her blossoming, fruit-bearing pear tree—her symbol of life, fertility, and freedom—"desecrated" by her grandmother, so Roselily thinks of flowers choked to death; she feels like a rat cornered. Even the veil she wears reminds her of a kind of servitude that she longs to be free of. It is the same kind to which Janie Crawford is subjected. All Logan wants Janie to be is his maid, his cook, and a laborer on his farm; all Jody wants her to be is "Mrs. Mayor Starks" whose "place is in de home" and the humble clerk in his store. The religion of the man whom Roselily is marrying requires, like Jody demands of Janie, that she wear her hair covered, that she separate herself from the men, and that she take her place in the home. But this is Roselily's only chance to be respectable, to achieve status and prestige, and to provide a better life for her children. Despite her misgivings, her feelings of entrapment, she marries the man, and she will go to live in Chicago, have more children regardless of her wishes, and *endure.*

Alice Walker's Myrna in **"Really, *Doesn't* Crime Pay?"** another story from *In Love and Trouble,* also endures, despite her aspirations to be a writer. Like Janie during her marriage to Jody, Myrna is placed on a pedestal by her hardworking husband, Ruel. And she aspires to be the perfect wife and lady—keeping house, cooking meals, painting her face, polishing her fingernails, visiting the shopping center daily buying hats she would not dream of wearing, dresses already headed for the Goodwill, and shoes that will mold and mildew in her closet. Then she meets Mordecai Rich who praises her for her intelligence and creativity. Mordecai is an aspiring writer, "a vagabond, scribbling down impressions of the South, from no solid place, going to none." As Jody Starks and Tea Cake do for Janie, Mordecai promises Myrna love and excitement. She gives herself to him completely. Not only do they engage in passionate love-making, but Myrna shares with Mordecai her interest in writing and the volumes of stories that she has drafted but has kept hidden from Ruel. Unlike Janie, however, Myrna does not leave with Mordecai, instead, one day, he suddenly disappears. And later, Myrna reads one of her stories in a magazine, "filled out and switched about," authored by Mordecai Rich. Thereafter, she suffers a nervous breakdown, attempts to kill Ruel with a chain saw, and spends some time in a mental institution.

Unlike Roselily, Myrna does, in her own way, fight against her entrapment. Myrna's most important act of rebellion, her only sense of freedom, rests in taking the Pill. Ruel desperately wants a child, and he struggles very hard to make Myrna conceive. She consents to his every wish. She even visits the doctor at Ruel's request to see about "speeding up the conception of the child." But she never tells Ruel that she "religiously" takes the Pill, and this engenders in her a feeling of triumph over him, a sense of independent choice. At the end of the story, Myrna exults in her deceptively won freedom:

> It is the only spot of humor in my entire day, when I am gulping that little yellow tablet and washing it down with soda pop or tea. . . . When he is quite, quite tired of me I will tell him how long I've relied on the security of the Pill.

Meridian Hill, the central character of Alice Walker's novel *Meridian,* begins her life, like Janie, Roselily, and Myrna, as a woman with few choices. Meridian, however, bears a special relationship to Janie Crawford because, unlike Roselily and Myrna, Janie and Meridian become women who make options for themselves, who finally choose a life of their own. In Janie's story and in Meridian's story, we see Black women developing a consciousness, an awareness, which allows them to arrive at a deepened sense of self and to grow stronger by speaking from and for that self. They thus are able to take control of their own destiny. Both Janie and Meridian then are involved in a quest for identity. Each woman struggles to affirm the "self" which she knows exists beneath the false images imposed upon her because she is Black and female. Janie's search is deeply personal, her vision intensely romantic. She seeks and finally finds a sense of fulfillment through fusion with another "self." Meridian, however, possesses a deeply social and moral vision. Her story emanates from a broader social and political context than does Janie's. As Mary Helen Washington notes, Meridian "evolves from a woman trapped by racial and sexual oppression to revolutionary figure, effecting action and strategy to bring freedom to herself and other poor disenfranchised Blacks in the South."

Against her wishes, the teenaged Meridian, like the sixteen-year-old Janie, is forced into an unfulfilling marriage. Meridian becomes pregnant; she reluctantly marries Eddie, the father of her child, and makes an effort at being a "proper" wife and mother. Finding this role confining and intolerable, she harbors thoughts of killing her child; then she contemplates suicide rather than harm her own baby. Finally, her marriage ends, and she gives her child away believing she is saving both lives. From this point, Meridian moves through college and the Civil Rights Movement into a revolutionary group where she discovers that she cannot kill for the Revolution. Her spirit broken, she begins a sort of physical degeneration. She loses her hair, dons a cap and dungarees, lives alone in small rooms in small southern towns trying to find her own health while she helps the Black people in these towns find power. She is followed by Truman Held, a man whom she sincerely loves but whom she must finally reject in an effort to get a hold of her own life.

Like Janie Crawford, Meridian Hill leaves the men in her life to search for fulfillment as a human being. While Janie abandons Logan and the memory of Jody, journeys to the horizon with Tea Cake, and finds a satisfying love, Meridian leaves Eddie and Truman, turns inward, and travels back through many generations to free herself. She identifies with her mother's great-grandmother, a slave but also an artist who became famous and bought her freedom by painting lasting decorations on barns. She remembers her father's grandmother, the mystical and high-spirited Feather Mae, and she, like Feather Mae, experiences an ecstatic communion with the past atop the Sacred Serpent, an Indian burial mound. At college Meridian learns about the slave woman and storyteller Louvinie and the Sojourner. She also expresses deep sensitivity for her own mother who, through suffering and sacrifice, fulfilled her dreams of becoming a school teacher. Such an anchor in her ancestral past gives Meridian a sense of strength and continuity, a knowledge of herself as a creative human being, which helps to fortify and to free her from a need for dependence on another person in her quest for identity.

Through the total range of her experiences, Meridian creates a new self—an androgynous self; she is transformed, as symbolized by the wasting illness from which she recovers and returns "to the world cleansed of sickness." Meridian's androgynous quality, expressed in physically androgynous features, is communicated through a passage near the end of the novel when she visits a prison and the inmates ask, "Who was that person? That man / woman person with a shaved part in close-cut hair? A man's blunt face and thighs, a woman's breast?" Here, Meridian appears as a symbol of one who has creatively united the masculine and feminine opposites and achieved a state of unconscious wholeness. As she leaves Truman for the last time, he recognizes the change in her:

> What he *felt* was that something in her was exactly the same as she had always been and as he had, finally, succeeded in knowing her. That was the part he might now sense but could not see. He would never see "his" Meridian again. The new part had grown out of the old, though, and that was reassuring. This part of her, new, sure and ready, even eager, for the world, he knew he must meet again and recognize for its true value at some future time.

Janie Crawford does not reach the androgynous state that Meridian achieves. Janie longs for it, as symbolized by her mystical experience of the pear tree, an androgynous symbol with roots sinking into the feminine earth and branches stretching forth to the masculine sky. For Janie, the tree represents a loving harmony between the masculine and feminine forces of nature, a union which she desires to attain. Throughout her story, she seeks this unity, this wholeness. But she relies first on Logan and Jody and then on Tea Cake rather than searching within herself to realize it. Finally, she kills Tea Cake in self-defense and thereby frees herself. Through this symbolic act, Janie breaks the cycle of dependency set in motion by her grandmother. Janie ends her story alone, settling down in her own private room, at peace with herself, wrapped in loving memories of Tea Cake. But her experience of happiness is still tied to him. Significantly neither Zora nor Alice endorses isolation as a way of life, but each of their protagonists finds it necessary to be alone in order to achieve insight and growth. At the end of the novel, Janie, alone in her room, is prepared to embark upon the inward voyage that Meridian undertakes. We might even say that Meridian Hill finishes the struggle that Janie Crawford begins, for the end of *Their Eyes Were Watching God* marks the beginning of another story, a story which Alice Walker takes up and completes in Meridian. Thus, Alice Walker further reveals her strong dedication to accomplishing the task to which Zora Neale Hurston, her sister writer, had earlier devoted her creative energy.

"A people must define itself" writes Ralph Ellison in *Shadow and Act.* It is thus the duty of the American Black woman to dispel the myths and burst the stereotypes surrounding her character, personality, and experience. Zora Neale Hurston and Alice Walker are two of the several Black women writers who have sought to fulfill this task. In their literary works, we hear the Black woman speak. She speaks in a loud voice—with power and with fervor, but always with compassion and grace—as she defines, affirms, and preserves in literature the essential humanity of her own group.

Philip M. Royster (essay date Winter 1986)

SOURCE: "In Search of Our Fathers' Arms: Alice Walker's Persona of the Alienated Darling," in *Black American Literature Forum,* Vol. 20, No. 4, Winter, 1986, pp. 347-70.

[*In the following essay, Royster discusses the complicated relationship between Walker and her audience and asserts that Walker's female protagonists are representations of Walker's perceptions of herself.*]

Alice Walker's third novel, *The Color Purple,* is fueling controversy in many black American communities. Afro-American novelist/critic David Bradley recalls "sens[ing] that *The Color Purple* was going to be ground zero at a Hiroshima of controversy." Some women have found it difficult to lay the book down unfinished; some men have bellowed with rage while reading it (as well as afterwards). It appears that Walker's depiction of violent black men who physically and psychologically abuse their wives and children is one of the poles of the controversy and that her depiction of lesbianism is another.

Many critics have praised the novel, especially for its use of a black dialect that reviewers laud in such terms as "positively poetic," "eloquent," and "masterful." A reviewer in the *New Yorker* labeled the novel "fiction of the highest order." Peter Prescott called it "an American novel of permanent importance." A *Publishers Weekly* reviewer considers the book "stunning and brilliantly conceived"; Mel Watkins regards the novel as "striking and consummately well-written"; and Dinitia Smith believes that "at least half the book is superb, it places . . . [Walker] in the company of Faulkner."

Yet, not all of those who have read the novel have liked it, including many black women. David Bradley observes that "one black poet, Sonia Sanchez, criticized Alice Walker's theme of black male brutality as an overemphasis. Another black woman told me *The Color Purple* was 'a begging kind of piece' and she was 'getting tired of being beat over the head with this women's lib stuff, and this whole black woman/black man, "Lord have mercy on us po' sisters," kind of thing' in Alice Walker's work." One of the strongest responses to the novel has come from Trudier Harris, who believes the novel should be ignored because of its portrayal of a protagonist that is not merely idiosyncratic but unrealistic, and because the book's portrayal of domestic violence is based on unwholesome stereotypes of black folk and their communities that appeal to spectator readers.

This polarization of responses to *The Color Purple* may be better understood by focusing attention on Walker's expressed fictive and nonfictive attitudes towards her role as a writer, her intended audience, and the issues of sexuality and aggression.

Walker has committed her efforts to at least two great social movements that have stimulated the alteration of consciousness in the last half of the twentieth century: the Civil Rights Movement and the Women's Liberation Movement. Walker's involvement with these movements both generates and reflects her intention, first articulated in 1973, to champion as a writer the causes of black people, especially black women: "I am preoccupied with the spiritual survival, the survival *whole,* of my people. But beyond that, I am committed to exploring the oppressions, the insanities, the loyalties, and the triumphs of black women."

In a 1984 interview, Walker revealed that, since childhood, she has seen herself as a writer who rescues: "'I was brought up to try to see what was wrong and right it. Since I am a writer, writing is how I right it.'" Walker's fiction confronts such issues as racism, intraracism, sexism, neocolonialism, and imperialism in order to transform both society and the individual. She expressed her commitment to change in 1973 with the affirmation: "I believe in change: change personal, and change in society." In *The Color Purple,* she seems to be preoccupied with the task of overcoming black male sexist exploitation of black women.

Yet, along with this commitment to change, Walker holds other attitudes that have the potential to frustrate her goals. She indirectly announced one such attitude in *Revolutionary Petunias & Other Poems* through a persona who articulates the position of an outcast to the social order: "Be nobody's darling; / Be an outcast. / Qualified to live / Among your dead." The concerns of this fictive persona resound in Walker's nonfictive voices, but in the nonfiction the speaker expresses a need to be both somebody's darling (that somebody is usually an older man) and an outcast (who uses her art as a means to rescue victims). The personas in both her fiction and nonfiction also experience feelings of inadequacy as rescuers, and they appear to be both infatuated with and plagued by notions concerning suicide, death, and the dead. (Although Walker seems to consider herself to be a medium, she simultaneously articulates perennial fantasies concerning suicide.)

Walker's perception of herself as a writer who is a social outcast apparently began after her brother blinded one of her eyes with a bb gun when she was eight years old: "I believe . . . that it was from this period—from my solitary, lonely position, the position of an outcast—that I began really to see people and things, really to notice relationships and to learn to be patient enough to care about how they turned out.

I no longer felt like the little girl I was. I felt old, and because I felt I was unpleasant to look at, filled with shame. I retreated into solitude, and read stories and began to write poems." The accident seems to have led Walker to feel both alienated from her environment and perceptive of people and their lives. Her confidence in her insight undoubtedly helped to prepare her for the role of a rescuer, yet the fact that she no longer felt like a little girl engendered attitudes that would ultimately frustrate her goal. Her experiences of the loss of her childhood, the shame of a disfiguring scar, and social inadequacy would soon give rise, in her writing, to voices with tones of resentment, anger, and bitterness, on the one hand, and voices that articulate the desire to feel again like a little girl (or a darling to older men), on the other. The speaker of one of her poems that appears in *The American Poetry Review* expresses something of the intensity of Walker's alienation when she asserts: "I find my own / small person / a standing self / against the world." One of the comforts for the outcast persona is her as-yet-unending search for father figures with whom to be a darling. This search influences Walker's fictions, which portray women with frustrated psychosexual attitudes towards men (Ruth towards Grange, Meridian towards both Eddie and Truman, and Celie towards both Alfonso and Albert), and colors her expressed nonfictional attitudes concerning men.

The issue of audience identification is especially important in a multi-cultural society in which one culture creates institutions that exploit, manipulate, and dominate other cultures. What a writer understands of her own relationships to the dialectical tensions between the exploiter and the exploited, the oppressor and the oppressed, or the persecutor and the victim is important. Does the writer see herself as the rescuer or champion of the exploited, uncontaminated herself by oppression or oppressive values; does she regard herself as being involved in the circle of the victims; or is she drawn unwittingly into the circle of the persecutors? Frantz Fanon articulates some of the issues for the "native intellectual" struggling with the influence of the "colonial bourgeoisie" in *The Wretched of the Earth.* These issues influence the writer's fictive and nonfictive voices and the reader's interpretations of the writer's texts, so despite the pitfalls yawning as one leaps from a writer's recorded assertions and perceptions to a theory for understanding that writer's fiction, it is urgent to examine Walker's attitudes towards her audience. Moreover, examining her written perceptions of and attitudes towards her past experiences allows one to better understand her handling of the concepts of sexuality and aggression. It permits the critic to create a bridge of understanding that joins the writer, with her work, to more of her readers.

If Walker is an alienated writer who wants to rescue others by changing society, she needs an audience. Yet in a recent interview with Claudia Tate, Walker expresses contradictory attitudes towards the issue of audience. "I'm always happy to have an audience," Walker remarks. ". . . otherwise it would be very lonely and futile." But she adds that, although she is willing to, she usually does not consider the audience before writing. Rather, she writes what she thinks and feels, and does not worry whether or not she finds an audience. She says that writing is not about finding an audience but "expanding myself as much as I can and seeing myself in as many roles and situations as possible." However, earlier in the conversation she expresses the belief that "black women instinctively feel a need to connect with their audience, to be direct, to build a readership for us all. . . ." By "us" she seems to mean black folk, because she goes on to say that "none of us will survive except in very distorted ways if we have to depend on white publishers and white readers forever. And white critics." Although she feels that she needs black readers, she believes that the "main problem" for black writers is that "black people, generally speaking, don't read."

If Walker's intention in writing *The Color Purple* was to lessen the oppression of black women by black men, a reasonable question is: To whom is the work directed—black men, black women, or both? Who is going to be responsible for ending sexist exploitation, and who is going to determine the means to that end? Walker's reaction to criticism of *The Color Purple* reveals that she is not satisfied with the responses from at least one segment of her audience: "'I just always expected people to understand. Black men, because of their oppression, I always thought, would understand. So the criticism that I have had from black men, especially, who don't want me to write about these things, I'm just amazed.'" Walker's disappointment with criticism by black men suggests that she intends for them to be sitting in the audience before her stage waiting to be moved by her performance. Also, they could be looking over her shoulder to provide critical direction and approval as she writes. Whether or not black males make up both stage and critical audiences, a discrepancy exists between authorial intention and audience reaction. My work with Alice Walker's writings suggests that her recorded attitudes towards segments of her intended audience make it difficult for her to communicate effectively with them.

There is a revealing irony concerning Walker's perception of herself as an outcast: After she was partially blinded, Walker became alienated from a group already shunted to the edge of the social order—Southern black sharecroppers. After telling the story of her mother's being denied government flour because her hand-me-down clothes were better than the clothes worn by the white woman who distributed the flour, Walker asserts, "Outcasts to be used and humiliated by the larger society, the Southern black sharecropper and poor farmer clung to his own kind and to a religion that had been given to pacify him as a slave but which he soon transformed into an antidote against bitterness." Walker perceives herself

as an outcast of those whom she regards as having themselves been cast out.

Despite this doubled burden of alienated feelings, Walker, in 1970, spoke of wanting very consciously to write to blacks from the rural South. Desiring to be a poet whose work derives from the Southern rural experience, she asserted that she "want[ed] to write poetry that is understood by one's people, not by the Queen of England." From a comment in 1971 it is clear that Walker feels a moral commitment to communicate to her stage or listening audience of people with whom she shares roots, for she asserts that "it is unfair to the people we expect to reach to give them a beautiful poem if they are unable to read it." The title of the essay from which this quote is taken, **"Duties of the Black Revolutionary Artist,"** reinforces the notion that it is Walker's intention not merely to communicate with but also to rescue victims. Thus, it appears that Walker is alienated from the group she wants to rescue.

Along with wanting to help the poor, Walker attacks the new black middle class for forsaking its rescuing responsibilities by manifesting selfishly materialistic rather than altruistic and radical concerns. Yet this purportedly irresponsible class is the one to which Walker belongs not by birth but by education and occupation. In short, she here repeats the pattern, established as a child, of feeling alienated from the class with whom she shares an identity.

The theme of the alienated rescuer becomes more strident in a 1973 interview, in which Walker articulates more of her perceptions of the role of a responsible writer: "The writer . . . must be free to explore, otherwise she or he will never discover what is needed (by everyone) to be known. This means, very often, finding oneself considered 'unacceptable' by masses of people who think that the writer's obligation is not to explore or to challenge, but to second the masses' motions, whatever they are. Yet the gift of loneliness is sometimes a radical vision of society or one's people that has not previously been taken into account." These remarks suggest more than Walker may have realized. Is the voice that of a sturdy, no-nonsense revolutionary or of a victim of her own past and her romantic ideals? Her assertion that everyone needs to know what an artist discovers seems presumptuous and paternalistic (or should that be maternalistic?). The fact that she passively accepts (or actively invites) being cast out ("unacceptable") and lonely, as if she has no options, suggests that she feels like a victim of the very people she is supposed to be rescuing. Although Walker seems to be tough on leadership that approves the actions of its following, in 1979 she would dedicate a collection of her poems to her romantic ideal of a *"quiet man [who] always said, 'Let the people decide.'"*

It seems clear that her alienation is not so much a product of her writing career as her writing career is a response to the alienation that she has entertained since childhood. Walker's courting of her own alienation is even more apparent in a 1973 interview, in which she defended her right to live in Mississippi with her white husband (the couple later divorced): "Otherwise, I'd just as soon leave. If society (black or white) says, Then you must be isolated, an outcast—then I will be a hermit. Friends and relatives may desert me, but the dead . . . are a captive audience." The persona here readily embraces the role of the outcast.

As to the question of Walker's adequacy as a rescuer of others, a substantial case could be constructed from her own admissions to argue to the contrary. For example, she asserts that, "always a rather moody, periodically depressed person, after two years in Mississippi I became—as I had occasionally been as a young adult—suicidal." In 1973, she confides, "the threat of self-destruction plagued me as it never had before." Although Walker had moved to Mississippi to help rescue sharecroppers and other victims as part of her commitment to the Civil Rights Movement, it appears that she herself stood in need of a helping hand. David Bradley calls our attention to Walker's having observed that "writing poems . . . is my way of celebrating with the world that I have not committed suicide the day before." While in Mississippi, Walker also felt inadequate in her rescuing role as mother: "I . . . found motherhood onerous, a threat to my writing."

Walker traces the source of her urge to commit suicide to what appears to be guilt concerning the inadequacy of her work in the Movement: "I believe that part of my depression came out of anguish that I was not more violent than I was. . . . The burden of a nonviolent, pacifist philosophy in a violent, nonpacifist society caused me to feel, almost always, as if I had not done enough." Walker's comment suggests that she had not assimilated the fundamental precepts of Gandhi's Satyagraha, the "soul-force" or "truth-force" which gives one power to end persecution and oppression by inflicting suffering not on "the opponent but on one's self." Accustomed to practicing self-denial, Gandhi knew how to withstand this suffering without feeling like a victim or a persecutor, and he became a successful rescuer; Walker lacked Gandhi's special talents. Gandhi also reminds those who would struggle against oppressive violence that "by using similar means we can get only the same thing that they got." That is, instead of remaining a faithful rescuer of victims, one would become a persecutor were one to adopt the violent means of the persecutor. Alice Walker's languishing for the want of more violent means suggests that she has been inadequately prepared to be a rescuer of victims. Permitting suffering to be inflicted on oneself is more difficult for many people than inflicting it on others; to withstand, one must practice informed self-denial. Attention to the past exposes the shortcomings of violent would-be rescuers. Gandhi says that the "belief that there is no connection between the means and the end is a great

mistake. Through that mistake even men who have been considered religious have committed grievous crimes."

Walker's comments in 1976 suggest that she may be becoming both more sensitive to and yet more alienated from black folk: "Writing this now, in New York City, it is impossible not to feel that black people who are poor are lost completely in the American political and economic system, and that black people and white people who are not have been turned to stone. Our moral leaders have been murdered, our children worship power and drugs, our official leadership is frequently a joke, usually merely oppressive. Our chosen and most respected soul-singer—part of whose unspoken duty is to remind us who we are—has become a blonde." Here it is not merely the Southern black sharecropper but all of America's poor blacks who are cast out, and their outcast plight is no longer mitigated by adaptations of their "slave" religion, for now they are completely lost. Other blacks (and whites) she accuses of being insensitive; the children (the future) worship false gods; adequate leaders have been assassinated, and those leaders who remain are bankrupt. To cap it all, Aretha Franklin has betrayed black folk and their culture by dyeing her hair. This is Walker's perception of black people, the ones she wants to rescue by bringing them the truth that all of them need to know.

Influencing her recorded perception of the folk is Walker's tendency to over-generalize by creating large categories and then describing the contents of those categories in ways that suggest, reflect, and undoubtedly encourage hopelessness. Walker's attitudes towards black folk suggest more about who she is and the way she writes than they do about who black folk are. If it is true that everywhere she looks she sees the worst, she may be projecting onto the backs of the folk something of her own consciousness, and if that is the case, then she is using black people for her own scapegoat victims. In other words, just as Gandhi, the spiritual and philosophical father of the nonviolent philosophy of the Civil Rights Movement, had forewarned, the would-be rescuer has become the persecutor, not of her persecutors but of the very victims she is committed to rescuing.

Walker would articulate more of her perceptions of black people in 1977, when she asserted that life in America had destroyed racial solidarity in Northern cities and reduced her to doubting whether she could survive being assaulted by a black person:

> The bond of black kinship—so sturdy, so resilient—
> has finally been broken in the cities of the North.
> There is no mutual caring, no trust. Even the rhetoric of revolutionary peoplehood is hissed out threateningly. The endearment "sister" is easily replaced with "bitch." My fear is past grief, and if I were ever attacked or robbed by another black person I doubt

I'd recover. This thought itself scares me. There is also the knowledge that just as I'm afraid of them, because I no longer know what behavior to expect, they're afraid of me. Of all the vile things that have happened to us in America, this fear of each other is to me the most unbearable, the most humiliating.

In this passage Walker sounds more like a victim than a rescuer: The racial bond is broken, and she fears for her own well-being. I do not wish to overlook the issues of Walker's right to her feelings and of violence among the oppressed (it is a well-known truth that victims adopt the world view of their persecutors), but adequate rescuers are not intimidated by that violence. Nor are they intimidated by their own fear of violence, for even if the rescuer experiences fear, adequacy is maintained by suffering privately, as did Martin Luther King, Jr., rather than by sowing seeds of panic in the passions of the populace. Again, Walker's response reflects her alienation from the oppressed.

In her interview with Claudia Tate, Walker, while discussing the judgment needed to improve the interpersonal relationships between black men and women as portrayed in Shange's *for colored girls . . . ,* asserts: "Judgment is crucial because judgment is lacking in black people these days." She must have sensed the inflammatory potential of this remark because she attempts to clarify it by distinguishing her meaning to be a regret that the community will no longer come to the rescue of women who are accosted by dirty-minded men. Both the remark and the clarification arise from the fantasies of an alienated darling who blames the folk for the misery of the group and who avoids assuming responsibility for herself. Walker's voice becomes even more strident when she chews on her notion that the community neglects its writers because it does not respect itself: "If the black community fails to support its own writers, it will never have the knowledge of itself that will make it great. And for foolish, frivolous and totally misinformed reasons—going directly back to its profound laziness about the written message as opposed to one that's sung—it will continue to blunder along, throwing away this one and that one, and never hearing or using what is being said." Undoubtedly such attitudes helped to distance Walker from her black community. Black folk may be less misinformed than Walker's comments suggest. How many of them would rush to catch pearls cast by someone who is not merely terrified of them but also believes them to be profoundly lazy and without judgment? This is one instance among many when it becomes difficult to distinguish Walker's voice from those of the bourgeoisie that has colonized her people.

Walker articulates the chasm she perceives between herself and black Americans in her 1984 interview with David Bradley: "'I've been so out of favor with black people, I figure if I can take that, I can be out of favor with anybody. In some ways, I'm just now becoming a writer who is directed toward "my" people. My audience is really more my spirit helpers.'" Walker is here referring to the dead, such as Langston Hughes, with whom she believes herself to be in contact through such media as dreams. Walker's statement is ambiguous with regard to whether the "spirit helpers" and black people are critical or stage audiences. Apparently, she believes that her "spirit helpers" are part of the critical audience looking over her shoulder, but black people form a stage audience ("toward 'my' people"). A less favorable interpretation would be that the "spirit helpers" are also her stage audience. But if that is the case, then she has abandoned all of her notions of the writer's social responsibility, possibly to fulfill her outcast's vision of becoming "Qualified to live / Among your dead."

After considering Alice Walker's assertions of alienation from black people, it is indeed ironic to examine her approval, in 1971, of Coretta King's vision that black women who feel compassion, love justice, and have resisted embitterment will become leaders of mankind. Walker says of Mrs. King:

> . . . she says something that I feel is particularly true: "Women, in general, are not a part of the corruption of the past, so they can give a new kind of leadership, a new image for mankind. But if they are going to be bitter or vindictive they are not going to be able to do this. But they're capable of tremendous compassion, love, and forgiveness, which if they use it, can make this a better world. When you think of what some black women have gone through, and then look at how beautiful they still are! It is incredible that they still believe in the values of the race, that they have retained a love of justice, that they can still feel the deepest compassion, not only for themselves but for anybody who is oppressed; this is a kind of miracle, something we have that we must preserve and pass on."

Coretta King is drawing a picture of a female rescuer of the race who is adequate for her role; that is, one who maintains it without switching to the roles of either victim or persecutor. Although Walker admires the image, she does not appear to be cut of that cloth. King might be speaking indirectly of her perceptions of Walker, challenging the writer to rise above them.

But Walker does not use King's ideal to measure herself; rather, she challenges the ideal with her own feminist concern: "I want to know her opinion of why black women have been antagonistic toward women's liberation. As a black woman myself, I say, I do not understand this because black women among all women have been oppressed almost beyond recognition—oppressed by *everyone*." Walker's complaint suggests that she perceives a psychic distance between herself and the community of black women, who, generally speaking (and this was even more true in 1971), are unwilling to join a white women's movement. Walker's emotional generalization that everyone oppresses black women, one of her hobbyhorses, is an exaggeration that reflects her alienation: Accustomed to viewing herself as an outcast, Walker here places black women generally in opposition to everyone else.

By 1973 Walker apparently had found an ally in Barbara Sizemore, after the latter's assertion that nationalist organizers, such as Amiri Baraka, keep black women in inferior positions in their organizations. Both Walker and Sizemore shared a vision of black women more radical than most in 1973, for, even at an American college conference on black women, Walker was to experience considerable distance between herself and most of the other black women present: "It was at the Radcliffe symposium that I saw that black women are more loyal to black men than they are to themselves, a dangerous state of affairs that has its logical end in self-destructive behavior." Often, Walker's nonfictive assertions emphasize the worst in people and groups, and she then proceeds to inflate the consequences of her perceptions. Her remarks on the loyalty of black women to black men is interesting in the light of her hankering to be the darling of older men and her bitterness towards younger ones. It is difficult to refrain from wondering whether the political rhetoric masks such basic feelings as envy, resentment, and anger, for if the women Walker maligns actually feel loyalty towards black men (or anyone else, for that matter), they have achieved something that cannot be found in Walker's writing. Her warning of the self-destruction in store for black women may be little more than a projection onto them of her own suicidal urges.

In an article that appeared the following year (1974), Walker would articulate more explicitly the complaint, camouflaged with epithets that assert that black women manipulate or destroy black men, against black women's playing the role as America's "mules":

> Black women are called, in the folklore that so aptly identifies one's status in society, "the *mule* of the world," because we have been handed the burdens that everyone else—*everyone* else—refused to carry. We have also been called "Matriarchs," "Superwomen," and "Mean and Evil Bitches." Not to mention "Castraters" and "Sapphire's Mama." When we have pleaded for understanding, our character has been distorted; when we have asked for simple caring, we have been handed empty inspirational appellations, then stuck in the farthest corner. When we have asked for love, we have been given children. In short, even our plainer gifts, our labors of fidelity and love, have been knocked down our throats. To be an artist and a black woman, even to-

day, lowers our status in many respects, rather than raises it: and yet, artists we will be.

Walker seems to be saying more emphatically that everyone exploits black women no matter what those women do to appease their persecutors. Her concerns over the status of black women writers and her perception of the plight of black women seem like caricatures that might be captioned, "Poor me."

In 1974, Walker also attended a conference of the National Black Feminist Organization and reported somewhat defensively: "We sat together and talked and knew no one would think, or say, 'Your thoughts are dangerous to black unity and a threat to black men.' Instead, all the women understood that we gathered together to assure understanding among black women, and that understanding among women is not a threat to anyone who intends to treat women fairly." Angry with reporters from black newspapers for not covering the conference meetings, Walker chides the black press by appealing to the model of black participation, support, and coverage of women's issues and meetings established by Frederick Douglass and his famous newspaper the *North Star:* "... *his* newspaper would have been pleased to cover our conference.... He understood that it is not incumbent upon the slave to make sure her or his uprising is appropriate or 'correct.' It is the nature of the oppressed to rise against oppression. Period. Women who wanted their rights did not frighten him, politically or socially, because he knew his own rights were not diminished by theirs." Walker rejects the concepts of appropriateness and correctness here and in her fiction (through the protagonist, Meridian, for example) because she believes they have been used to keep black women in check. She reassures those well-intentioned black men disturbed with the fear that the organization of black women will drive a wedge deeper into the split between black men and black women. On the other hand, she is also warning black male chauvinists that their dominance is coming to an end.

She is less convincing when she chooses to browbeat black women into supporting her concerns: "To the extent that black women dissociate themselves from the women's movement, they abandon their responsibilities to women throughout the world." Appealing to the women's sense of guilt, Walker seems determined to distract the women from whatever else they are doing so that they can do what *she* thinks best. The punitive rhetoric, with its emotional appeal, undoubtedly fails to bring Walker any closer to many black folk, especially black women, who are not about to open the door to someone else giving orders. This seemingly radical persona stands in stark contrast to the romantic ideal of the patient and compassionate revolutionary to whom she dedicates the poems of *Good Night, Willie Lee.* As the dedication suggests, intelligent and competent organizers enable people to get where the people want to go, at their own pace, without haranguing or condemning them, and with respect for the right of each to self-determination.

Walker's assertions concerning criticism of black women are sometimes blatantly contradictory. For example, she demurely states that one of her "great weaknesses, which I am beginning to recognize more clearly than ever around the Michele Wallace book, is a deep reluctance to criticize other black women." Yet when she returns to the subject of *Black Macho* . . . , she attacks the book with enough zest and zeal to suggest that she is not unfamiliar with a critical posture towards black women. (Also, compare this assertion of reluctance with the opinions quoted above concerning the soul singer who became a blonde and regarding black women who are loyal to black men.)

On the other hand, in 1984, when David Bradley criticized her for failing to be as tough on black women as on black men, Walker responded not merely by excusing black women's weaknesses but also by arguing that the motives of women are less reprehensible than those of men: "'But I am really aware that they are under two layers of oppression and that even though everybody, the men and the women, get [sic] twisted terribly, the women have less choice than the men. And the things that they do, the bad choices that they make, are not done out of meanness, out of a need to take stuff out on people.'" The persona is clever enough to reach for feminist rhetoric, "two layers of oppression" (as if black men have not been and are not still sexually and racially exploited by black women and white people), but she destroys the credibility of her position with feminist (or would this be womanist?) psychology: the assertion of gender-determined meanness. Of course, behind this image of meanness stands an old folk image that Walker caricatures for the reader. Black folklore and street talk are full of images of "mean and evil" black men and black women. Some people have called them devils or criminals and have wanted to roast them or at least put them in jail, but black folk brought up to understand their own culture know that *this* "mean and evil" has little to do with the mean and evil of the white folk. The individuals black folk label as "mean and evil" are usually in rebellion from a white power structure and its values (check out Miles Davis, for example, or Pilate Dead). In the lore, mean and evil black folk were primarily self-determining blacks who brooked no exploitation, manipulation, or dependency. Gender-determined meanness exists only as a joke among the folk who know and as a means for projection for those who don't. A woman might say, "Niggers are mean!" (she is discussing the merits of black men or, to be more precise, the black men that she has encountered); what she means is, "I can't find one to do as I tell him." Wise women know that they are finding language to express their frustration, not uncovering the emotional anatomy of the opposite sex. (I don't

wish to ignore the issue of mutual violence between the sexes, but that is another matter.)

In 1980 Walker would applaud the coming out of the closet of black lesbians, reflected by the publication of *Conditions: Five. The Black Women's Issue,* which also includes the work of non-lesbian writers. The attitudes that engender this support certainly must bring her closer to black lesbian women and the liberal-minded, but, undoubtedly, they aggravate the already troubled waters with a large number of black folk who possess more conservative, often homophobic values. Walker's accepting attitude towards lesbianism apparently influences her depiction of the affair between Celie and Shug in *The Color Purple.*

Yet despite Walker's liberal thinking, when she comes to champion a cause that has long been a concern for most black people—the intraracism against dark, black women—, she does not refrain from exposing her pessimistic vision of the future of the race: "To me, the black black woman is our essential mother—the blacker she is the more us she is—and to see the hatred that is turned on her is enough to make me despair, almost entirely, of our future as a people." This is not the first time for Walker's despairing, nor, I suspect, will it be her last. It is important to note that she is losing hope for an audience about and to whom she writes. The problems in communication between Walker and black folk may have something to do with this defeatist attitude that seems to filter her vision. It is also important not to overlook Walker's judgment of women based on their color. Although she appears to be arguing against intraracism, in actuality her proposition that the darker a black woman the closer she is to being the "essential mother" of the race can only serve to fan the fires of rancor and recrimination that have been raging among black people of different shades at least since slavery days. Walker's proposition, whether or not she is aware of it, has the effect of becoming a thinly cloaked attack on Afro-American mulattoes; it shunts them aside (or places them on a lower rung of Walker's ladder of blackness) as the outcast bastards of the slave plantation's white adulterers and fornicators. Like Walker's notion that black women suffer more and are less guilty than black men, her intraracial remarks constitute a persecutory proposition, elevating one victim, casting down another, and dividing the race.

A contrast with another black woman novelist might serve to expose the gratuitous character of Walker's reasoning. Toni Morrison has also considered the issue of intraracism and has come up with a proposition, within the plotting of her fourth novel, *Tar Baby,* which does not carry the invidious intent that lies beneath Walker's assertion. Morrison argues that some women of the race do not maintain the "ancient properties," the personal psychological characteristics that allow a woman to value caring for the well-being of the black family and the black race and to exhibit a healthy acceptance of her own sexuality. It is not the color of one's skin that determines this in Morrison's novel (although the mulatto character, Jadine, does have problems with her womanhood traceable to, among other sources, white reactions to her skin color) but, rather, whether or not a woman has first learned to be a daughter—that is, to love and to respect the mothers, mother figures, and parents responsible for her nurturing. Morrison argues that, if a woman learns to be a daughter, then she will be able to be a wife to a black man and a mother to black children and a nurturer and preserver of black people. Were one to initiate a search for the "essential mothers" with whom Walker seems to be concerned, skin color might prove a less dependable criterion than the characteristics identified by Morrison.

One might, moreover, question whether Walker seriously believes what she has articulated. For example, would her intraracial proposition hold true for men also? If so, then how is one to understand Walker's marriage (now terminated) to a white man or her relationships with light-skinned black men? Are the latter any less "essential" than dark-skinned black men (such as her father)? Or perhaps men don't qualify for entering the pantheon of racial "essentials." Walker continues her crusade on behalf of dark-skinned black women when she attacks black male political leaders who seem to prefer light-skinned women to dark: "For the dark-skinned black woman it comes as a series of disappointments and embarrassments that the wives of virtually all black leaders . . . appear to have been chosen for the nearness of their complexions to white alone."

What Wallace Thurman called intraracism is a corollary of America's white racism. The slaves and their descendants have been taught to get as close to whiteness as possible, in as many ways as possible. Blacks have taught each other to "marry up"; that is, to marry lighter-skinned blacks (if whites were unattainable or unwanted), a practice that has been called by blacks themselves "putting a little color into the race." In reaction to this value preference and its consequences, blacks (and whites, for somewhat different reasons) who feel admiration, covetousness, jealousy, or envy have scapegoated mulattoes. Intraracism is divisive, and it is disheartening to see Walker engaged in it.

The distance some black folk feel from Alice Walker may be a reflection of her involvement with white feminists. Whatever that involvement has been, she seems to be discovering some of the wisdom about working with whites that many other folk in the struggle have been teaching each other (or learning the hard way) for generations:

> . . . in America white women who are truly feminist—for whom racism is inherently an impossibility—are largely outnumbered by *average* white women for whom racism, inasmuch as it assures

white privilege, is an accepted way of life. Naturally, many of these women, to be trendy, will leap to the feminist banner. . . . What was required of women of color was to learn to distinguish between who was the real feminist and who was not, and to exert energy in feminist collaborations only when there is little risk of wasting it. The rigors of this discernment will inevitably keep throwing women of color back upon themselves. . . .

As the Laguna of Leslie Silko's *Ceremony* lament the loss of Little Sister (the mother of the novel's protagonist, Tayo) to the corrupted and degrading embrace of exploitative white men and their culture, so do black folk fear that their young angry women, afflicted with the victim's alienation from her own self as well as her oppressed group and its roots, will squander the energy and future of the clan or tribe in a futile search for liberation among the very people responsible for and benefiting from the oppression of the race. The wisdom of the folk suggests that most white women will sleep with white men, despite the movement for gay liberation. To expect these white women to act for the benefit of black people by wresting political and economic power from white men and redistributing that power to black folk (along with white women?) seems to be unrealistic. Toni Morrison (bless her soul for not biting her tongue) characterizes white feminism as a family fight in which it is unwise for outsiders to become involved ("What the Black Woman Thinks"). Although most folk want to see an end to sexual exploitation, many still believe that the real battle lines will be drawn over racial and class exploitation. Walker's continual search for the real feminist seems somewhat unsophisticated in the light of the history and experience of black and white contact in struggle. One might indeed lament that her "women of color" have to be thrown "back upon themselves." It makes them seem to be reactionary assimilationists rather than assertive leaders with vision and direction for the future of black women and black people. To be assertive, visionary leaders of black people, black women may have to feel a greater loyalty towards black men (about whom they know) than towards "women throughout the world" (about whom they know little), and this is precisely the possibility that Walker has gone on record as lamenting.

Undoubtedly, Walker's alienation from black men influences her portrayal of them in fiction. Her audiences may achieve greater tolerance of her perceptions of men if they consider Walker's portrayal of male characters as part of the aftermath of the childhood accident in which she was blinded in one eye after her brother shot her with a bb gun. David Bradley asserts that "after that accident, she felt her family had failed her, especially her father. She felt he had ceased to favor her, and, as a child, blamed him for the poverty that kept her from receiving adequate medical care. He also, she implies, whipped and imprisoned her sister, who had shown too much interest in boys. . . . In company with her brothers, her father had failed to 'give me male models I could respect.'" Walker's disenchantment sounds like that of a child who no longer feels like her father's darling. She seems to be at odds with her father, her brothers, and her family. Walker is more explicit about her disenchantment in an article first published in 1975: "I desperately needed my father and brothers to give me male models I could respect, because white men . . . offered man as dominator, as killer, and always as hypocrite. My father failed because he copied the hypocrisy. And my brothers—except for one—never understood they must represent half the world to me, as I must represent the other half to them." Walker's assertion of a mutual need between men and women to reflect the opposite half of the world is discordant with her disapproval of the loyalty some black women feel towards black men. Her perception that there was an absence of adequate young-adult male images within her childhood influences her literary portrayals of young black males: The central characters are flat stereotypes depicting, as Bradley notes, images of malevolence or impotence. Also, one might ask whether Walker's alienated perception of the males in her family was involved with her decision to marry a white man, despite her articulation of a problem with the image of the white male.

Walker's father died in 1973, before she had effected a reconciliation with him, and his death aggravated her alienation before it propelled her toward confronting it. She told David Bradley: "'You know, his death was harder than I had thought at the time. We were so estranged that when I heard—I was in an airport somewhere—I didn't think I felt anything. It was years later that I really felt it. We had a wonderful reconciliation after he died.'" Walker's estrangement seems to date from her childhood accident. It also appears that her hardheartedness towards her father prevented her grieving for him until quite a while after his death. The year 1973 also marks Walker's last year in Mississippi, when she continued her struggles against depression and the urge to commit suicide: "My salvation that last year was a black woman psychiatrist who had also grown up in the South. Though she encouraged me to talk about whether or not I had loved and/ or understood my father, I became increasingly aware that I was holding myself responsible for the conditions of black people in America. Unable to murder the oppressors, I sat in a book-lined study and wrote about lives. . . ." The correspondence between the issue that Walker holds against herself and that which precipitated her alienation from her father is startling: She feels just as inadequate at rescuing black people as she felt he was inadequate at rescuing her after the childhood accident.

As the concerns of her therapist suggest, Walker seems ignorant of her father's life. It may be this ignorance that she tried to relieve on the visit to her father's grave that she reports in the Bradley interview: "'I didn't cry when he died, but that

summer I was in terrible shape. And I went to Georgia and I went to the cemetery and I laid down on top of his grave. I wanted to see what he could see, if he could look up. And I started to cry. And all the knottedness that had been in our relationship dissolved. And we're fine now.'" Since Walker elsewhere says that it took years for her to allow herself to grieve for her father, it is difficult to take literally this assertion of dissolved knottedness. Moreover, this account seems to undercut her 1975 statement concerning her father's sexism: "It was not until I became a student of women's liberation ideology that I could understand and forgive my father." The persona of the poem **"Good Night, Willie Lee, I'll See You in the Morning"** insists that there is real forgiveness of the father and a "healing / of all our wounds," but the more the persona speaks of forgiveness the less assured the reader feels that Walker's fundamental attitude towards her father has changed, especially when one considers her fictive portrayal of men. Yet it is certain that finding ways to forgive her father has been a continuing concern of Alice Walker's.

In 1975 she had not yet laid to rest the ghost of her father. She reveals that she perceives older men as father figures: "Dr. Benton, a friend of Zora [Neale Hurston]'s and a practicing M.D. in Fort Pierce, is one of those old, good-looking men whom I always have trouble not liking. (It no longer bothers me that I may be constantly searching for father figures; by this time, I have found several and dearly enjoyed them all.)." Speaking of Langston Hughes and Arna Bontemps in 1971, Walker observed that "*We must cherish our old men.*" And, speaking of old men as a category, she notes, "I love old men." The persona's attitudes and attachments to older men suggest that she may be in search of someone with whom she can play the role of darling, even daughter, to complete a circle involving a father figure that she abandoned in childhood in the aftermath of an accident. Elderly black men are portrayed with at least approval and often veneration because she liked her grandfathers who to her appeared to be gentle, in contrast to younger adult black males. Walker says, "'I knew both my grandfathers and they were just doting, indulgent, sweet old men. I just loved them both and they were crazy about me.'" An ongoing effect of her childhood accident seems to be that she sees younger men (who would be in the age range that her father was when she became alienated from him and her brothers) with a jaundiced eye.

Walker's attitude towards her father is further uncovered by the connections she draws between a dream she had of him while she was in Cuba (during which he returned to look at her with something missing in his eyes) and her meeting with a Cuban revolutionary, Pablo Diaz, once a poor sugar cane cutter who had risen to the role of an "official spokesperson for the Cuban Institute for Friendship Among Peoples." Of Diaz she says, "Helping to throw off his own oppressors obviously had given him a pride in himself that nothing else could, and as he talked, I saw in his eyes a quality my own father's eyes had sometimes lacked: the absolute assurance that he was a man whose words—because he had helped destroy a way of life he despised—would always be heard, with respect, by his children." Walker's response to the Cuban revolutionary exposes circular and emotional reasoning: She may not respect her father because, since he did not bring about the end to his own oppression, he did not afford any assurance that what he said would be respected. Walker might be paraphrased, "I don't respect you because you don't expect me to respect you"; or, more to the point, "I don't respect you because you have not fulfilled my expectations." It appears that in her nonfictive assertions concerning her father, Walker plays the role of a victim who has become angry and bitter because the person she expects to rescue her is himself a victim (as well as a persecutor). (This attitude is similar to that she expresses when she attacks the judgment of the black community that will not protect black women accosted by black men.) She will not bear the sight of her father's anguish; she will not bear its weight on her consciousness. And his anguish is all the more unbearable because Walker, as a child, naturally expected him to be her protector, her comforter, her inspiration, her rescuer. Undoubtedly, one should not expect an eight-year-old, gripped by the physical and psychic trauma of impending blindness, to cope with the imperfection of her father (and also her older brothers). Moreover, to his plight as a sharecropper, one must add whatever may have been his personal shortcomings in order to get an accurate picture of the child's confrontation with his inadequacies. Walker was not merely disappointed but also frustrated by her father's anguish: She could not rescue him or make him into what she wanted or expected him to be, just as she has been unable to rescue black people. In other words, her continual rejection and condemnation of black people because they are either victims, persecutors, or inadequate rescuers may be, indeed, a reflection of her unresolved attitudes towards her father. Walker's suicidal impulses may be the result of her feeling like a child who is unable to be a daughter and a darling because no one appears (or remains) adequate to be the father she discarded as a child. Like a pendulum, Walker's recorded attitudes swing slowly back and forth between a victim's suicidal depression and a persecutor's deadly anger and thirst for revenge. The personas of the adult Walker continue to reject the father of her youth (all young men) waiting for her in her dreams and search out older men who fit her perceptions of her grandfathers, who appear to be adequate enough to rescue her, and for whom she can be a darling. She may be in search of not so much our mothers' gardens as our fathers' protecting arms.

If one accepts this insight, it is easy to explain the system of the characterization of Ruth, Grange, and Brownfield (as well as the other major characters of *The Third Life of Grange Copeland*); Meridian, the protagonist of *Meridian*; and Celie, the protagonist of *The Color Purple.* The major female char-acters are masks for Walker's perceptions of herself. None of them has an adequate relationship with a male character. The adult women do not enjoy sex with males. The last two novels end with protagonists who are certain never again to allow the possibility of sexual contact with a male. Alice Walker cannot afford to allow her protagonists to enjoy male sexuality, not merely because those protagonists believe that males, by nature, are inadequate humans (e.g., Celie's ridiculing of male genitalia along with her image of men as frogs or losers) but also because all the males with the potential for sexual relations with Walker's protagonists may be masks for her father.

For all Celie knew when Alfonso was raping her, he may as well have been her father. As a stepfather, no matter how inadequate, he is a parental figure. It is important to note that Celie allows herself to be repeatedly raped by this man, yet she protects Nettie so that Alfonso never touches her. One would have to give Celie much less credit for adequate human faculties than I do to think that she could know enough to protect Nettie but be too stupid to protect herself from Alfonso. And then she goes to Albert and plays the same game—"You go ahead and get away, Nettie, I'll stay back and let him abuse me. You wouldn't want him to do this awful thing to you; we both can see how terrible it is, but one of us must satisfy this male, and I think that I am the one who deserves to, probably because my esteem for myself is so low." Or something like that. (Friends with whom I have argued this issue are quick to assert the low self-esteem of Celie. Admitted, obviously, by definition. What I believe is interesting is not the psychological realism of the literary characterization, but the relationships that can be drawn between the characterization and Walker's perceptions of herself and her experiences.) Albert, Celie's husband, plays the same big-/mean-daddy role with Celie that Alfonso does: He beats her, forces her to work, ruts with her, and uses her as bait for Nettie. Later, Celie expresses some of her pent-up rage when she realizes that she wants to kill Albert and when she almost succeeds with a curse she lays on him. Appropriate to the attitudes of the novel, the malevolent Alfonso dies while screwing a child wife. Celie is up for only violent, abusive, and manipulative sexual relationships with father figures or parental figures to justify the anger and sublimate the desires of the alienated darling in search of a father. Celie never achieves mutual sexual equality with anyone. Even Shug, like Alfonso and Albert, takes advantage of her role as Celie's rescuer (that, along with her age, makes her more like a mother or parent). Shug successfully corners off the emotionally crippled Celie for sexual purposes and manipulates her into sitting on the porch (Hurston's Janie Starks knew better) while Shug chases around the country after her sexual fancies. Celie's homosexuality is clearly portrayed not as congenital but as a predilection or pathology that results from being the victim of not merely male but also father figure abusiveness: She is too afraid of her father to look at boys; she expresses a desire for only one person; and she seems unaware of the sexuality of other women.

I could go on with this, but the drift of the argument should be clear: Alice Walker's fictional characterizations include thinly disguised representations of perceptions of herself and her family that began in childhood. Unwittingly, she masquerades these perceptions, primarily the products of fantasies of sexuality and aggression, as the creations of a mature adult awareness, and she is then surprised by the responses of her intended audience, for whom she expresses more contempt than respect. She seems unaware that her readers may be reacting to their perceptions and intuitions of her feelings of hostility toward and alienation from them, and that those feelings unavoidably interfere with her ability to speak effectively to her audience. Feeling like an outcast of her own community, she has flirted and engaged herself with whites, undoubtedly searching for the acceptance and affirmation that she did not find at home, but she has discovered that they will not relinquish their racism, and so she appears to be searching for a way to return. If so, then the next critical step for black folk is to open their arms and embrace Alice Walker, to reassert the strength of the extended family, the unity of the tribe, with an acceptance and understanding that quells all anguish, including that which stems from the recognition that one bears the very evils one would extirpate from the social order—racism, sexism, and colorist values.

The rapprochement may be more easily secured by those who recognize that Walker's alienation is not unusual. With his depiction of the marginal man stranded between two cultures of a social order, Milton Gordon seems to be describing a pattern in Walker's life:

> . . . most frequently he is a member of a minority group attracted by the subsociety and subculture of the dominant or majority group in the national society of which he is a part. Frustrated and not fully accepted by the broader social world he wished to enter, ambivalent in his attitude towards the more restricted social world to which he has ancestral rights, and beset by conflicting cultural standards, he develops, according to the classic conception, personality traits of insecurity, moodiness, hypersensitivity, excessive self-consciousness, and nervous strain.

Without this rapprochement it may be impossible for Alice Walker to achieve her goal of rescuing black people, especially black women.

Barbara T. Christian (essay date 1986)

SOURCE: "We Are the Ones That We Have Been Waiting For: Political Content in Alice Walker's Novels," in *Women's Studies International Forum,* Vol. 9, No. 4, 1986, pp. 421-26.

[*In the following essay, Christian discusses the interdependence of individual and societal change in Walker's novels.*]

> Because women are expected to keep silent about
> their close escapes I will not keep silent.
>   —(Walker, 1979)

There is no question that Alice Walker's works are directed towards effecting social change, that she is a writer with political intent. Black women writers have little choice in this regard. Even if they could manage blindness, deafness to the state of black people, their status, as black, female, writer, a triple affliction, would, at some point, force them to at least consider the effect of societal forces on the lives of individuals. I make this bold-faced statement at the beginning of this essay on political content in Walker's novels, because it seems to me that our supposedly most radical avant garde critics seem to consist upon the unimportance of external reality, that the text ought to be dispersed, deconstructed—that writers do not mean what they write, do not even know what they write, that language is devoid of meaning, and is primarily a system of signs that refer to other signs rather than to anything that exists. Probably many of these critics would agree, if they thought they could say it aloud, that the best text would be silence, and that such a term as a political writer is a backward reactionary one.

I am particularly concerned with emphasizing my disagreement with this point of view, since I believe it would demolish much of the tradition (a bad word, I am told) of Afro-American writers, who have always had to refer to that reality out there which has its all too real foot on their necks. Further, for women, whatever their race, who have been silenced for so long, the very essence of this supposedly radical literary theory would reduce their words to sound and fury without meaning. It strikes me ironic that as groups who have traditionally been silenced begin to 'penetrate' the literary market, we learn that neither the world nor meaning exists. That a text is but a reference to other texts.

Like many other black women writers, Walker intends her works to effect something in the world. That is why she speaks and that is why she writes. But in her work, intention is not the only political factor. The process of political changing, the envisioning of social transforming is central to her work. Her forms, themes, imagery, critiques are marked by her belief in a coherent yet developing philosophy of life (an ideology in other words), which has some relationship to external reality. Her works are not merely *her* fictions, they are her fictions in relation to the world.

The core of her works is clearly her focus on black women, on the freedom allowed them as an indicator of the health of our entire society. This focus may seem a simple one. But if one considers the reality of black women's conditions in American society, her focus must involve a complexity of vision, if that condition is to be probed. In looking at what it means to be a black woman in the world, one must confront the vortex of sexism, racism, poverty so integrated that the parts of the whole can hardly be separated.

Many of Walker's literary ancestors had attempted to illuminate one part of this vortex, racism, primarily because of the tremendous oppression black women and men have suffered because of their race. But in so doing these writers have not *consciously* probed the salient fact, that racism is most invidiously expressed in sexist terms and that often the forms used most effectively by racist institutions are based on this interrelationship. Thus, the slave was to relate to the master, the black to the white, as woman was to relate to man, in a submissive, obedient manner essentially, as a role to the *real* person, who was master, white, male. I wrote about this construct in *Black Women Novelists* by analysing the patriarchal plantation system, the major ideology that buttressed American slavery. And last year, I discussed this interrelationship as an underlying theme in all of black women's fiction, though often unconsciously perceived by the writers themselves.

But Walker is certainly *conscious* about demonstrating the relationship between these two oppressions. One reason why her maternal ancestors had not approached this interrelationship was their fear that the other, the powerful other, whites, were listening, could read their published works, and that any critique of the behavior of black people would further be used by whites to further oppress the race. Walker, however, insists on placing black people at the center of her work both as subject and as audience. In portraying the sexism that exists in black communities and demonstrating its relationship, though not source in racism, she is speaking to her community about itself and its many participants. Walker's focus is itself an important political one, a breaking of silence which overthrows the oppressive stance fostered by racism, that white people are all that is important, that they are to blame for everything, that black people have no responsibility to themselves, their families, their institutions. Like Audre Lorde, another contemporary Afro-American woman poet, Walker proclaims that speaking the truth is necessary to survival, especially for those of us who were not meant to survive.

Walker's critiquing of her own community, her demonstration of the relationship between sexism and racism is already focal in her first novel, *The Third Life of Grange Copeland* which was published in 1970. At a time when the prominent black writers of the day emphasized confrontation between the beleaguered black community and the powerful white society, Walker's novel showed how that confrontation affects the relationships between black women, men, and children in other words the family. If the family is the core of the community, within which values are nurtured, the place where black people relate to each other on the most intimate level, then one needs to look at that interaction in order to discuss political reality, political possibility. As in her other two novels, *Meridian* and *The Color Purple,* Walker traces the development of three generations of a black family. In contrast to her second and third, however the focus in *Grange Copeland* is on the Copeland men, their mistaken acceptance of the definition of maleness as power, an attribute they cannot possibly attain and how that results in their brutalization of their wives and children.

This subject was certainly a taboo one in the early 1970s since black writers were intent on idealizing nationhood. What Walker did was to show how racism is capable of distorting the individual's relationship to his own kin, because he is encouraged to blame everything on the white folks and not accept responsibility for his own actions. No nationhood was possible if violence in the family persisted. Too, she does not hesitate to expose the destruction of black women by their own relations. But Walker also shows the coming to consciousness of Grange Copeland in this novel, his awareness that his resistance against whites must begin with his love of himself and his own family. This is a part of the novel that many who condemn it for its pessimism refuse to acknowledge, stunned as they are by a critique that they do not wish to confront. Yet this coming to consciousness is an essential part of every Walker novel—an integral part of her political statement.

Walker's first novel is an indicator of her political stance, but also of her insights into political process. As in her other two novels, *Grange Copeland* also analyses how economic struggle is linked to racism and sexism for the people she focuses on are southern sharecroppers. Her protagonists must contend with the restrictiveness of the economic order, of capitalism on their lives, even as they do not understand its nature. The effects of capitalism on the southern black family cannot be understood only in terms of the present. Thus all her novels span generations, in other words, are rooted in history.

> **Walker's first novel is an indicator of her political stance, but also of her insights into political process. As in her other two novels, *Grange Copeland* also analyses how economic struggle is linked to racism and sexism for the people she focuses on are southern sharecroppers.**
> **—*Barbara T. Christian***

The process by which Walker interweaves the overall history of the Copeland family with the story of each generation of that family is an important aspect of her political vision. She uses quilting, a Southern womanist form, as a model for her first novel. Just as her maternal ancestors took bits of waste material and transformed them into patterned works, at once useful and beautiful, so Walker stitches together motifs repeated in each generation into a coherent pattern. Thus we are able to see how essential the motifs of racist terror and sexual violence are to the pattern of this family's history. Only when Grange learns to love himself and his granddaughter Ruth is the destructive pattern changed and a regenerative pattern begun. Even so the force of the previous history is so strong that the old pattern of destruction threatens the new one, as Brownfield Copeland attempts to destroy his father, Grange. By concluding the novel with the appearance of Civil Rights workers, Walker suggests the necessity not only for the personal change that Grange Copeland undergoes, but also that the pattern of this quilt will not be changed for long unless social change begins to occur.

Paradoxically, although Walker uses a womanist form in her first novel, the adult Copeland women are destroyed precisely because they do not understand the social forces that are arrayed against them as black women. Convinced by their culture that they can be 'the perfect wife' regardless of their economic and social context, they are defeated by the men in their own families, as well as by white society. Walker courageously opposes the widespread belief that black women always 'endure,' as she shows how terrifying are the oppressions that assail them. Such a portrayal was practically heresy in 1970, when black women were being continually exalted for their superhuman ability to survive anything, the implication being that they did not need, as urgently as others, relief from their condition. Although Margaret and Mem Copeland are destroyed, Ruth, the girl-woman of the Copelands' third generation has the possibility of surviving for she is given by her grandfather the knowledge about her culture and about white society that she will need. As importantly, she has a greater possibility of 'surviving whole' because a social movement against racism may affect her life.

This historical dimension which is prevalent not only in *Grange Copeland* but in all of Walker's novels enables her to analyse the process by which the social order becomes oppressive, particularly of black women while giving her the space to show how they come to consciousness about the nature of their condition. Paradoxically, even as she focuses on the intimate relationships between black women and men, black parents and children, black women and black women, she is able to relate the quality of these relationships to the larger sweep of history. And her novels show, through this historical dimension, not only the repression that blacks have suffered but also their resistance to it. Thus a knowledge of their own history is one source for the coming to conscious-

ness that her protagonists go through, a reminder that black people before them, black women before them have resisted powerful attempts of dehumanization. History, too, is an impetus for black women, a source of their understanding of their right to be themselves whatever the prevailing black ideology may be, as well as an indicator of the often painful process through which they must go to retain their integrity as human beings. Since much of the 'history' that is written omits black women, Walker and her sisters who write are reclaiming that history even as they create visions of new alternatives. And in so doing, they are primary political actors.

> 'They were women then
> My mamma's generation
> Husky of voice—stout of
> Step
> With fists as well as
> Hands'

Meridian, Walker's second novel, is an even more graphic illustration of the importance of herstory to black women's lives. One of the novel's major themes is both a rich critique of the ideology of black motherhood in this country and a celebration of the true meanings of motherhood. By tracing the history of black people, not through battles or legislation, but in terms of the lives of mothers, Walker demonstrates how motherhood is 'an angle of seeing life,' of valuing all life, of resisting all that might destroy it—in other words that motherhood is not merely a biological state but an attitude towards life.

Even as she probes the meaning of motherhood, Walker's use of herstory also allows her to highlight the insidious ways in which both black and white society restrict, punish individual mothers even as they canonize motherhood. The political meaning of this analysis is tantamount to the freeing of woman, who solely has the potential of being a mother, and who has, for much of the world's history, been reduced to that role. Walker then, extends the definition of womanhood beyond the restrictive definition of biological motherhood, even as she beautifully expands the meaning of that state.

But Walker also extends the true meaning of mother, of cherishing life, to that of the revolutionary. For the novel *Meridian* relates this attitude to the spiritual/political principles of the Civil Rights movement, a social movement opposed to violence, the destruction of life, even as it had violence inflicted upon its members by the ruling classes. Meridian poses a major political question: 'When is it right to kill? Why isn't revolutionary murder, murder?' How does the acceptance of the culture of violence effect those who struggle for positive social transformation. 'What would the music be like?' It is a question critical to our world when revolutions sometimes self-destruct, and when sometimes the only actual change after a political revolution is a changing of the guards. Walker of course does not fully resolve the question but she does probe its meaning reminding us that those who consider killing in order to effect change must prepare themselves to go through their own personal revolution—that social change is impossible without personal change. The flawed Meridian pursues the question of revolutionary violence in the novel, an issue she can perceive, because from her point of view she has violated life at its deepest level. Because she feels guilt about giving up her son to others and about aborting her second pregnancy, Meridian is propelled on a search for spiritual and political health. Having sinned against biological motherhood, she becomes a mother by 'expanding her mind with action' which is directed toward the preservation of all life.

Meridian's form is itself a graphic image of revolution. It is both circular and ascending, the meaning of the word *meridian,* as Walker intersects the personal histories of Meridian, Truman and Lynne, actors in the Civil Rights movement, with the collective history of black people. Within this form, Walker carefully connects bits and pieces of these histories, as she creates an even more intricate quilt in this second novel. The meridian-like movement of the novel indicates a process of coming to consciousness for Meridian, which Truman at the end of the novel, can use as a source of inspiration and process if he is to become whole. In *Meridian* then, Walker suggests a process for all those who seek social change. Meridian must go backward in time in order to move forward beyond the point that she is at, continually seeking the connections between her personal history and communal history. It is through this process that Walker the writer is able to show the interrelationship of sexism, racism and economic deprivation not only on individuals and their families but also *on the political movements they create.* And how, as well, these areas of oppression must be struggled through, rather than ignored or talked out of existence. Only then is ascension possible.

> *The Nature of this Flower Is to Bloom*
> Rebellious. Living.
> Against the Elemental Crush.
> A Song of Color
> Blooming
> For Deserving Eyes.
> Blooming Gloriously
> For its Self.
> *Revolutionary Petunia.*

The forms that Walker creates then have political content. Perhaps, even more than *Meridian,* the form of her most recent novel, *The Color Purple* is dramatically political, for she employs a technique that is both associated with every day life and with women. *The Color Purple* is written entirely in letters. Not only is this a *tour de force* for Walker, the novelist, letters along with diaries were the only forms

allowed women to record their herstory. Letters both express Celie's view of herself and her view of the world even as they show her development from a victimized girl to a woman who becomes strong enough to change her condition and to love herself. Letters are both a source of subjective information, Celie's feelings about herself, and objective information, the world in which she moves. Letters proclaim the woman-centered focus of this novel, a political statement in itself.

> **[Walker's] exposing of incest in *The Color Purple* has precipitated more discussion within her community on sexism than ever before, as Walker insists that black people adhere to the value of life for black women.**
> **—*Barbara T. Christian***

Also Walker distinguishes her woman protagonist as a black women by her language. Like Walker's other two novels, *Color Purple* traces three generations of a family, most emphatically this time from a woman's point of view. Like *Grange Copeland* the novel is a story about a rural Southern family, though not sharecroppers but small landowners. But *Color Purple* is distinguished from these other two novels by its use of black folk language which too develops in complexity as Celie becomes stronger, more articulate, older. By using this language in contrast to standard English, Walker affirms the value of Afro-American culture. This is no small political assertion. Attempts are always made to discredit the language of a people in order to discredit them; for it is in their language that a people's values are expressed. If there is any significant idea (and there are many) that Walker has learned from her literary maternal ancestor Zora Neale Hurston, it is this one.

Perhaps the most obvious measure of *The Color Purple's* political direction is the novel's focus on sexism within the black community. This is not a new subject for Walker. All her work exposes how sexism, is, tragically, a part of black mores, a question of power in the black community as it is in all other human cultures we know. But in *The Color Purple,* Walker protests incest, a taboo subject in the black community. Just as she approached in 1970 the taboo subject of family violence in *Grange Copeland,* in 1976 the myth of black motherhood and the idea that revolutionary violence should at least be questioned in *Meridian,* in 1983 Walker again approached a taboo subject among black ideologues. Her exposing of incest in *The Color Purple* has precipitated more discussion within her community on sexism than ever before, as Walker insists that black people adhere to the value of life for black women. By critiquing her community she affirms our right to take responsibility for ourselves, by speaking to her community as her audience, she demonstrates how central black people are to her vision.

As if breaking the silence about incest in black families were not enough, the intrepid Walker gives *Color Purple* a distinctly womanist thrust by having Celie triumph over brutality, wife-beating, incest—through her sisters—through Shug who becomes her lover and friend, through Nellie her blood sister who writes letters to her from Africa, and whose letters she finally can answer, and through Sophie, her sister-in-law who resists her husband as well as white peoples' attempts to beat her down. Again Walker explores another taboo subject, for physical as well as spiritual love between women is the core of the novel. By presenting this love as natural and freeing, Walker protests homophobia in the black community. Sisterhood among women is *Color Purple's* theme and form as Walker proclaims bonding among black women as a necessary ingredient if we are to be free.

Walker, however does not ignore racism among women. Through Sophie's experience with the Mayor's wife which results in this black woman being jailed and taken away from her children, Walker questions whether sisterhood across racial lines is possible until white women descend from the unnatural pedestal they stand on and eliminate racism in themselves. But Walker also insists that sexism, though affected by racism is not derived from it. Nellie's sections in Africa has as one of their focus, the sexism African women are afflicted with as Walker exposes another taboo subject amongst black ideologues. Nellie's sections also emphasize the impact of colonialism and imperialism on African peoples as Walker protests in one bold stroke the doctrine of white supremacy and capitalist expansion.

But *Color Purple* goes beyond the protest of sexism, racism, and homophobia. Perhaps the novel's most significant contribution to Walker's expanding political vision is the pivotal role the erotic plays in Celie's movement toward freedom. The title of the novel itself is a celebration of the beauty, the pleasure of living and how that celebration is at the core of spiritual and political growth. It is through Celie's awareness of her right to the passion, creativity, satisfaction possible in life that she empowers herself. Once she experiences the erotic, the sharing of joy, she fights for her right to participate in it. Celie's story beautifully exemplifies Audre Lorde's words in her essay 'The Uses of the Erotic, the Erotic as Power':

> In touch with the erotic I become less willing to accept powerlessness or those other supplied states of being which are not native to one such as resignation, despair, self-effacement, depression, self-denial.

Like Lorde, Celie comes to *demand* from all of her life—her

relationships, her work, whatever she is engaged in—that deep satisfaction. In guiding her to that knowledge Shug, her friend and lover, helps Celie to initiate change in all these aspects of her life. And in changing herself, Celie helps to change her entire community. Political change in *The Color Purple* occurs because of life-affirmation. From my point of view then one of the most important political statements of *Color Purple* is its emphasis on the right to happiness for even the most oppressed of us all, for poor black women, and that our happiness can be imagined, pursued, achieved through the growing strength of the community of black women:

> We are the Ones We have been Waiting for.

From her first novel, *The Third Life of Grange Copeland* to her most recent, *The Color Purple,* Walker shows how lasting political change is impossible without personal transformation. But she also emphasizes in her work that personal change is inevitably linked to a community of changers. The individual cannot effect lasting change for the self without some corresponding societal change. And for Walker, personal change is most indelibly achieved through the process of working for change with others.

In *Grange Copeland,* change begins to occur for the Copeland family when Grange, like so many others, goes North, the traditional escape for Southern blacks since slavery. When he discovers, as did so many others, the ineffectiveness of this solution he begins to work for change in his granddaughter's life in the South. But though his personal transformation has meaning, he is killed by the system he opposes. In ending the novel with Civil Rights workers, a growing community of changers, Walker suggests that other Granges are beginning to come together in their need and desire to change their society. Walker's second novel *Meridian* explores that historical development for the novel is as much about the principles of the Civil Rights and Black Power movements as it is about her characters. Meridian, her major protagonist, both affirms and challenges the underlying concepts of these movements of the 60s. As a black woman, as a black mother, she struggles to be free within herself even as she encounters sexism, elitism, violence within the Movement. The themes of *The Color Purple* build on Meridian's pilgrimage to freedom, for Walker's most recent novel explores basic tenets of the women's movement of the 1970s. Thus she protests violence against women and racist violence among women, while celebrating the bonding that women must develop in their struggles to achieve selfhood. Too, she expands feminist thought by placing the erotic, the right to satisfaction in women's lives at the center of the novel. Black women loving each together and working together are the community of changers in *The Color Purple,* through which individual black women and men come to demand and experience more of life.

Walker therefore scrutinizes historical movements that have had significant effects on the lives of black women. In celebrating these movements she both celebrates and critiques them. Walker's peculiar sound as a political writer has much to do with her contrariness, her willingness at all turns to challenge the fashionable beliefs of the day, to examine them in the light of black women's herstory, of her own experiences, and of dearly won principles that she has previously challenged and absorbed. It is significant that 'the survival whole' of black people which Walker focused on in *Grange Copeland* is extended to the value of life she illuminated in *Meridian* and is further developed into the relationship between freedom and happiness in *Color Purple,* particularly for her women characters. While Margaret Copeland and men are destroyed in *The Third Life of Grange Copeland,* Meridian 'expands her mind with action.' But in pursuit of spiritual health, Meridian goes through a period of 'madness,' paralysis of the body, then self-abnegation. Celie completes the cycle of Walker's women. Like Mem Copeland she is physically abused; like Meridian she goes through a painful period of healing. Celie however comes to full bloom in her entire self, physically and spiritually.

Survival whole—the value of all life—the right to happiness—these are increments in an ever-expanding philosophy of Walker's fiction. And for her, these goals can only be imagined as possible, pursued, and believed in, if we take responsibility for ourselves, and undergo the process of struggle historically, personally and collectively necessary to make ourselves physically, passionately, spiritually healthy. Only then can we achieve a sense of the oneness of creation, as symbolized by the color purple. Further, for Walker, black women must do this for themselves and each other, if the unnatural hierarchies of sexism, racism, and economic exploitation are to be eliminated: 'We are the ones we have been waiting for.'

Susan Willis (essay date 1987)

SOURCE: "Alice Walker's Women," in *Specifying: Black Women Writing the American Experience,* The University of Wisconsin Press, 1987, pp. 110-28.

[*In the following essay, Willis discusses the women of Walker's fiction, in particular Meridian, and their relationship to their history and community. She asserts that revolution can only succeed when an individual commits herself to the community.*]

> Be nobody's darling
> Be an outcast.
> Take the contradictions
> Of your life

> And wrap around
> You like a shawl,
> To parry stones
> To keep you warm.

> What the black Southern writer
> inherits as a natural right is
> a sense of community.

The strength of Alice Walker's writing derives from the author's inexorable recognition of her place in history; the sensitivity of her work, from her profound sense of community; its beauty, from her commitment to the future. Many readers associate Alice Walker with her most recent novel, *The Color Purple,* for which she won a Pulitzer Prize. But the best place to begin to define the whole of her writing is with the semiautobiographical novel, *Meridian.* In that novel I suggest we first consider a very minor character: "Wile Chile." For "Wile Chile" is not gratuitous, not an aberrant whim on the part of the author, but an epigrammatic representation of all the women Walker brings to life. I think this is how Walker intended it, precisely because she begins telling about Meridian by describing her confrontation with "Wile Chile," a thirteen-year-old ghetto urchin, who from the age of about five or six, when she was first spotted, has fed and clothed herself out of garbage cans. More slippery than a "greased pig" and as wary as any stray, the Wild Child is virtually uncatchable. When it becomes obvious that the Wild Child is pregnant, Meridian takes it upon herself to bring her into the fold. Baiting her with glass beads and cigarettes, she eventually catches "Wile Chile," leads her back to the campus, bathes and feeds her, then sets about finding a home for her. However, Meridian's role as mother comes to an abrupt end when "Wile Chile" escapes and bolts into the street where she is struck by a speeding car.

If we consider the story of "Wile Chile" against the events that shape Meridian's development from childhood (the daughter of schoolteachers), through college, into the Civil Rights movement and finally to embark on her own more radical commitment to revolutionary praxis, the two pages devoted to the Wild Child seem at most a colorful digression. Her only language comprised of obscenities and farts, "Wile Chile" is Meridian's social antithesis. Nevertheless, the story of "Wile Chile" is central to our understanding of *Meridian* and the woman whose name is the title of this book, for it includes certain basic features, present in different forms in all the anecdotal incidents that make up the novel and through which Meridian herself must struggle in the process of her self-affirmation.

When Meridian drags the stomach-heavy "Wile Chile" back to her room, she puts herself in the role of mother and enacts a mode of mothering that smacks of liberal bourgeois sentimentality. On the other hand, "Wile Chile"'s own impending motherhood represents absolute abandonment to biological contingency. These are only two of the many versions of womanhood that the problem of mothering will provoke in the book. Although Meridian and "Wile Chile" do not share a common social ground, they come together on one point, and that is the possibility of being made pregnant. For "Wile Chile" and Meridian both, conception articulates oppression, to which "Wile Chile" succumbs and against which Meridian struggles to discover whether it is possible for a black woman to emerge as a self and at the same time fulfill the burdens of motherhood.

The story of "Wile Chile" also raises the question of Meridian's relationship to the academic institution and the black community that surrounds the university. Her outrageous behavior causes Meridian (and the reader) to reflect on the function of the university as a social institution whose primary role is to assimilate bright young black women, who might otherwise be dangerously marginal, to a dominant white culture. "Wile Chile"'s unpermissible language draws attention to the tremendous pressures also placed on Meridian to become a "lady" patterned after white European cultural norms. This is not a cosmetic transformation, but one that separates the individual from her class and community and forever inscribes her within the bourgeois world. That the university serves bourgeois class interests is dramatized when Saxon College students and members of the local black community attempt to hold "Wile Chile"'s funeral on the campus. Barred from entering the university, the funeral procession is isolated and defined as "other" in the same way that the local neighborhood, which ought to be the university's community of concern, is instead its ghetto.

In *Meridian,* childbearing is consistently linked to images of murder and suicide. In this, the figure of the Wild Child is as much a paradigm for the book's main characters, Meridian and Lynne, as it is for another minor anecdotal figure, Fast Mary. As the students at Saxon College tell it, Fast Mary secretly gave birth in a tower room, chopped her newborn babe to bits, and washed it down the toilet. When her attempt to conceal the birth fails, her parents lock her up in a room without windows where Fast Mary subsequently hangs herself. In posing the contradictory social constraints that demand simultaneously that a woman be both a virgin and sexually active, the parable of Fast Mary prefigures the emotional tension Meridian herself will experience as a mother, expressing it in fantasies of murder and suicide. The tales of "Wile Chile" and Fast Mary also pose the problem of the individual's relationship to the group. Fast Mary's inability to call on her sister students and her final definitive isolation at the hands of her parents raise questions Meridian will also confront: is there a community of support? And is communication possible between such a community and the individual who is seen as a social iconoclast?

The problem of communication, and specifically the question of language, is at the heart of another of *Meridian's* anecdotal characters: Louvinie, a slave woman from West Africa whose parents excelled in a particular form of storytelling, one designed to ensnare anyone guilty of having committed a crime. Louvinie's duties as a slave are to cook and mind the master's children. The latter includes her own superb mastery of the art of storytelling, which for Louvinie, as for all oppressed peoples, functions to keep traditional culture alive and to provide a context for radical social practice. The radical potential of language is abundantly clear when the master's weakhearted young son dies of heart failure in the middle of one of Louvinie's gruesome tales.

At the level of overt content, the story of Louvinie focuses on the function of language; in its structure, it reproduces the features associated in the book with motherhood. Louvinie, who does not have children of her own, nevertheless functions as a mother to the master's offspring. She, like "Wile Chile," Fast Mary, even Meridian and Lynne, kills the child defined structurally as her own. In more narrow terms, Louvinie provides a model closer to the way Meridian will resolve her life. Her actual childlessness suggests in asexual terms Meridian's choice not to be fertile and bear children. Moreover, when Louvinie murders the child in her charge it is clearly a politically contestatory act, which is not the case for either "Wile Chile" or Fast Mary—but is true for Meridian when she chooses to abort her child.

Louvinie's punishment rejoins the problem of language, as the master cuts out her tongue. Louvinie's response is to bury her tongue under a small magnolia tree, which, generations later, grows to be the largest magnolia in the country and stands at the center of Saxon College. As a natural metaphor, the tree is in opposition to the two social institutions—the plantation and the university—and suggests an alternative to their definition of black history and language. Just as the university excludes women like "Wile Chile," so too does it seek to silence black folk culture typified by Louvinie's stories. The magnolia casts the university in stark relief, exposes its version of history as a lie, its use of language as collaborative with the forces of domination.

The magnolia also provides a figural bridge linking the struggle of black women from slavery to the present. In the past, it offered a hiding place for escaped slaves and in the present its enormous trunk and branches provide a platform for classes. Named The Sojourner, the magnolia conjures up the presence of another leader of black women, who, like Louvinie, used language in the struggle for liberation. In this way, Walker builds a network of women, some mythic like Louvinie, some real like Sojourner Truth, as the context for Meridian's affirmation and radicalization.

As the stories of "Wile Chile" and Fast Mary demonstrate,

anecdotes are the basic narrative units in Walker's fiction. They reveal how Walker has managed to keep the storytelling tradition among black people alive in the era of the written narrative. The anecdotes are pedagogical. They allow the reader to experience the same structural features, recast with each telling, in a different historical and social setting. Each telling demands that the college students (and the reader) examine and define their relationship to the group in a more profound way than in the explicitly political gatherings where each is asked to state what she will do for the revolution. In this way, Walker defines story writing in the radical tradition that storytelling has had among black people.

It is not surprising that language is crucial to Meridian's process of becoming. From slavery to the present, black women have spoken out against their oppression, and when possible, written their version of history. However, their narratives have fared less well in the hands of publishers and the reading public than those written by black men. Only very recently and with the growing interest in writers like Morrison, Marshall, and Walker have black women enjoyed better access to recognized channels of communication outside those of home and church. As testament to the very long struggle for recognition waged by black women and the deep oppression out of which their struggle began, the literature is full of characters like Hurston's Janie Woods, whose husband sees and uses her like a "mule" and will not allow her to speak, to Walker's most recent female character, Celie, in ***The Color Purple,*** also denied a voice, who out of desperation for meaningful dialogue writes letters to God. For black women writers, the problem of finding a viable literary language—outside of the male canon defined predominantly by Richard Wright—has generated a variety of literary strategies. Morrison's solution was to develop a highly metaphorical language, whereas for Walker the solution has been the anecdotal narrative, which because of its relationship to storytelling and the family more closely approximates a woman's linguistic practice than does Morrison's very stylized discourse.

The fact is no black woman has ever been without language, not even the tongueless Louvinie, who uses the magical preparation and planting of her tongue to speak louder and longer than words. The question of language is not meaningful except in relation to the community. Louvinie's example affirms that the community of struggle will always exist and that the actions of a single black woman join the network of all. In contrast, "Wile Chile" represents a negation of the individual's need for community. With language reduced to farts and swears, hers is a one-way communication whose every enunciation denies integration with the group and proclaims her absolute marginality. Contrary to the Wild Child's self-destructive marginality, Meridian must define a form of oneness with herself that will allow her to speak and work with the community and at the same time will prevent be-

coming submerged by it. Meridian's quest for a language and a praxis is analogous to Walker's work as a writer, which demands both distance from and integration with the people.

When, in the book's first chapter, Meridian is asked if she could kill for the revolution, she finds herself unable to make the required revolutionary affirmation and defines instead what will be her more difficult form of revolutionary praxis: "I'll go back to the people." People means the South, the small towns, the communities for whom the Civil Rights movement passed by too quickly to transform embedded racist and sexist practices. In this, she is the antithesis of "Wile Chile," who never was a part of any community and hence can never return to one.

Meridian's decision is her way of defining the single most common feature in fiction by black women writers: that of return to the community. From Zora Neale Hurston's *Their Eyes Were Watching God,* to the recent novels by Toni Morrison, the trajectory of departure and return is the common means for describing a woman's development and structuring the novel. In every instance, return raises the fundamental question of whether a community of support exists and what will be the individual's relationship to it.

For Morrison's Sula, return articulates the tragic plight of an extremely sensitive and perceptive black woman, in many ways ahead of her time, who goes to college, sees the world and a fair number of men, only to find herself dispossessed of place. Although the community of her girlhood has undergone economic progress, neither the town's new golf course nor its convalescent hospital testify to deep social transformation. Sula returns home to find her girlhood friend deeply stigmatized by male sexual domination. Traumatized by his abandonment, she has become a sterile shell living out a life whose only excuse is her moral and economic enslavement to her children. There is no community of possibility for Sula, who dies alone with her dreams and aspirations—a halcyon symbol of a future womanhood that can never be the basis for a community in this society.

Walker's rendering of return involves elements present in both Hurston's tale of Janie Woods and Morrison's account of Sula, but set in an entirely different context: the Civil Rights movement, which historically was not a factor for Hurston and geographically does not significantly enter into Morrison's tales, which are usually set in the Midwest. Only in Walker, a writer of the Southern black experience, do we come to understand how psychically important the Civil Rights movement was—not that it solved anything, but it definitely marks the moment after which nothing can ever be the same. Meridian's mission is to help discover the shape of the future.

Return is the developmental imperative in all Walker's novels, where the journey over geographic space is a metaphor for personal growth and, in a larger sense, historical transformation. In her first novel, *The Third Life of Grange Copeland,* Walker's conception of geographic space embodies a dialectical understanding of history. When Grange Copeland abandons wife and child to seek self and fortune in New York City, he leaves behind a rural community historically representative of the plantation system for the North and the industrial mode. The third moment of the dialectic is marked by Grange's return to the South, not as a penniless sharecropper, but with money in his pocket to buy his own land. The farm Grange brings into being suggests Walker's vision of a very different basis for black community, one that has experienced and transcended two forms of enslavement: first to the plantation, then to wage labor. In Walker's vision of the future, property ownership will not be for the purpose of accumulation as it is under capitalism, but will provide for the satisfaction of basic human material and spiritual needs.

The epic of Grange Copeland is doubly transformational in that the character who will bear his experience into the future (both of the distant past that Grange passes along in the form of folktales and of the more recent past that Grange has directly known) is not a male heir, as more traditional literature might have it, but his granddaughter, whose coming-of-age is marked by sit-ins, voter registration, and the speeches of Martin Luther King, Jr. His own life marred by his struggle against bigotry, his own acts of violence, and the terrible racism and sexism of which he has been both a victim and an agent, Grange cannot be the embodiment of the future. Rather, some great moment of rupture from the past is needed, and this Walker achieves in the transition from the male to the female principle. The novel ends on a note of affirmation—but not without uncertainty over the shape of the future. Ruth, Grange's granddaughter, is an adolescent and her future as well as the post-Civil Rights black community in the South cannot yet be told, but is, like the sixteen-year-old Ruth, on the threshold of its becoming.

In geographic strokes less broad, Walker's most recent novel, *The Color Purple,* also articulates personal and historical transition. In it, Celie is married as an adolescent to a man who makes her cook and keep house, tend the fields and look after his unruly children from a previous marriage, and who pretty much conceives of her as a "mule." Celie's abuse is deepened by the fact that before marriage she had already been repeatedly raped by the man she calls "father" and made to bear his children only to have them taken from her soon after birth. If there is to be any transformation in this book, its starting point is the absolute rock bottom of a woman's economic and sexual enslavement in a male-dominated and racist society.

The possibility of Celie's transformation is brought about by her journey away from the rural backwater and to the big city, Memphis, where she comes to support herself—not by means of wage labor (it is clear that Walker sees no hope for liberation in the transition to the industrial mode)—by means of learning a trade that is both artistic and necessary. She designs and sews custom pants.

If Celie's transformation is to be thorough, it must be not just economic, but sexual as well. Celie's ability to question what would otherwise be her "lot in life" and to break with her passive acceptance of her husband's domination is made possible by her friendship and eventual lesbian relationship with a black blues singer, Shug Avery. Unlike the monstrous inequality between husband and wife, theirs is a reciprocal relationship—Celie giving of herself to heal the sick and exhausted Shug (even though Celie's husband has for years been enamored of the singer), and Shug giving of herself, patiently and lovingly teaching Celie to know the joys of her own body and to follow the intuition of her mind. Neither the economics of pants-making nor the sexuality of lesbianism represents modes of enslavement as do the economics of industrial capitalism and the sexuality of male-dominated heterosexual relationships. At book's end Celie is neither seen as a pantsmaker in the way one might see an autoworker as a particular species of human, nor as a lesbian lover the way one sees a wife and mother.

Out of Walker's three novels, *The Color Purple* defines return in the most auspicious terms and offers not a prescription for but a suggestion of what a nonsexist, nonracist community might be. No longer a voiceless chattel to her man, Celie is able to converse with her husband. Having undergone liberation in both economic and sexual terms, she is for the first time perceived not as a domestic slave or the means toward male sexual gratification but as a whole woman: witty, resourceful, caring, wise, sensitive, and sensual. And her home—the site of an open and extended family where family and friends merge—suggests the basis for a wholly new community. The Fourth of July picnic that concludes the book and reunites Celie with her sister and children redefines the traditional family group in the context of a radically transformed household.

For Meridian, the autobiographical embodiment of Walker herself, coming of age in the sixties does not offer a free ticket, but provides an atmosphere of confrontation and the questioning of contradiction with which the individual must grapple.

—*Susan Willis*

Of all of Walker's novels, *Meridian* offers the clearest view of the process of radicalization. For Meridian, the autobiographical embodiment of Walker herself, coming of age in the sixties does not offer a free ticket, but provides an atmosphere of confrontation and the questioning of contradiction with which the individual must grapple. Early in the book it becomes clear that one of the most profound ideologies to be confronted and transcended is the acceptance of mystical explanations for political realities. Meridian's childhood is steeped in Indian lore, the walls of her room papered with photographs of the great Indian leaders from Sitting Bull and Crazy Horse to the romanticized Hiawatha. Moreover, her father's farm includes an ancient Indian burial mound, its crest shaped like a serpent, where, in the coil of its tail, Meridian achieves a state of "ecstasy." Absorbed in a dizzying spin, she feels herself lifted out of her body while all around her—family and countryside—are caught up in the spinning whirlpool of her consciousness. It is not odd that Walker focuses on mystical experience. After all, this is a book about the sixties whose counterculture opened the door to more than one form of mysticism. It is also not strange that Meridian's mystical experience derives from Native American culture, given the long cohistorical relationship between blacks and Indians in the southeastern United States (their radical union goes back to the time of cimarrons and Seminoles).

However, ecstasy is not the answer. Although Meridian will learn from the mystical experience, it will not be sufficient to her life's work to rely on the practice of retreat into the ecstatic trance. What, then, of the historic link between Indians and blacks? If, in the course of the book, Meridian learns to transcend ecstasy, is this a denial of her (and her people's) relationship to the Indian people?

Definitely not. The book's epigraph gives another way of defining Meridian's relationship to Native Americans, which the great lesson taught by her radicalization will bring into reality. Taken from *Black Elk Speaks,* this is the epigraph:

> I did not know then how much was ended. When I look back now . . . I can still see the butchered women and children lying heaped and scattered all along the crooked gulch as plain as when I saw them with eyes still young. And I can see that something else died there in the bloody mud, and was buried in the blizzard. A people's dream died there. It was a beautiful dream . . . the nation's hoop is broken and scattered. There is no center any longer, and the sacred tree is dead.

Black Elk's words remember the massacre of Wounded Knee, which for Indian people was the brutal cancellation of their way of life. The dream Black Elk refers to is the vision he, as a holy man, had of his people and their world: "The leaves on the trees, the grasses on the hills and in the valleys, the waters in the creeks and in the rivers and the lakes, the four-legged and the two-legged and the wings of the air—all danced together to the music of the stallion's song."

This is a vision of a community of man and nature, which Black Elk, as a holy man, must bring into being—not individually, but through the collective practice of the group. As he sees it, the nation is a "hoop" and "Everything an Indian does is in a circle, and that is because the Power of the World always works in circles, and everything tries to be round." These are images of a community's wholeness, which Meridian takes as her political paradigm—not the particulars of Indian culture; not the beads that hippies grafted on their white middle-class identities, not the swoons of ecstasy—but the Indian view of community, in which the holy man or seer is not marginal, but integral to the group. So when Meridian says she will "go back to the people" and when she leads them in demonstration against racist practices, she enacts Black Elk's formula for praxis. As an intellectual and a political activist, she understands that the individual's inspiration for social change can only be realized through the group's collective activity.

By far the greatest test of Meridian's radicalization is to overcome the social and sexual categories ascribed to all women, and black women in particular. Because she does not choose the lesbian alternative as Celie does in *The Color Purple,* Meridian's struggle is within and against heterosexual relationships. As Walker describes it, the two most fundamental categories of womanhood defined under male-dominated heterosexuality are bitches and wives. The first category is composed of white women; the second is made up of black women and is essentially the same as saying "mothers." The bitch in the book is Lynne, who in many ways is Meridian's antithetical parallel. A white woman, from the North, Jewish, a student and fellow Civil Rights worker, Lynne is the third factor in a triangular love relationship that includes Meridian and Truman, also a Civil Rights worker and the man both Lynne and Meridian love. The tension produced by love and jealousy is the ground on which Walker examines social categories and defines the process through which Meridian eventually liberates herself from male sexual domination.

Meridian begins her adult life a high-school dropout and teenage mother married to a restaurant busboy. Motherhood for Meridian is fraught with contradictory impulses. Caressing her child's body, she imagines that her fingers have scratched his flesh to the bone. At other times, she thinks of drowning her baby; when not fantasizing her child's murder, she dreams of suicide. Murder and suicide are the emotional articulation of social realities. This is the experience of futility—the mother's purposelessness as an individual, whose only function is to add yet another little body to the massive black underclass, and the child's bankrupt future, another faceless menial laborer.

In contrast to the futility is the one moment—equally profound for its singularity—when Meridian beholds her child with loving wonderment and sees him as a spontaneous, unasked-for gift, absolutely unique and whole. In response to the possibility for her child's selfhood and in recognition of her own desperate need to redefine her life's course, Meridian chooses to give her child away when, as if by miracle, her high IQ makes her a college candidate. In relinquishing her child, Meridian recognizes her relationship to the history of black motherhood, which, under slavery, defined the black woman's struggle to keep her children as a radical act, making the mother liable for a beating or worse; as well as to the time of freedom, which, in giving black women the right to keep their children, provided the fetters of enslavement to poverty and sexism. Meridian's mother is very much a part of this tradition. Although morally outraged at her daughter's decision to "abandon" her child, the mother exemplifies the plight of black mothers, "buried alive, walled away from her own life, brick by brick" with the birth of each successive child.

In giving her child away, Meridian makes it clear that mothering, as it has been defined by heterosexual relationships in racist society, is the single most insurmountable obstacle to a black woman's self-affirmation. Only by refusing ever to be a mother in the particular can she carve out a new social function, which includes a form of mothering, but in the larger sense of an individual's caring for her community. We get a sense of what this might involve when Meridian first appears in the novel leading a band of children in demonstration. But for the most part, Meridian's practice is less an indication of future possibilities and more a critique of the way heterosexual relationships have individualized a woman's relationship to *her* children, making them *her* property. This is the mother-child relationship that Meridian violently denies for herself when, becoming pregnant for a second time, she chooses to abort her lover's baby. Her decision is also a dramatic refutation of Truman's overtly male-chauvinist invitation to "have [his] beautiful black babies" for the revolution. For Meridian, the subsequent decision to have her tubes tied represents another step in the direction toward a new form of womanhood where heterosexuality will not be the means toward oppression but a mode within which sexual partners will one day set each other free. But for the time being, her espousal of a selfless, nunlike celibacy suggests that the day is a long way off.

For Lynne, however, heterosexuality, complicated by the pressures on the biracial couple in a racist society, leads not to liberation and the affirmation of a new social mode, but rather the rock-bottom debasement of self. Notwithstanding her marriage to Truman, Lynne will always be the white bitch, and notwithstanding their child's African name, Camara, the mulatto does not represent a hope for a nonracist future. This is because American society—before, during, and after Civil

Rights—remains racist and sexist. Camara's brutal murder graphically puts an end to any liberal thoughts about a new, hybridized society of the future. The death of this child—and all the book's children, either by abortion or murder—dramatizes Walker's radical intuition that the future as something positive and new cannot be produced out of genetic or personal terms, but demands, as Black Elk saw it, the selfless involvement of the individual with the community. When Truman criticizes Meridian for never having loved him, she responds, "I set you free." Meridian has chosen to relinquish personal and sexual relationships, which in this society cannot help but be the means and form of a woman's oppression, as a way of advancing her own struggle—and that of her loved ones—toward their liberation.

For the most part, Walker's writing is not figural, but there is in *Meridian* one very important metaphor, whose function is to synthesize the many levels of Meridian's struggle. This is the significance of Meridian's sickness, which goes by no medical name but is characterized by dizziness, temporary blindness, swooning faints, loss of hair, paralysis, and general bodily weakness. The illness strikes Meridian immediately after she first sees the Wild Child. Because many of the symptoms coincide with her childhood experiences of mystical ecstasy, the illness is a link between her early confrontation with cultural ideology and her later struggle as an adult against social and sexual oppression, typified by the plight of the Wild Child. The illness allows the reader to perceive at the level of experience the absolute energy-draining work of political praxis, as with each demonstration Meridian must struggle to regain her vanquished strength, patiently forcing her paralyzed limbs to work again. Meridian's trademark, a visored cap to cover her baldness, articulates the contradictory notions attached to a black woman's hair—her crowning glory and sign of sexuality—for which the head rag was both a proclamation and refutation. With each confrontation with white male authority—be it under the abortionist's knife or facing down an army tank—Meridian's swoon and faint proclaim not surrender but absolute commitment to the struggle. Coming back to consciousness, Meridian awakens to find the struggle—an ongoing process—renewed on a higher, more exacting level.

At the novel's conclusion, Walker gives us to understand that Meridian has mastered not the whole struggle but herself in that struggle. Rid of the sickness, her woolly head restored, she discards her cap and packs her bag to set out once again on the road to confrontation. Although one individual's coming to grips with self can be a lesson for others, it cannot be their solution. The novel closes on Truman, dizzily crawling into Meridian's sleeping bag, pulling her cap upon his head, and accepting for himself the long process of her struggle. The transition from Meridian to Truman lifts the book out of its sexual polarization and suggests that everyone regardless of socially ascribed sex roles, must work to deessentialize sex. Now it will be Truman who works for the community and in its care to bring the collective dream into being.

Although not by his choosing, Truman, at book's end, is no longer capable of being perceived either as a lover or a father. The course of Meridian's struggle to liberate herself from sexually prescribed categories has been the means for Truman's unwitting relinquishment of positions from which men have traditionally exerted domination. The transcendence of sexual domination undermines other forms of domination including racism, but this does not mean that race itself has been neutralized. Rather, blackness is affirmed. Meridian's new crop of woolly hair testifies directly to her renewal as a black woman. Nor has transcendence brought about Meridian's separation from the community, whose coherent presence has always been the novel's core. In contrast to the strength of the black presence, white people enter *Meridian* incidentally and are always perceived as individuals, bereft of any relationship with their own community. Almost freakish in their singularity and behavior, white people in general closely approximate their symbolic representation in the form of a mummified white woman, a sideshow attraction, whose husband carts her from town to town earning money off her exhibition.

Walker's affirmation of blackness uses racially specific traits not to define a form of black racism but to delineate the look of a class. Black is the color of the underclass. And all Walker's women are peasants, from Celie in *The Color Purple,* to Ruth's mother and grandmother in *The Third Life of Grange Copeland* and Meridian's female forebears. Bound to the land and their husbands (or fathers), worn by toil in the fields and the demands of childbearing, these women are the underclass of the underclass. This is why literacy and education are so crucial to the way Walker depicts the process of liberation. Her radical understanding of education lies at the heart of literacy campaigns from revolutionary Angola to Grenada and Nicaragua. Clearly, the ability to raise questions, to objectify contradictions, is only possible when Celie begins writing her letters. Similarly, for Meridian, education (notwithstanding its inspiration in liberalism) and the academic institution (notwithstanding its foundation in elitism) offer the means for confronting social and sexual contradictions that she, as a black teenage mother, would not have been able to articulate—either for herself or anyone else.

Walker elaborated on the importance of class and the role of women in class politics in a workshop on black women writers held at Yale University (spring 1982). She stressed the significance of rediscovering Agnes Smedley, particularly Smedley's description of Chinese women during the years of the Revolution. Both Smedley and Walker would agree that the radical transformation of society can only be achieved when the bottom-most rung attains liberation; in fact, the wellspring of revolution is the rebellion of the peasant class.

This is the great historical lesson of revolution in the twentieth century from China to Cuba and Central America. And it lies at the heart of all Smedley's "sketches" of women revolutionaries, who, when their class background and education more closely approximate Meridian's, must, like Walker's character, turn to the people and be one with their struggle. The individual who becomes separate from the peasantry is truly lost, like Walker's Lynne, who never outgrew her liberal background and the tendency to see black people as works of art; and Smedley's the "Living Dead," women reclaimed by the aristocracy and abandoned to opium dreams or so traumatized by the White Terror that they wander about dazed.

There is a great deal of similarity between the real-life Smedley and the fictional Meridian—and her autobiographical inspiration, Walker herself. Smedley, born in the South (Missouri), was also a peasant woman. Her childhood grounded in poverty, she, although white, knew a form of enslavement when, at the age of eleven, she was hired out as a domestic. Education and, later, leftist politics were her way up and out of poverty, just as writing was her way back to the people. Always an advocate of feminism, both in journalism and in fiction, Smedley, like Walker, depicts the contradictions of womanhood as they relate to abortion, birth control, and mothering. Finally, although Smedley's chosen community was revolutionary China, her relationship to that community as a foreigner and an intellectual bears striking similarity to Meridian's relationship to her community.

Perhaps the best way to characterize all three—Smedley, Meridian, and Walker—is with the title of one of Walker's collections of poems: *Revolutionary Petunias.* It captures the spirit of revolutionary women both in beauty and in struggle. Certainly, there was a great deal of flamboyance in Agnes Smedley as she donned a Red Army uniform and marched into Xi'an. Rather than a simplistic identification with the Communist forces, her act was intended to draw the attention of the world press (which it did) and to articulate a joyous celebration of struggle (which it still does) in the linguistics of gesture and playacting often used by women in lieu of those modes of communication, like speech and writing, that have been traditionally defined by male discourse. This is a form of revolutionary praxis very like the moment when Meridian, at the head of a pack of kids, faces down the town militia and a World War II tank. Not to be confused with flower children and the politics of counterculture, "Revolutionary Petunias" are those women, who, with grace, strength, and imagination, have put their lives on the line.

J. Charles Washington (essay date Spring 1988)

SOURCE: "Positive Black Male Images in Alice Walker's

Fiction," in *Obsidian II,* Vol. 3, No. 1, Spring, 1988, pp. 23-48.

[*In the following essay, Washington asserts that Walker does present some positive black male images in her work, and that her criticism of black men and women is in the spirit of helping them to grow and improve.*]

Now that the controversy over Alice Walker's Pulitzer Prize-winning novel **The Color Purple** has subsided, it might be worthwhile to re-examine her fiction, specifically, the short stories, in an attempt to resolve the issue of her purported attack on Black males. In particular, her critics charged her with presenting a grossly negative image of Black men, who were portrayed as mean, cruel, or violent, entirely without redeeming qualities. In a review of the film of the novel, the *Washington Post* of February 5, 1986, stated: "But what is being heatedly discussed is the characterization of Black males as cruel, unaffectionate, domineering slap-happy oafs." Gloria Steinem, a major source of these discussions, writes in the June 1982, issue of *Ms.* magazine, that "a disproportionate number of her (Walker's) hurtful, negative reviews have been by Black men."

This "disproportionate number" is significant, but only because, according to Trudier Harris, "black women critics have . . . been reluctant to offer . . . criticisms of it." The reason for this reluctance, Harris explains, is that "To complain about the novel is to commit treason against Black women writers, yet there is much in it that deserves complaint." With a tone that reveals the high degree of distress and frustration she feels, Harris complains not only about the negative, unrealistic and stereotypical portraits of Black men and women the novel presents, but also about its overall thematic development:

> The novel gives validity to all the white racist's notions of pathology in Black communities. For these spectator readers, Black fathers and father-figures are viewed as being immoral, sexually unrestrained. Black males and females form units without the benefit of marriage, or they easily dissolve marriages in order to form less structured, more promiscuous relationships. Black men beat their wives—or attempt to—and neglect, ignore, or abuse their children. When they cannot control their wives through beatings, they violently dispatch them.

Thus Harris's article suggests that the objections to Walker's portraits of Black men are not limited to Black men.

Though this charge came about primarily as a result of the novel, negative male characters appeared in Walker's work long before its publication. Her first novel, **The Third Life of Grange Copeland,** published in 1970, some 13 years be-

fore **Purple,** is a good example, yet many of those who cried the loudest seem to have taken no notice of this work. Perhaps the best-known voice in the chorus of Walker critics belongs to novelist David Bradley (author of *The Chaneysville Incident*). Interestingly, he does not object to the male images in **Purple,** but in a long article written for the June 8, 1984, issue of the *New York Times Magazine,* he expresses dismay at "some of the things" he finds in Walker's collection of essays **In Search of Our Mothers' Gardens,** which lends further support to the criticism and controversy the novel aroused and, because of his reputation as a novelist and critic, gives his article a quasi official stamp of approval:

> But there is much that dismays me. Some of these things can be written off as polemical excess. . . . But other excesses are more troubling because they form, it seems, a pattern indicating Alice Walker has a *high level of enmity toward Black men* [emphasis added].

As part of his support for this contention, Bradley cites Walker's "dismissal and disdain" of individual Black male writers such as Richard Wright and Jean Toomer.

An examination of Walker's works reveals what many of her critics have failed to see: that they also contain positive Black male images. Bradley, in the *New York Times Magazine* piece, comments on the positive types of Black male characters he has observed:

> Black men in Alice Walker's fiction . . . seem capable of goodness only when they become old like Grange Copeland, or paralyzed and feminized, like Truman Held. If they are not thus rendered symbolically impotent, they are figures of malevolence, like Ruth's murderous father, Brownfield. . . .

However, depending on how one looks at them, that is, the moral/social standard one uses, there are other positive male characters in Walker's fiction who do not fall into these categories. In contrast to the negative label connoting characters who are inherently evil, positive as used here means that there is within them the potential for growth, development and change. This is not to say, however, that they are without human flaws. Such characters are found in several of the short stories in Walker's first collection **In Love and Trouble.** Her presentation of both negative and positive Black male images, then, would seem to indicate that she is not carrying a feminist banner (or "womanist," her term for a Black feminist) with which she intentionally flagellates Black men.

Having established that Walker hates Black men, and apparently well versed in Freudian psychology, it seems natural that Bradley would locate the cause of Walker's enmity within her family, that is, in her hatred for her father. Similar to his handling of Walker's alleged dismissal of Toomer, however, Bradley chooses particular words of Walker to prove *his* point, when the truth is otherwise. Building his case against her, he cites her disparaging remarks about Toomer the man, which moreover had to do with racism not sexism, while de-emphasizing her favorable remarks about his work. In fact, what Walker does in *Mothers' Gardens* is castigate Toomer for his racial ambivalence, while praising his work highly, concluding with: "*I love it (Cane) passionately;* could not possibly exist without it."

Similarly, Bradley presents only half the truth regarding Walker's feelings about her father, ignoring the significance of the change in them that occurred later in her life. For though in her youth she did harbor strong resentment against her father, blaming him for her family's poverty, as an adult she came to realize that "he was a poor man exploited by the rural middleclass rich, like millions of peasants the world over."

The charge against Walker cannot be supported, for it is based on far too simplistic a view of an artist. Though her work is woman-centered, its wider focus is on the struggle of Black people—men and women—to re-claim their own lives. As she writes in *Mothers' Gardens,* "I am preoccupied with the spiritual survival, the survival *whole* of my people. But beyond that, I am committed to exploring the insanities, the loyalties, and the triumphs of Black women." Her exclusive concentration on what used to be called the weaker sex who, if no longer as weak as they once were, are still the most oppressed in society does not mean that she is anti-male, but that she has less time and energy to devote to exploring more fully the problems of men or the common causes of the oppression of both.

This commitment to Black women—itself an act of love—no less than her treatment of Black men, is a likely basis of the negative criticism Walker has received. For much of it is an expression of homophobia triggered by any notion of women loving women. In the eyes of some readers, male and female, its "logical" conclusion is lesbianism equated with a virulent hatred of men. Many of these individuals became convinced of the correctness of their reasoning when in *Purple* Walker not only presents a lesbian relationship but also shows it to be extremely fulfilling.

What these readers fail—or refuse—to realize, however, is that for all of the suffering and violence Celie experiences from Black men, she does not grow to hate them; in fact, her eventual rejection of them is no more permanent than her brief flirtation with lesbianism. Both are simply steps in the process of learning to love herself and finding her own identity, which is the author's main concern. Of equal significance to her is the means of strategy by which this growth takes place—that is, women loving and reaching out to sup-

port each other. The strategy is not fail-safe. Some errors are expected, but if they occur, the author implies, the moral risk is worth the human gain.

It is clear that Walker's commitment to women has nothing to do with sex at all. And the same can be said of the homophobia that fuels the controversy. On the contrary, both have everything to do with power—women's gain and men's loss of it. For their own empowerment and control of their own destiny, women must commit themselves to each other and to creating their own identity. The failure "to define ourselves," Audre Lorde writes in *Sister Outsider,* is that "we will be defined by others—for their use and to our detriment." Homophobia, the handmaiden of sexism, becomes a useful tool in men's efforts to define and control women. Additionally, Lorde writes, "the red herring of lesbian baiting is being used . . . to obscure the true face of facism/sexism."

Far from being a purely emotional reaction, homophobia reveals itself to have a political dimension, seen in the efficacious role it plays in maintaining power or the status quo. Frequently it is used by some men who attempt to rule Black women by fear, who threaten them with emotional rejection: "'Their poetry wasn't too bad but I couldn't take all those lezzies.'" Ishmael Reed, the novelist who has rightfully often decried the degeneration of Black males in American society, is not above this kind of emotional blackmail if, faced with competition from a Black female, it contributes to his own personal gain. Complaining that he had sold only eight thousand copies of his last book, Reed is reported to have said, "if he had been a *black lesbian poet* [emphasis added] he would have sold many more."

This complex nexus of cause and effect, of power struggles and political ploys underlying the often turbulent relations between Black men and women lies at the heart of Walker's works. Out of it emerges the negative criticism she has received. It is inevitable that she would arouse hostility, for in her struggle to help Black men and women overcome the oppression that binds them, she refuses to be intimidated or ruled by anything other than her own conscience.

We should pause here to note exactly what "oppression" means in Walker's works. Her target is not racism itself, but the Black men and women whom it affects, not society, but the lives of her characters. Recounting human tragedies because the characters themselves are largely responsible for their own fate, though their fate may have its being in racism, Walker's fiction explores a much more personal kind of oppression: that which the individual inflicts on himself or on another individual. The good to be derived from this central focus Walker explains in *Mothers' Gardens* in her analysis of what she feels is a major failing of Black writing:

It seems to me that black writing has suffered because even black critics have assumed that a book that deals with relationships between members of a black family—or between a man and a woman—is less important than one that has white people as primary antagonists. The consequence of this is that many of our books by 'major' writers . . . tell us little about the culture, history, or future, imagination, fantasies, and so on, of black people, and a lot about isolated (often improbable) or limited encounters with a nonspecific white world.

Unlike the books of these "major" writers, Walker's works tell us a great deal about the lives of Black people, and it is ironic that her reward has often been controversy and harsh criticism. Her persistence in the face of it springs from her commitment to truth and honesty. Like most Black artists concerned about freeing Black people from their past mistakes, she too believes that "the truth shall set you free." In *Black Women Writers,* Barbara Christian writes that "there is a sense in which the 'forbidden' in the society is consistently approached by Walker as a possible route to truth." In contrast to many Black writers who are reluctant to criticize Black males because they fear it will exacerbate an already precarious situation between Black men and women, the "forbidden" Walker exposes is the role Black men, both the positive and negative types, have played in the oppression of Black women.

Examples of the purely negative type of Black male abound in Walker's work, among them the men in *The Color Purple*; however, . . . one of the most glaring examples is the younger Grange Copeland, hero of *The Third Life*.
—*J. Charles Washington*

Examples of the purely negative type of Black male abound in Walker's work, among them the men in *The Color Purple*; however, as mentioned, one of the most glaring examples is the younger Grange Copeland, hero of *The Third Life,* of whom Barbara Christian writes in *Black Women Writers:* "Grange Copeland hates himself because he is powerless, as opposed to powerful, the definition of maleness for him. His reaction is to prove his power by inflicting violence on the women around him." The cyclical nature of this phenomenon is seen in the life of Grange's son Brownfield, perhaps the most monstrous character in all of Walker's fiction, who brutalizes his children and his wife and then murders her.

The role played by the positive type of Black male found in *In Love and Trouble* is no less destructive on the lives of Black women, for it often means only a change in the kind of violence inflicted; that is, emotional violence predominates

over the physical kind. But there is a major difference in the men who cause the oppression, and it is this distinction which allows us to label them positive rather than negative and which supplies the hope that change is possible. While the men in *Purple* and *Third Life* shock us with their unspeakable cruelty and violence not only because they are fully aware of their immoral behavior but also because they often revel in and enjoy inflicting pain, the men in *In Love and Trouble* are never monsters of this type. On the contrary, they are at all times human beings who reveal a variety of human strengths and weaknesses.

The positive classification also depends on the perspective from which one views them. For instance, Ruel, the antagonist/-husband in **"Really, Doesn't Crime Pay,"** who fails to recognize his wife's ambition to write or her need for her own identity because he only sees her as a housewife is, in my view, not a negative character. A product of the social mores of his time stemming from the morally sanctioned patriarchal tradition which fostered them, he is as much a victim as his wife of a seemingly permanent mind-set in society which neither of them created and which will bind them until they realize that they must set themselves free. Similarly, while it may be considered immoral by some, a man who marries for money, in this case at the invitation of the female, as Jerome Washington does in **"Her Sweet Jerome,"** is no more negative than a woman who does the same. To label him such would require applying to him the same pernicious double standard of which women have always been victim.

A second significant cause of the oppression of the Black women in these stories, as it relates to their interaction with Black men, is their mistaken definition of themselves as women. Their own blindness about themselves and about what they can and must do for themselves is given strong emphasis, which is another important sign that Walker is searching for the truth, and that her interest is in finding causes, not assessing blame. The female protagonist of **"Really, Doesn't Crime Pay,"** for example, is spiritually and emotionally imprisoned by her husband's limited definition of her humanity and sits waiting deliverance from her life of useless dissipation, completely unaware that what she desires most lies within her own power—that, in other words, she must be the agent of her own deliverance. Such behavior on the women's part does not correlate with positive male characters. It does mean, however, that the men's behavior is no worse than that of the women, their alleged victims. They are in fact equally responsible for their problems and for the suffering they inflict on each other.

A particularly effective example of a Black woman whose attempt to free herself goes awry because, ironically, she tries to reverse roles and play the one her husband had played is that of Margaret Copeland, wife of Grange. After years of suffering his adultery and brutality, she resorts to a similar kind of immorality as she begins sleeping around with a number of men, among them Shipley, the white man for whom her husband works and by whom she has a baby. Her eventual suicide, then, is the result of both her victimization by her husband and significantly, of her own guilt feelings about her immoral behavior and illegitimate half-white child.

Similarly, many of the women in *In Love and Trouble* share culpability in their own downfall, and this fact plays an important part in softening the negative image of their Black men. For though it is not always the case, and a man or woman must bear responsibility for his/her immoral behavior no matter what the circumstances, the men's role in the oppression of these women is often aided by the women's contribution to or willful participation in—sometimes, even, a masochistic invitation of—their own victimization.

The variety of problems and character types found in these stories is perhaps the most convincing evidence of Walker's preoccupation with presenting the full range of Black humanity—"the survival whole" of her people—as seen in the individual lives of her characters. To reiterate, what we are seeing, then, is not a common theme of oppression, but a multiplicity of themes based on the individuals' responses to it. Like her female characters, the Black male characters are shown to be individual human beings. Regarding them as such, one will find among them several positive Black male images or characters, which is the thesis of this essay. Because most of the stories have female protagonists and male antagonists, in such a case the selection of stories has to be based on those in which the male antagonists are sufficiently developed to give a substantial view of their characters. From this group, two have been selected for examination: **"Really, Doesn't Crime Pay"** and **"To Hell with Dying."**

Even though this essay concentrates on the Black male, to understand and appreciate the total picture or truth that Walker offers requires an equally close scrutiny of the female characters, as well as the plot and language of the stories. For, as indicated, it is the interaction between the male and female, reflected in the interrelatedness of literary elements, that allows us to see the not always blameless victimization of the Black female as well as the not always villainous actions of the Black male, but the common humanity of both.

"Really, Doesn't Crime Pay" takes place within the pages of Myrna's writing notebook. "Myrna" is never used within the story itself. To identify her, the name appears in parentheses only as an undertitle.

On the surface, the notebook entries tell about Myrna's desire to be a writer and her dissatisfaction with her life as a housewife. Spending her days in idleness and useless dissipation—she does not have to work—she falls prey to a young Black charlatan or amateur writer, Mordecai Rich, who se-

duces and then abandons her, leading to an emotional breakdown. One day while sitting in the doctor's office, she discovers that he has published under his own name one of her stories that she had given him. Later that night while in bed, she attempts to murder her husband Ruel, who had ridiculed her desire to be a writer, insisting instead that she have a child and become a housewife.

On a deeper level, the story is a tragedy about a young Black woman who has talent but who lacks the understanding, courage and know-how to break the restrictions placed on her and to create the meaningful identity she craves and needs. Her insecurity about her talent and her own self-worth resulting in extreme self-hatred, leads to her victimization by Mordecai and to her attempted murder of her husband, whom she blames for her plight and to whom she transfers her frustration and hatred.

Myrna's entries in her notebook are significant in revealing her character and exposing the tragic nature of her situation. Walker skillfully establishes the interrelatedness of the literary elements of theme, character and plot. Allowing us to see inside Myrna's head and heart, we observe more than twenty years of rage and anger bottled up there, which is more than enough to drive anyone mad. Since the entries in her notebook are both the plot as well as samples of her writing, what they also allow us to see is not only the quality of her writing and the sensitivity and talent required to produce it, but also the tragic waste of them and her life due to her failure to act or to attempt to solve the dilemma she faced.

The house where she spends her days of idleness is like a prison to her. There she fritters away the hours with her jars and bottles of cosmetics, symbolizing her spiritual decay, indulging herself; "her hands—in Herbessence nailsoak, polish, lotions and creams." Although she still writes, and has done so for some twenty years, her doubt about her talent and her unwilling acceptance of the role society has created for her are seen in her words, "I am not a serious writer. . . ." Her feelings about herself begin to change after she meets Mordecai Rich, whose flattery helps banish her insecurity. After showing him some of her work, she says, "Mordecai Rich praised me for my intelligence, my sensitivity, the depth of the work he had seen." What Walker shows us here is the self-doubt which causes Myrna to act contrary to her own moral instincts and which is the basis of her vulnerability; for she understands quite clearly what or whom she is up against. Recognizing Mordecai Rich for what he is, she says, "I think Mordecai Rich has about as much heart as a dirt-eating toad." It is this vulnerability, specifically, her need for praise and recognition, that cause her to succumb to him; after he reads a story of hers, this thought runs through her mind:

> If he says one good thing about what I've written, I

promised myself, I will go to bed with him. (How else could I repay him? All I owned in any supply were my jars of cold cream!)

So devoid of self-esteem that she feels the jars of cold cream are all she possesses of value, since she cannot give them to him, she resorts to sex as an expression of her gratitude. For if all else fails, sex is always considered a valuable commodity. Myrna kept her word by giving herself to Mordecai, and the effect was immediate, albeit, regrettably, ephemeral:

He took me in his arms, right there in the grape arbor. . . . After that, a miracle happened. Under Mordecai's fingers my body opened like a flower and carefully bloomed. . . .

Walker never lets the reader forget that Myrna is conscious or fully aware of her acts. In fact, it is this awareness on her part that makes her appear less sympathetic, and the man with whom she commits adultery less villainous, in the readers' eyes. The above passage, for instance, concludes with Myrna's thought, "And it was strange as well as wonderful. For I don't think love had anything to do with this at all." What increases the antipathy toward her even more, however, is her use of her week-long sexual encounter with Mordecai, unknown to her husband, of course, as a way of striking back at him for his failure to recognize her need: "I gloat over this knowledge. Now Ruel will find out that I am not a womb without a brain that can be bought with Japanese bathtubs and shopping sprees."

Putting all her hope for a change in her life in Mordecai, she declares, "The moment of my deliverance is at hand." He abandons her, however, and soon thereafter she begins to reveal signs of an emotional breakdown. As her condition worsens, Ruel tells her she acts as if her mind is asleep, to which she makes the mental notes: "Nothing will wake it but a letter from Mordecai telling me to pack my bags and fly to New York." Clearly, this indicates the confusion in her mind about what change is needed to bring about the happiness she craves. This change is not an external one, although new scenes, sights and surroundings would no doubt help alleviate her mental depression. What she actually requires is a fundamental modification in the way she thinks about herself. Thus, it is not Ruel alone who needs to know that she is not "a womb without a mind," but she too must realize that she has the capability of being both "womb" and "brain"—both a housewife and artist; in separating the two or failing to see the alternative available to her, she commits the same kind of error that Ruel makes. Complementing this confusion in her mind is another serious mistake on her part: her lack of self-involvement in changing her condition. And so she sits waiting for deliverance, expecting Mordecai to do for her what only she can do for herself.

That Walker sees the solution to Myrna's problems as one of her own making is found in *Mothers' Garden,* in the author's analysis of the escape route by which Black women have traditionally sought and succeeded in securing their spiritual survival. This route, based on an intuitive sense which enabled them to know how to get what they needed, was their flexibility combined with an enormous capacity for work: this enabled them to be both worker and creator, both wife and artist. Using her mother, who bore and raised eight children, as an example, Walker first explains that many of the stories she writes are her mother's stories; then she adds:

But the telling of these stories . . . was not the only way my mother showed herself as an artist. . . . My mother adorned with flowers whatever shabby house we were forced to live in. And not just your typical straggly country stand of zinnias, either. She planted ambitious gardens . . . with over fifty different varieties of plants that bloom(ed) profusely from early March until late November.

The conclusion of this anecdote illustrates the enormous will and energy required to maintain the garden:

Before she left home for the fields, she watered her flowers, chopped up the grass, and laid out new beds. When she returned from the fields she might divide clumps of beds, dig a cold pit, uproot and replant roses, or prune branches from her taller bushes or trees—until night came and it was too dark to see.

With this as the norm, one can see how far from it Myrna is. Not compelled to work to support herself, her life of ease, which would have given her ample time for self-development, cannot be compared to the lives of drudgery of the generation of Black women to which Walker's mother belongs. Myrna's easy life is of little consequence, however, for in addition to her fragile emotional nature and her blindness about the deeper cause of her problem, she lacks the pragmatism which would have enabled her to find a solution to her problem. Without it, acting instead in response to her feelings of self-hatred, she continues to destroy the life she has by contemplating suicide and by commiting cruelty against her husband. Interestingly, no critic, male or female, has commented on the cruelty and violence this female character inflicts on her husband, actions which make her no less negative than some of the males in Walker's works. After release from the hospital, where she has recovered from her breakdown, she resumes her life of uselessness and idleness. She also continues to deceive her husband, who still hopes for the birth of a child, by religiously taking birth control pills. Illustrating her enjoyment of the pain she inflicts on him, it is, she says, "the only spot of humor in my entire day when I am gulping that little yellow tablet. . . ." Her spiritual death, then, is seen not only in these acts of cruelty, but also in her refusal to give birth to life. As for her sterility and failure to come to grips with her life, she says:

> I go to the new shopping mall *twice a day now* [emphasis added]; once in the morning and once in the afternoon, or at night. I buy hats I would not dream of wearing, or even owning.

In her analysis of this story, Barbara Christian, writing in *The Black Scholar,* concludes that what I regard as Myrna's cruelty to her husband is part of her way of "securing her freedom," based on what appears to be a well thought-out strategy of "contrariness." Myrna happened upon this strategy, Christian continues, through her "discovery of the magnificance of the manipulation of words. . . ." In such a case, one wonders why Myrna did not begin to recognize or gain more faith in her own writing ability after the publication of her story that Mordecai had plagiarized. Other parts of this strategy of "yessing them to death" are her lies about trying to conceive a child while her husband exhausts himself every night trying to impregnate her, as well as her acceptance of his advice to go on frequent shopping sprees. I strongly disagree with this interpretation, for the evidence drawn from the story itself leads to the conclusion that Myrna's condition renders her incapable of rational thought, and that, instead, her reaction is a purely emotional one typifying the destructiveness of the individual who suffers from an identity problem.

Christian also says that Myrna's strategy "secures some small victory, but it is a victory achieved from the position of weakness." What must be emphasized here, however, is not the "victory" but the "weakness," specifically, her weakness of character; for her actions produce no change in her life, certainly not the crucial one she hopes for. This same weakness casts suspicion on her declaration that one day she will leave her husband. It is highly unlikely that she ever will because she has learned nothing from her experiences. At the end of the story, the clearest sign of her total capitulation is her complete abandonment of her writing.

Ruel, Myrna's husband, is cast in the traditional mold. A solid, lower middle-class type, he is a 40-year-old Korean war veteran who works in a store and raises a hundred acres of peanuts. Steady, immovable and unchanging like the earth he cultivates, he clings to life in the same small southern town in which he was born and reared. In fact, he has traveled beyond its confines only once when he went off to war. Though he claims the experience broadened him, especially his two months of European leave, it did not change him or affect his thinking in any fundamental way. Because his character had already been shaped by the values of a Southern tradition hundreds of years old, the brief, passing moment in Europe did not—indeed, could not—penetrate the deeper core of his being. Referring to these values as "the web of conventions that is the South," Barbara Christian states that "they

have much to do with the conduct of relationships—man and woman, young and old, black and white. . . ." The reflection of this, as well as the unchanging nature of these values, is seen in Ruel's ideas of what married life entails, that is, the fixed roles that marriage partners must play, which are the same ones he learned in childhood, passed down to him from his father. It must be noted, however, that these values are not limited to the South, for they are the foundation of the patriarchal tradition known and practiced throughout the world.

Men of this type do not permit their wives to work, as he does not, even though in his case, it may mean that he has to work two jobs to supply his wife with the things he thinks she needs or wants. Not just a reflection of the male ego, this social pattern is in keeping with the men's expectation that the freedom and time it gives their women will enable them to more easily perform their "duty" as wives and mothers. Seeing this duty as the only appropriate one for a female, Ruel naturally thinks that his wife's writing is "a lot of foolish vulgar stuff" and that she is "peculiar" for wanting to do it. This "unnatural" desire of hers is a threat to him, for its exposure to the public will cause him embarrassment. Conversely, the traditional role he urges on her will confirm his normalcy and masculinity. And so, whenever she mentions the subject of writing, "he brings up having a baby or going shopping. . . ."

When Mordecai Rich appears, Ruel is slightly jealous but does not feel threatened. How could he be disturbed by such "a skinny black tramp," when he, Ruel, is all an ideal husband should be, which is how he sees himself. However, it is his preoccupation with himself, with his own needs and self-image, that blinds him to the needs of his wife. Failing to see his own shortcomings, he readily dismisses the signs of her distress because he cannot see that she has a problem. Failing to do so, he would never believe that he might possibly be implicated in its cause. For this reason too, he only begins to notice her and to feel that something is wrong with his life after Mordecai abandons her and the signs of her oncoming nervous breakdown are too obvious to be ignored.

What we see in this couple, then, is an identically matched pair of individuals with an interesting kind of incompatibility that renders them incapable of helping each other. Both, therefore, share the blame for the deterioration or destruction of their relationship. In both individuals, the root of the problem is not immorality, but fundamental character flaws. In Ruel's case, it is his selfishness or egocentrism based on his belief that what is good or right for him is also good enough for his wife. It must be re-emphasized, however, that his behaviour, which is typical of many men everywhere and therefore universal, has its basis in the mores of the patriarchal tradition, a tradition which regrettably makes little allowance for the spiritual needs of women.

Because he is a plain, common, everyday type who is unaware of any other tradition or set of values and therefore blameless, Ruel is not a negative character. In contrast to his wife, even his faults are virtues. For though he is preoccupied with his own image and his own life, it is devoted to and expressive of his love for her. Therefore, he is never cruel, brutal or violent. Rather, his life is characterized by hard work, as he struggles to provide her with a decent home to live in and other material possessions she needs or wants. Mindful of his role and image as provider, he feels ashamed of the wooden house he purchased for his wife, with its toilet in the yard. Constantly trying to improve their life, he dreams of a better home for her, telling her, "One day we'll have a new house of brick, with a Japanese bath." Finally, it is ironic that what Myrna considers his greatest fault, his insistence that she have a child, is in fact the greatest expression of his love for her, since he believes, as most men and women do, that a child will cure her illness and provide her with the self-fulfillment she needs.

It is not only his moral fiber and love that establishes Ruel as a positive male image, but also his innocence. All of these qualities produce the sympathy we feel for him. Such a solid, respectable person could not be the monster his wife makes him out to be. Such a decent person does not deserve to be the cuckhold she makes of him or the victim of the cruel tricks she plays on him. Even after Myrna's attempt to murder him, it is clear that he never understands her, or the real source of their problem. Rather, Ruel blames Mordecai, "cursing [him] for messing up his life." After Myrna's recovery, Ruel makes repeated attempts to impregnate her, never once suspecting that she is deliberately thwarting conception of the child he desperately wants. When she fails to become pregnant, he sends her to a gynecologist. When this step also fails to produce the desired result, he finally learns one irrelevant fact: irrelevant because it will not change him either: As Myrna says, "He knows now that I intend to say yes until he is completely exhausted."

Lacking knowledge of himself and therefore incapable of changing, Ruel faces a hopeless situation. But what he represents is an important part of what Walker wishes to show us. Even such basically good men as Ruel are often unwitting contributors to the destruction of relationships between Black men and women.

As David Bradley notes in his *New York Times Magazine* article, Walker's stories with older men protagonists (in their sixties onward) contain overwhelmingly positive Black male images. This change results from a major shift in theme. Sexual or marital relations between Black men and women, with all the attendant stress and pain they entail, are not the central focus. Rather, the author's interest is in presenting the experiences of the old as a legacy for the young, as she explains in *Mothers' Gardens*: "Next to them (Black women),

I place old people—male and female—who persist in their beauty in spite of everything. How do they do this, knowing what they do? Having lived what they lived. It is a mystery, and so it lures me into their lives."

Because many of Walker's stories are based on her own experiences (or, vicariously, on those of her mother), those about older men are a necessary part of the evidence that shows she does not hate Black men. How could she, after having learned in her youth the kindness and love these men are capable of giving? If she views younger men with less charity than she extends the older ones, it is because she sees the Black male's development as having a predictable, unchanging pattern. That is, their aggressiveness and penchant for violence begins in the adult years, reaches its peak in the middle years and recedes in the later years. In Bradley's *New York Times Magazines* article, she comments on this phenomenon by saying, "One theory is that men don't start to mature until they're 40"; and then she amplifies her point by explaining:

> I knew both my grandfathers, and they were just doting, indulgent, sweet old men. I just loved them both and they were crazy about me. However, as young men, middle-aged men, they were . . . brutal. One grandfather knocked my grandmother out of a window. He beat one of his children so severely that the child had epilepsy. Just a horrible, horrible man. But when I knew him, he was a sensitive, considerate man.

The point, then, is that because Walker understands Black men and knows what they are capable of, she can criticize younger men without hating them and praise older men for the positive image, which is their legacy.

The one story of this kind in *In Love and Trouble* is **"To Hell with Dying,"** the first story Walker ever wrote, her first published one, and her "most autobiographical." "It is autobiographical though, in fact, none of it happened. The *love* happened." It is easy to understand why it was so successful, for it is a beautiful story, suffused throughout with love and rendered in poetic language. Described by Walker as a story "about an old man saved from death countless times by the love of his neighbor's children," it is as much, if not more, about what the old man's love does for the neighbor's female child, who narrates the story. And since it is about love, it is much more about life than death, as the title indicates.

At the beginning of the story the main character, Mr. Sweet Little, is about 70; the unnamed female child narrator is about 4; at the end, he is 90, and she is 24. In the span of twenty years, the living out of a lifetime love affair occurs as he moves from old age to death, and she from early childhood to adulthood.

As the story begins, when she is still a young child, the relationship between them has the aura of a sexual relationship between a man and a woman. Walker creates this sexual feeling, which shimmers just beneath the surface of the story, apart from but parallel to the poetic language. It remains only a feeling, however, because the love between the old man and young girl is pure and wholesome.

The plot itself is simple. Mr. Sweet, a diabetic and alcoholic, periodically falls ill, sinking so low that everyone believes he is dying. Each time, however, he is revived or saved by the ministrations of the narrator, who, taken to his home by her parents, climbs on his bed and kisses and hugs him. This ritual, which her older brothers and sisters had performed before her, was always initiated by her father's call, "To hell with dying, man; these children want Mr. Sweet." These revivals occurred when Mr. Sweet was in his 70s. In his 80s, he lived a peaceful life and was no longer threatened by death. The narrator had grown up and was away from home studying at the university. When he was 90, she was summoned home because Mr. Sweet was again near death. As she had so often done in childhood, she tried to save him, but this time he did die, leaving her with the gift of his spirit and with the realization that he had been her first love.

In any relationship, sexual or otherwise, what is important is the giving, co-equally and unreservedly. However, if Mr. Sweet gives more than the narrator, which seems to be the case, that is entirely appropriate; for far more important than the needs of the old man, whose life is nearly over, are those of the young girl, whose life is just beginning. What he gives her, among other things, and what she needs at this stage of her life, is a sense of her own self-worth, of her own self-esteem. He makes her feel that she is physically attractive and, significantly, has the power to control her own destiny.

Because Mr. Sweet's frightening bouts with death always occurred when he was in bed and usually at night or early morning, it was necessary for the girl to exercise her healing powers there. This structuring of the situation, which conjures up the thought of the restorative powers of sex, contributes to the feeling of a sexual relationship between them. The physical contact between them also strengthens this feeling: "'To hell with dying. . .' was my cue to throw myself upon the bed and kiss Mr. Sweet all around the whiskers and under the eyes and around the collar of his nightshirt were he smelled so strongly of all sorts of things. . . ." This particular healing event, which the narrator recalls as the first time she actually remembered participating in one of Mr. Sweet's "revivals," occurred when she was seven, an age at which she would have been conscious of sex and sexual differences. A final detail of this ritual is its privacy and intimacy: "My parents would leave the room to just the three of us [her brother was with her, although she invariably did the reviving]; Mr. Sweet . . . would be propped up in bed . . . with me sitting and lying

on his shoulder and along his chest." Her sexual awakening and love are further seen in her wish that she had been old enough to be the woman Mr. Sweet had really loved but lost when he was forced to marry his wife, Miss Mary.

There is a strong connection between the sexual mood, the plot and the general theme of solutions to problems in relationships between Black men and women. This relationship between the little girl and the old man, which bears such a strong resemblance to and contains all the usual ingredients of normal man/woman relationships except for sex, acts as a model for those in which sex is the primary—in many cases, the only—factor. The conclusion to be drawn or the lesson it teaches is nothing new but bears repeating. If men and women would base their relationship on love above all else, these relationships might be much more successful. The sexual ingredient could only increase this likelihood by cementing the bond between them because it would be an addition to, not a substitute for, the love they already have for each other.

The gift of love the girl gave the old man, reflected in the numerous times she retrieved him from the brink of death, was matched in kind by gifts he gave her. First, his response to her, which may not have been as miraculous as it seems, gave her a tremendous sense of power. Usually occurring during or after his bouts of drinking, these frequent brushes with death may have been attributable to the alcohol, in combination with his diabetes, or to the self-pity induced by it. They may also have been a plea for attention or love, especially after his wife died. That they were not entirely spontaneous, that their cause was more emotional than physical, is seen because they were often preceded by certain recognizable signs, such as his crying while playing his guitar. On one occasion, as he was leaving the narrator's house after having displayed the tell-tale signs, her mother noted that "we'd better sleep light that night for probably we'd have to go over to Mr. Sweet before daylight. And we did."

Whatever the cause, the attacks appeared to be real, so real, in fact, that the doctor was usually called. Other than as part of what makes the story intriguing, however, the reality or cause of them is not important. What is significant is the mystery of death, paralleling Walker's comment that the events of the story are not real, only the love. More specifically, she shows us a way of conquering death or giving it a human dimension by treating it as a normal part of life. To get the point across, she gives us a child's perspective of death as an ordinary event, even fun, which has an ordinary cure, love. In contrast is the usual adult perspective of death as something horrible, and based on their supposed superior knowledge of causes and cures, they presume to exert control over it but cannot. In the end they are as confounded and perplexed as ever by its mystery.

The certainty of death's arrival, even though the threat of it had occurred no less than ten times, and of the narrator's ability to thwart it, set her and her family apart from the rest of the community: "All the neighbors knew to come to our house if something was wrong with Mr. Sweet. . . ." This responsibility placed great stress on the young girl, for, as she says, "these deaths upset me fearfully, and the thought of how much depended on me . . . made me nervous." It should be noted, however, that the fear she expresses is more of failure than of death itself. But she did not fail, and the success she always had, as well as the feeling of power and accomplishment it gave her, served to increase her feeling of self-esteem; at the same time, the "fun" and love she associated with the revivals helped remove her fear of death.

> It did not occur to us that we were doing anything special; we had not learned that death was final when it did come. We thought nothing of triumphing over it so many times, and in fact became a trifle contemptuous of people who let themselves be carried away. It did not occur to us that if our own father had been dying we could not have stopped it, that Mr. Sweet was the only person over whom we had power.

In addition, Mr. Sweet also helped increase the girl's sense of self-esteem by making her feel that she was physically attractive. While this is important generally, it was particularly so to a young girl, whose fate was decided by the beauty of face and body, as well as by her own attitude toward it. The blemish she possessed, a low hairline, which may have led her to have negative feelings about herself, was removed by the power of Mr. Sweet's touch, quite by accident, it seems: "Looking into my eyes he would . . . run a scratchy old finger all around my hairline, which was rather low, down nearly to my eyebrows, and made some people say I looked like a baby monkey." Through the power of his voice, as well as his overall attitude toward and treatment of her, he did even more to make her feel physically attractive: "Mr. Sweet used to call me princess, and *I believed it* [emphasis added]. He made me feel pretty at five and six, and simply outrageously devastating at the blazing age of eight and a half."

What made Mr. Sweet so likeable to the narrator as a child was his difference from other adults she knew: "Toward all of us children he was very kind, and had the grace to be shy with us, which is unusual in grownups." This difference affected her because Mr. Sweet's behavior gave her a more positive image of adults, specifically, males, than the ones she had usually known. The children also liked him because he was capable of becoming one of them, treating them as if they were equals. An expert guitar player who loved to sing, sometimes, when he was "feeling good," he would dance around the yard and play with them. As much as for what he did, they liked him for the way he looked: "He was a tall thinnish man with kinky hair going dead white. He was a

dark brown, his eyes were very squinty sort of bluish. . . ." Not only did Mr. Sweet's actions help increase the children's tolerance for adults, but the fact that he, their ideal playmate, was an old man also helped remove the barrier between youth and old age: "We never felt anything of Mr. Sweet's age when we played with him. We loved his wrinkles and would draw some on our brows to be like him." As a boy, the narrator's brother was most affected by the positive image of Mr. Sweet: "What he would do while I talked to Mr. Sweet was pretend to play the guitar, in fact pretend that he was a young version of Mr. Sweet. . . ."

Uncertainty exists about the effect Mr. Sweet's drinking had on his bouts with death and about its effect on his life in general. There is no doubt, however, that the children considered it a plus: "His ability to be drunk and sober at the same time made him an ideal playmate. . . ." The fact that her mother "never held his drunkenness against him" also seems to suggest that she did not consider him immoral for doing it. Moreover, while it may have been a reflection of some flaw in his character, it was not an overwhelmingly controlling force in his life. Though he did often give in to it, he always remained its master: "Although Mr. Sweet would sometimes lose complete or nearly complete control of his head and neck so that he would loll in his chair, his mind remained strangely acute and his speech not too affected."

A stronger, more ominous force operated on his life, but it did not destroy him completely either: "Mr. Sweet had been ambitious as a boy, wanted to be a doctor or lawyer or sailor, only to find that black men fare better if they did not. Since he could not become one of these things he turned to fishing as his only earnest career. . . ." What this suggests about his character is that he is a man who remained spiritually alive in spite of the racism he faced, over which he had no control. The spiritual aliveness, symbolized by his love of and ability to create music—"playing the guitar [was] his only claim to doing anything extraordinarily well"—enabled him to recognize and take advantage of other alternatives. From these, he made his own choice, which meant that, as with his drinking, he controlled his life. Moreover, he had learned early the uselessness of blaming fate for his problems and accepted responsibility for his own actions, for in most cases fate had nothing to do with them. He, not fate, had impregnated Miss Mary and therefore had had to marry her, even though he had been in love with another woman. He was not sure that Joe Lee, her "baby," was his own child, but he accepted the consequences of his actions, as she defended them, and did what he had to do by marrying her.

Finally, his tendency to remain in control of his own life is seen in his relationship to death. He was able to defeat death so often, which is perhaps the most important of his gifts to the narrator, because he was not ready to die. Her mother invariably shed tears whenever Mr. Sweet lay dying, the narrator states, "although she knew the death was not necessarily the last one *unless Mr. Sweet really wanted it to be*" [emphasis added].

All of these gifts of love from him to her were matched by her continuing love for him, which endured throughout her adult life and extended even beyond his death. A sign of this love was the attention she showered on him whenever she could, even though he was now in no danger of dying:

> When Mr. Sweet was in his eighties I was studying in the university many miles from home. I saw him whenever I went home, but he was never on the verge of dying. . . . By this time he not only had a moustache but a long flowing snowwhite beard, which I loved and combed and braided for hours. He was very peaceful, fragile, gentle. . . .

On his ninetieth birthday, Mr. Sweet decided that he was ready to die, but not before he gave the narrator, who rushed home to see him, his final gifts of love. Perhaps the most valuable of these is the beauty of his dying. Shorn of ugliness and fear because of the kind of man he was and by the closeness to him of those who loved and cared for him, it occurs "in a shack overgrown with yellow roses" making the "air heavy and sweet and very peaceful." Having successfully performed the revival ritual so many times in the past, though now a grown woman and aware her effort must surely fail, the narrator, transported back to those earlier times, is tempted to try it again. But, and here is noted another valuable lesson this dying brings, it will be a vain attempt. This lesson is brought home to her by the realization of the passage of time and hence the inevitability of death, reflected in the faces of her own parents, "who also looked old and frail." Her father is a willing participant, intoning the familiar line he had uttered so many times before. She, too, does her part, as Mr. Sweet does his, tracing her hairline with his finger. But it did not work this time, because Mr. Sweet had made up his mind that he was ready to die: "I closed my eyes when his finger halted above my ear, his hand stayed cupped around my cheek. When I opened my eyes, sure that I had reached him in time, his were closed."

After his death his final gift to her was his spirit, symbolized by his guitar. "He had asked them months before to give it to me; he had known that even if I came next time he would not be able to respond in the old way." Ironically unaware of his importance to her, the narrator states that Mr. Sweet gave her his guitar because "he did not want to feel that my trip home had been for nothing." On the contrary, the significance of his life and death, which she now fully realizes, is summed up in the final paragraph of the story:

> The old guitar! I plucked the strings, hummed "Sweet Georgia Brown." *The magic of Mr. Sweet lingered still in the cool steel box* [emphasis added]. Through the window I could catch the fragrant delicate scent of tender yellow roses. The man on the . . . bed . . . had been my first love.

The moral emphasis found in Alice Walker's works reveals her adherence to two different but similar traditions of art, the classical Greek and the ancient African, both of which form the basis of the Afro-American or Black Aesthetic. The Greeks had confidence in the immense power of art "as a molding or formative agent in developing human feelings and motivations"; and according to Leopold Senghor, "all African art has at least three characteristics: that is, art is functional, collective and committing or committed." Thus, Walker's works demonstrate her love for her people, both men and women, for, reflecting the ideals of both of these traditions, these works are predicated on the belief that man is inherently good and that, therefore, if flaws in his character exist, through the use of art that educates they can be removed and the personality restored to health. Rather than being a sign of enmity toward Black men, then, her criticism of them and of Black women is the strongest reflection of this love. She gives praise where praise is due; however, her strong moral sense, courage and commitment to truth and honesty will not allow her to shrink from criticizing where criticism is due, in order that future improvement can be made. This look toward the future, seen in her desire to bring harmony between men and women by improving human character, echoes the most distinctive ideal of the classical tradition—"to complete human potentiality in the light of the highest standard of excellence or nobility."

Alice Hall Petry (essay date Winter 1989)

SOURCE: "Alice Walker: The Achievement of the Short Fiction," in *Modern Language Studies,* Vol. XIX, No. 1, Winter, 1989, pp. 12-27.

[*In the following essay, Hall Petry discusses the differences between the short stories of Walker's* In Love and Trouble *and her stories in* You Can't Keep a Good Woman Down, *asserting that the stories in the first collection are much stronger than those in the second.*]

There's nothing quite like a Pulitzer Prize to draw attention to a little known writer. And for Alice Walker, one of the few black writers of the mid-'60s to remain steadily productive for the two ensuing decades, the enormous success of 1982's *The Color Purple* has generated critical interest in a literary career that has been, even if not widely noted, at the very least worthy of note. As a poet (*Once,* 1968; *Revolutionary Petunias,* 1973) and a novelist (*The Third Life of Grange Copeland,* 1970; *Meridian,* 1976), Walker has always had a small but enthusiastic following, while her many essays, published in black- and feminist-oriented magazines (e.g., *Essence, Ms.*), have likewise kept her name current, albeit in rather limited circles. The Pulitzer Prize has changed this situation, qualitatively and perhaps permanently. Walker's name is now a household word, and a reconsideration of her literary canon, that all but inevitable Pulitzer perk, is well underway. An integral part of this phenomenon would be the reappraisal of her short fiction. Walker's two collections of short stories—1973's *In Love & Trouble* and 1981's *You Can't Keep a Good Woman Down*—are now available as attractive paperbacks and selling briskly, we are told. But a serious critical examination of her short stories—whether of particular tales, the individual volumes, or the entire canon— has yet to occur. Hence this essay. As a general over-view, it seeks to evaluate Walker's achievement as a short story writer while probing a fundamental question raised by so many reviewers of the two volumes: why is *You Can't Keep a Good Woman Down* so consistently less satisfying than the earlier *In Love & Trouble*? How has Alice Walker managed to undermine so completely that latest-and-best formula so dear to book reviewers? The answer, as we shall see, is partly a matter of conception and partly one of technique; and it suggests further that Walker's unevenness thus far as a writer of short fiction—her capacity to produce stories that are sometimes extraordinarily good, at other times startlingly weak— places her at a career watershed. At this critical juncture, Alice Walker could so refine her art as to become one of the finest writers of American short fiction in this century.

She could just as easily not.

One key to understanding the disparate natures of *In Love & Trouble* and *You Can't Keep a Good Woman Down* is their epigraphs. *In Love & Trouble* offers two. The first epigraph, a page-long extract from *The Concubine* by Elechi Amadi, depicts a girl, Ahurole, who is prone to fits of sobbing and "alarmingly irrational fits of argument": "From all this her parents easily guessed that she was being unduly influenced by agwu, her personal spirit." It is not until the end of the extract that Amadi mentions casually that "Ahurole was engaged to Ekwueme when she was eight days old." In light of what follows in the collection, it is a most suitable epigraph: the women in this early volume truly are "in love and trouble" due in large measure to the roles, relationships, and self-images imposed upon them by a society which knows little and cares less about them as individuals. A marriage arranged in infancy perfectly embodies this situation; and the shock engendered by Amadi's final sentence is only heightened as one reads *In Love & Trouble* and comes to realize that the concubinage depicted in his novel, far from being a bizarre, pagan, foreign phenomenon, is practiced in only slightly modified form in contemporary—especially black—America. In the opening story of *In Love & Trouble,* "Roselily," the overworked title character marries the unnamed Black Mus-

lim from Chicago in part to give her three illegitimate children a better chance in life, and in part to obtain for herself some measure of social and economic security; but it is not really a relationship she chooses to enter freely, as is conveyed by her barely listening to her wedding ceremony—a service which triggers images not of romance but of bondage. Even ten-year-old Myop, the sole character of the vignette "**The Flowers,**" has her childhood—and, ultimately, her attitudes towards her self and her world—shattered by the blunt social reality of lynching: as much as she would love to spend her life all alone collecting flowers, from the moment she accidentally gets her heel caught in the skull of a decapitated lynching victim it is clear that, for their own survival, black females like Myop must be part of a group that includes males. Hence the plethora of bad marriages (whether legal unions or informal liaisons) in Walker's fiction; hence also the mental anguish suffered by most of her women characters, who engage in such unladylike acts as attacking their husbands with chain saws (**"Really, *Doesn't* Crime Pay?,"** *IL & T*) or setting fire to themselves (**"Her Sweet Jerome,"** *IL&T*). Must be that pesky agwu again—a diagnosis which is symptomatic of society's refusal to face the fact that women become homicidal/suicidal, or hire rootworkers to avenge social snubs (**"The Revenge of Hannah Kemhuff,"** *IL&T*), or lock themselves up in convents (**"The Diary of an African Nun,"** *IL&T*) not because of agwus, or because they are mentally or emotionally deficient, but because they are responding to the stress of situations not of their own making. Certainly marriage offers these women nothing, and neither does religion, be it Christianity, the Black Muslim faith, or voodoo. That these traditional twin sources of comfort and stability cause nothing but "trouble" for Walker's characters might lead one to expect a decidedly depressing volume of short stories; but in fact *In Love & Trouble* is very upbeat. Walker manages to counterbalance the oppressive subject matter of virtually all these 13 stories by maintaining the undercurrent of hope first introduced in the volume's second epigraph, a passage from Rainer Maria Rilke's *Letters to a Young Poet:* ". . . we must hold to what is difficult; everything in Nature grows and defends itself in its own way and is characteristically and spontaneously itself, seeks at all costs to be so and against all opposition." For Walker as for Rilke, opposition is not necessarily insurmountable: struggles and crises can lead to growth, to the nurturing of the self; and indeed most of the women of *In Love & Trouble,* sensing this, do try desperately to face their situations and deal with them—even if to do so may make them seem insane, or ignorant, or anti-social.

The sole epigraph of *You Can't Keep* lacks the relevance and subtlety of those of *In Love & Trouble:* "It is harder to kill something that is spiritually alive than it is to bring the dead back to life." Fine words from Herr Hesse, but unfortunately they don't have much to do with the fourteen stories in the collection. Few characters in *You Can't Keep* would qualify as "spiritually alive" according to most informed standards. We are shown a lot of self-absorbed artistes (the jazz-poet of **"The Lover,"** the authoress of **"Fame,"** the sculpture student of **"A Sudden Trip Home in the Spring"**), plus rather too many equally self-absorbed would-be radicals (**"Advancing Luna—and Ida B. Wells," "Source," "Laurel"**), plus a series of women—usually referred to generically as "she"—who engage in seemingly interminable monologues on pornography, abortion, sadomasochism, and rape (**"Coming Apart," "Porn," "A Letter of the Times, or Should This Sado-Masochism Be Saved?"**). These women are dull. And, unlike the situation in *In Love & Trouble,* the blame can't really be placed on males, those perennial targets of Alice Walker's acid wit. No, the problem with the women of *You Can't Keep* is that they are successful. Unlike the ladies of *In Love & Trouble,* who seem always to be struggling, to be growing, those of *You Can't Keep* have all advanced to a higher plane, personally and socially: as Barbara Christian observes, there truly is a clear progression between the two volumes, from an emphasis on "trouble" to an emphasis on self-assertiveness. The women of *You Can't Keep* embody the product, not the process: where a mother in *In Love & Trouble* (**"Everyday Use"**) can only fantasize about appearing on *The Tonight Show,* a woman of *You Can't Keep* (**"Nineteen Fifty-Five"**) actually does it! Gracie Mae Still meets Johnny! Similarly, a dying old lady in *In Love & Trouble* (**"The Welcome Table"**) is literally thrown out of a segregated white church, but in *You Can't Keep* (**"Source"**) two black women get to sit in an integrated Anchorage bar! With real Eskimos! Trudier Harris is quite correct that, compared to those of *In Love & Trouble,* the women of *You Can't Keep* seem superficial, static: "Free to make choices, they find themselves free to do nothing or to drift"—and they do, with Walker apparently not realizing that in fiction (as in life) the journey, not the arrival, is what interests. Men and marriage, those two bugaboos of *In Love & Trouble* responsible for thwarting women's careers (**"Really, *Doesn't* Crime Pay?"**), mutilating hapless schoolgirls (**"The Child Who Favored Daughter"**), and advocating anti-white violence (**"Her Sweet Jerome"**), at least brought out the strength and imagination of the women they victimized, and the women's struggles engross the reader. In contrast, the men of *You Can't Keep* have declined, both as people and as fictional characters, in an inverse relationship to the women's success. Most of the volume's male characters barely materialize; the few who do appear are milquetoast, from the pudgy, racist lawyer/rapist/lover Bubba of **"How Did I Get Away with Killing One of the Biggest Lawyers in the State? It Was Easy"**; to Ellis, the Jewish gigolo from Brooklyn who inexplicably dazzles the supposedly cool jazz-poet heroine of **"The Lover"**; to Laurel, he of the giant pink ears who (again inexplicably) dazzles the black radical journalist in **"Laurel."** And many of the male characters in *You Can't Keep* meet sorry ends—not unlike the women of *In Love & Trouble*: Bubba is shot to death by his schoolgirl victim; the shopworn

Ellis gets dumped; poor Laurel winds up in a coma, only to emerge brain-damaged. Curiously, we don't miss them; instead, we miss the kinds of conflicts and personal/social revelations which fully-realized, reasonably healthy male characters can impart to fiction.

For men, either directly or through the children they father, are a vital part of love; and it is love, as the soap operatic title of *In Love & Trouble* suggests, which is most operative in that early volume. It assumes various forms. It may be the love between a parent and child, surely the most consistently positive type of love in Walker's fiction. It is her love for her dying baby which impels Rannie Toomer to chase a urinating mare in a rainstorm so as to collect **"Strong Horse Tea,"** a folk medicine. It is her love for her daughter Dee that enables Mama to call her "Wangero Leewanika Kemanjo" in acknowledgment of her new Afro identity, but her equally strong love for her other child, the passive Maggie, which enables her to resist Dee/Wangero's demand for old quilts (Maggie's wedding present) to decorate her apartment (**"Everyday Use"**). Then again, the love of *In Love & Trouble* may be between a woman and God (**"The Welcome Table"**); and it may even have an erotic dimension, as with the sexually-repressed black nun of **"The Diary of an African Nun"** who yearns for her "pale lover," Christ. And granted, the love of *In Love & Trouble* is often distorted, even perverse: a father lops off his daughter's breasts in part because he confuses her with his dead sister, whom he both loved and loathed (**"The Child Who Favored Daughter"**); a young black girl and her middle-aged French teacher, the guilt-ridden survivor of the holocaust, fantasize about each other but never interact (**"We Drink the Wine in France"**); a dumpy hairdresser stabs and burns her husband's Black Power pamphlets as if they were his mistress: "Trash!' she cried over and over . . . 'I kill you! I kill you!'" (**"Her Sweet Jerome"**). But in one form or another, love is the single most palpable force in *In Love & Trouble.* This is not the case in *You Can't Keep,* and the volume suffers accordingly.

What happened to love in the later collection? Consider the case of **"Laurel."** What does that supposedly "together" black radical narrator see in wimpy Laurel? Easy answer: his "frazzled but beautifully fitting jeans": "It occurred to me that I could not look at Laurel without wanting to make love with him." As the black radical and her mousy lover engage in "acrobatics of a sexual sort" on Atlanta's public benches, it is clear that "love" is not an issue in this story: these characters have simply fallen in lust. And as a result, the reader finds it impossible to be concerned about the ostensible theme of the story: the ways in which segregation thwarts human relationships. Who cares that segregation "was keeping us from strolling off to a clean, cheap hotel" when all they wanted was a roll in the sack? Likewise, the husband and wife of **"Coming Apart,"** who speak almost ad nauseum on the subjects of pornography and sadomasochism, seem to feel nothing for each other: they are simply spokespersons for particular attitudes regarding contemporary sexual mores, and ample justification for Mootry-Ikerionwu's observation that characterization is definitely not Alice Walker's strong suit. Without love, without warmth, this ostensible Everywife and Everyhusband connect literally only when they are copulating; and as a result Walker's statements regarding the sexual exploitation of women, far from being enriched by the personal touch of seeing how it affects one typical marriage, collapses into a dry lecture punctuated by clumsy plugs for consciousness-raising essays by Audre Lorde, Luisah Teish, and Tracy A. Gardner. Similarly, its title notwithstanding, **"The Lover"** has nothing to do with love. The story's liberated heroine, having left her husband and child for a summer at an artists' colony in New England, decides—just like that—to have an affair with the lupine Ellis: "when she had first seen him she had thought . . . 'my lover,' and had liked, deep down inside, the illicit sound of it. She had never had a lover; he would be her first. Afterwards, she would be truly a woman of her time." Apparently this story was meant to be a study of how one woman—educated, intelligent, creative—uses her newly-liberated sensuality to explore her sense of womanhood, her marriage, her career as a jazz poet. But the one-night-stand quality of her relationship with Ellis, not to mention the inappropriateness of him as a "lover"—he likes to become sexually involved each summer "with talkative women who wrote for *Esquire* and the *New York Times*" because they "made it possible for him to be included in the proper tennis sets and swimming parties at the Colony"—makes the story's heroine seem like a fool. And that points to a major problem with *You Can't Keep a Good Woman Down:* whereas the stories of *In Love & Trouble* move the reader to tears, to shock, to thought, those of the latter volume too often move him to guffaws. Too bad they weren't meant to be humorous.

One would think that a writer of Alice Walker's stature and experience would be aware that, since time began, the reduction of love to fornication has been the basis of jokes, from the ridiculous to the sublime. And whether they come across as comic caricatures (*vide* Laurel and Ellis), examples of bathroom humor, or zany parodies, the characters, subject matter, and writing style of most of the stories in *You Can't Keep a Good Woman Down* leave the reader with a she's-gotta-be-kidding attitude that effectively undercuts its very serious intentions. Consider the subject matter. In stories like **"Porn," "A Letter of the Times,"** and **"Coming Apart,"** Walker *attacks* pornography, sado-masochism, and violence against women by *discussing* them: it's a technique that many writers have used, but it can backfire by (1) appealing to the prurient interests of some readers, (2) imparting excitement to the forbidden topic, or (3) discussing the controversial subject matter so much that it becomes noncontroversial, unshocking; and without the "edge" of controversy, these serious topics often seem to be treated satirically—even when

that is not the case. This is what happens in many stories in *You Can't Keep,* and the problem is compounded by the weak characters. The story **"Coming Apart"** is a good example: the husband dashes home from his bourgeois desk job to sit in the john and masturbate while drooling over the "Jivemates" in *Jiveboy* magazine. None of this shocks: we see so many references to genitalia and elimination in *You Can't Keep* that they seem as mundane as mailing a letter. Worse, the husband himself (called "he" to emphasize his role as Typical Male) comes across as a rather dense, naughty adolescent boy. He is so clearly suffering from a terminal case of the Peter Pan syndrome that it's impossible to believe that he'd respond with "That girl's onto something" when his equally-vapid wife (called "she") reads him yet another anti-pornography essay from her library of black feminist sociological tracts. Walker's-gotta-be-kidding, but she isn't. Likewise, the story **"Fame"** has a streak of crudity that leaves the reader wondering how to respond. For the most part, **"Fame"** consists of the ruminations of one Andrea Clement White (Walker always uses all three names), a wildly successful and universally admired writer who returns to her old college to receive her one-hundred-and-eleventh major award. She doesn't much like her former (Caucasian) colleagues or the banquet they are giving her, as her thoughts on the imminent award speech testifies:

> "This little lady has done . . ." Would he have said "This little man . . ."? But of course not. No man wanted to be called little. He thought it referred to his penis. But to say "little lady" made men think of virgins. Tight, tiny pussies, and moments of rape. (Walker's ellipses)

As Andrea Clement White degenerates from Famous Author to a character type from farce—the salty-tongued granny, the sweet old lady with the dirty mind—everything Walker was trying to say about identity, success, black pride has dissipated. We keep waiting for Walker to wink, to say that **"Fame"** is a satire; but it isn't.

The reader's uncertainty about how to respond to *You Can't Keep a Good Woman Down* is not dispelled by the writing style of many of the stories. Funny thing about lust: when you confuse it with love and try to write about it passionately, the result sounds curiously like parody. The following passage from **"Porn"** reads like a Harlequin romance:

> She was aflame with desire for him.

> On those evenings when all the children [from the respective previous marriages] were with their other parents, he would arrive at the apartment at seven. They would walk hand in hand to a Chinese restaurant a mile away. They would laugh and drink and eat and touch hands and knees over and under the

table. They would come home. Smoke a joint. He would put music on. She would run water in the tub with lots of bubbles. In the bath they would lick and suck each other, in blissful delight. They would admire the rich candle glow on their wet, delectably earth-toned skins. Sniff the incense—the odor of sandal and redwood. He would carry her in to bed.

Music. Emotion. Sensation. Presence.
Satisfaction like rivers
flowing and silver.

Except for the use of controlled substances and the licking and sucking, this is pure Barbara Cartland. Likewise, the narrator's passion for Laurel (in the story of the same name) makes one blush—over the writing: "I thought of his musical speech and his scent of apples and May wine with varying degrees of regret and tenderness"; their "week of passion" had been "magical, memorable, but far too brief."

One might be inclined to excuse these examples on the grounds that love (or lust, or whatever) tends naturally towards purple prose. Unfortunately, however, similar excesses undermine *You Can't Keep* even when the characters' hormones are in check. Here is Andrea Clement White once again, musing on her professional achievements while awaiting the award at her banquet:

If she was famous, she wondered fretfully . . . , why didn't she *feel* famous? She had made money . . . Lots of money. Thousands upon thousands of dollars. She had seen her work accepted around the world, welcomed even, which was more than she'd ever dreamed possible for it. And yet—there remained an emptiness, no, an ache, which told her she had not achieved what she had set out to achieve.

The theme is stale; worse, the writing itself is trite, clichéd; and frankly one wonders how anyone with so unoriginal a mind could be receiving her one hundred and eleventh major award. The same triteness mars **"A Sudden Trip Home in the Spring,"** in which Sarah Davis, a black scholarship student at northern Cresselton College, is "immersed in Camusian philosophy, versed in many languages" and the close personal friend of the small-eyed, milky-legged, dirty-necked blonde daughter of "one of the richest men in the world." Sarah is BWOC at Cresselton: "She was popular"; "Her friends beamed love and envy upon her"; her white tennis partners think that she walks "'Like a gazelle.'" There is a momentary suggestion that Sarah takes her situation and her classmates with a grain of salt ("She was interesting, 'beautiful,' only because they had no idea what made her, charming only because they had no idea from where she came"), but this theme and tone are quickly abandoned as the tale lapses into a curiously un-black reworking of the you-can't-

go-home-again concept. If irony is what Walker has in mind, it certainly doesn't come through; and the over-all impression one gets from **"A Sudden Trip"** is that, like her 1973 biography of Langston Hughes, this is an earnest story intended for adolescent readers who appreciate simplistic themes, characters, and writing styles.

The mature reader's uncertainty over how to respond to **"A Sudden Trip"** takes on a new wrinkle when one considers that Sarah Davis's prototype was another black scholarship student from rural Georgia attending an exclusive northern college: Alice Walker. The least effective, most seemingly comic heroines in Walker's short fiction were inspired by Walker herself. These predominate in *You Can't Keep a Good Woman Down.*

Walker has never denied that there are some autobiographical dimensions to her stories. When **"Advancing Luna— and Ida B. Wells"** was first published in *Ms.* magazine, Walker included a disclaimer that "Luna and Freddie Pye are composite characters, and their names are made up. This is a fictionalized account suggested by a number of real events"; and John O'Brien's 1973 interview with Walker offers further details. Similarly, Walker in a 1981 interview with Kristin Brewer discusses the autobiographical basis of her earliest story, 1967's **"To Hell with Dying"** (*IL&T*). Anyone familiar with Walker's personal life will see the significance of the references to Sarah Lawrence, the doorless first apartment in New York, and the job at the Welfare Department in **"Advancing Luna"** (*YCK*); or the stay at a New England artists' colony in **"The Lover"** (*YCK*); or the marriage to a New York Jew, the baby girl, the novel, and the house in the segregated South in **"Laurel"** (*YCK*). There is nothing inherently wrong with using oneself as the prototype for a story's character; the problem is that the writer tends, of course, to present his fictionalized self in the most flattering—even fantastic—light possible; and too readily that self assumes a larger role in the story than may be warranted by the exigencies of plot and characterization. Consider **"Advancing Luna,"** in which the speaker—who is "difficult to distinguish from Walker herself"—takes over the story like kudzu. We really don't need to hear all about her ex-boyfriends, her getting "high on wine and grass" with a Gene Autry lookalike who paints teeth on fruit, or her adventures in glamorous Africa ("I was taken on rides down the Nile as a matter of course"). Her palpable self-absorption and self-congratulation draw the story's focus away from its titular heroine, poor Luna—the selfless victim of interracial rape who ostensibly is an adoring friend and confidante of the narrator. The reader's immediate response (after confusion) is that the story is really quite funny— and with that response, all of Walker's serious commentary on rape, miscegenation, and segregation have dissipated. We see the same inadvertently comic, Walker-inspired heroine in **"Laurel"** and **"The Lover."** In the latter, the jazz poet "had reached the point of being generally pleased with herself," and no wonder. What with her "carefully selected tall sandals and her naturally tall hair, which stood in an elegant black afro with exactly seven strands of silver hair," and her "creamy brown" things and "curvaceous and strong legs," she is able to stop meals the way other women stop traffic: "If she came late to the dining room and stood in the doorway a moment longer than necessary—looking about for a place to sit after she had her tray—for that moment the noise from the cutlery already in use was still." (Really, who could blame Ellis for wanting her so?) If only there were an element of self-mockery in **"The Lover"**; if only Walker were being ironic in **"A Sudden Trip"**; if only she were lampooning the shopworn notion of the successful but unsatisfied celebrity in **"Fame"**; if only she were parodying romantic writing styles (and thereby puncturing those "love affairs" undertaken purely to prove one's "sexual liberation") in stories like **"Porn," "Laurel,"** and **"The Lover."** But there is absolutely nothing in Alice Walker's interviews, nothing in her many personal essays, nothing in her friends' and colleagues' reviews of her books, nothing anywhere to suggest that she is being anything but dead serious in *You Can't Keep a Good Woman Down.*

What is especially unfortunate about the unintentional humor of *You Can't Keep* is that Walker is quite capable of handling her material very effectively; in several stories, for example, she excels at narrative technique. Consider **"How Did I Get Away with Killing One of the Biggest Lawyers in the State? It Was Easy"** (*YCK*). At first glance, the narrative voice seems untenable: how is it that a poor little black girl from Poultry Street writes such perfect English? (Placed entirely in quotation marks, the story is "written" by her.) We learn the answer at the end of the story: having murdered Bubba, the white lawyer who became her lover after raping her, the narrator/confessor stole all the money from his office safe and used it to finance her college education. Hence her flawless English, and the irony of her "confession": there is no repentance here, and no reader can blame her. The point of view also is consistent and effective. The same cannot be said of the long and rambling **"Source,"** which unfortunately occupies the second most prominent position in *You Can't Keep*—the very end. It has no identifiable point of view, and suffers accordingly. **"Source"** would have been far more effective had Walker utilized what has been identified as her "ruminative style": "a meandering yet disciplined meditation." It is seen in those stories (first-person or otherwise) which essentially record one character's impressions or thoughts, such as **"Fame"** (*YCK*), **"Roselily"** (*IL&T*), and **"The Diary of an African Nun"** (*IL&T*). The sometimes staccato, sometimes discursive third-person narration of **"Roselily"**— "She feels old. Yoked."—is reminiscent of E.A. Robinson's account of another dubious love affair, **"Eros Turannos"** ("She fears him, and will always ask / What fated her to choose him"). Likewise, the barely-restrained first-person narration of **"The Diary of an African Nun"** is very evocative of Li

Po's "The River-Merchant's Wife: A Letter," and it comes as no surprise that Walker attributes her fondness for short literary forms to the Oriental poetry she has loved since college. Also effective is the shifting point of view: the black father's and black daughter's disparate attitudes towards her affair with a married white man is conveyed by the alternating perspectives of **"The Child Who Favored Daughter"** (*IL&T*). This rhythmic technique is usually identified as cinematic, but it also owes much to the blues, as Walker herself is well aware.

This blues quality in the narrative points to the bases of several of her best stories: the oral tradition. Whereas stories based on Walker's own experiences tend, as noted, to be overwritten and hence inadvertently comic, her most memorable tales are often inspired by incidents which were told to her— be they actual accounts (e.g., **"The Revenge of Hannah Kemhuff"** [*IL&T*] depicts her mother's rebuff by a white woman while trying to obtain government food during the Depression) or black folk tales (e.g., **"Strong Horse Tea"**). A particularly striking example is **"The Welcome Table"** (*IL&T*): having been ejected bodily from an all-white church, an old black lady meets Christ on a local road, walks and talks with him, and then is found frozen to death, with eyewitnesses left wondering why she had been walking down that cold road all alone, talking to herself. It could be right out of Stith Thompson. The importance of the oral tradition in Walker's stories is further evident in direct addresses to the reader ("you know how sick [my husband] makes me now when he grins'" [**"Really, *Doesn't* Crime Pay?,"** *IL&T*]) and parenthetical asides ("I scrooched down as small as I could at the corner of Tante Rosie's table, smiling at her so she wouldn't feel embarrassed or afraid" [**"The Revenge of Hannah Kemhuff,"** *IL&T*]). The oral quality of Walker's stories is as old as folk tales, ballads, and slave narratives, and as new as Joan Didion, who shares with Walker a flair for using insane or criminal female narrators: compare Maria in *Play It as It Lays* with the would-be chain saw murderess in **"Really, *Doesn't* Crime Pay?"** (*IL&T*) or the coolly-detached killer of **"How Did I Get Away with Killing. . ."** (*YCK*). Curiously, when the teller of the tale is an emotionally-stable omniscient narrator, the oral tale techniques tends to backfire. For example, the narrator's remark at the opening of **"Elethia"** (*YCK*)—"A certain perverse experience shaped Elethia's life, and made it possible for it to be true that she carried with her at all times a small apothecary jar of ashes"—sounds regrettably like a voice-over by John-Boy Walton.

Clearly the oral tradition is a mixed blessing for Walker's fiction; but it is a particular liability when, as in so many folk tales and ballads, there is a paucity of exposition. Consider **"Entertaining God"** (*IL&T*), in which a little boy worships a gorilla he has stolen from the Bronx Zoo. The story would make no sense to a reader unfamiliar with Flannery

O'Connor's *Wise Blood,* and where a lack of preliminary information tends to draw the reader into O'Connor's novel, it alienates him in **"Entertaining God"**: the story comes across as a disjointed, fragmentary, aborted novella. Another *Wise Blood*-inspired story, **"Elethia"** (in which a character with a habit of lurking about museums steals a mummy which proves to be a stuffed black man), does not fare much better. Similarly, as Chester J. Fontenot points out, **"The Diary of an African Nun"** (*IL&T*), although "only six pages in length, . . . contains material for a novella." Expanded to that length, **"The Diary"** could take an honorable place alongside another first-person account by a disenchanted nun, *The Nun's Story*—assuming, of course, that Walker did not turn it into a series of socioeconomic lectures disguised as chatty personal letters as she did with African missionary Nettie's letters in *The Color Purple.* Lack of exposition can be extreme in Walker's short stories. Consider this extract from **"Porn"** (*YCK*): "They met. Liked each other. Wrote five or six letters over the next seven years. Married other people. Had children. Lived in different cities. Divorced. Met again to discover they now shared a city and lived barely three miles apart." How is the reader to respond to this? Is Walker making a statement about the predictability, the lamentable sameness of the lives lived in the ostensibly individuality-minded 1970s? Or is she just disinclined to write out the details? The more one reads *You Can't Keep,* the more one tends (albeit reluctantly) towards the latter.

Walker's disinclination for exposition, and the concomitant impression that many of her stories are outlines or fragments of longer works, is particularly evident in a technique which mars even her strongest efforts; a marked preference for "telling" over "showing." This often takes the form of summaries littered with adjectives. In **"Advancing Luna"** (*YCK*), for example, the narrator waxes nostalgic over her life with Luna in New York: "our relationship, always marked by mutual respect, evolved into a warm and comfortable friendship which provided a stability and comfort we both needed at that time." But since, as noted earlier, the narrator comes across as vapid and self-absorbed, and since the only impressions she provides of Luna are rife with contempt for this greasy-haired, Clearasil-daubed, poor-little-rich-white-girl from Cleveland, the narrator's paean to their mutual warmth and friendship sounds ridiculous. No wonder critic Katha Pollitt stated outright that she "never believed for a minute" that the narrator and Luna were close friends. Even more unfortunate is Walker's habit of telling the reader what the story is about, of making sure that he doesn't overlook a single theme. For example, in **"The Abortion"** (*YCK*), the heroine Imani, who is just getting over a traumatic abortion, attends the memorial service of a local girl, Holly Monroe, who had been shot to death while returning home from her high school graduation. Lest we miss the point, Walker spells it out for us: "every black girl of a certain vulnerable age *was* Holly Monroe. And an even deeper truth was that Holly

Monroe was herself [i.e., Imani]. Herself shot down, aborted on the eve of becoming herself." Similarly transparent, here is one of the last remarks in the story **"Source"** (*YCK*). It is spoken by Irene, the former teacher in a federally-funded adult education program, to her ex-hippie friend, Anastasia/Tranquility: "'I was looking toward "government" for help; you were looking to Source [a California guru]. In both cases, it was the wrong direction—*any* direction that is away from ourselves is the wrong direction.'" The irony of their parallel situations is quite clear without having Irene articulate her epiphany in an Anchorage bar. Even at the level of charactonyms, Walker "tells" things to her reader. We've already noted the over-used "he"/"she" device for underscoring sex roles, but even personal names are pressed into service. For example, any reasonably perceptive reader of the vignette **"The Flowers"** (*IL&T*) will quickly understand the story's theme: that one first experiences reality in all its harshness while far from home, physically and/or experientially; one's immediate surroundings are comparatively "innocent." The reader would pick up on the innocence of nearsightedness even if the main character, ten-year-old Myop, hadn't been named after myopia. Likewise, **"The Child Who Favored Daughter"** is actually marred by having the father kill his daughter because he confuses her with his dead sister named "Daughter." The hints of incest, the unclear cross-generational identities, and the murky Freudian undercurrents are sufficiently obvious without the daughter/Daughter element: it begins to smack of Abbott and Costello's "Who's on First?" routine after just a few pages. Alice Walker's preference for telling over showing suggests a mistrust of her readers, or her texts, or both.

One might reasonably ask how a professional writer with twenty years' experience could seem so unsure about her materials and/or her audience, could have such uneven judgment regarding fictional technique, could seem so strained or defensive in her short stories. Part of the answer may be that she is a cross-generic writer. Leslie Stephen felt that newspaper writing was lethal for a fiction writer, and perhaps the same may be said for journalistic writing—especially when the magazine's target readership is a special interest group. Whatever the case, as a short story writer Alice Walker seems to alternate between (1) presenting editorials as fiction, (2) experimenting with the short story as a recognized literary form, and (3) rather self-consciously writing "conventional" short stories. At best, the results are mixed.

The magazine editorials which masquerade as short stories are among Walker's least successful efforts. The classic example of this is **"Coming Apart"** (*YCK*). It began as the introduction to a chapter on violence against third world women in *Take Back the Night;* then, with the title of **"A Fable,"** it ended up in *Ms.* magazine, for which Walker happened to be a contributing editor; and now, unrevised, it is being marketed as a short story in *You Can't Keep a Good*

Woman Down. The volume contains several stories which occupy this No Man's Land between journalism and fiction: **"Advancing Luna," "Porn," "A Letter of the Times"**—and, somewhat less transparently, **"Elethia," "Petunias,"** and **"Source"**—all exist so that Walker (or a mouthpiece character) can make some statement about pornography, racism, politics, sado-masochism, the Search for Self, whatever. Perhaps these "stories" have some impact when read in isolation, months apart, in a magazine such as *Ms.;* but when packaged as a collection of short stories they are predictable and pedantic. The omniscient narrators and mouthpiece characters rarely get off their soap-boxes; too often they resort to lecturing other characters or the reader. Consider this appraisal of the husband in **"Coming Apart"**: "What he has refused to see . . . is that where white women are depicted in pornography as 'objects,' black women are depicted as animals. Where white women are depicted at least as human beings, black women are depicted as shit." The insistence upon the points Walker is trying to make would be appropriate for editorials or magazine essays, but it doesn't wash in a short story.

Those stories in which Walker attempts to experiment with what is commonly held to be "the short story" are a bit stronger, although they often have that fragmentary, unpolished quality alluded to earlier. Frequently the experimental pieces are very short: **"Petunias"** (*YCK*) is a one-page diary entry by a woman blown up by her Vietnam veteran son; it is entirely in italics, as are **"The Flowers"** (*IL&T*) and **"Elethia"** (*YCK*). As Mel Watkins notes in the *New York Times Book Review,* Alice Walker's shorter pieces tend to be "thin as fiction," and he is probably correct to classify them as that short story offshoot, "prose poems." Longer pieces also can be experimental. For example, **"Roselily"** (*IL&T*) utilizes a point/counterpoint format, alternating fragments of the wedding ceremony with the thoughts of the bride: the phrase "to join this man and this woman" triggers "She thinks of ropes, chains, handcuffs, his religion." The irony is as heavy-handed as the imagery, but the device does work in this story. Experimentation with structure just as often fails, however. **"Entertaining God"** (*IL&T*) offers three discrete cinematic scenes—one of the boy and the gorilla, another (evidently a flashback) of his father, and a third of his mother, a librarian turned radical poet; but the scenes never really connect. Perhaps it was meant to be what Walker has termed (in reference to *Meridian*) a "crazy quilt story," but if so the quilting pieces never do form a pattern. The same quality of uncertainty and incompletion is evident in **"Advancing Luna,"** which offers four—count 'em, four—separate endings with such pretentious titles as "Afterwords, Afterwards, Second Thoughts," "Discarded Notes," and "Imaginary Knowledge." Apparently meant to be thought-provoking, instead they suggest that Walker is indecisive about why she even wrote the story—or, what is worse, is resorting to experimentation as an end in itself.

In light of all this, one might expect Walker's more "conventional" stories to be uniformly stronger than the essay/story hybrids or the experimental efforts, but such is not always the case. All too often, conventionality brings out the banal, the sentimental, and the contrived in Alice Walker. Not surprisingly, two of her earliest stories—**"To Hell with Dying"** (*IL&T*) and **"A Sudden Trip Home in the Spring"** (*YCK*)—are very conventional in terms of structure, characterization, and action. In each, a young woman returns to her rural Southern home from college up North at the death of an elderly loved one. Old Mr. Sweet in **"To Hell with Dying"** is a sort of dipsomaniac Uncle Remus, wrinkled and white-haired, with the obligatory whiskers, a nightshirt redolent of liniment, and a fondness for singing "Sweet Georgia Brown" to the narrator, who helps to "revive" him during his periodic fake deathbed scenes. In short, he is very much the sentimentalized "old darky" character that Walker challenged so vigorously in **"Elethia,"** that O'Connoresque tale of the grinning, stuffed Uncle Albert in the white man's restaurant window. Sarah Davis, the heroine of the equally sentimental **"A Sudden Trip,"** summarizes what she learned by attending her estranged father's funeral: "'sometimes you can want something a whole lot, only to find out later that it wasn't what you *needed* at all.'" Is it any wonder that black writer Ishmael Reed has called Walker "'the colored Norman Rockwell'"?

Her sentimental streak has been noted by many of her commentators (Jerry H. Bryant admits to a lump in his throat), and Walker herself acknowledges she is "nostalgic for the solidarity and sharing a modest existence can sometimes bring." Perhaps it does have a place in some of the stories from early in her career. But it seems frankly incongruous in the work of a woman who prides herself on being a hard-hitting realist, and it poses particular problems in her handling of the stories' endings. The potentially incisive **"Fame"** is all but ruined when the tough-as-nails Andrea Clement White melts at hearing a little black girl sing a slave song. Likewise, **"The Lover"** (*YCK*) ends with the jazz poet heroine in a reverie: she "lay in bed next day dreaming of all the faraway countries, daring adventures, passionate lovers still to be found." Perhaps in part to avoid these final lapses into sentimentality, Walker sometimes doesn't "end" her stories: she leaves them "open." It can be a very effective technique in stories such as **"Strong Horse Tea"** (*IL&T*) or **"The Child Who Favored Daughter"** (*IL&T*), where the pain is underscored by the lack—indeed, the impossibility—of resolution in the character's situations. Probably Walker's strongest non-sentimental endings belong to three of the most conventional stories: **"The Revenge of Hannah Kemhuff"** (*IL&T*), **"Nineteen Fifty-Five"** (*YCK*), and **"Source"** (*YCK*). In **"The Revenge,"** Mrs. Sarah Marie Sadler Holley, fearing that a black rootworker will be able to use them in spells against her, stores her feces "in barrels and plastic bags in the upstairs closets" rather than trust "the earthen secrecy of the water mains." Her psychotic behavior turns her husband against her, and she lets herself die in a chilling dénouement that would do Miss Emily Grangerford proud. Walker has used the psychology of guilt and fear in lieu of the Jesus-fixed-her-but-good attitude held by Hannah's prototype, Walker's mother, and the refusal to sentimentalize enhances the story. Likewise, **"Nineteen Fifty-Five,"** a strong story with which to open *You Can't Keep* but atypical of the volume, is a sort of docudrama tracing the career of Elvis Presley (Traynor) through the eyes of blues great Big Mama Thornton (Gracie Mae Still). Still never does understand this sleepy-eyed white man or his alien world, and her reaction to seeing his funeral on television—"One day this is going to be a pitiful country, I thought"—is the perfect conclusion to the story. No sentiment, no commentary. Finally, **"Source"** offers a surprisingly non-sentimental ending to an insistently nostalgia-soaked story. Whether they are grooving in a Marin County commune with Peace, Calm, and Bliss (didn't nostalgia for the '60s end with *Easy Rider?*) or getting it together in the '70s in an Anchorage bar (sort of "*The Big Chill* Goes Alaskan"), the story of Irene and Anastasia/Tranquility has little for anyone. But the ending of the story—that is, after the now-reconciled heroines have hugged "knee against knee, thigh against thigh, breast against breast, neck nestled against neck"—is quite provocative: a group of tourists, peering through the mists, believe they are seeing Mt. McKinley: "They were not. It was yet another, nearer, mountain's very large feet, its massive ankles wreathed in clouds, that they took such pleasure in." Suggestive without being saccharine, and ironic without that "tinge of cynicism" which undercuts so many of Walker's endings, it is an ideal fade-out conclusion to a collection that, with varying degrees of success, seeks to pose questions, to raise issues, to offer no pat answers.

The strengths and weaknesses of *In Love & Trouble* and *You Can't Keep a Good Woman Down* offer little clue as to the direction Alice Walker will take as a writer of short fiction in years to come. Surely she will continue to write short stories: Walker personally believes that women are best suited to fiction of limited scope—David Bradley points out that this is "the kind of sexist comment a male critic would be pilloried for making"—and she feels further that, as her career progresses, her writing has been "always moving toward more and more clarity and directness." The often fragmentary and rambling tales of *You Can't Keep* published eight years after the moving and tightly constructed *In Love & Trouble,* would suggest that this is not the case. At this point in her career as a short story writer, one wishes that Walker would acknowledge the validity of Katha Pollitt's appraisal of *You Can't Keep*: "Only the most coolly abstract and rigorously intellectual writer" can achieve what Walker attempts in this recent volume, but unfortunately that is not what she is like: "As a storyteller she is impassioned, sprawling, emotional, lushly evocative, steeped in place, in memory, in the compelling power of narrative itself. A lavishly gifted writer,

in other words—but not of this sort of book." What Alice Walker needs is to take a step backward: to return to the folk tale formats, the painful exploration of interpersonal relationships, the naturally graceful style that made her earlier collection of short stories, the durable *In Love & Trouble,* so very fine. Touch base, lady.

Robert James Butler (essay date Summer 1993)

SOURCE: "Alice Walker's Vision of the South in *The Third Life of Grange Copeland,*" in *African American Review,* Vol. 27, No. 2, Summer, 1993, pp. 192-204.

[*In the following essay, Butler discusses Walker's complicated portrayal of the South in* The Third Life of Grange Copeland, *in which she uses each life to show a different aspect of the South.*]

> Two-heading was dying out, he lamented. "Folks what can look at things in more than one way is done got rare."

In **"The Black Writer and the Southern Experience,"** Alice Walker defines her response to the South in a richly ambivalent way. Although she stresses that she does not intend to "romanticize Southern black country life" and is quick to point out that she "hated" the South, "generally," when growing up in rural Georgia, she nevertheless emphasizes that Southern black writers have "enormous richness and beauty to draw from." This "double vision" of the South is at the center of most of her fiction and is given extremely complex treatment in her best work. While Walker can remember with considerable resentment the larger white world composed of "evil greedy men" who paid her sharecropper father three hundred dollars for twelve months of labor while working him "to death," she can also call vividly to mind the "sense of *community*" which gave blacks a way of coping with and sometimes transcending the hardships of such a racist society. Although she emphatically states that she is not "nostalgic . . . for lost poverty," she can also lyrically recall the beauties of the Southern land, "loving the earth so much that one longs to taste it and sometimes does." Even the Southern black religious traditions, which she consciously rejected as a college student because she saw them with one part of her mind as "a white man's palliative," she values in another way because her people "had made [religion] into something at once simple and noble," an "antidote against bitterness."

Walker's ambivalence, therefore, is a rich and complex mode of vision, a way of seeing her Southern background which prevents her from either naïvely romanticizing the South or reducing it to an oversimplified vision of despair and resentment. Ambivalence, or what Grange Copeland might call "two-heading," allows Walker to tell the full truth about her experience in the South. Avoiding the "blindness" created by her awareness of the injustices done to blacks in the South, she is able to draw "a great deal of positive material" from her outwardly "'underprivileged'" background. Indeed, she stresses that her status as a black Southern writer endows her with special advantages:

> No one could wish for a more advantageous heritage than that bequeathed to the black writer in the South: a compassion for the earth, a trust in humanity beyond our knowledge of evil, and an abiding sense of justice. We inherit a great responsibility as well, for we must give voice to centuries not only of silent bitterness and hate but also of neighborly kindness and sustaining love.

Walker's sense of herself as both a black and a Southern writer, then, enables her to participate in a literary tradition containing a richness of vision which she finds missing in the mainstream of American literature. In **"Saving the Life That Is Your Own: The Importance of Models in the Artist's Life,"** she expresses a distaste for the overall pessimism of modern American literature. She claims that "the gloom of defeat is thick" in twentieth-century American literature because "American writers tended to end their books and their characters' lives as if there were no better existence for which to struggle." But because Southern black experience is rooted in both "struggle" and "some kind of larger freedom" resulting from such struggle, the black writer is able to overcome the despair which enervates so much modern literature. African American writers, therefore, participate in a literary tradition which is distinctive for both its lucid criticism of modern life and its special ability to recover human value and thus make important affirmations which give black American literature a unique vitality and resonance.

The single work which best expresses Walker's powerful ambivalence toward Southern life is her first novel, *The Third Life of Grange Copeland,* a book notable for its vitality and its resonance.
—Robert James Butler

The single work which best expresses Walker's powerful ambivalence toward Southern life is her first novel, *The Third Life of Grange Copeland,* a book notable for its vitality and its resonance. Walker's complex vision of the South can be seen in her development of the novel's three main characters—Brownfield, Ruth, and Grange Copeland. While Brownfield is a terrifying example of how the South can physically enslave and spiritually cripple black people, Ruth's story offers considerable hope because she is able to leave the

South, rejecting the racist world which destroys Brownfield and, in so doing, move toward a larger, freer world which offers her fresh possibilities. Grange Copeland's narrative points out some of the positive features of Southern black life. He returns to Georgia after an unsuccessful journey north to find the things he needs for his identity—a sense of place and a feeling of family and community, what Michael Cooke has called "intimacy." Although the narratives, taken in isolation, do not express the author's whole vision of Southern life, together they offer a series of interrelated perspectives which capture Walker's richly ambivalent vision of the South. While Grange's story in isolation might suggest a glib romanticizing of the black South and while the stories of Ruth and Brownfield might suggest an equally simplistic debunking of black Southern life, all three narratives constitute what Walker has called "the richness of the black writer's experience in the South."

Brownfield's narrative concentrates all that is negative about Southern culture: He is cruelly victimized by the extreme racism and poverty of the Georgia backwoods world in which he is born and raised. As his name clearly suggests, his is a case of blighted growth; he is a person who has been physically and emotionally withered by the nearly pathological environment which surrounds him. By the end of the novel, he is portrayed as "a human being . . . completely destroyed" by the worst features of rural Southern life—ignorance, poverty, racism, and violence. Appropriately, one of the earliest images of him in the novel describes him as undernourished and diseased, his head covered with tatter sores, his legs afflicted with tomato sores, and his armpits filled with boils running with pus. As his narrative develops, these images of disease coalesce into a frightening metaphor which dramatizes how Brownfield is infected and eventually destroyed by a racist world which systematically deprives him of human nourishment.

This is particularly true of the way in which the system of Southern sharecropping destroys his family by enslaving them to the land which would otherwise nourish them. Because Brownfield's father Grange cannot make an adequate living for his family, his ego is gradually eroded, until he comes to see himself as a "stone," a "robot," and a "cipher." He therefore fails as a husband and a father, driving his wife to suicide and withdrawing emotionally from his son. The net effect on Brownfield is to engrave deep emotional scars into his character which ultimately stunt his growth. After being abandoned by Grange and losing his mother shortly afterwards, Brownfield is frozen into a condition of Southern servitude. His efforts to establish a new life fail to materialize because his loss of family and the destruction of self-esteem caused by a racist environment trap him in a kind of moral vacuum:

> He was expected to raise himself up on air, which was all that was left after his work for others. Others

who were always within their rights to pay practically nothing for his labor. He was never able to do more than exist on air; he was never able to build on it, and was never able to have any land of his own; and was never able to set his woman up in style, which more than anything else was what he wanted to do.

Literally cheated out of land and morally dispossessed of a human foundation for his life, Brownfield is ironically condemned to repeat his father's failures. As he realizes not long after being abandoned by Grange, " . . . his own life was becoming a repetition of his father's." His efforts to go north result in "weeks of indecisive wandering," eventually bringing him to a small Georgia town where he forms a debilitating relationship with Josie, one of his father's discarded lovers. When he does discover a fruitful relationship with Mem, their marriage is ruined by the same factors which destroyed his parents' marriage. The "warm, life-giving circle" of their life together is gradually dissolved by "the shadow of eternal bondage" which eroded his father's self-esteem. Bound like his father by "the chain that held him to the land," Brownfield too becomes neurotically jealous of his wife and degrades her to the point where he can recover part of his ego by feeling superior to her. Like his father, who pushed his wife into suicide because he could not bear loving her and could not adequately support her, Brownfield murders Mem because a social environment that strips him of manhood cancels out his love for her. Forced by an oppressively racist society to "plow a furrow his father had laid," Brownfield is indeed a "brown field," a crop that has failed to mature and bear fruit because his life has been deprived of necessary nutrients.

Like his five-year-old daughter, who is slowly poisoned by the arsenic she uses to dust the cotton crop in order to protect it from boll weevils, he is gradually victimized by a uniquely Southern system of segregation and sharecropping which infects his life. He eventually becomes exactly what his social environment wants him to be—an extension of its most pathological impulses. Indeed, Brownfield not only comes to accept the South but develops a perverse love of the world which dehumanizes him. Thus, he blankly accepts the impoverished roles extended to him by his Southern environment and makes no attempt either to rebel against these roles or to seek a better world:

> He had no faith that any other place would be better. He fitted himself into the slot in which he found himself; for fun he poured oil into the streams to kill the fish and tickled his own vanity by drowning cats.

A normal boy early in the novel, Brownfield becomes the book's most degraded character, for in accepting his "place" in Southern society, he degenerates into a killer of families and a poisoner of innocent life.

If Brownfield's narrative dramatizes Walker's most severe criticisms of the South, the story of his daughter Ruth qualifies this pessimistic vision by providing an alternative to the meaninglessness of Brownfield's life. Even though Ruth spends her formative years in the same environment which poisoned her father, she is able to protect herself with a number of antidotes because she develops a consciousness of Southern life which makes her aware of both its strengths and dangers. She is thus able to empower herself with some of the strengths of black folk culture in the Deep South and is also able to imagine her life in terms which transcend the South, ultimately leaving it for a larger world which offers her new possibilities. Whereas Brownfield's life travels a deterministic circle of futility (all his efforts to gain physical and emotional distance from the racist South fail), Ruth's story is existential in outlook. It involves a process of awakening and liberation. Like the slave narratives, which Walker has described as a part of a literary tradition where "escape for the body and freedom for the soul went together," Ruth's story is a flight from twentieth-century forms of Southern bondage. Her consciousness distills all that is good in her Southern black traditions and allows her to imagine a broader world beyond the South. As a result, she is able to create "a way out of no way." Like the Biblical Ruth, she finds herself an alien in a strange land, but, unlike Ruth, she can find her way to a kind of promised land, a new space offering fresh possibilities.

A crucial part of her liberation is contained in the fact that she does not grow up in the kind of spiritual and emotional vacuum which blighted Brownfield's life. Although she has had to face the physical poverty and racism which characterize her father's existence, she gains the benefit of the family life he was deprived of, and this puts her in contact with nourishing cultural and personal values. In contrast to Brownfield, who spins in futile circles because he "was expected to raise himself up on air," Ruth is raised by a mother whom she comes to regard as "a saint," someone who makes heroic efforts to meet her human needs. Although Mem literally gives up her life opposing Brownfield's acceptance of his "place" in Southern society, she succeeds in moving the family to a town where Ruth, for a time at least, has the benefit of a real house and formal schooling. More importantly, Mem provides Ruth with a powerful role model, for she is a woman who maintains her human dignity in a dehumanizing environment. Like the women whom Walker describes in *In Search of Our Mother's Gardens* who provided her with role models, Mem is an "exquisite butterfly trapped in an evil honey." By "inheriting" her mother's "vibrant, creative spirit," Ruth comes to transcend the limitations which white society seeks to impose on black women.

After Mem is murdered—literally by Brownfield and symbolically by the Southern society he comes to love and represent—Ruth is taken in by Grange, who becomes her surrogate father. From the moment of her birth, Grange sees Ruth as unique and beautiful, someone who almost magically appears in the midst of an environment which is harsh and ugly. Marveling at Ruth as a newborn child, he exclaims, "'Out of all kinds of shit comes something soft, clean, and sweet smellin'.'" From this point on, Grange dedicates himself to protecting Ruth from the foulness of the Southern environment into which she was born, and he commits himself to nurturing that which is "sweet" and "clean" in her. He provides her with a "snug house" in which to live and also gives her for the first time in her life an adequate supply of nourishing food.

More importantly, he nourishes her mind and soul. He forbids her to work in the cotton fields which have helped to destroy Brownfield's life, telling her, "'You not some kind of field hand!'" and he arranges for her to attend school. But in an important way he also becomes her teacher, instructing her in "the realities of life," drawing material from his own wide experience and his extensive knowledge of black folklore. His retelling of folktales from the black South provides her with a vivid sense of a mythic hero—the trickster "who could talk himself out of any situation." She thus learns from an early age a lesson which her father never acquired—that words and intelligence, not raw violence, have the power to transform experience by creating understanding and control over life. When listening to Grange sing blues music, she likewise feels "kin to something very old, a musical tradition arising out of the black South which transforms suffering into a kind of human triumph rooted in what Ralph Ellison has called a "near tragic, near comic lyricism."

By connecting Ruth to the life-giving tradition of the black folk art of the South, Grange provides her with the time-tested values which will help her to survive and even triumph over the racist world which destroys so many other people in the novel. His recounting episodes from black history reinforces in her mind the crucial idea that black people established a strong and viable culture in the South, despite the efforts of the dominant society to destroy that culture. His accounts of his personal past, especially from his boyhood, also bring to life in Ruth's consciousness "all sorts of encounters with dead folks and spirits and occasionally the Holy Ghost." In other words, his stories give her vital access to an imaginatively rich, emotionally potent world—precisely the kind of world which the psychologically underdeveloped Brownfield never becomes aware of. As Ruth grows older, Grange also teaches her about the world beyond the South. He steals books from the white library which open her mind and stimulate her imagination—books about mythology, geography, Africa, and romantic rebellion. He also reads her episodes from the Bible, especially the story of Exodus, again empowering her with the compelling myth of an oppressed people who triumph over circumstance through the strength of their will and spirit.

Although he twice offers her his farm, which would root her deeply to the South he has come to accept as his home, Grange loves Ruth enough to prepare her for the most dramatic action of her life, her flight from the South. Late in the novel, when Ruth asks him about her future, he tells her, "'We got this farm. We can stay here till kingdom come.'" But by this point in her life she feels stifled by the segregated South and tells him, "'I'm not going to be a hermit. I want to get away from here someday.'" The same fences which provide Grange with a sense of security Ruth perceives as encroachments.

The final third of the novel, therefore, deals with Ruth's increasing dissatisfaction with the rural South and her desire to move toward a larger, broader world which her protean identity needs. This struggle finally takes the form of her gaining independence from Brownfield and everything he represents about the South. A man who "had enslaved his own family," as well as himself, he is intent on taking Ruth back after he has been released from prison. When he encounters Ruth late in the novel as she walks to school, he shouts at her, "'You belongs to me, just like my chickens or my hogs.'" "'You need shooting,'" she defiantly replies. Rejecting the crippling roles imposed on her mother and grandmother by Southern society, she observes that "'I'm not yours.'"

As the novel draws to its close, Ruth, with Grange's help, achieves her independence from her father and Southern life in general. It becomes increasingly clear to Grange that the only way to protect Ruth from Brownfield is to encourage her to leave the South, for the full weight of Southern law is in favor of returning her to Brownfield, whom Judge Harry regards as her "'*real* daddy.'" Grange, therefore, centers his life on helping "to prepare Ruth for some great and herculean task"—her emancipation from Southern slavery and her pursuit of a new life. He buys her an automobile on her sixteenth birthday and begins saving money which she will use for college. He ultimately sacrifices his own life to save her from Brownfield, for he is killed by the police after shooting Brownfield when the court takes Ruth away from him.

The novel ends on a painful note of ambivalence. Southern injustice erupts in violence which takes Grange's life, yet his death frees Ruth for a new life of expanded possibilities. By the conclusion of the book, Ruth is poised for flight into a fast-changing world which will transform her. Observing the nightly television news, she becomes fascinated by "pictures of students marching" as they work toward a more open and fluid society. Even the Georgia backwater in which she has been raised shows dramatic evidence of real change—voter registration campaigns, interracial marriage, and the beginnings of integration.

But the novel strongly implies that Ruth will not stay long in the South because her own protean self requires more space and possibility than the South at this point in its history can provide. Eager to "'rise up'" in life, she dreams of going north. As she tells Grange, "'I want to get away from here someday. . . . I think maybe I'll go North, like you did. . . .'" Later she thinks vaguely of journeying to Africa. The exact physical direction of her life is not made clear, nor could it be. Like many African American heroic figures such as Frederick Douglass and the persona of Richard Wright's *Black Boy,* she has a lucid notion of the Southern places she must leave but keeps an indeterminate vision of the open space to which she will move. Like the Jews in Exodus, whose story Grange has told her "for perhaps the hundredth time," she must leave an all-too-real Egypt in order to quest for a mythic "Promised Land."

The third major narrative in the novel incorporates the visions of the South implicit in the other two narratives and offers one more critically important perspective on the South. Whereas Grange Copeland's "first" life powerfully reinforces the bleakly pessimistic view of the South implicit in Brownfield's narrative, and his "second" life is very similar in certain ways to Ruth's story, because it is a flight from the slavery of the segregated South, Grange's "third" life contains an important element missing in the other two narratives—his remarkable return to the South, which regenerates him as a human being. It is this return, like Celie's return to Georgia at the end of *The Color Purple,* which underscores Walker's most affirmative vision of the South. In returning to Baker County, Grange achieves "his total triumph over life's failures," creating a new place for himself by transforming the racist society which has withered Brownfield into a genuine "home" which nurtures Ruth and also causes him to be "a reborn man." Like the hero described in Joseph Campbell's *Hero with a Thousand Faces,* Grange attains truly heroic status by a three-part journey involving the leaving of a settled, known world; the experiencing of tests in an unknown world; and the returning home with a new mode of consciousness which transforms his life and the lives of others.

Walker, who knew the most brutal features of the rural South firsthand, is careful not to romanticize the South to which Grange returns. She emphasizes that Grange goes back to Georgia not because of a sudden nostalgia for magnolias and wisteria but simply because the circumstances of his life have made him a Southerner, for better or for worse: ". . . though he hated it as much as any place else, where he was born would always be home for him. Georgia would be home for him, and every other place foreign." Crucial to Grange's creation of a new home for himself in the South is his securing of land. Using the money he obtained in various devious ways in the North and the money he gets from Josie's sale of the Dew Drop Inn, he builds a farm which constitutes "a sanctu-ary" from the white world which has victimized him economically and poisoned him with hatred. As his name suggests, he is able to "cope" with his "land" so that he can build a "grange" or farm which will nourish himself and others. This "refuge" not only provides him with food from his garden and a livelihood from his sale of crops but, more importantly, gives him the independence and freedom he needs to assume meaningful roles which his earlier life lacked: ". . . he had come back to Baker County, because it was home, and to Josie, because she was the only person in the world who loved him. . . ."

Accepting the love from Josie which he had earlier rejected because he found it "possessive," he marries her shortly after returning from the North, thus embracing the role of husband. In this way he transforms her Dew Drop Inn from the whorehouse which was a grotesque parody of a human community into a real place of love between a man and a woman. Not long after this he begins to assume the role of father when he assists Mem in the delivery of Ruth on Christmas Day, a time when Brownfield is too drunk to be of much use to his family. After Brownfield murders Mem, Grange fully undertakes the role of father, providing Ruth with the love and care which he was unable to extend to Brownfield in his "first" life. In all these ways Grange is able to create a small but vital black community separated from the larger white world intent on destroying the black family.

Grange's journey north failed him because it poisoned him with the same kind of hatred which damaged his previous life in the South. His Northern experiences are revealed in the terrifying epiphany when he gloats over stealing a white woman's money while watching her drown in Central Park Lake. The whole experience becomes a grotesque inversion of a religious conversion, very much like Bigger Thomas's killing of Mary Dalton in *Native Son.* Like Bigger, who feels a grisly sort of "new life" when he savors the death of Mary Dalton, Grange feels "alive and liberated for the first time in his life" as he contemplates the image of withdrawing his hand from the drowning woman. He thus commits in a different form the same sin which brought his "first" life in the South to such a disturbing close. Just as Grange is partly responsible for the deaths of his wife and stepchild, whom he abandons when he is no longer able to cope with the societally induced hatred which poisons all of his human relationships, so too does he abandon the pregnant white woman when societally induced hatred causes her to call him a "nigger." Withdrawing his hand from her also echoes an earlier gesture of withdrawing his hand from his son shortly before he abandons him. Just as his hand "nearly touche[s]" the woman's in Central Park, his hand has earlier "stopped just before it reached [Brownfield's] cheek." In both cases his withdrawal of human sympathy from people is a clear index of how Grange has been emotionally damaged by the racist society in which he lives.

The South and North, therefore, are portrayed in Grange's first two lives as dehumanized and dehumanizing environments. But whereas the South has turned him into a "stone" and a "robot," the North converts him into the kind of invisible man classically described in African American literature by Du Bois and Ellison:

> He was, perhaps, no longer regarded merely as a "thing"; what was even more cruel to him was that to the people he met and passed daily he was not even in existence! The South had made him miserable, with nerve endings raw from continual surveillance from contemptuous eyes, but they *knew he was there*. Their very disdain proved it. The North put him into solitary confinement where he had to manufacture his own hostile stares in order to see himself. . . . Each day he had to say his name to himself over and over again to shut out the silence.

Although both environments pose severe threats to his humanity, Grange finally chooses the South over the North because he is humanly visible to Southerners, whereas Northern society is completely blind to him. Although Southern whites regard blacks with "contemptuous eyes" which distort their vision, they at least focus upon blacks as human beings; the white Northerners Grange meets would reduce blacks to complete anonymity. Thus, Grange experiences a condition of "solitary confinement" in the North but in the South is given the opportunity to feel the "sense of *community*" which Walker has extolled in her essays as a particularly important feature of Southern black life.

It is Grange's achievement of a "home" in Georgia which provides him with a genuine human conversion. He returns to Baker County with disturbing vestiges of his first two lives, fits of depression which lead him to contemplate suicide and express an "impersonal cruelty" which frightens Ruth. But his recovery of the meaningful roles of husband, father, and farmer lead to his regeneration, providing him with a "third" life. Josie's love, though flawed, is deeply experienced for a while, and Ruth is able, with "the magic of her hugs and kisses," to bring him out of his bouts of suicidal depression. As the novel develops, he admits to Ruth that she has "'thaw[ed]'" the "'numbness'" in him. Whereas early in the book Grange seems "devoid of any emotion . . . except that of bewilderment" and whereas in the middle of the book he is blinded by a nearly demonic hatred of whites, he finally becomes a fully developed, even heroic, person because of his recovery of a "home" in the black South.

Walker, however, consciously avoids idealizing Grange's Southern home. As the novel's ending makes clear, it is a small oasis of human love surrounded by the same kind of Southern racism which has blighted the lives of scores of black people in the novel. Southern courts continue to mete out injustice, and Southern violence continues to take the lives of innocent people, most notably Fred Hill, who is murdered when his son attempts to integrate a previously all white school. And as Ruth's narrative demonstrates, even Grange's home has its restrictive features. Although such a pastoral "refuge" satisfies Grange with a sense of place and continuity with the past, Walker clearly endorses Ruth's desire to leave it for the open space which her young spirit desires. Grange's story may contradict Thomas Wolfe's notion that you can't go home again, but Ruth's story emphasizes the fact that staying home or returning home for good can stifle certain kinds of people. Although Grange's Southern home provides Ruth with an essential foundation for human growth, ultimately she must leave that home if she is to continue to grow.

As Alice Walker has observed in *In Search of Our Mother's Gardens,* her sense of reality is inherently dialectical:

> "I believe that the truth of any subject comes out when all sides of the story are put together, and all their different meanings make one new one. Each writer writes the missing parts of the other writer's story. And the whole story is what I'm after."

The Third Life of Grange Copeland succeeds as a novel because it consciously avoids an oversimplified vision which expresses only one "side" of Southern life. Artfully mixing its three main narratives in order to include the "missing parts" absent from any single narrative, the novel suggests a "whole truth" about the South which is complex and many-sided. The book thus remains true to its author's deepest prompting and her most profound sense of her Southern black heritage.

Judy Mann (review date 16 January 1994)

SOURCE: "Victims of Tradition," in *Washington Post Book World,* January 16, 1994, p. 4.

[*In the following review, Mann praises Walker's and Pratibha Parmar's attempt to illuminate the prevalence of female genital mutilation in Africa, but faults the book for a slow start.*]

The World Health Organization estimates that some 80 million women living today have undergone an ancient and excruciatingly painful ritual known as genital mutilation. It is widely practiced in Egypt, the Sudan and the Horn of Africa—by rigidly patriarchal cultures. Pretexts marshalled to defend the practice range from religion and hygiene to cultural traditions. But the true reason this humiliating, dangerous practice continues is to ensure that women will remain virgins until marriage, and to maintain control over women by destroying their ability to enjoy sex. Mutilated women are turned into sexual vessels for men, many of whom believe the procedure enhances their own enjoyment.

The age at which girls are mutilated—from infancy to post-puberty—and the degree of mutilation varies widely between tribal cultures. Symbolic circumcision involves a ritual nicking of the clitoris to draw blood. Pharaonic circumcision, the most extreme form, involves the scraping away of the clitoris and the inner labia. Then, in a procedure known as infibulation, the outer labia are stitched together with sutures of catgut and with acacia thorns, leaving a hole the size of a pencil for the passage of urine and menses. After the outer labia are sewn up, the girl's legs are bound together from the hips to the ankles and she is forced to lie still on her back for several weeks until the labia grow together, forming a permanent closure over the vagina. At her marriage ceremony she is cut open again with a knife or sharp stone by her husband or mother-in-law.

When the United States first joined the hunger relief effort in Somalia—where 90 percent of the women have undergone Pharaonic circumcision—I wrote a column suggesting that we use American relief efforts to carrot-and-stick a campaign to wipe out female genital mutilation in that country.

The morning my column appeared, I received a phone call from a Somali woman working for a health organization in Washington. She said that women in her country were working to eradicate the practice and they needed help from women in the international community. I learned that my caller was a physician.

I also learned that she had undergone Pharaonic circumcision as a child.

This was the end of my illusions about female genital mutilation. It wasn't a ritual tribal practice in the abstract. It had been done to someone real: a voice on the telephone. I understood at that moment that the mutilation of women involved me.

In countries where circumcision is performed, it is taboo to talk about it. In the West, we are too horrified or ignorant to talk about it. Those of us who do know about it often think of it as something done only to primitive women living in mudhuts. Our silence is a psychological device for marginalizing the horror and separating ourselves from it—and it contributes to the shameful international indifference that allows it to continue.

Alice Walker and Pratibha Parmar aren't having any part of this global denial. Walker, who won a Pulitzer Prize in 1983 for her novel *The Color Purple* first wrote about female circumcision and its impact on a girl, in her novel *Possessing the Secret of Joy.* She has collaborated with Parmar, a Lon-don-based feminist filmmaker, on a documentary to confront world public opinion—to compel civilized countries to acknowledge that female genital mutilation is nothing less than ritual torture of girls—and to enlist international support to eradicate it. Their book, *Warrior Marks,* is the story of how they made the documentary, and the people and circumstances they encountered in Senegal, The Gambia and Burkina Faso.

They are deeply affecting when they write about the emotional toll in working with this practice. They understand that the price for girls goes beyond the loss of clitoral sexual pleasure. They lose their trust in their mothers who dare not defy the weight of tradition and so hand their unsuspecting daughters over to the circumcisers. Mutilation is almost always done by women, often in the most unsanitary conditions imaginable. The child is not anesthetized nor does she have access to antibiotics to fight the deadly infections that frequently result.

The documentary crew was allowed to film a "coming out ceremony," in which a group of Gambian girls who had been circumcised two weeks before returned from the bush to their village. "They looked totally stunned, bewildered, in shock and total despair," writes Parmar. "For a few minutes I just stared, and suddenly their expressions hit me with such force that I felt tears begin to roll down my cheeks . . . [But] I had to direct the crew and couldn't give in to this pain, not now.

"It was so sad to see the light gone from their beautiful eyes, to see their drawn faces. In the last two weeks, they had been catapulted into adulthood with great violence."

Warrior Marks is not an easy book to read, partly because the topic is so tough to handle. But it is also slow to get off the ground. The beginning is padded with laundry-list correspondence and journal entries that have to do primarily with the tedious logistical problems of doing a documentary—and tedious problems make for tedious reading. Walker writes one section, "Alice's Journey," and Parmar writes another, "Pratibha's Journey." Since they have witnessed many of the same events, there is much repetition and the reader is left wondering if she's lost her place. People who appear to be important to the writers' lives are mentioned in journal entries but not fully identified, producing irritating mysteries. The writers make the alarming assertion that circumcisions are being performed within immigrant communities in the U.S.—but they do not document the facts. The book does not get rolling until about a third of the way through, when the filmmakers arrive in Africa and begin interviewing women who are resisting the practice.

These are voices of hope, and one of the most important contributions *Warrior Marks* can make is to introduce women in the West to the courageous feminists in Africa who are mounting educational and health campaigns to drive this practice back into the Stone Age. Theirs is a war that can be won—and this should inspire Western women to pressure their governments to support eradication campaigns. Ten years ago, few people dared to talk about female genital mutilation. It is still ignored by the men who control the international aid machine. Both the United Nations Children's Fund and the U.S. Agency for International Development released reports on the children in developing countries shortly before Christmas and neither mentioned female genital mutilation and the resulting death rates of female children or women in childbirth.

Despite the efforts of Walker, Parmar and others, female genital mutilation remains a taboo subject. There has been more international attention devoted to the severing of John Wayne Bobbitt's penis than to the genital mutilation of tens of millions of women. *Warrior Marks* is a piercing howl into that silence, and it's a howl we need to hear.

Victoria A. Brownworth (review date September-October 1994)

SOURCE: A review of *Warrior Marks,* in *Lambda Book Report,* Vol. 4, No. 6, September-October, 1994, p. 37.

[*In the following review, Brownworth praises* Warrior Marks *by Walker and Pratibha Parmar for exploring the reasons that female genital mutilation and other forms of mutilation are allowed to continue.*]

In 1989, while living part of the time in London, I reported on a series of cases of young girls who had been kidnapped and sexually mutilated in and around the city. But unlike other sex crimes I had reported on, these attacks were not at the hands of strangers. Each of these young girls had been mutilated at the request of her family.

I had been aware of the practice of so-called female circumcision since college when it had been a primary focus of the first International Tribunal on Crimes Against Women. But before the girls in London, I had never seen the face of genital mutilation close-up. And until I spoke with a Somali woman gynecologist at a London clinic, I never truly understood what was being done to these young girls in London and how their lives were forever altered.

Reading *Warrior Marks* created the same sense of horror and rage I felt in that London clinic. Alice Walker and Pratibha Parmar, a Pulitzer Prize-winning African-AmerIndian writer and internationally known Indian lesbian filmmaker, embarked on a joint project to document female genital mutilation in Africa.

Warrior Marks is a record of that process and the making of Parmar's film. Letters, diary entries, poems, interviews and photographs from both women all combine to provide an indelible image of the mutilation of millions of the world's women and girls. Girls as young as a month old to women as old as thirty are taken away, often into the bush, where they have their clitorises and inner and outer labia cut or ripped away. The ritual is done manually, with no anesthetic. Because there are arteries that flow in and near the clitoris, sometimes girls bleed to death.

In some areas, what remains of the genitalia is stitched together or pinned together with thorns in a process called infibulation. Small holes are left for urine and menstrual flows, but infections are commonplace. Before or on a young woman's wedding night, she is slit open again to allow penetration by her husband. When I was in London, where both female circumcision and infibulation have been illegal since 1985, doctors would not perform this process; it was done (again without benefit of anesthesia) by aunts or mothers with a razor blade or knife.

Walker and Parmar present very different commentary, both mesmerizing. Walker ties the practice to the range of mutilations women across the globe suffer at the hands of patriarchal influence. Parmar's responses are less poetic, less intellectualized than Walker's—she is simply raw with the images. Both women, in very different ways, discuss how fragile they are made by their experience. Both of them (and most of the women on their crew) end up getting injured and/or sick; Parmar has nightmares, Walker, insomnia. Walker talks about nearly going off her head from the horror, Parmar calls her lover in London and cries to her.

The images are cataclysmic, oppressive, dramatic, insufferable. Walker's feminism pours out on the page like a kind of healing salve for these tortured girls. Parmar, whose films have spoken eloquently of the oppressions of Indian women, and lesbians and gay men, worries that she won't be able to get the images she needs to tell the story properly.

Warrior Marks is as chilling as it is visionary. Walker and Parmar lead us like brave guides into the charnel house. But they show us not only the terrible horrors: AIDS spread when the same knife is used on 20 or 30 girls at a time; women sexually maimed for life, often dying in childbirth or even from infections caused by menstruation; women who escape the mutilation banished from their families. They also show us the valiant women (and some men) struggling to eradicate the ritual through education and political movements, the faces of the youngest girls who may possibly escape, the words of mothers who insist they will not allow their daughters to be mutilated.

Female genital mutilation has been allowed to continue under the rubric of "culture." But as Walker so simply and astutely notes, "there is a difference between torture and culture." Lesbian and gay men have been tormented under the same guise of heterosexual "culture." *Warrior Marks* provides valuable insight for the queer community, as Walker and Parmar each explore the reasons this mutilation and others are allowed to thrive. Female genital mutilation is the most primal form of sexual oppression. *Warrior Marks* is a book every queer must read.

Tobe Levin (review date Fall 1994)

SOURCE: A review of *Warrior Marks,* in *NWSA Journal,* Vol. 6, No. 3, Fall, 1994, pp. 511-14.

[*In the following review, Levin admits the importance of stopping the practice of female genital mutilation, but asserts that* Warrior Marks, *by Walker and Pratibha Parmar shows a lack of understanding of cultural differences.*]

Media attention to the issue of female genital mutilation is essential if this practice is to be stopped. An activist in Germany since 1977, I believe in the power of exposure and so I say, Thank you, Alice, and Thank you, Pratibha, for releasing your book and film, *Warrior Marks.* Premiering in Washington, DC, in November 1993, the film concerns 100 million of the world's females. In an April interview with Ghanaian activist Efua Dorkenoo, I learned it affects "6,000 each day, 2 million each year." The crisis needs airing, Efua told me.

Yet "I know how painful exposure is," Alice Walker says in the video's opening vignette. "It is something I've had to face every day of my life, beginning with my first look in the mirror each morning!" Thus, "in a deliberate effort to stand with the mutilated women, not beyond them," Walker offers as a leitmotif the analogy to her visual maiming, what she came to identify, once having become a "consciously feminist adult," as "a patriarchal wound." As a girl, she hadn't received the gift Santa Claus brought her brothers: guns. The one who customarily bullied her aimed at Alice standing on the roof of the garage, his copper pellet blinding her.

Alice narrates "Like the Pupil of an Eye: Genital Mutilation and the Sexual Blinding of Women" while we watch an excised girls' coming-out ceremony in Dar Salamay, The Gambia. Barren women's club members dance in front of the children, ranging from 4 to 11 years of age, the expressions on their faces freighted with symbolic import. Although we cannot reach behind those eyes, the sadness speaks, discomfort shows. To Pratibha, who was there, "they looked totally stunned, bewildered, in shock and total despair," although she admits in print that "their feelings were unimaginable to [her]." I would share such caution, but no doubt the drawn

blankness of the suffering girls contrasts—and conflicts—with the jubilation all around them.

The youngsters, excised two weeks before, also walk with difficulty. The book's longest section called "Journeys" gives the women's movement symbolic status. The narrative of P.K., borrowed from Awa Thiam's *Black Sisters, Speak Out: Feminism and Oppression in Black Africa* (originally *La Parole aux Nègresses*), includes this motif and is the video's heart. "I did not know what excision was," P.K. tells us, "but on several occasions I had seen recently excised girls walking . . . like little bent old ladies [trying to balance] rulers between their ankles. . . . I can tell you it was not a pretty sight." This we see, as Parmar's camera focuses on the shuffle characteristic of the genitally mutilated. "The expression on the faces of the excised girls . . . aroused my fears," P.K. continues. The viewers' angst stirs as well, our empathy and outrage reaching out to the twelve-year-old "in the throes of endless agony, torn apart both physically and psychologically." The dancer Richelle represents her suffering, simultaneously expressing the joy of the body intact and the horror of the organ cut. "It was the rule that girls my age did not weep in this situation," P.K. adds. "[But] I broke the rule . . . with tears and screams of pain."

How can mothers ignore this pain and, using Alice Walker's term, "collaborate" with patriarchy? As Linda Weil-Curiel, the French lawyer for Malian Aminata Diop (the first girl to apply for political asylum on the basis of specific gender risk—of mutilation), tells Alice Walker in the book "Parents are always excused for what they do to their children. So when I read [*Possessing the Secret of Joy*], I was fearful. . . . Each time I turned the page, I was wondering: When will the excuse for the parents come? And I am very, very happy to tell you I never found that excuse, and I thank you for it."

Do *I* want to make "excuses" for these mothers, these behaviors? I hope not, yet we campaigners need to understand them and their fears. Like right-wing women in the West, traditional females link their survival to male power, and this can be, under the circumstances, a comprehensible strategy. Concerned with the Sudan, where 82% of women are infibulated, Ellen Gruenbaum argues that women who perpetuate practices painful and dangerous to their daughters and inhibit their own sexual gratification "must be understood in the context of their social and economic vulnerability in a strongly patriarchal society. . . . Effective change can only come in the context of a women's movement oriented toward the basic social problems affecting women, particularly their economic dependency, educational disadvantages, and obstacles to employment." Walker, in an interview sequence not in the video, acknowledges this financial base: "[in] a culture in which men will not marry you unless you have been mutilated and there is no other work you can do and you are . . . considered a prostitute if you are not mutilated, you face a very big problem. Women mutilate their daughters because they really are looking down the road to a time when the daughter will . . . marry and at least have a roof . . . and food." Poverty, to many African activists, is the prime issue, and, consequently, transforming individual awareness cannot free the masses of women from genital mutilation.

Nonetheless, **Warrior Marks** argues strongly that mutilation is child abuse and must be opposed like other customarily exercised but admittedly harmful practices—for instance slavery and battering. The epigraph reads: "'What is the fundamental question one must ask of the world? . . . *Why is the child crying*?'" Excerpted from **Possessing the Secret of Joy**, this answer ties Walker's empathy to her identifying with the suffering young person she once was. "It could have been me . . . passing through this slave house three hundred years ago, mutilated and infibulated," she recounts in the final interview on Gorée Island at the House of Slaves. "It's remarkable," she goes on, "that the [children's] suffering . . . is the thing . . . least considered. Children cry in pain and terror . . . yet their elders . . . just assume they will forget." She concludes on tape, "Do we have a responsibility to stop the torture of children we say we love, or not? . . . or are we like the midwife who said that when she's cutting the child and the child screams she doesn't hear it? Are we expected to be deaf?"

No, we aren't, and there is a most powerful argument for international solidarity. Efua Dorkenoo, the head of London-based FORWARD International, notes that a play she wrote along with mutilated refugee women could not be performed. Her coauthors told her, "Efua, if we put this . . . on, we will be killed." Many of us outsiders are not so threatened. At the very least we will be perceived as meddling, our gravest risk to be labeled arrogant or insulting. Admittedly, words which avoid degrading the victims are hard to find. Renaming them "warriors" and "survivors" doesn't really do the trick. Even the term "mutilation" has been criticized, and neutral words have eluded the most skillful pens. Witness Walker's use of "brainwashed" and "indoctrinated"; two initiates were "programmed to say nothing they felt." I perceive in these comments not only outrage but a specifically American blindness to aspects of cultural difference I attribute in part to monolinguality and the devaluation of intimate experience in foreign cultures. The fact that neither Walker nor Parmar resided for a considerable period in the societies they portray proves a handicap. For instance, in their original proposal, they expect to film people "talking . . . about their sexual and psychological experiences of genital mutilation"; they are surprised when Aminata Diop tells them her language has no words to discuss the topic. They seem genuinely taken aback on encountering a culture of silence.

I also find slightly irritating the inevitable lacunae in the work of people new to the field. Although I applaud the urgency

and speed with which author and film maker took an idea and transformed it into media, it is simply not true of the international movement, as Pratibha notes, that "except for the writings and voices of a handful of white feminists over the last decade or so, there has been a deafening silence." As far back as 1986, Dr. Lilian Passmore Sanderson, under the auspices of the Anti-Slavery Society for the Protection of Human Rights, published *Female Genital Mutilation; Excision and Infibulation,* a bibliography containing seventy densely filled pages.

Nonetheless, I urge you to see the video and read the book. Show the film to your classes. . . . Join the chorus of African women shown demonstrating in the film. "We condemn FGM!" they shout. When asked why, they explain: that evening, February 1, 1992, a councillor in Brent had raised a motion to legalize "female circumcision," arguing that British women too might benefit from it. "We feel very strongly about this," Bisi Adeleya-Fayemi tells the camera, "it is child abuse and degrades women." And nurse-midwife Comfort I. Ottah adds, "I helped a little girl who came to me and asked why? Why hadn't the government protected her from her parents? This is not culture. This is torture."

Claire Messud (review date 11 November 1994)

SOURCE: "Ancient Spirits," in *TLS,* No. 4780, November 11, 1994, p. 19.

[*In the following review, Messud states that while many of Walker's earlier short stories are skillful, her later stories are more like memoirs or essays which uphold a political agenda rather than art.*]

None of the pieces in **The Complete Stories of Alice Walker** is new: the book is a combined reprinting of her two earlier collections, **You Can't Keep A Good Woman Down** and **In Love and Trouble.** It seems perhaps premature, given Walker's relative youth, to have deemed these two books the sum total of her short fiction output, and cynical readers might here spy a marketing strategy designed to dupe fans into buying duplicate copies of the stories unawares. The collection does, however, afford the opportunity to read again the work Walker produced before **The Color Purple** brought her immense success and she began to focus more particularly on the novel form. The short story is at once elastic and rigid, and Walker reveals her ability to stretch it to its limits, as well as her occasional failure to gauge where it will break. The stories here are a varied lot, reflecting the times in which they were written and the particular cultural heritage out of which Walker writes. Whether successful or not, they are all personal works of art, written with self-awareness and integrity.

This can be a mixed blessing. The stories are at their strongest when they are least overtly self-conscious. **"The Revenge of Hannah Kemhuff"**, for example, bears the weight of Walker's family history (a story her mother told her) and of her ethnicity (the traditional power of voodoo in Southern black culture), but it carries these things lightly. The story, almost fabular, is engaging and memorable, telling of the curse put on a white woman by the black woman she had wronged many years before. Walker has written that, when working on the story, "I had that wonderful feeling writers get sometimes, not very often, of being with a great many people, ancient spirits, all very happy to see me consulting and acknowledging them." It is a feeling subtly but powerfully conveyed in the fabric of the story; and it is also present in a number of other pieces, among them **"Strong Horse Tea"** (also about a witch-doctor), **"To Hell With Dying"** and **"Elethia"**.

All but one of these are from Walker's first collection, which was, overall, very fine. The remaining one, **"Elethia"**, though it is a marvellous tale, is a patchy piece of prose. It opens, "A certain perverse experience shaped Elethia's life, and made it possible for it to be true that she carried with her at all times a small apothecary jar of ashes." This sentence is dreadful in its failure, in the carelessness that has allowed the bunching of meaningless words ("made it possible for it to be true") at its core. In a short story, such a lapse is nearly irredeemable, and yet, only a few pages later, Walker's prose crackles with life: "They used to beat him severe trying to make him forget the past and grin and act like a nigger. Whenever you saw somebody acting like a nigger, Albert said, you could be sure he seriously disremembered his past."

The stories that made up the second collection rarely offer such strong writing. Manifestations of a more relentless self-consciousness, they are frequently signs of Walker's political involvement at the expense of her art. While individual stories like **"Fame"**, about an elderly black woman writer fed up with receiving awards, allows moments of levity or irony, many are closer to memoirs or essays—like the uniquely awful **"Coming Apart"**, a pedantic introduction to a collection of essays on pornography which Walker subsequently called a short story. They strive bluntly to work out issues rather than to tell tales. In bulk, the tone of these later stories is often both self-righteous and confused, as Walker thinks through her observations on black identity, abortion, sex, feminism, the politics of black on white rape . . . often without drawing any notable conclusions. By doing her thinking out loud, she allows the reader neither the space to think for herself nor the luxury of literary enjoyment. Nor is the carelessness of **"Elethia"**'s opening sentence singular; the wholly ominous beginning of a lengthy, wandering, weak story entitled **"Source"** reads, "It was during the year of her first depressing brush with government antipoverty programs that San Francisco began to haunt Irene". Neither enticing nor

grammatical, it wears its preachiness like a red flag, and would be enough to deter even Walker's most ardent supporters.

Addressing the Black Students Association at her alma mater, Sarah Lawrence College, in 1971, Walker said:

> The truest and most enduring impulse I have is simply to write. . . . My major advice to young artists would be that they shut themselves up somewhere away from all debates about who they are and what color they are and just turn out paintings and poems and stories and novels."

But she went on "of course the kind of artist we are required to be cannot do this. Our people are waiting. But there must be an awareness of . . . what is practical and what is designed ultimately to paralyse our talents. For example, it is unfair to the people we expect to reach to give them a beautiful poem if they are unable to read it."

Although uttered at the time when Walker was writing some of her best stories, this extraordinary statement may explain what went wrong later. It seems to condone the production of second-rate art out of political motivation. It is not clear why it would not be possible, desirable or fair to create the most beautiful poems, then teach people to read them, rather than to patronize one's audience with unsubtle and unsophisticated work.

Apparently as a result of this misguided conviction, Alice Walker's later stories do not bear out the promise of her earlier ones. Perhaps her concentration over the past decade on the novel rather than the short story has been a wise decision. But it would be a pity to think that she would not again produce short narratives like **"The Revenge of Hannah Kemhuff"**.

Alyson R. Buckman (essay date Summer 1995)

SOURCE: "The Body as a Site of Colonization: Alice Walker's *Possessing the Secret of Joy*," in *Journal of American Culture*, Vol. 18, No. 2, Summer, 1995, pp. 89-94.

[*In the following essay, Buckman analyzes how the body can become a site of colonization, and the different methods of resistance as shown in Walker's* Possessing the Secret of Joy.]

Imperialism is an economic, political, institutional, and cultural phenomenon that has been practiced by power elites in relation to the masses of the United States, especially in relation to Native Americans, blacks, women, and immigrant groups such as Asians. Although the term is generally used to describe the control of one nation over the political, cultural, or economic life of another, it may be extended to include internal, as well as external, colonialism. The colonial relationship is one of domination and subordination among groups and is constructed primarily on notions of difference; it is established and maintained in order to serve the interests of the dominant group, fortifying its position and eroding choice for non-elites through force, authority, influence, and dominance. Elites include those in positions of influence and power, i.e., those who have access to resources that enable them to dominate in the creation of policy and culture: religious, political, and economic leaders; educators; artists; publishers; and professional associations, such as the American Medical Association.

The colonial relationship is not only physical, but psychic and cultural as well. Ideology occupies a dialectical relation to legislation, economics, and culture: it arises from and contributes to a system of exclusionary power relations. Those colonized have less access to resources as they are subordinated economically and politically; what resources they do have are tenuous as their bodies, which have become commodities, are dispensable in a surplus labor force. Imaging is one tool used to justify this exclusion and subordination, constructing those colonized as deserving of their lower status.

For instance, Charles Murray's "Model Minority" thesis is used to image blacks as lazy and socially parasitic in comparison to model Asians; if they wanted to live up to their Lockean social contract and take individual responsibility for their welfare, they could. The only reason blacks form a disproportionate number of the unemployed is that they are just too lazy to go out and get a job; instead, they live off of whites. Such propaganda as this reinforces stereotypes conducive to retaining elites in power. Violence is often a result of such imaging; these stereotypes and ideologies often promote physical as well as psychic violence, such as low self-esteem and despair, within and against non-elites. Incidents such as those of Bernhard Goetz, Rodney King, Vincent Chin, Bensonhurst, and the Los Angeles riots are an (il)logical result.

The image-making process is thus a vital part of how domination is (de)constructed. bell hooks and other authors agree that control over the image-making process is a vital part of systems of domination; while hooks specifically discusses racial domination, this is true for gender, sexual, and economic domination as well. Hegemonic discourse must therefore be disrupted and transformed as part of the process of decolonization; those who are dominated must be able to see themselves "oppositionally, to imagine, describe, and invent ourselves in ways that are liberatory." For example, in order to fight against their economic status as the lowest paid workers in America and their status as the primary victims of sterilization abuse and abortion, black women must take control

of the image-making process as part of revolutionary activity.

One example of this taking control is Alice Walker's *Possessing the Secret of Joy*; this text functions as an example of revolutionary action against the oppression of those colonized by the imperialist gaze. The female body and the African body are exposed as sites of colonization by power elites; the ritual of female genital mutilation and the AIDS epidemic are both imaged as means to oppression. However, in Walker's text these bodies also become sites of resistance to domination by power elites. In addition, the power relations in this text are not simplistically demarcated in a binary of colonized versus colonizer/good versus evil. Walker posits a complex system of power relations in which those oppressed themselves become oppressors through hegemonic systems.

The female body is revealed as a site of male and national colonization through the ritual clitoridectomy and infibulation that the protagonist, Tashi/Evelyn Johnson, undergoes. Walker bases the experience of her fictional character upon fact. Genital mutilation impacts upon approximately 100 million women worldwide; this is a procedure generally covered by the comparatively innocuous term "female circumcision." This mutilation ranges from knicking the clitoris to infibulation (the excising of all external genitalia and the sewing shut of the vulva—except for a tiny opening barely large enough to allow the passage of very small quantities of blood and urine). The girls and young women who undergo this procedure sometimes die, and medical complications, such as infections and problematic labors, frequently result.

The procedure is based on a variety of reasons dependent on the culture; aesthetic, social, hygienic, and moral values in varying combinations form the basis of this practice. In Olinkan culture (the fictional setting of Walker's *Possessing the Secret of Joy*) as in other cultures, the practice is based on a desire to limit women's sexuality and increase male pleasure. Without the clitoridectomy and infibulation, the woman is imaged as dirty, masculine, and whorish; the general belief is that the genitalia of the "uncircumcised" woman will continue to grow and become masculine, enabling her to satisfy herself. She is generally unable to marry, thus affecting her economic status as well.

For those faced with conflict between traditional and colonial influence, the ritual of genital mutilation gains added significance as a means of resisting tribal colonization. Tashi is a native African woman who is sensitive to the threat posed her people by outside colonizers. When her village is destroyed by a rubber manufacturer from England, Tashi engages in the revolutionary activity of embracing traditional tribal rituals; it is her way of resisting tribal erasure. And, indeed, this activity is sanctioned by a revolutionary figure known only as "Our Leader" (it is against colonial law to mention the man's name out loud), who bears considerable likeness to the Kenyan leader Jomo Kenyatta. Kenyatta, too, encouraged Africans to return to tribal rituals, such as female genital mutilation, as part of anti-colonial activity. The body is the only means of resistance left, as everything else has been stripped away by the foreign colonizers. Tashi narrates,

> I had taken off my gingham Mother Hubbard [that the missionaries had given the women of the tribe to wear]. My breasts were bare. What was left of my dress now rode negligently about my loins. . . . We had been stripped of everything but our black skins. Here and there a defiant cheek bore the mark of our withered tribe. These marks gave me courage. I wanted such a mark for myself.

However, although Tashi willingly requested to be "bathed" by the tsunga M'Lissa ("bathed" is a euphemism for the ritual; tsunga is a word Walker coined to describe the woman who performs the ritual), she did not realize what, precisely, was involved. This is partly due to the fact that discussing the ritual is taboo; it is enshrouded in a silence that helps to keep the practice intact. She did not realize either the physical or psychic damage that would result from the ritual.

Once a woman who took pleasure in her body, Tashi is embarrassed by the shuffling walk and odor that are characteristic results of the procedure (her menstrual period takes ten days and some of the blood is unable to get out due to the smallness of the vaginal opening); in addition, neither she nor Adam, her husband, could ever again experience the sexual pleasure they had before the operation. The operation ensures that the woman will have no pleasure through vaginal intercourse, and Adam, a non-tribal American male, does not enjoy either the blood or the pain that results for Tashi from forcing the vaginal opening wider. A part of Tashi's self hides away after the ritual ceremony; she is no longer the woman she once was.

Two other examples of genital mutilation are given to the reader to underscore the prevalence and pain of this practice: that of Dura, Tashi's older sister, and that of M'Lissa, the tsunga. Dura's experience is key as it forms part of Tashi's post-ritual madness. A hemophiliac, Dura died as a result of the ritual performed at M'Lissa's hands. After this traumatic occurrence, Tashi experiences a sort of amnesia related to her ensuing madness; when she overcomes this amnesia, a vital part of her cure is effected. This part of the cure entails naming her and her sister's oppression; Dura's death is named a murder which, in addition to the traumatic effects of the ritual upon Tashi, must be revenged. And the person upon whom vengeance must be visited is the one who performed the ceremony and the one praised as a national treasure: M'Lissa.

M'Lissa is also a victim of genital mutilation. She drags her left leg behind her, as the tendons were severed during the operation. M'Lissa's mother (the tsunga at the time) had attempted to simply knick M'Lissa's clitoris; the male witch doctor, however, was vigilant and, perceiving a violation of the ceremony, performed a thorough clitoridectomy and infibulation himself. As M'Lissa bucked under the razor-sharp stone, he also cut the tendons in her left leg.

Although M'Lissa is a victim, the reader is not persuaded to empathize with her plight. Although her body is marked and experienced as a site of male domination, she becomes the next tsunga and thus becomes complicitous with the patriarchy. She learns to stop feeling and becomes callous in the performance of her "duty." As this ritual is her livelihood, she decides to ensure her own autonomy at the expense of other women, women whom she sees as fools. She believes the women themselves to be the agents of their own domination; in her eyes, if women are stupid enough to obey this tradition, then they deserve everything they get as a result. Tashi puts this sort of belief as follows, describing its consequences: "'If you lie to yourself about your own pain, you will be killed by those who will claim you enjoyed it.'"

In looking at the female body as a site of colonization in this text, then, a few points are clear. First, those who are colonized may also act as colonizers. This is true of both the tribal leaders who encourage genital mutilation and the tsunga M'Lissa. As the leaders are subordinated to English colonial authority, so, too, do they subordinate women to their own authority, limited as it may be. As Audre Lorde writes, genital mutilation "is not a cultural affair as the late Jomo Kenyatta insisted. It is a crime against black women." Nationalism does not excuse oppression.

Second, Walker avoids easy binary oppositions of male/female, colonizer/colonized, white/black, European/African, and good/evil. This second point is further developed through the use of Adam and his sister, Olivia. While Adam and Olivia are both black Americans and, thus, victims of oppression themselves, they are also agents of colonization. As part of a missionary family (their mother, father, and aunt acted as missionaries to the Olinkans until the village was destroyed), they are seen as outsiders and, more importantly, as cultural TNT by the Olinkans. The mores (concerning religion, clothing, education, sexuality, beauty, et cetera) that Adam and Olivia's family had brought to the tribe are seen as the means to colonization that they are. Tashi phrases this discourse in the following way in a conversation with Olivia before she leaves for the ritual:

> They are right, I said to her from my great height astride the donkey, who say you and your family are the white people's wedge. . . . All I care about now is the struggle for our people, I said. You are a for-

eigner. Any day you like, you and your family can ship yourselves back home. . . . Who are you and your people never to accept us as we are? Never to imitate any of our ways? It is always we who have to change. . . . You are black, but you are not like us. We look at you and your people with pity, I said. You barely have your own black skin, and it is fading. . . . You don't even know what you've lost! And the nerve of you, to bring us a God someone else chose for you!

In this quote we can see the complexities of both intranational and international colonization for both America and Africa. Here we have two African-Americans who have accepted a religion, foreign to their ancestry, that was once used as a justification for slavery; in turn, they are asking Africans to replace their beliefs with this same religion. We have a woman who comes from and represents a patriarchal background, in religious as well as other American ideologies, begging another woman not to submit to a patriarchal tradition. And we have a woman who, in asserting and celebrating her tribal identity, is victimized by that tribal belief system.

Walker also complicates the male/female binary. For example, the character of Adam provides further complexities. As a colonizer, Adam acts as religious, male, and American figures of domination. The moment at which Tashi spiritually left their relationship, she tells us, is when Adam, a progressive minister, refused to give a sermon on female suffering as evidenced in Tashi's mutilation; he had lectured on the suffering of Christ, and Tashi believed he should lecture on the suffering of women like herself as well.

> I grew agitated each time he touched on the suffering of Jesus. . . . I am a great lover of Jesus, and always have been. Still, I began to see how the constant focus on the suffering of Jesus alone excludes the suffering of others from one's view. . . . Was woman herself not the tree of life? And was she not crucified? Not in some age no one even remembers, but right now, daily, in many lands on earth? . . . One sermon, I begged him. One discussion with your followers about what was done to me. . . . He said the congregation would be embarrassed to discuss something so private and that, in any case, he would be ashamed to do so.

Adam has the power to help revolutionize understanding of structures of domination, yet he refuses this possibility and becomes complicitous in maintaining a disempowering silence.

However, he, too, is hurt by the system of oppression. Although men are not victims of sexism in the way that women are, there are ways in which they are adversely affected by it;

many men experience the pain of their mothers, sisters, and daughters as they encounter sexism, often experiencing the ramifications of colonization with them. Specifically, Adam acts as an anchor to Tashi's psychically unbalanced life. He is the caretaker, for instance, when Tashi unconsciously slashes rings around her ankles. He remains with her throughout her voluntary commitments to a mental hospital and her episodic rages. He is also unable to have intercourse with his wife and thus experiences some of the same rupture in sexuality as Tashi does. Thus, the way in which her body has been colonized as a site of subordination has affected his own existence as well.

Another male, Benny, is also hurt by the colonization of Tashi's female body. Benny is the son of Tashi and Adam, and his trip through the birth canal was impeded by Tashi's infibulation; the vaginal opening was not large enough and part of Benny's brain was crushed during labor. As a result, Benny was born retarded. Although he functions fairly well, he cannot remember things and constantly has to take notes on conversations and instructions. Benny is also affected by Tashi's emotional disturbances, constantly rebuffed by the emotional wall surrounding his mother. Although he tries to snuggle up to her, both symbolically and literally, she pushes him away. Benny, although an American male, is clearly not aligned with the colonizer.

To complicate things even further, the male body becomes a site of colonization as the text proceeds; this occurs through the representation of the African AIDS epidemic. While women and children form the background to the AIDS ward, Hartford, a young African male, is foregrounded as an AIDS victim. It is Hartford who reveals to the audience one version of how the AIDS epidemic began. Hartford was recruited to work for a medical laboratory in Africa, first as a hunter of green monkeys and then as a decapitator of those same monkeys. Through his narrative (and Walker's notes, which follow the main text), Germans, Dutch, Americans, Australians, and New Zealanders are all implicated in the beginnings of the AIDS epidemic, as the white technicians use these monkeys in an attempt to find a cure for polio. However, some of the vaccine was contaminated and disseminated within the African population, which was used as a test subject.

This version of the AIDS epidemic corresponds, at least in part, to information that Tom Curtis, a journalist, has uncovered about the origins of the disease. Between 1957 and 1960, Curtis has discovered, at least 325,000, and perhaps more than a half million, people received an oral polio vaccine in equatorial Africa—which was then the Belgian Congo, Burundi, and Rwanda; this section of Africa is now the epicenter of the epidemic. The polio virus was nourished on monkey kidneys, some of which were infected with monkey viruses. While researchers knew about some of these viruses, others were unknown to them; as a result, they could not be screened out of the vaccines. However, the oral vaccine was apparently used prematurely in the Congo, as Dr. Hilary Koprowski competed with Dr. Albert Sabin to be the first to produce the favored polio vaccine. The successful polio immunization of the caretakers of 150 chimpanzees (who were test subjects for the vaccine) became the basis for mass trials in Africa.

In both Curtis and Hartford's narratives, the African body becomes a site of domination; Africans form a disposable supply of test subjects for Western doctors and technicians. In other myths of the origins of AIDS that Walker touches on, the intellectuals among the AIDS victims reach the conclusion that "it must have been an experiment, like the one conducted on black men in Alabama, who were injected with the virus that causes syphilis, then studied as they sickened and died. The kind of experiment that would not have been hazarded on European or white American subjects." This narrative, in conjunction with Hartford's testimony, clearly depicts the African body as a site of colonization.

The AIDS and genital mutilation narratives clearly posit the body, specifically male and female African bodies, as a site of both international and intranational colonization. Both Western and male ideologies posit the Other (African, female) as a commodity whose definition should be fixed by the power elite; after all, the Other is inferior to the dominant self and can be readily displaced within the system of power. This power differential is incorporated through colonial law, tribal traditions and leadership, economics, and cultural products such as image production. However, this system, which produces psychic and physical violence, can be disrupted through the image-making process and the rejection of silence; both are integral parts of revolutionary activity, and both are used in Walker's text.

In discussing a ritual that is traditionally taboo and in verbalizing a creation myth for AIDS that is vehemently denied by dominant groups, Walker deconstructs the silence that helps to empower these groups and disempower the Other. In addition, Walker constructs empowering images of the colonized, enabling the Other to transcend objectification and become subject. Part of this quest for transcendence is constituted by history.

Although Frantz Fanon in *Black Skin, White Masks* turns his back on the past in favor of the present and future, it seems to me that the three are necessarily related as history (and, by implication, memory) can act as a witness against oppression; I am, of course, not referring to histories written by the power elite. If the colonized refuse to forget the past, then they also refuse to be complicitous in their oppression, as it will not be forgotten. As bell hooks writes, "Memory sustains a spirit of resistance. Too many red and black people live in a state of forgetfulness, embracing a colonized mind so that they can better assimilate into the white world." While history may be painful, the Other can, in remembering, deconstruct the history of the colonizer and its falsifying representation of the colonized. Memory can then act as a catalyst against oppression.

Tashi's ability to gain control over her memory and accuse those responsible for her psychic and physical trauma and for Dura's death is the key to her recovery from madness and her growth in agency. Whereas previously her madness was self-defeating, once she gains control over her memory and is able to identify those who have oppressed her and other women, she is able to once again experience agency. Militancy is chosen over madness. Tashi returns to Africa and murders M'Lissa, enacting revenge for scores of women. Her act is not only against M'Lissa, however; M'Lissa has become a "national monument" and, in her act against M'Lissa, Tashi acts against the patriarchy that would subdue womanhood.

That this is not an individual act of aggression with limited consequences is evidenced by the demonstrations of African and Muslim women (also victims of genital mutilation) once Tashi is placed on trial. Professional women visit the president to ask for an appeal of Tashi's death sentence while other women stand vigil outside the jail in solidarity with Tashi, even as they are faced with men physically and verbally abusing them. While M'Lissa was a monument to the patriarchy, Tashi becomes a heroine to oppressed and subjugated women worldwide. These women testify to her status at her execution as well, enacting a pageant of solidarity. The last thing that Tashi sees, which explicates the meaning of her actions, is a banner reading "*RESISTANCE* IS THE SECRET OF JOY!" (original emphasis).

Not only does Walker image the body as victim, as a site of colonization, but she shows how the status of victim and Other can be transcended to that of agent and subject. Relations of oppression are also complexly imaged. In unmasking systems of domination, many authors are accused of not taking the next logical step and proposing a new solution; this is not the case with Walker. Her text acts as a revolutionary manifesto for dismantling systems of domination. As such, her text is that of a radical. To simply strive for social and economic equality with white men or to simply combat racism is not enough, although liberal and conservative ideology might propose these as solutions for sexism, racism, and classism. Instead, the complete system must be overturned. And the first step is overcoming the silence that empowers dominant groups; this is part of an overall resistance that might very well be the key to the secret of joy.

Francine Prose (review date 2 January 1996)

SOURCE: "Celebrity and Other Complaints," in *Washington Post Book World,* January 2, 1996, p. 5.

[*In the following review, Prose criticizes the boasting and complaining tone of Walker's* The Same River Twice, *a book comprised of essays, interviews, fan letters, and other writings.*]

Whenever someone in our family lamented what might have seemed to others an enviable excess (too much work, too much travel, too many social obligations) my late father-in-law, who in old age was hard of hearing, used to shout at the top of his lungs, "Are you boasting or complaining?" Almost every page of *The Same River Twice* may make the most polite and patient readers long to ask Alice Walker that aggressively sensible question—and at pretty much the same volume.

The Same River Twice is a deeply peculiar compendium of diary entries, fan letters, accolades, reviews, admiring essays and interviews, a film synopsis and a screenplay. Most of these documents relate to the transformation of Walker's novel, *The Color Purple,* into the film directed by Steven Spielberg—a film that shares the book's title but not (according to its author) its subtexts and subtleties. Not only was the process of filming the novel fraught with complication, but so was Walker's personal life during that same period, a decade ago. Her mother was critically ill, she herself was suffering from Lyme disease, and her "partner of many struggling but overall happy years" has just informed her that her distraction and sexual inattention had driven him to have an affair with a former lover.

> **The Same River Twice is a deeply peculiar compendium of diary entries, fan letters, accolades, reviews, admiring essays and interviews, a film synopsis and a screenplay.**
> **—Francine Prose**

Certainly there have been many writers who have (or could have, if they'd been alive) complained about the tasteless hash that Hollywood made of their fiction. Tolstoy, Faulkner, Dickens, Fitzgerald, Flaubert—the brightest stars in our literary firmament—should by all rights rise from the grave, en masse, to decry unfortunate casting choices and faux happy endings. Our sympathies go out to these writers, as they do to anyone enduring the ordinary human disasters of illness and heartbreak, the suffering Alice Walker describes in these pages.

But Walker seems to have so lost touch with the lives and sensibilities of ordinary humans that she apparently cannot hear how her complaints (so often indistinguishable from boasts) might sound to the less fortunate, who have been less generously favored by greatness. It's clear that Walker has legions of worshipful fans; one section of the book comprises their adoring letters: "I am a lover, not only of *The Color Purple,* but just about everything you have written. The depth of sensitivity and struggle that you bring to your characters amazes me still. Your essays . . . touch me beyond belief. I understand you more as a person, a human being, with every reading."

Such devotion may not ask its object to temper brilliance with modesty, to leaven profundity with humility. But the unconverted may find their good moods beginning to sour early in the book, when Walker confides in her diary (and in us): "'Fame' exhausts me . . . I am still tired from being 'recognized' by the Pulitzer Prize. I am sent countless manuscripts to read, books to endorse, there are invitations and award offerings that I couldn't begin to accept."

Many, I'm sure, will be charmed by the New-Age daffiness that is partly at fault for Walker's Lyme disease—she was bitten by ticks while lying "on the earth in worship" as is her "habit as a born-again pagan." A similar faith persuades her to face the premiere of the Spielberg film armed with a magic wand: "It is over a foot long with a handle made of black walnut and with almost a two-inch crystal on the end . . . I think my magic wand helped, and afterward Gloria [Steinem] and Mort [Zuckerman] came up and we hugged."

But won't some readers be taken aback by Walker's sense of her own importance, her mission—a conviction that at moments seems to border on the egomaniacal? It's one thing to have mixed feelings about the film version of one's novel. It's quite another to congratulate one's self on the fact that "because I followed love and joyous curiosity through the twists and turns of the labyrinth . . . I did find all the women in *The Color Purple,* who together are the sacred feminine that, because of the accessibility of the film, can be beamed across a world desperate for its return." A song written for the film is "a signal of affirmation that women could hum to each other coast to coast . . . an immeasurable gift to the bonding of women." She seems to feel that her work—had it been more widely read—could have reduced the violence in contemporary society. Even her refusal to let the film be shown in South Africa (still then under the rule of apartheid) strikes an almost comically wrong note: "Can you imagine how much I want to share *The Color Purple* with my brothers and sisters of South Africa? . . . What joy it would be to imagine Winnie and Nelson sitting in front of their VCR, laughing, crying, smiling, sighing, or even being appalled."

Perhaps the problem is that Alice Walker has been too ready to believe the passionate fan letters of the sort that appear in the book, letters from readers so touchingly eager to understand her "as a person." And one can only hope that these fans will be deeply moved by the section documenting Walker's struggle to recover the "3 percent share of the gross" promised by her contract and her reluctant willingness to "settle for three million." I know that I kept hearing my father-in-law's voice, his honest, working-class scorn for those guilty of the cardinal sin he called "crying all the way to the bank."

FURTHER READING

Criticism

Allan, Tuzyline Jita. "Womanism Revisited: Women and the (Ab)Use of Power in *The Color Purple*." In *Feminist Nightmares: Women at Odds,* edited by Susan Ostrov Weisser and Jennifer Fleischner, pp. 88-105, New York: New York University Press, 1994.
> Discusses the negative aspects of female power in Walker's *The Color Purple.*

Baker, Jr., Houston A. and Charlotte Pierce-Baker. "Patches: Quilts and Community in Alice Walker's 'Everyday Use.'" *Southern Review* 21, No. 3 (July 1985): 706-20.
> Compares the art of quilting in Walker's "Everyday Use" to overcoming chaos by skillfully stitching life's fragments.

Carter, Nancy Corson. "Claiming the Bittersweet Matrix: Alice Walker, Sandra Cisneros, and Adrienne Rich." *Critique* XXXV, No. 4 (Summer 1994): 195-204.
> Discusses the journey of the artist as portrayed in Walker's *In Search of Our Mothers' Gardens,* Sandra Cisneros's *The House of Mango Street,* and Adrienne Rich's *Your Native Land, Your Life: Poems.*

Dieke, Ikenna. "Toward a Monistic Idealism: The Thematics of Alice Walker's *The Temple of My Familiar.*" *African American Review* 26, No. 3 (Fall 1992): 507-14.
> Discusses interdependency and the universal chain of being in Walker's *The Temple of My Familiar.*

Digby, Joan. "From Walker to Spielberg: Transformations of *The Color Purple.*" In *Novel Images: Literature in Performance,* edited by Peter Reynolds, pp. 157-74, London: Routledge, 1993.
> Compares and contrasts Walker's novel *The Color Purple* to the film based on the novel directed by Steven Spielberg.

Estes, David C. "Alice Walker's 'Strong Horse Tea': Folk Cures for the Dispossessed." *Southern Folklore* 50, No. 3 (1993): 213-29.
> Analyzes the place of folk medicine in the African-American tradition, especially as it relates to women, in Walker's "Strong Horse Tea."

Harris, Norman. "*Meridian:* Answers in the Black Church." In his *Connecting Times: The Sixties in Afro-American Fiction,* pp. 98-119, Jackson, MS: University Press of Mississippi, 1988.
> Discusses three themes found in Walker's *Meridian,* including "(1) a form of parental and institutional socialization that does not connect the individual to his or her history, (2) problems within relationships between black men and women, and (3) the ascendancy of the black power movement (nationalism) and the diminution of the civil rights movement (integration)."

Hernton, Calvin C. "Who's Afraid of Alice Walker?" In his *The Sexual Mountain and Black Women Writers,* pp. 1-36, New York: Anchor Press, 1987.
> Asserts that Walker's *The Color Purple* is basically a slave narrative, and discusses the fear generated by the novel because of its treatment of black men.

Hite, Molly. "Romance, Marginality, Matrilineage: *The Color Purple.*" In her *The Other Side of the Story: Structures and Strategies of Contemporary Feminist Narrative,* pp. 103-26, Ithaca, NY: Cornell University Press, 1989.
> Compares Walker's *The Color Purple* to Zora Neale Hurston's *Their Eyes Were Watching God* and discusses how the two novels relate to literary tradition.

Hollister, Michael. "Tradition in Alice Walker's 'To Hell with Dying.'" *Studies in Short Fiction* 26, No. 1 (Winter 1989): 90-4.
> Offers a review of Walker's "To Hell with Dying" saying that the story "derives emotional power from universalist values, archetypal imagery, and recurrent rhythms."

Jamison-Hall, Angelene. "She's Just Too Womanish for Them: Alice Walker and *The Color Purple.*" In *Censored Books: Critical Viewpoints,* edited by Nicholas J. Karolides, Lee Burress, and John M. Kean, pp. 191-200, Metachun, NJ: The Scarecrow Press, Inc., 1993.
> Asserts that people are uncomfortable with Walker's *The Color Purple* because in it she is "womanish," resisting convention and insisting on exploring new levels.

Karrer, Wolfgang. "Nostalgia, Amnesia, and Grandmothers: The Uses of Memory in Albert Murray, Sabine Ulibarri, Paula Gunn Allen, and Alice Walker." In *Memory, Narrative, and Identity: New Essays in Ethnic American Literatures,* edited by Amritjit Singh, Joseph T. Skerrett, Jr., and Robert E.

Hogan, pp. 128-44, Boston: Northeastern University Press, 1994.

> Discusses the use of recall and amnesia in several works, including Walker's *The Temple of My Familiar.*

McKay, Nellie Y. "Alice Walker's 'Advancing Luna—and Ida B. Wells': A Struggle Toward Sisterhood." In *Rape and Representation,* edited by Lynn A. Higgins and Brenda R. Silver, pp. 248-60, New York: Columbia University Press, 1991.

> Discusses the issues of rape, power, and the relationships between black and white women as seen in Walker's "Advancing Luna—and Ida B. Wells."

Marvin, Thomas F. "'Preachin' the Blues': Bessie Smith's Secular Religion and Alice Walker's *The Color Purple.*" *African American Review* 28, No. 3 (Fall 1994): 411-21.

> Discusses the role of Shug Avery as a catalyst to Celie's metamorphosis from a passive victim to a confident woman in Walker's *The Color Purple.*

Mason, Jr., Theodore O. "Alice Walker's *The Third Life of Grange Copeland:* The Dynamics of Enclosure." *Callaloo* 12, No. 2 (Spring 1989): 297-309.

> Discusses the use of both physical and fictive enclosure in Walker's work, especially *The Third Life of Grange Copeland.*

Nadel, Alan. "Reading the Body: Alice Walker's *Meridian* and the Archeology of Self." *Modern Fiction Studies* 34, No. 1 (Spring 1988): 55-68.

> States that Walker's "*Meridian* is a lesson in the power of language, the power to retain as well as to distort, to affect as well as to deny."

Selzer, Linda. "Race and Domesticity in *The Color Purple.*" *African American Review* 29, No. 1 (Spring 1995): 67-82.

> Analyzes the relationship between public and private discourse in Walker's *The Color Purple.*

Wall, Wendy. "Lettered Bodies and Corporeal Texts in *The Color Purple.*" *Studies in American Fiction* 16, No. 1 (Spring 1988): 83-97.

> Asserts that the letters in Walker's *The Color Purple* act as a second body and give Celie a voice against the power structure.

Waters-Dawson, Emma. "From Victim to Victor: Walker's Women in *The Color Purple.*" In *The Aching Hearth: Family Violence in Life and Literature,* edited by Sara Munson Deats, Ph.D. and Lagretta Tallent Lenker, M.S., pp. 255-68, New York: Insight Books, 1991.

> Discusses how the black women of Walker's *The Color Purple* overcome victimization through self-love and a reliance on the tradition of their maternal ancestors.

Additional coverage of Walker's life and career is contained in the following sources published by Gale: *Authors and Artists for Young Adults,* **Vol. 3;** *Bestsellers,* **Vol. 89:4;** *Black Literature Criticism; Black Writers,* **Vol. 2;** *Concise Dictionary of American Literary Biography,* **1968-1988;** *Contemporary Authors,* **Vols. 37-40R;** *Contemporary Authors New Revision Series,* **Vols. 9, 27, and 49;** *DISCovering Authors; DISCovering Authors Modules: Most Studied Novelists, Multicultural Authors, Novelists, Poets,* **and** *Popular Fiction and Genre Authors; Dictionary of Literary Biography,* **Vols. 6, 33, and 143;** *Major Twentieth Century Writers; Something About the Author,* **Vol. 31; and** *Short Story Criticism,* **Vol. 5.**

□ Contemporary Literary Criticism

Indexes

Literary Criticism Series
Cumulative Author Index
Cumulative Topic Index
Cumulative Nationality Index
Title Index, Volume 103

How to Use This Index

The main references

list all author entries in the following Gale Literary Criticism series:

BLC = Black Literature Criticism
CLC = Contemporary Literary Criticism
CLR = Children's Literature Review
CMLC = Classical and Medieval Literature Criticism
DA = DISCovering Authors
DAB = DISCovering Authors: British
DAC = DISCovering Authors: Canadian
DAM = DISCovering Authors Modules
 DRAM = dramatists; **MST** = most-studied
 authors; **MULT** = multicultural authors; **NOV** =
 novelists; **POET** = poets; **POP** = popular/genre
 writers; **DC** = Drama Criticism
HLC = Hispanic Literature Criticism
LC = Literature Criticism from 1400 to 1800
NCLC = Nineteenth-Century Literature Criticism
PC = Poetry Criticism
SSC = Short Story Criticism
TCLC = Twentieth-Century Literary Criticism
WLC = World Literature Criticism, 1500 to the Present

The cross-references

list all author entries in the following Gale biographical and literary sources:

AAYA = Authors & Artists for Young Adults
AITN = Authors in the News
BEST = Bestsellers
BW = Black Writers
CA = Contemporary Authors
CAAS = Contemporary Authors Autobiography Series
CABS = Contemporary Authors Bibliographical Series
CANR = Contemporary Authors New Revision Series
CAP = Contemporary Authors Permanent Series
CDALB = Concise Dictionary of American Literary Biography
CDBLB = Concise Dictionary of British Literary Biography

DLB = Dictionary of Literary Biography
DLBD = Dictionary of Literary Biography Documentary Series
DLBY = Dictionary of Literary Biography Yearbook
HW = Hispanic Writers
JRDA = Junior DISCovering Authors
MAICYA = Major Authors and Illustrators for Children and Young Adults
MTCW = Major 20th-Century Writers
NNAL = Native North American Literature
SAAS = Something about the Author Autobiography Series
SATA = Something about the Author
YABC = Yesterday's Authors of Books for Children

Literary Criticism Series
Cumulative Author Index

Abasiyanik, Sait Faik 1906-1954
See Sait Faik
See also CA 123
Abbey, Edward 1927-1989 .... **CLC 36, 59**
See also CA 45-48; 128; CANR 2, 41
Abbott, Lee K(ittredge) 1947- .... **CLC 48**
See also CA 124; CANR 51; DLB 130
Abe, Kobo 1924-1993**CLC 8, 22, 53, 81; DAM NOV**
See also CA 65-68; 140; CANR 24, 60; DLB 182; MTCW
Abelard, Peter c. 1079-c. 1142 ...... **CMLC 11**
See also DLB 115
Abell, Kjeld 1901-1961 .... **CLC 15**
See also CA 111
Abish, Walter 1931- .... **CLC 22**
See also CA 101; CANR 37; DLB 130
Abrahams, Peter (Henry) 1919- .... **CLC 4**
See also BW 1; CA 57-60; CANR 26; DLB 117; MTCW
Abrams, M(eyer) H(oward) 1912- ... **CLC 24**
See also CA 57-60; CANR 13, 33; DLB 67
Abse, Dannie 1923- .. **CLC 7, 29; DAB; DAM POET**
See also CA 53-56; CAAS 1; CANR 4, 46; DLB 27
Achebe, (Albert) Chinua(lumogu) 1930-**C L C 1, 3, 5, 7, 11, 26, 51, 75; BLC; DA; DAB; DAC; DAM MST, MULT, NOV; WLC**
See also AAYA 15; BW 2; CA 1-4R; CANR 6, 26, 47; CLR 20; DLB 117; MAICYA; MTCW; SATA 40; SATA-Brief 38
Acker, Kathy 1948- .... **CLC 45**
See also CA 117; 122; CANR 55
Ackroyd, Peter 1949- .... **CLC 34, 52**
See also CA 123; 127; CANR 51; DLB 155; INT 127
Acorn, Milton 1923- .... **CLC 15; DAC**
See also CA 103; DLB 53; INT 103
Adamov, Arthur 1908-1970**CLC 4, 25; DAM DRAM**
See also CA 17-18; 25-28R; CAP 2; MTCW
Adams, Alice (Boyd) 1926-**CLC 6, 13, 46; SSC 24**
See also CA 81-84; CANR 26, 53; DLBY 86; INT CANR-26; MTCW
Adams, Andy 1859-1935 .... **TCLC 56**
See also YABC 1
Adams, Douglas (Noel) 1952- .... **CLC 27, 60; DAM POP**
See also AAYA 4; BEST 89:3; CA 106; CANR 34; DLBY 83; JRDA
Adams, Francis 1862-1893 .... **NCLC 33**
Adams, Henry (Brooks) 1838-1918 **TCLC 4, 52; DA; DAB; DAC; DAM MST**
See also CA 104; 133; DLB 12, 47
Adams, Richard (George) 1920-**CLC 4, 5, 18; DAM NOV**
See also AAYA 16; AITN 1, 2; CA 49-52; CANR 3, 35; CLR 20; JRDA; MAICYA; MTCW; SATA 7, 69
Adamson, Joy(-Friederike Victoria) 1910-1980 **CLC 17**
See also CA 69-72; 93-96; CANR 22; MTCW;

SATA 11; SATA-Obit 22
Adcock, Fleur 1934- .... **CLC 41**
See also CA 25-28R; CAAS 23; CANR 11, 34; DLB 40
Addams, Charles (Samuel) 1912-1988**CLC 30**
See also CA 61-64; 126; CANR 12
Addison, Joseph 1672-1719 .... **LC 18**
See also CDBLB 1660-1789; DLB 101
Adler, Alfred (F.) 1870-1937 .... **TCLC 61**
See also CA 119
Adler, C(arole) S(chwerdtfeger) 1932- .. **C L C 35**
See also AAYA 4; CA 89-92; CANR 19, 40; JRDA; MAICYA; SAAS 15; SATA 26, 63
Adler, Renata 1938- .... **CLC 8, 31**
See also CA 49-52; CANR 5, 22, 52; MTCW
Ady, Endre 1877-1919 .... **TCLC 11**
See also CA 107
Afton, Effie
See Harper, Frances Ellen Watkins
Agapida, Fray Antonio
See Irving, Washington
Agee, James (Rufus) 1909-1955 **TCLC 1, 19; DAM NOV**
See also AITN 1; CA 108; 148; CDALB 1941-1968; DLB 2, 26, 152
Aghill, Gordon
See Silverberg, Robert
Agnon, S(hmuel) Y(osef Halevi) 1888-1970 **CLC 4, 8, 14**
See also CA 17-18; 25-28R; CANR 60; CAP 2; MTCW
Agrippa von Nettesheim, Henry Cornelius 1486-1535 .... **LC 27**
Aherne, Owen
See Cassill, R(onald) V(erlin)
Ai 1947- .... **CLC 4, 14, 69**
See also CA 85-88; CAAS 13; DLB 120
Aickman, Robert (Fordyce) 1914-1981 . **C L C 57**
See also CA 5-8R; CANR 3
Aiken, Conrad (Potter) 1889-1973**CLC 1, 3, 5, 10, 52; DAM NOV, POET; SSC 9**
See also CA 5-8R; 45-48; CANR 4, 60; CDALB 1929-1941; DLB 9, 45, 102; MTCW; SATA 3, 30
Aiken, Joan (Delano) 1924- .... **CLC 35**
See also AAYA 1; CA 9-12R; CANR 4, 23, 34; CLR 1, 19; DLB 161; JRDA; MAICYA; MTCW; SAAS 1; SATA 2, 30, 73
Ainsworth, William Harrison 1805-1882 **NCLC 13**
See also DLB 21; SATA 24
Aitmatov, Chingiz (Torekulovich) 1928-**C L C 71**
See also CA 103; CANR 38; MTCW; SATA 56
Akers, Floyd
See Baum, L(yman) Frank
Akhmadulina, Bella Akhatovna 1937- .. **C L C 53; DAM POET**
See also CA 65-68

Akhmatova, Anna 1888-1966**CLC 11, 25, 64; DAM POET; PC 2**
See also CA 19-20; 25-28R; CANR 35; CAP 1; MTCW
Aksakov, Sergei Timofeyvich 1791-1859 **NCLC 2**
Aksenov, Vassily
See Aksyonov, Vassily (Pavlovich)
Aksyonov, Vassily (Pavlovich) 1932-**CLC 22, 37, 101**
See also CA 53-56; CANR 12, 48
Akutagawa, Ryunosuke 1892-1927 **TCLC 16**
See also CA 117; 154
Alain 1868-1951 .... **TCLC 41**
Alain-Fournier .... **TCLC 6**
See also Fournier, Henri Alban
See also DLB 65
Alarcon, Pedro Antonio de 1833-1891**NCLC 1**
Alas (y Urena), Leopoldo (Enrique Garcia) 1852-1901 .... **TCLC 29**
See also CA 113; 131; HW
Albee, Edward (Franklin III) 1928-**CLC 1, 2, 3, 5, 9, 11, 13, 25, 53, 86; DA; DAB; DAC; DAM DRAM, MST; WLC**
See also AITN 1; CA 5-8R; CABS 3; CANR 8, 54; CDALB 1941-1968; DLB 7; INT CANR-8; MTCW
Alberti, Rafael 1902- .... **CLC 7**
See also CA 85-88; DLB 108
Albert the Great 1200(?)-1280 ...... **CMLC 16**
See also DLB 115
Alcala-Galiano, Juan Valera y
See Valera y Alcala-Galiano, Juan
Alcott, Amos Bronson 1799-1888 .... **NCLC 1**
See also DLB 1
Alcott, Louisa May 1832-1888 . **NCLC 6, 58; DA; DAB; DAC; DAM MST, NOV; SSC 27; WLC**
See also AAYA 20; CDALB 1865-1917; CLR 1, 38; DLB 1, 42, 79; DLBD 14; JRDA; MAICYA; YABC 1
Aldanov, M. A.
See Aldanov, Mark (Alexandrovich)
Aldanov, Mark (Alexandrovich) 1886(?)-1957 **TCLC 23**
See also CA 118
Aldington, Richard 1892-1962 .... **CLC 49**
See also CA 85-88; CANR 45; DLB 20, 36, 100, 149
Aldiss, Brian W(ilson) 1925- . **CLC 5, 14, 40; DAM NOV**
See also CA 5-8R; CAAS 2; CANR 5, 28; DLB 14; MTCW; SATA 34
Alegria, Claribel 1924-**CLC 75; DAM MULT**
See also CA 131; CAAS 15; DLB 145; HW
Alegria, Fernando 1918-**CLC 57**
See also CA 9-12R; CANR 5, 32; HW
Aleichem, Sholom .... **TCLC 1, 35**
See also Rabinovitch, Sholem
Aleixandre, Vicente 1898-1984 ... **CLC 9, 36; DAM POET; PC 15**
See also CA 85-88; 114; CANR 26; DLB 108; HW; MTCW
Alepoudelis, Odysseus

See Celan, Paul
See also CA 85-88; CANR 33, 61; MTCW

Anwar, Chairil 1922-1949 .... **TCLC 22**
See also CA 121

Apollinaire, Guillaume 1880-1918**TCLC 3, 8, 51; DAM POET; PC 7**
See also Kostrowitzki, Wilhelm Apollinaris de
See also CA 152

Appelfeld, Aharon 1932- .... **CLC 23, 47**
See also CA 112; 133

Apple, Max (Isaac) 1941-.............. **CLC 9, 33**
See also CA 81-84; CANR 19, 54; DLB 130

Appleman, Philip (Dean) 1926-........ **CLC 51**
See also CA 13-16R; CAAS 18; CANR 6, 29, 56

Appleton, Lawrence
See Lovecraft, H(oward) P(hillips)

Apteryx
See Eliot, T(homas) S(tearns)

Apuleius, (Lucius Madaurensis) 125(?)-175(?)
CMLC 1

Aquin, Hubert 1929-1977 .... **CLC 15**
See also CA 105; DLB 53

Aragon, Louis 1897-1982 ..**CLC 3, 22; DAM NOV, POET**
See also CA 69-72; 108; CANR 28; DLB 72; MTCW

Arany, Janos 1817-1882.................**NCLC 34**

Arbuthnot, John 1667-1735 .... **LC 1**
See also DLB 101

Archer, Herbert Winslow
See Mencken, H(enry) L(ouis)

Archer, Jeffrey (Howard) 1940- ..... **CLC 28; DAM POP**
See also AAYA 16; BEST 89:3; CA 77-80; CANR 22, 52; INT CANR-22

Archer, Jules 1915-.......................... **CLC 12**
See also CA 9-12R; CANR 6; SAAS 5; SATA 4, 85

Archer, Lee
See Ellison, Harlan (Jay)

Arden, John 1930-**CLC 6, 13, 15; DAM DRAM**
See also CA 13-16R; CAAS 4; CANR 31; DLB 13; MTCW

Arenas, Reinaldo 1943-1990 .**CLC 41; DAM MULT; HLC**
See also CA 124; 128; 133; DLB 145; HW

Arendt, Hannah 1906-1975 .... **CLC 66, 98**
See also CA 17-20R; 61-64; CANR 26, 60; MTCW

Aretino, Pietro 1492-1556 .... **LC 12**

Arghezi, Tudor .... **CLC 80**
See also Theodorescu, Ion N.

Arguedas, Jose Maria 1911-1969 **CLC 10, 18**
See also CA 89-92; DLB 113; HW

Argueta, Manlio 1936-...................... **CLC 31**
See also CA 131; DLB 145; HW

Ariosto, Ludovico 1474-1533 .... **LC 6**

Aristides
See Epstein, Joseph

Aristophanes 450B.C.-385B.C.**CMLC 4; DA; DAB; DAC; DAM DRAM, MST; DC 2; WLCS**
See also DLB 176

Arlt, Roberto (Godofredo Christophersen) 1900-1942**TCLC 29; DAM MULT; HLC**
See also CA 123; 131; HW

Armah, Ayi Kwei 1939-**CLC 5, 33; BLC; DAM MULT, POET**
See also BW 1; CA 61-64; CANR 21; DLB 117; MTCW

Armatrading, Joan 1950- .... **CLC 17**
See also CA 114

Arnette, Robert
See Silverberg, Robert

Arnim, Achim von (Ludwig Joachim von Arnim) 1781-1831 .... **NCLC 5**
See also DLB 90

Arnim, Bettina von 1785-1859 .... **NCLC 38**
See also DLB 90

Arnold, Matthew 1822-1888**NCLC 6, 29; DA; DAB; DAC; DAM MST, POET; PC 5; WLC**
See also CDBLB 1832-1890; DLB 32, 57

Arnold, Thomas 1795-1842 ....**NCLC 18**
See also DLB 55

Arnow, Harriette (Louisa) Simpson 1908-1986
CLC 2, 7, 18
See also CA 9-12R; 118; CANR 14; DLB 6; MTCW; SATA 42; SATA-Obit 47

Arp, Hans
See Arp, Jean

Arp, Jean 1887-1966 ....**CLC 5**
See also CA 81-84; 25-28R; CANR 42

Arrabal
See Arrabal, Fernando

Arrabal, Fernando 1932-.... **CLC 2, 9, 18, 58**
See also CA 9-12R; CANR 15

Arrick, Fran .... **CLC 30**
See also Gaberman, Judie Angell

Artaud, Antonin (Marie Joseph) 1896-1948
TCLC 3, 36; DAM DRAM
See also CA 104; 149

Arthur, Ruth M(abel) 1905-1979 ......**CLC 12**
See also CA 9-12R; 85-88; CANR 4; SATA 7, 26

Artsybashev, Mikhail (Petrovich) 1878-1927
TCLC 31

Arundel, Honor (Morfydd) 1919-1973**CLC 17**
See also CA 21-22; 41-44R; CAP 2; CLR 35; SATA 4; SATA-Obit 24

Arzner, Dorothy 1897-1979 ....**CLC 98**

Asch, Sholem 1880-1957 .... **TCLC 3**
See also CA 105

Ash, Shalom
See Asch, Sholem

Ashbery, John (Lawrence) 1927-**CLC 2, 3, 4, 6, 9, 13, 15, 25, 41, 77; DAM POET**
See also CA 5-8R; CANR 9, 37; DLB 5, 165; DLBY 81; INT CANR-9; MTCW

Ashdown, Clifford
See Freeman, R(ichard) Austin

Ashe, Gordon
See Creasey, John

Ashton-Warner, Sylvia (Constance) 1908-1984
CLC 19
See also CA 69-72; 112; CANR 29; MTCW

Asimov, Isaac 1920-1992 **CLC 1, 3, 9, 19, 26, 76, 92; DAM POP**
See also AAYA 13; BEST 90:2; CA 1-4R; 137; CANR 2, 19, 36, 60; CLR 12; DLB 8; DLBY 92; INT CANR-19; JRDA; MAICYA; MTCW; SATA 1, 26, 74

Assis, Joaquim Maria Machado de
See Machado de Assis, Joaquim Maria

Astley, Thea (Beatrice May) 1925- ...**CLC 41**
See also CA 65-68; CANR 11, 43

Aston, James
See White, T(erence) H(anbury)

Asturias, Miguel Angel 1899-1974 **CLC 3, 8, 13; DAM MULT, NOV; HLC**
See also CA 25-28; 49-52; CANR 32; CAP 2; DLB 113; HW; MTCW

Atares, Carlos Saura
See Saura (Atares), Carlos

Atheling, William

See Pound, Ezra (Weston Loomis)

Atheling, William, Jr.
See Blish, James (Benjamin)

Atherton, Gertrude (Franklin Horn) 1857-1948
TCLC 2
See also CA 104; 155; DLB 9, 78

Atherton, Lucius
See Masters, Edgar Lee

Atkins, Jack
See Harris, Mark

Atkinson, Kate ....**CLC 99**

Attaway, William (Alexander) 1911-1986
CLC 92; BLC; DAM MULT
See also BW 2; CA 143; DLB 76

Atticus
See Fleming, Ian (Lancaster)

Atwood, Margaret (Eleanor) 1939-**CLC 2, 3, 4, 8, 13, 15, 25, 44, 84; DA; DAB; DAC; DAM MST, NOV, POET; PC 8; SSC 2; WLC**
See also AAYA 12; BEST 89:2; CA 49-52; CANR 3, 24, 33, 59; DLB 53; INT CANR-24; MTCW; SATA 50

Aubigny, Pierre d'
See Mencken, H(enry) L(ouis)

Aubin, Penelope 1685-1731(?)............... **LC 9**
See also DLB 39

Auchincloss, Louis (Stanton) 1917-**CLC 4, 6, 9, 18, 45; DAM NOV; SSC 22**
See also CA 1-4R; CANR 6, 29, 55; DLB 2; DLBY 80; INT CANR-29; MTCW

Auden, W(ystan) H(ugh) 1907-1973**CLC 1, 2, 3, 4, 6, 9, 11, 14, 43; DA; DAB; DAC; DAM DRAM, MST, POET; PC 1; WLC**
See also AAYA 18; CA 9-12R; 45-48; CANR 5, 61; CDBLB 1914-1945; DLB 10, 20; MTCW

Audiberti, Jacques 1900-1965**CLC 38; DAM DRAM**
See also CA 25-28R

Audubon, John James 1785-1851 ..**NCLC 47**

Auel, Jean M(arie) 1936-**CLC 31; DAM POP**
See also AAYA 7; BEST 90:4; CA 103; CANR 21; INT CANR-21; SATA 91

Auerbach, Erich 1892-1957............ **TCLC 43**
See also CA 118; 155

Augier, Emile 1820-1889 ....**NCLC 31**

August, John
See De Voto, Bernard (Augustine)

Augustine, St. 354-430 .... **CMLC 6; DAB**

Aurelius
See Bourne, Randolph S(illiman)

Aurobindo, Sri 1872-1950 .... **TCLC 63**

Austen, Jane 1775-1817 **NCLC 1, 13, 19, 33, 51; DA; DAB; DAC; DAM MST, NOV; WLC**
See also AAYA 19; CDBLB 1789-1832; DLB 116

Auster, Paul 1947- ....**CLC 47**
See also CA 69-72; CANR 23, 52

Austin, Frank
See Faust, Frederick (Schiller)

Austin, Mary (Hunter) 1868-1934 . **TCLC 25**
See also CA 109; DLB 9, 78

Autran Dourado, Waldomiro
See Dourado, (Waldomiro Freitas) Autran

Averroes 1126-1198 .... **CMLC 7**
See also DLB 115

Avicenna 980-1037.........................**CMLC 16**
See also DLB 115

Avison, Margaret 1918- **CLC 2, 4, 97; DAC; DAM POET**
See also CA 17-20R; DLB 53; MTCW

2; DAB; DAM DRAM
See also CA 104; 136; CDBLB 1890-1914;
CLR 16; DLB 10, 141, 156; MAICYA;
YABC 1

Barrington, Michael
See Moorcock, Michael (John)

Barrol, Grady
See Bograd, Larry

Barry, Mike
See Malzberg, Barry N(athaniel)

Barry, Philip 1896-1949 .... **TCLC 11**
See also CA 109; DLB 7

Bart, Andre Schwarz
See Schwarz-Bart, Andre

Barth, John (Simmons) 1930-**CLC 1, 2, 3, 5, 7,
9, 10, 14, 27, 51, 89; DAM NOV; SSC 10**
See also AITN 1, 2; CA 1-4R; CABS 1; CANR
5, 23, 49; DLB 2; MTCW

Barthelme, Donald 1931-1989**CLC 1, 2, 3, 5, 6,
8, 13, 23, 46, 59; DAM NOV; SSC 2**
See also CA 21-24R; 129; CANR 20, 58; DLB
2; DLBY 80, 89; MTCW; SATA 7; SATA-
Obit 62

Barthelme, Frederick 1943- .... **CLC 36**
See also CA 114; 122; DLBY 85; INT 122

Barthes, Roland (Gerard) 1915-1980**CLC 24,
83**
See also CA 130; 97-100; MTCW

Barzun, Jacques (Martin) 1907- ...... **CLC 51**
See also CA 61-64; CANR 22

Bashevis, Isaac
See Singer, Isaac Bashevis

Bashkirtseff, Marie 1859-1884 .... **NCLC 27**

Basho
See Matsuo Basho

Bass, Kingsley B., Jr.
See Bullins, Ed

Bass, Rick 1958- .... **CLC 79**
See also CA 126; CANR 53

Bassani, Giorgio 1916-........................**CLC 9**
See also CA 65-68; CANR 33; DLB 128, 177;
MTCW

Bastos, Augusto (Antonio) Roa
See Roa Bastos, Augusto (Antonio)

Bataille, Georges 1897-1962............. **CLC 29**
See also CA 101; 89-92

Bates, H(erbert) E(rnest) 1905-1974**CLC 46;
DAB; DAM POP; SSC 10**
See also CA 93-96; 45-48; CANR 34; DLB 162;
MTCW

Bauchart
See Camus, Albert

Baudelaire, Charles 1821-1867 **NCLC 6, 29,
55; DA; DAB; DAC; DAM MST, POET;
PC 1; SSC 18; WLC**

Baudrillard, Jean 1929-.................... **CLC 60**

Baum, L(yman) Frank 1856-1919 ... **TCLC 7**
See also CA 108; 133; CLR 15; DLB 22; JRDA;
MAICYA; MTCW; SATA 18

Baum, Louis F.
See Baum, L(yman) Frank

Baumbach, Jonathan 1933-.......... **CLC 6, 23**
See also CA 13-16R; CAAS 5; CANR 12;
DLBY 80; INT CANR-12; MTCW

Bausch, Richard (Carl) 1945- .... **CLC 51**
See also CA 101; CAAS 14; CANR 43, 61; DLB
130

Baxter, Charles 1947-**CLC 45, 78; DAM POP**
See also CA 57-60; CANR 40; DLB 130

Baxter, George Owen
See Faust, Frederick (Schiller)

Baxter, James K(eir) 1926-1972 .... **CLC 14**
See also CA 77-80

Baxter, John
See Hunt, E(verette) Howard, (Jr.)

Bayer, Sylvia
See Glassco, John

Baynton, Barbara 1857-1929 .... **TCLC 57**

Beagle, Peter S(oyer) 1939- ....**CLC 7**
See also CA 9-12R; CANR 4, 51; DLBY 80;
INT CANR-4; SATA 60

Bean, Normal
See Burroughs, Edgar Rice

Beard, Charles A(ustin) 1874-1948 **TCLC 15**
See also CA 115; DLB 17; SATA 18

Beardsley, Aubrey 1872-1898 .... **NCLC 6**

Beattie, Ann 1947-**CLC 8, 13, 18, 40, 63; DAM
NOV, POP; SSC 11**
See also BEST 90:2; CA 81-84; CANR 53;
DLBY 82; MTCW

Beattie, James 1735-1803 .... **NCLC 25**
See also DLB 109

Beauchamp, Kathleen Mansfield 1888-1923
See Mansfield, Katherine
See also CA 104; 134; DA; DAC; DAM MST

Beaumarchais, Pierre-Augustin Caron de 1732-
1799 .... **DC 4**
See also DAM DRAM

Beaumont, Francis 1584(?)-1616**LC 33; DC 6**
See also CDBLB Before 1660; DLB 58, 121

**Beauvoir, Simone (Lucie Ernestine Marie
Bertrand) de** 1908-1986**CLC 1, 2, 4, 8, 14,
31, 44, 50, 71; DA; DAB; DAC; DAM MST,
NOV; WLC**
See also CA 9-12R; 118; CANR 28, 61; DLB
72; DLBY 86; MTCW

Becker, Carl (Lotus) 1873-1945 ..... **TCLC 63**
See also CA 157; DLB 17

Becker, Jurek 1937-1997 .... **CLC 7, 19**
See also CA 85-88; 157; CANR 60; DLB 75

Becker, Walter 1950-........................**CLC 26**

Beckett, Samuel (Barclay) 1906-1989 **CLC 1,
2, 3, 4, 6, 9, 10, 11, 14, 18, 29, 57, 59, 83;
DA; DAB; DAC; DAM DRAM, MST,
NOV; SSC 16; WLC**
See also CA 5-8R; 130; CANR 33, 61; CDBLB
1945-1960; DLB 13, 15; DLBY 90; MTCW

Beckford, William 1760-1844 .... **NCLC 16**
See also DLB 39

Beckman, Gunnel 1910-.................... **CLC 26**
See also CA 33-36R; CANR 15; CLR 25;
MAICYA; SAAS 9; SATA 6

Becque, Henri 1837-1899 .... **NCLC 3**

Beddoes, Thomas Lovell 1803-1849 **NCLC 3**
See also DLB 96

Bede c. 673-735 .... **CMLC 20**
See also DLB 146

Bedford, Donald F.
See Fearing, Kenneth (Flexner)

Beecher, Catharine Esther 1800-1878 N C L C
30
See also DLB 1

Beecher, John 1904-1980 .... **CLC 6**
See also AITN 1; CA 5-8R; 105; CANR 8

Beer, Johann 1655-1700 .... **LC 5**
See also DLB 168

Beer, Patricia 1924-............................**CLC 58**
See also CA 61-64; CANR 13, 46; DLB 40

Beerbohm, Max
See Beerbohm, (Henry) Max(imilian)

Beerbohm, (Henry) Max(imilian) 1872-1956
TCLC 1, 24
See also CA 104; 154; DLB 34, 100

Beer-Hofmann, Richard 1866-1945**TCLC 60**
See also DLB 81

Begiebing, Robert J(ohn) 1946- .... **CLC 70**

See also CA 122; CANR 40

Behan, Brendan 1923-1964 **CLC 1, 8, 11, 15,
79; DAM DRAM**
See also CA 73-76; CANR 33; CDBLB 1945-
1960; DLB 13; MTCW

Behn, Aphra 1640(?)-1689**LC 1, 30; DA; DAB;
DAC; DAM DRAM, MST, NOV, POET;
DC 4; PC 13; WLC**
See also DLB 39, 80, 131

Behrman, S(amuel) N(athaniel) 1893-1973
CLC 40
See also CA 13-16; 45-48; CAP 1; DLB 7, 44

Belasco, David 1853-1931 .... **TCLC 3**
See also CA 104; DLB 7

Belcheva, Elisaveta 1893- ....**CLC 10**
See also Bagryana, Elisaveta

Beldone, Phil "Cheech"
See Ellison, Harlan (Jay)

Beleno
See Azuela, Mariano

Belinski, Vissarion Grigoryevich 1811-1848
NCLC 5

Belitt, Ben 1911- ....**CLC 22**
See also CA 13-16R; CAAS 4; CANR 7; DLB
5

Bell, Gertrude 1868-1926 .... **TCLC 67**
See also DLB 174

Bell, James Madison 1826-1902 ... **TCLC 43;
BLC; DAM MULT**
See also BW 1; CA 122; 124; DLB 50

Bell, Madison Smartt 1957-...... **CLC 41, 102**
See also CA 111; CANR 28, 54

Bell, Marvin (Hartley) 1937-**CLC 8, 31; DAM
POET**
See also CA 21-24R; CAAS 14; CANR 59; DLB
5; MTCW

Bell, W. L. D.
See Mencken, H(enry) L(ouis)

Bellamy, Atwood C.
See Mencken, H(enry) L(ouis)

Bellamy, Edward 1850-1898 .... **NCLC 4**
See also DLB 12

Bellin, Edward J.
See Kuttner, Henry

**Belloc, (Joseph) Hilaire (Pierre Sebastien Rene
Swanton)** 1870-1953 **TCLC 7, 18; DAM
POET**
See also CA 106; 152; DLB 19, 100, 141, 174;
YABC 1

Belloc, Joseph Peter Rene Hilaire
See Belloc, (Joseph) Hilaire (Pierre Sebastien
Rene Swanton)

Belloc, Joseph Pierre Hilaire
See Belloc, (Joseph) Hilaire (Pierre Sebastien
Rene Swanton)

Belloc, M. A.
See Lowndes, Marie Adelaide (Belloc)

Bellow, Saul 1915-**CLC 1, 2, 3, 6, 8, 10, 13, 15,
25, 33, 34, 63, 79; DA; DAB; DAC; DAM
MST, NOV, POP; SSC 14; WLC**
See also AITN 2; BEST 89:3; CA 5-8R; CABS
1; CANR 29, 53; CDALB 1941-1968; DLB
2, 28; DLBD 3; DLBY 82; MTCW

Belser, Reimond Karel Maria de 1929-
See Ruyslinck, Ward
See also CA 152

Bely, Andrey .... **TCLC 7; PC 11**
See also Bugayev, Boris Nikolayevich

Benary, Margot
See Benary-Isbert, Margot

Benary-Isbert, Margot 1889-1979 ....**CLC 12**
See also CA 5-8R; 89-92; CANR 4; CLR 12;
MAICYA; SATA 2; SATA-Obit 21

See also AAYA 11; CA 104; 132; DLB 8; MTCW; SATA 41

Burroughs, William S(eward) 1914-CLC 1, 2, 5, 15, 22, 42, 75; DA; DAB; DAC; DAM MST, NOV, POP; WLC
See also AITN 2; CA 9-12R; CANR 20, 52; DLB 2, 8, 16, 152; DLBY 81; MTCW

Burton, Richard F. 1821-1890 .... NCLC 42
See also DLB 55

Busch, Frederick 1941- ..... CLC 7, 10, 18, 47
See also CA 33-36R; CAAS 1; CANR 45; DLB 6

Bush, Ronald 1946- .... CLC 34
See also CA 136

Bustos, F(rancisco)
See Borges, Jorge Luis

Bustos Domecq, H(onorio)
See Bioy Casares, Adolfo; Borges, Jorge Luis

Butler, Octavia E(stelle) 1947-CLC 38; DAM MULT, POP
See also AAYA 18; BW 2; CA 73-76; CANR 12, 24, 38; DLB 33; MTCW; SATA 84

Butler, Robert Olen (Jr.) 1945-CLC 81; DAM POP
See also CA 112; DLB 173; INT 112

Butler, Samuel 1612-1680 .... LC 16
See also DLB 101, 126

Butler, Samuel 1835-1902 . TCLC 1, 33; DA; DAB; DAC; DAM MST, NOV; WLC
See also CA 143; CDBLB 1890-1914; DLB 18, 57, 174

Butler, Walter C.
See Faust, Frederick (Schiller)

Butor, Michel (Marie Francois) 1926-CLC 1, 3, 8, 11, 15
See also CA 9-12R; CANR 33; DLB 83; MTCW

Buzo, Alexander (John) 1944- .... CLC 61
See also CA 97-100; CANR 17, 39

Buzzati, Dino 1906-1972 .... CLC 36
See also CA 33-36R; DLB 177

Byars, Betsy (Cromer) 1928-............ CLC 35
See also AAYA 19; CA 33-36R; CANR 18, 36, 57; CLR 1, 16; DLB 52; INT CANR-18; JRDA; MAICYA; MTCW; SAAS 1; SATA 4, 46, 80

Byatt, A(ntonia) S(usan Drabble) 1936-C L C 19, 65; DAM NOV, POP
See also CA 13-16R; CANR 13, 33, 50; DLB 14; MTCW

Byrne, David 1952-........................... CLC 26
See also CA 127

Byrne, John Keyes 1926-
See Leonard, Hugh
See also CA 102; INT 102

Byron, George Gordon (Noel) 1788-1824 NCLC 2, 12; DA; DAB; DAC; DAM MST, POET; PC 16; WLC
See also CDBLB 1789-1832; DLB 96, 110

Byron, Robert 1905-1941 .... TCLC 67

C. 3. 3.
See Wilde, Oscar (Fingal O'Flahertie Wills)

Caballero, Fernan 1796-1877 .... NCLC 10

Cabell, Branch
See Cabell, James Branch

Cabell, James Branch 1879-1958 .... TCLC 6
See also CA 105; 152; DLB 9, 78

Cable, George Washington 1844-1925 T C L C 4; SSC 4
See also CA 104; 155; DLB 12, 74; DLBD 13

Cabral de Melo Neto, Joao 1920- ... CLC 76; DAM MULT
See also CA 151

Cabrera Infante, G(uillermo) 1929- . CLC 5,

25, 45; DAM MULT; HLC
See also CA 85-88; CANR 29; DLB 113; HW; MTCW

Cade, Toni
See Bambara, Toni Cade

Cadmus and Harmonia
See Buchan, John

Caedmon fl. 658-680 .... CMLC 7
See also DLB 146

Caeiro, Alberto
See Pessoa, Fernando (Antonio Nogueira)

Cage, John (Milton, Jr.) 1912- .... CLC 41
See also CA 13-16R; CANR 9; INT CANR-9

Cahan, Abraham 1860-1951 .... TCLC 71
See also CA 108; 154; DLB 9, 25, 28

Cain, G.
See Cabrera Infante, G(uillermo)

Cain, Guillermo
See Cabrera Infante, G(uillermo)

Cain, James M(allahan) 1892-1977CLC 3, 11, 28
See also AITN 1; CA 17-20R; 73-76; CANR 8, 34, 61; MTCW

Caine, Mark
See Raphael, Frederic (Michael)

Calasso, Roberto 1941- .... CLC 81
See also CA 143

Calderon de la Barca, Pedro 1600-1681 .. L C 23; DC 3

Caldwell, Erskine (Preston) 1903-1987CLC 1, 8, 14, 50, 60; DAM NOV; SSC 19
See also AITN 1; CA 1-4R; 121; CAAS 1; CANR 2, 33; DLB 9, 86; MTCW

Caldwell, (Janet Miriam) Taylor (Holland) 1900-1985CLC 2, 28, 39; DAM NOV, POP
See also CA 5-8R; 116; CANR 5

Calhoun, John Caldwell 1782-1850NCLC 15
See also DLB 3

Calisher, Hortense 1911-CLC 2, 4, 8, 38; DAM NOV; SSC 15
See also CA 1-4R; CANR 1, 22; DLB 2; INT CANR-22; MTCW

Callaghan, Morley Edward 1903-1990CLC 3, 14, 41, 65; DAC; DAM MST
See also CA 9-12R; 132; CANR 33; DLB 68; MTCW

Callimachus c. 305B.C.-c. 240B.C. CMLC 18
See also DLB 176

Calvin, John 1509-1564 .... LC 37

Calvino, Italo 1923-1985CLC 5, 8, 11, 22, 33, 39, 73; DAM NOV; SSC 3
See also CA 85-88; 116; CANR 23, 61; MTCW

Cameron, Carey 1952- .... CLC 59
See also CA 135

Cameron, Peter 1959- .... CLC 44
See also CA 125; CANR 50

Campana, Dino 1885-1932 .... TCLC 20
See also CA 117; DLB 114

Campanella, Tommaso 1568-1639 ...... LC 32

Campbell, John W(ood, Jr.) 1910-1971 C L C 32
See also CA 21-22; 29-32R; CANR 34; CAP 2; DLB 8; MTCW

Campbell, Joseph 1904-1987 .... CLC 69
See also AAYA 3; BEST 89:2; CA 1-4R; 124; CANR 3, 28, 61; MTCW

Campbell, Maria 1940- .... CLC 85; DAC
See also CA 102; CANR 54; NNAL

Campbell, (John) Ramsey 1946-CLC 42; SSC 19
See also CA 57-60; CANR 7; INT CANR-7

Campbell, (Ignatius) Roy (Dunnachie) 1901-1957 .... TCLC 5

See also CA 104; 155; DLB 20

Campbell, Thomas 1777-1844 .... NCLC 19
See also DLB 93; 144

Campbell, Wilfred .... TCLC 9
See also Campbell, William

Campbell, William 1858(?)-1918
See Campbell, Wilfred
See also CA 106; DLB 92

Campion, Jane .... CLC 95
See also CA 138

Campos, Alvaro de
See Pessoa, Fernando (Antonio Nogueira)

Camus, Albert 1913-1960CLC 1, 2, 4, 9, 11, 14, 32, 63, 69; DA; DAB; DAC; DAM DRAM, MST, NOV; DC 2; SSC 9; WLC
See also CA 89-92; DLB 72; MTCW

Canby, Vincent 1924- .... CLC 13
See also CA 81-84

Cancale
See Desnos, Robert

Canetti, Elias 1905-1994CLC 3, 14, 25, 75, 86
See also CA 21-24R; 146; CANR 23, 61; DLB 85, 124; MTCW

Canin, Ethan 1960- .... CLC 55
See also CA 131; 135

Cannon, Curt
See Hunter, Evan

Cape, Judith
See Page, P(atricia) K(athleen)

Capek, Karel 1890-1938 ... TCLC 6, 37; DA; DAB; DAC; DAM DRAM, MST, NOV; DC 1; WLC
See also CA 104; 140

Capote, Truman 1924-1984CLC 1, 3, 8, 13, 19, 34, 38, 58; DA; DAB; DAC; DAM MST, NOV, POP; SSC 2; WLC
See also CA 5-8R; 113; CANR 18; CDALB 1941-1968; DLB 2; DLBY 80, 84; MTCW; SATA 91

Capra, Frank 1897-1991 .... CLC 16
See also CA 61-64; 135

Caputo, Philip 1941- .... CLC 32
See also CA 73-76; CANR 40

Card, Orson Scott 1951-CLC 44, 47, 50; DAM POP
See also AAYA 11; CA 102; CANR 27, 47; INT CANR-27; MTCW; SATA 83

Cardenal, Ernesto 1925- .... CLC 31; DAM MULT, POET; HLC
See also CA 49-52; CANR 2, 32; HW; MTCW

Cardozo, Benjamin N(athan) 1870-1938 TCLC 65
See also CA 117

Carducci, Giosue 1835-1907 .... TCLC 32

Carew, Thomas 1595(?)-1640 .... LC 13
See also DLB 126

Carey, Ernestine Gilbreth 1908- ...... CLC 17
See also CA 5-8R; SATA 2

Carey, Peter 1943- .... CLC 40, 55, 96
See also CA 123; 127; CANR 53; INT 127; MTCW; SATA 94

Carleton, William 1794-1869 .... NCLC 3
See also DLB 159

Carlisle, Henry (Coffin) 1926- .... CLC 33
See also CA 13-16R; CANR 15

Carlsen, Chris
See Holdstock, Robert P.

Carlson, Ron(ald F.) 1947- .... CLC 54
See also CA 105; CANR 27

Carlyle, Thomas 1795-1881 .. NCLC 22; DA; DAB; DAC; DAM MST
See also CDBLB 1789-1832; DLB 55; 144

Carman, (William) Bliss 1861-1929 TCLC 7;

6, 105

Char, Rene(-Emile) 1907-1988CLC **9, 11, 14, 55; DAM POET**
See also CA 13-16R; 124; CANR 32; MTCW
Charby, Jay
See Ellison, Harlan (Jay)
Chardin, Pierre Teilhard de
See Teilhard de Chardin, (Marie Joseph) Pierre
Charles I 1600-1649 .... **LC 13**
Charyn, Jerome 1937-............... CLC **5, 8, 18**
See also CA 5-8R; CAAS 1; CANR 7, 61;
DLBY 83; MTCW
Chase, Mary (Coyle) 1907-1981 .... **DC 1**
See also CA 77-80; 105; SATA 17; SATA-Obit
29
Chase, Mary Ellen 1887-1973 ....CLC **2**
See also CA 13-16; 41-44R; CAP 1; SATA 10
Chase, Nicholas
See Hyde, Anthony
Chateaubriand, Francois Rene de 1768-1848
NCLC 3
See also DLB 119
Chatterje, Sarat Chandra 1876-1936(?)
See Chatterji, Saratchandra
See also CA 109
Chatterji, Bankim Chandra 1838-1894NCLC
19
Chatterji, Saratchandra .... **TCLC 13**
See also Chatterje, Sarat Chandra
Chatterton, Thomas 1752-1770 .LC **3; DAM POET**
See also DLB 109
Chatwin, (Charles) Bruce 1940-1989CLC **28, 57, 59; DAM POP**
See also AAYA 4; BEST 90:1; CA 85-88; 127
Chaucer, Daniel
See Ford, Ford Madox
Chaucer, Geoffrey 1340(?)-1400 LC **17; DA; DAB; DAC; DAM MST, POET; PC 19; WLCS**
See also CDBLB Before 1660; DLB 146
Chaviaras, Strates 1935-
See Haviaras, Stratis
See also CA 105
Chayefsky, Paddy .... **CLC 23**
See also Chayefsky, Sidney
See also DLB 7, 44; DLBY 81
Chayefsky, Sidney 1923-1981
See Chayefsky, Paddy
See also CA 9-12R; 104; CANR 18; DAM
DRAM
Chedid, Andree 1920- .... **CLC 47**
See also CA 145
Cheever, John 1912-1982 CLC **3, 7, 8, 11, 15, 25, 64; DA; DAB; DAC; DAM MST, NOV, POP; SSC 1; WLC**
See also CA 5-8R; 106; CABS 1; CANR 5, 27;
CDALB 1941-1968; DLB 2, 102; DLBY 80,
82; INT CANR-5; MTCW
Cheever, Susan 1943- .... **CLC 18, 48**
See also CA 103; CANR 27, 51; DLBY 82; INT
CANR-27
Chekhonte, Antosha
See Chekhov, Anton (Pavlovich)
Chekhov, Anton (Pavlovich) 1860-1904TCLC
**3, 10, 31, 55; DA; DAB; DAC; DAM
MST; SSC 2; WLC**
See also CA 104; 124; SATA 90
Chernyshevsky, Nikolay Gavrilovich 1828-1889
NCLC 1
Cherry, Carolyn Janice 1942-
See Cherryh, C. J.
See also CA 65-68; CANR 10

Cherryh, C. J. .... **CLC 35**
See also Cherry, Carolyn Janice
See also DLBY 80; SATA 93
Chesnutt, Charles W(addell) 1858-1932
TCLC 5, 39; BLC; DAM MULT; SSC 7
See also BW 1; CA 106; 125; DLB 12, 50, 78;
MTCW
Chester, Alfred 1929(?)-1971 .... **CLC 49**
See also CA 33-36R; DLB 130
Chesterton, G(ilbert) K(eith) 1874-1936
TCLC 1, 6, 64; DAM NOV, POET; SSC 1
See also CA 104; 132; CDBLB 1914-1945;
DLB 10, 19, 34, 70, 98, 149, 178; MTCW;
SATA 27
Chiang Pin-chin 1904-1986
See Ding Ling
See also CA 118
Ch'ien Chung-shu 1910- .... **CLC 22**
See also CA 130; MTCW
Child, L. Maria
See Child, Lydia Maria
Child, Lydia Maria 1802-1880 .... **NCLC 6**
See also DLB 1, 74; SATA 67
Child, Mrs.
See Child, Lydia Maria
Child, Philip 1898-1978 .... **CLC 19, 68**
See also CA 13-14; CAP 1; SATA 47
Childers, (Robert) Erskine 1870-1922 T C L C
65
See also CA 113; 153; DLB 70
Childress, Alice 1920-1994CLC **12, 15, 86, 96;
BLC; DAM DRAM, MULT, NOV; DC 4**
See also AAYA 8; BW 2; CA 45-48; 146; CANR
3, 27, 50; CLR 14; DLB 7, 38; JRDA;
MAICYA; MTCW; SATA 7, 48, 81
Chin, Frank (Chew, Jr.) 1940- .... **DC 7**
See also CA 33-36R; DAM MULT
Chislett, (Margaret) Anne 1943-.......**CLC 34**
See also CA 151
Chitty, Thomas Willes 1926- .... **CLC 11**
See also Hinde, Thomas
See also CA 5-8R
Chivers, Thomas Holley 1809-1858NCLC **49**
See also DLB 3
Chomette, Rene Lucien 1898-1981
See Clair, Rene
See also CA 103
Chopin, Kate TCLC **5, 14; DA; DAB; SSC 8;
WLCS**
See also Chopin, Katherine
See also CDALB 1865-1917; DLB 12, 78
Chopin, Katherine 1851-1904
See Chopin, Kate
See also CA 104; 122; DAC; DAM MST, NOV
Chretien de Troyes c. 12th cent. -..CMLC **10**
Christie
See Ichikawa, Kon
Christie, Agatha (Mary Clarissa) 1890-1976
CLC **1, 6, 8, 12, 39, 48; DAB; DAC; DAM
NOV**
See also AAYA 9; AITN 1, 2; CA 17-20R; 61-
64; CANR 10, 37; CDBLB 1914-1945; DLB
13, 77; MTCW; SATA 36
Christie, (Ann) Philippa
See Pearce, Philippa
See also CA 5-8R; CANR 4
Christine de Pizan 1365(?)-1431(?) ...... **LC 9**
Chubb, Elmer
See Masters, Edgar Lee
Chulkov, Mikhail Dmitrievich 1743-1792LC **2**
See also DLB 150
Churchill, Caryl 1938- ..... CLC **31, 55; DC 5**
See also CA 102; CANR 22, 46; DLB 13;

MTCW
Churchill, Charles 1731-1764 .... **LC 3**
See also DLB 109
Chute, Carolyn 1947- .... **CLC 39**
See also CA 123
Ciardi, John (Anthony) 1916-1986 . CLC **10, 40, 44; DAM POET**
See also CA 5-8R; 118; CAAS 2; CANR 5, 33;
CLR 19; DLB 5; DLBY 86; INT CANR-5;
MAICYA; MTCW; SATA 1, 65; SATA-Obit
46
Cicero, Marcus Tullius 106B.C.-43B.C.
CMLC 3
Cimino, Michael 1943- .... **CLC 16**
See also CA 105
Cioran, E(mil) M. 1911-1995 .... **CLC 64**
See also CA 25-28R; 149
Cisneros, Sandra 1954-CLC **69; DAM MULT;
HLC**
See also AAYA 9; CA 131; DLB 122, 152; HW
Cixous, Helene 1937- .... **CLC 92**
See also CA 126; CANR 55; DLB 83; MTCW
Clair, Rene .... **CLC 20**
See also Chomette, Rene Lucien
Clampitt, Amy 1920-1994 ..... CLC **32; PC 19**
See also CA 110; 146; CANR 29; DLB 105
Clancy, Thomas L., Jr. 1947-
See Clancy, Tom
See also CA 125; 131; INT 131; MTCW
Clancy, Tom .... CLC **45; DAM NOV, POP**
See also Clancy, Thomas L., Jr.
See also AAYA 9; BEST 89:1, 90:1
Clare, John 1793-1864 NCLC **9; DAB; DAM
POET**
See also DLB 55, 96
Clarin
See Alas (y Urena), Leopoldo (Enrique Garcia)
Clark, Al C.
See Goines, Donald
Clark, (Robert) Brian 1932-............. **CLC 29**
See also CA 41-44R
Clark, Curt
See Westlake, Donald E(dwin)
Clark, Eleanor 1913-1996 .... CLC **5, 19**
See also CA 9-12R; 151; CANR 41; DLB 6
Clark, J. P.
See Clark, John Pepper
See also DLB 117
Clark, John Pepper 1935-.......CLC **38; BLC;
DAM DRAM, MULT; DC 5**
See also Clark, J. P.
See also BW 1; CA 65-68; CANR 16
Clark, M. R.
See Clark, Mavis Thorpe
Clark, Mavis Thorpe 1909- .... **CLC 12**
See also CA 57-60; CANR 8, 37; CLR 30;
MAICYA; SAAS 5; SATA 8, 74
Clark, Walter Van Tilburg 1909-1971CLC **28**
See also CA 9-12R; 33-36R; DLB 9; SATA 8
Clarke, Arthur C(harles) 1917-CLC **1, 4, 13, 18, 35; DAM POP; SSC 3**
See also AAYA 4; CA 1-4R; CANR 2, 28, 55;
JRDA; MAICYA; MTCW; SATA 13, 70
Clarke, Austin 1896-1974 ....CLC **6, 9; DAM
POET**
See also CA 29-32; 49-52; CAP 2; DLB 10, 20
Clarke, Austin C(hesterfield) 1934-CLC **8, 53;
BLC; DAC; DAM MULT**
See also BW 1; CA 25-28R; CAAS 16; CANR
14, 32; DLB 53, 125
Clarke, Gillian 1937-........................ **CLC 61**
See also CA 106; DLB 40
Clarke, Marcus (Andrew Hislop) 1846-1881

de Beauvoir, Simone (Lucie Ernestine Marie
    Bertrand)
    See Beauvoir, Simone (Lucie Ernestine Marie
        Bertrand) de
de Brissac, Malcolm
    See Dickinson, Peter (Malcolm)
de Chardin, Pierre Teilhard
    See Teilhard de Chardin, (Marie Joseph) Pierre
Dee, John 1527-1608 .... LC 20
Deer, Sandra 1940- .... CLC 45
De Ferrari, Gabriella 1941- .... CLC 65
    See also CA 146
Defoe, Daniel 1660(?)-1731 LC 1; DA; DAB;
    DAC; DAM MST, NOV; WLC
    See also CDBLB 1660-1789; DLB 39, 95, 101;
        JRDA; MAICYA; SATA 22
de Gourmont, Remy(-Marie-Charles)
    See Gourmont, Remy (-Marie-Charles) de
de Hartog, Jan 1914- .... CLC 19
    See also CA 1-4R; CANR 1
de Hostos, E. M.
    See Hostos (y Bonilla), Eugenio Maria de
de Hostos, Eugenio M.
    See Hostos (y Bonilla), Eugenio Maria de
Deighton, Len .... CLC 4, 7, 22, 46
    See also Deighton, Leonard Cyril
    See also AAYA 6; BEST 89:2; CDBLB 1960 to
        Present; DLB 87
Deighton, Leonard Cyril 1929-
    See Deighton, Len
    See also CA 9-12R; CANR 19, 33; DAM NOV,
        POP; MTCW
Dekker, Thomas 1572(?)-1632 .. LC 22; DAM
    DRAM
    See also CDBLB Before 1660; DLB 62, 172
Delafield, E. M. 1890-1943 .... TCLC 61
    See also Dashwood, Edmee Elizabeth Monica
        de la Pasture
    See also DLB 34
de la Mare, Walter (John) 1873-1956TCLC 4,
    53; DAB; DAC; DAM MST, POET; SSC
    14; WLC
    See also CDBLB 1914-1945; CLR 23; DLB
        162; SATA 16
Delaney, Franey
    See O'Hara, John (Henry)
Delaney, Shelagh 1939-CLC 29; DAM DRAM
    See also CA 17-20R; CANR 30; CDBLB 1960
        to Present; DLB 13; MTCW
Delany, Mary (Granville Pendarves) 1700-1788
    LC 12
Delany, Samuel R(ay, Jr.) 1942-CLC 8, 14, 38;
    BLC; DAM MULT
    See also BW 2; CA 81-84; CANR 27, 43; DLB
        8, 33; MTCW
De La Ramee, (Marie) Louise 1839-1908
    See Ouida
    See also SATA 20
de la Roche, Mazo 1879-1961 .... CLC 14
    See also CA 85-88; CANR 30; DLB 68; SATA
        64
De La Salle, Innocent
    See Hartmann, Sadakichi
Delbanco, Nicholas (Franklin) 1942- CLC 6,
    13
    See also CA 17-20R; CAAS 2; CANR 29, 55;
        DLB 6
del Castillo, Michel 1933- .... CLC 38
    See also CA 109
Deledda, Grazia (Cosima) 1875(?)-1936
    TCLC 23
    See also CA 123
Delibes, Miguel .... CLC 8, 18

See also Delibes Setien, Miguel
Delibes Setien, Miguel 1920-
    See Delibes, Miguel
    See also CA 45-48; CANR 1, 32; HW; MTCW
DeLillo, Don 1936- CLC 8, 10, 13, 27, 39, 54,
    76; DAM NOV, POP
    See also BEST 89:1; CA 81-84; CANR 21; DLB
        6, 173; MTCW
de Lisser, H. G.
    See De Lisser, H(erbert) G(eorge)
    See also DLB 117
De Lisser, H(erbert) G(eorge) 1878-1944
    TCLC 12
    See also de Lisser, H. G.
    See also BW 2; CA 109; 152
Deloria, Vine (Victor), Jr. 1933- ..... CLC 21;
    DAM MULT
    See also CA 53-56; CANR 5, 20, 48; DLB 175;
        MTCW; NNAL; SATA 21
Del Vecchio, John M(ichael) 1947- ...CLC 29
    See also CA 110; DLBD 9
de Man, Paul (Adolph Michel) 1919-1983
    CLC 55
    See also CA 128; 111; CANR 61; DLB 67;
        MTCW
De Marinis, Rick 1934- .... CLC 54
    See also CA 57-60; CAAS 24; CANR 9, 25, 50
Dembry, R. Emmet
    See Murfree, Mary Noailles
Demby, William 1922-. CLC 53; BLC; DAM
    MULT
    See also BW 1; CA 81-84; DLB 33
de Menton, Francisco
    See Chin, Frank (Chew, Jr.)
Demijohn, Thom
    See Disch, Thomas M(ichael)
de Montherlant, Henry (Milon)
    See Montherlant, Henry (Milon) de
Demosthenes 384B.C.-322B.C. ...... CMLC 13
    See also DLB 176
de Natale, Francine
    See Malzberg, Barry N(athaniel)
Denby, Edwin (Orr) 1903-1983 .... CLC 48
    See also CA 138; 110
Denis, Julio
    See Cortazar, Julio
Denmark, Harrison
    See Zelazny, Roger (Joseph)
Dennis, John 1658-1734 .... LC 11
    See also DLB 101
Dennis, Nigel (Forbes) 1912-1989 .... CLC 8
    See also CA 25-28R; 129; DLB 13, 15; MTCW
Dent, Lester 1904(?)-1959 .... TCLC 72
    See also CA 112
De Palma, Brian (Russell) 1940- .... CLC 20
    See also CA 109
De Quincey, Thomas 1785-1859 .... NCLC 4
    See also CDBLB 1789-1832; DLB 110; 144
Deren, Eleanora 1908(?)-1961
    See Deren, Maya
    See also CA 111
Deren, Maya 1917-1961 .... CLC 16, 102
    See also Deren, Eleanora
Derleth, August (William) 1909-1971CLC 31
    See also CA 1-4R; 29-32R; CANR 4; DLB 9;
        SATA 5
Der Nister 1884-1950 .... TCLC 56
de Routisie, Albert
    See Aragon, Louis
Derrida, Jacques 1930- .... CLC 24, 87
    See also CA 124; 127
Derry Down Derry
    See Lear, Edward

Dersonnes, Jacques
    See Simenon, Georges (Jacques Christian)
Desai, Anita 1937-CLC 19, 37, 97; DAB; DAM
    NOV
    See also CA 81-84; CANR 33, 53; MTCW;
        SATA 63
de Saint-Luc, Jean
    See Glassco, John
de Saint Roman, Arnaud
    See Aragon, Louis
Descartes, Rene 1596-1650 .... LC 20, 35
De Sica, Vittorio 1901(?)-1974 .... CLC 20
    See also CA 117
Desnos, Robert 1900-1945 .... TCLC 22
    See also CA 121; 151
Destouches, Louis-Ferdinand 1894-1961C L C
    9, 15
    See also Celine, Louis-Ferdinand
    See also CA 85-88; CANR 28; MTCW
de Tolignac, Gaston
    See Griffith, D(avid Lewelyn) W(ark)
Deutsch, Babette 1895-1982 .... CLC 18
    See also CA 1-4R; 108; CANR 4; DLB 45;
        SATA 1; SATA-Obit 33
Devenant, William 1606-1649 .... LC 13
Devkota, Laxmiprasad 1909-1959 . TCLC 23
    See also CA 123
De Voto, Bernard (Augustine) 1897-1955
    TCLC 29
    See also CA 113; DLB 9
De Vries, Peter 1910-1993 CLC 1, 2, 3, 7, 10,
    28, 46; DAM NOV
    See also CA 17-20R; 142; CANR 41; DLB 6;
        DLBY 82; MTCW
Dexter, John
    See Bradley, Marion Zimmer
Dexter, Martin
    See Faust, Frederick (Schiller)
Dexter, Pete 1943-... CLC 34, 55; DAM POP
    See also BEST 89:2; CA 127; 131; INT 131;
        MTCW
Diamano, Silmang
    See Senghor, Leopold Sedar
Diamond, Neil 1941- .... CLC 30
    See also CA 108
Diaz del Castillo, Bernal 1496-1584 ... LC 31
di Bassetto, Corno
    See Shaw, George Bernard
Dick, Philip K(indred) 1928-1982CLC 10, 30,
    72; DAM NOV, POP
    See also CA 49-52; 106; CANR 2, 16; DLB 8;
        MTCW
Dickens, Charles (John Huffam) 1812-1870
    NCLC 3, 8, 18, 26, 37, 50; DA; DAB; DAC;
    DAM MST, NOV; SSC 17; WLC
    See also CDBLB 1832-1890; DLB 21, 55, 70,
        159, 166; JRDA; MAICYA; SATA 15
Dickey, James (Lafayette) 1923-1997 CLC 1,
    2, 4, 7, 10, 15, 47; DAM NOV, POET, POP
    See also AITN 1, 2; CA 9-12R; 156; CABS 2;
        CANR 10, 48, 61; CDALB 1968-1988; DLB
        5; DLBD 7; DLBY 82, 93, 96; INT CANR-
        10; MTCW
Dickey, William 1928-1994 .... CLC 3, 28
    See also CA 9-12R; 145; CANR 24; DLB 5
Dickinson, Charles 1951- .... CLC 49
    See also CA 128
Dickinson, Emily (Elizabeth) 1830-1886
    NCLC 21; DA; DAB; DAC; DAM MST,
    POET; PC 1; WLC
    See also AAYA 22; CDALB 1865-1917; DLB
        1; SATA 29
Dickinson, Peter (Malcolm) 1927-CLC 12, 35

See also AAYA 9; CA 41-44R; CANR 31, 58; CLR 29; DLB 87, 161; JRDA; MAICYA; SATA 5, 62

Dickson, Carr
See Carr, John Dickson

Dickson, Carter
See Carr, John Dickson

Diderot, Denis 1713-1784 .... **LC 26**

Didion, Joan 1934-CLC 1, 3, 8, 14, 32; DAM NOV
See also AITN 1; CA 5-8R; CANR 14, 52; CDALB 1968-1988; DLB 2, 173; DLBY 81, 86; MTCW

Dietrich, Robert
See Hunt, E(verette) Howard, (Jr.)

Dillard, Annie 1945- . CLC 9, 60; DAM NOV
See also AAYA 6; CA 49-52; CANR 3, 43; DLBY 80; MTCW; SATA 10

Dillard, R(ichard) H(enry) W(ilde) 1937-
CLC 5
See also CA 21-24R; CAAS 7; CANR 10; DLB 5

Dillon, Eilis 1920-1994 .... **CLC 17**
See also CA 9-12R; 147; CAAS 3; CANR 4, 38; CLR 26; MAICYA; SATA 2, 74; SATA-Obit 83

Dimont, Penelope
See Mortimer, Penelope (Ruth)

Dinesen, Isak .... CLC 10, 29, 95; SSC 7
See also Blixen, Karen (Christentze Dinesen)

Ding Ling .... **CLC 68**
See also Chiang Pin-chin

Disch, Thomas M(ichael) 1940- ... **CLC 7, 36**
See also AAYA 17; CA 21-24R; CAAS 4; CANR 17, 36, 54; CLR 18; DLB 8; MAICYA; MTCW; SAAS 15; SATA 92

Disch, Tom
See Disch, Thomas M(ichael)

d'Isly, Georges
See Simenon, Georges (Jacques Christian)

Disraeli, Benjamin 1804-1881 .... NCLC 2, 39
See also DLB 21, 55

Ditcum, Steve
See Crumb, R(obert)

Dixon, Paige
See Corcoran, Barbara

Dixon, Stephen 1936- .... CLC 52; SSC 16
See also CA 89-92; CANR 17, 40, 54; DLB 130

Dobell, Sydney Thompson 1824-1874 N C L C 43
See also DLB 32

Doblin, Alfred .... TCLC 13
See also Doeblin, Alfred

Dobrolyubov, Nikolai Alexandrovich 1836-1861
NCLC 5

Dobyns, Stephen 1941- .... CLC 37
See also CA 45-48; CANR 2, 18

Doctorow, E(dgar) L(aurence) 1931- CLC 6, 11, 15, 18, 37, 44, 65; DAM NOV, POP
See also AAYA 22; AITN 2; BEST 89:3; CA 45-48; CANR 2, 33, 51; CDALB 1968-1988; DLB 2, 28, 173; DLBY 80; MTCW

Dodgson, Charles Lutwidge 1832-1898
See Carroll, Lewis
See also CLR 2; DA; DAB; DAC; DAM MST, NOV, POET; MAICYA; YABC 2

Dodson, Owen (Vincent) 1914-1983 CLC 79; BLC; DAM MULT
See also BW 1; CA 65-68; 110; CANR 24; DLB 76

Doeblin, Alfred 1878-1957 .... TCLC 13
See also Doblin, Alfred
See also CA 110; 141; DLB 66

Doerr, Harriet 1910- .... CLC 34
See also CA 117; 122; CANR 47; INT 122

Domecq, H(onorio) Bustos
See Bioy Casares, Adolfo; Borges, Jorge Luis

Domini, Rey
See Lorde, Audre (Geraldine)

Dominique
See Proust, (Valentin-Louis-George-Eugene-) Marcel

Don, A
See Stephen, Leslie

Donaldson, Stephen R. 1947- CLC 46; DAM POP
See also CA 89-92; CANR 13, 55; INT CANR-13

Donleavy, J(ames) P(atrick) 1926-CLC 1, 4, 6, 10, 45
See also AITN 2; CA 9-12R; CANR 24, 49; DLB 6, 173; INT CANR-24; MTCW

Donne, John 1572-1631LC 10, 24; DA; DAB; DAC; DAM MST, POET; PC 1
See also CDBLB Before 1660; DLB 121, 151

Donnell, David 1939(?)- .... CLC 34

Donoghue, P. S.
See Hunt, E(verette) Howard, (Jr.)

Donoso (Yanez), Jose 1924-1996CLC 4, 8, 11, 32, 99; DAM MULT; HLC
See also CA 81-84; 155; CANR 32; DLB 113; HW; MTCW

Donovan, John 1928-1992 .... CLC 35
See also AAYA 20; CA 97-100; 137; CLR 3; MAICYA; SATA 72; SATA-Brief 29

Don Roberto
See Cunninghame Graham, R(obert) B(ontine)

Doolittle, Hilda 1886-1961CLC 3, 8, 14, 31, 34, 73; DA; DAC; DAM MST, POET; PC 5; WLC
See also H. D.
See also CA 97-100; CANR 35; DLB 4, 45; MTCW

Dorfman, Ariel 1942- .... CLC 48, 77; DAM MULT; HLC
See also CA 124; 130; HW; INT 130

Dorn, Edward (Merton) 1929- ... CLC 10, 18
See also CA 93-96; CANR 42; DLB 5; INT 93-96

Dorsan, Luc
See Simenon, Georges (Jacques Christian)

Dorsange, Jean
See Simenon, Georges (Jacques Christian)

Dos Passos, John (Roderigo) 1896-1970 C L C 1, 4, 8, 11, 15, 25, 34, 82; DA; DAB; DAC; DAM MST, NOV; WLC
See also CA 1-4R; 29-32R; CANR 3; CDALB 1929-1941; DLB 4, 9; DLBD 1, 15; DLBY 96; MTCW

Dossage, Jean
See Simenon, Georges (Jacques Christian)

Dostoevsky, Fedor Mikhailovich 1821-1881
NCLC 2, 7, 21, 33, 43; DA; DAB; DAC; DAM MST, NOV; SSC 2; WLC

Doughty, Charles M(ontagu) 1843-1926
TCLC 27
See also CA 115; DLB 19, 57, 174

Douglas, Ellen .... CLC 73
See also Haxton, Josephine Ayres; Williamson, Ellen Douglas

Douglas, Gavin 1475(?)-1522 .... LC 20

Douglas, Keith 1920-1944 .... TCLC 40
See also DLB 27

Douglas, Leonard
See Bradbury, Ray (Douglas)

Douglas, Michael

See Crichton, (John) Michael

Douglas, Norman 1868-1952 .... TCLC 68

Douglass, Frederick 1817(?)-1895NCLC 7, 55; BLC; DA; DAC; DAM MST, MULT; WLC
See also CDALB 1640-1865; DLB 1, 43, 50, 79; SATA 29

Dourado, (Waldomiro Freitas) Autran 1926-
CLC 23, 60
See also CA 25-28R; CANR 34

Dourado, Waldomiro Autran
See Dourado, (Waldomiro Freitas) Autran

Dove, Rita (Frances) 1952-CLC 50, 81; DAM MULT, POET; PC 6
See also BW 2; CA 109; CAAS 19; CANR 27, 42; DLB 120

Dowell, Coleman 1925-1985 .... CLC 60
See also CA 25-28R; 117; CANR 10; DLB 130

Dowson, Ernest (Christopher) 1867-1900
TCLC 4
See also CA 105; 150; DLB 19, 135

Doyle, A. Conan
See Doyle, Arthur Conan

Doyle, Arthur Conan 1859-1930TCLC 7; DA; DAB; DAC; DAM MST, NOV; SSC 12; WLC
See also AAYA 14; CA 104; 122; CDBLB 1890-1914; DLB 18, 70, 156, 178; MTCW; SATA 24

Doyle, Conan
See Doyle, Arthur Conan

Doyle, John
See Graves, Robert (von Ranke)

Doyle, Roddy 1958(?)- .... CLC 81
See also AAYA 14; CA 143

Doyle, Sir A. Conan
See Doyle, Arthur Conan

Doyle, Sir Arthur Conan
See Doyle, Arthur Conan

Dr. A
See Asimov, Isaac; Silverstein, Alvin

Drabble, Margaret 1939-CLC 2, 3, 5, 8, 10, 22, 53; DAB; DAC; DAM MST, NOV, POP
See also CA 13-16R; CANR 18, 35; CDBLB 1960 to Present; DLB 14, 155; MTCW; SATA 48

Drapier, M. B.
See Swift, Jonathan

Drayham, James
See Mencken, H(enry) L(ouis)

Drayton, Michael 1563-1631 .... LC 8

Dreadstone, Carl
See Campbell, (John) Ramsey

Dreiser, Theodore (Herman Albert) 1871-1945
TCLC 10, 18, 35; DA; DAC; DAM MST, NOV; WLC
See also CA 106; 132; CDALB 1865-1917; DLB 9, 12, 102, 137; DLBD 1; MTCW

Drexler, Rosalyn 1926- .... CLC 2, 6
See also CA 81-84

Dreyer, Carl Theodor 1889-1968 ...... CLC 16
See also CA 116

Drieu la Rochelle, Pierre(-Eugene) 1893-1945
TCLC 21
See also CA 117; DLB 72

Drinkwater, John 1882-1937 .... TCLC 57
See also CA 109; 149; DLB 10, 19, 149

Drop Shot
See Cable, George Washington

Droste-Hulshoff, Annette Freiin von 1797-1848
NCLC 3
See also DLB 133

Drummond, Walter
See Silverberg, Robert

Drummond, William Henry 1854-1907 TCLC
25
See also DLB 92
Drummond de Andrade, Carlos 1902-1987
CLC 18
See also Andrade, Carlos Drummond de
See also CA 132; 123
Drury, Allen (Stuart) 1918- .... CLC 37
See also CA 57-60; CANR 18, 52; INT CANR-
18
Dryden, John 1631-1700 LC 3, 21; DA; DAB;
DAC; DAM DRAM, MST, POET; DC 3;
WLC
See also CDBLB 1660-1789; DLB 80, 101, 131
Duberman, Martin 1930- .... CLC 8
See also CA 1-4R; CANR 2
Dubie, Norman (Evans) 1945- .... CLC 36
See also CA 69-72; CANR 12; DLB 120
Du Bois, W(illiam) E(dward) B(urghardt) 1868-
1963 CLC 1, 2, 13, 64, 96; BLC; DA; DAC;
DAM MST, MULT, NOV; WLC
See also BW 1; CA 85-88; CANR 34; CDALB
1865-1917; DLB 47, 50, 91; MTCW; SATA
42
Dubus, Andre 1936- CLC 13, 36, 97; SSC 15
See also CA 21-24R; CANR 17; DLB 130; INT
CANR-17
Duca Minimo
See D'Annunzio, Gabriele
Ducharme, Rejean 1941- .... CLC 74
See also DLB 60
Duclos, Charles Pinot 1704-1772 .... LC 1
Dudek, Louis 1918- .... CLC 11, 19
See also CA 45-48; CAAS 14; CANR 1; DLB
88
Duerrenmatt, Friedrich 1921-1990 CLC 1, 4,
8, 11, 15, 43, 102; DAM DRAM
See also CA 17-20R; CANR 33; DLB 69, 124;
MTCW
Duffy, Bruce (?)- .... CLC 50
Duffy, Maureen 1933- .... CLC 37
See also CA 25-28R; CANR 33; DLB 14;
MTCW
Dugan, Alan 1923- .... CLC 2, 6
See also CA 81-84; DLB 5
du Gard, Roger Martin
See Martin du Gard, Roger
Duhamel, Georges 1884-1966 .... CLC 8
See also CA 81-84; 25-28R; CANR 35; DLB
65; MTCW
Dujardin, Edouard (Emile Louis) 1861-1949
TCLC 13
See also CA 109; DLB 123
Dulles, John Foster 1888-1959 .... TCLC 72
See also CA 115; 149
Dumas, Alexandre (Davy de la Pailleterie)
1802-1870... NCLC 11; DA; DAB; DAC;
DAM MST, NOV; WLC
See also DLB 119; SATA 18
Dumas, Alexandre 1824-1895 NCLC 9; DC 1
See also AAYA 22
Dumas, Claudine
See Malzberg, Barry N(athaniel)
Dumas, Henry L. 1934-1968 .... CLC 6, 62
See also BW 1; CA 85-88; DLB 41
du Maurier, Daphne 1907-1989 CLC 6, 11, 59;
DAB; DAC; DAM MST, POP; SSC 18
See also CA 5-8R; 128; CANR 6, 55; MTCW;
SATA 27; SATA-Obit 60
Dunbar, Paul Laurence 1872-1906 . TCLC 2,
12; BLC; DA; DAC; DAM MST, MULT,
POET; PC 5; SSC 8; WLC
See also BW 1; CA 104; 124; CDALB 1865-

1917; DLB 50, 54, 78; SATA 34
Dunbar, William 1460(?)-1530(?) .... LC 20
See also DLB 132, 146
Duncan, Dora Angela
See Duncan, Isadora
Duncan, Isadora 1877(?)-1927 .... TCLC 68
See also CA 118; 149
Duncan, Lois 1934- .... CLC 26
See also AAYA 4; CA 1-4R; CANR 2, 23, 36;
CLR 29; JRDA; MAICYA; SAAS 2; SATA
1, 36, 75
Duncan, Robert (Edward) 1919-1988 CLC 1,
2, 4, 7, 15, 41, 55; DAM POET; PC 2
See also CA 9-12R; 124; CANR 28; DLB 5,
16; MTCW
Duncan, Sara Jeannette 1861-1922 TCLC 60
See also CA 157; DLB 92
Dunlap, William 1766-1839 .... NCLC 2
See also DLB 30, 37, 59
Dunn, Douglas (Eaglesham) 1942- CLC 6, 40
See also CA 45-48; CANR 2, 33; DLB 40;
MTCW
Dunn, Katherine (Karen) 1945- .... CLC 71
See also CA 33-36R
Dunn, Stephen 1939- .... CLC 36
See also CA 33-36R; CANR 12, 48, 53; DLB
105
Dunne, Finley Peter 1867-1936 ...... TCLC 28
See also CA 108; DLB 11, 23
Dunne, John Gregory 1932- .... CLC 28
See also CA 25-28R; CANR 14, 50; DLBY 80
Dunsany, Edward John Moreton Drax Plunkett
1878-1957
See Dunsany, Lord
See also CA 104; 148; DLB 10
Dunsany, Lord .... TCLC 2, 59
See also Dunsany, Edward John Moreton Drax
Plunkett
See also DLB 77, 153, 156
du Perry, Jean
See Simenon, Georges (Jacques Christian)
Durang, Christopher (Ferdinand) 1949- C L C
27, 38
See also CA 105; CANR 50
Duras, Marguerite 1914-1996 CLC 3, 6, 11, 20,
34, 40, 68, 100
See also CA 25-28R; 151; CANR 50; DLB 83;
MTCW
Durban, (Rosa) Pam 1947- .... CLC 39
See also CA 123
Durcan, Paul 1944- CLC 43, 70; DAM POET
See also CA 134
Durkheim, Emile 1858-1917 .... TCLC 55
Durrell, Lawrence (George) 1912-1990 C L C
1, 4, 6, 8, 13, 27, 41; DAM NOV
See also CA 9-12R; 132; CANR 40; CDBLB
1945-1960; DLB 15, 27; DLBY 90; MTCW
Durrenmatt, Friedrich
See Duerrenmatt, Friedrich
Dutt, Toru 1856-1877 .... NCLC 29
Dwight, Timothy 1752-1817 .... NCLC 13
See also DLB 37
Dworkin, Andrea 1946- .... CLC 43
See also CA 77-80; CAAS 21; CANR 16, 39;
INT CANR-16; MTCW
Dwyer, Deanna
See Koontz, Dean R(ay)
Dwyer, K. R.
See Koontz, Dean R(ay)
Dylan, Bob 1941- .... CLC 3, 4, 6, 12, 77
See also CA 41-44R; DLB 16
Eagleton, Terence (Francis) 1943-
See Eagleton, Terry

See also CA 57-60; CANR 7, 23; MTCW
Eagleton, Terry .... CLC 63
See also Eagleton, Terence (Francis)
Early, Jack
See Scoppettone, Sandra
East, Michael
See West, Morris L(anglo)
Eastaway, Edward
See Thomas, (Philip) Edward
Eastlake, William (Derry) 1917-1997 . CLC 8
See also CA 5-8R; 158; CAAS 1; CANR 5; DLB
6; INT CANR-5
Eastman, Charles A(lexander) 1858-1939
TCLC 55; DAM MULT
See also DLB 175; NNAL; YABC 1
Eberhart, Richard (Ghormley) 1904- CLC 3,
11, 19, 56; DAM POET
See also CA 1-4R; CANR 2; CDALB 1941-
1968; DLB 48; MTCW
Eberstadt, Fernanda 1960- .... CLC 39
See also CA 136
Echegaray (y Eizaguirre), Jose (Maria Waldo)
1832-1916 ....
TCLC 4
See also CA 104; CANR 32; HW; MTCW
Echeverria, (Jose) Esteban (Antonino) 1805-
1851 .... NCLC 18
Echo
See Proust, (Valentin-Louis-George-Eugene-)
Marcel
Eckert, Allan W. 1931- .... CLC 17
See also AAYA 18; CA 13-16R; CANR 14, 45;
INT CANR-14; SAAS 21; SATA 29, 91;
SATA-Brief 27
Eckhart, Meister 1260(?)-1328(?) ... CMLC 9
See also DLB 115
Eckmar, F. R.
See de Hartog, Jan
Eco, Umberto 1932- CLC 28, 60; DAM NOV,
POP
See also BEST 90:1; CA 77-80; CANR 12, 33,
55; MTCW
Eddison, E(ric) R(ucker) 1882-1945 TCLC 15
See also CA 109; 156
Eddy, Mary (Morse) Baker 1821-1910 T C L C
71
See also CA 113
Edel, (Joseph) Leon 1907- .... CLC 29, 34
See also CA 1-4R; CANR 1, 22; DLB 103; INT
CANR-22
Eden, Emily 1797-1869 .... NCLC 10
Edgar, David 1948-... CLC 42; DAM DRAM
See also CA 57-60; CANR 12, 61; DLB 13;
MTCW
Edgerton, Clyde (Carlyle) 1944- ..... CLC 39
See also AAYA 17; CA 118; 134; INT 134
Edgeworth, Maria 1768-1849 ....NCLC 1, 51
See also DLB 116, 159, 163; SATA 21
Edmonds, Paul
See Kuttner, Henry
Edmonds, Walter D(umaux) 1903- .. CLC 35
See also CA 5-8R; CANR 2; DLB 9; MAICYA;
SAAS 4; SATA 1, 27
Edmondson, Wallace
See Ellison, Harlan (Jay)
Edson, Russell .... CLC 13
See also CA 33-36R
Edwards, Bronwen Elizabeth
See Rose, Wendy
Edwards, G(erald) B(asil) 1899-1976 CLC 25
See also CA 110
Edwards, Gus 1939- .... CLC 43
See also CA 108; INT 108

Edwards, Jonathan 1703-1758 ..... **LC 7; DA; DAC; DAM MST**
See also DLB 24

Efron, Marina Ivanovna Tsvetaeva
See Tsvetaeva (Efron), Marina (Ivanovna)

Ehle, John (Marsden, Jr.) 1925- ...... **CLC 27**
See also CA 9-12R

Ehrenbourg, Ilya (Grigoryevich)
See Ehrenburg, Ilya (Grigoryevich)

Ehrenburg, Ilya (Grigoryevich) 1891-1967 **CLC 18, 34, 62**
See also CA 102; 25-28R

Ehrenburg, Ilyo (Grigoryevich)
See Ehrenburg, Ilya (Grigoryevich)

Eich, Guenter 1907-1972 .... **CLC 15**
See also CA 111; 93-96; DLB 69, 124

Eichendorff, Joseph Freiherr von 1788-1857 **NCLC 8**
See also DLB 90

Eigner, Larry .... **CLC 9**
See also Eigner, Laurence (Joel)
See also CAAS 23; DLB 5

Eigner, Laurence (Joel) 1927-1996
See Eigner, Larry
See also CA 9-12R; 151; CANR 6

Einstein, Albert 1879-1955 .... **TCLC 65**
See also CA 121; 133; MTCW

Eiseley, Loren Corey 1907-1977 .... **CLC 7**
See also AAYA 5; CA 1-4R; 73-76; CANR 6

Eisenstadt, Jill 1963- .... **CLC 50**
See also CA 140

Eisenstein, Sergei (Mikhailovich) 1898-1948 **TCLC 57**
See also CA 114; 149

Eisner, Simon
See Kornbluth, C(yril) M.

Ekeloef, (Bengt) Gunnar 1907-1968 **CLC 27; DAM POET**
See also CA 123; 25-28R

Ekelof, (Bengt) Gunnar
See Ekeloef, (Bengt) Gunnar

Ekwensi, C. O. D.
See Ekwensi, Cyprian (Odiatu Duaka)

Ekwensi, Cyprian (Odiatu Duaka) 1921- **CLC 4; BLC; DAM MULT**
See also BW 2; CA 29-32R; CANR 18, 42; DLB 117; MTCW; SATA 66

Elaine .... **TCLC 18**
See also Leverson, Ada

El Crummo
See Crumb, R(obert)

Elia
See Lamb, Charles

Eliade, Mircea 1907-1986 .... **CLC 19**
See also CA 65-68; 119; CANR 30; MTCW

Eliot, A. D.
See Jewett, (Theodora) Sarah Orne

Eliot, Alice
See Jewett, (Theodora) Sarah Orne

Eliot, Dan
See Silverberg, Robert

Eliot, George 1819-1880 **NCLC 4, 13, 23, 41, 49; DA; DAB; DAC; DAM MST, NOV; WLC**
See also CDBLB 1832-1890; DLB 21, 35, 55

Eliot, John 1604-1690 .... **LC 5**
See also DLB 24

Eliot, T(homas) S(tearns) 1888-1965 **CLC 1, 2, 3, 6, 9, 10, 13, 15, 24, 34, 41, 55, 57; DA; DAB; DAC; DAM DRAM, MST, POET; PC 5; WLC 2**
See also CA 5-8R; 25-28R; CANR 41; CDALB 1929-1941; DLB 7, 10, 45, 63; DLBY 88;

MTCW

Elizabeth 1866-1941 .... **TCLC 41**

Elkin, Stanley L(awrence) 1930-1995 **CLC 4, 6, 9, 14, 27, 51, 91; DAM NOV, POP; SSC 12**
See also CA 9-12R; 148; CANR 8, 46; DLB 2, 28; DLBY 80; INT CANR-8; MTCW

Elledge, Scott .... **CLC 34**

Elliot, Don
See Silverberg, Robert

Elliott, Don
See Silverberg, Robert

Elliott, George P(aul) 1918-1980 .... **CLC 2**
See also CA 1-4R; 97-100; CANR 2

Elliott, Janice 1931- .... **CLC 47**
See also CA 13-16R; CANR 8, 29; DLB 14

Elliott, Sumner Locke 1917-1991 ..... **CLC 38**
See also CA 5-8R; 134; CANR 2, 21

Elliott, William
See Bradbury, Ray (Douglas)

Ellis, A. E. .... **CLC 7**

Ellis, Alice Thomas .... **CLC 40**
See also Haycraft, Anna

Ellis, Bret Easton 1964- ... **CLC 39, 71; DAM POP**
See also AAYA 2; CA 118; 123; CANR 51; INT 123

Ellis, (Henry) Havelock 1859-1939 **TCLC 14**
See also CA 109

Ellis, Landon
See Ellison, Harlan (Jay)

Ellis, Trey 1962- .... **CLC 55**
See also CA 146

Ellison, Harlan (Jay) 1934- ... **CLC 1, 13, 42; DAM POP; SSC 14**
See also CA 5-8R; CANR 5, 46; DLB 8; INT CANR-5; MTCW

Ellison, Ralph (Waldo) 1914-1994 **CLC 1, 3, 11, 54, 86; BLC; DA; DAB; DAC; DAM MST, MULT, NOV; SSC 26; WLC**
See also AAYA 19; BW 1; CA 9-12R; 145; CANR 24, 53; CDALB 1941-1968; DLB 2, 76; DLBY 94; MTCW

Ellmann, Lucy (Elizabeth) 1956- ...... **CLC 61**
See also CA 128

Ellmann, Richard (David) 1918-1987 **CLC 50**
See also BEST 89:2; CA 1-4R; 122; CANR 2, 28, 61; DLB 103; DLBY 87; MTCW

Elman, Richard 1934- .... **CLC 19**
See also CA 17-20R; CAAS 3; CANR 47

Elron
See Hubbard, L(afayette) Ron(ald)

Eluard, Paul .... **TCLC 7, 41**
See also Grindel, Eugene

Elyot, Sir Thomas 1490(?)-1546 .... **LC 11**

Elytis, Odysseus 1911-1996 **CLC 15, 49, 100; DAM POET**
See also CA 102; 151; MTCW

Emecheta, (Florence Onye) Buchi 1944- **CLC 14, 48; BLC; DAM MULT**
See also BW 2; CA 81-84; CANR 27; DLB 117; MTCW; SATA 66

Emerson, Ralph Waldo 1803-1882 . **NCLC 1, 38; DA; DAB; DAC; DAM MST, POET; PC 18; WLC**
See also CDALB 1640-1865; DLB 1, 59, 73

Eminescu, Mihail 1850-1889 .... **NCLC 33**

Empson, William 1906-1984 **CLC 3, 8, 19, 33, 34**
See also CA 17-20R; 112; CANR 31, 61; DLB 20; MTCW

Enchi Fumiko (Ueda) 1905-1986 ...... **CLC 31**
See also CA 129; 121

Ende, Michael (Andreas Helmuth) 1929-1995 **CLC 31**
See also CA 118; 124; 149; CANR 36; CLR 14; DLB 75; MAICYA; SATA 61; SATA-Brief 42; SATA-Obit 86

Endo, Shusaku 1923-1996 **CLC 7, 14, 19, 54, 99; DAM NOV**
See also CA 29-32R; 153; CANR 21, 54; DLB 182; MTCW

Engel, Marian 1933-1985 .... **CLC 36**
See also CA 25-28R; CANR 12; DLB 53; INT CANR-12

Engelhardt, Frederick
See Hubbard, L(afayette) Ron(ald)

Enright, D(ennis) J(oseph) 1920- **CLC 4, 8, 31**
See also CA 1-4R; CANR 1, 42; DLB 27; SATA 25

Enzensberger, Hans Magnus 1929- .. **CLC 43**
See also CA 116; 119

Ephron, Nora 1941- .... **CLC 17, 31**
See also AITN 2; CA 65-68; CANR 12, 39

Epicurus 341B.C.-270B.C. .... **CMLC 21**
See also DLB 176

Epsilon
See Betjeman, John

Epstein, Daniel Mark 1948- .... **CLC 7**
See also CA 49-52; CANR 2, 53

Epstein, Jacob 1956- .... **CLC 19**
See also CA 114

Epstein, Joseph 1937- .... **CLC 39**
See also CA 112; 119; CANR 50

Epstein, Leslie 1938- .... **CLC 27**
See also CA 73-76; CAAS 12; CANR 23

Equiano, Olaudah 1745(?)-1797 **LC 16; BLC; DAM MULT**
See also DLB 37, 50

Erasmus, Desiderius 1469(?)-1536 ..... **LC 16**

Erdman, Paul E(mil) 1932- .... **CLC 25**
See also AITN 1; CA 61-64; CANR 13, 43

Erdrich, Louise 1954- ..... **CLC 39, 54; DAM MULT, NOV, POP**
See also AAYA 10; BEST 89:1; CA 114; CANR 41; DLB 152, 175; MTCW; NNAL; SATA 94

Erenburg, Ilya (Grigoryevich)
See Ehrenburg, Ilya (Grigoryevich)

Erickson, Stephen Michael 1950-
See Erickson, Steve
See also CA 129

Erickson, Steve 1950- .... **CLC 64**
See also Erickson, Stephen Michael
See also CANR 60

Ericson, Walter
See Fast, Howard (Melvin)

Eriksson, Buntel
See Bergman, (Ernst) Ingmar

Ernaux, Annie 1940- .... **CLC 88**
See also CA 147

Eschenbach, Wolfram von
See Wolfram von Eschenbach

Eseki, Bruno
See Mphahlele, Ezekiel

Esenin, Sergei (Alexandrovich) 1895-1925 **TCLC 4**
See also CA 104

Eshleman, Clayton 1935- .... **CLC 7**
See also CA 33-36R; CAAS 6; DLB 5

Espriella, Don Manuel Alvarez
See Southey, Robert

Espriu, Salvador 1913-1985 .... **CLC 9**
See also CA 154; 115; DLB 134

Espronceda, Jose de 1808-1842 ..... **NCLC 39**

Esse, James

Franklin, (Stella Maraia Sarah) Miles 1879-1954 .... TCLC 7
See also CA 104

Fraser, (Lady) Antonia (Pakenham) 1932-
CLC 32
See also CA 85-88; CANR 44; MTCW; SATA-Brief 32

Fraser, George MacDonald 1925- ...... CLC 7
See also CA 45-48; CANR 2, 48

Fraser, Sylvia 1935- .... CLC 64
See also CA 45-48; CANR 1, 16, 60

Frayn, Michael 1933-CLC 3, 7, 31, 47; DAM
DRAM, NOV
See also CA 5-8R; CANR 30; DLB 13, 14;
MTCW

Fraze, Candida (Merrill) 1945- .... CLC 50
See also CA 126

Frazer, J(ames) G(eorge) 1854-1941TCLC 32
See also CA 118

Frazer, Robert Caine
See Creasey, John

Frazer, Sir James George
See Frazer, J(ames) G(eorge)

Frazier, Ian 1951- .... CLC 46
See also CA 130; CANR 54

Frederic, Harold 1856-1898 .... NCLC 10
See also DLB 12, 23; DLBD 13

Frederick, John
See Faust, Frederick (Schiller)

Frederick the Great 1712-1786 .... LC 14

Fredro, Aleksander 1793-1876 .... NCLC 8

Freeling, Nicolas 1927- .... CLC 38
See also CA 49-52; CAAS 12; CANR 1, 17, 50; DLB 87

Freeman, Douglas Southall 1886-1953T C L C
11
See also CA 109; DLB 17

Freeman, Judith 1946- .... CLC 55
See also CA 148

Freeman, Mary Eleanor Wilkins 1852-1930
TCLC 9; SSC 1
See also CA 106; DLB 12, 78

Freeman, R(ichard) Austin 1862-1943T C L C
21
See also CA 113; DLB 70

French, Albert 1943- .... CLC 86

French, Marilyn 1929-CLC 10, 18, 60; DAM
DRAM, NOV, POP
See also CA 69-72; CANR 3, 31; INT CANR-31; MTCW

French, Paul
See Asimov, Isaac

Freneau, Philip Morin 1752-1832.... NCLC 1
See also DLB 37, 43

Freud, Sigmund 1856-1939 .... TCLC 52
See also CA 115; 133; MTCW

Friedan, Betty (Naomi) 1921- .... CLC 74
See also CA 65-68; CANR 18, 45; MTCW

Friedlander, Saul 1932- .... CLC 90
See also CA 117; 130

Friedman, B(ernard) H(arper) 1926-. CLC 7
See also CA 1-4R; CANR 3, 48

Friedman, Bruce Jay 1930- ...... CLC 3, 5, 56
See also CA 9-12R; CANR 25, 52; DLB 2, 28;
INT CANR-25

Friel, Brian 1929- .... CLC 5, 42, 59
See also CA 21-24R; CANR 33; DLB 13;
MTCW

Friis-Baastad, Babbis Ellinor 1921-1970C L C
12
See also CA 17-20R; 134; SATA 7

Frisch, Max (Rudolf) 1911-1991CLC 3, 9, 14,
18, 32, 44; DAM DRAM, NOV

See also CA 85-88; 134; CANR 32; DLB 69,
124; MTCW

Fromentin, Eugene (Samuel Auguste) 1820-1876 .... NCLC 10
See also DLB 123

Frost, Frederick
See Faust, Frederick (Schiller)

Frost, Robert (Lee) 1874-1963CLC 1, 3, 4, 9,
10, 13, 15, 26, 34, 44; DA; DAB; DAC;
DAM MST, POET; PC 1; WLC
See also AAYA 21; CA 89-92; CANR 33;
CDALB 1917-1929; DLB 54; DLBD 7;
MTCW; SATA 14

Froude, James Anthony 1818-1894NCLC 43
See also DLB 18, 57, 144

Froy, Herald
See Waterhouse, Keith (Spencer)

Fry, Christopher 1907- CLC 2, 10, 14; DAM
DRAM
See also CA 17-20R; CAAS 23; CANR 9, 30;
DLB 13; MTCW; SATA 66

Frye, (Herman) Northrop 1912-1991CLC 24,
70
See also CA 5-8R; 133; CANR 8, 37; DLB 67,
68; MTCW

Fuchs, Daniel 1909-1993 .... CLC 8, 22
See also CA 81-84; 142; CAAS 5; CANR 40;
DLB 9, 26, 28; DLBY 93

Fuchs, Daniel 1934- .... CLC 34
See also CA 37-40R; CANR 14, 48

Fuentes, Carlos 1928-CLC 3, 8, 10, 13, 22, 41,
60; DA; DAB; DAC; DAM MST, MULT,
NOV; HLC; SSC 24; WLC
See also AAYA 4; AITN 2; CA 69-72; CANR
10, 32; DLB 113; HW; MTCW

Fuentes, Gregorio Lopez y
See Lopez y Fuentes, Gregorio

Fugard, (Harold) Athol 1932-CLC 5,9,14,25,
40, 80; DAM DRAM; DC 3
See also AAYA 17; CA 85-88; CANR 32, 54;
MTCW

Fugard, Sheila 1932- .... CLC 48
See also CA 125

Fuller, Charles (H., Jr.) 1939-CLC 25; BLC;
DAM DRAM, MULT; DC 1
See also BW 2; CA 108; 112; DLB 38; INT 112;
MTCW

Fuller, John (Leopold) 1937- .... CLC 62
See also CA 21-24R; CANR 9, 44; DLB 40

Fuller, Margaret .... NCLC 5, 50
See also Ossoli, Sarah Margaret (Fuller
marchesa d')

Fuller, Roy (Broadbent) 1912-1991CLC 4, 28
See also CA 5-8R; 135; CAAS 10; CANR 53;
DLB 15, 20; SATA 87

Fulton, Alice 1952- .... CLC 52
See also CA 116; CANR 57

Furphy, Joseph 1843-1912 .... TCLC 25

Fussell, Paul 1924- .... CLC 74
See also BEST 90:1; CA 17-20R; CANR 8, 21,
35; INT CANR-21; MTCW

Futabatei, Shimei 1864-1909 .... TCLC 44
See also DLB 180

Futrelle, Jacques 1875-1912 .... TCLC 19
See also CA 113; 155

Gaboriau, Emile 1835-1873 .... NCLC 14

Gadda, Carlo Emilio 1893-1973 .... CLC 11
See also CA 89-92; DLB 177

Gaddis, William 1922- CLC 1, 3, 6, 8, 10, 19,
43, 86
See also CA 17-20R; CANR 21, 48; DLB 2;
MTCW

Gage, Walter
See Inge, William (Motter)

Gaines, Ernest J(ames) 1933- CLC 3, 11, 18,
86; BLC; DAM MULT
See also AAYA 18; AITN 1; BW 2; CA 9-12R;
CANR 6, 24, 42; CDALB 1968-1988; DLB
2, 33, 152; DLBY 80; MTCW; SATA 86

Gaitskill, Mary 1954- .... CLC 69
See also CA 128; CANR 61

Galdos, Benito Perez
See Perez Galdos, Benito

Gale, Zona 1874-1938TCLC 7; DAM DRAM
See also CA 105; 153; DLB 9, 78

Galeano, Eduardo (Hughes) 1940- .. CLC 72
See also CA 29-32R; CANR 13, 32; HW

Galiano, Juan Valera y Alcala
See Valera y Alcala-Galiano, Juan

Gallagher, Tess 1943- ...... CLC 18, 63; DAM
POET; PC 9
See also CA 106; DLB 120

Gallant, Mavis 1922- ... CLC 7, 18, 38; DAC;
DAM MST; SSC 5
See also CA 69-72; CANR 29; DLB 53; MTCW

Gallant, Roy A(rthur) 1924- .... CLC 17
See also CA 5-8R; CANR 4, 29, 54; CLR 30;
MAICYA; SATA 4, 68

Gallico, Paul (William) 1897-1976 ..... CLC 2
See also AITN 1; CA 5-8R; 69-72; CANR 23;
DLB 9, 171; MAICYA; SATA 13

Gallo, Max Louis 1932- .... CLC 95
See also CA 85-88

Gallois, Lucien
See Desnos, Robert

Gallup, Ralph
See Whitemore, Hugh (John)

Galsworthy, John 1867-1933TCLC 1, 45; DA;
DAB; DAC; DAM DRAM, MST, NOV;
SSC 22; WLC 2
See also CA 104; 141; CDBLB 1890-1914;
DLB 10, 34, 98, 162

Galt, John 1779-1839 .... NCLC 1
See also DLB 99, 116, 159

Galvin, James 1951- .... CLC 38
See also CA 108; CANR 26

Gamboa, Federico 1864-1939 .... TCLC 36

Gandhi, M. K.
See Gandhi, Mohandas Karamchand

Gandhi, Mahatma
See Gandhi, Mohandas Karamchand

Gandhi, Mohandas Karamchand 1869-1948
TCLC 59; DAM MULT
See also CA 121; 132; MTCW

Gann, Ernest Kellogg 1910-1991 ..... CLC 23
See also AITN 1; CA 1-4R; 136; CANR 1

Garcia, Cristina 1958- .... CLC 76
See also CA 141

Garcia Lorca, Federico 1898-1936TCLC 1, 7,
49; DA; DAB; DAC; DAM DRAM, MST,
MULT, POET; DC 2; HLC; PC 3; WLC
See also CA 104; 131; DLB 108; HW; MTCW

Garcia Marquez, Gabriel (Jose) 1928-CLC 2,
3, 8, 10, 15, 27, 47, 55, 68; DA; DAB; DAC;
DAM MST, MULT, NOV, POP; HLC; SSC
8; WLC
See also AAYA 3; BEST 89:1, 90:4; CA 33-
36R; CANR 10, 28, 50; DLB 113; HW;
MTCW

Gard, Janice
See Latham, Jean Lee

Gard, Roger Martin du
See Martin du Gard, Roger

Gardam, Jane 1928- .... CLC 43
See also CA 49-52; CANR 2, 18, 33, 54; CLR
12; DLB 14, 161; MAICYA; MTCW; SAAS

See also AITN 1; CA 5-8R; CABS 1; CANR 8, 42; DLB 2, 28; DLBY 80; INT CANR-8; MTCW
Hellman, Lillian (Florence) 1906-1984CLC 2, 4, 8, 14, 18, 34, 44, 52; DAM DRAM; DC 1
See also AITN 1, 2; CA 13-16R; 112; CANR 33; DLB 7; DLBY 84; MTCW
Helprin, Mark 1947-CLC 7, 10, 22, 32; DAM NOV, POP
See also CA 81-84; CANR 47; DLBY 85; MTCW
Helvetius, Claude-Adrien 1715-1771 . LC 26
Helyar, Jane Penelope Josephine 1933-
See Poole, Josephine
See also CA 21-24R; CANR 10, 26; SATA 82
Hemans, Felicia 1793-1835 .... NCLC 29
See also DLB 96
Hemingway, Ernest (Miller) 1899-1961 C L C 1, 3, 6, 8, 10, 13, 19, 30, 34, 39, 41, 44, 50, 61, 80; DA; DAB; DAC; DAM MST, NOV; SSC 25; WLC
See also AAYA 19; CA 77-80; CANR 34; CDALB 1917-1929; DLB 4, 9, 102; DLBD 1, 15; DLBY 81, 87, 96; MTCW
Hempel, Amy 1951- .... CLC 39
See also CA 118; 137
Henderson, F. C.
See Mencken, H(enry) L(ouis)
Henderson, Sylvia
See Ashton-Warner, Sylvia (Constance)
Henley, Beth .... CLC 23; DC 6
See also Henley, Elizabeth Becker
See also CABS 3; DLBY 86
Henley, Elizabeth Becker 1952-
See Henley, Beth
See also CA 107; CANR 32; DAM DRAM, MST; MTCW
Henley, William Ernest 1849-1903 .. TCLC 8
See also CA 105; DLB 19
Hennissart, Martha
See Lathen, Emma
See also CA 85-88
Henry, O. .... TCLC 1, 19; SSC 5; WLC
.See also Porter, William Sydney
Henry, Patrick 1736-1799 .... LC 25
Henryson, Robert 1430(?)-1506(?) ..... LC 20
See also DLB 146
Henry VIII 1491-1547 .... LC 10
Henschke, Alfred
See Klabund
Hentoff, Nat(han Irving) 1925- .... CLC 26
See also AAYA 4; CA 1-4R; CAAS 6; CANR 5, 25; CLR 1; INT CANR-25; JRDA; MAICYA; SATA 42, 69; SATA-Brief 27
Heppenstall, (John) Rayner 1911-1981 . C L C 10
See also CA 1-4R; 103; CANR 29
Heraclitus c. 540B.C.-c. 450B.C. .... CMLC 22
See also DLB 176
Herbert, Frank (Patrick) 1920-1986 CLC 12, 23, 35, 44, 85; DAM POP
See also AAYA 21; CA 53-56; 118; CANR 5, 43; DLB 8; INT CANR-5; MTCW; SATA 9, 37; SATA-Obit 47
Herbert, George 1593-1633 ..... LC 24; DAB; DAM POET; PC 4
See also CDBLB Before 1660; DLB 126
Herbert, Zbigniew 1924- ...CLC 9, 43; DAM POET
See also CA 89-92; CANR 36; MTCW
Herbst, Josephine (Frey) 1897-1969 CLC 34
See also CA 5-8R; 25-28R; DLB 9
Hergesheimer, Joseph 1880-1954... TCLC 11

See also CA 109; DLB 102, 9
Herlihy, James Leo 1927-1993 .... CLC 6
See also CA 1-4R; 143; CANR 2
Hermogenes fl. c. 175- .... CMLC 6
Hernandez, Jose 1834-1886 .... NCLC 17
Herodotus c. 484B.C.-429B.C. ...... CMLC 17
See also DLB 176
Herrick, Robert 1591-1674LC 13; DA; DAB; DAC; DAM MST, POP; PC 9
See also DLB 126
Herring, Guilles
See Somerville, Edith
Herriot, James 1916-1995CLC 12; DAM POP
See also Wight, James Alfred
See also AAYA 1; CA 148; CANR 40; SATA 86
Herrmann, Dorothy 1941- .... CLC 44
See also CA 107
Herrmann, Taffy
See Herrmann, Dorothy
Hersey, John (Richard) 1914-1993CLC 1, 2, 7, 9, 40, 81, 97; DAM POP
See also CA 17-20R; 140; CANR 33; DLB 6; MTCW; SATA 25; SATA-Obit 76
Herzen, Aleksandr Ivanovich 1812-1870 NCLC 10, 61
Herzl, Theodor 1860-1904 .... TCLC 36
Herzog, Werner 1942- .... CLC 16
See also CA 89-92
Hesiod c. 8th cent. B.C.- .... CMLC 5
See also DLB 176
Hesse, Hermann 1877-1962CLC 1, 2, 3, 6, 11, 17, 25, 69; DA; DAB; DAC; DAM MST, NOV; SSC 9; WLC
See also CA 17-18; CAP 2; DLB 66; MTCW; SATA 50
Hewes, Cady
See De Voto, Bernard (Augustine)
Heyen, William 1940- .... CLC 13, 18
See also CA 33-36R; CAAS 9; DLB 5
Heyerdahl, Thor 1914- .... CLC 26
See also CA 5-8R; CANR 5, 22; MTCW; SATA 2, 52
Heym, Georg (Theodor Franz Arthur) 1887-1912 .... TCLC 9
See also CA 106
Heym, Stefan 1913- .... CLC 41
See also CA 9-12R; CANR 4; DLB 69
Heyse, Paul (Johann Ludwig von) 1830-1914 TCLC 8
See also CA 104; DLB 129
Heyward, (Edwin) DuBose 1885-1940 T C L C 59
See also CA 108; 157; DLB 7, 9, 45; SATA 21
Hibbert, Eleanor Alice Burford 1906-1993 CLC 7; DAM POP
See also BEST 90:4; CA 17-20R; 140; CANR 9, 28, 59; SATA 2; SATA-Obit 74
Hichens, Robert S. 1864-1950 .... TCLC 64
See also DLB 153
Higgins, George V(incent) 1939-CLC 4, 7, 10, 18
See also CA 77-80; CAAS 5; CANR 17, 51; DLB 2; DLBY 81; INT CANR-17; MTCW
Higginson, Thomas Wentworth 1823-1911 TCLC 36
See also DLB 1, 64
Highet, Helen
See MacInnes, Helen (Clark)
Highsmith, (Mary) Patricia 1921-1995CLC 2, 4, 14, 42, 102; DAM NOV, POP
See also CA 1-4R; 147; CANR 1, 20, 48; MTCW

Highwater, Jamake (Mamake) 1942(?)- C L C 12
See also AAYA 7; CA 65-68; CAAS 7; CANR 10, 34; CLR 17; DLB 52; DLBY 85; JRDA; MAICYA; SATA 32, 69; SATA-Brief 30
Highway, Tomson 1951-CLC 92; DAC; DAM MULT
See also CA 151; NNAL
Higuchi, Ichiyo 1872-1896 .... NCLC 49
Hijuelos, Oscar 1951- CLC 65; DAM MULT, POP; HLC
See also BEST 90:1; CA 123; CANR 50; DLB 145; HW
Hikmet, Nazim 1902(?)-1963 .... CLC 40
See also CA 141; 93-96
Hildegard von Bingen 1098-1179 . CMLC 20
See also DLB 148
Hildesheimer, Wolfgang 1916-1991 . CLC 49
See also CA 101; 135; DLB 69, 124
Hill, Geoffrey (William) 1932- CLC 5, 8, 18, 45; DAM POET
See also CA 81-84; CANR 21; CDBLB 1960 to Present; DLB 40; MTCW
Hill, George Roy 1921- .... CLC 26
See also CA 110; 122
Hill, John
See Koontz, Dean R(ay)
Hill, Susan (Elizabeth) 1942- . CLC 4; DAB; DAM MST, NOV
See also CA 33-36R; CANR 29; DLB 14, 139; MTCW
Hillerman, Tony 1925- ..CLC 62; DAM POP
See also AAYA 6; BEST 89:1; CA 29-32R; CANR 21, 42; SATA 6
Hillesum, Etty 1914-1943 .... TCLC 49
See also CA 137
Hilliard, Noel (Harvey) 1929- .... CLC 15
See also CA 9-12R; CANR 7
Hillis, Rick 1956- .... CLC 66
See also CA 134
Hilton, James 1900-1954 .... TCLC 21
See also CA 108; DLB 34, 77; SATA 34
Himes, Chester (Bomar) 1909-1984CLC 2, 4, 7, 18, 58; BLC; DAM MULT
See also BW 2; CA 25-28R; 114; CANR 22; DLB 2, 76, 143; MTCW
Hinde, Thomas ....CLC 6, 11
See also Chitty, Thomas Willes
Hindin, Nathan
See Bloch, Robert (Albert)
Hine, (William) Daryl 1936- .... CLC 15
See also CA 1-4R; CAAS 15; CANR 1, 20; DLB 60
Hinkson, Katharine Tynan
See Tynan, Katharine
Hinton, S(usan) E(loise) 1950- CLC 30; DA; DAB; DAC; DAM MST, NOV
See also AAYA 2; CA 81-84; CANR 32; CLR 3, 23;.JRDA; MAICYA; MTCW; SATA 19, 58
Hippius, Zinaida .... TCLC 9
See also Gippius, Zinaida (Nikolayevna)
Hiraoka, Kimitake 1925-1970
See Mishima, Yukio
See also CA 97-100; 29-32R; DAM DRAM; MTCW
Hirsch, E(ric) D(onald), Jr. 1928-.... CLC 79
See also CA 25-28R; CANR 27, 51; DLB 67; INT CANR-27; MTCW
Hirsch, Edward 1950- .... CLC 31, 50
See also CA 104; CANR 20, 42; DLB 120
Hitchcock, Alfred (Joseph) 1899-1980CLC 16
See also AAYA 22; CA 97-100; SATA 27;

See Howells, William Dean

Howells, William Dean 1837-1920TCLC 7, 17, 41
See also CA 104; 134; CDALB 1865-1917; DLB 12, 64, 74, 79

Howes, Barbara 1914-1996 .... CLC 15
See also CA 9-12R; 151; CAAS 3; CANR 53; SATA 5

Hrabal, Bohumil 1914-1997 .... CLC 13, 67
See also CA 106; 156; CAAS 12; CANR 57

Hsun, Lu
See Lu Hsun

Hubbard, L(afayette) Ron(ald) 1911-1986
CLC 43; DAM POP
See also CA 77-80; 118; CANR 52

Huch, Ricarda (Octavia) 1864-1947TCLC 13
See also CA 111; DLB 66

Huddle, David 1942- .... CLC 49
See also CA 57-60; CAAS 20; DLB 130

Hudson, Jeffrey
See Crichton, (John) Michael

Hudson, W(illiam) H(enry) 1841-1922 T C L C 29
See also CA 115; DLB 98, 153, 174; SATA 35

Hueffer, Ford Madox
See Ford, Ford Madox

Hughart, Barry 1934- .... CLC 39
See also CA 137

Hughes, Colin
See Creasey, John

Hughes, David (John) 1930- .... CLC 48
See also CA 116; 129; DLB 14

Hughes, Edward James
See Hughes, Ted
See also DAM MST, POET

Hughes, (James) Langston 1902-1967CLC 1, 5, 10, 15, 35, 44; BLC; DA; DAB; DAC; DAM DRAM, MST, MULT, POET; DC 3; PC 1; SSC 6; WLC
See also AAYA 12; BW 1; CA 1-4R; 25-28R; CANR 1, 34; CDALB 1929-1941; CLR 17; DLB 4, 7, 48, 51, 86; JRDA; MAICYA; MTCW; SATA 4, 33

Hughes, Richard (Arthur Warren) 1900-1976
CLC 1, 11; DAM NOV
See also CA 5-8R; 65-68; CANR 4; DLB 15, 161; MTCW; SATA 8; SATA-Obit 25

Hughes, Ted 1930- CLC 2, 4, 9, 14, 37; DAB; DAC; PC 7
See also Hughes, Edward James
See also CA 1-4R; CANR 1, 33; CLR 3; DLB 40, 161;MAICYA; MTCW; SATA 49; SATA-Brief 27

Hugo, Richard F(ranklin) 1923-1982 CLC 6, 18, 32; DAM POET
See also CA 49-52; 108; CANR 3; DLB 5

Hugo, Victor (Marie) 1802-1885NCLC 3, 10, 21; DA; DAB; DAC; DAM DRAM, MST, NOV, POET; PC 17; WLC
See also DLB 119; SATA 47

Huidobro, Vicente
See Huidobro Fernandez, Vicente Garcia

Huidobro Fernandez, Vicente Garcia 1893-1948 .... TCLC 31
See also CA 131; HW

Hulme, Keri 1947- .... CLC 39
See also CA 125; INT 125

Hulme, T(homas) E(rnest) 1883-1917 T C L C 21
See also CA 117; DLB 19

Hume, David 1711-1776 .... LC 7
See also DLB 104

Humphrey, William 1924- .... CLC 45

See also CA 77-80; DLB 6

Humphreys, Emyr Owen 1919- .... CLC 47
See also CA 5-8R; CANR 3, 24; DLB 15

Humphreys, Josephine 1945- ..... CLC 34, 57
See also CA 121; 127; INT 127

Huneker, James Gibbons 1857-1921TCLC 65
See also DLB 71

Hungerford, Pixie
See Brinsmead, H(esba) F(ay)

Hunt, E(verette) Howard, (Jr.) 1918- . CLC 3
See also AITN 1; CA 45-48; CANR 2, 47

Hunt, Kyle
See Creasey, John

Hunt, (James Henry) Leigh 1784-1859N C L C 1; DAM POET

Hunt, Marsha 1946- .... CLC 70
See also BW 2; CA 143

Hunt, Violet 1866-1942 .... TCLC 53
See also DLB 162

Hunter, E. Waldo
See Sturgeon, Theodore (Hamilton)

Hunter, Evan 1926- . CLC 11, 31; DAM POP
See also CA 5-8R; CANR 5, 38; DLBY 82; INT CANR-5; MTCW; SATA 25

Hunter, Kristin (Eggleston) 1931- .... CLC 35
See also AITN 1; BW 1; CA 13-16R; CANR 13; CLR 3; DLB 33; INT CANR-13; MAICYA; SAAS 10; SATA 12

Hunter, Mollie 1922- .... CLC 21
See also McIlwraith, Maureen Mollie Hunter
See also AAYA 13; CANR 37; CLR 25; DLB 161; JRDA; MAICYA; SAAS 7; SATA 54

Hunter, Robert (?)-1734 .... LC 7

Hurston, Zora Neale 1903-1960CLC 7, 30, 61; BLC; DA; DAC; DAM MST, MULT, NOV; SSC 4; WLCS
See also AAYA 15; BW 1; CA 85-88; CANR 61; DLB 51, 86; MTCW

Huston, John (Marcellus) 1906-1987 CLC 20
See also CA 73-76; 123; CANR 34; DLB 26

Hustvedt, Siri 1955- .... CLC 76
See also CA 137

Hutten, Ulrich von 1488-1523 .... LC 16
See also DLB 179

Huxley, Aldous (Leonard) 1894-1963 CLC 1, 3, 4, 5, 8, 11, 18, 35, 79; DA; DAB; DAC; DAM MST, NOV; WLC
See also AAYA 11; CA 85-88; CANR 44; CDBLB 1914-1945; DLB 36, 100, 162; MTCW; SATA 63

Huysmans, Charles Marie Georges 1848-1907
See Huysmans, Joris-Karl
See also CA 104

Huysmans, Joris-Karl .... TCLC 7, 69
See also Huysmans, Charles Marie Georges
See also DLB 123

Hwang, David Henry 1957-...CLC 55; DAM DRAM; DC 4
See also CA 127; 132; INT 132

Hyde, Anthony 1946- ....CLC 42
See also CA 136

Hyde, Margaret O(ldroyd) 1917- ..... CLC 21
See also CA 1-4R; CANR 1, 36; CLR 23; JRDA; MAICYA; SAAS 8; SATA 1, 42, 76

Hynes, James 1956(?)-....................... CLC 65

Ian, Janis 1951- .... CLC 21
See also CA 105

Ibanez, Vicente Blasco
See Blasco Ibanez, Vicente

Ibarguengoitia, Jorge 1928-1983 ...... CLC 37
See also CA 124; 113; HW

Ibsen, Henrik (Johan) 1828-1906 TCLC 2, 8, 16, 37, 52; DA; DAB; DAC; DAM DRAM,

MST; DC 2; WLC
See also CA 104; 141

Ibuse Masuji 1898-1993 .... CLC 22
See also CA 127; 141; DLB 180

Ichikawa, Kon 1915- .... CLC 20
See also CA 121

Idle, Eric 1943- .... CLC 21
See also Monty Python
See also CA 116; CANR 35

Ignatow, David 1914- .... CLC 4, 7, 14, 40
See also CA 9-12R; CAAS 3; CANR 31, 57; DLB 5

Ihimaera, Witi 1944- .... CLC 46
See also CA 77-80

Ilf, Ilya .... TCLC 21
See also Fainzilberg, Ilya Arnoldovich

Illyes, Gyula 1902-1983 .... PC 16
See also CA 114; 109

Immermann, Karl (Lebrecht) 1796-1840
NCLC 4, 49
See also DLB 133

Inchbald, Elizabeth 1753-1821 ...... NCLC 62
See also DLB 39, 89

Inclan, Ramon (Maria) del Valle
See Valle-Inclan, Ramon (Maria) del

Infante, G(uillermo) Cabrera
See Cabrera Infante, G(uillermo)

Ingalls, Rachel (Holmes) 1940- .... CLC 42
See also CA 123; 127

Ingamells, Rex 1913-1955 .... TCLC 35

Inge, William (Motter) 1913-1973 CLC 1, 8, 19; DAM DRAM
See also CA 9-12R; CDALB 1941-1968; DLB 7; MTCW

Ingelow, Jean 1820-1897 .... NCLC 39
See also DLB 35, 163; SATA 33

Ingram, Willis J.
See Harris, Mark

Innaurato, Albert (F.) 1948(?)- .. CLC 21, 60
See also CA 115; 122; INT 122

Innes, Michael
See Stewart, J(ohn) I(nnes) M(ackintosh)

Ionesco, Eugene 1909-1994CLC 1, 4, 6, 9, 11, 15, 41, 86; DA; DAB; DAC; DAM DRAM, MST; WLC
See also CA 9-12R; 144; CANR 55; MTCW; SATA 7; SATA-Obit 79

Iqbal, Muhammad 1873-1938 .... TCLC 28

Ireland, Patrick
See O'Doherty, Brian

Iron, Ralph
See Schreiner, Olive (Emilie Albertina)

Irving, John (Winslow) 1942-CLC 13, 23, 38; DAM NOV, POP
See also AAYA 8; BEST 89:3; CA 25-28R; CANR 28; DLB 6; DLBY 82; MTCW

Irving, Washington 1783-1859 . NCLC 2, 19; DA; DAB; DAM MST; SSC 2; WLC
See also CDALB 1640-1865; DLB 3, 11, 30, 59, 73, 74; YABC 2

Irwin, P. K.
See Page, P(atricia) K(athleen)

Isaacs, Susan 1943-........ CLC 32; DAM POP
See also BEST 89:1; CA 89-92; CANR 20, 41; INT CANR-20; MTCW

Isherwood, Christopher (William Bradshaw) 1904-1986.... CLC 1, 9, 11, 14, 44; DAM DRAM, NOV
See also CA 13-16R; 117; CANR 35; DLB 15; DLBY 86; MTCW

Ishiguro, Kazuo 1954- CLC 27, 56, 59; DAM NOV
See also BEST 90:2; CA 120; CANR 49;

Author Index

See also CDBLB 1660-1789; DLB 39, 95, 104, 142

Johnson, Uwe 1934-1984 .. CLC **5, 10, 15, 40**
See also CA 1-4R; 112; CANR 1, 39; DLB 75; MTCW

Johnston, George (Benson) 1913- .... CLC **51**
See also CA 1-4R; CANR 5, 20; DLB 88

Johnston, Jennifer 1930- .... CLC **7**
See also CA 85-88; DLB 14

Jolley, (Monica) Elizabeth 1923-CLC **46; SSC 19**
See also CA 127; CAAS 13; CANR 59

Jones, Arthur Llewellyn 1863-1947
See Machen, Arthur
See also CA 104

Jones, D(ouglas) G(ordon) 1929- ..... CLC **10**
See also CA 29-32R; CANR 13; DLB 53

Jones, David (Michael) 1895-1974CLC **2, 4, 7, 13, 42**
See also CA 9-12R; 53-56; CANR 28; CDBLB 1945-1960; DLB 20, 100; MTCW

Jones, David Robert 1947-
See Bowie, David
See also CA 103

Jones, Diana Wynne 1934- .... CLC **26**
See also AAYA 12; CA 49-52; CANR 4, 26, 56; CLR 23; DLB 161; JRDA; MAICYA; SAAS 7; SATA 9, 70

Jones, Edward P. 1950- .... CLC **76**
See also BW 2; CA 142

Jones, Gayl 1949- ...... CLC **6, 9; BLC; DAM MULT**
See also BW 2; CA 77-80; CANR 27; DLB 33; MTCW

Jones, James 1921-1977 ...... CLC **1, 3, 10, 39**
See also AITN 1, 2; CA 1-4R; 69-72; CANR 6; DLB 2, 143; MTCW

Jones, John J.
See Lovecraft, H(oward) P(hillips)

Jones, LeRoi .... CLC **1, 2, 3, 5, 10, 14**
See also Baraka, Amiri

Jones, Louis B. .... CLC **65**
See also CA 141

Jones, Madison (Percy, Jr.) 1925- .... CLC **4**
See also CA 13-16R; CAAS 11; CANR 7, 54; DLB 152

Jones, Mervyn 1922- .... CLC **10, 52**
See also CA 45-48; CAAS 5; CANR 1; MTCW

Jones, Mick 1956(?)- .... CLC **30**

Jones, Nettie (Pearl) 1941- .... CLC **34**
See also BW 2; CA 137; CAAS 20

Jones, Preston 1936-1979 .... CLC **10**
See also CA 73-76; 89-92; DLB 7

Jones, Robert F(rancis) 1934- ....CLC **7**
See also CA 49-52; CANR 2, 61

Jones, Rod 1953-................................ CLC **50**
See also CA 128

Jones, Terence Graham Parry 1942- CLC **21**
See also Jones, Terry; Monty Python
See also CA 112; 116; CANR 35; INT 116

Jones, Terry
See Jones, Terence Graham Parry
See also SATA 67; SATA-Brief 51

Jones, Thom 1945(?)- .... CLC **81**
See also CA 157

Jong, Erica 1942- CLC **4, 6, 8, 18, 83; DAM NOV, POP**
See also AITN 1; BEST 90:2; CA 73-76; CANR 26, 52; DLB 2, 5, 28, 152; INT CANR-26; MTCW

Jonson, Ben(jamin) 1572(?)-1637 .. LC **6, 33; DA; DAB; DAC; DAM DRAM, MST, POET; DC 4; PC 17; WLC**

See also CDBLB Before 1660; DLB 62, 121

Jordan, June 1936- .... CLC **5, 11, 23; DAM MULT, POET**
See also AAYA 2; BW 2; CA 33-36R; CANR 25; CLR 10; DLB 38; MAICYA; MTCW; SATA 4

Jordan, Pat(rick M.) 1941- .... CLC **37**
See also CA 33-36R

Jorgensen, Ivar
See Ellison, Harlan (Jay)

Jorgenson, Ivar
See Silverberg, Robert

Josephus, Flavius c. 37-100 .... CMLC **13**

Josipovici, Gabriel 1940- .... CLC **6, 43**
See also CA 37-40R; CAAS 8; CANR 47; DLB 14

Joubert, Joseph 1754-1824 .... NCLC **9**

Jouve, Pierre Jean 1887-1976 ....CLC **47**
See also CA 65-68

Joyce, James (Augustine Aloysius) 1882-1941 TCLC **3, 8, 16, 35, 52; DA; DAB; DAC; DAM MST, NOV, POET; SSC 26; WLC**
See also CA 104; 126; CDBLB 1914-1945; DLB 10, 19, 36, 162; MTCW

Jozsef, Attila 1905-1937 .... TCLC **22**
See also CA 116

Juana Ines de la Cruz 1651(?)-1695 ..... LC **5**

Judd, Cyril
See Kornbluth, C(yril) M.; Pohl, Frederik

Julian of Norwich 1342(?)-1416(?) .... LC **6**
See also DLB 146

Juniper, Alex
See Hospital, Janette Turner

Junius
See Luxemburg, Rosa

Just, Ward (Swift) 1935- .... CLC **4, 27**
See also CA 25-28R; CANR 32; INT CANR-32

Justice, Donald (Rodney) 1925- .. CLC **6, 19, 102; DAM POET**
See also CA 5-8R; CANR 26, 54; DLBY 83; INT CANR-26

Juvenal c. 55-c. 127 .... CMLC **8**

Juvenis
See Bourne, Randolph S(illiman)

Kacew, Romain 1914-1980
See Gary, Romain
See also CA 108; 102

Kadare, Ismail 1936- ....CLC **52**

Kadohata, Cynthia ....CLC **59**
See also CA 140

Kafka, Franz 1883-1924TCLC **2, 6, 13, 29, 47, 53; DA; DAB; DAC; DAM MST, NOV; SSC 5; WLC**
See also CA 105; 126; DLB 81; MTCW

Kahanovitsch, Pinkhes
See Der Nister

Kahn, Roger 1927- ....CLC **30**
See also CA 25-28R; CANR 44; DLB 171; SATA 37

Kain, Saul
See Sassoon, Siegfried (Lorraine)

Kaiser, Georg 1878-1945 .... TCLC **9**
See also CA 106; DLB 124

Kaletski, Alexander 1946- ....CLC **39**
See also CA 118; 143

Kalidasa fl. c. 400- .... CMLC **9**

Kallman, Chester (Simon) 1921-1975 CLC **2**
See also CA 45-48; 53-56; CANR 3

Kaminsky, Melvin 1926-
See Brooks, Mel
See also CA 65-68; CANR 16

Kaminsky, Stuart M(elvin) 1934- ..... CLC **59**

See also CA 73-76; CANR 29, 53

Kane, Francis
See Robbins, Harold

Kane, Paul
See Simon, Paul (Frederick)

Kane, Wilson
See Bloch, Robert (Albert)

Kanin, Garson 1912- .... CLC **22**
See also AITN 1; CA 5-8R; CANR 7; DLB 7

Kaniuk, Yoram 1930- .... CLC **19**
See also CA 134

Kant, Immanuel 1724-1804 ....NCLC **27**
See also DLB 94

Kantor, MacKinlay 1904-1977 ....CLC **7**
See also CA 61-64; 73-76; CANR 60; DLB 9, 102

Kaplan, David Michael 1946- .... CLC **50**

Kaplan, James 1951- .... CLC **59**
See also CA 135

Karageorge, Michael
See Anderson, Poul (William)

Karamzin, Nikolai Mikhailovich 1766-1826 NCLC **3**
See also DLB 150

Karapanou, Margarita 1946- .... CLC **13**
See also CA 101

Karinthy, Frigyes 1887-1938 .... TCLC **47**

Karl, Frederick R(obert) 1927- .... CLC **34**
See also CA 5-8R; CANR 3, 44

Kastel, Warren
See Silverberg, Robert

Kataev, Evgeny Petrovich 1903-1942
See Petrov, Evgeny
See also CA 120

Kataphusin
See Ruskin, John

Katz, Steve 1935-............................... CLC **47**
See also CA 25-28R; CAAS 14; CANR 12; DLBY 83

Kauffman, Janet 1945- .... CLC **42**
See also CA 117; CANR 43; DLBY 86

Kaufman, Bob (Garnell) 1925-1986 CLC **49**
See also BW 1; CA 41-44R; 118; CANR 22; DLB 16, 41

Kaufman, George S. 1889-1961CLC **38; DAM DRAM**
See also CA 108; 93-96; DLB 7; INT 108

Kaufman, Sue .... CLC **3, 8**
See also Barondess, Sue K(aufman)

Kavafis, Konstantinos Petrou 1863-1933
See Cavafy, C(onstantine) P(eter)
See also CA 104

Kavan, Anna 1901-1968 .... CLC **5, 13, 82**
See also CA 5-8R; CANR 6, 57; MTCW

Kavanagh, Dan
See Barnes, Julian (Patrick)

Kavanagh, Patrick (Joseph) 1904-1967 C L C **22**
See also CA 123; 25-28R; DLB 15, 20; MTCW

Kawabata, Yasunari 1899-1972 CLC **2, 5, 9, 18; DAM MULT; SSC 17**
See also CA 93-96; 33-36R; DLB 180

Kaye, M(ary) M(argaret) 1909- .... CLC **28**
See also CA 89-92; CANR 24, 60; MTCW; SATA 62

Kaye, Mollie
See Kaye, M(ary) M(argaret)

Kaye-Smith, Sheila 1887-1956 .... TCLC **20**
See also CA 118; DLB 36

Kaymor, Patrice Maguilene
See Senghor, Leopold Sedar

Kazan, Elia 1909- .... CLC **6, 16, 63**
See also CA 21-24R; CANR 32

See Irving, Washington

Olesha, Yuri (Karlovich) 1899-1960 ... **CLC 8**
See also CA 85-88

Oliphant, Laurence 1829(?)-1888 .. **NCLC 47**
See also DLB 18, 166

Oliphant, Margaret (Oliphant Wilson) 1828-1897 .... **NCLC 11, 61; SSC 25**
See also DLB 18, 159

Oliver, Mary 1935- .... **CLC 19, 34, 98**
See also CA 21-24R; CANR 9, 43; DLB 5

Olivier, Laurence (Kerr) 1907-1989 **CLC 20**
See also CA 111; 150; 129

Olsen, Tillie 1913-**CLC 4, 13; DA; DAB; DAC; DAM MST; SSC 11**
See also CA 1-4R; CANR 1, 43; DLB 28; DLBY 80; MTCW

Olson, Charles (John) 1910-1970**CLC 1, 2, 5, 6, 9, 11, 29; DAM POET; PC 19**
See also CA 13-16; 25-28R; CABS 2; CANR 35, 61; CAP 1; DLB 5, 16; MTCW

Olson, Toby 1937- .... **CLC 28**
See also CA 65-68; CANR 9, 31

Olyesha, Yuri
See Olesha, Yuri (Karlovich)

Ondaatje, (Philip) Michael 1943-**CLC 14, 29, 51, 76; DAB; DAC; DAM MST**
See also CA 77-80; CANR 42; DLB 60

Oneal, Elizabeth 1934-
See Oneal, Zibby
See also CA 106; CANR 28; MAICYA; SATA 30, 82

Oneal, Zibby .... **CLC 30**
See also Oneal, Elizabeth
See also AAYA 5; CLR 13; JRDA

O'Neill, Eugene (Gladstone) 1888-1953**TCLC 1, 6, 27, 49; DA; DAB; DAC; DAM DRAM, MST; WLC**
See also AITN 1; CA 110; 132; CDALB 1929-1941; DLB 7; MTCW

Onetti, Juan Carlos 1909-1994 ... **CLC 7, 10; DAM MULT, NOV; SSC 23**
See also CA 85-88; 145; CANR 32; DLB 113; HW; MTCW

O Nuallain, Brian 1911-1966
See O'Brien, Flann
See also CA 21-22; 25-28R; CAP 2

Oppen, George 1908-1984 ...... **CLC 7, 13, 34**
See also CA 13-16R; 113; CANR 8; DLB 5, 165

Oppenheim, E(dward) Phillips 1866-1946 **TCLC 45**
See also CA 111; DLB 70

Origen c. 185-c. 254 .... **CMLC 19**

Orlovitz, Gil 1918-1973 .... **CLC 22**
See also CA 77-80; 45-48; DLB 2, 5

Orris
See Ingelow, Jean

Ortega y Gasset, Jose 1883-1955 .... **TCLC 9; DAM MULT; HLC**
See also CA 106; 130; HW; MTCW

Ortese, Anna Maria 1914- .... **CLC 89**
See also DLB 177

Ortiz, Simon J(oseph) 1941-.. **CLC 45; DAM MULT, POET; PC 17**
See also CA 134; DLB 120, 175; NNAL

Orton, Joe .... **CLC 4, 13, 43; DC 3**
See Orton, John Kingsley
See also CDBLB 1960 to Present; DLB 13

Orton, John Kingsley 1933-1967
See Orton, Joe
See also CA 85-88; CANR 35; DAM DRAM; MTCW

Orwell, George **TCLC 2, 6, 15, 31, 51; DAB;**

WLC
See Blair, Eric (Arthur)
See also CDBLB 1945-1960; DLB 15, 98

Osborne, David
See Silverberg, Robert

Osborne, George
See Silverberg, Robert

Osborne, John (James) 1929-1994**CLC 1, 2, 5, 11, 45; DA; DAB; DAC; DAM DRAM, MST; WLC**
See also CA 13-16R; 147; CANR 21, 56; CDBLB 1945-1960; DLB 13; MTCW

Osborne, Lawrence 1958- .... **CLC 50**

Oshima, Nagisa 1932- .... **CLC 20**
See also CA 116; 121

Oskison, John Milton 1874-1947 . **TCLC 35; DAM MULT**
See also CA 144; DLB 175; NNAL

Ossoli, Sarah Margaret (Fuller marchesa d') 1810-1850
See Fuller, Margaret
See also SATA 25

Ostrovsky, Alexander 1823-1886**NCLC 30, 57**

Otero, Blas de 1916-1979 .... **CLC 11**
See also CA 89-92; DLB 134

Otto, Whitney 1955- .... **CLC 70**
See also CA 140

Ouida .... **TCLC 43**
See also De La Ramee, (Marie) Louise
See also DLB 18, 156

Ousmane, Sembene 1923- .... **CLC 66; BLC**
See also BW 1; CA 117; 125; MTCW

Ovid 43B.C.-18(?)**CMLC 7; DAM POET; PC 2**

Owen, Hugh
See Faust, Frederick (Schiller)

Owen, Wilfred (Edward Salter) 1893-1918 **TCLC 5, 27; DA; DAB; DAC; DAM MST, POET; PC 19; WLC**
See also CA 104; 141; CDBLB 1914-1945; DLB 20

Owens, Rochelle 1936- .... **CLC 8**
See also CA 17-20R; CAAS 2; CANR 39

Oz, Amos 1939-**CLC 5, 8, 11, 27, 33, 54; DAM NOV**
See also CA 53-56; CANR 27, 47; MTCW

Ozick, Cynthia 1928- **CLC 3, 7, 28, 62; DAM NOV, POP; SSC 15**
See also BEST 90:1; CA 17-20R; CANR 23, 58; DLB 28, 152; DLBY 82; INT CANR-23; MTCW

Ozu, Yasujiro 1903-1963 .... **CLC 16**
See also CA 112

Pacheco, C.
See Pessoa, Fernando (Antonio Nogueira)

Pa Chin .... **CLC 18**
See also Li Fei-kan

Pack, Robert 1929- .... **CLC 13**
See also CA 1-4R; CANR 3, 44; DLB 5

Padgett, Lewis
See Kuttner, Henry

Padilla (Lorenzo), Heberto 1932- ..... **CLC 38**
See also AITN 1; CA 123; 131; HW

Page, Jimmy 1944- .... **CLC 12**

Page, Louise 1955-.............................. **CLC 40**
See also CA 140

Page, P(atricia) K(athleen) 1916- **CLC 7, 18; DAC; DAM MST; PC 12**
See also CA 53-56; CANR 4, 22; DLB 68; MTCW

Page, Thomas Nelson 1853-1922 .... **SSC 23**
See also CA 118; DLB 12, 78; DLBD 13

Paget, Violet 1856-1935

See Lee, Vernon
See also CA 104

Paget-Lowe, Henry
See Lovecraft, H(oward) P(hillips)

Paglia, Camille (Anna) 1947- .... **CLC 68**
See also CA 140

Paige, Richard
See Koontz, Dean R(ay)

Paine, Thomas 1737-1809 .... **NCLC 62**
See also CDALB 1640-1865; DLB 31, 43, 73, 158

Pakenham, Antonia
See Fraser, (Lady) Antonia (Pakenham)

Palamas, Kostes 1859-1943 .... **TCLC 5**
See also CA 105

Palazzeschi, Aldo 1885-1974 .... **CLC 11**
See also CA 89-92; 53-56; DLB 114

Paley, Grace 1922-**CLC 4, 6, 37; DAM POP; SSC 8**
See also CA 25-28R; CANR 13, 46; DLB 28; INT CANR-13; MTCW

Palin, Michael (Edward) 1943- .... **CLC 21**
See also Monty Python
See also CA 107; CANR 35: SATA 67

Palliser, Charles 1947- .... **CLC 65**
See also CA 136

Palma, Ricardo 1833-1919 .... **TCLC 29**

Pancake, Breece Dexter 1952-1979
See Pancake, Breece D'J
See also CA 123; 109

Pancake, Breece D'J .... **CLC 29**
See also Pancake, Breece Dexter
See also DLB 130

Panko, Rudy
See Gogol, Nikolai (Vasilyevich)

Papadiamantis, Alexandros 1851-1911**T C L C 29**

Papadiamantopoulos, Johannes 1856-1910
See Moreas, Jean
See also CA 117

Papini, Giovanni 1881-1956 .... **TCLC 22**
See also CA 121

Paracelsus 1493-1541 .... **LC 14**
See also DLB 179

Parasol, Peter
See Stevens, Wallace

Pareto, Vilfredo 1848-1923 .... **TCLC 69**

Parfenie, Maria
See Codrescu, Andrei

Parini, Jay (Lee) 1948- .... **CLC 54**
See also CA 97-100; CAAS 16; CANR 32

Park, Jordan
See Kornbluth, C(yril) M.; Pohl, Frederik

Park, Robert E(zra) 1864-1944 ...... **TCLC 73**
See also CA 122

Parker, Bert
See Ellison, Harlan (Jay)

Parker, Dorothy (Rothschild) 1893-1967**C L C 15, 68; DAM POET; SSC 2**
See also CA 19-20; 25-28R; CAP 2; DLB 11, 45, 86; MTCW

Parker, Robert B(rown) 1932-**CLC 27; DAM NOV, POP**
See also BEST 89:4; CA 49-52; CANR 1, 26, 52; INT CANR-26; MTCW

Parkin, Frank 1940- .... **CLC 43**
See also CA 147

Parkman, Francis, Jr. 1823-1893 ... **NCLC 12**
See also DLB 1, 30

Parks, Gordon (Alexander Buchanan) 1912-**CLC 1, 16; BLC; DAM MULT**
See also AITN 2; BW 2; CA 41-44R; CANR 26; DLB 33; SATA 8

Parmenides c. 515B.C.-c. 450B.C. **CMLC 22**
See also DLB 176
Parnell, Thomas 1679-1718 .... **LC 3**
See also DLB 94
Parra, Nicanor 1914- ...... **CLC 2, 102; DAM MULT; HLC**
See also CA 85-88; CANR 32; HW; MTCW
Parrish, Mary Frances
See Fisher, M(ary) F(rances) K(ennedy)
Parson
See Coleridge, Samuel Taylor
Parson Lot
See Kingsley, Charles
Partridge, Anthony
See Oppenheim, E(dward) Phillips
Pascal, Blaise 1623-1662 .... **LC 35**
Pascoli, Giovanni 1855-1912 .... **TCLC 45**
Pasolini, Pier Paolo 1922-1975**CLC 20, 37; PC 17**
See also CA 93-96; 61-64; DLB 128, 177; MTCW
Pasquini
See Silone, Ignazio
Pastan, Linda (Olenik) 1932- **CLC 27; DAM POET**
See also CA 61-64; CANR 18, 40, 61; DLB 5
Pasternak, Boris (Leonidovich) 1890-1960 **CLC 7, 10, 18, 63; DA; DAB; DAC; DAM MST, NOV, POET; PC 6; WLC**
See also CA 127; 116; MTCW
Patchen, Kenneth 1911-1972 ... **CLC 1, 2, 18; DAM POET**
See also CA 1-4R; 33-36R; CANR 3, 35; DLB 16, 48; MTCW
Pater, Walter (Horatio) 1839-1894 .. **NCLC 7**
See also CDBLB 1832-1890; DLB 57, 156
Paterson, A(ndrew) B(arton) 1864-1941 **TCLC 32**
See also CA 155
Paterson, Katherine (Womeldorf) 1932-**C L C 12, 30**
See also AAYA 1; CA 21-24R; CANR 28, 59; CLR 7; DLB 52; JRDA; MAICYA; MTCW; SATA 13, 53, 92
Patmore, Coventry Kersey Dighton 1823-1896 **NCLC 9**
See also DLB 35, 98
Paton, Alan (Stewart) 1903-1988 **CLC 4, 10, 25, 55; DA; DAB; DAC; DAM MST, NOV; WLC**
See also CA 13-16; 125; CANR 22; CAP 1; MTCW; SATA 11; SATA-Obit 56
Paton Walsh, Gillian 1937-
See Walsh, Jill Paton
See also CANR 38; JRDA; MAICYA; SAAS 3; SATA 4, 72
Paulding, James Kirke 1778-1860 ... **NCLC 2**
See also DLB 3, 59, 74
Paulin, Thomas Neilson 1949-
See Paulin, Tom
See also CA 123; 128
Paulin, Tom .... **CLC 37**
See also Paulin, Thomas Neilson
See also DLB 40
Paustovsky, Konstantin (Georgievich) 1892-1968 .... **CLC 40**
See also CA 93-96; 25-28R
Pavese, Cesare 1908-1950 ... **TCLC 3; PC 13; SSC 19**
See also CA 104; DLB 128, 177
Pavic, Milorad 1929- .... **CLC 60**
See also CA 136; DLB 181
Payne, Alan

See Jakes, John (William)
Paz, Gil
See Lugones, Leopoldo
Paz, Octavio 1914-**CLC 3, 4, 6, 10, 19, 51, 65; DA; DAB; DAC; DAM MST, MULT, POET; HLC; PC 1; WLC**
See also CA 73-76; CANR 32; DLBY 90; HW; MTCW
p'Bitek, Okot 1931-1982**CLC 96; BLC; DAM MULT**
See also BW 2; CA 124; 107; DLB 125; MTCW
Peacock, Molly 1947- .... **CLC 60**
See also CA 103; CAAS 21; CANR 52; DLB 120
Peacock, Thomas Love 1785-1866 . **NCLC 22**
See also DLB 96, 116
Peake, Mervyn 1911-1968 .... **CLC 7, 54**
See also CA 5-8R; 25-28R; CANR 3; DLB 15, 160; MTCW; SATA 23
Pearce, Philippa ....**CLC 21**
See also Christie, (Ann) Philippa
See also CLR 9; DLB 161; MAICYA; SATA 1, 67
Pearl, Eric
See Elman, Richard
Pearson, T(homas) R(eid) 1956- ....**CLC 39**
See also CA 120; 130; INT 130
Peck, Dale 1967- .... **CLC 81**
See also CA 146
Peck, John 1941- .... **CLC 3**
See also CA 49-52; CANR 3
Peck, Richard (Wayne) 1934-............**CLC 21**
See also AAYA 1; CA 85-88; CANR 19, 38; CLR 15; INT CANR-19; JRDA; MAICYA; SAAS 2; SATA 18, 55
Peck, Robert Newton 1928- ..... **CLC 17; DA; DAC; DAM MST**
See also AAYA 3; CA 81-84; CANR 31; CLR 45; JRDA; MAICYA; SAAS 1; SATA 21, 62
Peckinpah, (David) Sam(uel) 1925-1984**C L C 20**
See also CA 109; 114
Pedersen, Knut 1859-1952
See Hamsun, Knut
See also CA 104; 119; MTCW
Peeslake, Gaffer
See Durrell, Lawrence (George)
Peguy, Charles Pierre 1873-1914 ... **TCLC 10**
See also CA 107
Pena, Ramon del Valle y
See Valle-Inclan, Ramon (Maria) del
Pendennis, Arthur Esquir
See Thackeray, William Makepeace
Penn, William 1644-1718 .... **LC 25**
See also DLB 24
Pepys, Samuel 1633-1703 **LC 11; DA; DAB; DAC; DAM MST; WLC**
See also CDBLB 1660-1789; DLB 101
Percy, Walker 1916-1990**CLC 2, 3, 6, 8, 14, 18, 47, 65; DAM NOV, POP**
See also CA 1-4R; 131; CANR 1, 23; DLB 2; DLBY 80, 90; MTCW
Perec, Georges 1936-1982 .... **CLC 56**
See also CA 141; DLB 83
Pereda (y Sanchez de Porrua), Jose Maria de 1833-1906 .... **TCLC 16**
See also CA 117
Pereda y Porrua, Jose Maria de
See Pereda (y Sanchez de Porrua), Jose Maria de
Peregoy, George Weems
See Mencken, H(enry) L(ouis)
Perelman, S(idney) J(oseph) 1904-1979 **C L C**

3, 5, 9, 15, 23, 44, 49; DAM DRAM
See also AITN 1, 2; CA 73-76; 89-92; CANR 18; DLB 11, 44; MTCW
Peret, Benjamin 1899-1959 .... **TCLC 20**
See also CA 117
Peretz, Isaac Loeb 1851(?)-1915 .. **TCLC 16; SSC 26**
See also CA 109
Peretz, Yitzkhok Leibush
See Peretz, Isaac Loeb
Perez Galdos, Benito 1843-1920 .... **TCLC 27**
See also CA 125; 153; HW
Perrault, Charles 1628-1703 .... **LC 2**
See also MAICYA; SATA 25
Perry, Brighton
See Sherwood, Robert E(mmet)
Perse, St.-John .... **CLC 4, 11, 46**
See also Leger, (Marie-Rene Auguste) Alexis Saint-Leger
Perutz, Leo 1882-1957 .... **TCLC 60**
See also DLB 81
Peseenz, Tulio F.
See Lopez y Fuentes, Gregorio
Pesetsky, Bette 1932- ....**CLC 28**
See also CA 133; DLB 130
Peshkov, Alexei Maximovich 1868-1936
See Gorky, Maxim
See also CA 105; 141; DA; DAC; DAM DRAM, MST, NOV
Pessoa, Fernando (Antonio Nogueira) 1888-1935 .... **TCLC 27; HLC**
See also CA 125
Peterkin, Julia Mood 1880-1961 .... **CLC 31**
See also CA 102; DLB 9
Peters, Joan K(aren) 1945-..................**CLC 39**
See also CA 158
Peters, Robert L(ouis) 1924- .... **CLC 7**
See also CA 13-16R; CAAS 8; DLB 105
Petofi, Sandor 1823-1849 .... **NCLC 21**
Petrakis, Harry Mark 1923- .... **CLC 3**
See also CA 9-12R; CANR 4, 30
Petrarch 1304-1374 **CMLC 20; DAM POET; PC 8**
Petrov, Evgeny .... **TCLC 21**
See also Kataev, Evgeny Petrovich
Petry, Ann (Lane) 1908-1997 ... **CLC 1, 7, 18**
See also BW 1; CA 5-8R; 157; CAAS 6; CANR 4, 46; CLR 12; DLB 76; JRDA; MAICYA; MTCW; SATA 5; SATA-Obit 94
Petursson, Halligrimur 1614-1674 .... **LC 8**
Philips, Katherine 1632-1664 .... **LC 30**
See also DLB 131
Philipson, Morris H. 1926- .... **CLC 53**
See also CA 1-4R; CANR 4
Phillips, Caryl 1958- . **CLC 96; DAM MULT**
See also BW 2; CA 141; DLB 157
Phillips, David Graham 1867-1911 **TCLC 44**
See also CA 108; DLB 9, 12
Phillips, Jack
See Sandburg, Carl (August)
Phillips, Jayne Anne 1952-**CLC 15, 33; SSC 16**
See also CA 101; CANR 24, 50; DLBY 80; INT CANR-24; MTCW
Phillips, Richard
See Dick, Philip K(indred)
Phillips, Robert (Schaeffer) 1938- .... **CLC 28**
See also CA 17-20R; CAAS 13; CANR 8; DLB 105
Phillips, Ward
See Lovecraft, H(oward) P(hillips)
Piccolo, Lucio 1901-1969 .... **CLC 13**
See also CA 97-100; DLB 114
Pickthall, Marjorie L(owry) C(hristie) 1883-

See Mencken, H(enry) L(ouis)

Thompson, Francis Joseph 1859-1907TCLC 4
  See also CA 104; CDBLB 1890-1914; DLB 19

Thompson, Hunter S(tockton) 1939- CLC 9,
  17, 40; DAM POP
  See also BEST 89:1; CA 17-20R; CANR 23,
  46; MTCW

Thompson, James Myers
  See Thompson, Jim (Myers)

Thompson, Jim (Myers) 1906-1977(?)CLC 69
  See also CA 140

Thompson, Judith .... **CLC 39**

Thomson, James 1700-1748 LC 16, 29; DAM
  POET
  See also DLB 95

Thomson, James 1834-1882 NCLC 18; DAM
  POET
  See also DLB 35

Thoreau, Henry David 1817-1862NCLC 7, 21,
  61; DA; DAB; DAC; DAM MST; WLC
  See also CDALB 1640-1865; DLB 1

Thornton, Hall
  See Silverberg, Robert

Thucydides c. 455B.C.-399B.C. ...... **CMLC 17**
  See also DLB 176

Thurber, James (Grover) 1894-1961 CLC 5,
  11, 25; DA; DAB; DAC; DAM DRAM,
  MST, NOV; SSC 1
  See also CA 73-76; CANR 17, 39; CDALB
  1929-1941; DLB 4, 11, 22, 102; MAICYA;
  MTCW; SATA 13

Thurman, Wallace (Henry) 1902-1934T C L C
  6; BLC; DAM MULT
  See also BW 1; CA 104; 124; DLB 51

Ticheburn, Cheviot
  See Ainsworth, William Harrison

Tieck, (Johann) Ludwig 1773-1853 NCLC 5,
  46
  See also DLB 90

Tiger, Derry
  See Ellison, Harlan (Jay)

Tilghman, Christopher 1948(?)- ...... **CLC 65**

Tillinghast, Richard (Williford) 1940-CLC 29
  See also CA 29-32R; CAAS 23; CANR 26, 51

Timrod, Henry 1828-1867 .... **NCLC 25**
  See also DLB 3

Tindall, Gillian 1938- .... **CLC 7**
  See also CA 21-24R; CANR 11

Tiptree, James, Jr. .... **CLC 48, 50**
  See also Sheldon, Alice Hastings Bradley
  See also DLB 8

Titmarsh, Michael Angelo
  See Thackeray, William Makepeace

Tocqueville, Alexis (Charles Henri Maurice
  Clerel Comte) 1805-1859 ...NCLC 7, 63

Tolkien, J(ohn) R(onald) R(euel) 1892-1973
  CLC 1, 2, 3, 8, 12, 38; DA; DAB; DAC;
  DAM MST, NOV, POP; WLC
  See also AAYA 10; AITN 1; CA 17-18; 45-48;
  CANR 36; CAP 2; CDBLB 1914-1945; DLB
  15, 160; JRDA; MAICYA; MTCW; SATA 2,
  32; SATA-Obit 24

Toller, Ernst 1893-1939 .... **TCLC 10**
  See also CA 107; DLB 124

Tolson, M. B.
  See Tolson, Melvin B(eaunorus)

Tolson, Melvin B(eaunorus) 1898(?)-1966
  CLC 36; BLC; DAM MULT, POET
  See also BW 1; CA 124; 89-92; DLB 48, 76

Tolstoi, Aleksei Nikolaevich
  See Tolstoy, Alexey Nikolaevich

Tolstoy, Alexey Nikolaevich 1882-1945T C L C
  18

See also CA 107; 158

Tolstoy, Count Leo
  See Tolstoy, Leo (Nikolaevich)

Tolstoy, Leo (Nikolaevich) 1828-1910TCLC 4,
  11, 17, 28, 44; DA; DAB; DAC; DAM MST,
  NOV; SSC 9; WLC
  See also CA 104; 123; SATA 26

Tomasi di Lampedusa, Giuseppe 1896-1957
  See Lampedusa, Giuseppe (Tomasi) di
  See also CA 111

Tomlin, Lily .... **CLC 17**
  See also Tomlin, Mary Jean

Tomlin, Mary Jean 1939(?)-
  See Tomlin, Lily
  See also CA 117

Tomlinson, (Alfred) Charles 1927-CLC 2, 4, 6,
  13, 45; DAM POET; PC 17
  See also CA 5-8R; CANR 33; DLB 40

Tomlinson, H(enry) M(ajor) 1873-1958TCLC
  71
  See also CA 118; DLB 36, 100

Tonson, Jacob
  See Bennett, (Enoch) Arnold

Toole, John Kennedy 1937-1969 CLC 19, 64
  See also CA 104; DLBY 81

Toomer, Jean 1894-1967 .... CLC 1, 4, 13, 22;
  BLC; DAM MULT; PC 7; SSC 1; WLCS
  See also BW 1; CA 85-88; CDALB 1917-1929;
  DLB 45, 51; MTCW

Torley, Luke
  See Blish, James (Benjamin)

Tornimparte, Alessandra
  See Ginzburg, Natalia

Torre, Raoul della
  See Mencken, H(enry) L(ouis)

Torrey, E(dwin) Fuller 1937- .... **CLC 34**
  See also CA 119

Torsvan, Ben Traven
  See Traven, B.

Torsvan, Benno Traven
  See Traven, B.

Torsvan, Berick Traven
  See Traven, B.

Torsvan, Berwick Traven
  See Traven, B.

Torsvan, Bruno Traven
  See Traven, B.

Torsvan, Traven
  See Traven, B.

Tournier, Michel (Edouard) 1924-CLC 6, 23,
  36, 95
  See also CA 49-52; CANR 3, 36; DLB 83;
  MTCW; SATA 23

Tournimparte, Alessandra
  See Ginzburg, Natalia

Towers, Ivar
  See Kornbluth, C(yril) M.

Towne, Robert (Burton) 1936(?)-...... **CLC 87**
  See also CA 108; DLB 44

Townsend, Sue 1946- .... CLC 61; DAB; DAC
  See also CA 119; 127; INT 127; MTCW; SATA
  55, 93; SATA-Brief 48

Townshend, Peter (Dennis Blandford) 1945-
  CLC 17, 42
  See also CA 107

Tozzi, Federigo 1883-1920 .... **TCLC 31**

Traill, Catharine Parr 1802-1899 ..NCLC 31
  See also DLB 99

Trakl, Georg 1887-1914 .... **TCLC 5**
  See also CA 104

Transtroemer, Tomas (Goesta) 1931-CLC 52,
  65; DAM POET
  See also CA 117; 129; CAAS 17

Transtromer, Tomas Gosta
  See Transtroemer, Tomas (Goesta)

Traven, B. (?)-1969 .... **CLC 8, 11**
  See also CA 19-20; 25-28R; CAP 2; DLB 9,
  56; MTCW

Treitel, Jonathan 1959- .... **CLC 70**

Tremain, Rose 1943- .... **CLC 42**
  See also CA 97-100; CANR 44; DLB 14

Tremblay, Michel 1942- CLC 29, 102; DAC;
  DAM MST
  See also CA 116; 128; DLB 60; MTCW

Trevanian .... **CLC 29**
  See also Whitaker, Rod(ney)

Trevor, Glen
  See Hilton, James

Trevor, William 1928- ..CLC 7, 9, 14, 25, 71;
  SSC 21
  See also Cox, William Trevor
  See also DLB 14, 139

Trifonov, Yuri (Valentinovich) 1925-1981
  CLC 45
  See also CA 126; 103; MTCW

Trilling, Lionel 1905-1975 ...... CLC 9, 11, 24
  See also CA 9-12R; 61-64; CANR 10; DLB 28,
  63; INT CANR-10; MTCW

Trimball, W. H.
  See Mencken, H(enry) L(ouis)

Tristan
  See Gomez de la Serna, Ramon

Tristram
  See Housman, A(lfred) E(dward)

Trogdon, William (Lewis) 1939-
  See Heat-Moon, William Least
  See also CA 115; 119; CANR 47; INT 119

Trollope, Anthony 1815-1882NCLC 6, 33; DA;
  DAB; DAC; DAM MST, NOV; WLC
  See also CDBLB 1832-1890; DLB 21, 57, 159;
  SATA 22

Trollope, Frances 1779-1863 .... NCLC 30
  See also DLB 21, 166

Trotsky, Leon 1879-1940 .... **TCLC 22**
  See also CA 118

Trotter (Cockburn), Catharine 1679-1749L C
  8
  See also DLB 84

Trout, Kilgore
  See Farmer, Philip Jose

Trow, George W. S. 1943- .... **CLC 52**
  See also CA 126

Troyat, Henri 1911- .... **CLC 23**
  See also CA 45-48; CANR 2, 33; MTCW

Trudeau, G(arretson) B(eekman) 1948-
  See Trudeau, Garry B.
  See also CA 81-84; CANR 31; SATA 35

Trudeau, Garry B. .... **CLC 12**
  See also Trudeau, G(arretson) B(eekman)
  See also AAYA 10; AITN 2

Truffaut, Francois 1932-1984 .. CLC 20, 101
  See also CA 81-84; 113; CANR 34

Trumbo, Dalton 1905-1976 .... **CLC 19**
  See also CA 21-24R; 69-72; CANR 10; DLB
  26

Trumbull, John 1750-1831 .... NCLC 30
  See also DLB 31

Trundlett, Helen B.
  See Eliot, T(homas) S(tearns)

Tryon, Thomas 1926-1991 . CLC 3, 11; DAM
  POP
  See also AITN 1; CA 29-32R; 135; CANR 32;
  MTCW

Tryon, Tom
  See Tryon, Thomas

Ts'ao Hsueh-ch'in 1715(?)-1763 .... **LC 1**

See also CA 1-4R; CAAS 7; CANR 1, 33; CDBLB 1960 to Present; DLB 13; MTCW
Wesley, Richard (Errol) 1945- .... **CLC 7**
See also BW 1; CA 57-60; CANR 27; DLB 38
Wessel, Johan Herman 1742-1785 .... **LC 7**
West, Anthony (Panther) 1914-1987 **CLC 50**
See also CA 45-48; 124; CANR 3, 19; DLB 15
West, C. P.
See Wodehouse, P(elham) G(renville)
West, (Mary) Jessamyn 1902-1984**CLC 7, 17**
See also CA 9-12R; 112; CANR 27; DLB 6; DLBY 84; MTCW; SATA-Obit 37
West, Morris L(anglo) 1916- .... **CLC 6, 33**
See also CA 5-8R; CANR 24, 49; MTCW
West, Nathanael 1903-1940 **TCLC 1, 14, 44; SSC 16**
See also CA 104; 125; CDALB 1929-1941; DLB 4, 9, 28; MTCW
West, Owen
See Koontz, Dean R(ay)
West, Paul 1930- .... **CLC 7, 14, 96**
See also CA 13-16R; CAAS 7; CANR 22, 53; DLB 14; INT CANR-22
West, Rebecca 1892-1983 ... **CLC 7, 9, 31, 50**
See also CA 5-8R; 109; CANR 19; DLB 36; DLBY 83; MTCW
Westall, Robert (Atkinson) 1929-1993**CLC 17**
See also AAYA 12; CA 69-72; 141; CANR 18; CLR 13; JRDA; MAICYA; SAAS 2; SATA 23, 69; SATA-Obit 75
Westlake, Donald E(dwin) 1933- **CLC 7, 33; DAM POP**
See also CA 17-20R; CAAS 13; CANR 16, 44; INT CANR-16
Westmacott, Mary
See Christie, Agatha (Mary Clarissa)
Weston, Allen
See Norton, Andre
Wetcheek, J. L.
See Feuchtwanger, Lion
Wetering, Janwillem van de
See van de Wetering, Janwillem
Wetherell, Elizabeth
See Warner, Susan (Bogert)
Whale, James 1889-1957 .... **TCLC 63**
Whalen, Philip 1923- .... **CLC 6, 29**
See also CA 9-12R; CANR 5, 39; DLB 16
Wharton, Edith (Newbold Jones) 1862-1937 **TCLC 3, 9, 27, 53; DA; DAB; DAC; DAM MST, NOV; SSC 6; WLC**
See also CA 104; 132; CDALB 1865-1917; DLB 4, 9, 12, 78; DLBD 13; MTCW
Wharton, James
See Mencken, H(enry) L(ouis)
Wharton, William (a pseudonym)CLC 18, 37
See also CA 93-96; DLBY 80; INT 93-96
Wheatley (Peters), Phillis 1754(?)-1784**LC 3; BLC; DA; DAC; DAM MST, MULT, POET; PC 3; WLC**
See also CDALB 1640-1865; DLB 31, 50
Wheelock, John Hall 1886-1978 ...... **CLC 14**
See also CA 13-16R; 77-80; CANR 14; DLB 45
White, E(lwyn) B(rooks) 1899-1985 **CLC 10, 34, 39; DAM POP**
See also AITN 2; CA 13-16R; 116; CANR 16, 37; CLR 1, 21; DLB 11, 22; MAICYA; MTCW; SATA 2, 29; SATA-Obit 44
White, Edmund (Valentine III) 1940-**CLC 27; DAM POP**
See also AAYA 7; CA 45-48; CANR 3, 19, 36; MTCW
White, Patrick (Victor Martindale) 1912-1990

CLC 3, 4, 5, 7, 9, 18, 65, 69
See also CA 81-84; 132; CANR 43; MTCW
White, Phyllis Dorothy James 1920-
See James, P. D.
See also CA 21-24R; CANR 17, 43; DAM POP; MTCW
White, T(erence) H(anbury) 1906-1964 **C L C 30**
See also AAYA 22; CA 73-76; CANR 37; DLB 160; JRDA; MAICYA; SATA 12
White, Terence de Vere 1912-1994 ...**CLC 49**
See also CA 49-52; 145; CANR 3
White, Walter F(rancis) 1893-1955 **TCLC 15**
See also White, Walter
See also BW 1; CA 115; 124; DLB 51
White, William Hale 1831-1913
See Rutherford, Mark
See also CA 121
Whitehead, E(dward) A(nthony) 1933-**CLC 5**
See also CA 65-68; CANR 58
Whitemore, Hugh (John) 1936- ....**CLC 37**
See also CA 132; INT 132
Whitman, Sarah Helen (Power) 1803-1878 **NCLC 19**
See also DLB 1
Whitman, Walt(er) 1819-1892.. **NCLC 4, 31; DA; DAB; DAC; DAM MST, POET; PC 3; WLC**
See also CDALB 1640-1865; DLB 3, 64; SATA 20
Whitney, Phyllis A(yame) 1903- ..... **CLC 42; DAM POP**
See also AITN 2; BEST 90:3; CA 1-4R; CANR 3, 25, 38, 60; JRDA; MAICYA; SATA 1, 30
Whittemore, (Edward) Reed (Jr.) 1919-**CLC 4**
See also CA 9-12R; CAAS 8; CANR 4; DLB 5
Whittier, John Greenleaf 1807-1892**NCLC 8, 59**
See also DLB 1
Whittlebot, Hernia
See Coward, Noel (Peirce)
Wicker, Thomas Grey 1926-
See Wicker, Tom
See also CA 65-68; CANR 21, 46
Wicker, Tom ....**CLC 7**
See also Wicker, Thomas Grey
Wideman, John Edgar 1941- **CLC 5, 34, 36, 67; BLC; DAM MULT**
See also BW 2; CA 85-88; CANR 14, 42; DLB 33, 143
Wiebe, Rudy (Henry) 1934- .. **CLC 6, 11, 14; DAC; DAM MST**
See also CA 37-40R; CANR 42; DLB 60
Wieland, Christoph Martin 1733-1813**N C L C 17**
See also DLB 97
Wiene, Robert 1881-1938 .... **TCLC 56**
Wieners, John 1934-............................**CLC 7**
See also CA 13-16R; DLB 16
Wiesel, Elie(zer) 1928- **CLC 3, 5, 11, 37; DA; DAB; DAC; DAM MST, NOV; WLCS 2:855-57, 854**
See also AAYA 7; AITN 1; CA 5-8R; CAAS 4; CANR 8, 40; DLB 83; DLBY 87; INT CANR-8; MTCW; SATA 56
Wiggins, Marianne 1947- ....**CLC 57**
See also BEST 89:3; CA 130; CANR 60
Wight, James Alfred 1916-
See Herriot, James
See also CA 77-80; SATA 55; SATA-Brief 44
Wilbur, Richard (Purdy) 1921-**CLC 3, 6, 9, 14, 53; DA; DAB; DAC; DAM MST, POET**
See also CA 1-4R; CABS 2; CANR 2, 29; DLB

5, 169; INT CANR-29; MTCW; SATA 9
Wild, Peter 1940- .... **CLC 14**
See also CA 37-40R; DLB 5
Wilde, Oscar (Fingal O'Flahertie Wills) 1854(?)-1900**TCLC 1, 8, 23, 41; DA; DAB; DAC; DAM DRAM, MST, NOV; SSC 11; WLC**
See also CA 104; 119; CDBLB 1890-1914; DLB 10, 19, 34, 57, 141, 156; SATA 24
Wilder, Billy .... **CLC 20**
See also Wilder, Samuel
See also DLB 26
Wilder, Samuel 1906-
See Wilder, Billy
See also CA 89-92
Wilder, Thornton (Niven) 1897-1975**CLC 1, 5, 6, 10, 15, 35, 82; DA; DAB; DAC; DAM DRAM, MST, NOV; DC 1; WLC**
See also AITN 2; CA 13-16R; 61-64; CANR 40; DLB 4, 7, 9; MTCW
Wilding, Michael 1942-..................... **CLC 73**
See also CA 104; CANR 24, 49
Wiley, Richard 1944- .... **CLC 44**
See also CA 121; 129
Wilhelm, Kate ....**CLC 7**
See also Wilhelm, Katie Gertrude
See also AAYA 20; CAAS 5; DLB 8; INT CANR-17
Wilhelm, Katie Gertrude 1928-
See Wilhelm, Kate
See also CA 37-40R; CANR 17, 36, 60; MTCW
Wilkins, Mary
See Freeman, Mary Eleanor Wilkins
Willard, Nancy 1936- .... **CLC 7, 37**
See also CA 89-92; CANR 10, 39; CLR 5; DLB 5, 52; MAICYA; MTCW; SATA 37, 71; SATA-Brief 30
Williams, C(harles) K(enneth) 1936-**CLC 33, 56; DAM POET**
See also CA 37-40R; CAAS 26; CANR 57; DLB 5
Williams, Charles
See Collier, James L(incoln)
Williams, Charles (Walter Stansby) 1886-1945 **TCLC 1, 11**
See also CA 104; DLB 100, 153
Williams, (George) Emlyn 1905-1987**CLC 15; DAM DRAM**
See also CA 104; 123; CANR 36; DLB 10, 77; MTCW
Williams, Hugo 1942-........................ **CLC 42**
See also CA 17-20R; CANR 45; DLB 40
Williams, J. Walker
See Wodehouse, P(elham) G(renville)
Williams, John A(lfred) 1925- ..... **CLC 5, 13; BLC; DAM MULT**
See also BW 2; CA 53-56; CAAS 3; CANR 6, 26, 51; DLB 2, 33; INT CANR-6
Williams, Jonathan (Chamberlain) 1929-**CLC 13**
See also CA 9-12R; CAAS 12; CANR 8; DLB 5
Williams, Joy 1944- .... **CLC 31**
See also CA 41-44R; CANR 22, 48
Williams, Norman 1952- .... **CLC 39**
See also CA 118
Williams, Sherley Anne 1944-**CLC 89; BLC; DAM MULT, POET**
See also BW 2; CA 73-76; CANR 25; DLB 41; INT CANR-25; SATA 78
Williams, Shirley
See Williams, Sherley Anne
Williams, Tennessee 1911-1983**CLC 1, 2, 5, 7,**

Literary Criticism Series
Cumulative Topic Index

This index lists all topic entries in Gale's *Classical and Medieval Literature Criticism, Contemporary Literary Criticism, Literature Criticism from 1400 to 1800, Nineteenth-Century Literature Criticism,* and *Twentieth-Century Literary Criticism.*

Topic Index

Contemporary Literary Criticism
Cumulative Nationality Index

Nationality Index

Nationality Index

Nationality Index

Title Index